Christianity

DIARMAID MacCULLOCH

Christianity

The First Three Thousand Years

VIKING

For Philip Kennedy

Faithful friend, who has managed to persist in affirming a
Christian story

VIKING
Published by the Penguin Group
Penguin Group (USA) Inc., 375 Hudson Street,
New York, New York 10014, U.S.A.
Penguin Group (Canada), 90 Eglinton Avenue East, Suite 700,
Toronto, Ontario, Canada M4P 2Y3
(a division of Pearson Penguin Canada Inc.)
Penguin Books Ltd, 80 Strand, London WC2R 0RL, England
Penguin Ireland, 25 St. Stephen's Green, Dublin 2, Ireland
(a division of Penguin Books Ltd)
Penguin Books Australia Ltd, 250 Camberwell Road, Camberwell,
Victoria 3124, Australia
(a division of Pearson Australia Group Pty Ltd)
Penguin Books India Pvt Ltd, 11 Community Centre, Panchsheel Park,
New Delhi – 110 017, India
Penguin Group (NZ), 67 Apollo Drive, Rosedale, North Shore 0632,
New Zealand (a division of Pearson New Zealand Ltd)
Penguin Books (South Africa) (Pty) Ltd, 24 Sturdee Avenue,
Rosebank, Johannesburg 2196, South Africa

Penguin Books Ltd, Registered Offices:
80 Strand, London WC2R 0RL, England

First American edition
Published in 2010 by Viking Penguin,
a member of Penguin Group (USA) Inc.

1   3   5   7   9   10   8   6   4   2

Published in Great Britain as A History of Christianity by Allen Lane, an imprint of Penguin Books Ltd.

Illustration credits appear on pages xi–xiv.

Library of Congress Cataloging-in-Publication Data

MacCulloch, Diarmaid.
Christianity : the first three thousand years / Diarmaid MacCulloch.
p. cm.
Includes bibliographical references and index.
ISBN 978-0-670-02126-0
1. Church history. I. Title.
BR145.3.M33 2010
270—dc22
2009040184

Printed in the United States of America

Contents

PART IV

The Unpredictable Rise of Rome (300–1300)

PART V

Orthodoxy: The Imperial Faith (451–1800)

PART VII

God in the Dock (1492–present)

List of Illustrations

Every effort has been made to contact all copyright holders. The publishers will be happy to make good in future editions any errors or omissions brought to their attention.

Endpapers: Jacopo Tintoretto, *The Crucifixion*, 1565 (detail). Scuola Grande di San Rocco, Venice. Photo: The Bridgeman Art Library

List of Maps

Acknowledgements

Such a hubristic enterprise as a single-volume history of quite a lot of history floats on a sea of friendship and help. As ever, Stuart Proffitt has been the prince of editors, combining encouragement, critical judgement and a relish for getting prose exactly right, and Joy de Menil and Kathryn Court have also provided thorough and invaluable editorial comment from across the Atlantic. Unflappable and assiduous in their help in preparing the text have been Sam Baddeley, Lesley Levene, Cecilia Mackay and Huub Stegeman. My literary agent, Felicity Bryan, once more had the ability to envisage me writing this book when I might have felt faint-hearted, and has always been there to cheer me on. Many professional colleagues have shown generosity in their conversation and replies to importunacies as I have been constructing the book; some of them have even taken on the penitential task of reading drafts of the text. I am indebted to them all, but particularly to Sam Baddeley, Sebastian Brock, James Carleton Paget, Andrew Chandler, Eamon Duffy, Craig Harline, Philip Kennedy, Judith Maltby, Andrew Pettegree, Miri Rubin, John Wolffe and Hugh Wybrew. I am also grateful for advice on particular points to Sarah Apetrei, Kwabena Asamoah-Gyadu, Pier Giorgio Borbone, Michael Bourdeaux, Frank Bremer, Michael Chisholm, Tom Earle, Massimo Firpo, Peter Groves, Ahmad Gunny, Peter Jackson, Ian Ker, Sangkeun Kim, Graeme Murdock, Matteo Nicolini-Zani, Martin Palmer, Mark Schaan, Bettina Schmidt, Andrew Spicer, Dom Marie-Robert Torczynski, Dom Gabriel van Dijck, Steve Watts, Philip Weller and Jonathan Yonan, and to Pier Giorgio Borbone, Joel Cabrita and John Edwards for permission to quote unpublished material. Remaining imperfections are of course my responsibility and not theirs.

My colleagues in the Theology Faculty and the Humanities Division of the University of Oxford made researching for and writing this book much easier by their forbearance and flexibility in agreeing to my having an extended period of unpaid leave to create it, and I am especially grateful to the Rev. Dr Charlotte Methuen for being my alter ego in the university during this period. It has been a privilege to be a member of a university where there are so many seminars and lectures on offer to give glimpses of specialist wisdom across the whole span of Christian history, and I am grateful to all the convenors and lecturers who have given me a hospitable welcome when, as a bogus asylum seeker, I have sought self-improvement on their shore. As ever, Oxford's wonderfully rich library resources and benevolent librarians have been a luxury at my disposal, and I am particularly appreciative of the help of Alan Brown. As festive companions and encouragers in this venture, my colleagues in the running of the *Journal of Ecclesiastical History* have been exemplary: Martin Brett, James Carleton Paget, Christine Linehan and Anne Waites.

Colleagues in a different enterprise have been all those involved in making the BBC television series which has accompanied the writing of this book, a mammoth operation which has brought much fun and many varied expeditions round the world. Among the very many involved in that process, I particularly thank Gillian Bancroft, Jean-Claude Bragard, Kathryn Blennerhassett, Nick Holden-Sim, Mike Jackson, Roger Lucas, Erin Mactague, Lucy Robinson, Sian Salt, Graham Veevers and Michael Wakelin. Both projects spanned a new time in my life. I am especially in Sam Baddeley's debt for his friendship and shrewd advice. Support, morale-boosting or wise words have also come from Mark Achurch, Isabel and Rosa Gerenstein, Peter and Bea Groves, Gaynor Humphrey, Philip Kennedy, Craig Leaper, Judith Maltby, Jane Upperton and Allen Young, to name the principals among legion.

Diarmaid MacCulloch
St Cross College, Oxford
Passiontide 2009

Organized Christianity came into existence, and exists, to preserve a treasure, a command to be executed, a promise to be repeated, a mission to be fulfilled. This treasure belongs to past, present, and future; it is potential, yet active; an object of contemplation, yet the inspiration of right conduct. An unfathomable mystery, it must be related to all knowledge. And in their endeavours to guard and transmit their trust, its guardians have raised the most perplexing issues. They have caused endless destruction of life in the name of universal peace. They have built up the most realistic of political systems in the effort to establish a kingdom not of this world. In the exploration of the recesses of the soul, they have developed the arts and sciences, and constructed theories of the universe. And, in their desire to satisfy the deepest needs of mankind, they have raised up against themselves the visions, prophecies, and extravagances of excitable and obstinate men, and the dislike of many sensible men.

The treasure which has caused all this activity was cast into the world with a few simple sentences. 'Thou shalt love the Lord thy God and thy neighbour as thyself. What shall it profit a man if he shall gain the whole world and lose his own soul?' And again, 'God so loved the world that he gave his only begotten Son, that whosoever believeth in Him should not perish but have everlasting life. No one cometh to the Father, save by Me. Take, eat; this is my body.' And again, 'Go and preach the Kingdom of God. Feed my sheep. Thou art Peter, and upon this rock will I build my Church. Peace I leave with you, my peace I give unto you. I have come not to bring peace, but a sword.'

Maurice Powicke, 'The Christian Life', in *The Legacy of the Middle Ages* (Oxford, 1926)

Introduction

In seventeenth-century England, there lived a country parson called Samuel Crossman. A rather reluctant Anglican of Puritan outlook, he spent most of his ministry in a small Gloucestershire parish, whose chief hamlet is delightfully called Easter Compton, though briefly at the end of his life he was Dean of Bristol Cathedral. Crossman wrote a handful of devotional poems, one of which, in a most unusual metre, is a work of genius. Beginning 'My song is Love unknown', it ends the tale of Jesus's arrest, trial, death and burial with an exclamation of quiet joy that this suffering so long before had shaped the life of Mr Crossman in his little English parsonage:

> Here might I stay and sing,
>   No story so divine;
> Never was love, dear King!
>   Never was grief like Thine.
>   This is my Friend,
>   In Whose sweet praise
>   I all my days
>   Could gladly spend.[1]

The intimacy of Crossman's lines hints at the degree to which Christianity is, at root, a personality cult. Its central message is the story of a person, Jesus, whom Christians believe is also the Christ (from a Greek word meaning 'Anointed One'): an aspect of the God who was, is and ever shall be, yet who is at the same time a human being, set in historic time. Christians believe that they can still meet this human being in a fashion comparable to the experience of the disciples who walked with him in Galilee and saw him die on the Cross. They are convinced that this meeting transforms lives, as has been evident in the experience of other Christians across the centuries. This book is their story.

There are two thousand years' worth of Christian stories to tell, which may seem a daunting task for historians who are used to modern European professional expectations that a true scholar knows a lot about not very much. Yet two millennia are not very much. Christianity has to be seen as a young religion, far younger than, for instance, Taoism, Buddhism, Hinduism or its own parent, Judaism, and it occupies a small fraction of the lived experience of what is so far a very short-lived species. I have given the book a subtitle which invites the reader to consider whether Christianity has a future (the indications, it must be said, can hardly be other than affirmative); yet it also points to the fact that what became Christian ideas have a human past in the minds of people who lived before the time of Jesus Christ. As well as telling stories, my book asks questions. It tries to avoid giving too many answers, since this habit has been one of the great vices of organized religion. Some readers may find it sceptical, but as my old doctoral supervisor Sir Geoffrey Elton once remarked in my hearing, if historians are not sceptical, they are nothing.[2]

The book conceives the overall structure of Christian history differently, I believe, from any of its predecessors. Within the cluster of beliefs making up Christian faith is an instability which comes from a twofold ancestry. Far from being simply the pristine, innovative teachings of Jesus Christ, it draws on two much more ancient cultural wellsprings, Greece and Israel. The story must therefore begin more than a millennium before Jesus, among the ancient Greeks and the Jews, two races which alike thought that they had a uniquely privileged place in the world's history. The extraordinary cultural achievements in art, philosophy and science of the ancient Greeks gave them good reason to think this. More surprising is the fact that the Jews' constant experience of misfortune did not kill their faith in their own destiny. Instead it drove them to conceive of their God not simply as all-powerful, but as passionately concerned with their response to him, in anger as well as in love. Such an intensely personal deity, they began to assert, was nevertheless the God for all humanity. He was very different from the supreme deity who emerged from Greek philosophy in the thought of Plato: all-perfect, therefore immune to change and devoid of the passion which denotes change. The first generations of Christians were Jews who lived in a world shaped by Greek elite culture. They had to try to fit together these two irreconcilable visions of God, and the results have never been and never can be a stable answer to an unending question.

After the period of Jesus's life and its immediate aftermath, as I try to explain in Part II of this book, the history of Christianity can only be a unified narrative for around three centuries before it begins to diverge into language-families: Latin-speakers, Greek-speakers and those speaking Oriental languages (the chief among them being of course Jesus Christ himself). As a result, after the three or four centuries which followed the birth of Jesus, the story of Christianity told here is divided three ways. One split emerged because a section of Christianity, the Church within the Roman Empire, found itself suddenly receiving patronage and increasingly unquestioning support from the successors of the emperors who had formerly persecuted it. Those to the east of that empire did not. Within the imperial Church, there was a further division between those who, when looking for a formal language in which to express themselves, habitually chose Greek and those who turned to Latin. This tripartite split became institutionalized after the Council of Chalcedon in 451, and the three tales can thereafter be told with little overlap until around 1700.

First is the Christianity which in the early centuries one would have expected to become dominant, that of the Middle Eastern homeland of Jesus. The Christians of the Middle East spoke a language akin to the Aramaic spoken by Jesus himself, the language which developed into Syriac, and very early they began developing an identity which diverged from the Greek-speakers who first dominated most of the great Christian centres of the Roman Empire to the west. Many of these Syriac Christians were on the margins of the empire. When, at Chalcedon, a Roman emperor sought to impose a solution to a difficult theological problem – how to talk of the divine and human natures of Jesus Christ – most Syrians rejected his solution, though they radically disagreed among themselves as to why they were rejecting it, taking precisely opposite views, which are most precisely if inelegantly described as 'Miaphysite' and 'Dyophysite'. We will find Miaphysite and Dyophysite Syriac Christians performing remarkable feats of mission in north-east Africa, India and East Asia, although their story was also profoundly and destructively altered by the coming of a new monotheism from the same Semitic homeland, Islam. Still in the eighth century of the Christian era, the great new city of Baghdad would have been a more likely capital for worldwide Christianity than Rome. The extraordinary accident of the irruption of Islam is the chief reason why Christian history turned in another direction.

The second story is that of the Western, Latin-speaking Church, which came to look to the Bishop of Rome, and within which he became an unchallenged leader. In the Latin West, the prominence of the Bishop of

Rome, already often referred to as *papa* ('Pope'), was becoming apparent during the fourth century, as the emperors abandoned Rome, and he was increasingly left to his own devices at a time when more and more power was flowing into the hands of churchmen. After this Western story has reached the point in the fourteenth century when the papal project of monarchy ran into difficulties, we move eastwards to meet the third story, of Orthodoxy. Like Rome, the Orthodox are the heirs of the Roman Empire, but whereas Western Latin Christians emerged out of the ruins of the western half of that empire, the Greek-speaking Eastern Church was shaped by the continuing rule of the Eastern emperor. Just when it seemed doomed to decay after the fall of Byzantium to the Ottomans, a new variety of Orthodoxy far to the north began revealing its potential as leader among the Orthodox: I outline the development of Russian Christianity. The Western Latin story resumes with the Reformation and Counter-Reformation, which tore the Western Church into fragments, but which also launched Christianity as the first world faith. From 1700, the three stories converge once more, as the world was united by the expansion of Western Christian empires. Despite their present variety, modern Christianities are more closely in touch than they have been since the first generations of Christians in the first-century Middle East.

I seek to give due weight in these narratives to the tangled and often tragic story of the relations between Christianity and its mother-monotheism, Judaism, as well as with its monotheistic younger cousin, Islam. For most of its existence, Christianity has been the most intolerant of world faiths, doing its best to eliminate all competitors, with Judaism a qualified exception, for which (thanks to some thoughts from Augustine of Hippo) it found space to serve its own theological and social purposes. Even now, by no means all sections of the Christian world have undergone the mutation of believing unequivocally in tolerating or accepting any partnership with other belief systems. In particular I highlight the huge consequences when the fifteenth- and sixteenth-century monarchs of the Iberian peninsula (Spain and Portugal) re-invented their multi-faith society as a Christian monopoly and then exported that single-minded form of Christianity to other parts of the world. I develop the theme which became (rather to my surprise) a ground-bass of the narrative in my previous book, *Reformation*: the destruction of Spanish Judaism and Islam after 1492 had a major role in developing new forms of Christianity which challenged much of the early Church's package of ideas, and also in fostering the mindset which led in the seventeenth and eighteenth centuries to the Enlightenment in Western culture. Here I examine the role of nineteenth- and twentieth-century European Christian empires in creating a reaction of fundamentalist intolerance within other modern world faiths, principally Islam, Judaism and Hinduism.

Deeply embedded in Christian tradition is a vocabulary of 'repentance' and 'conversion', both words which mean 'turning around'. So this book describes some of the ways in which individuals were turned around by Christianity, but also the ways in which they could turn around what Christianity meant. We will meet Paul of Tarsus, suddenly struck down by what he heard as a universal message for all human beings, who then quarrelled fiercely with other disciples of Jesus who saw their Lord as a Messiah sent only to the Jews. There is Augustine of Hippo, the brilliant teacher whose life was turned around by reading Paul, and who, more than a thousand years later, deeply influenced another troubled, brilliant academic called Martin Luther. There is Constantine, the soldier who hacked his way to total control of the Roman Empire and became convinced that the Christian God had destined him to do so – for Constantine, his side of the bargain was to turn Christians from a harried, suppressed cult, accused of ruining the empire, into the most favoured and privileged of all Roman religions.

In the old city of Jerusalem is a medieval church which stands on the site of the basilica that the Emperor Constantine and his mother built over the likely site of the death, burial and resurrection of Christ.[3] Within the walls of what the Western Churches call the Church of the Holy Sepulchre (the Orthodox give it an entirely different name, the *Anastasis*, Resurrection), the results of Constantine's decision are played out daily in the epically bad behaviour of the various fragments of the imperial Christian Church whose adherents worship in the building. I have witnessed early one December morning the instructive spectacle of two rival ancient liturgies noisily proceeding simultaneously above the empty tomb of the Saviour himself, on opposite faces of the ugly and perilously decayed nineteenth-century Sepulchre shrine. It was a perfect juxtaposition of Chalcedonian and non-Chalcedonian Christianity, as the serenity of a Latin Mass with full organ struggled against the spirited chanting of the Miaphysite Copts (see Plate 21). I particularly enjoyed the moment when the bearer of the Coptic censer swept with brio around the shrine to the very frontier of the rival liturgy and sent his cloud of incense billowing into the heretical Latin West. The extremes of Christianity result from its seizing the most profound and extreme passions of humanity. Its story cannot be a mere abstract tale of theology or historical change.

The central text of Christianity is the Bible, as mysterious and labyrinthine a library as that portrayed by Umberto Eco in *The Name of the Rose*. It has two parts, the Tanakh (the Hebrew scriptures), which Christians retained as their 'Old Testament', and a new set of books, the 'New Testament', concentrating on the life, death, resurrection and immediate after-effects of Jesus Christ. It describes ancient encounters with God which are far from straightforward. God knows who God is, as he once remarked to Moses out of the fire of a burning bush. Jewish and Christian traditions want to say at the same time that God has a personal relationship with individual human beings and that he is also beyond all naming, all characterization. Such a paradox will lead to a constant urge to describe the indescribable, and that is what the Bible tries to do. It does not have all the answers, and – a point many forget – only once does it claim to do so, in one of the last writings to squeeze into the biblical canon, known as Paul's second epistle to Timothy.[4] The Bible speaks with many voices, including shouts of anger against God. It tells stories which it does not pretend ever happened, in order to express profound truths, such as we read in the books of Jonah and Job. It is also full of criticism of Church tradition, in the class of writings known as prophecy, which spend much of their energy in denouncing the clergy and the clerical teaching of their day. This should provide a healthy warning to all those who aspire to tell other people what to do on the basis of the Bible.

From the biblical text, a great variety of Christian and pre-Christian themes re-emerge periodically in new guises. In Ethiopia, Miaphysite Christianity returned to the practices of mainstream Judaism, borrowing features of worship and life-practice (such as circumcision and refraining from eating pork) which shocked sixteenth-century Jesuits coming from Counter-Reformation Europe. One of the most numerically successful movements of modern Christianity, Pentecostalism, has centred its appeal on a particular form of communication with the divine, speaking in tongues, which was severely mistrusted by Paul of Tarsus and which (despite the understandable claims of Pentecostals to the contrary) has very little precedent in Christian practice between the first and the nineteenth centuries CE.

A much more frequent recurrence has been that basic theme of the founder so far never fulfilled, the imminence of the Last Days – for some reason, a particularly common theme in Western rather than Eastern

Christianity. In the medieval West, it was usually the property of the powerless, but it became mainstream in sixteenth-century Europe's Reformation, playing a major part in launching warfare and revolution. After the nineteenth-century addition of particular sub-themes, premillennialism and the 'Rapture' of the saved, it has come to play an equal part in American conservative evangelical Protestantism, and it has spread throughout Asia, South America and Africa wherever Western Pentecostalism has taken root and become an indigenous religion. It is not surprising that so many have sought the Last Days. The writing and telling of history is bedevilled by two human neuroses: horror at the desperate shapelessness and seeming lack of pattern in events, and regret for a lost golden age, a moment of happiness when all was well. Put these together and you have an urge to create elaborate patterns to make sense of things and to create a situation where the golden age is just waiting to spring to life again. This is the impulse which makes King Arthur's knights sleep under certain mountains, ready to bring deliverance, or creates the fascination with the Knights Templar and occult conspiracy which propelled *The Da Vinci Code* into best-seller lists.

Repeatedly the Bible has come to mean salvation to a particular people or cultural grouping by saving not merely their souls, but their language, and hence their very identity. So it was, for example, for the people of Wales, through the Bible published for the first time in good literary Welsh by the Protestant Bishop William Morgan in 1588. Morgan's Bible preserved the special character of Welsh culture in the face of the superior resources and colonial self-confidence of the English, and it also ensured, against all likelihood in the early Reformation, that the religious expression of the Welsh became overwhelmingly Protestant.[5] So it was too for Koreans at the end of the nineteenth century, when the Korean Bible translation revived their alphabet and became a symbol of their national pride, sustaining them through Japanese repression and paving the way for the extraordinary success of Christianity in Korea over the last half-century. And one of the reasons for the obstinate survival and now huge revival of Orthodox Christianity has been a story (largely unknown in the Christian West) of biblical translation, undertaken by the Russian Orthodox Church for an astonishing variety of language groups in Eastern Europe and the area of the former Soviet Union.

The Bible thus embodies not a tradition, but many traditions. Self-styled 'Traditionalists' often forget that the nature of tradition is not that of a humanly manufactured mechanical or architectural structure with a constant outline and form, but rather that of a plant, pulsing with life and continually changing shape while keeping the same ultimate identity. The Bible's authority for Christians lies in the fact they have a special relationship with it that can never be altered, like the relationship of parent and child. This does not deny relationships with other books which may be both deep and long-lasting, and it does not necessarily make the parental relationship easy or pleasant. It is simply of a different kind, and can never be abrogated. Once we see this, much modern neurosis about the authority of the Bible can be laid aside. Maybe the Bible can be taken seriously rather than literally.

Books are the storehouses for human ideas. Three great religions which come from the Middle East centre their practice on a sacred book and are indeed frequently known as Religions of the Book: Judaism, Christianity, Islam. This book about the people of a book therefore necessarily discusses ideas. Many readers may want to see it as a narrative: students and scholars may find it helpful to test how social and political history both breed and are transformed by theology. Ideas, once born, often develop lives of their own within human history, and they need to be understood in their own terms as they interact with societies and structures. Christianity in its first five centuries was in many respects a dialogue between Judaism and Graeco-Roman philosophy, trying to solve such problems as how a human being might also be God, or how one might sensibly describe three manifestations of the one Christian God, which came to be known collectively as the Trinity. After much ill-tempered debate on such matters, the outcome of the Council of Chalcedon in 451 was dictated by political circumstances and did not carry the whole Christian world with it. The schisms which followed were made permanent by the political bitterness aroused by the Western Crusades of the High Middle Ages, their transmutation into attacks on Eastern Christians and their eventual failure either to recapture the Holy Land or to defend Eastern Christianity against Islam. All these cataclysmic human events stemmed from an idea constructed by a council of bishops.

The Bible of the Church was itself a disputed text at least until late in the second century of the Christian era. But even when Christians had argued their way to a consensus as to which texts should be included in the Bible and which should not, they encountered a problem common to all Peoples of the Book. Judaism, Christianity and Islam have all discovered that the text between the covers cannot provide all the answers. Hence the growth of a vast array of pronouncements, interpretations and pragmatic solutions to new problems which formed bodies of tradition in various parts of Christianity. As early as the fourth century CE, a respected Christian authority in the eastern Mediterranean, Basil of Caesarea, was saying that some traditions were as important and authoritative as the Bible itself. It was one of the big issues of the European Reformation, whether any of this tradition beyond scripture should be regarded as part of the essential kit of being a Christian. Roman Catholics said yes – the official Church was the guardian of the tradition and must be obeyed in all things. Protestants said no – most of the tradition was part of the confidence trick played on ordinary Christians by the Church, diverting them from the glorious simplicity of the biblical message. Protestants were not consistent on this, for otherwise they could not justify aspects of their own Christianity not found in scripture, like the universal baptism of infants. Radicals who believed in scripture alone criticized them as hypocrites, with some justice.

All the world faiths which have known long-term success have shown a remarkable capacity to mutate, and Christianity is no exception, which is why one underlying message of this history is its sheer variety. Many Christians do not like being reminded of Christianity's capacity to develop, particularly those who are in charge of the various religious institutions which call themselves Churches, but that is the reality and has been from the beginning. This was a marginal branch of Judaism whose founder left no known written works. Jesus seems to have maintained that the trumpet would sound for the end of time very soon, and in a major break with the culture around him, he told his followers to leave the dead to bury their own dead (see p. 90). Maybe he wrote nothing because he did not feel that it was worth it, in the short time left to humanity. Remarkably quickly, his followers seemed to question the idea that history was about to end: they collected and preserved stories about the founder in a newly invented form of written text, the codex (the modern book format). They survived a major crisis of confidence at the end of the first century when the Last Days did not arrive – perhaps one of the greatest turning points in the Christian story, although we know very little about it. Christianity emerged from it a very different institution from the movement created by its founder or even its first great apostle, Paul.

Since from the beginning, radical change and transmutation were part of the story, the succeeding millennia provide plenty of further examples. After three centuries of tension and confrontation with Roman imperial power, the counter-cultural sect mutated into the agent of settled government and preserved Graeco-Roman civilization in the West when that government collapsed. In nineteenth-century America, marginal Christians created a frontier religion with its own new sacred book, the basis of the Church of Jesus Christ of Latter-Day Saints (the Mormons). The astonishing growth of the Mormons is as much part of the modern story of Christianity as that of Orthodoxy, Roman Catholicism or Protestantism, however fiercely conventionally conceived Christianity may deny the Mormons the name Christian. So are later extensions of the Christian core identity, such as the Kimbanguists of central Africa or the Unification Church founded by the Korean Rev. Sun Myung Moon. Such transformations have always been unpredictable. In Korea, an extraordinarily successful Presbyterian (Reformed Protestant) Church now lectures Reformed Protestants in Europe on how to be true to the sixteenth-century European Reformer John Calvin, while this same Korean Church expresses its faith in hymns borrowed from the radically anti-Calvinist Protestantism of Methodism. What is more, many Korean Christians manage to be intensely patriotic, while worshipping in churches which are careful reproductions of the Protestant church architecture of the Midwestern United States (see Plate 68).

The passions which have gone into the construction of a world faith are if nothing else the catalyst for extraordinary human creativity in literature, music, architecture and art. To seek an understanding of Christianity is to see Jesus Christ in the mosaics and icons of Byzantium, or in the harshly lit features of the man on the road to Emmaus as Caravaggio painted him (see Plate 18). Looking up at the heavily gilt ceiling of Santa Maria Maggiore in Rome, one should realize that all its gold was melted down from temples across the Atlantic Ocean, sent as a tribute to the Christian God and to the Catholic Church by the King of Spain, the theft accompanied or justified by frequent misuse of the name of Christ. The sound of Christian passion is heard in the hymns of John and Charles Wesley, bringing pride, self-confidence and divine purpose to the lives of poor and humble people struggling to make sense of a new industrial society in Georgian Britain. It shapes the sublime abstractions of the organ music of Johann Sebastian Bach. During the drab and mendacious tyranny of the German Democratic Republic, a Bach organ recital could pack out a church with people seeking something which spoke to them of objectivity, integrity and serene authenticity. All manifestations of Christian consciousness need to be taken seriously: from a craving to understand the ultimate purpose of God, which has produced terrifying visions of the Last Days, to the instinct to comfortable sociability, which has led to cricket on the Anglican vicarage lawn (see Plates 12 and 52).

This is emphatically a personal view of the sweep of Christian history, so I make no apology for stating my own position in the story: the reader of a book which pontificates on religion has a right to know. I come from a background in which the Church was a three-generation family business, and from a childhood spent in the rectory of an Anglican country parish, a world not unlike that of the Rev. Samuel Crossman, of which I have the happiest memories. I was brought up in the presence of the Bible, and I remember with affection what it was like to hold a dogmatic position on the statements of Christian belief. I would now describe myself as a candid friend of Christianity. I still appreciate the seriousness which a religious mentality brings to the mystery and misery of human existence, and I appreciate the solemnity of religious liturgy as a way of confronting these problems. I live with the puzzle of wondering how something so apparently crazy can be so captivating to millions of other members of my species. It is in part to answer that question for myself that I seek out the history of this world faith, alongside those of humankind's countless other expressions of religious belief and practice. Maybe some familiar with theological jargon will with charity regard this as an apophatic form of the Christian faith.

I make no pronouncement as to whether Christianity, or indeed any religious belief, is 'true'. This is a necessary self-denying ordinance. Is Shakespeare's *Hamlet* 'true'? It never happened, but it seems to me to be much more 'true', full of meaning and significance for human beings, than the reality of the breakfast I ate this morning, which was certainly 'true' in a banal sense. Christianity's claim to truth is absolutely central to it over much of the past two thousand years, and much of this history is dedicated to tracing the varieties of this claim and the competition between them. But historians do not possess a prerogative to pronounce on the truth of the existence of God itself, any more than do (for example) biologists. There is, however, an important aspect of Christianity on which it is the occupation of historians to speak: the *story* of Christianity is undeniably true, in that it is part of human history. Historical truth can be just as exciting and satisfying as any fictional style of construction, because it represents the flotsam from a host of individual stories of human beings like ourselves. Most of them are beyond recall or can only be tantalizingly glimpsed, with the aid of the techniques which historians have built up over the last three centuries.

It has been calculated, for instance, that in the half-acre of one English village churchyard, Widford in Hertfordshire, there are more than five thousand corpses, laid to rest over at least nine centuries. We could never know as much as the names of more than a few hundred of them, let alone much else about them, and there is a special excitement in gathering up the fragments of past lives where we can.[6]

I hope that this book will help readers stand back from Christianity, whether they love it or hate it, or are simply curious about it, and see it in the round. The book is self-evidently not a work of primary-source research; rather, it tries to synthesize the current state of historical scholarship across the world. It also seeks to be a reflection on it, a way of interpreting that scholarship for a larger audience which is often bewildered by what is happening to Christianity and misunderstands how present structures and beliefs have evolved. It can be no more than a series of suggestions to give shape to the past, but the suggestions are not random. At some points in it, I have developed further the text of my previous book, *Reformation*, which was an attempt to tell part of this wider story, but which led me on to this attempt to put shapes on the greater picture. My aim is to tell as clearly as possible an immensely complicated and varied tale, in ways which others will enjoy and find plausible. Furthermore, I am not ashamed to affirm that although modern historians have no special capacity to be arbiters of the truth or otherwise of religion, they still have a moral task. They should seek to promote sanity and to curb the rhetoric which breeds fanaticism. There is no surer basis for fanaticism than bad history, which is invariably history oversimplified.

I have been given great privileges in my career, which now demand their price. I have enjoyed the precious opportunity of research, teaching and discussion in the understanding and serene environment of world-class universities, Cambridge and Oxford. Many may think of such settings as an ivory-tower retreat from reality, and they will have some justification for their opinion if those within the university do not extend the discussion out beyond its walls. That is what I seek to do here. Equally, I feel immensely privileged to have been trained as a professional historian, because my training is a call to discipline my strong feelings of both affection and anger towards my own inheritance. That training may help me tell a story which readers can consider fair and sympathetic, even if they have very different personal standpoints on what Christianity means and what it is worth. My aim has been to seek out what I see as the good in the varied forms of the Christian faith, while pointing clearly to what I think is foolish and dangerous in them. Religious belief can be very close to madness. It has brought human beings to acts of criminal folly as well as to the highest achievements of goodness, creativity and generosity. I tell the story of both extremes. If this risibly ambitious project can at least help to dispel the myths and misrepresentations which fuel folly, then I will believe my task to have been more than worthwhile.

CONVENTIONS

Most primary-source quotations in English are in modern spelling, but where I have quoted translations made by other people from other languages, I have not altered the gender-skewed language common in English usage up to the 1980s. I am more of a devotee of capital letters than is common today; in English convention, they are symbols of what is special, or different, and, in the context of this book, of what links the profane and the sacred world. The Mass and the Rood need capitals; both their devotees and those who hated them would agree on that. So do the Bible, the Eucharist, Saviour, the Blessed Virgin and the Persons of the Trinity. The body of the faithful in a particular city in the early Church, or in a particular region, or the worldwide organization called the Church, all deserve a capital, although a building called a church does not. The Bishop of Exeter needs a capital, as does the Earl of Salisbury, but bishops and earls as a whole do not. My decisions on this have been arbitrary, but I hope that they are at least internally consistent.

My general practice with place names has been to give the most helpful usage, whether ancient or modern, sometimes with the alternative modern or ancient usage in brackets and with alternatives given in the index. The common English versions of overseas place names (such as Brunswick, Hesse, Milan or Munich) are also used. Readers will be aware that the islands embracing England, Ireland, Scotland and Wales have commonly been known as the British Isles. This title no longer pleases all their inhabitants, particularly those in the Republic of Ireland (a matter to which this descendant of Scottish Protestants is sensitive), and a more neutral as well as more accurate description is 'the Atlantic Isles', which is used at various places throughout this book. I am aware that Portuguese-speakers have long used the phrase to describe entirely different islands, and indeed that Spaniards use it for yet a third collection; I hope that I may crave their joint indulgence for my arbitrary choice. Naturally the political entity called Great Britain, which existed between 1707 and 1922, and later in modified form, will be referred to as such where appropriate, and I use 'British Isles' in relation to that relatively brief period too.

Personal names of individuals are generally given in the birth-language which they would have spoken, except in the case of certain major figures, such as rulers or clergy (like the emperors Justinian and Charles V, the kings of the Polish-Lithuanian Commonwealth or John Calvin), who were addressed in several languages by various groups among their subjects or colleagues. Many readers will be aware of the Dutch convention of writing down names such as 'Pieterszoon' as 'Pietersz'; I hope that they will forgive me if I extend these, to avoid confusion for others. Similarly in regard to Hungarian names, I am not using the Hungarian convention of putting first name after surname, so I will speak of Miklós Horthy, not Horthy Miklós. Otherwise the usage of other cultures in their word order for personal names is respected, so Mao Zedong appears thus.

In the notes and bibliography, I generally try to cite the English translation of any work written originally in another language, where that is possible. I avoid cluttering the main text too much with birth and death dates for people mentioned, except where it seems helpful; otherwise the reader will find them in the index. I employ the 'Common Era' usage in dating, since it avoids value judgements about the status of Christianity relative to other systems of faith. Dates unless otherwise stated are 'Common Era' (CE), the system which Christians have customarily called 'Anno Domini' or AD. Dates before 1 CE are given as BCE ('before the Common Era'), which is equivalent to BC. I have tried to avoid names which are offensive to those to whom they have been applied, which means that readers may encounter unfamiliar usages, so I speak of 'Miaphysites' and 'Dyophysites' rather than 'Monophysites' or 'Nestorians', or the 'Catholic Apostolic Church' rather than the 'Irvingites'. Some may sneer at this as 'political correctness'. When I was young, my parents were insistent on the importance of being courteous and respectful of other people's opinions and I am saddened that these undramatic virtues have now been relabelled in an unfriendly spirit. I hope that non-Christian readers will forgive me if for simplicity's sake I often call the Tanakh of Judaism the Old Testament, in parallel to the Christian New Testament. Biblical references are given in the chapter-and-verse form which Christians had evolved by the sixteenth century, so the third chapter of John's Gospel, at the fourteenth verse, becomes

John 3.14, and the first of two letters written by Paul to the Corinthians, the second chapter at the tenth verse, becomes I Corinthians 2.10. Biblical quotations are taken from the Revised Standard Version of the Bible unless otherwise stated.

PART I

A Millennium of Beginnings
(1000 BCE–100 CE)

I

Greece and Rome

(*c.* 1000 BCE–100 CE)

GREEK BEGINNINGS

Why begin in Greece and not in a stable in Bethlehem of Judaea? Because in the beginning was the Word. The Evangelist John's Gospel narrative of Jesus the Christ has no Christmas stable; it opens with a chant or hymn in which 'Word' is a Greek word, *logos*. The Word, says John, was God, and became human flesh and dwelt among us, full of grace and truth.[1]

This *logos* means far more than simply 'word': *logos* is the story itself. *Logos* echoes with significances which give voice to the restlessness and tension embodied in the Christian message. It means not so much a single particle of speech, but the whole act of speech, or the thought behind the speech, and from there its meanings spill outwards into conversation, narrative, musing, meaning, reason, report, rumour, even pretence. John goes on to name this *logos* as a man who makes known his Father God: his name is Jesus Christ. So there we read a second Greek word: Christ. To the very ordinary Jewish name of this man, Joshua/Yeshua (which has also ended up in a Greek form, 'Jesus'), his followers added '*Christos*' as a second name, after he had been executed on a cross.[2] It is notable that they felt it necessary to make this Greek translation of a Hebrew word, 'Messiah', or 'Anointed One', when they sought to describe the special, foreordained character of their Joshua. In life, the carpenter's son who died on the Cross would certainly have known Greek-speakers well, but they were the folks in the town down the road from his own Jewish hometown of Nazareth: other people, not his people. The name 'Christ' underlines the importance of Greek culture from the earliest days of Christianity, as Christians struggled to find out what their message was and how the message should be proclaimed. So the words '*logos*' and '*Christos*' tell us what a tangle of Greek and Jewish ideas and memories underlies the construction of Christianity.

How, then, did Greeks become so involved in the story of a man who was named after the Jewish folk hero Joshua and whom many saw as fulfilling a Jewish tradition of 'Anointed One', saviour of the Jewish people? We must follow the Greeks back to the stories they told of themselves, in lands which they had made home some two millennia before Joshua the Anointed One was born: mountainous peninsulas, inlets and islands which are the modern state of Greece, together with the coast now the western fringe of the Turkish Republic. Around 1400 BCE, one grouping among the Greek people was organized and wealthy enough to create a number of settlements with monumental palaces, fortifications and tombs. Chief among them was the hill-city of Mycenae in the near-island of southern Greece known as the Peloponnese, the centre of an empire which for a couple of centuries was capable of wielding power as far as the great island of Crete. Around 1200 BCE there was a sudden catastrophe, whose nature is still mysterious, which was contemporary with destruction and a collapse of culture which affected many other societies in the eastern Mediterranean; three centuries followed which have been termed a 'Dark Age'. Mycenae was overwhelmed and left in ruins, never again to be a major power. But its name was not forgotten. Mycenae was celebrated by a Greek poet who knew very little about it, but who managed to make its memory into the primary cultural experience first of Greeks, then of all peoples in the Mediterranean and then of the world which has taken on the culture of the West.[3]

To talk of this 'poet' is no more than convention. There are two epic poems, the *Iliad* and the *Odyssey*, traditionally ascribed to a single author called 'Homer'. It is certain that Homer lived long after Mycenae's fall around 1200 BCE – certainly not less than four hundred years later. Yet this writer or writers or band of professional singers who created the two surviving epics drew on centuries of songs and stories about that lost world. They deal with one military campaign, probably reflecting some real conflict of the remote past, in which Greeks besieged and destroyed the non-Greek city of Troy in Asia Minor (the modern Turkey). There follow the adventures of one Greek hero, Odysseus, in an agonizingly prolonged ten-year journey home. The two epics, which took shape in recitation some time in the eighth or seventh century BCE, became central to a Greek's sense of being Greek – which is strange, because the Trojan enemies are depicted as no different in their culture from the Greeks besieging them. In Asia Minor, Greeks lived close to several other peoples like the Trojans, and although in

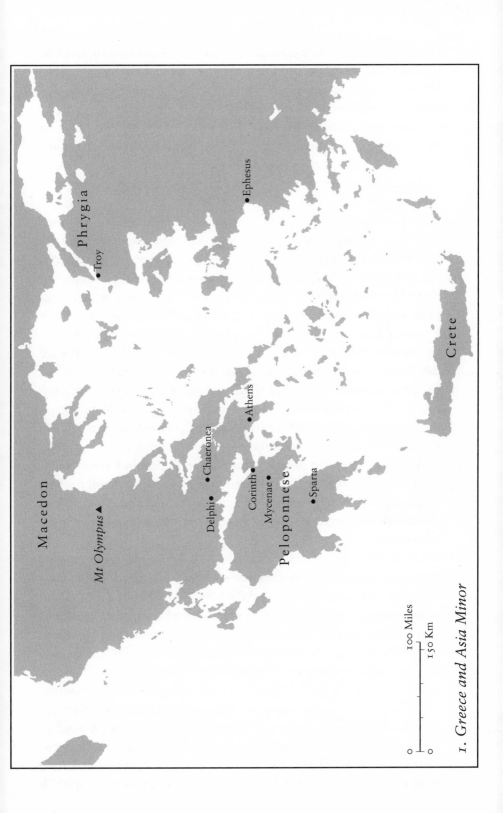

1. *Greece and Asia Minor*

formal terms they loftily regarded all non-Greeks as *barbaroi*, speakers of languages which sounded as meaningless as a baby's 'ba-ba' babble, they were in fact keenly interested in other sophisticated cultures, particularly in two great powers which affected them: the Persian (Iranian) Empire, which came to dominate their eastern flank and rule many of their cities, and south across the Mediterranean the Egyptian Empire, whose ancient civilization stimulated their jealous imitation and made them keen to annex and exploit its agreeably mysterious reserves of knowledge.

Despite their strong sense of common identity, summed up in their word *Hellas* ('Greekdom'), Greeks never achieved (and mostly did not seek to create) a single independent political structure on the gigantic scale of Persia or Egypt. They seem to have had a real preference for living in and therefore identifying with small city-states, which made perfect sense in their fragmented and mountainous heartland, but which they also replicated in flatlands in colonies around the Mediterranean. Greeks recognized each other as Greek by their language, which afforded them their common knowledge of Homer's epics, together with religious sites, temples and ceremonies which were seen as common property. Chief among the ceremonies were competitive games held to honour their chief god, Zeus, and his companions at Olympia below the mountain of Zeus's father, Kronos; there were lesser games elsewhere which likewise embodied the intense spirit of competition in Greek society. Further north was Delphi, shrine and oracle of the god Apollo, whose prophetess, dizzy and raving on volcanic fumes rising from a rock fissure, chanted riddles which any Greek might turn into guidance on worries private or public.

So, like Jews, Greeks made their religion central to their identity; and they were also the people of a book – more precisely, two books – their common cultural property. Like Jews, they borrowed a particular method of writing down their literature from the Phoenicians, a seafaring people with whom they had much commercial contact: an alphabetic script. Throughout the world, the earliest and some of the most long-lasting writing systems have been pictogrammic: so a tree could be represented by the picture of a tree. By contrast, alphabetic scripts abandon pictograms and represent particular sounds of speech with one constant symbol, and the sound symbols can be combined to build up particular words – so instead of hundreds of picture symbols, there can be a small, easily learned set of symbols: generally twenty-two basic symbols in both Greek and Hebrew, twenty-six in modern English. It was in the Greek alphabet that the earliest known Christian texts were written, and the overwhelming majority of Christians until the Roman Catholic world missions of the sixteenth century experienced their sacred scriptures in some alphabetic form. Indeed, the last book of the New Testament, Revelation, repeatedly uses a metaphor drawn from the alphabet to describe Jesus: he is Alpha and Omega, the first and the last letters of the Greek alphabet, the beginning and the end.[4]

But there the cultural similarities between Jews and Greeks end: their religious outlooks were significantly different. Like most ancient societies, Greeks inherited a collection of stories about a variety of gods which they welded into an untidy description of a divine family, headed by Zeus; the Homeric legends drew on this body of myth. The gods are constantly present in the *Iliad* and *Odyssey*, an intrusive and often disruptive force in human lives: often fickle, petty, partisan, passionate, competitive – in other words, rather like Greeks themselves. It was no accident that Greek art portrayed gods and humans in similar ways, as it moved beyond its imitation of Egyptian monumental sculpture of the human form. Without knowing something of the complex iconography of this art, one would be hard put to tell the beauty of the foppish would-be dictator Alcibiades from the beauty of the god Apollo, or distinguish the nobility of the Athenian politician Pericles from that of a bearded god. The portrayal of human beings tended away from the personal towards the abstract, which suggested that human beings could indeed embody abstract qualities like nobility, just as much as could the gods. Moreover, Greek art exhibits a fascination with the human form; it is the overwhelming subject of Greek sculpture, the form in which gods as well as humans are portrayed to the exclusion of any other representational possibility.[5] The fascination extended to a cult of the living and breathing body beautiful, at least in male form, which in turn led to an insistence on athletes performing in the nude in Greek competitive games; this peculiarity baffled and horrified most other cultures, and rather embarrassed the Romans, who later tried to make themselves as much as possible the heirs of Greek culture.

Greek gods are rather human; so may humans be rather like gods, and go on trying to be as like them as possible? The remarkable self-confidence of Greek culture, the creativity, resourcefulness and originality and the consequent achievements which have been borrowed by Christian culture, have much to do with this attitude to the gods embedded in the Homeric epics. It is very different from the way in which the Jews came to speak of the remote majesty of their one God, the all-powerful creator, who (at relentless length) angrily reminded the afflicted Job how little a lone created being like him understood divine purposes; who dismissed Moses's question 'What is your name?' with a terrifying cosmic growl out of a burning bush in the desert, 'I WILL BE WHO I WILL BE'.[6] The name of the God of Israel is No Name.

Greeks could not be accused of marginalizing religion, for Greek cities were not dominated visually by palaces, as they had been in Mycenaean culture; instead they focused themselves around temples. Such temples will be familiar from that iconic and exceptionally splendid example in Athens, the Parthenon of the goddess Pallas Athene, and the most superficial examination of their layout will reveal that however monumental Greek temples appear, their chief function was not to house a large worshipping congregation, but to house a particular god, like the shrine-churches dedicated to an individual holy figure which Christians built later. Temples were served by priests, who performed local rituals for a god or gods in approved customary fashion, but who were not normally seen as a caste apart from the rest of the population. They were doing a job on behalf of the community, rather like other officials of the city, who might collect taxes or regulate the market. So Greek religion was a set of stories belonging to the entire community, rather than a set of well-bounded statements about ultimate moral and philosophical values, and it was not policed by a self-perpetuating elite entrusted with any task of propagating or enforcing it.

Such a system is not hospitable to the idea of heresy, to which (as we will see) certain varieties of Christianity have consistently been attracted. It is true that Socrates, one of the greatest of Greek philosophers, was tried and executed in 399 BCE after accusations that his disbelief in his society's gods (and his rhetoric generally) corrupted young people, but Socrates lived in a time of huge political crisis and he could be seen as a threat to Athenians' hard-won democracy (see pp. 30–31). Generally Greeks' esteem for their gods did not place limits on their hunger to make sense of the world around them, and they could see that stories about the gods left unanswered many questions about being and reality. Maybe answers could be extracted by trying to make as tidy a system as possible out of the stories: the first surviving Greek literature in prose is a varied set of records of these traditional stories, 'mythographies'. The poet Hesiod, writing in the same era as Homer, created an epic, *Theogony*, which later generations regarded with gratitude as the most accessible effort at making sense of the tangle.

Within the common Greek culture, then, was an urge to understand

and create a systematic structure of sacred knowledge which ordered their everyday life. Greeks so esteemed Homer's two epics that they extended this quest to the Homeric stories. A volume of commentary was developed on what they were really about, under the narrative surface. Greek curiosity created the literary notion of allegory: a story in literature which must be read as conveying a deeper meaning or meanings than is at first apparent, with the task of a commentator to tease out such meanings. Much later, first Jews and then Christians treated their sacred writings in the same way. Greeks were convinced that the learning of a race as ancient as the Egyptians must conceal wisdom which ought to be shared more widely, and when they eventually encountered Jewish literature, they likewise found its antiquity impressive. But they were not afraid to turn from the past to search anew for wisdom for themselves. That search for wisdom they entrusted to people whom they defined as lovers of wisdom: philosophers.

Some concerns of philosophers were not new. Long before in Babylon and Egypt, let alone in cultures which have left no written records as far north as the isles of Shetland, people spent a good deal of time considering the skies above them; the movements of stars and planets had practical relevance to the passage of time in their farming and religious observances. Greek philosophy was far more all-encompassing, and its obsession with questioning, classifying and speculating has little parallel in the earlier cultures of which the Greeks had knowledge. The fact that Greeks adopted an alphabetic script has often been seen as one of the stimuli to their achievements in philosophy, since it is rather easier to convey abstract ideas in the easily learned handful of symbols in alphabets than in the multiple pictorial symbols of pictogrammic script. But that hardly explains why Phoenicians or Jews were not stimulated by their own alphabetic writing systems to produce anything like the intellectual adventures of the Greeks.

A better answer must lie in the peculiar history of the Greeks which emerged from their early geography: that proliferation of tiny independent communities eventually scattered from Spain to Asia Minor. Each of these was a *polis* – another of those Greek words like *logos* which at first sight seems easy to translate into English, in this case as 'city'. Even if the meaning of the word is given one more layer of sophistication as 'city-state', the translation is inadequate to convey the resonance of *polis*, with the same sort of difficulty one might find in speaking of the resonance of the English word 'home'. *Polis* was more than the cluster of houses around a temple which was its visible embodiment and gave it its name. The *polis* included the surrounding mountains, fields, woods, shrines, as far as its frontiers; it was the collective mind of the community who made it up, and whose daily interactions and efforts at making decisions came to constitute 'politics'. We will need to consider the politics of the *polis* at some length to understand just why the Greeks made their remarkable contribution to shaping the West and the versions of Christianity which it created.

In the end, the mega-states of Macedonia and then Rome swallowed up the freedom of these *poleis*. Nevertheless, more than a millennium after Homer's time, the life of the Greek *polis* still represented an ideal even for those Mediterranean societies which had turned to Christianity. In the words of the great twentieth-century philosopher-historian R. G. Collingwood: 'Deep in the mind of every Roman, as in the mind of every Greek, was the unquestioned conviction which Aristotle put into words: that what raised man above the level of barbarism . . . to live well instead of merely living, was his membership of an actual, physical city.'[7] When Christians first described their own collective identity, with its customs, structures and officer-bearers, they used the Greek word *ekklēsia*, which has passed hardly modified into Latin and its successor languages. Greek-speaking Jews before the Christians had used the same word to speak of Israel. *Ekklēsia* is already common in the Greek New Testament: there it means 'Church', but it is borrowed from Greek political vocabulary, where it signified the assembly of citizens of the *polis* who met to make decisions.

So the *ekklēsia* represents the *polis*, a local identity within the greater whole of Christianity or Christendom, just as the Greek *polis* represented the local identity of the greater whole *Hellas*, 'Greekdom'. Yet the Christian *ekklēsia* has become more complicated, because the word can also describe the universal Church, the equivalent of *Hellas*, as well as the local – not to mention the fragments of universal Christianity with particular identities which call themselves 'Church', and even the buildings which house all these different entities. There is a further interesting dimension of the word. If the *ekklēsia* is the embodiment of the city or *polis* of God, lurking in the word *ekklēsia* is the idea that the faithful have a collective responsibility for decisions about the future of the *polis*, just as the people of a *polis* did in ancient Greece. This creates a tension with another borrowing from Greek which has passed into several northern European languages, and which appears in English as the word 'church' or in Scots English as 'kirk'. This started life as an adjective which emerged in late Greek, *kuriakē*, 'belonging to the Lord', and because of that, it emphasizes the authority of the master, rather than the decision of those assembled. The tension between these perspectives has run through the history of *ecclēsia*/kirk, and is with Christians still.

The original Greek association of *polis* and *ekklēsia* emerged out of political and social turmoil in an age which, thanks to modern historians' urge to label periods of time, has been given the collective description 'Archaic Greece' (roughly 800–500 BCE).[8] Most Archaic city-states were initially ruled by groups of noblemen, but during those three centuries, many governing elites faced challenges from those who saw them as misgoverning. The common Greek institution of slavery for non-paid debt created a steadily more divided society and undermined the ability of cities to defend themselves with armies of free inhabitants. Population rise strained resources. That was one reason why particular cities sent off citizens to found replica cities, colonies, in new areas of the Mediterranean – Massalia or Massilia (Marseilles) in the south of France, for instance, was one of the earliest of those colonies, founded from the Ionian city of Phocaea far away on the west coast of Asia Minor. Even that safety valve did not end trouble, which at various stages in different places resulted in the overthrow of existing regimes. In the interests of avoiding chaos and restoring stability, power generally came into the hands of a single individual, styled a *tyrannos*. Originally without the present sinister connotation of 'tyrant', this term simply described a ruler who could not appeal to any traditional legitimacy. The first recorded seizure of power by a *tyrannos* took place in Corinth in the 650s BCE.

Such political coups were hardly unprecedented in human history, but most ancient cultures disguised them with some sort of appeal to a higher divine approval: witness the way in which the books of Samuel in the Hebrew scriptures present the usurper David's takeover from the dynasty of Saul as God's deliberate abandonment of the old king for his disobedience.[9] Perhaps there were simply too many sudden political disruptions in the various city-states of Archaic Greece to make divine involvement plausible; so if a *tyrannos* was to exercise authority without any traditional or religious justification, there would have to be some other basis for government. The solution which the Greeks adopted held great significance for the future. The inhabitants of the *polis* who had acquiesced in the upheaval would decide on laws with which their community would be governed. This was a radically new way of conceiving power. Even where a Greek *polis* gave credit to some particular named person as its lawgiver, whether legendary or real – the name is Solon in Athens, and Lycurgus in Sparta – this still meant that a human being had made decisions about structuring justice and government without any especial involvement of the gods. The great lawmakers of other cultures had claimed divine authority for their law codes, like King Hammurabi in Babylon of the eighteenth century BCE, or Moses, whom the Jews portrayed as bringing God's detailed instructions down from a mountain with the full panoply of thunder, fire and cloud, his face unnaturally transfigured with light.[10] The self-confidence which is such a recurrent feature of Greek culture meant that Greeks could make laws without such theatrics. The *tyrannos* was (or should be) subject to those laws like everyone else.[11]

It is unsurprising that not all *tyrannoi* consistently agreed with this proposition, and their regimes did not generally last long before they were removed. That led to the culminating step in the evolution of the independent Greek *polis*: cities moved to a form of government in which every male citizen over the age of thirty meeting in the *ekklēsia* had a voice in policymaking (once more, like 'politics', the word 'policy' is a derivative of *polis*). The system, new in the recorded history of Asian, African or European civilization, was called democracy: rule by ordinary people (or rule by the mob, if one was feeling sour about the idea). A lead was taken by Athens, one of the most centrally positioned, dramatically sited and generally flamboyant of Greek cities, where, in 510 BCE, two years of civil war after the overthrow of a *tyrannos* culminated in the establishment of a democracy. This is often seen as one of the key symbolic dates in the transition from the Archaic to the 'Classical' period in Greek history, during which Greek democracy enjoyed two centuries of extraordinary achievement which has remained central to the Mediterranean and then the Western cultural experience.[12] It was the democratic institutions of Athens which caught the imagination of subsequent generations, and turned the city into something of a theme park of the Greek Way of Life, long after the comparatively brief period during which Athenian democracy had actually functioned. The general Classical fascination with Athens may be one reason why virtually no Greek poetry which is not Athenian has survived from an extraordinarily creative period in the sixth and fifth centuries BCE.[13]

Democracies such as that of Athens notoriously had their limits. Many of the great and wealthy families in city-states had survived ejection from power and continued to be a significant force in public affairs, as great families always will. They were particularly dominant in office-holding in Athens, where their continuing aristocratic ethos meant that snobbery and respect for elite lifestyles always competed with the democratic impulse. Democracy gave no role to half the population: women, who in a culture which took far more interest in the emotional and intellectual relationships formed between males, were generally secluded in the domestic sphere – in the funeral oration for the great Athenian Pericles, it was said that the greatest Athenian woman was she who was spoken about least by men, whether in praise or criticism.[14] Given that life expectancy was low, a threshold of thirty years of age for participation also excluded a majority of males. Democratic participation excluded all Greeks who were not born citizens of the *polis* in which they now lived, and participation also relied on the body of enfranchised citizens having enough leisure time to listen to debates on policy and then take a part in decision-making. This required a large body of slaves to do a great deal of work for citizens, and naturally slaves had no useful opinions. Take all these factors together and perhaps only around a fifth of the adult inhabitants of proudly democratic Classical Athens could actually be described as active citizens: those who were considered best to represent the community of the *polis*. Nevertheless, with all these caveats, large numbers of ordinary people who were not privileged by birth or divine favour were indeed charged with responsibility for their own future and the future of their community.

This was a frightening responsibility. Could frail human beings bear the emotional load? This is surely one of the chief reasons why the Greeks searched for meaning in cosmos and society with an intensity unparalleled elsewhere in Mediterranean civilization, and why they were more inclined than others to detach that search from structures of traditional religion. Philosophers involved themselves intimately in debate about what society should be like and how it should govern itself. Some did this through deliberately aggressive and paradoxical distancing from everyday life, brutally to present reality to their fellow citizens, particularly the complacently wealthy. So Diogenes of Sinope, whom the philosopher Plato nicknamed 'Socrates gone mad', became a wandering beggar and, when infesting Athens with his presence, he slept in a large wine jar (he was sufficiently appreciated by the citizenry that when a teenage vandal broke his jar the *ekklēsia* is said to have bought him a replacement and to have had the boy flogged). His lifestyle was an enacted reminder that although human beings were rational animals, they were still animals – he was nicknamed 'the dog', from which his admirers and imitators took the name Cynics ('those like dogs').

Christianity has at various stages produced saints in his mould, holy fools and others openly contemptuous of worldly wealth, although they have rarely shared Diogenes's propensity for masturbation in public as a symbol of detachment from conventional values.[15]

At the other extreme, there were philosophers who plunged into practical politics. Followers of the mystical mathematician Pythagoras seized power in a number of Greek cities in south Italy during the late sixth and the fifth centuries BCE, but they generally do not seem to have made a great success of their activism, which included an alarming tendency to live by intricate binding rules – this, not surprisingly, caused violent resentment among fellow citizens who did not share their obsessions.[16] Most philosophers would not take such risks, and saw their calling as to offer comment on and analysis of the society around them, as part of a wider exploration of humanity and its environment. Much of their comment was openly critical. Patterns were provided by three philosophers who taught in Athens: Socrates (c. 469–399 BCE), Plato (428/7–348/7 BCE) and Aristotle (384–322 BCE). This trio are foundational to the Western philosophical tradition, first Greek, then Roman. Christians inherited Graeco-Roman culture and thought, and when they have talked about questions of faith or morals or have tried to make sense of their sacred books, it has taken an extraordinary effort of will and original imagination to avoid doing so in ways already created by the Greeks. It was particularly difficult in the early centuries, when Christianity was so much dominated by the Classical thought-world around it, at the very time when it was having to do a great deal of hard thinking as to what it actually believed.

Socrates wrote nothing himself and we hear his voice mediated through writings of his pupil and admirer Plato, mostly in dialogue form. While he was teaching in Athens, his was an insistently and infuriatingly questioning voice, embodying the conviction that questions can never cease to be asked if human beings are to battle with any success against the constant affliction of public and private problems. At Socrates's trial, Plato portrays the philosopher as insisting in his speech of defence that 'the unexamined life is not worth living'.[17] It was Socrates's questioning of the half-century-old Athenian democracy which was a major cause of his trial and execution; his trial is the central event around which Plato's dialogues are focused, making it as much a trial of Athenian society and thought as it was of Socrates. The grotesque absurdity of killing a man who was arguably Athens's greatest citizen on charges of blasphemy and immorality impelled Plato to see a discussion of politics as one facet of discussions of justice, the nature of morality and divine purpose – in fact to see the two discussions as interchangeable. Western religion and philosophy have remained in the shadow of those exchanges: Western culture has borrowed the insistence of Socrates that priority should be given over received wisdom to logical argument and rational procession of thought, and the Western version of the Christian tradition is especially prone to this Socratic principle. Yet he was also to find his most mischievous disciple in a nineteenth-century Danish Lutheran who overturned even the systematic pursuit of rationality: Søren Kierkegaard (see pp. 833–5).

Plato's influence on Christianity was equally profound in two other directions. First, his view of reality and authenticity propelled one basic impulse in Christianity, to look beyond the immediate and everyday to the universal or ultimate. In his dialogue *The Republic*, he represents Socrates as telling a story which in more than one sense illuminates the Platonic view of the human condition. Prisoners are chained in a cave, facing a wall; their bonds are fixed in such a way that the wall is all they can see. Behind them a great fire roars, but between them and the fire is a walkway, on which people parade a series of objects, such as carved images of animals or humans, whose shadows fall on the wall under the prisoners' gaze. The bearers pronounce the names of the objects as they pass and the echoes of the names bounce off the wall. All the prisoners can experience, therefore, are shadows and echoes. That is what they understand to be reality. If any of them are released, the brightness of the sun's real light is blinding, and makes their sight of any of the real objects less convincing than the shadows which they have come to know so well, and the echoing names which they have heard.[18] Human life is an imprisonment in the cave. The particular phenomena we perceive in our lives are shadows of their ideal 'Forms', which represent truer and higher versions of reality than the ones which we can readily know. We should not be content with these shadows. An individual human soul should do its best to find its way back to the Forms which lie behind the world of our clouded senses, because there we may find *aretē* – excellence or virtue. The path is through the intellect. 'Excellence [*aretē*] of soul' is our chief purpose or direction, because beyond even the Forms is the Supreme Soul, who is God and who is ultimate *aretē*.

Plato's second major contribution to Christian discussion is his conception of what God's nature encompasses: oneness and goodness. Plato took his cue from Socrates's radical rethinking on the traditional Greek range of gods (the 'pantheon'), looked beyond it and made ethics central to his discussion of divinity. The pantheon portrayed in both Greek myth and the Homeric epics can hardly be said to exemplify virtue: the origins of the gods in particular make up an extraordinary catalogue of horrors and violence. Hesiod's *Theogony* named the first divinity as Chaos; among the divinities who emerged from him, representing the cosmos spawned out of chaos, was Gaia, the Earth. Gaia's son Ouranos/ Uranus (the Sky) incestuously mated with his mother and had twelve children, whom he forced back into Gaia's womb; Gaia's youngest son, Kronos/Cronus, castrated his father, Ouranos, before in turn committing incest with his sister and attempting to murder all their children. How unlike the home life of the Christian Trinity. Matters only marginally improved in the generation of Zeus. If one were compiling a school report on the behaviour of the Olympian gods, it would have to include comments on their lack of moral responsibility, consistent pity or compassion.

Greeks generally looked on this disconcerting lack of moral predictability among their divinities with cheerful resignation and did their best to secure the best bargain available from them by due ceremonial observances at home or in temples or shrines. Now Plato presented a very different picture of the ultimate God. His perspective looking beyond the traditional pantheon has a further dimension, which does actually in effect limit the way in which he envisaged the goodness of God. Although Plato's supreme God is unlike the fickle, jealous, quarrelsome gods of the Greek pantheon, his God is distanced from compassion for human tragedy, because compassion is a passion or emotion. For Plato, the character of true deity is not merely goodness, but also oneness. Although Plato nowhere explicitly draws the conclusion from that oneness, it points to the proposition that God also represents perfection. Being perfect, the supreme God is also without passions, since passions involve change from one mood to another, and it is in the nature of perfection that it cannot change. This passionless perfection contrasts with the passion, compassion and constant intervention of Israel's God, despite the fact that both the Platonic and the Hebrew views of God stress transcendence. There is a difficulty in envisaging how Plato's God could create the sort of changeable, imperfect, messy world in which we live – indeed, have any meaningful contact with it. Even the created wholeness of the Forms would most appropriately have been created by one other than the God who is the Supreme Soul: perhaps an image of the Supreme Soul, an image which Plato describes in one of the most influential of his dialogues, *Timaeus*, as a craftsman or artificer (*demiourgos*, from which comes the English term 'demiurge').[19] Creation was likely to extend away from God in a hierarchy of emanations from the supreme reality of the divine.

Plato's discussion of God fed into the commonplaces of discussion of divinity in the ancient world, and that, as we will see, became a problem for Christians as they tried to talk about their faith. But equally influential was the work of Plato's pupil Aristotle. He was led in a very different direction in his quest for truth. While Plato had sought for reality in the ideals beyond the particular – feeling, for instance, that an ultimate Form of 'treeness' was more real than any individual tree – Aristotle sought for reality in individual and observable objects. He classified different sorts of tree. For him, the path to knowledge lay in searching out as much information and opinion as possible about the objects and forms which exist and can be described in the world of human senses. The difference can be seen by comparing the ways in which the two philosophers approached that perennial Greek preoccupation, government. Plato in his *Republic* presents an elite-dominated, authoritarian society. Although apparently an ideal, it directly confronts, indeed subverts, the Athenian democracy which Plato had observed descending, through its petty politicking and distorted judgement, into authorizing the execution of Socrates. No one sane has sought to replicate Plato's picture of government in the real world – although some insane societies have warmed to his recommendation that the activities of musicians should be curbed and all poets expelled. One hopes that Plato did not intend it to be more than a mirror for societies, including his own, to contemplate.[20] By contrast, Aristotle organized a research team to gather data on as many different existing governments as possible from which to produce potted descriptions of them. Only one remains, rediscovered in the nineteenth century, and, as luck would have it, it is the description of the constitution of Athens.[21]

This was characteristic of Aristotle's approach. He applied the same technique to all branches of knowledge, from subjects like biology and physics to theories of literature and rhetoric (the art of public speaking and debate). Equally, he discussed abstract matters such as logic, meaning and causation in a series of texts which, being placed in his collected works after his treatise on physics, were given the functional label *meta ta physica*, 'After *The Physics*'. And so the name of metaphysics, the study of the nature of reality, was born in an accident. Aristotle's work therefore resembles a gigantic filing system, and what survives to us from it is not in the polished form of dialogues, like most of Plato's writings, but lecture notes taken down by his pupils and assistants. Those unnamed assistants, had they known it, were wielding an intoxicating power over the future, because for two thousand years after his death Aristotle would set the way in which Christians and Muslims alike shaped their thoughts about the best way to organize and think about the physical world, about the arts and the pursuit of virtue.

The Christian Church began by being suspicious about Aristotle, preferring the otherworldliness of Plato's thought, but there was no other scheme for understanding the organization of the world as remotely comprehensive as his. When Christians were faced with making theological comments on natural subjects like biology or the animal kingdom, they turned to Aristotle, just as Christian theologians today may turn to modern science to inform themselves about matters in which they are not technically expert. The result was, for instance, that two millennia after the death of this non-Christian philosopher two monks in a monastery somewhere in northern Europe might consider an argument settled if one of them could assert, 'Well, Aristotle says . . .' Right down to the seventeenth century, Christian debate about faith and the world involved a debate between two Greek ghosts, Plato and Aristotle, who had never heard the name of Jesus Christ. Aristotle fuelled the great renewal of Christian scholarship in the Western Church in the twelfth and thirteenth centuries (see pp. 398–9), and even in the last twenty years the leaders of the Catholic Church in Rome have reaffirmed the synthesis of Christianity and Aristotelian thought which Thomas Aquinas devised at that time.

The Greek experiment with direct democracy had other creative results. One was the creation of drama, the foundation of the Western tradition of theatre, which, like the various athletic competitions of Greek culture such as the Olympic Games (see p. 22), grew out of public religious ceremonies. An audience at an open-air Greek theatre, sitting massed in the sun, characteristically overlooking a panoramic landscape stretching behind the stage, was given the chance to ponder extreme versions of the sort of situations on which they might find themselves voting in the assembly of the *polis*. Because of its immediacy theatre, even more than philosophy, confronts and crystallizes the most profound dilemmas in human life, and it may provide perverse comfort in revealing that dilemmas have no solutions, as human misery is played out against the indifference of the cosmos, in the same way that the landscape stretches behind the Greek theatre stage and dwarfs it. From Athens in particular, a series of writers in an astonishingly brief period of little more than a century, from the early fifth to the beginning of the fourth centuries BCE, created the classic works of this theatrical tradition. Aeschylus, Sophocles and Euripides explored the depths of human tragedy and folly, in ways which have never been surpassed. In the second half of the same period, Aristophanes wrote comedies which often poked outrageous fun at the very Athenian audiences who watched and enjoyed them. They knew that they had to laugh at themselves if they were to remain sane – and indeed, as we will see, the effort of sanity and balance proved too much even for the Athenians.

Another way in which Greeks could explore means of understanding and controlling their world was to build up experience by studying the past. Out of their urge to comprehend came a tradition of historical writing which has become particularly associated with the culture of the Christian West; this book stands in that tradition, and it is worth the reader seeing how historical writing originated. The impulse seems to have started in the Greek cities of the coast of Asia Minor, which were forced to take a particular interest in the affairs of 'barbarians' because of the inescapable fact that they were ruled by the Persian Empire. They began gathering data about their neighbours, describing their differences, sometimes even with sympathy or admiration. A crucial stage came when the Persian Empire started coming into conflict with the city-states of mainland Greece, which it saw as encouraging its own Greek subjects to rebel. Full-scale war broke out and lasted over a half-century from 499 BCE. It ended in the defeat of Persia, one of the most powerful polities that the world had so far seen, by a coalition of Greek city-states led by Athens. Greek democracy and the culture that went with it were saved.

One Greek from Asia Minor, Herodotos of Halikarnassos, decided to write a work which would climax in an account of these Persian Wars, the greatest known clash between Greek and non-Greek, but it would also encompass all that he could find out about other peoples and places, which he would try to visit in person (often he succeeded). He called this enterprise a *historia*: an inquiry, in which any form of knowledge he could gather might contribute towards the great whole. Hesiod and the 'mythographers' had developed the method to understand the stories of the gods, but we know of no one before Herodotos who had tried to gather memories and documents together on such a scale to tell a connected story about the past. It was a very brave undertaking: the Persian Wars had finished around the time of his birth and had been over for more than a generation by the time he was writing. We owe Herodotos so much that, for all his unreliability and untidiness, it would be unjust to pick up the gibe made about him by some ancient authors who, following the lead of a prolonged and peevish attack on him by the later historian Plutarch, claimed that he was the Father of Lies rather than the Father of History.[22] Plutarch's anger with him stemmed from the fact that Herodotos was too entranced by the glorious mess of history to turn it into edifying and improving stories for the young. Modern historians should sympathize with Herodotos's engaging unwillingness to ignore the inconvenient, or to mistake moralizing for morality.

Herodotos's work in history was taken further by Thucydides, a leading Athenian whose career in his city's affairs was ruined by a further round of warfare during the later fifth century BCE, this time among the Greeks themselves. This 'Peloponnesian War' was as great a disaster for Athenian confidence and self-respect as the Persian Wars had been a triumph, and it ultimately destroyed their power. The defeat of Persia left Athens at the head of a victorious group of city-states, the Delian League. The Athenians yielded to the temptation of using their leading role to turn the League into an empire for themselves. Their sudden access of wealth and power stimulated and funded some of their most striking achievements in art, but it also attracted jealousy and resentment, especially from the rival *polis* of Sparta. Sparta was very different from Athens: a small minority of its people ruled a conquered and cowed population through military force and deliberately sustained terror, keeping themselves in permanent armed readiness by means of a tradition of brutal training for their male elite.[23] When Plato, an Athenian alienated from his own democratic culture, portrayed his authoritarian and supposedly 'beautiful city' in *The Republic*, his Athenian readers would have recognized his mixture of fascination with and repulsion from Sparta, that other version of Greek identity.

The Athenians' increasingly selfish and greedy behaviour in the Delian League encouraged Sparta to intervene against them, paradoxically as the defender of Greek liberties. After a bitter twenty-seven years of war (431–404 BCE), Sparta and its allies left Athenian power shattered. One victim of events was Thucydides, a general forced into exile after being involved in defeat – according to his own account, a disgrace which he did not deserve. He used his two decades of enforced leisure to ponder why such a catastrophe had befallen him and his fellow Athenians. He decided to write an account of what had happened, spending his time and wealth on travelling to find out as much as possible about the detailed circumstances of the prolonged tragedy. His startlingly original idea was to look for deep underlying causes for the catastrophe. They had emerged not from the whims and fancies of a single individual, as Herodotos might have told the story, or from a clash in lovers' passion and divine tantrums, as Homer had portrayed the cause of the Trojan War, but from the collective corruption of an entire society. The Athenians had been brought low by their pride and decline in political morality. Like the view of humanity presented in the cynical governmental structures of Plato's *Republic*, this was a bleak assessment of the true potential of human nature and the flaws of Athenian democracy, born of bitter experience; and although it was an emphatically moral view of history, it was not one which especially involved divine intervention – if at all.[24]

Thucydides had grasped that vital historical insight that groups of people behave differently and have different motivations from individual human beings, and that they often behave far more discreditably than individuals. He saw his task as the production of a history which was a work of art, as cool, balanced and perfectly structured as a Greek temple. Such harmony might clash with the need to depict accurately the messiness and randomness of the ways in which chance interacts with human motivation and collective folly. There is a struggle in the knotty prose of Thucydides between the reporting of events and the deployment of rhetoric, both in his own meditations and in the fictional speeches he allotted to various participants in events, but that struggle is apparent in any work of history which seeks to move on beyond chronology towards analysis. Perhaps it is not surprising that in such a novel undertaking his history has come down to us unfinished, yet he remains the greatest historian that the ancient world produced and an example to all those who have written history since his time.

HELLENISTIC GREECE

If Thucydides had known the fate of his society half a century after his death, he might well have observed that fourth-century Greeks, still rent by wars between states and quarrels within cities, deserved the Macedonians. This non-Greek kingdom lay to the north of mainland Greece; King Philip II of Macedon launched a war of conquest southwards and in 338 BCE sealed his control of the Greek peninsula in a close-run but decisive victory over combined Greek forces at Chaeronea. Philip's murder by a bodyguard drawn into the tangle of his homosexual love life resulted in the succession of the King's twenty-year-old son as Alexander III. Alexander took the expansionist traditions of the Macedonian royal house to extraordinary lengths, earning him posterity's nickname of 'the Great': his eastward conquests overwhelmed both the Persian Empire and Egypt and took him and his armies as far as northern India, all before his death aged only thirty-two. Alexander brought destruction and misery to great swathes of the Balkans, Egypt and Asia; yet he achieved much more of lasting significance than most of the sadistic megalomaniacs whose sudden conquests over the next sixteen hundred years down to the time of Timur (see pp. 273–5) swept through the same lands. He and his father had immersed themselves in Greek modes of life and social or intellectual assumptions, far beyond their ready adoption of same-sex love. Alexander transformed modes of thought and culture for the Near East and for Egypt in ways which were still the norms for that world in the time of Jesus Christ. His imperial style much impressed those later imperial conquerors, the Romans, who treated his cultural legacy with reverence and created an enduring empire in his mould.[25]

It was hardly surprising that Alexander's overextended empire could not survive as a political unit when he died. His Greek and Macedonian generals manoeuvred and fought each other until they had divided the empire up and established themselves as monarchs rather like the rulers whom Alexander had defeated, semi-divine potentates with armies and tax-collecting bureaucracies. There was even a Macedonian soldier, Ptolemy *Sōtēr* ('the Saviour'), as the new Pharaoh of Egypt, founder of the latest in the long series of Pharaonic dynasties, whose last descendant the Romans eventually swept away. These semi-Greek inheritors of ancient non-Greek tradition followed Alexander in founding new cities or refounding old ones, complete with temples in Greek style and theatres where Greek drama was performed. Little local imitations of the Classical Greek *polis* sprouted and survived for centuries as far away as the Himalayas in the east. So the Afghan city of Kandahar is called by a disguised version of the name which Alexander and his admirers gave to a scatter of cities across his conquests: Alexandria. The greatest Alexandria of all arose in the Nile Delta in Egypt, the port-city which Alexander himself had founded from a tiny village and named. Thanks to Ptolemy, it was equipped with a famous academy of higher learning – the ancient equivalent of the medieval and modern university – and the most splendid library in the ancient world, a symbol of how Greek learning and curiosity had taken new roots in an alien setting. To remain

Greek in the setting of an ancient culture before whose antiquity and sophistication even Greek self-confidence faltered was to indulge in an almost adolescent act of self-assertion. It was in this Alexandria that many of the most self-conscious decisions were made about what was important among the works of Greek literature and what was not, forming a literary 'canon', a repertoire of acceptable classics which Christianity inherited and which have shaped our own view of what Greek civilization was like.[26]

So Alexandria became one of the most important cultural exchange points in the Mediterranean, and it was a major force in changing the nature of what it was to be Greek. Nineteenth-century scholars started calling this world created in the wake of Alexander's conflicts 'Hellenistic', to show how Greek it was, but also in order to differentiate it from the Greece which had gone before it.[27] Classical Greece, however briefly, had fostered democracy, while here were states which were undisguised dictatorships. Their rulers took on divine trappings which Greeks had long ago rejected, but which Philip II had revived for himself; Alexander had turned this strategy into a major programme of identification with a variety of Greek and oriental divinities.[28] Even when the newly minted monarchs wore their Greek guises, they usurped forms of worship which the Greeks had reserved for the Olympian gods alone. Never again did the Greek *polis* enjoy the true independence which was its ideal. The new Hellenistic cities remained little elite colonies, rather as two millennia later British colonial officials created imitations of an English village from Surrey when they wanted somewhere to relax in the India of Queen-Empress Victoria.

These cities stood side by side with the more ancient cultures conquered by the Macedonian generals, and there were untidy accommodations between the different worlds: an unstable mixture of repulsion, incomprehension and mutual exploration and exploitation. A much enriched variety of encounters in religion and culture was paired with a steep decline in political choice for the inhabitants of these *poleis*. What independence of action they experienced was no more than administering themselves and organizing taxes for their royal masters. There was a degree of sham in this Greek culture, at least as compared with the great days of Classical Athens. It may be because of this that there was a gradual closing down on the exuberant creativity which had been so prominent in Classical Greece. A strain of pessimism began to run through Hellenistic culture, redolent of Plato's pessimism about everyday things, his sense of their unreality and worthlessness.[29]

If philosophers could no longer hope to alter the policies of cities by influencing the thought of the people in the marketplace, and monarchs seemed impervious to the instruction of the most cultivated tutors, philosophy might as well concentrate on the inward life of the individual which no mighty ruler might tamper with. It became concerned with the proper cultivation of the self. At the most extreme, some took up the label of 'Cynic', cherishing the memory of Diogenes of Sinope and his purposefully antisocial behaviour (which had included telling Alexander the Great to step sideways out of his sunlight); others admired a contemporary of Philip and Alexander, Pyrrhon of Elis, who advised that it was best to refrain from making any judgements at all. Another contemporary, Epicurus, saw the pursuit of happiness as life's ultimate goal: that Epicurean affirmation is echoed in the American Declaration of Independence, curiously omitting the original qualification that happiness consists in the attainment of inner tranquillity. Zeno, teaching in the *Stoa* ('Porch') in Athens, inspired 'Stoics' to strive to conquer their passions, and to make sure that the inevitable miseries of life did as little as possible to hurt them.

Against such an intellectual background, where the everyday world was of little account to the true idealist, curiosity expressed in practical creativity was no longer much valued. There was little follow-up to the remarkable advances seen in Classical Greece in the understanding of technology, medicine and geography. When the steam engine was invented in Alexandria about a hundred years after the birth of Jesus Christ, it remained a toy, and the ancient world failed to make the breakthrough in energy resources which occurred in England seventeen centuries later. Abundant slave labour, after all, blunted the need for any major advance in technology. Yet in the realm of ideas, philosophy and religious practice, Hellenistic civilization created a meeting place for Greek and oriental culture, which made it easy and natural for Jewish and then non-Jewish followers of Jesus Christ to take what they wanted from the ragbag of Greek thought which any moderately educated inhabitant of the Middle East would encounter in everyday conversation.

ROME AND THE COMING OF THE ROMAN EMPIRE

By the time Jesus Christ was born in Palestine, the Hellenistic world was being ruled by another wave of imperial conquerors, who had come from the west, but who did little to challenge the cultural superiority of the society which they had found – quite the reverse. Their rule, unlike Alexander's, lasted for centuries, and the memory of it has haunted Christianity ever since. Rome was a city whose sense of destiny was all the greater because no one could have predicted the effect of such an insignificant place on the wider world. Strabo, the Greek historian and geographer, who died just before Jesus embarked on his public ministry, shrewdly observed that Rome's sheer lack of resources made its people acutely aware that their only assets were their energies in war and their determination to survive; the city had few natural endowments apart from timber and river transport to recommend it and, sited in the centre of the Italian peninsula, it was not even on any international trade route. It lacked any strong natural defences and, as it grew, its local agriculture would have been quite inadequate to support its population had it not acquired new territory.[30]

It was around the mid-eighth century BCE that Rome became a walled city with a king, rather like a *polis* in archaic Greece.[31] The monarchy was overthrown in 509 BCE and thereafter the Romans had such a pathological fear of the idea of kingship that no one bore the title 'King of the Romans' again until a Christian ruler from what is now Germany reinvented it a millennium and a half later, far from Rome and therefore deaf to the ancient taboo. There followed a generation of conflict between an aristocracy (the patricians) and the people (plebeians), just as in Greece. However, the result of this war was opposite to the outcome in Greek city-states like Athens or Corinth: the aristocrats won and the constitution of the Republic (*res publica*) which they developed influenced Roman forms of government down to the end of the empire. The plebeians lost whatever power they had possessed under the monarchy; there were still popular assemblies, but their role was without substance. Real power lay with two consuls, officers chosen annually from among the patricians, and with the Senate, an assembly of patricians; even here, junior senators had little say in the running of affairs. Ordinary people had influence on policy only through the popularly elected tribunes, who were honoured and sacrosanct during their year of office. Tribunes looked after the legal rights of the people, and even in the later Republic, when popular rights had dwindled still further, they still vetoed legislation proposed by the Senate.

Otherwise, the Roman Republic starkly contrasted with the development of democracy in the Athenian mould. Its unequal balance appealed greatly to aristocrats in Christian societies, once Christian societies came into existence, and we will meet several such 'Republics' (or, in an alternative English translation, 'Commonwealths') as alternatives to monarchy, in both Latin and Orthodox Christendom: Venice, Novgorod, Poland-Lithuania, the seventeenth-century England of Oliver Cromwell. The Roman Republic's difference from developed Greek city-states probably arose because of Rome's continual yearning to expand: a state more or less permanently at war either to maintain or to expand its frontiers could not afford the luxury of real democracy. Why was Rome's expansion so remarkably successful? Plenty of other states produced dramatic expansion, but survived for no more than a few generations or a couple of centuries at most. The western part of the Roman state survived for twelve hundred years, and in its eastern form the Roman Empire had a further thousand years of life after that. The answer probably lies in another contrast with Greece: the Romans had very little sense of racial exclusiveness. They gave away Roman citizenship to deserving foreigners – by deserving, they would mean those who had something to offer them in return, if only grateful collaboration. Occasionally whole areas would be granted citizenship. It was even possible for slaves to make the leap from being non-persons to being citizens, simply by a formal ceremony before a magistrate, or by provision in their owners' wills.[32]

Where this highly original view of citizenship came from is not clear; it must have evolved during the struggle for power between the patricians and the plebeians after the fall of the kings. In any case, the effect was to give an ever-widening circle of people a vested interest in the survival of Rome. That became clear in one dramatic case in the first century of the Common Era, when a Jewish tent-maker called Paul, from Tarsus, far away from Rome in Asia Minor, could proudly say that he was a Roman citizen, knowing that this status protected him against the local powers threatening him. It might have been his pride in this status of universal citizen which first suggested to Paul that the Jewish prophet who had seized his allegiance in a vision had a message for all people and not just the Jews.

The story of the Roman Republic is one of steady expansion throughout the Mediterranean. Rome must have had contact with Greeks from
its earliest days, but it started casting interested and acquisitive eyes on
the Greek mainland during the second century BCE. Rome's eventual
conquest of Greece and the Near East, still ruled by Seleucid descendants
of one of Alexander the Great's generals, was not planned: initially
friendly relations gradually deteriorated until the Republic lurched into
war with the Seleucid king Antiochos III from 192 to 188 BCE. As a
result Rome became the master of Greece and soon the Romans extended
their encirclement of the Mediterranean basin with their conquest of the
Ptolemaic monarchy of Egypt. The paradoxical cliché (no less true for
being so) about the consequence of this advance was suavely expressed
in Latin by the Emperor Augustus's admirer the Roman poet Horace:
'Greece, the captive, made her savage victor captive, and brought the arts
into rustic Latium.'[33] The relationship was always edgy, its awkwardness
symbolized by newly imperial Rome's adoption of a convenient fiction
that it had been founded by descendants of Aeneas, a refugee from Troy,
that archetypal foe of the Greeks in the Homeric epics. So through the
Romans' triumph in the East, Troy had finally triumphed over the
Greeks. Nevertheless the Romans became fascinated by Greek culture
and philosophy, which complemented their own highly developed skills
in military affairs, administration and matters of law. Greek became
just as much an international language as Latin for the Roman Empire.
Indeed, it was the *lingua franca* of the Middle East in the time of Jesus,
and it was the language which, in a rather vulgar marketplace form,
most Christians spoke in everyday life during the Church's first two
centuries of existence. By the sixth and seventh centuries, Greek was
ousting Latin as the official language of the surviving Eastern Roman
Empire, with the strong encouragement of the Christian Church. That
was an achievement unparalleled among languages of supposedly
defeated peoples, and a tribute to Hellenistic cultural vitality and adaptability long after the end of the various Hellenistic monarchies.

The Roman rule which Jesus experienced had undergone a great
transition, from Republic to imperial monarchy. It is surprising that the
Republic had postponed trouble for so long, but its structures proved
increasingly inadequate to cope with running its bloated empire. Rising
poverty, land hunger and an accumulated popular sense of injustice
came to a head around 100 BCE. Seventy years of misery and intermittent
civil war followed, ending with the defeat of one party boss by another
in 31 BCE, when Octavian won a naval victory at Actium against Mark

Antony and his ally the Ptolemaic queen of Egypt, Cleopatra. Octavian, adopted heir of the assassinated general and dictator Julius Caesar, achieved supreme power within the Roman state in a series of unscrupulous manoeuvres; he now had to hang on to his power and bring back peace to the shattered state. His lasting success came through meticulous adherence to all the old forms of the Republican constitution. The Senate and the two annual consuls continued to function for centuries – in fact a Roman Senate modelled on that of old Rome was still convening in Constantinople until the extinction of this New Rome in 1453.[34]

Behind the façade, Octavian carried out a revolution in government. Careful to avoid the hated title of King, he arranged that the Senate should give him the harmless-sounding title of First Citizen (*princeps*), while renaming himself Augustus, a symbol of a fresh start after the wretchedness of civil war. This is the name we find used for him in the Christian scriptures, the New Testament. To show his good intentions, Augustus also graciously accepted the office of tribune, the only officer in the old constitution who still commanded any affection among ordinary people, but he also assumed a traditional military title of honour which Julius Caesar had held, commander – *imperator*. Now he was the first of the Roman emperors, with a succession which lasted until 1453. This was the title that mattered: it signified his control of the army, which had traditionally bestowed the honour by acclamation, the real basis for imperial power from now on. The virtually perpetual warfare which so dominated the Roman past meant that the best justification for holding power in the Republic had been a track record of military success: hence the importance of the *imperator* title. Augustus made sure that his various publicists magnified a personal record as a military commander which was in reality decidedly unimpressive.[35]

Ordinary people raised few objections to Augustus's new role as *imperator*; they had little nostalgia for the Roman Republic, which had done nothing for seven decades but produce misery. As far as they were concerned, the old forms had been a sham anyway, so what difference would it make if Augustus elaborated the pretence through traditional titles and institutions? He paid particular attention to beautifying Rome. Central to various symbols of his achievements was a monumental 'Altar of Peace' (*Ara pacis*) voted him by a grateful (or at least politically realistic) Senate, which can still be admired in Rome, albeit now on a new site chosen by that latter-day failed Augustus, Benito Mussolini. The theme of peace was well chosen: most Romans were more interested in the fact that Augustus brought them peace and prosperity than they were in the Republic. For all that his own military prowess was dubious, Augustus and his successors tore down political frontiers all round the Mediterranean, and by controlling piracy, they made it comparatively safe and easy to travel from one end of the sea to the other. The first great exponent of a worldwide Christianity, the Apostle Paul, made the most of this, and so would the Christian faith as a whole. Without the general peace brought by Roman power, Christianity's westward spread would have been far more unlikely.

Yet the new order of politics was deeply depressing for the battered remains of the old Roman upper classes. They were no more taken in than anyone else by the Emperor's Republican window-dressing. They had done well out of the old Republic, and they had the sense to see that they could do well out of Augustus's regime, but they felt the humiliation deeply. Worst of all was the increasing reverence paid to Augustus. He did not actually claim divine honours, but he raised no objection to a system of honours in which offerings and sacrifices were made to his *genius*, the sacred force or guardian spirit which guided his personality and actions; Roman religion had already accommodated the habit of paying divine honours to such abstractions.[36] After Augustus's death, his successors in any case did declare him a god, and subsequent emperors saw the usefulness of this: the consecration of a predecessor as divine gave the living emperor prestige and legitimacy as well as glorifying the dead. Some of Augustus's successors explicitly assumed the role of a god in their lifetimes, and although this was politically risky at first, by the late third century it had become routine for emperors to claim divine status. Aristocratic Romans resented worshipping a man who had once been a colleague. A note of regret for the past, of merely grudging respect for the emperor, runs through much literature of the early empire, particularly in the surviving work of the first-century-CE historian Tacitus. It was no coincidence that, as in Hellenistic culture, Stoicism became one of the most influential philosophical stances in Rome. As long as the western part of the Roman Empire lasted, this regret never wholly left the old aristocracy – or the newly rich, who were anxious to take on aristocratic manners and attitudes.

So, over the next two centuries and more, divine honours were paid to a political leader whose position in the empire often came from a nakedly brutal seizure of power. This divine leader attached himself to the traditional gods of Rome (a pantheon rather like that of the Greeks). For many aristocratic Romans there would now be a complex of emotions associated with this amalgam of the political and the divine. Traditional duty demanded that they take their part in ancient cults: the worship of the pantheon and the priesthoods associated with it were inseparable from Roman identity, and pride in that identity might trump any quasi-Republican distaste for the honours accorded the emperor. Beyond the elite, there was no reason why enthusiasm for the old gods should die among the mass of ordinary Romans.[37] The imperial cult itself is testimony to the continuing appeal of the Roman pantheon, as otherwise it would not have been worth the investment. But the powerful were now well advised to keep an eye on how the emperor treated the many religions of his subjects. Whatever religion any individual emperor chose to favour would arouse the same set of associations between politics and the world beyond as the imperial cult encouraged by Augustus. There were plenty of unofficial competitors to the Roman pantheon, now that gods of all names and descriptions were able to take holiday trips along the sailing routes of a Mediterranean Sea united by Roman military might. Fertility cults in plenty arrived from the East, or more reflective religions like Iranian Mithraism, which described life as a great struggle between light and darkness, good and evil. Among the contenders for the notice of emperors and the Roman people, few people at first noticed or took seriously a newly emerged eccentric little Jewish sect on the fringes of the synagogues.

2

Israel

(*c.* 1000 BCE–100 CE)

A PEOPLE AND THEIR LAND

Along the south-eastern end of the Mediterranean coast lies a land difficult to name. In a very remote past it was called Canaan, but its later turbulent history left it with two names, Israel and Palestine, both of which are in use today, and both of which carry a heavy weight of emotion and contested identity. For one people, the Jews, the land is the Promised Land, granted to them in solemn pronouncements made by God to a succession of their forefathers; Jews are so called from what was originally the southern part of it, Judah or in Greek Judaea, which contrived to keep its independence from great empires longer than its rival northern kingdom, which had arrogated to itself the name of Israel. Christians have their own name for Palestine or Israel: they call it the Holy Land, because Jesus Christ was born and died here. He was executed outside the city of Jerusalem, once briefly the capital of a united kingdom of Israel. The name Jerusalem (often called Zion after its citadel) echoes through the sacred songs of the Jews, in accents of longing or joy, and Christians have sung the same texts.

Jerusalem has preserved its ancient and medieval walls intact, and even with the extensions to their area made in the Roman period, the old city usually surprises those who visit it for the first time by how small it is. Yet great human longing and passions are focused on that small compass. Medieval Christians made maps of the world with Jerusalem at the centre, and it is the setting for one of the most ancient and revered shrines of Islam, built on the site of the Temple which long before had been the centre of Jewish worship. So Jerusalem is resonant for all three linked monotheistic faiths, often with tragic consequences as they have fought each other to gain exclusive control over this small city.[1] Jerusalem is the contested heart of Palestine or Israel, whose modest overall extent, no more than 150 miles by 100 miles when undivided, belies its importance in the history of the world. Those without some idea of its geography and climate will not fully understand the sacred scriptures of Judaism and Christianity, whose horizons it sets.

For all its small area, its geography is complicated. The coast has few decent harbours, and other peoples than the Children of Israel tended to dominate the ones that did exist, so the Jews never became seafarers (and generally made rather negative references to the sea and its creatures in their sacred writings). Along the coast runs a wide fertile plain, backed to the east by a north–south spine of hills which in the north become mountains; Jerusalem sits in the middle of the hill country. Before the hills rise to mountains in the north, they curve to the coast, enclosing the Kishon river valley running down to the sea. Through this curve of hills there is only one major north–south pass, guarded by an ancient strongpoint now called Megiddo. This is the chief passage point for land traffic from Egypt north-east to all the lands of the Middle East and beyond, especially the successive civilizations which rose and fell around the great rivers of Iraq, the Tigris and Euphrates. It is not surprising, therefore, that the great powers of the ancient world repeatedly fought over such a strategic place. This geographical accident has given the Holy Land a major international importance, to its inhabitants' misfortune. Such was the accumulated weight of memory of those contests between great powers at Megiddo that it came to symbolize the place of ultimate battles: Christians will know it better from their own sacred writings as Armageddon, singled out by the writer of Revelation as the setting for the ultimate cosmic conflict between the forces of evil and divine goodness.[2]

On its long eastern flank, the spine of hills falls away into the spectacular valley of the Jordan river, which flows from north to south. That river boundary was rich with symbolism for the Jews, who remembered it as the barrier which they had to cross into their Promised Land. Towards the river's northern end is a major lake, the Sea of Galilee, around which lay the communities which were home to Jesus and his early disciples. At its southern end, the river does something very strange: it flows into and ends in the Dead Sea, a huge landlocked lake, much bigger than the Sea of Galilee. Here the heat of the arid, rocky valley is such that millions of gallons of Jordan water rushing into the lake evaporate, needing no other outlet and leaving the water so exceptionally salty as to bear up the most helpless of non-swimmers. Water is indeed a constant concern throughout Israel/Palestine: deserts stretch to the south into the Sinai peninsula and to the east beyond the

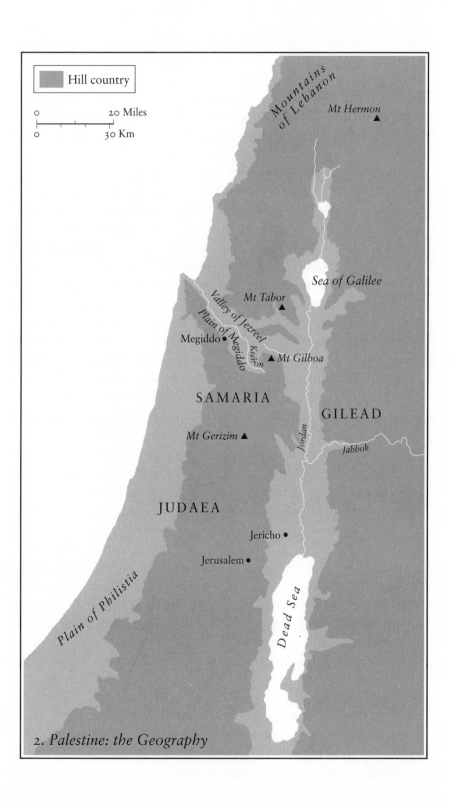

Hill country

o   20 Miles
o   30 Km

Mountains of Lebanon

▲ Mt Hermon

Sea of Galilee

Mt Tabor ▲

Valley of Jezreel

Plain of Megiddo

Megiddo ●

Kishon

▲ Mt Gilboa

SAMARIA

GILEAD

Mt Gerizim ▲

Jordan

Jabbok

JUDAEA

Jericho ●

Jerusalem ●

Plain of Philistia

Dead Sea

2. *Palestine: the Geography*

hills of Transjordan, and the further south one travels anywhere in the land, the less rain there is. Most winds bearing rain come west from the sea, and winds from the eastern deserts bear a deadly, parching heat. Summer is a time to dread: spring harvest time is over and there is always the fear that no rain will fall to make the next year's growth possible. The generally fragile fertility of the soil is a preoccupation of its people; it was one of the distinctive features of the Jews that they became fiercely opposed to rival religions stressing a concern with fertility, while at the same time they stubbornly maintained their attachment to their complex, difficult territory. Their holy books told them how they had fought to win it, trusting in ancient promises of God, how they had lost it and won it once more. These were the stories which Jesus learned in his childhood village in Galilee.

The Hebrew sacred books give a detailed picture of the history of the Israelites and their lineage, right back to the first humans created by God. The relationship of this detail to history as practised and understood by modern historians raises deeply felt arguments about the 'reliability' of sacred literature: hence any discussion of that history is a delicate matter, and no doubt many will contest the following attempt to reconstruct it.[3] The first book of scripture, Genesis, has accounts of leaders who have come to be known as Patriarchs, beginning with Abram, who is pictured as coming from Ur in what is now Iraq and receiving a repeated promise from God that his descendants will receive the land, symbolized by a new name given him by God, Abraham, 'Father of Multitudes'.[4] Around Abraham's rackety grandson Jacob are woven several engaging tales of outrageous cheating and deceit, and they culminate in an all-night wrestling match with a mysterious stranger who overcomes Jacob and is able to give him another new name, Israel, meaning 'He who strives with God'.[5] Out of that fight in the darkness, with one who revealed the power of God and was God, began the generations of the Children of Israel. Few peoples united by a religion have proclaimed by their very name that they struggle against the one whom they worship. The relationship of God with Israel is intense, personal, conflicted. Those who follow Israel and the religions which spring from his wrestling match that night are being told that even through their harshest and most wretched experiences of fighting with those they love most deeply, they are being given some glimpse of how they relate to God.

Using the Bible's own internal points of reference, the promises to the Patriarchs would have been made in a period around 1800 BCE. But this raises problems, even if one simply reads the whole biblical text attentively. One silence is significant: there is very little reference to the Patriarchs in the pronouncements of 'later' great prophets like Jeremiah, Hosea or the first prophet known as Isaiah, whose prophetic words date from the eighth and seventh centuries BCE. It is as if these supposedly basic stories of Israel's origins a thousand years before were largely missing from the consciousness of Jeremiah, Hosea and Isaiah, whereas references to the Patriarchs appear abundantly in material which is of sixth-century or later date. The logic of this is that the stories of the Patriarchs, as we now meet them in the biblical text, *post-date* rather than predate the first great Hebrew prophets of the eighth and seventh centuries, even though various stories embedded in the Book of Genesis are undoubtedly very ancient.[6]

It is also striking that certain incidents in the stories of the Patriarchs mirror incidents which took place in a more definitely 'historical' context, six centuries after 1800. Obvious lurid examples are the duplicated threats of gang rape to guests in a city (with dire consequences for the perpetrators), to be found in both Genesis 19 and Judges 19. Similarly the Children of Israel, with a carelessness that Lady Bracknell would have deplored, twice put to the sword the unfortunate city of Shechem, once in Genesis 34 and again in Judges 9. Another problem: the patri-archal narratives contain one or two references to Philistines, who come from a later period of history, and there are many more to a people who are close relatives of the Patriarchs, called Aramaeans – Abraham is very precisely given a kinship to the Aramaeans in one family tree.[7] The settlement of Aramaeans in areas reasonably close to the land of Canaan/ Israel/Palestine was a gradual process, but other historical evidence shows that it cannot have begun any earlier than 1200 BCE, and that was a very different era from the supposed time of the Patriarchs; their arrival was in a time which followed a further great upheaval in the story of the Children of Israel.[8] Altogether, the chronology of the Book of Genesis simply does not add up as a historical narrative when it is placed in a reliably historical wider context.

Genesis and the four books that follow are traditionally known as the Pentateuch ('five scrolls'), because, beginning with the final chapters in Genesis, they share a theme which is the tale of this new upheaval: Israel's journey into Egypt and subsequent liberation to travel once more north-eastwards. The journey to Egypt led to some 430 years during which the descendants of Israel and Joseph lived under the rule of the Egyptian Pharaohs. While the narrative passes over those four centuries in complete silence, there follows a richly detailed saga of mass migration or 'Exodus' out of Egypt, with the aim of seizing the land of Canaan promised by Israel's God to the Patriarchs of the Book of Genesis. In the course of this Exodus, God provides formidably precise sets of regulations for everyday life and also for furnishing and running a temple – a temple which in the event did not rise in Israel for another couple of centuries. Once more, there are problems in relating this disjointed account to much evidence in external history or archaeology. Yet at the heart of the Egypt and Exodus story is something which no subsequent Israelite fantasist would have wished to make up, because it is an embarrassment: the hero and leader of the Exodus, the man presented as writing the Pentateuch itself, has a name which is not only non-Jewish but actually Egyptian: Moses.[9] Moses's name is therefore a clue to connect a people who ended up in the land of Canaan/Israel/Palestine with a mass movement of people out of Egypt. Maybe the Egyptian migrants were only a small part of that later population, who then contributed their story of exodus to the greater identity of the people, whom we can now meet in their Promised Land in the Books of Joshua and Judges.

The Book of Judges at last provides stories which begin to sit more robustly and extensively amid conventional historical and archaeological evidence, and that evidence fits into the period 1200–1050 BCE. The Israel revealed in this biblical text is not yet a monarchy but a confederation of peoples ruled by 'Judges', leaders in peace and war who are portrayed as being individually chosen by God, but who do not rule in hereditary succession. Israel is engaged in constant struggle with other peoples of the land, and in fact never finally dislodges them all, a rueful and realistic underlying theme within the book. The writer of Judges is much concerned with a threat to the Children of Israel from one of these peoples, the Philistines. Philistines in fact bequeathed their name to the land and therefore built into the word 'Palestine' is a reminiscence of Israel's enemies. But the Philistines also performed a service to Israel, because they securely date the Book of Judges by their presence in its narrative. Sources discovered by modern archaeologists reveal that the Philistines did not just fight Israel but also came into frequent conflict with the Egyptian Empire. Consequently they left abundant traces in Egyptian records, which show the Philistines came over the sea from the west and occupied the coastal zone of Palestine between 1200 and 1050, as part of the same widespread disruption which had destroyed Mycenae (see p. 20).

Victorian archaeologists discovered the first known non-biblical mention of 'Israel', in an inscription on a stone victory monument created for the Egyptian Pharaoh Merneptah in 1216 BCE. In the course of his (possibly overblown) account of a successful military campaign in Canaan, listing his achievements there, he claims that 'Israel is laid waste, its seed is not'. Significantly the Pharaoh's inscription uses a different set of hieroglyphic conventions for 'Israel' from those which describe specific cities in Canaan and this suggests that 'Israel' is not conceived of as a place but as a people. Yet in the minds of the Egyptian monument-reading public, this people is clearly expected to be associated with 'seed', or grain. So we could conclude that 'Israel' was then known as a people of farmers perhaps scattered throughout the wider territory of Canaan, but that already they possessed a common name which could identify them.[10] The Book of Judges consistently tells Israel's story in reference to the one God, who called the people of Israel (with intermittent success) to be faithful to his commands. This probably reflects the reality that Israel's identity stemmed from their religion: maybe religion is all they had to unite them, rather than ethnicity or common origins.

From an early period, the Children of Israel were also called 'Hebrews' – usually (even in the Tanakh itself) by those who did not think much of them. The word is well authenticated beyond the Bible; it appears as '*Habiru*' in a wide variety of times and places from Egypt to Mesopotamia (modern Iraq). What is striking about these other references is that they seem to concern a social rather than an ethnic grouping, and their context invariably suggests people who were uprooted and on the edges of other societies, people of little account except for their nuisance value.[11] That is a plausible origin for the peoples who gathered as 'Israel' under the rule of the Judges in the land of Canaan/Israel. They were those who had been marginalized: nomads, semi-nomads, the dispossessed who now began to find ways of settling down and building new lives. While such people were not unique to this area, something remarkable seems to have happened to the groups of *Habiru* who massed in Canaan from the late thirteenth century BCE, whether from Egypt or elsewhere: they constructed a new identity, sealed by a God who was not necessarily to be associated with older establishments or older shrines. It would be natural for the worshippers of this God to begin a long process of refashioning a patchwork of ancient stories from their varied previous homes into a plausible single story of common ancestors, among whom may be numbered Abram/Abraham and Jacob/Israel. It was significant that these Patriarchs had experienced their God changing their names.

Perhaps the *Habiru* felt that this was what was happening to them: God was giving them a new identity.

And who was this God? Here some of the Pentateuch's references to the religion of the Patriarchs and of Moses are fascinating precisely because they do not all seem to be the result of later fabrication: they are untidy and anomalous, preserved out of respect for their antiquity despite their inconvenience. There is, for instance, a curious silence: only one mention of priesthood in Genesis, despite Israel's later institution of an elaborate priesthood, and that reference is very puzzling and untypical (the appearance of Melchizedek, who appears to be a Canaanite high priest, in Genesis 14).[12] Altars are built which seem to have little connection with any idea of sacrifice, despite Israel's later careful provision for sacrifice in a temple (for instance, Genesis 12.7–9; 13.18; 26.25). There is frequent and uninhibited mention of sacred trees and stones, which do not figure in later Jewish cultic practice. Most interesting is a series of references to gods associated with particular Patriarchs. So we have the 'Fear' of Isaac the son of Abraham (Genesis 31.53), the 'Mighty One' of Jacob (Genesis 49.24) and perhaps the 'Shield' of Abraham (Genesis 15.1). At Genesis 31.53 a dispute involving Jacob is settled by appealing to the judgement of the disputing parties' respective personal gods, the God of Abraham and the God of Nahor, with Jacob sealing the deal with an oath to the Fear of his father, Isaac.[13]

When contrasting the religions of the Greeks and the Jews (see pp. 23–4), we noted the moment when Moses found that a bush burning in the desert gave him a revelation about these personal gods. The God of Abraham, the God of Isaac, the God of Jacob, speaking in the bush, called himself by a single name that is not a name, 'I will be who I will be', which is an explanation of a name used thousands of times throughout the Hebrew scripture, *Yahweh*.[14] By itself, the story gives no reason to suppose that these personal gods had previously been linked by a single name. In effect the story tells of the recognition of a new god, and that point is underlined on a further occasion when God says to Moses about Abraham, Isaac and Jacob that 'by my name [Yahweh] I did not make myself known to them'.[15] What more likely than that such a dramatic change was indeed the result of personal revelation (personal inspiration, if you prefer), either to Moses or to someone else? This was a God whose cult was not tied to a particular sacred place, unlike the old Canaanite cults in the land which the Israelites sought to conquer in the time of the Judges. Instead this God revealed his identity in the context of individual human lives, in all their changeability and battles with the divine – to wanderers like Abraham, Isaac, Jacob and Moses.[16] Around such a personal god, who announced a new identity for himself, the dispossessed, the migrants, the *Habiru*, could themselves find comfort and a new identity.

It has been worth exploring this first historic appearance of Israel and Yahweh in some detail, because it is likely to have been the source of the unique flexibility, adaptability and capacity to develop which became the characteristic of Judaism into the early Christian era and then became an inheritance for Christians and Muslims as well. Over the next century the circumstances of Israel changed dramatically, so that towards the end of the eleventh century BCE a judge and successful military campaigner named Saul took on the trappings of monarchy familiar in other contemporary kingdoms. The development was not universally popular in Israel, as can be seen from the ambiguities and discrepancies in the accounts of the change preserved in the Books of Samuel: they contain a sour note about kingship which, many centuries later, was destined to help some Christians become republicans.[17] In any case, Saul's rule was overthrown by a charismatic young courtier, David, who greatly extended the power of the kingdom and seized for the first time for Israel the strategically important city of Jerusalem, which now embarked on its career as one of the most resonant names in world history.

It is likely to have been an astute political move for the usurper-king to choose this city as a new capital in an effort to head off jealousy between rival groupings in Israel. It was a natural political consequence that he lent respectability to his venture by relocating in Jerusalem a cultic symbol of Yahweh, a sacred wooden chest known as the Ark of the Covenant. This has attracted much subsequent speculation and fascination in both Judaism and Christianity, partly because we have no reliable notion of what the chest originally contained, but principally because of its subsequent mysterious and undatable disappearance.[18] The Ethiopian Christian Church later made its own heroic if implausible effort to solve the problem (see pp. 243–4). King David has remained the greatest hero in the history of Israel; to him was ascribed authorship of all the 150 songs or liturgical hymns which have become welded into a single book as the psalms, even though many of them are patently of much later date. In the first century CE it was important for the early Christians to establish that their Anointed One Jesus had an actual family kinship with the ancient hero, allowing Jesus to be called 'Son of David' (see pp. 78–82).[19] It was the work of David's actual son, King Solomon, to build a temple in the newly conquered Jerusalem, to be a fitting home for the Ark of the Covenant. This temple began to outdo any rival sacred cultic sites created or inherited by the religion of Yahweh, and it produced much of the psalmody later attributed to Solomon's father; elaborate music was a prominent feature of the new cultic observance which was now created in Jerusalem.

During the long reign of Solomon (*c.* 970–*c.* 930 BCE) the kingdom of Israel reached its greatest extent, and it might even have been seen as a regional power, a status which later biblical writers living in less glorious days did nothing to diminish. In the many bad times that followed, there was deep nostalgia for this brief brilliant flourish of Israel's power and a longing for it to return. Around the turn of the first millennium BCE, therefore, Israel acquired much of the potential profile of later Judaism. These thousand years of Jewish history between David and Jesus Christ the 'Son of David' are also effectively the first millennium of Christian history, for that span of time established key notions which would shape Christian thinking and imagery: for instance, the central importance of the kingdom of God's chosen one David and of the Temple in Jerusalem. There took shape a history of divinely foreordained salvation for the Jewish people, shot through with retribution for their constant backsliding and misunderstanding of God's purposes. From a different perspective, the same history is a story of a struggle to establish that Yahweh was one supreme God, with neither effective rivals nor companions (for instance, a female consort).[20] The literature of the Hebrew scriptures was produced by the victors in that struggle, although the editors of it were often too respectful of the ancient texts which they had inherited entirely to eliminate rival voices. We have already met examples of this respectful preservation in the text of the Book of Genesis (see pp. 54–5).

Solomon's empire quickly split on his death into two kingdoms, southern Judah and northern Israel, whose union had even in David's time appeared fragile; the bitterness of the rift led to constant warfare of varying intensity between them. It must have been a grave disappointment for those who had seen the Davidic monarchy as the culmination of Yahweh's purposes. While Judah kept the Solomonic capital of Jerusalem with its Temple, the kings of Israel had to retreat to the northern city of Samaria. With their control of the strategic pass of Megiddo, they were more exposed to the commerce and activities of great powers to the south and north, so they were more cosmopolitan and more inclined to take an interest in other cultures and religions than were the rather introverted rulers of Judah, who resentfully guarded their

Jerusalem Temple for Yahweh. Nevertheless both kingdoms produced kings prepared to experiment with the gods of more powerful people who might be allies or overlords.

The time of the Judges and then of David and Solomon had coincided with weakness in Egypt and an Assyrian monarchy which was preoccupied in another direction; these circumstances may have afforded opportunity for the brief success of the united kingdom of Israel. From the mid-eighth century, the Mesopotamian empire of Assyria was ready to intervene more actively in Palestine/Israel, enjoying a third phase in a long history of military success which now spread its power from the Persian Gulf to the frontiers of Egypt. To judge by the inscriptions and imagery of their victory monuments, the Assyrians delighted in the use of terror and punitive sadism to seal their military success. The rise of this horrifying new threat to the north inevitably affected Israel, the northern kingdom, more than Judah. As both the Bible and Assyrian records confirm, Israel suffered frontal assault and destruction by the Assyrians around 722 BCE; thousands of its people were exiled and its political organization disappeared for ever.[21] That left the kingdom of Judah standing alone, delivered from total conquest because the Assyrians were distracted by revolts elsewhere, a historical accident which the biblical chroniclers naturally interpreted in terms of divine deliverance. Judah survived for another century and a half, but once more Palestine/Israel had become the object of land-grabbing by external powers and, apart from the century-long interlude of the Hasmonean regime from 167 BCE (see pp. 65–71), that has been the case until modern times. This new reality would have a major impact on Judaism.

The gathering crisis for the two kingdoms in the ninth and eighth centuries reinforced the role in Jewish culture and society of figures who presented themselves as mouthpieces of Yahweh, carrying urgent messages for his people: the prophets. The modern meaning of the word 'prophecy', relating it to the future, may mislead; in Greek, *prophēteia* means the gift of interpreting the will of the gods. As ancient Middle Eastern archives rediscovered from the nineteenth century onwards have revealed, Israel was not the only ancient society in the region in which prophets played a major role: long before, in the eighteenth century BCE, they can be found in the Mesopotamian Babylonian kingdom of Mari, and they also appear among the Jews' then contemporary enemy Assyria. Yet the peculiar circumstances of Israel's history and the consequent preservation of documents by and about the Israelite prophets conspire to give them a special and enduring place first in the history of

Judaism, then of Christianity.[22] The prophets' primary job was to talk about the present, not the future, and there had been such prophets in Israel before this period – yet apparently not so ready as the new generation to confront people of power. Some prophetic concerns were now with external enemies: various threats to Jewish existence from the succession of great powers, provoking generally all-too-accurate prophetic warnings of imminent danger – one might consider such warnings as contributions to foreign policy debate. Yet prophets just as much feared internal enemies who would betray Yahweh and contaminate his worship by promoting inappropriate sacred places, or by stressing the theme of fertility so prominent in the widely flourishing cult of the fertility god Baal and in Canaanite worship generally. A classic conflict of the mid-ninth century was that with Queen Jezebel, a Phoenician princess who brought the worship of Baal with her on her marriage to King Ahab of Israel. She had to face the wrath of the prophet Elijah, whose name ('Yahweh is my God') economically encapsulated his agenda. In one of Elijah's clashes with Ahab and Jezebel, Yahweh dramatically ended a long drought, showing that Elijah's God could see off any fertility god if he so chose. Both Elijah and Jezebel in their confrontations indulged in massacres of prophets who adhered to the other side, the casualties reputedly running into hundreds.[23]

While only a few remnants of the pronouncements of Elijah or his fellow prophets of the ninth century survive embedded in later stories, the biblical record of eighth-century prophets (Amos, Hosea, Micah, the first Isaiah) probably represents the earliest sustained sequences in the Hebrew scriptures in something like their original form: these are impassioned, individual voices, not a careful editorial compilation from patches of earlier prose. Because there is so little surviving precedent, it is difficult to be certain how much of what they said was new or innovative, but the desperate nature of their times would suggest that they did bring a new message for the people of Yahweh. The prophets say much about their call to prophecy, which was not a career choice but generally associated with tension and trauma. So Amos is torn away from his prosperous Judaean farm to go north into hostile territory, still hotly denying that he is really a prophet, and Hosea finds that his wretched marriage shows him something of the faithlessness of Israel, to the extent that he will even say that the Lord ordered him to embark on this matrimonial disaster.[24]

The voice of these prophets is the singular 'I', but it is a very different singularity from the purposeful whimsicality of Diogenes in later Athens (see pp. 29–30). They speak of their loneliness and express their sense of bitter distance from the official religion of their day. They even attack the Temple cult of Jerusalem, although the first of a series of prophets known as Isaiah is contradictory on this, both condemning the Temple and its sacrificial routine, and also finding an intense spiritual experience of Yahweh amid its ceremonies.[25] Such inconsistency is less important than the common feature of such prophecy: rather than attacking individuals, it indicts all society. Previous prophets, especially those at the royal Court, had been employed to curse foreigners and invoke peace for the nation. The eighth-century prophets had scant message of peace for Israel. If any consolation could be offered, it was in the survival of no more than a few. So the first Isaiah, against the dire background of Assyrian attacks on Judah in the later eighth century, imitated Elijah by enacting prophecy in a name and called his child Shear-jashub, 'A remnant shall return'.[26]

By all the rules of ancient statecraft, the fact of external threat and eventual conquest should have erased Israel's national identity and religion, as sooner or later it repeatedly erased every other national identity created by a state structure in the Middle East. Uniquely in Israel, this was not the case. The nation's commitment to Yahweh, probably forged out of very miscellaneous materials, survived the destruction first of the northern kingdom and then finally, in 586 BCE, of the southern kingdom as well. This achievement owed much to the insights of the prophets of Judah and Israel. Either through their individual genius or through divine revelation, the eighth-century prophets understood the international situation, with its constant threats of annihilation by Assyrian military might, and perceived that the only thing which could save their people from long-term annihilation was that obedience to Yahweh for which Elijah and his fellow prophets had fought in the previous century. And Yahweh was powerful enough to decide the course of history – occasionally these prophets were prepared to proclaim that he was lord of universal history and of nations beyond their own. It was an astonishing claim for this people who were apparently helpless before the great empires of their day:

> . . . many peoples shall come, and say:
>   'Come, let us go up to the mountain of the LORD [Yahweh],
>   to the house of the God of Jacob;
>   that he may teach us his ways
>   and that we may walk in his paths'.

For out of Zion shall go forth the law,
and the word of the LORD from Jerusalem.
He shall judge between the nations,
and shall decide for many peoples;
and they shall beat their swords into ploughshares
and their spears into pruning hooks;
nation shall not lift up sword against nation,
neither shall they learn war any more.[27]

The prophets were not the only people who contributed to the refashioning of the national cult during the eighth century. After the destruction of the northern kingdom, the people of Judah brooded on the recent catastrophe and on how to defend what was left. Their fierce debate about the future was played out in an appeal to the past – in fact, a large-scale reinterpretation and invention of the past. What we know of the story can be gleaned through the history written by the winners in the struggle, preserved for us in the second Books of Kings and Chronicles. The kingdom's political turbulence culminated in a coup d'état which around 640 BCE killed King Amon of Judah and installed his young son Josiah as a puppet ruler. As the boy grew up, his energy and zeal were harnessed to push forward a reform programme which, in the way of such innovations in the ancient world, was presented as the rediscovery of a venerable document: a code of law, attributed to Moses himself. With impeccable timing, this set out regulations, particularly for sacrifice, which had not been applicable at the time of the Exodus from Egypt, but which were judged extremely relevant to the age of Josiah. In its present developed form, the law code is to be found in the Pentateuch as the Book of Deuteronomy (this name 'second law' was provided by Greek translators of the Hebrew scriptures). Significantly the place of its discovery was the Temple in Jerusalem, and the lucky find was made by the High Priest of the Temple.[28]

Throughout the Deuteronomic Code, there is an emphasis on the pure worship of Yahweh alone, and it orders its devout readers to be savage to those within Israel who might suggest religious deviations – even the closest of relatives and friends, even one's own son or wife: '[Y]our hand shall be first against him to put him to death, and afterwards the hand of all the people.'[29] It also emphasizes the idea of 'covenant', a treaty: Yahweh has made a covenant with his people and it is up to them to keep its conditions. In the more developed vision of this idea, texts written later than this period such as those incorporated in the Book of

Genesis would emphasize that Abraham was the first to receive the covenant and had been told to ensure that his male descendants were circumcised as a sign of their faithfulness to it, but Deuteronomy concentrates on the covenant as it was made with Moses, when God gave Ten Commandments on Mount Horeb (Sinai) as the centrepiece of an intricate set of laws.[30] There were more laws to come in a period much later than Josiah's reign, but they were likewise back-projected to the time of Moses. For the moment, the Deuteronomic reform was no doubt encouraged by the fact that Josiah's innovations coincided with a decline in Assyrian power: surely a sign of divine favour.[31]

The angry, precise legislative programme of the Deuteronomic party extended beyond the book itself into a wholesale rewriting of Jewish history. In an operation of remarkable scholarly and literary creativity which probably involved many collaborators working over several decades, older documents were edited and incorporated into a series of books (Joshua, Judges, Samuel, Kings, Jeremiah) which carefully told the story of Israel's triumphs and tragedies in relation to its faithfulness to Yahweh. The coherence of this literature can be detected not merely in its deployment of that central notion, but even in the language idioms which it uses. This remarkable programme was given practical expression in the gleeful destruction of cultic objects and of any sacred places within Judah which might rival the Jerusalem Temple, but besides a drastic simplification of the Jewish sacred landscape, the reform achieved something unusual in the religions of the time. In much the same era that Homer's epics began taking on their own particular significance as the central works of literature for all Greeks, the Jews likewise began to focus their religious identity on the contents of a book. Probably to start with, there was only one copy of the Deuteronomic Code for consultation and solemn public recitation, but together with the literature that it inspired, it was an increasingly indispensable point of reference for the religion of Yahweh. That proved to be of huge importance when a new catastrophe befell the Jews.

The southern kingdom had managed to withstand assaults from the Assyrians. If this had been more by luck than judgement, that is not how the historians in the Deuteronomic tradition saw matters; it was the result of faithfulness to God's commands. The luck, however, did not last – or the faithfulness faltered. As Assyrian power collapsed at the end of the seventh century BCE, it was replaced by a new Middle Eastern power, based in Babylon, showing a fierce pride in the previous empire which had ruled from that city long before. The Babylonians, in alliance with other powers, sacked the Assyrian capital, Nineveh, in 612 BCE. It was not many years before Judah found itself overwhelmed by Babylonian armies, and after its last king rebelled against subject status, around 586 BCE the Babylonians sacked the already shattered city, destroyed the Temple and carried off many people from Judah to exile in Babylon. Those exiled are likely to have been community leaders; those left behind were apparently mostly of little account. The exiles were not allowed to return until Babylon itself was conquered by the Persian ruler Cyrus in 539. Not all Jews did go home then, and many formed a community in Babylon which for centuries continued to be one of the most important centres of Judaism outside the homeland.

THE EXILE AND AFTER

This renewed catastrophe was a key event in the history of the people of Israel. Maybe if the exile in Babylon had lasted more than half a century, the impetus to preserve and enhance a Jewish identity might have been lost, but as it was the exiles who returned were able to rebuild the Temple in Jerusalem; it was reconsecrated in 516 BCE. There could be no independent native monarchy now, for the rebuilding was thanks to the generous spirit of the new conqueror Cyrus and his successors. So the Temple and its priesthood became the absolute centre of Jewish identity, as well as being the only significant institution in Jerusalem, and remained so for the next half-millennium. Those who rebuilt the Temple were helped by the exiles who had remained in Babylon, but by contrast and significantly, they refused help from local people who had not been deported in this or previous disasters, and who may have also included exiles whom the Babylonians had brought to Palestine from elsewhere. The exiles and their descendants continued to feel condescension or hostility to these others as 'the people of the land', a people who had not shared in the sufferings of God's chosen people – had not sat by the waters of Babylon and wept remembering Zion.[32] Many of these despised people built a rival temple on Mount Gerizim in the central Palestinian territory known as Samaria, and hence they were called Samaritans (a word of contempt to Jews); in very reduced numbers, they still live round their sacred mountain now. Much later, Jesus told a characteristically provocative story about a Samaritan who was kinder than any of the representatives of Jewish respectable society, and one Gospel writer also portrays Jesus as having mightily impressed the

Samaritan community after a friendly and candid encounter with one of their women.[33]

The voice of the former exiles and the continuing exiled community in Babylon, who jointly regarded themselves as the true representatives of mainstream Judaism, was now heard in the increasing volume of sacred writings added in this 'Second Temple' period. Their preoccupations and the results of their new experiences went on permanently to colour Jewish religion. For instance, it may have been the fact that the scene of their exile was Babylon on the River Euphrates that led them to cherish the idea that the Patriarch Abram had come to their Promised Land from Ur, a city then near the mouth of the Tigris and Euphrates rivers. They learned ancient tales, like the story well known throughout the Middle East about a great flood, and incorporated them in their own narrative of the ancient past. Jews still in Babylon picked up an interest in the long Babylonian tradition of observing and speculating on the stars and planets, and began contributing their own thoughts to the subject. More profoundly, post-Exilic Jews puzzled about how a loving God could have allowed the destruction of his Temple and the apparent overturning of all his promises to his people. One answer was to try to let God off the hook by conceiving of a being who devoted his time to thwarting God's purposes: he was called the Adversary, *Hassatan*, and although he was a fairly insignificant nuisance in the Hebrew scriptures, he grew in status in later Jewish literature, particularly among writers who were influenced by other religious cultures which spoke of powerful demonic figures. Hassatan caught the imagination of the Christian sect, and by the time that the Christian Book of Revelation was written, he had become a figure of cosmic significance now called Satan, depicted as the final adversary for God in the End Time.[34]

Judaism was nevertheless reluctant to make too much of any rival to God, having put such effort into affirming his sole and cosmic power. Some Jews felt that any questioning of or search for understanding of their tragedy was impious as well as a waste of energy. This is the message in the Book of Job, a tale which is the classic cry of pain and anger against unjust suffering, and which provides Satan's first major debut in biblical literature. Job's suffering arises not out of anything that he has done, for he is one of God's most loyal servants; it results from a peculiar and apparently heartless wager between God and Satan about his loyalty. It can only be resolved when Job fully submits to the mysterious will of God. A later writer nicknamed *Qoheleth*, the

'Preacher' or 'Teacher' (Greeks tried to translate this as 'Ecclesiastes'), approached the same problem in a different way. Dispensing with any story as a vehicle for what he wanted to say, he made a series of observations which form one of the most compelling and unexpected expressions in any sacred literature of resignation at the futility of human existence:

All things are full of weariness; a man cannot utter it; the eye is not satisfied with seeing, nor the ear filled with hearing. What has been is what will be, and what has been done is what will be done, and there is nothing new under the sun ... In much wisdom is much vexation, and he who increases knowledge increases sorrow.

Qoheleth's smile at human folly is chillier than that of the Greek Cynics or Stoics; at the end, it falls away and dims into a description of the decay of old age moving towards the grave. Yahweh provides no comfort, but 'the spirit returns to God who gave it. Vanity of vanities, says the Preacher; all is vanity.'[35]

But this was not the only mood in post-Exilic Jewish literature. It was capable of directly contradicting Job and Qoheleth, with calls to activism in leading a morally upright life, such as those in the Book of Proverbs, whose cosy assertions of the value of everyday goodness have provided material for settled Jewish or Christian societies ever since. Writers seeking to rebuild Israel gave unambiguous answers to the great question aroused by Jewish experiences after 586. They created new sets of laws and careful restorations and extensions of past ceremonial practice in the Temple, taking care that most of it was represented as a return to ancient decrees of the Lord from before the Exile. They stated in ever more extreme terms the message of separation which had been the centrepiece of the Deuteronomistic reform movement; now they had the catastrophe of the Babylonian captivity to ram home the point that Yahweh wanted obedience to his law and had severely punished the nation for not providing that obedience. Never again should Israel make the same mistake.

On this principle was founded the continuing existence and development of Judaism. Like its daughter religion, Christianity, Judaism has often fostered the idea that it has an exclusive approach to the divine. Yet this claim to exclusivity was coupled with a remarkable new feature of Yahweh's religion – or perhaps really a return to its miscellaneous origins amid the displaced people of the *Habiru*. From this period under Persian rule comes an acceptance that it was not necessary to be born a

Jew to enter the Jewish faith: what was necessary was to accept fully the customs of the Jews, including the rite of genital circumcision performed on all Jewish males. One could then be accepted as a convert ('proselyte', from a Greek word meaning 'stranger' or 'foreigner living in the land'). It was enough to accept the story which Judaism told: so in theory, Judaism could become a universal religion. Jews did not generally take that logical step of thought. It was left first to Christianity and then to Islam to make it a great theme of their faith.[36]

In the centuries after the return from Babylon, the Jews in Palestine were repeatedly faced with the same prospect of more powerful cultures overwhelming their own and overpowering them. Most disturbing was the coming of Hellenistic kingdoms, after Alexander the Great burst into the eastern Mediterranean in the 330s (see pp. 37–40). First, the Ptolemaic Pharaohs of Egypt ruled the land, and then (from 198 BCE) the Seleucids of Syria. The worst confrontation between Jewish identity and the Greek world surrounding it exploded into open violence when their second Seleucid overlord, King Antiochos IV (who boastfully called himself *Epiphanēs* or 'Manifestation'), tried to force Greek customs on to the Jews and attacked the religious life centred on the Temple in Jerusalem. From 167 BCE the Jews rebelled against him, first under the leadership of Judas Maccabeus. With the unpromising exception of Judah's rebellion against Babylonian rule before the Exile, it was the first time that Jews had ever risen against any of their varied foreign masters over the previous centuries. The Maccabean rebels suffered terribly in this war, but they did succeed in winning independence for Judaea under a dynasty of native rulers, known from an earlier ancestor as the Hasmoneans. These descendants of heroes in the war of independence now formed a succession of high priests for the Jerusalem Temple.

During this period Judaea could claim to be a significant power in the Middle East, in a manner previously achieved in Jewish history only by the Solomonic kingdom (and Solomon's prestige might well have been exaggerated in Jewish historical writing). For a moment it looked as if God was finally satisfied with his people; and they did not forget the lesson that rebellion might pay off, a memory which was to have dire consequences in the rebellions against the Roman Empire (see pp. 106–11). Protestant Christians are not generally familiar with the Books of Maccabees, because in the sixteenth-century Reformation they were among the works sidelined from the Bible and relegated to the so-called Apocrypha (see page 68). Judaism takes a very different view of them: these are among the most important stories of Jewish history, the centrepiece, for instance, of the great festival of Hanukkah. It is possible that two hymns to be found in the Christian New Testament and much used in Christian liturgy, Mary's song (the *Magnificat*) and the thanksgiving of John the Baptist's father, Zechariah (the *Benedictus*), are lightly adapted victory songs associated with the Maccabees.[37]

It is at this period that Jews were first described by the Greek *Ioudaios*, a word which could be applied to all Jewish people who looked to the life of the Jerusalem Temple, whether they lived in Judaea or not.[38] Many now were far away. Both the Jews' long history of military misfortunes and their energy and enterprise had resulted in a Jewish dispersal far beyond Palestine or the remaining Jewish community in Babylon. All around the seaports of the Mediterranean there developed Jewish communities which honoured Jerusalem and which, if they could, joined pilgrimages to the Temple, which was becoming one of the most important goals for religious journeyings in the ancient world. In their everyday lives, far from Jerusalem, Jews kept their sense of identity and community in meeting places which significantly had a Greek name, synagogue.

Synagogues were remarkable institutions, with little other parallel in the ancient world. They were not temples, because with the exception of a few insignificant rival institutions Jewish sacrifice now took place only in the Jerusalem Temple, yet from the start synagogues seem to have had a religious function. The first evidence of them comes from Jewish inscriptions in Greek in Egypt, where they are at first and even as late as the fourth century called a 'prayer house' – *proseuchē* – rather than *synagogē*, which neutrally means 'an assembly'.[39] So synagogues were the setting for prayer and the reading of sacred scripture, but they also provided a focus for the general activities of the community – especially education. This was not just education for an elite, as was the case in Greek society, but education for everyone in the Jewish community; and it had a strong moral emphasis, unlike the concentration on cultic practice in the many other religions of the Mediterranean world. Judaism could make claim to providing a philosophy of life as well as a series of observances and customs for approaching the divine, an unusual feature in ancient religion. The life of the synagogue and the assumptions of a well-instructed, well-ordered and uniformly observant community that it fostered furnished an attractive and distinctive model which Christianity later readily imitated as it developed its own separate institutions.[40]

If worship in the synagogue centred on the reading of God's word from written texts, this demanded that there should be common consent throughout the Jewish community in the Mediterranean as to what could and could not be read. The long process of creating and re-editing texts now approached something like completion, and a number of books, twenty-four in all, came to be recognized as having a special status. It is difficult to say exactly when this happened: in Jewish tradition the decision is said to have been made in a 'Great Assembly' in 450 BCE, but that is a fairly typical historical back-projection of a process which was probably gradual and incremental. In fact it must have been completed at a much later date, especially since some books within the collection, like the prophecies of Daniel, patently cannot be as old as the fifth century BCE, whatever superficial claims they make to a particular antiquity. The Jewish historian Josephus, writing soon after the death of Jesus Christ, provides the first known reference to a particular number, twenty-two, but the first reference to the choice of the twenty-four is in a work known as IV Ezra (confusingly contained in a larger work commonly known as II Esdras). By its content IV Ezra can be dated as late as the time of the Roman Emperor Domitian, towards the end of the first century CE, just a little later than Josephus. This reference also makes clear that a larger number of other books, supposedly seventy, were no longer to be treated as having the same degree of authority as the twenty-four.[41]

The whole collection of authorized and privileged texts came to be known by a Hebrew word, *Tanakh*. This was actually a symbolic acronym formed from the three initial Hebrew letters of the three category names of books it contained: Law, Prophets and Writings. The last is a rather vague catch-all term for history, psalms and writings containing wise sayings, and the categories are not altogether helpful as concepts: books which are mainly historical are to be found among both Prophets and Writings, while Job and Qoheleth nestle among the Writings, despite their prophetic brutality towards the sort of common-sense advice for coping with everyday life which is represented by the Wisdom literature of the Writings – works like the Book of Proverbs, for example.

The Tanakh is recognizable to Christians as their Old Testament, albeit arranged in a different order. Beyond it, reflecting and in some cases obviously including the symbolic seventy rejected books, are a series of texts which neither Jews nor Christians afforded the same special status, but which have had a large influence on both religious traditions. Some of these books were actually added to the Tanakh by Jews in Greek-speaking settings such as Alexandria (see p. 69), and hence the early Christians, also Greek-speaking, regarded them as having the full status of God's word. During the fourth century CE doubts began to be expressed by some Christian commentators, who gave them the description 'apocrypha' ('hidden things'). In the sixteenth-century Reformation of the Western Church, Protestants made a definite decision to exclude them from what Christians term the 'canon' of recognized scripture.[42] For Protestants, this had the useful effect of undercutting various doctrines held by that part of the Western Church still loyal to the pope, doctrines which could find biblical warrant only within books of the Apocrypha. Martin Luther duly fished these extra books out of the general assemblage of scripture, yet he kept them in an appendix to his German Bible of 1534, and the Church of England allowed some samples of them to be read in public worship; other Protestants dropped them altogether.

Still further out than the Apocrypha in terms of biblical respectability are a great number of texts which vary in date from the second century BCE to the first CE. Christian scholars give them the loaded title of 'Inter-Testamental literature', works falling between what Christians call the Old and New Testaments – clearly not a term which has any meaning within the Jewish tradition. Within this literature there is a preoccupation with telling the story of the Last Days, when the wretchedness and suffering of Israel in the present would be given a glorious reward and God's purposes made clear: this genre of text is called 'apocalyptic' (from the Greek for 'revelation'), and the Tanakh admitted one set of examples of it, some sections of the Book of Daniel.[43] Like Daniel, many of these books make a bid for the respectability of age by taking the name of some biblical worthy recognizable from the Tanakh: for instance, various books reach way beyond the Patriarchs to claim the authorship of Enoch, father of Methuselah. For one of these books, the gamble on antiquity has paid off in Christian history: I Enoch is explicitly quoted by one obscure writer called Jude, whose epistle did manage to worm its way into the New Testament canon, and I Enoch is also treated as mainstream inspired scripture by the Christian Church of Ethiopia.[44] An interesting variety of Christian traditions and assumptions is based on this array of books; they were largely forgotten in mainstream Christianity, yet they were part of the mental furniture of the generation of Jesus and his disciples.

One of the most significant Jewish communities formed in the Egyptian seaport city which remained as Alexander's most spectacular single memorial, Alexandria: a symbol of the success of Hellenistic culture throughout the eastern Mediterranean. By the time of Jesus there may have been a million Jews there, the largest single community of Jews outside Palestine, and they were kept from dominating city politics only by the exclusive practices of their religion.[45] Naturally in such a wealthy and prosperous community, it was a great temptation to take on the ways of the surrounding world: a Greek world. At least a century before hatred of all things Greek pushed Judas Maccabeus and his fellows into open rebellion against Antiochos, the Jews of Alexandria commonly spoke Greek instead of Hebrew, to the extent that they were forced to translate their sacred books into Greek to make sure that they did not lose touch with the meaning. The name given to this collection of translations (together with the Apocrypha books in Greek which Hellenized Jews themselves added) was an indication of how proud Greek-speaking Jews were of their achievement; it became known as the Septuagint, from the Latin word for seventy. This was a reference to the seventy-two translators who, legend said, had produced it in seventy-two days, and who were themselves an image of the seventy elders who had been with Moses on the sacred mountain during the Exodus.[46] Jews later lost their enthusiasm for the translation and abandoned it for others when Christians wholeheartedly adopted it.

In general these Hellenized Jews were much more interested in winning respect from Greeks for their culture than Greeks were interested in Judaism. They found that Greek reaction to what the translation revealed of Hebrew sacred literature posed problems: Greeks respected such ancient writings, but were also puzzled that a God who was supposed to be so powerful would do strange things like walk in the Garden of Eden or indulge in arguments with earthly men like Lot or Jonah. Many Jews came to feel that such apparent embarrassments in their stories must conceal deeper layers of truth and so must be allegories. Greeks had after all already applied this idea of allegorical meaning to their own myths and to the writings of Homer (see pp. 24–5), and the allegorical approach became naturalized among Alexandrian Jews in the biblical commentaries of Jesus Christ's Jewish contemporary the scholar and historian Philo.[47] When a Christian community eventually became established alongside the Alexandrian Jewish community, it was much influenced by Philo's allegorical method.

Powerful currents of opinion within Judaism also continued to suggest modifications of aspects of Jewish belief if there seemed to be valuable material in the religions of others. Following Greek thought, Jews embraced the concept of nothingness, and that gave them a new

perspective on creation. II Maccabees, a work of the Apocrypha probably written in the second century BCE, is the first in Jewish literature
to insist that God did not make creation 'out of things that existed',
unformed, chaotic material, but summoned creation out of nothing.[48]
This was important for Christians later, as they struggled to find a
convincing way of expressing their conviction that God could remain
divine while entering the world which he had created. Greek discussion
of nothingness helped to change Jewish views on beginnings; Jewish
thinkers also borrowed ideas to help them understand the end of human
life and its aftermath. On the whole, before the time of the Maccabees,
Jewish discussion of God had shown little interest in the nature of the
afterlife; Judaism was concerned with this life and with interpreting
the many tragedies that happened to people on earth. Because of this,
the Tanakh does not have all that much to say about death and what
comes after. What it does say, particularly in texts written before the
Babylonian exile, suggests that human life comes to an end and, for all
but a few exceptional people, that is it.

A new impulse to develop ideas about the afterlife seems to have been
provoked by the terrible deaths of some of the heroes of the Maccabean
war of independence, discussed in detail with pious horror in the histories of the wars. Surely such heroism deserved a particularly lavish
reward? Some argued that God would grant back the martyrs bodily
resurrection in this life, but inconveniently this failed to happen. Perhaps,
then, the resurrection of the martyrs would be in a life to come, and
the reward should be specific to individual suffering; this implied the
prolonging of a recognizable personal existence.[49] No doubt the era of
the Maccabees was not the first time that this fairly obvious train of
argument had occurred to thoughtful Jews, but now they could listen to
voices in other religious or philosophical traditions which might give
shape to the idea. The most readily available vocabulary and central
concept was actually Greek and had been particularly developed by
Plato: he talked of individual humans as having a soul, which might
reflect a divine force beyond itself.

The first Jewish texts to say much about the soul therefore appear in
the Hellenistic period, in 'Inter-Testamental literature' dating after the
closure of the Tanakh, like the so-called *Wisdom of Solomon*, probably
written between the mid-second century BCE and the early first century
BCE.[50] The Book of Daniel (or at least most of its text) managed to find
a place in the Tanakh, but likewise it is almost certain to have been
written as late as the second century. It is unprecedented in Jewish sacred

literature in spelling out the idea of an individual resurrection of a soul in a transformed body in the afterlife – though still not for everyone![51] Naturally all these developments within Judaism were highly controversial and provoked continuing argument; yet by the time Christians were beginning to construct their own literature, their writers clearly found such talk of the individual soul and of resurrection completely natural, and it became the basis of that Christian concern with the afterlife which sometimes has bordered on the obsessional.

It was the Hasmonean dynasty, significant power players in the eastern Mediterranean in the wake of the successful revolt of the Maccabees, which first established official contacts between Judaea and the Romans, during the second century BCE. At that stage, Rome was far away, a possible ally against the hated Seleucids, and relations remained friendly for about a century, until the Romans invaded Judaea in 63 BCE as part of their mopping-up operations around the conquest of their real prizes, the Seleucid and Egyptian empires. A mixture of deportees from this latest catastrophe for the Jews, together with generations of traders making the best of a bad situation, created an increasingly large and flourishing Jewish community in Rome itself, concentrated in the downtown area across the River Tiber from the main city (Trastevere), where the Basilica of St Peter now stands (the first Christian groups in Rome probably emerged from this Jewish quarter). In Judaea, finding no convincing or compliant Hasmonean candidates for a Jewish throne, in 37 BCE the Romans displaced the last Hasmonean ruler and replaced him with a relative by marriage, who reigned for more than three decades. This puppet king, an outsider whose forebears came from the territory to the south of Judaea which the Romans called Idumea (Edom), was Herod, 'the Great'.

Herod rebuilt the Temple with unprecedented magnificence, making it one of the largest sacred complexes in the ancient world; the quality of his masonry in the visible surviving sections of its monumental precinct wall can still be admired. Yet he got little thanks from his subjects, who were equally ungrateful for his attempt to please them with such foreign innovations as Greek-style public sporting contests, gladiatorial combats or horse racing in newly built arenas.[52] Complications continued after Herod's death in 4 BCE because his sons took the extensive territories which the Romans had allowed him to build up and divided them between themselves. During the first century CE the Romans experimented with a mixture of indirect rule through various members of the Herodian family and direct imperial rule of parts of Palestine through a Roman official – Pontius Pilate was one of these. Within Judaea itself, there were at least four identities for Judaism, Sadducees, Pharisees, Essenes, Zealots, and probably many lesser sects. Even though they tolerated each other's existence, each saw itself as the most authentic expression of Jewish identity.[53] Perhaps one way to understand the differences between them is to realize that they took distinguishable stances towards the Hellenistic world ruled over by the Romans, and towards all the temptations away from Jewish tradition that it embodied: they represented different degrees of distance or accommodation.

The Sadducees provided the elite which ran the Temple. They had done well out of successive regimes, both Jewish and non-Jewish, and they continued to do well when the Romans were in charge. It was therefore not surprising that they were the most flexible of our four groups in relation to outsiders. For them, it was enough to keep the basic commands of the Law in the scriptures and not to add the complex additional regulations which governed the everyday life of the Pharisees and made Pharisee life obviously distinct from the world of non-Jews around them. Significantly, being conservatives and minimalists in their view of Jewish doctrine, Sadducees had little time for the comparatively recently evolved discussion of the afterlife; Jesus is portrayed as on one occasion teasing Sadducees on this subject, to the pleasure of some Pharisees, and the writer of Acts tells a story of the Apostle Paul making a bid for Pharisee sympathy on the subject against the Sadducees when he was in a dangerous situation.[54] Both Jesus and Paul can be identified by their backgrounds as closer to the Pharisees than to any other religious grouping, though it is unlikely that Jesus had anything like the pungent command of everyday Greek which is evident in Paul's surviving letters and which marked Paul out as part of the dispersed and Hellenized Jewish population – the *diaspora* which could now be found all round the Mediterranean and into the Middle East.

For the group known as the Essenes, however, even the distinctiveness which the Pharisees maintained was not enough to keep them from pollution in semi-colonial Palestine. The Essenes left ordinary society by setting up their own separate communities, usually well away from others, with their own literature and their own traditions of persecution by other Jews. Sometimes it has been suggested that the early Christians were close to the Essenes, but that seems unlikely. Essene separation from the rest of Judaism was a matter of principle, whereas the eventual Christian separation was a result of Christianity's failure to become the leading force within the Judaism of the first century CE, and Christians became eager to move out into the world beyond Palestine, as we will see (see pp. 108–11).[55] The Zealots held a militant version of the same Essene theme of separation: for them, the only solution to the humiliation of Roman rule over the Jewish homeland was to take up Maccabean traditions of violent resistance, and it was they who gave impetus to the successive disastrous revolts which by the mid-second century CE had shattered Jewish life in Palestine (see pp. 106–9).

Out of that destruction emerged a group which at first seemed just another minority answer to the problem of Jewish identity. Now it did much towards the permanent shaping of that identity, as well as becoming a world religion in its own right. The Jewish sect which became Christianity borrowed the sacred literature created by the Jews and shaped Christian belief in its founder-Messiah along lines already present in the sacred books of the Tanakh. Christian history thereafter is shot through with and shaped by the stories of the Tanakh – they became particularly useful when Christians allied with monarchies, for the Christian New Testament has little to do with kings, while the Old Testament has much to say about them. When Christians created a sacred book of two 'Testaments', they turned their brand-new belief system into one which could stand on an ancient sacred tradition and claim to be the most ancient religion of all. Muslims likewise took over this claim to antiquity, remaining conscious of the two older assemblies of books, but Muslims replaced the authority of the two Testaments with a further book which became their supreme revelation of God's word, the Qur'an. For Christians, that revelation had already appeared in the Jew Jesus of Nazareth.

PART II

One Church, One Faith, One Lord?

(4 BCE–451 CE)

3

A Crucified Messiah

(4 BCE–100 CE)

BEGINNINGS

And so to Bethlehem of Judaea, where Jesus was born in a stable because there was no room at the inn. Or perhaps not. We learn of these events within four books of the Christian 'New Testament', credited with authorship by early followers of Jesus called Matthew, Mark, Luke and John. They shine four different spotlights on the life, death and resurrection of Jesus Christ, and, as we will see, all four were probably written not less than half a century after his death (see pp. 84–5 and 102–3). They are collectively called the Gospels, a word which started life as the Greek for 'good news', *evaggelion*. Significantly, the first Latin Christians did not seek an exact equivalent in their own language and simply slurred the word with a Latin lilt into *evangelium*. Many modern languages have in turn borrowed from the Latin: hence, in English, 'evangelist' and 'evangelical'. Far away from Mediterranean society in England, during what we misleadingly used to call the Dark Ages, Anglo-Saxon scholars were more adventurous than the early Christian Latin-speakers: they considered the etymology of the original Greek and came up with their word 'Godspell', once more meaning 'good news' – Gospel.

This care to find a special name for the books of Matthew, Mark, Luke and John reflects their oddness. Biographies were not rare in the ancient world and the Gospels do have many features in common with non-Christian examples. Yet these Christian books are an unusually 'down-market' variety of biography, in which ordinary people reflect on their experience of Jesus, where the powerful and the beautiful generally stay on the sidelines of the story, and where it is often the poor, the ill-educated and the disreputable whose encounters with God are most vividly described.[1] In the Gospels, events in historic time astonishingly fuse with events beyond time; it is often impossible to define a distinction between the two. The only other books specifically to be called Gospels apart from the canonical four are their literary rivals or imitators, written solely by Christians for the same purpose: to tell stories about the life and resurrection of Jesus. The so-called 'Gospel of Thomas' is one of the better known, since its collection of sayings attributed to Jesus resembles more than most the four Gospels contained in the New Testament. By transfer, 'Gospel' describes the whole message contained in all the biblical books, not just in the Gospels: the multiform, restless story of good news which is Christianity.

It is important to realize that a book of good news is not the same as straightforward reported news, or its more aged and academically respectable relative, history. The writer Jan Morris once recalled being advised by the Sudanese Minister of National Guidance, soon after the Second World War, that as a foreign correspondent she should try to report 'thrilling, attractive and good news, corresponding, where possible, with the truth'. That might sound cynical, but Ms Morris felt that the minister, an austere man, spoke more wisely than might at first appear, and she fruitfully bore it in mind in her career in journalism.[2] The minister's words provide a model of how we might approach the Gospels in a spirit which goes beyond cynicism. We may pare away the non-historical from the probably historical elements in Christian sacred literature, but that is in order better to understand the motives and preoccupations which led to the shape of the good news constructed by the first generations of Christians. Nowhere is that more apparent than in the stories of the birth of Jesus.

Only two out of four Gospels, Matthew and Luke, have narratives of this birth in Bethlehem at the end of the reign of King Herod the Great (73–4 BCE), and outside those narratives, there is much to direct the alert reader to a contrary story. John's Gospel is most explicit when it records arguments among people in Jerusalem, once Jesus had grown up and his teaching was making a stir: some sceptics pointed out that Jesus came from the northern district of Galilee, whereas the prophet Micah had foretold that the Jews' Anointed One, the Messiah, would come from Bethlehem in Judaea, in the south.[3] The other three Gospels – even the Gospels with stories of his birth in Bethlehem – repeatedly refer to Jesus as coming from Galilee, or more precisely from the village of Nazareth in Galilee. In fact outside the text of the two birth narratives, the Gospels do not refer to Jesus being born in Bethlehem, nor does any other book of the New Testament.

Luke's birth narrative, the more elaborate, explains that Jesus's parents travelled from Nazareth to Bethlehem at the time of Jesus's birth because they had to comply with the residence terms of a Roman imperial census for tax purposes, 'because he was of the house and lineage of David'.[4] This does not ring true: the idea is based on Luke's ancestor list for Jesus, designed to show that he was linked to King David a thousand years before, which was a matter of no concern whatsoever to Roman bureaucrats. Implausibilities multiply: the Roman authorities would not have held a census in a client kingdom of the empire such as Herod's, and in any case there is no record elsewhere of such an empire-wide census, which would certainly have left traces around the Mediterranean. The story seems to embody a confusion with a well-attested Roman imperial census which certainly did happen, but in 6 CE, far too late for the birth of Jesus, and long remembered as a traumatic event because it was the first real taste of what direct Roman rule meant for Judaea.[5] The suspicion therefore arises that someone writing a good deal later, rather hazy about the chronology of decades before, has been fairly cavalier with the story of Jesus's birth, for reasons other than retrieving events as they actually happened. This suspicion grows when one observes how little the birth and infancy narratives have to do with the later story of Jesus's public ministry, death and resurrection, which occupies all four Gospels; nowhere do these Gospels refer back to the tales of birth and infancy, which suggests that the bulk of their texts were written before these particular stories. We must conclude that beside the likelihood that Christmas did not happen at Christmas, it did not happen in Bethlehem.

Why, then, were the stories created? One motive for locating the birth in Bethlehem might be precisely to settle the argument noted in John's Gospel about Jesus's status as Messiah of his people Israel: it answered the sceptics who pointed out the problem with Micah's prophecy. But there is much else to these stories, all reflecting the deepening conviction among followers of Christ that this particular birth had profound cosmic importance. Matthew's and Luke's preoccupations diverge – one would not realize from listening to the harmonization of fragments of them in Christian Christmas celebrations that the Gospels agree in hardly any detail about Jesus's infancy. The narrators intend to recall more ancient stories in the minds of the hearers by applying them to the coming of Jesus the Christ. So Matthew raises an echo of Moses by sending Jesus and his parents in flight to Egypt from the murderous King Herod: once more, a birth is imperilled, innocent children are killed by a worldly ruler, and yet the one child survives in Egypt to be a deliverer for Israel.

Matthew and Luke provide two ancestor lists for Jesus which agree very little in the personnel involved and whose distinct patterns seem to have different preoccupations.[6] Christians quickly felt uncomfortable about these divergent families, producing explanations which, as recorded by the early-third-century scholar Julius Africanus ('the African'), are masterpieces of far-fetched genealogical speculation.[7] Matthew's list unconventionally includes descent through women, unlike Luke's; a strange bunch those women are, all associated with eyebrow-raising sexual circumstances and also, Jesus's mother, Mary, excepted, with non-Jews. The messages here seem to be that Jesus (and maybe also the circumstances of his birth) transcends petty conventions of behaviour in Jewish society, and also that even while he is a Jew, his destiny is confirmed as a universal one, not simply for the benefit of Jews.[8] The same thoughts run through the whole Gospel narrative which is given Matthew's name: of all the Gospel writers, he is the most concerned to define how far and in what ways the Christian community for whom he is writing can depart from Jewish tradition while still observing its spirit. His Jesus says that he has come to 'fulfil' Jewish Law, not 'abolish' it, and piles up quotations from the Law, only to plunge far beyond them in rigour, punctuating his thrusts with the repeated phrase 'But I say to you . . .'[9] Whoever added Matthew's infancy narrative shared the agenda of the main creator of the Gospel. The messages would be understood and appreciated by the Christian congregation which first heard Matthew's text recited or chanted in its worship.

Furthermore, Matthew's and Luke's ancestor lists are in their present form pointless. They claim to show that Jesus could be described as the Son of David; in fact Luke goes further, taking Jesus back to Adam, the first man. Yet they do this by tracing David's line down to Jesus's father, Joseph. Both then defeat their purpose by implying that Joseph was not actually the father of Jesus. Matthew does it by abruptly ending the genealogical mantra 'father of' after the generation of 'Jacob the father of Joseph', continuing 'Joseph the husband of Mary, of whom Jesus was born'. Luke is more directly indecorous by calling Jesus 'the son (as was supposed) of Joseph'.[10] These rather lame phrases cannot be other than emendations of the rival texts, designed to accommodate the rapidly growing conviction of Christians that Jesus's mother, Mary, was a virgin in human terms and became with child by the Holy Spirit. Matthew describes the announcement of the miraculous birth as being made to Joseph, but Luke gives the experience to Mary, and it is striking that

Christian devotion and Christian art have overwhelmingly concentrated on Luke's account of an 'Annunciation' to Mary and have ignored Joseph's equal revelation. It is a surprising reversal of the normal priority offered to men's experience in the ancient world, and it reflects the early growth of a complex of Christian emotional and devotional needs attached to Mary and her role in Christ's story. In the centuries which followed, Christians went further, coming to insist that Jesus's mother remained a virgin throughout her life. A proclamation of Mary's perpetual virginity meant commentators clumsily making the best that they could of clear references in the biblical text to Jesus's brothers and sisters, who were certainly not conceived by the Holy Spirit (see p. 597).

This tangle of preoccupations with Mary's virginity centres on Matthew's quotation from a Greek version of words of the prophet Isaiah in the Septuagint (see p. 69): 'Behold, a virgin shall conceive and bear a son, and his name shall be called Emmanuel'. This alters or refines the meaning of Isaiah's original Hebrew: where the prophet had talked only of 'a young woman' conceiving and bearing a son, the Septuagint projected 'young woman' into the Greek word for 'virgin' (*parthenos*).[11] This Christian use of the Septuagint was either cause or result of changing perspectives on Jesus, which emerged out of what is likely to have been a cacophony of opinions and assertions among his first followers, trying to make sense of the extraordinary impact of this Jewish teacher. Most of the cacophony is lost to us because it does not survive in written form, but we can glimpse in the biblical text one view of Jesus as the coming Messiah from David's line, or as another Moses, the ancient Deliverer. These perspectives were not lost, but voices emerged to acclaim Jesus as having a Father who was divinity itself, and these voices are now those overwhelmingly dominant in the New Testament.

The Tanakh had on rare occasions referred to Israel's God as Father, but the idea sprouts mightily within the New Testament, where Jesus is portrayed as constantly referring to God as Father. He actually produces one of his most remarkable innovations by calling God '*abba*', an Aramaic word equivalent to 'Dad', which had never been used to address God before in Jewish tradition, and whose peculiar novelty was attested by being kept in its Aramaic form in the Greek text of the New Testament. There is further proof that this notion of an intimate Fatherhood between God and humanity is a basic layer of Jesus's message: he goes beyond self-reference. In 'The Lord's Prayer', which lies at the heart of Christian approaches to God, he tells his disciples to pray to *their* Father in Heaven – though the followers address God not as *abba* but by the ordinary Greek word for 'father', *patēr*.[12]

The birth and infancy narratives in the Gospels therefore provide an excellent example of the way in which those biblical accounts which are hardly historical in themselves reveal a great deal about the historical circumstances in which they were created. But much of the history of the Gospels themselves is history of the time after the life of Jesus himself. What can we know of Jesus's life, death and original message? There is some shakiness even about dating, but that might be expected for a man who came from an obscure corner of the ancient world and whose death seemed at first a matter of little consequence amid the great affairs of the empire. Nearly two centuries later, Julius Africanus, one of the first great scholars of the ancient world to be a Christian, tried to piece together a coherent chronology for Christian events. He placed the Saviour's birth in a year which he reckoned as the 5,500th from Creation; this calculation became embedded in the work of later historians, such as the sixth-century Dionysius Exiguus ('the Short'), who has often wrongly stolen credit from Julius for fixing the first Year of the Lord (*annus Domini*). Alas, Julius's figures were themselves wrong, because they were based on a misdating of the death of King Herod the Great, making it three years too late.[13] The significance of this is that both Matthew's and Luke's infancy narratives place Jesus's birth in the final year or so of Herod's reign, and Herod's death actually took place in 4 BCE.[14] Assuming (although it is a large and even illogical assumption) that we can place more faith in the infancy narratives' chronological fix on Jesus's birth than in their general claims for a birth in Bethlehem, it is likely that Jesus was born in that same year, 4 BCE.

THE ADULT JESUS:
A PUBLIC CAMPAIGN

Once we leave the birth and childhood stories and leap over the almost total silence in all four Gospel narratives about Jesus's next two decades of life, we reach the brief but crowded action of his campaign or 'ministry' of public preaching, teaching and healing, and we find much more circumstantial narratives. This story of good news nevertheless still bristles with problems of historical interpretation. One date alone looks fairly secure: Luke's Gospel carefully places the beginning of a parallel ministry by John 'the Baptist', said to be a cousin of Jesus, in the year 28–9 CE; Jesus himself underwent a baptism in the River Jordan at the hands of John.[15] This immediately preceded Jesus's own independent appearance on the public stage; Jesus's campaign may have been something of a rival movement, given the vigorous assertions of Jesus's superiority to John to be found in all the Gospels.[16] Luke asserts that Jesus was about thirty when he began his public ministry: this indicates that the death of Jesus took place some time between 29 and 32 CE, depending on how many years he was engaged in his proclamation, and assuming his birth some time around 4 BCE.[17] The Gospels do not give a definite answer as to whether Jesus's ministry lasted for one year (John) or three (Matthew, Mark and Luke), or where its main focus lay within the Holy Land. The Gospels of Matthew, Mark and Luke speak of a ministry spent mostly in Galilee in the north, with a final southward journey to Jerusalem; the evangelist John, by contrast, deals mostly with activity in the south, Judaea, focusing especially on the city and the Temple.

Scholars from a Western Christian or Enlightenment background have now spent more than two centuries trying to reach through the filters of the four Gospels and the letters of Paul to find a 'real' Jesus and an 'authentic' version of what he actually said: it has been perhaps the most thoroughgoing and sophisticated analysis of any set of texts in the history of human thought. Many Christians have found the accumulation of this scholarly activity distressing and destructive, but after all that sifting, there is much that we can say about what Jesus preached. Naturally we are inclined to ask what was 'new' or 'original' in what he said, but that question may be misguided and distort what was important in his teaching; not only were there a good many wandering teachers like him at the time, but it may have been precisely the ideas he shared with his contemporaries and predecessors which were most significant at the time and first won a hearing through their familiarity. One of his central commands is a commonplace of ancient philosophy, and is a conclusion at which most world religions eventually arrive: 'whatever you wish that men would do to you, do so to them' – what has come to be known as the Golden Rule.[18]

Nevertheless it is worth listening for the voice of Jesus, particularly in the three Gospels which develop common material and edit it in their own ways. Of the three, Mark's text is generally held to be the earliest, with separate forms of development and use of additional material in Matthew and Luke. They are all likely to have been written in the last

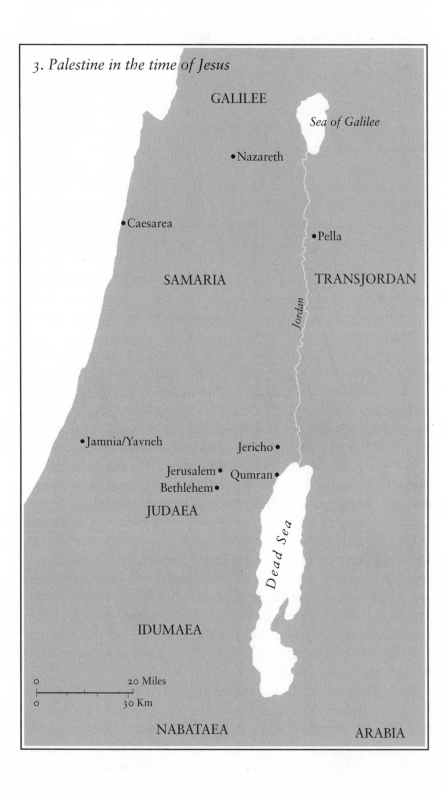

3. *Palestine in the time of Jesus*

GALILEE

Sea of Galilee

•Nazareth

•Caesarea

•Pella

SAMARIA   TRANSJORDAN

Jordan

•Jamnia/Yavneh   Jericho •

Jerusalem •   Qumran •
Bethlehem •

JUDAEA

Dead Sea

IDUMAEA

20 Miles

30 Km

NABATAEA   ARABIA

three decades of the first century, around half a century after Jesus died, but certainly no later than that, since they are already beginning to be quoted in other Christian texts datable not much later than 200 CE. They seem to have been based on earlier collections of sayings of Jesus; they represent selections by different Christian communities anxious to put boundaries on the stories of good news about Jesus's life and resurrection, and also to bring their own perspectives to the good news. The three Gospels are together known as the 'Synoptic' Gospels to distinguish them from the Gospel of John, which was probably written a decade or two later than they were; the three present the basic story of Jesus in a similar way, quite differently from John's narrative – so they 'see together', the root meaning of the Greek *synopsis*.[19]

To a surprising degree, the Synoptic Gospels reveal distinctive quirks of speech in Jesus's sayings which suggest an individual voice. One very common and very Semitic peculiarity, for instance, is found more than a hundred times in these three Gospels: Jesus has a trick of setting one proposition against an opposed proposition. So Mark has Jesus saying, 'With men it is impossible, but not with God; for all things are possible with God.' The likelihood that this was how Jesus spoke is strengthened by the fact that Luke seems to dislike the literary form, perhaps finding it inelegant, and from time to time he weakens Mark's original formulation – in this case down to 'What is impossible with men is possible with God.'[20] The form has its precedents in the Hebrew literature which Jesus would have known, but it is noticeable that those previous examples tend to have a stress on the first element, while Jesus mostly stresses the second. This suggests an urgency to his message, a punchiness which would make each saying easy to remember and recite long after listeners had first heard it shouted in public.[21]

Another quirk is Jesus's frequent and apparently unprecedented use of the emphatic Hebrew and Aramaic exclamation 'Amen!' before he makes a solemn pronouncement: 'Amen I say to you . . .' The word was considered so important that it was preserved in its original form in the Greek biblical text; in sixteenth- and seventeenth-century versions of the English Bible, it becomes 'verily'. John's Gospel develops the peculiarity even further than the Synoptics by customarily doubling it – 'Amen Amen I say to you . . .', which is probably gilding the lily in the interests of John's exalted view of Jesus Christ as cosmic Saviour.[22] The effect is rather like Dr Samuel Johnson's famous characteristic phrase 'Depend upon it, Sir . . .' as he launched on some particularly final or crushing remark: it is intended to emphasize the uniquely personal authority of the speaker, and it may be contrasted significantly with the reported-speech construction of a phrase which had been much used in the Tanakh, 'Thus says the Lord'. Jesus in the Gospels is his own authority. He is, after all, the one who has seized the intimate word *abba* and used it when speaking to God.

Along with this sense that Jesus has a prerogative to speak with greater power than that of the ancient prophets, one hears irony, indirectness in his voice, particularly in a mysterious phrase of his which continues to provoke debate among biblical scholars, 'the Son of Man'. Jesus in the Synoptic Gospels virtually never calls himself 'Son of God', though he does in John (see p. 103). He repeatedly uses this other phrase: for instance, 'The sabbath was made for man, not man for the sabbath: so the Son of Man is Lord even of the sabbath.'[23] All four Gospels record the usage frequently, though there is no overlap at all between the Synoptic Gospels' sayings of Jesus which include it and the sayings in John's Gospel. This may suggest that John created 'sayings of Jesus' for his own purposes. In the extensive surviving writings of the Apostle Paul about Jesus, the phrase never occurs – nor does it recur beyond scriptural texts over the next few centuries in the works of Christian writers, for whom it would have been less than helpful as they debated how Jesus Christ could be both human and divine. Those silences make 'the Son of Man' all the more striking as it rings through the Gospels, virtually exclusively in the reported words of Jesus.[24] It echoes a use of a phrase, 'One like a son of man', in the Book of Daniel, a work about two centuries older than Jesus's time, where the reference is to one who takes up an everlasting reign to replace the demonic kingdoms of the physical world.[25] Therefore it points to a Jesus who saw himself and proclaimed himself as the Messiah whom Jews expected – but in a curious, oblique way. There is no positive evidence that anyone in the age of Jesus would have recognized 'Son of Man' as a special title – in fact there is not much evidence in the Gospels that Jesus used any particular title for himself, whatever others called him. Rather 'Son of Man' may reflect in Greek a phrase in Aramaic (Jesus's everyday language) meaning 'someone like me', sometimes with the sense that this meaning extends to the group who have the privilege of listening to what Jesus is saying – 'people like us'.[26]

It is always difficult to catch irony and humour across a gap of centuries; but if evanescent tints remain in the phrase 'Son of Man', they are much clearer in another distinctive and engaging feature of Jesus's discourses, the miniature stories or 'parables' which illuminate aspects of his message. There is nothing like the parables in the writings of Jewish spiritual teachers (rabbis) before Jesus used them; interestingly, they emerge as a literary form in later Judaism only after Jesus's death. Was this form of Jesus's teaching so successful that it impressed and influenced even Jews who did not become his followers?[27] Because the parables are stories, they have woven themselves into general memory more than any other aspects of Jesus's message: the Good Samaritan; the Wise and the Foolish Virgins; the bad and good use of talents – a word which has itself been enriched thanks to the parable of the Talents, whose original reference was simply to coins called talents and not to gifts of personality. They resonate with the sense of a single voice, not least because of all the odd, counter-intuitive things which happen in them.

Nevertheless, many of Jesus's parables would have had all the more impact because they drew on existing stories which ordinary people knew: for instance, the contemporary Alexandrian Jewish tale of a rich man's funeral and a poor man's funeral and the reversal of their fortunes in the next world, which lies behind the different narrative thrusts of two well-known parables, the Great Man's Rejected Supper and the parable of Dives ('Rich Man' in Latin) and Lazarus the beggar.[28] Originally these pointed little stories were directed to a particular audience and situation: so Mark and then Matthew and Luke developing Mark's text record one parable about wicked tenants who murder the son of their landlord, and they specifically say that it was told 'against' and in the presence of the leaders of the Temple in Jerusalem, provoking their fury.[29] In some cases, such as the story of the great man who stages a banquet which is then rejected by the guests, it looks as if the Gospel writers took a parable story from one specific original context and gave it a new one, even expanding and complicating the story to get a new meaning across which would be helpful to later generations in the emerging Church.[30]

The overwhelming preoccupation in the parables, despite their various accretions after Jesus's time, is a message about a coming kingdom which will overwhelm all the normal expectations of Israel and take its establishment figures by surprise. People must be watchful for this final event, which is inevitably going to catch them unawares: so both the wise and the foolish virgins snatch a nap before the bridegroom arrives, but the wise virgins have provided ample oil for their lamps of celebration, still burning when they need to wake up.[31] In a gem of sarcasm, Jesus points out that a householder would not have left his house to be broken into if he had been informed of the burglar's intended hour of arrival – 'for the Son of man is coming at an unexpected hour'. How extraordinary to compare the fulfilling of God's purposes to an act of criminality, even violence![32] Much celebration and joy run through these stories, which tell of feasts and wedding banquets, yet also custom, common sense and even natural justice are at times ruthlessly ignored: labourers in a vineyard who have done a full day's work are told to stop complaining when they get the same wage as latecomers who only put in an hour.[33] The coming kingdom will make up its own rules. The later Church found this an uncomfortable message as it settled down to make sense of people's everyday lives.

This sense that all the rules have changed is to be found in many of the sayings attributed to Jesus, particularly those which in Matthew's and Luke's Gospels have been gathered into an anthology, known from Matthew's version of it as the Sermon on the Mount (Luke's shorter version actually places the event on a plain, not a mountain, but somehow that setting has never captured Christians' imagination to the same extent).[34] It begins with a dramatic collection of blessings on those whom the world would call unfortunate, such as the poor, the hungry, those weeping, those who are widely hated. All these will have their fortunes precisely reversed. These 'Beatitudes' have remained as a subversive tug at the sleeve for churchmen in the centuries during which they have had too much worldly comfort, an encouragement for the oppressed, and even a stimulus to many Christians to seek out deprivation and practise humility – an inspiration to monks and friars in later centuries, as we will see. Jesus's breaking of conventions continues after the Beatitudes: traditional sayings are quoted, such as the admirable 'You shall not kill; and whoever kills shall be liable to judgement', and then they are put on the rack or disconcertingly extended to their logical conclusion. So physical killing ought indeed to be condemned, but so should all people angry with their brother who then turn the anger into verbal violence; they shall be liable to the Hell of fire.[35] There is much punishing fire flickering round the preacher's words. There is nothing gentle, meek or mild about the driving force behind these stabbing inversions of normal expectations. They form a code of life which is a chorus of love directed to the loveless or unlovable, of painful honesty expressing itself with embarrassing directness, of joyful rejection of any counsel suggesting careful self-regard or prudence. That, apparently, is what the Kingdom of God is like.

Jesus's preoccupation with the imminent kingdom is clear not only in all this material, and in his reference to Daniel's 'Son of Man', but also in 'The Lord's Prayer' which he taught his followers and which is embedded in different versions in both versions of the Sermon anthology.[36] The prayer moves straight from addressing the Father in Heaven to the plea 'Thy kingdom come'. It is also shown to belong to the earliest strata of the Gospel material even in its Greek form, because one of its petitions includes an adjective whose meaning has baffled Christians ever since: 'epiousios', a very rare word indeed in Greek. The puzzling character of the word is not apparent in its common English translation, which suggests a very ordinary request, 'Give us this day our *daily* bread'. Yet epiousios does not mean 'daily', but something like 'of extra substance', or at a stretch 'for the morrow'. The first Roman Catholic attempt to translate 'The Lord's Prayer' into English from the Latin Vulgate in the late sixteenth century courageously recognized the problem, but also sidestepped it simply by borrowing a Latin word as 'supersubstantial'; not surprisingly, 'give us this day our super-substantial bread' never caught on as a popular phrase in prayer. If we can assign any meaning to epiousios, it may point to the new time of the coming kingdom: there must be a new provision when God's people are hungry in this new time – yet the provision for the morrow must come now, because the kingdom is about to arrive.[37]

The evidence for Jesus's concentration on the imminence of the coming kingdom piles up, all the more strikingly because within decades of Jesus's death the Church began to have second thoughts on just how imminent it might be. The Apostle Paul hardly ever recorded what Jesus had actually taught, so it is all the more notable that he records as a 'word of the Lord' that 'the Lord himself will descend from Heaven with a cry of command, with the archangel's call, and with the sound of the trumpet of God' – phrases echoed (probably a few decades after Paul wrote) in Matthew's Gospel.[38] Jesus gathered around him twelve special disciples or 'Apostles' as the central figures in his public ministry: twelve was the number of the long-dispersed tribes of Israel, a sign that the fractured past and present were to be made perfect. Reportedly after Jesus's death, a new Apostle called Matthias was appointed out of two possible candidates to make up the Twelve, since Judas, one of the original Apostles, had betrayed Jesus to the authorities and then killed himself.[39] The fact that after that, most of the Twelve had little recorded impact on the early Christian story makes it all the more noticeable that the Jesus narratives in the Gospels still give such a prominent place to the selection of the Twelve and their role in his ministry.

So Jesus was convinced of his special mission to preach a message from God which centred on an imminent transformation of the world, yet he spoke of himself with deliberate irony and ambiguity, and used a delicate humour that is revealed in the content of some of his sayings. He spoke of his special place in a divine plan, looked forward to a last judgement in which he would play a leading part, yet also saw that the way to this final conclusion might result in suffering and death both for himself and for his followers. He made crowds laugh. He shocked or excited them with irreverent comments on authority; so he caricatured rival religious teachers 'straining out a gnat and swallowing a camel'. He produced outrageous inversions of normality – 'Leave the dead to bury their own dead,' Jesus said to a man who wanted to postpone becoming his disciple in order to see to his father's funeral.[40] This saying is clearly authentic, since Gospel writers felt bound to preserve it even though it outrages every pious norm of the ancient world and a universal human instinct; moreover, Christianity has stonily ignored the command throughout its subsequent history. Jesus puzzled people with references which apparently needed spelling out in private even to his closest followers.[41] He had power: around him, as with many charismatic leaders over the centuries, there gathered stories of exceptional healings, miracles of providing food and drink, even raising apparent corpses from the dead. For a large part of Christian history, these miracles have provided much of the fascination of Jesus for those drawn to his story, though for three centuries they have increasingly aroused unease or intellectual conflict for Christians formed by the Enlightenment of the West.

Still, Jesus was a Jew immersed in the traditions that constituted the identity of his fellow Jews. He is recorded as taking a cavalier attitude to the Jewish Law or obeying its demands in ways which seem capricious, which caused anxious debate for generations about how far Christians should imitate him, and which are still puzzling after much very sophisticated modern analysis of the mixture. Maybe the answer is that Jesus did not care a great deal about being consistent on the issue, given his concentration on the imminent coming of the kingdom, in which all laws would be made anew. So he was not especially worried about special observance of the Jewish weekly holy day (the Sabbath), or various rules for ritual purity, but he cared a great deal about oaths, in particular about an agreement to enter marriage. In this respect Jesus was more hard line than regular Jewish practice embodied in the Law of Moses – too hard line indeed for the Church's later comfort. We can tell that an absolute prohibition of divorce was one of his foundation principles, since Jesus's posthumous Apostle and interpreter Paul of Tarsus (see pp. 97–102) went out of his way to contradict the unconditional 'commandment from the Lord' on this matter, and one of the Gospel writers similarly nervously modified the 'no divorce' command to allow for the circumstance of adultery.[42]

CRUCIFIXION AND RESURRECTION

Certainly Jesus cared profoundly about the Temple in Jerusalem. His intense feelings about it made him predict its destruction, and apparently his own ability to rebuild it in three days. He provoked a disturbance in it, protesting at what he saw as its misuse for commerce and profit, and it was the goal of his last fatal public appearances. Then he was arrested in Jerusalem, put on trial and executed along with two common criminals on a hill outside the city, by the ghastly Roman custom of crucifixion. It is a sequence of events – the 'Passion', so called from the Latin verb to suffer, *pateor* – which forms the dramatic culmination of the Gospels' account of his public ministry. There is indeed more high drama in the Passion than in the accounts of Jesus's subsequent resurrection and renewed appearances to his disciples. At the beginning of that story of humiliation, torture and death, on the night that he was betrayed to Temple and Roman authorities, is the account of his 'last supper' with the Twelve. On that occasion, not merely the Synoptic Gospels but also Paul of Tarsus, in a reminiscence of the actual earthly life of Jesus very rare in Paul's writings, record that he took bread and wine, broke the bread, gave thanks and gave them to his disciples. It was a meal taken amid the Jewish festival of the Passover, the joyful season when the Jews remembered their liberation from Egypt (see pp. 51–2). Indeed, perhaps the group was celebrating the Passover meal itself.

The death of Jesus became inextricably linked in the minds first of the witnesses, then of the later Church, with the lamb killed for a blood-soaked sacrifice in the Passover ceremonies. Jesus spoke of the bread of the supper as his body and the wine as his blood. A rich mixture of thought associations with death, sacrifice and thanksgiving for deliverance from disaster has flowed from that evening meal, into the supper drama which Christians have made the centre of their worship and have called the Eucharist. That is still the everyday Greek word for 'thanks'. There is endless and probably irresolvable debate about how this ritual meal might have related to pre-Christian Jewish worship customs and ritual thanksgivings. What is clear is that there was nothing quite like it in previous tradition. From the earliest time of its institution, it involved a recital of the words of Jesus which ordered his followers to do it in remembrance of him, and it was done as a re-enactment of that 'last supper' which Jesus had shared with his Twelve before his arrest.[43] The power and mystery of the Eucharist, linking the crucified Saviour to those who break bread and drink wine ever afterwards, has provoked intense devotion, gratitude and joy among Christians, yet also deep anger and bitterness when they argue about what it means.

These Passion narratives are probably the earliest continuous material in the Gospels, a set of stories first formulated for public recital in the various communities which compiled their own accounts of his life, sufferings and resurrection. Unlike the two infancy narratives, their details have much circumstantial overlap and feel like real events, but in their present shape they are also designed to make sense of something which came to be a real problem for the later Church. The Romans killed Jesus, however much the Temple establishment, in fury and fear at the nature of his preaching, had prompted them to do so. Jesus had said nothing more outrageous about the religion of the Jews than other wild representatives of Judaism had proclaimed either before him or in his own time. His was not a theological but a political threat to the fragile stability of the region. Non-Jews killed a potential Jewish leader, as they had killed the Maccabean heroes long before. This was emphasized by the title inextricably associated with the stories of Jesus's last hours and said to have been affixed to his cross: 'King of the Jews'. Like 'Son of Man', this was not a title for which the later Christian Church found any use and so its survival in the tradition is all the more instructive. That 'King of the Jews' phrase is an inescapable repeated refrain through the Passion narratives, even despite the embarrassment which it was to cause Christians in the fraught political situation which emerged a few decades after that death on the Cross.

Most Christians did not want to be enemies of the Roman Empire and they soon sought to play down the role of the Romans in the story. So the Passion narratives shifted the blame on to the Jewish authorities, and the local representative of Roman authority – a coarse-grained soldier called Pontius Pilate – was portrayed as inquisitive and bewildered, cross-questioning the seditious prisoner before him as if Jesus were an equal and making every effort to get him off the hook. The evangelist John pictured the Jews as being forced by legal circumstance to hand over a man condemned for blasphemy to the Roman authorities if they were to secure the death sentence for him which they ardently sought.[44] That is implausible, considering that three decades later the Jerusalem High Priest was directly responsible for the execution of Jesus's brother James, then leader of the Christians in Jerusalem. Additionally, the evangelist Matthew shifted blame for Jesus's death (with satisfying drama, though without any legal force) to the Jewish crowds, who in his narrative roared out, 'His blood be on us, and on our children!'[45] The Christian Church has drawn much out of Matthew's literary decision. It would have been better for the moral health of Christianity if the blame had stayed with Pilate.

If that lingering and humiliating death on the Cross had been the end of the story, then the tale of Jesus would have remained embedded in Judaism. Jesus might have made it into the history books, even inspired a new departure in Jewish faith, but there would have been little likelihood of a separated or wider religion. Jesus's public ministry had been to Jews; otherwise he made some forays into the territory of their despised cousins the Samaritans and Mark and Matthew once record him straying out of this Judaic world, into 'the region of Tyre and Sidon', where he met his match in wit with a Greek-speaking 'Canaanite' woman desperate for him to cure her mentally disturbed daughter.[46] Jesus spoke Aramaic as his first language. As the encounter with the Canaanite woman seems to indicate, and is in any case to be expected, he could speak marketplace Greek when he needed to, but that knowledge has left no trace even where one might expect it, in the filtered versions of his story in the Greek New Testament. Jesus left no writings – in fact the only record of his writing is of some doodles in the dirt as a diversion in a tricky situation, and we have no idea what might have been read in them on that day which saved the life of a woman taken in adultery.[47]

What the Gospels tell us happened after the Crucifixion was the ultimate good news: Jesus came back to human life after three days in the tomb. Somehow a criminal's death and defeat on the Cross, 'Good Friday', as Christians came to call it, were transformed by his followers into a triumph of life over death, and the Passion narratives ended with the story of Easter Resurrection. This Resurrection is not a matter which historians can authenticate; it is a different sort of truth, or statement about truth. It is the most troubling, difficult affirmation in Christianity, but over twenty centuries Christians have thought it central to their faith. Easter is the earliest Christian festival, and it was for its celebration that the Passion narratives were created by the first Christians.

Belief in the truth of the Resurrection story and in Jesus's power to overcome death has made Christians act over twenty centuries in the most heroic, joyful, beautiful and terrible ways. And the fact that Christianity's Jesus is the resurrected Christ makes a vital point about the misfit between the Jesus whose teachings we have excavated and the Church which came after him. It mattered much less to the first Christ-followers after the Resurrection what Jesus had said than what he did and was doing now, and who he was (or whom people thought him to be). And as he emerged in the first Christian writings, they now thought him to be a Greek *Christos*, not a Jewish Messiah – even though Greek-speakers beyond the Jewish milieu hardly understood what a *Christos* was, and quickly assumed that it was some sort of personal name.[48] Historians might take comfort from the fact that nowhere in the New Testament is there a description of the Resurrection: it was beyond the capacity or the intention of the writers to describe it, and all they described were its effects. The New Testament is thus a literature with a blank at its centre; yet this blank is also its intense focus.

The beginning of the long Christian conversation lies in the chorus of assertions in the writings of the New Testament that after Jesus's death his tomb was found empty. He repeatedly appeared to those who had known him, in ways which confused and contradicted the laws of physics: he showed witnesses that he could be touched and felt and could be watched eating grilled fish, but he also appeared and disappeared regardless of doors or any normal means of exit and entrance. Many who at first found such claims absurd when others made them are reported as having being convinced when they had the same experience. Luke's Gospel ends with one of the most apparently naturalistic-sounding and circumstantial of these encounters: a conversation between a stranger and two former disciples, Peter and Cleopas, on the road from Jerusalem to a village called Emmaus. It was only later, over a meal in Emmaus, that Peter and Cleopas recognized Jesus for who he was.[49] The seventeenth-century Italian artist Caravaggio, in two of his most disturbing and exciting paintings, projected the astonishment and delight of that encounter into an ordinary room in his own time, but he also made it clear that this was a story with as many echoes as the stories in the infancy narratives (see Plate 18).

The most casual viewer of Caravaggio's paintings can see what the artist recognized in the biblical narrative: the meal of recognition at Emmaus is transparently the Church's breaking of bread and wine, echoing the Last Supper or Eucharist of the Passion narratives. All

Eucharists are celebrations of the man resurrected from the dead, who meets his disciples at a most unlikely time and place, just as he did at Emmaus, which was among the most unlikely of settings for such an encounter. For one dimension of the story is that Emmaus may not have been a real place near Jerusalem at all in first-century Judaea. Two centuries before, it certainly had been a real place: the site of the first victory of the Maccabean heroes over the enemies of Israel, where 'all the Gentiles will know that there is one who redeems and saves Israel'.[50] In terms of the Gospel story, Emmaus was beyond time, but it was the natural setting for the disciples to meet the one who had eclipsed the sufferings of the Maccabees in order to redeem the new Israel before the face of all people.

After some time (the accounts are contradictory, implying either a few days or forty) Jesus removed his presence from his disciples – was taken up or carried into Heaven, as two of the Gospel writers put it. Later Christians commonly called this departure the Ascension, and on occasion its final last moment has been portrayed endearingly literally in Christian art, when all that can be seen are Christ's feet disappearing into a cloud.[51] Historians are never going to make sense of these reports, unless like some of those who first heard them they choose to regard them as simply ludicrous. Nevertheless they can hardly fail to note the extraordinary galvanizing energy of those who spread the story after their experience of Resurrection and Ascension, and they can reconstruct something of the resulting birth of the Christian Church, even if the story can never be more than fragmentary. Whether through some mass delusion, some colossal act of wishful thinking, or through witness to a power or force beyond any definition known to Western historical analysis, those who had known Jesus in life and had felt the shattering disappointment of his death proclaimed that he lived still, that he loved them still, and that he was to return to earth from the Heaven which he had now entered, to love and save from destruction all who acknowledged him as Lord.[52]

It is hardly surprising that in the two millennia of Christian history since these profound surprises and mysteries, Christianity has been a perpetual argument about meaning and reality. Readers of this book may become bewildered, bored or irritated by my extended discussions of the theological niceties which once aroused such passions among Christians; but no history of Christianity which tries to sidle past its theological disputes will make sense. The problem is simple in its utter complexity: how can a human being be God? Christians can be passionately convinced that they meet a fellow human in Jesus who is God, but they may not like the implications of this: how can God be involved in the unhygienic messiness of everyday life and remain God? There are basic problems of human dirt, waste and decay from which devotion recoils – yet without dirt, where is the real humanity of Christ, which tears other humans away from despair and oblivion towards joy and life? The variety of answers to these questions dominated the development of the Church in its first five centuries, and at no time have those who call themselves Christians reached unanimity on the puzzles. And the disagreements were not academic in any sense of the word; they were matters of eternal life or eternal death. We will meet a crowd butchering a bishop who had signed up to the wrong solution; we will find Christians burning other Christians alive over matters which now seem no more than points to debate in a university seminar. We should try to understand why these people of past societies were so angry, frightened and sadistic, even if we cannot sympathize with them. That will mean encountering a crowded menu of theology, centring on the Lord Jesus Christ.

'Lord' – the Greek word *Kyrios* – resounds so much through the Bible that my old concordance of words occurring in the Bible, compiled by the magnificently obsessive eighteenth-century Scotsman Alexander Cruden, takes eight pages in three columns of tiny print to list all the usages of 'Lord' through Old and New Testaments. Nearly all relate to divine figures: first in the Old Testament as a translation via Greek of the Hebrew words for the name of God, and then throughout the New Testament, directly and newly for Jesus Christ. All the New Testament writings are written with this consciousness in mind: Jesus is Lord, the word for God. Probably none of these texts were written by anyone who had known Jesus in person, though some have taken the names of people who did. Those now thought to be written first – in other words, before the Gospels which narrate the ministry of Jesus – were the work of a man who came to an intense relationship with Jesus Christ a year or two after the Lord's Ascension. He was called Saul, which after his turn to Christianity he changed to Paul; he was a businessman, by trade a tent-maker, from a Mediterranean port called Tarsos or Tarsus, hundreds of miles north of Palestine in what is now Turkey.

NEW DIRECTIONS: PAUL OF TARSUS

Saul was a devout and soundly educated Jew in the Pharisaic tradition, reflecting the great centuries-long dispersal of the Jewish people because he spoke as his first language not Jesus's Aramaic but Greek, the common (*koinē*) Greek of the marketplace and quayside. This vigorous, non-literary, everyday Greek was the style in which virtually all the New Testament was written and the earliest surviving parts are a series of letters which Paul wrote to various congregations of Christ-followers. Some of these letters survive in lightly edited form, seven in number in their present arrangement, alongside slightly later pastiches of the authentic letters which have also taken Paul's name.[53] The Church knows them as 'epistles', from the Greek word *epistolē*, which reflects the character they have come to assume in Christian tradition as 'commands' or 'commissions', not simply as messages. We meet Paul too in the text of a slightly later work in the biblical canon. It is called the Acts of the Apostles, and presents itself in its introduction as having been written by the author of the Gospel of Luke, though in the course of its tales of the adventures of Paul and of other early Christian activists, Acts has something of the feel of a historical novel. Acts is eager to play down the fact that Paul was often to be found in confrontations with the earlier leaders of the Church, and that his message had distinctive qualities. It also has to be said that the Paul of Acts does not always sound like the Paul of his own letters (letters which are never actually mentioned in Acts). The general excitement of the stories in Acts has frequently eclipsed the considerably more personally complex Paul to be met in his own words.[54]

The tent-maker from Tarsus turned from active hatred of Christianity to become the most prominent of its early spokespeople whose memory has survived. The circumstances of this conversion as described in Acts are dramatic; it came in the wake of his watching and approving of the stoning to death in Jerusalem of Stephen, the first known martyr for Christ after Christ's death, some time in the early 30s CE. Maybe it was the effect of witnessing this violence which produced such a violent reaction in Saul. As he travelled on the road to Damascus, 'suddenly a light from heaven flashed about him. And he fell to the ground and heard a voice saying to him, "Saul, Saul, why do you persecute me?" '[55] It was Jesus himself speaking. Such was the trauma of this vision that Saul temporarily lost his sight and was struck dumb for several days.

Paul's own account in his letter to the Churches in the Roman province of Galatia (in central Asia Minor) is more reticent. It merely says that God 'was pleased to reveal his Son to me', and that his good news had came to him 'through a revelation of Jesus Christ', but even this reference is coupled with the notice of a dramatic new direction for the proclamation of the good news: Paul claims that God had set him aside to preach Christ 'among the Gentiles' – that is, non-Jews. Paul also says that he did not consult any of the existing Jewish leaders of the Jesus movement in Jerusalem, or indeed any 'flesh and blood'. He went away to Arabia to preach Christ, then three years passed before his first encounter in Jerusalem with two of the original Twelve, Peter (whom he calls Cephas) and the leader of the Jerusalem Church, James.[56]

Acts says nothing of that first mission to Arabia, and the suspicion occurs that it was not a great success – though maybe this country remote from Tarsus and Jerusalem was also the crucial setting in which Paul's extraordinary version of the Jesus message took shape. Paul's journeys which we know about from Acts, some of which are also attested in his surviving letters, take him in an entirely opposite direction: the eastern Mediterranean, and finally to Rome, the scene of his death some time in the mid-60s CE. It was a momentous change, which in the long term was to turn Christianity from a faith of the Semitic East into something very different, in which the heirs of Greek and Latin civilization determined the way in which the Christ story was told and interpreted. For Paul was not merely a Jew: he was one of those countless subjects of the Roman Empire who had obtained grants of citizenship and could consider themselves privileged people entitled to the consideration of the emperor in Rome. It is noticeable that in geographical references throughout his letters, he refers as a matter of course to the names set up by the Romans for their various provinces throughout the empire.[57] When Paul was put on trial by a provincial tribunal in Palestine (according to Acts, because he had brought a non-Jew into the Temple in Jerusalem), he insisted on appealing to the emperor, though his appeal did not do any more than buy him a good deal of time to spread his message more widely before his eventual execution in Rome. He took pride in the title he had conferred on himself: 'an Apostle to the Gentiles'.[58]

In reality, Paul's move towards the Gentile world may at first have been partial and cautious. The Book of Acts does portray him preaching in fully Gentile settings, although the most famous of such encounters, in the centre of Athens, is not presented as having much result. Yet

Paul's authentic letters take for granted a very detailed knowledge of Jewish tradition in their readers, which does not suggest that his congregations were made up of converts recruited at random from the general Classical public. It is far more likely that in making his approaches to the Gentile world, Paul was helped by a particular feature of many synagogue communities in the Mediterranean world: in addition to those members of the synagogue who were identified as Jews, through birth and the physical mark of circumcision, there were groups of non-Jews who had consciously bought into the faith of Judaism. The writer of Acts calls them by various terms, one of which is 'God-fearers' or 'God-reverers' (*theosebeis*), and he makes them an important part of Paul's audience.

Some commentators on Acts have doubted the historical reality of this category *theosebēs*, but in 1976 archaeological excavations at Aphrodisias, in what is now south-west Turkey, revealed an inscription belonging to a synagogue from the third century CE in which that same word was used in a list of benefactors of the building: the set of names was arranged separately from Jewish names and represented only slightly less than half of the total number of donors. So at least this synagogue boasted a substantial proportion of people emotionally committed to Judaism and its tradition, yet still part of a wider world. Paul himself does not use the word *theosebēs* in his letters, but his epistle to Christians in Galatia is by implication directed exactly to such an audience: pressure is being brought on them to be circumcised, indicating that they are not already but are still knowledgeable enough about Judaism to be expected to appreciate Paul's detailed references to Jewish sacred literature and beliefs.[59] They might be ready to listen to a message which was both radically different from what they had heard before and yet clearly had a relationship to it, a relationship expressed with a passion and urgency appropriate for a final age.

One wonders what Paul was preaching when he started out. His surviving writings are virtually empty of what the earthly Jesus had taught – teaching (in Aramaic) which would have naturally been passed on to him by 'flesh and blood', if he had consulted them – and the silence contrasts significantly with the fact that he is regularly prepared to quote the Tanakh. A person, and not a system, had captured him in the mysterious events on the road to Damascus. The person was Christ and Lord: the two titles expressed slightly different aspects of who Jesus was for Paul. Jesus is Christ (the Anointed) because he has been chosen to fulfil God's plan, and Lord because his place in God's plan gives him eternal dominion and power.[60] The distinction is not a rigid one; but Paul tended in his letters to talk of Jesus as 'Christ' when he was making statements and as 'Lord' when he was pleading with his readers or ordering them to do something. He associated the title 'Christ' with the work of God accomplished on the Cross – no longer a political Messiah or 'Anointed One' to save the people of Israel. He saw Jesus the Lord as the one to whom Christians owe obedience and so he associated the title 'Lord' with the obedient implementing of this work in the life of the Church.[61]

Paul knew much in his previous belief system about obedience to the Law, and one senses him struggling with his inheritance of Law in ways that are never wholly coherent. In his letter to the Christians in Rome, one can read that the Law brings wrath and sin, but also that it is holy.[62] Most striking of all is Paul's repeated insistence that traditional Jewish genital circumcision counts for no more than lack of circumcision, beside keeping the commandments of God. Surely he could not ignore the clear message of the Tanakh that circumcision was indeed one of the commandments of God? It seems that for him, even more than for Jesus, Law was good, Law was bad – he was as fond of a strong paradox as was Martin Luther fifteen centuries later, and perhaps that is why the two men's minds met. But this seeming incoherence may be explained by the completeness of his traumatic Damascus road experience: he had rejected what was good, his Jewish heritage, for something incomparably better – Christ. An intimate meeting with Christ was a better way of being 'righteous', a word at the centre of a cluster of words which he uses with the same root in the verb *dikaioun*, 'to be made righteous' or, in the form made famous by Protestants in the sixteenth-century Reformation, 'to be justified'. The biblical scholar E. P. Sanders has expressed the sense of a grace coming from outside ourselves by coining a memorably clunky phrase, 'be righteoused' – reconciled once more to God.[63] Adam, the first man, sinned so completely that no law had power to deal with the universal sin that resulted; neither he nor his descendants could be 'righteoused' through their own efforts, however much they might feel the pain and wretchedness of the Fall away from Eden. Only Christ could repair the damage, and the core of Paul's message was to point to Christ and our need for total faith in him; salvation to eternal life comes through Christ alone. Paul managed to find a prophet of the Tanakh to sum up what he wanted to say: 'the righteousness of God is revealed through faith for faith, as it is written "he who through faith is righteous shall live"'.[64]

Thus for the purposes of being 'righteoused', the Law was irrelevant; yet Paul could not bear to see all the Law disappear. For those who were righteoused, it might have its uses, guiding a true obedience for Christ-followers which was just as attainable for Jews as non-Jews.[65] Obedience is a theme to which Paul obsessively returns. He speaks of Christ's followers as being like slaves, wives, debtors, younger sons, coheirs: the relationship of the believer to Christ can become so intimate that he can speak of it in terms of one personality absorbing another – one of his characteristic phrases is that believers are 'in Christ'. This is all the more extraordinary since the starting point of this faith is an individual human being in recent historic time, not some abstract Platonic Supreme Soul. And yet Paul presented this Jesus as he had experienced him: a risen, transcendent figure whose earthly life was secondary to what happened as a result of his death. He pointed back to the catastrophe brought about by Adam's disobedience, and then to Christ's triumph over this catastrophe: 'As in Adam all die, so also in Christ shall all be made alive'.[66]

Since all believers are given new life in Christ, they are part of the same community, the Church. Paul already used the word 'Church' in two senses, to describe both the local gatherings of Christ-followers in their communities and the body which unites them all through their relationship to Christ. The Church is distinguished wherever its particular congregations meet by a common meal, which Paul described as echoing and remembering actions of Jesus Christ at the Last Supper.[67] Everywhere the Church is united by baptism, a once-for-all ceremony of washing the believer with water. Nothing else is able to bring unity to the followers of Christ, because they are so varied – Jews, non-Jews, slaves, freemen, men, women – and also so various, in the gifts for action (*charismata*) which God has given them. 'For by one Spirit we were all baptized into one body – Jews or Greeks, slaves or free – and all were made to drink of one Spirit.'[68]

We are now hearing of a third party beside 'God' and 'Christ': the 'Spirit'. It was a word familiar to any Jew, already echoing through the Tanakh from its very opening sentences, when, before completed creation, 'the earth was without form and void, and darkness was upon the face of the deep; and the Spirit of God was moving over the face of the waters'.[69] Paul is constantly speaking of this Spirit, and questions arise as to how it relates to Christ – indeed, these questions occupied the Church for the next five centuries and the answers then hammered out have often been contested since. Rather than see the questions as a problem, Paul and the communities to whom he was writing would no doubt have said that all he was doing was trying to express a reality which they had found in their midst. Indeed, one of Paul's motives for writing to the Church at Corinth was that they were celebrating their experience of the Spirit in ways which he found imprudent; he sent them an extended health warning on this theme (I Corinthians 14), particularly the practice of speaking ecstatically in unknown 'languages'. The power of the Spirit was like a volcano under the community, showing itself in forms ranging from such spectacular displays to the everyday. The Spirit might perfect or express our prayers with sighs too deep for words, yet might also use us like ventriloquists' dolls, making us echo Jesus's cry to his Father, *Abba!*, and make it our own.[70] In one of the earliest stories in the Book of Acts (2.1–13), it took over the reconstituted Twelve Apostles and made them speak the languages of all those who heard, on the Jewish feast which was known by Hellenized Jews as Pentecost. Eighteen centuries later, Christians would remember that first Pentecost of the Church and make something new of it (see pp. 912–13).

Entering Paul's theological world in his letters is rather like jumping on a moving merry-go-round: the point of entry hardly matters. It is an intensely painted set of portraits of how a Christian community works and what a Christian community signifies – but one has to remember that it is only one vision of Christian community. It has curiously little interest in the life and teaching of its founder, concentrating instead on the effect of his death and resurrection in God's cosmic plan. The individual, living in Christ, is never his own person. Love, participation, indwelling bind all together: such relationships transcend the usual human bonds of marriage, family ties or social status, which are allowed to survive precisely because they are irrelevant to the categories of the new age to come. The Christian future was to present many alternative situations and possibilities.

THE GOSPEL OF JOHN
AND REVELATION

Paul was not alone in his development of a Christ message which strayed away from Jesus's own emphases. Some very similar themes are to be found in the fourth Gospel, John, which is thought to have been written rather later than the Synoptic Gospels, some time around the turn of the first and second centuries CE. Perhaps it should be seen as a fruitful meditation on the tradition which the Synoptics were creating.[71] John has much information about Jesus which is not to be found in Matthew, Mark and Luke. He seems genuinely to supplement their picture of Jesus's life; yet that is not John's main purpose, and his information is put to uses other than those in the Synoptics. He portrays from the outset a Jesus who, in the Gospel's great opening hymn, is already fully identified with the pre-existing Word which was with God: John's Gospel narrative is a progressive glorification of this figure, to the Cross and beyond. John's Jesus, in the course of his majestic discourses, sets himself up in great metaphoric statements prefixed by 'I am', mystically seven in number like the days of creation. He is Bread, Light, Door, Shepherd, Resurrection/Life, Way/Truth/Life, Vine.[72] He repeatedly refers to himself as the Son of God, which he does only once (and then only by implication) in the Synoptics, though they frequently put this title into the mouth of others.[73] This Johannine Christ says little about forgiving one's enemies, which is such a strong theme in the Synoptics. His pronouncements about himself might seem arrogant, even insuffer-able, to those who could not accept them; they might be interpreted as a voice solemnly speaking through a man who is possessed. The Spirit of whom Paul speaks is also a constant presence in this Gospel, from the moment that John the Baptist sees it descending on Jesus in his baptism in the River Jordan.[74]

The tradition of John's Gospel is reflected in a number of minor letters which have also taken the name of John as author, and it may be seen as evidence of another strand within the non-Jewish communities which in parallel to those chiefly influenced by Paul were spreading beyond the Jewish matrix of the Church. A strange poetic work known as Revelation now forms the last book of the New Testament, an open letter addressed to a number of named Church communities in what today is southern Turkey. It is likely to have been written in the time of the Emperor Domitian (81–96 CE) and to be the product of Christian fury at his brutal campaign to strengthen the cult of emperor worship. Like much inter-Testamental literature (see p. 68), it is an 'apocalypse' (the Greek for 'revelation'): a vision of cosmic struggles in the End Time and of a triumphant judgement of God. Its author is also called John, and may be a contemporary of the Gospel writer (from whom he is distinguished by being called 'the Divine'); his crude Greek style is very different, as are his preoccupations.

Brooding on the Roman government's maltreatment of Christians,

John the Divine delighted in constructing a picture of the Roman Empire's collapse which would have been familiar to pre-Christian Jewish writers in the apocalyptic tradition. He described Rome in a frequent Jewish shorthand for tyrannical power, 'Babylon'. Significantly, John the Divine is the only New Testament writer uninhibitedly and without qualification to use the provocative title of 'king' for Christ. There are plenty of New Testament references to the Kingdom of God, or Christ as the King of the Jews, or the King of Israel; but those are not the same at all. The early Christians were scared of what the Roman authorities might think if they started calling Christ a king; after all, Jesus was crucified because he was said to have claimed to be just that, 'King of the Jews'. So the rest of the New Testament seems almost to be avoiding the idea; modern Western Christians, who tend to talk a lot about Christ as king (see pp. 931–41), generally do not notice this. When two eighteenth-century English Evangelicals, John Cennick and Charles Wesley, wrote what has become a widely loved hymn, 'Lo, he comes with clouds descending', they drew most of its rich kingly imagery from Revelation:

> Yea, Amen! let all adore Thee,
> High on Thine eternal throne;
> Saviour, take the power and glory,
> Claim the kingdom for Thine own;
> O come quickly! O come quickly! O come quickly!
> Everlasting God, come down!

So Revelation is the great exception: the one book of the New Testament which positively relishes the subversiveness of the Christian faith. It is not surprising that, through the ages of Christian history, again and again this book has inspired oppressed peoples to rise up and destroy their oppressors. Such emphases frequently alarmed Christians and hindered Revelation's entry into full acceptance in the biblical family; but what probably saved the book was the major aspect of its picture of Jesus Christ which did resonate with Paul's writings and with John's Gospel. Once more, Jesus is a figure of cosmic significance, the Lamb who at the end of worldly time sits upon the throne. For John's first readers, this Lamb would be resonant of the sacrifice in the Jewish Passover, and would therefore lead them to a tangle of thoughts about the Last Supper which was their first Eucharist. Significantly, together with God the Almighty, the Lamb has replaced any need for a Temple in the city which is the New Jerusalem.[75] For by the time that John the

Divine was writing, the relationship of Christ-followers to the Old Jerusalem had radically changed: the future of Christianity was to move away from Jerusalem.

Paul has a good deal to say about the communities of Christ-followers, mostly from a Jewish background, who looked to the leaders of the Church based in Jerusalem after the death of Jesus and his removal from earthly life. As we have noted (see p. 98), the most important among these leaders was at first James the brother of Jesus. When the Jewish authorities executed James in 62 CE on charges of breaking the Jewish Law, his place was taken by another 'kinsman' of the Lord, Simeon. If the gathering of Christ-followers in Jerusalem had intended to become the mainstream expression of Judaism, they had failed, because they remained a minority grouping on the edge of the religious life in the city and in Palestine generally. Nevertheless, among the emerging Christ-followers they had a good deal of prestige because of their leaders' intimate connection with Jesus. Paul was constrained to admit when writing to the Corinthians that these men had experienced Resurrection appearances of the Lord before his own, in an order which he is careful to make clear – first Peter, then James.[76] Indeed, Paul repeatedly urges the Churches to whom he writes around the Mediterranean to send funds to the Jerusalem Church, in the same way that Jews made a contribution to the Temple. This implies that the institution of the Jerusalem Church was beginning to take the place of the old Temple in the esteem of Christ's followers, and it is not surprising that Paul would have to respect it. Yet he represented the growing number of communities which placed their trust in Christ as Lord far away from Jerusalem around the Mediterranean world: communities which had grown in circumstances which will probably always remain obscure, despite the brilliant flashes of light or apparent light which illuminate their origins in Paul's epistles and the Book of Acts.

The separate inspiration of much of Paul's message (a matter which, as we have seen, he himself emphasized) was bound to bring tensions with the Jerusalem leadership, and in fact there were bitter clashes hinted at even in the emollient prose of the Book of Acts. A furious passage in Paul's letter to the Galatians reveals the real seriousness of the quarrel, as Paul accused his opponents, including Jesus's disciple Peter, one of the original Twelve, of cowardice, inconsistency and hypocrisy.[77] At stake was an issue which would trouble Christ-followers for 150 years: how far should they move from the Jewish tradition if, like Paul, they preached the good news of Christ's kingdom to non-Jews? Questions of deep symbolism arose: should converts accept such features of Jewish life as circumcision, strict adherence to the Law of Moses and abstention from food defiled by association with pagan worship (that would include virtually all meat sold in the non-Jewish world)? Paul would allow only that Christians should not eat food which they knew had been publicly offered to idols, and otherwise not make much of a fuss about wares on sale in the market or about the dishes at a non-believer's table.[78]

One might have expected that the result of this would be the development of two branches of Christianity in fundamental disagreement with one another about their relationship with the parent Judaism: there would be a Jewish Church looking to the tradition represented by James and a Gentile Church treasuring the writings of Paul and John. In fact this is not so. There is one epistle in the New Testament which has been given James's name, and which does represent a rather different view of the Christian life and the role of the Law from that of Paul, but otherwise all Christians alive today are the heirs of the Church which Paul created. The other type of Christianity once headed by the brother of the Lord has disappeared. How did this happen? A great political crisis intervened to transform the situation.

THE JEWISH REVOLT AND THE END OF JERUSALEM

In 66 CE a Jewish revolt broke out in Palestine which drew its inspiration from the traditions of Jewish self-assertion and rage against outside interference which looked back to the heroic era of Judas Maccabeus (see pp. 65–6). The comforts provided by Roman rule were not enough to persuade everyone in the Jewish community that they should outweigh the constant reminder from the Roman authorities that Jews were not masters of their own destinies. The rebels eventually took control in Jerusalem and massacred the Sadducee elite, whom they regarded as collaborators with the Romans. The Jewish Christian Church, interestingly, fled from the city; it was distant enough from the world of Jewish nationalism to wish to keep out of this struggle. The result of the revolt was in the long term probably inevitable: the Romans could not afford to lose their grip on this corner of the Mediterranean and they put a huge effort into crushing the rebels. In the course of the capture of Jerusalem, whether by accident or by design, the great Temple complex went up in flames, never to be restored; its site lay as a wasteland for centuries.[79] Jewish fury accumulated at this highly unusual destruction of one of the Mediterranean world's most renowned shrines and in 132–5 they rose again in revolt. Now the Romans erased the name of Jerusalem from the map and created a city, Aelia Capitolina. It took its name with deliberate offensiveness from a new temple of Jupiter, the chief god of the Roman pantheon as worshipped on the Capitoline Hill in Rome itself (the temple was built apparently on a site which encompassed the place of Jesus's crucifixion and burial, although this was probably coincidental). So Aelia Capitolina was not even intended to be a Greek city; it was a Roman colony.[80]

After the revolt of 66–70 no substantial Christian community returned to Aelia/Jerusalem until the fourth century. The Jewish-led Christ-followers regrouped in the town of Pella in the upper Jordan valley and maintained contact with other like-minded Jewish Christian communities in the Middle East. Their refusal to become associated with the second great Jewish revolt of 132–5 cost them dear in terms of violence from their fellow Jews, who regarded them as traitors, but even when the crushing of the rebellion brought them relief, their future was one of gradual decline. No longer did they have the prestige of a centre in the sacred city of Jerusalem. The fourth-century Roman scholar Jerome came across surviving Jewish-Christian communities when he moved to live in the East, and he translated their 'Gospel according to the Hebrews' into Latin, but after that they faded from history. The Church of Paul, which had originally seemed the daughter of the Jerusalem Church, rejected the lineal heirs of the Jerusalem Church as imperfect Christians. Soon it regarded their ancient self-deprecating name of Ebionites ('the poor' in Hebrew: an echo of Jesus's blessing on the poor in the Sermon on the Mount) as the description of a heretical sect. Interestingly, the later Christian historian Eusebius claims that the Ebionites rejected the idea of the Virgin Birth of Jesus. That may well have been because, unlike Greek-speaking Christians, they knew that the notion was based on a Greek misreading of Isaiah's Hebrew prophecy (see p. 81).[81]

The catastrophe for Jerusalem had another important effect: it left the Jewish intelligentsia determined to make their peace with the Roman authorities, to preserve their religion and to give it a more coherent identity. Like the Jewish Christ-followers, the surviving leaders of mainstream Judaism were forced to regroup away from the former capital and the Romans concentrated them on a former estate of the Herodian

royal family at the town of Jamnia (Yavneh), near the coast.[82] Here
tradition says that this gathering was very influential in giving Judaism
a unity of religious belief which it had not previously possessed; it hardly
matters whether or not the story was really that simple, because the
end result was indeed a much more clearly circumscribed identity for
Judaism. The Sadducee leadership was dead or discredited, and so it was
the Pharisee group which shaped the future of this ancient monotheistic
faith, producing an ever-expanding volume of commentary on the
Tanakh and a body of regulations to give a sense of precise boundaries
to Jews in their everyday life. That was compensation for the tragedy
that they could no longer look to the Temple to provide identity and
purpose. Temple sacrifice ended for ever; what was left was the first
religious tradition which could have taken the phrase which later became
so important to Muslims and called itself the People of the Book. Instead
of the Temple, the synagogues were now destined to carry the whole life
and devotional activity of the Jewish people.

It is interesting to see this development reflected in the Gospels. If any
section of the Jewish nation had been responsible for the train of events
leading up to the death of Jesus, it had been the Temple establishment
of Sadducees, but the Pharisees come in for far more abuse recorded by
the Gospel writers, often in the mouth of Jesus, despite the fact that
Jesus seems to have resembled the Pharisees in much of his teaching and
outlook. When the Gospels were compiled in the last decades of the first
century, the descendants of the Pharisees, the leaders at Jamnia, were a
living force, unlike the Sadducees, and many Christian communities had
become strongly opposed to them. John's exalted Christ, echoing the
exaltation of Christ in the writings of Paul, is emancipated from any
concern for Jewish sensibilities about his identity, and in John's picture
of Jesus's life, 'the Jews' repeatedly and often menacingly prowl around
the Jesus story as if they had no organic connection with the carpenter's
son from Nazareth.[83]

The growing coherence in Judaism, the narrowing in variety of Jewish
belief, meant that by the end of the first century CE a break between
Christianity and Judaism was more and more likely: a symptom of that
is John the Divine's readiness to replace the Temple with the Lamb
Jesus.[84] In many communities, the break probably occurred two or more
decades earlier. Christ-followers had taken a decisive step away from
Judaism by offering worship specifically to Jesus: there was no precedent
in the tradition for this in Judaism, even though Jews had commonly
recognized and celebrated the existence of supernatural beings like

angels or the personified Wisdom of God.[85] Moreover, at some very early stage, Christians celebrated their main worship on a different day: the day following the Jewish Sabbath. Many Christian cultures refer to it by its pagan Roman name, Sunday, but in many languages other than English it is called the Lord's Day, as it was the day on which the Lord had risen from the dead, according to the accounts in the Gospel Passion narratives.[86] And central to worship for Christians was that meal in which they shared bread and wine. By the beginning of the second century at least, we find Ignatius, leader or 'bishop' in the Christian community of Antioch, calling this 'Eucharist'.[87]

In everyday life, the Roman imperial authorities unwittingly encouraged the process of separation between Jews and Christians by imposing a punitive tax in place of the voluntary contributions which Jews had once paid to the Jerusalem Temple. For Roman bureaucrats, therefore, it became important to know who was and was not a Jew. Despite all the Jewish rebellions, tax-paying Jews continued to enjoy a status as an officially recognized religion (*religio licita*). In fact, despite the brutality with which Rome crushed various Jewish rebellions both in Palestine and beyond, it is remarkable that the Romans continued to regard Judaism with such respect and forbearance – most notably in adopting the Jewish division of the week into seven days rather than the traditional Roman eight, probably in the same century that they destroyed the Temple.[88] Christians who finally broke their links with the parent culture would find no such recognition from the Roman government, although it also meant that they avoided the special tax, and they may have been anxious to avoid association with the 'guilt' of the Jews in the rebellion of 66–70 as well. Interestingly, such was Christians' sense of alienation from the Jewish world that they made no attempt to cling on to that privileged status.[89]

Thanks to these developments, and to the energy of Paul's work in reaching out to the non-Jewish world, the movement which had started as a Jewish sect decisively shifted away from its Palestinian home, and all the sacred writings which form the New Testament were written in Greek. The Christ revealed in the letters of Paul, the Gospel of John and the Book of Revelation, much more than in the Gospels of Matthew, Mark and Luke, was a cosmic ruler and his followers must conquer the whole world. For Paul, that meant setting his sights westwards across the Mediterranean Sea, to the capital of the empire of which he was a citizen, Rome. But very early on, other preachers of Christ looked east, to the capital of the Persian king at Ctesiphon in what is now Iraq, or even beyond, to the remote cultures with which the Mediterranean world traded, far to the east in India and maybe further. Paul had apparently met failure in his first mission to Arabia; these others did not, as we will see.

If the new religion had remained focused on the Middle East, there were obvious contenders among Roman imperial cities to replace the lost Jerusalem in its significance for the followers of Christ. There was Alexandria, capital of Egypt, home to the largest single Jewish community beyond Palestine itself, and there was also Antioch of Syria, the old Seleucid capital, still then the chief city in Rome's eastern imperial provinces. It was in fact in Antioch, according to the Book of Acts, that colonial Latin-speakers coined a word for Christ-followers (in no friendly spirit) – *Christiani*.[90] This name 'Christian' has a double remoteness from its Jewish roots. Surprisingly in view of its origin in the Greek eastern Mediterranean and amid the Semitic culture of Syria, the word has a distinctively Latin rather than Greek form, and yet it also points to the Jewish founder not by his name, Joshua, but by that Greek translation of Messiah, *Christos*. With its Latin development of a Greek word summing up a Jewish life-story, this very name 'Christian' embodies a violent century which had set Rome against Jerusalem, and the word has resonated down nearly two thousand years, during which Christianity in turn has set itself against its surviving parent, Judaism. 'Christian' embodies the two languages which became the vehicle for talking about Christianity within the Roman Empire: Latin and Greek, the respective languages of Western Catholicism and Greek Orthodoxy.

Rome owes its exceptional historic position in the Church to the Roman Empire – not merely the simple fact of the city's status as the imperial capital, resonant throughout the Mediterranean world and beyond, but the actions of first-century emperors: the sack of Jerusalem and two executions of key early Christian figures, the Apostles Peter and Paul, in Rome itself. When Jerusalem was wrecked by the Roman expeditionary force in 70 CE and the oldest and most prominent community of Christians was permanently dispersed, Peter and Paul had probably been dead for around half a decade, apparently victims of a persecution whipped up in Rome by the Emperor Nero. The Book of Acts says much about Paul's journey to Rome under arrest, and previously one of his most important letters had been written to Christians already living there. Scripture says nothing to link Peter and his death to Rome, and the suspicion does linger that the story of Peter's martyrdom there was a fiction based retrospectively on the undoubted death of Paul in the city. Nevertheless there are strong witnesses in tradition and archaeology that at least as early as the mid-second century the Christians of Rome were confidently asserting that Peter was buried among their dead, in a cemetery across the Tiber beyond the western suburbs of Rome.[91]

The leadership of the Western Church went on to build on that memory or claimed memory over a thousand years, to create one of Christianity's most noble and dangerous visions, the Roman papacy. Their building was literal, in the massive shape of the Basilica of St Peter above Peter's supposed grave site, a building which we will repeatedly encounter in Christian history. The city of Rome is now the centre of the largest branch of Christian faith, which styles itself the Catholic Church, but we should remember that this is an oddity: Rome was, after all, the capital of the empire which killed Christ. Without the tragedy of the destruction of Jerusalem, Rome might never have taken the unique place which it has held in the story of Western Christian faith. But no one would have realized this even two centuries after the death of Jesus Christ; and for centuries more there was as much likelihood of Christianity spreading as strongly east as west from the ruins of Jerusalem, to become the religion of Baghdad rather than of Rome. That is why the next stage of this story will take us east, rather than in the westward and northward directions so often chosen by the historians of Christianity.

4

Boundaries Defined
(50 CE–300)

SHAPING THE CHURCH

According to legend, nearly three centuries after the Crucifixion a Roman emperor's mother called Helena headed an archaeological expedition to Jerusalem which, with a spectacular good fortune rare in modern archaeology, quickly achieved its precise goal: the rediscovery of the wooden cross on which Jesus had died (see pp. 193–4). Later archaeologists have been less easily rewarded in searches for material remains of the earliest Christians. Christianity had no specific ethnic or social base, and to begin with it was a movement too insignificant to leave artefacts or even much trace in literary sources outside those which Christians themselves created. So if we want to get a picture of who Christians were and what their lives were like, we are forced to meet them virtually exclusively through their documents (see Plate 1). Indeed, one of the earliest known definitely Christian artefacts is a fragment of text bearing two little patches of John's Gospel; the style of its handwriting suggests a date in the second century CE, perhaps within decades of the first composition of the Gospel.[1] Even then, we have to remember that the vast majority of early Christian texts have perished, and despite many new archaeological finds, there is a bias among those that survived towards texts which later forms of Christianity found acceptable. One expert on the period has recently estimated that around 85 per cent of second-century Christian texts of which existing sources make mention have gone missing, and that total itself can only represent a fraction of what there once was.[2] The documents which do survive conspire to hide their rooting in historic contexts; this makes them a gift to biblical literalists, who care little for history.

The series of letters generally agreed to come from Paul's own hand are characterized by very specific references to situations, mostly of conflict, and by references to named people, often including a little description to give us some sense of those who were important in their communities, at least in the eyes of Paul. So to the Christians in Rome, he sends greetings to a long list, including 'Epaenetus, who was the first convert in Asia for Christ . . . Mary, who has worked hard among you . . . Andronicus and Junias, my kinsmen and my fellow prisoners . . . Ampliatus, my beloved in the Lord . . .'[3] The most striking feature of the correspondence is the locations of its recipients: in busy Graeco-Roman towns, commercial centres throughout the eastern half of the Mediterranean as far as Rome, and including people like Epaenetus, who had much experience of travel. By contrast, the story of Jesus told in the Gospels had been played out in a rural and largely non-Greek environment, where villages within an easy day's journey of each other could naively be described by the writers as cities and where only the denouement of the story took place in a real city, Jerusalem. Now Paul, the Apostle of the Gentiles, divided up the world he perceived around him into city, sea and wilderness (II Corinthians 11.26), and despite his pride in his Jewish roots, he unselfconsciously divided the people of that world into Greeks and barbarians (Romans 1.14).

One significant and at first sight puzzling peculiarity actually emphasizes Paul's break with Jesus's first followers in Palestine. His letters have a preoccupation with personal means of support, which he links directly to one of his few quotations of the Lord Jesus. Characteristically, he takes a contrary line to the Lord. Jesus had said that 'those who proclaim the gospel should get their living by the gospel': that is, they deserve support from others.[4] Paul emphasizes that he has not done this: he tells us that he has supported himself, although in what seems to be an attempt to face down criticism, he proclaims his contradiction of Jesus's practice as a privilege renounced rather than an obligation spurned. He makes no bones about saying 'keep away from any brother who is living in idleness and not in accord with the tradition *that you received from us*'. So much for Jesus and his wandering Twelve. Paul was on the side of busy people who valued hard work and took a pride in the reward that they got from it: tent-makers of the world, unite.[5] Christianity had become a religion for urban commercial centres, for speakers of common Greek who might see the whole Mediterranean as their home and might well have moved around it a good deal – Paul's restless journeyings are unlikely to have been unique. The communities associated with him included such figures as Gaius, wealthy enough to be 'host to me and the whole Church', or Erastus, a man prominent as 'the city treasurer' in the great city of Corinth.[6] Although there is not much sign that Christianity had yet made inroads on 'old money' – the aristocratic elites of Mediterranean society – it was already gathering people across a wide spectrum of social status, and it is not surprising that differences of wealth and public esteem produced tensions and arguments.

Two examples involve food, but have much wider implications. The earliest specific description of Christianity's later central ritual meal, the taking of bread and wine in the Eucharist, is found in Paul's writings to the Corinthians, because this meal of unity had caused trouble there. Some had been withdrawing from the general congregation in order to eat in a separate group and Paul made it clear that it was the wealthy who were at fault. He emphasized that all must eat together.[7] That tension can be laid alongside another concern already noted (see p. 106): some in the congregation at Corinth worried about banqueting with non-Christian friends who might offer them food offered to idols. Paul's proposed compromise solution allowed such Christians to maintain their private social links with the non-Christian elites of the city, while keeping public solidarity with less affluent Christians because they had avoided public contact with civic ritual.[8]

This set a significant pattern for the future: Christianity was not usually going to make a radical challenge to existing social distinctions. The reason was that Paul and his followers assumed that the world was going to come to an end soon and so there was not much point in trying to improve it by radical action. That attitude has recurred among some of the apocalyptically minded in later ages, although others have drawn precisely the opposite conclusion. Nevertheless, while sharing Jesus's belief in the imminent end, Paul drew very different conclusions from that prospect: in present conditions, 'every one should remain in the state in which he was called'.[9] He made notably little reference in his letters to the 'kingdom of God', that concept of a radical turn to world history which had meant so much to Jesus and had accompanied his challenge to so many existing social conventions. Paul was a citizen of the Roman Empire, here and now, emphasizing without Jesus's witty ambiguity that everyone must 'be subject to the governing authorities. For there is no authority except from God, and those that exist have been instituted by God.' His command to obedience had a great future in Christian conversations with the powerful.[10]

Paul's solutions to the two food problems preserved a delicate balance between equality in the sight of God and inequality in the sight of humanity. So in his famous declaration to the Galatians, equality within the Church remained an equality in spiritual status, looking forward to eternal life: 'neither Jew nor Greek . . . neither slave nor free . . . neither male nor female, for you are all one in Jesus Christ' – but not in the everyday life of the present world.[11] Certainly he was aware that in the complex religious make-up of the eastern Mediterranean, there were cults which held ritual meals like the Christian Eucharist, and he was determined that Christian groups celebrating their Eucharist should not be mistaken for them. Hence his insistence that there should be no link between the 'cup of the Lord and the cup of demons', the 'table of the Lord and the table of demons'.[12] The balance he struck represented a tension between a wish to keep the gatherings of Christians exclusive and a wish to keep the new religion's frontiers open in order to make more converts. This undercurrent of instability remained through the centuries during which the Church was identified with all society and has never wholly disappeared from Christian consciousness.

Paul's acceptance of the secular status quo had especial implications for two groups whose liberation has over the last quarter-millennium sparked conflict worldwide, but especially within Western Christianity: slaves and women. One short letter of Paul from a Roman prison to a fellow Christian called Philemon is undoubtedly genuine, since it contains no useful discussion of doctrine and can only have been preserved for its biographical information about the Apostle. It centres on the future of Onesimus, a slave to Philemon. He had recently been serving Paul in imprisonment and the letter contains a none-too-subtle hint that Paul would appreciate continuing to enjoy the benefit of Onesimus's service. There is no suggestion that he should be freed, only that now he could be 'more than a slave' to Philemon; and certainly there is no question of consulting Onesimus about his own wishes. The Epistle to Philemon is a Christian foundation document in the justification of slavery.[13]

Slavery was, after all, an indispensable institution in ancient society. A Christian writer from a generation later than Paul, who bore the name of Jesus's disciple Peter but who is unlikely to have been the same man, wrote a miniature treatise which became one of the epistles accepted into the New Testament. It told house-slaves to compare their sufferings to the unjust sufferings of Christ, in order that they should bear injustice as Christ had done. That did not say much about the writer's expectations that Christian slave owners would be better than any others, and it followed a strong command to 'be subject to every human institution'.[14] In the early second century, when the Church's leadership was beginning to be concentrated in the hands of single individuals styled bishops (see pp. 130–37), Bishop Ignatius of Antioch observed in a letter to his fellow bishop Polycarp of Smyrna that slaves should not take advantage of their membership in the Christian community, but live as better slaves, now to the glory of God – and his opinion was that it would be inappropriate to use church funds to help slaves buy their freedom. By the fourth century, Christian writers like Bishop Ambrose of Milan or Bishop Augustine of Hippo were providing even more robust defences of the idea of slavery than non-Christian philosophers had done before them – 'the lower the station in life, the more exalted the virtue', was Ambrose's rather unctuous opinion.[15]

If the coming of Christianity thus made little significant difference to the position of slaves, there are plenty of signs that Christians began by giving women a newly active role and official functions in Church life, then gradually moved to a more conventional subordination to male authority.[16] The Gospel narratives give a prominence to women in the Jesus movement unusual in ancient society; this culminates in the extraordinary part which they play in Matthew's, Mark's and John's accounts of the human discovery of the Resurrection. All three evangelists make women the first witnesses to the empty tomb and resurrection of Jesus; this is despite the fact that in Jewish Law women could not be considered as valid witnesses. The most prominent named woman, first in all three accounts, is Mary Magdalene ('from Magdala' in Galilee). She was a close associate of Jesus in his public ministry and has continued to arouse a set of variously motivated fascinations among Christians throughout the ages. Some overexcited modern commentators and mediocre novelists have even elevated her (on no good ancient evidence) to the status of Jesus's wife.

The Gospels' threefold affirmation of Mary Magdalene's Resurrection experience can account for a good deal of the subsequent interest in her, but it is also apparent that she became a symbol of resistance to the way in which the authority structures of the Church began to crystallize exclusively in the hands of men. Feminist theologians have naturally found this of great interest, but it is worth noting that elsewhere the status of Mary Magdalene is repeatedly shown as being supported by some men against other men. The Gospel of Thomas, which of all such Gospel pastiches beyond the New Testament most resembles the four 'mainstream' Gospels in its content and its likely dating to the late first century, describes a confrontation between Mary Magdalene and the Apostle Peter, in which Jesus intervenes on her behalf to reproach Peter.

This theme of arguments between the Magdalene and Peter occurs elsewhere. The Gospel of Mary, for instance, is a 'gnostic' work probably of the second century and represents a fairly even-tempered attempt at conversation with non-gnostic Christians. Here, Jesus's disciple Levi is presented as exclaiming to Peter, 'if the Saviour made her worthy, who are you then to reject her? Certainly the Saviour knows her very well. That is why he loved her more than us.'[17]

Paul is apparently inconsistent about the status of women. In his seven authentic letters, various women are named as office holders: amid the large number of people whom he lists as sending greetings to the Romans are Phoebe the deacon (administrative officer or assistant) in the Church of Cenchreae (a port near Corinth), Prisca, a 'fellow worker' and Tryphaena and Tryphosa, 'workers in the Lord' – descriptions also applied to men in the same passage. Most strikingly, there is Junia, a female 'apostle', so described alongside another 'apostle' with a male name – this was considered such an appalling anomaly by many later readers of Romans that Junia's name was frequently changed to a male form in the recopying of manuscripts, or simply regarded without any justification as a man's name. Early biblical commentators, given a strong lead by the great fourth-century preaching Bishop of Constantinople John Chrysostom, were honourably prepared to acknowledge the surprising femininity of Junia, but then there was a sudden turn in the writings of Giles of Rome in the thirteenth century, which was only rectified during the twentieth century. Likewise, historians have tended to view Phoebe's status as that of a 'deaconess'; yet this is probably reading back from the third and fourth centuries, when female deacons were restricted to roles necessarily reserved for women, like looking after scantily clad female candidates in services of baptism. First- and second-century Christians may not have made such a distinction between male and female deacons or the part that either played in the life of the Church.[18]

While Paul thus provides evidence about the roles that women were playing in positions of authority in Christian communities, his list of witnesses to Resurrection appearances significantly contrasts with that of three Gospels, by not including any women at all. He also insists in his first letter to the Corinthians on a hierarchical scheme in which God is the head of Christ, Christ the head of men and a husband the head of his wife: quite a contrast to his proclamation of Christian equality for all. That leads to a passage notable for its confusion of argument, in which he tells women to cover their heads when prophesying, yet elsewhere when addressing the same community in Corinth, he forbids women to speak in worship at all.[19] This was not a stable position and a second generation was bound to move to clarify it. Paul's admirers evidently decided to place increasing emphasis on his hierarchical view of Christian relationships and on his awareness of the scrutiny of Christian communities by non-Christians.

Perhaps this was not surprising as hopes of Christ's imminent return began to fade in the later first century and Christians began to realize that they must create structures which might have to last for a generation or more amid a world of non-believers. The change is visible in a series of further epistles which, although they assume the name of Paul, display a distinctive vocabulary and a mechanically intensive reuse of phrases from his writings. They should be thought of as commentaries on or tributes to his impact and teaching. Two which are now given addresses to Churches in Colossae and Ephesus are very closely related: Ephesians contains a patchwork of words and phrases from Colossians and from authentic letters of Paul, to the extent that it seems to be a devout attempt to provide a digest of Paul's message.[20] Three other epistles, supposedly addressed to Paul's close associates Timothy and Titus, seem to be circular letters to Church communities in Paul's tradition, hence their common collective designation as the 'Pastoral Epistles'.

What is striking in this literature is the way in which the idea that the end is at hand, so prominent in Paul's letters, has faded from view. The author of Ephesians is prepared to talk about 'the coming ages', which seems to mean a long time on this earth.[21] Nowhere is this shift more perceptible than in one feature of these documents, also to be found in the first of the two epistles attributed to Peter, which also takes many cues from Ephesians: sets of rules for conducting a human household, which in the sixteenth century Martin Luther styled *Haustafeln*, 'tables of household duties'. What is particularly remarkable about the *Haustafeln* is that they include commands to children 'that they may live long in the land': the Church must now consider the next generation and its earthly future.[22] Indeed, the writer to Timothy tells women that their salvation comes from having children (not a text to find favour with countless generations of women in the monastic life in later centuries).[23] These lists repeat the commonplace Hellenistic wisdom of their day, but they give it a gloss from Paul's argument that the relationship of husband to wife is like Christ's relationship to his Church: '[T]he husband is head of the wife as Christ is head of the Church, his body, and is himself its Saviour.'[24] Now the various gradations of status and authority to be found in the world are to shape the way in which Christians conceive their faith. And there is an extra consideration, connected to the Pastoral Epistles' insistence that Church leaders must be beyond reproach outside the community as well as inside it.[25] The Church is worried about its public image and concerned to show that it is not a subversive organization threatening the well-being of society, 'that the word of God may not be discredited'.[26] As we have seen (see pp. 103–5), the only dissident voice against this frank quest for respectability is to be found in that very unusual entrant into the Christian New Testament, the Book of Revelation.

In just two respects are the first Christians recorded as having been consciously different from their neighbours. First, they were much more rigorous about matters of sex than the prevailing attitudes in the Roman Empire; they did not forget their founder's fierce disapproval of divorce. Although with Paul's encouragement Christians did move to make some exceptions to Jesus's absolute ban (see pp. 90–91), their concerns to restrict such exceptions are in sharp contrast to the relative ease with which either party in a non-Christian Roman marriage could declare the relationship to be at an end. Likewise, abortion and the abandonment of unwanted children were accepted as regrettable necessities in Roman society, but, like the Jews before them, Christians were insistent that these practices were completely unacceptable. Even those Christian writers who were constructing arguments to show how much Christians fitted into normal society made no effort to hide this deliberate difference.[27] Paul's contribution was once more ambiguous. A celibate himself, he was of the opinion that marriage was something of a concession to human frailty, to save from fornication those who could not be continent, so it was better to marry than to burn with lust. Many Christian commentators, mostly fellow celibates, later warmed to this joyless theme. Yet in the same passage Paul said something more positive: that both husband and wife have mutually conceded each other power over each other's bodies. This gives a positive motive for Christian counter-cultural opposition to divorce, but it is also striking in its affirmation of mutuality in marriage. That message has struggled to be heard through most of Christian history.[28]

The other challenge to the norms of imperial society might seem to contradict even more strongly everything that we have said about Christian acceptance of the existing social order. In the Book of Acts there is an apparently circumstantial account of the Jerusalem congregation selling all the private property that its members owned in order to create a common fund for the community.[29] However, this is unlikely to have happened. The story is probably a creation of the writer's, designed to illustrate the theological point that this community was the New Israel; in the old Israel, there had supposedly been a system of 'Jubilee', a year in which all land should go back to the family to which it had originally belonged and during which all slaves should be released.[30] Probably even that original idea had never been implemented, simply remaining a pious hope, but the writer of Acts did not know that and he was making the Jerusalem Church re-enact the Jubilee of God's chosen people. Even if one decides to believe that the attempt was actually made (and it is just possible that it was), the story is frank in its admission that the scheme did not work, and two people who cheated the system were struck dead for their disobedience. Christian communism thereafter lapsed for nearly three centuries until the new counter-cultural impulse of monasticism appeared, in very different circumstances.

One has always to remember that throughout the New Testament we are hearing one side of an argument. When the writer to Timothy insists with irritating fussiness that 'I permit no woman to teach or to have authority over men; she is to keep silent', we can be sure that there were women doing precisely the opposite, who were probably not slow in asserting their own point of view.[31] But their voices are lost, or concealed in texts modified much later. Up to the end of the first century, it is virtually impossible to get any perspective on the first Christian Churches other than that of writings contained in the New Testament, however much we would like to have a clearer picture of why and how conversions took place. There is a silence of about six crucial decades, during which so many different spirals of development would have been taking place away from the teachings of the Messiah, who had apparently left no written record. A handful of Christian writings can be dated to around the time of the latest writings now contained in the Christian New Testament, at the beginning of the second century, and these give us glimpses of communities whose priorities were not those of the Churches which had known Paul. For instance, one very early book about church life and organization called the *Didachē* ('Teaching') tells us a good deal about the worship used in the community whose life the writer was seeking to regulate, perhaps some time at the turn of the first and second centuries. It is much closer both to earlier Jewish prayers and to forms to be found in later Jewish liturgy than is perceptible in other early Christian liturgies.[32] And for all Paul's hatred of idleness, he would have been infuriated by the *Didachē*'s assertion that it is necessary for us to work to ransom our sins.[33]

Even in the communities of Paul's tradition, we have noted change and development in the way in which Christians talked about their faith. Elsewhere, there was a whole range of possibilities for the future shape of this new religion, and no certainty as to whether any single mainstream would emerge. We have already seen how the accident of the destruction of Jerusalem had been the beginning of the end for one major possible future (see pp. 106–11). Once the Christians expanded beyond Palestine, they were meeting cultures very different from that of Judaism, especially within the Graeco-Roman world. Many converts would be people with a decent Greek education; it was only natural for them to understand what was taught them by reference to the thought of Greek philosophers. Jews had found it difficult enough to understand how the man Jesus could also be God; for Greeks, who looked to the writings of Plato to shape their understanding of God's nature, it was more difficult still. How could a Jewish carpenter's son, who had died with a cry of agony on a gallows, really be the God who was without change or passions, and whose perfection demanded no division of his substance? There were many different answers to these questions; many claimed to have particular knowledge (*gnōsis* in Greek) of the truth. As early as the end of the second century, one leader destined to be seen as defining mainstream Christianity, Irenaeus, Bishop of Lyons, grouped such alternative Christianities together under a common label, talking about *gnōstikē hairesis* ('a choice to claim knowledge'), with adherents who were *gnōstikoi*. A seventeenth-century Cambridge scholar, Henry More, turned this into an English word, 'gnosticism'.[34] For all the dangers of accepting a label born in hostility, there is still usefulness in discussing these various tendencies together. Gnosticism represented an alternative future for the Church. It is probably no exaggeration to say that wherever there were Christians in the second-century world, a good many of them could have been labelled *gnōstikoi* by the likes of Irenaeus.

ALTERNATIVE IDENTITIES: GNOSTICISM, MARCIONISM

Getting to know gnostics has become much easier over the last century thanks to significant archaeological discoveries, the flagship of which was at Nag Hammadi in the Egyptian desert in 1945, when a field-labourer came across a pottery jar containing fifty-two fourth-century texts in the Egyptian language Coptic.[35] They are all likely to have been translations from much older texts in other languages, principally Greek, since one of them is a section from Plato's *Republic*. Previously we had known of gnosticism through the hostile filter of such biased commentators as Bishop Irenaeus; now we can meet it in its own words. In a set of movements or tangles of thought with such variety, a search for the origins of gnosticism is unlikely to produce one answer. Much of gnosticism is a dialogue with Judaism – that is particularly true of the documents from Nag Hammadi – but the dialogue partners were not necessarily Greek. A frequent mark of gnostic attitudes was their dualism, envisaging a cosmic struggle between matched forces of good and evil, darkness and light, and that might suggest acquaintance with the dualism of Zoroastrian religion in Iran (Persia). It would be possible to argue for influence from as far away as India, in the complex of religions now known as Hinduism; after all, Alexander the Great had set Greeks into contact with India, and Roman traders continued a flourishing commerce that far east. Not all texts which belong to the gnostic literary family concern themselves with Christian problems, but despite assertions to the contrary, there seems little evidence that they predate Christianity itself.[36] Amid the different belief systems, some attributed to individuals such as Simon Magus, Cerinthus, Saturninus or Carpocrates, it is worth drawing together common tendencies.

Implicit in most gnostic systems was a distrust of the Jewish account of creation. This suggests that gnostic beliefs were likely to emerge in places with a Jewish presence and gnostics were people who found the Jewish message hard to take – maybe actually renegade Jews. Gnosticism was a creed for cultural frontiers, for instance, where Judaism interacted with Greek culture, as in Alexandria.[37] But anyone imbued with a Greek cast of enquiring mind might raise questions about Jewish insistence that God's creation is good: if that is so, why is there so much suffering and misery in the world? Why is the human body such a decaying vessel, so vulnerable even amid the beauty of youth to disease and petty lusts? Platonic assumptions about the unreality of human life, or prevailing Stoic platitudes about the need to rise above everyday suffering, could conspire with dualism from the East to produce a plausible answer: what we experience with our physical senses is mere illusion, a pale reflection of spiritual reality. If the world of senses is such an inferior state of being, then it could not possibly have been created by a supreme God. Yet the Tanakh said that it had been.

From such questions and answers, there could follow a train of

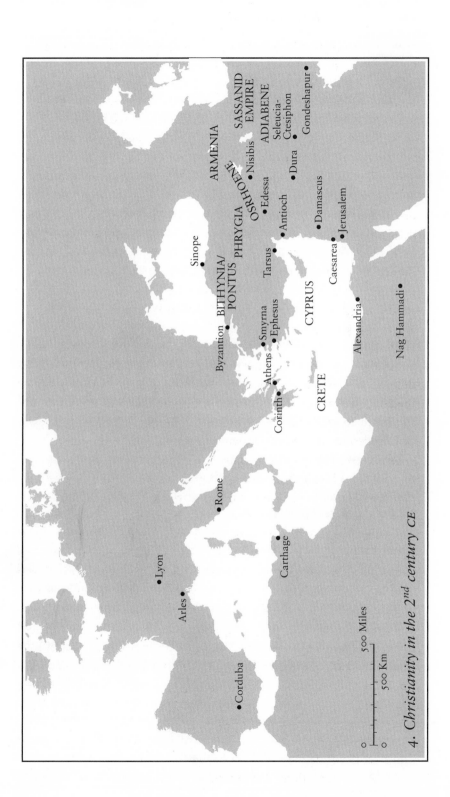

4. *Christianity in the 2nd century CE*

thought perceptible in various forms in many gnostic documents. First, if the God of the Jews who created the material world said that he was the true and only God, he was either a fool or a liar. At best he can be described in Plato's term as a 'demiurge' (see pp. 32–33), and beyond him there must be a First Cause of all that is real, the true God. Jesus Christ revealed the true God to humanity, so he can have nothing to do with the Creator God of the Jews. Knowledge of the true God is a way to contemplate the original harmony of the cosmos before the disaster represented by the creation of the physical world. That harmony is so distant and distinct from physical creation that it involves a complicated hierarchy of beings or realities (lovingly described in mind-numbing detail and variety in different gnostic systems). Those capable of perceiving this harmony and hierarchy are often said to have been granted that privilege by a fate external to themselves: a predestination. It is these people – gnostics – whom Jesus Christ has come to save. And who is Jesus? If there can be no true union between the world of spirit and the world of matter, then the cosmic Christ of the gnostics can never truly have taken flesh by a human woman, and he can never have felt what fleshly people feel – particularly human suffering. His Passion and Resurrection in history were therefore not fleshly events, even if they seemed so; they were heavenly play-acting (the doctrine known as Docetism, from the Greek verb *dokein*, 'to seem').

Equally, the real nature of the gnostic has no solidarity with the flesh of the human body; we should 'be one of those who pass by', as the Gospel of Thomas phrases it.[38] Mortal flesh must be mortified because it is despicable – or, on the contrary, the soul might be regarded as so independent of the body that the most wildly earthly excesses would not imperil its salvation. Hostile 'mainstream' Christian commentators probably took much more relish in contemplating such excesses than was justified by practice among gnostic believers. Their prurient accounts are to be taken with more than a pinch of salt. In the fourth century, Epiphanius/Epiphanios, an energetically unpleasant Cypriot bishop and heresy hunter, described gnostic rites parodying the Eucharist with the use of semen and menstrual blood.[39] In fact, the austere, ascetic strain in gnosticism is far more reliably attested than any licentiousness, and that makes it unwise to rebrand gnostic belief as a more generous-minded, less authoritarian alternative to the Christianity which eventually became mainstream. Still less plausible is a view of gnostic belief as a form of proto-feminism.[40] Gnostic hatred of the body would match very uneasily with some modern emphases on the liberating power of sexuality or feminism's physical celebration of all that it is to be female.

It is nevertheless the case that gnostics opposed the authority structures then evolving in parts of the Church, particularly in relation to
one important issue: martyrdom. As we will see (see Chapter 5), this
was a crucial issue in a Church which, from the death of its founder
onwards, repeatedly faced bouts of persecution from the authorities of
both the Roman and the Sassanian empires. One might have expected
gnostic contempt for the flesh to lead gnostics to sacrifice it in martyrdom
as did other Christians, but evidently they did not think the body worth
sacrificing. Not only is there a total absence of stories of gnostic martyrs,
but there is positive evidence that gnostics opposed martyrdom as a
regrettable self-indulgence and were angry that some Christian leaders
encouraged it. A text discovered at Nag Hammadi, *The Testimony of
Truth*, sneers at 'foolish people, thinking in their heart that if only they
confess in words, "We are Christians" . . . while giving themselves over
to a human death', they will achieve salvation. The *Apocalypse of Peter*,
also recovered from Nag Hammadi, says that bishops and deacons
who send little ones to their death will be punished. And the recently
rediscovered *Gospel of Judas*, which probably assumed Judas's name to
shock followers of the bishops, condemns the Apostles as leading the
Christian crowds astray to be sacrifices upon an altar. Small wonder
that the Church whose leaders came to regard themselves as successors
to the Apostles, and which increasingly celebrated martyrs for Christ,
loathed gnostics so much.[41]

Gnostic contempt for the flesh ran against the whole tendency of
Jewish religion, with its earthy affirmation of created things and its
insistence on God's personal relationship with his chosen people.
Because of this distancing from Judaism, it was extremely easy for
Christians to see the logic of pursuing gnostic solutions to the problem
which had exercised Paul so much: how much of the Jewish heritage to
jettison from the new faith. The gnostics included people of sophistication and learning – the complexity and frequent obscurity of their
literature impressively demonstrated that – and arguably they had a
more intellectually satisfying solution to the problem of evil in the world
than the mainstream Christian Church has ever been able to provide.
Evil simply exists; life is a battle between good and evil, in a material
world wholly beyond the concern of the true God.

Rather distinct from gnostic concerns was the contemporary approach
to Christian identity adopted by a Christian thinker of the early second
century named Marcion. Son of the Bishop of Sinope on the Black Sea,

he was successful in the shipping business and used this wealth to pursue a career of theological exploration. After he had come to Rome about 140, he was eventually expelled by the Church there when the full radicalism of his approach to the faith became apparent. Like gnostics, with whom he has often been wrongly identified, he was determined to pull Christianity away from its Jewish roots. He saw the writings of Paul as his chief weapon, but moving on from Paul's own conflicted relationship with Judaism, he came to the same conclusion as gnostics in saying that the created world must be a worthless sham and Jesus's flesh an illusion; his Passion and death should be blamed on the Creator Demiurge. In characteristically Greek fashion, Marcion found the Tanakh in its Greek form crude and offensive – 'Jewish myths', in a phrase of the Epistle to Titus, which he would have attributed to the Apostle Paul.[42] He saw the Creator God of the Jews as a God of judgement, rather than the God of love whom he saw perfectly revealed in Jesus Christ. Christ had died to satisfy the Creator God.

It is not easy to reconstruct Marcion's biblical writings and commentary, since they were largely destroyed by his enemies, but it is clear that he was a literalist who despised any figurative or allegorical interpretation of scripture and rather took the first apparent sense. If that sense clashed with his own sense of true religion, he simply rejected the text. The result was that all the Tanakh had to go, even though Marcion still drew on its prophecies to complete his picture of the saving work of Christ. What remained of the New Testament was a collection of Paul's letters (probably the collection which he inherited), together with a version of Luke's Gospel. Perhaps he simply chose this because Luke was the Gospel with which he had grown up, but it may have been because Luke's constant references to the Spirit in the story of Christ and the life of the Church appealed to him, or because of Luke's evident association with Paul through Luke's authorship of the Acts of the Apostles.[43] To hammer home his anti-Jewish and ultra-Pauline message, he added a book of *Antitheses*, pointing out the difference in approach between his selection of scripture and the Hebrew sacred books. He was no isolated eccentric: references to Christians opposing Marcion come from places as far apart as France and Syria, so it is clear that his teachings had a widespread effect, and there is evidence that congregations with Marcionite beliefs survived until as late as the tenth century in what are now the borderlands of Iran and Afghanistan.[44] Marcion fascinated the great German Lutheran Church historian of the nineteenth and twentieth centuries, Adolf von Harnack, and it must be said that there are curious resemblances in Marcion's thought to the spiritual progress of Martin Luther: the revulsion against the idea of a God of judgement, the contrast between Law and Gospel, the fascination with Paul and the single-minded search for a core message within the inheritance of sacred writings.[45]

CANON, CREED, MINISTRY, CATHOLICITY

Gnosticism and Marcionism offered two possible futures for the Jesus cult. A gnostic Christianity would have bred immense diversity of belief; indeed, because of gnosticism's general hospitality to mixtures of doctrine, Christianity might have drained into the sands of a generalized new religiosity within the Roman Empire if gnostic beliefs had become dominant within it. By contrast, a Church in which Marcion prevailed would have been a very tidy organization, given boundaries by the new master, just as Paul and the Pauline communities before him had sought to fence themselves in. The Christianity which emerged in reaction to these two possibilities adopted the same strategy as Marcion: it sought to define, to create a uniformity of belief and practice, just as contemporary Judaism was doing at the same time in reaction to the disaster of Jerusalem's fall. That demanded a concept of the Church as one wherever it was: a universal version of Christianity which had taken up Paul's mission to the Gentiles and combined it with much of the rhetoric and terminology of ancient Israel to express its wider unity. From an ordinary Greek adjective for 'general', 'whole' or 'universal', *katholikos/ē*, there developed a term of great resonance for Christianity, despite the fact that the word is not to be found in the Bible. Bishop Ignatius of Antioch provides the first known use in his letter written to the Christians of Smyrna, in the early second century, but he evidently expected his readers to be familiar with it; he certainly did not bother to explain exactly what he meant by 'the whole' (*katholikē*) Church.[46]

This was a momentous development. Christians have never since abandoned their rhetoric of unity, despite their general inability to sustain it at any stage in the reality of history. Yet they have gone on trying, and have used three main tools to build a 'Catholic' faith: developing an agreed list of authoritative sacred texts (a 'canon' of scripture, from the Greek for 'straight rod' or 'rule'); forming creeds;

embodying authority in ministers set aside for the purpose. It is easy (and traditional) to tell the history of all three developments in the early Church as a story of convergence and synthesis, but that story has left many casualties along the way. The last of the three has in fact proved one of the major forces to divide Christianity, as rival systems of ministry split or made their own claims to exclusive Catholic authority; almost equally divisive has been the question of what creeds should actually say. If we seek one explanation of why 'Catholic' Christianity so successfully elbowed aside both the gnostic alternatives and the tidy-mindedness of Marcion, it is to its sacred literature that we should point: its formation of a text which still remains the anchor of Christian belief, and which is held in common throughout the many varieties of Christian Churches.

To begin with, Christians had the Jewish Tanakh, obsessively re-directed in its reference towards their efforts to grapple with the meaning of the life and death of Jesus, and when they spoke of 'scripture' at the beginning of the second century CE, it is the Tanakh that they meant. By the end of that same century, 'scripture' was a more complicated word, because by then many Christians would include in the term a new series of books, a 'New Testament' of exclusively Christian works. The construction of a canon of scripture to stand in this New Testament alongside the Tanakh was a gradual process, even given the spur that Marcion was proposing to do the same thing. It is likely that the first collection of biblical 'New Testament' books which would be familiar to modern Christians was made in the middle of the second century, but that is not the same as saying that it was universally accepted by Christians straight away.[47] The earliest surviving complete list of books that we would recognize as the New Testament comes as late as 367 CE, laid down in a pastoral letter written by Athanasius, the Bishop of Alexandria. Even then, parts of the Church continued to argue whether it was really necessary to have four Gospels which did not always agree with each other, and some Churches went on into the fifth century using a harmony (in Greek, *Diatessaron*) combining all four, produced by the Syrian writer Tatian at the end of the second century (see pp. 181–2). Besides this, some books drifted in and out of the canon: the Church in Corinth long treasured as scripture the first of two epistles written to them by the Roman Church leader Clement (see pp. 132–3), and elsewhere the strongly anti-Jewish Epistle of Barnabas enjoyed lasting influence.[48] Some Christian communities in the eastern Mediterranean regarded the Book of Revelation with suspicion as late as the fifth century.

What this meant was that from now on there was a large literature of books excluded from the mainstream, both Jewish and Christian in origin, taking the form of 'Gospels', 'Apocalypses', 'Acts' and the like. A few, mainly the oldest, were gathered in the approved secondary character of 'apocrypha' (see pp. 67–8), but others flitted in and out of Christian consciousness, particularly if they provided a good story or memorable images or information not otherwise found in canonical scripture. Thus the name of Mary's mother and Jesus's grandmother, Anna or Anne, is only provided in the excluded books, first the work which is termed the 'Infancy Gospel [*Protevangelium*] of James'. Likewise the ox and the ass commonly thought of as fixtures of Jesus's birth in the stable in Bethlehem appear only in a text from as late as the eighth or ninth century, although it probably reflects earlier lost apocryphal books (see Plate 25). The same is true of accounts of the beheading of St Paul or of St Peter's martyrdom: according to the apocryphal *Acts of Peter*, Peter apparently insisted on being crucified upside down so that his death would be more debasing than that of his Lord. Popular awareness of this vanishing literature was therefore sustained through the vivid pictures which these stories continued to stimulate in Christian art – in the case of the ox and the ass, down to the Christmas cards and carols of the present day.[49]

The advantage of credal statements was that almost anyone was capable of learning them quickly to standardize belief and put up barriers against speculation or what was likely to be a boundless set of disagreements about what the Christian scriptures actually meant. New believers had probably been given such formulae at baptism from the earliest days of Christ-following; several can be traced embedded in the texts of the epistles both of Paul and of others. However, in the second century these creeds took on a new aggressive tone in response to the growing diversity of Christian belief. Take, for instance, a credal statement set down by Bishop Irenaeus of Lyons in a work of instruction written in Greek in the late second century and now preserved only in an Armenian translation: for ease of remembering, it is fashioned into three articles, dealing with three aspects of the Christian encounter with the divine:

God the Father, uncreated, beyond grasp, invisible, one God the maker of all; this is the first and foremost article of our faith. But the second article is the Word of God, the Son of God, Christ Jesus our Lord, who was shown forth by the prophets according to the design of their prophecy and according to the manner in which the Father disposed; and through Him were made all things whatsoever. He also, in the end of times ... became a man among men, visible and tangible, in order to abolish death and bring to light life, and bring about the communion of God and man. And the third article is the Holy Spirit, through whom the prophets prophesied and the patriarchs were taught about God ... and who in the end of times has been poured forth in a new manner upon humanity over all the earth, renewing man to God.[50]

This creed contains much less matter than subsequent creeds, which were concerned to exclude other challenges to the Church's identity, yet practically every clause in it hits at gnostic attitudes. No gnostic could have asserted that God made everything, or that Jesus was 'tangible', or that the Spirit had inspired Hebrew prophets and taught the Jews about God.

Above all, there must be a universally recognized single authority in the Church able to take decisions: to choose sacred texts for canonical status or compare the content of local creeds in Churches for a uniform direction in teaching. Such a Church would be 'Catholic' indeed. The second century saw a marked increase in the authority and coherence of the Church's ordained ministry. By 200 CE there was a mainstream Catholic Church which took for granted the existence of a threefold ministry of bishop, priest and deacon, and there would be few challenges to this pattern for the next thirteen hundred years. When the pattern was indeed challenged in the sixteenth-century Reformation in the Western Church, those arguing about the nature of ministry looked for proof of their respective opposing viewpoints in the earliest years of the Church, and in the end no party could find complete satisfaction in the evidence. Let us discover why.

It was not surprising that the Jerusalem Church had a single leading figure in the wake of the death of Jesus, since it was Jesus's own brother, James. He seems to have presided over apostles; they included the remaining figures from the original Twelve but also numbered others awarded this description. The leadership in Jerusalem under James had a group of elders as well: the Greek is *presbyteroi*, which would descend into the English 'priests', as well into other terms which much later took on polemical overtones, 'presbyters' and 'presbytery'. In addition to these, there was a group of seven deacons: the word is the ordinary Greek for servant, *diakonos*.[51] So it is tempting to see in this the equivalent in embryo of the later grades of bishop, priest and deacon. A similar picture emerges from one of the earliest major Christian centres, Antioch in Syria, when Antioch re-emerges at the end of the first century, after a hiatus in surviving documentation. At this stage, the Church in Antioch had a single leader, overseer or 'bishop' (*episkopos*), just like the (by then dispersed) community in Jerusalem: Ignatius – interestingly, a man with a Latin name, in the same way that the enduring Antiochene nickname for Christ-followers, *Christiani*, was a Latin rather than Greek idiom (see p. 110). Ignatius was also assisted by presbyters and deacons. It might seem that the later Catholic case for ministerial order is clinched by such foundational examples, but the full story is to be found elsewhere.

Antioch and Jerusalem seem to have found their models for ministry in the organization of the Jewish Temple and its hierarchy, as one might expect from Christian centres so much resonating with the Palestinian past. The Church elsewhere had spread in more Hellenized settings mainly through the work of Paul and his sympathizers, and all sorts of patterns of ministry emerge from casual references in various epistles and in Acts. Talk of *charismata*, gifts of the Spirit, is frequent, and these gifts were not confined to the Apostles, posing problems in regulating them (see pp. 101–2). Paul and his admirers list gifts of the Spirit more than once, and comparing such lists as those in I Corinthians 12 and Ephesians 4, it is clear that they vary. They should not be considered as rigid technical terms, merely as ways of organizing a mission which constantly demanded improvisation without much possibility of guidance from the past.

Gradually, however, the similar situations which the work of mission produced tended towards standardization of language. The words *presbyteros* (elder) and *episkopos* (overseer) are found scattered throughout the epistles and Acts, but it is quite clear that at this early stage they often described the same people interchangeably: so, for instance, in Acts 20 Paul is said to have addressed himself to the *presbyteroi* of Ephesus, but to have told them that the Holy Spirit had made them pastors or bishops (*episkopoi*) over their Church. There is a useful comparison to be made with another effort at improvising oversight in mission conditions: John Wesley's structuring of Methodism in eighteenth-century Great Britain and North America, where a mobile 'itinerant' ministry grew up alongside a settled and locally based one, called local preachers. A similar stage can be detected in the late-first-century Church: a mobile ministry included those known as apostles and prophets, the local ministry in particular places consisted of a grade known interchangeably as bishops or presbyters, together with a separate grade of deacons, who assisted in performing the Eucharist, the central Christian ritual act, and also in the day-to-day running of church affairs.

It was perhaps not surprising that a mobile and a local ministry should sometimes come into conflict: they represented two different ways of presenting authority handed down from the Apostles, and each form of minister might have their own charisma. This tension is represented in the *Didachē* (see p. 120), which lays down instructions for detecting false prophets who might turn up in a community, and also reminds its readers that the local ministry should be given just as much honour as the mobile ministry: 'despise them not: for these are they which are honoured of you with the prophets and teachers'.[52] It does not take much imagination to see why a community should have felt it necessary to commit such thoughts to writing. How would this tension be resolved? Ultimately the mobile ministry disappeared from the mainstream Church, leaving the local ministry as the only accepted form.

This was probably inevitable as the Church began to settle down around local centres which had their own traditions and way of life, and as wandering teachers with dangerous charisma brought with them the sort of variety of belief and teaching which one finds in the gnostic literature. Despite the comparative brevity of its history, the 'Catholic' Church took its cue from Paul in talking a great deal about 'tradition', continuity. This theme was prominent in an influential document of about 100 CE, a letter sent to the Church at Corinth. Arguments at Corinth had led to the congregation dismissing their leaders and appointing others. Clement, a leader of the Church in Rome, wrote to protest in the most solemn terms, not because the congregation was deviating in any way in belief, but simply because it was endangering a God-given line of authority from the Apostles, who first preached the Gospel which they received directly from Jesus, himself 'sent from God'. Break this link, said Clement, and the appointed worship of God is endangered; by implication, succession is the only way of making sure that doctrine remains the same in Corinth and in Rome and throughout the whole Church. In a creative misquotation, Clement called in aid the prophet Isaiah and made him the mouthpiece for God's pronouncement 'I will establish their bishops in righteousness and their deacons in faith.'[53] This is the first surviving formulation of an idea of apostolic succession in Christian ministry. The Corinthians listened and restored their old leaders, so it was also the first known occasion that a Roman cleric had successfully influenced the life of another Church: a moment with much significance for the future of Christianity generally.

Clement actually took as given the twofold order of bishop/presbyter, which can also be seen in the *Didachē*, even though most sources are agreed in regarding him as Bishop in Rome. Another tract from Rome, not much later than the time of Clement, the book by Hermas known as the *Shepherd*, also talks of a collegiate ministry of presbyter-bishops, even though the final version of the *Shepherd* was written when Hermas's brother Pius was Bishop of Rome. This suggests that a twofold and threefold view of ministry could coexist; yet the elevation of one leading bishop figure above other presbyters was virtually complete by the end of the second century. One powerful force in this development was the prestige enjoyed in all parts of the Church by the seven letters written to various Churches and to Bishop Polycarp of Smyrna by Ignatius, Bishop of Antioch. They relate to his journey from Antioch to Rome following his arrest just after 100 CE and were written in the certain expectation (indeed joyful hope) that he would die as a martyr.[54]

In these letters Ignatius spoke much of his concern at what are recognizable as forms of gnostic belief, including docetic views of Christ's Passion. To combat this, he emphasized the reality of both Christ's divinity and his humanity, which he saw best expressed in the Church's continuing celebration of the Eucharist. But how could this doctrine be guaranteed? Ignatius pointed to what he saw as a standard of doctrine set by the beliefs affirmed by the Church in Rome, which he knew would be the city of his martyrdom; it is worth noting that he made no mention of the Bishop of Rome, simply of the Church. He linked with this the role in each community of the bishop, who should be the one person in every place responsible for handing on the faith and guarding against deviation. The bishop, after all, presided at the Eucharist and should be the automatic source of authority: 'You must all follow the bishop as Jesus Christ [followed] the Father . . . Let no one do anything apart from the bishop that has to do with the Church. Let that be regarded as a valid Eucharist which is held under the bishop or to whomever he entrusts it. Wherever the bishop appears, there let the congregation be; just as wherever Jesus Christ is, there is the whole [*katholikē*] Church.'[55]

The cynical might say that it was easy for Ignatius to take this line, since there was already one bishop in Antioch and his name was Ignatius. Noticeably, a letter written by his correspondent and fellow martyr Bishop Polycarp of Smyrna does not claim that Polycarp had a similar status as monarchical bishop in his city Church: it describes a collegiate grouping of presbyters there with a grade of deacons and an order of widows.[56] But in this contest of martyrs, it was Ignatius's passionate account of a monarchical episcopal ministry which set the pattern for the future. That may be because he was deliberately talking in priestly language familiar to converts to Christianity from outside Judaism, who were used to the round of civic religion in the temples of Mediterranean cities.[57] His arguments in any case combined with a discussion of apostolic succession by yet another reputed martyr, Clement of Rome. The advantages of a monarchical leadership were clear: it was much more straightforward for one person to act as a focus for the Church in this way, to resist any widening of its beliefs, just as it made more sense for one person to preside over a community's Eucharist than it did for a committee to do so. If Churches started taking this line on the nature of ecclesiastical authority, it is easy to see why the alternative authority embodied in the mobile ministry should come to seem unnecessary and even a threat to the good order of the Church.

It must be significant that there is no surviving debate about the gradual domination of Church affairs in each community by one man in apostolic succession (monarchical episcopacy), with the notable exception, as we have seen, of gnostic texts. The early Christians were not afraid to commit their disagreements with each other to writing, and their disagreements have survived, but not in this case. Soon, big churches had many presbyters under the bishop's authority: deacons were the bishops' assistants, occasionally themselves rising to be bishops, but never being made presbyters. Much later, the distinctive role of the deacon diminished, and late in the Roman Empire there were already examples of the diaconate being used as the first step in a successful clerical career through the order of presbyters, up to the rank of bishop, just like the various career grades in the Roman civil service.

Amid these developments of a 'Catholic' episcopate in the second century, the episcopal leaders of certain cities stood out as especial figures of authority, what would later be called patriarchs: in the East the predictable centres of Antioch and Alexandria (equally predictably by this stage, not Jerusalem). In the West was Rome. Here in the imperial capital one of the two great martyrs of the first generation who had died there, Christ's Apostle Peter, was later credited not only with having died there but also with having been the city's first monarchical bishop.[58] In early centuries Peter and Paul were given more or less equal veneration in Rome, and in early Christian art they were commonly paired together, but in Rome manifestly the balance has now drastically shifted towards Peter. The pope occupies the episcopal throne of Peter; he holds sway in the Catholic Church from a miniature state centring on a vast basilican church built above Peter's shrine. Although Paul is honourably enshrined in a major basilica (San Paolo fuori le Mura), it is sited in a formerly malaria-infested plain, a mile beyond the walls of Rome, and the average tourist could be forgiven for not noticing that the Apostle of the Gentiles had much to do with the city. That was the case long before the catastrophic fire which destroyed most of the historic interest of Paul's shrine-church in 1823 – and it is significant that much of the previous fascination of that church lay in the fact that, in contrast to the strenuous construction history of St Peter's Basilica, no one had bothered to rebuild or much alter St Paul's-outside-the-Walls since its first enlargement in the 380s. Its neglect in the late medieval period was not the least among the scandals of fifteenth-century Rome.[59]

Paul's epistles are the oldest surviving documents in the Christian tradition. They shaped the theology of the Christianity which survived as mainstream, and the theology of the Latin West especially reflects Paul's preoccupations, which had brought him into serious conflict with his fellow Apostle Peter (see pp. 105–6). Tensions between the two are also reflected in early apocryphal Christian books.[60] By contrast with Paul's literary achievement, we have already noted Peter as being credited with two short epistles in the New Testament which are so different in character that at least one of them cannot be by him, and in any case no one has regarded either of them as especially significant in the life of the Church. Yet Peter has taken the limelight in Rome. The fading of Paul from popular devotional consciousness and from much share in the charisma of Rome is one of the great puzzles of Christian history, but it is obvious that part of the answer to the puzzle lies in a vast expansion of the power and prestige of the Bishops of Rome.

Some time in the 160s a shrine was built for Peter at the place of his burial, perhaps to commemorate a hundred years passing since his death. The remains of it, directly under the high altar of the present basilica, were recovered during the twentieth century in a sensational series of archaeological investigations.[61] The shrine was a modest structure, but its very existence in a public urban cemetery speaks of a community determined to stake its claim to an open existence in the capital. It is unclear whether Peter had actually played the role of bishop in the Church in Rome, even if he did indeed die in the city, and the names traditionally provided for his successor bishops up to the end of the first century are no more than names. They are probably the result of later second-century back-projection to create a history for the episcopal succession in the era when episcopal succession had become significant.

Even in the second century, the evidence suggests that Bishops of Rome were part of a team of presbyters who might also be considered as having the authority of bishops, in a diverse and loosely organized city Church, and what particular prestige and authority were enjoyed by the Church in Rome was a matter of its collective identity.[62]

The second-century Roman Church's numbers were substantial, but still it formed a tiny proportion of the city's population, and at that time and for some decades to come it revealed its origins as a community of immigrants by the fact that its language was not Latin but Greek. There is one survival of Greek in the liturgy of the Western Church: a Greek prayer so venerable (though not to be found in the text of scripture) that even after the Church in Rome changed to Latin, Western congregations continued to chant it. The threefold *Kyrie Eleison, Christe Eleison, Kyrie Eleison* ('Lord have mercy, Christ have mercy, Lord have mercy') is so intensely used in Orthodox liturgy that its repetition can almost sound like a mantra; in the Western Church its appearance is much more restricted, but it is one of the fixtures in the preparatory sections of the Eucharist, the inspiration for much sacred music over the centuries. It is a powerful reminder of the era when the 'Catholic' Church throughout the Mediterranean was united by a common language.

The switch to Latin in Christian Rome may have been made by one of the bishops at the end of the century, Victor (189–99).[63] He may indeed have been the first monarchical bishop in Rome; he was one of that generation of Church leaders, like Irenaeus in Lyons and Demetrius in Alexandria, intent on creating a Church with a single source of episcopal authority and a single doctrinal standard which would be affirmed by other bishops elsewhere (see pp. 129–30). It was Victor, with the encouragement of Irenaeus, who narrowed the diversity of belief which a Bishop of Rome would consider acceptable, by ending the long-standing custom of sending Eucharistic bread and wine which he had consecrated to a variety of Christian communities in the city – including Valentinian gnostics, Montanists and various exponents of Monarchian views on the Trinity (see pp. 145–6).[64] This was in effect a punitive action; as such, it was a pioneering form of a favourite device in later centuries, excommunication – cutting off offenders from fellowship with the Christians in a particular place. Nothing could better illustrate the new formal role of the bishop as teacher and guardian of discipline. Successive bishops emphasized their unifying role in the vastness of the city by visiting the various places of Christian worship in turn; during the third century, as more churches achieved permanent sites instead of congregations casually meeting in Christian houses, this became the basis of a liturgical rota of 'stational' papal visits which still survives in the liturgical year in Rome. Many other bishops in large and potentially divided cities followed the Bishop of Rome's example later.[65]

Already, therefore, during the third century, the Bishop of Rome was consolidating a role which was likely to give him a special prominence in Western Churches. The first surviving use of the title *'papa'* in Rome occurs in the time of Bishop Marcellinus (296–304), in a funerary inscription for his deacon Severus in one of the catacombs in the city.[66] There was, after all, no other Church in the West which could lay claim to the burial place of two Apostles and pilgrimage was beginning to draw Christians to Rome. The surroundings of St Peter's original shrine are covered in early graffiti from pilgrims, and although these are not easily datable, there are similar graffiti in a shrine out on the Via Appia to the south-east of the city, below the present Church of San Sebastiano. This roadside shrine seems to have sheltered the remains of both Peter and Paul for some time after persecutions of Christians in the mid-third century: the names and the often ill-spelled forms of expression used in the graffiti there suggest that they were made by visitors to the city, and quite humble visitors too.[67]

The only possible rival to the position of Rome was the Church of the North African coast, which was probably the first major centre of Latin-speaking Christianity, but North Africa, despite its many martyrs in the late second and third centuries, did not possess any counterweight to two Apostles. It was a dispute in 256 between Bishop Stephen of Rome and the leading Bishop of North Africa, Cyprian of Carthage, that produced a Roman bishop's first-known appeal to Matthew 16.18: Christ's pronouncement to Peter that 'on this rock I will build my Church' might be seen as conferring particular authority on Peter's presumed successor in Rome (see pp. 173–6). This was a claim which met with modified rapture in North Africa, and which likewise would at the time have been greeted with polite scepticism in the eastern Mediterranean. Rome's place in the Christian Church remained subject to many accidents of history, as we will discover.

MONTANISM: PROPHECY RENEWED AND SUPPRESSED

The disappearance of charismatic wandering Christian teachers or prophets and the assertion of the authority of bishops were probably sealed by the Catholic Church's confrontation in the later second century with a movement known as Montanism or 'the New Prophecy'. Montanus was a native of Phrygia in the mountains of Asia Minor, which was already emerging as one of the earliest centres of Christian numerical strength and enthusiasm during the second century. Asia Minor was, after all, the setting for the prophetic poem of John the Divine, and the hesitant reception of his Book of Revelation into the New Testament may reflect ecclesiastical worries about this recurrent theme of prophecy among Christians in Asia Minor. Like so many converts, Montanus passionately proclaimed his enthusiasm for his new-found faith, but that extended (at a date uncertain, but probably around 165) into announcements that he had new revelations from the Holy Spirit to add to the Christian message. It was not so much the content of these messages that worried the existing Christian leadership of the area as the challenge which they posed to their authority. By what right did this man with no commission, in no apostolic succession, speak new truths of the faith and sweep crowds along with him in his excitement?

What made matters worse was that Montanus was accompanied by female prophetesses who spoke in states of ecstasy. The position of women leadership in the Church had steadily diminished over the previous century, and this combination of female assertiveness and prophecy seemed dangerously reminiscent of the female seers at ancient cultic centres: the worst possible resonance for a cult seeking to demonstrate its separation from other religions. So the Church in Asia was riven: was Montanus a blessing or a danger? Both sides appealed to other Churches around the Mediterranean, and to the great distress of the Montanists, they found themselves condemned by Eleutherius, the Bishop of Rome. As is often the case, opposition and hostility drove them into ever wilder statements about their own mission; their total and final exclusion from the Catholic Church by a council of bishops was sadly inevitable after this. Elsewhere in the Christian world, only in North Africa, which came to have a tradition of high-temperature Christianity, did their passionate commitment to the Holy Spirit find a lasting sympathy among prominent Christian activists, especially the distinguished early-third-century Christian writer Tertullian (see pp. 144–7). Yet in their Phrygian homeland, the Montanists persisted obstinately until at least the sixth century. Then in 550 the morale of the proud descendants of the 'New Prophecy' was finally broken when the Byzantine Emperor Justinian sent in his troops to wreck their great shrine of the founder-prophets in the now-venerable Montanist stronghold at Pepouza. Eventually even Pepouza's whereabouts were forgotten and only recently has the enthusiasm of researchers revealed its probable site.[68] Yet less than a century after the imperial vandalism at Pepouza a new 'New Prophecy' began tearing at the fabric of the Byzantine Empire, as Muslim armies swept north from Mecca and beat at the frontiers of Asia Minor. Maybe there were still Montanists in Asia Minor to welcome the fervour of the new arrivals.

While the Montanists early on became firmly convinced that they were about to see the New Jerusalem descend on earth at Pepouza, their enthusiasm contrasted sharply with the Catholic Church's general abandonment of Paul's original conviction that the Lord Christ would soon be returning. Generally in the next few centuries, such beliefs were to be found in marginal Christian groups. Among the Montanists' contemporaries in the mainstream leadership, only Bishop Irenaeus of Lyons showed positive enthusiasm for a vision of the world's last days coming in his lifetime, and his views on this caused such embarrassment to the next generations of Christians that their original expression in Greek has entirely disappeared and even many of the manuscript copies of its Latin translation censor out its passages on this subject. The Latin translation of what Irenaeus had said turned up only in the late sixteenth century and was then equally embarrassing to the Counter-Reformation Church of Rome, which was not pleased to find one of the bastions of the Catholic faith saying the same sorts of things as contemporary radical Protestants.[69]

One might regard the Montanist emphasis on new revelations of the Spirit as a natural reaction to the gradual closing of the New Testament canon, but there was little that could actually be described as heretical in what they said. The problem was one of authority. The Church leadership's strong reaction against Montanus might reflect tensions between the urban Christianity of the late first century, which was gradually evolving leadership around one man in a city congregation, and a new expansion of Christian enthusiasm out in rural backwaters.[70] The Church was settling on one model of authority in monarchical episcopacy and the threefold ministry; the Montanists placed against that the random gift of prophecy. The two models have a long history of conflict in the subsequent Christian centuries: the significance of the Montanist episode is that this is the first time the clash appears. Later it would be seen in the first Protestant rebels against Rome, in the radicals beyond the Protestants, in Methodists and Millerites, in Pentecostals and African-initiated Churches; we will meet them all. And one should not forget the other conflict which has returned as an active issue in the Church after two millennia, well summed up in the dark warning of a Victorian clergyman-professor in a reference work still useful in many respects: 'If Montanism had triumphed, Christian doctrine would have been developed, not under the superintendence of the church teachers most esteemed for wisdom, but usually of wild and excitable women.'[71]

Gnosticism and Montanism thus both had a marked effect on the Church, causing it to shut doors on all sorts of possibilities for new Christian identities. The most dramatic effect of the fight against gnosticism was to halt Christianity's march away from its Jewish roots, that process which had begun so early and had dominated its life in the first century. From the earliest days Christians had searched the Tanakh in their anxiety to find pre-echoes of their own passionate convictions about the God-Man Jesus Christ. Now even more self-consciously, in quotations in its literature and in the reading of sacred texts in communal worship, the Church vigorously reaffirmed the worth of what it called the Old Testament alongside the New. Nevertheless the new episcopal guardians of doctrine were still faced with the problem of presenting their faith in an urban culture which stretched all round the Mediterranean and beyond the bounds of the Roman Empire, dominated by highly literate elites steeped in Greek learning, literature and ways of thinking. Paul of Tarsus had probably not experienced a conventional advanced education; there is certainly no trace of it in his literary style or the content or shape of his writings. He does not even bother mentioning philosophy; indeed, it attracts precisely one mention in the New Testament, where, in the words of Paul's admirer who wrote Colossians, it is dismissed as 'empty deceit'.[72]

A hundred years later, such a cavalier approach would not do. A good education was becoming more common among prominent Christians and that would affect their view of their faith. They had now accepted many of the social values of this world; they had also rejected some of the more extreme ways in which gnostics had adapted the Christian message to other systems of thought. That left large questions about the relationship of the Catholic Church to Greek and Roman high culture, which in the work of a series of authors from the later years of the first century CE reached a new peak of literary creativity and self-conscious pride in the Greek cultural past, conventionally now called the 'Second Sophistic'. It was not surprising that thoughtful Christians who listened to the self-confident voices which dominated cultured conversations in the world around them went on to find ways of drawing on the best of this culture for their own purposes. But the problems were great. Could one call on Plato or Aristotle or their new interpreters in contemporary society to help in preaching the Gospel? The Second Sophistic offered wisdom which owed nothing to the Christian revelation in scripture; was its wisdom then worthless? A series of highly intelligent and thoughtful Christians thought that the answers to these questions were obvious: the Greek inheritance was indispensable to the Church. In their efforts to harness it to the Christian message, they can be said to have created or manufactured Christian teaching on a heroic scale, and for good or ill the Church universal has never ceased to look back at and build on what they achieved.

JUSTIN, IRENAEUS, TERTULLIAN

A series of Christians tackled these questions during the second century, without closing them down. Christianity has never ceased to debate the relationship between truth revealed from God in sacred text and the restless exploration of truth by human reason, which on a Christian account is itself a gift of God. It is a mark of how far Christianity had spread by the second century that some of the most prominent in the writings which have survived to us – Justin, Irenaeus, Tertullian – worked mainly in Rome and Churches of the western Mediterranean. Two others – Clement of Alexandria and Origen – came from the great intellectual and commercial centre of Alexandria. Nevertheless all of them except Tertullian thought and wrote in Greek: this was still the common currency of the Church throughout the Mediterranean, even in the Latin-speaking West, which is an indication that Western Christianity was still largely dominated by an urban population maintaining ready links with the Greek East. Indeed, Justin and Irenaeus revealed this continuing mobility and interconnectedness in Christianity by their move from eastern to western cities in the empire.

Justin was born in Samaria and tells us how he came to Christian faith in a little piece of autobiography which is also a parable of his position in the revelation/reason debate – in fact it may be no more than a parable. He tells us that he travelled to Ephesus for his higher education and had a series of disappointments. He started predictably enough with a tutor in the most influential philosophy of the age, Stoicism, but that tutor could tell Justin nothing about God: Stoicism, after all, was designed to cultivate and regulate the self rather than illuminate the nature of God. Justin had no more luck with an exponent of Aristotle, who was mainly concerned with fixing a fee for his services – perhaps a dig at the practical and systematizing concerns of Aristotelianism. A Pythagorean was no help to him, because he demanded that Justin should first become expert in music, astronomy and geometry before contemplating the mysteries which these skills illustrated. Finally Justin went to a Platonist and found satisfaction in what he learned – but then, in a field near the Ephesus seashore, he met an old man who culminated a long conversation by speaking to him of the Hebrew prophets who had foretold Christ.[73] Justin's journey was complete. His clinching point in the saga was that the wisdom of the prophets was older than that of the Greeks, and in an age which was inclined to see oldest as best, this was the most promising argument open to any exponent of the new faith in Christ. Yet Justin never ceased to wear his philosopher's cloak (*pallium*), as distinctive a mark of identity as the modern Christian clerical collar – or perhaps a better analogy would be with the gown and square cap of the properly dressed Oxford don, since to wear the cloak was to make a claim to be a teacher in a school for advanced students. It was also a dramatic and continual visual sign in his everyday life and in his teaching that Justin was committed to the proposition that two traditions might speak as one.

Because Justin valued the whole of his spiritual exploration, he was concerned to explain his newly acquired Christian faith to those outside its boundaries in terms that they would understand; he was chief among a series of 'Apologists' who, in the second century, opened a dialogue with the culture around them in order to show that Christianity was superior to the elite wisdom of the age. In particular, he was happy to explain the mysterious relationship of Jesus Christ to God the Father in terms which would make sense to intelligent Greeks puzzled by Christian claims. He deployed one of the commonplace terms used alike by Platonists, Stoics and Hellenized Jews influenced by the Jewish scholar of the first century CE Philo of Alexandria when they discussed divinity: Word (*Logos*), already the keynote theme of the hymn which so sonorously opens John's Gospel. For Justin, God the Father corresponded to Plato's discussion of a supreme Being. Justin wanted to say with the mainstream Church against gnosticism that this supreme God had created the material world, and he tried to get over the problem of relating the two by seeing the Logos as a mediator between them. This Logos had been glimpsed by the Hebrew prophets, but also by great philosophers like Plato, thus happily enrolled among Christian witnesses. The Logos was seen finally and completely in Jesus Christ, a being other than the Father, but derived from him with the fullness and intimacy of a flame which lights one torch from another: torchlight from torchlight, in a phrase which was embedded in the fourth century in the doctrinal statement which is now called the Nicene Creed.[74]

Such use of 'Logos' was popular among second-century theologians, and is to be found in Justin's younger contemporary, Irenaeus. Probably from Smyrna on the west coast of Asia Minor, Irenaeus travelled first to Rome for study and then to southern France and the city of Lyons. Persecution devastated the Christian Church there in 177, and among those killed was the bishop, Pothinus, so Irenaeus took his place. His career as a writer was shaped by the practical concerns of a father in God for a flock troubled both by official harassment and by alternatives offered by gnostic belief. He was not an innovative thinker like Justin, but, as one might expect from someone in his position, he defended Christianity against gnosticism just as Ignatius of Antioch had done, by emphasizing the tradition which the bishop embodied, such as the credal statements already noticed (see pp. 129–30). As we have already seen (see p. 121), Irenaeus took the word *hairesis* ('self-chosen opinion'), used in the latest epistles in the New Testament in the sense of 'sect', and reapplied it to the whole spectrum of gnostic belief. He thereby implied that he was condemning a single if many-headed movement. Progressing from speaking of sectarianism, he was popularizing a concept with a prosperous future in Christian consciousness: heresy. It was the natural counterpart of his concept of a united 'Catholic' Christianity with a single leadership.

Irenaeus saw the vital centre of Catholic Christianity as the Eucharist, which could not be separated from the leadership role of the bishop who presided over it. He was determined to stress the importance of flesh and matter which he saw proclaimed in the Eucharist, and which gnostics rejected. Accordingly Irenaeus followed Justin in seeing God's purpose unfold through all human history. The Old Testament was the central text on that history – so much for Marcion's dismissal of it –

and Irenaeus delighted in stressing the symmetries or 'recapitulations' which its text revealed: thus the fall of the first man, Adam, was remedied by the second Adam, Christ, rising from the dead; the disobedience of the woman Eve remedied by the obedience of the woman Mary; the fateful role of the Tree of Life in the Garden of Eden was remedied by the Tree of Life which was Christ's cross.[75] Such symmetries appealed to a culture fascinated by the poetry of numbers and geometry, and they make sense of the lively confidence with which both Justin and Irenaeus looked, on the basis of Revelation 20, to a coming earthly thousand-year rule of God's chosen (a *millennium*, hence the belief in such an event being known as millenarianism). Even though most other influential voices in the Church now found such apocalyptic themes embarrassing, the confidence which Justin and Irenaeus expressed is logical: one would expect God's final purpose to be expressed in his created world, since the doctrine of recapitulation showed that this is where his plans had worked out before.

Tertullian is the first known major Christian theologian who thought and wrote in Latin. He came from the important North African city of Carthage, which in the third and second centuries BCE had nearly succeeded in ending the steady rise of the Roman Republic. Its conquest, destruction and refoundation as a Roman colony had been so thorough-going that it was now a centre of Latin culture, with its own flourishing schools of advanced education; it is likely that a Latin-speaking Christian Church emerged first here rather than in Rome. The city's links with Rome were close, for it was the centre of the North African grain export trade, vital to the Roman emperors in their constant task of keeping their huge capital city supplied with free bread. The Christian Churches of Carthage and Rome followed this pattern of trade in maintaining close if not always friendly links. Tertullian had much to do with controversies which had Rome as their main stage.

Although much remains disputed about Tertullian's life and back-ground, his writings reveal a man who had received a first-class Latin education. He showed his debt to the Classical tradition in the brilliance of his Latin literary style, which sparkles through his numerous theologi-cal and controversial works with all the verve and energy of a very talented and very bad-tempered high-class journalist. Unlike Justin, he affected to despise the Classical tradition, coining the rhetorical question which sums up the preoccupation of second-century Catholic theo-logians, 'What has Athens to do with Jerusalem?'[76] But he could never escape it: he was a maverick Roman intellectual who spent his life in rebellion, in the end, even against the Catholic Church itself, because he became a champion of the Montanists in their schism. Despite the break, his memory was treasured in the North African Church, which repeatedly demonstrated the chafing against settled authority which the Montanists had already exhibited.

This paradoxical rebel could in one work bitterly abuse the Bishop of Rome for his laxity in enforcing what Tertullian saw as proper Christian rigour in moral standards, yet elsewhere write movingly of the honour which attached to the role of bishops in apostolic succession, including Rome itself.[77] Supporters of Marcion, advocates of infant baptism, collaborators with imperial power, opponents of Montanism, all came under the lash of his pen. Tertullian suggested that the human soul is transmitted by parents to their children and is therefore inescapably associated with continuing human sin: this doctrine of 'traducianism' underlay the pessimistic view of the human condition and its imprisonment in original sin which was presented in an extreme form by that later theological giant from North Africa, Augustine of Hippo (see pp. 306–9).

Amid all that controversy, Tertullian fashioned much of the language which Latin Christians were destined to use to discuss the perplexities of their faith. He dealt combatively with a most perplexing problem which had evolved out of the Church's sense, perceptible already in the writings of Paul, that the one God is experienced in three aspects, as Father, Son and Spirit – creator, redeemer and strengthener. But what was the relationship between them? Oneness in divinity was somehow reflected in threeness – indeed, one would need a word to express that idea of threeness. It is to be found for the first time in Tertullian's writings, although probably he did not invent it: *Trinitas*. His discussion comes mainly in a typically abusive pamphlet which he wrote against a Christian from Asia Minor called Praxeas.[78] Praxeas represented an important school of thought within second-century Christianity called Monarchianism, which was a reaction against the 'Logos' language used by theologians like Justin. Justin was so concerned to stress the difference in the role of Father and Son that he had gone as far as to talk of the Logos as 'other than the God who made all', although he was quick to try to cover himself by adding, 'I mean in number not in mind'.[79] This did not save him from accusations that theologians like him were endangering the basic Christian idea of the unity of God; but in turn those 'Monarchians' who stressed unity were in danger of losing any concept of distinctiveness between Father, Son and Spirit. So it was not merely Tertullian who became deeply concerned at their assertions.

Monarchian models of God could take two forms. One, 'Adoptionist Monarchianism', explained the nature of Christ by saying that he had been adopted by God as Son, although he was a man; he was only God in the sense that the Father's power rested in his human form. Some early writers such as Hermas in his book the *Shepherd* had taken this view without being singled out for condemnation, but late-second-century Monarchians like Theodotus, who came to Rome from Byzantion, took the idea much further. For him, Jesus was a man like other men apart from his miraculous birth; at his baptism in the Jordan, the Holy Spirit had descended on him and given him the power to work miracles, but that did not mean that he became God. Because of this emphasis on the power of the Holy Spirit in Jesus's 'promotion', this view is sometimes called *dynamic* (from the Greek *dynamis,* 'power').

The other Monarchian approach was 'modalist', so called because it saw the names of Father, Son and Holy Spirit as corresponding merely to different aspects or modes of the same divine being, playing transitory parts in succession, like an actor on the Classical stage donning a theatrical mask to denote a tragic or a comic role. The Latin word for this theatrical mask was *'persona'*. That root word for the English word 'person' underlines the difficulty of talking about the Trinity, because in later Christian discussion, far from describing a series of temporary roles, the idea of 'person' was instead attached to the individual and unchanging natures of Father, Son or Spirit, in a view of the Trinity which represented (among other things) the defeat of the Monarchian viewpoint. Modalist Monarchianism is often known as 'Sabellianism', commemorating an otherwise obscure late-second-century exponent of the idea, and a term of abuse which has been flung around at various periods in Church circles with about as much discrimination as Senator Joe McCarthy once used the word 'Communist'.

The Roman authorities eventually condemned both forms of Monarchianism at the turn of the second and third centuries, but three successive Roman bishops had hesitated to do so, a symptom of the way in which earlier Christianity had not been prepared to shut down a plurality of ways of viewing its most difficult theological problems.[80] Monarchian ideas were not going to disappear; they were an inevitable consequence of a faith which wants to talk about God as both one and three. In particular, many Christians associated one Greek word with Monarchian thinkers: *homoousios*, meaning 'of one substance', which could be applied to the intimate and direct relationship of Father and Son. Now it sits apparently innocently in the Nicene Creed recited by millions in every Eucharist, but once it rang alarm bells for many Christians, especially in the East. Its use seemed to endanger the separate identities of the three persons of the Trinity, since it had been used by Monarchians in the third century, in particular Paul of Samosata, a Syrian Christian who had been deposed as Bishop of Antioch on an enjoyably ripe variety of scandalous charges. For that reason, *homoousios* proved to be capable of tearing the Christian world apart in the fourth century, as we will see (see pp. 211–22).

ALEXANDRIAN THEOLOGIANS: CLEMENT AND ORIGEN

Among Alexandrian theologians there developed the closest relationship with Greek philosophy which early Christianity achieved without entirely losing contact with the developing mainstream of the Church. This was hardly surprising, since the Christian schools in which Clement of Alexandria and Origen taught were outcrops of the most famous centres of higher education in the ancient world. Jews, Greeks and Egyptians had lived side by side in Alexandria for centuries; it was natural that gnosticism should flourish here and that its boundary with Christianity should be very permeable. Clement was not at all shy of annexing the word *gnōsis* ('knowledge') from his rivals, and he was very ready to defend a proposition that 'The man of understanding and perspicacity is . . . a Gnostic', or to speak of Christians living 'perfectly and gnostically'.[81] In the eyes of many later unsympathetic writers, both he and Origen had stepped over the borders which could be considered orthodox for Christianity. It is no coincidence that many of Clement's and Origen's writings are lost to us. When one manuscript might be the only source of a particular work and might easily crumble to dust in obscurity if someone did not think it worth copying, quiet ecclesiastical censorship could make sure that many works of these dangerous and audacious masters remained uncopied and so disappeared from sight.

About 190, Clement, a much-travelled scholarly Christian convert, succeeded a now obscure teacher called Pantaenus as the most prominent leader in the Christian schools of Alexandria. Twelve years later, he was caught up in a crisis of persecution far away from Alexandria in the Cappadocian city of Caesarea in Asia Minor; here he looked after the harassed Christian community and even brought new people into it.[82]

Yet even after he had proved his pastoral abilities in a desperate situation, his writings show that he regarded knowledge not merely as a useful intellectual tool of analysis for a Christian but as the door to a higher form of Christian spiritual life. Like Plato, whom he much admired, he believed that knowledge increases one's moral worth. There is an intellectual elitism both in his writings and in those of Origen which many Christians found unhealthy.

Any survey of Clement's teaching will reveal a great gulf between his concerns and those of the gnosticism we have described. He does speak as gnostics do of a special tradition handed down to his own teachers, but the tradition comes from the Apostles 'Peter and James, John and Paul', a collective, not some single gnostic authority. It is also firmly based on all scripture, Old and New Testaments.[83] He emphasizes the Christian doctrine of creation and the positive value of our life on earth, presenting earthly existence as a journey towards knowledge of God, the result of hard work and moral progress. Salvation did not come through some random external gift, as many gnostics might assert; knowledge of God was found both in scripture and in such achievements of the human intellect as the writings of Aristotle and Plato: 'Philosophy is a preparation, making ready the way for him who is being perfected by Christ.'[84] Clement was so concerned to stress the Christian progress in holiness that he saw each individual's journey as continuing after physical death: 'after he has reached the final ascent in the flesh, he still continues to advance'.[85] He spoke of these further advances in afterlife in terms of the cosmic hierarchies which would have been familiar to gnostics, but he also spoke of this progress as a fiery purging – not the fires of Hell, but (borrowing a concept from Stoicism) a fire of wisdom.[86] An opportunity for further purging was a comforting doctrine for those who feared a sudden death which might leave them helpless before God without adequate preparation; the concept bore rich fruit in Christian thought. In the course of centuries it flowered into the complex family of ideas about the afterlife which the medieval Western Church called Purgatory (see pp. 555–8).

Since Clement made so central the idea of moral progress, he wrote much about the way in which the Christian life should be lived on a day-to-day basis; he was one of the earliest Christian writers on what would now be called moral theology. He discussed worldly wealth, a very necessary concern in a Church where there were more and more wealthy people, but one rendered slightly problematic by Jesus having told a rich man to go and sell all he had before becoming a follower.

Clement pointed out that 'He who has cast away his worldly abundance can still be rich in passions even though his substance is gone . . . A man must say goodbye, then, to the injurious things he has, not to those that can actually contribute to his advantage if he knows the right use of them.'[87] In defending a Christian's responsible stewardship of riches, he provided an extended framework for Christian views of money and possessions for centuries to come. Like any Stoic teacher, but framing his discussion in biblical terms as well as in commonplaces familiar to well-educated Alexandrians, he laid down principles of moderation in eating and drinking for those who had enough money to leave moderation behind. He was also concerned to affirm the value of human sexuality, which, like gnostics, many mainstream writers viewed as too contemptible, fallen and dangerous to merit their consideration. However, he did so with a very particular agenda, which is indebted to the more-or-less scientific notions of the non-Christian Aristotle more than it is to the Tanakh or to Paul. Emphatically Clement did not base justifications for marriage on romantic love, but on the necessity for procreating children: he was capable of saying 'to have sex for any other purpose other than to produce children is to violate nature'. One might call this the Alexandrian rule, and it still lies behind many of the assumptions of official moral theology in the Roman Catholic Church.[88]

Origen succeeded Clement in the Christian school of Alexandria: a boy from a devout Christian household, thrust into a leading role while still in his late teens by that major imperial persecution in 202 which drove Clement to Cappadocia. From then on, his life was a constant intellectual exercise: research, presenting his faith to inquisitive non-Christians, and acting as a one-man academic task force in various theological rows throughout the eastern Mediterranean. We know a good deal about him thanks to a biography by his great admirer the fourth-century historian Eusebius of Caesarea. Origen's fiery nature led him to near-destruction in 202, as he was saved for his later work in the Church only by his mother's hard-headed decision to hide all his clothes when he wished to run out into the street and proclaim himself a Christian. Embarrassment won out over heroism.[89]

Later his combativeness made Origen many enemies, not least his bishop, Demetrius, who was doing his best to pull together the Church in Egypt, laying the foundations of a formidable ecclesiastical machine which later made the Bishopric of Alexandria one of the major powers in the Church. It was not surprising that Demetrius felt himself sorely tried by this independent-minded thinker who followed Clement's line

that what really mattered in the Christian life was the pursuit of knowledge. Demetrius and Origen clashed over what the Bishop rightly saw
as successive acts of insubordination while Origen was visiting admirers
in the Palestinian Church. First they asked Origen to preach, though he
was only a layman, and on a later occasion they ineptly tried to get
round this problem by securing his ordination as presbyter without
reference back to Alexandria. This second incident led to a complete
breach with Demetrius, and Origen retired to Caesarea in Palestine to
continue his scholarly work, handsomely funded by a wealthy admirer;
Eusebius's account of these unfortunate events betrays a certain embarrassment.[90] Origen's thirst for martyrdom came close to formal fulfilment when he died as a result of brutal maltreatment in one of the
mid-third-century persecutions.

Origen's importance was twofold as biblical scholar and speculative
theologian, in which roles he exhibited interestingly different talents. As
a biblical scholar, he had no previous Christian rival. He set standards
and directions for the giant task which was already occupying the
Church, of redirecting the Tanakh to illuminating the significance of
Jesus Christ in the divine plan: creating the text of the Bible as Christians
now know it. His biblical commentaries became foundational for later
understanding of the Christian sacred texts.[91] Origen's biblical work
showed a concern for exactness and faithfulness to received texts, something very necessary in an age when the text was still uncertain in many
details; on that was based the exuberant adventure of the imagination
which was his theology. As we will see, his theological work contains
statements of extraordinary boldness, though often presented simply as
theoretical suggestions for solving a particular problem. So radical were
some of these that a whole group of his ideas were labelled 'Origenism'
and condemned at a council at Alexandria a century and a half after his
death, in 400. Origen's thought and speculations have nevertheless gone
on quietly fermenting in Christian imaginations ever since his time,
providing a counterpoint to those who have seen him as a bad influence
on Christianity. We will discover his admirers more than once setting
their thinking over against the formidable Augustine of Hippo (see
pp. 315–16 and 601–2).

Much of Origen's work consequently remains in fragments, though
censorship cannot account for the loss of most of his unchallengeably
admirable work, the crown of his biblical labours, the *Hexapla*. This
was a sixfold transcription of the Tanakh in six different columns side
by side, apparently beginning with the Hebrew text and a transliteration

of it into Greek alongside four variant Greek translations, including the Septuagint. This columnar arrangement, which had precedents in official documents, but is likely never to have been used before in a book, was partly designed for use in the still-continuing theological debates with Judaism over the meaning of the sacred text of the Tanakh. There are various explanations of why there might have been different Greek versions of the Tanakh – the most obvious being that there simply were – but by the second century one possibility is that Jews had ceased to trust their Septuagint Greek version of scripture precisely because Christians habitually used it. We have noted one instance of this in relation to the virginity of Mary (see p. 81), a good illustration of why Jews might turn to more-literal translations. It is a mark of how far Christianity and Judaism had now drifted apart that Origen, the greatest of third-century Christian biblical scholars, was hesitant in his grasp of Hebrew. But still the result was staggering: an unprecedented tool of reference, occupying perhaps forty manuscript books when it was complete – one of Christianity's first works of scholarship and a remarkably innovative project in anyone's terms. The fragments gathered by an unusually accomplished Victorian editor fill two printed volumes, and more have turned up since in archaeological digs.[92]

How should a firmly established Christian biblical text now be used? Origen turned his attention to biblical commentaries, the first major collection to survive in Christian history. He affected to despise Greek thought, unlike his master Clement, but in reality he was just as voracious a consumer of its heritage; he used Aristotelian method in his arguments and he brooded on the legacy of discussion of divine truths to be found in Plato and the Stoics.[93] That meant that when he read the Bible, he shared Greek or Hellenistic Jewish scepticism that some parts of it bore much significant literal meaning. Looking at the Genesis account of creation, 'who is so silly as to believe that God, after the manner of a farmer, planted a paradise eastward in Eden, and set in it a visible and palpable tree of life, of such a sort that anyone who tasted its fruit with his bodily teeth would gain life?' Origen might be saddened to find that seventeen hundred years later, millions of Christians are that silly. He would try to tell them that such things were true, because all parts of the scriptures were divinely inspired truth, but they should not be read as if they were historical events, like the rise and fall of Persian dynasties. He insisted that this rule should even be applied within the text of the Gospels.[94]

In viewing the biblical text in this way Origen followed Clement in relishing the use of an 'allegorical' method of understanding the meaning of literary texts, which by then had a long history in Greek scholarship. This is how learned Greeks had read Homer (see pp. 24–5) and how learned Alexandrian Jews like Philo had read the Tanakh. Allegorical readers of scripture saw it as having several layers of meaning. The innermost meanings, hidden behind the literal sense of the words on the page, were not only the most profound, but also only available to those with eyes to see. Once more we meet that Alexandrian Christian elitism already encountered in Clement. Allegorical approaches to scripture proved very influential throughout Christianity, because they were hugely useful in allowing Christians to think new thoughts, or to adapt very old thoughts into their faith which derived from sources beyond the obvious meaning of their Old and New Testaments. The Latin West tended to have more reservations early on, but the great Augustine of Hippo found allegory useful, and subsequent commentators in the Western Church frequently threw caution to the winds in their enthusiasm for proving truths which were not otherwise self-evident. There were contrary currents in the East too: the Syrian city of Antioch was home to theologians who were inclined to read the Bible as a literal historical record. The contrast in approach between Alexandria and Antioch, not merely to the Bible but to a whole range of theological issues, resulted in the long term in some ugly power struggles in the Eastern Churches, as we will see (see pp. 222–37).

Origen's preoccupation with the classic concerns of Greek philosophy was as apparent in his work on systematic theology as in his biblical commentaries. Particularly in his book entitled *On First Principles*, one of the first attempts at a universal summary of a single Christian tradition, he grappled with the old Platonic problem of how a passionless, indivisible, changeless supreme God communicates with this transitory world. For Origen as for Justin, the bridge was the Logos, and like Justin Origen could be quite bold in terming the Logos 'a second God', even tending towards making this Logos-figure subordinate to or on a lower level than the supreme God, whose creature he is – a doctrine known as subordinationism.[95] In concentrating on explaining this relationship of Father and Son, Origen had little to say about the Holy Spirit, who, he could quite boldly say, was inferior to the Son. As far as Origen was concerned, the main role of the Holy Spirit was to bring strength to those who were full members of the Church. He frankly admitted that there were questions about the person and work of the Spirit which puzzled him and which still needed clarification by the Church.[96] Few early Christian writers had much to say about the Spirit in the unhappy aftermath of expelling the Montanists, with their particular devotion to the Spirit.

One of the boldest parts of Origen's theological scheme is his suggestion as to how to relate the Fall and the Incarnation. He says that God created inferior spirits with free will and that they had abused this gift, following the example of a ringleader – Satan. The degree of their fall then determined which part of the cosmic order they occupied, from angels through humankind to demons. It is thus our duty to use our free will to remedy the mistake which we had made in this fall (the reality of which was allegorized in the story of Adam and Eve). Like Clement before him, Origen asserted that humankind will be saved through its own efforts with the help of Christ, through purging which goes on past human death. He could not accept that humankind or creation was totally fallen, as that would destroy all moral responsibility: 'A totally wicked being could not be censured, only pitied as a poor wretch'.[97]

Origen tried to explain this proposition with yet more adventurousness. He suggested that amid the catastrophe of the Fall, one soul alone had not fallen, and that it was this soul which the Logos entered when finally he decided that he must come himself to save humankind.[98] The point of this idea was to safeguard Christ's free will in his earthly life: he enjoyed the free will granted to that soul, so he was making real choices, not playing a Docetic charade, as gnostics maintained. Thus our free will also has value, because it is seen most perfectly in Christ, and it is a gift for us to use properly. The whole scheme was intended to affirm the majesty of God, as Plato and Paul had done, but also to affirm the dignity of humankind. Divine majesty and human dignity have never been easy concepts for Christianity to balance. This was a very different approach to the radical pessimism about the human condition which has come to dominate Western Christianity, especially thanks to Augustine of Hippo. But Origen had not finished with his startling speculation. Since the first fall was universal, so all, including Satan himself, have the chance to work back towards God's original purpose. All will be saved, since all come from God.[99]

Predictably given this proposition, Origen had no time for Irenaeus's and Justin's millenarian vision of a selection of saints ruling in triumph in an End Time, and he bequeathed his scepticism to the Greek Churches in general. Yet the Church in both East and West turned its back on Origen's vision of a universal salvation. Such a notion was indeed hard to square with some of the Gospels' records of Jesus talking of final separation between sheep and goats. By rejecting it, Christianity was committing itself to the idea that God has made eternal choices, separating all people into the saved and the damned, although the debate continued as to when and through whom this separation comes about – human or divine initiative? Perhaps if Catholic Christianity was to maintain the character which had been apparent from its earliest days as a religion hungry for souls, this drawing back from universal salvation was inevitable: could there be urgency in a mission to win converts if the end of time and the cosmos inevitably saw the return of all things to their creator? Origen might say that the purpose of proclaiming Christianity was to proclaim truth and wisdom, regardless of any initiative like an escape from damnation. For the Church as a whole, this delight in wisdom was not enough. Salvation mattered more. And large sections of the Church were now about to pursue a different sort of universalism: an engagement with secular power, which would take Christianity from being the Church of the outsiders and the despised into the heart of politics, and towards the domination of all society.

5

The Prince: Ally or Enemy?
(100–300)

THE CHURCH AND THE ROMAN
EMPIRE (100–200)

It took the Romans some time to distinguish between Christians and the other quarrelling segments of Judaism, but once Jews and Christians had separated, Christianity could not hope for any sort of official recognition. Normally the Roman authorities were tolerant of the religions in their conquered territories; as long as a religion had a tradition behind it, they could accept it as having some vague relationship to the official gods of Rome. All that they demanded was that subjects of the empire accept in turn some sort of allegiance to the official cult of the emperors, alive and dead. Even Judaism, an exceptionally exclusive religion which refused to make this concession, with an awkward insistence on regarding every other religion as untrue, could be accepted because it had a long pedigree (see p. 109). Christianity had no such tradition to excuse it, despite the claim by many of its exponents that it could share the antiquity of the Hebrew prophets. Particularly when its episcopal or Catholic form, with its increasingly fixed canon of scripture and carefully constructed creeds, began shouldering aside gnostic forms of Christian belief, Christianity made exclusive claims for its three-in-one God. That attitude is already aggressively promoted in its earliest surviving literature, the letters of Paul. At the beginning of his letter to the Romans, he develops at some length the idea that all religion directed away from the true God and towards 'images resembling mortal man or birds or animals or reptiles' is a perversion, a theme which he goes on to elaborate in the most lurid terms that a Jewish tent-maker from Tarsus could imagine.[1]

The unnerving self-confidence of Christians and their view of every other form of religion as demonic contrasted with the comfortable openness to variety normal in contemporary religious belief. The only exception Christians made was for Judaism, despite their increasingly tense relations with it; and unlike Judaism, they seemed actively to be aiming for total monopoly of the religious market.[2] Greek-speaking Christians, like Jews before them, called all non-Christians who were not Jews 'Hellenes', a word to which a sneer was attached, but it was probably during the third century that Western Latin-speaking Christians developed their own contemptuous term for this same category: *pagani*. The word means 'country folk', and the usual explanation is that urban Christians looked down on rural folk who stuck like backwoodsmen to traditional cults. More likely is that the word was army slang for 'non-combatants': non-Christians had not enrolled in the army of Christ, as Christians did in baptism.[3] Christians cut across the normal courtesies of observing the imperial cult and that made them a potential force for disruption in Roman life. Indeed, the language they used in their enthusiasm for their saviour seems almost to be borrowed from the language which the imperial cult was developing in the lifetime of Jesus. So a Greek inscription found in Ephesus calls Julius Caesar 'god made manifest'; the Emperor Augustus's birthday was called 'good news' and his arrival in a city the *'parousia'* – exactly the same word which Christians used for Christ's expected return.[4] It would be easy for sensitive Romans to hear such Christian usages as deliberate and aggressive plagiarism.

For the authorities, one feature of the Christians' exclusivity was particularly alarming: their frequently negative attitude to military service. No Christian of the first three centuries CE would fit easily into the army, since military life automatically demanded as routine attendance at official sacrifices as today it demands salutes to the flag and parades. The legacy of Christian sacred literature to state violence was contradictory. On the one hand there was the demonstrative imperial loyalty of Paul of Tarsus, alongside the memory of the victories won by the Maccabees and the frequent militancy described in the Tanakh, which centred on a land won by military conquest. On the other was the Saviour who had made forgiveness his watchword and who had rebuked his defender Peter for using a sword. Such uncertain messages made for perplexity: the debates produced a number of martyr stories of Christian soldiers who suffered because they refused to conform to military discipline, most of which were probably fabricated in an effort to encourage waverers to keep to a principled line. A more complicated fabrication was the story promulgated by Bishop Apollinaris of Hieropolis in Phrygia (Asia Minor) that the Emperor Marcus Aurelius (reigned 161–80) had recently recruited a legion of Christian soldiers, who saved him from defeat not by their military prowess, but by successfully praying for a strategically placed storm on the River Danube (conveniently for Apollinaris, a location a long way away from Phrygia).[5]

Apollinaris's confident report of what was no doubt a pious rumour clearly reflected Christians' anxiety to have their cake and eat it: to demonstrate their active and useful loyalty to an exceptionally capable and respected emperor (who was in reality hostile to them), while keeping within guidelines of acceptable Christian behaviour. The Roman priest Hippolytus was the probable author of a pioneering guide to Christian life of around 200 entitled *Apostolic Tradition*. One of its surviving versions, now preserved only in a variant of Coptic but probably closest to the original Greek text on this point, deals fairly ineptly with the problem when listing occupations which were acceptable or unacceptable for Christian membership. It stipulates that soldiers could be admitted to the Church only on condition that they do not kill or take the military oath. Hippolytus, however, was a notoriously crotchety moralist who inclined to extremes, and versions of his text preserved in other languages than Coptic modify his unrealistic demand.[6] Against his hard line, it is worth placing a funerary inscription to a man from Phrygia called Aurelius Mannos, who made no bones about proclaiming both his Christianity and his profession as a soldier. His monument commemorated his death in the 290s, at a time when the imperial authorities were about to stage their greatest confrontation yet with the Christian Church.[7]

As Christian communities established themselves as recognizable communities in cities, they often did not endear themselves to people. This was not because they lived austere lifestyles which made a painful contrast to a world of debauchery and luxury around them; that is a later Christian caricature which ignores the austere and world-denying character of much Greek thought in the early empire. Nor was it because they indulged in much public proclamation or systematic soliciting of converts, in the manner of modern Evangelicals. After the descriptions of such activity in the New Testament, there is very little indication that early Christians continued as flamboyant public proclaimers of the Gospel, unless they were cornered in time of persecution. What really offended was the opposite: Christian secretiveness and obstinate separation into their own world.

For Christians, such separation was inevitable, given their sense of the falsity of all other religions: ancient life was saturated with observances of traditional religion, and to play any part in ordinary life was to risk pollution, particularly in public office. Christians generally avoided public baths; and the full enormity of this refusal can only be appreciated if one visits the surviving public baths of Eastern Europe or the Middle East and sees the way in which they serve as centres of social life, politics and gossip. One interesting exception is the popular story that John the Divine once entered a public bathhouse, but when he noticed the gnostic Cerinthus there, he fled screaming, terrified that God in his anger might cause the bath roof to fall in.[8] Yet even this enjoyable tall tale describes a visit to the baths which proved less than successful, and it might have been intended as a warning about the sort of people that one might find there. The consequence may have been that Christians smelled less sweet than their non-Christian neighbours.

The separate nature of Christian life is symbolized in a puzzling peculiarity of their literature: with remarkable consistency, they recorded their sacred writings not in the conventional form of the scroll, like their Jewish predecessors and like everyone else in the ancient world, but in gatherings of sheets of parchment or paper in the form of our modern book (the technical Latin name is *codex*, and that has no Greek equivalent word, telling us something significant about its origins).[9] Why this was so has been the subject of much debate. Before the Christians made it so universal, the codex form had been used for scribbling jottings in low-status notebooks. It is possible that material which became one of the first Gospels was scribbled in this form and that this accident gave the codex a special status in liturgy, when the words of the Lord were solemnly recited. Another possible explanation lies in the Christian insistence that the new good news of Jesus Christ was foretold in the ancient writings of the prophets, an argument which was embedded in the Gospel texts themselves and which we have noted, for instance, as a central plank of Christian apologetics in the writings of Justin Martyr (see p. 142). This impulse might result in a constant need to flick between one text and another, Gospel and prophecy, and that is much easier to do in little books laid side by side than in scrolls. The contrast between Judaism, the religion of the scroll, and Christianity, the religion of the book, would have been evident in their liturgies when the codex of scripture was used as a performed chanted text. The surviving fragments of early biblical texts have a set of consistent abbreviations singling out sacred words, the most frequent being the especially reverenced name 'Jesus'. One would have to be specially informed to know how to interpret these abbreviations (known as sacred terms, *nomina sacra*), for they do not occur in other literary works (see Plate 1).[10] Maybe they were sung in a special way when the text was chanted liturgically.

Christians also jealously guarded their ceremonies of Baptism and Eucharist from the uninitiated. It is indeed one of the peculiarities of their surviving literature from the first century CE (mostly the books of the New Testament) that although it talks a great deal about Baptism, it almost seems deliberately to avoid mention of the Eucharist – after Paul's description of the Eucharist when writing to the Corinthians in the mid-first century, and the parallel descriptions in the Gospels, there is hardly any reference to it except in the writings of Ignatius of Antioch and the *Didachē*, both perhaps from the beginning of the second century (see p. 120). As a result, these ceremonies were thoroughly misunderstood by intelligent and sensitive Roman observers. There arose reports of incest from their talk of love-feasts, of cannibalism from the language of eating and drinking body and blood. As they attracted converts, many unsympathetic outsiders became convinced that Christian success must be the result of erotic magic, strong enough to tear wives away from non-Christian husbands; after all, a number of Christian accounts of martyrdom did indeed describe women leaving their husbands or fiancés for Christian life or death. The second-century African comic novelist Apuleius, who clearly detested Christianity, described an adulterous Christian wife as turning to an old witch to regain the love of her wronged and furious husband – but the scheme went wrong and a murderous ghost goaded the poor man into suicide.[11]

It was a small step from such suspicion and righteous indignation to violence and riots. It was equally understandable that the Roman authorities, paranoid about any secret organizations, sought to suppress troublemakers who wasted taxpayers' money by provoking disturbances of the peace. In the early days of the spread of Christianity, the first Christians in cities had usually begun proclaiming their 'good news' within the Jewish communities, and when they did so, they often provoked violence from angry Jews. One of the first mentions of a Christian presence in Rome, for instance, is a remark by the second-century historian Suetonius that the Emperor Claudius (reigned 41–54 CE) expelled the Roman Jews for rioting 'at the instigation of Chrestus' – probably a garbled reference to Christian preaching within synagogue communities, a decade or more after the crucifixion of Christ.[12]

Yet the separateness and dogmatism of the early Christians were as much strengths as weaknesses; they produced a continuing stream of converts. This inward-looking community could attract people seeking certainty and comfort, not least in a physical sense. Christians looked after their poor – that was after all one of the main duties of one of their three orders of ministry, the deacons – and they provided a decent burial for their members, a matter of great significance in the ancient world. It may be that the first official status for a Christian Church community was registration as a burial club: a considerable irony in view of Jesus's dismissive remark, 'Leave the dead to bury their own dead.' Outside the periods of persecution, which, however brutal while they lasted, were extremely episodic until the last savagery under Diocletian (see pp. 175–6), the normal interaction between a Roman official and a Christian leader would have been to transact bureaucracy around cemeteries. Burial remained an important function within any Christian community: when seventeen staff of the Christian Church in the city of Cirta (now Constantine in Algeria) were arrested and interrogated during the last great persecution of Christians in 303–4, six of those listed were gravediggers, and there were other gravediggers unnamed.[13]

In Rome, towards the end of the second century, the Church was already acquiring rights to excavate tunnels for burial in the soft tufa stone of the region, the first Christian catacombs – not refuges from persecution, as pious Counter-Reformation Catholics assumed in the sixteenth century, just places for decent and eternal rest (see Plate 2). The whole system of catacombs in Rome (named after one particular complex of tunnels beside the Appian Way in a sunken valley, *In catac-umbas*, knowledge of which survived when all the others were forgotten) eventually extended over sixty-eight square miles and house an estimated 875,000 burials made between the second and ninth centuries.[14] What is interesting about the earliest of these burials is the relative lack of social or status differentiation in them: bishops had no more distinguished graves than others, apart from a simple marble plaque to record basic details such as a name. This was a sign of a sense of commonality, where poor and powerful might be all one in the sight of the Saviour. The picture was already changing by the mid-third century, when it becomes apparent that wealthier members of the Church wanted to make more of an artistic splash with elaborate wall paintings or expensive sculpted stone coffins.[15] The upper classes were beginning to arrive at church.

The Christian sense of certainty in belief was especially concentrated in their celebration of constancy in suffering, even to death. From time to time, they faced mob harassment and official persecution, which in the worst cases ended in public executions preceded by prolonged torture and ritual humiliation, the victims stripped naked in front of a gleeful crowd in sporting arenas. Among the early victims were such Christian leaders as Peter, Paul, Ignatius of Antioch and Polycarp of Smyrna, a very old man when he died around 155 and the first Christian to be recorded as having been burned alive. That grisly fate Christians later visited on each other a good deal once they gained access to power, yet alongside a continuing Christian inclination to persecute other Christians, there has survived an intense celebration of martyrdom. The first people whom Christians recognized as saints (that is, people with a sure prospect of Heaven) were victims of persecution who died in agony rather than deny their Saviour, who had died for them in agony on the Cross. Such a death, if suffered in the right spirit (not an easy matter to judge), guarantees entry into Heaven. We have seen how many gnostics questioned this cult of death: it was an important part of their objections to the Church of the Catholic bishops (see p. 125).

The attractive feature of a martyr's death was that it was open to anyone, regardless of social status or talent. Women were martyred alongside men, slaves alongside free persons. The necessary ability was to die bravely and with dignity, turning the agony and humiliation into shame and instruction for the spectators. Martyrs' bones were treasured and their burial places became the first Christian shrines. From the end of the third century onwards, even while martyrdoms were still being suffered, there is evidence of Christians wanting to be buried near such tombs.[16] The stories of the martyrs were lovingly preserved as an example to others; the earliest datable document from the Latin-speaking Church in the West is an account from 180 of martyrdom in North Africa, in a village called Scillium or Scilla.[17] Characteristically, these accounts include what sound like authentic transcriptions of conversations between victims and persecutors, so the reader could learn by imitation, as one might in modern times learn a foreign language through listening to dialogues on CD or tape. So Speratus, one of those Scillitan martyrs, retorted in echoes of the Gospels when Saturninus, the proconsul of Africa, demanded that he swear by the *genius* (guardian spirit) of the emperor:

I do not recognize the empire of this world; but rather I serve that God, whom no man has seen nor can see. I have not stolen, but if I buy anything, I pay the tax, because I recognize my Lord, the King of Kings and Emperor of all peoples.

When a great deal of later inauthentic imitation has been sifted out, the most compelling of these accounts are more than just edifying guides to do-it-yourself sainthood: they preserve portraits of people in the most extreme of situations, the circumstances of which have released them to behave well beyond convention. Most surprising is the journal of sufferings written in the first decade of the third century by an unusually well-educated, spirited (and Montanist) North African martyr called Perpetua. One of the most remarkable pieces of writing by a woman surviving from the ancient world, its content caused problems to both its editors and to subsequent conventionally minded devotees because it was shot through with her determined individuality and self-assertion. She did not simply defy the authorities but went against the expectations of everyday society (including, of course, Christian everyday society) by disobeying her father, who desperately wanted her to abandon her faith:

'Father', I said, 'for the sake of argument, do you see this vase, or whatever you want to call it, lying here?'
    And he said, 'Yes, I see it'.
    And I said to him, 'Can you call it by any other name than what it is?'
    And he said 'No, you can't'.
    'So', I said, 'I cannot call myself anything other than what I am – a Christian'.
    Merely hearing this word upset my father greatly. He threw himself at me with such violence that it seemed he wanted to tear my eyes out . . .'[18]

In that charged encounter is a characteristic moment of tension for Christianity: how does one form of authority relate to another, and which is going to prevail? Perpetua was disobedient not just to her father but to the institutional Catholic Church which later enrolled her among its martyrs, because she was a Montanist. Some of the most remarkable passages in her account occur in her description of the second and third dreams or visions that she had in her prison cell. She saw her younger brother Dinocrates, who had died of cancer at the age of seven without being baptized as a Christian, in a dark place, very hot and thirsty, and just out of reach of a cooling pool of water. She prayed for him. In the third dream, she watched him drink from the pool, and 'play joyfully as young children do'; the cancerous growth in his face melted away. Perpetua did not comment on this vision of release, but the likelihood is that she would not have needed to for the contemporary readership she envisaged. What she was saying was that, through prayer, she had been granted the power to release the dead from suffering because of her faith in the 'New Prophecy'. Dinocrates needed no institutional Church or cleric to remedy his lack of sacramental grace.

But perhaps the most agonizing moral choice of all for Perpetua was whether to be a martyr or a good mother. In choosing to affirm her faith and face imprisonment and death, she was forced to abandon her suckling baby. There followed a miserable alternation of separation and return of the child, in which in the end she was told in her prison cell that her baby no longer wanted her breasts. Seldom do we read a Christian text which so brutally exposes what a Christian commitment might mean: it returns us to the terrifying story of Genesis 22, when God commanded the Patriarch Abraham to make a human sacrifice of his own young son, Isaac, and only countermanded the order as the butcher's knife was raised. In counterpoint to the Church's pronounced drive towards conformity with society's often perfectly reasonable expectations, which we have noted as such a characteristic feature of the later literature in the New Testament (see pp. 114–18), Christian obedience repeatedly plays a troubling wild card. It is the Apostle Peter's impudent retort to the angry high priest of the Jerusalem Temple, recorded in Acts 5.29: 'We must obey God rather than men.' Not so long after Perpetua brutally confounded her father's natural expectations and set herself up as the agent of God's forgiveness, bishops including Peter's self-styled successor in Rome would come to find themselves cast in the role of the high priest: furious at the disobedience of Christians to their own authority and in the end even condemning Christians to death, as once Peter had been by the Roman authorities.

More often than such incidents of dramatic intensity as Perpetua's sufferings, persecution petered out rather inconclusively, as the Roman authorities felt that they had better things to do than to try and wipe out a group of troublesome fanatics. One little instance of this untidiness is preserved among the papers of a highly cultivated and conscientious Roman provincial administrator, the younger Pliny, writing to his equally urbane and thoughtful emperor, Trajan. Pliny, newly appointed about 112 to sort out the chaotic affairs of the province of Bithynia in Asia Minor, found among a host of other problems a strong and aggressive body of Christians, which was emptying the temples and ruining local trade by following Paul's old recommendation and boycotting sales of meat previously offered in sacrifice. Pliny rounded up Christians who had been anonymously denounced to him and he interrogated under torture some who appeared important, but he was puzzled as to what to do next with people who seemed to him deluded but comparatively harmless. He asked for advice from Trajan, whose reply was soothing but hardly much help, since his most definite advice was to ignore anonymous denunciations about anyone, 'a very bad example and unworthy of our time'.[19]

There must have been many encounters like this in the first and second centuries, and there was no central organization in what persecution there was. It came about as the result of some personal initiative, like the pogrom unleashed in Rome in the 60s CE by the increasingly unbalanced Emperor Nero (Christians were not the only victims of his megalomaniac caprice), or the angry response of some local provincial governor to a particular outbreak of trouble. At the end of the second century, this random response began to change because of the sheer visibility of Christianity around the empire. By then, it had established itself throughout the Mediterranean world and into the Middle East. It is impossible to estimate the numbers of converts involved; Pliny's experience in Bithynia would suggest that in Asia Minor at least, right at the beginning of the second century, Christians could form an economically significant part of the population. That likelihood of a precocious Christian presence there is reinforced by the prominent part played by Asia Minor in the theological ferment already discussed (see Ch. 4) and by archaeological finds which show that during the third century Christians in Asia Minor were putting up blatantly Christian tombstones, presumably in public places – generations before the appearance of similar openly Christian material in provincial settings elsewhere.[20]

Beyond Asia Minor, Christian communities were probably quite small, particularly in the West outside Rome, and even there their numbers were dwarfed by the immense scale of the city. What was impressive, and increasingly noticed by non-Christians, was not so much the numbers of any one community but the geographical spread of the Church throughout the empire and beyond, and its sense of community. We have no definite witness to Christianity in Britain before the early fourth century, and not much from the far end of the Mediterranean in Spain, but from the late second and early third centuries there is evidence elsewhere of well-established communities, invariably with an episcopal organization which had been in existence for some time. This is true, for instance, in North Africa around Carthage, in Alexandria and in the south of France at Lyons. Fragments preserved from letters of the late-second-century Bishop Dionysius of Corinth shed sudden shafts of light on Christian Churches in Athens, Crete and Pontus (a section of the southern coast of the Black Sea).[21]

The largest cities of the empire produced the largest and most important Christian communities – Rome, Antioch, Alexandria, Carthage –

and while Rome pointed back to an authentic presence of the Apostles Peter and Paul in its early past, others which had not had an episcopal organization or were founded later on are likely to have confected lists in which a line of bishops could be traced back to Apostles of the first generation. Athens, for instance, pointed to Paul's convert Dionysius the Areopagite (usefully mentioned in Acts 17.34), while Alexandria claimed foundation by the evangelist Mark himself. The genuineness of such claims is less important than the witness they give to the way in which apostolic succession had now established itself as a vital idea in the thinking of the Church, and to the self-confidence which these communities could feel in the ownership of a common tradition which involved many others. In what may be the earliest datable Christian sculpted inscription, a self-composed epitaph from before 216, Abercius, Bishop of Phrygian Hieropolis, in the next generation from Bishop Apollinaris, proudly describes his Mediterranean adventures in terms of the travels of Paul of Tarsus. It is notable that among the places he describes, Judaea and Jerusalem do not figure. The Catholic Church had already rewritten the history of its past and there was no longer much need for Jerusalem to play an active role in it.[22]

By the late second century, intelligent non-Christians had started to realize the significance of this self-confidence. Christianity was beginning to offer a complete alternative to the culture and assumptions of the Roman establishment, an establishment which had never felt thus threatened by the teeming ancient cults of the provinces, or even by Judaism. Christianity had no national base; it was as open to those who wished to work hard to enter it as Roman citizenship itself. It talked much of new covenant, new law, amid all its selective annexation of a Jewish past. Was it really trying to create a new citizenship for its own purposes, to create an empire within an empire? This was certainly the opinion of one well-educated late-second-century traditionalist called Celsus, who wrote a bitter attack on Christianity, probably somewhere in the eastern Mediterranean. This has been preserved for us only because it is embedded in the text of a Christian answer written by Origen some seventy years later – a useful recurrent accident in the history of Christian polemic which has preserved many texts which would otherwise have disappeared.[23]

Celsus felt that certainty was unattainable in religious matters, but he loved the old gods of Rome because they were the pillars of the society which he loved. Probably aware of Justin Martyr's claims for Christianity's antiquity, he emphasized its novelty among religions. He deplored the superstition of Eastern mystery cults as much as he deplored Christian stupidity in paying divine honours to a recently executed Palestinian carpenter. Yet if Christian belief was stupid, it was particularly dangerous because of its worldwide coherence: it was a conspiracy, and one which Celsus saw as especially aimed at impressionable young people. The result of Christian propaganda would be to leave the emperor defenceless, 'while earthly things would come into the power of the most lawless and savage barbarians.'[24]

THIRD-CENTURY IMPERIAL CRISIS

When Celsus wrote these words, about 180, they would have had a new and terrible significance for his Roman readers. During the second century, the empire ceased to expand; it reached its maximum extent under the Emperor Trajan (reigned 98–117), who annexed new territories in what are now Romania and Iraq. After that, the people on the frontiers began pushing back, which meant that Roman emperors from now onwards faced a constant battle to keep their borders secure. Over many centuries, people after people pushed westwards from the interior of Asia, and now a new phase in this long process caused disruption among the tribes in central Europe, forcing them in turn to look westwards and southwards for refuge, inside Rome's territories. When the Danube froze in the winter of 166–7, it was a particular disaster for the empire, giving thousands of the Langobardi a chance to cross over and devastate Rome's central European provinces. On the eastern Roman frontier, matters became even more serious in the early third century. A new dynasty in Iran, the Sassanians, regained Iranian independence from their neighbours the Parthians, and they were determined to take revenge on the world of Greece and Rome for the humiliations inflicted on Iran centuries before by Athens and the Hellenistic monarchs after Alexander the Great (see pp. 35–40). The dynasty's founder, Shah (King) Ardashir, made his intention plain by additionally taking the name of the ancient Iranian king and conqueror Darius. In 260 Ardashir's son Shapur achieved the ultimate humiliation for the Romans by taking the Emperor Valerian prisoner in battle; Valerian died in captivity.[25]

All this might not have been so disastrous if the empire had contrived to remain united under capable rulers. Although more than one first-century emperor had been broken by the psychological strain of ruling the greatest empire in Western history and had descended into megalomania, the empire later enjoyed a succession of exceptionally able and wise rulers in the dynasties of the Flavians and Antonines (69–192). Then the last of the Antonines, Commodus, had reverted to the pattern of insanity and was eventually murdered by his mistress Marcia to stop him murdering her (she was a Christian, a circumstance which furnished the great eighteenth-century historian Edward Gibbon with one of his best feline passages at Christianity's expense).[26] From the chaos and civil war that ensued during 192 there emerged as emperor an army officer from North Africa, Septimius Severus. His sons who succeeded him on the imperial throne displayed his ruthless brutality without his political good sense, and from Septimius's death at York in 211 to Diocletian's seizure of supreme power in 284, hardly a single Roman emperor died a natural death. It was a terrible time for the empire: a mute tribute is how little we know about these decades.

The failure of leadership bred trouble throughout the political system. The short-lived Severan dynasty had been based on a military coup d'état and so were most of the succeeding regimes well into the fourth century. Such emperors could not appeal to any traditional legitimacy and were therefore increasingly dependent of the goodwill of the army. 'Be harmonious, enrich the soldiers, and scorn all other men,' Severus urged his sons on his deathbed; they listened to clauses two and three of his advice.[27] The army's needs, both in the constant frontier wars and in equally bitter civil wars, became all-important: to pay for the soldiers, taxation soared, and many people fled their towns and villages, turning to banditry. This in turn created a problem of internal policing which could be met only by reinforcing the army: a vicious circle. Misery was increased by rampant inflation, caused by reckless imperial currency debasement, and many parts of society reverted to a barter economy as a result.

It is a tribute to the strength of the Roman Empire that it survived the third-century crisis at all. Survive it did, unlike the Parthian Empire in its parallel crisis; indeed, in the East, there was still a Roman emperor more than a thousand years later. But the price of this survival was that imperial government became the ancient equivalent of a police state. This was intensified rather than remedied when Diocletian restored long-term stability to the economy and in some measure to politics after 284. All this spelled ruin for the delicate balance of city life which had been the basis of Classical civilization since the great days of the Greek *poleis*. Wealthy citizens had voluntarily accepted the round of civic office, seeing to the construction of beautiful buildings, roads, water supplies, bridges; it was a necessary demonstration of public spirit. Now few were willing to engage in such undertakings, and the imperial authorities had either to force people to take on public office or to send in their own bureaucrats to do the work with the backing of troops. A melancholy symptom of the new situation was the fact that when third-century Roman cities showed energy in building, it was often to put up defensive city walls, partly constructed out of civic buildings torn down for the purpose. Archaeologists have noted a particularly sinister feature of many of these new schemes of fortification: they enclosed only part of the city, the official headquarters and the wealthy areas. The old spirit of civic solidarity had withered.[28]

The end of the autonomous culture of the *polis* had profound consequences for religion. Traditional cults were linked with local identities: in towns and cities, with the self-government which had helped to sustain them. The decline of traditional religion can be measured through archaeology in smaller numbers of votive offerings at temples, falling temple incomes and, in some areas, an end to new votive inscriptions.[29] Even without Christianity, religious culture would have changed. The usurping dynasty of the Severans set a significant pattern, bolstering their dubious regime by encouraging the identification of different territorial gods as facets of one supreme God, then identifying themselves with this single figure: Septimius Severus became particularly associated with the Egyptian god Serapis, but he also allowed his emperor cult to be fixed on any other local god who might command reverence in a particular area.[30]

This new religiosity was not simply a matter of official cult or imperial pressure. The third century has been seen as an 'age of anxiety', when people were driven to find comfort in religion.[31] The idea has been challenged, but the surviving writings of the literate elites do show a new interest in personal religion, remote from the traditionalist respect for the old gods and the cultured cynicism which in easier times had been the received wisdom for aristocrats like Celsus. The worship of the sun became steadily more dominant, a natural universal symbol to choose in the brilliant sunshine of the Mediterranean. So Christianity was not the only religion to talk of oneness, to offer strict tests for initiation or to expect the result of these to be a morally regulated life with a continuing theme of purification. The sun cult of Mithraism, imported from the East like Christianity, had this character, and it is not surprising that Christians felt a particular bitterness towards Mithras.[32]

Mithraism predated Christianity in its appearance in the empire, but the growth of Christianity now also made it possible to consider initiating a cult which would be a conscious rival to the Christian faith and which, in the fashion of Christians like Justin Martyr, might make an effort to combine ritual observance with a serious and systematic interest in the great questions of Classical philosophy. Christians had tried to engage philosophers; now philosophers would have to decide on their attitude to Christianity. At the beginning of the third century Philostratus, tame philosopher in the household of Septimius Severus's wife, Julia Domna, wrote a biography of Apollonius of Tyana, an austere, ascetic philosopher who had been born about the time of Jesus Christ's crucifixion. He presented Apollonius as a performer of miracles and a spiritual healer, like Christ, but Apollonius's story ended without crucifixion or suffering. After a spirited confrontation with the Emperor Domitian (also a bête noire of Christian writers), he had avoided the tyrant's rage through an unspectacularly discreet exit from the imperial Court. In contrast to this unfussy practicality, he later demonstrated extraordinary powers when he was able to enjoy watching Domitian's murder in Rome by long-distance vision in Ephesus. It hardly matters how much truth or fiction there is in Apollonius's biography (though the fictional element is very evident); it is valuable in revealing what someone in the age of Septimius Severus felt was the most admirable possible portrait of a philosopher, and it is also very striking that Philostratus never once mentions Christianity in his writing. Apollonius was intended to upstage Christ, and he excited fury among Christians – the Christian historian Eusebius of Caesarea wrote an attack on him a century later.[33]

Intelligent people were now regarding it as respectable to take an interest in the sort of wonder-working which Philostratus described Apollonius as practising. They were also increasingly drawn to forms of philosophy which wore a religious and even magical aspect. Stoicism lost the intellectual dominance which in the second century had led an emperor, Marcus Aurelius, to become one of its most interesting and important exponents. Now the intellectual fashion was for Neoplatonism, a development from Plato's thought which emphasized its religious character. The greatest Neoplatonist teacher was Plotinus (c. 205–70). Accounts of him include what seems the first recognizable description in Western history of acute dyslexia, which probably explains why he was a reluctant writer; his inspirational oral teachings were mediated to a rapidly growing circle of admiring intellectuals through his somewhat self-important biographer and editor Porphyry, who published Plotinus's works at the beginning of the fourth century.[34]

Plotinus was a younger contemporary of Origen in the advanced schools of Alexandria and his picture of the supreme God has resemblances to Origen's. He spoke in a trinitarian fashion of a divine nature consisting of an ultimate One, of Intelligence and of the Soul. The first represented absolute perfection, the second was an image of the first but was capable of being known by our inferior senses, and the third was a spirit which infused the world and was therefore capable of being diverse, in contrast to the perfection of the One and of Intelligence. In this scheme, there was no Christ figure to be incarnate; it was the task of the individual soul by ecstatic contemplation of the divine to restore the harmony lost in the world, an ecstasy so rare that Plotinus himself admitted to achieving it only four times in his life. Neoplatonism was largely independent of the old religious forms, though it could coexist perfectly happily with traditional gods, by enrolling them as manifestations of Intelligence. Porphyry's writings encouraged this tendency, which was yet another force uniting the religions of the Mediterranean. Christian thinkers over many centuries were not exempt from the fascination of Neoplatonism, and we will repeatedly encounter its effects.

Christianity faced an equally powerful challenge from a new religion with the same Semitic background from which it had itself emerged, in the teachings of a new prophet called Mani. He was born around 216 near Seleucia-Ctesiphon, capital of the increasingly troubled and feeble Parthian Empire, of whose ruling house he was a minor relative. As a boy he witnessed the Parthians fall to the Persians, but he managed initially to gain favour from the new rulers before they turned against him and threw him in prison, where he died in 276 or 277. His travels, meanwhile, had taken him as far as India, at much the same time as Syriac Christianity was also gaining a foothold in the East; he encountered Buddhism and Hinduism to range alongside his previous knowledge of Christianity in both its gnostic and its Catholic varieties. Maybe it was his consciousness of the collapse of his family's world which prompted Mani to create a new synthesis of all the religions which bordered his homeland. Clearly there was a demand for such syntheses in societies full of myriad cross-cultural encounters, because his efforts attracted huge success.

Mani combined all the religions which he respected with his own experience of revelation into a new 'Manichaean' cult. Like gnostic dualism before it, this provided a convincingly stark account of the world's suffering, portraying it as the symptom of an unending struggle between matched forces of good and evil. Jesus occupied a very important place in Mani's scheme of divinity: indeed, he habitually referred to himself as the 'Apostle of Jesus Christ', as Paul of Tarsus had done before him. For him Jesus was judge at the last, and a divine healer and teacher, who, as in so many gnostic cosmic constructions of his role in salvation, had no real human body: physical matter was a prison for individual spirits which sought their home in Heaven. So Mani's Jesus spoke in strong paradoxes: 'Amen, I was seized; Amen again, I was not seized . . . Amen, I suffered; Amen again, I did not suffer.'[35]

Mani's teachings equalled the spread of Eastern Christianity in time and geography, taking Manichaean faith as far as the shores of China as well as into the Roman Empire.[36] Christians in the eastern Mediterranean in particular found his teachings as fascinating as previously they had the ideas of gnostic teachers, while the traditionalist Emperor Diocletian (reigned 284–305) loathed Manichees as much as he did the Christians, initiating a policy of burning them alive, even before he and his colleagues had yielded to the impulse to begin brutal persecution of Christianity.[37] Discoveries of Greek, Syriac and Coptic papyri from the 1990s onwards at an Egyptian oasis, now called Ismant el-Kharab but anciently containing the small town of Kellis, have suddenly revealed fourth-century Manichees in a new light. There they had the appearance of a variant on Christianity, regarding themselves as a Church within the town, with a community life, officers and almost certainly a monastery around which their religious life probably revolved. Among the documents are two boards bearing word lists of key Manichaean phrases in Syriac with Coptic translations, revealing the sense of a commonality in this Coptic- and Greek-speaking community with Manichees a thousand miles away in Syria, rather reminiscent of Catholic Christianity's own worldwide vision.[38] No wonder the episcopal Christian Church loathed the Manichees so much and sought to eliminate them as competitors once it got the chance. It never challenged Diocletian's provision for burning Manichees alive; indeed, centuries later the Western Latin Church imitated and extended Diocletian's policy to apply it to other Christian 'heretics'.

FROM PERSECUTION TO
PERSECUTION (250–300)

Celsus had made it clear that it was now impossible for the Roman authorities to ignore Christianity. By the end of the second century, this religion from an obscure eastern province was beginning to find a presence even in the imperial palace. Marcia, the Emperor Commodus's mistress and instigator of his murder, might seem a rather disconcerting pioneer patroness of Christians at Court, but it is noticeable that the first identifiably Christian gravestones for members of the imperial household date from only just after Commodus's death.[39] In their wake come rather less lurid connections to the imperial family: Julia Mamaea, mother to the Emperor Severus Alexander (great-nephew of Septimius Severus), was clearly interested in Christianity, inviting Origen to talk with her about the faith, and the aggressive Roman priest Hippolytus was courtly enough to dedicate a treatise on the Resurrection (now mostly lost) either to her or to another prominent imperial lady.[40] The young Severus Alexander is said, admittedly by a patchily reliable source, to have commissioned statues of Christ and Abraham for his private place of prayer alongside statues of Apollonius of Tyana, Alexander and deceased and deified imperial ancestors. This is the first recorded figure-sculpture of the Saviour in Christian history, although given its eclectic setting, with Christ reduced to a semi-divine celebrity, it forms a rather dubious precedent for the later flowering of Christian sculptural art.[41] On both sides there is a sense of ambiguity. Christians were torn between their traditional exclusivity and a strong desire to please the powerful (even when the powerful offended Christian prejudices against graven images by sculpting Christ), while prominent Romans were caught between interest in and suspicion of Christian intentions.

The situation was bound to produce extremes of fortune. An edict of Septimius Severus in 202 had forbidden conversions to either Christianity or Judaism, and that had been significant in promoting persecution during his reign and those of his sons. When the usurper Maximinus Thrax murdered Severus Alexander and seized his throne in 235, the brief interval of favour for Christians came to a sudden end.[42] Then, in the mid-third century, Christian subjects of the Roman emperor found themselves persecuted for the first time on an empire-wide scale on imperial initiative. The new earnestness and personal commitment to religion among non-Christian elites spelled trouble in any case for Christians, but the situation came to a head in the 240s, which historically aware Romans would realize marked a thousand years from the foundation of the city of Rome. It was a time for citizens to contemplate the history of their beloved empire, a depressing prospect for the conservative-minded succession of army officers who fought their way to the imperial throne.

Trajan Decius, an energetic senator and provincial governor who seized power as emperor in 249, felt this keenly. He attributed the empire's troubles on the morrow of its thousandth year squarely to the anger of the old gods that their sacrifices were being neglected – as we have seen (see pp. 167–8), he was right. For Decius the solution was simple: enforce sacrifices on every citizen, man, woman and child, or at least the head of a household in the name of all its members – a radical intensification of a traditional practice whereby emperors ordered every community to offer sacrifices on their accession. It was obvious that the group which had most systematically avoided sacrifices in the empire was the Christians, and the confrontation which now took place turned a pitiless spotlight on an intransigence which had often previously been unobtrusive. In 250 the new imperial policy was implemented with bureaucratic efficiency. Those who sacrificed were issued with certificates of proof, some of which have been preserved for us in the rubbish pits and desert sands of Egypt.[43] The order was coupled with punishment, usually imprisonment but in some cases death, for those who refused. Two later emperors, Trebonianus Gallus and Valerian, revived the policy in 252 and 257 between their many other preoccupations, and persecution was only abandoned in 260 by Gallienus, son and successor of the hapless Persian prisoner Valerian, because the empire faced so many other pressing dangers. But in the previous decade, the Christian Church had been severely damaged, not so much in terms of death and suffering, because few died outside a small group of leaders, but in terms of morale.

The truth is that the overwhelming majority of Christians gave way. This might have been predicted, because the same thing had happened when, for instance, Pliny the Younger had arrested Bithynian Christians back in 112. It was only natural to wish to obey the emperor: that most Christians felt a deep reverence for the empire is obvious from their leading writers' confused and contradictory statements about the limits on obedience to it.[44] Moreover, the Church as a whole was not used to persecution, or certainly not a systematic campaign directed from the centre. Trouble did not end when persecution ended and the leadership began picking up the pieces. The bishops' authority was at stake. Some bishops had followed the Lord's command recorded in John's Gospel to suffer martyrdom bravely and had been killed (including the Bishops of Antioch, Jerusalem and Rome). Others had followed the Lord's precisely contradictory advice to be found in Matthew's Gospel to flee from city to city; they included such important figures as the Bishops of Carthage and Alexandria.[45]

Those who had fled were likely to come in for criticism from those who had stayed and suffered for their faith; from the Roman technical legal term for someone who pleads guilty as accused in court, these steadfast Christians were termed 'confessors'. Confessors provided the troubled Church with an alternative sort of authority based on their sufferings, particularly when arguments began about how and how much to forgive those Christians who had given way to imperial orders – the so-called 'lapsed'. Many of the lapsed flocked to the confessors to gain pardon and re-entry to the Church, and the bishops did not like this at all. Especially important disputes broke out in Rome and Carthage over the issue of forgiveness. Faced with both defiance from some confessors and the election of a rival bishop, Bishop Cyprian of Carthage engaged in pamphlet warfare, producing statements about the role of a bishop in the Church which were long to outlive this particular dispute. He came to see authority for forgiveness of sins as vested in the bishop and he stressed that the bishop was the focus for unity in the whole Catholic Church, a successor of the Apostles in every diocese. It was another stage in the discussion which Ignatius, Clement and Irenaeus had begun. In Rome the argument was mainly over whether there could be any forgiveness at all for those who had lapsed. The priest Novatian, a hardliner on this issue, opposed the election of his colleague Cornelius as bishop, since Cornelius held that forgiveness was possible at the hands of a bishop. The Church in Rome was bitterly divided as to whom to support. Cyprian and Cornelius, who had arrived at similar conclusions about the powers of a bishop, allied with each other and the supporters of Novatian found themselves an isolated minority.

Matters became worse when, in their initial enthusiasm, the Novatianists started making new Christian converts in North Africa as well as in Rome. When many of their sympathizers decided that the division had gone too far, and the newly baptized applied to rejoin the Catholic Church in communion with Cyprian and Cornelius, Carthage and Rome were faced with the problem of deciding the terms. Was Novatianist baptism valid? Cyprian thought not, but a new Bishop of Rome, Stephen, wishing to be conciliatory to those who were coming in, disagreed with him. Now a furious argument broke out between them, partly an expression of Rome's growing feeling that the North African bishops were inclined to think too well of their own position in the Western Church. Stephen not only called Cyprian Antichrist, but in seeking to clinch the rightness of his own opinion, he appealed to Christ's punning proclamation in Matthew's Gospel 'Thou art Peter, and on this rock I will build my Church' (Matthew 16.18).[46] It is the first time known to us that the text had been thus used by a Bishop of Rome; this row in 256 represents another significant step in Rome's gradual rise to prominence. In the end, North Africa and Rome agreed to differ on the issue of baptism, the North Africans saying that valid baptism could take place only within the Christian community which is the Church, the Romans saying that the sacrament belonged to Christ, not to the Church, and that therefore it was valid whoever performed it if it was done in the right form and with the right intentions.

Comparative peace then descended on the Church for several decades, and it is likely that the steady expansion of Christian numbers was one significant factor in the decline of traditional religious institutions during that period (see p. 168). In 272 the Church even called in the Emperor Aurelian for legal support in a long-running effort to evict the obstinate deposed Bishop of Antioch, Paul of Samosata, who had refused to end his occupation of the cathedral church complex in Antioch: the first recorded imperial intervention in Christian affairs. Nevertheless there followed the most serious bout of persecution yet, designed to wipe out Christianity in the empire, led by the reforming Emperor Diocletian. Diocletian made it his life's work to restore the glory of the old Rome, and although the oppressive bureaucracy and relentless quest for uniformity which emerged from his efforts were very different from the early empire, he was determined to honour the old gods: he distrusted all religious novelty, not just Christianity. Only gradually did his undemonstrative religious conservatism turn into active persecution of Christians.

In the last decade of the third century Diocletian became increasingly influenced by a clique of army officers from Rome's Adriatic provinces in the Balkans, headed by Galerius, one of the colleagues whom Diocletian had chosen to help him govern the empire. Gradually this rabidly anti-Christian group, some of them enthusiasts for Neoplatonism, persuaded Diocletian to follow his inclinations and from 303 a full-scale attack was launched on the Christians, beginning with clergy. Churches were torn down, sacrifices ordered and Christian sacred texts confiscated. Persecution was not so intense in the West, where Diocletian's colleague Constantius had some sympathy with Christianity, but elsewhere pressure intensified after Diocletian retired from public life in 305. Although this 'Great Persecution' proved to be the last in the history of the Roman Empire and ended two decades later with an extraordinary turnaround in the Church's fortunes, it was far more savage than most previous assaults on Christianity; nearly half all recorded martyrdoms in the early Church period are datable to this period.[47] Moreover, as we will see in Chapter 6, the eventual end of persecution left in its wake the same welter of internal quarrels as the mid-century persecutions by Decius and his successors.

KINGS AND CHRISTIANS: SYRIA, ARMENIA

This was a moment of dire danger for Christianity in the Roman Empire. Anyone capable of taking a wide view over the Mediterranean world in 303 would have been justified in concluding that it represented a final set-piece conflict between the traditional alliance of Graeco-Roman religion and politics and an organization which had made an unsuccessful bid to transform the empire and was now suffering the consequences. But Christianity was not merely a prisoner of the Roman world. Eastwards of Rome's Mediterranean provinces, something remarkable had happened a century before: the religion of the carpenter's son and the tent-maker Roman citizen had entered an alliance with a monarch. So, for the first time, it experienced what it was like to be established and promoted by the powerful. In cultures beyond the empire, Christianity expressed itself in other languages than Greek or Latin. These Christians might have very different priorities and perspectives from those within the Roman imperial frontiers and they went on to produce Christian traditions very different in character. They survive today, reminding the heirs of Greece and Rome that Christianity began as a religion of the Middle East and was as likely to move east as west. In Chapters 7 and 8 we will trace their stories into the fifteenth century, before taking up the stories of the Latin, Greek and Slavic Churches. To do this is a necessary reminder of the sheer variety of Christianity from its earliest

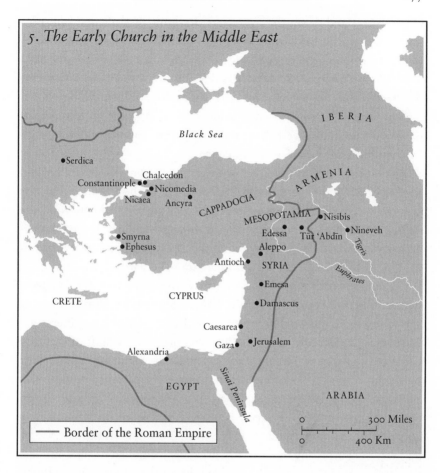

5. The Early Church in the Middle East

days: a vital lesson to learn for modern Christians who wish to impose a uniformity on Christian belief and practice which has never in fact existed.

The Holy Land in which Christianity emerged represents the southern-most end of a Semitic cultural zone stretching more than seven hundred miles from the desert of Sinai on the borders of Egypt up to the Taurus Mountains, which shield the plateaux of Armenia. In its northern region, it is crossed by the two great rivers Tigris and Euphrates, which flow down to the south-east, giving fertility and prosperity to Mesopotamia ('the land between the rivers') and into the Persian Gulf. The Romans gave the name 'Syria' to the whole region, Palestine included; today it is politically divided between Israel, Palestine, Jordan, Syria, Lebanon, northern Iraq and eastern Turkey, and its present state of tension is nothing new. It has always been the area's economic fortune and political misfortune to look both west across the Mediterranean and east to

Central Asia and down the two rivers. In terms of trade and transport it is a fulcrum for sea routes west, land routes to the south into Africa and the beginning of trails eastward through the Asian steppes, then already established over centuries as the 'Silk Road' to China. Politically, the Tigris and Euphrates formed a much-contested boundary for a historic series of opposed great powers and cultures – in the time of the early Christians, westwards was the Roman Empire, eastwards the Parthians and later the Sassanian Persians.

Even at the height of Roman success in spreading its power beyond the Euphrates in the second century CE, much of the Syrian region was only very superficially part of the Graeco-Roman world. Beyond the dignified Classical architecture of government buildings and the politeness of Hellenized city elites who did their best to ape the glory days of Athens, Latin and Greek would fade from the ear and the babble of voices in the street was dominated by some variant of the language which Jesus had spoken: Aramaic. Languages like it became known as Syriac and there was originally a single alphabetic script for its literature: Estrangela. Eventually, after the fifth century, the turmoil of war and Christian controversy (see pp. 220–40) made the Euphrates a fairly fixed border for centuries. That heightened the sense of difference between east and west Syria either side of the river. As a consequence there developed two ways of reading the Syriac language, written in divergent scripts derived from Estrangela: Serto in the west, Nestorian in the east.[48]

It was not surprising that Syriac Christians continued to have intimate ties with Judaism. The region provided the natural routes for Jews who wanted to travel to Jerusalem from Mesopotamia in the Parthian and Sassanian empires, where Babylon continued to sustain the large and cultured Jewish community which had arrived at the time of the Exile (see pp. 61–3). The rulers of one small kingdom to the east of the River Tigris, Adiabene (in the region of the modern Iraqi city of Arbil), were actually converted to Judaism by Jewish merchants in the first century and gave active assistance to the rebels in the Jewish revolt of 66–70 CE.[49] With such encouragement, there was a lively Jewish presence throughout the region, so Christianity arrived early. Following the precedent of the *Didachē*, which was compiled somewhere in the Syriac region (see p. 120), the liturgy of the Syriac Church continued to have a much more Jewish character than elsewhere.[50] There was soon a Bible in Syriac, whose developed form in the fifth century was called the *Peshitta*, a word meaning 'simple' or 'current' (rather as the developed Latin Bible of the fourth century was called 'common' or 'Vulgate'), the

Syriac Old Testament part of which may have been independently created by Syriac-speaking Jews.[51]

A small Hellenistic Syrian city called Dura Europos on the banks of the Euphrates was destroyed by the Sassanians around 256–7 after a century of Roman military occupation.[52] Abandoned for ever, it proved a sensationally well-preserved paradise for twentieth-century archaeologists. Its unfortunate inhabitants are unlikely to feel much posthumous compensation for their disaster in the current fame of their city, which centres on the twin revelation of the world's oldest known surviving synagogue and oldest known surviving Christian church building, both preserved when buried in earth defences in the final siege, some decades after their original construction. Both buildings are additionally famous for their wall paintings. The Jewish paintings, a cycle of scenes from the Tanakh, are rather finer than their Christian counterparts. Their very existence is an instructive surprise in view of the later Jewish consensus against representations of the sacred, although being paintings technically they do not violate the Second Commandment's prohibition of graven or sculptured images.[53]

The Christian church at Dura had been converted from a courtyard house and in plan is therefore very unlike the churches of later Christianity anywhere in the world. Like many of the developed churches of the next few centuries, it does have separate chambers for congregational worship and for the initiation rite of baptism, together with a separate space for those who are still under instruction (the 'catechumens'), but there is one remarkable oddity, making it different from any subsequent Christian church building before some of the more radical products of the Protestant Reformation thirteen hundred years later: there is apparently no substantial architectural provision for an altar for the Eucharist.[54] The subjects of the paintings in the various rooms contrast with those of the synagogue in being derived from the New Testament, including Christ as the Good Shepherd, one of the first favourites in Christian art generally, and the three Marys about to investigate Christ's tomb after the Resurrection. Absent is the representation which modern Christians might expect, but which was nowhere to be found in Christian cultures before the fifth century: Christ hanging on the Cross, the Crucifixion. Christ in the art of the early Church was shown in his human life or sprung to new life – never dead, in the fashion of the crucifixions which were to become so universal in the art of the later Western Church.

One of the other little border kingdoms of Syria, Osrhoene, had its capital at Edessa (now Urfa in Turkey), which in fact provides the earliest record of a Christian church building, predating the existing remains at Dura Europos. We know that it was destroyed in a flood in 201.[55] The Romans conquered Osrhoene and made it part of the empire in the 240s, but before that its kings had let Christianity flourish. Later Syrian Christians celebrated this in the legend of King Abgar V of Osrhoene, who back in the first century was supposed to have received a portrait of Jesus Christ from the Saviour himself and to have corresponded with him. The fourth-century Greek historian Eusebius took a great interest in Abgar, preserving the supposed correspondence, although apparently as yet unaware of the portrait, and the elaborated legend gained an extraordinary popularity westwards far beyond Syria. Partly this was because it remedied an embarrassing deficiency in the story of early Christianity, a lack of an intimate connection with any monarchy. That was probably why Eusebius discussed Abgar, exultant chronicler as he was of the Emperor Constantine I's new alliance with the Church, and in general a writer little excited by the Church on the eastern fringe of the empire.[56] Equally, as the cult of relics gathered pace in the fourth and fifth centuries, there was sheer fascination for many devout Christians in the idea of a relic provided by Christ himself. In an elaborated version of the story, this portrait became the first of many Christian displays of a miraculous imprint of an image on cloth, which naturally possessed impressive powers as a result. Later, in 944, now known as the *Mandylion* (towel) of Edessa, the healing cloth was taken to Constantinople. Later still, taking the story even further west, it was linked to another mysterious expanse of cloth now preserved in Turin Cathedral as the shroud of Christ, despite the likelihood that this admittedly remarkable object was created in medieval Europe.[57]

The most bizarre outcrop of the Abgar legend was its redeployment in the interest of medieval and Tudor monarchs far away in England. Under his Latin name Lucius, King in Britium, the Latin name for the fortress-hill looming over the city of Edessa, Abgar became by creative misunderstanding King Lucius of Britannia, welcoming early Christian missionaries to what would become England's green and pleasant land. Although the heroic error seems in the beginning to have been the fault of an author in the entourage of a sixth-century pope in Rome, the story became much beloved by early English Protestants when they were looking for an origin for the English Church which did not involve the annoying intervention of Augustine of Canterbury's mission from Pope Gregory I (see pp. 334–9), but the Abgar legend was more generally pressed into polemical service by a remarkable variety of combative clergy in the English Reformation.[58] This was a far cry from its original purpose as a self-serving story for the Syriac Church, designed to testify to its early and royal origins. That story probably reached its full elaboration at a time when Syriac bishops and local leaders were hoping to curry favour with or impress late Roman emperors in Constantinople. The legend's back-dating to the first century CE was helped by the fact that most kings from the dynasty of Osrhoene were called Abgar. If the story of the Edessan monarchs' favour to the Church has any plausible chronological setting, it was probably Abgar VIII 'the Great' (177–212), not the first-century Abgar V, who first gave Christianity an established place in Edessa at the end of the second century, following the precedent of the royal conversions to Judaism in Adiabene 150 years before.[59]

But there was much more to the Church of Edessa and Syria beyond it than just the elaborated legend of a towel. Its legacy to the universal Church was many-sided, not always to the comfort of Christians to the west. At the same time as generations of bishops and scholars from Ignatius to Origen were shaping Christian belief within the imperial Catholic Church, individual voices were emerging in Syriac Christianity which frequently earned suspicion and condemnation from neighbours to the west. The first major personality of the Syriac Church for whom there is reasonably certain dating was a combative Christian convert from Mesopotamia who, in the mid-second century, travelled as far as Rome for study, and who was known in Greek and Latin as Tatian. Tatian followed Justin Martyr (who was his teacher in Rome) in writing a vigorous defence of Christianity's antiquity which won grudging praise from Catholic Christians – 'the best and most useful of all his treatises,' said Eusebius nearly two centuries later – but his independence of mind led to accusations that he was an exponent of the gnostic system of Valentinus.[60] This was probably a smear, intended to discredit him, for Tatian was responsible for another major enterprise, the harmonization (*Diatessaron*) of the four canonical Gospels. This might seem a controversial enterprise, but in the very fact that he chose the four accepted by the emerging mainstream Church, Tatian showed just how far he was from the gnostic proliferation of Gospel accounts.

Many found the *Diatessaron* useful. A parchment fragment of it has been recovered from the ruins of Dura and some version of a Gospel harmony survived long enough to be translated into Arabic and Persian perhaps five centuries later.[61] Although in the end the prestige of the four originals would overcome Tatian's synthesis of them, many Christians at the time found it difficult to see why they should use four discrepant versions of the same good news. In an era when at least one Syrian Church in the north-east corner of the Mediterranean was in any case using an entirely different Gospel from the canonical four, it made sense to try to create a single definitive version for liturgical use.[62] A consolidated Gospel message was also a weapon against Marcion's minimalist view of Christian sacred texts – given that so much of Syrian Christianity was still unusually close to its Jewish origins, Marcion's anti-Jewish views were particularly disruptive in Syria.[63] Despite Tatian's impeccably anti-Marcionist line, subsequent Christian censorship has not allowed Tatian's harmonized Gospel text or indeed most of his other writings to come down to us complete. The worst that one can say of his individuality on the evidence available was that he was enthusiastic for the sort of world-denying lifestyle which in the next century crystallized into monasticism. His second-century assertion of ascetic values is one of the signs that we should look behind the common story of monastic origins in Egypt and give the credit to Syria. Tatian's problem was that, in terms of the subsequent writing of Christian history, he was in the wrong place at the wrong time.[64]

More definitely at odds with the Catholic Church developing to the west was Bar-Daisan (Bardesanes in Greek), from a generation after Tatian in the later second century. Some sources assert that, like Tatian before him, he created his own version of the Gospels (if it ever existed, it is now completely lost), and although he was another bitter opponent of Marcion, he was also accused of heresy by later authors. He certainly denied what became the mainstream Christian doctrine that the body is resurrected along with the immortal soul, and in a linked train of thought, he denied the bodily sufferings of Christ in his Crucifixion. It was small wonder that in the fourth century the much more self-consciously orthodox Syrian theologian Ephrem looked back on Bar-Daisan as 'the teacher of Mani'.[65] Yet Ephrem gave credit to his heretical predecessor in one very significant respect: he admitted to having borrowed rhythms and melodies from Bar-Daisan's hymns, adding to them new and theologically correct words, on the grounds that their beauty 'still beguiled the hearts of men'.[66]

This highlights one of the most significant features of Syrian Christianity: it was a pioneer in creating a repertoire of church music, hymnody and chant. Although hardly anything of Bar-Daisan's pioneering hymns survives except through the hostile filter of Ephrem, hymns are preserved from Syria in a collection known as the Odes of Solomon which are likely to be second century in date. One of them gives what may be the first reference beyond the biblical text to Mary the mother of Jesus as a virgin mother, and they pioneer a characteristic feature of Syrian Christianity, reference to the Holy Spirit as female. Grammatically, after all, *ruha*, the Syriac word for spirit, is feminine, although later Christians found this disconcerting and from around 400 CE arbitrarily redefined the word as masculine in grammatical gender.[67] Ephrem himself triumphantly used metrical verse for a major part of his writings, whether polemic or spiritual, and he wrote hundreds of hymns, often to be sung in the liturgy complementing the chanting of scripture, and they were widely translated from an early date for use in other Eastern Churches. Here he sings the praise of the Festival of Christmas in images of a riot of wealth, hospitality and also – audaciously, but just like Jesus before him – wild looting:

> Behold, the First-Born has opened His feast-day for us
> like a treasure-house. This one day,
> the [most] perfect in the year, alone opens
> this treasure-house. Come, let us prosper
> and become rich from it before it is closed.
> Blessed are the vigilant who plunder from it
> the spoils of life. It is a great disgrace
> if one sees his neighbour
> carrying away treasures, yet he in the treasure-house
> reposes and sleeps to come out empty-handed.
> On this feast let everyone garland
> the door of his heart. May the Holy Spirit
> desire to enter in its door to dwell
> and sanctify. For behold, She moves about
> to all the doors [to see] where She may dwell.[68]

Ephrem's musical precedent remains one of the most widely appreciated (if not always acknowledged) legacies of Syrian Christianity. His achievement prompted the writing of hymns in Greek, and the result has been that all Eastern liturgy has become far more based on poetry and hymns than the liturgy of the Western Latin Church. The Syriac musical tradition contains hymns sung in vigorous repetitive metre, a very different sound from that of the Greek or Russian Orthodox tradition. Moreover, preserved in the worship of Syriac Orthodox Christians from Edessa, who were expelled in the 1920s and are now living just over the border in the Syrian city of Aleppo, there is a distinctive form of liturgical music in chant and hymns. This is a proud heritage for the descendants of the refugees in Aleppo who have formed the Church of St George; it is likely to represent a living tradition from the oldest known musical performance in Christian history.[69]

But music is only part of the Syriac legacy. Music is an aspect of worship. In the Syrian Churches, principally the Church known as the Church of the East (about which we will have much more to say in Chapters 7 and 8), but also parts of the Church which over the centuries have accepted the authority of the Catholic Church of the West, there remains a regularly used form of prayer for the Eucharist which is the most reliably ancient of any in Christianity. Today this prayer is the heart of a structure of eucharistic worship for the Church's year and for ceremonies such as baptism and ordination which is known as the Liturgy of Addai and Mari. That lends it an association with those whom the Syrian Church reveres as its founders, but there is little doubt that it was the form of eucharistic prayer used in the Church of Edessa and it may be as early as the late second century. Nothing else preserved from anywhere in the Christian world has survived the austere scrutiny of modern liturgical scholars, to be authenticated as a form of worship that would have been familiar to very early Christians week by week.[70] It is a rare privilege to have been welcomed as I was to a congregation of exiled Christians from Baghdad in their refuge in Damascus, still mourning those murdered in the latest agonies of the Syriac Church, and to know that words were being solemnly sung as so many centuries ago they had first been chanted in Edessa:

Your majesty, O Lord, a thousand thousand heavenly beings worship, and myriad myriads of angels, hosts of spiritual beings, ministers of fire and spirit with cherubim and holy seraphim, glorify your name, crying out and glorifying, 'Holy, holy, holy, God almighty, Heaven and earth are full of his glories' . . .

Since Syrians lived either side of the shifting frontier between Rome and its eastern neighbours, the Church was naturally as liable to spread eastwards as westwards. At the beginning of the third century, Bar-Daisan could speak of Christian communities in the sprawling regions of Central Asia which now form such ex-Soviet Republics as Turkmenistan and Uzbekistan, while from further south Christian graves have been found on Kharg Island in the Persian Gulf which can be dated to the mid-third century. The Parthians showed little hostility to this new religion, but there was a significant shift with the founding of the Sassanian Empire in the 220s; the first restored shah, Ardashir, was the grandson of a high priest of the Zoroastrian faith and a Zoroastrian restoration became a keynote of the new empire's drive to restore Iranian tradition.[71] Relations between episcopal Christians and Manichaeans were tense enough, but that was because they had much in common in the role which they assigned to Jesus Christ. Zoroastrianism, by contrast, was an ancient religion which looked with contempt on the Christian revelation and its developing doctrine of the Trinity. Like Manichaeism, it was a dualist faith, but it was not the dualism which led Manichees and gnostics to regard the world and matter as evil. The Zoroastrian dualist struggle was between being and non-being, in which the world created by the 'Wise Lord' (Ahura Mazda) was the forum for a struggle between the creator and an uncreated 'Evil Spirit' (Ahriman). The Zoroastrians' experience of the world was therefore shot through with divinity; Zoroastrians made animal sacrifices to Ahura Mazda and paid reverence to fire. They despised Christian and Manichaean asceticism, which were developing in Syria just as the Sassanians seized power.[72]

A confrontation became more and more likely as Christian numbers in the Sassanian Empire grew, just as they were growing in the Roman Empire through the third century. Refugees crossed the frontier from the Roman Empire, fleeing the imperial persecutions, and there were also huge groups of prisoners from successful Sassanian military campaigns; a mixture of Greek-speakers and Syrians in numbers running into thousands, so that the shah settled them in newly built cities. One of these places, Gondeshapur (in south-west Iran, also anciently known as Beit Lapat), developed a school of higher education where the medium of instruction was Syriac. This was destined to become a major centre of Christian scholarship (see p. 246). By around 290 there was a bishop based in the Sassanian capital, Seleucia-Ctesiphon, very near the modern Baghdad, whose successors increasingly took on the role of presiding bishop in the East beyond the Roman frontier. These bishops faced a problem in uniting two different language groups of Christians under a single authority. Tensions developed between Greek- and Syrian-speaking Christians, and they underlined the fact that the Sassanians could easily treat both groups as an alien threat to their rule. That tension became acute after Constantine established his alliance with Christian bishops at the beginning of the fourth century. Now it was easy for successive shahs to see Christianity as a fifth column for Rome.

In the third century the Sassanian shahs had occasionally put some of their Christian subjects to death, although in that era the Sassanians were even more hostile to the newly developing religion of the Manichees.[73] In the fourth century the Church faced much greater trials. From the beginning of the 340s Bishop Simeon (Shem'on) of Seleucia-Ctesiphon led opposition to separate taxation for the Christian community in the Sassanian Empire, and that provoked Shah Shapur II to a massacre of the bishop and a hundred of his clergy. The Shah's anger and fear persisted in a persecution whose atrocities outdid anything that the Romans had achieved in their third-century attacks on the Church. There was a sickening attention to prolonging individual suffering which has rarely been equalled in the history of persecuting Christians until the concentrated Japanese persecutions of the early seventeenth century (see pp. 707–9). The situation was so dire that the bishopric in the Sassanian capital remained vacant until the beginning of the fifth century.[74] When we consider the astonishing acts of ascetic self-destructiveness by western Syrian monks in the fourth century and later (see pp. 206–9), it is worth remembering that they would be acutely aware of the grotesque sufferings inflicted on countless Christians over the border in the Sassanian Empire during these grim years.

To the north of Syria lay the kingdom of Armenia, protected over the centuries by its rugged geography from much direct interference from its powerful neighbours. Although its dominant cultural influences had long been from Iran, it had also over the centuries reached a comfortable understanding with the Romans, allowing them to believe that it was a Roman client state, to the extent that some of the coins of the Emperor Augustus could proclaim the propaganda message 'Armenia has been captured'.[75] The Romans, reluctant to take on the expense of governing such a difficult and remote area, were happy not to interfere too much. The early stages of Christian contact with the kingdom are obscure, but there are plausible stories of Syrian missions to it during the second and third centuries.[76] These predate the more widely circulated story of the founding bishop, Gregory the Illuminator (or 'Enlightener'), which describes a dramatic turnaround for Christianity as a result of the conflicted relationship between the saint, a minor member of the royal family brought up a Christian in exile in the Roman province of Cappadocia in Asia Minor, and his distant cousin Trdat.

Trdat, known to the Romans as Tiridates, became king of Armenia in the 280s or 290s with the support of the Emperor Diocletian, and at first he followed Diocletian's increasingly hostile policies towards Christianity. In the conversion story, it was after suffering acute mental disorder that the new king turned to Gregory for counsel, having previously subjected him to savage torture. The King then ordered his people, including the priesthood of the old religion, to convert en masse to Christianity, in a year which is uncertain but most calculations place in the decade before the Roman Emperor Constantine's victory at the Milvian Bridge in 312. Trdat reputedly went further than Constantine's new favour shown to the Church, ordering his people to become Christian en masse.[77] Such wholesale conversion cannot have been as straightforward as the story implies, but it did represent the beginning of a passionate melding of Christianity and Armenian identity. Members of Gregory's family succeeded him in the newly established bishopric, which received its succession from the Church of Cappadocia, in which he had grown up. A century after the conversion, a new Armenian alphabetic script was devised by a scholar-monk, Mesrop Maštoc'. Within a few decades there was a complete Bible in Armenian, adding one or two more books than those accepted into the canon of the imperial Church. It was a foundation document for Armenian literary culture, even more than Homer was for the Greeks.[78]

When it looked beyond its frontiers, the Armenian Church began by cherishing its links with Cappadocia and the Roman Empire. Christianity was a force pulling Armenia out of its previous careful balance between Rome and the Eastern powers. While Roman emperors had now taken the same action as Armenian monarchs in establishing Christianity as the official Church, the Sassanian shahs were persecuting Christians in their lands with increasing frequency, and during the fifth century, they made a concentrated effort to conquer Armenia and destroy its adopted faith in favour of their own Zoroastrianism. That only served to link Armenian and Christian identity all the more intimately, but the Armenian Church remained distinctive in character. It broke with the imperial Church after the Council of Chalcedon (see pp. 226–8), but there were other local elements of difference. One incident in the Gregory legend seeks to account for a curious feature of Armenian worship which has persisted in its homeland to the present day: every church has a space reserved for the ritual killing of animals at the end of worship. This is said to derive from the compromise Gregory reached with the existing priesthood: if they became Christian priests, he allowed them to continue with these traditional sacrifices, which would afterwards be eaten communally.[79]

In 303, as persecution of Christians gathered momentum in the empire, the last thing anyone would have expected was for the Church to enter an alliance with the Roman state in any way comparable with what had happened in Osrhoene or Armenia. Yet between the military campaigns of Constantine I and the end of the fourth century, the alliance became so complete that it governed the way that the Greek and Latin Christian traditions thought of themselves through to the twentieth century. Europe became a self-proclaimed Christian society, although often in ways remote from the challenges to human assumptions posed by Jesus's teachings in his Sermon on the Mount (see p. 88). Only now are the long centuries of 'Christendom' apparently coming to an end and the consequences of this new stage in Christian life have yet fully to be assessed.

6

The Imperial Church
(300–451)

CONSTANTINE AND THE GOD
OF BATTLES

The year 306 was crucial for the Christian Church. It was then that the senior emperor in the west, Constantius I, died at the British military headquarters at Eboracum or York (the second Roman emperor to do so). The army there proclaimed his son Constantine emperor. In 293 Diocletian had instituted a team of four emperors under his leadership (the 'Tetrarchy'), with a senior and a junior emperor in east and west, in the hope that it would make the empire more manageable and stable; in fact, after he retired in 305, he had to watch the Tetrarchy trigger further civil war. Following a series of complex manoeuvres, in 312 Constantine led his army to face the army of his rival, Maxentius, at the Milvian Bridge, which crossed the River Tiber and was barring his passage into Rome. During what became a crushing victory for Constantine, his troops bore on their shields a new Christian symbol: the Chi Rho ☧, the first two letters of Christ's name in Greek combined as a monogram.[1] This striking device, with no precedent in scripture or early Christian tradition, was now to become an all-pervasive symbol of an imperial Christianity, soon even on the small change of imperial coinage jingling in the wallets of the emperor's subjects throughout his lands.

The following year, Constantine and the Eastern emperor, Licinius, his ally for the time being, made a joint declaration at Milan proclaiming equal toleration for Christians and non-Christians, which no doubt reflected a policy which Constantine had already been operating in the western half of the empire.[2] When Constantine won further victories against his rival emperors still persecuting the Church in the East, he ordered his troops to say a prayer to the God of the Christians. Over the next decade, Constantine's alliance with Licinius cooled and they eventually clashed in open war. Now that Constantine was so obviously favouring Christianity, it was perhaps understandable that Licinius turned on prominent Christians at his Court. The Christian chronicler Eusebius of Caesarea, a fervent admirer of Constantine, came to produce the narrative which tells us most of what we know about these turbulent years, and revising his previous positive account of Licinius, he now had an excuse to portray Constantine's former colleague as the last great enemy of the Christian faith in the tradition of Valerian and Diocletian.[3] Certainly Licinius's defeat and murder in 324 ended any immediate possibility of a new violent assault on the Church. The crisis which had begun in 303 with Diocletian's persecution was now decisively resolved.

Over the century and a half from Constantine's military victory in 312, emperors, armies, clergy, monks and excited mobs of ordinary Christians all contributed to a complex of decisions on which version of Christian doctrine was to capture the allegiance of the rulers of the world in the West and in Constantinople. The culmination of this process was a great council of Church leaders at Chalcedon in 451, under the control of a Roman emperor and his wife. We have already seen mainstream Christianity based on a series of exclusions and narrowing of options: Jewish Christians, gnostics, Montanists, Monarchians were all declared outside the boundaries. Chalcedon was to mark a new stage in this process of exclusion. As a result, after 451 many Christians who owed their allegiance to the Church of Antioch, that same Church where Bishop Ignatius had first used the word 'Catholic', were to find themselves on the wrong side of the line. We will meet these excluded folk in Chapters 7 and 8, but first we will see how the new imperial Church asserted itself as the one version of Christian truth for the world to follow, and, in the process, created a great deal of that truth for the first time.

What lay behind the Church's remarkable reversal of fortune in the Roman Empire? Constantine has often been seen as undergoing a 'conversion' to Christianity. This is an unfortunate word, because it has all sorts of modern overtones which conceal the fact that Constantine's religious experience was like nothing which would today be recognized as a conversion. It is worth remembering Septimius Severus, that other unscrupulous military commander who turned emperor a century earlier. Severus had promoted the cult of Serapis, encouraged the idea that Serapis represented a single supreme deity and then reaped the benefit by identifying himself with that God as a way of strengthening his monarchy. Constantine had learned enough about the jealous nature of this God not to make the mistake of trying to merge imperial and divine identities, but their association was still intimate. Most obviously, and for reasons which will probably remain hidden from us, the Emperor associated the Christian God with the military successes which had destroyed all his rivals, from Maxentius to Licinius. For Constantine, this God was not gentle Jesus meek and mild, commanding that enemies should be loved and forgiven seventy times seven; he was a God of Battles. Constantine himself told Eusebius of Caesarea that one of the crucial experiences in his Milvian Bridge victory had been a vision of 'a cross of light in the heavens, above the sun, and an inscription, CONQUER BY THIS'.[4] The association of the sun and the Cross was no accident. A military leader and a ruthless politician rather than an abstract thinker, Constantine was probably not very clear about the difference between a universal sun cult and the Christian God – at least to start with. As he began showering privileges on the Christian clergy, it is unlikely that many of them considered whether the Emperor should be given a theological cross-examination before they accepted their unexpected gifts. What interested Constantine was the Christian God rather than the Christians. It would hardly have been worth his while from a political point of view to court favour from Christians, for, however one calculates their numbers, they were still a decided minority in the empire, and noticeably weak in those crucial power blocs, the army and the Western aristocracy. A simple grant of toleration would have been enough to delight the battered Church.

Constantine went much further than that. There is no doubt that he came to a deeply personal if rather capricious involvement in the Christian faith; according to Eusebius, he regularly delivered sermons to his no doubt slightly embarrassed courtiers.[5] Over his reign, he gave the Church an equal place alongside the traditional official cults and lavished wealth on it. Christianity could now embark on its long intoxication with architecture, previously a necessarily restricted passion. Among his many other donations were fifty monumental copies of the Bible commissioned from Bishop Eusebius's specialist scriptorium in Caesarea: an extraordinary expenditure on creating de luxe written texts, for which the parchment alone would have required the death of around five thousand cows (so much for Christian disapproval of animal sacrifice). It is possible that two splendidly written Bibles of very early date, now called respectively the Codex Vaticanus and the Codex Sinaiticus after their historic homes, are survivors from this gift.[6] The Emperor favoured Christians in senior positions and went as far as being baptized just before his death. There were hesitations: the designs on imperial coinage were always a barometer of official policy and propaganda preoccupations because they were frequently changed, and some mints were still producing coins with non-Christian sacred subjects as late in his reign as 323.[7] Traditionalists in Italy would have been pleased by Constantine building a new temple dedicated to the imperial cult, but the lion's share of imperial patronage was now going to the Christians, and at the same time many temples were being stripped of precious metals at imperial command.[8]

Most striking of all Constantine's symbolic associations with the new religion was his founding of a new capital for his empire. He had no emotional investment in the city of Rome. It is likely that he had hardly if ever visited it before his victory at the Milvian Bridge, and he found the city problematic. Its ruling class was unsympathetic to his new faith and clung to their ancient temples, and it was difficult to change the face of the city itself with monumental building for his new-found friends.[9] Instead he looked to the eastern part of the empire to create a city which would be peculiarly his own, and would also mark his victory over the former ruler in the East, Licinius.[10] He had considered refounding the city of Troy, original home of Aeneas, the legendary founder of Rome, as his New Rome, but this association with pre-Christian Roman origins did not prove enough of an incentive.[11] The site Constantine chose was an ancient city enjoying a superb strategic site at the entrance to the Black Sea and the command of trade routes east and west: Byzantion. He renamed the city after himself, as previous emperors had done in imitation of Alexander's precedent: Constantinople. The old name persisted, eventually modified in academic Latin to Byzantium. It was destined to provide a new identity for the Eastern Roman state, whose capital it remained over the next millennium, in what has commonly become known in history as the Byzantine Empire.[12] But for countless numbers of people of the eastern Mediterranean over that millennium and beyond, Constantinople would simply be 'the City', the dominant presence in their society, their religious practice and their hopes for the future.

Constantine quadrupled Byzantium in size, and although virtually none of the buildings which he provided survive, the Great Palace of the emperors remained on the same site from its first completion in 330 until the death of the last emperor in 1453. This new Rome reflected the new situation of tolerance for all, but with Christianity more equal than others. Traditional religion was put in a subordinate place: the core centres of worship were Christian churches of great magnificence. They included a church in which Constantine proposed to gather the bodies of all twelve Apostles to accompany his own corpse: a mark of how he now saw his role in the Christian story, although the coffins alongside his own had to remain mainly symbolic in default of enough relics of the Twelve.[13] For the most part the city churches were not exactly congregational or parish churches. They were designed like the contemporary temples of non-Christians with specific dedications or commemorations in mind, to concentrate on a particular saint or aspect of the Christian holiness. One of the greatest, close to the Imperial Palace, was dedicated to Holy Peace (*Hagia Eirēnē*). It was soon outclassed when Constantine's son put up an even greater church right beside it dedicated to the Holy Wisdom (*Hagia Sophia*), whose successor building was to have a special destiny in Christian history, as we will discover. So Christian life in Constantinople straight away became based on a rhythm of 'stational' visits to individual churches at special times, the clergy linking them by processions which became a characteristic feature of worship in the city. To live in Constantinople was to be in the middle of a perpetual pilgrimage.[14]

Constantine's vigorous annexation of the Christian past for imperial purposes in Rome and Byzantium also bore fruit in a remarkable enterprise which was a huge boost to the growing Christian urge to visit sacred places: the recreation of a Christian Holy Land centred on Jerusalem.[15] Palestine had been a backwater of the empire since its miserable century of rebellion and destruction from 66 CE. The former Jerusalem was a small city with a Roman name, Aelia Capitolina, some evocative ruins on the former Temple site, and a modest number of Christians who had unobtrusively returned to live around the area. In the middle years of Constantine's reign its provincial tranquillity began to be interrupted, much to the delight of its ambitious bishop, Macarius, who was pressing for appropriate honour to be done to the true home of Christianity. The bishop clearly attracted the Emperor's attention by some skilled self-promotion at the great Council of Nicaea in 325. He returned home armed with instructions to start an expensive programme of church-building, the preparations for which revealed a sensational double find beneath the stately imperial Capitoline temple built by Hadrian (see p. 107). What emerged was the exact site of Christ's crucifixion and the tomb in which the Saviour had been laid. It is possible that there had been a continuous Christian tradition as to the whereabouts of these sites and that therefore there was not much revealing to be done.[16] Less plausibly, it was not long before the Jerusalem Church was announcing that the actual wood of the Cross had also been rediscovered, and within a quarter-century another enterprising Bishop of Jerusalem, named Cyril, was linking that discovery to an undoubted historic event: a state visit to the Holy City in 327 by Constantine's mother, the dowager Empress Helena.

Helena may not have found the wood of the Cross (certainly no one at the time said that she did), but her presence was important enough – important from the imperial family's point of view, in demonstrating their Christian piety in the wake of the unfortunate and unexplained recent sudden deaths of the Emperor's wife and eldest son, and vital to the Church in Jerusalem as a direct imperial endorsement of a new centre of world pilgrimage. It took nearly a century for pilgrimage to Jerusalem to gather momentum, partly because of the expense, but partly because not everyone was enthusiastic either for pilgrimage or for this particular destination. Eusebius's comments on developments in Jerusalem are reserved, including the lofty remark in his later years that 'to think that the formerly established metropolis of the Jews in Palestine is the city of God is not only base, but even impious – the mark of exceedingly petty thinking' – a remarkably risky statement in view of the enthusiasm of his imperial patrons for the Jerusalem project.[17] One has to remember that Eusebius was bishop of a neighbouring Palestinian city, Caesarea, and the metropolitan (presiding bishop) within the whole province of Palestine, so he was not inclined to look favourably on his junior episcopal colleague's archaeological good fortune and all that stemmed from it. His comments continued to be echoed by such diverse major figures of the later fourth century Church as the brilliant preacher Bishop John Chrysostom, the scholar Jerome and the monk-theologian Gregory of Nyssa, who, after some unfortunate experiences when visiting the city, commented sourly that pilgrimage suggested that the Holy Spirit was unable to reach his native Cappadocia and could only be found in Jerusalem.[18]

That for many people was of course precisely and triumphantly what it did suggest. Scepticism was generally drowned out by the eagerness of people seeking an exceptional and guaranteed experience of holiness, healing, comfort – increasingly a self-fulfilling prophecy as the crowds swelled, to the delight of the souvenir traders and night-time entertainment industry in the Holy City.[19] There was now a proliferation of relics of the wood of the Cross. Earlier the usual Christian visual symbol for Christ had been a fish, since the Greek word for 'fish', *ichthys*, could be turned into an acrostic for the initial letters of a Greek phrase, 'Jesus Christ, Son of God, Saviour', or similar devotional variants. Now the fish was far outclassed not only by the new imperial Chi-Rho monogram referring to the same word, but also by the Cross. Crosses had featured little in public Christian art outside written texts before the time of Constantine; now they could even be found as motifs in jewellery.[20] Pilgrimage, from having played a seemingly minor role in Christian life, was now launched as one of its major activities. The life of Judaism had once revolved around one great pilgrimage: to Jerusalem. For Christians, Jerusalem would be only the principal star of a galaxy of holy places that has never since ceased to proliferate. Shrines have come and gone, but some, like Jerusalem itself, or Rome in the West, have never lost their appeal to the Christian faithful.

Jerusalem and the spectacularly large Church of the Holy Sepulchre begun by Constantine became host to a liturgical round which sought to take pilgrims on a journey alongside Jesus Christ through the events of his last sufferings in Jerusalem, his crucifixion and resurrection. Already in the 380s the Jerusalem liturgy had arrived at a state of elaboration lovingly described by an exotic visitor, Egeria, a member of one of the first western European communities of nuns, who had travelled all the way from the Atlantic coast of Spain (we are lucky that a single manuscript of her account written for her sisters turned up in Italy in 1884).[21] Interestingly, it is clear from Egeria's description that the Church authorities made little attempt to commemorate the other events of Jesus's life which associated him more positively with the old life of Jerusalem, such as his presentation in the Temple in adolescence, or his angry expulsion of the moneychangers from the Temple. Any liturgical reminiscences around these events might have provided opportunities for Jews to make unwelcome polemical points, and they would also have compromised one of the best-attested predictions of the Saviour himself, that not one stone of the Temple would remain on another.[22] The silence continued in later centuries, during which the site of the Temple remained a wilderness; its rehabilitation awaited those who listened to the prophet Muhammad (see pp. 255–61).

According to Luke's Gospel, the Mother of God celebrated her pregnancy with a song praising God for putting down the mighty from their seat and sending the rich empty away.[23] Now Christianity was becoming the religion of the powerful and it was entering what might be seen as an increasingly cosy alliance with high society. Power in the Graeco-Roman world lay in cities. Christians had acknowledged this by making them their own centres of power as they gradually created the uniform system of leadership by bishops and when they identified their leading bishops as 'metropolitans': those who presided over the Christian community of a 'metropolis'. This became so much a habit in both the Roman and the Greek Churches that when Rome started sending missionaries into northern Europe during the sixth and later centuries, it still encouraged bishops to find cities as bases and take their title from them, although there were hardly any communities recognizable as cities.

Even in the second century, long before the alliance with Constantine, the Apologists and Logos-theologians were witnessing to Christian willingness to express itself in the terms of conventional Classical culture (see pp. 141–3). Eventually the Latin and Greek Churches became so identified with the Graeco-Roman world that within living memory in the Christian West, almost fifteen hundred years after the disappearance of the last Western Roman emperor, schoolboys and schoolgirls learned Latin as a necessary qualification for entry in any subject to two of England's leading universities. The crucial stage in this extraordinary cultural saga was the reign of Constantine. The historian Eusebius of Caesarea so identified Constantine's purposes with God's purposes that he saw the Roman Empire as the culmination of history, the final stage before the end of the world. Gone was any expectation of a thousand-year rule of the saints, which he felt to be a deplorable falsehood, associated with the Book of Revelation, which he mistrusted. But this Christian historian felt very differently about the nature of the empire from the great Latin historians of the past, such as Tacitus or Suetonius. The city of Rome meant little to him and he took a comparatively restrained interest in its history; the empire had become something greater, more universal in God's plan.[24]

Significantly, imperial Christianity came to follow the political division of the empire which had originally been established by its archenemy Diocletian, when he split the administration of his empire between east and west, with a dividing line running through central Europe to the west of the Balkans, and a separation of North Africa and Egypt. In Europe, that boundary is very largely that existing today between Orthodox and Catholic societies, with fairly minor adjustments, even to the division of Slavic peoples between Orthodoxy and Catholicism. Moreover, the Church started using a technical administrative term which Diocletian had adopted for the twelve subdivisions he created in the empire: 'diocese'. In the Western Latin Church, this has become the term for an area under the control of a bishop. The

Churches of Orthodox tradition reserve it for the territories of the whole group of bishops who look to a particular metropolitan or patriarch, such as the Orthodox Patriarch of Antioch, or the Bishop of Constantinople, who is now known as the Oecumenical Patriarch. For the area presided over by a single bishop, they use a word which the West has redeployed for much smaller pastoral units served by a single priest: the *parochia* or parish. The West has another term equivalent to diocese, from a Latin word for a chair, *sedes*, which comes into English as 'see'.

This new vocabulary reflected the fact that the role of a bishop had been radically transformed now that he was not the leader of a small intimate grouping which might be scarcely larger than a household. That was what the Pastoral Epistles (see pp. 118–19) had described when they considered how a bishop should lead his people, but now the situation had radically changed. Willy-nilly, but mostly without much protest, bishops were becoming more like official magistrates, because their Church was being embraced by the power of the empire. Less than a century before, the heap of charges against Bishop Paul of Samosata had included the complaint that he had sat on a throne like a 'ruler of the world'; now all bishops did this.[25] The idea of a seated bishop presiding over the liturgy but also pronouncing on matters of belief and adjudicating everyday disputes, became so basic to Western Christian ideas of what a bishop represented that the Church annexed a second Latin word for 'chair', *cathedra*, previously associated with teachers in higher education, and used it for the city church in which the bishop's principal chair could be found: his cathedral. The buildings which the Church now put up for the worship of their great congregations reflected the bishops' role as politicians and statesmen: churches borrowed their form not from the temples of the Classical world, which were not designed for large congregations, and which in any case had inappropriate associations with sacrifice to idols, but instead from the secular world of administration.

The model chosen was the audience hall of a secular ruler, called from its royal associations a *basilica*. Conventionally it was a rectangular chamber big enough to hold large numbers, with an entrance through one of the long sides to face the chair of the presiding magistrate or ruler, often housed in a semicircular apse in the other long wall. Interestingly, although the new Christian basilicas took this architectural form, they made two radical modifications to it. One of the earliest examples of this major re-envisioning of the basilican plan can still be seen in Rome at Constantine's church now dedicated to St John Lateran, and it is splendidly instanced in the slightly later pair of basilicas dedicated to Sant' Apollinare in Ravenna (see Plate 4), but there are countless others. The plan was applied in a remarkably uniform fashion throughout the imperial Church, and indeed beyond its borders as far away as the Church in Ethiopia in its early years. The first Christian innovation was, wherever possible, to 'orient' the building: that is, to lay out its long axis west to east, with an apsidal end at the east to contain the eucharistic table or altar with the bishop's chair behind it. There are a host of biblical justifications for east–west orientation, from the eastern entrance of the Garden of Eden leading to the Tree of Life (Genesis 3.24) to the angel of Revelation 7.2 who rises from the east and gives safe passage to the chosen – but one feels that none of them would have had a decisive architectural effect without the plain fact that the sun rises in the east, regardless of the Bible and its preoccupations. Second, instead of an entrance in a long side wall, the west gable of a Christian basilica now housed the entrance. So those coming into the building had their gaze directed throughout its length, both to the bishop's chair and to the altar in front of it, which increasingly frequently contained or stood over the remains of some Christian martyr from the heroic era of persecution.

The purpose of this replanning was to turn the basilica into a pathway towards all that was most holy and authoritative in Christian life: the pure worship of God. If it is in the fourth century that we first get substantial numbers of surviving Christian church buildings, it is also from this period that we first have substantial evidence about the worship for which they had been designed as theatres. Despite the efforts of much liturgical scholarship, it is remarkably difficult to get a coherent picture of what Christian worship looked like or felt like before the time of Constantine; throughout the Christian world, probably only the present-day liturgy of the Syriac Churches is anything like a form which predates that period (see p. 184). In a brilliant miniature study, the twentieth-century liturgical scholar R. P. C. Hanson indeed established that in general, up to the end of the third century, bishops were free to improvise a form of words around set themes which would be considered appropriate for the great drama of the Eucharist. They were after all the Church's teachers, as their *cathedra* chair came to symbolize, and they could be trusted to include the right material. In the fourth century the situation changed: the liturgy, like the buildings in which it was celebrated, became more fixed and structured. From that era onwards, architecture and manuscript evidence come together for the first time to offer a flood of light on these matters at the heart of Christian experience.[26]

Armed with this combination of knowledge, we could enter a basilica to look eastwards towards the table of the Lord's death and resurrection. We would remember the martyred servant of Christ whose bones were incorporated in it, and who by his or her suffering had a place guaranteed close to the Lord in Heaven. In the great services of the Church's year, we would also see the living representative of God on earth, the bishop sitting in his chair, flanked by his clergy. This was a model of the Court of Heaven; and naturally everyone at the time would expect splendour at a Court. It was an age when clergy began to dress to reflect their special status as the servants of the King of Heaven. The copes, chasubles, mitres, maniples, fans, bells, censers of solemn ceremony throughout the Church from East to West were all borrowed from the daily observances of imperial and royal households. Anything less would have been a penny-pinching insult to God.

Although the Church celebrated God's banquet, the Eucharist, by annexing countless symbols of worldly triumph, there remained a difference from imperial feasting. The triumphal atmosphere was edged with the memory that the Eucharist was a meal of 'Last Supper' which had led directly to Christ's suffering and death, and which had then been re-enacted in joy in the presence of the risen Christ at that table in the village of Emmaus (see pp. 94–5). The Cross which was now becoming universally familiar as a visual symbol of Jerusalem, of crucifixion and resurrection, was never far from the portraits of the imperious Christ staring down from the walls on his servants celebrating below. And like the imperial Court, some people must be excluded from the festivities because they were not authorized to enter. Those who had not fulfilled the requirements for baptism and were still under instruction (*catechēsis*) were the 'catechumens'. They were dismissed before the Eucharist began and restricted to the entrance area of the church, which often developed as a separate chamber at the west end of the basilican building.

And for all Christians, there was a time of preparation before the great festivals which became longer and more elaborate in direct proportion to the elaboration of the festivals themselves. From early days, the time of anxiety and tragedy which led up to the Resurrection was marked out by abstinence and vigil. By a natural progression of ideas, this was linked to the story in the Synoptic Gospels that Christ had retreated from his active life and ministry into the desert for forty days and nights. It was the perfect time of the liturgical year for catechumens to spend a last rigorous preparation before their triumphal reception into the Church during the celebration of Easter. This forty-day period, first explicitly mentioned without much fanfare in the Canons of the Council of Nicaea and therefore probably of long standing, was the season which in English is known as Lent.[27] Christ's birth and the celebration of the Christ Child's adoration by non-Jewish astrologers (his 'showing forth' or 'Epiphany') came over the next centuries also to be observed with a similar introductory period of fasting and austerity, during which the faithful could act out their longing for the Saviour's arrival or 'Advent'. That forty-day season would make all the more joyful the Christmas and Epiphany festivals at the darkest time of the calendar, when the days were at their shortest, as the release came at last from the time of preparation.

THE BEGINNINGS OF MONASTICISM

It seemed that episcopal authority had now triumphed in the Church. But worshippers at the Eucharist, seeing the bishop seated before them with his presbyters, might be aware that there was an alternative source of power and spirituality in the Church: an institution which had only gradually emerged during the third century. The closer the Church came to society, the more obvious were the tensions with some of its founder's messages about the rejection of convention and the abandonment of worldly wealth. Human societies are based on the human tendency to want things, and are geared to satisfying those wants: possessions or facilities to bring ease and personal satisfaction. The results are frequently disappointing, and always terminate in the embarrassing non sequitur of death. It is not surprising that many have sought a radical alternative, a mode of life which is in itself a criticism of ordinary society. Worldly goods, cravings and self-centred personal priorities are to be avoided, so that their accompanying frustrations and failures can be transcended. The assumption is that such transcendence has a goal beyond the human lifespan, the goal which some term God. The movement known as monasticism is a way of structuring this impulse.

Something like monastic systems are found at the margins of several world faiths – Jains, Taoists, Hindus and Muslims – but Buddhism and Christianity have made monasticism a central force within their religious activity. It is more surprising that Christianity should make monasteries part of its tradition than that monasticism should have developed in Buddhism, for Christianity affirms the positive value of physical human flesh in the incarnation of Christ, while Buddhism has at its centre nothingness and the annihilation of the self. Christianity's parent religion, Judaism, is actively hostile to celibacy, one of monasticism's chief institutions, and Jewish groups which practised a form of monasticism are fairly marginal in Jewish history: the Essenes and the shadowy sect of the Therapeutae mentioned by the Jewish historian Philo. Descriptions of monasticism are notable by their absence in both Old and New Testaments, and we have seen that the one recorded attempt in Christianity's first generation to practise community of goods was short-lived, if indeed it happened at all (see pp. 119–20).

The spiritual writer A. M. Allchin called one episode in monastic history 'the silent rebellion', and this happy phrase can be more widely applied.[28] All Christian monasticism is an implied criticism of the Church's decision to become a large-scale and inclusive organization. In its early years, the Christian Church was a small community which found it easy to guard its character as an elite consisting of spiritual athletes proclaiming the Lord's coming again. Later, the gnostic impulse in Christianity encouraged this tendency, pushing Christians in the direction of austerity and self-denial, just like much contemporary non-Christian philosophy. The stance became increasingly hard to maintain as Christian communities grew and all sorts of people began flocking in; even the long process of instruction and preparation for baptism and admission to communion then customary for converts and born Christians alike could not prevent this process. There were arguments about this in Rome as early as the end of the second century, when the austere priest Hippolytus (see p. 172) furiously attacked his bishop, Callistus, for what he regarded as laxity in imposing penances on Church members who had fallen into serious sin.[29] At the root of this quarrel, which resulted in Hippolytus severing his links with the mainstream Church, was the issue of whether the Church of Christ was an assembly of saints, hand-picked by God for salvation, or a mixed assembly of saints and sinners. The same dilemma lay behind the schisms of the Novationists, Melitians and Donatists in the third and fourth centuries (see pp. 174–5 and p. 212), and it was all the more obvious when Christians generally ceased to have the opportunity to be martyred at the hands of non-Christians after the time of Constantine.

It was probably inevitable that the hardliners from Hippolytus to Donatus should lose the argument and leave the mainstream, since from its beginnings, at least as described in the Book of Acts, Christianity had a voracious appetite for converts. If the sort of rigorous moral standards which the purists wanted were applied, there would hardly be anyone left in the Church. But might there be a solution short of schism for those who wanted something more? The impulse to separate while remaining in communion with the mainstream Christian body is already perceptible during the third century, before the great surprise of Constantine's 'conversion'. Underlining the uneasy relationship between monasticism and the mainstream Church, its origins are in the lands from which gnostic Christianity had also emerged: the eastern borderlands of the Roman Empire in Syria, and in Egypt. Moreover, the first moves to founding monastic communities were made at much the same time as the emergence of that new rival to Christianity, Manichaeism, with its ethos of despising physical flesh. It may be that the famous austerities of Christian monks (see pp. 206–8) were imitations of similar feats of spiritual endurance by Indian holy men and that Manichees were responsible for bringing the idea westwards into the Christian world.

One text, known as *The Acts of Thomas*, hovered on the borders of acceptability in Christian sacred literature until the sixteenth century, when the Council of Trent (justifiably in its own terms) dismissed the book as heretical. Purporting to describe the life of Thomas, one of Christ's original Apostles, its preoccupations suggest a much later date than Thomas's time, probably early third century, so much later than the so-called Gospel of Thomas (see p. 78). Nevertheless, like that probably late-first-century text, *Acts* belongs to the Christian penumbra of gnostic works, and it is likely to have been written in Syria, at much the same time that the Syrian theologian Tatian was praising a life of abstinence and austerity (see pp. 181–2). Amid its descriptions of Thomas's adventures on his mission to India are fervent commendations of celibacy: the Apostle's first major move was to persuade two newlyweds to refrain from sexual relations. On another occasion, his eloquence on the subject of 'filthy intercourse' was such that the wife of an Indian prince repelled her husband with the equivalent of pleading a headache.[30] The testimonies in this work and in Tatian's writings to the emergence of an ascetic (world-denying) impulse come at much the same time as the first evidence of organized celibate life inside the mainstream Church. Likewise, this was in Syria. Groups of enthusiasts called Sons (or Daughters) of the Covenant vowed themselves to poverty and chastity, but they avoided any taint of gnostic separation by devoting themselves to a life of service to other Christians under the direction of the local bishop. Their role in the Syrian Church continued for several centuries alongside developed monasticism.[31]

In Egypt there is a similar ambiguity about the first monastic institutions. It is worth noting that the richest modern find of gnostic literature, from Nag Hammadi, came from a Christian monastic community of fourth-century date. Egypt was peculiarly suited to a Christian withdrawal from the world because of its distinctive geography: its narrow fertile strip along the Nile, backed by great stretches of desert, means that it is easy literally to walk out of civilization into wilderness. It was here towards the end of the third century that the monastic movement first securely tied itself into the developed Church of the bishops and left a continuous history in conventional Christian sources, through the lives of two powerful personalities who could be presented as founder-figures: Antony and Pachomius, representatives respectively of two different forms of monastic life, that of the hermit and that of the community. The reality was more complicated. Much of this story of origins was an effort by Egyptian monks to claim priority for themselves in the monastic movement, in the face of their competitors and probable predecessors in Syria. Yet without such founding myths, it might have been less easy to integrate the new movement into the Church.

In fact the biography of Antony written by the great fourth-century Bishop of Alexandria Athanasius makes it clear that he was not the first Christian hermit; from his boyhood in the 250s and 260s, Antony was already seeking out in fascination individual Christians in neighbouring villages who had taken to a solitary life or practised an ascetic discipline.[32] Eventually his desire to live a Christian life out of touch with anyone else led him into the desert or wilderness: from the Greek for wilderness, *erēmos*, comes the word 'hermit'. After twenty years of solitude, Antony was faced with a new problem: hordes of people were coming out to join him in the desert. Diocletian's persecution of Christians and the sheer burden of taxation in ordinary society were powerful incentives to flee into the wilderness. As persecution ceased, not everyone wanted to go to such an extreme. So the community life already in existence in Syria found its parallel in Egypt, where groups of people withdrew from the world in the middle of the world, founding what were in effect specialized new villages in the fertile river zone: the first monasteries. They owed their existence principally to Pachomius, a soldier who converted to Christianity during the Great Persecution, impressed by Christians' ready support for suffering fellow Christians even if they had not previously known them.

Life in the army was self-selecting and communal, with clear boundaries and conventions, and it may be that the ex-soldier Pachomius drew on that experience when he devised a simple set of common rules for hermits to preserve their solitude while becoming members of a common group living together. An example of the practical good sense of his arrangements was the stipulation that seniority in his communities was acquired simply by the date at which the individual joined. This would be important when those joining began to include people from the upper end of the social scale, who might seek to perpetuate their status.[33] Notably, Pachomius set up his first community not in the desert, but in the deserted houses of a village which he found conveniently abandoned close to the bank of the Nile. A second takeover of a deserted village followed; one might therefore see Pachomius's movement as an effective way of remedying third-century social disruption, to which the growing tax burdens had significantly contributed. Pachomius's sister is given the credit for founding female communities along similar lines, with a programme of manual work and study of scripture.[34]

Remarkably soon, the word *monachos* ('monk') gained its specialized religious meaning in Greek: the earliest known use is in a secular petition in an Egyptian papyrus dating from 324.[35] There is a significant curiosity in the implication of this word, because the Greek/Latin *monachos/monachus* means a single, special or solitary person, but a truly solitary way of life is not the most common form of monasticism. Nor was that first-designated Egyptian *monachos* living in a wilderness, since the reason that we know about him is that he was a passer-by in a village street who stepped in and helped to break up a fight. Historically, most Christian monks and nuns have lived in community, ever since the time of Pachomius, rather than becoming hermits. Indeed, *'monachus'* with its cognates is a particularly inappropriate piece of Christian lexical imperialism when it is applied to Buddhism, whose concept of monasticism, the *Sangha*, centres firmly on community, and where hermits are even more in a minority than among Christian monks.

It is perhaps difficult for modern observers of Christianity, who accept hermits, monasteries and nunneries as a traditional feature of Christianity, to see that this acceptance was not inevitable. The Church might well have seen the 'silent rebellion' as a threat, not simply because of the dubious and possibly gnostic origins of monasticism, but because the most 'orthodox' of hermits, simply by his style of life, denied the whole basis on which the Church had come to be organized, the eucharistic community presided over by the bishop. Indeed, that worry was translated by the Eastern Church authorities into a vague menace called 'Messalianism', a deviant enthusiasm for emphasizing one's own spiritual experience in asceticism rather than valuing the Church's sacraments – and the 'Messalian' accusation frequently hung over early ascetics or ascetic communities.[36] How could Antony receive the Eucharist out in the desert, and how therefore did he relate to the authority of the bishop? Moreover, he was not part of the dominant Greek culture of the urban Church – he did not even speak Greek, but the native Egyptian language, Coptic. Pachomius came from an even humbler Coptic background.[37] As it happened, Antony amply proved himself in the eyes of the Church authorities, first by leaving his isolation during Diocletian's persecution to comfort suffering Christians in Alexandria. He then became a great friend of Bishop Athanasius of Alexandria, who wrote an admiring biography of him, which has been described as 'the most read book in the Christian world after the Bible': a risky claim, but certainly in the right order of magnitude.[38]

Athanasius painted a portrait of Antony which suited his own purposes: an ascetic who was soundly opposed to Athanasius's opponents, the Arians (see pp. 211–22), and was a firm supporter of bishops such as Athanasius himself. The biography was specifically addressed to monks beyond Egypt; the bishop's aim was a triumphant assertion of Egypt's spiritual prowess, providing a model for all monastic life. Its first half was a dramatic account of the solitary's twenty years of lonely struggle with demons of the desert, often in the shape of wild animals, snakes and scorpions; worse still, in the form of a seductive woman. At the end of the first great contest, the Devil, deranged in his exhaustion and frustration, was reduced to the shape of a little black boy from Ethiopia, and Antony was able to sneer at the 'despicable wretch . . . black of mind, and . . . a frustrated child'. That was an unfortunate literary conceit, since many early monks in imitation came to use the same image for the Prince of Darkness, with a conscious racism directed towards Africans: a backhanded compliment to the success of Athanasius's work, and not the best of stereotypes for promoting good relations with the Church of Ethiopia.[39] It was not the last time that Christians would associate black races with evil and fallenness (see pp. 867–8).

If anything bonded monasticism into the episcopally ordered Church, it was this pioneering hagiography ('saint-writing') from one of the most powerful bishops of the fourth century. It also established Egyptian monasticism in its image of desert solitude, encapsulated in that paradoxical word '*monachos*', and equally in Athanasius's gleeful paradox that 'the desert was made a city by monks'.[40] The image was a significant and useful one, because Christian cities were presided over by bishops; it was a symbol of victory over the Devil's city and his rebellion against the purposes of God (not to mention the purposes of God's bishops). As a description of the origins and development of monasticism, however, it was to a large extent a fabrication. Athanasius deliberately emphasized the desert as he told Antony's story, and the accidents of later history have subsequently reinforced his distortion: when Egyptian and Syrian Christianity faced being marginalized by conquering Islam (see pp. 261–7), it was indeed the remoter desert monasteries which were best placed to preserve monastic life and culture, and hence the common description of the spiritual literature from this society as being written by 'the Desert Fathers'. But that does not represent the earlier reality of the fourth- and fifth-century Church or the place of monasticism in it: far more part of the everyday experience of urban and farming landscapes.

The power of monks and hermits was dependent on their reputation in following Antony's heroic austerity. They had the inspiration of Christ's words in the Beatitudes (see p. 88), but there were also more contemporary reasons propelling them. Like the ascetics of Syria, they would know of the terrible continuing sufferings of Christians in the fourth-century Sassanian Empire, and they would also be uncomfortably aware that such suffering was no longer available in the Roman Empire. In default of any more martyrdoms provided by Roman imperial power, they martyred their bodies themselves, and thus they annexed the esteem which martyrs had already gained among the Christian faithful. They were extending the category of sainthood. There was quite conscious competition in this between Egyptians and Syrians, what Athanasius in his biography was happy to describe as 'a noble contest'.[41] During the fourth century, Egyptian hermits and monks became famous for their self-denial, vying like athletes in such exercises for God's glory as standing day and night, or eating no cooked food for years on end.[42] This spirit was equalled in Palestine and Syria, where monks and hermits performed terrifying feats of endurance and punishment of their worldly bodies by squeezing into small spaces or living in filth. Jerome, the Latin scholar-immigrant to the East who had tried their lifestyle and did not take to it (see p. 295), did his best to put them down with the comment that Syrian monks were as much concerned for the dirtiness of their bodies as with the cleanliness of their hearts.[43] Syrians would probably have retorted that in view of the continuing appalling sufferings of their

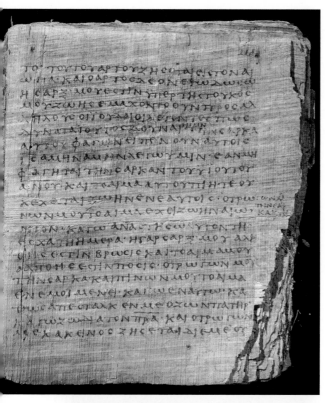

1. Bodmer Papyrus 66, discovered in Egypt in 1952, is a virtually complete text of John's Gospel, probably *c.* 200 CE. Page NB (2) begins in the middle of 7.52 ('Search and you will see that no prophet is to rise from Galilee') and covers some of Chapter 8, but omits the story of the woman taken in adultery (7.53–8.11), as do many early MSS of John. The third line has one of the characteristic Christian Greek abbreviations for a sacred name (*nomen sacrum*): IC for *Iesous*.

2. The catacomb of Callixtus, on the Appian Way outside Rome, the main Christian cemetery in third- and fourth-century Rome, depicted in 1870 two decades after its rediscovery. The area covered is around 90 acres and probably half a million people were buried there over four centuries, including nine popes and three bishops during the third century. Visible is the circular stone table on which burned oil lamps beside the tomb of Pope Cornelius, who died in exile in 253.

3. The stump of the pillar (the rest was chipped away by pilgrims) on which Simeon 'Stylites' spent around forty years until his death in 459, at the centre of the Basilica of Qal'at Sam'an (Simeon's Castle), constructed by the Emperor Zeno in less than two decades after 476, now in northern Syria. Around the pillar-base are traces of a drain from the pillar's plumbing system.

4. The Church now called Sant' Apollinare Nuovo, Ravenna, was built as the Chapel Royal of the Arian King Theodoric the Ostrogoth (reigned 471–526). It is one of the finest examples of a basilica from the early Church, but it was built not for Catholic but for Arian worship. The main tier of mosaics with saints processing east dates from its Catholic reconsecration in the late sixth century; the nearest are doctored survivors from Theodoric's time.

Hagia Sophia, the emblematic 'Great Church' of world Orthodoxy, though a mosque since
453, was rebuilt by the Emperor Justinian in an astonishing five years after its basilican
predecessor was wrecked in riots in 532. This view of the eastern parts reveals the exuberant
intricacy of the semidomes which support the great central dome, above the imperial galleries
from which the Court viewed the liturgy. The Qur'anic inscriptions on circular boards are
nineteenth century.

(*left*) 6. The library pagoda of Ta Qin,
near Wuchun, central China, forms part
of a Dyophysite Christian monastery site
dating from the seventh century, now a
Buddhist temple.

(*right*) 7. Stele of 781 CE celebrating the
first 150 years of Dyophysite Christianity
in China, now in the Forest of Stelae in the
imperial city of Xi'an. 279 cm tall, it has
inscriptions in Chinese and some in Syriac,
emphasizing the benefits of Christianity
for the Empire and commemorating the
leaders of the Christian community. At
its head, the cross floats above the Taoist
lotus blossom, clouds and dragons.
Discovered by Jesuits in the seventeenth
century, it may have come from Ta Qin
monastery.

8. Ireland had never been part of the Roman Empire, but after the Western Empire's fall it became one of the most important refuges of Latin Christianity. These sixth-century stone 'beehive' huts housed the monks who lived on the island of Skellig Michael overlooking the Atlantic Ocean off the Irish coast, in what was the westernmost outpost of Christianity. The Archangel Michael is the patron saint of high places.

9. Bet Giyorgis (St George's Church), Lalibela, Ethiopia. Dating of these buildings cut from the living rock is uncertain, but it is likely to be no later than the thirteenth century. Beside the church in its trench is an open-air baptismal pool.

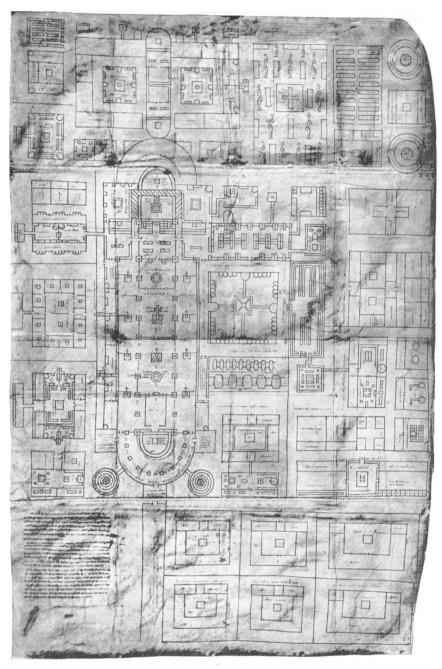

10. An extraordinary survival in the library of the Swiss Abbey of Sankt Gallen (for which it was commissioned) is a ninth-century plan for an ideal Abbey, which did indeed become the standard plan for Benedictine monasteries. To the left (north of the square central cloister yard) is the church with its many altars; to the east of the cloister is the dormitory and warming-house (later one would also expect the chapter-house here). To the south are the dining-hall (refectory) and kitchens, to the west, cellars and larders. Around are a host of lesser buildings and gardens to service the community and house guests.

(*above*) 11. Work on St Vitus Cathedral, Prague, stopped in the fifteenth-century Hussite crisis, and the building was still a torso when it was here depicted in 1793. Completion, like that of Cologne Cathedral truncated by the Reformation began amid the Romantic admiration for Gothic in the mid nineteenth century and was achieved by enthusiastic Czech nationalists in the 1920s.

(*left*) 12. The *Nuremberg Chronicle* (1493) was one of the most successful and ambitious works of early printed publishing. It played to the interests of potential reading public, one of which the end of the world. Here the Archangel Michael fights with demons, while below a demon advises a richly dressed Christian preacher. One man ignores the preacher and reaches out to the cosmic struggle. Albrecht Dürer, who went on to produce some of the most famous of Christian apocalyptic images, was apprenticed in the workshop which produced this picture.

3. The third rebuilding of the Abbey church of Cluny, completed in the early twelfth century, made it the largest church in the world for four centuries thereafter. It survived intact until the French Revolution, after which it was demolished piecemeal for its materials. Only a minor transept remains.

. Equally destructive had been the Scottish Reformation from the 1560s, which had no use for Scotland's cathedrals if they did not become parish churches. The most splendid, St Andrews, seat of Scotland's premier archbishopric and also an Augustinian monastery, was soon reduced to its present sad state – here seen from the west, with the ghost of its great cloister. To the east rears the tower of the equally ruinous eleventh-century parish church of St Regulus.

15. Ignatius Loyola, founder of the Society of Jesus, portrayed here in 1556, the year of his death, by Jacopino del Conte (1510–98); the picture still hangs in the study of the General of the Society.

16. Don Antonio Manuel ne Vunda, descended from the pre-eminent religious family of pre-Christian Kongo, was sent by King Alvaro II of this now devout Christian African kingdom as ambassador to the Holy See. He died in Rome in 1608, and the then very exotic African dignitary was buried and commemorated in the church of Santa Maria Maggiore.

17. Fernando Álvarez de Toledo y Pimentel, 3rd Duke of Alba, was a ruthless governor of the Netherlands (1567–73) on behalf of Philip II of Spain. Although his thousand-plus executions included Catholic leaders of the uprising against Spain, his conduct, such as these deaths in Bruges portrayed by Franz Hogenberg (1540–c. 1590), came to symbolize Spanish Catholic cruelty and identified the cause of resistance with Protestantism.

fellow Syrians at the hands of the Sassanians (see pp. 185–6), they had rather more grasp of what martyrdom meant than he did.

One Syrian word for monk is *abila*, 'mourner'. One of the many Christian spiritual writers who sought to borrow respectability for his works by placing them under the name of the much-honoured Ephrem the Syrian maintained that Jesus had cried but never laughed, and so 'laughter is the beginning of the destruction of the soul'.[44] Nevertheless, it was in this same Syrian setting in the fifth century that there evolved a particular form of sacred self-ridicule or critique of society's conventions: the tradition of the Holy Fool. It was a specialized form of denying the world. Behind its Syrian origins lurked a Greek archetype from before the coming of Christianity: Diogenes of Sinope (see pp. 29–30). The first well-known reviver of Diogenes's deliberate attempt to flout all convention was Simeon, who came to be known in Syrian as *Salus* ('foolish'). Simeon outdid Diogenes in active rudeness: when he arrived in the city of Emesa (now Homs in Syria), he dragged a dead dog around, threw nuts at women during church services and gleefully rushed naked into the women's section of the city bathhouse ('as if for the glory of God', his biographer optimistically commented). Not unnaturally he caused considerable offence, then somewhat illogically himself took offence at a group of girls who mocked him, miraculously leaving a number of them permanently cross-eyed. His affectionate chronicler a century later was Leontius, a Cypriot bishop. Bishops are not normally associated with antisocial behaviour; perhaps Leontius was writing in the same satirical spirit as Dean Swift. Certainly Diogenes 'the dog' lurked in some of Leontius's literary allusions – not least in the dead dog hanging from Simeon's belt. The Holy Fool was destined to have a long history in the Orthodox tradition (although for some reason the Serbs never took to him). His extrovert craziness is an interesting counterpoint or safety valve to the ethos of prayerful silence and traditional solemnity which is so much part of Orthodox identity. Not all Orthodox theologians have been very comfortable with that contrast.[45]

One of the most extraordinary practices adopted by some ascetics in Syria was to spend years on end exposed on top of a specially built stone column, living on a wicker platform which resembled the basket of a modern hot-air balloon. This form of devotion was pioneered in the early fifth century by another Simeon, therefore nicknamed the Stylite ('pillar-dweller'). Once established on his column, he reputedly never descended from it before his death. Since the column was successively

extended in height to some sixty feet, special arrangements were presumably made for the alterations; while detailed investigation has solved one
obvious practical question by revealing evidence that this and subsequent
pillars were en suite. Otherwise, Simeon's frugal needs were met by an
eager entourage of admirers who hoisted food up to him from the
ground. His pillar survives in part, surrounded by a massive ruined
basilica in the Syrian hill country beyond Aleppo, within sight of the
modern border with Turkey. The column has literally been eaten away
by its devotees, who over centuries chipped off small portions which
they then ground to powder and swallowed for healing purposes. The
remnant, now whittled down to man height from its original sixty feet,
resembles a well-sucked lollipop (see Plate 3).

Over the next seven centuries, around 120 people imitated Simeon's
initiative in Syria and Asia Minor. They were like living ladders to
Heaven, and even if hermits, they were far from remote. St Simeon
himself had chosen one of the most elevated sites in his portion of
northern Syria next to a major road, dominating the view for scores of
miles, and preaching twice a day.[46] Stylites often became major players
in Church politics, shouting down their theological pronouncements
from their little elevated balconies to the expectant crowds below, or
giving personalized advice to those favoured enough to climb the ladder
and join them on their platform. There was little love lost between some
rival pillars of different theological persuasions. Simeon the younger
Stylite (521–97) is rather implausibly said to have insisted on spending
his infancy on a junior pillar, but there is no doubt that he eventually
graduated to a full-scale pillar near Antioch, of which there are remnants
even more substantial than those of his elder namesake. It was possible
for pilgrims to get there without too much trouble from the city, making
for an edifying day out. Simeon does not seem to have protested while
a large expensive church (whose ruins also still survive) was being built
round his pillar, thus making this ragged hermit into a bizarre living
relic, sole exhibit in a Christian zoo.[47] It is plausible that one of the most
important symbols of Islam, the minaret, was inspired by the sight of
the later representatives of these Syrian Christian holy men summoning
the faithful to worship God from their pillars. The first known minaret,
after all, was part of the great Ummayad mosque in Damascus, well
within the cultural zone of the Stylites.

Pillar-dwelling made it briefly into the Balkans, but in the climate of
Europe westwards, it proved impracticable. Likewise in Asia Minor the
winters were much harsher than further south, and even most ascetics

were inclined to community life rather than the individualism of Antony or Simeon. It was here that most of the monastic rules were devised which form the basis of modern Eastern monasticism. Chief among their formulators was the monk Basil, who, unlike many talented theologians, combined wisdom and practicality, so that his influence was decisive not only in monastic life but also in one of the greatest doctrinal crises of the fourth century (see p. 218). He has come to be called 'the Great', and he was one of the first to set a pattern which became a norm in the Eastern Churches (see p. 437): he was first a monk, but was then chosen as bishop of his native Caesarea in Cappadocia, the modern Kayseri in Turkey. Basil, then, can be given much of the credit for uniting the charisma of monk and bishop, one of the potential problems for the fourth-century Church. He had gentle but firm words discouraging the hermit lifestyle in favour of community: 'the solitary life has one aim, the service of the needs of the individual. But this is plainly in conflict with the law of love, which the apostle fulfilled when he sought not his own advantage but that of the many, that they might be saved.'[48] Basil's rules for monastic life were imitated and adapted to local conditions in the West, when only a few decades later Western Christians began experimenting for themselves with the monastic life (see pp. 312–18).

Basil's importance for the future of monasticism was equalled by that of his contemporary and acquaintance Evagrius/Evagrios, from the province of Pontus on the southern shores of the Black Sea (hence 'Evagrius Ponticus'), who travelled far from his homeland and a later popular ministry in Constantinople to become a monk in the deserts to the west of the Nile Delta. He and Basil were among the first monks to turn to writing alongside the physical struggles through which ascetics built up their spiritual life, yet the writings of Evagrius illustrate once more how uncomfortably the monastic movement might sit within the structures of the Christian Church. He was an admirer of Origen, and consequently suspect to many; in fact 150 years after Origen was first posthumously condemned by a Church council in 400, the same fate befell Evagrius, accused of 'Origenism' alongside Origen himself and condemned by the fifth Council of Constantinople in 553 (see p. 327). What made Evagrius's ideas particularly suspect later was his distinctive pronouncement that the highest level of contemplation could produce no image or form when it reached to the divine, in order that a true union with God could take place: 'Never give a shape to the divine as such when you pray, nor allow your mind to be imprinted by any form, but go immaterial to the Immaterial and you will understand.'[49] By the eighth and ninth centuries, that sounded dangerously like fuel for the image-haters, the 'Iconoclasts' (see pp. 442–56), and Evagrius's memory gained renewed condemnation. It has taken the work of modern scholars to recover much of his work from Armenian or Syriac manuscripts and reassess him as one of the greatest founding fathers of Christian spiritual writing. His immediate impact was profound, and his ideas quietly worked away among communities of monks able to transmit them if only by word of mouth from generation to generation.

Even when it was impolitic to admire, let alone name, Evagrius, his descriptions of progress in the spiritual life could not be and were not ignored, because they resonated in the experience of generations of monks to come. Like so many others, he started on a road of inner exploration: a pattern in which the ascetic faced struggles and torments, to arrive at a state of serenity (*apatheia*) and then a final state achieved by the true master of the spirit, for which Evagrius was not afraid to use the resonant word *gnosis*. In all this Evagrius pointed, like a physician prescribing a programme of exercise, to an essential frame for spiritual progress: a rhythm of each day in structured monastic life, the orderly recital from the Psalms of David followed by a short time of silent prayer (in his case, a hundred times a day), and meditation on the Bible, which provided the seedbed in which prayer could grow. He was a strong believer in the human ability to receive God's generosity and mercy and grow in grace: 'we come into [this] life possessing all the seeds of the virtues. And just as tears fall with the seeds, so with the sheaves there is joy.' In an echo of Origen's universalism, he repeatedly asserted that even those suffering in Hell kept those imperishable seeds of virtue. No wonder his Church decided that he was dangerous.[50]

The very fact of the deliberate competition between Egyptian and Syrian monks in striving for holiness demonstrates their consciousness of the wider world; they were far from detached from the life and concerns of the Church. Monks and monastic leaders now often complicated political struggles and exercised power in ways which seem far from the Saviour's admonitions to humility, love and forgiveness. First in the Eastern and then the Western Church, they proved to be key players in theological confrontations, beginning with the struggles which erupted in the wake of Constantine's new ecclesiastical alliance.

CONSTANTINE, ARIUS AND THE ONE GOD (306–25)

Very quickly the Emperor Constantine I learned to his cost that Christians were inclined to imperil the unity which their religion proclaimed. The first instance of this came as a result of the Great Persecution: renewed quarrels about how to heal the wounds to the Church's self-esteem. In Egypt, hardliners were so shocked at the Bishop of Alexandria's willingness to forgive the repentant lapsed that around 306 one of them, Bishop Melitius of Lycopolis, founded his own rival clerical hierarchy, which disrupted the Church in Alexandria for decades.[51] An even more serious split took place in the North African Church, where equally issues of forgiveness were combined with the problem of who had legitimate authority to forgive. A disputed episcopal election took place in Carthage, product of complicated arguments about who had done what in the crisis, combined with personality clashes. The Churches in Rome and elsewhere recognized Caecilian as bishop – one of the prices of recognition being his abandonment of the view of baptism which Cyprian had upheld independently in North Africa (see pp. 174–5). The opposition, furious at what they saw as this final proof of Caecilian's unworthiness, rallied behind the rival bishop, Donatus. The centuries-long Donatist schism in the North African Church had begun.[52]

Constantine's interventions in this intractable dispute have a remarkably personal quality, as the ruler of one of the most powerful empires in world history suddenly found himself confronted with subjects who appealed to a higher principle than his power. The dissidents were of course used to doing so, but the Emperor had not expected such ingratitude after he had ended the Great Persecution. If he knew nothing else about the Christian God, he knew that God was One. Oneness was in any case a convenient emphasis for the emperor who had destroyed Diocletian's Tetrarchy to replace it with his own single power, but there is more to the annoyance and apprehension apparent in Constantine's official correspondence than cynical political calculation. Anything which challenged the unity of the Church was likely to offend the supreme One God, and that might end his run of favour to the Emperor. Faced with petitions from the Donatists, in 313 Constantine made a decision of great significance for the future. Rather than make a judgement for the Christians with the help of the traditional imperial legal system, as the non-Christian Emperor Aurelian had once done before him (see p. 175), he would use the expertise of Church leaders, asking them to bring the matter 'to a fitting conclusion'.[53] So he adapted the North African Church's well-established practice of submitting disputes to councils of bishops, with the difference that now for the first time they were gathered from right across the Mediterranean.

Constantine's first summons of a council was to Rome, in 313. The Donatists ignored the result, since it went against them; so Constantine tried again the following year, this time summoning an even more widely recruited council to the city of Arles in what is now southern France. The bishops, travelling on imperial passes, even included three from the remote province of Britannia, one of the first indications of Christian activity in that island. Once more the council did not succeed in appeasing the Donatists, and in the course of much muddled negotiation with Donatist leaders, the Emperor was provoked into ordering troops to enforce their return to the mainstream Church. The first official persecution of Christians by Christians thus came within a year or two of the Church's first official recognition, and its results were as divisive as previous persecutions by non-Christian emperors. Most Donatists stayed out and stayed loyal to their own independent hierarchy, nursing new grudges against the North African Church, which remained in communion with the rest of the Christian Mediterranean Churches and which thus arrogated to itself the title of Catholic. The split was never healed, and it remained a source of weakness in North African Christianity for centuries until the Church there faded away (see p. 277).

The councils of Rome and Arles were thus not a promising precedent, but over the next century the use of councils to resolve Church disputes became firmly established as a mechanism of Church life. It represented a notable concession by the commander of Rome's army to the officers of God's army, and it meant that throughout the rest of the long history of the Catholic Church and beyond, the principle persisted that its bishops had a power and jurisdiction independent of the emperors. Rulers and Church leaders continued to work out this complicated and conflicted relationship. What was nevertheless now apparent was that the Catholic Church had become an imperial Church, its fortunes linked to those of emperors who commanded armies, to sustain or extend their power in the ways that armies do. That had implications for Christians who lived beyond the boundaries of the Roman Empire in territories where they or their ruler might regard the empire as an enemy. They might well also feel that about the imperial Church.

Constantine next sponsored a council in an attempt (again not blessed with short-term success) to solve a dispute sparked in the Church of Alexandria. This was yet another episode, and in many ways one of the most decisive, in the long debates about Christology (that is, discussion of the nature and significance of Jesus Christ), and the relationship between Father and Son. An austere and talented priest there called Arius was concerned to make his presentation of the Christian faith intellectually respectable to his contemporaries. To achieve this, he would have to wrestle with the old Platonic problem of the nature of God. If God is eternal and unknowable as Plato pictured him, Jesus Christ cannot be in the same sense God, since we know of him and of his deeds through the Gospels. This means, since the supreme God is one, that Christ must in some respect come after and be other than the Father, even if we accept that he was created or begotten before all worlds. Arius's opponents accused him of using as a slogan 'There was when he was not'.[54] Moreover, since the Father is indivisible, he cannot have created the Son out of himself; if the Son was created before all things, it would therefore logically follow that he was created out of nothing.

Here, then, was Arius's Christ: inferior or subordinate to the Father (as indeed Origen and other earlier writers had been inclined to say), and created by the Father out of nothing. In many respects, Arius was the heir of Origen and should be thought of as among theologians of Alexandrian outlook. It has been argued that Arius was not merely preoccupied by logic and that he had a warm concern to present Christians with a picture of a Saviour who was like them and participated in human struggles towards virtue; his Christ was part of the created order, not simply an image of God.[55] Arius certainly found an affectionate following among ordinary Alexandrians, whom he taught simple songs about his ideas. Whatever his motives, by around 318 he had provoked an infuriated opposition in Alexandria, including his bishop, Alexander. Alexander would not be the last bishop to turn the fact that one of his clergy was a rather more acute thinker than himself into a matter of ecclesiastical discipline. His feelings cannot have been eased by the fact that Arius seems to have been previously associated with the rigorist schism of Melitius of Lycopolis.[56]

Finding himself condemned by a synod (local council) of Egyptian bishops, Arius appealed to a significantly large number of friends further afield, not least the wily and politically minded Bishop of Nicomedia, a city which, until the founding of Constantinople, had been the Eastern imperial capital. The bishop was called Eusebius, not to be confused with his contemporary the historian who was Bishop of Caesarea – *Eusebios* ('pious') was then a common name among Christians. The Bishop of Nicomedia was in a powerful position to rally support for Arius, so the dispute began overtaking the entire Church in the eastern Mediterranean. Constantine was now consolidating his power in the East after eliminating his last imperial rival, Licinius, and he was determined to reunite the warring churchmen. His instinct was to try the tactics of a decade earlier as at Arles, summoning a council of bishops to solve the dispute, but his first plans in 324 to summon a council to the city of Ancyra were pre-empted by Arius's enemies, who seized the chance of the death of the Bishop of Antioch to gather there, both to choose one of their supporters as the new bishop for that key diocese and once more to condemn Arius's views. They also issued what they claimed was a definitive creed: a precedent for many more official statements which would make the same claim.[57]

Furious, Constantine now summoned a council at which nothing could go amiss.[58] He chose the city of Nicaea (now the pleasant lakeside town of Iznik, still contained in its grand imperial walls), conveniently near his headquarters at Nicomedia. He told the delegates that they would enjoy the climate and also, with a hint of menace, that he intended to 'be present as a spectator and participator in those things which will be done': the first time in Christian history that this had happened. Some think that he actually presided at the council. It was he, probably on the recommendation of his ecclesiastical adviser, a Spanish bishop, Hosius or Ossius of Cordova, who proposed a most significant clause in the creed which emerged as the council's agreed pronouncement: the statement that the Son was 'of one substance' (*homoousios*) with the Father. Faced with the awe-inspiring presence of the emperor of the known world, there could be little opposition to this: only two bishops are recorded as standing out against it. A large accumulation of other matters controversial in the life of the Church were discussed at this council. They included precedence among the leading bishops, a prohibition on moneylending among the clergy and over-hasty promotion of recent converts to the episcopate, the reconciliation of schismatics, even a ban on voluntary eunuchs being ordained as clergy. There was much for subsequent ecclesiastical lawyers to pore over and argue about. Thanks to the Emperor's forceful role as travel agent, the council had attracted unprecedented attendance and geographical coverage among its participants; the traditional but mystically inspired number of 318 delegates is probably not far wrong. Nicaea has always been regarded as one of the milestones in the history of the Church, and reckoned as the first council to be styled 'general' or 'oecumenical'.[59] As we will see, that status did not win ready consent, and twelve hundred years later there once more emerged Christian Churches which looked askance at the work and consequences of Nicaea (see p. 624).

COUNCILS AND DISSIDENTS FROM NICAEA TO CHALCEDON

Arius himself faded from public life and, although pardoned by Constantine, eventually died obscurely, reputedly as the result of an acute attack of dysentery in a latrine in Constantinople, which circumstance afforded his enemies some unchristian pleasure, and was eventually commemorated with exemplary lack of charity in the Orthodox liturgy.[60] He had tried to exercise the sort of independence of mind and as a teacher which had been possible in the Alexandria of Origen's day, but which was becoming dangerous in an age when bishops were seeking to monopolize control of instruction; nevertheless, he had raised questions which would not go away. There were problems with the word *homoousios* (the *Homoousion*). To begin with, and most troublingly, it was not a word used in the Bible. Second, it had a history, which we have already touched on when discussing the Monarchian disputes (see pp. 146–7). Arius had asserted to his bishop that it expressed the views of the hated Manichaeans about Christ's nature, and it is likely that his known detestation of the term was a major factor in dragging it into the new creed. Likewise for Eusebius of Nicomedia, it was a word tainted by the likes of Paul of Samosata, and he spared no effort to place like-minded bishops in positions of power over the next decades. The campaign to get rid of the *Homoousion* from Christian credal statements split the Church in the empire for another half-century and more.[61]

Constantine was initially furious with Eusebius of Nicomedia for his obstructiveness, but he may have come to realize that the *Homoousion* which he had effectively imposed at Nicaea was an obstacle to his aim of unity in the Church. He may also have been galvanized by accusations of misconduct, substantiated or trumped up by the Eusebians, against

Eustathius, Bishop of Antioch, a key figure among the voting majority at Nicaea.[62] So Eusebius and his sympathizers were remarkably successful in building up influence with the Emperor in his last years – the most remarkable feature having been the pardon granted to Arius – and they also gained support from a succession of emperors who came after him in the East when the imperial power was divided once more. At the height of their success they managed to harry and make fugitives out of most of their opponents in the Church's leadership. Chief among these was Athanasius, Bishop of Alexandria, who allied ruthlessness to an acute theological mind. Athanasius was fixedly determined to defend the doctrinal consensus on the nature of divinity achieved at Nicaea (although it is noticeable that even he was very cautious about using the term *homoousios* until around 350). He had an ear for a memorable phrase which would stick in the mind: the equality of Son and Father was 'like the sight of two eyes'.[63] At the heart of his thinking was a potent and paradoxical idea which he inherited from Irenaeus, one that has been much echoed since, particularly in the Orthodox world, and sums up the fascination of Christianity's idea of an incarnate God: the Son of God 'has made us sons of the Father, and deified men by becoming himself man'.[64] Athanasius was also a genius at categorizing in order to damn: he styled all those who disagreed with him 'Arians', and the term has stuck. In the end, many of his opponents in the next generation were prepared to wear the label with pride.[65]

In the course of the struggle, some Arians became ever more extreme, saying that the Son was actually *unlike* the Father (hence their being called 'Anomoeans' in Greek, or 'Dissimilarians' in Latin). In reaction, a middle party was concerned to unite as much of the Church as it could, and backed the formulation of creeds which said merely that the Son is 'like' the Father (from which comes the party's name 'Homoean', from the Greek word *homoios* for 'like'). Its greatest triumph was to win the backing of the Emperor Constantius II, who through his military victories reunited the whole empire, and who was therefore able in 359, after much negotiation and previous drafting, to dictate a Homoean formula to two councils representing East and West. This statement, an effort to settle the dispute once and for all, was named the Creed of Ariminum after the Western council which was steamrollered into accepting it. In the end it failed to stick, and survived only as a rallying statement of those who came to think of themselves as Arians.[66]

Maybe the Homoean formula of Ariminum would have succeeded in uniting the Church if Constantius had not unexpectedly died in his mid-forties in 361. He had been leading an army to defend himself against his cousin, the Caesar Julian, who was propelled by Constantius's death as sole emperor on to the imperial throne. Christianity was now thrown into confusion as Julian, whom Christians subsequently angrily labelled 'the Apostate', startlingly abandoned the Christian faith. He had been brought up a Christian under the tutelage of Eusebius of Nicomedia, but had come to be sickened by what he regarded as Christianity's absurd claims, and he discreetly developed a deep fascination for Neoplatonism and the worship of the sun; he may have been initiated into the worship of Mithras.[67] He was a subtle and reflective man, perhaps too much of a philosopher for his own good, and he employed the devastatingly effective strategy against Christianity of standing back from its disputes to let it fight its internal battles without a referee, a mark of how quickly the emperor had become a crucial player in the Church's disputes. There was widespread support for his reversing the humiliation of traditional cults, and some violence against Christians, which seems to have included the lynching of George, the recently arrived Bishop of Alexandria, although it is not clear whether partisans of the previous bishop, Athanasius, were in fact the main perpetrators of this outrage.[68]

Only Julian's early death on campaign on the empire's eastern borders in 363 restored the alliance of imperial throne and imperial Church. Not everyone said that the spear that killed him had been wielded by enemy forces, and there was indiscreet rejoicing in the city of Antioch, whose Christian majority had been a particular source of distress to him.[69] This was Athanasius's moment of opportunity, particularly since his rival George was now dead. The Homoeans were in disarray; the theological radicalism of the Anomoeans concentrated the minds of their opponents, while Julian's exposure of Christian insecurity made the more statesmanlike leaders of the Eastern Churches realize that they must find a new middle way. Among them was a group whom the Cypriot Bishop Epiphanius, an even more assiduous labeller of undesirables than Athanasius, christened the 'semi-Arians'. They shifted the language at issue, trying to avoid further argument by rallying the Church to a word which differed from *homoousios* by one *iota*: so they declared that the Son and the Father are not 'the same in essence' but *similar* in essence (*homoiousios*).[70]

Fortunately for Athanasius and his scheming, the semi-Arians included some of the most reflective and constructive theologians of their day. Chief among them was a trio who have come to be known as the Cappadocian Fathers. The monk-bishop Basil of Caesarea ('the Great') we have already met (see p. 209): he said sadly about the state of the controversy that it was like a naval battle fought at night in a storm, with crews and soldiers fighting among themselves, often in purely selfish power struggles, heedless of orders from above and fighting for mastery even while their ship foundered.[71] Associated with him were his brother, Gregory of Nyssa, and their lifelong friend, Gregory of Nazianzus. Athanasius and the remaining champions of the *homoousios* view now found them unexpected allies, and the Cappadocian Fathers provided a way of speaking about the Trinity which would create a balance between threeness and oneness.[72]

The problem for many Eastern leaders had been their uncertainty about the philosophical implications of the word *ousia* (essence, or substance). The eventual solution to their worries was to take a different Greek word, *hypostasis*, which previously had been used with little distinction in meaning from *ousia*, and assign to the two different words two different technical meanings.[73] As a result of this verbal pact, the Trinity consists of three equal *hypostaseis* in one *ousia*: three equal Persons (Father, Son, Holy Spirit) sharing one Essence or Substance (Trinity or Godhead). The arbitrariness of this decision, for all its practical convenience, will be realized by comparing the Greek word *hypostasis*, 'that which lies under', with its nearest equivalent in Latin, *substantia*. From now on, when used in reference to the new trinitarian formula, these synonyms in Greek and Latin were corralled in opposite theological categories, like families divided by a frontier in some political act of partition beyond their control. A more exact Greek equivalent than *hypostasis* for the Latin *persona* would have been *prosōpon*, since both words mean in their respective languages 'theatrical mask'; and in fact theologians in the tradition of Antioch did indeed use *prosōpon* in preference to *hypostasis*, further confusing the international theological tangle. It was not surprising that Western Latin-speaking Christians were inclined over the next few centuries to feel that the Greeks were too clever by half; but a great deal of this suspicion was the result of clumsy translation of intricate theological texts on both sides. We will meet other examples.

The disintegration of the Arian party in the East was completed by a political revolution in 378: the Eastern emperor, Valens, an upholder of the Homoean settlement of 359, was killed in a major Roman defeat on the frontier at Adrianople (to the west of Constantinople), and the Western emperor, Gratian, sent a retired Spanish general to sort out the resulting chaos as the Emperor Theodosius I. Theodosius had no sympathy for the Arians, reflecting the general Latin and Western impatience with Greek scruples about language; he convened a council at Constantinople in 381 at which Arian defeat was inevitable, and Nicaea's formulae would definitively be vindicated. In the same year, a Western 'council' at Aquileia in north-east Italy, actually little more than a rigged trial, condemned and deposed the remaining recalcitrant Western Homoean leaders.[74] This first Council of Constantinople saw the formulation of the fully developed creed which is now misleadingly known as the Nicene, and has come to be liturgically recited at the Eucharist in Churches of both Eastern and Western tradition. The main imperial Churches in the Latin West and Greek East, but also the Armenians and Syrians on the imperial frontier, all agreed on the outcome: Jesus Christ the Son of God is not created and is equal to the Father in the Trinity. At much the same time, the creed which came to be known as the Apostles' Creed was evolved in the West, embodying the same theology in shorter form.

The Council of Constantinople not only outlawed Arianism from the imperial Church, but also blocked two other directions in which the doctrine of the Trinity might have been led. The first came to be known (for reasons still obscure) after an Eastern Church leader called Macedonius, but the 'Macedonians' are more accurately described by their nickname of Pneumatomachi ('fighters against the Spirit'), because their development of subordinationist ideas took them in a different direction from Arius. While accepting the Nicene proposition of the equality of Father and Son, they denied the equal status of the Holy Spirit in the Godhead, seeing the Spirit as the pinnacle of the created order. This was not a proposition without precedent or contemporary respectability. Origen had been vague on the exact status of the Holy Spirit (see pp. 152–3), and even the most respected contemporary Latin theologian from the Western Church, Hilary of Poitiers, was notably tight-lipped on the subject, observing that the Bible never actually called this Spirit 'God' and following suit by his own silence.[75] The Council of Nicaea, preoccupied by Father and Son, had not extended its quarrels to the Spirit, and so it was not surprising that a large question remained for judgement in 381.

The second initiative to be crushed in 381 was ironically an effort to combat Arianism by a distinguished Lebanese theologian who became Bishop of Laodicea, Apollinaris, who was a great admirer of Athanasius, to the extent that some of his writings were subsequently attributed to the great Alexandrian, causing much confusion among the faithful.[76]

Apollinaris wanted to emphasize Christ's divinity and hence the truth of the *Homoousion*, Christ's consubstantiality with the Father, by saying that in Jesus Christ there had indeed been a human body and soul, but rather than possessing a human mind 'changeable and enslaved to filthy thoughts', the Divine Logos had simply assumed flesh. The danger of this anti-Arian enthusiasm was therefore that any real idea of Christ's humanity would be lost – an example of the difficulty of sustaining the balance between the two truths which most Christians passionately wished to affirm: that Jesus Christ was both divine and human.[77]

The Council of Constantinople thus radically narrowed the boundaries of acceptable belief in the Church, creating a single imperial Christianity backed up by military force. It was one half of a profound transformation in Christian status in the empire in the 380s. The declaration of Constantine and Licinius at Milan back in 313 had proclaimed general toleration. That had been a reaffirmation of traditional Roman practice, with the one great exception of Christianity, which had leapt from persecuted to favoured religion. Now 'Catholic' Christianity was given monopoly status, not just against its own Christian rivals but against all traditional religion: ancient priesthoods lost all privileges and temples were ordered to be closed even in the most remote districts. The process began with a decree in Constantinople in 380, but politics intervened to accelerate the new situation. In 392 a barbarian general of the Roman army named Arbogast backed a coup d'état in which the legitimate Western emperor, Valentinian II, was murdered and replaced with a modest and competent academic of traditionalist sympathies named Eugenius.

Moves to restore honour and equal treatment to the old religions had not got very far when, in 394, Theodosius intervened from the East and destroyed the usurping regime. His conclusion, naturally enough, was that his policy, already launched in the East, should be extended throughout the empire. The Olympic Games were no longer celebrated after 393. Further decrees after his death banned non-Christians from service in the army, imperial administration or at Court.[78] This was backed up by ruthless action: some of the most beautiful and famous sacred places of antiquity went up in flames, together with a host of lesser shrines. Monks were prominent agitators in the crowds which exulted in the destruction, and dire consequences are always likely to follow rampaging mobs. Perhaps the most repulsive case was the death in 415 of the Neoplatonist philosopher Hypatia, so well respected for her learning that she had overcome the normal prejudices of men to win pre-eminence in the Alexandrian schools. Christian mobs were persuaded that she was instrumental in preventing the Prefect of Egypt from ending a quarrel with Bishop Cyril of Alexandria, so she was dragged from her carriage, publicly humiliated, tortured and murdered. The perpetrators went unpunished. It was a permanent stain on the episcopate of Cyril and few Christian historians have had the heart to excuse it.[79] Nearly fifteen hundred years later, the breezy Anglican clerical novelist Charles Kingsley used Hypatia's story to annoy Roman Catholics, casting them in a none-too-veiled parallel in the role of the intolerant Alexandrian killers.

Although Arian Christianity was now harried to extinction in the imperial Church, significantly where imperial repression could not follow, across the northern frontier, it flourished – among the 'barbarian' tribes known as the Goths and their relatives the Vandals. Eusebius of Nicomedia had proved that he was not merely a politician with short-term goals when he had encouraged a mission to the Goths, led by one of their own called Ulfila. Ulfila translated the Bible into his native language, though he omitted to translate the Books of Kings on the grounds that their content was too warlike and might give the Goths ideas.[80] It was not a stratagem crowned with success: the Goths remained enthusiastic for war, as the Roman Empire was to find out to its cost, and they came to see their theological difference from the imperial Church as an expression of their racial and cultural difference. When they eventually occupied large sections of the former Western Empire, they kept their faith intact and unsullied by Nicene Christianity for a long time (see pp. 323–4). Arianism might well have formed the future of Western Christianity.

It will be immediately obvious, even from this brief summary of the Arian entanglement, how much imperial politics now affected Church affairs; but the emperors were deeply involved not so much because of their own religious convictions (though these might play a significant part), but because so many other people cared so much about the issues. Naturally clergy were passionately involved, and it is difficult to disentangle their righteous longing to assert the truth from their consciousness that the clerical immunities and privileges granted Christian clergy by Constantine and his successors were only available to those who had succeeded in convincing the emperors that they were the authentic voice of imperial Christianity. The play of forces was in more than one direction: emperors had no choice but to steer the Church to preserve their own rule, while few in the Church seem to have perceived the moral dangers involved when mobs took up theology and armies marched in the name of the Christian God. It may seem baffling now that such apparently rarefied disputes could have aroused the sort of passion now largely confined to the aftermath of a football match. Yet quite apart from the propensity of human beings to become irrationally tribal about the most obscure matters, we need to remember that ordinary Christians experienced their God through the Church's liturgy and in a devotional intensity which seized them in holy places. Once they had experienced the divine in such particular settings, having absorbed one set of explanations about what the divine was, anything from outside which disrupted those explanations threatened their access to divine power. That would provide ample reason for the stirring of rage and fear.

MIAPHYSITES AND NESTORIUS

The entanglement of politics, popular passion and theology is even more painfully apparent in a new set of disputes which go under the name of the Miaphysite or Monophysite controversy. In these, the focus of theological debate shifted away from the relationship of Son to Father, as in Arianism, or of Spirit to the Trinity as a whole, as in the views of the Pneumatomachi. Now the argument was about the way in which Christ combined both human and divine natures – that issue which the ultra-Athanasian Apollinaris had already raised, to his eventual misfortune. Behind the theological debate lay several hidden agendas which were as much to do with power politics as with theology. Once Jerusalem had been eliminated, the Church in the eastern Mediterranean had looked to two great cities, Antioch in Syria and Alexandria, the seats of major 'metropolitan' bishops or patriarchs with jurisdiction over other bishops. Now added to this was the new power of the Bishop of Constantinople, which the bishops in more long-standing Churches resented, particularly as Constantinople preened itself on the title 'the new Rome', and had made sure that this was officially affirmed at the council in 381, to general annoyance. Three times in seventy years after the Council of Constantinople, successive Bishops of Alexandria contributed to the downfall of successive Bishops of Constantinople.[81] Since the Bishopric of Jerusalem had also greatly benefited from its promotion under Constantine and his mother as a centre of pilgrimage (see pp. 193–5), the Bishops of Jerusalem had ambitions to match their guardianship of the greatest shrine of the Saviour. All these four cities would therefore be jostling for power at the same time as they fought to establish what the most adequate view of Christ's humanity and divinity might be. Alongside them was the Bishop of Rome, increasingly assertive of his charismatic position as successor of Peter (see pp. 290–94), yet also generally slightly marginal to the cut and thrust of Greek theological debate in the eastern Mediterranean.

The basic theological differences lay between Alexandrian and Antiochene viewpoints. Theologians do not always behave like successfully trained sports teams, but there were clear differences in approach between Christian scholars in the two cities; we have already noted the greater literalism of Antiochene comment on the text of the Bible (see p. 152). At issue once more was the question of Christology: that three-centuries-old puzzle of how a human life in Palestine could relate to a cosmic saviour, or more exactly be a single person who was both human and cosmic saviour. Now the Arian controversy had been settled by asserting that Christ was of one substance with the Father, what did that say about his human substance – as seen in his tears, his anger, his jokes, his breaking of ordinary bread and wine in an upper room? How far should one distinguish the human Christ from the divine Christ? Successive theologians associated with Antioch offered their own answer, first Diodore, Bishop of Tarsus, and then his student Theodore, a forceful and subtle theologian, and a native Antiochene, who became Bishop of Mopsuestia (now dwindled to a small Turkish village called Yacapinar).

Alexandrian theologians, following Origen's line, tended to stress the distinctness of the three persons of the Trinity, so they were reluctant to stress a further distinctness within the person of Christ. Diodore and Theodore, familiar with an Antiochene literal and historical reading of the Gospel lives of Jesus, were ready to emphasize the real humanity of Christ; they also tended to stress the oneness of the whole trinitarian Godhead, so they were much more prepared to talk of two natures in Christ, truly human and truly divine, in a way which Alexandrians were inclined to think blasphemous. As an image to explain these different positions, the Alexandrian view of Christ's humanity and divinity contained in a single Person has been likened (although not by Alexandrians themselves) to a vessel which contains wine and water, perfectly and inextricably mixed, in contrast to the view of Theodore and his associates, where the vessel of Christ's person could be said to contain two natures as it might oil and water, mingling but not mixing.

Diodore and Theodore were particularly galvanized to defend their point of view by their horror at Apollinaris's assertion that Christ was indwelled by the Logos, which replaced a human mind in him. They determinedly affirmed Christ's real human nature alongside his divinity. For Theodore, it was vital to remember that Christ was the Second Adam, who had effected human redemption by offering himself as a true human being – that emphasis lay behind the frenetically self-destructive attitudes of contemporary Syrian monks towards their bodies, determined to get as close as was possible to the self-denial of the human Jesus. God had become a particular man, not humanity in general, Theodore insisted: 'to say that God indwells everything has been agreed to be the height of absurdity, and to circumscribe his essence is out of the question. So it would be naïve in the extreme to say that the indwelling [of God in Jesus] was a matter of essence.' It was therefore vital to keep the distinction between the man Jesus, despite his 'outstanding inclination to the good', and the eternal Word, which partook of the essence of the Godhead.[82]

The real flashpoint came in 428, when an energetic and tactless priest called Nestorius was chosen as Bishop of Constantinople. Nestorius was a devoted admirer of Theodore, having been his pupil in Antioch. His promotion did not please Bishop Cyril, successor to Athanasius in a line of resourceful and power-conscious politician-bishops of Alexandria, a prelate whom we have already met in connection with the lynching of the philosopher Hypatia (see pp. 220–21). Cyril, though unlikely to have been a pleasant man to know, was more than simply an unscrupulous party boss.[83] When he contemplated his Saviour Jesus, he could see only God, mercifully offering his presence to sinful humanity, especially every time the Church offered Christ's flesh and blood in the bread and wine of the Eucharist; why otherwise had Cyril's much-revered predecessor Athanasius fought so hard for an equality of Persons in the Trinity? Encouraged by a theological work which he thought was by Athanasius but (disastrously) was actually by Apollinaris of Laodicea, Cyril could see no reason to make a distinction between two words which for him both referred to the 'person' and 'nature' of Jesus Christ: these were the term used by the Cappadocian Fathers for 'person', *hypostasis*, and a word for 'nature', *physis*.[84] By contrast, and offensively to Cyril's ears, Theodore and those who thought like him spoke of two *physeis* in Jesus Christ, and made a distinction between those two natures and the one person, the theatrical mask, *prosōpon*.[85]

The Bishop of Alexandria was particularly outraged when Nestorius aggressively promoted his Antiochene views by attacking a widely popular title of honour for the Virgin Mary: *Theotokos*, or Bearer of God. Devotion to Mary was now becoming prominent throughout the Roman Empire: enthusiasts for the Nicene settlement of doctrine encouraged it, as a way of safeguarding Christ's divinity against Arianism, since it emphasized the unique favour granted his earthly mother. It was true that such Marian enthusiasm had developed in the Syrian Church precociously quickly (see pp. 182–3), but Nestorius's concern to distinguish the two natures of Christ outweighed this in his desire to be clear about what her role should be and how it should be described. Provoked in his new home of Constantinople by hearing a devotional sermon on Mary which he regarded as fatuous, he snappily responded that talk of *Theotokos* was nonsense: 'The Word of God is the creator of time, he is not created within time'. He was in effect saying that the title could only be used if one simultaneously balanced it by calling Mary *Anthrōpotokos*, Bearer of a Human, and he insinuated that those who overpraised Mary were reviving the worship of a mother-goddess.[86] Even many educated in the Antiochene tradition blanched at his reckless precision. Various victims of Nestorius's sharp tongue and reforming zeal rallied to the cause, and with grim satisfaction Cyril exploited a groundswell of devout indignation against his rival bishop.[87]

The ensuing row once more plunged the entire Eastern Church into a bewildering welter of intrigue and complication which drew in the Eastern emperor, in sheer self-defence, to stop his empire being ripped apart. After a council at Ephesus in 431 and negotiations over the next two years, Theodosius II forced a compromise on the opposing sides. It vindicated the title *Theotokos*, ruined Nestorius's career for good and left 'Nestorian' theology permanently condemned, but it also left many supporters of Cyril's theology outraged that their own theology had not been fully vindicated with the full triumphalism that they would have wished. The death of Cyril in 444 did nothing to diminish their militancy. Their discontent was given practical expression in further political manoeuvres led by Cyril's aggressive admirer and successor, Bishop Dioscorus, which culminated in a second Council of Ephesus (449), humiliating all opponents of Alexandrian claims and outlawing all talk of two natures in Christ.

Such was the Alexandrians' determination to assert their position that this council ignored a statement of the Western view on the natures of Christ presented by delegates from Leo, the Bishop of Rome (the 'Tome' of Leo). This infuriated and permanently alienated a see which had been

Alexandria's long-term ally against other Eastern bishoprics; yet the fault was not entirely on the Alexandrians' side. The Pope had not quite understood Nestorius's position aright, and it was easy for the hypersensitive to see in the 'Tome' an affirmation that there were two agents in Christ. Leo and indeed the later Roman Church always maintained the absolute authority of his statement, a stance which was now becoming a habit in Rome, but the fact that Leo himself later wrote a revised statement on the same subject for an Eastern audience probably indicates that he privately recognized its shortcomings. In the words of one of the latest studies of his thought, the 'Tome' 'contributed to bitter divisions which continued for sixteen centuries'.[88]

Once more a political revolution intervened and proved the downfall of the Alexandrian party. A palace coup on the death of Theodosius in 450 brought to power his formidable sister, Pulcheria, a bitter enemy of the 'one-nature' theologians who had found political backing in Constantinople. She selected Marcian as a biddable husband for herself to occupy the imperial throne (biddable enough to respect her previous vows of chastity), and in 451 the new regime with Marcian as emperor called a council to a city where the imperial troops could keep an eye on what was going on: Chalcedon, near Constantinople. The main concern at Chalcedon was to persuade as many people as possible to accept a middle-of-the-road settlement. The council accepted as orthodoxy the 'Tome' presented to Ephesus by Pope Leo's envoys two years before, and it constructed a carefully balanced definition of how to view the mystery of Christ: 'the same perfect in divinity and perfect in humanity, the same truly God and truly man, of a rational soul and a body; consubstantial with the Father as regards his divinity, and the same consubstantial with us as regards his humanity . . .' This still remains the standard measure for discussion of the person of Christ, in Churches otherwise as diverse as Greek, Romanian and Slavic Orthodox, Roman Catholics, Anglicans and mainstream Protestants. So, like Nicaea in 325, 451 remains an important moment in the consolidation of Christian doctrine into a single package for much of the Church.[89]

But by no means all. The Chalcedonian agreement centred on a formula of compromise. Although it talked of the Union of Two Natures, and took care to give explicit mention of *Theotokos*, it largely followed Nestorius's viewpoint about 'two natures', 'the distinction of natures being in no way abolished because of the union'.[90] Meanwhile, to satisfy his enemies, the unhappy former Bishop of Constantinople was condemned once more: an ecclesiastical stitch-up, dictated by imperial power. Nestorius was already completely isolated from public affairs, in a remote Egyptian location (which the Egyptian government still uses for a high-security prison); he endured his humiliation at the hands of his enemies with stoicism. He is reputed to have died the day before a message arrived inviting him to participate in the Council of Chalcedon; regardless of this impulse to reconciliation, the Emperor then ordered Nestorius's writings burned, and children bearing his name were rebaptized and renamed. His last and most extensive work, written in prison, a dignified defence of all that he had done, was only rediscovered in a manuscript in 1889, in the library of the East Syrian Patriarch, whose Church's separate status originated in its unhappiness with the results of Chalcedon.[91]

The Chalcedonian Definition certainly proved to have staying power, unlike the Homoean compromise solution to the Arian dispute at Ariminum in 359, but it still won much less acceptance than the credal formula of Constantinople from 381. In the manner of many politically inspired middle-of-the-road settlements, it left bitter discontents on either side in the Eastern Churches. On the one hand were those who adhered to a more robust affirmation of two natures in Christ and who felt that Nestorius had been treated with outrageous injustice. These protestors were labelled Nestorians by their opponents, and the Churches which they eventually formed have habitually been so styled by outsiders ever since. It would be truer to their origins, and more considerate to their self-esteem, to call them Theodoreans, since Theodore of Mopsuestia was the prime source of their theological stance and Nestorius hardly figured in their minds as a founding father. In view of their insistence on two (*dyo*) natures in Christ, they could with justice be called 'Dyophysites', and we will trace their subsequent history primarily as 'the Church of the East' using this label.

By contrast, on the other side the history of the winners has likewise given those who treasure the memory of Cyril and his campaign against Nestorius a label which they still resent: 'Monophysites' (*monos* and *physis* = single nature). This latter group of Churches has always been insistent on claiming that title prized among Eastern Churches: 'Orthodox'. In an age where both Churches of the Greek, Romanian and Slavic Orthodox traditions and the various Catholic and Protestant heirs of the Western Latin Church have increasingly sought to end ancient bitterness, these sensitivities have been respected, and the label 'Monophysite' has widely been replaced by 'Miaphysite'. That derives from a phrase for 'one nature' (*mia physis*) which Bishop Cyril habitually and undeniably

used, in writings which retained a wide esteem in both Greek East and
Latin West. I will respect that change of usage, although Miaphysites
themselves might brush it aside as an unnecessary vindication of their
obvious claim to Orthodoxy.[92] Nevertheless, to use the 'Miaphysite'
label is to point to the fact that Cyril was not crudely talking about 'one
nature' in Christ; he would have said that Christ's nature might be
single, but it was also composite. The difference between two Greek
words for 'one' may seem small, but in a millennium and a half of
brooding on ancient insults, it can mean a great deal. In the next chapters, we will follow the adventures of those Churches whose rejection
of the Chalcedonian formula from either point of view led them into
extraordinary histories of Christian mission, endurance and suffering.
There is a common assumption among those Christians who are heirs
of either Eastern or Western European theology that Chalcedon settled
everything, at least for a thousand years. The stories which we are about
to follow show how mistaken this is.

PART III

Vanishing Futures:
East and South
(451–1500)

7

Defying Chalcedon: Asia and Africa
(451–622)

MIAPHYSITE CHRISTIANITY AND
ITS MISSIONS

Modern globalization has produced a dialogue between world religious faiths which in the last century or so has become something of an international industry. But this is a rediscovery for Christians and not a novelty: there were once Christianities which had little choice but to talk to believers in other world religions, because they were surrounded on all sides by them and often at their mercy. These Christians neverthe-less travelled thousands of miles east of Jerusalem and brought a Chris-tian message at least as far as the China Sea and the Indian Ocean. One of those encounters produced a tale which went on to unite Christians everywhere in enjoyment of it for something like a millennium, though now it has almost been forgotten in the form which those Christians knew. It is nothing less than the story of Gautama Buddha, turned into a Christian novel about a hermit and a young prince, Barlaam and Josaphat. Barlaam converts the prince to the true faith, but that true faith is no longer Buddha's revelation, but Christianity – while the Buddha has become a Christian hermit in the desert of Sinai, though his prince is still from a royal house of India.[1]

How can this extraordinary cultural chameleon have been conceived? What seems to have happened is that a version of the Sanskrit original life of Buddha, probably translated into Arabic in Baghdad, fell into the hands of a Georgian monk some time in the ninth century. He was so charmed by the story that he rewrote it in Georgian in Christian form as *Balavariani*, and fellow monks who spoke different languages also loved it and moved it into their own tongues. When it made its way into Greek, it took on a spurious authorship and plenty of pious quotations from the safely Orthodox giant of theology and philosophy John of

Damascus to lend it respectability and increase its selling power, and now it was *The Life of Barlaam and Joasaph*. The two heroes became saints, with their own feast days, hymns and anthems. Small bony fragments of St Josaphat acquired in the East by Venetian merchants can be seen in a church in Antwerp.

The tale's travels had by no means ended. It spread from the Byzantine Empire through western Europe and south via Egypt: one could pick up copies of it in Latin, Hebrew, Old Norse, Old Russian, Ethiopic, medieval Catalan, Portuguese, Icelandic, Italian, French and English. The pioneering English printer William Caxton showed his usual commercial good sense when, in 1483, he chose to print it in his new translation of the great collection of saints' lives known as *The Golden Legend*, and Shakespeare used an episode from it in *The Merchant of Venice*. Perhaps we can appreciate just how far the Eastern Christian legacy eventually reached if we join the cultured English Roundhead military commander Thomas Fairfax, third Lord Fairfax of Cameron, in his Yorkshire study in the 1650s. Smarting from the end of his military career after a principled quarrel with Oliver Cromwell, Fairfax pulled his Latin or Greek Barlaam from his bookshelves and whiled away his retirement with his own English translation, some 204 folio pages long. Puritan (and Chalcedonian) Yorkshire was a long way from the home of the Buddha, and Fairfax would have had no idea of his debt to that long-dead Georgian monk.[2]

All this was thanks to the large number of Eastern Christians who hated the decisions of the Council of Chalcedon and decided to ignore or oppose them. It took a long time for those who felt like this to make a formal break with the Church authorities who had accepted the council's pronouncements. Of the two opposite points of view excluded by Chalcedon, Miaphysitism and Dyophysite 'Nestorianism', it was the Miaphysites who most worried the emperors in Constantinople. The Miaphysites' power base, Alexandria, was one of the most important cities in the Eastern Empire, essential to the grain supply which kept the population of Constantinople in compliant mood, and Miaphysites continued to have support in the capital itself. Already at the Council of Chalcedon, the Egyptian bishops present insisted that if they signed its Definition, they faced death back home, and it soon became clear that they were not exaggerating. Alexandria was, after all, the city which had lynched Hypatia forty years before.

The council had infuriated opinion in Alexandria by deposing its bishop, Dioscorus, a punishment for his prominence in the group who had disruptively proclaimed 'one-nature' theology as orthodoxy at the previous Council of Ephesus in 449 (see pp. 225–6). The Emperor Marcian and his wife, Pulcheria, were determined to find a pliable successor for Dioscorus. They brought pressure to bear on the Alexandrian clergy, which led to the election of one of Dioscorus's assistant clergy, Proterius, but the new bishop found his position steadily eroded. On Marcian's death in 457, he was left defenceless. A mob who regarded him as a traitor to Dioscorus pursued him into the baptistery of a city church, butchered him and six of his clergy, and paraded the bleeding corpses round the city: all in the name of the *mia physis* of Jesus Christ.[3] The emperor's authority in Egypt never fully recovered from this appalling incident: increasingly a majority in the Egyptian Church as well as other strongholds of Miaphysitism denounced Chalcedonian Christians as 'Dyophysites' and sneered at them as 'the emperor's people' – Melchites.[4] The word 'Melchite' has had a complicated later history, and now various Churches of Orthodox tradition in communion with the pope in Rome are happy to use it to label themselves, but it thus started life as a term of abuse as poisonous as 'collaborator' in the aftermath of Nazi occupation in the Europe of the 1940s.

From now on Egyptian Christianity increasingly worshipped God in the native language of Egypt, Coptic. The Church had long been ready to use various Coptic dialects, liberally seeded with loanwords from Greek, and already in the third century Coptic was being written in a version of Greek script, developed specifically for translating the Christian scriptures. The prestige of Antony, Pachomius and the ascetic movement sealed the respectability of Coptic in Christian life and worship, and it developed a considerable literature both of translated and original devotional texts, both mainstream Christian and unorthodox.[5] Now Coptic language and distinctive culture were becoming badges of difference from the Greek Christianity of the Church in Constantinople. There was a tendency all round the eastern Mediterranean for 'Melchites' to be concentrated in urban, affluent outposts of Greek society, while anti-Chalcedonian views on either side increasingly found strength in other communities.

The leaders of the Miaphysite cause across the empire still loudly proclaimed their loyalty to the imperial throne, and there is no reason to doubt that most were sincere. Their loyalty was certainly worth trying to secure. For two centuries and more a succession of emperors in Constantinople desperately tried to devise ever more intricate theological formulae which would reconcile the Miaphysites to the imperial Church, preferably but not necessarily preserving the essence of the Chalcedonian settlement. In doing so, they constantly imperilled their relations with the Western Latin Church. It was only natural that the Eastern emperors had shifted their political priorities away from the western half of the old empire as that disintegrated. In 410 had come the sack of Rome itself by barbarian armies: a deep humiliation for Romans proud of their history, even if the city had long ceased to be the capital for the emperors. In 451 there had still been an emperor in the West – more or less – but in 476 the barbarian rulers who were taking over so much of the former western territories of Rome allowed the last emperor to reign for no more than a few months of his teenage years before consigning to oblivion both the boy and the increasingly wraith-like imperial succession in the West.

Now that the Eastern Empire stood alone, it often paid little attention to the opinions or outraged representations of the leading bishop in the surviving Western Church, the pope in Rome. A series of popes, increasingly assertive in the Church (see pp. 322–9), took it as axiomatic that their sainted predecessor Leo had said the last word on the subject of the natures in Jesus Christ in his 'Tome', delivered to the unreceptive Miaphysite bishops at Ephesus in 449 (see pp. 225–6). Rome measured every turn of policy in Constantinople by how much it seemed to honour the 'Tome', and popes could not appreciate the multitude of political and military considerations preoccupying Eastern emperors when they contemplated questions of Christology. As a result, from 482 until 519, Rome and Constantinople were in formal schism because the Byzantine Emperor Zeno and his bishop, Acacius, in the capital backed a formula of reunion (*Henotikon*) with the Miaphysites: it contained fresh condemnations of Nestorius (an easy target), praised key documents from Cyril's attack on him, but in a manner deeply offensive to Rome remained silent on the 'Tome of Leo', which the Miaphysite party at Ephesus had treated with such contempt.[6] It took a change of emperor in 518 to put an end to the *Henotikon* and the 'Acacian schism'. Justin I was an illiterate Latin-speaking soldier from a Western background who had an instinctive respect for the Bishop of Rome and he abruptly speeded up negotiations for reconciliation which had been languishing for years.[7]

The emperors' preoccupation with the Miaphysites is all the more understandable since, not just in Egypt but throughout the Eastern Empire, there continued to be Miaphysites hostile to the work of the Council of Chalcedon. Western Syria and Asia Minor were full of them.

The Emperor Zeno, himself a native of south-west Asia Minor, tried posthumously to recruit the celebrated pillar-dweller Simeon Stylites (see pp. 207–8) as a champion of the Chalcedonian deal, and he rapidly and vigorously promoted Simeon's cult. Within a couple of decades of the hermit's death, Zeno was pouring money and labour into the building of what was then the largest church in the Middle East to shelter the Stylite's pillar at its heart.[8] The church's magnificent surviving ruins still testify to Zeno's anxiety to bring back Syrian Miaphysites into the fold of Chalcedon, but although Simeon's cult flourished in the region, the Chalcedonian cause did not. The most impressive and articulate theologian of the early sixth century was Severus, who came from what is now south-western Turkey. He was so firm in his Miaphysite views that at first he rejected the *Henotikon* as an unsatisfactory compromise, until the prospect of the Bishopric of Antioch changed his mind. His hold on that powerful see ended with the theological revolution of 518, but from his exile among friends in the safety of Egypt, Severus remained a powerful voice as the factions struggled for dominance at the imperial Court. In 527 there came to the throne one of the most significant emperors in the history of Byzantium: Justinian, nephew and adopted son of Justin, who was destined to do so much to transform the former Eastern Roman Empire (see pp. 429–31). He was torn between his wish to preserve the fragile agreement of 519 with Rome and his continuing awareness of Miaphysite partisanship in the East – not least from his energetic and unconventional wife, Theodora, who became an active sympathizer with the Miaphysite cause, very ready to express her own opinions and act on them.

Some extraordinary double messages began emerging from the imperial Court.[9] Justinian sought repeatedly to make concessions to the Miaphysites, but also fitfully treated them as dangerous rebels, and remained open to advice or active intervention from the pope. In 535 and 536 there were starkly contrasting choices to fill key bishoprics: following Theodora's intervention in the episcopal election in Alexandria, an avowed Miaphysite called Theodosius became bishop there. Yet in Constantinople, Bishop Anthimus, a Miaphysite sympathizer, was forced out after Pope Agapetus, who happened to have travelled east on a diplomatic mission to the Emperor, directly lobbied Justinian for his removal. The exiled Bishop Severus was faced with condemnation by a synod of pro-Chalcedonian bishops; against a background of increasing repression and even executions of Miaphysite sympathizers, he made a decision with great significance for the future. He gave his blessing to discreet consecrations of bishops who would be reliable Miaphysites: a complete parallel succession to their rivals backed by the Emperor. When Theodosius was likewise swiftly deprived of the see of Alexandria in 536, the Empress secretly made sure that he had a safe refuge in Constantinople, and, like Severus, Bishop Theodosius began to build up a Miaphysite alternative to the Chalcedonian Church.

The Empress's protégés even began spreading Miaphysite Christianity beyond the formal boundaries of the empire. To the south of Egypt, the King of Nobatia (a northern kingdom of Nubia) was converted in the 540s, turning what had previously been a small cult into a Court religion. Christianity eventually spread eastwards through much of what is now Sudan, halfway to the Niger as far as Darfur, and remnants of it survived in one Nubian kingdom into the eighteenth century. Archaeology has revealed the ruins of superb churches, some of which have preserved extensive remains of wall paintings in a tradition created over several centuries depicting biblical scenes, saints or leading bishops.[10] Like the Copts, Nubian Christians achieved a blend of Greek culture with their own, using both Greek and their vernacular in their worship. Fragments of manuscripts reveal that they shared the common devotion of eastern Mediterranean Christianity to St George, a shadowy figure who may have died in persecutions of the late fourth century, but who gained huge popularity as a Christian martyr who was also a soldier.[11] In an age when the frontiers of the various great powers were increasingly unstable and life was insecure and frightening, the thought of a military protector in Heaven was a particular comfort.

A further triumph for the Miaphysites came on the eastern border of the empire in Syria, where an Arab people known as the Ghassānids had migrated from the south of the Arabian peninsula and set up a formidable independent kingdom. This stretched all the way from southern Syria along the borders of the Holy Land to the Gulf of Aqaba (Eilat) at the north-eastern end of the Red Sea, and its military strength made it a crucial buffer state for Byzantium against the Sassanians, though the relationship was troubled and often fractured, because the Ghassānids, on their initial conversion to Christianity, set their faces firmly against the decrees of Chalcedon.[12] When the Ghassānid ruler Arethas demanded bishops to organize a Church for his people, once more the Empress Theodora took an active but clandestine role in supplying clergy ordained by Bishop Theodosius to minister to them.

One of these clergy was a charismatic eastern Syrian called Jacob Baradeus, who had already achieved spectacular missionary success in remote parts of Asia Minor, and whose Latinized second name comes from a no doubt originally jocular reference to his incessant travelling: it means 'the man who has a horse-cloth'.[13] While the Empress was alive, she contained the threat of Miaphysite confrontation with the imperial authorities. After her death, in 548, despite Justinian's continuing efforts to find a formula to heal the splits in the Church, Miaphysite defiance of the Court became systematic: Jacob and other Miaphysites sought to create an alternative episcopal hierarchy both among the Ghassānids and elsewhere.[14] Travelling often in disguise, Jacob undertook a prodigious programme of ordinations and consecrations of bishops which extended across the imperial border into Ghassānid territory and further into the Sassanian Empire. He created a Syrian Miaphysite Church which is often called Jacobite in acknowledgement of his founding energy, but which also insists on Orthodoxy in its official title, the Syriac Orthodox Church.[15] Its eucharistic liturgy is named after St James of Jerusalem, brother of the Lord, embodying the proud claim of the Church to reach back to the Semitic fountainhead of Christianity. At the heart of the liturgy, the prayer of consecration celebrates the first three General Councils of the Church, Nicaea, Constantinople and Ephesus, and name-checks an impressive array of orthodox Fathers of the Church before the disruption of Chalcedon, with special mention of the 'exalted and firm tower', Cyril of Alexandria.

This anti-Chalcedonian version of Orthodoxy came to dominate a centre of monastic life in the mountainous region of Tūr 'Abdīn, in what is now south-east Turkey. Tūr 'Abdīn contained (and, against formidable odds, still contains) monasteries of comparable importance to those which later emerged for Greek Orthodoxy on Mount Athos (see p. 470). Monastic life flourished generally among both Syrian and Arab Christians; their monks built settlements which were as much fortresses as monasteries, complete with towers, as elaborate and impressive structures as those being built at the same time inside the Byzantine Empire. The commentator most familiar with the Ghassānids has seen their Christianity as a 'religion of monks', yet with the coming of Islam, this chapter of Christian monasticism and its buildings has been almost entirely lost. Archaeology may still recover a great deal.[16]

The warrior traditions of the Ghassānids attracted them to yet another soldier-martyr like George: his name was Sergius and he had been killed in Syria during Diocletian's Great Persecution. They developed a fierce devotion to him and he became patron saint among the Arabs. His cult spread through the Byzantine Empire as well, encouraged by patronage from Justinian, who was only too ready to win esteem among his Eastern subjects by judicious investment in church-building in honour of this popular martyr. Sergius came habitually to be associated in partnership and iconography with his fellow soldier-martyr Bacchus, in a union so close as to be described as that of 'lovers', which has bequeathed an interesting image of same-sex love to Eastern Christianity, even though it has rarely felt able fully to explore the possible implications.[17] Even a Zoroastrian monarch, the brutal Sassanian Shah Khusrau II (reigned 590–628), realized the strategic advantage of showing respect to St Sergius when he began expanding his conquests westwards into Byzantine Christian territories. Khusrau is reported as having twice made offerings at Sergius's shrine at the Ghassānid city of Sergiopolis (Resafa in Syria), first after winning back his throne from a rival with Byzantine military help in 591 and then in thanksgiving for his Byzantine wife's successful childbirth; he also rebuilt the shrine after it had been burned down by Christians opposed to the Miaphysites.[18]

Across the imperial border to the north, there was also suspicion of the work of the Council of Chalcedon in the various kingdoms of Georgia and Armenia, none of which had been represented in the council's discussions. One monarchy among those which ruled Georgia, K'art'li, which the Romans called Georgian Iberia, officially converted to Christianity not long after the Armenians in the early fourth century. A century later, a member of that same royal house of K'art'li proved to be a major force in prompting hostility to Chalcedon among the Georgians. In his teenage years, the prince was sent to Constantinople as an official hostage for K'art'li's alliance with the Roman Empire, and he was brought up at the imperial Court in the turbulent years which witnessed the abrupt twists and turns in theological supremacy around the Council of Ephesus in 431 (see pp. 225–6). He took the name Peter when he turned to the monastic life in Palestine, where, despite extensive travels around the Middle East, he spent most of his life. He briefly became a bishop in Maiuma in what is now the Gaza Strip, as well as founding the first Georgian monastery in the city of Jerusalem. A great admirer of Cyril of Alexandria, Peter was infuriated when Juvenal, Bishop of Jerusalem, abandoned his support for Alexandrian theology (Juvenal literally crossed the floor from one party to another at the Council of Chalcedon); Peter's reputation as an ascetic lent authority to his bitter denunciations of Chalcedon.[19] His uncompromising Miaphysite views have been problematic for the later Georgian Church to square with its devotion to Peter the Iberian as one of the premier national saints – for the Georgians eventually agreed to recognize the Chalcedonian Definition, although it took until the beginning of the seventh century, long after Peter's time.[20]

By contrast, the Armenians specifically declared themselves against Chalcedon in the sixth century and have never been reconciled to its formulae since. They saw its language as expressing unacceptable novelties, partly because, like the Georgians, their normal word for 'nature' was closely related to the Iranian root-word for 'foundation', 'root' or 'origin' – so any description of Christ as having two natures, even the qualified definition of Chalcedon, sounded like blasphemous nonsense to them. They took care to construct their own Armenian theological vocabulary on the basis of Greek writings from an impeccable succession of theologians from the Cappadocian Fathers to Cyril of Alexandria – all dating before the taint of Chalcedon.[21] In fact, the Armenian Church was so concerned to build up an arsenal of Christian literature to guarantee its own view of orthodoxy that it undertook a sustained programme of translating classic Greek and Syriac theological manuscripts. This has proved an immense service to modern students of the ancient Church, because thanks to accidental destruction or deliberate censorship of the originals, often these Armenian translations are the only texts surviving.[22]

Armenian liturgy came to incorporate a distinctive feature which was a permanent reminder of the conflicts of the fifth and sixth centuries. Characteristic of Eastern Christian worship generally, used in every service, is the chanting of a plea for mercy, 'Holy God, Holy and Strong, Holy and Immortal, have mercy upon us' – the *Trisagion* ('Thrice-Holy').[23] There is no common consent among the wide spectrum of Christians who use this chant as to whether it is addressed to the whole Trinity of the Godhead, as its threefold shape might suggest, or to Christ alone. Peter the Fuller, a late-fifth-century Miaphysite monk from Constantinople, made the latter assumption. That led him to express his theology in liturgical form by adding to the *Trisagion* the phrase 'crucified for us' – so the Second Person of the triune God is liturgically acclaimed as having been crucified.

This central statement of a theological movement known as 'Theopaschism' was controversial even among Miaphysites, causing major divisions in their ranks, although it is pleasing to note that around the time of Peter the Fuller the Miaphysite poet Isaac of Antioch wrote eloquently and at epic length celebrating a parrot who had learned to sing the *Trisagion* with Peter's additional phrase.[24] The imperial Church in Constantinople eventually rejected the addition, but the Armenians defiantly adopted it into their liturgical practice; so every congregation in the Armenian Church continues in this solemn prayer to affirm the intimacy of relationship of divine and human in Christ. As the Church's season of liturgical year moves round, they replace the phrase with others commemorating Christ's human birth and resurrection, still addressing these commemorations to 'Holy God'. With Peter the Fuller's phrase in mind, devotion, literature and art in both Armenia and Georgia assigned a special significance to the Cross. In Armenia, one of the most familiar monuments of sculpture is a quadrilateral stone bearing carvings of the Cross in forms of extreme elaboration and variety in treatment.[25]

ETHIOPIA: THE CHRISTIANITY OF 'UNION'

The most remarkable and exotic triumph of the Miaphysite cause around the Byzantine Empire was far to the south even beyond Nubia, in Ethiopia. The origins of Christianity in this remote and mountainous area are not clear, beyond a mysterious self-contained story in the Book of Acts of an encounter in Judaea between Philip, one of the first Christian leaders in Jerusalem, and a eunuch servant of the 'Queen of Ethiopia', who was fascinated to hear that Jewish prophecy had been fulfilled in the coming of Christ.[26] The first historical accounts are from the fourth century, and make it clear that Christian approaches came not southwards from Egypt but from the east across the Red Sea, via Ethiopia's long-standing trade contacts with Arabia and ultimately Syria. It was a Syrian merchant, Frumentius, who is credited with converting Ezana, the Negus (king or emperor) of the powerful northern Ethiopian state of Aksum. Certainly Ezana's coins witness to a conversion no less dramatic and personal than Constantine's: they change motifs from traditional symbols of a crescent and two stars to a cross. Ezana has left a surviving inscription in Greek announcing his renunciation of his status as son of the Ethiopian war god, putting himself instead under the care of the Trinity.

An energetic monarch determined to secure immortal memory in this world as in the next, Ezana was responsible for beginning a tradition of monumental religious sculpture in the city of Aksum which is breathtaking, though now difficult to interpret: scores of monolithic stelae

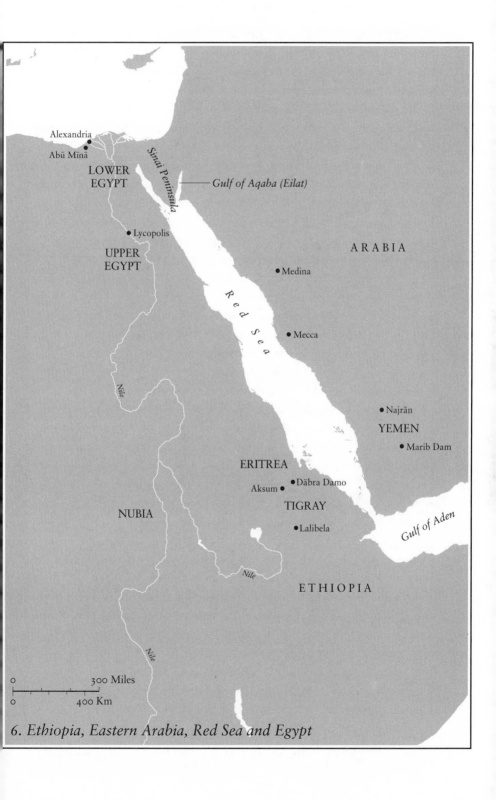

Alexandria
Abū Mīnā

LOWER
EGYPT

Sinai Peninsula

————— *Gulf of Aqaba (Eilat)*

Lycopolis

UPPER
EGYPT

A R A B I A

Medina

Red Sea

Mecca

Nile

Najrān

YEMEN

Marib Dam

ERITREA

Däbra Damo

Aksum

TIGRAY

Gulf of Aden

NUBIA

Lalibela

Nile

E T H I O P I A

0   300 Miles
0   400 Km

6. Ethiopia, Eastern Arabia, Red Sea and Egypt

(upright monoliths) imitating tower-like buildings with multiple doors and windows. Some of them are immense: one, probably originally more than a hundred feet high and which may have fallen down almost as soon as it was put up, is among the biggest single stones ever quarried in the ancient world.[27] There is no good reason to doubt the story that it was also Ezana who made contact with the Church in Alexandria, asking no less a divine than Bishop Athanasius to supply his people with a bishop. Thus from a very early date comes that peculiar Ethiopian arrangement which persisted for sixteen hundred years, as late as 1951: the presiding bishop (*abun*) in the Church of Ethiopia was never a native Ethiopian, but an import from the Coptic Church hundreds of miles to the north, and there was rarely any other bishop present in the whole country.[28]

This has meant that the *abun* rarely had much real power or initiative in a Church to which he came usually as an elderly stranger with a different native language. Authority was displaced elsewhere, to monarchs and to abbots of monasteries; monasticism seems to have arrived early in the Church in Ethiopia and quickly gained royal patronage. Around these leaders are still numerous hereditary dynasties of non-monastic clergy who, over the centuries, might swarm in their thousands to seek ordination on the *abun*'s rare visits to their area. The education of these priests, deacons and cantors might not extend far beyond a detailed knowledge of how to perform the liturgy, but that was a formidable intellectual acquisition in itself. They were ordinary folk who thus shaped their religion into that of a whole people rather than simply the property of a royal elite. Over the centuries of trials and bizarre disasters to afflict the Ethiopian Church, they are the constant underlying force which has preserved its unique life against the odds.

King Ezana may have renounced traditional gods, but the worship of the Church over which he first presided has remained unique and unmistakably African in character. Since church buildings are often temple-like in character rather than congregational spaces, much of the liturgy is conducted in the open air, accompanied by a variety of drums and percussive and stringed instruments, and with the principal clergy and musicians shaded from the weather by elaborately decorated umbrellas. Instead of church bells, sonorous echoes struck on stones hanging from trees summon worshippers to prayer (see Plate 20). The Church's liturgical chant, inseparable from its worship, is attributed to the sixth-century Court musician Yared. According to legend, his genius rather backfired on him when Gabra Maskel, the then king of Aksum, was so entranced by Yared's singing that he failed to notice that the spear on which he was leaning had pierced the singer's foot. Yared himself was (perhaps diplomatically) too absorbed in his own art to comment.[29]

It was not surprising that during the controversies of the fifth and sixth centuries, this Church, which derived its fragile link to the wider episcopal succession via Alexandria, followed the Egyptian Church into the Miaphysite camp. One of the concepts which remain central in Ethiopian theology is *täwahedo*, 'union' of humanity and divinity in the Saviour who took flesh. Nevertheless, despite the crucial role of the *abun*, the Ethiopian Church did not become Coptic in character. Far more all-pervasive were its links with the Semitic world, already evident before the coming of Christianity in Ethiopian language and even place names in the coastal regions of Tigray and Eritrea.[30] It was one of those Semitic languages, Ge'ez, which became the liturgical and theological language of the Ethiopian Church, and remains so, even though it is not otherwise in current use. The arrival of Miaphysite faith is also connected to the Semitic world, because in legend it is associated with 'Nine Saints' of mostly Syriac background, who are said to have arrived as refugees from Chalcedonian persecution in the late fifth century and to have been instrumental in establishing the Ethiopian monastic system.

Ethiopia's Semitic links are also apparent in the unique fascination with Judaism which has developed in its Christianity. This is reminiscent of the distinctively close relationship with Judaism in early Syriac Christianity (see pp. 178–9), but over a much longer period the character has become much more pronounced in Ethiopia. This may not originally have arisen so much from direct contacts with Jews as from Ethiopian pride in that foundation episode in the Book of Acts, in which Christianity's Jewish heritage already lies at the heart of the story of Philip and the eunuch. Meditation on this during the passing of centuries in the isolation of Africa has made that seed grow into a major theme in a Church which honours the Jewish Sabbath, practises circumcision (female as well as male, unlike the Jews), and makes its members obey Jewish dietary laws. External sources as early as the thirteenth century record the Church as treasuring an object which was claimed to be the Ark of the Covenant once housed in the Temple in Jerusalem. The report that the Ark was decorated with crosses does present problems for this provenance, given that, if genuine, it had been constructed a millennium before the Crucifixion.[31] At its extreme, the preoccupation with the Hebrew past in Ethiopian Christianity has produced a grouping of peoples first attested in Ethiopia in the fourteenth century, who have been styled by other Ethiopians *Falasha*, 'Strangers', but who call themselves *Beta Israel* ('House of Israel') because they claim full Jewish identity. In recent years, most of the *Beta Israel* have emigrated to the State of Israel.[32]

Central to the complex of associations with Israel and Judaism is a foundational work of Ethiopian literature, the *Kebra Nagast*, the 'Book of the Glory of Kings'. It is this work, difficult to date and composite in character, which sets out the origins of the Ethiopian monarchy in the union of King Solomon of Israel and the Queen of Sheba, that legendary ruler of a Yemeni kingdom whom the Tanakh had recorded as visiting Jerusalem in great splendour. What is now considered to be a late addition to the accounts in the *Kebra Nagast* is the story that their son Menelik, the first Ethiopian king, brought the Ark, or *tabot*, back to Ethiopia, where it is kept to this day in a chapel in Aksum. Every Ethiopian church has a much-venerated representation of the *tabot* in its sanctuary. Quite when the *tabot* at Aksum became so important in Ethiopian devotion is controversial. The latest historian to consider the confused and partial evidence places it as late as the end of the sixteenth century, when recent Islamic destruction and bruising contacts with the wider Christian world made the Ethiopian Church particularly concerned to assert its special character and enrich its existing Jewish traditions (see pp. 711–12).[33]

The original form of the *Kebra Nagast* is certainly much older, and it may relate to a period in the sixth century when Aksum was at one of its peaks of power. This formidable Christian empire under King Kaleb then had an intimate concern with the land of the Queen of Sheba, the Yemen. The active role which Ethiopia now seized in the politics of Yemen and Arabia was one of the great might-have-beens of history, and would certainly explain the later fascination in Ethiopia with Solomon and the Queen of Sheba. In the early years of the sixth century, Miaphysite Christian refugees from the Byzantine Empire gathered in the Yemeni city of Najrān (now in south-west Saudi Arabia), attracted by an existing Christian community, and the city became a major centre for Miaphysite Christianity. In 523 or 524 its population suffered a horrific massacre at the hands of their overlord, Yusuf as'ar Yath'ar of the Yemeni kingdom of Himyar; in the previous century, his family had converted to Judaism and his campaigns were expressions of his own militant zeal for recreating Israel in Arabia. King Kaleb of Ethiopia, already provoked by Yusuf's killing of Ethiopian soldiers, forcefully intervened across the Red Sea after this outrage and defeated and killed Yusuf.[34]

With Ethiopian backing, a local Miaphysite ruler, Abraha, now came to establish a kingdom in southern Arabia which had Miaphysite Christianity as its state religion. This might have become the future of the Arabian peninsula, had it not been for a major disaster of engineering: in the 570s, the ancient and famous Marib dam, on which the agricultural prosperity of the region depended, and which had undergone thorough repair under King Abraha, nevertheless suffered a catastrophic failure. After more than a thousand years of existence, it was never rebuilt until modern times. A complex and wealthy society which had flourished on the irrigation provided by the dam was ruined for ever, and with the collapsing dam must have perished much of the credibility of Christianity throughout Arabia. Five hundred miles to the north, in the same decade that the dam failed, there was born an Arab destined to be a new prophet: Muhammad (see pp. 255–9). The memory of the end of the Marib dam, when Sheba's gardens were replaced 'with others that yielded bitter fruit', was still traumatic enough to win a mention in Muhammad's revelations in the Qur'an, where the disaster was described as a punishment from God for Sheba's faithlessness.[35] But before we meet the new prophet and the impact of his faith on the world, we must turn to the other dissidence against Chalcedon: the Church of the East, the Dyophysite heirs of Theodore of Mopsuestia.

THE CHURCH OF THE EAST (451–622)

At the time of the Council of Chalcedon, with Nestorius declared a non-person despite the council's quiet acceptance of much of his theology, matters looked dire for defiant Dyophysites. They had no power base in the Byzantine Empire comparable to Miaphysite Alexandria, and even eastwards beyond the imperial frontier there was no secure refuge for them among Syrian Christians in the Sassanian Empire. The mid-fifth century saw renewed pogroms of Christians by the Zoroastrian authorities. In the worst sequence under Shah Yazdgerd II, what is now the Iraqi city of Kirkuk witnessed the slaughter of ten bishops and reputedly 153,000 Christians (a biblically symbolic number for a figure which was clearly still grotesquely large). Nevertheless, persecution was not a consistent Sassanian policy, and the Church survived and consolidated; because the Byzantine Empire reaffirmed Chalcedonian Christianity or tried to woo the Miaphysites, it was not surprising that east Syrian Christianity took on an increasingly explicit commitment to the Dyophysite cause.

A significant shift took place in 489, when the Byzantine Emperor Zeno in his drive to placate Miaphysites finally closed the School of the Persians in the city of Edessa (now Urfa in Turkey). This had been the major centre of higher education for Christians throughout the East, both within and beyond the empire, but now a school was established little more than 150 miles eastwards in Sassanian territory, in the city of Nisibis (now Nusaybin in the extreme south-east of Turkey), ready to take on the duty of training Dyophysite clergy. In Nisibis Greek works could be translated and expounded to Syriac-speakers: the Church was concerned to preserve even the works of pre-Christian Greek philosophy so that they could be used as intellectual tools for arguments with Chalcedonian and Miaphysite Christians. This was of huge importance for a wider future (see pp. 266–7). Moreover, the flow of knowledge to Nisibis was not just from the west. It was a Christian scholar from Nisibis, Severus, with a Persian surname, Sebokht, abbot and bishop of a monastery on the Euphrates, who in the mid-seventh century first described a system of mathematical signs invented by Indians, which were then absorbed into Islamic culture and are therefore known to us as Arabic numerals.[36]

The scholars of Nisibis did not have a monopoly of Christian higher education; the most important other centre was far to the south, in the settler city of Gondeshapur. In the time of the unusually tolerant and cultured Shah Khusrau I (reigned 531–79), a contemporary of the Byzantine Emperor Justinian, the Christian school in Gondeshapur was promoted into a centre of general learning, with a richly augmented library whose holdings united such widely separated cultures as Greece and India. Syriac remained the chief medium of instruction in this school. If anything helped to integrate Syriac Christianity into Sassanian elite life after its traumatic sufferings, it was the role of Gondeshapur in providing a series of skilled physicians who were Dyophysite Christians, and who became doctors first to the shahs and later to Islamic rulers in Seleucia-Ctesiphon. It was only the founding of Baghdad and its schools two centuries later which outshone the importance of Gondeshapur for learning and the preservation of ancient culture; but now Baghdad's predecessor, the once-famous centre of power and scholarship, has been utterly eclipsed, and its scanty visible ruins near a little Iranian village have never even been excavated.[37]

Dyophysite Christianity also spread south of the great empires, into the peninsula of Arabia, where there had long been tribes embracing Christianity. There were strong contrary influences here to turn the existing Christian presence towards Miaphysite belief, thanks to external powers like the Miaphysite Ethiopians and Ghassānids, and we have seen those having an effect on local rulers in Sheba (see pp. 244–5). Yet political rivalries meant that by no means all Arab Christians were going to follow suit; in fact, some embraced Dyophysite Christianity precisely because the Ghassānids believed the opposite. What was significant about this dual character of Christian activity in Arabia was how little Arabian Christians were inclined to identify with the imperial Church of Chalcedon: they set their sights on Semitic versions of the faith. The trade routes to Syria, southwards to Arabia and the Red Sea, which Ghassānid power kept open and secure, brought Syrian theology and worship into the peninsula. One paradoxical trace of that is the presence of a substantial number of Syriac loanwords in the text of Arabian Christianity's nemesis, the Qur'an; these probably derive from Muhammad's knowledge of Jewish and Christian sacred texts in that language. This is a hint that, as elsewhere in the Christianity which had Syriac roots, the liturgical and scriptural language of Arabian Christianity remained Syriac rather than the Arabian vernacular of the region.[38]

By the sixth century, therefore, the Church of the East was fully established, both in its independence of any bishop in the Byzantine Empire and in its firm adherence to the theology condemned at Chalcedon. Its principal bishop or patriarch, normally resident in one of the great cities of the Sassanian Empire, was known as the Catholicos, 'universal bishop' – a title as reasonable as the high claims of the Bishops of Rome or Constantinople, considering the wide areas and increasing numbers of Christians who looked to this bishop as their chief pastor. As much as the 'Melchite' Chalcedonians or the Miaphysites, its spiritual life was sustained by a rapid expansion of monastic life. Many monasteries in the East had fallen into disarray during the troubles of the later fifth century, and in 571 one powerful monastic personality, Abraham of Kashkar, created a set of rules to restore discipline to their life. When his successor in the Great Monastery in the Izla Mountains above Nisibis, Abbot Dadisho, augmented Abraham's rule seventeen years later, he firmly stated a test of doctrinal purity: anyone who 'does not accept the Orthodox fathers Mar Diodore [of Tarsus], Mar Theodore [of Mopsuestia] and Mar Nestorius shall be unknown to our community'.[39] Monasteries among the Dyophysites were strengthened through the military success of the Sassanian Shah Khusrau II in areas of the Byzantine Empire along the eastern Mediterranean. For a couple of decades from 605 the Shah had control of the hills of Tūr 'Abdīn, where the

monasteries had previously been divided between Melchite and Miaphysite communities (see p. 237). From this date, some monastic communities of Dyophysites held on to their places in Tūr 'Abdīn, and it
was not until after 1838 that the last monks from the Church of the
East left this enclave of extraordinary Christian sanctity.[40]

The Church of the East was now travelling astonishing distances away
from the heartlands of the previous Christian centuries: eastwards along
land and sea routes which connected the Roman and Sassanian worlds
with China and India – and noticeably without any political support.
To begin with, it must have been something like a chaplaincy for expatri-
ates, but it was also a mission which could draw on the natural articulacy
and propensity for salesmanship which made Syrian merchants so successful across Asia. During the fourth and fifth centuries the east Syrians
reached out beyond the Sassanian Empire and established Christian
outposts among the peoples of Central Asia, and over the next centuries
they moved steadily onwards in their activities, which means that in
such unexpected places as the mountains and plains around Samarqand,
so long the territory of Islam, it is possible to have the shock of encountering the sight of carved medieval crosses or inscriptions in Syriac.[41]

One of the Syrians' earliest extensions of the Christian faith was to
India. The 'Mar Thoma' Church there treasures a claim to have been
founded by the Apostle Thomas, which is not beyond the bounds of
possibility, given the evidence that archaeology has revealed of vigorous
trade between the Roman Empire and India in the first century CE.
Traditions about Thomas certainly already triggered an early-third-
century apocryphal Syrian account of his deeds in the subcontinent (see
p. 202). By the fourth century there was a sufficiently organized Church
in the Malabar Coast in south-west India (what is now Kerala) that
arrangements were made to put it under the authority of the bishop in
one of the main trading ports in the Sassanian Empire, Rew Ardashir
(now Bushehr on the Persian Gulf).[42] A century later, a Christian writer
from Alexandria called Cosmas took a nickname from his extraordinary
travels around India – Indicopleustes, 'voyager to India' – though the
traveller was also an eyewitness of King Kaleb of Ethiopia's momentous
campaign in the Yemen in the 520s (see pp. 244–5). Despite coming
from Egypt, Cosmas Indicopleustes was a Dyophysite, steeped in the
writings of Theodore of Mopsuestia and Diodore of Tarsus, and he
sneered at the recent 'schismatical Father', the exiled Bishop Theodosius
of Alexandria. He was proud of the Church of the East, which had
spread its faith from Persia to Churches in India and even Sri Lanka,

rejoicing that his travels had shown him how the whole earth was 'still being filled, and that the gospel is preached throughout all the world'. It is a pity from the point of view of modern historians that his one surviving work devotes itself primarily to cosmological questions centring on the failed proposition that the world is flat, but we still need to be grateful for its incidental remarks on the world that Cosmas actually knew; we have so little other evidence.[43]

The 'Thomas Christians' settled down to a comfortable relationship with the non-Christian elites and society round them. Besides a number of carved stone crosses, the earliest datable artefacts of their history are five copper plates which record tax privileges and corporate rights granted them by local monarchs and rulers in the eighth and ninth centuries.[44] Their lifestyle, despite various individual customs, became very similar to that of their Hindu neighbours; they found a rather respectable niche in Indian society. They were never totally cut off either from their Dyophysite co-religionists in the Middle East or indeed from the Church further west. One of the most remarkable contacts may have been with ninth-century England, where several versions of *The Anglo-Saxon Chronicle* report that a prominent Anglo-Saxon courtier called Sigehelm was sent by the great King Alfred of Wessex on a pilgrimage to the tomb of St Thomas in India.[45] It was only in the sixteenth century that the Thomas Christians' ancient place in Indian society became a disadvantage, when they re-encountered armed and aggressive Western Catholic Christians, who were unsympathetic both to their cultural compromises and to their 'Nestorian' heresies, and who then did much to destroy their distinctive way of life and the records of their history (see pp. 704–5).

Consistently, the Church of the East remained united by adhering to its Syrian roots, displaying the vigorous individuality which Syriac Christianity had exhibited from its earliest years. It gloried in its difference from the misguided Christianities further west. Everywhere it went, it treasured the memory of the prophet Jonah (one of the Bible's most entertaining explicit fictions). Most Christians honoured him as a symbol of the Resurrection because of his three days spent in the belly of the great fish, but the Church of the East remembered that the point of his sojourn in the fish was that Jonah had been unsuccessfully trying to avoid God's call to preach salvation to the Assyrians' hated city Nineveh – and now there was a Christian bishop of the Church of the East in Nineveh, to complete Jonah's work! A theology of two natures in Christ kept the Church of the East faithful to the emphasis in Theodore of

Mopsuestia's teaching that Christ in his human nature was the Second Adam. As such, he was a true pattern for all sons and daughters of Adam, so that human beings could do their best to imitate the holiness of Christ. Such belief did lead monks in the Syrian tradition into their extraordinary self-punishments to achieve such imitation, but it also represents an optimistic pole of the Christian spectrum of beliefs in human worth, potential and capacity, because if Jesus had a whole human nature, it must by definition be good, and logically all human nature began by being good, whatever its subsequent corruptions. This was a contrast with the savage pessimism that has often emerged from Latin Western Christianity, following Augustine of Hippo's emphasis on original sin (see pp. 306–9).

That outlook continued to illuminate the theology of the Church of the East. It was unimpressed and uninhibited by the condemnations which such teachings had received in the imperial Church around 400, and equally unimpressed by the imperial Church's later condemnation of the monk and spiritual writer Evagrius Ponticus (see pp. 209–10). Much of Evagrius's work is now preserved only in Syriac translation, the Greek originals having been deliberately destroyed.[46] Isaac, a seventh-century monk from Qatar who briefly held the resonant title Bishop of Nineveh, took up the notion which Evagrius had derived from the writings of that audacious Alexandrian Origen that in the end all will be saved. He saw divine love even in the fire of Hell, which prepared humanity for a future ecstasy:

out of it the wealth of His love and power and wisdom will become known all the more – and so will the insistent might of the waves of His goodness. It is not [the way of] the compassionate Maker to create rational beings in order to deliver them over mercilessly to unending affliction . . . for things of which He knew even before they were fashioned.[47]

In the writings of Isaac's successor in the eighth century, the monk John of Dalyatha, the Syriac emphasis on bodily penance was pressed to an extreme as forming a road back to the original purity of human nature. John proclaimed that through humility and contemplation (especially while prostrate), a monk could unite his purged nature not simply with all creation, but also with his creator, to achieve a vision of the glory of God himself: 'in the same way that fire shows its operation to the eyes, so God shows his glory to rational beings who are pure'. John went so far as to deny that a layperson could experience the mystical union with God which resulted from such self-purging: 'Christ cannot live with the world . . . but always, he comes to the soul's home and visits her to live in her, if she is empty of all that is of the world.' As so often in the history of Christianity, when mystics try to explain their experience of transcendence, the results are not just difficult for those beyond to understand, but seem to overstep the mark between creator and created. John's teachings were condemned by a synod of the Church of the East soon after his death, but they continued to hold a fascination for mystics, and much of what he said would be echoed in later centuries in other settings.[48]

There was one remarkable aspect of the Church of the East's faithfulness to a single tradition. The Miaphysites, thanks to various political successes and alliances with power at crucial stages of their history, were ready to develop their culture and theology in such diverse languages as Armenian, Georgian, Coptic, Nubian and Ge'ez, and retained no common language as a point of reference. By contrast, although the Dyophysite Church did indeed likewise translate many of its biblical, liturgical and other texts into the languages of the East, it still hung on to Syriac as a common liturgical and theological language in the most exotic of settings, as far east as China, using the 'Nestorian' script developed out of the original Syriac Estrangela. Unlike most alphabetic scripts, neither this Nestorian script nor its western Syrian counterpart (Serto) developed a cursive or minuscule form for rapid writing, so it was possible for readers over several centuries to follow and understand very ancient texts written in it. It has been suggested that this is one of the reasons why Syriac Christianity has changed so little in its long existence.[49] Yet the common Syriac language of the Church was a source of weakness as well as of strength and stability. It meant that in the many cultures which the Eastern Christians encountered, Dyophysite Christians were destined to remain a minority with an alien lingua franca – far more alien than the use of the imperial language Latin in the Western Church. Worse still for their general popularity, often they were a minority with some social status and special privileges. They nowhere achieved the critical mass necessary to become the dominant culture.

Crucially, in contrast to the Miaphysites in Ethiopia, Nubia and Armenia, the Church of the East never permanently captured the allegiance of any royal family, despite the frequently important role played by Eastern Christians in various royal and princely Courts. Only once in this period did the Church of the East come close to any such prospect, and the result was in the long term a disaster for it – fateful indeed for all Christianity, as we will see. The opportunity came in the violent end to the reign of the Sassanian Shah Khusrau II in 628. He was murdered by his own son, Crown Prince Shiroi, who took the precaution of murdering all Khusrau's other male children as potential rivals, and took the name Kavad II. Kavad was backed in his palace coup by several prominent Dyophysite Christian families, and because his father's military successes against the Byzantine Empire had dramatically extended Sassanian territories westward, for the first time in the Sassanian Empire's history it is likely that a majority of the Shah's subjects were Christian.[50] Already the late Khusrau, whose two successive wives were both Christian, had shown fitful strategic favour to the Church (see p. 238). Now there was a moment when the new shah or his successors might well have decided to make the sort of turnaround to Christianity which had seized Trdat, Constantine and Ezana.

The new reign proved to be brief, as Shah Kavad died only a few months after his coup, but significant goodwill gestures to Christians and their advance into the centre of action in the empire continued. Kavad had quickly ordered that a new Catholicos should be chosen for the Church, ending a hiatus of twenty years in which Shah Khusrau had prevented the office being filled. The man singled out, Ishoyahb II, proved an outstanding diplomat of wide vision who gave official encouragement to those taking Christianity into China. He sent a delegation to the Chinese Tang emperor led by a bishop whom the Chinese called Alopen. Alopen was well received on his arrival in 635. The occasion was long remembered and celebrated by Chinese Christians, for it led to the foundation of the first of several monasteries in China, with official encouragement, and in no less a setting than the then Chinese imperial capital, Chang'an (now Xi'an). The library pagoda on the site of one once-celebrated monastery rebuilt a century or so later still survives in Zhouzhi, forty-five miles south-west of Xi'an (see Plate 6). Despite the site's centuries of later use by Taoists and then Buddhists, the building still bears the Chinese name which signified both Christianity and the world of the eastern Mediterranean, *Ta Qin*, and although local people had always remembered its Christian origins through the centuries, their significance was not more widely recognized until the 1930s. The pagoda stands proudly on a hillside; remarkably and surely significantly, it is within easy sight of the next hill, on which stands the famous Taoist Louguan Temple, much favoured as a centre of higher education by the early Tang emperors in those years when the Church of the East flourished here. Here is a tangible link to the Chinese community of the Church of the East, which although long lost now was destined to persist over seven centuries. In the former Japanese capital of Kyoto, recent investigations suggest that there too one surviving ancient temple started life as a building of the Church of the East. Mongolia is yielding parallel finds. These unexpected rediscoveries may not be the last.[51]

There were equally promising moves for the Church of the East towards the west and Byzantium. One of Khusrau II's most significant trophies in his campaigns against the Byzantines had been not territory but a prime Christian relic: no less an object than the True Cross, which had somehow appeared in Jerusalem in the fourth century during the city's self-promotion as a holy place (see pp. 193–4). To the fury and humiliation of the Byzantine Emperor Heraclius, the Shah seized the Cross from Jerusalem when he sacked the city in 614. Yet Khusrau treated it with respect, entrusting it to his Christian wife; it then became a prime bargaining counter in diplomacy when the new Sassanian Queen Boran, recognizing reality in the wake of Heraclius's successful counterattacks, sought a peace settlement with Byzantium. The Sassanian peace delegation which returned the True Cross was led by Patriarch Ishoyahb, and in 630 he had a satisfaction unprecedented in the history of the Dyophysites when he celebrated the Eucharist according to the rites of his Church in the city of Berrhoea (now Aleppo) in the presence of the Byzantine Emperor and of Chalcedonian bishops. The treaty was a triumph for Heraclius too, for it enabled him to parade his relic back in what remained of Byzantine Jerusalem after its comprehensive trashing by the Sassanian armies.[52]

This climax of peace between the two traditional enemy great powers in fact proved a sad irrelevance to the future. Kavad II's murder of his father, Khusrau II, swiftly followed by his own death, had poisonously destabilized Sassanian Court politics, leading to a procession of short-lived rulers struggling to maintain their position, while the constant frontier warfare with the Byzantines devastated the Middle East and weakened both imperial armies. Moreover, the clash of the two empires brought destruction to lesser Christian military powers, principally the Miaphysite Ghassānids, who for more than a century had kept the Byzantines in touch with events in Arabia and had brought security to the region. The Ghassānids could have alerted the Byzantines to the early formation of a new military power which had appeared quite unexpectedly from the south: the armies of Islam. The arrival of the Muslims proved terminal for the Sassanians. Within a decade in the 640s, the three-centuries-old empire was in ruins. Yazdgerd III, last ruling Sassanian shah, defeated and murdered, was buried not with Zoroastrian rites but by a bishop of the Church of the East; his son and heir fled all the way to China. There he was treated with respect, and one of his acts was to found the second monastery for Dyophysite Christianity to be sited in the capital, Chang'an.[53] Yet this royal favour had all come all too late for the Church of the East. Now Christianity everywhere faced the consequences of the new prophecy from Arabia – consequences which are still unravelling in our own time.

8

Islam: The Great Realignment
(622–1500)

MUHAMMAD AND THE COMING
OF ISLAM

In the late sixth century, at the time of the birth of Muhammad in the city of Mecca (Makkah in Arabic), three varieties of religious belief confronted each other in the Arabian peninsula. Over the previous century, Judaism and Christianity (itself bitterly divided, as we have seen) had been locked in murderous clashes. Both despised the traditional cults of the region, which amid their considerable variety boasted one of the Middle East's ancient centres of pilgrimage at Mecca, around a sacred black stone contained in the shrine known as the Ka'aba. For centuries the shrine at Mecca had been of merely local importance, far outshone by the Temple of the Jews in Jerusalem, whose cult Christians had in good measure renewed by their pilgrimage in honour of Christ's crucifixion and resurrection, while leaving the actual site of the Jerusalem Temple dishonoured and waste. Then in the fifth century one prominent family of Mecca had vigorously promoted their local shrine and set it on the road to fame and prosperity. A proud descendant of that family, born around 570, was the merchant Muhammad.[1]

Arabia was a society very conscious of the ecological disaster caused by the failure of the dam at Marib (see p. 245). Travellers in the southwest of the peninsula could see for themselves a dying society apparently unable to save itself, after centuries of wealth and fame throughout the region. Religious conflict, ancestral pride in Mecca, the compromised state of the Jerusalem sacred site, God's judgement and power over his people: all were there for a sensitive mind and a poetic genius to contemplate and sculpt into a single message. To appreciate this historical context makes it easier to understand the effect and character of Muhammad's proclamation of Islam (a word meaning 'submission'), but it does not explain the man himself or his revelations, any more than the historian can give a satisfactory explanation of the story of Jesus Christ's resurrection. What remains for scholars of Islam to achieve is the equivalent of Western Christian culture's patientanalysis of the documents at the heart of Christian faith, to gain a clearer picture of the society and thought-world in which the Qur'an was created.[2]

Muhammad's revelations of words from God only began for him in middle age, in 610, while he was on one of his regular expeditions to a cave outside Mecca, to retreat from his daily cares into meditation. As revelations continued, he would dictate the words he had heard to an ever-growing body of disciples, through years of struggle in which he and his followers (Muslims) saw their fortunes transformed. At first they were a beleaguered group suffering oppression and expulsion – their moment of withdrawal ('Hijra') from Mecca to Yathrib (Medina) in 622 CE has become the basis of Islamic dating. Within Muhammad's lifetime – he is generally said to have died in 632 CE – Muslims in Mecca had become a victorious and self-confident community which now needed regulation for its life. Both these experiences are reflected in pronouncements which, during the next century and a half, came to be a fixed and written text – still known despite its written form as 'that which is to be recited', or *Qur'an*. In contrast to the similar transition in fortunes for the followers of Christ witnessed in the Gospels, Acts and Epistles of the New Testament, the Muslims from their earliest days won their survival at least partly by physical force of arms, another phase in the struggles which had convulsed the peninsula over the past century, and their subsequent extraordinary expansion was inseparable from military conquest. Little more than half a century after the first convulsions in Mecca, the Dyophysite Patriarch Henanisho I had the courage to point this out to 'Abd al-Malik, then Islamic caliph (that is, the leader who claimed to be successor to Muhammad). The Caliph asked him to give his opinion of Islam. The Patriarch replied, 'It is a power that was established by the sword and not a faith confirmed by divine miracles, like Christianity and like the old law of Moses.'[3]

This is not the whole story – in fact forced conversions were not at all the rule in early Islam, even while it was extending its reach by military campaigns. At the centre of Muhammad's achievement was the extraordinary poetry which enshrined his revelations. Muslim sources have often ascribed the Qur'an's power to its exceptional beauty in the

Arabic language, and the Qur'an does not translate well, particularly into English. Conversion to Islam can therefore be a deeply felt aesthetic experience that rarely occurs in Christian accounts of conversion, which are generally the source rather than the result of a Christian experience of beauty. It is perhaps for that reason that from the beginning Islam has set its face against any further representation of the divine in pictures, since the divine beauty is already represented in the words of the Qur'an. It has often been said that the Qur'an plays the role in Islam which the incarnate Son has traditionally done in Christianity: a final revelation of God. It is nevertheless in the nature of poetry to send out resonances of meaning beyond the capacity of prose, and for that reason the proclamation of the finality of the Qur'an has always been qualified by the possibility of multiple meanings in its text. It has become as subject to the possibility of intricate reinterpretation and meditation as its predecessors in sacred scripture – all the more because, in most forms, Islamic societies have not developed the equivalent of the Christian hierarchy of clergy who might champion a single meaning.

The Qur'an is strikingly preoccupied with the two monotheisms which Muhammad had known from his boyhood, Judaism and Christianity. He was concerned to proclaim a new unity of religion through 'the God' (al-ilah, subsequently abbreviated as Allah) who had been the focus of the shrine cult at Mecca, but otherwise Muhammad spoke contemptuously of Arabian traditional cults, and he was very aware of the sacred books which had previously spoken of one God, the Tanakh and the Christian New Testament. His concern for them, and indeed stringent criticism of their content and their over-credulous readers, is particularly evident in the early suras (sections) of the Qur'an. In its present arrangement, after an initial proclamation of God, who is given the titles of mercy and compassion traditional in Arabian religion, the Qur'an passes to a long sura which takes its name of 'The Cow' from its references to stories of Moses and the Children of Israel in their Exodus from Egypt. The name of Mary, the mother of Jesus, occurs almost twice as often in the Qur'an as in the New Testament, and she gives her name to one of its suras. By contrast, there is one silence in the Qur'an which is startling once it is noticed: the name of Paul of Tarsus. Such naming and silence may have been the emphases of the Jewish 'Ebionite' Christians long before (see p. 107); and that provokes interesting reflection.

Far from speaking of a new message, Muhammad proclaimed Islam as the original truth which later centuries had obscured. Christian apologists in the second century had made the same claim for their message in relation to Judaism. His theme of oneness is a clear contrast with the Christian quarrels about the nature of Christ which Chalcedon had failed to heal. In a much-discussed and not conclusively understood verse of the Qur'an, God is represented as telling the Christians 'believe in God and his messengers and do not speak of a "Trinity" . . . God is only one God, He is far above having a Son.'[4] There is much in modern Muslim practice which would have been familiar to seventh-century Christians, and which is likely to have been borrowed from the Christian practice which Muhammad observed: the fast of Ramadan has the intensity of early Christian observance of Lent, and the characteristic prostration of Muslim prayer was then normal in the Christian Middle East, where it still survives in some traditional Christian communities. Prayer mats, still one of the most familiar features of the mosque today, were extensively used by Christian monks as far apart as Syria and Northumbria or Ireland before the coming of Islam, and they are reflected in the aptly nicknamed 'carpet' pages of intricate interlace and geometry to be found in great manuscripts of the early West such as the Lindisfarne Gospels.[5] We have already observed that the pillar-dwellers of Syriac Christianity may have inspired the minaret (see p. 208). Saints proliferated in fourth- to seventh-century Christianity. Many of them were taken straight over by Islam and remain the focus of Islamic cults to the present day, while Islam in most of its manifestations over the centuries has delighted in celebrating new holy men with similar honours of festival and pilgrimage.[6]

Reading the Qur'an quickly makes it apparent that Muhammad's relationship with Judaism was more conflicted than his relationship with Christianity, perhaps because it was more intimate.[7] It is possible to interpret his image of himself and his destiny as the last in the succession of Hebrew prophets, and his initial mission as a resolve to restore a monotheism concentrated on the Jerusalem Temple, which Christians had compromised. To begin with, Muhammad instructed his followers to pray facing Jerusalem, and he only altered the direction of prayer to Mecca after a murderous disagreement with the Jews of Medina. From that moment, the possibility of a united movement of Jews and followers of Muhammad ended and the Muslims formed their own single community (*ummah*).[8] That concept of a united *ummah* has survived all subsequent divisions in Islam, including the great and so far permanent rupture between Sunni and Shī'a, but alongside it has been the concept of various People of the Book. These were the faiths which, unlike adherents of traditional Arabian cults formerly rivalling the Meccan cult of *al-ilah*, were to be allowed to persist in their flawed but genuine understanding of God's truth: 'The [Muslim] believers, the Jews, the Christians, and the Sabians [an Arabian monotheism] – all those who believe in God and the Last Day and do good – will have their rewards with the Lord'.[9]

This was of great importance for the future as Muslims began to make an astonishing series of conquests in the decades after Muhammad's death. The Prophet had not apparently envisaged or provided for this eventuality, even though his own career had been full of conflict, in which Muhammad had been a much more aggressive participant than had Jesus when facing violence in his own ministry. Muslims now occupied much of the world that over the previous six centuries had become Christian, including its earliest historic centres, and they have continued to occupy it ever since. In the end that decisively moved the centre of Christian gravity westwards. The military crisis caused by the late-sixth-century wars between the Byzantine and Sassanian empires, and the short-sighted destruction by those war-locked empires of the various Christian buffer states along their borders (see pp. 253–4), gave a perfect opportunity for the armies to sweep first north out of Arabia, then east and west into Byzantine and Sassanian territory. Christianity's internal divisions made the task easier: there were plenty of Miaphysite or Dyophysite Christians who had no especial affection for the Chalcedonian rulers in Constantinople, and equally, plenty of Christians who had little time for Zoroastrian Sassanians, and who did not defend them against the new masters. In Egypt, for example, excavations at one of its greatest international Christian shrines, that of St Menas at Abū Mīnā, have revealed how suddenly Greek documents disappeared from the life of the community when the Muslim armies arrived. The last Greek receipts for the wine harvest scribbled on pottery are precisely for the invasion year of 641, and from then on the Coptic Church was entirely in charge at the shrine.[10]

The Muslim conquerors did little to explain their faith to their new subjects or to convert them to it. It might have been possible for Christians initially to regard these newcomers as a peculiar sort of Arian Christian sect, while Dyophysites would note with approval that they gave honour to the Virgin Mary without tolerating a cult of her. So the sudden irruption of the Muslims might be a catastrophe, but it could be endured for the time being, particularly if it brought quieter times than the campaigns of Heraclius. The result was one of the most rapid shifts of power in history.[11] Between 634 and 637, three battles crippled the armies of Byzantium and the Sassanians. In February 638, only eight years after the Emperor Heraclius had triumphantly restored the True Cross to Christian Jerusalem, the city fell to Muslim forces after a year's siege; it was in any case a shadow of its former self, devastated only a quarter-century earlier by the Sassanian Shah Khusrau II. Sophronios, the Melchite or Chalcedonian Patriarch of Jerusalem, insisted on making the surrender in person to the Caliph Umar.

Umar entered the city in deliberate humility in plain robes, riding on a camel, and he treated the new conquest with equally deliberate forbearance. He knew that he was fulfilling the design of the Prophet in doing so, because the conquest of Jerusalem was no incidental military victory. Umar signified the triumph of Islam on the vacant site of the Temple by building a mosque above the ruins. In doing so, the Caliph achieved what the Emperor Julian the Apostate (see p. 217) had planned long before: to restore honour and splendour to this long-desecrated sacred site which Christians had deliberately spurned, and whose memory had been so vital for Muhammad. In the early 690s the Caliph 'Abd al-Malik outdid Umar's first monument with an extraordinary domed structure, now often called the Mosque of Umar – a double error, since it was built neither as a mosque nor by Umar. The function of this 'Dome of the Rock' seems originally to have been to mark the victory of Muhammad's revelation over Christianity, by creating a building which would be as impressive as anything that Christianity had put up – the Caliph would have known the reputation of the Church of Hagia Sophia in Constantinople, then already a century and a half old (see pp. 429–31). The Dome of the Rock bears the earliest datable set of texts from the Qur'an, including the famous rebuke to those who worship the Trinity, and it exhibits the earliest datable use of the word 'Muslim'. Even though it reversed Christian mistreatment of the Temple, it was probably built by Christian craftsmen, and its architectural forms are derived from those of Byzantium.[12]

Really this was logical. What the Dome of the Rock proclaimed was the arrival of a new empire which would replace the surviving Christian empire of the Byzantines; the city of Constantinople was now the goal of what seemed an unstoppable programme of conquest. Islam did not succeed in this ultimate aim – yet. In 678, after five years of repeated attacks, the Byzantine Emperor Constantine IV finally repulsed the besiegers, but other Islamic armies pressed on to the furthest coasts of North Africa. From their conquest of Alexandria and all Egypt by 641, they took a half-century of hard fighting to reach the Straits of Gibraltar, but then they went on to seize virtually the entire Iberian peninsula: they were checked in their advance northwards only in central France at a battle near Poitiers in 732 or 733. The two Christian victories at Constantinople and in France between them preserved a Europe in which Christianity remained dominant, and as a result the centre of energy and unfettered development and change in the Christian world decisively shifted west from its old Eastern centres. By contrast, a crushing Islamic victory over Chinese armies in what is now Kyrgyzstan in 751 laid open Central Asia to Islam, bringing eventual ruin to the Church of the East.

ISLAM AND THE EAST

In the Middle East and around the African shore of the Mediterranean most Christians would now have to live with a new reality: they had lost their position at the centre of society. The new situation was at its most extreme in Arabia itself, where Muslims put into practice what was said to have been one of Muhammad's deathbed commands and set about eliminating Christianity from the peninsula. After a century or so, there were only a few Christian communities left. In a symbolic annexation which echoes similar architectural appropriations by Christians from predecessor sacred buildings, the eighth-century Great Mosque in Sana'a in the Yemen incorporates columns from the demolished cathedral built there two centuries before by the Miaphysite ruler Abraha (see pp. 244–5). It may be the result of a policy of thorough Islamic destruction that no trace remains of a Bible in Arabic which can be dated to the era of flourishing Christianity before the coming of Islam; on the other hand, given the Syriac character of the Arabian Churches before, maybe it had never existed.[13]

Elsewhere, there was no such extreme policy of suppression, and in fact in most of the societies newly dominated by Islam two or more centuries passed before there was anything like a Muslim majority. Although to begin with there was no effort to fill the cities with Muslim converts, wherever a church or cathedral was a prominent central building, it was likely to become the main mosque. It was natural that many Christians should assume that the Arab conquests signalled the end of the world, and there was much excited writing to that effect, but, as has so far proved the case in Christian history, apocalypse was postponed and everyday life took over.[14] Someone would have to do practical deals with the conquerors. In default of action from the shattered secular authorities, a number of Christian bishops followed the example of Sophronios's surrender to Caliph Umar I in Jerusalem and negotiated permanent settlements. Regardless of the era in which they were actually concluded, conventionally these came to be known collectively as the Pact or Covenant (*dhimma*) of Umar; this referred to a second caliph called Umar (reigned 717–20), though the attribution may have been retrospective. The Pact had its precedent already in the Sassanian Empire. Christians and Jews as People of the Book (and later, by extensions of dubious logic but practical utility, other significant religious minorities) were organized into separate communities or *millets*, defined by their common practice of the same religion, which was guaranteed as protected as long as it was primarily practised in private. They were given a specified tax burden and their second-class status was defined as that of a *dhimmi* (a non-Muslim protected under a *dhimma*).

The conquerors thus remained a military and governing elite, aloof from their conquered populations, having to concentrate their scattered forces through their huge new dominions in garrisons. They were a good deal less interested in Christian beliefs than the Christians were in them. Christians learned about Islam, not always with great accuracy, in order to denounce it and justify themselves against it. Significantly, the terms in which they denounced the new prophecy were similar to the insults which they directed towards other Christians who disagreed with them and whom they styled heretics. This is not how they talked about Zoroastrianism, or the defeated cults of the old Roman Empire.[15] Whether Christians found themselves oppressed in the new situation depended on the personality and outlook of the Muslim authorities. At various times discrimination was deliberately burdensome: so under a number of governors and caliphs of the Umayyad dynasty, who were the first conquerors and who ruled from Damascus in the seventh and eighth centuries, Christians faced the destruction of churches and the strict enforcement of a host of petty humiliations and restrictions, while under the last great Abbasid Caliph Al-Mutawakkil (reigned 847–61) they were forced to wear distinctive clothing in yellow – an anticipation of a measure which, in later centuries, Christian societies would take against their Jewish minorities in Europe.[16]

At other times under rulers of wider sympathies, second-class status might mean as much privilege and flexibility as it had done under the Sassanians. Some of the Umayyads found themselves charmed by the cultures which they had conquered, so that archaeologists in Palestine and Syria have revealed an astonishing flourishing of Christian-style figural art under their rule. Even in Umayyad palaces the mosaic floors may luxuriate in satyrs and cupids, and, contrary to any picture of consistent destruction, there was an outburst of church-building complete with rich figural mosaics datable to after the Arab invasions.[17] One Dyophysite bishop wrote in 649, soon after the Muslim conquest, that 'these Arabs fight not against our Christian religion; nay, rather they defend our faith, they revere our priests and Saints, and they make gifts to our churches and monasteries'.[18]

Monasteries were nevertheless going to have a hard time surviving in this new world, particularly in the cities, and in the long term the more remote monasteries stood the best chance of survival. Muslims were torn between the general cultural respect for ascetic holy men in the Middle East, attested in the Qur'an itself, and other pronouncements of the Qur'an which condemn monks as dangerous charlatans.[19] One device for protection against negative opinions was to create stories which provided a comfortingly warm picture of relationships between monks and the Prophet. This was possible because around the text of the Qur'an there grew a great range of traditional stories (known as a hadīth) which deal with matters on which the Qur'an is not sufficiently explicit. So it was supposed to have been a Miaphysite monk, Bahīrā, who recognized Muhammad's special destiny in his youth, long before he had received any revelations.[20] One famous monastery below Mount Sinai refounded by Justinian and later dedicated to St Catherine of Alexandria reinforced the security created by its isolation and inaccessibility by adroitly injecting into Islamic tradition a hadīth that Muhammad himself had granted protection to the community – this was duly backed up by a document in the monastery archives of St Catherine, autographed with the Prophet's own hand (literally, a picture of his hand).[21] In the era of the tolerant Egyptian Islamic dynasty of the Fatimids, St Catherine's showed further prudence by actually constructing a mosque within its precincts, which still exists complete with minaret, although it is sealed up and is in any case not properly oriented towards Mecca, as a mosque should be.

One of the most influential theologians for Byzantine Orthodoxy in the years around 700 (see pp. 447–8) spent all his life as a subject of the Umayyad caliph in Damascus, and he was indeed ethnically an Arab, as his family name, Mansūr, revealed; he has come to be known as John of Damascus. John enjoyed the privileges of a traditional elite which had made a smooth transition from the old regime to the new: his grandfather, Mansūr ibn Sargūn, a Chalcedonian Christian, had been the last governor of the city on behalf of the Byzantine emperor, while John's father was a high-ranking official in Umayyad administration. John grew up alongside the future Caliph Al-Yazīd, and assumed the hereditary family place in public office as chief councillor, though later in life, after political disgrace, he withdrew into the celebrated monastery of St Sabas near Jerusalem. His intimacy with the elite of the new dispensation did not prevent him from writing combatively against Islam and even calling it 'forerunner of the Antichrist'.[22]

Chalcedonian Orthodoxy like John's was obviously going to be at a long-term disadvantage once the protection of the Byzantine armies had been removed. Jerusalem and its shrine of the Holy Sepulchre remained one stronghold of Melchite Orthodoxy amid the Miaphysite and Dyophysite majority. It would not be too cynical to suggest that this was understandable, given the continuing flow of Chalcedonian pilgrims into Palestine from the empire and even further west; they would not appreciate being received at the holy places of Bethlehem and Jerusalem by Christians whom they regarded as heretics. The same applied to the great monastery in Sinai, hugely popular in the Byzantine world despite the difficulty of getting there, long before St Catherine's bones were found on Mount Sinai above it. The Burning Bush flourishing within its walls, said to be the same in which God had appeared to Moses (see p. 54), recalled the Virgin who had likewise in Chalcedonian eyes sheltered the Godhead, and the monastery always remained loyal to Chalcedonian Orthodoxy, looking to the Melchite patriarch in Jerusalem rather than the Miaphysite Copts to its west.

Elsewhere, neither Miaphysites nor Dyophysites had much reason to look back with regret on the disappearance of the imperial power and its Church. When the Abbasid dynasty overthrew the Umayyads in 750, they moved the centre of government in the caliphate into Mesopotamia, where from 762 they designed a new capital with no links to previous imperial histories. Baghdad replaced both Damascus and Seleucia-Ctesiphon as the key city of the Middle East. In the battle for prominence among the various factions of Christianity, that shift eastwards would inevitably favour the Dyophysite 'Church of the East' against the Melchites and Miaphysites, and the Abbasids gave an unprecedented official jurisdiction to the Dyophysite patriarch over all Christians in their caliphate, which stretched from Egypt into Central Asia.

This was not an unmixed blessing. The political importance of the patriarchate meant that caliphs took a personal and official interest in

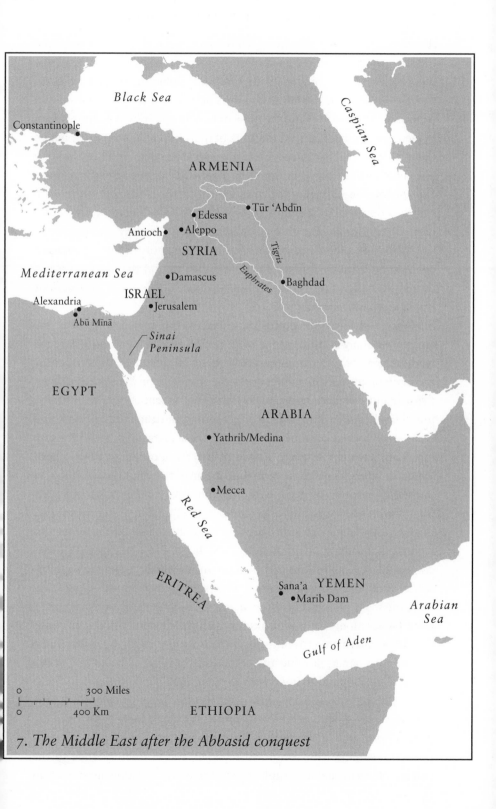

Black Sea

Constantinople

ARMENIA

Caspian Sea

•Tūr ʿAbdīn

•Edessa

Antioch• •Aleppo

SYRIA

Tigris

Euphrates

•Baghdad

Mediterranean Sea

•Damascus

ISRAEL

Alexandria
•
Abū Mīnā

•Jerusalem

Sinai
Peninsula

EGYPT

ARABIA

•Yathrib/Medina

•Mecca

Red Sea

ERITREA

Sana'a
•
•Marib Dam

YEMEN

Arabian
Sea

Gulf of Aden

0   300 Miles

0   400 Km

ETHIOPIA

7. *The Middle East after the Abbasid conquest*

the election of new patriarchs, who had no choice but to live in the capital. Just as under the Sassanians, a succession of Dyophysite Christians became Court physicians to Muslim caliphs, and equally that was not necessarily beneficial in its consequences: Christian physicians might be more interested in using the patriarchate for their own purposes than in securing the more general interests of the Church. Yet the value which the Abbasid caliphs placed on the medical services of the Christian physicians was a major reason why Baghdad became the setting for a new institution of higher learning which, from its foundation in 832, came to outshine the schools of Nisibis and Gondeshapur. Christians particularly dominated its specializations in astronomy and medicine. The Abbasid caliphate was interested in drawing on all the resources of pre-Islamic learning that might be useful to it, and the chief source of this was the literature preserved by the Church of the East, translations from Greek into Syriac.

Now an industry of retranslation began, this time into Arabic: the structured analysis and science of Aristotle, the dialogues of Plato, the medical texts of Galen and the followers of Hippocrates, the geography and cosmology of Ptolemy were only the star items on the library shelves. Most famous of these translators was the ninth-century Christian Court physician Hunayn ibn 'Ishāq, director of the caliphate's library and nicknamed 'prince of translators'. It was these texts, translated yet again into Latin, which were the source of the reimport of swathes of lost Classical knowledge into Latin Europe in later centuries. Among so much else turned into Arabic, the charming tale of Barlaam and Josaphat, which had started life as the story of the Buddha, passed westwards through this factory of translation (see pp. 231–2).[23] The scale of this feverish acquisition of knowledge, the huge size of Islamic libraries compared with collections in the Christian West and the general sophistication of Abbasid administration were such that, from the eighth century, the mass of texts encouraged a new copying technology imported from China along the trade routes which the Eastern Christians dominated: instead of papyrus or expensive parchment, cloth rags were transformed into paper, durable and comparatively easy to make and cheap as a writing material to cope with the demand.[24]

The late eighth and early ninth centuries were promising times for the Church of the East, aided by the fact that through forty years from the 780s its patriarch, Timothy I, was an outstanding diplomat in his dealings with caliphs who continued to be erratic in their attitude to the Church. It has been suggested that in his time around a quarter of all the world's Christians saw Timothy as their spiritual leader – probably as many as looked to the then pope in the decaying city of Rome, far away in the West.[25] The Patriarch's Church increasingly looked east beyond the Abbasid borders. The vigour of Church life combined with the increasing awareness of the Dyophysite bishops that they had less and less room for manoeuvre within the caliphate: conversions from Islam were forbidden and other potential converts who were not People of the Book were diminishing in numbers, so the Church would have to look elsewhere to spread its message. Patriarch Timothy is known to have consecrated a bishop for Tibet, at a time when its Buddhist identity was still in flux, and he could look much further east than that, to the Christian Church which had flourished there for more than a century.[26]

THE CHURCH IN CHINA

The Chinese Empire had been ruled since 618 by the Tang dynasty, which in the years of its power and prosperity was ready to give a place to any religion which did not seem to threaten its security, providing Bishop Alopen with the opportunity for success on his mission of 635 (see pp. 252–3). Christianity's fortunes in China thereafter were mixed, depending on the whims or foreign policies of successive emperors, but in the mid-eighth century, thanks to the patronage of one general victorious in civil wars, Christians found themselves over several decades in a position of advantage in China which would not be repeated for some centuries. It was from this hopeful time that there survives one of the most remarkable and beautiful monuments of the Church of the East: a black limestone stele standing nearly ten feet tall, which caused justifiable excitement among the Jesuits of a later Christian mission when, in the early 1620s, they learned of its rediscovery (on a site now unknown, but very possibly that of the identifiable Ta Qin monastery in Zhouzhi (see Plate 7). Dated 781, surmounted by dragons and a cross and bearing inscriptions in Chinese and Estrangela, it is a silkily expressed commemoration of imperial favour shown towards the Christians since 635, culminating in their present protector, General Guo Ziyi. Besides its detailed if inevitably politically selective account of that history, it boldly recites a statement of Christian faith in Chinese, commendations of the faith, and poetry in praise of the triune God and of Christ 'divided in nature', with allusions to imperial literature which stake a bold claim for Christianity as the best expression of the universe's underlying principle, the Tao. With the stele's proud enunciation of various ecclesiastical dignitaries alongside emperors and imperial officials, there could be no better symbol of the integration of the Dyophysite Christian community into imperial life. The first and last visual impression that it leaves in its present setting in Xi'an's 'Forest of Stelae' is just how alike are all the other monuments around it.[27]

There are many more traces of the Church of the East's real attempt to explain the Christian message in terms which would make sense to people in this alien culture. From their first arrival in China, Christians seemed to have realized that it would be a good strategy to use language familiar to Chinese from Taoism, as the stele from 781 now at Xi'an witnessed. Taoism, after all, had a vision of the original goodness of human nature which was congenial to Dyophysites emphasizing the whole humanity of Christ's separate human nature alongside his divinity. Yet Dyophysite Christians were also ready to model themselves on another faith which the Chinese recognized as having come from beyond their borders, but which was by now well established and widely respected: Buddhism. So Alopen and his successors presented their faith in the form of sutras, discourses in Buddhist style, and they had no inhibitions in presenting Buddhism as a form of truth, albeit one which needed extending. So Alopen, drawing on the specialized titles of honour of the Buddhists, had written in his *Jesus Messiah Sutra*:

All the buddhas as well as kinnaras and the superintending-devas and arhans can see the Lord of Heaven. No human being, however, has ever seen the Lord of Heaven . . . All the buddhas flow and flux by virtue of this very wind, while in this world, there is no place where the wind does not reach.

Here, there seems to be a real attempt to suggest that the teachings of Buddhism are in a literal sense inspired by the Holy Spirit. Elsewhere in his *Discourse on the oneness of the Ruler of the Universe*, Alopen observed that, thanks to the Devil, '[i]t has become impossible for a human being to understand the truth and attain "liberation from sorrow"' – the latter phrase simply being a Chinese Buddhist term which in turn translated the Sanskrit for liberation, one of many such familiar terms which the missionaries deployed to arouse recognition in their audiences. And in his *Lord of the Universe's discourse on almsgiving*, Alopen could warm to the Lord of the Universe's chosen theme so much that he raised the real possibility of salvation beyond those who recite the creeds of Christianity:

Therefore, you who have already embraced the faith, OR you who do all kinds of meritorious deeds, OR who will walk in his way with an honest heart, shall all enter heaven and remain in that abode of happiness for ever and ever.[28]

All this suggests a faith which, to a degree highly unusual in Christian history, allowed itself to listen to other great interpretations of the divine. Perhaps this was inevitable. Christianity's previous encounter with ancient, sophisticated wisdom had been with Plato and Aristotle; and that encounter had transformed it in the second century CE. Now, for the first time, it was meeting a variety of highly developed religious systems, in a situation where it had no power of coercion. Moreover, the Church of the East pushed forward its frontiers through Syrian merchants, who were renowned throughout Asia for their bargaining skills. Can it be any surprise that the result was a form of Christianity which delighted in theological give and take?

The problem for the Dyophysites of China was that integration into Chinese society also meant dependence on power within it. As so often in the history of the Church of the East, the years of good fortune were comparatively brief. During the mid-ninth century the Emperor Wuzong turned against all religions which he regarded as foreign and the Church suffered accordingly. When the Tang dynasty finally collapsed in 907, the western trade routes which remained the lifeline of the Church were closed and the possibility of renewal through missions for the time being came to an end. But only for the time being. Three centuries later the accidents of history nevertheless offered a second chance for the Church of the East in China, because of its persisting ancient presence in Central Asia, and maybe in China too. Once more the Church came close to achieving what Islam was able to make permanent: winning the allegiance of successful military dynasties. The near-miss took place among the Mongols: the last in a centuries-long sequence of Central Asian nomadic peoples whose migrations shaped the history of both Asia and Europe, and, with it, the future of the Christian religion.

THE MONGOLS: NEW HOPE
AND CATASTROPHE

The Mongols' rise among the various peoples of the steppes was comparatively sudden at the end of the twelfth century. They had their own religious system, which described the way in which sky and earth combined in cosmic consciousness, as do male and female; they also believed that souls animated both people and animals, and survived after death. Given their nomadic lifestyle close to one of the world's greatest trade routes, they had nevertheless long been familiar with and genially interested in a wide spectrum of other people's religious beliefs, and they were inclined to give an ear to any religious ideas which took their fancy – Chinese Taoism and Confucianism, Islam, Buddhism and Dyophysite Christianity were the principal wares on offer.[29] When in 1007 Christianity gained its first success among the Mongols, it was thanks to the long-dead Syrian St Sergius – a tribute to how this hugely popular military saint had impressed himself on imaginations far away from the site of his Roman martyrdom seven centuries before (see pp. 237–8). Sergius had power, and the Mongols became increasingly interested in power. Perhaps also these warriors who relied for their success on their close bonding found Sergius's intimate relationship with his soldier-companion Bacchus a good model for their own warfare.

It was indeed to one of the most powerful rulers among the Mongols that Sergius appeared in a vision. In or around 1007, the Mongol Khan of the Keraits, adrift in a snowstorm, became convinced that he would die lost and alone, but the saint promised deliverance in return for conversion, and deliverance from the blizzard duly arrived. The Dyophysite clergy who then received the large numbers of Keraits trooping into baptism in the wake of their hugely relieved khan were, with characteristic flexibility, creative in their tolerance of existing Mongol religious beliefs. They were happy to preside over the solemn corporate drinking of mares' milk blessed on their altar by the Khan himself. Amid the immensity of the Central and East Asian steppes, with few clergy of any persuasion to badger their beliefs into tidiness, Mongols preserved a comfortable mixture of Christianity and tradition. It is clear from archaeological finds that they enjoyed wearing Christian crosses, though they might enliven these with such symbols as the Indian swastika which Buddhists had brought them. Some of their rulers took Christian names;

the greatest Mongol ruler of them all, Temüjin, who in 1206 was proclaimed 'Genghis Khan' ('Ruler of the Ocean'), had been the vassal of a Christian Kerait khan and married his overlord's Christian niece.[30] It was through Temüjin's leadership that, in the space of a few decades, the Mongols became a world power to terrify people from the Mediterranean to the China Sea. His successors were convinced that they had been destined for world supremacy, and for a while it looked as if they were right.[31]

This was a moment when the immense conquests of Genghis and his successors might have promoted an official Dyophysite Christianity throughout Asia from the Black Sea to the China Sea. During the thirteenth century, the Turkic people in Inner Mongolia known as the Önggüds mostly became Christian, including their royal family, and they remained so for more than a century. As a result of Genghis's carefully planned set of alliances with Christian Kerait Mongol princesses, a series of Great Khans had Christian mothers, including Kublai Khan, who in the years up to 1279 fought his way to become the first Yuan emperor of China. Under Kublai Khan, Dyophysite Christians returned to the centre of power in China. After nearly three centuries in which their presence had been scarcely perceptible, they revealed themselves from generations of outward profession of other Chinese religions which had official favour. Yet the old pattern repeated itself. The Yuan rulers of China quickly conformed themselves to the rich and ancient culture which they had seized and, worse still, successive Yuan monarchs showed themselves steadily more incompetent to rule. Their overthrow by the fiercely xenophobic native Ming dynasty in 1368 was a bad blow to Christianity in the empire. It still had yet to interest more than a minority of Chinese. It is perhaps appropriate that the only apparent modern linguistic survival of the Syriac missions in the Far East is the word for 'tomb', *qavra*, used by the Turco-Mongol people known as the Uyghur, in the Xinjiang Autonomous Region of China.[32]

So in neither of its great missionary ventures did the Church of the East achieve enough indigenous support to make an open stand against whatever the emperor decreed. By the time that a new wave of Western Latin Christians arrived from Europe in the sixteenth century, Christian faith and practice had once more virtually disappeared – at least in public. What has become evident in recent years in the countryside beyond the former imperial capital Xi'an, around that extraordinary survival the Ta Qin monastery pagoda, is the likelihood that a consciousness of the Christian tradition and even a Christianity disguised as

Taoism did persist. After the Catholic missions of the sixteenth and seventeenth centuries, this small area became and remains a stronghold of rural Chinese Catholicism, Catholic parish churches now peppering the skyline as they might do in southern Europe. Maybe this was not the only place in China which was home to such a survival. Maybe secret Christians remained to welcome the first Western missionaries, as they did in later centuries after later persecutions, and there are many remarkable possibilities still to be investigated in the history of Chinese Christianity.[33]

The Mongols' conquests turned west as well. They finally shattered the power of the already declining Abbasid dynasty; their leader in this was Il-Khan ('Subordinate Khan') Hülagü, whose principal wife belonged to the Church of the East. That was a happy circumstance for the Christians of Baghdad, who were the only community whom the Mongols spared massacre when the city fell in 1258; indeed the Mongols gave the Catholicos one of the caliphs' palaces in which to establish his headquarters and cathedral complex.[34] Now the Il-Khan established a new Mongol dynasty in Iran. It was not just the Dyophysites who had real expectations of a new Christian empire based on the dubious authority of these spectacularly brutal warriors. Hope flared up among Western Latin Christians, whose Middle Eastern Crusades against Muslim powers were looking increasingly hopeless (see pp. 384–6). The results were some epic Christian ventures into unknown territories to investigate the new diplomatic possibilities, led by a formidable set of missionaries from an innovative Latin organization, the Order of Franciscan Friars (see pp. 402–4).[35]

In the early 1250s, the great Crusader-king of France, Louis IX, was inspired to send William of Rubruck, a sharp-eyed Franciscan, as an emissary to the Great Khan Möngke in Central Asia. William recorded his travels in an absorbingly interesting journal of one of the most remarkable diplomatic exploits in this unprecedented episode of Western exploration.[36] Just as enterprising and exotic visitors in the other direction, in 1285 and 1287–8, were successive envoys of the Il-Khan Arghun: first a Chinese Christian official of Kublai Khan and then a Dyophysite monk of Mongol descent called Rabban Sauma, who successively travelled to Constantinople, to the pope in Rome and then westwards all the way to the kings of England and France. In turn, Sauma's visit inspired fresh Franciscan efforts to penetrate Central Asia in the name of Chalcedonian Christianity. One result was the erection in the 1290s of a Gothic-style cathedral of the Western Latin rite in the improbable setting of Inner Mongolia, where its foundations have been excavated at the site of the city of Olon Sume. The Franciscan friar responsible travelled on to China, where he spent most of his time pestering Dyophysite Christians to become Chalcedonians.[37] By that time, optimism on either side was running out.

It was becoming clear that the Mongols were not going to fulfil the hopes which Christian strategists placed in them – that might have been obvious from the beginning, if their ghastly toll of millions of people and even animals massacred on an industrial scale had been taken into account. The Mongols were unimpressed by their increasing acquaintance with Christian rivalries, which had not previously been apparent in Mongol homelands in Dyophysite Central Asia, and, as always, they had their own priorities. William of Rubruck commented with rueful humour after his meeting with the Great Khan Möngke on the chances of converting the great man: 'If I had possessed the power to work miracles, as Moses did, he might perhaps have humbled himself.'[38] Already a train of events in the 1250s had begun the downfall of Christianity in Central Asia, signalling the end of any possibility of a tame Christian Mongol empire. First was the conversion to Islam of Berke, one of the royal family of the Mongol grouping known as the Kipchak Khanate or Golden Horde, in what is now southern Russia (see pp. 510–11). In 1256 Berke murdered his Christian nephew in order to take power as Kipchak Khan, and although the Mongol Il-Khans of Iran were still apparently riding high on military conquest, Berke allied with the enemies of the Il-Khans, the Islamic rulers (Mamluks) of Egypt. It was a dangerous split in Mongol solidarity, which was fatally prolonged by an accident: the death of the Great Khan Möngke far away in Mongolia. Mongol leaders returned to their heartland to choose his successor, leaving their forces in a weakened state, and the Mamluks were able to inflict a crushing defeat at 'Ayn Jālūt in the Holy Land in 1260.[39]

This was the first check on Mongol power, and the beginning of steady decline for the Il-Khans of Iran, who themselves turned away from their alliance with Christianity when they realized that Christian Europe had more important priorities than giving them support, and that Christian Europe was in any case less impressive in military terms than it liked to think. The future lay with those Mongol rulers increasingly committed to Islam. The fortunes of the Church of the East plummeted still further with the rise to power from the mid-fourteenth century of the Mongol warlord Timur or Tamerlane, intent on restoring

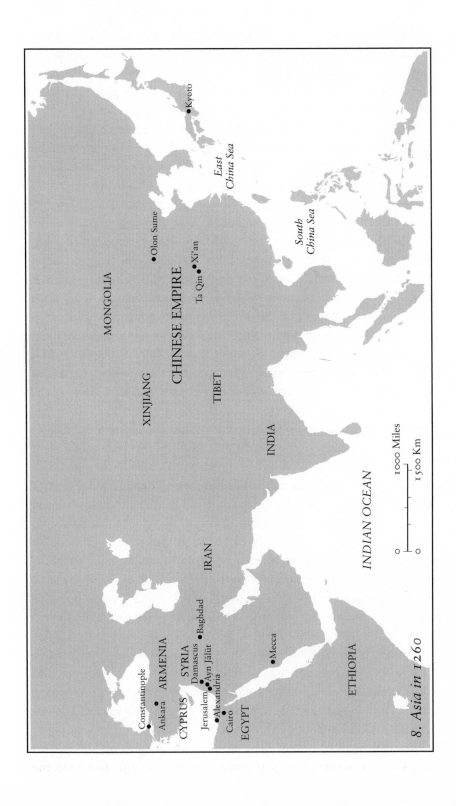

8. Asia in 1260

Constantinople
Ankara
ARMENIA
CYPRUS
SYRIA
Damascus
Jerusalem
Alexandria
Cairo
EGYPT
Ayn Jālūt
Baghdad
IRAN
Mecca
ETHIOPIA
INDIAN OCEAN
INDIA
TIBET
XINJIANG
MONGOLIA
CHINESE EMPIRE
Ta Qin
Xi'an
Olon Sume
Kyoto
East
China Sea
South
China Sea

1000 Miles
1500 Km

the glory of Mongol power from its fractured state. Timur's conquests extended from the Black Sea to Afghanistan and the Persian Gulf. His systematic cruelty and will to destruction made the Mongol khans' massacres in previous centuries look half-hearted. His mountainous piles of skulls are no picturesque myth. While Timur had no compunction in attacking other Muslim rulers, including eliminating the Il-Khans, Muslims generally fared better in his conquests, and it was Christianity in vast swathes of its former eastern strongholds which chiefly suffered.[40]

Timur's orgies of destruction hit Christian populations in Central Asia which had already been terribly reduced by the advance of the plague which western Europe would come to know in 1348–9 as the Black Death. From now on, outside the comparative safety of India, the story of the Church of the East recedes to the efforts by disparate enclaves to cling on to existence in the face of Islamic dominance, usually in remote upland areas out of sight of the authorities. Even when Timur found no successors in his cruelty and the Mongol threat receded, the growing power of the Ottoman Turks (see p. 483) continued the pressure on non-Muslims. In an increasingly hostile Islamic world, embittered at the memory of the alien outrage of the Western Crusades, the ancient privileged place of Christians at the Courts of monarchs disappeared.

The Miaphysite Church of Armenia suffered like the Dyophysites from the calamities of the fourteenth century. The last independent Armenian kingdom, in Cilicia in south-west Turkey, fell to Mamluk forces in 1375 and more than two centuries of struggle for Christian survival followed. The Armenians had centuries of experience in being buffeted by neighbouring great powers and they were long used to migrating away from disaster. These desperate years sent more of them travelling through eastern Europe as far away as Poland, let alone whatever refuge they could find in Asia – but as with the Jews in diaspora, their sufferings sharpened their skills in commerce and negotiation, skills which they were ready to apply to their religious troubles. From the fourteenth century, at odds theologically with both their Byzantine neighbours and the Church of the East, they showed an enterprising interest in alliance with the Church of Rome, despite the problems caused by memories of Chalcedon, and this produced some lasting results, despite the intense divisions which it also created among Armenian Christians.

Pope John XXII, an energetic though not uncontroversial pontiff (reigned 1316–34), showed particular interest in the plight of the

Armenians and the prospect of bringing them into the Catholic fold. He sustained the missions of friars (both Franciscans and Dominicans) into Central Asia which had begun in the thirteenth century. Some of the warmest contacts which the friars made were with migrant Armenian communities in Iran and on the steppes; the earliest translations of recent Latin theologians like the Dominican Thomas Aquinas (see pp. 412–15) into any other language were into Armenian. One group of Armenian monks in Asia actually remodelled their monastic life on Dominican lines and accepted Roman obedience, taking a Latin name which also proclaimed their pride in their Armenian heritage as the Fratres Unitores of the congregation of St Gregory the Illuminator (see pp. 186–7). Similar Church unions took place in eastern Europe in the fifteenth century, in which Armenian congregations kept their liturgy and distinctive devotional practices, while acknowledging papal primacy as 'Uniates'. These unions provided the model for later similar arrangements which Rome made with many other groups in the Counter-Reformation (see pp. 533–5). Not everyone was delighted by these moves to unity on Rome's terms: the Armenian hierarchy clinging on in the Armenian heartland furiously opposed union with the papacy and the word 'Uniate' has often carried an abusive flavour. A Miaphysite Catholicate continued in very difficult circumstances to sustain the independent life of the Church from the cathedral in the former Armenian capital city of Ējmiacin or Vałaršapat.[41]

In the same period, the Dyophysite Church of the East developed its own strategies for survival. In a move of pragmatic desperation, it diverged from the universal tradition of Eastern Christianity and increasingly abandoned artistic representations of sacred subjects, especially in paintings or statues; they were likely to attract vandalism from Muslims. The Dyophysites had in any case always rejected crucifixes, which suggested to them a confusion of the natures of Jesus making God suffer on the Cross; so their crosses were bare to symbolize the resurrected Christ (ironically, the Miaphysite Armenians favoured the same bare cross, for their own opposite theological reasons). Friar William of Rubruck had been scandalized in the 1250s when a Dyophysite Christian in Central Asia saw a silver crucifix 'in the French style' and wrenched the figure of Christ off it.[42] When Protestant missionaries arrived in the Ottoman Empire in the nineteenth century, they were surprised and delighted by the Nestorians' lack of images and declared the Church of the East 'the Protestants of Asia'. By then the Dyophysites were only too pleased to cooperate with the blithe misapprehensions of new potential allies, for the medieval and early modern periods had proved by no means to be the nadir of the Church's fortunes. They were experiencing fresh disasters which, in the last century and a half, have afflicted both the Church of the East and the Church of Armenia with some of the worst stories of martyrdom in Christian history (see pp. 854–5 and 923–4).[43]

ISLAM AND THE
AFRICAN CHURCHES

The story of Christianity in Africa into the early modern period is likewise one of defensiveness and decline nearly everywhere, leading inexorably to its complete extinction along the North African coast and in Nubia. The North African Church, the first stronghold of Latin Christianity, the home of Tertullian, Cyprian and Augustine of Hippo, should be given credit for surviving the Arab conquest of the 690s for some five centuries in certain areas, but it never recovered its unity after the bitterness of fourth- and fifth-century divisions between the Donatists and the Catholic elite which was in communion with the wider Mediterranean Church (see pp. 303–5). Eventually in the twelfth century the rigidly intolerant Almohad dynasty insisted on mass conversion of both Jews and Christians. It is probably significant that the Church seems to have remained at least formally Latin-speaking: gravestones have been discovered south of Tripoli which as late as the eleventh century do their best to use Latin, though '*vixit*' ('lived') has become '*bixit*', and '*vitam*' ('life') '*bitam*'.[44] This use of speech which represented a vanished governing class rather than the Berber language contrasts with the Copts' maintenance of their vernacular in Egypt, but also with the fact that the Copts were sufficiently numerous and part of mainstream Egyptian society that in the end they adopted Arabic as their devotional and liturgical language as well as for everyday conversation.

In similar circumstances to the Church of the East, the Coptic patriarchs were made to live in the newly founded Arab capitals in Egypt: first at Fustāt and then nearby Cairo, after the Fatimid dynasty of caliphs created it in the late tenth century. The Miaphysite faith of the Copts meant that their Muslim overlords did not identify them with the Byzantine Empire and generally treated them with tolerance. Wholly exceptional was an episode of persecution under Caliph al-Hākim from 1004 to 1013, which included the destruction of the Church of the Holy Sepulchre in Jerusalem – one of the sparks of the eleventh-century impulse of Latin Christians to reconquer the Holy Land (see pp. 381–9). Hākim's atypical actions should not be attributed to Islam as much as to insanity, which eventually led him to proclaim himself as Allah, whereupon he was murdered by outraged fellow Muslims.[45]

Greater and irreversible troubles came when the Latin Crusades began and were followed by Mongol advances. The Mamluks, who seized power in Egypt in 1250, were a caste of men captured for military service, so they drew their identity from their defence of Islam against its enemies. Even though Coptic Christians had little sympathy either with crusading Western Christians, who regarded them as heretics, or with Mongols, who favoured Nestorians heretical in Miaphysite eyes, it was now easy for Egyptian Muslims and their rulers to regard any Christian as a fifth columnist, especially when Crusaders and Mongols turned to actual invasion of Egypt during the thirteenth century. Just as in Central Asia, the fourteenth century proved the turning point into decline for the Coptic cause in Egypt, though not here into extinction. There was a particularly terrifying sequence of anti-Christian pogroms in 1354, when churches were torn down and both Jews and Christians were forced by mobs to recite the Islamic profession of faith, or be burned to death; unlike previous outbreaks there was little refuge, since the terror extended throughout the land, not just to Cairo.[46] Christians were forced out of most of the best land in Egypt, 'exiles in their own country'.[47] In a desperate and temporary move in the fifteenth century, the Church agreed to a union with the Latin Western Church, at a time when the Byzantine emperor was trying to arrange a similar deal with Rome for Greek Orthodoxy at the Council of Florence, but the Copts soon realized that they would gain little benefit from it.[48] Their survival over the next three centuries was through their own efforts and the stubborn maintenance of ancient traditions in their monasteries, most of which could survive only in the most remote or poverty-stricken locations.

While Christianity throughout North Africa, Egypt and Asia succumbed almost universally to Islamic rule, Ethiopia stood out as still a Christian monarchy, protected by its rugged geography and distance from the Muslim heartlands, but now rarely a major player in the politics of the Red Sea and Arabia, and never wholly secure. In the tenth century, Ethiopia faced a devastating revolt by a chieftainess, Gudit or Judith, who is said to have made it the business of her rebels to cause as much destruction as possible to the churches and Christian life of the kingdom. Certainly only the most remote buildings survive from an earlier date, most spectacularly the ancient cliff-top monastery of Däbra Damo in the Aksum region; this was one of the earliest foundations of Ethiopian monasticism, whose church, perched on a cliff top above a high hill, is still only accessible by scaling the cliff face clinging to a cable. Such troubles, and the near-obliteration of Ethiopia's historical record from the time of Gudit and before, make any attempt to reconstruct Ethiopian Christian history speculative, and a junk heap of romantic misconceptions demands a degree of critical ruthlessness in dealing with what evidence we have. The fragmentary truth looks remarkable enough.

At some periods Ethiopia was almost completely cut off from other Christians and might even have been without any *abun* sent from Alexandria to link it to the worldwide apostolic succession of bishops. Its available theological literature was selective and haphazard in character – so the Ethiopians came to treat the book known as I Enoch as part of the scriptural canon when it had lost respectability anywhere else, and indeed I Enoch played a special part in Ethiopian tradition by providing material for the foundation for the royal epic, the *Kebra Nagast* (see p. 244).[49] Naturally prominent was a Miaphysite doctrinal anthology, named the *Qerellos* after the main content extracted from the works of Cyril of Alexandria, but despite this link with one part of the wider Christian world, it was small wonder that the preoccupations and character of Ethiopian faith developed on very individual (not to say eccentric) lines. It was the Ethiopians, for instance, who meditated on various Coptic apocryphal accounts of Pontius Pilate and decided that the Roman governor who presided over Christ's crucifixion should become a Confessor of the Church, to be celebrated in their sacred art and given a feast day in June and a star place in the liturgy at Epiphany, the greatest feast of the year, when the priest intoned a phrase from the Psalms which was also an echo of his words: 'I will wash my hands in innocence'. The Copts and Ethiopians did not forget Pilate's complicity in the death of Christ, but in retelling his story they made him realize the full extent of his guilt, and they brought a symmetry to his fate by making him die on a cross, like the trio whom he had killed at Golgotha on the day that the sun hid its face. Thus Ethiopia's royal Church found a unique way of assuaging the prolonged Christian embarrassment that the life of Christ had been played out far from the contemporary institutions of worldly power.[50]

It is to a new dynasty, the Zagwe kings (1137–1270), that Ethiopian

Christianity attributes a cluster of Christian monuments which are as haunting and astonishing as the earlier stelae of Aksum: the twelve churches of the Zagwe capital city of Lalibela, cut from the living rock (see Plate 9). What is now a small rural town was renamed after a Zagwe king who reigned at the turn of the twelfth and thirteenth centuries, to whom these extraordinary buildings are attributed. In fact, they must have taken much longer to construct than Lalibela's reign alone; some may be much earlier and may have survived the havoc attributed to Gudit through their indestructibility. It is said that King Lalibela conceived the idea of recreating Jerusalem in his capital after a visit to the Holy Land, in an effort to compensate for the renewed fall of the Holy City to Muslim armies in 1187 (see p. 385). As so often in Ethiopian history, it is impossible to know whether centuries of subsequent meditation, wishful thinking and purposeful political rebranding have overlaid whatever original scheme was intended at Lalibela, to produce its present rich skein of associations with Jerusalem – the Church of Golgotha now includes two tombs designated respectively for Jesus Christ and King Lalibela, and the Church of the Holy Sepulchre lies at the heart of the Lalibela complex.[51] What is clear is that this wave of new monuments to Ethiopian Christian confidence was followed by a major expansion of Christian life in a renewal of monasticism. Monks founded their communities for the first time in the central highlands, usually deliberately seizing pre-Christian holy sites, and they displayed all the heroic feats of ascetic self-denial which had been pioneered in Syria and Egypt. They were at the heart of two centuries and more which were another golden age of Ethiopian Christianity, as well as one of its greatest periods of contention and struggle.[52]

At the end of the thirteenth century, another dynasty supplanted the Zagwe, and between its founder, Yekuno Amlak (reigned 1270–85), and his grandson Amdä Seyon (reigned 1314–44), it came to restore the military might of Ethiopia. It appears that the Egyptian Coptic Church was affronted at the usurpation and refused to supply an *abun*, so for some considerable time the Ethiopians had to resort to bishops from Syria to preserve their episcopal succession.[53] Such internationally expressed doubts needed addressing and a sustained campaign began to plug the dynasty into ancient history, with the aid of King Solomon: Amdä Seyon's name ('Pillar of Zion') was no casual reference. It may thus be that this was the stage at which the Ethiopian Church's identification with Israel really began to become distinctive. The existence of the *Kebra Nagast* may have been the inspiration for this stratagem, and it is likely that its present literary form dates largely to around 1300.[54]

Later tradition represents a vital element in Negus Yekuno's support as his understanding with the chief activist in the expansion of monasteries, the monk from Däbra Damo, Iyäsus Mo'a ('Jesus has prevailed'). It is a plausible but also a convenient story, since the monks were to prove a constant source of difficulty for the 'Solomonic' dynasty, through their independent charismatic authority and individual opinions. The chief disciple of Iyäsus Mo'a, Täklä Haymanot ('Plant of Faith'), was a formidable ascetic, said to have spent a considerable proportion of his life standing on one leg in his monastic cell, feeding on one seed brought by a bird once a year. When the other leg atrophied away, God rewarded the monk with an array of wings.[55] We can take these stories as a shorthand indication for a religious leader with an intimidating arsenal of power. Täklä Haymanot was the first in a series of monks to become a key figure at Court, as the Echage (*ečägé*). This official came to exercise the sort of power over Church life and government which might have been the *abun*'s, if the *abun* had not been an elderly Egyptian.

Tensions soon evolved between monarchy and monastery, whose new vigour naturally looked on existing Ethiopian institutions with reforming zeal, and did not always welcome the new close association between the Court and some leading monks. One vexed issue has continued to agitate Christians throughout Africa to the present day: polygamy versus monogamy (see pp. 883–5). The Church was anxious to outlaw polygamy, which, despite having a perfectly respectable presence in the Tanakh, is clearly unacceptable in the New Testament. Ethiopian monarchs conformed to African tradition and habitually took several wives: the monk BäSälotä Mika'él had the temerity to denounce Negus Amdä Seyon himself for both polygamy and an array of concubines, and it is noticeable that the Kebra Nagast insists on monogamy for Christians.[56] The monarchy stilled much of the criticism with generous grants of land to leading monasteries, and it did not give up polygamy. Neither did most of the Ethiopian laity, who virtually all accepted that the price of their maintenance of polygamy was that they would not get married in church, and that between marriage and final bereavement from their partners they would face exclusion from the Eucharist. They made something positive of their exclusion by turning it to the enthusiastic ritual practice of fasting.[57]

Parties developed among the monks and particular groups of monasteries, which were something like the orders of monks which evolved

in the twelfth-century Western Church (see pp. 389–93). Particularly
important over several centuries from the early fourteenth was the
northern grouping known as the House of Ewostatewos, named after a
monk who ended his life an exile, travelling extensively beyond his
country as far as Miaphysite Armenia. Despite this unusual cosmopolitanism in their founder-hero, admirers of Ewostatewos concentrated
their devotion on a peculiarly Ethiopian issue reflecting the Church's
exploration of Judaism: the observance of the Jewish Sabbath as well
as the Christian Sunday. This aroused opposition, especially from
Christians encouraged by Alexandrian-born *abuns* who knew the practice of the wider Church. Among a number of wooden inscriptions
from Lalibela dubiously attributed to King Lalibela himself, the longest
contains praise of Sunday; this probably tells us nothing about that
particular king's attitude to the subject, but may be taken as a contribution to the debate at some date which is uncertain.[58] At issue
was how far the Ethiopian Church was prepared to travel in its own
direction and ignore what links it had with the wider world: monks of
the House of Ewostatewos rejected ordination by the *abun*, and it is
possible that they might have ended up as separate from their parent
Christianity as that other independent-minded Ethiopian movement, the
Falasha (see pp. 243–4).

The triumph of the Sabbath was sealed by devoted advocacy from
one of Ethiopia's most remarkable monarchs, Zar'a Ya'qob (reigned
1434–68), who combined military success with intense piety, himself
writing works of Christian instruction for his subjects. Thanks to Zar'a
Ya'qob, Ethiopia's effective rule extended once more to the coast of the
Red Sea, and despite the Negus's pride in the special character of Ethiopian devotion, he was intensely aware of his links with a wider world;
he took the regnal name Constantine. There was a great sensation in
Europe when a delegation of two monks from the Ethiopian monastery
in Jerusalem arrived in 1441 at the Pope's council at Florence (see
pp. 492–3) and uttered the name of their far-distant monarch – this
was the same council which also received representations from the
beleaguered Copts. Zar'a Ya'qob also derived great spiritual comfort
from an unlikely source, a short popular work of devotion called *The
Miracles of Mary*, which seems to have been compiled for use in Marian
shrines in France in the twelfth century; having gained great popularity
in western Europe, it had been translated into Arabic and then into
Ethiopic. The Negus made it a mandatory work of devotion for his
clergy: a strange stray from an alien world which he nevertheless found

a useful tool in moulding his people to a single style of faith, and Marian devotion was hugely reinforced in the Ethiopian Church.[59] Less indebted to French devotional style was Zar'a Ya'qob's decree that all his subjects should be tattooed on their foreheads with the words 'Father, Son and Holy Spirit' and on their right and left hands respectively 'I deny the Devil' and 'I am a servant of Mary'. Ethiopian Christian tattooing still characteristically features a cross in blue on the chin or the forehead.[60]

Zar'a Ya'qob was determined that religious divisions should not undermine his newly extended empire, and key to this was a full understanding between the Solomonic monarchy and the awkward monks of the House of Ewostatewos. This was achieved at a major council of the Ethiopian Church summoned to the Negus's newly founded monastery of Däbra Mitmaq in 1449, at which the main agreement was that both the Sabbath and Sunday should henceforth be observed. In return, monks of the House of Ewostatewos agreed to be reconciled to the *abun* and accept ordination at his hands; so the forces of Ethiopian particularism were not terminally separated from the Church's link to the wider Christian world. It was an important moment for the future of Ethiopian Christianity, a moment nevertheless when, in continuing to observe the Sabbath, it explicitly separated itself from the devotional practice of the Church it knew best, the Miaphysite Church of Alexandria.

The Council of Däbra Mitmaq was a triumph for the Negus himself, the zenith of one of the most prosperous and self-confident eras in the empire's existence. His last years were troubled, as (in a pattern which would be repeated in Ethiopian history) this exceptionally talented man descended into paranoia and obsessive brutality. He became a recluse; his drive to regulate his Church, his hostility to any Judaism beyond the extent of his own ordinances and his determination to eradicate traditional non-Christian religion all led him into a spree of punishment killings. Among the victims accused of betraying their Christian faith were one of his wives and several of his children, flogged to death. After the Negus's own death, the movement away from the wider Church might have proceeded further, as powerful voices continued to question the role of the Egyptian *abun* in the Church, but in 1477 a further council of the Church presided over by his son reaffirmed this ancient link with the Patriarch of Alexandria. The fifteenth century thus set patterns and boundaries for Ethiopian Christianity which survived into modern times. Yet those links to a wider Catholicity were still to a Christianity which rejected the Roman imperial Church's conclusions at Chalcedon. This was a matter of great significance when the wider world erupted into the remoteness of Ethiopia in the sixteenth century, during one of the worst tests and most terrible times in its history (see pp. 711–12).

The Western bishops at the Council of Florence had not expected to hear of a king of Ethiopia called Zar'a Ya'qob, but they did know (or thought they knew) of a priest-king in the East called Prester John. Since the twelfth-century Crusades had first brought intensified contacts between Europe and the Middle East, there had been tales of this mighty Christian ruler who would be an ally for hard-pressed Latin Europeans against the threat of Islam. Some placed him in India, others, vague about geography beyond their own world, further north in Asia – this drew on the reality of Muslim defeats by Mongol khans in twelfth-century Central Asia who were in fact adherents of Buddhism, a religion which meant nothing to western Europeans. Friar William of Rubruck, one of the few to know better, had commented sourly in the 1260s that the stories about Prester John were all the fault of the Nestorians (Dyophysites), who were prone to 'create big rumours out of nothing'.[61]

At the Council of Florence in 1441, it was the reality of Ethiopia, a remote but powerful Christian monarchy south beyond Egypt, that encouraged new European excitement about Prester John. Prester John went on prompting optimism for a turn for the better in Christian fortunes; in addition to two hundred known manuscripts of the Latin letter written by the imaginary king between the twelfth and seventeenth centuries, there were fourteen early printed editions of the letter up to 1565, and large numbers of translations into vernacular European languages.[62] Nevertheless, in cold practical results, Prester John turned out to be a disappointing myth, and what it chiefly revealed was just how little Western Chalcedonian Christians knew about centuries of Christian struggle, scholarship, sanctity and heroism in another world. Western Christianity, heir to Chalcedon, Reformation and Counter-Reformation, still has a long way to go before the balance is fully righted.

Western Christians have forgotten that before the coming of Islam utterly transformed the situation in the eastern Mediterranean and Asia, there was a good chance that the centre of gravity of Christian faith might have moved east to Iraq rather than west to Rome. Instead, the ancient Christianity of the East was nearly everywhere faced with a destiny of contraction in numbers, suffering and martyrdom which still continues. But there was one practical consequence of the fifteenth-century Latin delusion that Prester John might unite with Western

Christians. The myth generated an optimism which had a vital galvanizing effect on Latin Christianity, so it played a part in that surprising
new expansion worldwide which from the end of the fifteenth century
led Western Catholicism and Protestantism to become the dominant
form of the Christian faith into modern times (see Chapter 17). It is
towards Rome that we now turn, to begin exploring how this unlikely
turn of events took place.

PART IV

The Unpredictable Rise
of Rome
(300–1300)

9

The Making of Latin Christianity
(300–500)

THE ROME OF THE POPES (300–400)

Two bishops in the universal Church still use an ancient Latin title which started as a child's word of affection for its father: '*Papa*' or, in English, 'Pope'. One is the Coptic Patriarch of Alexandria, supposedly a successor to the Gospel writer Mark, and certainly successor to Cyril, Dioscorus and the brutally murdered Proterius. The other is the Bishop of Rome, only slightly less supposedly a successor to the Apostle Peter, and leader of the largest single grouping within world Christianity. Of all the various Christian understandings of the word 'Catholic', the most commonly used is a description for the Church over which the pope in Rome presides, and with that usage there go claims for an overriding and objective authority among all other Christian bodies, which the contemporary papacy has so far done nothing to repudiate.[1] A more neutral description of the 'Catholic Church' would be 'the Western Church of the Latin Rite'. The point of this admittedly cumbersome label is that it acknowledges the equal historic status of the various Churches of Orthodoxy in eastern Europe and the Middle East, whom we have still to meet, not to mention the various Churches of Asia and Africa which decided after the fifth century to ignore or repudiate the Chalcedonian Definition of the nature of Jesus Christ.

We now explore how this Latin-speaking Christianity evolved and flourished in western Europe up to the fourteenth century, when the pope's steady accumulation of authority began to falter. That was followed by a crisis in the sixteenth century, when much of Western Christianity with a Latin heritage broke away from its acknowledgement of the pope's leadership and gained yet another label as 'Protestantism'. The surviving Church under the Roman obedience still sustains one of the world's oldest monarchies, based on the claim to succeed Peter as Bishop of Rome and to be the guardian of his tomb. As we have noted (see pp. 134–5), such a claim bore the price of a gradual marginalization of the memory of Rome's other apostolic martyr, whose death was more certainly placed in the city, Paul of Tarsus. But that change was part of a momentous shift in the story of Christianity. From being the poor relation of the Greek- and Semitic-speaking Churches of the East, Latin Christianity survived largely unscathed the eruption of Islam, and embarked on adventures which turned it into the first world faith. It should not be forgotten how unpredictable this outcome was.

Peter's charisma was the most useful resource at the disposal of Roman bishops as, from the third century, they increasingly claimed to be arbiters of doctrine in the wider Church. No pope before mid-fifth-century Leo the Great at the time of the Council of Chalcedon in 451, and virtually none after him, could claim the authority of being a major theologian, nor did the city prove to be a centre of lively theological discussion or controversy. It is significant that the one exception to this rule, the disputes over Monarchian views of Christ (see pp. 145–7), had occurred in the late second century while the Church in Rome's predominant language was still Greek and links to the East were still strong. After that, the two outstanding theologians writing in Latin up to the fifth century, Tertullian and Augustine, were both natives not of Italy but of North Africa. The pope's claim to a special place in the life of the universal Church came rather from the tombs of the Apostles, and from the end of the third century it was reinforced by a further accident of history.

The Emperor Diocletian's reorganization of the whole empire would not have seemed particularly relevant to the popes in Rome when it took place in the 290s; he was after all about to become one of the Church's most dangerous enemies. Nevertheless, it had a major and permanent effect on the city. Diocletian removed the real centre of imperial government to four other capitals more strategically placed for emperors to deal with the problematic northern and eastern frontiers of the empire – Nicomedia in Asia Minor, Sirmium in what is now Serbia, Mediolanum, the modern Milan, and Augusta Trevorum, the modern Trier. Emperors never again returned to Rome for extended residence. Once the Church became the ally and beneficiary of emperors rather than the victim of their persecution, that vacuum in secular power in the ancient capital meant that the Christian bishop was given an opportunity to expand his power and position. By the end of the fourth century this combination of advantages made it worthwhile for Greek Christians in their various intractable disputes to appeal to popes for support, the most outstanding example being the place of Pope Leo I's Tome at Chalcedon.

Constantine I mightily helped the process along when he gave Christianity official status. In Rome he nevertheless had a handicap: he was working within the restrictions of a city whose heritage of monuments and temples reflected the glory of Christianity's enemies. Even though Rome was no longer in any real sense his capital, Constantine gave the Church in the city a set of Christian buildings which in some important respects set patterns for the future of Christian architecture, and in others remained deeply idiosyncratic. In any case, their splendour formed a major element in the fascination which Rome came to exercise for Western Christians, and it is worth considering in some detail these buildings which so seized the imagination of generation on generation of pilgrims. First, the property inheritance of Constantine's wife, Fausta, enabled him to build one monumental church inside the city boundaries: a basilica dedicated to the Saviour which became and remains the cathedral of the Bishop of Rome, and was rededicated much later as St John Lateran. Many basilicas in centuries to come followed its plan and architectural forms at various levels of magnificence or modesty, but at the time this church was not on a prominent or especially visible site compared with the city's ancient architectural wonders, and the Emperor's other major Christian building projects had to be beyond the city walls.[2]

The sense of something radically new happening to Christianity in these other architectural gifts is accentuated by the fact that, in terms of Christian architecture, they were not much imitated. The gruesomely martyred deacon St Lawrence, who had won his martyr's crown in the mid-third century by being roasted alive, was honoured with a monumental building of U-shaped plan like a truncated Roman circus, forming a large covered cemetery for those wishing to benefit in death through burial close to this very popular saint.[3] The handful of circus-shaped churches of Constantine in Rome seemed to have been designed also just like the circuses of old Roman society as meeting places for great numbers of Christian believers, not just during the time of service. Perhaps they also provided a deliberate, triumphant reminiscence of the use to which circuses had occasionally been put: to torture and murder Christians before the new dispensation. The new regime was not shy of reminding Rome of the tally of past Christian martyrs, and their numbers were destined to swell a good deal in legend beyond those who had actually died.

Curiously, and surely significantly, Constantine seems to have done little for the martyred St Paul, at best modestly rehousing the saint at his rural shrine, but he gave sudden promotion to the cult of Peter far beyond the Apostle to the Gentiles, through a massive investment in what became the largest church in Rome. It was to survive until the sixteenth century, when its rebuilding had a momentous consequence (see pp. 608–9).[4] Like Constantine's work at St Lawrence's shrine, the Emperor's gift to Peter was not a conventional basilica or a congregational church or cathedral, but a huge structure intended for burials, funeral feasts and pilgrimages, all under the patronage of the saint. It eventually ended up with a plan in the shape of a T-cross, its altar in a semicircular apse at the junction-head of the T. A cruciform plan for a church building, although much developed by both East and West in different ways in later centuries, was unusual in the early Church, and although this plan of 'Old' St Peter's has often been taken as a reminiscence of Constantine's victory through the Cross, it was in fact an architectural accident. The head of the T was the original building, the shrine of Peter being located (with considerable difficulty because of the hillside site) at its centre point, in front of the altar-apse. Later, a monumental nave with two aisles on either side was added to the west, giving a vast space which, like the circus-shaped churches such as St Lawrence, was capable of holding thousands of people (see Plate 26).[5] We should imagine this aisled nave used as the ultra-pious multi-millionaire Pammachius did in the early 390s, commemorating the death of his wife with a vast banquet for a crowd of the poor, who filled the whole place, St Peter brooding benevolently over the gargantuan feast from his grave beyond to the east. Christian charity combined harmoniously with the public assertion of a great aristocratic family's place in the city.[6]

St Lawrence's and St Peter's churches thus witnessed to the newly Christian Emperor's special concern for death and honourable burial, a contrast to the attitude of the Saviour himself. War and death seem to have been Constantine's chief motives for interest in the Christian faith, although one might argue that his busyness in matters of burial stemmed from the title of Pontifex Maximus which he held as emperor. This high priest of Rome had traditionally been concerned with the administration of burials, so perhaps Constantine regarded his provision of Christian burial places as a reflection of that duty. Even with that possibility, it is still interesting that burial was the aspect of the high priest's duties which particularly exercised him. Constantine only ever attended Christian worship on very special occasions, as was the case with some of his successors as emperors right up to the end of the fourth century, so it is unsurprising that congregational churches were not his prime interest.[7] Besides his own burial church of the Twelve Apostles in Constantinople and his family's concern with the Holy Sepulchre in Jerusalem (see pp. 193–4), the Emperor built in all six funeral churches in Rome, capable of accommodating thousands of Christians in death as well as in life. They seem to have been a gift to his Christian subjects to parallel his gift of privileges solely granted to their clergy. Regardless of any personal considerations, the Emperor's generosity showed a lively awareness that the Christian religion (and therefore presumably its God) had long paid particular attention to providing properly for burial.[8]

The Emperor's preoccupation with death also encouraged a different variety of building which, by contrast, did have a long future in Christian architecture: circular-plan structures. These took their cue from a great non-Christian funeral building, the mausoleum of the emperors which Hadrian had built in Rome, back in the second century – it survives as the papal fortress known as the Castel Sant'Angelo. Constantine's own first projected tomb outside Rome, which actually came to house his mother, Helena, is circular in this fashion. A design associated with imperial death was therefore appropriate both for shrines to martyred saints, who won a crown worthy of an emperor in Heaven by their death on earth, and for the death to sin which every Christian experienced in baptism. The most famous example was the circular-plan structure which during the fourth century was built around the tomb in Jerusalem designated as that of Christ, as part of the giant 'martyrium' pilgrimage complex of the Holy Sepulchre.[9] There were eventually two such circular 'martyria' alongside the Basilica of St Peter commemorating particular saints, while beside the Cathedral Church of St John Lateran Constantine himself had built a spectacular circular baptistery centring on a sunken font; for most of the fourth century, it was the only place of baptism for the whole Church in Rome. It still stands, although the vastness of its eight-sided space is now reduced by a later inner ring of columns.[10]

The great new building at St Peter's was bound to be good news for the Bishop of Rome. The most significant pope to exploit the new possibilities was Damasus (366–84). After a highly discreditable election, in which his partisans slaughtered more than a hundred supporters of a rival candidate, and some very shaky years following that while he established his authority, Damasus sought to highlight the traditions and glory of his see.[11] He was the first pope to use the distant language favoured by the imperial bureaucracy in his correspondence. He took a keen interest in the process of making Rome and its suburbs into a Christian pilgrimage city, financing a series of handsomely sculpted inscriptions at the various holy sites in indifferent but lovingly and personally composed Latin verse, some of which survive. They gave accounts of the importance of each place, generally with details about them that improved generously on the scanty reality of genuine facts about early Christian Rome, while sometimes cheerfully admitting that there was not much to tell: 'Time was not able to preserve their names or their number' was his comment on one group of skeletons.[12]

One aim of this programme was to place a new emphasis on the role of Peter rather than the joint role of Peter and Paul in the Roman past. Moreover, it was in Damasus's time that Peter came to be regarded not merely as the founder of the Christian Church in Rome, but also as its first bishop.[13] Ironically, it was actually a North African bishop, point-scoring against his local Donatist opponents by stressing the North African Catholics' links to Rome, who is the first person known to have asserted on the basis of Matthew 16.17–19 that 'Peter was superior to the other apostles and alone received the keys of the kingdom, which were distributed by him to the rest'; yet significantly it was in the time of Damasus that this thought occurred to the North African, some time around 370.[14] All this promotion of Peter was not merely for the pope's greater glory; it was a conscious effort to show that Christianity had a past as glorious as anything that the old gods could offer. The faith adopted by Constantine and his successors was no longer an upstart, but could be a religion fit for gentlemen.

Damasus performed one other great service for Western Latin Christianity. In 382 he persuaded his secretary, a brilliant but quarrelsome scholar called Jerome, to begin a new translation of the Bible from Greek into Latin, to replace several often conflicting Latin versions from previous centuries. Like the saintly Bishop Cyril of Alexandria, Jerome is not a man to whom it is easy to warm, although he certainly had a powerful effect on various pious and wealthy ladies in late-fourth-century Rome. One feels that he was a man with a six-point plan for becoming a saint, taking in the papacy on the way. After Damasus's death Jerome abruptly relocated to Palestine, though the precise reasons for his departure from Rome have now somehow disappeared from the record. Soon afterwards, he wrote of his recently interrupted career in Rome: 'the entire city resounded with my praises. Nearly [sic] everyone agreed in judging me worthy of the highest priesthood [that is, the papacy]. Damasus, of blessed memory, spoke my words. I was called holy, humble, eloquent.'[15] An earlier venture to seek holiness with the fierce ascetics of the Syrian desert had not been a success, and after Jerome's withdrawal from Rome he spent his last years in a rather less demanding religious community near Bethlehem. There he continued with the round of scholarship which was his chief virtue, together with bitter feuding, which was not.

Jerome produced an interesting and important spin on the scholarly task which he enjoyed so much. Traditionally it had been an occupation associated with elite wealth, and even in the case of this monk in Bethlehem it was backed up with an expensive infrastructure of assistants and secretaries. Study and writing, he insinuated, were as demanding, difficult and heroically self-denying as any physical extravagance of Syrian monks, or even the drudgery of manual labour and craft which were the daily occupation of monastic communities in Egypt. He elaborated the thought with a certain self-pity:

If I were to weave a basket from rushes or to plait palm leaves, so that I might eat my bread in the sweat of my brow and work to fill my belly with a troubled mind, no-one would criticize me, no-one would reproach me. But now, since according to the word of the Savior I wish to store up the food that does not perish, I who have made authenticity my cause, I, a corrector of vice, am called a forger.[16]

The long-term result can be seen in the curiously discrepant portrayals of Jerome in medieval art (Spain especially bristles with examples, thanks to the devotion of the powerful and wealthy Spanish monastic order later named after him, the Jeronimites). Either he is portrayed in a lavishly equipped study, as a scholar absorbed in his reading and writing, or he is a wild-eyed hermit in the desert – precisely the career at which he had failed. In either case he is very often accompanied by a lion, who has actually arrived in the picture by mistake, thanks to a pious confusion of names, probably by medieval Western pilgrims in the Middle East. They would have been told of a popular Palestinian hermit-saint called Gerasimos, who had actually lived a generation later than Jerome (Hieronymus). Gerasimos's spectacular feats of ascetic self-denial attracted to himself the pre-Christian story of a good man who removed a thorn from a lion's paw and won its long-term friendship – or maybe indeed a lion had grown fond of the wild holy man. Lions apart, if Jerome had not been so successful in his campaign for sainthood, and in persuading future writers that it was as much of a self-sacrifice for a scholar to sit reading a book as it was for St Simeon to sit on top of his pillar in a Syrian desert, it might have been far more difficult for countless monks to justify the hours that they spent reading and enjoying ancient texts, and copying them out for the benefit of posterity. Ultimately the beneficiary was Western civilization.[17]

Besides this, there was Jerome's immediate and spectacular scholarly triumph: along with a fleet of biblical commentaries, he constructed a Latin biblical text so impressive in its scholarship and diction that it had an unchallenged place at the centre of Western culture for more than a thousand years. This Vulgate version (from the Latin *vulgata*, meaning 'generally known' or 'common'), was as great an achievement as Origen's work in producing a single Greek text a century and a half before (see pp. 150–52). Undeniably Jerome's Vulgate was a work of Latin literature, but there was nothing much like it in Latin literature which predated the arrival of Christianity. That was the problem for Damasus and his new breed of establishment Christians. They wanted to annex the glories of ancient Rome, but they had no time for the gods who were central to it. All through the fourth century arguments simmered between traditionalist aristocrats and Christian emperors, bishops and government officials about the fate of the historic and ancient statue of Victory which stood with its altar in the Senate building in the Forum of Rome. The statue and altar were removed by imperial order in 382, then a decade later the statue alone was only temporarily restored in the brief usurpation of Eugenius. This was in every sense a symbolic conflict and its resolution in Christians' favour coincided with Theodosius's imposition of a monopoly for Christianity after Eugenius's fall. Once the statue of Victory had gone from their midst, the senators took the hint: nearly all of them joined the Church with telling rapidity.

A RELIGION FIT FOR GENTLEMEN (300–400)

A Christianity fit for the Roman aristocracy now came to terms with aristocratic values, while doing what it felt necessary to modify them. Roman noblemen valued 'nobility' or 'distinction': so much for the Virgin Mary's *Magnificat*, celebrating the mighty being put down from their seats. The Roman elite also put a positive value on wealth, unlike the wanderer Jesus, who had told the poor that they were blessed and told a rich man to sell all he had. Churchmen squared this circle by encouraging the rich to give generously out of their good fortune to the poor, for almsgiving chimed in with their own priorities: bishops were aware of the advantages to themselves and to the prestige of the Church in general of being able to dispense generous charity to the poor. Augustine of Hippo, whom we will meet as the prime theologian of this new era in the Western Church, made an adroit appeal to aristocratic psychology in one of his sermons when he said that the poor who benefited could act as heavenly porters to the wealthy, using their gratitude to carry spiritual riches for their benefactors into the next life.[18] Other preachers and biblical commentators brought their own glosses or enrichments which went beyond such socially conventional rhetoric, into territory more problematic for a great nobleman. Christian talk of almsgiving often portrayed the poor who received charity not simply as porters but in much more intimate ways: as the children or friends of the givers, fellow servants to that higher master in Heaven, God himself, or even as the humble Christ himself. Preachers also often showed themselves aware that St Paul had said that those who did not work should not eat, but they delicately contradicted the Apostle by massing alternative texts or explaining that Paul's hard-headed remark concerned those poor healthy enough to work.[19]

The Church would also have to decide what it should keep from the literary culture so prized by wealthy and distinguished Romans. There was predictable hostility to such literature as the raunchy novels of Petronius or Apuleius, but Christians could not and would not dispense with that icon of Roman literature from the age of the first emperor, the poetry of Virgil. This was after all one of the most potent links between Rome and Greece, since Virgil's monumental epic poem told of the wanderings of Aeneas, both refugee from the Greek siege of Troy and ancestor of the founders of Rome. Elite culture was unthinkable without it. Luckily the great Augustan poet could be pictured as foretelling the coming of Christ in one of his Eclogues, where he spoke of the birth of a boy from a virgin who would usher in a golden age. Constantine I or his speechwriter had already noted this in one of the Emperor's very first speeches to Christians after his conversion to the faith. That was Virgil's passport to a central place in medieval Western Christian literature, symbolized by his role as Dante's guide through the underworld in the great fourteenth-century poem *Inferno*.[20] Dante's homage was anticipated in the fourth century by a conscientious Christian senator's daughter. Her resoundingly aristocratic name, Faltonia Betitia Proba, proclaimed her ancient lineage, but she was also blessed with a good education and a pride in the Roman past. She took it upon herself as a labour of love to meld together little fragments of Virgil's poetry into a sort of literary quilt (*cento* in Roman usage), using her quotations to retell the biblical stories of the Creation and the life of Christ. Jerome, stern biblical purist, was not impressed, but others, maybe in imitation of her, played this literary game in Christian interests.[21]

If Proba's work was ingenious, the lyric poetry of Prudentius (348–c. 413) might be said to be the first distinguished Latin verse written in the Christian tradition but not intended for the Church's liturgy; some has nevertheless been adapted into it as hymnody. Many will know Prudentius's majestic celebration of Christ's Incarnation which has become the hymn 'Of the Father's heart begotten, ere the world from chaos rose'.[22] That celebration of Jesus Christ as 'Alpha and Omega' is also a celebration of the Christ of the Nicene Creed, one substance with the Father. Prudentius, like Constantine's adviser Bishop Hosius, like Pope Damasus and the Emperor Theodosius, was a Spaniard. Spain (Hispania) was a bastion of resistance to attacks on the decisions of the Council of Nicaea, and the Latin-speaking Hispanic elite had a long tradition of deep pride in Roman institutions and history, back to the great second-century Spanish emperor, Trajan, and beyond.

That pride shines through the poetry of Prudentius, which he revealed in a single collection at the end of a distinguished career which had taken him to being a provincial governor. He entered the argument over the Senate's statue of Victory, urging Rome to celebrate its successes in war, hanging the trophies of victory in the Senate House, but to 'break the hideous ornaments that represent gods thou hast cast away' – so the empire's glorious history was beautified, not distorted, by jettisoning the falsehoods of the old gods. Yet Prudentius also wrote admiringly of Christianity's great enemy the Emperor Julian (see p. 217), paying generous tribute in his boyhood memory of a 'brave leader in arms, a lawgiver, famous for speech and action, one who cared for his country's welfare, but not for maintaining true religion'.[23] His most extended work was his *Peristephanon*, a roll call of Christian martyrs, singing of their terrible deaths and the places where pilgrims could now pursue their cults. Damasus's verse creations of a Roman and Christian history were put in the shade. In all Prudentius's verse, whose Latin has the sonorous clarity of some great monumental inscription on one of Rome's ancient buildings, there is not one mention of the new Rome, Constantinople.

Provincial administrators did not only become Christian poets; increasingly, they or their relatives became bishops, taking with them the mitres which were part of the uniform of officials at the imperial Court in Byzantium. The Church, particularly after the terminal crisis of the Western Empire in the early fifth century, became a safer prospect than the increasingly failing civil service for those aspiring to serve or direct their communities; often Roman noblemen would become bishops because they saw the office as the only way to protect what survived of the world they loved. Their prime role model came from the late fourth century, in the form of the imperial governor who became Bishop of Milan: Ambrose. Brought up a Christian but very much a gentleman, he was the son of the Praetorian Prefect (Governor-General) of the vast imperial province which included the modern France, England and Spain. This great aristocrat predictably embarked on a military career, equally predictably ending up as governor of the Italian province whose capital, Milan, was the chief imperial headquarters in the West.

Here, in 373 or 374, matters took an unexpected turn. The Christian population gathered to choose a new bishop and were bitterly divided between Nicenes and supporters of the Homoean compromise (see pp. 216–17). That is interesting proof that Christian communities still had genuine choices of leadership to make even in a key strategic city, but it also meant that the occasion threatened to turn into the sort of murderous riot which had marred Damasus's election as pope. Ambrose came along at the head of a detachment of troops to keep order and, as he was delivering some crisp military sentiments to the crowd, a child's voice pierced the church: 'Ambrose for Bishop!' It was the perfect solution; the mob took up the shout.[24] Consecrated bishop after an indecently hasty progress through baptism and ordination, Ambrose proved a remarkable success, at least in political terms. He was ruthless in dealing both with the opponents of Nicaea and with a series of Christian emperors. It was an extraordinary transformation of fortunes for Christianity that a man who might easily have become emperor himself now wielded the spiritual power of the Church against the most powerful ruler in the known world. The Church had come a long way from the days when the Roman authorities had seen it as a minor nuisance.

More extraordinary still was the fact that Ambrose consistently won. In 385 he refused to surrender a major church in the city to the anti-Nicene Homoeans, still a powerful force at Court under the young Western emperor, Valentinian II, despite the decisions of the Councils of Constantinople and Aquileia in 381 (see pp. 218–20). As the power struggle in the city continued, the following year Ambrose was inspired to an extraordinary act of self-assertion. He had commissioned another large new church and now let it be known that he himself would eventually be buried there at its heart, under the altar. There was no precedent for a living bishop to do this and not even Constantine had dared to provide such a place for his burial. What Ambrose was telling the imperial Court was that he expected to be a martyr and had made provision for a suitable commemoration of his martyrdom. Piling audacity on audacity, he then put workmen to dig up the floor in his newly built church, where they unearthed the bodies of two martyrs from the time of Nero's persecution, complete with names, Gervasius and Protasius, 'long unknown', and indeed the first martyrs ever known in the Church of Milan. Around the chief churches of the city, the bishop triumphantly paraded their impressively large blood-covered bones – perhaps, if this was indeed a genuine discovery, ochre-painted bones from prehistoric burials. Miraculous cures followed. The Homoeans could not compete, and their power in any case ended with the death of Valentinian.[25]

After these years of struggle, Ambrose was well prepared for self-assertion, or the assertion of the Church's power, against the pious Nicene Emperor Theodosius I. To our eyes, the results seem ambiguous. In two famously contrasting instances, Ambrose both forced the Emperor to cancel an order for compensation to a Jewish community in Mesopotamia whose synagogue had been burned down by militant Christians and, on the other hand, successfully ordered the Emperor to do penance for his vindictiveness in massacring the riotous inhabitants of Thessalonica (the modern Thessaloniki).[26] Both atrocities had taken place hundreds of miles from Milan, but this made it clear that a bishop of the Church universal could indeed be an international statesman. When Ambrose came to preach funeral sermons first for the young and rather ineffective Emperor Valentinian II and then for Theodosius, he had no compunction in ignoring all the conventions for praising such world leaders, presenting them as fallible, suffering human beings, and particularly emphasizing the humility of the great Theodosius.[27]

So it appeared in the 390s that the future lay with a Christian empire under strong rulers like Theodosius and strong bishops like Ambrose: a culmination of God's plan for the world and the beginning of a golden age, the vision of Constantine's historian Eusebius of Caesarea finally realized. This turned out to be a mirage. The Western Empire was overwhelmed by a series of invasions of 'barbarian' tribes from beyond the northern frontier; the most humiliating blow of all was the capture and sack of the city of Rome itself by a Visigoth army led by Alaric in 410. Sixty-six years later, mercenary troops of the boy-emperor Romulus Augustulus deposed him and came to a conveniently vague arrangement with the emperor in Constantinople, recognizing him as sole emperor. By that time, most of what had been the Western Roman Empire was under the control of barbarian kings, and although the Byzantines did go on to recapture much of the western Mediterranean, they did not hold on to those conquests for long. All this was the background to a long process of disengagement and separation within the imperial Church between East and West. The Western Latin Church now added to Damasus's assertion of its tradition and Ambrose's demonstration of how it could outface worldly power by finding a theologian who would give it its own voice and shape its thinking down to modern times: Augustine, Bishop of Hippo.

AUGUSTINE: SHAPER OF THE WESTERN CHURCH

Augustine was a Latin-speaking theologian who had little interest in Greek literature, only came to the Greek language late in life, read virtually nothing of Plato or Aristotle, and had very little influence on the Greek Church, which in fact came to look with profound disapproval on one aspect of his theological legacy, a modification of the Nicene Creed (see pp. 310–11).[28] By contrast, his impact on Western Christian thought can hardly be overstated; only his beloved example, Paul of Tarsus, has been more influential, and Westerners have generally seen Paul through Augustine's eyes. He is one of the few writers from the early Church era some of whose work can still be read for pleasure, particularly his remarkable and perhaps too revealing self-analysis in his *Confessions*, a gigantic prayer-narrative which is a direct conversation – I–Thou – with God. His life was played out against the background of the rise, final splendour and fall of the Christian Western Empire, but apart from these great political traumas, his life's work can be seen as a series of responses to conflicts both internal and external.

The first struggle was with himself. Who did he want to be and how would he find a truth which would satisfy him? He was brought up in the 350s and 360s in small-town North Africa. His father, Patricius (of whom he says little), was a non-Christian; his mother, Monica, a deeply pious if not very intellectual member of the Catholic Church. The relationship of mother and son was intense and often conflicted. Augustine reacted against her unsophisticated religion, and after his parents had scrimped and saved to send him to the School of Carthage, he was increasingly drawn by the excitements of university life to the philosophy and literature of Rome. The world was at his feet; he settled down with a mistress and she bore him a son whose name, Adeodatus ('Given by God'), may have been a reflection of the fact that the baby's arrival was evidently unplanned.[29] But even as Augustine began an exceptionally promising career as a teacher of rhetoric (the language study which lay at the heart of Latin culture, a ticket to success and perhaps a political career), he was becoming tormented by anxieties which remained his theological preoccupations all his life.

What was the source of evil and suffering in this world? This was the ancient religious question which the gnostics had tried to answer by picturing existence as an eternally dualistic struggle, and it was the gnostic religion of Augustine's day, Manichaeism, which first won his allegiance and held it for nine years. Yet increasingly he was dissatisfied by Manichaean belief, and as he pursued academic success in Rome and Milan he was haunted by doubts and anxieties about the nature of truth, reality and wisdom. As he ceased to find Manichaeism of use, he turned to Neoplatonist belief, but in Milan he also became fascinated by Bishop Ambrose. Here, for the first time, he met a Christian whose self-confident culture he could respect and whose sermons, sonorous and rich in their language, made up for the crudity and vulgarity of the Bible which had distressed the young Augustine. Even though he remained embarrassed by his mother's demonstrative piety (she had followed him to Milan), he now contemplated a faith which united the imperious nobleman in the pulpit with the elderly woman from a provincial backwater. The contradictory influences of career and Christian renunciation came to tear him apart and made him disgusted with his ambitions. To add to his pain, on his mother's urging, in 385 he broke with his mistress in order to make a good marriage. The woman went back to Africa, swearing to remain faithful to him – in the middle of his narrative of worldly renunciation in the *Confessions*, Augustine at least had the grace to record her resolution, even though he could not bring himself to name her. We may wonder what she felt as she slipped out of the life of the man who had been her companion for fifteen years, leaving behind her charming and talented teenage son to her lover's care.[30]

In a state bordering on nervous breakdown, and physically unwell, Augustine arrived in 386 at a crisis which was to bring him a new serenity and a new certainty. In his own account, the crucial prompting was the voice of a child overheard in a garden – children seem to have had a good sense of timing in Milan. The repetitive chant sounded to Augustine like '*tolle lege*' – 'take it and read'. The book Augustine had to hand was the Epistles of Paul, which he opened at random at the words of Romans 13, from what is now verses 13–14: 'put on the Lord Jesus Christ, and make no provision for the flesh, to gratify its desires . . .'[31] It was enough to bring him back fully to his mother's faith and it meant that his plans for marriage were abandoned for a life of celibacy. Another woman spurned: the fiancée has received no more consideration than the mistress from historians until modern times. On Augustine's announcement of the resolution of his torment, Monica 'was jubilant with triumph and glorified you . . . And you turned her sadness into rejoicing . . . far sweeter and more chaste than any she had hoped to find in children begotten of my flesh.' There is more than one way of interpreting this maternal triumph.[32] When, in later years, Augustine came to discuss the concept of original sin, that fatal flaw which in his theology all humans have inherited from the sin of Adam and Eve, he saw it as inseparable from the sexual act, which transmits sin from one generation to another. It was a view momentous in its consequences for the Western Church's attitude to sexuality.

Augustine found his conversion a liberation from torment. One element in his crisis had been the impact of meeting a fellow North African who had been thrown into a state of deep self-doubt and worry about his own successful administrative career by an encounter with Athanasius's *Life of Antony*.[33] Now Augustine determined on his own abandonment of ambition, leaving his teaching career to follow Antony's example – after a fashion, for his was to be the life of the desert minus the desert and plus a good library. His plan was to create a celibate religious community with cultivated friends back in his home town: a monastery which would bring the best of the culture of old Rome into a Christian context. This congenial scheme was soon ended by the turbulent Church politics of North Africa. Augustine's Catholic Christian Church was connected with the rest of the Mediterranean Church and with the imperial administration, but it was a minority in Africa, faced with the deep-rooted localism of the Donatists, cherishing grievances now a century old from the Great Persecution of Diocletian (see p. 211) and including some of the ablest theologians of the African Church.

From 387 the Donatists suddenly gained the advantage of political support from a local rebel ruler, Gildo, who established a regime semi-independent of the emperor. In 391 Augustine happened to visit the struggling Catholic congregation in the city of Hippo Regius (now Annaba in Algeria), the most important port of the province after Carthage. The bishop, an idiosyncratic but shrewd old Greek named Valerius, encouraged his flock to bully this brilliant stranger into being ordained priest and soon Augustine was coadjutor (assistant) bishop in the town. From Valerius's death until his own in 430, he remained Bishop of Hippo. All his theological writing was now done against a background of busy pastoral work and preaching for a Church in a world in collapse; much of it was in the form of sermons.[34] The next period in his life was dominated by the problem posed by the Donatists, in terms not just of politics but also of the challenges that their theology posed to the Catholics. Proud of their unblemished record in time of persecution, they proclaimed that the Church was a gathered pure community. Augustine thought that this was not what 'One, Holy and Catholic' meant. The Catholic Church was a Church not so much of the pure as those who tried or longed to be pure. Unlike the Donatists, it was in communion with a great mass of Christian communities throughout the known world. The Catholic Church was in fact what Augustine was not afraid to call 'the communion of the emperor'.[35]

In 398 the Donatists' run of luck ended when imperial troops destroyed Gildo's regime; now the Catholics found themselves in a position to dictate terms again. Over the previous decade, Augustine had done much to prepare for this moment, in cooperation with Aurelius, the statesmanlike Bishop of Carthage; now he tried to bring the Donatists back into the Catholic fold by negotiation. A series of conferences failed; the old bitterness lay too deep. Faced with government hostility and orders to conform, the Donatists remained defiant, and the behaviour of both sides began deteriorating in a miserable cycle of violence.[36] By 412 Augustine had lost patience and he backed harsh new government measures against the Donatists. He even provided theological reasons for the repression: he pointed out to one of his Donatist friends that Jesus had told a parable in which a host had filled up places at his banquet with an order, 'Compel them to come in'.[37] That meant that a Christian government had the duty to support the Church by punishing heresy and schism, and the unwilling adherence which this produced might be the start of a living faith. This was a side of Augustine's teaching which had much appeal to Christian regimes for centuries to come.

At the same time, Augustine was faced with the problem of explaining the Roman world's catastrophe. How could God's providence allow the collapse of the manifestly Christian Roman Empire, especially the sack of Rome by barbarian armies in 410? Naturally, traditionalists in religion were inclined to say that Rome's flirtation with the Christian Church was at the root of the problem, but even Christians could not understand how a heretical Arian like the Goth Alaric had been allowed to plunder Catholic Rome. Part of the Christian response was to argue from history. Paulus Orosius, a Spanish protégé of Augustine, wrote a *History against the Pagans*, designed to show from a brief survey of all world history that there had been worse disasters in pre-Christian times and that the coming of Christ had made all the difference to the peace of the world. However, Orosius's work seems thin stuff indeed compared with the response which Augustine was making at the same time: *The City of God* (*De Civitate Dei*). It was his most monumental work and it took him thirteen years from 413 to write.

Augustine starts with a consideration of Roman history and ridicules the old gods, but his preoccupation quickly becomes wider than the single disaster for Rome, or even the whole canvas of Roman history. It turns to the problem at the centre of Augustine's thought: what is the nature and cause of evil, and how does it relate to God's majesty and all-powerful goodness? For Augustine, evil is simply non-existence, 'the loss of good', since God and no other has given everything existence; all sin is a deliberate falling away from God towards nothingness, though to understand why this should happen is 'like trying to see darkness or hear silence'.[38] It was understandable that the ex-Manichee should thus distance himself from the notion previously at the centre of his belief, that evil was a positive force constantly struggling for mastery with the force of light, but as a definition of evil it has often been criticized. On a visit to Auschwitz-Birkenau or the killing fields of Campuchea, it is difficult not to feel that, in human experience at least, pure evil is more than pure nothingness; nor does Augustine seek to explain how a being created flawless comes to turn towards evil – in effect, to create it from nothing.[39]

Only halfway through the work, at the end of fourteen books, does Augustine explicitly begin to take up the theme of two cities: 'the earthly city glories in itself, the Heavenly City glories in the Lord'.[40] All the institutions which we know form part of a struggle between these two cities, a struggle which runs through all world history. If this is so, the idea of a Christian empire such as Eusebius of Caesarea had envisaged can never be a perfect reality on earth. No structure in this world, not even the Church itself, can without qualification be identified as the City of God, as biblical history itself demonstrated from the time of the first murderer: 'Cain founded a city, whereas Abel, as a pilgrim, did not found one. For the City of the saints is up above, although it produces citizens here below, and in their persons the City is on pilgrimage until the time of its kingdom comes.' Though this remains his principle, Augustine is occasionally incautious in expression, and does indeed identify the visible Church in the world with the Heavenly City.[41] Ironic-ally, much of the influence of *The City of God* over the next thousand years came from the eagerness of medieval churchmen to expand on this identification in their efforts to make the Church supreme on earth, equating the earthly city with opponents of ecclesiastical power like some of the Holy Roman Emperors.

Yet another side of Augustine's energies was occupied in the same years with a fierce controversy over the teachings of a British monk called Pelagius.[42] Upper-class circles in Rome, newly Christianized at the end of the fourth century, were anxious for spiritual direction and a number of 'holy men' hastened to supply the demand. After the abrupt departure of Jerome in 384, Pelagius had few major rivals. A central concern for him and his spiritual charges was to deal with the new established status of Christianity: were the affluent people among whom Pelagius ministered simply joining the Church as an easy option, without any real sense that they must transform their lives in the process?[43] Pelagius was particularly concerned at what he read of the earlier works of Augustine: Augustine's preoccupation with God's majesty seemed to leave humankind helpless puppets who could easily abandon all responsibility for their conduct. Augustine and other like-minded con-temporaries followed thoughts of Tertullian two centuries before and talked of humankind being wholly soiled by a guilt inherited from Adam which they termed 'original sin'. This likewise seemed to Pelagius to provide a false excuse for Christians passively to avoid making any moral effort. He was determined to say that our God-given natures are not so completely corrupt that we can do nothing towards our own salvation: 'That we are able to see with our eyes is no power of ours; but it is in our power that we make a good or a bad use of our eyes . . . the fact that we have the power of accomplishing every good thing by action, speech and thought comes from him who has endowed us with this possibility, and also assists it.'[44] The consequence was that Pelagius believed that the nature of a 'Holy Church' was based on the holiness of its members: exactly what the Donatists said about the Church, and so particularly liable to arouse Augustine's fury.[45]

As the controversy developed, Pelagius's followers pushed the implications of this further, to insist that although Adam sinned, this sin did not transmit itself through every generation as original sin, but was merely a bad example, which we can ignore if we choose. We can choose to turn to God. We have free will. Pelagius's views have often been presented as rather amiable, in contrast to the fierce pessimism in Augustine's view of our fallen state. This misses the point that Pelagius was a stern Puritan, whose teaching placed a terrifying responsibility on the shoulders of every human being to act according to the highest standards demanded by God. The world which he would have constructed on these principles would have been one vast monastery.[46] It would have been impossible to sustain the mixed human society of vice and virtue which Augustine presents in the 'City of God', where no Christian has the right to avoid everyday civic responsibilities in this fallen world, even to be a magistrate who is responsible for executing other human beings, precisely because we are all caught up in the consequences of Adam and Eve's fall in the Garden of Eden. Augustine's pessimism started as realism, the realism of a bishop protecting his flock amid the mess of the world. It is worth noticing that his first denunciations of Pelagius's theology came not in tracts written for fellow intellectuals, but in sermons for his own congregation.[47]

The sack of Rome in 410 produced a scatter of refugees throughout the Mediterranean and this began spreading the dispute beyond Pelagius's Roman circle. One enthusiastic follower of Pelagius, a lawyer named Celestius, arrived in North Africa and began expounding Pelagius's views to an extreme point where he left no possibility of affirming original sin. So he said that there was no sin to remit in baptism: 'sin is not born with a man, it is subsequently committed by the man; for it is shown to be a fault, not of nature, but of the human will'.[48] There could not have been a more sensitive issue to choose in North Africa, where much of the argument between Catholics and Donatists had centred on both sides' claim to be the true heir of Cyprian's third-century teaching on baptism as the only way to gain salvation. It was these statements of Celestius which first provoked Augustine's fury against the group of propositions which came to be labelled as Pelagianism; his relations with Pelagius himself did not descend to the same bitterness. Over the next few years, a complicated series of political moves and counter-moves raised the temperature to new heights; Augustine's crusade against the Pelagians eventually resulted in their defeat and the dismissal from Church office of all their highly placed supporters.

In the process, Augustine's thoughts about the nature of grace and salvation were pushed to ever more extreme positions, which can be traced both through *The City of God* and the long series of tracts which he wrote attacking Pelagian thought. Eventually he could say not simply that all human impulses to do good are a result of God's grace, but that it is an entirely arbitrary decision on the part of God as to who receives this grace. God has made the decision before all time, so some are foreordained to be saved through grace – a predestined group of the elect. The arbitrariness is fully justified by the monstrousness of Adam's original fall, in which we all have a part through original sin: Augustine repeatedly uses the terrible word 'lump' (*massa*) to describe humanity in its state of loss. It is a word to which he often returned, associating it with Latin words for 'loss', 'sin', 'filth'.[49] There was much criticism of this theology of grace at the time, and it has alternately repelled and fascinated both Catholic and Protestant down to the present day. One of Augustine's modern admirers and biographers, having wrestled with the man for a lifetime, is prepared bluntly to say that 'Augustinian predestination is not the doctrine of the Church but only the opinion of a distinguished Catholic theologian.'[50] Western theologians, Catholic and Protestant, would do well to ponder that. Eastern theologians, so influenced by the Eastern monastic tradition of spiritual endeavour which encompasses both Chalcedonians and non-Chalcedonians, have never found Augustine's approach to grace congenial. Contemporary opponents, in particular the clever and outspoken Pelagian aristocrat Julian, Bishop of Eclanum, pointed to Augustine's personal history and his involvement with the Manichees, with their dualist belief in the eternal struggle between equally balanced forces of good and evil.[51] Such critics said that this was the origin of both Augustine's pessimistic view of human nature and his emphasis on the role of sexual reproduction in transmitting the Fall.

It would probably do more justice to Augustine to say that he was heir to the world-denying impulses of Platonists and Stoics. Augustine's early grounding in Neoplatonism undoubtedly stayed with him; references to the heritage of Plato (of whose actual works he had in fact read little), and Platonic modes of thought, shape much of his writing. Amid many approving references to Plato in *The City of God*, he can assert at length that Platonists are near-Christians; 'that is why we rate the Platonists above the rest of the philosophers'.[52] This helps explain why

Plato remained close to the heart of Christian thinking through the medieval period, even when Christian thinkers began to be excited by their rediscovery of many lost works of Aristotle during the twelfth and thirteenth centuries (see pp. 398–9). Augustine did nothing to discourage Christians seeing God through Neoplatonic eyes. God in Platonic mode was transcendent, other, remote. When his image appeared in mosaic or painting, characteristically as the resurrected Christ the Judge of the Last Days, dominating a church building from the ceiling of the apse behind the altar in front of congregation and clergy, it was as a monarch whose stern gaze transfixed the viewer in awe, just as an earthly emperor would do on formal occasions.

That created all the more need for the Church to recognize a myriad of courtiers who could intercede with their imperial Saviour for ordinary humans seeking salvation or help in their everyday lives. These were the saints. Their ranks were increasingly extended beyond the ranks of the martyrs from persecution times, who had been honoured since the second century in pilgrimage centres such as that of St Peter in Rome. Now the martyrs were joined by a growing array of hermits, monks, even bishops, although not many people living their lives as layfolk in the everyday world were thus honoured. As we have noted when encountering fourth-century Christians worshipping in their new basilican churches (see pp. 197–9), the Court of Heaven with its hierarchy of angels and saints looked rather like the Court of Constantinople or Ravenna. People needed patrons in this world to get things done or merely to survive, and it was natural for them to assume that they would need them in the next world too. Moreover, friendship, *amicitia*, was a prominent aristocratic value for Romans, and it would be easy and attractive to see a saint as a useful friend in Heaven as well as a patron.[53] The convenience of such saint-patrons was that their demands were likely to be infrequent, while their good turns could be called on at any time. Sometimes the growth of belief in the saints has been seen as a superstition of the ignorant or half-converted, a stealthy return of the old gods in saintly disguise: this was a favourite theme of some humanists and Protestant reformers in the sixteenth-century West. In fact it is a logical outcome of the Platonic cast of Augustine's theology, and an echo of the hierarchies which Plato and his admirers saw as existing in the cosmos around the supreme God. It is no aberration that the majestic literary architecture of *The City of God* makes space in its final book for a series of accounts of contemporary miracles associated with the saints.[54]

Least openly controversial in form among Augustine's major works, but ultimately the source of more ecclesiastical conflict than anything else that he wrote, was his treatise on the Trinity, the most profound study of this central enigma of Christian faith which the Latin West had yet produced. Begun around 400, it was written in consciousness that debate on the Trinity in the East had in some measure been resolved. Augustine had an imperfect knowledge of the great clashes of the previous decades in the East about the Trinity, knowing nothing, for instance (and perhaps unfortunately), of the Council of Constantinople of 381 or the creed which it created – but he may have had some Latin translations of Gregory of Nazianzus's important Trinitarian discussions in Greek.[55] Whatever the source, he was inspired to develop a defence of the doctrine of three equal persons in one substance, which in its subtlety and daring both shaped the Western Church's thinking and helped to alienate Eastern Christians from the West.

Despite his increasing insistence on the fallen nature of humanity, Augustine discerned within humans an image of the Trinity, or at least analogies by which fallen humans might understand. First, Father, Son and Spirit could be represented respectively by three aspects of human consciousness:

the mind itself, its knowledge which is at once its offspring and self-derived 'word', and thirdly love. These three are one, and one single substance. The mind is no greater than its offspring, when its self-knowledge is equal to its being; nor than its love, when its self-love is equal to its knowledge and to its being.

He went on to present the analogy in a different form, with the persons of Father, Son and Spirit corresponding to three aspects of the human mind itself: respectively memory, understanding and will – in the same way, these were 'not three substances, but one substance'.[56]

For Greeks, this 'psychological' image of the Trinity ultimately proved unacceptable, largely because Augustine coupled with it a particular understanding of how the Spirit as love or will related to the other persons of the Trinity. We should note his description of memory and understanding – and so Father and Son – as 'embraced, while their enjoyment or their use depends on the application of will'.[57] Since the first formula of Nicaea in 325, the relationship of Son to Father had been described like that of physical son to parent: 'begotten' of the Father. The Spirit was not 'begotten' of the Father, and the word which had come to be chosen to define the Spirit's relationship to the Father was 'proceeding'. Augustine naturally did not want to challenge that, since 'proceeding' has a good biblical basis in a pronouncement of Jesus on the Spirit in John 15.26. But like anyone discussing the Trinity, he was faced with the way in which the language of 'proceeding' emphasized the lack of congruence between the Persons of the Trinity. Father and Son are necessarily defined by their interrelationship, but the name 'Spirit' seems to derive its individual character from its own nature, without association. Father and Son relate to each other in a different way from their joint relationship to the Spirit.

This thought raised the same problem faced by many other theologians of the late fourth century, in justifying the equal rather than subordinate status of the Spirit within the Trinity (see p. 219). Augustine decided that it would be wise to preserve the Spirit's equality by asserting that the Son participated in the Spirit's 'proceeding' from the Father. Had it not been the resurrected Jesus Christ, Son of God, who had said to the disciples, 'Receive the Holy Spirit' (John 20.22)? Through this double procession from Father and Son, the Spirit represented to humanity 'that mutual charity by which the Father and the Son love one another'.[58] Those who read Augustine later would nevertheless notice that the Nicene Creed of Constantinople of 381 said only that the Spirit 'proceeds from the Father'. Should this not be extended, on Augustine's analogy, to say that the Spirit 'proceeds from the Father *and the Son*'? Although there were respected Greek theologians who had used similar language to Augustine about double procession, the question came to split the imperial Church: we will see that while the West eventually agreed that this alteration should be made to the Creed, the alteration became a matter of high offence in the East (see p. 350). Augustine's reputation among Greeks suffered accordingly.

Modern Western readers may find it hard to understand Greek anger over the Augustinian view of the Trinity, while finding Augustine's view of human nature more difficult to condone, particularly if one reads the increasingly harsh later phases of his writings against the Pelagians. What we need to remember is that Augustine's bleak view of human nature and capabilities was formed against a background of the destruction of the world he loved. In one of the greatest disappointments ever experienced by the Church, the Western Roman Empire of the 390s, which had promised to be an image of God's kingdom on earth, disintegrated into chaos and futility. Augustine himself died in 430 during a siege of his beloved Hippo by the Arian Vandals, who captured all North Africa and bitterly persecuted the Catholic Church there for sixty years. He stands between the Classical world and a very different medieval society, sensing acutely that the world was getting old and feeble: a sense which did not desert Western Europe down to the seventeenth century.

EARLY MONASTICISM IN THE
WEST (400–500)

It was hardly surprising that the sudden sequence of great power and great disappointment for the imperial Church in the West inspired Western Christians to imitate the monastic life of the Eastern Church. Among the first was Martin, who became one of the most important saints in Western Latin devotion. An ex-soldier like the Egyptian pioneer Pachomius, he abandoned his military career in Gaul (France) to live a life apart from the world. Around him, probably in the year 361, there gathered the West's first known monastic community at what seems to have been an ancient local cultic site in a marshy valley, now called Ligugé; it was near the city of Pictavia (now Poitiers), which was already the seat of an important bishopric. Archaeological traces still remain of Martin's first community buildings at Ligugé, treasured by the monks who, after many vicissitudes, have returned to this place so resonant in the story of the religious life.[59] Not long afterwards, in 372, Martin was one of the first ascetics anywhere in the Church to be chosen as a bishop, in the Gaulish city far north of Poitiers called Civitas Turonum (now Tours). While bishop, he still lived as a monk, and his second monastic foundation near Tours was destined to fare rather better than Ligugé in its later monastic history: as Marmoutier, it remained one of the most famous and ancient abbeys in France until its near-total destruction in the French Revolution.

In his public career, Martin retained enough of his soldierliness to emerge as a notably aggressive campaigner for the elimination of the traditional religion still strong in rural areas of western Europe such as his. His ministry, played out against formidable opposition, was clearly dramatic. The outlines of it are now luridly obscured by a biography created by his fervent admirer Sulpicius Severus, who had not known Martin particularly well, but built on his fond memories of their meetings to produce a picture of a man with sensational powers. Martin, for instance, had on one occasion undermined a tree sacred to old gods, then stood in the path of its fall, but forced it to fall elsewhere by making the sign of the Cross. The audience loved it and, as a result, 'you may be sure salvation came to that region', Sulpicius said with satisfaction.[60] Perhaps a less miraculous explanation of such triumphs in the face of conflict is to be found in Martin's evident ability to fascinate young aristocrats from important Gallo-Roman families, which resulted in his drawing them into the religious life. In other situations we know of complaints that the monastic life deprived society of the public duties which noblemen were expected to perform, but the accretion of powerful friends cannot have done Martin's campaigns any harm. Sulpicius proudly pointed out that many of them went on to take up new public responsibilities, as bishops.[61]

People who had known Bishop Martin rather better than Sulpicius Severus were infuriated by his exuberant stories, but their opinions were drowned out in the course of time by the wild popularity of Sulpicius's book, which addressed the same spiritual market as Athanasius's *Life of Antony*. A story told by Sulpicius gave Western Christianity one of its most frequently used technical terms: chapel. Martin was said to have torn his military cloak in half to clothe a poor man, who was later revealed to him in a dream as Christ himself. The cut-down 'little cloak', *capella* in Latin, later became one of the most prized possessions of the Frankish barbarian rulers who succeeded Roman governors in Gaul (see pp. 323–5), and the series of small churches or temporary structures which sheltered this much-venerated relic were named after it: *capellae*. Thus the West gained its name for any private church of a monarch, and later just for any small church. What Sulpicius had achieved was a strident assertion that the Latin West could produce a holy man who was the equal of any wonder-worker or spiritual athlete in the East – yet another building block in the growing edifice of Western self-confidence. More than a millennium later, in 1483, a little boy was born on St Martin's day in north Germany, so he was given the name of the much-loved saint. His surname was Luther and he also left something of a mark on Western Christianity.[62]

Perhaps without the example of the country missions undertaken by Martin Luther's patron saint, north Germany would not have become Christian. Bishop Martin's work excited those who sought to preach their faith in similar areas where city life was either decaying or had never existed, and it can be no coincidence that now a number of individuals began taking missionary initiatives beyond Gaul and even beyond the empire. A common thread was that they had spent time in Gaul or even in Rome. North of the furthest imperial frontiers in Britain, an ascetic called Ninian established a mission around 400 in what is now south-west Scotland, reputedly building a church in stone, such a rare sight in the area that it was called the 'White House', *Candida Casa*. Ninian or one of his early successors dedicated this church in honour of Martin the Gaulish bishop, who had only very recently died; the site at Whithorn is still marked by the rather stolid ruins of a medieval cathedral, and it was probably the first Christian outpost north of Hadrian's Wall.[63] Much would follow in Ireland and Scotland which blew Christianity back across the North Sea into northern Europe (see pp. 333–44).

Just as in the East, the new monastic movement caused tensions and problems. A good deal of Jerome's troubles in Rome stemmed from his fervent promotion of asceticism among his aristocratic Roman patrons, provoking particular public hostility when one of his spiritual protégées, a young lady called Blesilla, apparently died as a result of fasting and generally excessive spiritual rigour. Jerome also aroused anger by a hostility to sex and even marriage which far exceeded even the general early Christian prudishness about sexuality. He and the Greek philosopher Pythagoras were jointly credited with a particularly chilling sentiment by one much-read later author, Vincent of Beauvais, the thirteenth-century Dominican friar who wrote the most widely esteemed compendium of knowledge of the high Middle Ages: 'One who loves his wife rather eagerly is an adulterer . . . all love for another man's wife is indeed shameful, but so is excessive love for one's own wife'.[64] Jerome was nevertheless able to draw on support from the general Christian assumptions of his day to rout theologians who felt differently. First, it was Helvidius, who took the plain meaning of scripture to say that Jesus patently had brothers and sisters, so therefore his mother, Mary, had enjoyed a normal family life rather than remaining perpetually virgin. It was then the turn of the kindly former monk Jovinian, who became repelled by ascetic practice – 'a new dogma against nature', he called it – and insisted that any baptized Christian, married, celibate or just single, had an equal chance of getting to Heaven.[65] By leading the campaigns to label these two for posterity as theological deviants, Jerome took a significant step in the long process, particularly pronounced in the Western Church, by which the celibate state came to be considered superior to marriage.

A more short-term tragedy was the debacle surrounding the efforts of Priscillian, a Spanish aristocrat, to establish his own form of the ascetic life. Such has been the embarrassed obfuscation around his career that it is not easy to recover what Priscillian actually believed, although it is likely that his rejection of the world went beyond mainstream ascetic preoccupations into some form of gnostic dualism. He certainly split the Spanish Church into opposing camps. Even so, it was not an encouraging precedent for later Christianity when, in 385, the usurping emperor in Gaul, Magnus Maximus, took over an ecclesiastical case against Priscillian; in an effort to build up support in the Christian establishment, Maximus had the ascetic leader and some of his close circle executed for heresy, the first time that this had happened within the Christian community. He was burned at the stake, the only Western Christian to be given the treatment which the pagan Emperor Diocletian had pre-scribed for heretics until the eleventh century. It is to Bishop Martin's great credit that he furiously protested against this act of tyranny, and to express his continuing disapproval, in a species of reverse miracle or sanctified work-to-rule, he announced that his spiritual powers were diminished by his own association with the crime, however marginal that had been. '[I]n curing the demoniacs, he took longer than he used to do,' Sulpicius noted, with uncharacteristic scrupulousness.[66]

Eastern and Western monasticism combined fruitfully in the monk John Cassian, who began his monastic life in Bethlehem around 380 and was then much impressed by the ascetic life of Egyptian monks when he moved to live with them. His subsequent writings are peppered with references to his time in Egypt, which may have lasted for as long as fifteen years. The turbulence of ecclesiastical politics in the Eastern Churches brought him west to Rome in 404 and thence (perhaps because of the sack of Rome six years later) into the comparative security of south-east Gaul, where the ancient port of Massilia (now Marseilles) still flourished. Here he founded new monastic communities, perhaps with a conscious agenda of improving on monasteries such as those founded by Bishop Martin of Tours – Cassian's writings do not suggest a great admiration of Sulpicius Severus's biography of Martin, and they also contain the distinct suggestion that Gaulish monks did not like getting their hands dirty.[67]

Cassian in fact became a controversial figure in the Western Church. His mentor in earlier years had been that great spiritual writer and monk who was increasingly a source of controversy, Evagrius Ponticus (see pp. 209–10); in other words, Cassian was an enthusiastic Origenist, with all that implied in an optimistic outlook on human capacity to cooperate with God and grow in the spiritual life. Cassian was aware that Evagrius's name was already suspect, and it is notable for its absence from his spiritual writings, but they develop an Evagrian theme of 'purity of heart' as the goal of monastic endeavour. Unlike another favourite term of Evagrius, 'passionlessness' or 'serenity', *apatheia*, which quickly aroused hostile criticism from Jerome among others, this was a safely biblical phrase, but it is clear from Cassian's writings that the aim of purifying the heart, like the aim of stripping out the passions from human consciousness, was to lead on to a union with the glorified, resurrected Christ. The vehicle for this was a life of unceasing prayer and contemplation.[68] Since Cassian's teaching and example inspired enthusiasm among the growing monastic communities of Gaul, the inheritance from Origen (not for the last time) provoked a confrontation with the theology of that great Westerner whose call to serve his Church had led him to turn away from monastic life: Augustine. The issue was the extreme version of predestination which had appeared in Augustine's writings in the later phases of his conflict with Pelagius.

It is doubtful whether Cassian and Augustine would have differed much in their everyday practice of an austere Christian life, but Augustine's view of grace offended Cassian's theology of salvation, grounded as it was in the rival tradition of Origen and Evagrius. Cassian, like Pelagius, wanted to give human beings a sense of responsibility for their progress towards God, and Augustine's picture of humans stranded helplessly in their 'lump of lostness' threatened this possibility.[69] He penned some fairly open and pointed criticisms of Augustine's assertions; he found a sympathetic audience among the monks of communities newly founded in south-eastern Gaul, for whom Cassian was a major inspiration and in many respects a founding father, and who have often been given a label intended to discredit their theology, 'Semi-Pelagians'. Augustine did have his admirers in Gaul: one monk, Prosper of Aquitaine, alerted the Bishop of Hippo to the controversy, and Augustine replied to his critics with two of his most savage treatises spelling out the logic of predestination. For many among the Gaulish monks, such statements transcended the bounds of acceptability.[70]

In particular, Vincent, a monk on the island of Lérins (Ile-Saint Honorat), admired much of Augustine's writings where he dealt with the Trinity and Christ's incarnation, but he also felt that on the subject of grace both Augustine and Prosper had gone beyond the bounds of doctrine as understood in the universal Church. He gave a definition of how doctrine should be judged properly Catholic or universal. It was what had been believed everywhere in the Church, always and by everyone ('*quod ubique, quod semper, quod ab omnibus creditum est*').[71] The formula has become a favourite of Catholic Christians, although the story of Christianity so far should give us a fair indication that, if applied with historical knowledge, it would leave a rather skeleton faith. Certainly it would exclude Augustine's theology of grace; yet it was Augustine whom the Western Church recognized as a saint, while ecclesiastical history left Cassian under a cloud of disapproval, like Origen and Evagrius before him. Nevertheless, Cassian's legacy went beyond controversy: he proved as important for Western monasticism as Evagrius in the East. Much as Cassian admired the Egyptian hermits, he felt that their life represented a way of perfection which was not for all, and that most ascetics should live in community. His instructions for such communities, principally set out in his *Institutes*, were of great influence on a later monk apparently born around 480, a half-century after Cassian's death. This monk, Benedict, admiring what Cassian had written, created a Rule which became the basis of Western monastic life.

Benedict is a shadowy figure who quickly attracted a good deal of legend, lovingly collected into a life by Pope Gregory I at the end of the sixth century. The implausibility of much of Gregory's narrative has led to suggestions that Benedict may not even have been a single individual, but a representative 'blessed one' (*Benedictus* in Latin), to whom a bundle of ideas came to be attributed as the 'Rule' of St Benedict, which was certainly compiled in the sixth century.[72] In fact we now know that the Rule draws heavily on a previous text called 'The Rule of the Master' (*Regula Magistri*), probably drawn up some decades before, at the beginning of the sixth century. The later Rule both prunes the text and adds material, and the result is itself the best evidence against Benedict's identity having been constructed from the collective efforts of some committee of monastic founders. His changes breathe the simplicity, common sense and practical wisdom of a single gifted individual, with a sense of terse style, and a gentler, less autocratic attitude than the Master to the community which an abbot must lead. He is notably kindlier than the Master in the treatment which he offers to monks who fall ill.[73]

This Rule was intended to guide a number of monastic communities in south Italy, principally the mountain-top house of Monte Cassino (so cruelly bombarded to rubble during an epic siege in the Second World War). In the opening chapter, both the Master and Benedict give honourable mention to the hermit's vocation, seeing it as a more heroic stage of asceticism than community life, but then Benedict takes over the Master's brutally contemptuous description of two other variants on the monastic life: groups of two or three living without a Rule, and those individual monks who wandered from place to place – the Rule regards them as parasites on settled communities. This attitude set a pattern which made Western monasticism distinctive, because the wandering holy man remained a common and widely honoured figure in the Eastern Churches. The Rule was there to describe how to construct a single community, living in obedience to its abbot and under the same Rule as communities round it, yet fully independent of any other. That remains the characteristic of Benedictine monasteries to this day.

The developed Rule's single-minded emphasis on obedience, including the corporal punishment which is one of the abbot's ultimate physical sanctions, may seem very alien to modern individualism, but the author is intent on creating a balance between the spiritual growth of each monk and the general peace and well-being of the community in which he lives. Discipline, in fact, proved to be one of the chief attractions of Benedictine monasteries, in an age enmired in terrifying lawlessness which longed for the lost order of Roman society. The Rule is comparatively brief: a skin of parchment would have sufficed to copy it out – its last clause points out that there is much more that might be said about being a monk. Because of its simplicity, it has proved very adaptable, forming the basis of much Western monastic life for both men and women to the present day in societies very different from the decaying Classical world of the sixth century. In particular, monks within the Benedictine tradition creatively adapted Benedict's twin commands to 'labour and pray' so that labour might include scholarship. The shade of Jerome, who had taken so much trouble to shape that thought (see pp. 295–6), would be gratified, and otherwise the story of Western Europe would have been very different. It is to the expansion of this Western Christian society from the ruins of the Western Roman Empire that we now turn.

10

Latin Christendom: New Frontiers (500–1000)

CHANGING ALLEGIANCES: ROME, BYZANTIUM AND OTHERS

The era spanning the collapse of the Western Roman Empire's political structures up to the tenth century, so often called the Dark Ages, was a rich and creative period in the development of the West, and 'early medieval' might describe it more neutrally and fairly. When did it begin? Something recognizable as Classical society survived in the western Mediterranean well after the Western Empire itself, only decisively changing in the later sixth century. The Roman aristocracy had been shattered by repeated wars in Italy, ironically mostly resulting from efforts by emperors in Constantinople to restore the old Italy under their own rule. Similar catastrophes crippled the old way of life in North Africa, leaving it weakened before Muslim onslaughts in the seventh century (see pp. 260–61). Perhaps most significantly, in the decades after 550, Latin culture came within a hair's breadth of extinction: the witness to that is the survival of datable manuscript copies of texts. The laborious process of copying manuscripts, the only way in which the fragile products of centuries of accumulating knowledge could be preserved, virtually came to an end, and would not be taken up again for two and a half centuries in the time of Charlemagne (see pp. 352–3). In the intervening period, much of Classical literature was lost to us for ever.

Politically, the area of the former empire was transformed into a series of 'barbarian' kingdoms, mostly ruled by Arian Goths, who preserved their Arianism as a mark of cultural distinction from the Catholic Christians of the old Latin world. The two cultures remained curiously separate side by side, with the Latin elite excluded from military service, paying tribute to Gothic leaders while preserving some shadowy rights

of property as 'hosts' to 'guests' who never actually got round to leaving.[1]
We have already noted that young Gallo-Roman noblemen are said to
have formed a disproportionate number of those joining the pioneer
monasteries of Bishop Martin of Tours in the late fourth century, and
that many of them went on to be bishops (see p. 313). Frequently bishops
of the Catholic Church were the only form of Latin authority left, since
the imperial civil service had collapsed. One suspects that capable and
energetic men who would previously have entered imperial service, or
who had indeed started out as officials in it, now entered the Church as
the main career option available to them, when in the East they still had
the option of imperial bureaucracy. The Western Church has remained
notable for the presence within its clerical ranks of a great many who
are interested in clear rules and tidy filing systems. Western canon
law was one of the West's intellectual achievements long before its
systematization in the twelfth century (see p. 377), and Western theology
has been characterized by a tidy-mindedness which reflects the bureaucratic precision of the Latin language: not always to the benefit of its
spirituality.

How would the Western Latin Church as a whole react to this new
situation? Would it look to the Greek East and identify itself wholeheartedly with the Byzantine attempt at reconquest? Would it disappear,
like all the other institutions of the old empire? Would it follow the
new configuration of power and melt into a series of Arian Churches,
separated into the various ethnic groupings which now occupied the
West? In fact the leadership of the Western Church chose a middle path
which was to prove of huge significance for its future. It continued to
stand aloof from the Arianism of the Gothic peoples, but it increasingly
distanced itself from Constantinople, and it developed an increasing
focus on the Bishop of Rome. This cautious approach to the new world
became apparent when, in 493, the Arian Ostrogoth military leader
Theoderic seized the city of Ravenna, at the head of the Adriatic, the
last capital of the Western emperors. He established his rule there ostensibly as a subordinate of the Byzantine emperor but in reality as an
independent monarch – one of such talent and capacity that even later
Byzantine chroniclers had to give him grudging credit.[2] Theoderic's
adoption of the sophisticated culture that he found is attested by a
handful of superb buildings which survive from his rule in Ravenna.
Among them is his own palace chapel, originally dedicated to the
Redeemer, but now known because of a later Catholic rededication, as
the 'new church' of St Apollinaris (Sant' Apollinare Nuovo – an older

church near Ravenna had previously borne the same dedication to the alleged first bishop of the city). This is the grandest church building ever built in Italy for a non-Catholic version of the Christian faith, for the Arian monarch intended it for Arian worship. What is immediately visually striking on entering it is that this is a church of classic Christian basilican form (see Plate 4). Clearly it was not commissioned for leaders who were disrespectful of established Christian tradition, or who regarded their faith as anything other than central to it. Yet closer inspection reveals some interestingly individual features.

Some of the mosaics in Sant' Apollinare are contemporary with its construction in the early sixth century. Two sequences depicting the Court of Theoderic and notables at his port city of Classis both now make no visual sense, as the figures have rather ineptly been replaced by abstract mosaic designs; these heroic portrayals of a heretical monarch and his retinue could not be allowed a place of honour in what had become a Catholic building. One intact sequence of original mosaic friezes, safely remote from the viewer at the very highest level of the walls, although it spans the whole length of the church on either side of the nave, seems to emphasize the Arian view of the nature of Christ. It tells stories of Jesus Christ's life on earth: on the north side of the church the miracle worker and teller of parables is depicted as a young beardless man, while on the south side, which shows the Passion and Resurrection, he is portrayed as older and bearded. So the Redeemer lives his life and grows and matures as a truly human being who suffers as a human and yet is resurrected for our sakes (see Plate 19). Theoderic thus proclaimed his Arian faith to the world with all the resources of Christian art and architecture. Despite bombing hits in both world wars of the twentieth century, Sant' Apollinare and the other Ostrogothic survivals in Ravenna are among the few witnesses to Arian culture and literature, when virtually everything else produced by the Arians has been deliberately erased from the record. Here we glimpse the splendour and richness of Arian Christianity, elsewhere so successfully obliterated by the medieval Latin Church of the West.

Alongside his lavish gifts to the Arian Church, Theoderic allowed the Catholic Church to flourish, and used the skills of Roman and Catholic aristocrats in his administration. The most distinguished and learned of them, Boethius, was also one of the least fortunate: his service at Court ended around 524 with his execution on charges of treasonous intrigue with the Byzantines. Yet he played a great part in shaping the future of Christian culture in the West. Boethius had a fluency in Greek which was increasingly rare in the West: he knew its literature widely and intimately. He had planned to undertake a major programme of translations of Plato and Aristotle into Latin; in the end he completed only a few of Aristotle's treatises on logic, but books which could provide a structured framework for clear thinking were precious enough amid the increasingly scarce resources of scholarship in the West. Equally significant was the treatise which Boethius wrote in prison while awaiting execution, *The Consolation of Philosophy*. There is not much that is Christian about the *Consolation*: it is the work of a man whose intellectual formation has been in Neoplatonism. Yet that was part of its value. It embedded Plato in Western thought for the next few centuries as surely as did the works of Augustine (and in the same fashion at one remove from Plato himself); the spirit of serenity in the face of death which it expressed was an impressive reminder to Western clergy and would-be scholars that the philosophers who had been ignorant of Christ were worth listening to with respect.

Theoderic and other 'barbarian' rulers who did not match his flamboyance could be seen as protectors of the Western Catholic Church against Byzantine emperors who, from the mid-fifth century, frequently alienated and angered Catholic leaders in the West. The Council of Chalcedon in 451 had brought Roman–Byzantine relations back from the brink of rupture (see pp. 225–7) and it was not coincidental that around that time the embattled Pope Leo I began regularly using a description of his office which proclaimed him with a modesty intended as a strident assertion of inherited historic authority, 'the unworthy heir of blessed Peter' (*indignus haeres beati Petri*). That formulation did have the additionally useful effect of suggesting that if a pope was indeed unworthy, he still enjoyed the charismatic inheritance of the Apostle, which later proved useful when popes might have to defend actions which looked discreditable.[3] In the aftermath of Chalcedon, with successive emperors desperately trying to placate their Miaphysite subjects and risking Chalcedon's hard-won agreement with the West, relations reached a new nadir in the formal 'Acacian' schism of East and West between 482 and 519 (see p. 234).

During this break, Pope Gelasius I (492–6) was an aggressive upholder of the Chalcedonian formula and, in what proved despite its brevity to be an energetic and long-remembered tenure of the papal throne, he tried to pull Constantinople back into line, in the tradition of Ambrose's consecrated bullying of the Emperor Theodosius. Among his various pronouncements, in 494 Gelasius argued in a letter to the Eastern emperor, Anastasius I, that God had provided two ruling authorities in the world, monarchs and bishops. They were charged to use their powers to work together to promote God's purposes for his people, but 'of these, the burden of the priests is greater in so far as they will have answer to the Lord for the kings of men themselves at the divine judgement'. The Pope paid all due deference to the emperor's worldly authority – unlike some of his successors in later centuries – but he asserted that the emperor ought to defer to the clergy in all matters concerning the faith.[4] Beyond the immediate occasion of these pronouncements during the schism, Gelasius had laid down a principle which in the West was respected by monarchs and much exploited and extended by future Church leaders, while in the East it never gained the same hold. Only occasionally did Eastern patriarchs get away with saying similar things to the emperor.

During the schism, there was another event of great significance for the future of western Europe: one powerful barbarian king within the former Western Empire turned his allegiance to Catholic Christianity. His power base was in northern Gaul and his name Clovis; he and his successors took their family name from his grandfather Merovech, to be styled 'Merovingians'. Becoming king of one branch of the Germanic people known as Franks in 481, Clovis proved to be a successful warlord who extended his family's power throughout the former provinces of Gaul – henceforward known as Francia, and more or less the area now represented by France. Like other Germanic leaders, he dallied with Arian Christianity, and members of his family certainly chose Arianism.[5] However, he married a Catholic wife, and he developed a devotion to the saint of the Catholic Church who had been first a soldier and then a bishop, Martin of Tours. The God of Martin won Clovis his victories, just as that same God had favoured Constantine two centuries before. The fascination of Rome and its local saintly champion tilted Clovis's beliefs towards his wife's faith.

Bishop Gregory, a great Gallo-Roman aristocrat who was Bishop of Tours, and therefore Martin's successor as well as the saint's devout partisan and biographer, records that Clovis was made a consul by the Byzantine Emperor Anastasius, an honour which Clovis lavishly celebrated in Martin's city of Tours – the date is complicated by problems in interpreting Gregory's account, but is likely to have been 493 or 503.[6] The grant of a consular title could not be a real assertion of Byzantine power, but it represented the Emperor's eagerness for alliance with an unexpected Catholic Christian ally against Arian rulers in the

West; consular dignity was still a potent link between an old world and a new. Over a period of 1,300 years after Clovis's conversion, eighteen monarchs of what became the kingdom of France were christened with his name, which in its French mutation of the Latin *Ludovicus* became 'Louis'. Now the Latin Church could look to a powerful military patron in the West who was neither an Eastern emperor of dubious orthodoxy nor a heretical Arian like Theoderic. It was a century more before the Visigothic kings of Spain withdrew their loyalty from their ancestral Arianism and embraced the Catholic faith which most of their Christian subjects had defiantly retained. The way in which the history of Catholic Christianity has been told obscures just what a near-miss Arian Christianity proved in the West. If the balance of preferences among barbarian monarchs had been swayed by the Spanish Visigoths rather than by Clovis of the Franks, European Christianity could have remained a decentralized Arianism rather than a Roman monarchy; and the consequences are incalculable. No wonder Clovis remained so celebrated.

At the heart of the Catholic victory was the dead bishop-saint Martin of Tours, now a trophy saint for the Merovingian dynasty. He had become a potent symbol of the triumph of Catholicism over Arianism as far away as Byzantine Italy and the late Arian Ostrogothic kingdom of Ravenna. In the 550s, when the Archbishop of Ravenna celebrated the Byzantine emperor's confiscation of the great Arian chapel royal in Ravenna (now Sant' Apollinare Nuovo) and converted it to a place of Catholic worship, he rededicated the building to Martin the Gaulish saint, even though the archbishop's imperial master in Constantinople could have furnished plenty of Eastern saintly champions against Arianism. It was a significant little gesture to demonstrate that the Western Church was not going to be digested into Eastern Christian practice, even after such a significant victory for Byzantine military power and Catholic Christianity as the reoccupation of Ravenna. In the nave wall mosaics of that church in Ravenna, Martin of Tours still proudly leads the procession of male saints towards the Saviour, even now the church itself has been inconsiderately rededicated to the local hero, St Apollinaris.[7]

The Frankish Merovingian dynasty survived far longer than any of its Arian or pagan rivals among the former barbarian peoples, and despite its later political divisions and misfortunes, it carried forward in the territories of Francia the sense of a political unit consecrated by a trio of great Catholic Christian saints. Besides Martin of Tours, there was a third-century bishop martyred in northern Gaul in the time of Decius,

Dionysius (in later French, Denis); he had been the first bishop of Lutetia, the city which was the forerunner of Paris, which Clovis had refounded as his capital on the island site of the old settlement. These two were joined by an extraordinary woman contemporary of Clovis, a nun called Genovefa (in later French, Geneviève), who had built a tomb for the martyr Denis and is said to have organized Lutetia's resistance to invading Huns in the mid-fifth century.[8] Towards the end of her life, she had a great personal influence on Clovis when Lutetia's surrender to his armies became inevitable. She probably played a part in his conversion and his new enthusiasm for Denis. When Genovefa died in 512, the Merovingian royal family guaranteed her instant promotion to sanctity by burying her in a new basilica which overlooked their island capital, and which signalled their new-found loyalty to Rome with its dedication to Peter and Paul. Geneviève's fame eventually saw to the church's rededication in her honour, and the chilly grandeur of its eighteenth-century successor is now secularized as Paris's Pantheon, a shrine to the very different intellectual and cultural achievements of Enlightenment France.

The three great Catholic saintly patrons of the Frankish dynasty thus comprised two bishops, one a monk who was an ex-soldier, together with a saint highly unusual at the time or indeed at any other: a woman who had pioneered the monastic life and also shown the qualities of a soldier. Geneviève the counsellor of a king would in the fifteenth century provide a role model for an equally strange model of female sanctity, Joan of Arc, peasant visionary, intimidating presence at the French Court and formidable military leader against the English. The alliance between these saints and a Christian Catholic monarchy of France remained one of the great political facts about Christianity in western Europe down to the nineteenth century, and later French monarchs came to glory in their title of 'the Most Christian King'. That title stood alongside another potent title which sprang from the eventual downfall of the Merovingians: the 'Holy Roman Emperor' (see pp. 349–50). Over centuries, the rivalry of these two sacred Christian monarchies repeatedly disturbed the peace of Europe. Until within living memory, French politics were still affected and embittered by an intense consciousness of the ancient French alliance between Church and Crown. The reputation of the Merovingians still enthrals many who prefer to construct the past through cloudy esoteric conspiracy theories rather than pay attention to the exciting realities of Christian history.

Another monarchy was also taking shape, in Rome. The end of the

Acacian schism in 519 produced renewed assertions of the pope's spiritual authority. It was a moment when the devout and Western-born Emperor Justin was especially eager to conciliate Rome, with the encouragement of his nephew and heir Justinian, who was himself already contemplating the restoration of a single united empire of East and West based on Constantinople. The then pope, Hormisdas (514–23), was determined to drive a hard bargain for restoring the two halves of the imperial Church to communion together. He demanded that the bishops of the Eastern Church should subscribe to a formula of agreement which would leave Rome in an unchallengeable position:

Christ built his Church on St Peter, and so in the apostolic see the Catholic faith has always been kept without stain. There is one communion defined by the Roman see, and in that I hope to be, following the apostolic see in everything and affirming everything decided thereby.[9]

The Patriarch of Constantinople managed to sidestep a full commitment to this statement of total surrender, but it was destined to have a long future in the armoury of the Bishops of Rome, both in later efforts to force reunion on a weakened Byzantine Church and in their own general self-image: the pronouncement of Papal Infallibility at the first Vatican Council of 1870 (see pp. 824–5) is inconceivable without this foundation.

It was clear to Catholic leaders in the West that Easterners were cold towards Hormisdas's formula and that the Emperor Justinian was still seeking to modify Chalcedon. Given that there was now so much cooperation between Catholic elites, Arian Western monarchs and moreover a Merovingian royal house committed to Catholic Christianity, there was modified rapture among Westerners when in 533 Justinian began his programme of reconquest in Italy, and in 536 publicly proclaimed his programme of reuniting the Mediterranean under Byzantine rule. Silverius, son to Pope Hormisdas, became pope in 536 with the backing of successive Ostrogoth monarchs in Ravenna, and so the papacy became irresistibly drawn into the military confrontation between Ravenna and Constantinople. When Justinian humiliated the Ostrogoths and made Ravenna his western capital, there was an eager potential successor, Vigilius, archdeacon to the Pope, waiting to supplant Silverius. As a result the new pope was a creature of the Emperor – soon, indeed, after an imperial invitation to Constantinople, his virtual prisoner.

Vigilius found that his new dignity had not brought him a free holiday on the Bosphorus, but had led him into a trap in which Justinian was still pursuing a formula to please Miaphysites and needed the pope's approval to the deal. Between 547 and 548 the hapless pope reluctantly added his agreement to imperial edicts ('Three Chapters') which included condemnations of three deceased theologians whose views were undoubtedly Dyophysite, but whom Chalcedon had specifically declared orthodox – among them was no less a figure than the great Theodore of Mopsuestia (see pp. 223–4). A Church council sitting in Constantinople in 553 endorsed the condemnations laid out in the Three Chapters, while blandly reaffirming Chalcedon and making the best of Vigilius's determined absence from its deliberations. Now Vigilius was caught between Western fury and the real prospect of being beaten up by the Emperor's thugs. After miserable wavering, in 554 he returned to his affirmation of the Three Chapters with their condemnations. He was spared from dire consequences in Rome only by dying on the journey home from Byzantium. So much for Gelasius's affirmation of clerical power, or for Hormisdas's stainless faith maintained by the apostolic see: a pope had committed himself to a major statement of heresy, coerced by an emperor.[10]

So, for the first time since the days of Constantine I, there was now a division in the Church leadership's attitude to the emperor. It was particularly difficult further west in Gaul and Spain to relish any contact with Byzantium: increasingly the survivors of the Classical world in the West would feel that if anything was to remain from the old culture, it would be dependent on those they had once dismissed as 'barbarians'. Arianism was weakening: the Byzantine conquests in Italy had dealt it a severe blow. Yet Justinian's military successes in Italy and North Africa in turn melted away through the ruinous wars of the later sixth century, leaving more scope for papal assertions of Rome's place in the Western Church. Unlike in the East, where Churches in the great cities had competing claims, there was no rival to the pope's position in the West, particularly as the Latin North African Church, once so self-assertive, was laid low by the seventh-century Arab invasions. The Church's constant search for a source of authority to solve its disputes encouraged the trend. For all the honour paid to great oecumenical councils like Nicaea and Chalcedon, the conflicts in their aftermaths, and the messy outcome of the council of 553, revealed the drawbacks in this method of decision-making.

The battered prestige of the Bishop of Rome was restored and then extended by the pontificate of Pope Gregory I (590–604), often known as 'the Great'. He was from the same wealthy, traditional administrative background as Ambrose two centuries before, and indeed he was Prefect of the City of Rome before becoming a monk in the city. Gregory was the first monk to become pope, although this was not monasticism as Pachomius or even Martin had known it: Gregory financed the foundation of the monastery which he entered, built on a family property within the city, and a later tradition asserted that his mother, Silvia, customarily sent him vegetables to his monastery on a silver dish.[11] This Roman aristocrat showed no enthusiasm for the claims of the surviving Roman emperor. For six years Gregory had represented the Church of Rome as a diplomat (apocrisiary) at the Byzantine Court; despite or perhaps because of this, he had no great affection for or high opinion of the Greeks. When at the end of the sixth century Byzantine power in Italy was shattered by a central European people known as Lombards, Gregory certainly did not see the Lombard victory as a baffling catastrophe, as many had seen Alaric's sack of Rome in 410. On the contrary, in 592–3 he presided over a separate peace with the Lombards, ignoring the Byzantine imperial representative in Ravenna. He strongly objected to the title of Oecumenical or Universal Patriarch which the Patriarch of Constantinople had used for the past century, particularly because its justification was that the patriarch was bishop in the Universal City of Constantinople, 'Universal' because it was capital of the empire. It may have been in order to highlight the pride embodied in the Oecumenical Patriarch's title that Gregory adopted one of aggressive self-deprecation, which his successors have used ever since: 'Servant of the servants of God'.[12]

Gregory did have a strong sense of urgency in his papacy, for the good reason that he believed that the end of the world was imminent. It was easy to assume this, amid the political upheavals and decay of the society which had brought his family their prestige and fortune.[13] If the Last Days were coming soon, it was essential that all Christians, not just monks, should prepare themselves for the end by reforming their lives; the clergy, chiefly himself, should be energetic in helping them do so. Gregory is the first writer whose work has survived who spends much time discussing how clergy should offer pastoral care and preach to laypeople: a very different clerical duty from the contemplative life of a monk, to which he had withdrawn before his election as pope. Gregory the former monk saw that this active ministry in the world might afford clergy the chance to make greater spiritual progress than in a monastery, precisely because it was so difficult to maintain contemplative serenity and an ability to expound good news amid the messiness of everyday life: 'When the mind, divided and torn, is drawn into so many and such weighty matters, when can it return to itself, so as to recollect itself in preaching and not to withdraw from rendering its ministry of preaching the word?'[14] As the Church increasingly emphasized the spiritual heroism of monks, this was a valuable affirmation that parish priests had their own spiritual challenges to face.

MISSIONS IN NORTHERN EUROPE (500–600)

It may also have been Gregory's concern to bring the world to as perfect a condition as possible before the Last Days which led him in 597 to launch a mission to a former island outpost of the Roman Empire, lost to Rome two centuries before in the tumult following the sack of Rome. When the Roman legions left the island in 410, it contained the two Roman provinces of Britannia Inferior and Superior, but four hundred years of settled Roman culture there had fallen away with remarkable rapidity. Now much of it was dominated by Germanic peoples – Angles, Saxons, Jutes – who had begun to migrate there in the last years of Roman rule and who by now had given the land a very different character. Gregory's dispatch of a mission to the English in Britannia marked a crucial stage in the Western Latin Church's change of direction away from Byzantium and towards the north and west. Once the Western Church had been the poor relation of the Greek East in terms of numbers and theological sophistication. It had been tied to the fortunes of an empire in increasing disarray and was then confronted by rulers with an alien variety of Christian faith. Now it was reaching out beyond the boundaries of the Roman imperial world. The Bishops of Rome, proclaimed the successors of Peter, were giving a new significance to the ancient city: Rome was to gain an empire of the mind greater than anything which Octavian had created by force of arms in the time of Jesus Christ.

The English mission was the first in which a Bishop of Rome had made any effort to extend the existing frontiers of Christianity. It is curious and probably significant that previous major Christian missionary efforts had nearly all been undertaken by people whom the imperial Chalcedonian Church labelled as heretics – Bishop Eusebius of

Nicomedia and the 'Arian' Ulfila to the northern 'barbarians', the Syriac Miaphysite Jacob Baradeus in the Middle East and the Syriac Dyophysites who spread Christianity into Arabia, Central Asia and (initially) to Ethiopia. The one substantial exception to this had been the initiatives of Celtic Britons, who were Catholic Christians, strongly influenced by the vigorous Catholic Church of Gaul. It was very important for the future shape of British Christian life that, like the Christians of Gaul, they decided to keep their literature and liturgy in the sacred language of the Catholic Western Church: Latin. From the late fourth century these Celtic Christians travelled beyond the frontiers of the decaying provinces of Britannia, into Hibernia (Ireland) and territories and islands to the north of Hadrian's Wall, lands where Germanic peoples had as yet made little impact. We have met one of them already, Ninian of Whithorn (see pp. 313–14), but he is a shadowy figure compared with a driven, tormented British eccentric called Patrick, who was probably a younger contemporary of Ninian's: Patrick and Ninian would both have been alive and active in Christian ministry when the great theologian Augustine was Bishop of Hippo. Patrick, unlike Ninian, is illuminated for us by his own account of his life, written in rough and confused Latin, but a wonderfully precious and rare survival.

Dating this text and Patrick's career is difficult, but it seems to fit into the first half of the fifth century, a generation after the death of Martin of Tours, a time when the Western Church was still much divided by the Pelagian controversy (see pp. 315–17): conflicts resound through what remains of Patrick's writing. Grandson of a priest, he tells us the name of his home town, 'Bannavemtaberniae', the identity of which has provoked much debate, but it was probably one of the little settlements along Hadrian's Wall.[15] As a teenager, he was captured and enslaved by raiders from Ireland, and after wanderings to Gaul and a return to his own people, he felt compelled to go back to Ireland to act as bishop, gathering up what remained from the mission of a previous bishop, Palladius. Both this and a subsequent letter reveal that Patrick faced a good deal of distressing opposition alike in Britain, southern Scotland and Ireland, much of which was from fellow Christians, but this opposition is left behind in subsequent legend. Patrick was to become Apostle to Ireland and eventually, through the worldwide wanderings of the Irish, a saint inspiring veneration throughout the modern Catholic Church – but his posthumous sway was to extend even further, since his years as a slave across the seas (and his reputation for having expelled snakes from Ireland) inspired countless Africans who also found themselves victims of enslavement by Europeans (see p. 714 and Plate 61).[16]

Patrick and his successors as bishops in Ireland faced a society very different even from the fragmented state of mainland Europe after the empire had disintegrated. The island had no central authority, or (importantly) any memory of one, and instead there was a large collection of groupings (*tuatha*) headed by dynastic leaders. Their power over kin and clients was based both on their ability to provide defence against other dynastic leaders and to intercede with supernatural powers for the prosperity of crops and cattle. To call these leaders kings may be misleading, since there could have been anything between 150 and 200 of them in the island at any one time. No Christian episcopate had previously had to cope with anything like this since the Church had first formed its alliance with the powerful. In puzzling out how the situation might become fruitful, the bishops realized that the Church could be rooted in Irish society by founding monasteries and nunneries.[17]

Patrick already spoke with pride of the 'sons and daughters of Scottic [Irish] chieftains . . . seen to become monks and virgins of Christ'.[18] That association with chieftains proved a way of providing for monastic foundations: in the state of Irish legal custom, it would have been impossible to provide for independent estates for monastic maintenance, as was the norm in the former empire, so monasteries became part of the joint estate of great families. As a result, there grew a network of Christian communities intimately involved in the life of each local dynastic grouping, fostering Christian life throughout the island all the more powerfully because monasteries were so enmeshed in the pride and pre-Christian traditions of each *tuath*. There was nothing fixed or enduring about many *tuatha*, and reflecting the itinerant character of much of Irish society, the Church developed the peculiar phenomenon of roving ecclesiastical families, in whom priesthood and care of churches descended from one generation to another; they carried with them in their migrations the stories of their founding saints, spreading the same cult to widely separated parts of the island.[19]

A surprising number of early Christian buildings can still be seen in the west of Ireland and its remote Atlantic islands, mostly monastic sites: drystone-built, straggly collections of cells and halls within enclosures, like the homes of the leaders who had provided for them. Also pleasingly numerous in survival and staggering in their extravagant beauty and sophistication are the art objects which served the sacred life of these communities: manuscripts illuminated and written in a beautiful and individual Latin script, bronze bells, metal crosiers, lovingly preserved despite the violent and destructive later history of Ireland because they became relics associated with early saints, just as important as their bones. Celtic Christian culture made a great deal of such sacred objects in its devotion. The inquisitive and gossipy historian Gerald of Wales in the twelfth century made special mention of this emphasis, saying that in Scotland, Ireland and Wales people were more afraid of breaking oaths taken on bells, crosiers and the like than they were of breaking oaths taken on Gospel books.[20]

Spiritually, Celtic monastic life was as intense as anything in the deserts of Egypt or the Middle East. Half-starved monks crouched against the gales high in the rocky cliffs of the Skellig Islands, and the terrifying beauty of the waters in front of them made them see the sun dance for joy over the Atlantic Ocean, as it celebrated the Lord's Resurrection on Easter Day (see Plate 8). They were actually capable of having contacts with Syrian or Egyptian Christians, at least through books which had started life at the furthest margins of the Byzantine Empire and had been brought west. It has been plausibly proposed that the astonishing intricacy of figural paintings to be found in such Celtic sacred manuscripts as the Gospel text known as *The Book of Durrow* (see Plate 23), and similar figures in Celtic sculpture of the same period, derive from the travels to Scotland and Ireland of a long-lost copy of a Syriac manuscript of the Gospel Harmony called the *Diatessaron*. Before these late-sixth-century artworks, there was very little attempt in Celtic art to portray the human figure; the sudden appearance suggests some external stimulus. Another copy of this same *Diatessaron* text, illuminated in the Syrian monastic enclave of Tūr 'Abdīn, has ended up in Florence, and despite dating from several centuries later than *The Book of Durrow*, it has a series of figures posed in precisely the same idiosyncratic way as some of *Durrow*'s key illustrations. Other features of Celtic Christian art, even that most emblematic of motifs the Celtic cross, can be shown to have precedents in the art of Coptic Christianity.[21]

These unpredictable links between the Middle East and furthest western Europe produced a Celtic theology which resonated at whatever distance with the tradition of Origen and Evagrius. Celtic monasteries took the same line as their fellow monks John Cassian and Vincent of Lérins in the struggle against Augustine of Hippo over grace (see pp. 315–17): they wanted to emphasize the importance of humans striving as best they could towards perfection. One Irish commentator writing in the margin of his manuscript of Jerome's *Preface to the Psalms* summed up the optimism behind their spiritual battles in those bleak windswept cells: 'It is in the nature of every man to do good and to avoid doing evil'.[22] Out of this theology of moral struggle came a distinctive Irish devotional practice which was to become a major feature of the whole Western Church. The Irish clergy developed a series of 'tariff books' for their own use. These were based on the idea not only that sin could be atoned for through penance, but that it was possible to work out exact scales of what penance was appropriate for what sin: tariffs of forgiveness. They saw the spiritual life as a constant series of little setbacks, laboriously compensated for before the next little lapse. They used their tariff books to help layfolk who were oppressed by guilt and shame.

When missionaries from Ireland and Scotland started spreading their faith in northern and central Europe in the seventh century, they brought tariff books with them; these were the first 'penitentials' or manuals of penance for clergy to use with their flocks. The idea was hugely popular – who would not jump at the chance of being able to do something concrete and specified, however hard, in order to lift a burden of guilt? It became the basis of the medieval Western Church's centuries-long system of penance: a practice whereby everyone repeatedly confessed their sins to a priest, who then consulted his book or his memory and awarded the necessary penance. Despite its success and acceptance into the Church's pastoral practice, the whole system directly contradicted Augustine's theology of grace, and that was to become an issue which helped permanently to split the Western Church in the sixteenth century Reformation, as we will see.[23]

The fact that this remote corner of Europe could have such a profound influence on the whole Church is testimony to the restless energy of Celtic Christians, for whom the sea was a series of trackways to their neighbours and cultures far beyond. They treasured a legend of St Brendan sailing to discover new lands to the west, which has long generated Irish pride in its anticipation of Christopher Columbus, and is certainly testimony to the openness of Celtic society to such a possibility. In the later sixth century one of the greatest of their monastic leaders, Columba or Colmcille ('Dove of the Church'), not only founded the monasteries of Durrow and Derry in central and northern Ireland, but also built an island monastery far to the north on the island of Iona, which remains one of the best-known sacred places in the Atlantic Isles; he frequently crossed the sea between his various foundations.[24] But adventurous as Columba was, he was still moving within a Gaelic Celtic world. One of his younger contemporaries, also Columba (but conventionally and conveniently distinguished from the elder as Columbanus), found a new and more challenging image for his travels: he would follow the biblical example of Abraham and travel to strange peoples to do the will of his God.

Columbanus's first journeys (probably in the 580s) were into Christian Gaul, where his foundation of monasteries was met with less than wholehearted gratitude by the existing episcopate. One liturgical issue which was to prove a recurrent source of annoyance between Celtic and non-Celtic Catholics was their disagreement about the date for celebrating Easter, that earliest and most important of Christian festivals. The tensions prompted Columbanus's move east, to what is now Switzerland, and they also indicate that he was not primarily undertaking missions to pagans: his journeys might be best seen as a campaign of renewal addressed to the wider and older Christian world which had originally fostered Irish Christianity. He could do this, of course, because of that foundational Celtic Christian decision to keep Latin as the language of its public worship and its Bible. Naturally where Columbanus found non-Christian customs still prevailing, he did something about it, having before him the model of the great Martin, who had demonstrated the power of the Christian God against all inferior competitors. The stories of his feats probably provided a handy distraction for his biographers from his confrontations with Frankish bishops. One of Columbanus's finest exploits was in Bregenz, where he was infuriated by the sight of an enormous barrel of beer being prepared by people in honour of their fierce god Woden. Columbanus had nothing against alcohol, but he did not want to see all that beer wasted on a false god, so he made a pre-emptive strike by blowing hard on the giant barrel. It exploded and Woden lost his beer. The crowds present were highly impressed that Columbanus's God could be so emphatically destructive and the mission benefited accordingly. From Switzerland Columbanus moved even further into the heartland of Western Christianity, into northern Italy, where he died in 615 at his newly built monastery at Bobbio.[25]

Columbanus had set a pattern of mission from Ireland and Scotland, and other Celtic monks extended his initiative still further by taking Christianity beyond the ghost of the imperial frontier into northern Europe. But now another mission had been launched in the opposite direction, from Rome itself, by Pope Gregory I. In 597, the year that Abbot Columba died far away in Iona, a party of monks and priests set

9. *Christian western Europe in the seventh century*

0   300 Miles

0   400 Km

Iona

SCOTLAND

Derry
Kells

Lindisfarne

HIBERNIA

BRITANNIA

Durrow

Eboracum (York)

Skellig
Islands

MERCIA

FRISIA

Londinium

WESSEX

Canterbury

Aachen

FRANCIA

BOHEMIA

Paris

Metz

Fleury

BAVARIA

Tours

Sankt Gallen

Bregenz

Aquileia

Milan

Massilia

Ravenna

ITALY

VISIGOTHIC KINGDOM

Rome

DUCHY OF
BENEVENTO

Corduba

out from Rome on the Pope's command; they were bound for the Atlantic Isles under the leadership of a monk from Gregory's monastery of St Andrew, called Augustine. There is a certain air of haste and improvisation about this mission to the Anglo-Saxons, which suggests that Pope Gregory may have been fired by a sudden enthusiasm for England. When the missionaries set out, not one of them spoke any variant of Anglo-Saxon, and Gregory's rather lame advice was to pick up some Frankish interpreters to help out in contacting the prospective flock.[26] The Anglo-Saxons preserved a self-congratulatory anecdote which is probably still the best-known memory of Gregory's interest in England: he was struck by the beauty of some English slave-boys in the market at Rome. On enquiring where they were from and being told that they were *Angli*, he commented that the name was appropriate to those who had angelic faces, and he elaborated that cheerful thought in a garland of further devout Latin puns. Traditionally Gregory's remarks have been summed up in a misquotation which is nevertheless apt: '*Non Angli sed angeli*', 'Not Angles, but angels'. This delightful tale would be a good motivation for the Pope's impulsiveness, so at base it might be true.[27]

Clearly Gregory had not learned much about the island to which his mission was launched. He envisaged his new Church rebuilding the structures of the old imperial provinces of Britannia Inferior and Superior, so there would be metropolitan bishops in the former colonial capitals of Londinium (London) and Eboracum (York), each with an apostolic flock of twelve bishops: all very tidy, and two hundred years out of date, given that England was now divided up among a series of Anglo-Saxon kingdoms, and that London was at a low ebb. Instead, the new Bishop Augustine recognized reality and established himself in the extreme south-east in Kent, the nearest kingdom to mainland Europe, where pagan King Ethelbert had married a Frankish Christian princess called Bertha, and where there was still a lively sense of the importance of the Roman past. The Kentish royal capital was a former Roman city now called Canterbury. When political power later shifted away from Kent, successive Anglo-Saxon bishops and archbishops in Augustine's line found advantages in being slightly at a distance from imperious monarchs in Wessex or Mercia, and stayed in Canterbury. Only much later did twelfth-century Angevin monarchs turn a revived city of London into their capital, also developing a palace immediately to its west in Westminster. The Archbishops of Canterbury then experimented with exploiting the possibilities of a newly acquired property in the heart of London itself, on the site of what is now the parish church of St Mary-le-Bow, but they soon changed tack. They thought it wise to develop a minor estate of theirs at Lambeth, which was a quick barge journey across the River Thames from Westminster, and the new palace there became their true centre of operations, rather than Canterbury itself. One late-twelfth-century archbishop even tried to fulfil Gregory's plan and move his cathedral to Lambeth, a scheme foiled only by his death on crusade.[28]

We are lucky to know a great deal about Augustine's English mission because of the brilliant and engaging *Ecclesiastical History* of Bede, a Northumbrian monk who lived a century after Augustine's mission (*c.* 672–735). Bede was the greatest historian of his age in all Europe, perhaps the greatest for many centuries either side of his own time. He was admirably honest in sorting out his varied sources; very often one can tell where he has got his material. Monks at Canterbury, for instance, supplied him with a great many formal documents, which lie at the core of his stories of Gregory and Augustine. He frequently tells us specifically the status and source of his information, and one can picture him on his eager quest for what would now be called oral history – 'The priest Deda . . . a most reliable authority . . . told me that one of the oldest inhabitants had described to him . . .', etc.[29] Bede is the equal of Thucydides in this respect, and a good deal less credulous than Herodotus (see pp. 35–6).

Despite his enthusiasm for Gregory's mission, Bede is honest enough to reveal that Augustine was not coming to a land empty of Christians. There was already a bishop in Canterbury, a Frankish chaplain of Queen Bertha's, and a functioning church, dedicated either by Franks or by earlier British Christians to St Martin of Tours. It is moving when visiting Canterbury to see part of its fabric still standing, incorporated in a modest medieval church building on the edge of the ancient city. It is worth realizing that bishops were not then treated like troubleshooters or roving ambassadors; they were there because a flock was there to be led.[30] Nor is it likely that Bishop Liudhard ministered simply to a tiny expat Frankish colony, for one curious fact must strike anyone reading the letters of Gregory to Augustine preserved by Bede. Certain purple passages on the subject of conversion are always quoted from them, but in reality a large proportion of Gregory's attention is taken up with discussing sex – to be more specific, ritual impurity. Gregory argued at great length against people who had been perplexing Augustine because of their strong opinions about what constituted sexual uncleanness among their contemporaries. These rigorists wanted to borrow Old Testament exclusions from participation in the Temple liturgy and apply them to pregnant women and the sexual relations of married couples.

Clearly such troublesome people were Christians, since non-Christians would have no interest in and presumably no knowledge of the Old Testament. The Roman missionaries were facing difficulties because they were coming up against a significant body of well-informed local Christians with different standards from themselves.[31] Only a few decades before the arrival of Augustine, the balance of power through lowland England had still been not with Saxon warlords but with Celtic British. Certainly the British population had not been wiped out or driven to the far west, as historians have often in the past assumed, but had stayed put, while proving rather more able and willing to learn Anglo-Saxon than the Anglo-Saxons were capable of learning Celtic languages (*plus ça change*).[32] Many of these Britons would be Christian to some degree: Christianity did not come as a startling novelty to the inhabitants of lowland England in 597. So what was different about Augustine's mission? Chiefly, but crucially, its emphasis on Roman obedience.

OBEDIENT ANGLO-SAXONS AND OTHER CONVERTS (600–800)

Augustine's missionary party tried to turn Canterbury into Rome and Kent into Italy. They built a monastery in Canterbury dedicated to Rome's premier saints, Peter and Paul, and that monastery (later rededicated to the missionary Augustine) stood outside the Roman walls of the Kentish capital, just like Rome's basilicas of St Peter and St Paul; Clovis had done the same thing outside Paris (see p. 325). The cathedral church which they also founded out of the ruins of a Roman church was dedicated as Christ Church, in direct imitation of the Lateran cathedral in Rome, a fact now obscured because the Bishop of Rome's cathedral has since been rededicated to St John. Even when the mission founded a second Kentish diocese at Rochester, the Roman theme continued: Rochester cathedral was dedicated to St Andrew after the basilica and monastery on the Caelian Hill, from which Augustine himself had come – especially significant because St Andrew's was the monastery which Pope Gregory had founded on his own family estate.[33] Nor was this reminiscence of Rome mere sentiment. Gregory sent Augustine a special liturgical stole, the *pallium*, a piece of official ecclesiastical dress borrowed from the garments worn by imperial officials. The gift was therefore a sign of subordination: Archbishops of Canterbury should receive their power from Rome ever after. In an interesting historical oversight, their coat of arms is still based on the Y-shape of the pallium, despite the Protestant Reformation of the sixteenth century.[34]

It took the next century from 597 to ensure Christianity's full sweep throughout the kingdoms occupying the former Britannia. Some kings were still non-Christian in the 680s and there were some notable changes of mind on the way. Nevertheless, Christianity finally gained a monopoly status which it had never enjoyed in Roman Britannia. Anglo-Saxon kings must have been influenced by the fact that Christianity was the religion of the Franks, who under the Merovingian successors of Clovis had emerged as the most powerful and admired of all the political units founded by Germanic migrants.[35] The Church could also be sensitive to the pride of newly Christianized rulers and noblemen, enabling them to marry new to old. In many places it allowed people to go on expressing their grief at death by filling graves with prized possessions of the dead, despite the fact that these would be put to shame by the gadgets available in the Christian Heaven. Even the great Christian holy man of northern England Cuthbert of Lindisfarne was given his grave goods to take with him; fragments of them removed from his burial place in Durham Cathedral can still be seen.[36] The Church encouraged royal families to extend their genealogies further beyond the Germanic god Woden, not to leave him out, but to go all the way back to biblical Adam. Bishops outshone non-Christian religious leaders with their splendid hospitality, the traditional mode of asserting one's social status. Wilfrid, an aristocratic Abbot of Ripon and Bishop of York, definitely no Puritan, threw a three-day party for high society in the 660s after dedicating what is now Ripon Cathedral: no doubt the occasion was a satisfying mixture of solid Anglo-Saxon cheer and delicate Roman canapés, if anyone was capable of remembering afterwards.[37]

By the tenth century, out of the diversity of these Christianized Anglo-Saxon kingdoms emerged one of the most coherent political units in Europe, a single monarchy of England, with a precociously centralized government which eventually fell like a ripe plum into the grateful hands of Norman carpetbaggers in 1066. The ideology of this remarkable kingdom was fuelled by the way in which Bede had depicted a single race called the English; his book, after all, was called 'The Ecclesiastical

History of the *gens Anglorum*' – 'people of the *Angli*'. Bede gave this 'people' a pride in their common and special identity, paradoxically based on their common loyalty to Rome. Pope Gregory I rather than Augustine is the hero of Bede's tale of the conversion of the English. Bede called not Augustine but Gregory the 'Apostle' of the English; and he was not creating this image, but reflecting a continuous veneration in England for Gregory.[38] In Bede's own day, the rest of western Europe would have considered this Gregory-mania a case of English eccentricity, for Gregory had actually ended his papacy under something of a cloud, unmourned by the people of Rome. The first life of Gregory was written by an Englishman in the early eighth century in the Northumbrian monastery of Whitby, and it was two centuries after Gregory's death before Rome caught up with his cult, enshrining the Pope alongside Ambrose, Jerome and Augustine as one of the 'Big Four' theologians of the earlier West, the four Latin Doctors.[39] It may be that the popularity of pictures of the Latin Doctors in medieval English churches – a favourite and of course appropriate subject for portrayal on pulpits – stemmed from the thought that one of the Doctors was Pope Gregory, who could be considered an honorary Englishman.

This 'Englishness' can be considered one of the most lasting and unexpected consequences of Augustine's mission, and the way that Bede told its story: the English achieved a political unity which, by contrast, the equally fervently Christian Irish never envisaged or sought for themselves until much later. Bede's narrative reflected the fact that the Church in England had already secured its unity under Roman obedience before the Anglo-Saxon kingdoms united. The crucial decade was the 670s, when a couple of councils of English bishops made decisions for the whole Church in the various kingdoms of England, first at Hertford in 673 and then at Hatfield in Yorkshire in 679.[40] Hertford gave shape and discipline to the English Church, beginning to set up a single system of written law for it to operate under, at a time when no king in England contemplated such an idea. At Hatfield, the bishops supported the Pope's condemnation of the continuing Byzantine efforts to conciliate Miaphysites, and also gave their assent to the 'double procession' of the Spirit from Father and Son, that proposition of Augustine's which so infuriated the Byzantine Church.

A paradoxical feature of these vigorous Anglo-Saxon affirmations of Western Latin theology was that the Archbishop of Canterbury presiding over the councils was a brilliant Greek, a scholar named Theodore who, like the Apostle Paul, came from Tarsus. Maybe Pope Vitalian had sent him to England because he was worried that Theodore might be disruptive in Rome, but it was still a remarkable reminder that England's links to a wider world were overwhelmingly thanks to the Church. One of Theodore's most important and energetic colleagues was the Abbot of St Augustine's Abbey in Canterbury, Hadrian, sent to England by the Pope more or less to keep an eye on the archbishop; Hadrian was just as exotic as Theodore, since he was a refugee from the now beleaguered Church in North Africa.[41] No one could accuse the English Church of being provincial. Because it maintained a loyalty to Rome untypical in the rest of Europe, that sense of difference enhanced a precocious belief among the English in their special destiny among their neighbours, both in the same islands and among the people of Europe. Thanks to Bede, and to the leadership of Archbishop Theodore, they could see themselves as a covenanted people like ancient Israel, a beacon for the Christian world.

Though Bede never explicitly made the connection, it would not be difficult to conceive of a single political unit called England as well as a religious entity. Israel was most at one with God in its covenanted status when it was united, and at its most glorious when that unity was under single monarchs, David and Solomon. Bede caused the English to meditate on Solomon in another of his works beside his *History*. For centuries his extended allegorical commentary on Solomon's Temple in Jerusalem enjoyed more popularity, and he might have been surprised and a little put out to learn that it is his *History* which is now chiefly remembered. Why was Solomon's Temple so important to Bede? Because it stood for him as one image in a pair of opposites, the other being the Tower of Babel. The Tower represented human pride, and pride led to a confusion of tongues. The Temple represented obedience to God's will, and it led to the healing of the terrible divisions of Babel. It foreshadowed the unity of tongues which Bede cheerfully anticipated coming very soon in history, in the Church of the Resurrection: that cosmic unity at the end of time might first be foreshadowed in England.[42]

Anglo-Saxon and Celtic Christians between them made the Atlantic Isles in the seventh and eighth centuries a prodigious powerhouse of Christian activity. Their energies flowed together in the islands themselves, in the founding of a network of new churches and monasteries, but they also followed the sea routes which Columbanus had pioneered into mainland Europe, conscious that they had received Christianity by mission and were determined to do the same for others. Their activities coincided with and were aided by an expansion of Frankish power north and east, into what are now the Low Countries and the territories of Germany commonly known as Saxony; they increasingly received more encouragement from the bishops of the Frankish Church and from local secular rulers than Columbanus had done. For Anglo-Saxons, the mission to Low Countries areas like Frisia was to people with a consciousness of a common ancestry, close trade links and variants on a language which would still be comprehensible either side of the North Sea; even beyond the Low Countries in Saxony, they came as cousins. They were given a cue by that most flamboyant of seventh-century Anglo-Saxon prelates, Bishop Wilfrid, who had a lucky break in that his very successful campaign of preaching in Frisia coincided with one of the best fishing catches in the North Sea for years. Then in the next generation there was Boniface, a monk of southern England who put to shame the bishops of Francia with his prodigious energy in extending the frontiers of the faith, and who was at the end both Archbishop of Mainz and a much-celebrated martyr for the Church, hacked to death in 754 by those same close relatives of the English in Frisia.[43]

These conversions sponsored by missionaries from Ninian through Patrick and Augustine far into central Europe were not conversions in the sense often demanded by evangelists in the twenty-first century, accepting Christ as personal Saviour in a great individual spiritual turn-around. In the medieval West, there were only one or two recorded examples of such experiences, taking their cue from the New Testament's description of what happened to the Apostle Paul. So Augustine of Hippo in the fourth century and Anselm of Canterbury in the twelfth do indeed write about spiritual struggles which sound like those of Paul on the Damascus Road: they talk of dramatic new decisions, realigning their whole personality. In the Reformation, Protestants picked up the same tradition, and since then personal conversion based on assent to an itemized package of doctrine has become almost a compulsory experience in some versions of Christianity. Yet from the fourth to the fourteenth centuries, one of the most successful periods in the expansion of the faith, when all Europe became Christian, people rarely talked about conversion in that sense. If they did, they generally meant something very different: they had already been Christians, but now they were becoming a monk or a nun.[44]

How, then, did the Western Church convert Europe piece by piece between the thousand years which separated Constantine I from the conversion of Lithuania in 1386? At the time, those who described the experience normally used more passive and more collective language than the word 'conversion': a people or a community 'accepted' or 'submitted to' the Christian God and his representatives on earth. This was language which came naturally: groups mattered more than single people, and within groups there was no such thing as social equality. Most people expected to spend their lives being given orders and showing deference, so when someone ordered dramatic change, it was a question of obeying rather than making a personal choice. Once they had obeyed, the religion which they met was as much a matter of conforming to a new set of forms of worship in their community as of embracing a new set of personal beliefs. Christian missionaries were just as much at home with worldly as with supernatural power. They expected people to be unequal, that was what God wanted, and inequality was there to be used for God's glory. Mass rallies were not their style; most evangelists were what we would call gentry or nobility, and they normally went straight to the top when preaching the faith. That way they could harvest a whole kingdom, at least as long as local rulers did not have second thoughts or take a better offer.

Above all, Christians everywhere had a big advantage in being associated with the ancient power that obsessed all Europe: imperial Rome. The Latin-speaking Church became a curator of *Romanitas*, Romanness. That was a paradox, since Jesus had been crucified by a Roman provincial governor and Peter by an emperor, but the cultural alliance stuck. By Bede's account, when discrepant methods of calculating Easter in the Atlantic Isles were debated at the Synod of Whitby in 664, King Oswy of Bernicia decided in favour of the Roman method over the Celtic because Peter was the guardian of the gates of Heaven and Columba of Iona was not.[45] Everyone wanted to be Roman: the memory of the empire stood for wealth, wine, central heating and filing systems, and its two languages, Latin and Greek, could link Armagh to Alexandria. But, as King Oswy's judgement showed, there was more to mission than simple material matters. People hungered for meaning; they were terrified of their own frailty. Famously, Bede told a story that when Oswy's father-in-law, King Edwin of Deira and Bernicia, was weighing up whether or not to become Christian in the 620s, one of his advisers reminded his master of the baffling brevity and inconsequentiality of human life: he compared it to a sparrow which swoops in suddenly through one door into the warm, brightly lit, noisy royal hall and then flies straight out through the other door, back to the darkness and storms outside.[46] Bede probably made the speech up, as historians did at the time, but he made it up because he thought that his readers would think it plausible. The troubled people of Europe sought not only good drains and elegant tableware, but a glimpse of the light which would make sense of their own brief flights out of the darkness. The missionaries of Christianity talked to them of love and forgiveness shaping the purposes of God, and there is no reason to believe that ordinary folk were too obtuse to perceive that this could be good news.

As the Anglo-Saxons travelled east into mainland Europe, so did their devotion to the papacy and their memory of how Augustine had brought them their faith. Even though Rome had done little of substance since Gregory to launch missions into new lands, the Anglo-Saxon missionaries were very fond of quoting the sections of Gregory's letters to Augustine which discussed ways of converting the heathen, and in that they set a pattern which still persists.[47] Celtic missionaries were less enthralled than the English by the mystique of Rome – they were hardly unique in western Europe in that – but they still cherished Latin as the language of the Church, and it is noticeable how many of the newly founded churches across Saxony were dedicated to St Peter.[48] The eighth and ninth centuries were a period in which the papacy was intent on asserting its dignity and special place in God's purpose, a mood not unconnected with the reality of its fragile position between two potentially threatening secular powers in Italy, Lombards to the north and Byzantines to the south.

Matters might have turned out differently, for in the seventh century, after a certain *froideur* in the era of Gregory the Great, papal contacts with Byzantium could be regarded as consolidating: eleven out of eighteen popes in the period 650–750 had a Greek or Eastern background.[49] There was still a sense among ordinary Christians and ordinary clergy that they were part of a single Mediterranean-wide Church. One proof positive of that is the way that, during the sixth, seventh and eighth centuries, fragments of Greek liturgical hymns and psalms were incorporated into various western Mediterranean worship traditions, often without even translating them into Latin, in a variety of settings, from Spain to Italy – Rome itself, Milan, Benevento.[50] One long-standing cause of theological alarm in Rome was neutralized in 680–81, when Constantinople hosted yet another major council of the Church (reckoned as the sixth held there). It finally reaffirmed the imperial Church's commitment to the decisions of Chalcedon against any attempt to placate Miaphysites in the empire, ending the so-called 'Monothelete' controversy (see pp. 441–2). Roman representatives joined Eastern bishops in condemning as heretical four Patriarchs of Constantinople and, more reluctantly, one former Roman pope, Honorius; his name was discreetly inserted in the middle of the list of patriarchs to minimize Roman embarrassment.[51]

Yet the Roman delegates at Constantinople would not have forgotten that the Monothelete clashes also produced one of the most appalling abuses of Byzantine power in 649, when Pope Martin I was arrested by imperial officials for presiding over a council in Rome opposing the Emperor's Monothelete theology. He died in remote exile in the Crimea in wretched circumstances, which have led him to be recognized as the last pope to die as a martyr – this time, uniquely at the hands of a Christian emperor. Such frictions meant that popes were alert for any signs of fresh doctrinal deviance in the East, and the eighth century soon brought them new alarms as the growing hostility to the devotional use of images – iconophobia and then iconoclasm – were promoted by successive Byzantine emperors from Leo III onwards (see pp. 442–56). It was not merely the issue itself which worried Rome, but the way in which these iconoclast emperors were prepared to order major changes in the everyday life of the Church, including in the Byzantine sphere of influence in Italy. That had implications for the authority of Peter's successor.

By contrast to the high-handed Easterners, with their fitful regard for Roman sensibilities, popes were well aware of the fund of goodwill towards the see of Peter in northern Europe, exemplified by no fewer than four Anglo-Saxon reigning monarchs who, between the seventh and ninth centuries, successively undertook the long journey to Rome. The pioneer less than a century after Augustine's arrival in England was Caedwalla, king of the predecessor kingdom of Wessex called Gewisse (c. 659–89), and he was followed later by Ine, King of Wessex (d. 726), and Coenred (d. c. 709) and Burgred (d. c. 874), both kings of Mercia in the English Midlands. All died there, and three of them, Caedwalla, Coenred and Ine, are known to have decided to abdicate and retire to the city permanently; the long love affair between English wealth and Italian sunshine had begun. But the English were too distant to be of much political use to the popes against Lombardy or Constantinople. They looked instead directly across the Alps to the powerful Franks. Frankish rulers in the second half of the seventh century had their own reasons for finding this a very convenient alliance.

CHARLEMAGNE, CAROLINGIANS AND A NEW ROMAN EMPIRE (800–1000)

In Francia, two and a half centuries of Merovingian Christian monarchy sputtered to an ignominious close in 751, when the titular and already powerless Merovingian King Childeric III was informed that he and his son had discovered a religious vocation, after which his hair was given a monastic tonsure and he spent the rest of his days confined in a monastery. A pioneering example of what proved to be a frequent Christian technique for disposing of inconvenient monarchs or politicians, both male and female (often inconvenient spouses too), this was the brainchild of a ruthless nobleman called Pippin and maybe also his elder brother, Carloman. Between them they had been the real rulers of Francia for some time, as the Court officials known as the 'Mayors of the Palace'; they were the sons of the great former mayor Charles Martel who had won the crucial victory against the Arabs at Poitiers in 732–3, turning back the Islamic advance into Europe (see p. 261).[52] Carloman and his family in turn were rapidly eliminated in a series of events which remain much more squalid and murky than chroniclers of the time were prepared to admit. The kingship of Pippin was a wholly illegitimate break with historic succession and, like David's coup d'état against Saul long before in Israel, it needed all the boosting it could get from divine power and sacred place.

Accordingly, the Frankish bishops invested the installation of the new King Pippin III with an unprecedented degree of ceremonial. Pippin paid especial devotion to the Merovingian royal saints, Martin of Tours and Denis, thus annexing that intimate relationship between dynasty and sanctity, while in subsequent decades his family unabashedly claimed continuity with the Merovingian glory days by christening their children with Merovingian names such as Louis (Clovis) or Lothar. Pippin further bolstered his saintly support by enlisting another celebrated former Bishop of Paris, Germanus (Germain), who appeared in a well-timed vision to a pious woman and ordered her to solicit the reburial of his remains in Paris and in greater splendour – Pippin devoutly obeyed with ostentatious ritual in the presence of many Frankish notables, and he also lavishly endowed the saint's monastery (St-Germain-des-Prés, then in countryside beyond Paris) with former Merovingian lands.[53] Pippin and Carloman thus linked the fortunes of their new political venture to major changes and reforms in the Church, particularly in backing great monastic communities who housed their powerful long-dead saintly allies.

In doing this, the new dynasts were only the most prominent and successful of a number of Frankish noblemen who saw their chance to increase their power as the Merovingian monarchy disintegrated, and who were happy to ally this project with the renewal of the Church, linking their own interests to the glory of God. Outstanding among them was Chrodegang, a great aristocrat and Merovingian palace official who, in the 740s, also became Bishop of Metz in what is now north-east France; he may have been the leading bishop in the anointing of Pippin in 751.[54] He energetically summoned councils of his clergy and imposed reforms on his diocese, including a strict code of rules for the clergy of his cathedral church. He set out a system which made their community life much more disciplined, like that of a monastery, but still left them free to exercise pastoral care in cathedral and diocese – a model much imitated later. Since the Greek word for a rule or measure is *kanōn*, the word 'canon' became increasingly commonly applied to members of such regulated bodies of clergy in cathedrals or other major churches.

Bishop Chrodegang also started an ambitious programme of church building and reconstruction in his city of Metz, aiming at making it a centre of sacred power, just as the dynasty of Pippin was enriching the sacred places of Paris. Significantly, when he introduced innovations to the liturgy (and liturgical music) used in his diocese, he justified them on the grounds that they were those used in Rome. Notably, for the first time in northern Europe, he organized 'stational' services around a rotation of the churches of Metz, just as Bishops of Rome had used stational liturgy to unite the Church in their city since the third century (see pp. 136–7). Chrodegang intended Metz to be a local symbol of the unity of the Church, a lesser reflection of Rome, just as the monk Augustine had done in Anglo-Saxon Kent in his mission from 597. Chrodegang even obtained bodies of certain saints from Rome to be rehoused in key monasteries of his diocese: another initiative then almost unprecedented north of the Alps, and a charitable act likely to secure him a great deal of goodwill from entrenched corporations which might otherwise have challenged his authority.[55] In his celebration of Rome in Metz, Chrodegang was closely reflecting the aims of his patron in the new dynasty – for a key component in Pippin's success, and of great significance for the future, was the fact that he too looked for support beyond the clergy of the Frankish Church, over the Alps to Rome.

As early as the 760s clerical chroniclers in Francia were assiduously cultivating the idea that the Pope had explicitly ordered and authorized Pippin's eviction of the Merovingian king (they also did their best to portray the last Merovingians as the sort of accident-prone unfortunates whom no divine insurer would underwrite).[56] There is no question that Pippin quickly won approval for his abrupt change of regime from Pope Zacharias, and Zacharias's immediate successor, Stephen II (752–7), reaped the reward of this affirmation. In 751, the year that Pippin presented King Childeric with his monastic vocation, the Lombards had finally ejected the Byzantine emperor's representative from Ravenna, and they overran the remaining Byzantine territories in Italy as far south as Rome. King Pippin recaptured these lands, but he did not return them to imperial government: instead (to the fury of the Byzantines) he gave them to Pope Stephen. His decision had consequences for the next thousand years; he had founded one of Europe's most enduring political units, the Papal States of central Italy, whose final dissolution in the nineteenth century still shapes the mindset of the modern papacy (see pp. 821–7).

The alliance between the Franks and the popes ripened. Chrodegang was a key negotiator for Pippin in Rome, eventually receiving the pallium and title of archbishop for his pains, while successive popes now kept a permanent representative at the Frankish Court, just as they had long done at the imperial Court in Constantinople.[57] The new relationship was precisely symbolized in a move no less revolutionary for being logical: Pope Hadrian I (772–95) changed the dating custom used by the popes. He began dating his administrative documents and correspondence not by the regnal year of the emperor in Constantinople, but by the year of his own period in office and by the regnal year of the King of the Franks. By now this was the son of Pippin, Charles, the first Frankish king to visit Rome, during the military campaign of 774 which crippled Lombard power. Charles's reign was long, 768 to 814, and history soon christened him Charles the Great, *Carolus Magnus* – Charlemagne.[58] Such was the historic power of his name that it passed beyond his frontier into the Magyar language of his family's enemies in Hungary as the word for king, *király* – and beyond that into Russian and other Slav languages as *korol'* and similar forms. It is significant nevertheless that these mostly Orthodox lands remembered him only as king and not as emperor – that was something of a linguistic put-down for the man who had imperial ambitions, which as far as Westerners and Western history were concerned were realized in 800.

Charles had come a long way from those Arian chieftains who had burst on western Europe to smash the central structures of the Roman Empire, as was apparent in his regular happy wallowings in the hot springs at his newly established capital of Aachen (Aix-la-Chapelle): he enjoyed the opportunity to play at being an ancient Roman provided by public bathing. In fact, he was obsessed with ancient Rome – but also a Rome which was Christian: had he not himself sworn mutual oaths with the Pope in the very presence of Peter in the crypt of the Apostle's basilica? Charlemagne's Christianity did not prevent him taking up arms against other Christians; Carolingian control over the new empire's nobility was based on the rewards of plunder which successful campaigns could produce, which meant fighting Saxons or Avars in the north and east, among whom Christianity had long had a presence. The best that could be done was persuade posterity that the conquered were either all pagans or Christian deviants needing renewal by the Frankish Church, and Carolingian chroniclers set their energies to doing just that: a necessary whitewashing of a new Christian empire.[59] For the result was a political unit which stretched beyond the Pyrenees to the south-west and into the heart of modern Germany. On Christmas Day 800, Pope Leo III crowned Charles as a Roman emperor, in Rome itself. The ceremony was not without its problems. The Pope who performed the coronation had supposedly miraculously recovered from a murderous assault in an attempted coup in Rome the previous year, in which he had been blinded and his tongue cut out. Both mutilation and recovery are questionable (though much celebrated by Charlemagne's clerical publicists), and they were by no means the most dubious part of Leo's reputation. What undoubtedly they did prove was the Pope's urgent need for political support from the most powerful man in western Europe. Leo was the only pope ever to kneel in homage to a Western emperor: his successors did not make the same mistake.[60]

More seriously, there was the problem of what the existing Roman Empire in Constantinople might think of this unwelcome *doppelgänger*. It might be possible to outflank the Byzantines; so Charlemagne put out diplomatic feelers to the great Islamic Abbasid caliph, Hārūn ar-Rashīd, far away in Baghdad. This led to the arrival from the East of a present for the new emperor, an elephant, which remained a delightfully exotic adornment at his Court for nine years.[61] In the same spirit of defiance, Charlemagne's advisers tried to brazen out the situation by claiming that the Byzantine throne was vacant since it was currently held by a woman, the Empress Irene (see pp. 448–51). The Empress was in fact a formidable ruler not to be trifled with – she had after all recently blinded her own son in the room where he had been born, in order to seize his power – and Charlemagne changed tack; he opened negotiations to marry her. The proposal had the unfortunate effect of precipitating her downfall at the hands of courtiers appalled at the prospective marriage, and Charlemagne now had no choice but to stress the role of his coronation by the Pope as the basis for his new imperial power. Equally, the Byzantines had little eventual choice but to recognize the new dispensation and the new empire in the West, though it took them twelve years to do so.[62]

It was probably in this final stage, right at the end of his reign, that Charlemagne issued a series of coins which must have caused awe and amazement at the time, and still have the power to astonish. As best they could, the imperial moneyers carved coin dies which imitated the coins of ancient Rome from half a millennium before.[63] This was an audacious annexation of the past: a Frankish monarch portrayed laureate and clean-shaven, as once Augustus had been, and bearing little resemblance to Charlemagne's real everyday dress and coiffeur. Charlemagne was creating a new empire of the West, but, unlike Augustus, he posed as the defender of Christianity like the Byzantine emperor. He had no hesitation in confronting the Byzantines on theological matters. During his reign a major cause of misunderstanding and ill-will was the matter of iconoclasm (destruction of images), resulting in some aggressive statements against the Eastern Church by Frankish bishops and theologians, at a council presided over by Charlemagne himself, in conscious imitation of Constantine (see pp. 449–50). Another issue was the promotion of that troublesome addition to the Nicene Creed, the *Filioque* or double procession in the Trinity of the Spirit from Father and Son, which had taken its cue from Augustine's writing on the Trinity (see pp. 310–11). Once more it was Charlemagne's Court which encouraged this development. Although the phrase seems first to have been added to the liturgical recitation of the creed in seventh-century Spain, it was given universal respectability in the Western Church because Charlemagne's chaplains introduced it to the worship of his Court at Aachen, and then his bishops defiantly defended it as orthodoxy in the public statements of a synod held there.[64] Much trouble was to follow from this apparently small liturgical innovation.

Like the Papal States which his father had brought into being, Charlemagne's new empire of the West was destined to persist in one form or another for a thousand years as one of the cornerstone institutions of

Europe. In the middle of the twelfth century, emperors began referring to it as the 'Holy' empire and later as the 'Holy Roman Empire', largely because they had come to experience problems with the successors of Leo. Although these subsequent popes had discovered that they had helped to create an institution impossible to control from Rome, the pope's participation in the empire's foundation had been a dramatic assertion of the papacy's new self-confidence in its cosmic role, and it signalled the returning vitality of the Latin West. Both these character-istics were reflected in documents which now emerged to prove that this new situation in fact reflected an ancient reality. We can call them forgeries, but our attitudes to such matters are conditioned by the humanist historical scholarship which emerged in Italy in the fifteenth century. That leads us to expect that our history must be based on carefully checked and authenticated evidence, or it simply cannot exist. For centuries before, though, people lived in societies which did not have enough documents to prove what they passionately believed to be true: the only solution was to create the missing documentation.[65]

In this spirit, there emerged one of the most significant forgeries in history: the so-called Donation of Constantine. The document claims to be the work of Constantine I; after reciting a story of his healing, conversion to Christianity and baptism at the hands of Pope Sylvester, it grants the Pope and all his successors not merely the honour of primacy over the universal Church but temporal power in the territories of the Western Empire, reserving to himself the empire ruled from Byzantium (see Plate 26). Its real date is problematic, but it is generally thought to predate the coronation of Charlemagne, which would have rendered the second part of the gift embarrassing, and to have been written in the late eighth century, in the atmosphere of papal tensions with the Byzantine Empire and of energetic Frankish Church reform.[66] The forged Donation much fired the imagination of later popes and clerical supporters of their power, who saw it as a manifesto for a world in which Christ's Church would be able to rule all society. It is possible to see that as a noble vision.

This process of creative rewriting of the papal past reached a peak under Nicholas I (858–67), a pope who faced major confrontations and even schism with the Byzantine Church over the control of new Christian missions in central Europe (see pp. 458–60), and who looked for support from Frankish rulers in doing so. Nicholas was assiduous in gathering strong papal assertions of Rome's authority, such as those of Gelasius (see pp. 322–3), but he also became aware of a hitherto-unsuspected collection of Western Church law (canon law), gathered not in Rome but probably during the course of a local ecclesiastical dispute in the Frankish Church. This was attributed to one Isidore, a figure obscured from more exact identification by the passing of centuries, and it ingeniously combined genuinely old documents with some brand-new confections. For purposes of its own, the collection emphasized the power of the pope to overrule or reverse any decision of a local Church council. The Pope found this collection of 'False Decretals' of pseudo-Isidore highly useful: its great attraction was that it suggested that the papacy could construct Church law for itself, without references to the deliberations of bishops gathered in general councils of the Church, which had been the real source of the crucial decisions on discipline and theology made in the fourth and fifth centuries.[67]

So it was in the years after 800 that the two cornerstones of the medieval world, empire and papacy, consolidated claims for the future by looking to the past. What followed has been compared to a later movement of rediscovering the Classical past which took shape in the fourteenth century, and so it has been called the Carolingian Renaissance (Carolingian after Charles himself). Charlemagne's buildings proclaimed his agenda much earlier than that exceptional coinage of his last years. When he made Aachen his capital, its octangular imperial private chapel, now the central limb of a spectacular later medieval cathedral, was a copy of the octagonal church of San Vitale, built in the time of the Emperor Justinian in Ravenna three centuries before. Charlemagne went to the trouble of bringing architectural fragments from Ravenna to adorn it (see Plate 28). Throughout the lands where Charlemagne had control, he and his associates built monumental churches. They symbolized the creative refashioning of the past which was so characteristic of this era, because they imitated forms and plans of basilican churches from the early Christian past, but developed them in new ways, for instance building monumental entrance chapels and towers at the west end of the basilica, to overwhelm those approaching with ecclesiastical splendour and a sense of the beginning of a journey into a sacred interior; these were the first dramatic entrance façades in Christian architecture.[68]

Charles also brought to an end the long haemorrhage of written information from the Classical world which had resulted from texts dying as a single manuscript witness disintegrated. He encouraged a massive programme of copying manuscripts, his scribes developing from earlier Merovingian experiments a special script for fast writing and easy reading, 'Carolingian minuscule'. This spread throughout western Europe and was so influential that it is the direct ancestor of the typeface at which you are looking now. Virtually nothing of the Classical literature or early Christian writing that had survived in the West appears to have been lost since that burst of copying in the ninth century, and in virtually every case the earliest known copy of their texts dates from this period.[69] This 'information explosion' was the basis of an attempt to remodel and instruct society on Christian lines. The Emperor's advisers drew up systems of law to regulate all society by what they saw as the commandments of God; among Charlemagne's favourite reading was Augustine's *City of God*. When he published a programme for reform of Church and laity, the *Admonitio Generalis*, he was happy to have himself compared with King Josiah of Judah, who had pleased God by finding and implementing the ancient book of the Law, and his programme also associated him with Moses, the original lawgiver.[70]

Drawing on the practical example of what Chrodegang had done a generation before in the diocese of Metz, Charlemagne pushed reform on the Church's life and worship practice throughout his dominions. At the royal and imperial monastery of Lorsch, where Chrodegang's brother had been the first abbot, there was even an ambitious attempt to produce a replacement for the Julian calendar, though in the end it did not have the long-term or worldwide impact achieved by Pope Gregory XIII's calendar reform eight centuries later.[71] Charlemagne's agents for this heroic programme of social engineering were of course clergy, the only people who could be expected to read and write. Most prominent among them was the scholar and poet Alcuin, an Englishman from Northumbria, who came to Francia only in his middle age in the 780s, but who won Charlemagne's respect and even friendship. Alcuin proved one of the most important architects of Charlemagne's renewal programme, bringing with him the range of learning which had made England such an exceptional region of the Western Church since the days of Bede half a century before and which now returned to enrich the new empire.

Yet in one respect Alcuin was an exception to prove a significant rule amid Charlemagne's clerical agents: he only ever became a deacon, and he was in formal terms never a monk, even when he was made an abbot late in life. Otherwise, overwhelmingly the agents of reform and change in the Carolingian world were monks, and they were members of monastic communities with a particular formation, decided by the Rule which St Benedict had pioneered in Italy in the sixth century (see pp. 317–18). There had long been other monastic Rules known in the Frankish territories. Why did Benedict's prevail? One major motivation arose from a dramatic act of theft. In the central Loire valley, at the heart of France, there was a monastery called Fleury. Its much later Romanesque church still stands, a monumental tribute to the prestige of an ancient monastic tradition and the product of a hugely successful pilgrimage based on that theft, which is also commemorated in Fleury's alternative name, Saint-Benoît-sur-Loire.

Towards the end of the seventh century the monks of Fleury had mounted an expedition far into the south of Italy, to Monte Cassino, and there they clandestinely excavated the body of Benedict himself, plus the corpse of his even more shadowy sister and fellow religious, Scholastica. The consecrated raiding party bore their swag of bones back in triumph to the Loire, and there Benedictine monks still tend them in a crypt in their great church, to the continuing mortification of the Benedictines of Monte Cassino. Benedict had not put up any resistance to his abduction, so it was reasonable to suppose that he approved of it, and thus he gave his formidable blessing to the whole people of Francia. The possession of his bones in Frankish lands was a major reason why first the Franks and then other peoples who admired Frankish Christianity adopted Benedict's Rule as the standard in monastic life. Emperor Louis 'the Pious', Charlemagne's son, sealed the process during the 810s by decreeing that all monasteries in his dominions should follow the Rule. Now it was to set monastic standards throughout Latin Europe.[72]

Charlemagne encouraged the Benedictines to reform older monastic communities which to his eyes were chaotic and decadent. The Emperor's policies reflected the existing esteem which the elite families of Europe felt for monasteries; indeed, from the time of Pippin, the Carolingians were ruthless in annexing monastic patronage from their noblemen, in a bid to consolidate their power. Emperors and noblemen competed to endow Benedictine monasteries with estates to free the monks from financial anxiety.[73] Why did they make these huge investments? Even though there is much to be cynical about in the establishment of the Carolingian Empire and its reforms, clergy brought these brutal politicians and warlords to a healthy sense of their own need for repentance and humility: the theme runs alongside and in counterpoint to the power politics of their era. Pippin directed his body to be buried face-down at the west door of the Abbey of St-Denis outside Paris. Charlemagne did then rather neutralize this gesture of abasement, transforming it into triumphant celebration by building on to the abbey church a huge example of the new fashion for 'westworks', a separate section of the church to the west of the people's nave, over his father's grave.

Nevertheless, the Emperor himself also felt the theme of humility very keenly and personally. He commissioned Alcuin to produce for him a private prayer book which committed him, despite his status as a lay-man, to a regular daily round of recitation of extracts from the psalms, especially those which were customarily used to express penitence, and to a detailed and specific confession of his sins. In his preface addressed to the Emperor, Alcuin reminded him of yet another monarch of the Old Testament, the author of the psalms, who was also a great sinner: David of Israel.[74] It is difficult to know how far this private humility extended, and where it became a political pose. For instance, in all the magnificent and numerous manuscripts which the Emperor com-missioned, there was no picture of the Emperor himself – but then, one of the barrage of reasons which the Carolingians produced for no longer regarding the Eastern emperors as Roman emperors was that the Byzan-tines had let pictures of themselves be offered veneration, a fatal sign of their pride.[75] Equally, humility could be a useful instrument of policy: if an emperor was forced to change his mind in some radical way, he had a ready-made method of performing his political U-turn in the Church's language of penitence and forgiveness.[76]

From whatever motives, imperial humility persisted amid the legacy of splendour from Charlemagne's extraordinary reign. It was a potent theme because the Church was pushing the same idea throughout Frankish society and expected Charlemagne's subjects to follow his example. The ninth century was a decisive era in extending the peniten-tial discipline brought by the Celtic monks in their missions to central Europe (see pp. 332–3). During the eighth century they and their admirers had radically changed the older Christian idea of confession as a single event in an individual's life, something like a second baptism, into an encounter with a priest to be repeated again and again. Now laity who confessed could expect to have to perform regular real penances for their regular real sins: fasting, or abstention from sex, with the penalties laid out in the Church's penitential books.[77]

This new regime of penitence caused a problem for Carolingian war-lords. Quite apart from a healthy sense of their own sinfulness in general, they were faced with the continuing Christian insistence on the profound sinfulness of war in particular. Any notion of absolute prohibition on soldiering had long disappeared, but killing in war was still regarded as inherently sinful. Penance offered a way of dealing with this on a regular basis, but it still left noblemen in a cleft stick: they constantly had to fight to survive and gain wealth, but the price was drastic physical self-punishment. It has been pointed out that if the Norman armies who won the Battle of Hastings in 1066 had carried out the penances which the contemporary penitentials laid down as atonement for their fighting, they would have been too physically weak to go on to conquer England.[78] There was a solution: monasteries could use their round of prayer to carry out these penances on behalf of the noblemen and warriors who had earned them. There was a weak concept of individuality in this society; in early medieval eyes, God would not mind who actually performed the penance demanded, as long as it was done. So the regular round of communal prayer demanded by Benedict's Rule was an excellent investment for the nobility; it saved them from the powers of Hell, which were as near and real as any invading army on their territory. Monasteries were fortresses against the Devil, the monks the garrison, armed with prayer.

The highest and most powerful form of prayer the Church could offer was the Eucharist. In this drama of salvation, a priest led his congregation to a personal encounter with the Lord Jesus himself, in transforming bread and wine into body and blood on the altar. From the fourth century, the Western Church had come to call it the Mass, from *missa*, a late Latin form of the word [*missio*,] a 'sending' – in the liturgy of the Roman Mass current until the twentieth century, the priest enigmatically dismissed the people with the curious phrase '*Ite missa est*', 'Go, it is the sending.' So as laity sought the prayer of priests, they especially wanted the power of the Mass. This changed both its character and that of monasteries and the prayer they offered. Monks had rarely been ordained priests in earlier centuries, but now they were ordained in order to increase the output of Masses in a monastic community. Accordingly, the Mass began to change from the weekly chanted celebration of Eucharist on which congregational life in the early Church had centred. Now it commonly became a spoken service, the 'Low Mass', to be said as often as possible, often with only a server as token congregation. Because a Mass needed an altar, side altars began multiplying in Charlemagne's abbey churches, so that many Low Masses could be said alongside the sung High Mass which remained the centrepiece for the whole community at the high altar.[79] This never happened in the Eastern Churches, where the service of Eucharist is still always sung, as are all other parts of the liturgy, sermons excepted. Hence that immediate contrast in visual impact which one feels entering Orthodox or traditional Catholic churches. In the Orthodox building, there will be one altar behind its iconostasis (see pp. 484–6); in the Catholic, the high altar has its attendant host of side altars, just as often visible in the main body of the building as in their own side chapels.

It was also in this era of monastic development that the Western Church began adapting its Latin liturgy to provide Masses which would give particular mention of the dead, for use at the time of a burial, or at intervals of time thereafter. They came to be called 'requiems', from the opening phrase sung or spoken as the service began, '*Requiem aeternam dona eis, Domine*', 'Eternal rest grant unto them, O Lord'. Although Orthodoxy also has its services for the dead, they are significantly not Eucharists. There is nothing in Orthodox liturgy quite like the purposeful concentration on the passage of death to be found in the developed Latin service of requiem Mass, with its black vestments, its dark-coloured candles and its sense of negotiating a perilous path. Nothing else has so effectively conveyed the fullness of the Church's power over the faithful. Through the centuries the liturgy of the requiem gained extra texts, a twelfth-century sequence forming one of Christian liturgy's starkest presentations of human horror at death, judgement and damnation, the *Libera me* and *Dies irae*. This has continued to inspire Western composers to some of their most dramatic musical settings, even as the temporal power of the Church has faded, as those who cherish the Requiems of Giuseppe Verdi, Gabriel Fauré or Maurice Duruflé will vividly remember:

Deliver me, O Lord, from eternal death on that fearful day,
when the heavens and the earth are moved,
when you come to judge the world with fire.
I am made to tremble and I fear, because of the judgment that will come,
  and also the coming wrath.
when the heavens and the earth are moved,
That day, day of wrath, calamity, and misery, day of great and exceeding
  bitterness,
when you come to judge the world with fire!

Carolingian monasteries were not merely concerned with fighting sin and death; they were useful as a means of cutting down the numbers of claimants to a noble family's lands. Send spare sons or daughters off to a convent, for what more honourable life could there be than that of a monk or nun? This was particularly valuable for women. During the early medieval period, the monastic life offered a golden opportunity for talented women of noble or royal families to lead an emancipated, active life as abbesses, exercising power which might otherwise be closed to them and avoiding the unwelcome burdens of marriage. In the privacy of a nunnery with a good library, they and their nuns, who also tended to be from elite families, might become as well educated as any monk. Working within the conventions of the society of their time, they played as great a part in the life of the Church at large as their male equivalents, the abbots, or indeed as bishops. In fact those abbesses presiding over the greatest houses came to wear the headgear worn by abbots and bishops which symbolized authority in the Church: the mitre.

The pioneers among royal abbesses actually predated Carolingian monarchy by a century and appeared far beyond the northern border of the Frankish realm. They were Anglo-Saxons, members of the Wuffingas, in the later seventh century the royal family of East Anglia. One of the first, Princess Aethelthryth (Etheldreda or Audrey), managed to remain a virgin through two royal marriages; she was latterly Queen Consort in Northumbria, before she separated from her long-suffering husband after twelve years and returned to her homeland in 673 to found her own double monastery for monks and nuns. She chose an island called Ely, protected by the expanses of fenland which formed the western frontier of her family's kingdom – maybe her abbey could be seen as part of its border defences – and she became its first abbess. Twenty years after her death, her entombed corpse continued to make its presence felt. Having triggered enough miracles to demonstrate sanctity, it was solemnly reburied in a shrine which attracted a growing stream of pilgrims to her island retreat, and Etheldreda's memory is still honoured by the Anglican Dean and Chapter who now cherish the magnificent Romanesque cathedral on its bracingly windswept scarp. Such royal princesses were invaluable in bringing a sacred character to their dynasties, now that kings were subject to the Church and could not fully play the role of cultic figures, as they had in pre-Christian religions.[80]

None of the roles of a Benedictine monastery just described – scholarship, eucharistic intercession or social engineering – had played any part or received any mention in the Rule of St Benedict. Nevertheless, because of them, the ninth to eleventh centuries were a golden age for monasteries of the Rule; the survival of European civilization would have been inconceivable without monasteries and nunneries. One ninth-century manuscript, which survives in its original home in the incomparable library of the Swiss Abbey of Sankt Gallen, contains the plan of an elaborate monastery which was created as an ideal rebuilding of the abbey. In it we see a layout which did indeed become standard for Benedictine houses for centuries: church, dining hall, dormitories and assembly hall (chapter house) grouped round a central cloister yard, with a host of lesser buildings and gardens around them to service the community (see Plate 10).[81] It is all very different from the haphazard collection of cells and buildings which formed earlier monastic enclosures such as those still surviving in the west of Ireland. The plan itself speaks of order, just like the Rule of Benedict, and the increasingly elaborate and majestic cycle of liturgy in the monastery church, in the midst of a world which, for very good reasons, neurotically sought order and reassurance. Such communities seemed indeed like the City of God: an image of Heaven. The vision of order and regularity which the Benedictines represented was just what the rulers of the Carolingian age were looking for. It is not surprising that people came to feel that regulars (clergy and people living under a monastic rule) were especially close to God, and that it was much more difficult for laypeople in the ordinary world to gain salvation. Later this produced a reaction among both secular clergy (those clergy not living under monastic discipline) and layfolk at large.

Charlemagne died in 814 and the empire which he had created did not long survive him as a single political unit. By 843 his family had divided the territories into three Frankish kingdoms. They and those who supplanted them on these thrones increasingly faced invasion from north and east by Vikings, Magyars, Slavs and Muslims; in the process, many of the struggling Christian outposts in northern Germany and Scandinavia which the emperors had encouraged, even beyond their borders, dwindled away, and only in the eleventh century was much done to revive them.[82] Just as damaging as these external threats for the successor rulers, if not worse, was the return of powerful rivals among the nobility, who carved out territories for themselves in the form of duchies. West Francia, the predecessor of the later kingdom of France, proved particularly vulnerable to such encroachments during the tenth and eleventh centuries, and consequently the Capetian kings in Paris who ousted the last Carolingians in 987 clung with particular devotion to the great royal saintly cults of the Merovingian and Carolingian past as potential for strengthening their position. Indeed, anyone possessing or seeking power continued trying to annex the power of the Church in great monasteries for their own political purposes.

Monasteries were equally anxious to find protectors, but they were also conscious that they had a reservoir of sacred power to dispense. The most successful were those who saw that the popes in Rome could be useful allies: the pattern was set by that long-established abbey in central France, Fleury, and was later hugely developed by the Abbey of Cluny, as we will discover (see pp. 363–6). The enterprise of the monks of Fleury was not limited to burgling Italian cemeteries; as early as the eighth century, Fleury drew on its de facto possession of the bones of Benedict to negotiate the right to appeal directly to the pope against any bishop in the Frankish Church, and during the ninth century the abbey continued to enhance this useful weapon through creative manuscript forgeries. Popes were not slow to reward Fleury's succession of conse-crated crimes with further privileges, and in 997 the abbey pulled off a triumphant coup: it gained papal recognition as the premier monastery in France and custodian of St Benedict. A subsequent pope in 1059 issued a similar privilege for Italy to the indignant monks of Monte Cassino, who now claimed that Benedict had not gone missing at all.[83]

This steadily increasing stream of papal benevolence reflected the fact that the flow of benefit was not in one direction only. An exclusive relationship with a flourishing Frankish monastery was good for papal prestige and influence over the Alps, at a time when the reputation of individual popes was, to put it charitably, not high. These were dismal years for the Bishops of Rome, at the mercy of powerful families in their city and rarely rising above their difficult situation. Edward Gibbon had some good clean anti-clerical Georgian fun describing the most notorious of them, John XII (reigned 955–63), descended from a lady of some notoriety named Marozia:

The bastard son, the grandson, and the great grandson of Marozia, a rare genealogy, were seated in the chair of St Peter, and it was at the age of nineteen years that the second of these became head of the Latin church. His youth and manhood were of a suitable complexion; and the nations of pilgrims could bear testimony to the charges that were urged against him in a Roman synod, and in the presence of [the Holy Roman Emperor] Otho the Great. As John XII had renounced the dress and decencies of his profession, the *soldier* may not perhaps be dishonoured by the wine which he drank, the blood that he spilt, the flames that he kindled, or the licentious pursuits of gaming and hunting. His open simony might be the consequence of distress: and his blasphemous invocation of Jupiter and Venus, if it be true, could not possibly be serious. But we read with some surprise, that the worthy grandson of Marozia lived in public adultery with the matrons of Rome: that the Lateran palace was turned into a school for prostitution, and that his rapes of virgins and widows had deterred the female pilgrims from visiting the tomb of St. Peter, lest, in the devout act, they should be violated by his successor.[84]

While the papacy languished, the Western Roman Empire recovered. The idea of empire persisted through its years of weakness, and during the tenth century it was given political reality once more in the eastern part of the old Carolingian dominions by Emperor Henry I (919–36) and his successor, Otto I (Gibbon's 'Otho the Great': 936–73). This Ottonian dynasty did its best to imitate the achievements of the first Western emperor, inspiring a spectacular new burst of creativity in architecture, art and manuscript illumination. In 972 the Emperor Otto II outdid the Carolingians: he married into the imperial family of Constantinople. His wife, Theophano, proved an effective governor for her son, who became emperor, behaved impeccably in her lavish endowment of monasteries as far north as the Low Countries, and did her utmost to bring the best of Eastern devotion to the West, including the dedication of major churches to Greek saints. Yet this initiative led nowhere. Theophano's young son, the Emperor Otto III, died in his early twenties in 1002, just as a marriage was being negotiated for him in Byzantium.[85]

Many in the West were pleased at the failure. One eleventh-century chronicler in Regensburg (in modern-day Germany) recorded with satisfaction the vision of a nun who saw the Empress Theophano pleading for forgiveness in shame for her sins, which he obligingly went on to specify as excessive luxury in clothing and customs, so corrupting to women of the West. Behind such misogyny lurked much greater differences between the Christian practice and belief of East and West. The fact that the Western Roman Empire continued to exist at all was a symbol that the two cultures had begun to take decisively different directions. There was steadily less understanding between the two sides, because communication between them was irregular, haphazard and often bad-tempered, and that meant that differences of theological outlook could fester: principally Charlemagne's addition of the *Filioque* to the Nicene Creed (see p. 350). Successive popes proved remarkably obstinate in resisting Carolingian pressure about the *Filioque*, showing that they were aware of the gravity with which Constantinople regarded the issue. Rome was one of the last places to adopt the *Filioque* into its liturgy, and eventually only did so in the early eleventh century, under pressure from the last Ottonian emperor, Henry II, who was campaigning against the Byzantines in Italy.

This was a sign that papal relations with the East were reaching a low ebb.[86] A formal break between Rome and Constantinople in 1054 (see p. 374), not seen as significant at the time, signalled not simply a new era in relations between the two, but the culmination of a process in which the papacy made its claim to a primacy in the whole Church ever more formal. This could not have been predicted when, a thousand years before, Peter had been killed in the imperial capital. After the new millennium in 1000, three centuries followed in which the dream of a universal Christian monarchy became central to the shape of Western Christianity, and almost seemed to be capable of becoming reality.

The West: Universal Emperor or Universal Pope?
(900–1200)

ABBOTS, WARRIORS AND POPES: CLUNY'S LEGACY

For a French provincial town with just over four thousand inhabitants, Cluny in Burgundy boasts more than its fair share of fine stone medieval houses, towers from a generous circuit of former town walls, and three church spires in its skyline. Yet the place is haunted by an absence, the nature of which becomes clear if one seeks out the most imposing of those church spires in the town centre, to find it topping a very peculiar building, a monumental empty Romanesque domed hall, soaringly and at first sight bafflingly tall in proportion to its floor area. To enter this medieval elevator shaft of space is to realize that it was part of something much bigger. It is in fact one single transept from what was between the eleventh and the sixteenth centuries the largest church building in the world (see Plate 13). The church's ancient splendour made it a symbol of all that the French Revolution hated and, after a mob sacked it in 1790, the shell was sold to a building contractor, who took three decades to pull it down, all except this sad, towering remnant. The Emperor Napoleon had a stud farm built over much of the empty site. Until those dismal years, the prodigious church proclaimed the importance of the abbey which had created it.

At the beginning, Cluny Abbey had not been unique. Its foundation in 909–10 coincided with a new phase in the constant urge to renewal in Western monastic life, but in character it differed little from the monasteries which the Carolingian reforms had produced. Bishops and aristocrats still thought that the best way to battle against monastic complacency and corruption was to devote huge resources in land and wealth to the creation of ever more splendid Benedictine houses. In the same era England witnessed a burst of parallel activity, vigorously supported by an expanding monarchy, and it might have been thought that England would lead European reform, as it had once led missions into northern Europe. The English were now precociously united under a single king. From the time of the pious and energetic King Alfred (reigned 871–99), the kings of Wessex had done their best to fight off invasion and occupation by Danish and Viking armies to create a version of Carolingian monarchy, just at the time when the Carolingians themselves were descending into quarrels and failure. Alfred's successors Aethelstan (reigned 924–39) and Edgar (reigned 944–75) achieved the united English kingdom anticipated in the Church of Augustine's mission and in the writings of Bede (see pp. 341–2). The uniting of England provoked an outburst of pride which might almost be styled nationalist, and which had a distinctive and galvanizing effect on the English Church.

Reforms in England were the work of a small group of great reformers whom King Edgar made bishops and archbishops. Aethelwold, a courtier of King Aethelstan, who had become a monk and from 963 was bishop in Edgar's royal capital of Winchester, was a scholar and dynamic teacher who inspired a series of decaying monasteries to adopt the Benedictine Rule as their standard of life, having himself translated that Rule from Latin into Old English. His unusual impact on the English Church left it one individual feature not often found elsewhere in Europe, and which was even extended after the Norman Conquest of 1066: the creation of cathedral churches which, up to Henry VIII's sixteenth-century dissolutions, were also monasteries, with a prior and monks instead of a dean and canons. The capital, Winchester, was itself one; another was Worcester, another Canterbury, though the cathedral canons of York 'Minster' never succumbed to reorganization into the monastic life.

Dunstan, who had been Abbot of Glastonbury when Aethelwold was there, was Archbishop of Canterbury from 959. He was both a great statesman, who presided over King Egbert's quasi-imperial coronation at Bath in 973, and a zealous promoter of Aethelwold's Benedictine project throughout the kingdom (engagingly if surprisingly, he also took an interest in personally annotating a manuscript of no-holds-barred erotic verse by the Latin poet Ovid, which still exists in the Bodleian Library in Oxford). Oswald of Worcester, a monk of Danish descent, was equally energetic in monastic foundations and refoundations across the English Midlands from Worcester to Ramsey; Edgar promoted him to the Archbishopric of York in 971. Notably, all these scholars were as concerned to write in Old English as in Latin, developing with pride a vernacular literary tradition which had most unusually been fostered by the writings of a king, Alfred of Wessex. That emphasis on the vernacular might well have altered the patterns of Christianity in northern Europe, if England rather than Cluny had proved to be the powerhouse of Christian change in the next century.[1]

Cluny's glory days came later than the English revival. The abbey outgrew the patronage of any one secular monarch or nobleman and proved far greater in its influence than the restrictions of a single kingdom. The founder, Duke Guillaume of Aquitaine, had endowed the abbey lavishly but made unusually few demands in return, in reward for which generosity monastic posterity gratefully entitled him 'the Pious'. A century after the foundation, a series of exceptionally shrewd and capable abbots built on this freedom of manoeuvre; they took their cue both from a provision in Duke Guillaume's founding charter placing them under the pope's special protection and from the example of Fleury, that much older Frankish monastery which, with exceptional and ruthless enterprise, had pioneered a special relationship with Rome (see p. 360). In 1024 Odilo, Abbot of Cluny from 994 to 1049, followed Fleury's example in gaining exclusive papal privileges; he also began major rebuilding and enlargement campaigns at the abbey, which by the end of the eleventh century produced the final version of the prodigy church (see Plate 13).[2]

One should never underestimate the significance of architecture in Christianity and particularly not in the era of reform which now emerged. There was a vast amount of church-building, precisely because to rebuild a church building was regarded as a sacramental sign of institutional and devotional renewal in the Church: each new church was a reform in stone. One chronicler from Cluny saw the Christian world as clothing itself with 'a white mantle of churches', having safely passed the watershed of 1000, when the end of the world might have been expected (Cluny made rather a fuss about this millennium, while it is not at all clear that others did).[3] Worship in the church of Cluny itself was renewed in spectacular style amid the builders' scaffolding. Its monk-clergy celebrated an unbroken round of Masses and offices, while the centrepiece of these subsidiary dramatic performances were High Masses unequalled elsewhere in their splendour and solemnity. Western Europeans marvelled at this offering to God, and when they hastened to imitate it by endowing their own versions of Cluny, the abbots of Cluny harnessed this enthusiasm in a new way. Rather than simply giving their blessing to new independent abbeys in the traditional Benedictine manner, they demanded that each foundation should form part of a new international organization run by the abbot of Cluny himself, as 'priories' to his abbey: they would form a Cluniac 'Order' – the first monastic organization to bear this title – in which the abbot would progress round the priories and priors would gather at the mother house on a regular basis.

Moreover, the abbots of Cluny discovered a special and appropriately international purpose for their growing spiritual empire. Unusually and surprisingly for a great monastery, they did not make their own church into a cult centre for any celebrated saint. Instead they looked to a shrine on the furthest south-western frontier of Catholic Christendom, in the city of Compostela on the Atlantic coast of north-west Spain. From the ninth century Compostela Cathedral had claimed that it housed the body of one of the original twelve Apostles: James, in Spanish Santiago. From all over Europe, devout people now sought to make the long and difficult journey to the remote Iberian city, and Cluny, strategically placed in Burgundy, began organizing these crowds along the roads of Europe; its priories were agencies and way stations for the journey. The Compostela pilgrimage was only the flagship in a great industry of travel to holy places in Europe which blossomed during the eleventh century. Most of the greatest surviving churches of the period were built as stages or goals on pilgrimage tracks, and their architectural patterns took their cue from Cluny. Entering the main entrance of St Etheldreda's Ely Cathedral, Mary Magdalene's Vézelay Abbey, the church of St-Sernin in Toulouse on the Compostela route, or Compostela Cathedral itself, is to see something of what the lost church of Cluny was like. The nave is a long, cavernously vaulted road taking the pilgrim on a journey to the high altar in the far distance, with around the altar a passageway (ambulatory) completing a circuit of the whole church building. The entrances of such churches are commonly topped by relief sculptures of Christ in majesty or God the Father judging all creation, a powerful reminder of the object of any pilgrimage: the distant goal of Heaven. They are among the greatest and most moving specimens of medieval sculptural art.

The expansion of pilgrimage was only one symptom of profound changes in Church and society which Cluny Abbey embodied. What happened in the eleventh century was a Reformation, but unlike the more familiar Reformation of the sixteenth century, it was not a rebellion in the ranks but directed from the top, resulting in the most magnificent single structure of government which Christianity has known. Whether

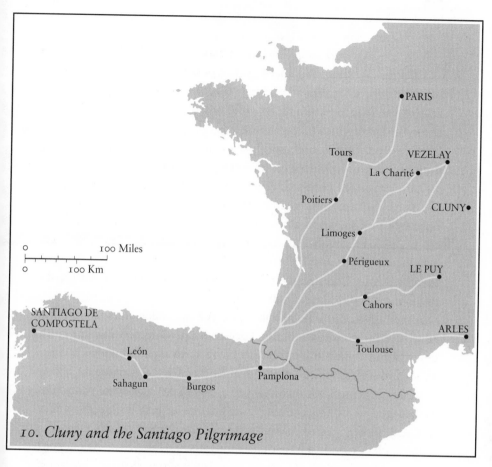

10. Cluny and the Santiago Pilgrimage

we approve of this achievement or not, it deserves the title of Reformation as much as the actions of Martin Luther and John Calvin, and we will not do it justice to see it, as later Protestants did, as a deliberate conspiracy by selfish clergy. The Church in the West was reacting creatively to change in the nature of power and wealth in the society to which it ministered. In the early medieval period, the chief way of gathering wealth was by warfare, yielding plunder and slaves; as we have seen, as late as the Carolingian period kings survived by giving handouts to their warlords (see p. 349). By the eleventh century this system was coming to an end. The change was symbolized by the collapse of Carolingian central authority in much of Europe over the previous century, which, whatever short-term disruptions it caused, was to lead to a new settled order in Western society. That was also encouraged by a gradual end to the wave of invasions of non-Christian peoples from north and east which had been a constant source of insecurity during the ninth and tenth centuries.

Nevertheless, most people would not have experienced the new system as a deliverance; it was characterized by new forms of exploitation. In a search for new sources of wealth, and with the prospect of greater stability in their territories, the nobility turned to squeezing revenues out of the lands which they controlled through more productive farming. Some of their enterprise was directed to expansion of cultivation – draining marshes, clearing forest – but whether in old or new farming communities, they regulated their land and the people on it ever more closely. From the tenth century many areas of Europe witnessed the purposeful creation of a network of new village settlements, with many more legal obligations on their newly gathered inhabitants. A large proportion of the rural population was reduced to serfdom: farmers became the property of their lords, with obligations to work on the newly intensive agricultural production.[4]

Economic productivity dramatically rose as a result. There were better food supplies and more wealth. Surplus wealth and the need for ready exchange in which to transfer it meant that money became a more important part of the economy than it had been for centuries. Trade naturally benefited from the new prosperity and the rulers of peoples on the margins of Christian Europe, drawn further into trading networks, saw the advantages of adopting the faith of their neighbours, in a remarkable series of parallel developments.[5] To the east, Poles, Hungarians and Czechs all began succumbing to Christian missions, although it was some time before their monarchs made decisions between Eastern and Western Christianity (see pp. 458–65). Likewise around 1000 Christianity began making renewed progress in Scandinavia – first a conversion in Denmark ordered by its king, Harald Bluetooth, around 960 under pressure from the Ottonian emperors, then a more gradual spread through what is now Norway and Sweden, even as far as remote Iceland. At the same time, the Christian nobility of Germany began casting covetous eyes on the non-Christian lands to their north-east around the Baltic, launching a counterpart to the wars of reconquest at the other end of Latin Christendom in Spain.

The transformation in farming production changed the nature of the Western Church's ministry in society, making it pay more attention to the needs and obligations of the humble and the relatively poor. The backbone of the early medieval Church had been the select group of monarchs and nobility who financed the growth of Benedictine monasteries and had themselves generally directed Church affairs. Probably in reaction to the newly emerging settlement patterns, the Church now spread its pastoral care throughout Europe in a dense network of what it called *parochiae*: parishes. Each of the new villages was expected to have a church. The ideal of a parish was a territorial unit which could offer literally everyday pastoral care for a universally Christian population; its area should be such that a parish priest could walk to its boundaries in an hour or two at most. That was certainly easily possible in the little Suffolk parish in which I grew up in the 1960s, where my father was the successor to a line of priests which dated back at least to this revolution in the Church's life in the eleventh century. From the eleventh century to the twentieth, the second half of Christianity's existence so far, the parish was the unit in which most Christians experienced their devotional life. Only now has that ceased to be the case.

As parishes were organized, it became apparent that there were new sources of wealth for churchmen as well as for secular landlords. The parish system covering the countryside gave the Church the chance to tax the new farming resources of Europe by demanding from its farmer-parishioners a scriptural tenth of agricultural produce, the tithe. Tithe was provided by many more of the laity than the old aristocratic elite, and was another incentive for extending the Church's pastoral concern much more widely. This had a large number of consequences, not least in the Church's attitude to sin. It certainly did not denounce as sinful the movement to enserf a large section of the population, any more than it had challenged slavery in the ancient world; that was hardly surprising, since very often great monasteries like Cluny were in the forefront of imposing serfdom on their tenants. But the clergy also became more alert to the possibilities of sin which wealth produced, and sought to protect their people from the consequences. It was during the twelfth century that avarice and the taking of interest on money (usury) became major themes for churchmen's moralizing alongside the most basic of human sins, pride.[6] As sins multiplied, so did the means of remedying sin. The great historian of medieval society Sir Richard Southern saw the extension of the clergy's pastoral care in the parishes as leading to a profound shift in the Western Church's theology of salvation and the afterlife.

The essence of Southern's argument is that in the earlier Benedictine era, the system of salvation had been geared to benefiting clergy and those wealthy enough to finance monks to pray for them and perform the very heavy penances demanded of the sinful, in order to avoid the pains of Hell. As the parish and tithe system developed, this older approach would not do: some other way must be devised to cope with the hopes and fears of a sinful population who could not afford such provision. This was where the idea of a middle state between Heaven and Hell, first envisaged in the theology of the Alexandrian theologians Clement and Origen at the turn of the second and third centuries, proved so useful and comforting. The instinct for justifying salvation by human effort, a constant thread from Origen through Evagrius and John Cassian, emerged once more to confront the 'grace alone' theology of Augustine. Few people can regard their drearily unspectacular sins as justifying hellfire, but most would agree with the Alexandrians that life on earth provides hardly enough time to remedy even those sins and enter Heaven without further purgation. Penance could be done in this middle state, which was time-limited, and which moreover had only one exit, not to Hell but to Paradise. By the 1170s, theologians observing this growth of popular theology of the afterlife had given it a name: Purgatory. Never a notion which gained currency in the Eastern world, despite its precedent in Greek-speaking theologians, Purgatory was to become one of the most important and in the end also one of the most contentious doctrines of the Western Latin Church.[7]

This was by no means the Church's only reaction to the new economy. One symptom of the reorganization of society's wealth was a great deal of local warfare as rival magnates competed to establish their positions and property rights, or used violence against humble people in order to squeeze revenue and labour obligations from them; this was the era in which a rash of castles began to appear across the continent, centres of military operations and refuges for noblemen. Churchmen in Francia reacted strongly in order to stop violence against their flocks (not to mention themselves and their own landed estates), appealing to the consciences of their communities to restore peace. They convened large gatherings, the first of which to be recorded was summoned by the Bishop of Le Puy in 975, in which the bishop threatened wrongdoers with excommunication and bullied those present into swearing an oath to keep the peace. The initiative was imitated by other bishops, who drew on their churches' collections of relics to reinforce their threats with the wrath of the saints.

So a 'Peace of God' movement was born throughout the Frankish dominions and beyond, east of the Rhine and south of the Pyrenees; eventually it even included a set of agreements about which days were legitimate for fighting. All sides benefited: thoughtful lords might be as relieved as the poor that the Church was providing an institutional setting where disputes could be resolved without the possibility of violence. It was striking that the Church was appealing to consciences right across the social spectrum, even if the net result was to confirm and strengthen the new order of society. It was an essential feature of the movement that crowds turned up to witness the proceedings; their numbers and their consent were as much part of the pressure put on recalcitrant magnates as the bones of the saints. Yet the notables spiritual and temporal were actors too. Odilo, most energetic of the abbots of Cluny, was among the Peace movement's leading advocates; soon kings and even the pope were involved in regulating these councils and agreements. The papacy's intervention was particularly significant for the future, because it pointed towards an inexorable conclusion: if a single problem occurred all over Europe, then it was best dealt with by a single authority.[8]

THE VICAR OF CHRIST: MARRIAGE, CELIBACY AND UNIVERSAL MONARCHY

The leadership of the Western Church was now doing its best to provide pastoral care in the everyday lives of its members, and part of the bargain was that it sought to hold everyone, rich and poor, to rigorous new standards of holiness. During the eleventh and twelfth centuries it did its best to gain more control over the most intimate part of human existence, sexual relationships and marriage; increasingly Church councils convened as part of the Peace movement began making orders which had nothing directly to do with peace, but regulated people's private lives.[9] The Church successfully fought to have marriage regarded as a sacrament: Augustine of Hippo had thus described it, in what was then a rather vague use of the word 'sacrament', but now precision was brought to the idea. Marriage became seen as one of seven sacraments which had been instituted by Christ himself, all marked with a sacred ceremony in church. A 'church wedding' had certainly not been known in the first few centuries of Church life; the laity were much slower (by several centuries) to accept this idea as the norm, and the efforts of some extremist theologians completely failed to impose the doctrine that the priest performed the marriage, rather than witnessing a contract between two people.

This sacramental view of marriage meant that the Western Church saw a union blessed in Church as indissoluble; there was no possibility of divorce – again, not a common view in the first few centuries before Augustine – and the best one could hope for was a declaration that (on a variety of grounds) a marriage had never actually existed and could be declared null. This remains an axiom of marriage law in the Roman Catholic Church, and rather more untidily in the Church of England.[10] At the same time, the Church much extended the number of relationships of affinity between relatives which could be considered incestuous and therefore a bar to marriage; churchmen took these well beyond what even contemporary theologians could have claimed were scriptural guidelines, so that in the end the great Council of the Church at the Lateran Palace in 1215 (see pp. 405–8) had to do some embarrassing backtracking to lessen the rigour.[11]

It is possible to be cynical and suggest that a principal motivation for this otherwise puzzling excess on affinity (a motivation, indeed, for the Church's general concern to regulate marriage) was a wish to see property left to churches rather than to a large range of possible heirs in the family. The more limits were placed on legal marriage, the more chance there was of there being no legal heir, so that land and wealth would be left to the Church, for the greater glory of God.[12] Another and wider perspective on this new concern for marriage and its boundaries would be to see it as yet another response to the new arrangements which were emerging for land ownership in eleventh-century society. If landed estates were to survive as economic units, it was important that they were not broken up by the old custom of letting all members of the family take their share. A new custom of 'eldest takes all' (primogeniture) became widely established by the twelfth century, and now the nobility could see the Church and its concern for legitimate marriage as a helpful clarification to identify the true heir under the law of primogeniture. Most readers will agree that the Church's new approach was preferable to forcible male castration, which was employed with distressing frequency by certain European noblemen in the eleventh century as a means of neutralizing potential competing founders of landed dynasties.[13]

Certainly it is true that churchmen were deeply concerned about the loss of ecclesiastical estates to possession by families; that had a further effect on the Church's regulation of marriage. Very many clergy at that time who were not monks customarily married. Married clergy might well found dynasties, and might therefore be inclined to make Church lands into their hereditary property, just as secular lords were doing at the same time. The result was a long battle to forbid marriage for all clergy, not just monks: to make them compulsorily celibate. There had been occasional efforts to achieve this before, and the Western Church had from the fourth century generally prevented higher clergy from being married, but in 1139 a second council to be called at the pope's residence in Rome, the Lateran Palace, declared all clerical marriages not only unlawful but invalid.

There was not merely the issue of land at stake. Celibacy set up a barrier between the clergy and laity, becoming the badge of clerical status; at a time when everyone was being called to be holy, celibacy guaranteed that clerics still stole a march in holiness on laypeople. The struggle for universal and compulsory clerical celibacy was bitter, but even in countries like England, where married clergy put up fierce resistance, the fight was largely over by the thirteenth century. The issue was thrown open again in the sixteenth-century Reformation, but in the intervening period, any woman who was the partner of a priest was a concubine and all their children were bastards. One pitiless view of such children among Church lawyers in the wake of the reforming Council of Pavia in 1022 was that they were automatically serfs of the Church, though there is little evidence that anyone took this very seriously.[14] More practically, during the next few centuries, bishops in some areas of the Church such as Switzerland were pleased to derive a substantial and reliable source of income from fining their parish clergy for keeping women as concubines.[15]

In many different ways, then, the clergy asserted their power to regulate the lives of the laity, as well as establish their distinction from laypeople, and they took major initiatives to seize and harness the profound changes in European society. They could only do this because, from the mid-eleventh century, a rather dim and occasionally deeply scandalous sequence of popes was replaced in Rome by successive capable and strong-willed reformers, inspired by what had been happening beyond the Alps. They drew on their predecessors' centuries of claims about their place in the Church, which had previously given the pope a position of great honour but not much real power. Popes had not appointed bishops; rulers like Charlemagne or the local bishops who were their creations had called councils to decide on Church law and policy, even contradicting papal opinions from time to time. When the Pope crowned Charlemagne in 800, it had been in practice if not in theory from a position of some weakness (see p. 349), and later Holy Roman Emperors had proved to have minds of their own. In fact it is a paradox, and an anticipation of the troubles which were now to afflict relations between pope and emperor, that the first pope who can be regarded as a reformer was a German imposed on Rome in 1046 as Clement II, after the Emperor Henry III had forcibly seen off the claims of three competing claimants to the papal title.[16]

However they arrived at their new situation, the reforming popes now constructed a view of their position which did not brook contradiction. The very name Clement was a manifesto, reminding the world that the first Clement had been a close successor of Peter. Pope Leo IX (reigned 1049–54) was in the final year of his pontificate responsible for the drastic step of excommunicating the Oecumenical Patriarch Michael Keroularios in his own cathedral in Constantinople. The immediate issue was a dispute about eucharistic bread. At some point after it had become apparent that East and West had begun drifting apart, in the years after Chalcedon, the Latin West had come to use unleavened bread (*azyma* in Greek) at the Eucharist. *Azyma* had the advantage of not dropping into crumbs when it was broken, a matter of some importance now that eucharistic bread was increasingly identified with the Body of the Lord – yet the Greeks (rightly) regarded this as yet another Western departure from early custom. Was such bread really bread at all?

Pope Leo sent his close friend Cardinal Humbert as negotiator with the Patriarch in 1054. Humbert was a former monk of Cluny who had recently been appointed archbishop in Sicily, an area of constant tension between Churches of Greek and Latin usage, and he was not inclined to diplomacy. Beginning with calculated rudeness to the Patriarch after their arrival in Constantinople, Humbert and his fellow envoys then appeared while worship was proceeding in the Great Church of Hagia Sophia. They strode through the congregation up to the altar and placed on it the Pope's declaration of excommunication, quitting the building with a ceremonial shaking of its dust from their feet, amid jeers from a hostile crowd. This was only a personal excommunication of the Patriarch and his associates, but unlike the Acacian schism of the late fifth century (see p. 234), Pope and Oecumenical Patriarch did not declare the excommunication revoked for another nine hundred years after the events of 1054, and even now in many areas the reconciliation between Orthodoxy and Western Catholicism is distinctly shaky.[17]

The pope who drew together all the strands of papal self-assertion in the eleventh century was Gregory VII (reigned 1073–85). Born Hildebrand, an Italian who became a monk, he was in papal service from the 1040s, so he was another major voice in the circle of Pope Leo IX alongside the Cluniac Humbert. Once pope, Gregory was free to pursue the programme of Church reform which now had all Europe as its canvas, and which, in a series of formal statements entered into his administrative register, was centred on a definition of the pope as universal monarch in a world where the Church would reign over all the rulers of the earth.[18] This one man's vision can be compared in its consequences over centuries with the vision of Karl Marx eight hundred years later; indeed, all the signs are that it will prove far longer-lasting in its effects. Popes had never before made such revolutionary universal claims. Not even the Donation of Constantine (see p. 351) would satisfy Gregory's agenda: it still represented a gift from a secular ruler to a pope, and that was the wrong way round, at a time when popes were increasingly bitterly clashing with successive emperors. Twice Gregory went so far as to excommunicate the king and future Emperor Henry IV in the course of an 'Investiture Controversy', a dispute which continued to rage through the twelfth century as to whether monarchs could present senior bishops with symbols of sacred office when they were appointed.

This was a straightforward struggle about who was going to exercise control in the Church. Famously in the first of their clashes, the Pope kept the excommunicate Henry waiting in penitential garb, allegedly barefoot, for three days in winter snow, at the castle of Canossa in northern Italy, before granting him absolution. Gregory's successors took a new title, more comprehensive than 'Vicar of Peter', more accurately to express his ideas: 'Vicar of Christ'. Not merely the successor of Peter, the pope was Christ's ambassador and representative on earth. His duty was to lead the task of making the world and the Church holy.[19] Gregory's humiliation of Henry was soon to be reversed, and the investiture controversy itself ended inconclusively in the early twelfth century, but similar issues flared up repeatedly later. In confrontations which sometimes became military campaigns, popes were able to wound the empire without effectively dominating it. As a result, Western Europe was not destined to become a single sacred state like the early Muslim caliphate, under either emperor or pope, but a constellation of jurisdictions, some of which threw off papal obedience in the sixteenth century.

One of the most poisonous confrontations between the Church's persistent claims and one of these monarchs was a dispute between King Henry II of England and his former Chancellor the Archbishop of Canterbury Thomas Becket, about whether the King's newly developing royal legal system could claim full jurisdiction over English clergy, at a time when the Church's canon law was far more comprehensively developed. A party of Henry's knights took the initiative in murdering Becket at the altar in his own cathedral in 1170. It was a disaster for the public image of the English monarchy, inspiring Henry's undeferential neighbour King William I of Scotland gleefully to found a monastery at Arbroath dedicated to Becket, only eight years after the archbishop's martyrdom. The monks of Christ Church Canterbury, who had never liked Becket in life, had plenty of reason to be grateful to him after his death, since he attracted a considerable pilgrimage cult to their cathedral, magnificently rebuilt to highlight his shrine.[20] Yet the English monarchy was no more permanently intimidated by papal claims to superior juris-diction than were later Holy Roman Emperors; the relationship re-mained always open to negotiation. The same was true of those devout heirs of the Merovingian monarchs and servants of St Denis, the kings of France, or indeed any of the monarchies of Europe who took on their own sacred trappings. In many kingdoms of Europe, particularly in Aragon, monarchs were known to assert their own semi-priestly charac-ter by themselves preaching sermons on great occasions, despite angry protests from senior churchmen.[21]

A universal monarchy, however notional, needed a complex central bureaucracy. The popes had earlier built up a permanent staff of assis-tant clergy, cardinals. They were so called from the Latin *cardo*, meaning a wedge rammed between timbers, for 'cardinals' were originally excep-tionally able or useful priests thrust into a church from outside – their appointment had systematically breached the early Church's (fairly breachable) convention that clergy should keep in the same place for life.[22] From the twelfth century these cardinals gained their own power, including the privilege of electing a new pope. Like every other European monarch, the Bishop of Rome found that he needed a Court (*Curia*); this would not only provide him with more personal and less independent attendants than the cardinals had become, but would also meet the ever-growing demand from the faithful of Europe that the pope must do business for them. So in the 1090s the crusader-pope, Urban II, formalized structures for his Curia which became permanent.

Rome's newly imposed importance in the everyday life of the Church meant that it was worth making the long journey there. A monastery might seek a privilege like Fleury's or Cluny's to stop interference from a local bishop; an illegitimate boy might need a dispensation to get round the Church's rules excluding bastards from the priesthood; a

nobleman, desperate for a legitimate heir under the rules of primogeniture, might need to have his childless marriage declared non-existent.
One petitioner in the time of Pope Innocent III in 1206 was an English
Augustinian canon, exercised because when he had been admitted to the
Augustinian Order he had taken on a new name, Augustine. He worried
that if people offered prayers for him as 'Augustine', the prayer would
not be as effective as if they had used his baptismal name of Henry, and
he wanted his old name back. Rome gravely assured him that since the
pope himself took a new name on assuming his office, there was no
cause for concern.[23]

Naturally the unified Church of Gregory's reforms needed a single
system of law by which universal justice could be given, and the twelfth
century was the first age when this began to be put in systematic form
as canon law. There had once been just such a system of universal law:
that of the Roman Empire. Now a great stimulus was the rediscovery in
Italy around 1070 of two copies of a compilation of imperial law, the
great *Digest* of Roman laws ordered by the Emperor Justinian (see
pp. 433–4); this prompted a flourishing of legal studies in Italy, especially in the city of Bologna.[24] If an emperor could once have gathered a
definitive volume of laws, so now could the Bishop of Rome. The chief
collection of existing laws and papal decisions which codifies canon law
comes from mid-twelfth-century Bologna, and goes under the name of
Gratian, about whom nothing else is known and who may only have
been the mastermind behind one draft of what remained an unwieldy
and disjointed document. Even though Gratian's *Decretum* only gained
official status from papal publication as late as 1917, from its earliest
days it was the basis of Roman canon law – not least because of the
vision which it embodied of a pyramid of Church authority culminating
in the pope. Gratian made much use of the earlier fictions of pseudo-
Isidore about papal authority (see pp. 351–2).[25] The *Decretum* and
canon law in general also specifically embodied that principle of the
Gregorian Revolution that there were two classes of Christians, clerical
celibates and laypeople. Only a century ago, this could still be pithily
spelled out in an official papal pronouncement: 'The Church is essentially an unequal society, that is, a society comprising two categories of
persons, the pastors and the flock, those who occupy a rank in the
different degrees of the hierarchy and the multitude of the faithful.'[26]
Given the new importance of canon law, it was no coincidence that
every pope of significance between 1159 and 1303 was trained primarily
as a canon lawyer.[27]

Bishops likewise developed their own administrations for local justice and Church order in their dioceses which reflected what was now happening centrally in Rome. The balance of local power in the Church between diocese and monastery was now tipping back in favour of bishops, after centuries in which abbots and indeed abbesses had characteristically been the leading figures in the Western Church. Diocesan bureaucracies were both symptom and cause of this. Kings and noblemen in Europe saw the usefulness of competent bishops to improve their own administration and drafted them into their own governments. Often this might take a bishop away from his duties in his diocese, so his administration might have to carry on without him. Usually it did so quite successfully, but an efficient office system is rarely spiritually inspiring. Even though they generally tried to be real fathers-in-God for their dioceses, bishops were increasingly trapped in a world of fixed routine – faced with demands from pope and lay rulers, and remote figures to their flocks. In the long term, it was not a healthy development, and it bred a constant succession of tensions between clergy and people with which episcopal systems have continued to struggle – most damagingly for the Western Church in the sixteenth-century Reformation.

Nevertheless, this age of growing episcopal power also left a staggering heritage of architectural beauty: the cathedrals of medieval Catholic Europe. The grandest church buildings of the Carolingian era were, as we have seen, virtually all built for the round of worship in monasteries. Given that the bishop and his diocese now had a new significance in the devotional lives of the faithful, the mother church of the diocese needed to be an outward and visible expression of that role. Very often, cathedrals were sited or resited in the expanding towns which were products of Europe's economic growth in the period. As a result, between the eleventh and thirteenth centuries, the cathedrals of Latin Europe were rebuilt on a huge scale, to the extent that one celebrated French historian, Georges Duby, dubbed this 'the age of the Cathedrals'.[28] It was by no means the case that great monasteries stopped building and rebuilding their great churches, but now they had rivals; on the whole, the accidents of European history, both in destruction and in well-intentioned rebuilding, have favoured the survival of medieval cathedrals rather than the most prodigious abbey churches. The archetypal specimens are in the region covered by France, although scarcely less splendid cathedrals are also to be found in England, where after 1066 Norman invaders did their best both to make a distinctive mark on the landscape and to pay off a debt of gratitude to the papacy for blessing their conquest of the realm (see pp. 382–3).

Symptomatic of that Anglo-French connection is the fact that the germ of a new architectural style for both cathedrals and monasteries, eventually spreading throughout Europe, is simultaneously to be found in major churches widely separated in this once-united cultural zone: Durham Cathedral, far to the north of England, and a rebuilt royal Abbey of St-Denis to the north of Paris, both under construction in the first half of the twelfth century. In these two enormous churches and then in many others, architects began tackling the technical challenge of engineering buildings which would reach to Heaven with an audacity not swiftly followed by their ignominious collapse. This was the style which ungrateful Italians of the fifteenth-century Renaissance christened 'Gothic', connecting it to barbarian peoples who by the age of the cathedrals had of course long vanished among the Catholic faithful.[29] Nothing could be further from the Dark Ages than a Gothic cathedral: it is suffused with light, which is designed to speak of the light of Christian truth to all who enter it. Abbot Suger of St-Denis, one of the pioneering patrons of this new style in the early twelfth century, had been seized by enthusiasm for the writings of Pseudo-Dionysius, mistaking that carefully obscured Eastern mystic for the martyred Gallo-Roman St Denis, patron of his own abbey. On the bronze doors of his lavish new enlargement of his abbey church, Suger arranged for an inscription of verses which encapsulated the way in which the anonymous Syriac Miaphysite associated the quality of physical light with the experience of spiritual enlightenment. A church of stone could be transformed:

> Bright is the noble work; but being nobly bright, the work
> Should brighten the minds so that they may travel,
> Through the true lights,
> to the True Light where Christ is the true door.[30]

Light in the churches of the Gothic architectural tradition was filtered through windows which were increasingly themselves huge sequences of pictures in stained glass, telling the divine story from Old and New Testament and beyond into the history of the Church. Stained glass became one of the most compelling though also one of the most vulnerable media for conveying the doctrine of the Western Church (see Plate 30). It has never played such an important role in Orthodoxy or the non-Chalcedonian Churches, whose church architecture never aspired to become a framework for windows in the fashion of the Gothic churches of the Latin West. Gothic windows grew ever greater in expanse and therefore posed ever greater problems for the engineer of a vast bulky building. Intricate schemes of stone buttressing like permanent open scaffolding for walls and ribs for stone-vaulted roofs were devised to take the stresses safely from ceiling, tower and spire to the ground. The semicircular arches of Romanesque architecture gave way (sometimes, all too literally) to arches composed of two arcs meeting at an apex in a point, so that the thrust could be absorbed more efficiently at the point, and arcades and windows could soar ever higher.

Above all were the church towers and pointed steeples which rose triumphantly higher than any other man-made structure in Catholic Europe; where they stood close to the palaces of kings or princes, no turret of the palace dared outstrip their closeness to the heavens. Even that great architectural historian Sir Nikolaus Pevsner, notoriously uncompromising champion of twentieth-century modernism in architecture, once observed in a moment of unusually lyrical concession that twentieth-century architects had 'not been able to create anything anywhere both as elegant and as powerful as a late medieval steeple'.[31] Perhaps the most perfect of all is the cathedral of Chartres, which, by a succession of miraculous escapes and the protection afforded by intense local pride, has preserved its twin spires, its sculpture and its stained glass almost unharmed from the twelfth and thirteenth centuries. Chartres Cathedral is a hymn to the glory of God and of the Mother of God, the shrine of whose tunic it was built to protect (so far, successfully). It rides its hill over the plains of northern France with no rival on the horizon, visible to its pilgrims further even than the bounds of the diocese ruled by its bishop (see Plate 31).[32]

The universality of the Gothic style is one of the symptoms of the way in which Gregory VII's vision of a single Catholic Church seized the Western Church in the two centuries after his turbulent tenure of the Throne of St Peter. Monarchs might resist the claims of the Bishop of Rome, bishops might ignore his authority when it suited them, but from the forests of Scandinavia to the cities of Spain cathedrals arose which did their best to ape the models provided by Chartres and St-Denis (see Plate 32). In their wake, the humblest parish church was likely to provide its own little local exuberance as far as its means would allow. The Gothic style is so characteristic of the Latin Catholic West that it comes as a visual shock to find it in alien settings, but there it is in the church which for many was the heart of the Christian world: the Church of the

Holy Sepulchre in Jerusalem, the shelter for the Crucifixion site and tomb of the Saviour. Equally surprising to a traveller to the eastern Mediterranean is to stumble on French Gothic cathedrals in the Levantine sunshine of the island of Cyprus, in the cities of Famagusta and Nicosia. Stripped of their present Muslim minarets, which come from a later and radically different phase of their existence, they could be transported to a town of northern Europe, and sit there without any sense of incongruity. How have such buildings got this far east? Their presence is the witness to one of the greatest but ultimately also the most tragic of all adventures within the life of the Western Latin Church: the Crusades.

THE AGE OF THE CRUSADES (1060–1200)

When Cluny Abbey fostered European pilgrimage to St James in Compostela, it was offering ordinary people the chance of access to holiness, like so much of the Gregorian Revolution. After all, the great attraction of pilgrimage was that it opened up the possibility of spiritual benefit to anyone who was capable of walking, hobbling, crawling or finding friends to carry them. But Cluny was also annexing to that thought another new and potent idea. St James had become the symbol of the fight-back of Christians in Spain against Islamic power. It is still possible in Hispanic cultures as far away as Central or South America to watch (as I have done in Mexico) Santiago's image triumphantly processed on horseback, with a second image, the corpse of a Muslim, pitched over his saddle.

The Cluniacs' investment in the pilgrimage routes to Compostela was a major influence on the balance of power between Christians and Islam in Spain. Thanks to the effective collapse of the Muslim caliphate of Cordoba in 1031, the Christian cause was becoming increasingly successful, and that was one reason why the crowds swelled across the pilgrimage trails to Spain. The order allied itself closely with the Christian kings of León-Castile and Aragon-Navarre who were winning victories against the Muslims. A network of Cluniac houses grew in Christian Spain, and among the Cluniac monks who came to lead the Church in Spain was one who rose to be primate of the Spanish Church as Archbishop of Toledo as well as papal legate (representative) in Spain:

Bernard, abbot of the chief Spanish model of Cluny, the monastery at Sahagún. The Cluniacs became familiar with the idea that God might wish Christians to initiate war against his enemies, and under Popes Gregory VII and Urban II, the latter of whom began his career as monk and then prior of Cluny, the Western Church took a dramatic new direction in its attitude to war.[33]

While Christian leaders had once simply tried to stop Christians from being soldiers (see pp. 156–7), now the Church came to see warfare as something it might use for its own purposes. The notion of holy war, crusade, entered Christianity in the eleventh century, and was directed against the religion which from its earliest days had spoken of holy war, Islam. The Carolingians had done their dubious best to present their campaigns in northern Europe as wars for Christianity (see p. 349), but the difference now was that Christian warfare could actually be seen as the means to win salvation. The first impulse in this was sparked by a spectacular if wholly unusual outrage: in 1009 the mentally unstable Caliph al-Hâkim of Egypt ordered the systematic demolition of Constantine's Basilica of the Holy Sepulchre in Jerusalem. Although the Caliph's campaign against Christianity was relatively short-lived, and a curtailed substitute building was completed in the 1040s, Christian indignation at the destruction gradually grew through the century. It was stimulated by the general growth in pilgrimage, but especially by the opening up of a new land route to Jerusalem via Hungary, which meant that more and more people witnessed the damaged site.[34]

Churchmen began suggesting that a solution to such grievances might be a reconquest of the Holy Land. But before that became a practical possibility, Christianity won a great victory in the central Mediterranean, in the island of Sicily, which had been contested between Muslims and Christians since the early days of Islam. The victorious armies were led by warriors whose ancestors had come from the north, a restless Scandinavian people whose northern origins were commemorated by their name, Normans. They carved out niches for themselves in widely separated parts of Europe: northern France ('Normandy'), as far east as the plains of what is now Ukraine and Russia, and most ambitiously, after 1066, the whole Anglo-Saxon kingdom of England. But the Normans' achievements in Italy were perhaps their most significant. The papacy had at first regarded their arrival as a threat, and Pope Leo IX had allied with Argyrus, governor of the Byzantine dominions in southern Italy. Leo also showed his interest in Sicily by appointing the increasingly influential Cardinal Humbert (see p. 374) as Archbishop of Sicily in 1050 – at the time, a purely symbolic gesture, since there was no Latin presence in the island, but one fraught with significance for the future.[35]

In the short term, the Pope's predictive powers seemed unimpressive: the Normans soundly defeated Argyrus in 1053 and took Leo prisoner after his disastrous rout in battle in south Italy. This unsurprisingly led to a spectacular reversal of policy by the Pope and his advisers (among whom Hildebrand and Humbert the Archbishop of Sicily were by now the most prominent). In 1059 the Pope recognized the Normans' new acquisition of wide territories in southern Italy, some of which were actually still in the hands of Muslims or Byzantines, and in 1066 there was to be a similar papal blessing for Duke William of Normandy's speculative invasion of England. Like the Franks before them, the Normans seemed to be a good investment for the papacy, and in Sicily they made spectacular conquests from 1060, setting up a Norman kingdom there which was to prove one of the most productive frontiers of cultural exchange between Byzantines, Muslims and Catholic Christians in the Mediterranean world. In 1063, in a gesture of thanks for a gift of four camels, Pope Alexander II sent the Norman King Roger of Sicily a banner which he intended should be associated with Roger's military victories. Gestures such as this were turning the conquest of a wealthy island into something more like a sacred cause. By the end of the century, both Muslim commentators and Pope Urban II were looking back on the Norman seizure of Sicily as a precedent for the greater campaign for the Holy Land itself.[36]

It was Gregory VII who first sought to turn Western indignation about the Holy Land into practical action. He tried and failed to launch a crusade to the Holy Land in 1074; no one believed his claim to have already gathered an army of 50,000 men, for it was not at all clear where they were all assembled.[37] His successor Urban II was a good deal more tactful and respectful of lay rulers than Gregory and did better – this despite the fact that there was no great immediate crisis to rally the West against Muslim aggression; in Spain, warfare continued to flicker on the frontier of the two religions, but that was nothing new. What Urban did have was a direct appeal for military help from the Byzantine Emperor Alexios Komnenos. It was by no means the first such request from Alexios, but now the Pope seized on it as an excuse for action. At a council of churchmen and magnates called to Clermont in France and in a flurry of papal letters accompanying it around 1095, Urban described renewed but completely imaginary atrocities against Christian pilgrims by Muslims in Jerusalem, so that he could arouse appropriate horror and action would follow. The effect was sensational: noblemen present hastened to raise their tenants to set out on a mission to avenge Christian wrongs in the East. In this state of heightened excitement, the Pope took time to consecrate the high altar of his old monastery of Cluny, dedicating the final enlargement of that gargantuan building; so the culmination of Cluny's glory can never be separated from the launch of the Crusades (see Plate 29).[38]

A great momentum had by now developed behind the papacy's assertions of its power. Noblemen and humble folk alike flocked on the proclaimed crusade because they were excited by the Pope's promise that this was a sure road to salvation. Urban made it clear that to die on crusade in a state of repentance and confession would guarantee immediate entry to Heaven, doing away with any necessity of penance after death: papal grants associated with this promise were the origins of the system of indulgences, later to cause such problems for the Western Church (see pp. 555–7). Not all the armies were led by kings or nobles, although that was generally the case with the forces which genuinely had the organization to make it to the Middle East. The Pope's message was now riding on currents of apocalyptic excitement which even the papacy could not control. The mainstream armies which he inspired did not behave as bestially as those raised by a charismatic preacher called Peter the Hermit. As they gathered in the cities of the Rhineland in 1096, they perpetrated Christianity's first large-scale massacres of Jews, since this was an identifiable group of non-Christians more accessible than Muslims to Western Europeans spoiling for a fight, and generally not able to put up much resistance. It would not be the last time that recruiting for Crusades led to such atrocities.[39]

Inhibitions in every section of the crusader army broke down at the climax of the expedition. In 1099 Western soldiers, exhausted but triumphant from winning the great city of Antioch after an epic siege, captured Jerusalem itself in a frenzied attack. Aware of a rapidly approaching Fatimid relief force, they indulged in hasty and vicious slaughter, and later more calculated executions of Jerusalem's Muslim and Jewish inhabitants and defenders. The scale of this massacre has been recently challenged,[40] but whatever qualifications one makes, it was savage enough to arouse astonishment and fury in the Islamic world. The Temple site, for the first time in its chequered history, became given over to Christian worship; the Al-Aqsa Mosque became a church, the Dome of the Rock a cathedral.

Muslims were bewildered at the sudden incursion of Western Europeans into the Middle East. In fact the crusading armies of this first
expedition had hit unawares on a moment of peculiar weakness and
disarray in Islamic states.[41] In that window of opportunity, Western
Europeans were able to establish a Latin kingdom in Jerusalem and a
territorial presence in the eastern Mediterranean which was only finally
extinguished when the Ottoman Turks completed their capture of the
island of Crete from the Venetians in 1669. By then the Holy Land itself
was long lost. Jerusalem had fallen in 1187 to the armies of the Kurdish
military hero Saladin (Salāh al-Dīn); its inhabitants were treated with
ostentatious magnanimity to contrast with the atrocities of 1099. It was
only temporarily restored to Christian rule between 1229 and 1244, and
in 1291 Islamic armies pushed Westerners out of their last strongholds
in Palestine.

Despite prodigious expenditure of heroism and resources over two
centuries, no crusade equalled the success of the first. The Latin kingdom, at its greatest extent approximately the size of the modern State
of Israel, was chronically unstable in government. That character in
itself was hardly much different from many of its prototypes in the Latin
West, but the kingdom was never a very robust political entity, relying
on a constant infusion of financial and military resources from Western
enthusiasts. One symptom of its provinciality and marginality was its
lack of any institution of Latin higher education such as were beginning
to emerge back home; moreover, no single holy figure emerged from its
society with sufficient charisma to join the growing list of saints of the
Western Church. The crusaders' initial success in 1099 was actually a
disastrous chimera; it held out the prospect that God would repeat his
favour, and the piling up of evidence to the contrary did not prevent the
triumph of hope over experience, prolonging the efforts to achieve
new victories. Ironically, as we will see, one of the most permanent
achievements of the crusaders was fatally to weaken the Christian empire
of the East. In 1204 a crusade which had begun with the aim of attacking
Muslim Egypt turned instead to Constantinople, had no hesitation in
sacking it and then set up a 'Latin' empire there. This catastrophe led to
deep bitterness among the Greeks against Westerners, which ruined the
chances for any scheme of religious reunion before the final destruction
of Byzantine power in 1453 (see pp. 475–7).

One of the effects of the Crusades was to establish an extraordinary
new variant on the monastic ideal. The hugely popular military saints
of the early Church – Sergius, Martin, George – had gained their sanctity

when they renounced earthly warfare; now the very act of being a soldier could create holiness. The mood is expressed in a fresco that can still be seen in the crypt of Auxerre Cathedral: here the Bishop of Auxerre, a protégé of Pope Urban II and himself active in the First Crusade, commissioned a picture of the end of time in which Christ himself was portrayed as a warrior on horseback. It was an image impossible to imagine in the early Church, and at the time it was still alien to the Greek East; at much the same time, a Greek visiting Spain was offended when he heard St James of Compostela referred to as a 'knight of Christ'.[42]

It was against such a background of changed assumptions that in the wake of the First Crusade there emerged monastic orders of warriors dedicated to fighting on behalf of Christianity, principally the Knights Templar and Knights Hospitaller. Their names reveal their agenda: the Hospitallers were named from their Hospital headquarters in Jerusalem, and the Templars from the Temple. The Templars built churches in the circular plan of what they thought was Herod's Temple, puzzlingly ignoring the fact that it had been destroyed by the Romans, and not realizing that the building that they were imitating was actually the Muslim Dome of the Rock (with an equally puzzling triumph of wishful thinking, they confidently identified the Al-Aqsa Mosque, standing beside the Dome of the Rock, as Solomon's Temple). Western architects were anxious to reproduce Herod's Temple, but could not or would not build the dome which was its whole architectural point. Such circular buildings can be seen all the way into northern Europe, notably as the lawyers' twelfth-century Temple Church in London – for the military orders gained extensive lands and local administrative houses (preceptories) right across the continent to finance their work.

Between 1307 and 1312, the entire Templar Order was suppressed, once it was clear that the Templars had no chance of contributing to a reconquest of the Holy Land. It was an understandable reaction both to their failure and to the apparent lack of purpose of their continuing wealth and power in estates which extended not merely through the eastern Mediterranean but as far west in Europe as Dublin. Admiring eleventh- and twelfth-century monarchs and noblemen had provided all these lands; now their descendants were inclined to feel that this had not been a wise investment. Nevertheless, the Templars' destruction was contrived out of confessions extracted under torture on charges of blasphemy and sexual deviance, apparently trumped up by Philip 'the Fair', a peculiarly unscrupulous French king. The dissolution of the order was carried out, not merely in France, with a degree of ruthless cruelty which can only inspire pity for both the humiliated survivors and those who were tortured and burned as heretics, from the Master downwards. Since the eighteenth century, their fate has also been the inspiration for a large amount of deranged conspiracy theory.[43] The Hospitallers managed to survive this crisis, and through the heroism of some of their rearguard actions against Islam from their bases in the eastern Mediterranean they continued to win Europe's respect into the seventeenth century.

A further military order, the Teutonic (that is, German) Knights, was alarmed by the fate of the Templars and reinvented itself after the Middle East defeats of the thirteenth century, relocating to northern Europe and recreating its Jerusalem hospital in great style not far from the Baltic coast at Marienburg (Malbork in Polish) on a branch of the River Vistula. Here the knights could fight against Europe's last surviving non-Christian power in Lithuania. Although not all Latin Christians admired their brutality and obvious interest in building up their own power, right into the fifteenth century there was a steady stream of volunteers to support them, not merely Germans, but from as far afield as England and France. The order created a series of colonies around the Baltic Sea which were as much culturally German as they were Christian, won at the expense of Christian Poland as well as of Lithuania. The Lithuanians' conversion to Latin Christianity in 1386 (see pp. 516–17) discomfited the order, robbing it of any real purpose, but it went on fighting to defend its very considerable economic and political interests against Poles and Lithuanians, despite the fact that the two peoples were now fully Catholic Christians owing allegiance to a single monarch. The effort earned the order crushing defeat from Polish-Lithuanian armies at Tannenberg in 1410, yet they did not disperse, and one fragment even survived the Protestant takeover of northern Germany in the sixteenth-century Reformation.[44]

Thus a form of holy warfare which had begun with Islam as its enemy ended up with Christians fighting Christians. There were plenty of precedents for this illogical development. Some of the earlier campaigns against Christians had been against deviants; from 1209, the Pope summoned crusaders against a threat to the Western Latin Church in southern France from a movement known as the 'pure' (in Greek, *Katharoi* or Cathars). Like Manichaeism facing the early Church (see pp. 170–71), the essence of Cathars' beliefs was dualist; they believed in the evil of material things and the necessity to transcend the physical in order to achieve spiritual purity. Their Greek name is one of many indications that this movement took its origin in the strain of dualist belief recurrent over many centuries in the Greek East, most recently in the Paulicians, who had been a presence in the Byzantine Empire since the eighth century, followed by the Bogomils (see p. 456). It may be that Catharism sprang from Latin contacts set up with Bogomils in Constantinople during the First Crusade. Certainly contemporaries made the connection with the East: the English word 'bugger' is derived from 'Bulgarian', and reflects the common canard of mainstream Christians against their opponents that heresy by its unnatural character leads to deviant sexuality. Cathars soon set up their own hierarchies of leaders in France, Italy and Germany: a direct criticism of the monolithic and powerful clerical structure created by the Gregorian Reform, for Cathar dualistic rejection of the flesh was a rejection of what could be seen as a fleshly hierarchy.[45]

The campaign to wipe out the Cathars soon turned into a war of conquest on behalf of the king and nobility of northern France. In its genocidal atrocity, this 'Albigensian Crusade' (the city of Albi was a Cathar centre, with its own Cathar bishop), ranks as one of the most discreditable episodes in Christian history; mass burnings at the stake were a regular feature of the crusaders' retribution against their enemies, who were by no means all Cathars.[46] During the thirteenth century, the idea of crusade reached its most strained interpretation when successive popes proclaimed crusades against their political opponents in Italy – chiefly the Holy Roman Emperor and his dynasty – and in the end, when the papacy itself splintered, even between rival claimants to the papal throne. Such campaigns dragged on intermittently until the 1370s. For the papacy, these were just as much a logical defence of the Church as crusades in the East, but it was not surprising that crowds did not rush to support the Holy Father, and that plenty of faithful Christians were perfectly ready to fight papal armies.[47]

What still did galvanize people to support crusades was the continued reality of threats from Islam, and as late as the sixteenth century there was real popular enthusiasm for crusading ventures to the East along the shifting frontier of the two faiths, now creeping westwards in the Balkans. One of the great Christian achievements of the fifteenth century was the successful defence of Belgrade against Ottoman Turkish armies in 1456, achieved by a combination of aristocratic-led armies and crowds of ordinary people aroused to fight for Christendom by charismatic preaching, just as had happened in the classic crusades of earlier centuries. Yet at the same time theologians began expressing increasing qualifications or doubts about the rightness of waging war on non-Christians. It was an important symbolic moment in 1567 when the then pope abolished the sale (though not the principle) of the indulgences which had taken their origins from the Crusades.[48] During the 1620s, the Medici Grand Duke of Florence made serious though in the end abortive preparations to demolish the Church of the Holy Sepulchre in Jerusalem and re-erect it stone by stone in his own capital city: to have done this in 1099 might have saved Western Europe a good deal of trouble.[49]

CISTERCIANS, CARTHUSIANS AND MARY (1100–1200)

It was not long before the triumph of Cluny came under challenge. In a world which seemed by contemporary standards newly awash with wealth, with the institutional Church a chief beneficiary, it was natural for many devout and serious Christians to react by emphasizing simplicity and self-denial. Catharism was one such reaction, but the twelfth century abounds with different examples of the mood, not least among monks. The crowds on pilgrimage and in the armies of the Crusades represented a new, more widely practised Western Christian spirituality; what did that say about the aristocratic ethos of the great monasteries, with their sprawling estates and hordes of servants? For many, Benedictine abbeys were no longer the perfect mirror of God's purpose for the world. Benedictine houses did not disappear – they were too powerful and well established – but alongside them came a large variety of new religious orders, seeking to change the direction of monasticism. What is significant is how few of the new orders were confined simply to one region of the Western Church. They expressed the continent-wide character of the huge changes which the Church experienced during the Gregorian reforms.

An explicit return to Benedictine roots came in the Cistercian Order, so called from its original house in Cîteaux (*Cistercium* in Latin) in Burgundy. Cistercian houses generally required endowment with lands on the same heroic scale as older Benedictine foundations, but they felt that contact with the sinful world had been their predecessors' downfall, so they sought lands far from centres of population, in wildernesses. There were advantages for donors in this: wildernesses were cheaper investments for benefactors than long-standing, well-cultivated estates – but the Cistercians did go to the length of creating wildernesses by destroying existing villages, sometimes not without a certain shamefacedness. One Cistercian chronicler of the foundation of his house during the 1220s at Heinrichau (now Henryków in south-west Poland) went to the extent of asserting that villagers who were victims of monastic cleansing went away of their own accord after a murderous community feud; the two murdered men 'mutually killed one another' apparently. Later monks of the house less scrupulously asserted that the founders of Heinrichau had come into a classic Cistercian wilderness.[50] This ruthlessness in the service of Christ is a mark of the militancy which the Cistercians brought to the religious life. They exhibited the new aggressiveness also to be seen in the crusading movement. Aggression was certainly one of the main characteristics of their most formidable early representative, Bernard of Clairvaux, and his electrifying preaching was influential in launching the Second Crusade in 1145.

Two years before those crusaders marched east, a Cistercian and former monk under Bernard had been elected pope as Eugenius III. By the end of the century, there were 530 Cistercian houses throughout Europe, tightly organized into a single structure centred on Cîteaux. This was as much of an international corporation as the Cluniacs who had provided its model, but in conscious rejection of Cluniac splendour, Cistercian churches everywhere were built in the same austere style, without elaborate ornament, particularly any figure sculpture. They were nevertheless stylistically innovative: theirs were among the first major buildings to follow the lead set in Durham and St-Denis, moving from the circular-arched style of the Romanesque to the more efficiently load-bearing pointed arch of Gothic engineering, perhaps because its aesthetic effects were more dependent on sheer beauty of form than on sculptural enrichment. The Cistercians made enemies, but their spiritual severity won them admiration, particularly because they made the benefits of monasticism available to all: by basing the everyday work of their houses on teams of lay brothers sworn to a simpler version of the monastic rule than the fully fledged monks, they opened the monastic life once more to illiterate people.

The Cistercians began to decline at the end of the thirteenth century, when their fall in popular esteem was registered by a drastic reduction in those willing to be lay brothers: the reasons lay in their dilemma of success. They farmed their estates with such energy and innovation, for instance pushing forward the commercial development of English sheep farming, that they made huge profits. Their technologically resilient Gothic architectural style had the potential to create ever more soaring buildings to express Western Europe's constant aim of making its churches images of the heights of Heaven, and Cistercian monumental austerity tended towards sheer architectural magnificence little less than other church buildings. There is a sad sermon in stone in the surviving dormitory of one of their monasteries in western England, Cleeve, where the huge thirteenth-century chamber, originally an open space where all the monks slept communally, was divided up in the fifteenth century by wooden partitions so that everyone could have his own private space; grooves and settings for the partitions can still be seen on the walls. The world which the Cistercians had rejected thus crept back, and their houses became little different from the monasteries which they had begun by criticizing. Yet repeatedly the order has sought to find new ways of returning to its original ideals, particularly after the shocks of the sixteenth-century Reformation and the chaos created for monasteries by the French Revolution.

Another late-eleventh-century religious order made a permanent success of monastic simplicity: the Carthusians. Like the Cistercians, they take their name from their first house, the Grande Chartreuse (*Maior Cartusia* in Latin; a Carthusian monastery was domesticated in English to 'Charterhouse'), but their inspiration is not so much the Benedictine tradition as a rediscovery of the monasticism of the East which had provided the first models for Western monasteries. A description bestowed on them by successive admiring popes was 'never reformed because never in need of reform' (*nunquam reformata quia nunquam deformata*). Their key to avoid the temptations to slackness which haunt every religious community is their resolve to preserve each monk in solitude in order to seek a greater intimacy with the divine. Each member of the community occupies his own walled-in cottage and garden within the monastery, only meeting his fellows for three periods of worship through the day. Their return to the earliest forms of monastic life meant that they would never be a numerous religious order, but Carthusians were always widely respected.

Carthusian austerity sometimes seemed excessive to outside authority. One fourteenth-century pope tried to force the order to allow monks to eat meat in times of ill-health and to modify their solitary lives in other ways, but such were their protests that he let them preserve their standards. A pleasing legend, but no more than a legend, perhaps created by a Carthusian with a sense of humour, says that His Holiness was intimidated by the rude health of the protest delegation, in which the youngest member was eighty-eight and the oldest ninety-five.[51] The reasons for such health became apparent in archaeological excavations on the rubbish pits of the London Charterhouse; the monks' meat-free diet was exceptionally varied by medieval standards, with fish, vegetables and a rich choice of fruit – grapes, figs, plums, sloes, mulberries, strawberries, walnuts – plus whatever they chose to grow in their individual gardens. Moreover, their plumbing was exemplary.[52]

Yet another product of the diversity of eleventh- and twelfth-century monasticism was the Augustinian movement, so called because it looked not to Benedict but to a series of statements and simple rules made by or attributed to Augustine of Hippo, for religious communities under his control.[53] The Augustinian Rule appealed because it was even more general and brief than the Rule of Benedict, and thus could be adapted for community life in a wide range of circumstances. The membership of each Augustinian community, as priests living under a Rule (*Regulum*), were known as Canons Regular, in contrast with the 'secular' canons of non-monastic cathedrals and colleges. Their priestly duties took them to places where they could provide pastoral care for the laity, so they had precisely the opposite attitude to the world from the Cistercians. They sought out newly developing towns; they planted their houses beside the castles and homes of the wealthy, often taking over existing large churches whose community life was in disarray. They were enthusiastically received because they satisfied a universal hunger for the prayers of holy people. Their communities rarely sought to be as large or wealthy as Benedictine or Cistercian houses, and so they supplied spiritual services at what seemed like cut-price rates: the gift of a field from a modestly prosperous knight, or a town tenement bequeathed by a merchant's widow; a few pence from a poor man's family at his deathbed. Moreover, they gave tangible benefits to the communities around them; they served in parishes or hospitals as priests.

The result of all this was an extraordinary degree of choice for a twelfth-century man or woman seeking to fulfil a monastic vocation, to find a community best to express his or her personal piety, or simply to find a congenial spiritual friend outside the pressures of the ordinary world. To take one instance, by the end of the twelfth century the two English East Anglian counties of Suffolk and Norfolk, prosperous and thickly populated by the standards of the time, boasted around eighty monasteries and nunneries, representing eight different orders, including the Benedictines, amid a population contained in about fifteen hundred parishes. An hour or two's walk would bring virtually everyone in East Anglia to the gates of a religious house.[54] Amid this great diversity, one devotional impulse caught them all up, but it was particularly prominent among the Cistercians. Although this order's initial steely singleness of purpose and austerity might make it seem reminiscent of modern Christian evangelistic campaigning organizations, today's evangelicals would find this aspect of the Cistercian outlook uncongenial: all their monasteries were dedicated to Mary, the Mother of God. In this, the Cistercians were riding the crest of a wave which, in the era of the Gregorian reforms, had swept through all Europe.

From the time of the Nestorian controversy (see pp. 222–8) Western theologians made one significant step beyond Eastern devotion to the God-bearer (*theotokos*). When they translated that contentious word, they generally pushed it into Latin phrases straightforwardly meaning 'Mother of God' (yet another issue about the West to irritate Greeks). A mother is a more powerful figure than a bearer, and the word is also likely to produce a preoccupation with gynaecological issues – for instance, the rows in fourth-century Rome in which Jerome had championed Mary's perpetual virginity (see p. 314).[55] Such thoughts blossomed in the eleventh century, when various circumstances combined to promote and enrich Marian devotion. For Gregorian reformers, the ever-Virgin was the perfect example of the chastity which underpinned their new ideal of universal clerical celibacy, and naturally this theme particularly appealed to monks. Rather later, as the threat from the Cathars grew intense, Mary seemed, against Cathar dualism, to be a guarantor that God could sanctify created and fleshly things as much as he could the Spirit, since it was in Mary that the Word was made flesh. This did have its problems, since the Cathars themselves were also caught up in the general rise of devotion to Mary, and simply insisted that she was not a human mother – after all, did she not lack a genealogy in the Bible?[56]

Quite apart from that annoyingly good point, the theme of motherhood continued to promote nervousness among Mary's Western devotees, precisely because of their new preoccupations with celibacy and the regulation of marriage. Mary's sexuality ought to be kept away from sin if the Incarnation was to be itself preserved from that taint. Two conclusions arose with long-lived implications for Mary's place in the Christian faith. First, a number of English Benedictine abbots conferred in the 1120s and, in their enthusiasm for the Mother of God, began promoting the idea that Mary had been conceived without the normal human correlation of concupiscence (lust); because her conception was immaculate, unspotted by sin, so was her flesh. The doctrine was controversial: Bernard of Clairvaux, one of the loudest advocates of devotion to Mary in his preaching, said flatly that the idea of Immaculate Conception was a novelty which Mary would not enjoy, and that no conception, not even hers, could be separated from carnal pleasure. The Immaculate Conception went on disturbing the tranquillity of Catholic theology as late as the Counter-Reformation, when not even the impulse to defend Mary against Protestant irreverence stilled the quarrels.[57]

Yet the doctrine chimed usefully with a devotional belief current in both East and West that Mary's flesh should not see the normal corruption of death, and it also creatively interracted with a notable and highly significant absence throughout the Christian world: any tradition of Mary's burial, tomb or bodily relics. The next stage was an accident waiting to happen: in the late 1150s, a mystically inclined nun in the Rhineland, Elizabeth of Schönau, experienced visions of Our Lady being taken into Heaven in bodily flesh. The account of these apparitions, enthusiastically written up by her clerical brother with convenient brevity, was within a few years a manuscript best-seller all over Europe, not least thanks to the international contacts of the Cistercians. The fully fledged doctrine of the bodily Assumption of Mary was born, out of all the gathering strands of less precise devotional opinion from centuries before.[58] The huge success of a theological innovation suggested by a semi-literate German female shows that Marian devotion was no abstract theological issue; it was fired by a popular hunger to love the Mother of God.

The very absence of Mary's corpse from this sinful world was useful, because it necessarily promoted intense fixations on images of her missing body. Churches which did not possess any relic of any significance – that was particularly likely in northern Europe – could trump the competition simply by commissioning a statue of Our Lady, which with luck, divine favour, local enthusiasm or assiduous salesmanship might produce evidence of its miraculous power and become the focus of pilgrimage. This represented a certain democratization of pilgrimage cults, since any parish church might be a setting for such an image, as much as any monastic house. Given such considerations, it was not surprising that Our Lady could upstage lesser saints even when their relics were present, and all over Europe from the eleventh century churches were rededicated away from local saints, or even international saints, in honour of the Mother of God. By the end of the thirteenth century, it was uncontroversial for a bishop to do as Peter Quinel, an energetic Bishop of Exeter, did in 1287, ordering every parish church in his large diocese to make sure that they displayed an image of the Blessed Virgin as well as an image of their church's patron saint.[59] The very fact that he could confidently expect action on such a matter was a proof of the way in which Gregory's vision of a well-functioning ecclesiastical machine engineered for the glory of God had scored massive successes. Bishop Quinel issued his order in an age when the Gregorian papacy had achieved its greatest successes and had showed how capable it could be of surmounting formidable new challenges. These challenges we must now explore.

12

A Church for All People?
(1100–1300)

THEOLOGY, HERESY, UNIVERSITIES
(1100–1300)

We have now met various expressions of the ways in which Western Europeans were searching for salvation in the anxious, busy Gregorian age: pilgrimages, crusades, new monastic initiatives (many more than are here described). A problem remained: the clerically dominated structure of Latin Western Christianity had not exhausted the yearning of layfolk to show that they were active participants in the Body of Christ which was his Church. Throughout Europe a growth of industry, particularly in manufacturing clothing, created a network of new towns, and the Church found it difficult to cope; its developing parish system and the finance on which the parish was based operated best in the more stable life of the countryside. Now many people found themselves faced with the excitement and terror of new situations, new structures of life; their uncertainties, hopes and fears were ready prey for clergy who might have their own emotional difficulties and quarrels with the clerical hierarchy. This has been a repeated problem for institutional Christianity in times of social upheaval.

Religious dissent had developed throughout Europe, particularly its most prosperous and disturbed parts, from the early eleventh century. The Church gave much of it the label heresy and in 1022 King Robert II of France set a precedent by returning to the Roman imperial custom of burning heretics at the stake. Modern examination of this case suggests that the unfortunate victims were not heretics even in the contemporary Church's sense, but were caught up in the King's struggle with a local magnate.[1] Others expressed opinions which had not previously been declared unorthodox, but which were now defined as outside acceptability. Such was the case with the theologian from Chartres Berengar of Tours (*c.* 999–1088), who expressed his unease with the increasing precision with which his contemporaries asserted that eucharistic bread and wine could become the body and blood of Christ (Berengar escaped the flames by a sequence of humiliating forced recantations and died in mutinous silence). Even the Cathars, to whose suppression the Church devoted so much energy, may have started merely by seeking a purer, less worldly form of ministry before official repression turned their sympathies towards visiting dualists from the eastern Mediterranean (see pp. 387–8).

Certainly other dissenters began in a perfectly orthodox fashion and were marginalized by circumstance. Such were the Waldensians, a movement started around 1170 in Lyons by a wealthy man called Valdes, who gave away all his wealth to the poor and ministered to a group who also valued poverty as the basis for Christian life.[2] Church authorities were not prepared to make a distinction between this affirmation of poverty and that of the dualist Cathars in the same region, and from 1184 a solemn papal pronouncement (a bull) condemned them both. The Waldensians went on expanding, but were increasingly estranged from the episcopate of the Church on one vital issue: they were convinced that every Christian had a vocation to preaching, and that fatally clashed with the clerical priorities of the Gregorian reforms.

Elsewhere, there were more extreme forms of dissent. From at least the beginning of the thirteenth century, self-appointed leaders roamed Europe preaching that individuals could meet God through an inner light; it might be that God's Spirit could be found in all things, in a form of pantheism. These very loosely organized and often totally independent 'Brethren of the Free Spirit' could whip up mass support in times of crisis, often announcing that such disruptions heralded the beginning of Christ's reign on earth; much of their excitement became mixed up with the later crusades and the increasingly hopeless struggle to defend the Latin Kingdom of Jerusalem. So it shaded off without an easily definable break into the religious innovation which previously had brought so much of the official structures into being.[3] The ferment of the age seemed in danger of slipping from the Church's control.

Nor in the 'Age of the Cathedrals' were Benedictine monasteries any longer at the heart of Europe's cultural activity. They had first been displaced by the rapid development during the eleventh century of schools of higher education attached to certain notable cathedrals. It was in such settings that the systematic study of Christian teaching was first undertaken, generating an increasingly diverse literature that explored the problems and questions which the propositions of Christianity generated, particularly in the form of commentary on that endlessly fascinating and diverse library of texts, the Bible. This organized exploration was christened 'theology', a concept essentially an invention of the Western Church: the word was first given currency in the 1120s by the Paris theologian Peter Abelard when he used it as title of a controversial discussion of Christian thought, his *Theologia Christiana*.[4]

At least such cathedral schools were part of the clerical institutions of the Church; in Italy, however, there were cities greater in size and wealth than anything in northern Europe and during the eleventh century they developed and financed their own schools. Their models were from outside the Christian world: they copied in a remarkably detailed fashion the institutions of higher education which Muslims had created for their own universal culture of intellectual enquiry, especially the great school of Al-Azhar in Cairo – now-familiar institutions like lectures, professors, qualifications called degrees.[5] These were the first Christian universities – Christian, but not under the control of the Church authorities. With the exception of one or two ecclesiastical foundations, the Italian universities resolutely kept their lay-dominated character for centuries to come, even when the pope came to license new foundations. In the case of such institutions as Bologna, following Islamic precedent, law rather than theology was the emphasis of study. Alongside them, some northern European cathedral schools also developed into universities: the University in Paris became the leading centre of theological exploration in twelfth-century Europe, and its Theology Faculty (later often known as the Sorbonne, after one of the university's leading colleges) continued to be much used by popes when they needed specialist expertise to pronounce on a disputed question. This advisory role was a completely new development in Christianity, and again it represented a borrowing from the way in which scholars of Islamic religious law advised rulers in the Muslim world.[6]

All these institutions fostered a new intellectual life: a new stage in the ancient dialogue between Plato and Aristotle; now Aristotle came to excite and inform those whose business was ideas. Previously Plato had dominated Christian thinking, albeit at one remove through Augustine of Hippo; only Boethius had dealt much with Aristotle's intellectual systems, but in any case Boethius had otherwise himself been soaked in the world view derived from Plato, and had been one of the major forces embedding it in Western Christianity (see pp. 309–10 and 321–2). Otherwise the West had known little of Aristotle's work. By contrast, scholars in the Islamic world and the Jewish communities whom the Muslims sheltered had direct knowledge of Aristotle, whose writings had been preserved largely by scholars of the Church of the East (see pp. 245–6 and 266). Gradually, Aristotle's texts reached the West. The first influx came through the Spanish Christian capture of Muslim Toledo and its libraries in 1085, and then much more through contacts established during the Crusades (one of their more positive results). Once they were translated into Latin, the effect was profound: Western thought, enriched afresh by manuscripts containing Classical learning, experienced another movement of renewal, which has been called the twelfth-century Renaissance. Despite much initial official hostility, Aristotle and his analytical approach to the world, his mastery of logical thought, confronted the Platonism of Christian theologians. A debate opened up, in dialogue also with Arab and Jewish commentators on ancient thought, discussing the old problem of how to relate the work of reason to the revealed truths of Christian faith.

All three religions of revelation confronted the same problem. Aristotle's categorizations might suggest that the world could be understood without that special divine grace of knowledge otherwise closed to human intelligence. Although the participants in this debate often bitterly disagreed with each other, to the extent that on occasion they would secure their opponents' condemnation as heretics, the movement can be summed up in the term 'scholasticism': that is, the thought and educational method of the *scholae*, the new university schools. In essence it was a way of building up knowledge through discussion: a method of *quaestiones*, assertion, denial, counter-assertion, and a final effort to harmonize the debate. It respected authorities, but this was an alarmingly and unpredictably expanding body of authorities who themselves might not agree. Scholasticism was disputatious, sceptical, analytical, and that remained the characteristic of Western intellectual exploration long after most Western intellectuals had parted company with scholasticism itself. And it had its precedent in the method used in Islamic higher education. It is a happy irony that one of the great expressions of the cultural unity of the Latin West, evolved in the age of the Crusades, had its roots in the culture which the West was trying to destroy.

By the end of the twelfth century, the Western Church was thus facing challenges both from heresy and from the potentially uncontrollable nature of scholastic thought, bred in new institutions, the universities. None of its existing structures seemed well adapted to the purpose, and its first reaction to the growth of heresy was to redouble repression, evidenced at its worst in the Albigensian Crusade (see pp. 387–8). Western Christianity exhibited an urge to punish itself which should not simply be attributed to the lurid imaginations of clergy. For instance, in the city of Perugia in central Italy, a startling new movement began in the troubled year of 1260: flagellants, crowds of the laity who indulged in communal ritual beatings as acts of penitence for the sins of the world and of themselves. They walked in their bloodstained processions from Italy over the Alps in midwinter, right through central Europe north-wards until they reached the furthest bounds of Poland. On the way they inspired reversals of local quarrels and miseries in festivals of forgiveness. One Italian chronicler enthused that 'almost all those in disagreement were returned to concord; usurers and thieves hastened to restore what they had taken away . . . captives were released and exiles were given permission to return to their homes'.[7] Whatever the reality of his vision of 1260, later episodes of mass flagellation were certainly not so benevolent, for, like the earlier campaigns to gather crusader armies, they were often associated with crowds turning in violence on Jewish communities. Yet the spontaneous character remained: these were outbreaks of religious fervour which the Church authorities had done nothing to inspire and which they often found frightening and sought to suppress. Such religious energies could as readily turn against the Church as be absorbed by it.

Punishment was thus directed to outsiders as well as to sinful Christians. One of the characteristics of Western Christianity between the eleventh and thirteenth centuries is its identification of various groups within the Western world as distinct, marginal and a constant potential threat to good order: principal among such groups were Jews, heretics, lepers and (curiously belatedly) homosexuals.[8] In 1321 there was panic all over France, ranging from poor folk to King Philip V himself, that lepers and Jews had combined together with the great external enemy, Islam, to overthrow all good order in Christendom by poisoning wells. Lepers (as if they had not enough misfortune) were victimized, tortured into confessions and burned at the stake, and the pogroms against Jews were no less horrific. Muslims were lucky enough to be out of reach on that occasion.[9] From the mid-twelfth century, a particularly persistent and pernicious community response to the occasional abuse and murder of children was to deflect guilt from Christians by blaming Jews for abducting the children for use in rituals. This so-called 'blood libel' frequently resulted in vicious attacks on Jewish communities. Sometimes higher clergy did their best to calm the community hysteria in such cases;

sometimes they allowed shrine-cults of the murdered victims to develop. Recurrences of the blood libel persisted into the twentieth century as a blemish on Christian attitudes to Jews, spreading from the West into Orthodoxy in later centuries.[10]

A PASTORAL REVOLUTION, FRIARS AND THE FOURTH LATERAN COUNCIL (1200–1260)

A more complex and positive response to dynamic popular movements emerged at the end of the twelfth century, although in the end it allied itself and indeed helped to structure this 'formation of a persecuting society'. It produced two great religious leaders, Dominic and Francis. They were utterly different personalities, but they founded in parallel the first two orders of friars (an English version of the word *fratres*, Latin for 'brothers'). In 1194 Dominic became a priest in a community in Osma in northern Spain, living under Augustine's Rule; he was drawn into campaigns across the Pyrenees to win back southern France from the Cathar heresy. The effort was having little success, and Dominic realized why: it was being led by churchmen who conducted their task like the great prelates they were, surrounded by attendants and all the magnificence of their rank. Nothing was less calculated to impress those familiar with Cathar expressions of contempt for Catholic corruption.

To this situation, Dominic brought the practicality and closeness to ordinary life of his Augustinian background. In 1215 he got official permission from one of the bishops in the area affected by the Cathars to start a new effort: a campaign of preaching in which he and his helpers would lead a life so simple and apostolic in poverty as to outdo the Cathars, and convince people that the official Church was a worthy vehicle for a message of love and forgiveness. Not only that, but his preachers would have the best education that he could devise to make even their simplest message intellectually tough. Though his efforts in southern France had little immediate success amid the ferocity of the Albigensian Crusade, his idea blossomed; unlike some of the other leaders of new movements in his age, he was intent on emphasizing his close loyalty to the pope, and Pope Honorius III took a personal interest in drafting the document which in 1217 named Dominic's new organization as an Order of Preachers – the only order, one contemporary noted, to take its name from its function.[11]

The new friars also quickly gained the nickname Dominicans, and otherwise Blackfriars, from the black hood which they wore with their white robe. They avoided holding property so that they would not build up wealth like the monastic orders; instead, they lived by begging from people in ordinary society (hence the alternative name of friars, 'mendicants', from the Latin verb for begging). This mobility in the world was a significant addition to the West's armoury of spiritual resources, recreating a form of monastic wandering which always remained common in the Eastern Churches, but which centuries before had been firmly discouraged for Western monks by no less a figure than St Benedict himself (see pp. 317–18). Yet significantly the Westerners still did not allow their holy men to wander at random, as did the Churches of Orthodoxy and further east. To avoid unseemly competition between different communities of friars, they came to work within agreed set boundaries or limits, which gained them yet another nickname, 'limiters'.

Their life of begging made the friars very vulnerable to their public. They would have to be in constant contact with the people to whom they ministered, always needing to justify their existence by service. Their task was to bring a message of good news and comfort to the whole Church. They were evangelists, showmen in church or market square, but they could also quietly hear confessions and so enter the individual fears and miseries of those who heard their message from the pulpit. They developed a special mission to the universities too, and gained a brilliant reputation as defenders of orthodoxy yet often as restlessly original thinkers. These talents earned them another specialization which has not done any favours to their later reputation. In the mopping-up operations which ended the Albigensian Crusade, Dominicans found employment as investigators in the tribunals known as inquisitions, and soon dominated inquisitions as they became the chief weapon against religious dissidence wherever it appeared in Europe. In a rueful division of their Latin name, some came to call them *Domini canes*, 'hounds of the Lord'.

It could not have been predicted that the fascinating and maddening eccentric Francis would end up creating a very similar organization to that of Dominic. He was brought up in Assisi, a hill town of central Italy which typified the new wealth of late-twelfth-century Europe, and his father was a well-to-do cloth merchant. It was the same sort of background as that of Valdes in Lyons, and Francis had the same reaction to it. In his twenties, he reached an emotional and spiritual crisis: he took it as his divine mission to turn upside down the central obsession of his father's world, the creation of wealth. The trigger was his attitude to lepers. His revulsion against them had been as intense as that which later caused their scapegoating in the 1321 persecution. Then he realized that the blessed biblical figures of Job and Lazarus had been lepers – it was he and not they who needed healing. He rushed up to a leper and folded the outcast in his arms. Now he would gather together people who would strip themselves of all possessions and would be outcasts for Christ.

So this playboy son of an Italian millionaire threw away his money, shouted the Christian message at birds in a graveyard, and threw the Church into a turmoil by saying that Christ was a down-and-out with no possessions. He might have been burned as a heretic. Luckily for his future, alongside his almost pathological nonconformity, Francis was deeply loyal to the Western Catholic tradition. Against the Cathars, who said that the world was evil, he passionately affirmed that all created things – Brother Sun, Sister Moon – were good, sharing the goodness of God's human incarnation in Christ. In his own body, Francis is the first person known to have suffered *stigmata*, fleshly wounds which followed the patterns of the wounds of the crucified Christ (see Plate 25). This echo of Paul's mysterious remark in Galatians 6.17, 'I bear on my body the marks of Jesus', has since been a recurrent phenomenon among ascetics of the Western Church. At the time, it may have been a response to the Cathars, who claimed purity and said that flesh was part of the world of evil. What greater symbol could there be than Francis's *stigmata* that the divine suffering condescended to descend into flesh?

Distressed at the failures of the Fifth Crusade in Egypt, in 1219 Francis travelled there to convert the Ayyubid sultan. The Muslims, familiar with unkempt holy men, though surprised at meeting a Latin Christian in this role, allowed him to move freely between the Christian and Egyptian military camps. Although he survived, his mission produced no results.[12] This was not the only setback for his charismatic ministry: many of the followers who had flocked to his message were beginning to organize themselves into another religious order, demanding a structure and everyday leadership. Francis, having no taste for such developments, quickly handed over the task to someone else. In the last weeks of his life in 1226 he dictated a *Testament* expressing his fears that his commitment to poverty would be sidelined by the newly institutionalized

'Franciscans'. In particular he warned against their large-scale campaign of building convents for themselves.

Francis was justified in his worries. Within little more than a decade of his death, a grand and expensive basilica had been built over his tomb in Assisi, its foundation stone laid by a pope, its great bulk jutting out like a prow to the promontory on which sprawled the town of his birth. Its magnificence was a strange comment on Francis's life and work. Yet it was also a testimony to the impact of a man whom many saw as an *alter Christus*, a second Christ bearing the same *stigmata*, his preaching to the birds a sign that a human being could speak once more with the beasts of the wild, as Adam and Eve had done before their fall into sin in the Garden of Eden. Francis had created the Franciscan Order despite himself. Like the Dominicans, his followers did embrace apostolic poverty; their cheap, roughly dyed clothing earned them the English nickname Greyfriars, though the actual colour of their habit is brown. Francis's own unlovely tunic, and that of his female colleague Clare, foundress of parallel communities for women, are lovingly preserved and displayed by the nuns of St Clare in Assisi, so amid the stateliness and beauty of Clare's thirteenth-century basilica, there is a perpetual reminder of what it means to live like the destitute. And perhaps it would make Francis smile that the Italian town of his birth is now officially 'twinned' with a city in California named after him, which has made a speciality of its own joyous adventures in human possibilities: San Francisco.

It was probably inevitable that Franciscans should become a formal religious order, because the anarchy prevailing among Francis's early supporters could seem more of a threat than a help to the official Church. Francis and his followers survived because they won the sympathy of one of the most statesmanlike of medieval popes: Innocent III (Pope 1198–1216). In so many ways, Innocent represents the culmination of the age of reform which we have seen begin in Cluny. He was from a well-known Italian family, the Conti, which had already produced one pope (and after his death would produce more, over a period of four centuries). He was trained in Bologna and Paris, so he combined a knowledge of canon law and theology; his theological schooling in Paris took place in a circle with a lively concern to draw practical lessons for everyday life and the organization of society from the Bible, and it became his concern to apply the power built up by the centralized papacy to such a purpose. He spent much of his energy as pope in confronting secular rulers who undermined that power, or harnessing the piety of others to papal purposes. It was Innocent who rallied noblemen and the King of France to attack the Cathars, although he did in the end blanch at the indiscriminate violence which he had unleashed. There was indeed much more to Innocent's vision of his role in the world than the promotion of his office; this power must be put to a purpose. Few Christian leaders have had such a transforming effect on their world.

Although not himself a monk, Innocent sought to hold the monastic orders to the highest standards, which he regarded as set by the Cistercians, and he was much preoccupied by efforts to reform Benedictine monasticism. Yet he had the imagination to see that the new movements brought something different and valuable to the religious life, so he was prepared to listen benevolently to bishops who were friendly towards the various groups of evangelists, many previously regarded with suspicion.[13] He saw the friars as one instrument of his newly reordered Church, as preachers and hearers of confessions. In 1215 he called a council to his Lateran Palace which represented a gathering of bishops unprecedented in number in the Western Church, although given his own view of his authority, the bishops were only there to discuss an agenda strictly set by the Pope and the Curia.[14]

This fourth Lateran Council embodied the Gregorian aim of imposing regulated holiness on the laity and ensuring uniformity in both belief and devotional practice. So the council ordered every Catholic Christian beyond early childhood to receive the eucharistic elements at Mass at least once a year (in practice usually only bread rather than both bread and wine), and prepare for that encounter through confession. There was nothing new in the council's stipulation that confession should be to one's own priest, or that both sides should preserve absolute secrecy in what was said, but what was new was the universality of the demand; it was an extraordinary attempt to get everyone to scrutinize their lives, with the aid of expert help. Priests were now expected as a matter of course to instruct as well as tend their flocks: manuals of instruction for pastoral care and preaching proliferated.

Crucial to this instruction was that the faithful should understand what they were doing when they received the Eucharist. The council therefore recommended one philosophical explanation for understanding the miracle of the Mass: it asserted that Christ's 'body and blood are truly contained in the sacrament of the altar under the forms of bread and wine, the bread and wine having been changed in substance, by God's power, into his body and blood'.[15] This was the doctrine generally known as 'transubstantiation', although notably the council asserted it rather than provided any detailed analysis, which meant that a good deal of latitude remained in eucharistic belief down to the Counter-Reformation. It is easy to confuse the doctrine of the 'Real Presence', the general devotional belief that the bread and wine of the Eucharist are to be identified with the body and blood of Christ, with the doctrine of transubstantiation, which is just one explanation of this miracle.

The council's recommended explanation is couched in terms borrowed from the philosopher Aristotle, whose abstractions of 'substance' and 'accidents', conceived without reference to the Semitic thought patterns of the Bible, are perhaps best illustrated with a concrete example. The substance of a sheep, which is its reality, its participation in the universal quality of being a sheep, is manifested in its gambolling on the hills, munching grass and baaing. Its accidents are things particular to any individual sheep: statistics of its weight, the curliness of its wool or the timbre of its baa. When the sheep dies, it ceases to gambol on the hills, munch grass and baa: its substance, its 'sheepiness', is instantly extinguished, and only the accidents remain – its corpse including its weight, curly wool or voice box – and they will gradually decay. They are not significant to its former sheepiness, which has ended with the extinguishing of its substance in death. It has ceased to be a sheep. So it is with transubstantiation from bread and wine into divine body and blood. Breadness and wineness have gone in substance, but something more, by divine providence, has happened: divine corporal substance has replaced them. Accidents of breadness and wineness remain, but they are mere accidents.

In making these momentous enactments, Innocent's council was not simply exercising clerical power by handing down arbitrary orders to layfolk; it was responding to and seeking to regulate a tide of devotion to the Eucharist which had already seized ordinary people. During the twelfth century (it is not clear originally where or when), a new liturgical custom became very common in the Mass. Clergy consecrating the eucharistic elements lifted high the bread and chalice of wine as they pronounced the Latin words which echoed what Jesus had said at the Last Supper, *Hoc est enim corpus meum*, 'For this is my body'. This 'elevation of the host' became a focus for the longing of the Catholic faithful to gaze upon the body of Christ: the dramatic high point of the Western Latin Mass.

From this, there developed a new theme in the Western Church's devotional repertoire. Celibate women might have their own reasons for being attracted to the thought that the Eucharist gave them real bodily contact with their Saviour, and it was an Augustinian nun who inspired a movement which over the next two centuries swept through Western Europe. In 1208 Juliana of the nunnery of Mount-Cornillon near Liège first experienced a vision of Christ in which he urged her to seek the establishment of a feast entirely focused on his body and blood, the consecrated elements of the Eucharist – a celebration of the universal Christian celebration. After a good deal of lobbying led by the Dominicans, Juliana posthumously achieved the extraordinary accolade of a papal decree by Urban IV in 1264, establishing her feast throughout the Church. A pope had never previously used a decree in this fashion, and it was an innovation which subsequent popes and bishops were initially hesitant to follow up.

The new feast day was to fall on a Thursday, since this was the day on which the Last Supper took place, but it could only be on a Thursday which was not overshadowed by either the solemnity of Holy Week or the already festive atmosphere of Easter. The nearest Thursday after the date of the Last Supper therefore became the first available Thursday after Eastertide, a cheerful time of year in late spring. Already in Pope Urban's decree, the feast was called *Corpus Christi* ('the body of Christ'): bread/body seemed to upstage wine/blood in this liturgical celebration, maybe because the laity were generally restricted in the West to taking bread and not wine when they received the Eucharist, but also because the eucharistic elevation of the host was associated with 'This is my body'. After a slow and patchy start, during the fourteenth century Corpus Christi became one of the most important feasts of the Church, and inspired many lay associations (gilds) devoted to promoting and maintaining it. The festival was popular because it provided a wonderful excuse to combine great services in church with public processions amid what was normally likely to be a season of good weather. It was a way to express pride in community life and of course simply to have fun. Cities, towns, villages, hamlets could expand the Church's central liturgical celebration until it embraced all their streets, markets and fields. There could be no better way of showing how the Church brought the love of Christ into every corner of Western life.[16]

There was another side to this universality of Catholic faith in Western Latin society. In order to ensure uniformity of belief among the faithful, the Lateran Council created procedures for inquisitions to try heretics. It is difficult for modern Westerners to feel any sort of empathy with the inquisitorial mind, but we need to understand that an inquisitor could see his role as an aspect of pastoral work. That was after all the central task for the Dominicans, who largely staffed the tribunals. The inquisitors' outlook has been likened to that of officials in the Cheka, early revolutionary Russia's secret police, where the aim was not merely to repress, but to change society for the better – there is often a fine line between idealism and sadism. A major part of an inquisition's task was always to impose penances, just as a priest did for a penitent in the confessional, though increasingly inquisitions developed prisons, in what was virtually forced religious enclosure, as a setting for those convicted to carry out their penances. When we leap from thinking of inquisitions to thinking of burnings at the stake, it is worth noting that the horrific level of burnings in the brutal atmosphere of the Albigensian Crusade was not sustained. In the period 1249–57, of 306 recorded penalties handed out by inquisitions, only twenty-one were burnings; secular courts were much more likely than inquisitors to impose death penalties.[17]

Pope Innocent's concern to discriminate between heretics and devotional organizations which might benefit the Church extended beyond the followers of Dominic and Francis. He carefully considered other evangelistic groups previously condemned, such as the Waldensians (see p. 397) or the similar Italian grouping called Humiliati ('the humbled'), whose origins he recognized as not dissimilar to those of the other mendicants. If their beliefs seemed compatible with official doctrine, he gave them recognition and a set of rules to create a manageable identity for them – the reconciled Waldensians were renamed 'Poor Catholics'. In fact for many Waldensians it was too late: they were by now too separate from the mainstream Church to wish to be assimilated, and they suffered centuries of persecution and clandestine existence before they found new sympathy and support (at the price of a good deal of rebranding, both of their past and their future) from sixteenth-century Protestants.[18] During the previous century, in parallel with Waldensians or Humiliati, individual women had set themselves apart for a life of celibate service and prayer without joining a nunnery; in northern Europe they were called beguines, a word of uncertain derivation. Their irregular status attracted predictable worry from the authorities, and increasingly they gathered for respectability or companionship in societies which owned buildings for communal life, 'beguinages' – although their status was always open to question (see p. 422).

Other groups succeeded in taking on formal organization in an order similar to Dominicans or Franciscans. The most surprising were the

Carmelites or Whitefriars.[19] Carmelites started their existence as an informal group of hermits living on Mount Carmel in the Latin Kingdom of Jerusalem, probably as refugees when Jerusalem was first recaptured by the Muslims in 1187. Conditions grew impossible for them when the whole kingdom collapsed, so they migrated westwards across the Mediterranean. After they reached Europe, they accounted for their odd history to a wary Church hierarchy by the drastically ingenious means of inventing an even more exotic origin, in the time of the Prophet Elijah, a much earlier enthusiast for Mount Carmel. Thus they became the only religious order ever to claim a pre-Christian past, as well as the only order of contemplative religious to take their origins among the Latin settlements of the East. Carmelite pseudo-history was ridiculed even at the time, particularly by the Dominicans. Although Dominican leaders had been involved in drawing up a rule for the new order which in 1247 turned the Carmelites into another grouping of friars, the Dominicans found themselves drawn into a number of turf wars with their protégés. They were particularly annoyed when the Carmelites proclaimed with renewed creativity that one of their number had a vision from Our Lady remarkably like a previous vision of her to a Dominican. She granted the Whitefriars identical powers to the Black-friars, to bless a part of their friar's habit which draped over their shoulders and was known as the scapular; now laity could wear it and derive spiritual privileges from it. Dominicans were not slow to point out the coincidence.[20]

Despite such scepticism, enough influential people chose to believe Carmelite fictions to ensure their survival as a respected section of the mendicant world. There was indeed a distinctive value in their stubborn adherence to their story of Elijah: because they kept their collective memory of contemplation on Mount Carmel, they brought to the West a love of wilderness which the Cistercians had at first possessed but were already losing. Carmelites appreciated the aesthetic beauty of wild nature with a relish which anticipates later European romanticism. In his first defence of the order in 1270, their Prior-General Nicholas Gallicus wrote with engaging delight:

I want to tell you of the joys of the solitary life. The beauty of the elements, the starry heavens and the planets ordered in perfect harmony, invite us to contemplate infinite wonders ... all our sisters the creatures strive in the solitude to fill our eyes, ears and feelings with their caresses. Their inexpressible beauty cries out in silence and invites us to praise the marvellous Creator.

In order to enjoy such divine pleasures, the Carmelites later had their donors create wildernesses for them, not to farm but simply for contemplation: the first wild gardens or sacred theme parks.[21]

Other enterprises were not so lucky. The Italian Order of Apostles, for instance, was founded in Parma by Gerardo Segarelli in the 1260s to promote apostolic poverty like the Franciscans, but in 1300 Segarelli was burned as a heretic by a Dominican inquisitor. Through the filter of viciously biased later accounts of his movement, we glimpse a man who was strikingly like Francis, who gained support from several Italian bishops, and who had no traceable heretical associations. The problem was that he came late in the day to the foundation of orders of friars. Dominicans and Franciscans treated him as unwelcome competition; a major council of the Church at Lyons in 1274 decided to suppress 'all forms of religious life and the mendicant Orders' founded after the fourth Lateran Council of 1215. While many Franciscans furiously debated among themselves about the justice of the council's narrowing of religious possibilities, the Order of Apostles actively resisted suppression and in 1290 its members were collectively condemned by the Pope. Soon afterwards, the Church started burning them.[22]

Segarelli and his order were not alone in their misfortunes. For all their founder's personal friendship with cardinals and even with one pope, Francis's followers included crowds who were more part of the wild underworld of thirteenth-century religion than of the establishment. His movement split between those who wished to remodel the order to make it more like the Dominicans, and 'Spirituals' who wished to reject all property, and by implication all ordered society, on the basis that Christ and his Apostles had no private possessions – that nagging truth embedded in the Gospels, which the Apostle Paul had first considered a problem (see p. 113). The Spirituals took up the teachings of a mystically minded south Italian Cistercian abbot of the previous century, Joachim of Fiore, whose broodings on the course of human history had convinced him that it was divided into three ages, dominated in turn by Father, Son and Holy Spirit; he thought that the third Age of the Spirit would begin in 1260 and would see the world given over to the monastic life.[23] Joachim's prophecies caused great excitement: in 1254, fifty years after his death and on the eve of the 1260 deadline, one ultra-enthusiast Franciscan proclaimed in Paris that Joachim's writings had replaced the Old and New Testaments as the 'Eternal Evangel' envisioned in the Book of Revelation (14.6). It was after all in 1260 that the flagellant movement first appeared in Europe. Joachim's thought continued to fascinate a great variety of Christians and ex-Christians down to modern times, including W. B. Yeats and D. H. Lawrence. Those who listen to the vapid rock anthem 'The Age of Aquarius' are catching a last echo of the twelfth-century Cistercian abbot whose vision was of a dawning new age.[24]

The wilder sections of the Spirituals became increasingly mixed up in the battles between popes, kings of France and Holy Roman Emperors; eventually Pope John XXII, a strong-minded and not always admirable cleric, was driven in 1318 to condemn the Spirituals as heretical. Four of them were burned at Marseilles for proclaiming that Christ had lived in absolute poverty; it was a sensitive issue, reflecting adversely on the clerical hierarchy's wealth and therefore on their power. The most extreme Spirituals, one of whose leaders noisily proclaimed his allegiance to the memory of the martyred Gerardo Segarelli, came to lead movements prepared to defy the Church even with physical violence; their resistance lost nothing in the telling of official chroniclers and produced savage repression.[25] Those Franciscans who escaped destruction continued to quarrel with each other about the interpretation of their founder's message of poverty, and it has been a characteristic of Franciscan community life that breakaway orders have continued to be founded to make a particular point about this. Even the depiction of Francis in painting is contentious; those versions of the order which particularly emphasized poverty or austerity made a point of commissioning pictures of the saint which portrayed him as especially gaunt and ragged. Franciscan oratory could still have alarmingly unpredictable results on crowds: the preaching of maverick Franciscans inspired one of the last crusades in Hungary in 1514–15, but also led to angry mobs turning not on Muslims but on the nobility and gentry who had failed to provide proper leadership against them. Both sides in that most terrible of Hungarian social upheavals turned to impaling their opponents, which seems a long way from Francis's gentle message.[26]

For all its divisions, the surviving Franciscan Order harnessed much of thirteenth-century Europe's religious energy. Like the Dominicans, Franciscans became deeply involved in the universities, and both orders made a point of siting their houses wherever there were people, so that one can often tell whether or not a settlement was important and wealthy in the High Middle Ages by seeing if any friaries were founded there. Unlike most monastic orders, friars welcomed laypeople into their

communities for spiritual counsel and discussion, and they usually deliberately built their dining halls in part of their site which would make it
easy for people to walk off the street to talk to them. They evolved a
distinctive form of church architecture: their spacious naves were preaching halls stripped of obstacles, often single wide chambers, so that
crowds could listen to sermons. Popular enthusiasm for mendicant
preaching meant that the style spread beyond the friars to produce a
large crop of 'hall churches' all over Europe, with single naves, or naves
with aisles of equal height, the pillars of the dividing arcades as slender
as was safe.

THOMAS AQUINAS: PHILOSOPHY
AND FAITH

The year 1260 did not bring the end of the world, as Joachim had
predicted and so many had expected. Those middle decades of the
thirteenth century did represent the culmination of the age which had
started with the reforms at Cluny, because they saw the crowning years
of the career of the Dominican theologian Thomas Aquinas. If Gregory
was the most decisive personality of the eleventh-century Church and
Bernard of Clairvaux its greatest preacher in the twelfth, then Aquinas's
system of thought, Thomism, in the thirteenth represents a defining
moment in the theology of the medieval West. He was the son of a
nobleman from Aquino in south Italy, but his career illustrates the
international flavour of the age, when a knowledge of Latin would be
enough to make one understood by everyone who mattered in society
from Stockholm to Seville. Having joined the Dominicans, he went on
to study and work not just in Italy but also in the universities of Paris
and Cologne. Aquinas's huge corpus of writings mark the height of
Western Europe's enthusiasm for Aristotle (who was for him simply
'the Philosopher'), and he encouraged the translation into Latin of all
Aristotle's works then known. After much opposition and misgivings
from theologians especially in the later thirteenth century, the work of
Aquinas had the eventual effect of ending the official Church's fears
about the challenge which Aristotle's thought appeared to present to
Christian faith.

Aquinas took as the ground of his work that the systems of thought
and reasonable analysis presented by Aristotle did not deny the central

place of faith, but illustrated, perhaps even proved, its truths. Aristotle's categories and discussion of 'forms' reflected the nature of the humanity which God had created, which had its form in a rational soul and was naturally inclined to act with reason. Nothing should be proposed which is contrary to our reason; this is the path to truth which God has given us, and it is to be used combatively, in argument and counter-argument, in order to form an intellectually acceptable conclusion, in the vigorous debating method of scholasticism which was a century old by Aquinas's time. It was in the process of approaching faith through reasoned argument that Aquinas found Aristotle so useful, particularly Aristotle's newly translated works on logic and metaphysics (see pp. 33–4). Building on Aristotle's idea that everything created must have a cause from which it receives its existence, he could construct a system in which everything that is and can be described is linked back in a chain of causation to God, the first cause of all things. This God is still primarily the 'Unmoved Mover', Plato's perfect, passionless God, so it would be a caricature to see Thomas as rejecting Plato in favour of Aristotle; he was using any intellectual resource at his disposal in order to create his system. It is seen at its fullest in Aquinas's great work the *Summa Theologiae* ('Sum Total of Theology' – often more commonly known as the *Summa Theologica*).[27]

The *Summa* deals with the most abstract questions of being and the nature of God, yet it also extends to very practical discussions of the way everyday life should be viewed, and how we should live as part of God's purpose. Through its questions and distinctions pushing to conclusions, it presents a harmonious view of God's earthly and heavenly creation, a structure in which the successors of Gregory VII could see themselves as the earthly peak of God's system. Thomas put limits on the use of reason in understanding this harmony. In the opening discussion of the *Summa*, he quickly led the reader to a conclusion which was that of the pseudonymous Dionysius the Areopagite long before, and which had become much more familiar among the theologians of Byzantium: 'It seems that we can use no words at all to refer to God'.[28] That may seem strange for a work which, in its standard English edition, runs to sixty-one volumes and which remained unfinished at Aquinas's death in 1274, but what this greatest of scholastic theologians understood was that all language about God had to employ the sideways glance, the analogy, the metaphor. So Aquinas's judgements on truth are presented as a summary of probabilities, of the balance of arguments:

something which those turning to his great work for certainties have not always appreciated.

Nowhere is Thomas's balance between the specific and the wordless more apparent than in a text of his encountered by countless more Catholics than have read the *Summa*, his great eucharistic hymn *Pange lingua* ('Sing, my tongue, the mystery of the glorious Body and precious Blood'). Aquinas wrote this as part of a devotional office for the new feast of Corpus Christi in 1264, at the request of Pope Urban IV himself. For centuries, the Catholic faithful have experienced the last two verses of *Pange lingua* in one of the most dramatic moments of theatre provided by Western Latin liturgy: Benediction of the Blessed Sacrament, the ultimate though belated expression of the fourth Lateran Council of 1215. This eucharistic devotion is peculiar to the Western Latin tradition. It developed from the Corpus Christi festival, whose only disadvantage in the eyes of medieval Westerners was that it was not enough of a good thing: it only happened once every twelve months. Through the rest of the Church's year there arose a custom of 'reservation of the Blessed Sacrament': part of the eucharistic bread consecrated in the Mass was 'reserved' from the service, and housed in a safe place, a 'tabernacle', enhanced in churches by ever more magnificent decoration and canopy work. Soon the reserved bread became known in common parlance simply as 'the Sacrament'. In its tabernacle (often also called the 'Sacrament House') it was available for worshippers to use as the focus for their adoration whenever they wished, and it became a popular custom for clergy to gather the devout in front of the tabernacle, to lead them in devotional prayer.

Three centuries and more after Aquinas's time, the Sacrament was not simply reserved in this fashion, but it became the focus and main actor in its own service, known as Benediction. In the most elaborated form of Benediction, the priest or deacon, splendidly vested, brings the consecrated bread out of its tabernacle and uses it to bless the worshippers before him. Slowly and reverently lifted from the altar, generally with the officiant's hands veiled to avoid direct contact with its container, the Sacrament is moved through the cross-pattern of the blessing, a spiritual symbol made emphatically physical. There can be no more powerful embodiment of the Western doctrine of Christ's 'Real Presence' in the eucharistic elements than this service of Benediction. As the priest prepares to gather up God's blessing in this way, those present sing Aquinas's *Tantum ergo*, the culminating verses of his *Pange lingua*:

Therefore we, before him bending,
this great Sacrament revere;
types and shadows have their ending,
for the newer rite is here;
faith, our outward sense befriending,
makes our inward vision clear.

Glory let us give, and blessing
to the Father and the Son,
honour, might and praise addressing,
while eternal ages run;
ever too his love confessing,
who from Both with Both is One.

'Faith, our outward sense befriending, makes our inward vision clear': there is the resolution to the puzzle posed by the *Summa*'s affirmation that no words may describe God. As the blessing is done, and the moment of climax falls away, the priest leads his flock in a prayer which is also by Aquinas:

O God, who under a wonderful sacrament has left us a remembrance of your passion: grant, we beseech you, that we may so venerate the holy mysteries of your body and blood, that we may evermore perceive within ourselves the fruit of your redemption.[29]

LOVE IN A COLD CLIMATE: PERSONAL DEVOTION AFTER 1200

Aquinas's praise of Jesus Christ in the Mass was written for a Latin Europe where the conditions of life for most people were worsening, and where the symbolism of a person who was also bread and wine, food and drink, had a bitter resonance. For nearly two centuries from around 1200, the climate of the northern hemisphere generally got colder. Europe's farming was inefficient, its food supplies unequally divided between those with power and those without. The new conditions brought misery to a population whose growth had for two centuries been pressing on the agricultural resources available. It is always risky to try and relate such background anxieties to religious belief, which can be shaped by many different considerations, but the

thirteenth century saw the flowering of a distinctively Western devotional pattern which concentrated on God as person, actively intervening in his creation, and on a more personal exposition of the human
reality of Christ and his Mother. It is true that this personal search
for God was already perceptible in the previous century. The great
eleventh-century theologian Anselm, Archbishop of Canterbury, wrote
alongside his works of formal logic and dialectic passionate meditations
on the beauty of God: 'Lord Jesus Christ, my redeemer, my mercy, my
salvation . . . how great is the leanness of my desire and abundant the
sweetness of your love.' In fact the Latin term '*meditatio*' seems first to
have been used to describe such a text in the decades after his death.
Anselm's meditations already circulated widely in his lifetime, and they
inspired much imitation (most of it attaching his name to new texts) in
the century after his death.[30]

Yet after 1200, within this pattern of search for the divine, there was
a greater concentration on the specific details of the life and death of
Christ. New themes emerged: Dominicans, culminating in Aquinas, built
up their own line of thought on the sufferings of Christ, and Aquinas
built up a logical case (which not all will find convincing) that Christ's
physical pains in his Crucifixion were greater than any experienced by
any other human being in history. There could be many motives in this
particular theological development. Just as in the developing cult of
Mary in the twelfth century, Dominican inquisitors facing Albigensians
might have an eye on the Cathar denial of physicality in the divine. Even
if that was one consideration, it has been suggested that the Dominicans
might also have been trying a theological put-down of their rivals the
Franciscans. Franciscans were inclined in Dominican eyes to over-stress
the closeness of their founder to the suffering Christ, up to and including
the reproduction in Francis's own body of Christ's *stigmata*, and it was
useful therefore to stress just how far even a Francis could fall short of
what the Lord had gone through.[31] Yet such considerations can only be
partial eddies within a wider phenomenon. Without the deepening
worries of so many about their sheer physical survival, the varied voices
which created these new perspectives on Christian worship and contemplation might not have been so readily heard: voices like Juliana of
Cornillon, who spearheaded a much more physical popular devotion to
Christ's body in the Eucharist (see p. 407), and besides the Dominicans,
generations of Franciscan preachers and theologians, inspired by Francis
himself.

Francis's search for God had a new perspective. Not only Anselm but Augustine of Hippo and Dionysius the Areopagite had seen God primarily as Plato's 'Unmoved Mover': so, after Francis's time, did Thomas Aquinas. But rather than perceiving God as this self-sufficient divine being, Francis saw a person: his Lord. Again and again, Francis calls God 'Lord God' (*Dominus Deus*). The Lord enters agreements – covenants – with his people, just as he did with the people of Israel (see pp. 60–61). As his side of the bargain in covenanting, he acts, rather than simply is.[32] His greatest action is in becoming truly human in Jesus Christ through his mother, Mary. Francis called people to see the ordinariness, the humanity, in Christ, in order that they could love and worship him better as God. It was Francis who built the first Christmas crib, complete with apocryphal ox and ass, as a devotional object in church.

Francis's personal view of God was echoed in an immensely popular and much-imitated early-fourteenth-century Franciscan work of devotion, long attributed to his disciple the Italian Franciscan theologian Bonaventure but now generally thought to have been written two generations later by another Italian Franciscan, John de Caulibus (hence the author is still often known as 'Pseudo-Bonaventure'). John wrote his *Meditations on the Life of Christ* to help a nun of the Franciscans' associated Order of Poor Clares in her contemplation of Christ's earthly life, presenting it as a series of eyewitness accounts interlaced with commentary and exhortation which all imaginatively extended the Gospel narratives, so that the reader might be inspired to imitate Christ in her or his own daily life. John rejoiced in the fact that the Gospel narratives had not aspired to include everything about Jesus, and so he could fill the gaps. Here, for instance, is his augmented account of the birth of the Saviour:

When the hour of truth had arrived, namely, midnight Sunday, the virgin arose and placed herself at the foot of a kind of column which was there. But Joseph was seated, morose because he had not been able to provide anything more fitting. He rose, picking up some hay from the manger and scattered it by our Lady's feet. Then he turned aside. Thereupon the Son of God, leaving his mother's womb without any breach or lesion was one moment inside the womb and next outside the womb on the hay at his mother's feet. At once his mother bent over, gathered him and tenderly hugged him. She placed him on her lap and instructed by the Holy Spirit, began an overall anointing wash with heaven filled milk of her breast. Then she wrapped him in her veil and laid him in a manger.[33]

The *Meditations* were so pictorial in character (and manuscripts of the text so frequently full of illustrations) that they were one major

stimulus to a newly individual and intimate sacred art which sought to
transcribe a visual reality into painting or sculpture – very different from
what had gone before in the West, let alone the carefully prescribed
traditions of Orthodox art.

The Franciscan devotional style – the celebration of the everyday
proclaimed in Francis's Christmas crib – was an inspiration for one of the
first artists in the Western tradition to be remembered as an individual
personality and to project a personal vision in his artistic achievement:
Giotto. One of Giotto's earliest commissions, in the last years of the
thirteenth century, was to oversee and take the leading role in painting
a sequence of frescoes in the basilica in Assisi dedicated to Francis and
his shrine. When in the Arena Chapel in Padua slightly later Giotto
painted the Nativity scene which de Caulibus would soon paint in words,
his vision was equally a projection beyond scripture: it has a realism
which at the time was revolutionary, but it also went beyond a snapshot
of the everyday (see Plate 25). Giotto's Nativity provides a scene for our
meditation as unobserved external observers and worshippers, just like
the Poor Clare nun reading her text. He portrays the intense gaze of a
young mother on her son, but the son fixes her with a gaze equally
intensely focused and beyond that of a newly born baby. The ox's eye is
also firmly fixed on the Virgin as it strains forward up to the manger with
the ass. This is a study of relationships which are familiar to us from our
daily lives, but in which the haloes of Mother and Son, and our knowledge
of the sacred story, pull us beyond our own experience, to the relationships of love which form the heart of Christianity's story of salvation.[34]

If we read John de Caulibus's *Meditations on the Life of Christ*,
what is immediately apparent is the concentration of their narrative
particularly on the extremes of Christ's earthly life: his infancy and
Passion. In this set of choices, de Caulibus was simply echoing much
contemporary preaching of his contemporaries in the Franciscan Order.
Infancy and Passion privilege the role of Mary, both in Christ's birth
and in her agony at his final sufferings. Once more, this Marian devotion
was a development from popular twelfth-century devotional themes (see
pp. 393–4) – but with a new element: it was in the later thirteenth
century that Mary too became not a benevolent but distant monarch, a
model for queen dowagers and empresses everywhere, but a wretchedly
mourning mother (see Plate 30). Indeed from the early fourteenth century she was commonly depicted throughout Europe as 'Our Lady of
Pity' or *Pietà*, cradling her dead son in her arms after he had been taken
down from the Cross.[35] Christ too was now first depicted in art not as

a King in Majesty or serene Good Shepherd, but as the 'Man of Sorrows', with the wounds of his crucifixion exposed and his face twisted in pain. The emphasis continued through the Reformation into sixteenth-century Protestantism, which centred on the death of Christ and his atoning work for humanity by his suffering.

This constant exposition of the Passion had an unfortunate side effect. To dwell on Christ's sufferings was liable to make worshippers turn their attention to those whom the Bible narrative principally blamed for causing the pain: the Jews. Franciscans were not slow to make the connection explicit, and in doing so, they complicated and darkened the already tense relationships between Jews and Christians. Augustine of Hippo had declared that God had allowed the Jews to survive all the disasters in their history to act as a sign and a warning to Christians. They should therefore be allowed to continue their community life within the Christian world, although without the full privileges of citizenship which Christians enjoyed: God only intended them to be converted en masse when he chose to bring the world to an end. So Jews continued to be the only non-Christian community formally tolerated in the Christian West, but their position was always fragile, and they were excluded from positions of power or mainstream wealth-creating activities. One result was that a significant number turned to moneylending at interest (usury), an activity which, thanks to half-understood prohibitions in the Tanakh, the Church prohibited to Christians. That trade could bring wealth to Jews, but certainly not popularity.[36]

It is true that the Franciscans had not pioneered or single-handedly invented the link between Jews and the Passion. The Western liturgy of Holy Week had been elaborating and intensifying the drama of Good Friday, the day of Jesus's death, for at least a century before their first appearance, and others had drawn their conclusions from the emotion of that liturgical experience.[37] Yet the tragedy remains: the heirs of the apostle of love, Francis, were among the chief sustainers of the growing hatred of Jews in medieval Western Europe. It was in this atmosphere that England pioneered Western Europe's first mass expulsion of Jews when, in 1289, Edward I's Parliament refused to help the King out of his war debts unless he rid the realm of all Jews; other rulers followed suit later. Such anti-Semitic ill-will continued to be balanced, in the untidy fashion of human affairs and with Augustine's lukewarm encouragement, by perfectly cordial or straightforward relations between Jews and Christians, but the impulse to harass or persecute Jews became a persistent feature of Western Christianity which it has only now properly confronted in the wake of terrible events in the twentieth century.[38] Jews were not the only group to be scapegoated: we have already noted (see pp. 400–401) the way that in bad times, lepers and homosexuals could also be seen as conspiring against Christian society.

The early fourteenth century added a new set of conspirators: Satan and his agents on earth, witches. Pope John XXII, a man much exercised by enemies and disruptors of the Church like the Spiritual Franciscans, crystallized a good deal of academic debate about magic and witchcraft which had been building up during the previous half-century. In 1320 he commissioned a team of theological experts to consider whether certain specific cases of malicious conjuring could be considered heresy, a controversial proposition generally previously denied by theologians, who had tended to treat magic, spells and meetings with the Devil as devilish illusions without substance. In the wake of the Pope's commission, six or seven years later he issued a bull, *Super illius specula*, which now proclaimed that any magical practices or contacts with demons were by their nature heretical and therefore came within the competence of inquisitions. This was one of those ideas which bide their time; for the moment witches were not much troubled by the Church's discipline, but more than a century later, with the aid of new publicists fired by their own obsessions, the Western Church and its Protestant successors were to initiate more than two centuries of active witch persecution (see pp. 686–8).[39]

It is pleasant to turn back from this aspect of medieval Western devotion to something very different: an intensification of personal mysticism, particularly among women recluses and religious. As with the emergence of a more personalized view of the Christian story among Western Christians generally, there were previous precedents. The most famous twelfth-century female mystic was Hildegard of Bingen, Abbess of Rupertsberg, who a generation before Joachim of Fiore recorded her visions and prophesied about the end of time, and whose writings cover a range of interests unusual at the time in male scholars let alone abbesses: cosmology, medicine, musical composition as well as theology. Hildegard was speaking and writing at the end of the age when women in monasteries were likely to have as good an access to scholarship as men. In her lifetime, the first universities were taking shape, all-male institutions which were to gather to them most of the intellectual activity of Western Latin culture. Perhaps that is why women were now so attracted to a mode of spirituality which was independent of formal intellectual training, but in which mind and imagination sought out the hiddenness of God, beyond doctrinal propositions or the argumentative clashes of scholasticism. Such mystics reversed the normal priorities of Western spirituality, which privileges the positive knowledge of God and affirms what Christian teaching positively says about him, to join Easterners in privileging silence and otherness. One of the best-known works to emerge from this tradition, an anonymous English fourteenth-century meditation probably by a country priest and called *The Cloud of Unknowing*, goes beyond Aquinas in quoting that mysterious and subversive fount of Eastern spirituality, Dionysius the Areopagite, when he says that 'the most godlike knowledge of God is that which is known by unknowing'.[40]

Other dimensions of mysticism freed the mystic from the centralizing impulse of the Church. Much of the writings which conveyed mystical experience was in various European vernaculars – the *Cloud of Unknowing* being one example – and so was directed towards those whose command of Latin, the international language of culture, was shaky or non-existent. Perhaps that was why mystics hit on themes which were familiar in Orthodox spirituality, but which had not been given nearly as much official encouragement by the Western Church. The mystic met God beyond the mediation of the male Church hierarchy, and in ways which can be remarkable metaphorical or imaginative appropriations of physical contact with the divine. Characteristic in mystical writings of the period are expressions which emphasize the human vulnerability, frailty, virginity of the subject, but which also celebrate the capacity of this frailty to unite with the divine. Not only women were attracted to these themes. One of the most remarkable mystical writings of the period is a Latin text by a Franciscan friar who was a spiritual adviser and scribe to a probably illiterate woman beguine in Vienna, Agnes Blannbekin (d. 1315); the work may be regarded as a joint venture in spiritual conversation between the two. The two hundred or so visions of Agnes which the friar recorded during the early 1290s make a good deal of use of the metaphor of clothing and unclothing to signify her contact with God (there are naked dancing nuns and friars in her Heaven). Her relish in the Feast of the Circumcision, which led her to imagine swallowing the foreskin of Christ, was one of the issues which raised a good deal of worry when the manuscript was first put into print in the eighteenth century. Agnes's visions were infused with everyday perceptions transformed into symbol; in one of them, Christ appeared to her in quick succession as a bishop, a chef, a pharmacist and the keeper of a general store.[41]

It is not surprising that in the age when official Christianity clashed with the Spiritual Franciscans, such mysticism, springing from free choices by individuals which might owe little to the priorities of the Church authorities, attracted hostile attention from inquisitors. One of the most well-known beguine mystics, Marguerite Porete, who wrote of her experiences in a work in French entitled *The Mirror of Simple Souls*, was burned in France as a 'Free Spirit' heretic in 1310: there was a fine line between such a fate and eventual honour in the Church. The German Dominican Meister Eckhart, an associate of Marguerite during his years in France, was similarly accused of heresy and died while inquisition proceedings against him were proceeding; yet because his works eventually escaped full condemnation, they remained widely influential. Eckhart, writing in vigorous and multi-layered German, introduced the idea that after abstracting the particular 'this' or 'that' and achieving 'detachment', *Gelassenheit*, the soul can meet God in the 'ground', *Grunt*, of all reality. There she can achieve an inseparable union with the divine, 'the unplumbed depth of God [which] has no name': 'Life can never be perfected till it returns to its productive source where life is one being that the soul receives when she dies right down to the "ground", that we may live in that life where there is one being.' It could be said (and Eckhart did say) that 'God begets His only begotten Son in the highest part of the soul.'[42]

At the other end of the scale of acceptance from Porete was Bridget of Sweden, a fourteenth-century Swedish noblewoman, who founded the monastic order for women and attendant priests which came to take her name; she derived the considerable detail of her foundation from a single vision of Christ, who had considerately spoken to her in Swedish. The Bridgettine Order became much favoured by Bridget's fellow nobility and monarchs all over northern Europe and came to represent late medieval piety at its most lavishly funded, intense and sophisticated. It is nevertheless noticeable that despite all this rich flowering of female spirituality, hardly any women were canonized (officially declared to be saints) in the two centuries after 1300. One of them was indeed Bridget, and the other her Italian contemporary and fellow visionary Catherine of Siena. Both canonizations were deeply controversial – in fact in the case of Bridget, the process had to be repeated three times.

One compelling motive for Catherine and Bridget achieving such exceptional promotion was that it suited the Vicar of Christ in the generations after their deaths. Prominent among the prophecies of both women was their insistence that the popes who had relocated from

Rome to Avignon in the early fourteenth century (see pp. 558–9) were destined to return to the city of St Peter: predictions whose fulfilment did not harm their chances of long-term favour from the papacy.[43] There was good reason for the popes who had returned to Rome to be grateful for such affirmations. Their claims in the Church were seriously challenged in this period, and were to be given more serious challenges still in the sixteenth-century Reformation. The consequences were profound for all Christianity, and take the story of the Western Church into new territory. Before exploring it, there is another story to tell. We will return to the East: to the Orthodox Churches, which never experienced any reformations like the two which convulsed the Western Church in the twelfth and sixteenth centuries, and which, in contrast to the project of papal monarchy, preserved and promoted the Roman imperial ideal in new forms, in new settings.

PART V

Orthodoxy: The Imperial Faith (451–1800)

13

Faith in a New Rome
(451–900)

A CHURCH TO SHAPE ORTHODOXY:
HAGIA SOPHIA

The charisma of the Bishops of Rome is twofold, springing from the tomb of St Peter and from Europe's equally long-standing fascination with Roman power and civilization. Gradually, in the series of accidents which we have followed from the first century to the thirteenth, Peter's successors revived the aspirations of Roman emperors to rule the world, and they managed to prevent the successors of the Emperor Charlemagne from gaining a monopoly on this monarchical role in the Christianity of the West. In Constantinople the balance was different. The newly promoted bishop of the city took advantage of a favourable conjunction of politics at the first Council of Constantinople in 381 (see pp. 218–20) to get himself 'the primacy of honour after the Bishop of Rome, because Constantinople is the new Rome',[1] while his Church did its best to trump Rome in apostolicity by declaring that it had been founded by the first-recruited among Christ's Apostles, Andrew. Even by early Christian standards, this was an implausible shot, and Andrew never really achieved much for his putative episcopal successors, the Patriarchs of Constantinople. Instead, the Byzantine emperors and the ideal of Christian governance which they represented became the vital distinguishing force in the Churches later known as Orthodox, long after the last emperor had died defending Constantinople in 1453.

Orthodox Christianity prides itself on its faithfulness to tradition: its majestic round of worship, woven into a texture of ancient music, sustained with carefully considered gesture and choreography amid a setting of painting following prescribed artistic convention, can be seen as reflecting the timelessness of Heaven. Its history has customarily been written with that self-image in mind, and in telling the Orthodox story there is a real problem in recovering the reality of personalities or events which at particular moments provided alternative routes to the future, and who have accordingly won a negative presentation from later Orthodox historians. It is a peculiarity of the Orthodox tradition of public worship that it contains hymns of hate, directed towards named individuals who are defined as heretical, all the way from Arius through Miaphysites, Dyophysites and Iconoclasts.[2] Take, for instance, these lines from the fifth sticheron (hymn) for Great Vespers on the Sunday after the Feast of the Ascension. In celebration of the first Council of Nicaea, the liturgy describes with relish (and one malevolent theological pun) the wretched end of Nicaea's arch-villain in fatal diarrhoea on the privy:

> Arius fell into the precipice of sin,
> Having shut his eyes so as not to see the light,
> And he was ripped asunder
> by a divine hook so that along with his entrails
> he forcibly emptied out
> all his essence [*ousia*!] and his soul,
> and was named another Judas
> both for his ideas and the manner of his death.

Such liturgical performance of hatred is embarrassing for modern ecumenical discussions among Eastern Christians when it is directed at cherished saints of one of the Churches participating, but it is probably to be preferred to the Western practice of burning heretics. There were very few burnings in the Byzantine Empire and they ceased soon after the West resumed burnings in the eleventh century, although in later centuries burnings resumed in Orthodox Muscovy – apparently first thanks to prompting from envoys of the Holy Roman Emperor in 1490.[3] In fact there was a long tradition in the Orthodox Church of leading churchmen criticizing burnings at the stake, which has little or no parallel in medieval Western Catholicism.[4] Once the Orthodox Churches of the East and the Balkans were in the hands of the Ottoman Turks, persecuting Christian heretics was in any case no longer a practical proposition for Orthodox Christians – but the hymns of hate remained, liturgical affirmations that there was one truth in Orthodoxy which had fought its way past a series of satanic temptations to error.

Continuity is not the same as changelessness. The Church of Constantinople and the Churches which sprang from it were wedded to imperial politics and the politics of the empire's successor-states: their spirituality has moved in rhythms set by these chances of history. The destruction of the empire in 1453 did not merely encourage the Church to cling fiercely to its evolved theological identity, denying that any other could be or had been possible; it also led Churches which escaped the catastrophe to reaffirm the role of sacred monarchy in the mould of Byzantium, and it was only at the end of the twentieth century that the last monarch of an Orthodox country was sent packing from his throne – the King of Greece, who happened to bear the name of both the first 'Orthodox' monarch and the last Byzantine monarch, Constantine. In post-Communist Orthodox cultures there are still rulers who aspire to something of the same role.

Orthodoxy has to a remarkable extent been moulded round one single church building, far more influential than even those crucial Western sacred places, the Basilica of St Peter in Rome and the Abbey Church of Cluny. This is the Cathedral of the Holy Wisdom (Hagia Sophia) in Constantinople, whose fabric has fared better than Cluny's, but whose fate as a church converted to a mosque encapsulates the traumas of Orthodox history (see Plate 5). It owes its present form to the partnership of a Latin-speaking boy from the Balkans and a former circus artist of dauntingly gymnastic sexual prowess: the Emperor Justinian I and his consort, Theodora.[5] We have already encountered this heroic if unlikely imperial couple as we have visited the stories both of the Western Church and of the Churches which rejected the Christological formula of Chalcedon after 451. Even before Justinian succeeded his Balkan-born soldier-uncle Justin in 527, they were contemplating the reuniting of the old empire through a twofold strategy of theological negotiation with Miaphysite enemies of Chalcedon and military conquests in East and West.

Justinian and Theodora were the last Christian monarchs before the nineteenth-century British Queen Victoria to wield an influence throughout all sections of the Christian world in their age, and their influence was far more personal and less purely symbolic than hers. It was Justinian who presided over the fifth Council of Constantinople in 553 when it condemned the theological tradition of Origen, sought to intensify the Church's rejection of the Dyophysites and in the process humiliated Pope Vigilius (see pp. 209–10 and 326–7); it was Theodora who provided patronage for those who secretly built up a Miaphysite Church hierarchy to challenge the Chalcedonians (see pp. 235–6). One would not realize how colourful their lives had been from the mosaic portraits of the pair as majestic and universal rulers, breaking iconographical convention to stand in pious harmony with their clergy and attendants in the very sanctuary of the imperial church of San Vitale in Ravenna (see Plate 27). The colour is revealed through the unusually triangulated writings of the Court historian Procopius (or Procopios). To balance his eloquent celebration of the Emperor's public achievements and buildings, Procopius vented his frustrations at his own courtliness by furtively penning a poisonous denunciation of Justinian and Theodora in a gossipy account of the same events, *The Secret History*, whose rediscovery by the pope's Vatican librarian in the seventeenth century much enhanced historical enjoyment of the period.[6]

Justinian's rebuilding of Hagia Sophia resulted from a political upheaval which nearly ended his rule only five years after his accession. His lavish expenditure and his vigorous pursuit of frontier wars, and the attendant taxation to pay for them, had united the active citizens of Constantinople in fury against him. In 532 the sporting factions of Greens and Blues, who played a leading part in city politics because they organized public entertainment in the capital's stadium, the Hippodrome, suspended their normal rivalry in an effort to overthrow Justinian, pushing one of his nephews into claiming imperial power. The crowds' shouts of 'Victory' (*Nika*) filled the city as they set fire to major buildings. Procopius maintained that, amid the blaze and panic, it was only Theodora's steely declaration to her husband that 'Royalty is a fine burial shroud' that steadied his nerve, pulled him back from flight and dispatched troops to slaughter the Nika rebels and hack their way to the submission of the city.[7] Around the shaken Emperor, much of the city lay in ruins, not least the two-centuries-old basilica of Hagia Sophia next to the Hippodrome and the palace.

Justinian now revealed his passion for building. With extraordinary speed he commissioned his architect to obliterate the remains of the old church. Its replacement would serve as cathedral of the city and symbol of unity in his empire, as well as a perpetual warning to future unruly crowds as it loomed over the Hippodrome. The overall design, completed and dedicated after only five years, outdid all previous precedents. It abandoned the basilican plan of its predecessor church and showcased a feature of imperial architecture which previously had rarely been more than a subsidiary theme in Christian building: the dome, a recreation of the canopy of Heaven. From the time of Constantine, domes had been used to roof circular or centrally planned Christian buildings which spoke primarily of the route to Heaven in death – mausoleum-churches for the burial of prominent people or baptisteries which witnessed Christians' death to sin (see p. 293). Here, the aim was different, creating a congregational space for emperor, patriarch and people which felt as if it encompassed the long east–west axis of a conventional basilica. This was achieved by building a dome of breathtaking width and height, pierced around its base by a row of windows through which shafts of light transfixed the church interior below; the dome seemed to float on two half-domes to east and west. They climaxed at the east in the altar, housed beyond them in a central semicircular (apsidal) sanctuary; that apse was topped by yet another half-dome. One sixth-century poet, Paul the Silentiary, tried to capture the effect: it 'is a great helmet, bending over on every side, like the radiant heavens . . . like the firmament that rests upon air'.[8]

Paul's verse was actually commemorating an early restoration of Hagia Sophia after earthquake damage; the dome partially collapsed again in 1346. Few churches could risk trying to match its daring and complicated architectural form; none of Justinian's many foundations or rebuildings of other churches followed its model in full. What Hagia Sophia did do was decisively to promote the central dome as the leading motif of architecture in the imperial Church of the East and in those Churches which later sought to identify with that tradition. Moreover, following the precedent of Hagia Sophia, the dome became a major Islamic feature in mosques, once mosques became covered spaces rather than open courtyards. When the dome was used in other Eastern church buildings, it generally once more appeared as in earlier Christian buildings in the midst of a central plan, and now most commonly it rode over the centre of a cross with equal arms – a Greek cross. This plan could be adapted to the use of quite small communities like rural parishes or minor monasteries and still convey the impression of celestial splendour. In a much later development, a screen called an *iconostasis* customarily shut off the altar (see pp. 484–5), but this was not how such church interiors were originally conceived for five centuries or more after Justinian's time.

Nowhere was the Orthodox combination of architecture, art and liturgy seen more splendidly than in Hagia Sophia, often simply known as the 'Great Church', although its present rather dismal internal state does credit neither to its original incarnation nor to the care lavished on it in its subsequent life as a mosque. There was a moment in 612 when Patriarch Sergios decreed a reduction in what he regarded as an excessive staff and ceremony in the cathedral: the trimmed establishment which he allowed amounted to eighty priests, 150 deacons, forty deaconesses, seventy subdeacons, 160 readers, twenty-five cantors and a hundred

doorkeepers.[9] Worshippers beyond this monstrous array of sacred courtiers could see Heaven above them in the dome and semi-domes. The
images, still relatively simple in the original decoration of Hagia Sophia,
became more and more elaborate. Those who looked up into the dome
above a congregation would normally see the image of Christ the Ruler
of All (the 'Pantocrator'), in glory and in judgement. They could also
gaze east, to the table where bread and wine were made holy, normally
presided over by the images of Christ's Mother, usually with her baby
son, God made flesh. All around these representations of divinity
enthroned and incarnate was more figural representation in mosaic or
wall painting, in schemes which grew fixed throughout Orthodoxy not
merely in arrangement but in content, all conceived as reflecting their
archetypes, just as a particular object might reflect its Platonic form. The
tiers representing rulers, saints, clergy, all in hierarchical but intimate
relationship to God and Mary the *Theotokos*, were a constant assurance
to the congregations who viewed them that God in his mercy allowed
such intimacy to human beings.

Interestingly, the ordering of saints in Byzantine church interiors does
not much reflect the passing of the seasons of Christian worship; they
tend instead to be grouped in categories, such as martyrs or virgins.[10]
The Church's year – Christmas, Easter, Ascension – tells a story which
progresses in linear fashion through the months, centring on the life of
Christ, and it is also punctuated by days commemorating particular
historic events in the lives of saints. The Eucharist, by contrast, is
timeless, reflecting the eternity of Heaven. It is that timelessness that the
artistic schemes of the Orthodox Churches characteristically invoke –
the only moment to which they point above the altar is the end of time,
when Christ reigns in glory, the moment in which every Eucharist
participates. Eastern congregations did not develop the attitude of the
Carolingian West that the Eucharist was something to privatize,
directing its power to particular ends and intentions, and therefore
capable of being shortened into a said form (see pp. 356–7). In the East,
the celebration was done because it needed to be done – at the worst times
in Orthodox history, it has been just about all that the Church has been
able to do. Moreover, from an early date, Eastern Christians seem to have
concluded that it was enough for worshippers to be present at the
Eucharist without receiving bread and wine. This seems to have been a
measure of the awe which attached to the experience of eating the body
and blood of Christ, which is how the Eucharist was now perceived.
Laypeople's reception of these elements became a very occasional, per-

haps once-yearly, experience, much earlier than the same development in the West. Indeed, in the late fourth century, Ambrose of Milan recorded his disapproval of this Eastern custom.[11]

The ordered worship of God was the means by which holiness could enfold everyone, under the protection of the great helmet of the dome above. The singing of the liturgy imitated the music of Heaven, with angels in the same choir alongside the worshippers, and much of that music was intended for processions, for all to sing. The tradition allowed for voices alone, without instruments, in contrast to the gradual medieval acceptance in the Latin West of musical instruments, as also far away in the Church of Ethiopia. The singing congregations were travelling towards holiness, protected in the fixed shape of the liturgy, bound into the processions which dominated not merely the drama of the Church but everyday life in the streets of Constantinople. Moments of entry and reception into the sacred precincts were of especial importance, not least to the emperor himself, and the goal was the drama of the Eucharist at God's altar. Music which began life in processions might end up having other uses. For instance, that most popular of Eastern musical acclamations the *Trisagion* (see pp. 239–40) was said to have been devised by a boy in the mid-fifth century as a comment on the penitential psalm that he was singing in procession, to pray for deliverance from a sequence of violent earth tremors. The chant's success in stilling the earthquakes embedded it in the liturgy and in the consciousness of Eastern Christians far beyond Byzantium.[12]

Worship in the Orthodox fashion came to propel first monks, then laypeople beyond the monasteries, towards an idea which over centuries became basic to Christian Orthodox spirituality: union with the divine, or *theosis* – dizzyingly for humanity, and alarmingly for many Western Christians, the word can be translated as 'deification'. The concept was likely to take the Christian believer in a very different direction from Augustine's Western emphasis on the great gulf between God and humanity created by original sin. It asserted that human society could be sanctified through the ministry and liturgy of the Church, and by the meditations of those who were prepared to enter such difficult and testing labour. What Justinian was doing in his major programme of building in the capital and the creation of a constant round of sacred ceremony around Hagia Sophia was to make himself and the imperial Court the focus of a society where every public activity which formerly had been part of the non-Christian structure of the empire was now made holy and consecrated to the service of God.

The first major project of Justinian's reign, the codification of half a millennium of imperial legal decisions, might at first seem remote from the agenda of sacralizing Byzantine society, but Justinian's collections and abridgements were a deliberately Christian reshaping of the heritage of law from the empire, much more conscious in that objective than the previous harmonization of Roman law by an earlier Christian emperor of the fourth century, Theodosius II. This codification was one of Justinian's most lasting legacies. In the West it disappeared for centuries along with the empire itself, but its rediscovery in the eleventh century played a significant part both in the Gregorian remoulding of society and the creation of the first Christian universities (see pp. 377–8 and 398), and it provided the basis for most Western legal systems devised thereafter. It also remained the foundation for Eastern imperial justice until the Byzantine Empire disappeared in 1453, but the price of its survival was its rapid translation into Greek.

There was no future for Latin in the empire of Justinian's successors, for in the eastern Mediterranean it had only ever been an interloping language imposed by colonial administrators from the West. The people of Byzantium continued to call themselves 'Romans' (and that is also what the Arabs called them and their homeland of Asia Minor – *Rhum*), but they did so in Greek: they were *Rhomaioi*. They also lost the inclination to enjoy literature in Latin, until much later, at a time of renewed cultural contacts in the thirteenth century, they found new Greek translations of Latin poetry and philosophy to read.[13] The draining of what was Roman or non-Christian from New Rome was one of the irreversible effects of Justinian's reign and its aftermath: in the century and a half from his death in 565, a new identity was created for society in the Eastern Empire which can be described as Byzantine.

It was not merely that Justinian's military campaigns brought ruin to traditional Roman society in his new conquests in Italy and North Africa (see p. 320); he also undermined much of what remained from the past in the East. In 529 the Emperor closed the Academy of Athens, which in the great days of the 'Second Sophistic' at the height of Roman imperial self-confidence (see pp. 140–41) had been a self-conscious refoundation of the ancient Academy of Aristotle, and which still upheld the tradition of Plato. It was also during Justinian's time, in 550–51, that another institution of higher education in Berytus (Beirut) was closed after a major earthquake devastated the city; only Alexandria was left as a centre of ancient non-Christian learning until the Islamic conquest. With such losses, education became more and more the prop-

erty of Christian clergy and reflected their priorities. Books were otherwise scarce, and one new sort of book became increasingly common:
florilegia, which were collections of short extracts from complete works
which would act as guides to a subject, particularly in religion. Usually
they were gathered with some particular theological agenda in mind.
Another sort of new book flourished too: in the model of the life of
Antony of Egypt (see pp. 205–6), hagiographies (biographies of saints,
their miracles and the wonders associated with their shrines) became the
staple fare of Byzantine reading.[14]

This was natural enough. The world felt increasingly out of human
control, and the best hope seemed to be found in the hairline cracks
between Heaven and earth provided by sacred places and holy people.
The later sixth century saw the Byzantine Empire increasingly on the
defensive on all fronts, with major losses in the western Mediterranean
territories that Justinian had won and the seizure of imperial territory
in the Balkans by Slavs and Avars. In 613 a Persian army encamped
within sight of the city across the waters of the Bosphorus. In 626 came
the greatest crisis yet, when a joint force of Avars, Slavs and Persians
besieged the city. In the absence of the Emperor Heraclius on campaign,
the Patriarch called together a procession of the whole civilian population bearing icons. During the siege, a woman, identified as the Virgin
Mary herself, was reputedly seen leading the defenders: it was a major
stimulus for the already lively cult of Mary in the Eastern Church.[15]

Heraclius, one of the greatest if often maligned heroes of the whole
Byzantine story, performed extraordinary feats in outfacing these cumulative military threats, and his accession in 610 marked the beginning
of an imperial dynasty which was to last throughout the seventh century.
Still there remains his greatest failure: in his preoccupation with defeating his enemies in east and west, Heraclius had missed the importance of the new invaders from the south, the Muslim Arabs. After the
defeat of a Byzantine army in 636, all its southern provinces were soon
lost, Jerusalem included. There was actually a six-year-period when
the Emperor Constans II, desperate to defend his western provinces,
abandoned Constantinople and took refuge with his Court in Sicily
before being murdered in 668 by courtiers infuriated by his drastic
efforts to secure revenue and his apparent intention to make this move
permanent; ever afterwards, his name was reviled and made into the
belittling 'Constans' rather than his baptismal 'Constantine'.[16]

The heirs of Heraclius did succeed in preventing the whole empire
from being swallowed up. Constantine IV beat off Muslim armies from

Constantinople itself in 678, saved by the city's formidable walls and by the innovative use of a terrifying incendiary device known as 'Greek fire' (whose composition was always successfully kept undisclosed, a true Byzantine secret weapon) to destroy Arab ships.[17] While in hindsight we can see this Byzantine victory as a decisive move blocking westwards Islamic advance into Europe for centuries, there would have been little reason to feel relief at the time. The miseries of repeated warfare were compounded by a long-drawn-out natural catastrophe: from the 540s a major plague spread westwards through the empire and beyond, and it recurred right through to the eighth century. Population plummeted, including in Constantinople itself, and the general impact can still be seen dramatically in Syria, until then an area of continuing vigorous Classical urban civilization, where town after town was sucked dry of life and was never reoccupied, leaving a series of ruins in semi-desert wilderness to the present day. Constantinople itself was a city of ruins, a ghost of its former self.[18] This weakening of both Byzantine and Sassanian society by the plague must have been another reason why the Arabs found it so easy to overwhelm such large areas of mighty empires. Archaeologists have noted a remarkable fall in the number of coins recovered from excavations datable to the period from around 650 to around 800: economic activity must have drained away.[19] A Mediterranean-wide society faced ruin; no wonder that Byzantium was ready to listen with respect and longing to those who sought to bring it closer to its God.

BYZANTINE SPIRITUALITY: MAXIMUS AND THE MYSTICAL TRADITION

Under the circumstances, the preservation of Byzantine culture in the empire was increasingly the business of the one vigorous and expanding institution outside the Court. Just as in the fragmented kingdoms of the West, monasteries became the safe-deposits and factories of learning, and also strongholds of interference in imperial policy. Increasingly, the imperial Church chose monks to be bishops: there were no Christian equivalents of the vanished Academy of Athens, and no schools of theology like those which the Emperor Zeno had expelled from Edessa in 489 (see pp. 245–6). So there was nowhere else but a monastery to learn how to defend the faith, or discuss with spiritual men how to exercise pastoral care. A series of major Church historians in the fifth century produced pen-portraits of some of the great champions of Nicene and Chalcedonian orthodoxy. Prominent among these figures were monks such as Basil of Caesarea, or even the Westerner Martin of Tours, who had bridged that gap which in the beginnings of monasticism might have seemed impossibly wide, combining monastic and episcopal vocations. As a result, by the eleventh century, it was overwhelmingly the convention in the East that bishops should always be monks, and so it has remained in Orthodoxy.[20] The convention has led to a two-track career for Orthodox clergy, for in complete contrast to the medieval West, clergy with no intention of hearing a call to either monasticism or the episcopate have customarily continued to follow the practice of the early Church; they have been married men with families, and minister to the laity in their local churches.

By Justinian's time, certain key monasteries were celebrated throughout the imperial East. The first Christian emperors had discouraged the foundation of monasteries in the capital itself, but the convention was breached in the mid-fifth century by Stoudios, a wealthy senator, who paid for a monastery on his own estate within the city walls. Bolstered by its possession of the head of John the Baptist, this Stoudite community was to prove a major force in the life of Constantinople for nearly a thousand years.[21] On the frontiers of the empire too, in lands soon lost to the Muslim Arabs, two of the most important early foundations have managed to survive all the disasters of later history to the present day. The monastery of St Sabas near Jerusalem was from its inception in the 480s a large community (the 'Great Lavra') with a fleet of subsidiary houses. The founder Sabas, a monk from Cappadocia, died in his nineties in Justinian's reign. More remote and older was the community of St Catherine on Mount Sinai, a far-flung beneficiary of Justinian's enthusiasm for church-building. Besides the massive granite walls of the monastery, the dry conditions have preserved extraordinary woodwork; there are monumental doors in the church from Justinian's time, and behind later panelling there lurk roof timbers preserved in their original setting, inscribed with memorials to the generosity of the Emperor and his covertly Miaphysite empress, Theodora, in refounding and fortifying this key Orthodox monastery.

In the wretchedly anxious era which followed Justinian, certain key monastic writers not greatly known or appreciated in the West until modern times created a spirituality distinctive to the Orthodox world.

St Catherine's was home to one of the most important shapers of Byzantine monasticism: its abbot John of the Ladder (*tis Klimakos*, Climacus), so called from the work of spirituality which he created, the *Ladder of Divine Ascent*. Climacus is as shadowy a figure as the Western St Benedict, who (since so little is certain about either of them) may have been a near-contemporary of his in the sixth century. Likewise Climacus is known only through his written work, which is not a monastic rule like Benedict's, but a collection of sayings conceived as a guide for monks. Its metaphor of progress in the ascetic life through the steps of a ladder is a characteristic feature of Christian mysticism in both East and West. Many mystics through the centuries have spoken and written about the impulse to move towards a goal, to travel onwards, even though frequently to the worldly eye they are people steeped in stillness and immobility. Stillness may be the goal; on the way, there is much labour.

The Ladder distils much from the past. That is another feature of mystical writing, which repeatedly sets up echoes of past works, many of which the author is most unlikely to have known directly (while on occasion, the same mystical themes emerge quite independently in very varied settings). Climacus's texts resonate with pronouncements of Egyptian ascetics, including Evagrius of Pontus (see pp. 209–10), at that stage not yet condemned as heretical, from whom Climacus takes the concept of *apatheia*, passionlessness or serenity, as one of the main ladder steps into the union with the divine in *theosis*. There is a sharp perceptiveness and even humour in Climacus's writings which is very personal. One of the most original of his themes, much repeated later, is his paradoxical insistence that mourning is the beginning of a Christian's divine joy: 'I am amazed at how that which is called *penthos* [mourning] and grief should contain joy and gladness interwoven within it, like honey in the comb'.[22] Orthodox monasteries still customarily have the *Ladder* read through during their meals in Lent.

In the next generation, another monk gave further lasting shape to Orthodox spirituality, and is indeed often regarded as the greatest theologian in the Byzantine tradition: Maximus or Maximos (*c.* 580–662), known as 'the Confessor' from the sufferings he endured at the end of his long life in defence of Chalcedonian Orthodoxy.[23] His writings could guide a monk in almost every aspect of his life – doctrine, ascetic practice, worship and the understanding of scripture – and all is suffused with Maximus's constant return to the theme of union with the divine. Like Climacus, Maximus did not seek to be original: he restated and enriched the message of the past, but his choices set directions for the future. One of his sources was Cyril of Alexandria – whom he chose to see as a firm defender of the theology on the natures of Christ which the Council of Chalcedon had later affirmed – and, once more, Origen and Evagrius rather more discreetly than was necessary in a previous generation. But Maximus also looked to a writer who went under the name of one of the few converts whom Paul of Tarsus is said to have made in Athens, Dionysius the Areopagite.[24] The books of this 'Pseudo-Dionysius' were in fact probably compiled in Syria around eighty years before Maximus's time, by a Christian steeped in Neoplatonist philosophy, and moreover a sympathizer with the Miaphysites – an irony in view of Maximus's strong Chalcedonianism.[25] In fact the career of Pseudo-Dionysius is remarkable: he is a constant presence behind the mystical writings of Orthodox Christianity, and from the ninth century, when his writings were translated into Latin by the Irish philosopher John Scotus Erigena, he became a powerful voice in a Western Latin mystical tradition as well.

Dionysius the Areopagite drew on the thought of Neoplatonists (see pp. 169–70) in his exploration of how divinity could intimately combine with humanity through a progress in purging, illumination and union. These stages are to be found in many subsequent treatments of mystical Christianity long after Maximus, and their origins in such a dubiously provenanced work are a testimony to the way in which Christian mysticism reaches beyond the careful boundaries drawn by the councils of the Church.[26] Dionysian theology was also Neoplatonic in its view of the cosmos as a series of hierarchies; it viewed these hierarchies not as an obstacle to God, but as the means of uniting the remoteness and unknowableness of God with the knowable particularity of lower creation, just as courtiers might be intermediaries for humble people to approach a monarch. God could be known in precisely opposite ways: by what could not be said about him (the 'apophatic' view of God) and what could be affirmed about him (the 'kataphatic' view). Pseudo-Dionysius, like so many writers in mystical traditions, loved expressing in terms of light the relationship between unknowable transcendence and the tiers of being which represented knowable divinity:

Hierarchy causes its members to be images of God in all respects, to be clear and spotless mirrors reflecting the glow of primordial light and indeed of God himself. It ensures that when its members have received this full and divine splendour, they can then pass on this light generously.[27]

Maximus eagerly absorbed these themes and applied them in much greater detail to many different aspects of spirituality and worship. For him, *theosis* or deification was the destination for human salvation, whose attainment Adam's sin in Eden had imperilled but not rendered impossible; in fact all the cosmos was created to arrive at deification. A ground-bass of Maximus's meditation on *theosis* is *Logos*, the word that is Word and echoes through so much ancient philosophy to re-echo in John's Gospel prologue and the writings of the first Apologists (see pp. 1 and 142–3). For Maximus, the central moment in the whole story of the cosmos was the coming of the Word in Flesh, a union of uncreated and created, and that was why the latter half of his career was devoted to a bitter public struggle to assert his own Chalcedonian understanding of what that meant. But there were so many depths to the meaning of *Logos* beyond this event of incarnation. God's creation contained multiple 'words', *logoi*, which were God's intentions for his creation, and the source of differentiation behind all created things: God the One and Simple designed his creation in multiplicity and complexity, so 'it is said that God knows all beings according to these *logoi* before their creation, since they are in him and with him; they are in God who is the truth of all'. Rational created beings were destined and commanded to move back to meet their God through their *logoi*.[28]

The *Logos* was thus to be met both in Jesus and in all creation; it was also to be met in scripture. In a remarkably physical picture of the 'Word', Maximus said, 'The Word is said to become "thick". . . because he for our sakes, who are coarse in respect to our mentality, accepted to become incarnate and to be expressed in letters, syllables and words, so that from all these he might draw us to himself.'[29] Maximus relished the approach to scripture that Origen had pioneered, seeing behind the veil of the literal meaning of the text a great sea of spiritual truths. Among their other gifts to the faithful, they could explain and give positive value to the literal discrepancies and oddities to be found throughout the sacred books. To seek after these meanings was yet another pathway back to the Creator, and it was a path directed by love. Love 'is the producer *par excellence* of deification'. By whatever route, the goal was 'to become living images of Christ, or rather to become identical with him or a copy, or even, perhaps, to become the Lord himself, unless this seems blasphemous to some'.[30] Repeatedly, Maximus referred to Christians as gods through grace.[31]

One can see why some Christians might indeed find this language hard to accept, but Maximus escaped any later censure and has remained a voice of authority in the Eastern Church. This was partly because of his passionate belief that the Church's liturgical ceremonies served as a chief means of deification: his writing is at its most personally intense in his celebration of the liturgy's spiritual riches. He ties every part of its observation into the ascent towards God, culminating in the reception of the eucharistic bread and wine in which 'God fills [communicants] entirely and leaves no part of them empty of his presence'.[32] So alongside all the instruction which he provided for the interior life of the individual monk, Maximus's greatest eloquence was reserved for the communal drama which bound together clergy and laity. Of equal importance was that through his writing and sufferings at the end of his life Maximus became a chief symbol of Orthodoxy's resistance to yet another attempt by the emperors to conciliate Miaphysite opinion in the Church by developing a common theology on the basis of Cyril of Alexandria.

Among the Emperor Heraclius's multiform efforts to defend and strengthen his empire, perhaps the most far-reaching, encouraged by Patriarch Sergius, was to promote a theological reconciliation of his warring subjects. The group of theologians chosen to find a solution to the empire's doctrinal disagreements sought to be true to Chalcedon in acknowledging that two natures (human and divine) came together in Christ, but in order to accommodate the Miaphysites, they suggested that once these natures had thus met, the natures gained a unity of activity or will (*energeia* or *thelēma*). Maximus was one of the chief voices opposing this 'Monenergism' or 'Monotheletism'. He said that God had too much respect for his creations, humans included, to allow the *Logos* to assume anything less than true created human nature in all its fullness: so the incarnate Christ must have had a fully human activity and fully human will. When Christ, in his agony in the Garden of Gethsemane, submitted to his Father with 'Nevertheless, not as I will, but as thou wilt', he was as a man using his human will to obey his divine will. This was a bold claim, based on a largely novel vision of the will as self-determination both rational and beyond conscious reason; no Greek philosopher, let alone theologian, had fully enunciated this before, or made the will so central to an understanding of Christ.[33] For his opposition, Maximus suffered appallingly on the orders of Emperor and Patriarch: the Confessor is said to have had his tongue cut out and his right hand amputated, to stop him speaking or writing.

For all their novelty, the intensively repeated arguments in Maximus's later writings, and his final maltreatment for his convictions, embedded them deep within Orthodoxy. The increasing desperation of the imperial authorities to reap political benefits from their Monothelete compromise in the face of Arab military successes led them into brutal measures, not

merely against Maximus but against Pope Martin (see p. 345); that did
more to harm than help the Monothelete cause. Maximus did not live
to see the final condemnation of Monotheletism at the sixth Council of
Constantinople in 680–81. The successful assertion of Christ's human
will is a theme which gives a human immediacy to the sufferings of the
Saviour – so much greater than those of the believer, but not separated
in kind from them. That conviction has strengthened many in the varied
sufferings of Orthodoxy in later centuries.[34]

SMASHING IMAGES:
THE ICONOCLASTIC CONTROVERSY
(726–843)

When the Monotheletes were defeated in 681, they pointed grimly to a
new setback for the empire as a sign of God's disapproval: a move
southwards by the Bulgars, another in that long sequence of peoples
who had drifted westwards from central Asia to seek a home in Europe.
In 680 Bulgars defeated Byzantine frontier forces and set up a new
headquarters at Pliska, in territory which forms part of the modern
Bulgaria. In the centuries afterwards, the Bulgars remained one of the
more uncomfortable recurrent problems for Byzantine emperors. But
the wrath of God on the empire seemed even more concentrated in the
menace of Islam, which despite the repulse of Arab armies from the walls
of Constantinople in 678 continued to threaten the imperial territories in
Asia Minor. It was natural to wonder whether elements in the faith
and practice of such successful warriors represented God's will for
the Christian Church; and this became the conviction of a military
commander whose grim persistence in the unending slog of protecting
Byzantine frontiers earned him the imperial throne in 717 as Leo III.

 Leo was known as 'the Isaurian' from his origins in a frontier province
of Asia Minor, and it may be that already here, in close proximity to
Islamic territories, he had become impressed with one aspect of Muslim
austerity, the consistent rejection of pictorial representations of the
divine. That contrasted significantly with a growing feature of devotion
in Byzantine religion: the importance and indeed divine power attributed
to images or icons. Islamic iconophobia, hatred of images, confronted
Byzantine iconophilia, and Islam seemed to be winning. God's message

was particularly emphatically conveyed in a spectacular episode of the volcanic and seismic activity so characteristic of the eastern Mediterranean. In 726 a massive eruption devastated the Santorini archipelago and resulted in an entire new island emerging in the sea nearby. Among Leo's advisers was the bishop of a city in Asia Minor, Constantine from Nakoleia, who is known even before the Santorini eruption to have remarked on the apparent inability of wonder-working icons to achieve much against Arab armies, and he was by no means the only bishop who thought like that.[35] Iconophobia could easily turn to destructive action: iconoclasm. Accordingly, Leo began to implement iconoclast policies.

The struggle which followed over more than a century was not simply inspired by Islam; it exposed one of the great fault lines within Christianity itself, reflecting its dual origins in Hebrew and Greek culture. The pre-Christian Greeks, as we have seen, regarded it as natural to portray the divine in human form, and their sculptural art was dominated by such depictions (see p. 23). After the Jews had struggled with the various cults around them, Judaism came to take precisely the opposite attitude. Although in certain cultural settings Jews were capable of producing sacred painting and even sculpture (see pp. 178–9), they had at the heart of their observance the statement in the Ten Commandments given by God to Moses (the 'Decalogue') that 'You shall not make for yourself a graven image, or any likeness of anything that is in heaven above, or that is in the earth beneath, or that is in the water under the earth; you shall not bow down to them or serve them'.[36] This does seem very categorical, and mainstream Christians, having decided after their struggles in the second century CE to retain the Tanakh as sacred scripture, could not ignore the Ten Commandments any more than Jews. Nevertheless, questions remained. Biblical commentators both Jewish and Christian noted that the prohibition on graven images is the longest and most verbose of the Commandments. Far from reinforcing its authority, that raised the possibility that it was not part of the foundation Commandments at all, but a subsidiary comment on God's first Commandment and basic prohibition, which went before it: 'I am the LORD your God, who brought you out of the land of Egypt, out of the house of bondage. You shall have no other gods before me.'

This raised a further possibility for Christians. They could not contemplate altering the total number of ten in the Commandments, which had been foundational for Judaism since at least the Deuteronomic period (see pp. 60–61), but they might renumber the Commandments. A renumbering would involve tucking the graven-image prohibition inside Commandment One, rather than making it a free-standing Commandment Two (that meant dividing up the Commandment against covetousness at the end of the sequence to preserve the number ten). This was the conclusion drawn by Augustine of Hippo, and in it he was followed by the entire Western Church down to the Reformation, when some (but, as we will see, not all) Protestants returned to the question and pointedly began numbering the Decalogue once more in the Jewish fashion, thus justifying their deep hostility to traditional ecclesiastical art (see pp. 618–19). In the Church which Augustine knew, where sculptural sacred art had been generally accepted since at least the time of Constantine and possibly before (see p. 172), it was natural to feel that everyday devotion told strongly against any fundamental divine prohibition on the graven image.[37]

One might have expected the Eastern Church, with its spectacular devotion to the sacred image, to take the same line as Augustine on numbering the Ten Commandments. However, it did not: it remained true to the biblical exegesis of Origen, who continued to be deeply (and rightly) respected as a commentator on scripture even when much of his theology lay under condemnation. Origen had noted the questions around the Commandments, but firmly maintained his stance alongside the Jews on the question of their numbering; so the graven-image prohibition stood as Commandment Two. Self-evidently, this had not inhibited the Easterners from creating a wealth of sacred art, but what they did was to observe the Commandment to the letter: their figural art was characteristically not graven (that is, sculpted) but was created on flat surfaces – the busy jewelled surfaces of wall and floor mosaics in glass and stone, and the paintings on wooden tablets which became the image *par excellence* for the Orthodox Church: the icon.[38]

It may be, as has recently been argued, that icons took their cue from the ancient tradition of painted funeral portraits for Egyptian mummies, a tradition taken over with enthusiasm by Egyptian Christians.[39] Certainly the saints in icons share much of the impact of those haunting Egyptian mummy portraits with their gaze intensely directed to the viewer, but Egyptian funerary custom seems inadequate to account for the general phenomenon of non-sculptural Eastern Christian art. It had a theological origin: it was an ingenious solution to the dilemma posed by the Second Commandment, and it was of course regarded as pure hypocrisy by the eighth-century iconoclasts, again on theological grounds. What else was at stake in the iconoclastic controversy? One of the problems in understanding the issues is that virtually all the iconoclasts' arguments of their case have been destroyed by the eventually victorious iconophiles. The sole major iconoclast statement to survive is from the council of iconoclast bishops called by the Emperor Constantine V to his Hieria Palace in 754; and this was preserved only in the proceedings of the later iconophile Council of Nicaea in 787 so that it could be systematically contradicted and condemned (the council sadistically forced one of the repentant former iconoclast bishops who had been present at Hieria to read it all out).[40] It has been plausibly suggested that behind the arguments over Church art was an argument about how to reach out to God's holiness. How does the divine relate to the human world?[41]

Iconoclasts said that we meet holiness in particular situations where the clergy represent us to God, such as in the Church's liturgy, so icons are at best irrelevant; they argued that icons cannot be holy, as no specific prayer of blessing is said over them by a cleric (probably as a result, a blessing of icons with designated prayers is Orthodox practice in modern times).[42] Iconoclasts shared their emphasis on the performance of the liturgy with their opponents, but they had nothing else to offer those for whom the liturgy had become impossibly grand and remote to satisfy every spiritual need. Iconophiles had more to offer. They thought that no officially sanctioned initiative is needed to bring something into the realm of the holy: the sacred can be freely encountered by everyone, because all that God has created is by nature sacred. Everyone can reach God through icons whenever they feel that God calls them.

That became both the salvation and the strength of icons through the years in which they were torn down in churches: the little wooden tablets could take refuge in the privacy of people's homes, and in this domestic space, it would often be mothers or grandmothers who exercised their customary power within the home to take the decision to save the image, and then impressed their love for this private source of divine power on their children. Equally, icons and their defence became associated with holy men who might owe little to the Church hierarchy and its compromises with the emperor's wishes: men who were ordinary yet extraordinary, who might wander from place to place, yet still claim the holiness of a monk or hermit. Monks and nuns who loved icons could ally with a movement rooted among laypeople to save images from the consequences of high clericalism and imperial policy.

To begin with, the campaign against imagery and icons probably did not amount to much, little more than a few token removals of prominent icons from imperial buildings and the application of a good deal of whitewash to mosaics. As Leo was succeeded by his equally iconophobic but much more theologically literate son Constantine V, further action was taken. One spectacular iconoclast-inspired church survives intact from Constantine's patronage in Constantinople, a rebuilding of Constantine I's Church of Hagia Eirene after an earthquake in the 740s – it was preserved later by the Ottoman invaders ignominiously as an armoury beside the Topkapi Palace, and its memorably cavernous space has more recently served as a concert hall. Here the semi-dome of the apse sheltering the altar is decorated with a huge and plain black mosaic cross on a gold mosaic background, instead of the usual panoply of mosaic figures (see Plate 34). This was a characteristic substitution in iconoclast art. The Cross meant a great deal to iconoclasts: it was a symbol not merely of Christ's death and resurrection, but of the conquest of the Churches in the East by Islam and the loss to Arab armies of Jerusalem together with Heraclius's painfully recovered True Cross (see pp. 253–4).[43] Crosses from this period still lurk in shadowy form under later figural mosaics in other churches besides Hagia Eirene.

The iconoclast emperors of the eighth century enjoyed a run of luck in their military campaigns, which must for the time being have vindicated their policies. They do seem to have been riding a widespread mood in Eastern Christianity, as is indicated by church mosaics excavated in what had now become Umayyad- and Abbasid-ruled Palestine. Some of these mosaics have been carefully altered to replace figured by non-figured designs. The dates of the original mosaics help to date the alterations to the decades beyond the second quarter of the eighth century – so the changes are contemporary with the iconoclastic campaigns of Leo's dynasty, but they are to be found beyond the Byzantine frontiers.[44] Equally, we know of a rather earlier iconoclastic movement beyond the north-east frontier of the empire in Armenia.[45] What is also clear is the high level of destruction; there are very few surviving icons in the Byzantine world dating before this period, the most notable collection being those preserved beyond the reach of the emperors at the monastery of St Catherine in Sinai.

However much popular support there was for iconophobia, the iconoclastic controversy badly damaged the empire. The policy caused deep offence in Rome, driving popes into increasingly close alliance with the Frankish monarchy (see p. 350). In the emperors' own dominions, it provoked much anger, bitterly dividing Byzantium during its continuing military emergencies. It is not surprising that monks were prominent in the iconophile opposition, because Constantine V was not merely a vigorously opinionated man, passionately fond of secular theatre and music, but he was also contemptuous of the monastic way of life. He took measures to restrict monasticism and executed a number of iconophile monks; one was whipped to death in Constantinople's Hippodrome.[46] His reward for this was his bad press in Byzantine historiography, despite his military achievements and the fact that he did much to rebuild Constantinople after a sequence of natural disasters.

Far away in St Sabas's monastery in Palestine, beyond the imperial frontiers, the greatly respected John of Damascus (see pp. 263–4), after a lifetime contemplating and criticizing Islam at close quarters, saw the developing conflict as a familiar struggle. If Muslims despised the veneration of the Cross, he asked in his dialogue with a straw-man Muslim opponent, how did they justify the veneration of a black stone in the Ka'aba?[47] John proved one of the most damaging propagandists against iconoclasm: he was among the acutest minds of his day, a philosopher formidable enough to stir intense admiration much later in Thomas Aquinas. Aquinas frequently quoted from John, claiming to have read a few pages from his works every day of his adult life, and he followed the Arab Christian divine in his discussion of images, as in so much else.[48] John was the last Eastern theologian to have a continuous impact on Western Christian thinking until modern times.

John was famed in the centuries that followed the triumph of his defence of images not merely as a theologian and preacher, but as a poet, and it was as a poet that he treasured images of all sorts, verbal and visual. They illuminate and intensify our vision of God, and indeed in relation to God they are essential, because of the ultimately unknowable quality of God. We can only know him through his activities, and through the created things which result from his energy: they provide the images by which we can take a sideways glance at the divine. So John not only defended icons as justified in the face of the Old Testament prohibitions, which he said applied only to the period before Christ, but he vigorously promoted their positive value. He followed in the tradition of Maximus the Confessor in seeing Chalcedon's balance between the human and the divine in Christ as showing how the divine could interpenetrate the created: 'The divine nature remains the same; the flesh created in time is quickened by a reason-endowed soul. Because of this I salute all remaining matter with reverence, because God has filled it with His grace and power.'[49]

John was the first champion of icons to set out another of those careful

Greek distinctions about words, rather as four centuries previously Basil the Great and the Cappadocian Fathers had worked out how to set up an acceptable vocabulary for the Trinity (see pp. 217–18). In this case, he separated a usage between absolute and relative worship. *Latreia*, worship as adoration, is appropriate only when offered to God; the veneration appropriate to God's creations is *proskynēsis*, which is that offered for instance to the emperor in Constantinople. Such created things 'are truly called gods, not by nature, but by adoption, just as red-hot iron is called fiery, not by its nature, but because it participates in the action of the fire'. It was *proskynēsis* which the worshipper at home or in church offered to an icon.[50] Long before this, that same Cappadocian Father, the Great Basil, had observed of an image of the emperor that the honour done to the image passes to the prototype: in the same way, the honour and prayers offered to the image of a saint could pass beyond it to the saint, and hence to God, the Creator of all things and Saviour of the saints in Heaven.[51] Behind John's distinction of words there lurked a workmanlike grasp of Aristotle's discussion of categories and causes, which he bequeathed to later defenders of icons. Naturally a created human being would have a different relationship to the first cause of all things than she or he would to other objects of creation which were capable of secondary causation – such as the emperor. If one accepted this vocabulary and Aristotelian framework, then devotion to visual images in Christianity was safe.[52]

Constantine V might nevertheless have carried the day and set patterns for his successor had it not been for the intervention of the Empress Irene, widow of his son Leo IV. Irene became regent for her son Constantine VI on Leo's death in 780. There was a long tradition in Byzantine history of imperial women intervening in political decisions which became theological decisions, even before Pulcheria, who had so shaped the Council of Chalcedon (see pp. 226–7), and Irene was not the last. Now she took the initiative in convening a council to authorize images once more. Her motives for switching imperial policy so drastically are impenetrable. Later, when the twenty-six-year-old Emperor Constantine showed signs of wishing to exercise real power, she ordered him to be blinded in the same palace chamber where she had given birth to him, leaving her free to become the first sole-ruling empress in Byzantine history. This does not suggest a contemplative spirit any more than it reveals a strong maternal instinct. Irene was determined to assert her will against the establishment in Church and Palace; after a first set of meetings had been taken over by iconoclast bishops and sympathetic troops, she followed the example of Constantine the Great nearly five centuries before and in 787 called the bishops together at the more easily controlled venue of Nicaea. The Patriarch – actually a hastily consecrated layman chosen for his hostility to iconoclasm – presided, but his proceedings were scrutinized closely by the Empress regent and her teenage (as yet unblinded) son. The council made official the distinction already set out by John of Damascus between *latreia* and *proskynēsis*.

It might have been supposed that this reaffirmation of images would have gratified the outraged Church authorities in the West – and indeed Pope Hadrian I gave an enthusiastic reception to the Acts of the second Council of Nicaea. This was one of the last occasions when a pope would thus hail the work of a patriarch in Constantinople, but in politics there were other realities to consider. In Francia, Charlemagne was shaping an empire for the West, based on his Frankish monarchy, and after his coronation, in 800, the relationship of this newly minted emperor with the holders of the ancient imperial title in the East was fraught (see pp. 349–50). Charlemagne's hostility to the imperial power in the East was sharpened by a disastrous Latin mistranslation of one part of the council's Acts: one of the bishops of the Church in Cyprus was represented as saying that he gave the same veneration to images as to the Trinity, when he had in fact been following the iconophile party line and said precisely the opposite. Charlemagne was impelled to condemn the theology of the East which promoted images, and he authorized theological statements which minimized the value of images; they have been known in history as the 'Caroline Books' (*Libri Carolini*). A council of Frankish bishops at Frankfurt am Main in 794 followed up their message with trenchant criticism of what it took to be Eastern misuse of images.[53]

This was a curious moment in the history of the Western Church. The iconophobic mood in Carolingian circles undoubtedly had a political dimension, which is for instance revealed when the *Libri Carolini* sneered at the presumption which had led Eastern emperors to commission images of themselves, subsequently attracting veneration: this was another good reason to claim that the Byzantines had forfeited their claim to imperial honour.[54] But there was a more profound unease in Western circles about images. A number of theologians with a background in Spain reacted to their closeness to the Islamic frontier in the same way as iconoclasts in the East, drawing the conclusion from Muslim success that God disapproved of images. One of them, Theodulf,

whom Charlemagne made Bishop of Orléans after the Council of Frankfurt, is now reckoned to be the author of the *Libri Carolini*.

Theodulf also became abbot of the powerful monastery at Fleury on
the Loire (see p. 354). Nearby there still stands the oratory which he
built for himself in his episcopal palace, and which is now the parish
church of a little village called Germigny-des-Prés. The golden mosaic
of the sanctuary apse semi-dome, revealed when plaster fell off it in the
nineteenth century, is an extraordinary treasure from Theodulf's time.
The style transports the viewer to Byzantium, but the theme does not –
not, at least, to anything which now survives in the Byzantine world. At
the centre is the hand of God – no superstitious representation of his
face – flanked by twin angels, who point to twin cherubs beneath them
covering the Ark of the Covenant with their wings; an inscription around
the apse exhorts the viewer to look on the Ark and pray for Theodulf.
There is a corresponding passage of biblical commentary on the Ark in
the *Libri Carolini*. Amid the tranquillity of the Loire valley, we are
unexpectedly pulled into the bitter theological debates between East and
West in the time of Charlemagne. We are viewing iconoclast art.[55]

The iconophobic mood soon passed in the West, because the later
Carolingians became alarmed at the extreme versions which their
patronage had encouraged. Particularly vehement was another Spaniard,
called Claudius, an energetic and widely read if not especially profound
or elegant biblical commentator. Charlemagne's son Louis 'the Pious'
made him bishop of the important Italian city of Turin around 816,
considering that his views might be useful for diplomatic negotiations
with the Eastern Emperor Leo V, who was now once more promoting
iconophobic policies. Claudius had little reverence for the papacy; he
frequently attacked all images of the human form, pilgrimages and relics
and the whole cult of the saints, and even veneration of the Cross, the
symbol which still meant so much to the Eastern iconoclasts – he actually
destroyed crosses in the churches of his diocese. In a sneer of portman-
teau offensiveness, he characterized pilgrims as 'ignorant sort of people
who in order to obtain eternal life, want to go straight to Rome, and
esteem any spiritual understanding of less account'. Despite condemnation by the Pope and censure by a synod of Frankish bishops, he died
unabashed and in possession of his diocese, still protected by his patron
the Frankish Emperor Louis, but a volume of hostile comment on his
works continued to swell, and he was increasingly seen as a heretic,
although his commentaries went on being read. Even in his lifetime,
Claudius recognized that he was going against the popular mood in his

diocese: pilgrimages and shrines were going to survive his biliousness, and the Frankish rulers would not stand against the tide.[56]

The medieval Western Church became as fixated on visual images as Easterners, and given its alternative numbering of the Ten Commandments, it had no inhibitions about continuing to develop a vigorous tradition of figural sculpture. Statues rather than icons became the centre of Latin Western devotion, particularly in cults of Our Lady (see pp. 394–5). Moreover, Westerners improved on the terminology of Nicaea, while still recognizing that subtleties could be expressed so much more neatly in Greek than in Latin: they replaced *proskynēsis* with another Greek word for veneration, *dulia*. By the thirteenth century, the growth of devotion to Mary, the Mother of God, in both East and West led John of Damascus's admirer Thomas Aquinas to formalize a further refinement: the concept of an exceptional sort of veneration, *hyperdulia*, offered to the greatest of God's creations, Mary, the mother of Jesus. It was only in the sixteenth century that Protestants who hated images rediscovered Claudius of Turin, the Council of Frankfurt and the *Libri Carolini*, and gleefully resurrected them to demonstrate that Protestantism was saying nothing new. The first printed edition of the Frankish bishop's *Libri Carolini* was published in 1549 by another reform-minded French bishop, Jean du Tillet; he was a friend of John Calvin, and Calvin was quick to exploit the sensational find. Roman Catholics lamely protested that Calvinists had made it up.[57]

The conclusions of Nicaea II therefore remained contested, partly because Empress Irene's rule proved controversial and in most respects unsuccessful, ending in her deposition and exile – her blinding of her son was certainly one element in her unpopularity, but her proposed marriage to Charlemagne (see pp. 349–50) seems to have been the last straw. From 813, the iconoclastic struggle resumed with even greater ferocity, after Emperor Leo V declared war on images and once more pulled down a key icon from the Great Palace.[58] The fury of the iconophile party revealed that the Church's reverence for the emperor remained conditional, even in Constantinople. Theodore the Stoudite (then abbot of the monastery of Stoudios, and a major reformer of monastic life) was emerging as the chief champion of icons, and he had no compunction in telling Leo 'Your responsibility, Emperor, is with affairs of state and military matters. Give your mind to these and leave the Church to its pastors and teachers.'[59] Theodore and a network of monks kept in touch with each other even after the Stoudite had been packed off into exile; they were confident of support from the Pope in the West, who remained determinedly cold to the Emperor's conciliatory overtures. Meanwhile, iconoclasm proved no more capable of delivering military success than the armies of Empress Irene. A particularly bitter blow came in 838 with the fall to Muslim armies of the major frontier city of Amorion in Asia Minor. The loss was long remembered in Byzantine folklore and song, and one cannot help thinking that this was partly thanks to its association with the last iconoclast emperor, Theophilos.

It was Theophilos's empress, Theodora, who finally reversed the iconoclastic policy, from motives which, like those of Irene, are now permanently obscured by grateful Orthodox hagiographers. Once Theophilos was dead, Theodora as regent ordered the Patriarch Methodios to restore the icons to the churches. The occasion of this restoration, the first Sunday in Lent, 11 March 843, is commemorated as one of the most significant feasts of the Eastern Church, the 'Triumph of Orthodoxy'. On that day icons are paraded around Orthodox churches with particular ceremony, and a document enshrining the ninth-century decision and composed about that time is solemnly read out. This *Synodicon* theatrically includes a list of the chief personalities who could be seen as the defenders of icons, each followed by the acclamation 'eternal memory!' The Empress, worried about the reputation of her son, made sure that the parallel list of those condemned in the *Synodikon* did not include his father, her husband, Theophilos, and that broad hint prevented any campaign of revenge attacks on iconoclasts, who continued to argue their case throughout the later ninth century, but never again enjoyed official patronage.

The two iconophile empresses had effectively closed down the possibility of alternative forms of worship in the Orthodox tradition. They made veneration of icons a compulsory part of it, an essential badge of Orthodox identity (see Plate 33). They and their supporters not merely pronounced on a question of aesthetic preference, but also transformed the nature of the art which the Eastern Church produced. The special nature of Orthodox icons was emphasized by the growth of a notion, much encouraged by these bitter disputes, that there was one quite exceptional class of art: *acheiropoieta*, images of Jesus not made by human hands, the archetype of which was the now-mysterious *Mandylion* given by Christ himself to King Abgar of Edessa (see pp. 180–81) – the developed form of the *Mandylion* legend probably dates from the years of iconoclastic controversy. Such objects certainly defeated the iconoclast argument that icons had not received a specific blessing by the Church: a specifically divine creation trumped any such cavils.[60]

One modern commentator crisply sums up what had happened during the iconoclast controversy: 'In the course of almost 180 years of debate, Greek theologians produced a radical change in the language with which they framed the icon. In so doing, they raised the status of the work of art to that of theology and the status of the artists to that of the theologian.'[61] Art had become not a means of individual human creative expression, but an acclamation of the corporate experience of the Church. It was something to be approached with meditation and an acute sense of tradition. A technical change furthered this. The earliest icons, for instance, two majestic sixth-century portraits of Christ and St Peter preserved in St Catherine's monastery on Mount Sinai – from one point of view, fine examples of late Roman naturalistic art – are executed in encaustic fashion, paint employing hot wax. By its nature, this technique encourages speed, an almost impressionistic technique, before the wax becomes unworkable, and in these works naturalism is an ally of individualistic talent. Quick decisions, boldness are at a premium. Later icons are executed in tempera, the mixing of colours in egg white. The technique encourages tiny strokes, meticulously applied with care and thought: a highly appropriate medium for meditation and careful attention to detail. The artist in tempera could rely on increasingly formal conventions for representation of the holy, turning all his individual skill to illuminate an increasingly elaborate set of conventions which carried choreographed theological messages.

Not all monks had opposed the destruction of images, but the leading figures in campaigning for their restoration apart from the empresses had been monks like Theodore the Stoudite. They were also energetic in placing the restoration in a wider context: the renewal and enriching of worship and its music in Constantinople. It was done just at the time when the Carolingians and their bishops were greatly enriching the liturgy of Francia, but with a different reference point, Rome. In a parallel fashion, Byzantium looked eastwards: the ninth-century renewal of the city's liturgical tradition drew inspiration from a source beyond itself, in Jerusalem. Now that the city was in the hands of Muslims, there was a natural desire to preserve its spiritual tradition from possible extinction, as the iconoclasts' devotion to the Cross had demonstrated. Many Palestinian monks found that, at the end of the eighth century, Muslim rule was becoming a good deal more burdensome than in the past and they moved inside the empire to practise their faith. Theodore was an admirer of Palestinian monk-saints like St Sabas, and the Stoudite monastery became a laboratory for experiments with the ceremonies and texts of the worship from the monasteries of Palestine. Soon the liturgies used by monasteries, lovingly commented on in treatises by a sequence of monks from the time of Maximus the Confessor onwards, merged with the liturgy of the Great Church of Hagia Sophia to create a liturgy for the whole Church.[62]

What the Palestinian monasteries offered the Church of Constantinople was a tradition of music and hymnody which has remained at the heart of Byzantine liturgy; it was also in Palestine that the eight musical modes were developed. They were not only now used in Constantinople, but were soon adopted by the Carolingians and the Western Church as a whole to organize its musical composition and chant, and so they stand at the origin of the whole Western musical tradition.[63] Previously the music of churches in Constantinople had been dominated by the set sung narrative sermon in verse known as the *kontakion*, a dialogue between chanter and choir or congregation who sing a refrain. Now only one *kontakion* is customarily sung in full, in praise of the Virgin on the fifth Saturday in Lent, known as the *Akathistos* ('unseated'), since it is given the particular honour of being the one part of the liturgy for which all must stand. The other *kontakia* which still appear in the liturgy are much abbreviated. The liturgical form of hymn which replaced the *kontakion* was the *canon*, a set of nine hymns. These sets of hymns originated in Palestinian monasteries as meditations on themes from the Bible which were performed in the liturgy; the nine climaxed in an ode to the *Theotokos*.

The canon is only one element making Orthodox liturgy a constant refraction of scriptural texts, a web of interpretations and elaborations, especially in the non-eucharistic liturgical offices in the morning and the evening. To quote fragments gives only a taste of the effect: here are two *kontakia* from the Divine Liturgy of St John Chrysostom, the first from the Sunday of the Prodigal Son, appropriately penitential in mood as the weeks approach Lent, the second sung during the days of festival in high summer commemorating the moment when Christ's Transfiguration revealed his face full of divine light, and he conversed with Moses and Elijah:[64]

I have foolishly run away, O Father, from your glory; I have squandered in evil deeds the riches you entrusted to me; therefore I offer you the words of the Prodigal: I have sinned before you, compassionate Father: take me now repentant and make me as one of your hired servants.

You were transfigured on the mountain, and your Disciples beheld your glory, O Christ God, as far as they were able; that when they saw you crucified they might know that your suffering was voluntary, and might proclaim to the world that you are truly the brightness of the Father.[65]

So the worshipping congregation which hears the first chant joins the Prodigal of Christ's parable in penitence (Luke 15.11–32). The worshippers in a different season stand besides the awed disciples on Mount Tabor, reassured that even those privileged first followers could only see Christ's divinity in part; they also look forward through the year from this moment of glory to the next commemoration of the Saviour's earthly death, which he had predicted for them on the high mountain. This slow liturgical dance through scripture means that, for better or worse, the Orthodox approach the Bible and its meaning with much less inclination to separate out the activity of biblical scholarship from meditation and the everyday practice of worship than is the case in the Western tradition.

The ninth-century 'Triumph of Orthodoxy' should not obscure the fact that a very different strand of Christianity persisted both in the empire and to the east in the Armenian lands. These dissenters were opposed far more radically to the official hierarchy than were the iconophile monks, nuns and layfolk to the iconoclast bishops. They were dualist in belief, like gnostics and Manichees, although it is difficult to see any direct links with the earlier dualism. It seems that like Marcion (see pp. 125–7), from their own reading of the Christian New Testament and Paul in particular, they built up their theologies of a deep gulf between flesh and spirit. As we have seen, there were actually Marcionites surviving far to the east of the Byzantine Empire at this period, but the new dualism looks independent of them too, and is first to be found in late-seventh-century Armenia. Their enemies gave them the contemptuous name Paulicians, possibly from an early founder, but it is also noticeable that their admiration for the Apostle Paul was strong enough for them to follow Marcion's example and cut down the canon of the New Testament by dropping the two epistles attributed to Peter. This was apparently because they were infuriated at the feline statement in II Peter 3.16 that in the epistles of Paul 'there are some things . . . hard to understand'.[66]

Logically in view of their belief that matter was created by evil, the Paulicians despised fleshly aspects of imperial religion such as the cult of Mary or of a physical ceremony of baptism. Naturally they were also iconophobes – unlike the Byzantine iconoclasts, they extended their hatred to the Cross itself – and like the iconoclasts, they seem to have attracted soldiers to their beliefs. Iconoclastic emperors such as

Constantine V saw no problem not merely in tolerating Paulicians but in recruiting them for military service. Even iconophile emperors recognized their worth as soldiers and later employed them on Byzantium's Balkan frontiers, thus unwittingly spreading their message westwards. By the ninth century, the group was dangerous enough to the imperial Church to provoke the Archbishop of Bulgaria into commissioning a refutation of their teachings, which did not prevent the development in tenth-century Bulgaria of a further dualist sect, much more ascetic in character, known from the name of their ninth-century founder as Bogomils (Bogomil means 'beloved of God' in Slavonic, and so in Greek would have been 'Theophilos'). The Bogomils rapidly spread through the empire, and it was a Bogomil, Basil, who around 1098 was one of the very few known victims of burning for heresy in Byzantium – maybe the last.[67] There was a grim symmetry to Basil's burning, both because burnings for heresy intensified in the West just when they were disappearing in the East, and also because the Bogomils seem to have been the inspiration for the similarly ascetic Cathars of the western Mediterranean, who during the thirteenth century, in the Albigensian Crusade, became the victims of one of the Latin Church's most ruthless ever persecutions (see p. 388).

This was an unexpected export for what had supposedly become such a monolithic Orthodox culture in Byzantium. The Bogomils have a modern legacy in the Balkans, apart from the now discredited supposition that a haunting collection of enigmatic intricately carved monolithic gravestones concentrated in Bosnia-Herzegovina are legacies of their culture. Although there are no reliable references to Bogomils in Bosnia after the thirteenth century, in 1990s Oxford I met a Bosnian refugee who claimed to be one, and such a consciousness among Bosnians reflects the part which the much-reconstructed memory of the Bogomils played in the ethnic conflicts which so appallingly wounded Bosnia in that decade (see pp. 1004–5). Amid the various claims to ethnic priority in the region was that of Bosnian Muslims who, if they were descended from Bogomils, could counter Orthodox or Catholic assertions that they were incomers imported by the Ottomans. Besides, Bosnians might take pride in the memory of an independent Church which had Bogomilism behind it, regardless of whether or not they were now Muslim. All sides were inclined to use the scanty and contested history of the Bogomils to further their various and incompatible arguments.[68]

PHOTIOS AND NEW MISSIONS TO THE WEST (850–900)

The extension of this story of religious dissidence into the Balkans opens up another dimension of ninth-century Byzantium which proved crucial in the formation of Orthodox identity: a sudden expansion of mission west into central Europe, both into areas which had formerly been Christian in the Roman Empire and into new territories beyond the old imperial frontiers. The development was the result both of a new vigour in the Byzantine Empire after years of struggle and of the vision of one man, Photios, who took charge as Patriarch at a time of continuing crisis. In the wake of the iconophile victory of 843, the bitterly divided Church desperately needed strong leadership, and it was not going to be provided by the compromised Patriarch Methodios, who lasted only four years before being deposed. His successor, Ignatios, did not look much more promising: a castrated imperial prince who was Empress Theodora's puppet nominee, and was accordingly dismissed when she was ousted from power in 856.[69]

In Ignatios's place, Photios came as a more obviously qualified choice. He was the son of a wealthy layman who had died in exile in wretched circumstances because of his iconophile commitment, and the great-nephew of the patriarch who had presided at the iconophile second Council of Nicaea; but besides the resonance provided by his family history, he was one of the most gifted and creative men ever to occupy the patriarchal throne. Photios was responsible for a literary work without parallel in the ancient world, a summary review of around four hundred works of Christian and pre-Christian literature which he had read in his first three decades of literate life – a feat of reading itself probably un-paralleled at the time.[70] Indeed, Photios's exceptional learning aroused suspicions among monks who accused him of being a closet pagan – it was claimed that he recited secular poetry under his breath during the liturgy. They also found it difficult to believe that a priest who, albeit celibate, was not a monk had any right to rule the Church, and their hostility combined with the anger of the former Patriarch, Ignatios, who proved to have remarkable staying power as a rival for the patriarchal throne.

These allied malices twice conspired to bring about Photios's deposition as patriarch, first in 867 in favour of a restored Ignatios, and finally in 886, after which his various enemies did their best to make sure that his historical record would look discreditable. The Eastern Church nevertheless eventually decided that he should be celebrated as a saint (adroitly linking his name in liturgical acclamations with that of his eunuch rival), and there is good reason for such an expression of gratitude.[71] Photios's periods of patriarchal power coincided fruitfully with the coming of a succession of capable emperors who did much to restore the fortunes of the empire after two hundred years of miseries. They founded a dynasty which lasted for almost two centuries, the first to be so long sustained in the history of the entire Roman Empire, and known as Macedonians, from the birthplace of Basil, the first of the line. He was a courtier-soldier of relatively humble Armenian descent who schemed and murdered his way to the throne in 867, and who already in 863 had been responsible for a crushing victory over the Arabs. Emperor Basil I and his successors patiently brought relative stability and even expansion beyond their frontiers, and notably they turned their main attention west rather than east, even though they also ably blocked further Islamic encroachments on the empire. Their revival of Byzantine fortunes paralleled the imperial Church's moves to expand the bounds of Orthodox religious practice, Photios's lasting legacy. Orthodoxy owes its present cultural extent to his initiatives, which partly account for the dismal reputation that this patriarch long enjoyed in the Christian West.

Photios had not long been patriarch when the papal throne was taken by Nicholas I, whom we have met encouraging an imaginative re-writing of the past in order to assert the special authority of Rome (see pp. 351–2). Pope Nicholas was only too ready to make trouble for the incumbent patriarch by listening to the complaints of ex-Patriarch Ignatios. Photios's deep scholarship did not extend to any knowledge of Latin, and to a degree unusual among previous patriarchs, he was out of sympathy with the Western Church. There were good reasons for tension between the two outsize egos now presiding over the Church in Rome and Constantinople: at stake was the future Christian alignment of a vast swathe of southern central Europe in the Balkans and along the Adriatic coast (Illyricum and Great Moravia), an area long lost to the empire. Through it ran the ancient division between East and West first made by the Emperor Diocletian at the end of the third century (see p. 196). At a time when Frankish Latin Christianity was extending itself in northern and central Europe (see p. 349), the Byzantines were spurred to take a new interest in spreading their version of the faith as well as looking to extend their territories; there could be no better way of dealing with troublesome people on their frontiers such as the Bulgars than to convert them to Byzantine faith.

During the 850s and 860s a momentous event took place showing the possibilities and dangers of alternative conversions; it must have stimulated the imperial Church's moves beyond the frontiers. The entire people of a powerful and strategically important kingdom to the north-east of the Black Sea, the Khazars, were led by their khan to convert to Judaism, and no amount of persuasion by some of Photios's ablest advocates of Christianity could change the Khan's mind – maybe he remembered that, a century before, a Khazar princess had become the wife of the iconoclast Emperor Constantine V, and Byzantium's turn to iconophilia appealed less than Judaism's consistent ban on images. The Court language of the Khazars remained Hebrew and their mass conver-sion became one of the most significant (though often overlooked) moments in Jewish history.[72] Beyond political considerations, mission was a matter in which Photios took a passionate and personal interest. He is generally now reckoned to have written the preface of a new law code (*Epanagōge* or 'Proclamation') issued by Emperor Basil I, which, in the course of its discussion of the relationship between imperial and ecclesiastical power in the empire, proclaimed that it was the duty of the patriarch to win over all unbelievers as well as to promote orthodoxy in belief.[73] Photios took advantage of Byzantine military success on the eastern frontiers to make repeated overtures to the estranged Miaphysite Church in Armenia, and it was not his fault that nothing ultimately came of his careful diplomacy and the remarkable degree of goodwill which he managed to engender.[74]

Photius's relationship with Rome was much less conciliatory – indeed, one element in his overtures to the Armenians was to seek support in his conflicts with the Pope. Pope Nicholas was very ready to intervene on the Byzantine frontier, and various rulers in the region were not slow to exploit the resultant possibilities of playing off the Christians of West and East against each other. Chief among them was the deviously talented Khan Boris of the Bulgars (reigned 853–89), whose first move was to seek an alliance with his Frankish western neighbour King Louis the German, with an eye to threatening both the Byzantines and another people on Bulgarian frontiers, the Moravians. The Byzantines could not tolerate such an alliance, and with the aid of a large army, they ensured that in 863 the Khan accepted Christian baptism at the hands of Byzantine rather than Latin clergy and took the baptismal name of the Byzantine Emperor Michael himself.[75] Boris nevertheless continued to indulge in diplomatic bargaining with the bishops of Old and New Rome over the future jurisdiction of his new Bulgarian Church, producing a poisonous atmosphere which resurrected various long-standing issues of contention, such as the increasing Western use of the *Filioque* clause in the Nicene creed. Photios's furious comments on this matter have been described as 'a delayed-action bomb' in the simmering confrontation which culminated in the excommunication of 1054 (see p. 374), anticipated in 867 when Photios and Nicholas personally excommunicated each other over the Bulgarian question.[76] Once more Eastern and Western Churches were in schism.

The issue was not resolved when Nicholas died that same year, but soon Rome found itself desperate for help from the Byzantine emperor amid attacks by Islamic forces in southern Italy. The result was that two successive councils, meeting in Constantinople in 869 and 879, followed Khan Boris-Michael's eventual inclination to put himself and his Bulgarian Church under Byzantine patronage; he was encouraged by terms which suited him, granting him an archbishop of his own, over whom he could in practice exercise everyday control. The second council was a particular triumph for Photios, who was now restored to the patriarchate after the death of his rival and temporary supplanter, Ignatios. Bathing in the approval of the Emperor for all his work in extending the jurisdiction of the Church of Constantinople, Photios was acclaimed by the council as Oecumenical Patriarch, parallel in authority to the pope. This did not increase Rome's enthusiasm for the resolution of difficulties by decisions in councils, but the two councils had sealed the permanent extension of Christianity into one of the Balkans' most powerful and long-lasting monarchies.

Another success for Photios's missionary strategy developed among the Slavic peoples of Great Moravia, whose ruler Rastislav (or Rostislav, reigned 846–70) had the same sorts of ambitions and diplomatic skills as Boris of Bulgaria. The results were as momentous as they were complicated, and they continue to provoke controversy and tussles between Eastern and Western Christians over who owns their history. Modern-day Moravia is firmly within the Roman Catholic cultural sphere, like its neighbours in Austria, Bohemia, Croatia and Slovakia, and it is understandable that in the delicate state of central European relations over recent decades arguments have been made that Rastislav's 'Great Moravian' domains extended much further into south-eastern Europe, in lands which now have a primarily Orthodox tradition. The agents of the conversion were from Byzantium, two brothers born in

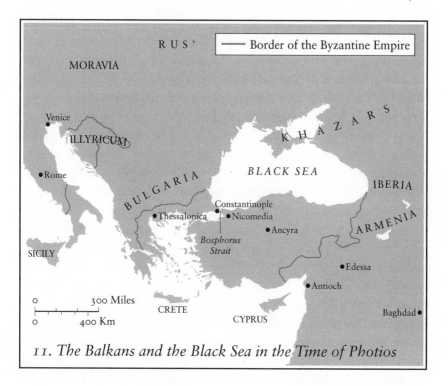

RUS'

MORAVIA

——— Border of the Byzantine Empire

Venice

ILLYRICUM

KHAZARS

Rome

BLACK SEA

IBERIA

BULGARIA

Constantinople

Thessalonica   Nicomedia

Ancyra

ARMENIA

Bosphorus
Strait

SICILY

Edessa

Antioch

0   300 Miles

0   400 Km

CRETE

CYPRUS

Baghdad

11. The Balkans and the Black Sea in the Time of Photios

the second most important city of the empire, Thessalonica (Thessaloniki), the port on the Aegean Sea. Growing up there, Constantine and Methodios would have known many Slavs, and Constantine in particular showed exceptional interest and ability in languages; he had been a student of Photios in the years before the scholar became patriarch, and Photios did not forget his talent.[77] The Patriarch used the brothers on that embassy to the Khan of the Khazars which sought to turn the Khan away from Judaism, but their lack of success did not prevent Photios launching them on a fresh expedition when Prince Rastislav asked for Byzantines to counter the influence of Frankish clergy operating in his territories.[78]

The evidence suggests that even before Rastislav's request, the brothers had embarked on an enterprise of great significance for the future: they devised an alphabet in which Slav language usage could be accurately conveyed. It was given the name Glagolitic, from an Old Slav word for 'sound' or 'verb'. Constantine and Methodios did more than create a method of writing, because they also put a great deal of thought into creating an abstract vocabulary out of Greek words which could be used to express the concepts which lie behind Christianity. The

Glagolitic alphabetic system is to say the least idiosyncratic, with only surreal resemblances to any other alphabetic form in existence, and when Bulgarians were looking for a way of writing their own version of Slavonic, it was an unappealing choice. They would be more familiar than the Moravians were with surviving antique inscriptions from the imperial past of their region, written in Greek. So it was probably in Bulgaria that, not long after the time of the two missionary brothers, another scholar devised a simpler alphabetic system, much more closely modelled on the uncial forms of the Greek alphabet.[79] It was named Cyrillic, in honour of Constantine, but in reference to the monastic name he adopted right at the end of his life, Cyril. That was an adroit piece of homage, which apart from the graceful tribute it embodied no doubt eased the new alphabet's acceptance in place of the holy pioneer's less user-friendly script.

Glagolitic did have a long-term survival, but mainly in relation to Slavonic liturgical texts. It was also adopted alongside Cyrillic for the Bulgarian liturgy by Khan Boris-Michael, who is likely to have seen the value of these innovative alphabets and the vernacular literature which they embodied as a way of keeping a convenient distance from both the Franks and also his eventual patrons in the Church of Constantinople. Both alphabets were specifically intended to promote the Christian faith. They and the Christianized Slavonic language which they represented were to be used not simply to produce translations of the Bible and of theologians from the earlier centuries of the Church, but with a much more innovative and controversial purpose. They made it possible to create a liturgy in the Slavonic language, translating it from the Greek rite of St John Chrysostom with which the brothers Constantine and Methodios were familiar. This was a direct challenge to the Frankish priests working in Moravia, who were leading their congregations in worship as they would do in their own territories, in Latin.

Although there was clearly East–West confrontation in the Moravian mission, there was a significant contrast with the Bulgarian situation, thanks to the diplomatic abilities of Constantine and Methodios. They were not themselves priests, and they deliberately set out to integrate their mission (albeit on their own terms) with the Church in Rome, seeking ordination for some of their followers from the Pope. While journeying to Rome, they attempted in Venice to defend their construction of a vernacular Slavonic liturgy, in a debate of which a rather partisan version survives in the Life of Constantine. Opponents objected that there were 'only three tongues worthy of praising God in the

Scriptures, Hebrew, Greek and Latin', on the grounds that these were the three languages affixed to Christ's cross. 'Falls not God's rain upon all equally? And shines not the sun also upon all?' retorted Constantine.[80]

Constantine's reception in Rome was much eased because he brought Pope Hadrian II a gift of fragments from the skeleton of Clement, one of the earliest of Hadrian's papal predecessors. With great foresight, Constantine had uncovered this lucky find during his otherwise unsuccessful time among the Khazars in the Black Sea region. Modern historians might spoil Constantine's pleasure by pointing out that the story of Pope Clement's exile to the Black Sea was actually a fifth-century confusion with the fate of another St Clement who probably really did die in the Black Sea region, but at the time Pope Hadrian was duly impressed and charmed into providing the necessary ordinations. A turning point in Church history was thus dependent on some wishful thinking and some misidentified bones.[81] Constantine spent his last months as the monk Cyril in Rome and when he died, in 869, he was buried appropriately in the already ancient Church of San Clemente – while equally appropriately and graciously, the last fragment of his body, otherwise destroyed during the Napoleonic occupation of Italy, was in the twentieth century given by Pope Paul VI for housing in a specially built Orthodox church in the saint's home city, Thessalonica or Thessaloniki.

Cyril's visit to Rome was a moment which suggested a more generous future for a Church in central Europe, leaving behind the ill-will between Nicholas and Photios. Pope Hadrian had his reasons for favouring three-way diplomacy, for he was aware that Frankish rulers had their own agendas which might not include all that much consideration for the interests of the papacy. He made Methodios his legate in central Europe, and even authorized the use of Slavonic vernacular in the liturgy, although he did ask that the scripture lessons should be read over first in Latin. The atmosphere of reconciliation did not last. Frankish rivals to Methodios's clergy were not forgiving and they forced the Byzantine missionaries eastwards until they took refuge in Bulgaria. From the Church's Bulgarian centre in Ohrid (now in the Former Yugoslav Republic of Macedonia), missionaries travelled west once more to reinforce Orthodox missions in a newly emerging kingdom, Serbia, and they took their grievances against Latin Westerners with them. Further west than Serbia, the Orthodox presence in the region between the Alps and the Carpathian mountains gradually weakened, although it was in Hungary that one crucial piece of cultural transmission took place, when the writings of John of Damascus were translated from Greek into Latin, spreading their influence permanently into the Western Church, and to Thomas Aquinas in particular (see p. 447).[82] In the long struggle between Orthodox and Catholic in central Europe, the line of cultural differentiation between Catholic Croats and Orthodox Serbs, which has so recently poisoned their relationship despite their common language, has ended up as not so different from that division of the empire originally set by Diocletian.

The great contribution to the Orthodox future from Cyril and Methodios (and, behind them, their patron Photios) was to establish the principle that the Greek language did not have a monopoly on Orthodox liturgy. So, from the late ninth century, Churches of Orthodoxy have diversified through a remarkable variety of language families and the cultures which those languages have shaped; in fact it is the Church's liturgy which has been the major force in deciding which languages should dominate cultures in various parts of the Orthodox world. Not all of these cultures are Slavonic: one of the largest Orthodox Churches has come to be that of Romania, which, as its name implies and the forms of its language make clear, cherishes a Latin past. It is not surprising that across such a tangle of different peoples and societies, Orthodox Churches have shown a considerable relish for quarrels over jurisdiction and consequent separations or schisms.

Yet that tangled history does not render totally absurd Orthodoxy's pride in its uniformity of doctrine. Schism is not the same as heresy. The doctrinal disagreements and affirmations from the time of Justinian to the Triumph of Orthodoxy have (partly by dint of a good deal of selective writing of Church history) produced a profound sense of common identity across cultures. They are bound together by the memory of the worship in the Great Church in Constantinople, by a common heritage in the theology of such exponents of *theosis* as Maximus the Confessor, and by the final crushing of iconoclasm in 843. As we have noted, that common heritage goes so far as to provide the worshipping congregation with corporate ways of ceremonially denouncing Christians who do not accept it: the ninth century, the era of the Triumph of Orthodoxy, was probably the time at which the Orthodox hymns of hate first entered the performance of the liturgy.[83] There is here a significant contrast with the Latin West. The sixteenth-century Reformation in the Western Church destroyed not merely the universality of Latin liturgy, a universality of language which did not exist in the East, and which indeed may have contributed to the frustrations behind the Reformation. It also ruptured the broad theological consensus in Western Christianity. By the time of that sixteenth-century explosion of dissent, the Byzantine Empire had perished, partly because of the inept and often malicious intervention of Western Latin Christians, which helped to destroy the institution so notably revived in the time of Photios and the Macedonian emperors.

14

Orthodoxy: More Than an Empire
(900–1700)

CRISES AND CRUSADERS (900–1200)

Around the millennium, Constantinople was the biggest city in the world that Europeans knew, with around 600,000 inhabitants. It surpassed Islam's greatest city, Baghdad, and dwarfed the Latin West's best attempts at urban life such as Rome or Venice, which at best might each muster a tenth of such numbers.[1] The scale of the area comprehended by the ancient and medieval walls still has the power to astonish as one walks across it: in societies which were overwhelmingly rural, the first experience of 'the City' must have been like a moon landing. The Byzantine Empire was strong and well defended; the emperor was the guarantor of an imperial gold coinage which astonishingly had remained the same in weight and fineness since the time of Constantine the Great, and which was the only gold currency then known in Europe – its name both in Greek and Latin spoke of strength and reliability, *nomisma* ('established'), *solidus* ('immovable'). In Western European heraldry, this coin survives symbolized by a golden disc, and in the macaronic Norman-French language of heralds, it is termed a 'bezant'.

The Macedonian emperors, who had been in power since 867, were very ready to employ mercenary soldiers who brought new tactics in warfare and helped Byzantium claw back territories long lost, as far east as Cyprus and Antioch of Syria. The Church of Constantinople was likewise expanding and self-confident. In the 960s and 970s the Macedonian dynasty won another great military success on the western front, annexing Bulgaria and for two centuries putting an end to the independence of its archbishop along with its monarchy. The Byzantine victory also brought defeat and death for Sviatoslav, the ruler of a pagan monarchy far to the north in Kiev, who had his own designs on Bulgaria. Through the conversion to Christianity of Sviatoslav's son Vladimir in 988, Orthodox Christianity was established in another new region, with momentous consequences for its future (see Chapter 15). In the far west, the Byzantines still controlled southern Italy, although 962 saw them lose their last stronghold in Sicily to Muslim rule. The self-confidence and practicality of the Macedonian emperors allowed them to make allies of people whom Chalcedonian Christians thought of as heretics: as they pushed eastwards into territories much depopulated in Cilicia and Armenia, they peopled them with Miaphysite Christian settlers and were happy to see them establish their own bishoprics, not subject to the patriarch in Constantinople. Leading Byzantine churchmen were furious at this move, unprecedented in imperial Christianity, but it was a useful balance for Muslims living on the frontiers, and it was a way of giving the deviant newcomers a good reason to invest in the future security of Byzantine rule.[2]

The recovery of nerve in society was nevertheless expressed in a vigorous affirmation of the institutions which had contributed to the Triumph of Orthodoxy and which now permanently shaped Byzantine religion. There was great attention to recording the ceremonial used at Court and in church. The definitive account of the formal life of the Byzantine Court was written as a guide for his heir by an exceptionally learned and reflective emperor, Constantine VII (reigned 945–59). He was known as *Porphyrogennētos* – 'born into the Purple' – to emphasize his legitimate imperial birth and status after his father's theologically controversial fourth marriage, and it was probably the contentious nature of his birth which made him give such attention to the proper order for formal ceremonies. By now Court ceremonial could not be separated from that of the Church, since all Church festivals of any significance needed the imperial presence, in procession, in the liturgy and afterwards as principal guest in a formal feast with the patriarch. Nearly all the earliest surviving manuscripts of the Byzantine liturgy date from the tenth century, even though they are copying much earlier texts: clearly there was an intense urge now to establish norms behind all these new texts.[3] At the end of the tenth century, the Emperor Basil II sponsored Symeon Metaphrastes ('the Translator') to lead a team of scholars in compiling a monthly catalogue or *Menologion* of saints' lives, which kept a peculiar authority among later compilations of saints, and around the same time an enthusiast for Constantinople's past collected all sorts of older materials to weld into an antiquarian guide to the city's monuments and treasures.[4]

The assertion of uniform values within the Orthodox Church and the new wealth in the tenth and eleventh centuries also led to a great investment in the institutions which had defended (or invented) the tradition so successfully in the years of conflict: the monasteries. Naturally much of this investment went into ancient well-established foundations, many of which were in the capital or in great cities, but as a result, the restlessness of the monastic spirit led to inspirational holy men moving out to find new wildernesses. This was a great age of colonization of 'holy mountains', the chief active survivor of which is the monastic republic of Mount Athos, a peninsula thrusting into the Aegean Sea in Greek Macedonia. Although a few hermits had been attracted to the Athonite peninsula's wild grandeur and isolation in earlier centuries, the Great Lavra, the most important among its monastic communities, was founded in 963, and after Greek-speaking communities had multiplied, other language groups from Eastern Churches also founded monasteries here. Subsequent historical shifts of fortune have propelled the Holy Mountain into one of the most important resources of Orthodoxy worldwide, now enjoying autonomy within the Republic of Greece. It is the only the state in the world with an entirely male population, including any animal or bird within human control.

The tensions within a period of success and expansion in monastic life were exemplified in the career and writings of Symeon (949–1022). He was known as 'the New Theologian' maybe originally sarcastically, but soon the nickname ranged him alongside the evangelist John and the fourth-century Gregory of Nazianzus. Coming from a background at the imperial Court, Symeon was twenty-eight when he entered the Stoudite monastery in the capital, but he was expelled as a misfit, for not obediently conforming to the monastic rule and for showing too great an attachment to a senior monk (eccentric enough to be considered a Holy Fool by some modern commentators), Symeon the Pious. When the younger Symeon moved to St Mamas's monastery outside Constantinople, his strong personality had a more positive effect and within a few years he had become abbot. After a quarter of a century his continuing ostentatious devotion to Symeon the Pious (he had set up an icon of his spiritual father, with a commemoration of his death date) and the very personal character of much of his preaching were too much for the Church hierarchy; his icons of Symeon were destroyed and he was exiled for the rest of his life.

Symeon's turbulent emotional career led him to deploy the traditional Orthodox themes of light and *theosis* in writing with a rare candour about his own spiritual experience, negative as well as positive; John Climacus's ancient emphasis on the tears of spiritual experience (see p. 438) gained a new intensity in his writings. Symeon's conflicts with the Church authorities led him to some radical thoughts. He emphasized the tradition of his day that monks who were not ordained could offer forgiveness to penitents, as part of a wider theme that 'ordination by men' was not the same as appointment by God through the Holy Spirit – not a comfortable theme for the Church hierarchy. Symeon was contemptuous of ordered scholarship in comparison with personal spiritual experience, singing that the Holy Spirit is sent

> . . . Not to lovers of glory,
> Not to rhetoricians, not to philosophers,
> Not to those who have studied Hellenistic writings . . .
> Not to those who speak eloquently and with refinement . . .
> But to the poor in spirit and life,
> To the pure in heart and body,
> Who speak and even more live simply.[5]

It is not surprising that such potentially disruptive notions, sitting very uneasily with obedience to properly constituted authority, long met with suspicion and censorship. Symeon's teaching was later to become a catalyst for major arguments about the nature of the monastic tradition in the fourteenth-century Hesychast controversy (see pp. 487–91). Yet Symeon the New Theologian's reputation as one of the most profound of Orthodox writers has now reached beyond a tradition of monastic admirers.

The reign of the Emperor Basil II, later famed as 'the Bulgar-slayer' for his conquest of Bulgaria, ended after nearly half a century in 1025. A highly capable and energetic ruler who can be given the chief credit for the conversion of the Principality of Kiev to Christianity (see pp. 506–8), he seemed to have left the empire more secure than ever, but there was one fatal problem: he never married, and he failed to produce an heir who might guarantee the long stability which his predecessors in the Macedonian dynasty had created. For more than half a century, the empire was once more disrupted by contention for supreme power, and the lack of firm leadership spread insecurity into provinces only recently annexed, especially in the Balkans. It was a momentous sign of weakness when, in the 1040s, the gold *nomisma* coin was debased for the first time in seven centuries.[6]

The international situation demanded a strong emperor in the mould of Basil, because in both West and East new powers fixed their eyes on the wealth and sophistication of Byzantium. Acquisitive-minded Latins, especially the Norman monarchy in Sicily and the Italian merchant-states of Venice and Genoa, were particularly concerned to extend their influence in the eastern Mediterranean trade routes. The Pope was fostering a crusader ideal which was increasingly looking eastwards for its fulfilment (see pp. 382–3). To the east, a new coalition of Muslim tribes under the leadership of a family of Turks called the Seljuks first overwhelmed the Muslim rulers of Baghdad and then swept into the eastern provinces of the Byzantine Empire; their Seljuk ruler took the title of *Sultan*, the Arabic for 'power'.

The most decisive battle in the Byzantine confrontation with the Seljuk Turks was at Manzikert in Asia Minor in 1071, at which the reigning Emperor Romanus was not only crushingly defeated, but suffered the humiliation of being taken prisoner. Even though he was treated graciously and released on the payment of a large ransom, there were major consequences. Asia Minor was increasingly undermined by Seljuk raids, and more and more territory passed out of Byzantine control. Most of the holy mountains which had become so important within Byzantine monasticism suffered badly in these invasions, with monks fleeing or being enslaved, and now Mount Athos, far away in secure Macedonia, was left gradually to emerge as the most significant among them. In 1081 the most successful of the imperial generals, Alexios Komnenos, seized power and established his dynasty on the throne, fighting on all fronts to save the empire from disintegration. As emperor, Alexios found that neither his family nor his army could be fully trusted in his struggles, and it may have been this insecurity which made him look beyond his frontiers for allies.[7] He repeatedly appealed to Western leaders for help against various enemies, and in 1095 for the first time he was given a serious hearing. It was this request which led Urban II to launch the publicity campaign which triggered the First Crusade (see pp. 383–4).

The Crusades proved a long-term disaster for the empire, despite the competence of Alexios and his Komnenian successors, who did their best to restore the fortunes of the Byzantine imperial machine during the twelfth century. If the gradual drifting apart of East and West had led to mutual incomprehension and hostility, their newly intimate contact frequently made relations even more tense. Even during the success of the First Crusade, the arrival of large armies from the West in Byzantine territory was alarming and disruptive, while Latins rapidly began fomenting a self-justifying tale back home that the Byzantines were treacherously sabotaging their own heroic efforts. That mutual ill-will strengthened as the Second Crusade from 1147 to 1149 failed to achieve its objectives in Palestine and Damascus. The whole miserable expedition was characterized by acute suspicion between Latins and Greeks and major indiscipline among crusader armies, whose remnants struggled back from the Holy Land to Western Europe taking their resentments with them. Some might have noted the contrast between this fiasco and Portuguese Christians' simultaneous capture of Lisbon from the Muslims with the help of another group of crusaders, operating as far from the Byzantines as it was possible to be in southern Europe. The worse the Latins behaved – and there was much worse to come – the more they peddled the notion that Byzantines were devious, effeminate and corrupt, and really deserved any unpleasantness that was done to them.

Problems ranged beyond the activities of the crusaders themselves. The growing claims of the papacy to universal monarchy were offensive not merely to the Oecumenical Patriarch, but to any Eastern churchman, since the East had remained closer to the older idea of the collective authority of bishops throughout the Church. With considerable justification, Easterners saw Westerners as innovators, while Latin diplomats raked up previous bombastic claims to authority from Rome all the way back to Pope Hormisdas in the sixth century (see p. 326). When a delegation of Greeks to the Holy Roman Emperor broke their journey at the Abbey of Monte Cassino in 1137, they observed to the monks that the Bishop of Rome behaved more like an emperor than a bishop.[8] At about the same time that the Western canon lawyer Gratian was compiling a law code which looked to the pope as the Universal Bishop, the greatest canon lawyer of the Eastern Empire, Balsamon (supplanted in his see of Antioch by a patriarch who owed allegiance to Rome after appointment by Latin crusaders), wrote bitterly about Western Christians in his own law compilation. He expanded words from Psalm 55: 'Their words are smoother than oil, Satan having hardened their hearts'.[9]

One symptom of the growing insecurity in the empire which went right back to the death of Basil II in 1025 was a new-found intolerance of any dissidence to the imperial Church. This contrasted with the more pragmatic attitude of the Macedonian imperial dynasty during the ninth century, but it was also a logical development of the urge to define and catalogue which had also characterized Orthodoxy under Macedonian rule. The first symptom of the new mood was a fatal weakening of the imperial policy of tolerance for Miaphysites in the eastern frontier provinces after Basil's death; when the new emperor abruptly ended tolerance in 1028 and did not restore it, the long-term consequences for the frontiers under Seljuk pressure were dire. We have already encountered the burning of the Bogomil Basil in the Hippodrome around the time of the First Crusade (see p. 456), and in the same era there occurred trials for heresy in Constantinople involving leading scholars of literature and theology, Michael Psellos and his student John the Italian (Italos). Psellos in the end escaped serious consequences, but Italos was not so fortunate; after repeated hearings of the case against him, from 1082 he was silenced and ended his days obscurely in a monastery.

There were political dimensions to the trials of Italos, since he was associated with the faction opposed to the Komnenos family's usurpation of the throne, and the collapse of Byzantine power in southern Italy rendered suspect his Italian background and links to the Normans in Sicily: the Emperor Alexios's daughter Anna Komnena, passionate partisan for her father and gifted historian of his reign, wrote scornfully of Italos's inept use of Greek. But there were more long-term issues at stake. Psellos and Italos were keenly interested in using Classical texts, particularly Plato, to illuminate Christianity. That aroused the same sort of fears which had dogged the Patriarch Photios in his enthusiasm for pre-Christian literature and philosophy (see p. 457). This same mood had surfaced in the anti-intellectualism of Symeon the New Theologian. How far could philosophy be of use to Christians?

The confrontation persisted. It claimed a fresh victim in a pupil of Italos, the theologian Eustratios, Metropolitan Bishop of Nicaea, who wrote commentaries on works of Aristotle. Eustratios had taken care to disassociate himself from the views of Italos, and the Emperor Alexios had specifically commissioned him because of his scholarship to prepare arguments against the Miaphysite theology of Armenian subjects of the empire. Yet the very fact that Eustratios used Classical dialectic in the manner of Aristotle to construct his case aroused hostility from his fellow clergy and, after a trial in 1117, the Emperor had him suspended from office. Interest in Plato and Aristotle did not die away in Constantinople, and the Komnenian age was notable for the diversity and variety of its literature – but as far as mainstream theology was concerned, a great contrast developed with the Latin West. On the eve of Western Europe's rediscovery of Aristotelian dialectic in scholasticism's creative exploitation of Classical learning (see pp. 398–9), the Byzantine authorities were turning away from the same intellectual resources. That mood intensified in some quarters of the Church to cause further disruption in the fourteenth century.[10]

The recurrent Byzantine pattern of centralized recovery followed by disintegration began another cycle with the death in 1180 of the great-nephew of Alexios, Manuel I Komnenos, after nearly four decades on the throne. Over the next half-century, the sequence of attempted seizures of power, rebellions and conspiracies came at a rate of around two a year.[11] The chaos provided an obvious opportunity for the Balkan and central European provinces of the empire to rebel and break away. Once more Bulgaria became an independent kingdom, Serbia also established itself as a monarchy under the long-lived Grand Župan (Prince) Stefan Nemanja (reigned 1166–96), while the King of Hungary overran the westernmost territories of the empire. Even so, most of the various self-promoted rulers in the Balkans continued to look to Constantinople for cultural models to dignify their regimes, giving out titles and offices which reflected the pattern of the Byzantine Court. When an independent Bulgarian patriarchate was established in the early thirteenth century in T'rnovo, then the capital of the Bulgarian kingdom, the city began being called the 'Third Rome' after Old and New Rome. It was a title which much later in the sixteenth century was to be revived for a Church in a new Orthodox world whose centre lay far to the north.[12] By that time, the Second Rome had fallen to the Ottoman Sultan. The roots of its fall lay in the disaster of the Fourth Crusade.

THE FOURTH CRUSADE AND ITS AFTERMATH (1204–1300)

Behind the course of the Fourth Crusade lay the ambitions of Venice for expansion in the eastern Mediterranean. The Venetians had been particularly energetic in securing trading privileges from the Byzantines. Eighty years before, they had provided a foretaste of future miseries in a crusading campaign of 1122–4 which centred on the capture of Muslim-held Tyre, but which also encompassed a great deal of raiding, mayhem and robbery in Byzantine territories around the Aegean, designed to force the Emperor into extending the concessions which they had already won. From Tyre they bore back in triumph to Venice a piece of marble on which Christ had once sat, and from Byzantine Chios the bones of St Isidore; their expedition ended with duly solemn praise of God in the *Te Deum*.[13] Now, in 1201, there were plans for a new crusade: a consortium of Western European crusaders struck an ambitious deal with Venice to build them a fleet and transport them to attack Cairo. It was a reasonable proposition if they wanted to knock out Islam's chief power and proceed to Jerusalem, and if there were no military operations in Palestine itself, the agreement would respect a truce of 1198 with the Ayyubid ruler in Damascus. However, those involved disastrously miscalculated: they could not hold fellow crusaders to the agreement for the fleet, and not enough people turned up to fill the horrifically expensive array of ships.

The Venetians were not going to lose their investment. They forced the crusaders uncomfortably camping out on the Lido to fulfil their bargain in a way that would suit Venetian interests. This involved an expedition not against Muslim Cairo, but against the great Christian power of Byzantium. The crusaders had already in their company a (not very impressive) young claimant to the Byzantine imperial throne, Alexios Angelos, and so the new scheme had a ghastly plausibility.[14] Pope Innocent III, originally an enthusiastic supporter of the enterprise, felt increasingly helpless at the march of events, partly thanks to the independent actions of his agent with the crusader armies, Cardinal Peter Capuano. Innocent watched horrified as in 1202 the crusaders wrecked the Adriatic city of Zara, which was actually under the over-lordship of a fellow crusader, the King of Hungary, but which had made the mistake of annoying the Venetians. Much worse followed: attacks on Constantinople in 1203 and 1204, horrible deaths in quick succession for a series of Byzantine emperors, including the little-regarded Alexios, the trashing of the Christian world's wealthiest and most cultured city – in short, countless incentives for centuries of Orthodox fury against Catholics.

With no very convincing Byzantine candidate for the throne left alive in the devastated city, the way lay open for an audacious new plan: the installation of Baldwin, Count of Flanders, a Latin Westerner, as Byzantine emperor, the distribution of large expanses of Byzantine terri-tories to crusader lords, and the formal union of the Church of Constan-tinople with the Church of Rome. Any notion of the armies moving east to win back the Latin Kingdom of Jerusalem its capital city was quietly forgotten. Innocent was now caught between his pleasure at the fulfil-ment of the ancient ambition of Rome to secure Church reunion on his own terms and profound misgivings about how this had been achieved. He had initially rejoiced that the capture of the city was an obvious prelude to the end of the world and the coming of Christ in glory, and even quoted at length from the apocalyptic writings of Joachim of Fiore to express his excitement, but he quickly changed his tune. 'By that from which we appeared to have profited up to now we are impoverished; and by that from which we believed we were above all else made the greater, we are reduced', he now lamented to Peter Capuano.[15] He was less than pleased that alongside the newly minted Latin Emperor Baldwin, the Venetians had elected fifteen canons as a Cathedral Chapter for Hagia Sophia without any reference to himself; the canons had in turn elected a Venetian as Patriarch of Constantinople.[16]

Even so, Innocent was not inclined to advocate the return of the city to heretical Greeks. His attitude to them was made plain in the fourth decree of his tame council called to the Lateran in 1215, 'On the pride of Greeks towards Latins': hardly the most apologetic of phrases after the mayhem visited on the city.[17] Drab practicalities began to occupy the Pope, notably the problem of looted relics – not so much the question of the ethics of looting them, as to how to authenticate them once they had arrived in Western Europe. Decree 62 of Innocent's Lateran Council forbade sales and ordered (completely ineffectively) that all newly appearing relics should be authenticated by the Vatican.[18] This flood of relics westwards affected all Europe. Far away from Byzantium on the north Norfolk coast, the priory of Bromholm found an end to its financial headaches when it installed the slightly ironically named 'Good Rood of Bromholm', a fragment of the True Cross filched from the emperor's private chapel in Constantinople, and a welcome stream of revenue from pilgrims followed.[19] This was small beer compared with the coup of the enthusiastic crusader King Louis IX of France, who (ignoring the orders of the fourth Lateran Council) bought from the Venetian pawnbroker of the hard-up Latin Emperor of Byzantium the actual Crown of Thorns worn by Christ at the Crucifixion. This was a major acquisition to equal the sacred relics accumulated by Louis's Merovingian predecessors, confirming that his Capetian dynasty had inherited all their anciently earned divine favour and sanctification – and what could be more appropriate for a saintly king (canonized as early as 1297) than possession of a crown more holy than his own? As display cabinet for the crown, Louis built the Sainte-Chapelle in the royal palace complex at the centre of Paris. The fury of the French Revolution spared enough that we can still marvel at its thrillingly soaring (though now empty) space and its exuberance in sculpture and glass.[20] Once the Latins had been expelled from Constantinople in 1261, duplicates of many of these purloined relics began to appear back in their original homes in the city and the Byzantines declared the restorations to be a series of miracles.[21]

The greater miracle was more gradual: a painstaking reconstruction of Byzantine society, but in a new and unprecedented mould. While the hated Latins still held 'the City', Byzantine leaders would have to rule from other cities of the shattered empire. Far away to the north-east on the Black Sea, members of the Komnenos family took over Trebizond, founding an 'empire' which continued to be independent (initially under Mongol protection against the Seljuks), even beyond the Ottoman capture of Constantinople, until 1461. At the other extreme of the pre-1204 empire, a nobleman related to the old imperial families set up a principality in the region of Epiros on the western Greek coast, but among all these new statelets, the city of Nicaea in the mountains of Asia Minor inland from the Sea of Marmara became the capital of what was the most convincingly imperial of the successor states. It enjoyed the very considerable advantage that a successor Greek Oecumenical Patriarch was installed there, alongside the imperial prince, whom he duly anointed as emperor.

It was eventually the rulers in Nicaea who recaptured Constantinople from the Latins in 1261. Successive popes loudly agitated for aid in restoring the deposed Latin emperor, but they had many other concerns, and the artificial construct of Latin Byzantium had few friends in the West: the Nicaean emperor actually drew on support from Venice's bitter commercial rival Genoa in recapturing the city.[22] A darkly intriguing find in modern Istanbul symbolizes the dead end of the Latin Empire of Byzantium. In 1967 a little chapel was discovered in excavating the lower layers of one of Istanbul's former monastic churches, now the mosque of Kalenderhane Camii. Its interior was filled with earth and its entrance blocked and plastered over with paintings; inside, on its walls were Western-style frescoes of the life of St Francis of Assisi, in fact the earliest now known, complete with the story of Francis preaching to the birds. Evidently when Franciscan friars fled the city, never to return, the chapel with its homage to a very newly minted Western saint was comprehensively consigned to oblivion.[23]

One can understand the depth of the feelings which went into that act if we consider the arrogance with which the Greek Church had been treated in some of the new Latin enclaves. In the Latin Kingdom of Cyprus, the suppression of Greek Church organization and general harassment of Greeks who used their traditional liturgy reached a nadir in 1231, when thirteen Greek monks were burned at the stake as heretics for upholding their traditional rejection of the Western use of unleavened bread in the Eucharist, and thus casting doubt on the validity of Latin Eucharists. The fact that this outrage took place during the breakdown of royal Cypriot authority in a civil war among the Latins hardly excuses it, and one can understand why a synod of the Oecumenical Patriarch defiantly denied validity to the Latin Eucharist two years later.[24] And it was during the thirteenth century that yet another issue was added to the sense of theological alienation between Greeks and Latins: the Western Church's elaboration of the doctrine of Purgatory (see pp. 369–70). When friars began expounding this doctrine in various theological disputations in the East, the Greeks with whom they were arguing correctly recognized the origins of the doctrine in the theology of Origen, and that was enough to make Latin talk of Purgatory seem a dangerous reversion to his heretical universalism.[25]

Even though Constantinople was restored to Byzantine control in 1261, the empire's political unity, that fundamental fact of Byzantine society from Constantine the Great onwards, never again became a reality. Trebizond and Epiros continued in independence; many of the Latin lords clung in their new enclaves in Greece, and the Venetians were only finally dislodged from the last of their eastern Mediterranean acquisitions, Crete, in 1669. An emperor was back in his palace in Constantinople, but few could forget that for all Michael Palaeologos's evident talent as military leader, ruler and diplomat, he had supplanted, blinded and imprisoned his young ward, John IV, in order to become emperor. After alienating many influential leaders in the Church and society by this act of cruelty, Michael VIII further infuriated a large number of his subjects by his steadfast pursuit of unity with the Western Latin Church, which he regarded not merely as a political necessity to consolidate imperial power, but as a divinely imposed duty. The hatred which his policy aroused pained and baffled him; the union of the Churches which his representatives carefully negotiated with the Pope and Western bishops at the Council of Lyons in 1274 was repudiated soon after his death.[26]

The balance of forces in Orthodox Christianity was never the same again after 1204. Orthodoxy beyond the Greeks could now fully emerge from the shadow of the empire which had once both created and constrained it. King Stefan *Prvovenčani* ('first-crowned') of the newly emerged state of Serbia first explored what privileges he might get from Innocent III, but he was deeply offended when the Pope changed his

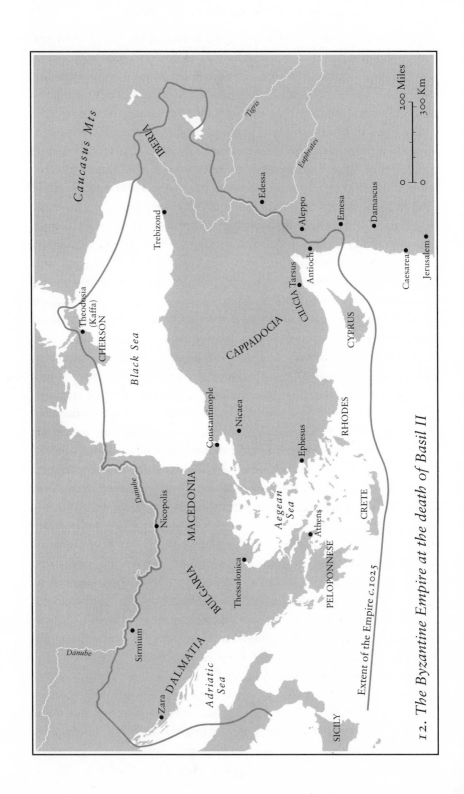

12. *The Byzantine Empire at the death of Basil II*

mind about granting him royal insignia. Although both Bulgaria and Serbia did eventually receive crowns from the papacy during the thirteenth century, the momentum of Orthodox practice was too strong to pull them back for long into the orbit of Latin Christianity. Both the newly consolidating Serbian monarchy and the Bulgarian monarchs (who were now calling themselves *tsars*, emperors) found it convenient to look to the patriarch in Nicaea for recognition of their respective Churches as autocephalous (self-governing). Mount Athos was a major influence in their turn towards Orthodoxy, and in Serbia the memory of one charismatic Athonite member of the princely family, Stefan Prvovenčani's brother Sava, was decisive. As a young man, Sava renounced his life at Court to become a monk on Mount Athos, where he was joined by his father, the former Grand Prince Stefan Nemanja. Together they refounded the derelict monastery of Chilandar (Hilander) on the mountain, and then Sava returned to organize religious life in a Byzantine mould in Serbia, becoming in 1219 the first archbishop of an autocephalous Church of Serbia.

Although Sava and his father might be seen as having renounced worldly ambition in turning to the monastic life, their status as churchmen had a vital political effect on their country. The monastery of Chilandar became an external focus for the unity of the Serbian state and a symbol of its links with the Orthodox East. The monarchy did not merely adopt Byzantine trappings of power but ostentatiously rooted out Bogomil heresy from its dominions – while around 1200 for the first time it also encouraged the use of the Serbian language in the inscriptions of Byzantine-style church paintings. Chilandar became the centre during the fourteenth and fifteenth centuries for a major enterprise of translating Greek theological and spiritual writings into a formal literary vernacular which would be generally comprehensible to the varied peoples who spoke Slavonic languages. Above all, Sava's immense spiritual prestige gave a continuing sacred quality to the Serbian royal dynasty amid the poisonous divisions of Serbian power politics. His memory became so much part of Serb identity that when the conquering Ottoman Turks wanted to humiliate and cow the Serbs in 1595, they dug up Sava's bones in Belgrade and publicly burned them.[27]

13. *The Byzantine Empire reunited under Michael Palaeologos*

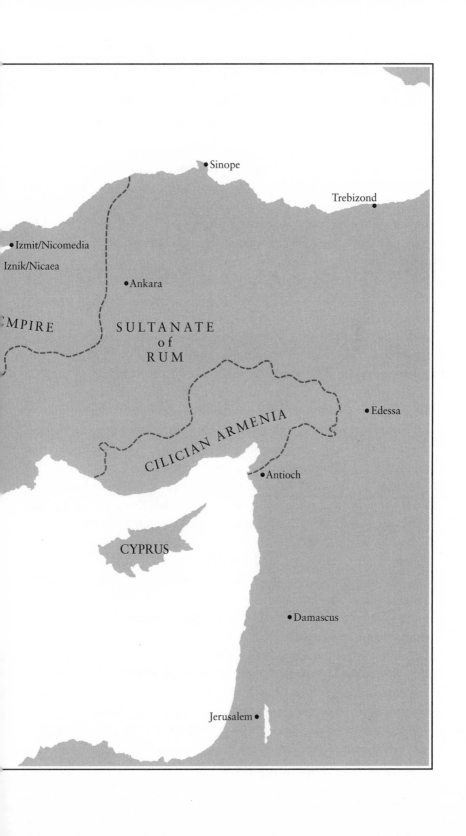

ORTHODOX RENAISSANCE, OTTOMANS AND HESYCHASM TRIUMPHANT (1300–1400)

This complex of stories after 1204 amounts to a reconfiguration of Orthodoxy. Certainly the emperors restored to Byzantium in 1261 kept an immense prestige despite their increasing powerlessness, right down to their dismal last years in the fifteenth century. Paradoxically, this was especially so among Melchite (that is, 'imperial') Christians living under Islamic rule and thus beyond Constantinople's control: for them, the emperor was a symbol of an overarching timeless authority, as they believed that God had greater plans for his creation than seemed possible in the present situation.[28] Nevertheless, Orthodox identity was no longer so closely tied to the survival of a political empire, and it was increasingly a matter for the Church to sustain. The Oecumenical Patriarch had been responsible for lending the princely claimant from Nicaea enough legitimacy to claim the imperial throne; that same patriarch had been the source of sacred guarantee for the new ecclesiastical independence of Bulgaria and Serbia, and the patriarch continued to provide his seal of approval to new Christian dioceses expanding far to the north of the imperial borders along the Volga, around the Black Sea and in the Caucasus. By the end of the fourteenth century, Patriarch Philotheos could write to the princes of Russia in terms which would have made Pope Innocent III blanch, although it is unlikely that his words came to the ears of anyone in Rome: 'Since God has appointed Our Humility as leader of all Christians found anywhere on the inhabited earth, as solicitor and guardian of their souls, all of them depend on me, the father and teacher of them all.'[29]

This was a strange reversal of fortunes for patriarch and emperor. The patriarch was bolstered by financial support from rulers beyond the old imperial frontiers who were impressed at least by the resonance of such claims. The magnificence and busy activity of the patriarchal household and the Great Church in Constantinople looked a good deal less threadbare than the increasingly curtailed ceremonial and financial embarrassment of the imperial Court next door.[30] Churches were lavishly redecorated or rebuilt, and they were hospitable to an adventurous renaissance in Byzantine art. Some of the most moving survivals are to be found in the church of Istanbul's Church of the Holy Redeemer in Chora, an exquisite monastic building lovingly restored from ruin after the expulsion of the Latins in 1261. Now its mosaics are exposed once more after their oblivion in the church's days as a mosque. Most are from the fourteenth century, and they bring a new quest to explore their subjects as human beings of passion and compassion; even Christ and his mother are softened from the imperial figures of earlier Byzantine convention (see Plate 22). We glimpse at the Holy Redeemer in Chora how Byzantine artists might have continued to explore some of the directions which an artistic and cultural renaissance began to take in Latin Europe in the same era, if the politics of the eastern Mediterranean had not curtailed the urge or the opportunity to consider new possibilities for Orthodox culture.

Over the early fourteenth century, the empire briefly revived after 1261 descended into renewed civil war and loss of territory, both in the west to the expansionist Orthodox monarchy in Serbia and in the east to a new branch of Turkish tribes who had carved out for themselves a principality in north-west Asia Minor and who survived a determined effort by the Byzantines to dislodge them in a significant victory in 1301. Their warlord leader was called Osman, and they took their name of Ottomans from him. During the fourteenth century, the Ottomans extended their power through Asia Minor and the Balkans, overwhelming the Bulgarians and encircling Byzantine territory. More and more Orthodox Christians found themselves under Islamic rule, and in an atmosphere of increasing intolerance for their religion, which might be seen as part of a general cultural mood in fourteenth-century Asia, North Africa and Europe (see pp. 275–8). Already in the 1330s, the shift to Islamic dominance seemed so irreversible that the Patriarch of Constantinople issued informal advice to Christians in Asia Minor that it would not necessarily imperil their salvation if they did not openly profess their faith.[31]

As before in Byzantine history, when secular administration decayed, monasteries flourished. Mount Athos, now the most prominent survivor of the holy mountains, remained independent of Ottoman rule until as late as 1423, assiduously cultivating the Muslim authorities which had by then encircled it for more than half a century. It is significant that, when given the choice in 1423, the Athonian monks preferred the Muslim overlordship of the sultan to a chance which they were offered of rule by the Venetians: the thought of Latin overlordship by the conquerors of 1204 was repulsive to them.[32] By then, the emperor had long been only one patron-monarch among many for the Athonian monasteries. Sava's foundation on Mount Athos had been one indication that already in the twelfth century it was becoming a focus for multiple Orthodox identities beyond its Greek origins. A proliferation of divinely sanctioned rulers were drawing their legitimacy from their Orthodox Churches, as far away as the Principality of Kiev and the rulers in Muscovy.

It was in this age that one of the most familiar features of the Orthodox church interior arrived at its developed form: the *iconostasis*, a wall-like barrier veiling altar and sanctuary area from worshippers. The word means 'stand for images', because now the barrier is covered in pictures of saints and sacred subjects, in patterns which have become fixed in order and positioning. Customarily the wall does not reach the ceiling, so that the sound of the clergy's liturgical chanting at the altar can clearly be heard above it and through its set of doors. It took a long time for the iconostasis to achieve its modern form. Both in East and West in the first centuries of church-building, there were low partitions inside churches to mark off the sanctuary area around the altar, and the different ways in which these partitions were developed is instructive. Western Latin churches developed their own taller screens to separate off the entire area containing clergy and liturgical singers (the 'choir' or 'chancel', plus the sanctuary area), and this was also a late development, encouraged by the intensification of eucharistic devotion in the thirteenth century. But the screens in Latin churches were generally open above waist-height to afford views of the high altar; they rarely presented themselves as solid walls in the Eastern manner, except in monastic or cathedral churches where clergy were carrying out their own round of liturgy in an enclosed space inside the church building. Universally, these new Western screens were associated with and carried above them carved figures of Christ hanging on the Cross or 'Rood', flanked by his grieving mother, Mary, and the new son whom Christ had assigned to her, John the Evangelist. Hence Western chancel screens are known as 'rood screens'.

The Orthodox development was entirely different, and it may be no coincidence that it happened in the same era, the thirteenth to fifteenth centuries, when Latin churches were completing the development of the rood screen. For Orthodox liturgy, the iconostasis encloses a set of actions rather than the whole area occupied by the clergy caste and assistants, although it does also mark a sanctuary area excluding lay-people without specific functions or permissions. It shelters and defines those liturgical actions only performed at the altar. When it first grew beyond the low barrier, it was known as a *templon*, and was enclosed only to waist-height, with open arcading above, so that the altar remained clearly visible to all at all times. What happened then was a gradual accretion of holy images which made a much more substantial solid screen. Some congregations concluded that it would be more reverent to veil the central parts of worship at the altar, and curtains filled the arcade spaces, to be pulled across at particular times. In other churches, icons were hung from the arcade, or against the curtains if they were now in place, and the screen now took on its character of an 'icon stand'.

Yet even if this might seem a visual barrier far more formidable than the average Western rood screen, it is quite the reverse to the eye of faith. Any representations of the sacred or of saints which appear in the decoration of a Western rood screen are incidental to the screen's character, below the figures of the rood group which crown it, Christ, Mary and John. Icons, by contrast, are of the essence of an iconostasis. Because each icon in its theologically appointed place reveals and refracts the vision of Heaven, the iconostasis becomes not so much a visual obstruction in the fashion of the Western rood screen, but is actually transparent, a gateway to Heaven, like the altar beyond it. It aids the spiritual eye to see something more real than that which it conceals from the human eye. Moreover, in developed form, the iconostasis is the culmination of a set of steps which symbolize the ascent of the soul towards heavenly joy. Those steps lead to a shallow platform before the iconostasis, on which much of the liturgy takes place, but it is also available for the congregation, excluded from physical entrance to the sanctuary, to venerate the icons of the iconostasis.

A gateway needs doors. The doors of the iconostasis are important: basic to the structure is a central entrance – the 'Beautiful Gates' – which, when open, affords the sight of the altar, and which is flanked by smaller doors – again, of course, all appropriately bearing their icons. Outside the time of worship, the doors are closed. Open or closed, they mark punctuation points in the liturgy which retains the processional quality so important in Byzantine worship from the earliest days of New Rome. The Beautiful Gates are principally reserved for the bishop, the side doors used liturgically by deacons (and therefore they often bear the images of sainted deacons such as the first martyr of the Christian faith, Stephen). Around the doors stand the other saints, prophets and festal scenes. These are dominated by images of Christ and his Mother, which may have their counterparts in different positions in the screen. The greatest development of the iconostasis and its structured decoration was to come in Russian Orthodoxy, but the overall concept and use were achieved in the empire before the fall of Constantinople.

It was a paradox of this age that despite all the wretchedness of the relationship between Latin and Greek Christianity in the wake of 1204, Latin and Orthodox cultures were now closer and more regularly in contact than they had been for half a millennium. Influences went in both directions, with Venice and its newly acquired colonies as one of the main conduits – literally in the case of a large number of art objects, which in Venice included not merely the famous four antique bronze horses stolen from Constantinople during the sack of the city, but a huge number of marble blocks and carvings which were shipped around the Greek coast and up the Adriatic to transform the exterior and interior of St Mark's Cathedral. Surprisingly in view of the distinctiveness of Orthodox worship, with its distinct liturgical models drawing on Eastern traditions attributed to St John Chrysostom, St Basil and St James, one of the greatest aspects of similarity remained in the liturgical chant which both Churches employed. In the charged atmosphere of the late twelfth or early thirteenth century, a Greek canon lawyer, John, Bishop of Kytros, could still say that the texts of chants and their melodies were common to East and West. In the next two centuries, Western musical innovations like polyphony could also be heard in Greek churches – indeed, Greek liturgical chant and Western plainsong probably did not sound especially different throughout the medieval period.[33] The real separation came with the trauma of the complete Ottoman conquest in 1453, when a great divergence in musical practice began. In particular, the Orthodox were never seized by the enthusiasm for the pipe organ which, in the era of Constantinople's fall, began its long dominance of the musical imagination of Western Christians.

Above all, in the realm of ideas, the two worlds spoke much more frequently to each other, albeit not always harmoniously. It was the first era in centuries in which Greeks began to read Latin texts, though there had always been a good deal more traffic in the other direction. One of the catalysts for exchange was the ultimately futile sequence of negotiations for reunion of the Churches which preoccupied thirteenth-century popes: one of the many papal friar-negotiators sent east, the Dominican William of Moerbecke, was highly important in extending Western knowledge of ancient scholarship because he collected Greek manuscripts and translated a variety of Greek authors, including Aristotle, into deliberately very literal Latin versions.[34] A few Easterners became interested in Western theologians whom the East had previously ignored, including the most prominent Westerner of them all, Augustine of Hippo. One Court protégé of Michael VIII Palaeologos, Manuel (monastic name Maximos) Planudes, translated Augustine's *De Trinitate* for the first time into Greek, and persisted with his efforts even when the Emperor's successor abandoned the policy of dialogue with the papacy. Naturally, that meant that he translated Augustine's views on *Filioque*, although in a puzzle which has not yet been resolved, he also wrote two treatises attacking the doctrine.[35]

The translation work of Planudes was not confined to theology; he ranged through Latin classics then completely forgotten in the East, such as Cicero, Boethius and even the less racy parts of Ovid's poetry. He was followed by a number of scholars who widened the range of texts on offer, including an extraordinary gamble in contemporary translation by brothers Prochoros and Demetrios Kydones: among their many other imaginative projects in the mid-fourteenth century, Demetrios undertook Greek versions of Aquinas's *Summa contra Gentiles* and *Summa Theologiae*. It was an acknowledgement unprecedented since the days of Justinian that other cultures could have major contributions to make to Byzantine society, but in many sections of the Church that was a deeply controversial and unacceptable idea.[36]

Amid the dismally deteriorating political situation in Constantinople, the Church was convulsed by a dispute about the validity of a style of mystical prayer known as Hesychasm. The principal combatants were Gregory Palamas, a monk of a community on Mount Athos who championed Hesychast spirituality, and Barlaam, an Orthodox monk from Calabria, the religious frontier land in Italy where Byzantine and Latin monasticism existed side by side. Hesychasm was only one of the issues which brought them into contention, but its results were the most far-reaching. The word 'Hesychasm' probably seems one of the more intimidating fragments of theological jargon to those first encountering it, but it simply comes from the Greek verb *hēsychazō*, 'to keep stillness' (or silence). Linked with the idea of stillness was the characteristic mystical idea of light as the vehicle of knowing God, or as a metaphor for the knowledge of God. Gregory Palamas maintained that in such practice of prayer, it is possible to reach a vision of divine light which reveals God's uncreated energy, which is the Holy Spirit. He pointed to the episode of transfiguration described in the Synoptic Gospels, where Jesus was with his disciples on Mount Tabor, and they could see that his face 'shone like the sun'.[37] The Transfiguration, already commemorated with greater elaboration in Orthodoxy than in the Latin West, therefore became a favourite Hesychast choice of subject for icons (see Plate 56).

Mystical themes have a habit of emerging in unpredictable circumstances as a counterpoint to various structured versions of Christian belief, so the Hesychast emphasis on silence and light is curiously reminiscent of a Christian movement remote in time and space from fourteenth-century Byzantium: the Quakerism which emerged in England during its seventeenth-century civil wars (see p. 653). The sharp contrast with the Quakers is in the way in which Hesychasm is rooted in specified devotional practices. Apart from contemplation of the icon, there are practical ways to structure still or silent prayer: appropriate physical posture and correct breathing are important, and one characteristic practice is to repeat a single devotional phrase, the most common of which came to be 'Lord Jesus Christ, Son of the living God, have mercy on me'. This phrase or variants on it became known as the 'Jesus Prayer'. Such set techniques are reminiscent of systematic Eastern approaches to prayer, from Buddhism to the Sūfīs of Islam, who themselves may have drawn on Indian spirituality. There may indeed be a direct relationship between the Hesychast approach and Sufism, though there remains controversy as to which way the influence travelled.[38]

Both the Hesychasts and their opponents appealed to the Orthodox past; in fact both were looking back to Maximus the Confessor, and beyond Maximus to that unknown writer who had borrowed the identity of Dionysius the Areopagite to lend respectability to his ideas (see p. 439). Barlaam wanted to defend his own understanding of monastic spirituality as being true to Orthodox tradition. For him, the assertions of Palamas ran counter to the apophatic insistence in Pseudo-Dionysius that God was unknowable in his essence. If so, it was foolish to suppose that, simply by concentrating in prayer, an individual could perceive something which was part of God's essence, the Holy Spirit itself. To expect to achieve this was to confuse creator and creation. There was a real risk that Hesychasts would forget all the dangers to which Maximus had pointed long before, allowing mystical experience to run out of control, and even wholly rejecting the control of reason in their search for God. Such excesses would jettison a tradition of purposeful meditation which ran back all the way to Evagrius of Pontus in the fourth century, and which Orthodox mystics had treasured ever since, even when the memory of Evagrius himself had been blackened.

Barlaam raised the name of various heresies, Bogimilism among them, and implied, not without some justification, that the Hesychasts were in danger of falling into the same excessive rigour and rejection of Christianity's setting in a fallen world. In retaliation, Palamas and his admirers said that Barlaam was a mere rationalist who was reducing any talk of God to the human capacity to grasp only what God was not. Palamas sneered at Barlaam's assertion that the great theologians of the early Church had used 'light' as a metaphor for knowledge and, echoing Symeon the New Theologian's dismissal of philosophy, he went so far as to praise a lack of instructed knowledge as something good in the spiritual life – close, indeed, to a condition for salvation, a bizarre position for one who wrote at intricate length on his chosen theological themes.[39]

Yet amid the various debates between Palamas and Barlaam about their own tradition, the recent emergence of Western theology in Byzantium fuelled their debate in unexpected ways. Palamas plundered Planudes's Greek translation of Augustine to expound his own ideas of the Holy Spirit as the mutual love between Father and Son, a concept which he would not have otherwise found in Orthodox theology, and he also quoted Augustine (unacknowledged) in arguing that the Spirit was the energy of God, the way in which the God unknown in essence still makes himself known in his creation.[40] These were tendentious borrowings for Palamas's own purposes. Augustine would have found bizarre the Palamite idea that an individual with bodily eyes can see the divine light on Mount Tabor. Augustine's own experience of the divine is witnessed by a famous description in his *Confessions* of the moment when, in conversation with his mother in a garden in Rome's port of Ostia, they had together reached out 'in thought' and 'touched the eternal wisdom' – but for one moment only, and emphatically as the end result of loving thought and discussion.[41]

Barlaam for his part read Thomas Aquinas as well as Pseudo-Dionysius, and because of his knowledge of Western theology, he was asked by the Patriarch of Constantinople to join in negotiations with papal delegates. In the course of these, Barlaam was prepared to affirm in the Western manner that it was permissible to speak of the Spirit proceeding from the Father and the Son, even though he loyally affirmed that the original version of the Creed of 381 should be recited without its Western addition.[42] Unsurprisingly, Palamas criticized him for defending Orthodox Christianity by Western Latin means – an irony, considering the innovations which Gregory himself was introducing into Orthodoxy from the same source. The mood in which Augustine could be seen as an ally in Orthodox disputes proved indeed to be short-lived. When Prochoros Kydones, who was one of Palamas's admirers as well as a translator from Latin, tried to use Augustine to defend his deceased master's theology, he was put on trial for heresy and excommunicated, and henceforward Augustine resumed his role as a non-person in the theology of the East.[43]

In the end, a Church council repeated previous vindications of Hesychasm in 1351, ten years after Barlaam had been condemned as a heretic. The condemnations of Barlaam became the last to be added to the anathemas or condemnations which are solemnly proclaimed in the Orthodox liturgy at the beginning of Lent. He ended his days in exile at the papal Court in Avignon, a convert to Western Latin Catholicism, and in his last years he performed a singular service to Western culture by teaching Greek to the great Italian poet Petrarch.[44] By contrast, Gregory Palamas had left behind any official worries about the dangers implicit in his spiritual teaching when he became Archbishop of Thessalonica, as part of a successful reaffirmation of imperial authority there against a powerful local faction backed by the Serbs.[45] In fact, in what might seem like overkill on the part of Palamas's supporters, the Patriarch of Constantinople canonized him in 1368, less than a decade after the Hesychast champion's death. Mount Athos had been a strong (though never unanimous) source of support for the Hesychasts, and the affirmation of Hesychasm brought Athos new prestige and a new wave of foundations there. Gradually the Holy Mountain was experiencing a rebalance of power and esteem with the patriarchate in the city.

It is not difficult to see why Palamas and the Hesychast movement should have triumphed in this dispute. He offered definable procedures for approaching the divine. It would be easy to take comfort from such apparently straightforward ways of coming close to God in an age when the political institutions of the Byzantine world presented a picture of decay and corruption, when all the known world faced the baffling terror of the Black Death (see pp. 552–4) and when Islam pressed ever closer. For their part, the Ottomans were well disposed to a movement which encouraged their new Christian subjects to introspection and political passivity. A theology which asserted that it was possible for Taborite divine light to be seen with bodily eyes appealed to a Church which had fought so fiercely to defend icons; icons had become precisely the vehicle for contemplation of divine light. Moreover, when Palamas and the Hesychasts discounted the place of reason in theology, they echoed prominent themes in the writings of Symeon the New Theologian, now widely respected in monastic circles.

Barlaam by contrast presented no more than many honest and clear-minded theologians have offered across centuries when confronted by populist movements in Christianity: an openness to alternative Christian points of view, qualification, critique and nuance. He could be caricatured as pro-Western, and his ultimate decision in frustration and desperation to submit to the pope lent plausibility to that accusation. Once his efforts to accommodate East and West and his accusations against Palamas were swept aside, the way was open for Hesychasm to become embedded in Orthodox tradition, and it is certainly the case that its techniques of meditation and prayer, particularly the Jesus Prayer at its heart, have nourished countless Christians in travail and in tranquillity ever since.

HOPES DESTROYED: CHURCH UNION, OTTOMAN CONQUEST (1400–1700)

Now 'the City' was shrunken and full of ruins, fields stretching between what had become villages sheltering within its ancient defences – though over all still loomed the Great Church and the ancient monuments of the New Rome. The last emperors of Constantinople survived as long as they did because of the strength of their city walls, and because between repeated Ottoman sieges, from the end of the fourteenth century, they had agreed to become vassals of the Ottoman sultan. They seemed to have little choice in this humiliation: their efforts to enlist the West produced repeated failures, fiascos and rebuffs. One emperor, John V Palaeologos, whose mother was an Italian princess, had in desperation actually made a personal submission to the Roman Church in 1355, but he had done nothing to enforce the change on his Church. Then the fact that from the Great Papal Schism of 1378 there were first two, then three claimants for the papacy (see p. 560) for the time being ruined any credibility that reunion schemes might have possessed in the East.

With ill timing, Westerners were nevertheless beginning to come to the uneasy realization that the Ottoman Turks presented a threat not merely to schismatic Eastern Christians but to themselves, now that the

Ottomans were pushing westwards into Greece, Serbia and Bulgaria. In the midst of the Great Schism, a major spasm of crusading zeal had a spectacularly wretched end. In 1396 there gathered what was possibly the largest crusader army ever, made up of knights from France, Germany and even remote England and Scotland, all led by the King of Hungary. It was soundly defeated while it was besieging the Danubian city of Nicopolis (Nikopol, in the modern Bulgaria); thousands were massacred by the Turks. The disaster prompted the Emperor Manuel II Palaeologos to travel as far west as England appealing for renewed help; he got much sympathy and won much esteem for his dignity and courtliness, but no practical assistance.

It was only when the efforts of the Council of Konstanz had restored unity to the Church of the West in 1417 (see pp. 560–61) that it was possible once more to investigate whether a plan of union might bring any advantage to Constantinople. By the 1430s, with Byzantium's second city of Thessalonica newly in Ottoman hands, the search for a settlement took on fresh urgency. The Western Church was still split between the Pope and a continuing council of clergy meeting at Basel which was seeking to assert conciliar authority against the Vatican, and both sides earnestly wooed the Emperor for union negotiations, seeing how much prestige would follow for the party which constructed the long-lost unity. In 1437 two rival Latin fleets set out for Constantinople to pick up Byzantine delegates for a council rendezvous, and in this peculiar ecclesiastical naval race, the papal fleet sailed into port a month in advance of the Basel party.

The Byzantine delegates, sensing that the Pope's support was rather more broadly based than that of his opponents, accepted the papal invitation, and were brought to the Pope's council, reconvened first in Ferrara and then in Florence. They were very serious in their intentions: the party from Constantinople numbered seven hundred, and included both the Patriarch Joseph and the Emperor John VIII Palaeologos. In fact such a widespread representation of contemporary Christianity had not been seen since the Council of Chalcedon in 451, and would not be seen again until the ecumenical meetings of the twentieth century. Among the welter of Eastern guests seeking help in their troubles who appeared at various times before the council's final dissolution in 1445 were representatives of the Georgian Church and other Churches of both the Chalcedonian and non-Chalcedonian East, plus the Miaphysite Copts of Egypt – and to everyone's astonishment, even a couple of Ethiopians appeared (see p. 282).[46]

In the end the results for Byzantium were illusory. The problem throughout the council was not new: the Latins were not prepared to make any substantial concessions even on the limited range of issues debated – the *Filioque* clause (this simple Latin word or three Greek words occupied discussions for six months), Purgatory, the use of unleavened bread, the wording of the prayer of consecration in the Eucharist and the powers of the papacy. Nevertheless, the emperor, worn down by the incessant wrangling and isolated by the death of the much-respected patriarch during the council proceedings, agreed to a formula of union in 1439. When he returned to Constantinople the following year, it proved impossible to gain any unanimity as to whether the city would accept the deal. For many Byzantines, there seemed little point in accepting what looked like a fresh humiliation after yet another Western army gathered by the Pope went down to defeat at Varna on the Black Sea in 1444.

After that, there was little hope left for the survival of 'the City'. Yet still in 1452 the last emperor, Constantine XI Palaeologos, eventually decided publicly to proclaim the union in Hagia Sophia: the pope's name was now included in the diptychs, the official lists of those for whom the Church prayed, both living and dead. That only intensified the quarrels which had raged in the city over the previous twelve years, and the deal never gained any wider recognition in the East. Far to the north, Muscovy had already repudiated it, in a move of great significance for the future of Russian Orthodoxy (see p. 518). Now there were only months left before the Ottomans closed in on Constantinople. The Emperor Constantine had at best eight thousand soldiers to defend it against Sultan Mehmet II's besieging army of more than sixty thousand, backed by many more miscellaneous supporters.[47] To call it a struggle of Muslims against Christians would ignore the fact that the majority of those fighting for the Sultan were Christian mercenaries.

The ancient walls were not breached. The crucial Ottoman breakthrough into the city was only possible because the Byzantines' Genoese general, Giovanni Giustiniani, badly wounded in fighting outside the city wall, insisted that one gate should be unlocked to let him back into the city and down to his ship. When an entrance had thus fatally been offered, the Ottoman forces poured in after his retreating party. The Emperor by contrast fought on until he was cut down – exactly how or where is uncertain, but the Ottomans made sure that they secured his corpse. The previous day, the packed congregation in Hagia Sophia had 'cried out . . . wailed and moaned' as the Emperor took his leave with due traditional ceremony from his last reception of the sacrament, before preparing himself for battle. On this final day, 29 May 1453, matins was still in progress in the Great Church at the summit of a city overwhelmed with murder, rape and looting, when the Ottoman soldiers battered down the massive door reserved for imperial processions and overwhelmed the worshippers during their defiant last act of divine praise. The Emperor's head was stuffed with straw and paraded around the cities of the Muslim world; his dynasty was scattered from the city of Constantine.[48]

Just before the wreck of 1204, the Arab gazetteer Ali ibn Abi Bakr al-Harawi had commented admiringly and wistfully that Constantinople was a 'city greater than its name! May God make it [an abode] for Islam by His grace and generosity, God the exalted willing.'[49] Now the Ottoman Sultan Mehmet had achieved that dream of Muslim conquerors since their first expansion out of Arabia. He had done what neither the Latin crusaders of 1204 nor the divided Greek successors to the shattered Komnenos inheritance had been able to do, and restore the boundaries of the Eastern Empire much as they had once been; there would be more Ottoman expansion to come. The shame and grief in Western Europe was immense and widespread, but despite the usual papal efforts to summon a crusade to attack the city, really there was nothing now to be done apart from mourn for the city and fight to stop the Ottomans moving any further west. So in 1455 the West's greatest living composer, Guillaume Dufay, far away in Italy in the service of the Duke of Savoy, composed four different polyphonic motets lamenting the end of Constantinople, to words which had been written in Naples. One of Dufay's motets dramatically reproaches God himself in the person of the Virgin Mary:

> Most piteous one, O fountain of all hope,
> father of the son whose weeping mother I am,
> I come to lay my plaint before your sovereign court
> about your power and Human Nature, which
> have now allowed such grievous harm to be
> Inflicted on my son, who has done me such honour.

And weaving around that cry of pain in French is the sonorous accusatory voice from a tenor in Latin, applying the Prophet Jeremiah's words about fallen Jerusalem familiar in the ceremonies of Holy Week: 'All her friends have dealt treacherously with her: among all her beloved, she hath none to comfort her.'[50]

18. *The Supper at Emmaus*, by Caravaggio (1571–1610), the first (1601) and more dramatic of two versions he painted. The meal of recognition at Emmaus is 'transparently the Church's breaking of bread and wine'.

19. Sant' Apollinare Nuovo, Ravenna: mosaics in the uppermost tier of the nave are early sixth century and seem to reflect an Arian view of Christ, with the young Christ of the north tier contrasting with the bearded Christ on the south. Here the younger Christ raises Lazarus.

(*above*) 20. A cleric of the Ethiopi[an] Orthodox Church rings the faithfu[l] worship, as his predecessors have [done] for fifteen hundred years and more [by] sounding resonant stone slabs.

(*left*) 21. The Coptic Orthodox (Egyptian Miaphysite) Church has proprietary rights over an altar on [the] western face of the Shrine of the H[oly] Sepulchre in Jerusalem. The Roma[n] Catholic Franciscans have the alta[r on] the other, eastern, face. Relations a[re] not close.

22. The mosaics commissioned by Theodore Metochites in the fourteenth-century restoration of the Church of the Holy Redeemer in Chora, Istanbul (Constantinople), are among the finest late flowerings of Byzantine art before the City's fall. This Christ in the inner narthex is accompanied by Mary in supplication (*deesis*).

23. The late sixth-century *Book of Durrow* is one of the first products of Celtic art to portray the human form, probably following an exemplar-manuscript from Syria. This page represents the symbol of the Evangelist Matthew, a human figure, at the beginning of his Gospel.

25. The fresco of the Nativity by Giotto (*c.* 1267–1337) forms part of the cycle of paintings decorating the Arena Chapel in Padua. There could be few better expressions of Giotto's union of artistic naturalism with the affective piety encouraged by St Francis.

24. St Francis receiving the stigmata from the crucified Saviour (1223); an anonymous thirteenth-century panel painting from Lucca.

26. A fresco on a grand scale in the Vatican Palace commissioned from Raphael's workshop by Pope Julius II (1503–13) illustrates the fictional tale of the Donation to the Pope by the Emperor Constantine – set in the nave of the Basilica of Old St Peter's Rome, which Julius was then engaged in demolishing.

(*above*) 27. The Byzantine Empress Theodora (*c.* 500–548) is depicted with her attendants in the sixth-century mosaics of the sanctuary area in the monastic church of San Vitale, Ravenna, confronting her husband Justinian across the sanctuary.

(*left*) 28. The rotunda of Aachen Cathedral, now effectively its nave, was the Palatine (imperial palace) Chapel built by Charlemagne, in imitation of San Vitale in Ravenna and incorporating pillars brought from it, in homage to a church associated with the Emperor Justinian. Pope Leo III consecrated it in 805. The western gallery arch contains Charlemagne's stone imperial throne, on later medieval steps.

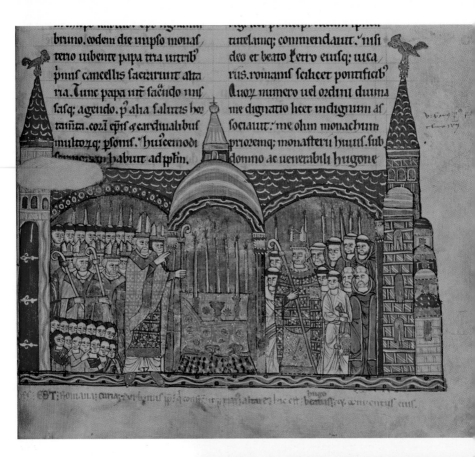

briuno. eodem die uipso monaf
terio uibente papa tria uitrib'
pmif cancellis faciarunt alta
ria. Tunc papa uit faciido unf
safq; agendo. p alia falutis ho
taiuta. cou epif g cardinalibuf
multoz q; pfomf. huicemodi
.... habuit ad pfm.

tutelamq; commendauit. nfi
deo et beato Petro euiq; uica
rius. romanif fcilicet pontificb'
Quoz numero uel ozdini diuina
me dignatio licet indignum af
fociauit. me olim monachum
prioremq; monafterii huuif. fub
domino ac uenerabili hugone

(*above*) 29. A twelfth-century
French manuscript depicts Pope
Urban II celebrating mass at the
final dedication of Cluny Abbey
church in November 1095, in the
course of his campaign to launch
the First Crusade.

(*right*) 30. Stained glass from a
Strasbourg workshop,
c. 1480, depicts the Mother of
Jesus mourning her son (*Mater
Dolorosa*). Blue is Mary's colour,
as is white for purity. Stained
glass is an artistic medium almost
exclusively found in the Western
Christian tradition.

. The Cathedral of Our Lady of Chartres, rebuilt after a fire of 1145, has preserved as its
incipal relic the sacred tunic of the Virgin Mary. This is how pilgrims from the north would
st have encountered the building, rising from the wheat-fields of northern France.

. Pilgrims have walked across Europe to the shrine of St James (Santiago) of Compostela
m the ninth century to the present day. The Cathedral is substantially the rebuilding
gun in 1075, though the skyline now reflects the later magnificence of Spanish Tridentine
tholicism.

33. Miniatures in the mid ninth-century Khludov Psalter illustrate Psalm 68 ('Let God arise and his enemies be scattered'). Those tormenting the crucified Christ are likened to iconoclasts whitewashing an icon of Christ. The sack of gold coins makes a point about the iconoclast heretics' love of money.

34. The stark interior of Hagia Eirene in Istanbul, rebuilt in the 740s by the iconoclast Emperor Constantine V, contrasts with the remaining sumptuous mosaics of nearby Hagia Sophia. It has paintings decorating its dome showing an array of armaments, relic of its centuries of use as an Ottoman arsenal, and above the site of its former altar is a plain black mosaic cross on a gold background, a rare survival from the Iconoclast period (726–843).

How did the Duke of Savoy react to this implicit reproach to himself alongside all other Western monarchs? It was the Serbian city of Belgrade, far to the west of Constantinople, which benefited from the wave of emotion generated by preachers and musical publicists like Dufay, for it was temporarily saved from Ottoman capture by desperate Western armies in a new expedition in 1456.[51] By then there was nothing to be done for 'the City' itself. A century later, in 1557, a scholar-librarian in Augsburg, Hieronymus Wolf, invented the Latin word which I use freely throughout this book to describe the culture of the Greek Orthodox East: he took the old Greek name of the city *Byzantion* to create the term *Byzantium*.[52] It took an external observer from the Renaissance West to formalize this description, with its resonances of a Christian culture whose roots were in the pre-Christian world – and for Wolf, the term referred to a culture, not an empire. By Wolf's time Byzantium had long ceased to be a living political reality, and it never would be again.

The people of Constantinople who could not flee did indeed suffer the fate which Guillaume Dufay had recalled from Jeremiah: like the people of Jerusalem long before them, they were sent off into slavery. But the Sultan wanted his new imperial capital brought to life; he could not leave the city as a wasteland. Almost immediately he began bringing in new people, and the majority of them were once again Christian and Greek. The Sultan realized that a vital encouragement as earnest of his good intentions would be to restore the Oecumenical Patriarchate, and within less than a year after the capture, he was able to choose a distinguished clergyman, George Scholarios, who now as a monk took the name Gennadios. Scholarios had been a delegate at the Council of Florence while still a layperson, because of his familiarity with Western theology and scholastic method; but usefully for the Sultan, the experience had turned him against the West and against the union with Rome in particular (naturally, Gennadios now made sure that the union was repudiated). One of the first things which the new patriarch did was to burn one of the most important writings of fifteenth-century Byzantium's most distinguished philosopher, Georgios Gemistos (who wrote under the pseudonym Plethon, suggesting both 'fullness' and Plato). What he objected to was Plethon's impassioned advocacy of Plato's philosophy and even of pre-Christian Greek religion.

Such censorship was understandable in the Patriarch's own terms, but it was an important signal about the future direction of Greek Orthodoxy. This was a time when the Renaissance of the West was reaching the height of its rediscovery of and enthusiasm for Classical literature and, through Plethon, Plato in particular (see p. 576); Plethon's surviving manuscripts found a safe home and much esteem in Western libraries.[53] As in literature, so in art. The growing naturalism of late Byzantine art, such as that wonderfully presented in the mosaics of the Holy Redeemer in Chora, was left behind. As significant as the fate of Plethon's manuscripts was the strange career of one of the most brilliant and original artists in sixteenth-century Christendom, Domenikos Theotokopoulos (1541–1614). Born in Crete, Theotokopoulos trained on the island as an icon painter, but he exploited the fact that Crete was still a colonial possession of the Republic of Venice to travel west and establish a career first in Venice, then in Rome and finally in Spain – though there is little evidence that he ever paid more than lip service to Western Catholicism. As he travelled, his style became more and more individual, leaving behind the tranquillity of the icon for stormily dramatic effects, his pictures full of glancing, restless light and brooding shadow, the figures often ghostly and elongated. This suited the dramatic tastes of some Western patrons, but throughout his long life of artistic productivity, the painter continued to inspire as much bewilderment as admiration – indeed, he still does. The only way that the Italians and Spaniards could find Theotokopoulos a meaningful place in their culture was to emphasize his otherness: they simply called him 'the Greek'. El Greco's wanderings far from his birthplace are a symptom of the way in which Orthodox culture could not now harbour any radical innovation in artistic style: the West found him difficult enough.

The Ottomans' treatment of Christian Constantinople followed patterns familiar since the earliest Arab conquests. A remorselessly increasing total of the main churches became mosques. Hagia Sophia was naturally among them, its domed skyline transformed by an unprecedented array of four minarets, and a century and a half after the conquest its magnificence inspired the then Sultan to build an equally gargantuan Islamic rival nearby, the Blue Mosque, deliberately built on the site of the old imperial palace and boasting even more minarets. Stretching away from this promontory of the city, a score of new mosques built over the following centuries paid their own architectural tribute to Eastern Christianity's lost and greatest church with their domes and semi-domes. The famous Stoudite monastery, with its venerable liturgical and musical tradition, was closed as soon as the city fell and nothing but the church building remained, turned like Hagia Sophia into a mosque; so now both the models for liturgical practice throughout the Orthodox world had vanished.[54] Throughout former Byzantine territories, as in Constantinople itself, the churches left in the hands of the Christians had to be lower in external profile than any nearby mosques, and church bells or clappers to summon congregations to worship were banned. This was part of an inexorable transformation of the landscape. The towers and extrovert façades of Christian churches were gradually dismantled, while the public presence of icons in wall niches and shrines – the architectural small change of a Christian world – faded away from the roadsides. As the traveller approached communities from villages to cities, minarets now dominated the horizon of roofs, just as the sound of worship was now the muezzin's call rather than the Christian clanging summons to prayer.[55]

As with landscape, so with people. The Christian population were given privileged but inferior and restricted *dhimmi* status (see p. 262) as a *millet* (distinct community) with the Oecumenical Patriarch at their head, and soon they found themselves ranged in Constantinople, Greece and Asia Minor alongside another rapidly growing group under a *dhimma*, Jews from Western Europe. Jews arrived here in their thousands from the 1490s after the expulsions from Spain and Portugal (see pp. 586–7), and they were welcomed by the Muslim authorities precisely because of their oppression by Christians. In Thessalonica, Jews remained a majority of the population until the arrival of huge numbers of Greek refugees in the tragic events of 1922–3 (see pp. 924–5), prior to an even greater catastrophe at the hands of the Nazis.[56] As had been the case throughout the gradual and piecemeal formation of the Ottoman territories in Asia Minor, the Ottoman Empire retained an extraordinary variety of cultures and jurisdictions, with no attempt being made to impose sharia or the customary law codes of Islam as an overall system (although in legal disputes which involved one Muslim contender, Islamic law would apply to the case).

When the Sultan recognized the Oecumenical Patriarch as head of all Orthodox Christians in the empire, it was a huge theoretical boost to the patriarch's power. Alongside him, Greeks who had prospered once more in the capital formed an elite of power brokers with the Ottoman authorities, and from their residence in the Phanar quarter of the city around the patriarch's headquarters, they were known as Phanariots. Such a narrowly restricted group existing on terms dictated by the conquerors was easily led into corruption and selfish exploitation of its position, and the Phanariots' Greek culture and pride in their past were constant potential sources of irritation to Orthodox such as Serbs, Bulgars or Romanians, who were also placed under the ultimate jurisdiction of the patriarch. Meanwhile the patriarch's supposed authority was constantly undermined by the fact that he was at the mercy of the sultan. The Ottoman administration frequently removed and replaced patriarchs, partly to weaken them, but partly because a fee was payable on the accession of a new patriarch, plus bribes from rival contenders. So in the century after 1595, thirty-one clergy were involved in fifty-five changes of patriarch.[57]

By their unstinting cooperation with the conquerors, the patriarchs saved their community from the worst possibilities of oppression. A major threat loomed in the 1520s, when leading Islamic lawyers (the 'ulema) tried to attack entrenched Christian privileges, arguing that because Constantinople had resisted attack by Mehmet and was then conquered, Christians were not entitled to their millet status. It took a great deal of secret negotiation between the Patriarch and the then Grand Vizier to Sultan Süleyman (reigned 1520–66), plus a great many bribes spread round the palace, to head off this threat. The Patriarch produced witnesses to the early days of the conquest, one of whom was 102 years old, and claimed to have been one of the soldiers in the siege.[58] The 'ulema were nevertheless much more successful in persuading Sultan Selim II in 1568–9 into a radical confiscation of monastic estates, an action reminiscent of and perhaps influenced by the contemporary Protestant dissolutions of monasteries in Western Europe, and a deeply damaging blow to the life of monastic communities. Mount Athos was much affected and it survived largely on the generosity of Orthodox rulers from the north.[59]

Within their community, the Orthodox authorities now had no very good means of exercising discipline apart from the punishment of excommunication. Between official prompting and popular opinion, excommunication gathered to it the power of folk disapproval; so that in Greek popular culture, with much informal encouragement from clerical writers, excommunicates were considered incapable of normal mortal decay at death. Instead, they became an undead creature called a tympaniaios, because the undecayed body of one of these unfortunates was said to become swollen until it was taut enough to be beaten like a drum. The only way of ridding the community of such a terrifying monster was by sprinkling the body or coffin with Orthodox holy water and a priestly rite of absolution. Thus did the clergy keep some control over their flocks, and demonstrate their power against both the local imam and interloping Roman Catholic missionaries.[60] Yet there was little they could do if a Christian converted to Islam, except to point out that the penalty for a reconversion of a convert Muslim to Christianity was death, by publicizing the martyrdoms which resulted from such reconversions. Missionary work was impossible, and the efforts of the patriarchate to provide a proper range of theological studies in the Patriarchal Academy in Constantinople, to equal the sort of higher education available in Western Europe, were fitful and constrained.

The result was a slow decline in the proportion of Orthodox Christians in the empire, perceptible from the late sixteenth century. Some became crypto-Christians, and generations were able to sustain such a life for extraordinary lengths of time. On the island of Cyprus, finally captured from the Venetians by the Turks in 1570, a large proportion of those who converted to Islam were said to be like a cloth in which cotton was covered with linen, making it look different on either side, so they were known as 'linen cotton' (*Linovamvakoi*). Such double allegiance survived right up to 1878, when the British ended Ottoman power on the island. There are similar stories of generations of crypto-Christians from Asia Minor numbering tens of thousands; even priests who functioned outwardly as mullahs.[61] Their passive survival was symptomatic of the general ethos of Orthodoxy in its great captivity. The instinct after 1453 was to preserve what it was possible to preserve in the face of repression and relegation of Christians to second-class status. The disaster only confirmed the end of the period of radical innovation in Orthodoxy, which had lasted from the iconoclast controversies of the eight and ninth centuries down to the affirmation of Hesychasm in 1351. It is worth speculating on how different the Orthodox mood might have been, how much openness to change and new theological speculation might have developed, if Byzantine Orthodoxy had not been so much on the defensive from the fourteenth century down to modern times.

From the mid-sixteenth century, Western Christians – Protestants as well as Roman Catholics, thanks to the great split of the Reformation – interested themselves afresh in their afflicted co-religionists in the East. Both sides of the fractured Western Church were looking for allies among the Orthodox for their own purposes, and hard-pressed Easterners often eagerly sought out their help. But there were major barriers to understanding or reconciliation: the long memory of 1204 overshadowed contacts with Roman Catholics which did not result in full submission to the pope's authority, and Protestant detestation of images – even the nuanced position of the Lutherans (see pp. 619–20) – was deeply offensive to the iconophile Orthodox.[62]

The one moment when the Church of Constantinople did find a leader who tried to seize the initiative and seek creative change only ended up confirming Orthodox Christians in their determination to defend their past: this was the ultimately tragic career of Cyril Lucaris (1572–1638). One great scholar of Orthodoxy, himself a bishop in the Orthodox tradition, has said of him that he was 'possibly the most brilliant man to have held office as patriarch since the days of St Photius'.[63] Lucaris was unusually cosmopolitan for a senior Orthodox churchman. He came from the island of Crete, then still ruled by the Venetians, and as a result he had access to Western higher education in the Republic of Venice's celebrated university at Padua. Padua was itself unusual in Western Europe because, despite the fierce Counter-Reformation Catholicism of the Italian peninsula, it was discreetly hospitable to Protestants; Lucaris gained further acquaintance with Protestantism as well as a different Orthodox world when he travelled far north to the Polish-Lithuanian Commonwealth in the 1590s. Here he witnessed the Ruthenian Orthodox Church submit to papal authority in the Union of Brest in 1596 (see pp. 534–5). The event appalled him, and he attributed it in part to the inferior education of Orthodox clergy, who were no match for the highly trained members of the Society of Jesus promoting the union. He began developing a sympathy for the Western Christians who also opposed the Roman Catholics, and in Poland that primarily meant Reformed (that is, non-Lutheran) Protestants.[64]

Back in the Mediterranean, in 1601 Lucaris was elected Patriarch of the small Melchite (Chalcedonian) Orthodox Church of Alexandria, an honour which a cousin of his had held before him, and in 1612 he was elected Oecumenical Patriarch in Constantinople, a tenure which was destined to be much interrupted and then brutally ended for political reasons. He became acquainted with a cultivated Dutch Reformed merchant and diplomat, Cornelius van Haga, and entered correspondence with one of the most respected leaders of international Reformed Protestantism, the Englishman George Abbot, Archbishop of Canterbury, whose family was much involved in the growing English trade with the Ottoman Empire. The two archbishops so far apart in geography and background saw a common interest: the fight against Roman Catholicism. They even considered the possibility of a Church reunited against the common enemy.

Abbot brought Lucaris to the attention of his king, James VI and I of Scotland and England, who with some justification regarded himself as an international Protestant statesman. King James was keenly interested in the reunion of Christendom, and back in his youth he had written and eventually published an epic poem celebrating the Christian naval victory over the Turks at the Battle of Lepanto in 1571.[65] With James's enthusiastic backing, the English government actually paid for a couple of Greek scholars to come and study in England, and one of them, Nathaniel Konopios, a fellow Cretan of Lucaris and future Metropolitan of Smyrna, is said to have drunk the first cup of coffee ever witnessed in the University of Oxford.[66] Such was Lucaris's sympathy for Reformed Protestant theologians, among whom John Calvin has often been taken as a representative figure, that he was soon to be known, in no complimentary spirit, as the 'Calvinist patriarch'.[67]

That cup of coffee which Konopios drank in Oxford – precedent for the huge intellectual liveliness of London coffee houses over the next century and a half – was alas one of the few lasting legacies of Lucaris's patriarchate, apart from a great deal of ill-will. Lucaris was a deeply pastorally minded bishop, distressed by what he saw as the ignorance and superstition of his flock, and by the obvious decline of his own Church. In 1627 he reopened the moribund Academy in Constantinople, providing it with a printing press staffed by a Greek printer trained in London. Within a few months Catholic missionaries of the Society of Jesus organized a mob to sack the printing office, but Lucaris persisted, sponsoring a translation of the New Testament into modern Greek. In 1629, in an effort to produce a point of instruction for the Greek Orthodox faithful and to introduce them to what he saw as the treasures of Western theology in a synthesis with Orthodox tradition, Lucaris published a *Confession of Faith*, which among other topics expounded a version of the Protestant doctrine of justification by faith alone and the Reformed development from it of predestination (see pp. 607–8 and 634). By now he had aroused a storm of opposition within his Church, much encouraged by the Jesuits, who sedulously presented him to the Ottoman authorities as a fifth columnist for foreign subversion; they spent a great deal of Rome's money in bribes to make the accusation stick. In 1638 the Patriarch was executed, condemned for supposedly encouraging Cossacks under Muscovite leadership to attack the empire. Relations between the Church of England and the Orthodox never completely lapsed after that, but neither did a pattern of opportunism born of political desperation on the Orthodox side, combined with a good deal of mutual theological incomprehension.[68]

Lucaris was one of those creative figures condemned to live at the wrong moment. His enemies fomented a poisonously anti-Protestant mood in the Orthodox Church, and the Jesuits sealed their triumph over

Lucaris as Greek Orthodoxy moved closer to Roman Catholicism during the seventeenth century, encouraged by steady investment by the Catholic monarchy of France, both commercial intervention and discreet royal diplomatic support of Eastern Christians within the Ottoman domains (see p. 715). In the sixteenth century, while the Ottomans remained a vigorous and expansive military power, Western ability to intervene in the eastern Mediterranean remained limited. Military achievements against the Ottomans were largely defensive, such as the defence of the Knights Hospitallers' headquarters of Malta in 1565 and the subsequent victory at Lepanto led by Catholic Habsburg forces. It was only at the end of the seventeenth century, after the great symbolic reversal of Ottoman fortunes when the Sultan's armies were beaten back from Vienna by Polish and Habsburg forces in 1683, that the situation began to change. By that time, alongside the former crusading powers in the West, a new Orthodox empire had emerged north of the Ottoman frontier, and that would change the dynamic of world Christianity once more.

15
Russia: The Third Rome
(900–1800)

A NEW THREAT TO CHRISTENDOM:
NORSEMEN, RUS' AND KIEV
(900–1240)

At the other extreme of ninth-century Europe from Constantinople, somewhere in southern England, perhaps at the Court of King Alfred of Wessex, a scribe sat puzzling his way through the task of translating into Anglo-Saxon a popular fifth-century Latin text about past world calamities: the *History against the Pagans* by Augustine of Hippo's Spanish admirer Paulus Orosius (see p. 305). Repeatedly in his text he found the concept of universal Christianity, and wondered how to translate it; he came up with a new Anglo-Saxon word, '*Cristendom*'.[1] Our scribe was inventing a term which his readership could use to express their part in the universality of a continent-wide culture focused on Jesus Christ. It had survived repeated disasters: the scribe took comfort from the fact that Orosius's Christendom had not been extinguished despite the calamities which the Spanish priest had experienced, and in fact he made his translation more determinedly cheerful than the original. In Orosius's day, various barbarian peoples had dismantled the Christian Western Empire and sacked Rome itself; now the scribe's optimistic tone defied the fact that Wessex was facing new barbarians, apparently intent on destroying everything that Christendom meant for England. The perpetrators sailed across the North Sea from Scandinavia, and in England they were called Norsemen, Danes or Vikings. They murdered kings, raped nuns, torched monasteries – one of their tortured and butchered victims, King Edmund of East Anglia, became such a symbol of those terrible times that he was long regarded as England's patron saint.

Christendom from west to east was united in its suffering at the hands of these people. Far to the east, the people of Constantinople also encountered Norsemen or Vikings, but knew them by a different Scandinavian word: Rus' or Rhos.[2] There too the word began as a name of terror; the Rus' were part of a single Scandinavian movement of restlessness, plunder and settlement which both sent the Norsemen to England and impelled these peoples into the plains of eastern Europe. They seem to have sailed there mainly from Sweden; among a variety of new settlements, they set up their headquarters far inland at a hilltop strategically sited beside a wide river. It was named in the local Slavic language Gorodishche, though to them it was Holmgardr; later the settlement which grew up nearby would be called the new city, or Novgorod.[3] In 860 the Rus' streamed southwards and laid siege to Constantinople itself. That imaginative ninth-century Patriarch of Constantinople, Photios, has left vivid descriptions of the horror sparked in the capital by their unexpected arrival, their plundering of the suburbs, their wild appearance and unknown language.

Photios's reaction was characteristically far-sighted: he proposed a religious solution for a political problem. He laid plans for a Christian mission to the Rus', just as he did for the troublesome Khazars or the Bulgars and Slavs. In 869 his missionary bishop to the Rus' found time to attend the first of two councils of Orthodox bishops in Constantinople which (to the fury of papal delegates present) pressed the case for the Bulgarian Church's links to the Byzantine Church (see p. 460).[4] Photios would have known that he was following a Western precedent. Earlier in the century, the English had also reached out to their Viking tormentors and tried to tame them by conversion; so did the Carolingian monarch Louis the Pious in northern Germany and southern Scandinavia. Of all these missions, the English were the most successful. Neither the Carolingians nor Photios's delegates achieved lasting results, although the discovery of contemporary Byzantine coins in excavations at Gorodishche does show that money passed hands by some means, peaceful or otherwise.[5] Nothing significant was heard of Christian activity in the lands of the Rus' for nearly another century, but the contacts between these remote regions and Byzantium grew and stabilized.

Norse power now spread hundreds of miles south from Gorodishche to the river system of the Dnieper, and in the mid-tenth century Norse leaders seized a settlement on the borders of the Khazar territories. It was at a confluence of rivers, and its easily defended hills were useful storage places for weapons and goods in transit: its name was Kiev or Ky'iv.[6] Its rulers, a clan group known in later histories as Rurikids from their supposed ancestor Rurik, were by now losing their Norse identity and taking Slav names; they established a brisk trade with the Byzantine Empire, and their fascination with the riches which they could steal or barter from Byzantium began to familiarize them with the culture of the imperial world. The Macedonian emperors began including warriors from Rus' among the mercenaries whom they gathered to fight on their frontiers: the first recorded instance is from 935, even before Kiev was in Norse hands.[7] Some objects recovered from Russian excavation layers datable to the tenth century are inscribed in Greek characters – informal scratches on pottery for the most part – but even more significantly, these finds are outnumbered by survivals of Cyrillic script – on pots, seals, tally sticks, sword blades.[8] So the Rus' and their Slavonic-speaking subjects were in touch not merely with Greeks, but with Bulgarian Christians, who with the encouragement of their rulers were at this time creating a Christian literature in a language and script which could be understood far to the north of their own lands.

It was against this background of contacts increasingly more about trade and less about violent plunder that in 957 a Rurikid princess, Olga, paid a ceremonial visit to Constantinople from Kiev. She was currently regent for her son Sviatoslav and the purpose of her visit was to complete her conversion to Christianity by receiving baptism. With ostentatious symbolism, Olga took the Christian name Yelena, after the reigning Byzantine empress, Helena. Her visit was a moment for the Byzantines to savour, and the occasion was written up in loving detail by Helena's husband, the Emperor Constantine VII, in his manual of imperial Court ceremonial – with one curious omission: he forgot to describe the baptism. That silence suggests that the expectations of the Byzantines and Olga from the visit were not in step, and her subsequent action indicates disappointment. She turned to the powerful Latin Roman Emperor Otto I to supply an alternative Christian mission, presumably to put diplomatic pressure on Constantinople, but once more expectations do not seem to have matched, and Otto quickly became lukewarm about her overture. Her son was not impressed by her incomplete efforts and, once he was in full control of his dominions, would not follow her into Christianity.[9] Sviatoslav had his own imperial ambitions, which led him to take an aggressive interest in the Christian khanate of Bulgaria. This brought him disaster. When Sviatoslav's armies overran Bulgaria, the Byzantine Emperor John I Tzimisces reacted with his own invasion and annexation of Bulgaria, and the Rurikid prince died on his retreat homewards in 972.

Sviatoslav's son and successor, Vladimir, now had no choice but to come to terms with Constantinople's military success, yet the new intimacy between his world and theirs also gave him a chance to exploit the internal struggles of the Byzantine imperial family. When the young Basil II succeeded John Tzimisces in 976, Basil faced rivals for the throne, including his co-emperor, who was his younger brother. To secure his position, he turned to the Prince of Kiev for substantial troop reinforcements, trading a promise of marriage to his sister, the imperial Princess Anna – a transaction regarded as demeaning an emperor's lawfully born daughter, and actually forbidden in regulations drawn up by his grandfather Constantine VII. Otto II of Saxony had already failed to secure the same Anna as a wife, but this deal went ahead: Basil's throne was secured, thanks to his bodyguards from Rus'.[10] The Byzantines continued to recruit elite warriors from the north, not merely from Rus' but directly from far-off Scandinavia; from the end of the tenth century, they referred to them as 'Varangians'. The name has often been wrongly back-projected on the first troublesome Norsemen who negotiated their way into Byzantine Christianity. The source of the confusion is the twelfth-century writer of the Kievan *Primary Chronicle*, who with little more to work on than a set of princely names from the remote past constructed much of the story of the first Rurikid princes, in an effort to tidy up the story of his people's reception of Christianity two centuries before his own time.[11]

Prince Vladimir was not going to let the remarkable and unprecedented gift of a Byzantine princess slip from him, and in 988, to reinforce his new alliance with the Emperor, he abruptly ordered the conversion of his people to Christianity, himself taking the baptismal name Basil (Vasilii in Russian) in allusion to his new brother-in-law. There is a well-known anecdote embedded in the *Primary Chronicle* that Vladimir hesitated not merely between adopting a Latin or a Greek form of Christianity, but between Islam and Judaism too, and that his envoys to Constantinople swayed the decision by reporting their awe and astonishment on entering the Great Church of Hagia Sophia: 'We no longer knew whether we were in heaven or earth.' Given the political circumstances, it is unlikely that Vladimir had any real hesitation in his Orthodox baptism, but it is a satisfying story for Orthodox Russia, rather reminiscent of the self-congratulatory foundation tale which the Anglo-Saxons told about Pope Gregory the Great and his English slave-boys (see p. 336).

And it does sum up two truths: Byzantine Christian culture had created the single most magnificent building in the European and West Asian world, and Kiev was now enthralled by Byzantine Christian culture. The feeling was not then reciprocated; Byzantine chroniclers are notably silent about the conversion of Vladimir and his imperial marriage, which they probably regarded as deeply demeaning for the dynasty.[12]

Once Vladimir had secured his bride from a distinctly reluctant Emperor Basil and brought her in triumph to Kiev, he provided her with a setting worthy of her heritage. Kiev soon boasted a stone-built palace complex and the beginnings of a proliferation of stone churches amid its fleet of wooden buildings, remaking the city in a Christian mould. Byzantine in style were the monumental architecture, mosaics and frescoes – naturally no statues – together with the liturgy which they sheltered, but individual features took on a local life of their own. The churches of Kiev and its imitators sprouted multiple domes or cupolas in a fashion which went beyond their more sober Byzantine models, perhaps because in the first instance timber buildings made this elaboration a more practical possibility, and then the developing architectural fashion gave a spur to stonemasons to reproduce the same effect. The first cathedral in Kiev, a wooden structure, had no fewer than thirteen cupolas, and it was not uncommon for the greater churches throughout Rus' to have seven, which could be given a rationale in a number of different symbolic interpretations of the number.[13] Likewise, over the course of time from its first development in the twelfth century, the iconostasis (see pp. 484–5) became an even more formidable feature in Russian churches than in the Greek tradition: where the Byzantine iconostasis customarily had three tiers of images of the saints, the Russian equivalent customarily had five by the fifteenth century, and as many as eight two centuries after that (see Plate 58).

This tendency to select particular themes from Byzantium and then develop them remorselessly was characteristic of what became Russian Orthodoxy. The first Kievan cathedral was unsurprisingly dedicated to the Holy Wisdom, but besides Hagia Sophia, another now long-vanished church of Constantinople worked particularly strikingly on the imaginations of the devout in Kiev. This was the shrine church of the Virgin of Blachernae, which since the sixth century had possessed the robe and miraculous icon of Mary the Virgin – both powerful defenders of the city against sieges and despicable iconoclasts over the centuries. The Virgin had allegedly given away her robe just before her death – what is in Eastern tradition called her Dormition, or falling asleep. In the

eleventh century, a Christian convert in Kiev is said to have had a
vision in which Mary commanded the building of a new church of the
Dormition, using holy fire to sear its proposed plan into the ground. So
this eleventh-century church in Kiev designed by God's own mother had
a particular significance for Rus'. Cathedrals of the Dormition appeared
all over the Russian world, each taking its distinctive (and, it must be
said, basically unimaginative) cuboid design from the original in Kiev.
The monumental Dormition cathedral built only a century later in
Vladimir-on-the-Kliazma is one of the most perfect and satisfying. The
imitations are the only way of gauging the appearance of the original,
since the Kiev exemplar, much rebuilt, had departed rather far from the
Virgin's blueprint by the time it was blown up by German soldiers in
1942. That last version of it now stands gloriously restored amid the
Monastery of the Caves complex.[14]

Kievan spiritual tradition likewise creatively augmented its inheritance
of saints from Byzantium. The first saints to be given honour in the
newly created Church were Boris and Gleb, two sons of Prince Vladimir.
A choice of royal founder-saints might seem predictable enough, but
Boris and Gleb could hardly have been classed as candidates for sainthood in earlier centuries. Their sanctity consisted in the nature of their
deaths: not exactly martyrdom for the faith, but political murder by
their half-brother Prince Sviatopolk in his effort to ensure that he
inherited power after Vladimir died in 1015. The real story of what
happened in a murky set of political manoeuvres is unclear and in
any case irrelevant to the spirit in which the murdered princes were
commemorated: they were reverenced because it was said that they had
refused to resist their murderers to avoid wider bloodshed, so their
suffering was both entirely innocent and inspired by compassion and
non-violence.[15]

Boris and Gleb can be seen as an example of a phenomenon common
in the popular religion of medieval northern Europe generally, Latin as
well as Orthodox: the feeling that those who met a violent and premature
end for no good reason deserved to be regarded as saints. In western
Europe, the authorities in Rome objected strongly to this idea – rightly
in terms of Christian tradition – and issued bitter if usually futile condemnations of such local cults.[16] The official reaction in Kiev was much
less hostile. That reflected a strand in Russian spirituality which
remained strong in later centuries: its 'kenotic' emphasis on the example
which Christ gave of his emptying of the self, his humiliation and
compassion for others. If Christ was passive, both in the modern usage

of the word and (in a closer sense to the original Latin verb *patior*, 'to suffer') accepting of his suffering, so followers of Christ should imitate his self-emptying. A parish priest in Moscow familiar with both East and West once observed to me that the Western reaction to a problem is to look for a solution; the Orthodox are more inclined to live with it.[17] It was easier for the Eastern tradition of 'synergy', or cooperation with divine grace, to warm to the theme of self-emptying than for Westerners drawing on Augustine of Hippo's crystallization of the doctrine that original sin had irredeemably tainted all human effort. Yet kenotic thinking has repeatedly crept back in Western Christianity. The last century's industrial production of innocent human death worldwide suggests that the theme has a Christian relevance wider than its original setting amid the frequent violence and cruelty of Russian history.

Linked to the kenotic concept of innocence and denial of self-esteem was the new popularity which from very early on an old genre of Eastern saint enjoyed in the Christianity of Kievan Rus', and which has endured into modern Russian Orthodoxy: the Holy Fool. Perhaps real Holy Fools capered their way up the trade routes of eastern Europe to Kiev, but it is more likely that they were discovered by Kievan monks in the pages of Byzantine and Bulgarian saints' lives, and the idea fused with the growing local devotion to innocence and unreason. The first recorded local fool was Isaakii (d. 1090), who thoroughly disrupted life in Kiev's Caves Monastery before lapsing into passive introspection as a hermit. The polarity in his career between foolery and contemplation is significant, because both approaches to the divine reveal an instinct to look beyond the rational in spirituality. In eleventh-century Byzantium the same mood inspired Symeon the New Theologian, and later it enthused the exponents of Hesychasm (see pp. 469 and 489). Hesychasm and the Jesus Prayer became important elements in Russian spiritual practice. Individual introspection and wild individual extroversion pointed to a common core in kenotic spirituality, and they both complemented the ordered corporate solemnity of the Orthodox liturgy.[18]

Although Kiev thus took so much of its culture and religious outlook from Constantinople, the official relationship was frequently tense, and as in other Orthodox Churches in the Balkans, the local leadership was often anxious to assert itself against the Oecumenical Patriarch, who in 1039 had sanctioned the creation of a bishopric in Kiev which would act as 'metropolitan', or regional leader, to all bishoprics which would subsequently be founded in the newly Christianized lands. The princes of Kiev continued the contacts with Latin monarchs pioneered by Princess

Olga; Prince Vladimir's son Jaroslav (reigned 1019–54) married six of
his children to Western princely families. One of those marriages to
Henry I of France in the 1020s introduced the Eastern name Philip to
the Capetian family, and successive dynasties of the French monarchy
continued to use it frequently in christening their children up to the
nineteenth century – at the present day, it is the second name of the
Orleanist pretender to the French throne. As relations between Constantinople and Rome deteriorated in the eleventh century, the same decline
did not necessarily hold for Kiev. It took some time to persuade Kievan
Christians that the Latins were heretics, a view which only became
plausible to them during the thirteenth century, once Latin bishops in
eastern Europe made it quite clear that they regarded the Church of
Kiev as heretical and started poaching on territories within its jurisdiction.[19] By that time, Rus' had been transformed by that same force which
so devastated Asian Christianity: the westwards sweep of the Mongols,
or, as they were known in northern Europe, the Tatars.

TATARS, LITHUANIA AND MUSCOVY (1240–1448)

The initial Mongol impact on Rus' was as catastrophic as in Asia. In
1240 they sacked Kiev in the course of a year's campaign in east–central
Europe, the furthest west their destructive forays ever took them. Their
assault in Hungary has been estimated to have caused the premature
death of around 15–20% of the population, obliterating a whole set of
relationships between Kievan Rus' and communities and networks of
trade on the trans-Danubian Hungarian plain. The disaster was decisive
in extinguishing the possibility that these links might have continued in
their previously vigorous development, to shift the boundaries of Latin
and Orthodox Christianity eastwards in central Europe.[20] Although Kiev
disappeared as a political force, its titular bishop, living in various
refuges in the region often far from Kiev, remained as Orthodox Metropolitan to the Christians of all Rus'. Now there was a Tatar power
dominating eastern Europe and exacting tribute from such political
entities as it allowed to survive. The wing of this nomad movement,
initially led by one of Genghis Khan's sons, which seized Rus' later came
to be known by Russian historians as the Golden Horde, but is more
accurately described as the Kipchak Khanate.[21]

To begin with, the Kipchak Khans kept their animist beliefs, but their people included many Turks, and they followed the general drift of Mongol leaders into Islam. Nevertheless, after their initial ferocity, the Tatars proved tolerant of Christianity, and allowed a bishopric to be established in their capital cities newly founded in the Volga basin (both successively called Saraï). They demanded little more than regular infusions of tribute and an equally valuable commodity: prayers for their khan from the Christian clergy. Overall, they interfered far less than other Muslims did with their Christian subjects, crucially making no effort to curb the Christian use of icons.[22] Christian leaders in Rus' advocating submission to Tatar rule could take their cue from the Byzantine emperors: Constantinople soon did its best to cultivate the new power, desperate for allies against the encroaching Ottomans, and worried about the interest which the pope and Latin Christian rulers were showing in alliances with Mongols. A series of illegitimate daughters of the Palaeologos emperors found themselves shipped off in marriage to Kipchak Khans. Most of the bishops of Saraï were Greek-speakers, and there seems to have been a deliberate system of alternation for metropolitan in Kiev between a cleric born in Rus' and a candidate brought from Greece. But by now the emperor was a remote figure whose practical power had never recovered from being shattered by the Latins in 1204. Was there a Christian power to whom the bishops of Rus' could turn for more effective support?

Urban life suffered terribly all over Rus'. The Mongol onslaught had wiped out whole communities, and those who survived fled the ruined towns and dispersed into safe forests, bewildered at the scale of the disaster. It was yet another reason for Orthodox Christians to meditate on suffering, but not everyone could claim the innocence of the sainted Boris and Gleb. Many presumed that God must be punishing them for their sins, and they turned to prayer, both for themselves and for those who died. They naturally looked to monks as the experts in prayer, and over the next two centuries at least a hundred monasteries were founded in the newly colonized lands, with the principal monks drawn from the noble families who were the natural leaders of frontier society.[23] But alongside this steady growth in the importance of monastic life, one great historic Christian city far to the north did survive the general wreck, and remained independent – Novgorod.

Novgorod could not ignore the new political configuration and paid tribute to the Tatars, but it came through the 1240s unscathed, simply because, for reasons of their own, the Tatars decided to abandon their

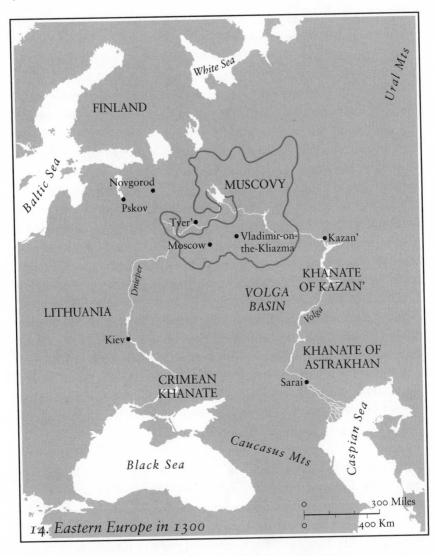

14. *Eastern Europe in 1300*

attack northwards. It continued to prosper mightily on trade, particularly its control of fur-trapping, and it built up its own northern empire with a reach from the Baltic to the Ural Mountains. In the twelfth century it had ejected its Kievan princes: the constitution which it then created was a republic of merchant families in which the bishop had more say than the nominal princes, and in which ordinary people might feel that they also played a part in at least commenting at public assemblies on policy. Because of this broad distribution of responsibility, the citizens of Novgorod valued literacy far more than anywhere else in the region, and a rich haul of birch-bark texts dating over four centuries has been rediscovered to testify to how widespread was literacy in city society. This remarkable urban organization was unique in Rus'. The city was in close contact with the German merchant confederation of towns and cities known as the Hanseatic League, whose constitutions were developing in the same fashion, with their overlord a Holy Roman Emperor whose authority was increasingly distant. Novgorod was so proudly conscious of its republican status that in the fifteenth century it even minted coins whose designs imitated those of Venice, that other great aristocratic republic so far away.[24]

The people of Novgorod and their neighbouring trading centre of Pskov shared the cosmopolitanism of the Hanseatic League, far more than settlements further east or south. The forest of city churches – eighty-three by 1500, a similar number to London – was enriched with art and monuments commissioned from artists living as far away as Germany or Serbia. One aspect of this contact with the west and south was that, in the fourteenth century, both Novgorod and Pskov became notably open to dissident religious movements which criticized the worldliness of the Church's leadership, a phenomenon not otherwise much known in Rus' in that era, but beginning to emerge in the Western Church.[25] Novgorod thus provided one model of what an Orthodox future for northern Europe might become: very different from the autocracies which came to be the background to Russian history. Novgorod was the first city to borrow from Bulgarian T'rnovo that resonant title with a long future in Russia, the 'Third Rome', but we will discover that the description was destined to move elsewhere.[26]

The fact that Novgorod did not shape the destiny of Russia was ultimately thanks to the rulers of a modest settlement called Moscow, hundreds of miles to its south-east. Hitherto little noticed in the affairs of Rus', in the later thirteenth century the ambitious rulers of Moscow began to make the most of their remoteness from Tatar interest or interference. They assiduously cultivated the Kipchak Khan, regularly visiting him and leaving their sons as hostages; right into the fifteenth century they paid tribute to the khan and customarily maintained prayers for him in the Church's liturgy. Similarly in the late fourteenth century, when Moscow started minting its own coinage, many of its coins bore Arabic inscriptions dutifully praying for long life for the khan.[27] Unsurprisingly, the princes of Moscow modelled many of their political institutions on those of Mongol society, but they also paraded their devotion to the Church traditions of Constantinople. By the fourteenth century, as their territories and influence expanded, the Tatars allowed them to take the title of Grand Prince, and across Europe rulers began hearing of this distant realm called Muscovy. Novgorod soon uncomfortably felt the rivalry of the Muscovite grand princes, while Muscovy among its various confrontations with neighbouring principalities, also fell into increasing tension with a growing power to the west, the grand princes of Lithuania.[28]

Of all the various powers in the Baltic region and the east to the Urals, an informed observer of east–central Europe in the late fourteenth century would have pointed to Lithuania as the most likely to emerge as supreme. The grand princes of Lithuania were the last major rulers in Europe to resist making a choice between the three great monotheisms, proudly keeping to their ancestral animist faith. They were vigorous and effective warlords who in the wake of the Mongol invasion preyed on the various shattered communities of the region, and over the late thirteenth and fourteenth centuries they extended their power to command the eastern European plains and mountain chains, from the Baltic eventually as far as the Black Sea. They proved as tolerant of Christians in their dominions as the Kipchak Khans had been, and the nobles (boyars) of Rus' were as happy to accept their overlordship as they had been that of the animist or Islamic khans.

The Grand Prince of Lithuania was anxious to unite as many traditions as possible in his vast domains. To his Latin-speaking elites he presented himself as '*dux magnus Litvanorum Russiaeque dominus et haeres naturalis*' – Grand Prince of the Lithuanians and Lord and Natural Successor of the Rus'. Yet his bureaucrats spoke a 'Ruthenian' form of Slavonic which reflected their familiarity with the liturgy of the Orthodox Church; some of his family looked to Orthodox Christianity to sustain them, and not only many of his boyars but most of his subjects were Orthodox Christians.[29] Soon it was natural for the Orthodox of the region to start looking to the Lithuanian capital, Vilnius, rather than the sad remnants of past magnificence at Kiev, which the metropolitan bishop now hardly ever visited; from 1363 Kiev itself was in the hands of the Lithuanians. Yet from the late thirteenth century the metropolitan based himself either in Moscow or Vladimir-on-the-Kliazma, which was also in Muscovite territory, and it became the ambition of the Muscovites to make this arrangement permanent. Throughout the fourteenth century, a contest took place between Muscovy and Lithuania as to who would host this key figure in the Christianity of Rus' – in effect, who really would be the 'Natural Successor of the Rus''. The Oecumenical Patriarch and emperor in Constantinople enjoyed the position of referees. That was a welcome boost to their fragile position, and a far cry from the condescension with which the Byzantines had greeted Vladimir of Kiev's conversion back in 988. The consequences of this century of manoeuvring are among the most important in the history of Russian Orthodoxy.

In the contest of Lithuania and Muscovy, the referees in Byzantium weighed the growing power of Lithuania against the fact that, by contrast with the ostentatious Orthodox piety of the grand princes in Moscow, the Lithuanian ruler was a non-Christian. The rhetorical advantage was with the Muscovites, and they exploited it fully. Metropolitan Peter of Kiev and all Rus' died in 1326 soon after taking up residence in Moscow. A cult of the 'miracle worker' rapidly grew up around him and he was declared a saint. This was a useful asset for Grand Prince Ivan Kalita when he persuaded Metropolitan Feognost, Peter's successor, likewise to settle in Moscow rather than in Vladimir-on-the-Kliazma. It did not do Moscow any harm that Metropolitan Peter had been treated badly in the Principality of Tver, a further rival to Muscovy, before his gratifyingly warm reception in Moscow, a point which Muscovite chroniclers laboured in their hagiography.[30] When the dome of Hagia Sophia in Constantinople partially collapsed in 1346, Grand Prince Semen (Simon) of Muscovy was quick to send money for the restoration fund to demonstrate his international position within the Orthodox world; likewise money flowed from the Grand Prince's dominions towards the monasteries of Mount Athos.[31] In 1371 Grand Prince Dmitrii Donskoi gave one of his sons the Christian name which the converted Vladimir of Kiev had taken at his baptism in 988, and in 1389 this boy became the first grand prince to bear the name Basil or Vasilii.

By contrast, Grand Prince Olgerd of Lithuania did not help his case when, in the late 1340s, he executed three Lithuanian Christians in Vilnius for refusing to eat meat during a period of Christian fasting. In outrage, Constantinople made sure that the dead men became the focus of a cult, since they were obvious modern martyrs for the faith in a manner more familiar in the early days of the Roman Empire, and the Oecumenical Patriarch secured their remains for his Great Church of Hagia Sophia. The Vilnius martyrs were not forgotten, and by the early fifteenth century they became a sign of the Christian unity of Constantinople and Muscovy. When in 1411 Emperor John VIII Palaeologos married a daughter of Vasilii II, Grand Prince of Muscovy, he sent Moscow a splendid specimen of the liturgical vestment known as a *sakkos* as a gift for Metropolitan Photios. It still exists, and it pointedly bears images of the Lithuanian martyrs alongside those of the Emperor and the Grand Prince.[32] By that time, the design was a symbol of how the conflict between Muscovy and Lithuania had eventually been resolved.

The course of the contest between Lithuania and Muscovy long swayed unpredictably. In 1352, with the outrage of the three martyrs still fresh in his mind, the Oecumenical Patriarch rejected Grand Prince Olgerd of Lithuania's nominee for metropolitan, and instead he chose a Muscovite closely related to the princely house. Diplomatic pressure on the Byzantine emperor from Lithuania's ally the Republic of Genoa (by now a major force sustaining Constantinople's fragile prosperity) then secured Olgerd a consolation prize in the shape of a metropolitan bishopric specifically consecrated for Lithuania alone. This was a controversial move which did not endure, but within a few years the undoubted fact that the metropolitan based in Moscow never took any personal interest in the western territories of the former Rus' led to Constantinople making a different appointment: a separate metropolitan for the region of Galicia, a former province of Kievan Rus' which had been annexed by the kingdom of Poland in 1349. From 1375 to 1378 there were even two rival Metropolitan Bishops of Kiev, both appointed by the Oecumenical Patriarch, but at the solicitation of Muscovy and Lithuania respectively: a strange if temporary anticipation of the Great Schism of Popes which was about to erupt in the Latin Church of the West (see p. 560).[33] The Orthodoxy of western Kievan Rus' was steadily diverging in character from that of Muscovy and the east, to the extent that it should be given a distinctive name as the Ruthenian Church.

The decisive factor in the contest came from the west. In his international diplomacy, the Grand Prince of Lithuania naturally had to consider Latin Christendom as well as the Orthodox world, far more than was necessary for the Grand Prince of Muscovy. Amid the steady expansion of Lithuanian frontiers, the Latin Christian Teutonic Knights were a continuing source of annoyance and harassment to the Lithuanians, continually crusading against the godless grand prince, and in the process helping themselves to a number of attractive territories and towns along the Baltic (see p. 387). By the second half of the fourteenth century, the strategic advantages of embracing one or other form of Christianity were becoming obvious to the rulers of Lithuania, but which Christianity should they choose? Grand Prince Jogaila for some time favoured the Orthodox option, which would after all unite him with most of his subjects. In the early 1380s he haggled for a marriage with the daughter of the principal Orthodox ruler in the north, the Prince of

Muscovy, Dmitrii Donskoi. But the problem with taking that course was that it would do nothing to lessen Lithuania's confrontation with the Teutonic Knights, who regarded Orthodox Christians as enemies to the Holy Father in Rome and little better than Lithuanian pagans. In any case, Jogaila was wary of giving too much power to the Orthodox nobility within his territories.

Much more promising for the Lithuanian prince was an alliance with Poland. The Poles were fellow victims of the Knights, but they were also uncompromisingly Catholic. Therefore they had as ready access as the Teutonic Order to the central institutions of the Roman Church and might offset the power of the Knights. They also had a dynastic problem: their ruler was not merely female but also a young girl. A deal with Jogaila was obvious, delivering Poland from the prospect of dynastic unions with a number of undesirably acquisitive royal suitors in central or western Europe. Accordingly, without much consultation with the eleven-year-old Queen Jadwiga, the Polish nobility agreed on her marriage to Jogaila (then approaching forty), and in 1386 they elected him king of Poland, after he had been baptized a Catholic Christian as Władysław Jagiełło. The union was purely personal through the Jagiellonian royal house, who doubled as Polish kings and Lithuanian grand princes, and it remained so into the late sixteenth century (see pp. 532–3). Nevertheless it committed the dynasty to the Catholic fold, despite the fact that, in the Grand Principality of Lithuania, Catholics were in a distinct minority.

This was a significant turning point for Orthodoxy and for the future of Rus'. The claim of the Lithuanian grand princes to be natural successors to the princes of Rus' now looked much less convincing even to their Ruthenian Orthodox subjects, let alone to anyone Orthodox further east, and the way was open for the prince of Muscovy to take on that role. There was now no question that the metropolitan bishop should make his principal residence anywhere other than Moscow, and in fact Cyprian, the Metropolitan of Kiev whom originally Jogaila had nominated, did take up residence there. His time in office, though interrupted, lasted till 1406, and he proved a notable champion of Orthodox tradition, encouraging the growth of monastic communities, giving his blessing to the spread of the Hesychast movement in them, and personally translating into Russian key works of monastic guidance such as the *Ladder* of John Climacus.[34] While Lithuania promoted the cause of Rome and looked with enthusiasm on the efforts of the Council of Florence to reunite Eastern and Western Christians under the pope,

Cyprian's successors in Moscow set their face against any such move, even if it meant opposing the emperor in Constantinople.

In 1438–9 Metropolitan Izydor, who had left Moscow to attend the Council of Florence soon after his appointment in 1436, loyally accepted the reunion deal hammered out at the council by Emperor John VIII Palaeologos (see pp. 492–3). When he arrived back in Moscow in 1441, the Grand Prince Vasilii II summarily declared him deposed and had him imprisoned; he proved to be the last Metropolitan of Kiev resident in Moscow appointed by the Oecumenical Patriarch in Constantinople.[35] Seven years later, Grand Prince Vasilii headed a Church council which chose Iona as a replacement metropolitan, without any reference to Constantinople. Just at the moment of this assertion of Vasilii II's power in the Church in the late 1440s, his coins began bearing a new title, 'Sovereign of all Rus'' or 'Sovereign of the whole Russian land'. The coins of his father Vasilii I (1389–1425) had used the phrase 'Grand Prince of all Rus'', in a clear imitation of the title of the Metropolitans of Kiev and all Rus'; now the new and unprecedented usage trumped the metropolitan's title in a fashion which some might style imperial. It was half a century before the grand princes dared to use the same title in documents which other rulers might see. Vasilii II had many other conflicts to deal with in his dominions at this time, one of which resulted in his being blinded by a relative, but the new title on the coinage seems rather more than coincidence, at the moment that Muscovy had broken with the ancient power of Constantinople in the name of preserving Orthodoxy.[36] The fall of 'The City' in 1453 only consolidated that break.

Behind this political struggle of the fourteenth and fifteenth centuries, an Orthodoxy was consolidating which both emphasized its roots in Byzantium and took on a distinctively local character. Rus' had virtually no centres of learning or scholarship to pursue its own answers to the puzzles raised by the Christian proclamation. What it did have were complex sets of rules and conventions in worship imported from Byzantine Christianity, the longing of ordinary folk to find ways to reach God amid the frequent harshness of their lives, and the capacity of the human imagination to range freely in solitude over a spiritual inheritance. It was inevitable that a Christianity formed in the sunshine of the Mediterranean and rooted amid very obvious remains from the cultures of Greece and Rome should assume a different complexion when it was adopted in Russia. This version of Orthodoxy was now the basis for Christian belief among a people with no reason to take an interest in

Classical culture. They lived amid the long darkness of winter cold, followed by spring seasons suddenly bringing life to the empty plains and great forests of north-eastern Europe, stretching towards the ferocious landscapes of the far north towards the Arctic Circle. Communities here could be tiny, vulnerable and widely separated; loneliness was part of everyday experience even more than is normal for human beings. Russian Christianity drew on the features of imported Orthodoxy which seemed valuable in such conditions.

The emphasis of Orthodoxy on corporate life, expressed in its liturgy and sacred music, appealed to medieval Russian society, for here people needed to cooperate to survive at all. Individualism was not a virtue unless it was in the celebratory, counter-cultural form exemplified by the Holy Fool, who could only exist because he knew which aspects of the strongly rule-bound society to overturn and mock, and thereby to reaffirm. Russian Orthodoxy was not a spirituality which valued new perspectives or original thoughts about the mysteries of faith: it looked for deepening of tradition, enrichment of the existing liturgy, enhanced insight through meditation. Reform meant recalling the life of the Church to previous standards. That was of course also the consistent rhetoric of the Western Latin tradition, but in the West the language of restoration disguised much more the steady creation of radical innovation, in a fashion which for Orthodoxy everywhere virtually ended with the acceptance of Hesychasm in the fourteenth century.

One sign of the way in which radical structural initiative now proved unwelcome in the Muscovite Church came in the Church's deliberate reshaping of a mission eastwards which was begun by the priest and monk Stefan (Stephen) Khrap. Galvanized by his conviction that the world would come to an end with the completion of a seventh millennium since Creation – dangerously near his own time – Stephen felt a call to spread the Christian message beyond the eastern frontier of the Muscovite lands, to within sight of the Ural Mountains. In 1376 he set out to establish his mission among the Komi people of the Perm' region, and achieved enough success for the Metropolitan to make him bishop (at the same time, significantly, his mission resulted in the Grand Prince of Muscovy replacing Novgorod as the overlord of that area). Like Cyril and Methodios, Stephen of Perm' created an alphabet for his converts and translated the Bible and liturgical texts for them, but times had changed. Despite the reverence which Stephen's memory inspired, the authorities in Moscow eventually decided that it was unhelpful to sanction another ecclesiastical language. After the region had been brought more firmly under the political control of the grand prince in the late fifteenth century, Church Slavonic replaced the local vernacular in Church life, and the use of Stephen's alphabet faded away.[37]

The dominant personality in the spiritual life of the Church in Rus' during the fourteenth century was not a metropolitan or a grand prince but the monk Sergei (Sergius) of Radonezh, a small town outside Moscow. Following the general impulse after the Mongol invasions to find refuge and found monasteries in remote forested areas, he created the Monastery (Lavra) of the Holy Trinity at a place later named after him, Sergiev-Posad, a couple of hours' walk from Radonezh. Like Antony in the Egyptian desert, Sergei had become a hermit, though in his case it was through circumstance: his brother abandoned their joint venture in monastic life, unable to endure the solitude, and left for Moscow. Sergei was content with his isolation, but again like Antony he found himself attracting many others to his forest clearing, hoping to imitate his way of life. In the end he took on the office of abbot and adopted the discipline used in the Stoudite monastery of Constantinople (see p. 451), which represented a much more rigorous and structured life than the rather loosely organized monastic foundations of Rus' in the Kievan era. Trinity Lavra was the inspiration for a renewal of Russian monastic life in a 'desert' mould.

Nevertheless, Sergei's preference for the life of a hermit was not forgotten, and encouraged others to follow his first example, to the extent that hermits remained much more common in the Russian Church than in the West. Their way of life was generally not much fenced in by a rule: the ordered monastic discipline of the Lavra became one end of a polarity in which, at the other extreme, wandering holy men represented a spirituality hardly in touch with the Church hierarchy. Such maverick figures had a personal charisma which, like that of prophets in the first days of the Christian Church (see pp. 131–2), gave them their own authority, and the institutionally ordered Church in Russia treated them with similar suspicion. Yet often encounters with such holy wanderers were the most intimate contacts with the Church experienced by the poor, not to mention by a wide variety of women in general across the social spectrum. One twentieth-century example of the type, Grigorii Rasputin, was to captivate no less a person than the Empress of All the Russias, to disastrous effect (see pp. 917–18). Russian Orthodoxy was in the course of time to develop some surprising identities, in which ordinary people reinterpreted their faith and worship in ways which made perfect sense to them, but took them further and further from the spiritual order and liturgical correctness envisaged by bishops and abbots. That trend was already perceptible in the fifteenth century, as the monastic movement inspired by Sergei began to grow and diversify.[38]

The pattern exemplified by Sergei's own life – the transition from hermit to abbot of a large community – was repeated all over Rus'. It had a practical utility in a perpetual frontier society which over several centuries saw settlements steadily expand north and east into remote areas: a hermit built his hut in a lonely place and made the place holy, later to be joined by others who created a monastery under some variant of a Stoudite rule. In turn, monks who felt ill at ease in that sort of communal discipline and life were likely to leave, to become hermits in an even more remote area, and perpetuate the cycle once more.[39] Thus did the monastic life spread – and with it also the political control which was increasingly monopolized in eastern and northern Rus' by the Grand Princes of Muscovy. The greatest of all monasteries, Sergei's Trinity Lavra (which in the course of time took on his name beside that of the Trinity as Sergiev-Posad), became enormously wealthy through its alliance with the grand prince. It became one of a ring of monasteries around Moscow which doubled as fortresses for him in case of foreign invasion or internal challenge.

The fourteenth and fifteenth centuries also set the art of Rus' and Muscovy in patterns for the Russian future, particularly the fact that it was almost exclusively the art of the Church. Artists took their models from the Church art of Byzantium, and showed virtually no interest in the rediscovery of pre-Christian Greek and Roman art which was at the same time transforming culture in the Latin Western Renaissance. Originality was not prized; genius was measured by the painterly eloquence and moral fervour with which the tradition could be presented. By the sixteenth century, a long-dead monk, Andrei Rublev (c. 1360–c. 1430), came to be seen as the greatest exponent of the style in fresco and in icon-painting – in 1551 his work was named in the Church legislation of the 'Council of a Hundred Chapters' (see p. 529) as definitive for Russian religious art. In view of that affirmation, it is unfortunate that only one of Rublev's various surviving works in Vladimir and Moscow can now definitively be said to be his, but it is a quite exceptional piece. This is an icon of the Trinity, now in the Tretyakov Gallery in Moscow, but up to the 1920s an eponymous icon at the Trinity Lavra at Sergiev-Posad, where it was regarded as second only in importance to the relics of St Sergius himself. In this work, monks of the Trinity Lavra could contemplate the dedication of their house to the Trinitarian mystery, refracted by Rublev in traditional Christian fashion through the three mysterious angel-visitors to whom the Patriarch Abraham had offered hospitality under the groves of Mamre. The Russian Orthodox Church declared Rublev a saint amid the millennium celebrations for the conversion of Prince Vladimir of Kiev in 1988. It was a proclamation of the centrality of sacred art to Russian Orthodox spirituality.[40]

MUSCOVY TRIUMPHANT (1448–1547)

The final collapse of the Byzantine Empire in 1453 had an ambiguous resonance in Moscow. To lose the holy places of Constantinople was a bitter blow, but the catastrophe did leave a useful vacuum in Orthodox leadership, for which the Muscovite leadership had been preparing over the previous century. Church and Court cooperated very closely in an increasingly autocratic system which presented the Grand Prince as the embodiment of God's will for the people of Rus'. The Grand Prince was effective in disposing of competitors: in 1478 he annexed the city-state of Novgorod, which had the effect of eliminating the model of a merchant republic from Russian society. The Hanseatic League regarded this annexation as a watershed in its relations with the East: it permanently withdrew the credit facilities which it had long extended to Novgorod and Pskov, for it did not trust the arbitrary rulers of Muscovy to be reliable financial partners. In a land where resources were perpetually scarce and the urge of the monarch to expand his dominions and power was consistently strong, the grand princes sought to gain as much control as they could over exploitable assets of manpower and finance. The Church hierarchy aided them by preaching the holiness of obedience to the prince with a thoroughness and zest which had little precedent in Byzantium, let alone Western Latin Christendom; but bishops and abbots did not forget that the Church had its own view of its destiny and purpose. The tension between these two agendas had a long future within Russian Orthodox Christianity.

The growing power of the Trinity-Sergius Lavra and the immense reverence paid to Sergei in the pilgrimage cult which began very shortly after his death in 1392 were not unconnected with the close ties which Sergei had developed to the Grand Prince of Muscovy, ties which were later strategically magnified by his hagiographers. It was said that he had blessed Grand Prince Dmitrii Donskoi when the Prince decided to attack his Tatar overlord; a victory in battle followed for Muscovy at Kulikovo in 1380. The reality of the blessing is dubious, and the victory was not such a turning point as it looked in subsequent Muscovite chronicles, but such doubts do not diminish the part that the narrative of the events played in constructing a new history for the Muscovite principality. During the fifteenth century, narratives of great saints of the Church lent their subjects' authority to the growing concentration of power in the hands of the grand princes.[41] Moscow's subservience to the Tatars was quietly forgotten: gone were the prayers for a Tatar khan which Muscovite coins had once borne, and in a wholesale rewriting of history, Muscovy's clerical chroniclers recast the Tatars as perpetual enemies of Muscovy. Two years after the annexation of Novgorod, Grand Prince Ivan III formally announced an end to the tribute which he and his predecessors had paid to the khans for two centuries. This was part of a wider appropriation of Byzantine pretensions: Ivan married a niece of the last Byzantine emperor and adopted the double-headed eagle once the symbol of Byzantine imperial power. Occasionally he would even use the title 'Emperor' – *Tsar* in Russian, in an echo of the imperial 'Caesar'.[42]

There was an urgent purpose to this hasty donning of imperial clothes. Measures needed to be taken to prepare for the end of the world, at a time when God had seen fit to destroy the former empire in Constantinople. In both Byzantium and West Asian Islam, much faith was placed in calculations that the seventh millennium since creation was about to be completed; this meant that the Last Days were due in the year equivalent to mid-1492–3 in the Common Era. It was such a firm conviction in educated Muscovite circles that the Church did not think to prepare any liturgical kalendars for the years after 1492; these kalendars were essential guides to knowing when the movable feast days of Orthodoxy should be celebrated in any given year. Given the absence of any end to the world in 1492, the task had to be hastily undertaken by Metropolitan Zosima himself. But as is usually the way with the non-appearance of the End Times, the disappointed made the best of their disappointment. God's mercy in sparing Muscovite society confirmed that he approved of the arrangements which Church and emperor were making for its future governance; it strengthened Muscovites in their sense of a divine imperial mission specifically entrusted to their polity.[43] Church-building flourished as it had done in western Europe in the wake of that successfully negotiated millennium End Time in 1000 (see p. 365): more stone churches were built in Russia during the sixteenth century than in the whole of the previous history of Rus'.[44]

This festival of church-building spanned complementary impulses. On the one hand, there was a gleeful reassertion of tradition. The grand princes encouraged their architects to scrutinize what survived from the pre-Tatar Kievan past and reproduce it, as in the rebuilt Cathedral of the Dormition in the Moscow Kremlin, actually designed in the 1470s by an Italian, but on the strict orders of his patron, Ivan III, conscientiously looking to the models of the already venerable Dormition cathedrals in Kiev and Vladimir-on-the-Kliazma. On the other hand, architects struck out in new directions, to emphasize the triumph of Orthodoxy in what was now the only major Orthodox Church not under an alien yoke, either Muslim or Western Catholic. Exuberant adaptations of the Byzantine style emerged – in the same era during which churches in the captive Greek Orthodox world ceased to dominate the landscape of their now Ottoman environment, Russia's churches aggressively bristled with gables and domes. The gables were named *kokoshniki* because of their resemblance to peasant women's headdresses – a metaphor which identified the Church with its humblest people. Towards the end of the sixteenth century, the domes took an 'onion' form which had previously only been seen in Orthodox manuscript pictures and small models of the Church of the Holy Sepulchre in Jerusalem. The onion dome was a fantasy improvement on the reality of that iconic domed building, but one which was to have far-reaching visual consequences for the Russian skyline, suddenly full of symbols of the New Jerusalem to come.[45]

It was against a background thus still seething with apocalyptic excitement that churchmen began referring to the Church in Rus' by the term previously adopted by the proud merchants and clergy of Novgorod for their own city: the 'Third Rome'. Now the phrase was revived to award the Russian Church a particular destiny ordained by God. The tsars always treated the idea with caution, since it might give clergymen too much power at their expense; by contrast, the Russian Church relentlessly propagated it in sermons and readings in the liturgy, and it had a deep appeal to ordinary folk, some of whom would later reject the tsars' religious policies when they forced innovation on the Church (see pp. 539–41).[46] The nature of the 'Third Rome' is most famously expounded in a letter to Grand Prince Vasilii III from Filofei, monk of a monastery in Pskov, written perhaps in the mid-1520s, and the theme is echoed in two of his other letters.

Amid a mixture of flattery and admonition, Filofei reminded his prince

of the shape of previous Christian history: the Church of Rome had
fallen away into heresy (he specified only the Apollinarian heresy, in a
clumsy reference to the *Filioque* controversy), while the Church of the
Second Rome in Constantinople had been overwhelmed by unbelievers
– Filofei recalled the last tragedy of the Turks breaking down the doors
of the churches with their axes in 1453. It was now the destiny of the
Church over which the Tsar presided, 'in the new, third Rome, your
mighty *tsarstvo'* [empire], to shine like the sun throughout the whole
universe, and to endure as long as the world endures: you are the only
Tsar for Christians in the whole world . . . Two Romes have fallen and
the third stands. A fourth will not be'.[47] It is worth emphasizing that in
none of his letters did Filofei identify the Third Rome specifically with
Moscow, the home of the Tsar; it was the whole Church of Rus' within
the grand prince's dominions which fulfilled this final role.

What is striking in this letter is its deeply clericalist character. Filofei's
threefold scheme of divine providence recalls the theories of Joachim of
Fiore, who had also envisaged an enduring third age, which he had seen
as dominated by monks (see pp. 410–12). Filofei is unlikely to have
known of Joachim: his exposition reflects the tendency of the Trinitarian
faith to think in threes, and his recommendations are severely practical
in their concern for the protection of monastic wealth and holy life,
without much apocalyptic flavour anywhere in the details of his programme.[48] He was writing against the background of a conflict among
the monks of Rus'. They took for granted that monks should be the
leaders of the new society of the grand prince; the quarrel between them
centred on the way in which monasticism might best reflect biblical
perfection, and how monks might best lead this project. The main issue
was the enormous wealth of the greater monasteries: it is not surprising
that a critique of such riches developed, since it is likely that by the
sixteenth century monasteries led by the Trinity-Sergius Lavra owned
around a quarter of Russia's cultivated land.[49] 'Possessors' defended
such monastic wealth, pointing out how monasteries could and did use
it for the relief and support of the poor; 'Non-Possessors' pointed to the
greater value of monastic poverty in forming the spirituality of monks,
and the need for monks to develop purity of heart rather than achieve
perfection in the liturgy.

The issues under contest were comparable to the unease about monastic wealth in late-twelfth-century Latin Europe, where they had been
to some extent resolved by the formation of the orders of friars (see
pp. 401–12). In Muscovy, there was no such compromise. The opposing

sides adopted as their symbolic champions Nil Sorskii and Iosif Volotskii, two leading fifteenth-century monks. We have to reassess them by filtering out much later polemical rewriting of their story: Russian liberals attributed to Nil an openness and tolerance of religious dissidence for which there is no actual evidence, while Russian Marxists saw the 'Non-Possessor' admirers of Nil as the 'progressive' party, on the grounds that the Muscovite princes eventually sided with their opponents, the 'Possessors', who honoured Iosif. In both interpretations, Iosif became a symbol of the monarchical autocracy which absorbed official Russian religion up to 1917. The two men do not in fact seem to have clashed during their lives; they were both advocates of Hesychasm, devotees of the great exponent of monasticism Sergei of Radonezh and firm advocates of the repression of religious dissidents, up to and including the death penalty.[50]

Among the scanty facts recoverable about Nil are that he visited Mount Athos in the late fifteenth century, and that on his return he founded a hermitage in the classic Russian style amid the swamps and forests of the Sora river in the far north-east; later his Non-Possessor admirers would be styled 'Trans-Volga Elders' in allusion to this location. Those writings which can be definitely attributed to him show him to be exceptionally learned for his time and deeply committed to the stillness of Hesychasm, about which he could write eloquently in ways whose appeal endured through later political storms. It was some of his later devotees who emphasized his championing of a hermit's life as best placed to achieve profound spiritual experience. They singled out Abbot Iosif as their opponent because one of Iosif's major achievements had been to create a new Rule to give a more rigorous structure for monastic community life. In reaction to attacks on Iosif, the defenders of monastic wealth in the mid-sixteenth century increasingly identified Nil as the inspiration for the movement which they now characterized as subversive of the good order of the Church, the Trans-Volgan group of monks and hermits. It is certainly true that Iosif's reputation was likely to appeal to the consolidating Church establishment, given his celebration of the value of the ordered liturgy and his renown as a gifted liturgical singer.[51]

Once more, there are worthwhile comparisons with the history of the medieval Western Church, where between the twelfth and sixteenth centuries a hierarchy intent on asserting clerical power and uniformity of practice and doctrine did its best to destroy any rivals or to define them as heretics. The sixteenth-century Muscovite Church came to treat the 'Non-Possessors' as dissidents when they were not, because it was in the process of condemning a wide spectrum of religious opinion, much of which similarly only challenged the Church once the Church met it with repression. Another and distinct late-fifteenth-century movement in eastern Europe was termed by later commentators 'the Judaizing heresy', and as so often in Russian history, most of what is known about it comes from those who opposed and suppressed it. Those who adhered to it apparently denied the reality of the Trinity, opposed icons and were critical of the existing clergy: three different grounds for the 'Judaizer' label. In the time of Grand Prince Ivan III, the movement had sympathizers in Court circles, including the Grand Prince's own daughter-in-law, the Moldavian princess Elena; caught up in the dynastic struggles after his death, she died in prison in 1505.[52] During the sixteenth century, the 'Judaizers' seem to have interacted fruitfully in Lithuania with those Reformation dissidents coming from the Western Latin tradition who also had doubts about the Trinity (see pp. 642–3).

One reason why Grand Prince Ivan and his successor at first resisted pressure from the metropolitan to persecute the 'Judaizers' may have been that the Court saw this rival party as allies in plans to trim the wealth of the monasteries, a plan which would have strengthened the monarchy at the expense of the Church's independent power. The same thought had, a hundred years before, led an English prince and his fellow noblemen to protect the dissident academic John Wyclif from the Western Church's anger, when he condemned the temporal wealth of the Church (see pp. 567–9). Soon it was also to be one motive in the promotion of the Protestant Reformation in western Europe. Indeed, the later stages of the dispute between Possessors and Non-Possessors may have been fuelled by knowledge that in the West from the 1520s onwards wholesale dissolutions of monasteries were taking place (see p. 628). At least one prominent monk among the Non-Possessors, Nil's disciple Vassian Patrikeev, urged that bishops should be put in charge of all Church lands, including those of the monasteries, which would have made Church wealth more readily available assets for the grand prince. Unlike his hero Nil Sorskii, Vassian really did argue for tolerance for religious dissidents.[53] Given that conjunction of ideas, it is not surprising that there were such bitter cries of heresy among the Possessors against both Judaizers and Non-Possessors; it was a convenient emphasis which may have helped to pull the grand princes into line behind their cause. The Possessors were naturally also careful to stress their reverence for the God-given power of the monarch.

Much of what the sixteenth-century Muscovite Church leadership condemned was simply the energy of popular devotion, creatively extending or modifying the liturgy to suit local needs, or experiencing its own unregulated encounters with the divine. This undergrowth of religious life could never wholly be contained by official weeding. After the mid-sixteenth century, the Church hierarchy deliberately restricted the number of those newly officially canonized as saints, and the candidates whom they chose tended to be drawn safely from the upper ranks of society. Into the vacuum poured a myriad of local cults, some of which became much more than local; so in 1579 it was the daughter of an ordinary soldier who discovered the hiding place in the newly Muscovite city of Kazan of an icon which became one of Russia's most revered images of the Mother of God.[54] And still the Holy Fools postured and agreeably shocked society with their consecrated antics. A sixteenth-century example of the breed, Vasilii (Basil) the Blessed, has been so centrally honoured in Russian devotion that the image of Moscow now most familiar worldwide is that of the church in Red Square containing his shrine, the Cathedral of the Intercession, now commonly known as St Basil's Cathedral. Appropriately it is an extraordinary culmination of Russian architectural posturing, and in it also lie the bones of a second and rather more obscure Holy Fool, Ioann 'Big Cap', whose speciality apart from his outsize head was apparently intimidating people with gnomic innuendoes.[55]

IVAN THE TERRIBLE AND THE NEW PATRIARCHATE (1547–98)

That anarchic fools should be honoured in Red Square is remarkable, because the Church of the Intercession was commissioned by the man who came to symbolize the dismal extremity of what Muscovite autocracy might mean: Ivan IV, known to anglophone history as 'the Terrible'.[56] Even by the poisonous standards of the Muscovite Court, few rulers have had an experience of brutality in their formative years appalling enough to equal Ivan's. A puppet ruler at the age of three on the sudden death of his father, Vasilii III in 1533, he experienced the probable death by poisoning of his mother when he was eight, after she had imprisoned, tortured and murdered a variety of dynastic rivals; at the age of thirteen he managed to secure the beating to death of the prince who had seized power after his mother, and who had humiliated him and his handicapped but much-loved younger brother. This was the beginning of a lifetime of exercising power through terror which intensified when the years of regency ended and Ivan assumed full power in 1547.[57]

It was not surprising that Ivan graduated from childhood sadism towards animals to the bestial treatment of anyone who might be regarded as getting in his way, and of many who were entirely innocent of any such possibility. The only countervailing influence during his unlovely upbringing was the Metropolitan Makarii, a 'Possessor' monk and a noted painter of icons, who did his best to recall the boy to the meaning of the Christian faith which he practised. As a result of the Metropolitan's intervention, and Ivan's frequent visits to the great holy places of Muscovy, the Grand Prince's career of tyranny, murder and power-seeking was shot through with an intense and justified concern for the welfare of his soul. It was also probably Makarii who prompted Ivan to be crowned in 1547 as Tsar, in a now permanent augmentation of the title of Grand Prince, although naturally Ivan retained the old title to emphasize his place as heir to all Rus'. Now there was a self-promoted Christian emperor in the East to rival the seven-centuries-old self-promotion of Charlemagne and his successors in the West.

For the first dozen or so years of his reign, the new tsar was intent, like many of his fellow European monarchs, on building up his personal power against any other power base in his dominions, but he ruled with the assistance of a competent set of advisers and set about a rational reordering of the temporal and Church government of Muscovy, codifying laws, reorganizing the army and presiding over that major reforming Church council 'of the Hundred Chapters' in 1551 which, among its other measures, elevated the art of Andrei Rublev into a universal standard (see pp. 521–2). One can only speculate how Ivan, after taking such an active role in Church affairs, would have reacted to Pope Pius IV's invitation to him in 1561 to send representatives to the Pope's parallel contemporary reforming Council at Trent; the Tsar never got to hear about it. The Catholic Poles, horrified at the prospect that their Muscovite enemies might receive any sort of hearing at Trent, blocked two successive papal envoys from travelling on to Moscow, to the extent of leaving the second of them in a Polish jail for two years.[58]

Ivan IV won decisive victories over the remaining Tatar khanates in the 1550s, and it was to commemorate these, in particular the capture of the Tatar city of Kazan in 1552, that he ordered the building of the

Red Square Cathedral of the Intercession. It is an extrovert symbol of the Tsar's joy in victory and his gratitude to Mary, the Mother of God, the Trinity and the various saints whose intercession he had successfully invoked against the Tatars. Ivan's eightfold victories provided a convenient historical accident which was imposed on all the biblical symbolism of the number eight and eight-plus-one already being exploited in the church architecture of Muscovy. So the building centres on an eight-sided church which becomes its own spire. This is surrounded by eight completely separate lesser churches, so that the ensemble is an eightfold star, or a pair of squares superimposed on each other – double the four corners of the earth or the four evangelists. In plan it seems rational and symmetrical, but no one except the architect and patron would ever have thought of it in terms of its plan. The exterior, so insistent in its monopoly on the viewer's attention, is intimidatingly original: each lesser church bears an onion dome in extravagantly contrasting decoration, all threatening to throttle the central spire which catapults above them. The effect would have been inconceivable in Byzantium. Inside, nothing could be further from the congregational space of either the early basilica or the Protestant architecture about to develop in the West than this intricately clustered honeycomb of shrines of thanksgiving. Sudden soaring interiors in their verticality assault the Heaven to which the insistent eightfold design is pointing the worshipper. They are capable of arousing both claustrophobia and vertigo.

Around 1560 Ivan's reign took a dark turn amid growing political crisis. The death of his first wife, whom he seems to have loved genuinely and deeply, was soon followed by the death of his brother and of Metropolitan Makarii. There was plenty in Ivan's previous career to anticipate the violence which he now unleashed, but the scale of it all was insane, worthy of the ancestors of the Tatars over whom he had triumphed – his second wife was indeed a daughter of one of the Tatar khans. Novgorod, once the republican alternative to Moscow's monarchical autocracy, especially suffered, with tens of thousands dying in a coldly calculated spree of pornographic violence. The Tsar's agents in atrocity, the *oprichniki*, were like a topsy-turvy version of a religious order: as they went about their inhuman business, they were robed in black cloaks and rode black horses, to which with equally black humour they attached dogs' heads and brushes to announce their role as guard dogs and cleansers. After 1572, Ivan abandoned the experiment in government by the *oprichniki* which had created this nightmare, but at his death, in 1584, he still left a country cowed and ruined.

As he rounded in turn on his *oprichniki* in 1573, the Tsar wrote a letter of bitter repentance (or dictated it – contrary to a long Russian historiographical tradition, it is not certain whether he was literate); it was addressed to the Abbot of Beloozero, one of the monasteries for which he had particular reverence. He threw himself on the mercy of the Church: 'I, a stinking hound, whom can I teach, what can I preach, and with what can I enlighten others?'[59] In the last phase of his reign, the Tsar poured resources into new monastic foundations in what is likely to have been an effort to assuage his spiritual anguish (exacerbated by his murder of his own son in 1581), confirming in his generosity the victory of the 'Possessors' in the Church. Yet his terror against a variety of hapless victims continued. Did he think that he was purging his people of their sins by the misery which he was inflicting on them? As his latest biographer sadly comments, echoing earlier Russian historians, he had become 'Lucifer, the star of the morning, who wanted to be God, and was expelled from the Heavens'.[60] This ghastly latter-day caricature of Justinian needed no Procopius to expose his crimes; they were there for all to see, with little more than his own attempt in Red Square at rivalling Justinian's Hagia Sophia to mitigate their dreadfulness.

In the reign of Ivan's son and successor, Feodor (Theodore) I, the Church of Muscovy gained a new title which mirrored the dynasty's assumption of imperial status; it became the Patriarchate of Moscow. The occasion was an unprecedented visit to northern Europe by the Oecumenical Patriarch Jeremias II, desperate to raise money for the Church of Constantinople. When Jeremias eventually reached Moscow in 1588, he was given a fine welcome, but after nearly a year of entertainment, it became clear to him that his parting might be even more considerably delayed if he did not give his blessing to a new promotion for the metropolitan to patriarch. Jeremias agreed: after all, his involvement in conferring this honour was a renewed acknowledgement that, like his predecessors in the fourteenth-century contests between Lithuania and Muscovy, he had the power and ultimate jurisdiction which made such decisions feasible.

One near-contemporary account of what happened suggests that Jeremias signed the document establishing the Moscow patriarchate without any clear idea of what it contained. This would have been just as well, since the text of it goes straight back to Filofei's letter to Vasilii III in describing the Russian Church as the Third Rome. It echoes Filofei's idea that Rome had fallen through Apollinarian heresy, while the Second Rome was now 'held by the grandsons of Hagar – the godless Turks.

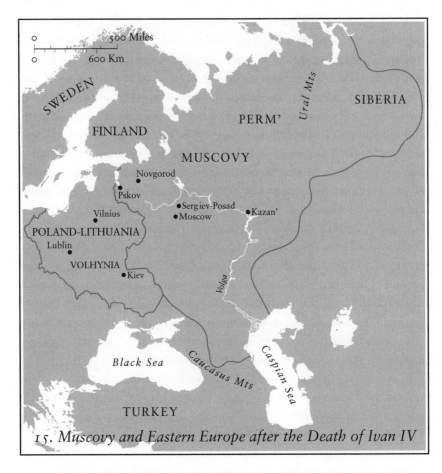

15. Muscovy and Eastern Europe after the Death of Ivan IV

Pious Tsar!', it continues, 'Your great Russian empire [*tsarstvo*], the third Rome, has surpassed them all in piety.'[61] If someone did actually translate this for him, Patriarch Jeremias would have to disregard the implied insult to the patriarchate of Constantinople and appreciate realities: Moscow was the only centre of power in the Orthodox Church which was free of Muslim rule. Moreover, another image of the new patriarchate would be in his mind. Regardless of whether it called itself the Third Rome, the Church of Moscow could be regarded in another light; looking to the five great patriarchates of the early Church, it could be seen as the replacement for one of the five, the now apostate patriarchate of Rome.

This was a very important consideration in 1589, for both secular and ecclesiastical power politics were building up to a major clash in eastern Europe. As in the past, the background was the confrontation between Poland-Lithuania and Muscovy. The Jagiellon dynasty of

Poland-Lithuania had built on their fourteenth-century manoeuvres to become one of the most successful political enterprises in eastern Europe, and particularly after Ivan IV's pathological wrecking of his own land, Poland-Lithuania's future looked very promising. In 1569, prompted to seek greater security by recent savage but inconclusive wars with Ivan IV, the Polish and Lithuanian nobilities – Catholic, Ruthenian Orthodox and Protestant – reached an agreement at Lublin with the last Jagiellon king, Sigismund II Augustus, to create a new set of political arrangements. Instead of a loose union dependent on the person of the king and his dynasty, there would be a closer association between the kingdom of Poland and the Grand Principality of Lithuania, in a Commonwealth (*Rzeczpospolita* in Polish) which would command greater resources and territory than any of its neighbours, and which carefully safeguarded the rights of its many noblemen against the monarchy. Such a vast unit included an extraordinary variety of religions, and it had done so even before the sixteenth-century Reformation had fragmented Western Christianity.

Given the commanding political position of the nobility, principally thanks to the fact that it would now collectively choose the monarchs of Poland-Lithuania by election, it was impossible to impose uniformity on the patchwork of the Commonwealth as many Western political authorities were trying to do, with varying degrees of success. Indeed, by the Confederation of Warsaw of 1573, the nobility extracted from a reluctant monarchy an enshrined right of religious toleration for nearly all the varieties of religions established in Poland-Lithuania, Lutheran and Reformed, even anti-Trinitarian Protestants (see pp. 643–4). In both halves of the Commonwealth, Protestantism made strong advances in the 1560s and 1570s, but mostly in a restricted social sphere of landowners and prosperous and educated people. By contrast, below that level, the vast mass of the population spread through the plains and forests remained little affected by these lively new movements. In the west of the Commonwealth that meant that they persisted in their Catholicism, while in the east, the Ukraine and Volhynia and much of Lithuania, they were mostly Ruthenian Orthodox. Even though King Sigismund Augustus and his successors of other dynasties were convinced Catholics, and welcomed the renewal of Catholicism which the Society of Jesus was bringing to their dominions from the 1560s (see pp. 678–9), they could see that there was still much potential advantage for the ruler of the Commonwealth in claiming to be the successor of Kievan Rus' rather than the new Orthodox tsar in Muscovy. How might the situation be resolved?

Of all the competitors for the religious allegiance of the population in the late sixteenth century, the Ruthenian Church was in most disarray. Disadvantaged by the Catholicism of its monarch (and so, for instance, forced against its will to accept the new calendar sponsored by Pope Gregory XIII in 1582), it was politically estranged from Moscow by political borders, looking instead to an independent metropolitan in Kiev, while its contact with the patriarch in Constantinople was almost non-existent. It had no equivalent of the revivalist movement of the Jesuits; it lacked the fierce commitment to preaching and theological argument in print which was the hallmark of both Lutheran and Reformed Protestantism, and the language of its liturgy and devotion was Old Church Slavonic, which, despite its ancient contribution to rooting Christianity in Slavic lands, now managed to be both increasingly regionalized in usage and remote from the Slavic language of ordinary people. Wholly exceptional was the achievement sponsored by the cultured and far-sighted Prince Konstantyn Ostroz'kyi, the most prominent nobleman of the Commonwealth still loyal to Orthodoxy: he founded an institute of higher learning at his chief town of Ostroh in western Ukraine, and in 1581 sponsored the printing of a Bible in Church Slavonic.[62]

It was not unexpected, then, that overall morale was low among the Ruthenian hierarchy. Perhaps surprisingly, it was not improved by that momentous journey of Patriarch Jeremias II to northern Europe in 1588–9. On his return from Moscow through the Ruthenian lands, anxious to assert his position in the light of the new arrangements for a patriarchate in Moscow, Jeremias alarmed the local bishops by reminding them of the powers of the Oecumenical Patriarch. As he demonstrated, these included weeding out and defrocking those clergy who had been twice married: those dispossessed numbered in their ranks no less a figure than Onysyfor, the Metropolitan of Kiev. Catholics noted the discontent with interest – the Ruthenian Bishop of L'viv begged his Catholic counterpart in 1589 to 'liberate [our] bishops from the slavery of the Patriarchs of Constantinople'.[63] Within seven years, the Polish-Lithuanian King Sigismund III had concluded a deal with the majority of Ruthenian bishops, and in 1596 the Ruthenian Bishop of Brest (himself also a great magnate and former castellan of the city, brought up as a Reformed Protestant) hosted an agreement on union. The model was the set of agreements in the fifteenth century around the Council of Florence. These had set up Churches which retained Eastern liturgical practice and married clergy, but which were nevertheless in communion with the pope and accepted his jurisdiction and the Western use of *Filioque* (see p. 276). Such Churches have often been referred to as 'Uniates', though generally the Churches of Ruthenian or other Orthodox origin in communion with Rome now prefer to term themselves 'Greek Catholics', the name bestowed on them by the Habsburg Empress Maria Theresa in 1774, to stress their equality of status with Roman Catholicism.[64]

Soon every Ruthenian diocese was headed by a bishop who accepted the Union of Brest, and there were hardly any dissident Orthodox bishops left in the Commonwealth. Nevertheless, the union faced problems from the beginning. Prince Ostroz'kyi had long cherished a vision of overall reunion of East and West, including the Protestants, with whom he had excellent relations, but he was infuriated by the terms which the Catholics laid down, since they gave no role to the Oecumenical Patriarch. In an open letter written even before the final deal was signed, he condemned 'the chief leaders of our faith, tempted by the glories of this world and blinded by their desire for pleasures' and menacingly added, 'When the salt has lost its savo[u]r it should be cast out and trampled underfoot.'[65] Passions ran very high: in 1623 the combative-spirited Greek Catholic Archbishop of Polock, Josaphat Kuncewicz, was murdered because, among other affronts, he had refused to allow Orthodox faithful who rejected the union to bury their dead in the parish graveyards which the Greek Catholics had taken over. Twenty years later the Pope declared him a martyr and beatified him; he is now a saint.[66] Meanwhile, as the Church of the Union fissured, in 1632 the Polish monarchy had given in to reality. A new king, Władyslaw IV, needed both to secure his own recognition from his elector-nobles and to consolidate the loyalty of his subjects in the face of a Muscovite invasion. To the fury of Rome but to the relief of moderates on both sides, he recognized the independent Orthodox hierarchy once more in 'Articles of Pacification'. From now on there were two hierarchies of Ruthenian Orthodox bishops side by side, one still Greek Catholic and loyal to Rome, the other answering to a metropolitan in Kiev in communion with Constantinople.[67]

The Orthodox Metropolitan of Kiev newly elected after this agreement in 1633 was a happy choice: Peter Mohyla. He came from one of the leading princely families in Moldavia, beyond the Commonwealth's borders to the south. With a Hungarian mother and experience of university study in France at the Sorbonne, he had the wide vision which the Orthodox Church of Kiev needed at this time. Like Prince

Konstantyn Ostroz'kyi before him, he cherished the hope that there could be a true union of Churches which would go beyond what he saw as Roman aggression: the Union of Brest, he remarked tartly, 'was not intended to save the Greek religion but to transform it into the Roman faith. Therefore it did not succeed.'[68] Mohyla's vision was of a Polish-Lithuanian Commonwealth which would become the supporter of a newly invigorated Orthodoxy: he was decidedly cool towards Muscovy and the claims of the patriarch in Moscow. He knew a great deal about Western Catholicism, and although he was especially familiar with the contemporary methods and writings of the Society of Jesus, he also produced a translation into contemporary literary Ukrainian of that Western devotional classic of the fifteenth century, Thomas à Kempis's *Imitation of Christ*, adapting it to his own Orthodox concerns, and diplomatically concealing the name of the original author to avoid the wrath of his Orthodox fellow clergy.[69]

One of Mohyla's most important and lasting achievements was the foundation of a new academy in Kiev, in the year before he became metropolitan. This was the equivalent of a Western university and was based on the institutions which the Jesuits had so successfully created throughout Catholic Europe as vehicles for their mission (see pp. 665–6). It had a brilliant future in giving Orthodox clergy the possibility of as good an education as anything in the West. Significantly, at the core of the foundation was a library of books mostly in Latin but also in German and other western European languages, many of which Mohyla presented himself; the foundation was unprecedented in eastern Europe (and alas, nearly all its books were destroyed in a fire in 1780). The aim was not to create a fifth column for Latin transformation of Orthodoxy, but to open up faltering Orthodox intellectual life to new possibilities.[70] The authorities in Rome, so hostile to the Articles of Pacification, recognized the quality of the new metropolitan, and Mohyla was able to promote serious though highly secret negotiations for a renewed union of Catholicism and Ruthenian Orthodoxy in Poland-Lithuania. They were proceeding promisingly even despite Mohyla's death in 1647, when all was abruptly ended by a political explosion in the Ukraine, the Kmel'nyts'kyi (Chmielnicki) rebellion of 1648. The future of all Orthodoxy was transformed, and we must take up the story of Muscovy once more to see how this unlikely turn of events took place.

FROM MUSCOVY TO RUSSIA
(1598–1800)

The eventual triumph of Moscow in the northern Orthodox world can be described as unlikely because at the end of the sixteenth century, while the Commonwealth of Poland-Lithuania seemed uniquely powerful in eastern Europe, it was conceivable that Muscovy would disappear altogether as a political unit. On the death of Ivan IV's son, Tsar Feodor I, in 1598, there was no obvious heir to the throne and civil war reduced the country to its 'Time of Troubles'. After a dozen years of fighting and opportunistic invasions by neighbouring states, the country had virtually ceased to exist: there were Swedish armies in the north and Polish armies penetrating as far east as Moscow. But from 1610 a movement of anger coalesced around princes of the Romanov family, cousins of the previous dynasty, and the occupying forces were painfully beaten back. In 1613 the teenaged Mikhail Romanov was declared tsar, the first in the dynasty which ruled until 1917. His father, Feodor Romanov, had been a victim of that old Byzantine political ploy of being forced to take irrevocable monastic vows, assuming the name in religion of Filaret. Rather than repudiate his vows and take the crown himself, Filaret was made patriarch once released from Polish imprisonment in 1619. Since the Patriarch then became the real ruler of Muscovy through a decade and a half of his son's reign, there could hardly have been a closer union of Church and throne. Deeply anti-Catholic after his Polish captivity, Filaret made sure that no innovation such as Mohyla was promoting in Kiev sullied the Church of Moscow, and he also steadily promoted the imposition of an even tighter autocracy on Muscovite society.

Such a regime was not likely to appeal to the Orthodox noble class of Lithuania, enjoying the remarkable political freedom of action which the Commonwealth had fostered, but there was a fatal flaw in their constitutional arrangements. One of the conditions of the Union of Lublin was a transfer of most of what is today the Republic of the Ukraine from Lithuania into the kingdom of Poland, including the city of Kiev itself. It confirmed existing political privileges to the nobilities of Poland and Lithuania, but did not so effectively grant rights to peoples of the Ukraine. They included the warlike people known as Cossacks, few of whom enjoyed noble status. Cossack political discontents combined with their fury both at what they saw as the violation of their

Orthodox faith in the Union of Brest and at the steadily more aggressive Counter-Reformation Catholicism of the Polish monarchy, especially under King Sigismund III (reigned 1587–1632). Patriarch Jeremias on his great visit of 1588–9 had encouraged lay activism by giving his blessing to religious gilds of Orthodox laymen, and these remodellings of medieval urban gilds proved very important in strengthening Orthodox consciousness and maintaining religious life in the virtual absence of an episcopal hierarchy. It was not a good idea for the monarchy to alienate the Cossacks, who provided one of the most effective fighting forces available to the Commonwealth.[71]

The situation boiled over in 1648, after five years during which fatally the Commonwealth had failed to pay its Cossack fighters. A bitter personal grievance led to the devoutly Orthodox Cossack Bohdan Kmel'nyts'kyi rallying a revolt against Polish rule. He proved an inspired leader in a struggle with both the Commonwealth and fellow Cossack leaders who sought some variety of renegotiation of the Union of Lublin. In the course of the fighting, Kmel'nyts'kyi came to ally directly with Muscovy in 1654: a move of huge significance for the future. Nearly two decades marked by exceptional atrocities left the Commonwealth shattered, perhaps a third of its population dead; it was the beginning of its long decline towards eighteenth-century partition and oblivion, and also the beginning of a long identity crisis between East and West for the Ukrainian people. By a treaty with the Tsar at Andrusovo in 1667, the Ukraine experienced its first partition, and Kiev was finally in the hands of Muscovy – the rest of the Ukraine followed a century later. From 1686, an extremely reluctant Oecumenical Patriarch had little choice but to accept the transfer of allegiance by the Metropolitan of Kiev to the Patriarch of Moscow. This in turn stimulated the Orthodox in Polish lands who could not stomach the link with Muscovy to declare a renewed allegiance to the Union of Brest: a move much encouraged by the authorities in Warsaw. With the important exception of this rejuvenated Greek Catholic Church, the Church of the Third Rome now dominated all Orthodoxy in northern Europe.[72]

The Ruthenian Orthodox people of Kiev who did not join the Greek Catholics still came from a very different cultural background to the Orthodox faithful of Moscow. They needed to adapt to a regime which abhorred the religious pluralism of the Commonwealth, and it must be said that they did so with some speed. The intellectual resources of the Mohyla Academy and other schools in the Ukraine were now at the service of the Tsar, and the academy was virtually the only long-term institute of higher education then available in Russia. Its scholars creatively rewrote history, so that now the standard accounts of Russian origins talked of the 'transfer' of Kievan rule to Moscow, and the Ukraine could be seen as 'Little Russia', alongside the 'Great Russia' of Muscovy and the 'White Russia' of Belarus.[73] At the same time, within Muscovy itself, the situation was far from static. A contest was taking place which was to deliver the Church into the hands of the Tsar, as well as causing lasting schism within Russian Orthodoxy.

The source of the conflict lay in a tsar and patriarch who both sought reform in the Church and initially cooperated in it: Tsar Aleksei (reigned 1645–76) and Nikon (Patriarch 1652–8). Even before Muscovy's military successes against Poland-Lithuania, Nikon was promoting a vision of Moscow as leader of Orthodox Christians throughout the world, a vision which would inevitably involve Church reform. Much of this was the type of tightened discipline for both clergy and laity that one might expect from a man who combined great energy with a thoroughly authoritarian temperament, but two other elements in his programme made for trouble. First, Nikon built on the clerical vision implicit in the 'Third Rome' ideology and extended it in a way that would have drawn sympathy from that eleventh-century bishop of the First Rome, Gregory VII. Indeed Nikon constructed his claims round that venerable Western forgery the Donation of Constantine (see p. 351): he proposed that the patriarch and not the tsar should be the chief power in the state, assuming the title *Veliki Gosudar* (Great Lord), which previously only tsars had used. It is not surprising that this near-suicidal self-assertion brought Nikon's patriarchate to a premature close and eventually led to his long-term imprisonment.[74] His defeat showed where the balance of power in Church and State was really going to lie between patriarch and tsar. This was about to be demonstrated all the more emphatically in the reign of Peter the Great.

Yet during Nikon's exercise of his patriarchate, he took a second initiative in liturgical reform which struck at the very heart of Russian tradition. In Russia, the details of Christian doctrine mattered much less to people than the details of Christian practice in worship. Popular religion based itself on the sacred drama which was the liturgical round controlled by the Church's kalendar, but Nikon was conscious that in many respects this drama had departed from the script set by the contemporary Church in Constantinople. Moreover, it was mixed up with a good deal of local ritual which he strongly suspected predated the arrival of Christianity, particularly since most of it seemed designed to enhance the gaiety of everyday life. He therefore announced reforms which he claimed were based on deep research into the most venerable of liturgical texts; in reality what he did was to take the most recent editions of Greek liturgical texts printed in Venice and have them translated into Church Slavonic.[75] This was enough to outrage many of the faithful, who were accustomed to thinking of the liturgy as an unchangeable ordinance of God.

In particular, Nikon courted disaster by insisting on an alteration in that most powerful of Christian visual sacramental actions, and that most frequently performed by clergy, the manual blessing. In 1667 a synod of the Church backed up earlier directives of Nikon ordering all Orthodox, clergy and laity alike, to make the sign of the cross with three fingers, symbolizing the Trinity, rather than with two, symbolizing the two natures of Christ.[76] Amid a welter of reforms which antagonized both clergy and congregations, this apparently trivial but salient symbol of change became the rallying point for a movement of resistance to centralized interference in personal devotion. The opposition drew on centuries of less than reverent obedience to the commands of the hierarchy, and popular lay dissidence combined with clerical outrage. In the matter of liturgical reform, Tsar Aleksei was at one with the deposed patriarch despite their otherwise complete breach, and he persisted in enforcing the changes. Intellectual leadership in the Church increasingly went to clergy trained in the Ukraine and to those who had visited Greece; both these groups were irredeemably tainted by Roman Catholic deviance in the perspective of traditionalist-minded clergy. Noncompliance was led by the priest Avvakum (Habbakuk), whose remarkable autobiography does not underplay his own saintly qualities.[77]

Avvakum possessed as formidable a will as Patriarch Nikon, and like Nikon he had started as a close friend of the Tsar. His talents and connections had brought him promotion as archpriest (dean) of a cathedral. After initially supporting the reforms – indeed personally smashing up carnival tambourines and masks and abducting two dancing bears – he took up the cause of tradition. He suffered for his leadership: for years on end he was imprisoned in a cellar, and eventually in 1682 he was burned at the stake.[78] This ghastly revival of a form of religious discipline by then obsolete in western Europe had a political rationale: in that year the Moscow military garrison allied with sympathizers of Avvakum briefly to seize the capital and humiliate the government of Princess Sophia, regent for her young son Peter. She soon ordered those who followed Avvakum to be punished in the same way, and over the next decade many others among them showed their defiance of heretical authority by setting fire to themselves. The movement of outrage and protest was coalescing into a series of sects which all saw themselves as the pure version of an official Church which had betrayed the faith; they came to be known as the Old Believers, a movement which gained vastly from protests against further changes in the Church during the eighteenth century, and which has survived all subsequent persecution to the present day.

Romanov autocracy was completed by Tsar Aleksei's son Peter I 'the Great', who defeated the rival northern power of Sweden, and humiliated and subverted the now declining Polish-Lithuanian Commonwealth. In 1721 Peter proclaimed himself Emperor of All the Russias, setting patterns for Russian expansion which through the eighteenth and nineteenth centuries created one of the largest empires the world had seen, stretching from eastern Europe to the Pacific. The transformation of Muscovy into a newly conceived empire was accomplished not merely by military conquest but by Peter's obsessive pursuit of Western skills and information, which he used to remould the culture of the governing elite. He saw to it that the pool of available knowledge was massively expanded. Before 1700, no more than about five hundred printed books had been published in Muscovy, most of them devotional works. By the time he died in 1725, there were around thirteen hundred more, 80 per cent of them on secular subjects. A large proportion of these were translations of foreign texts, and the Russian which emerged as the language of these books had a much expanded vocabulary – a significant portion of it being terms necessary for Peter's pride and joy, his newly founded Russian navy.[79] The brand-new capital which he designated to supplant Moscow, St Petersburg, was placed so that it was accessible to the sea routes west, and although it was full of churches, their architectural style, and that of the whole monumental stone-built city, was that of the Baroque of northern Europe, whose visual impact was becoming familiar from Dublin and Amsterdam to Stockholm and Vilnius.

Peter was one of the most secular of tsars. He demonstrated his lack of conventional piety by fashioning for himself a Court whose life was punctuated by revels featuring drink and debauchery which frequently spilled over into churches, misusing sacred vessels and poking fun at the liturgy.[80] He did not reject the whole of the Muscovite past: he bequeathed to his successors a conundrum of how they might balance and value a distinctive Russianness which united them with the vast majority of their subjects against their grasp on Western culture. Peter placed principal value on two inheritances: first, the ideology of unquestioning obedience to the tsar as the foundation of Russian identity, and second, the institution of serfdom, which he intensified and extended, just when the Western society which he so admired was undermining the premises on which it was based. Otherwise, the Church was in his eyes as much of an obstacle to the changes he was making as the Muscovite nobility whom he intimidated and forced to adopt Western ways and Western dress. With the memory of Patriarch Nikon's extravagant claims for power in his father's reign, he determined that never again would a tsar face a similar challenge from an ecclesiastical rival; the Church should concentrate on its preaching of obedience.

Patriarch Adrian died in 1700, after which his office remained vacant until, in 1721, Peter undertook a major reorganization of Church leadership which concentrated all its power in his hands. True to his Westernizing agenda, Peter had built up a team of clergy who had trained in Kiev at the Mohyla Academy, and it was one of their number, Feofan Prokopovich, made Bishop of Pskov, who drew up the new scheme of government, with the aid of advisory memoranda to the Tsar from a much-travelled English lawyer of mystical High Church Anglican outlook, Francis Lee. Prokopovich's own outlook can be gauged from the contents of his library of around three thousand books, three-quarters of which were of Lutheran origin.[81] Instead of the patriarch's rule, there would now be a twelve-strong 'College for Spiritual Affairs', presided over by an official appointed by the tsar, the chief procurator. It was reminiscent of the state-dominated Church government which had been in place in some Lutheran princely states of the Holy Roman Empire for the previous two centuries, but it was far more restrictive, since only the chief procurator could initiate business in the college.

When the College for Spiritual Affairs first met in 1721, the bishops present protested that its name was unprecedented in Russian Church history, and the Tsar was happy to give it a more resonant name which nevertheless in no way changed its nature or function: it became entitled the Holy Synod. While some of those who presided over the Holy Synod in the next two centuries were devout members of the Church (usually in the most darkly authoritarian mould of Orthodoxy), some had little religious belief, or, in the fashion of the Western Enlightenment, gained more spiritual satisfaction from Freemasonry. This was a source of grief and anger to many in the Russian Church, who came to have an obsessive hatred of Freemasonry partly as a result. Among the monarchs to whom the Holy Synod answered, one of the most long-reigning and effective of Peter the Great's successors was Catherine II (reigned 1762–96), a German princess who, despite her reception into the Orthodox Church, never moved far from her culturally Western and Lutheran background, except to befriend that apostle of Enlightenment scepticism Voltaire (see pp. 800–801). The Church was an organ of government, symbolized by Peter's decree of 1722 which required priests hearing sacramental confessions to disregard the sacred obligation of confidentiality and report any conspiracies or insulting talk about the tsar to the security officials of the state, under severe punishments for non-compliance.[82]

It is perhaps surprising that there was not more high-level protest against Peter's enactment of a state captivity for the Church's government, but after the humiliation of Patriarch Nikon and the savage official reaction to the Old Believers in the 1680s, there was little chance of any bishop raising further opposition. The clergy were in any case divided among themselves: there was resentment of the Ukrainian-trained clique around the Tsar, and there was also an increasingly bitter division among the clergy between the 'black' elite of monks, with a superior education and a career pointing towards the episcopate and higher Church administration, and the 'white' clergy, married and serving in the parishes. Peter introduced seminaries for clergy training, an institution familiar in Catholic and Protestant Churches to the west, but here they had a curriculum narrowly focusing on the theme of obedience and the selective version of Orthodox tradition which had survived the upheavals of the seventeenth century. Rarely in later centuries did they win much respect for their educational standards or indeed educational humanity, a reputation not mitigated by the memoirs of many former students. Since the seminaries were only open to the sons of clergy, they contributed very significantly to one of the growing characteristics of the 'white' clergy: they were turning into a self-perpetuating caste, marrying into other clerical families. They had their own culture, for good or ill. They might develop an intense commitment to the clerical vocation, or they might see it as more of a family business than the basis for any individual sense of commitment to a spiritual life. In addition, many of these seminary-trained children could not find jobs in the Church; overeducated, frustrated young clergy sons were to prove one of the hazards of life in nineteenth-century Russia.[83]

If anything saved Orthodoxy through its eighteenth-century period of unsympathetic leadership and low clerical morale, it was its profound hold over the lives and emotions of ordinary people, which contrasted

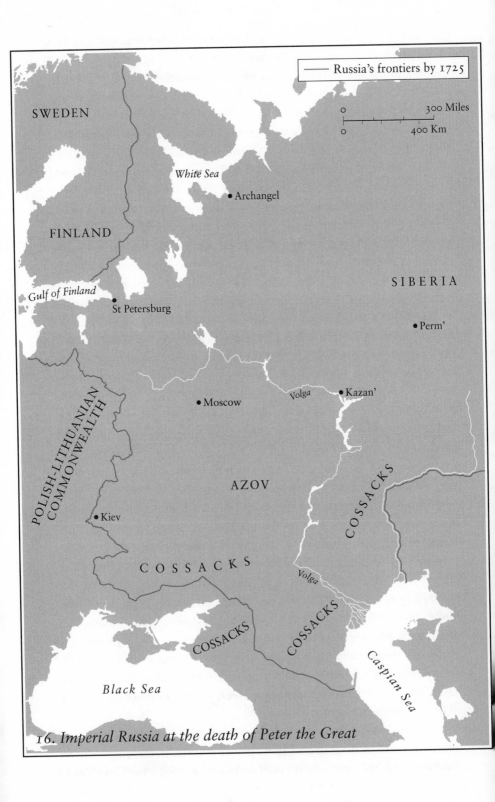

300 Miles

400 Km

SWEDEN

FINLAND

White Sea

• Archangel

SIBERIA

Gulf of Finland

St Petersburg

• Perm'

POLISH-LITHUANIAN
COMMONWEALTH

• Moscow

Volga

• Kazan'

AZOV

C O S S A C K S

• Kiev

C O S S A C K S

Volga

COSSACKS

COSSACKS

COSSACKS

Caspian Sea

Black Sea

16. Imperial Russia at the death of Peter the Great

with popular attitudes to state power. Russian society was exceptional in contemporary Christendom in the degree of separation between its government and its people. Authority and conformity were the watchwords of both the dynasty and the smallest village, but once local communities had paid their taxes to the tsar, raised troops for his armies, and weeded out troublemakers and criminals, they were left largely to their own devices and to their own traditions of making sense of their often desperately harsh environment.[84] Woven inextricably into their common experience were the practices of religion, perhaps the only area of most people's lives where it was possible to make genuine personal choices. Given the isolation of all Russians from much possibility of foreign influence apart from the tiny proportion who belonged to the elite, that meant some variant on Orthodox belief.

Laity who were unhappy at clerical inadequacies and repelled by innovation which could be associated with foreign influences had an alternative in the existing dissidence of the Old Believers, whose numbers and variety swelled during the eighteenth century. They preserved older traditions of worship and devotional styles which the authorities had repudiated, and their rejection of novelty was a rejection of all that they saw as not Russian. Some Old Believers refused to eat the tsars' recommended new staple food, the potato, because it was an import from the godless West – potatoes were generally hated among the Russian peasantry on their first arrival, before their value in making vodka became apparent. 'Tea, coffee, potatoes and tobacco had been cursed by Seven Ecumenical Councils' was one of the Old Believers' rallying cries, and at various times, dining forks, telephones and the railways were to suffer the same anathemas.[85]

Sometimes Russian dissidence spiralled off into the most alarmingly eccentric varieties of Christianity ever to emerge from meditation on the divine, usually fuelled by the belief which had once been the mainstay of the official Church, that the world was about to end and the Last Judgement was to come. Towards the end of the eighteenth century, a self-taught peasant leader, Kondratii Selivanov, founded a sect devoted to eliminating sexual lust from the human race. He based his teachings on a creative misunderstanding of particular proof texts in his Russian Bible, reading *Oskopitel'* (castrator) for *Iskupitel'* (Redeemer) when the New Testament speaks of Jesus, and reading God's command to the Israelites as *plotites'* (castrate yourselves) rather than *plodites'* (be fruitful). As a result, his followers, the *Skoptsy* ('castrated ones'), cut off their genitals or women their breasts to achieve purity. Despite persecution by

the appalled authorities in both tsarist and Soviet Russia, the sect persisted into the mid-twentieth century, when unaccountably it died out,
just before the arrival of the permissive era which might have provided
it with some justification. The *Skoptsy* were not alone in their self-
destructive impulse; in the late nineteenth century, one group of Old
Believers, apparently living perfectly peaceably and openly among their
neighbours, prevailed on one of their number to bury alive all of them
and their children, thus reviving the suicide traditions of the first Old
Believers in order to save their souls before the Last Days.[86]

Within the official Church, the entrenched traditions of popular
Orthodoxy survived the Church's institutional faults; so holy men and
women continued to seek stillness in Hesychasm, and to bring what
comfort they could to the troubled society around them. Some of the
best-loved saints in the Orthodox tradition come from this era. The
most celebrated is probably Serafim of Sarov (1759–1833), who lived
like Sergei of Radonezh before him in the classic style of Antony. Once,
after he had been senselessly attacked and permanently crippled by
bandits, he prayed alone for a thousand days, kneeling or standing on a
rock. Towards the end of his life he abandoned his solitary existence to
strengthen crowds of suppliants daily with his counsel and spiritual
pronouncements, like the Syrian stylites long before (see pp. 207–9).
'Achieve stillness and thousands around you will find salvation,' he
said.[87] It was in his era that a new Greek collection of classic devotional
texts from the fourteenth and fifteenth centuries came to present a sure
guide to the forms of prayer in the Hesychast tradition: the *Philokalia*
('Love of the Beautiful'), compiled by monks of Mount Athos and first
published in Venice in 1782. Only eleven years later, the Ukrainian
monk Paisii Velichkovskii produced the first Slavonic translation of this
work which became standard in the Orthodox world, and which was a
major force in reuniting Orthodox spirituality after the stresses and
divisions of the seventeenth and eighteenth centuries.

At the same time, the expanding Russian Empire gained an international vision for its version of Orthodoxy. It maintained its contacts
with Mount Athos, supporting monastic life on the Holy Mountain with
a generosity which saw a great flowering of Russian communities there
in the nineteenth century. But there was much more to the tsars' intervention in the Ottoman Empire, as it became apparent that the hold of
the Turkish sultan on his territories was beginning to weaken. During
the eighteenth century, throughout the Orthodox world still ruled by
Muslims in the Balkans and the East, Churches began looking with

increasing hope to this great power in the north which proclaimed its protection over them, whose Church still announced itself to be the Third Rome, and which pushed its armies ever further into the lands so long languishing in the hands of the Grandsons of Hagar. Soon in its efforts to fulfil its ambitions at the expense of the decaying Ottoman Empire, the Russian Empire would clash with heirs of the Western Reformation, with consequences disastrous for all those drawn into the contest. It is to the West that we now return, to trace the story which led Christendom to the events of 1914.

PART VI

Western Christianity Dismembered (1300–1800)

16

Perspectives on the True Church
(1300–1517)

THE CHURCH, DEATH AND
PURGATORY (1300–1500)

By the end of the thirteenth century, the Western Latin Church had created nearly all the structures which shaped it up to the Reformation era. Throughout Europe, from Ireland to the kingdoms of Hungary and Poland, from Sweden to Cyprus and Spain, Christians looked to the pope in Rome as their chief pastor. He looked further than that: newly aware of the possibilities of a wider world thanks to the Crusades and the Western Church's thirteenth-century missions into Central and East Asia (see pp. 275–6), the popes made large claims to be the focus of unity in all Christendom. Given the crusaders' failure to recapture former Christian lands except in the Iberian peninsula, these claims remained empty, but within its own world the Church was united by institutions whose ultimate appeal was to Rome: canon law, religious orders, indeed the whole network of parishes, dioceses and archdioceses which made a honeycomb of the map of Europe. European universities, which mostly owed their formal existence to a specific papal grant, embodied in their name their claim to 'universality', the fact that they taught a range of disciplines in a common curriculum embodying a common Latin European culture.

All literate Europeans who owed allegiance to this Church were united by the Latin language which separated the Western Church from its many Eastern counterparts, and which had once been the language of official power in the Roman Empire. Amid Europe's ruins of palaces, temples and monuments surviving from the Classical society digested by Christendom, it was possible to see the Church as the heir of the Roman emperors, but there was another contender, as was clear from a symbolic split in the inheritance of imperial titles between the popes and the monarchs who were heirs of Charlemagne. The Bishop of Rome was *Pontifex Maximus*, the priestly title once appropriated by the Emperor Augustus and his successors and then redeployed by the papacy, while the acknowledged senior among central Europe's princes and cities was an emperor, now calling himself both 'Holy' and 'Roman'. Amid all the symbols of Christian unity, this division symbolized the indecisive results of earlier clashes between popes and monarchs, such as the eleventh- and twelfth-century 'Investiture Controversy' (see pp. 375–6). The campaign to establish a universal papal monarchy had reached its height under Pope Innocent III, but never came close to achieving its aim. It sought a stability in society which could never be attained in practice, and which was mocked by the flux of human affairs. From the eleventh to the thirteenth centuries, the Church had at least been at the forefront of change. After that, the institutions which it had created proved increasingly inadequate to manage or confront new situations; and the outcome was the division of Europe in the sixteenth-century Reformation.

One major disruption came in the sudden catastrophe which afflicted all Europe in the years after 1348. Already by 1300, worsening economic conditions had probably made Europe's population growth level out, and people's general resistance to disease was weakened by a steadily less sustaining diet. There then appeared from the east a disease, now generally thought to be a variant of bubonic plague, which quickly came to be known as the Black Death. As if the Mongols had not intentionally spread enough death and destruction, it was a siege by plague-stricken Mongols from the Kipchak Khanate of a Genoese trading post in the Crimea in 1346 which first brought Europeans into contact with the Black Death. Genoese fleeing the horror instead took the disease first to Constantinople, then around the whole circuit of the Mediterranean. Knowledge of the plague sped before it; far to the north in Oslo in 1348, a group of worried townsfolk endowed an altar in their cathedral for St Sebastian, celebrated for warding off the plague. Sebastian did not put up an impressive performance.[1] Through several years, 1348–53, the effect of the Black Death in Europe was more thoroughgoing than any other recorded disaster: proportionally, it was far more destructive than the First World War, with perhaps as many as one in three of the population dying, and in some places up to two-thirds.

In Central Asia, this same plague hastened the ruin of the Church of the East during the fourteenth century (see p. 275). In Europe, the institutions of the Church had support from the political institutions around them, which ensured that overall survival would be easier, but the blow to society's morale was deep and bitter. One major emergency plague cemetery to have been systematically investigated, in East Smithfield in London, reveals the particular horror of the disease, that it disproportionately attacked those who were the symbols of adult vigour and sustainers of families in society. The peak age of death of those buried there whose ages could be estimated was between twenty-six and forty-five, and males were also revealed as more vulnerable than females.[2] The sheer concentration of sudden and squalid death underlined the fact already perceptible in less dire times that death's visitation did not exempt clergy; in fact unwittingly they probably helped to spread plague as they ministered to the dying. The Church was revealed as better at celebrating the end of catastrophe than preventing or halting it. Once the plague had begun retreating in intensity, there was a widespread impulse to build chapels and votive shrines on the part of survivors wanting to express their gratitude (and perhaps guilt) for their survival, but while plague still raged, there was an equally powerful impulse to seek someone to blame for God's anger: either oneself, collective sin in society or some external scapegoat.

All three thoughts united in a renewed and much grimmer version of the flagellant movement which had begun in Italy in 1260 (see p. 400) but now found widespread expression in northern Europe.[3] There was no trace of the earlier flagellants' emphasis on peace-making. On the contrary, outbreaks of flagellant activity became associated with quite exceptional anti-Semitic violence, which included the torturing and burning alive of Jews in groups. This was justified by accusations that Jews had poisoned wells and food supplies: the torture supplied the necessary confessions. In the Rhineland and in some other central European regions, Jewish communities were effectively wiped out; overall this was 'the most severe persecution of Jews before the twentieth century'.[4] By autumn 1349 Pope Clement VI, lobbied by alarmed monarchs, bishops and city authorities, issued a bull, *Inter sollicitudines*, which forbade flagellant processions, specifically linking them to anti-Jewish violence; he tried to confine religious flagellation to private houses, or exercises in churches supervised by clergy.[5] Certainly the Church came to take over and regularize a good deal of flagellant activity, so that in Italy the members of one major variety of gild, confraternity or religious association took the name '*battuti*' from their practice of penitential self-flagellation. In one small north Italian town called San Sepolcro, by 1400 practically every adult male belonged to one of several flagellant gilds, and this pattern might be paralleled elsewhere.[6] Yet renewed outbreaks of plague repeatedly broke through the Church's supervision, bringing renewed panic, renewed flouting of Pope Clement's prohibition on flagellant public processions and renewed troubles for the Jews.

The need for consolation in the wake of disaster intensified the personalized devotion which had grown up in the thirteenth century, and singled out the themes of suffering, the Passion and death. In northern Europe, new shrine cults of relics of Christ's blood sprang up. These were associated with the rising devotion to his body and blood in the Eucharist, but they took some time to gain acceptance. They always remained controversial, particularly because they were usually the result of unregulated local enthusiasms, and in any case they raised some awkward theological questions about the mechanism of transubstantiation. One of the earliest, Henry III's effort to start a Holy Blood cult in Westminster Abbey in the mid-thirteenth century, to rival King Louis IX's sensational acquisition of the Crown of Thorns in Paris (see p. 475), never aroused popular enthusiasm and rapidly faded away; it had appeared prematurely.[7] By contrast, after the Black Death, blood cults gathered momentum, and like so much else in Passion devotion they acquired an anti-Semitic edge, because they were often associated with stories that Jews had attacked wafers of eucharistic bread. So the anti-Semitism which had been such a feature of Western Christianity since the era of the early Crusades continued to intensify.

In 1290 in Paris a Jew had supposedly stabbed a eucharistic wafer with a knife and it started bleeding. Among the hundred or so blood cults which appeared over the next three centuries, mainly in the Holy Roman Empire, a majority involved a story of Jewish desecration. There were further stories of deliberate Jewish maltreatment of the host apart from the pilgrimage cults – some are likely to have reflected real assaults by angry Jews, themselves inspired, ironically, by the myth that such assaults had happened.[8] In an allied development, particularly in Iberia, Christ's earliest days also came often to be associated with the shedding of his blood through the Feast of the Circumcision: this happy celebration of Jesus's identification with his Jewish people, which so delighted the Viennese beguine Agnes Blannbekin, was turned into a Jewish assault on the child, rather like the atrocities against children imagined in the 'blood libel' against the Jews (see pp. 400–401). I remember the shock of seeing in the Museo de Arte Antica in Lisbon an example of one of these Circumcision paintings from an anonymous sixteenth-century

Portuguese master. Lying naked in the centre was the Christ Child, over whom stood a rabbi, bishop-like in a mitre, about to wield the knife (and interestingly wearing spectacles, symbolizing his distorted vision, an anti-Semitic visual cliché with a long life ahead of it). On the Child's right were Mary and Joseph, Joseph a befuddled but harmless old man, so a non-threatening sort of Jew, and Mary looking distinctly worried. On the other side stood as vicious a crowd of Jews as one could expect to meet, gleefully brandishing the Ten Commandments.

European society in the wake of the Black Death remained preoccupied by death and what to do about it. No wonder the eleventh- and twelfth-century development of the doctrine of Purgatory was one of the most successful and long-lasting theological ideas in the Western Church. It bred an intricate industry of prayer: a whole range of institutions and endowments, of which the most characteristic was the chantry, a foundation of invested money or landed revenues which provided finance for a priest to devote his time to singing Masses for the soul of the founder and anyone else that the founder cared to specify (since either separate buildings or distinct parts of a church were customarily set apart for this purpose, there is often confusion between the chantry foundation and the chantry chapel in which the foundation operated). Easing the passage of souls through Purgatory with the prayer of the Mass or simply with the prayers of good Christian folk addressed that age-long human sense of bafflement and helplessness in the face of death, for it suggested that there was indeed something constructive to be done for the dead. Moreover, while the dead were languishing in the penitential misery of Purgatory preparatory to being released to eternal joy, they might as well get on with showing some gratitude for the prayers of the living by returning prayer back to them for future use. It was a splendidly mutual system, and a particularly neat aspect was the developed institution of indulgences, which had originated in the first enthusiasm of the Crusades (see p. 384).[9]

To understand how indulgences were intended to work depends on linking together a number of assumptions about sin and the afterlife, each of which individually makes considerable sense. First is the principle which works very effectively in ordinary society, that a wrong requires restitution to the injured party. So God demands an action from a sinner to prove repentance for a sin. Second is the idea that Christ's virtues or merits are infinite since he is part of the Godhead, and they are therefore more than adequate for the purpose of saving the finite world from Adam's sin. Additional to Christ's spare merits are those of the saints, headed by his own mother, Mary: clearly these are worthy in the sight of God, since the saints are known to be in Heaven. Accordingly, this combined 'treasury of merit' is available to assist a faithful Christian's repentance. Since the pope is the Vicar of Christ on earth, it would be criminal meanness on his part not to dispense such a treasury to anxious Christians. The treasury of merit can then be granted to the faithful to shorten the time spent doing penance in Purgatory. That grant is an indulgence.

All these ideas were explicitly drawn together on the very eve of the Black Death in a bull of Pope Clement VI, *Unigenitus* ('The Only Begotten [Son of God]'), in 1343, by which time the Pope was seeking to rationalize a system of indulgence grants already well established, 'now for total, now for partial remission of punishment due for temporal sins'.[10] It was only natural for pious Christians to show gratitude for such an act of charity on the Church's part. Eventually their thanks-offerings became effectively a payment for the indulgence, although all indulgences were very careful to lay down proper conditions for use, particularly instructions to the purchasers to go to confession, and also, in a specialized form of welfare relief, free indulgences were offered to the destitute. There were good reasons to cherish indulgences and their sale: they were very useful for fund-raising for good causes, such as the rebuilding of churches or the support of the charitable homes for the elderly and infirm called hospitals (themselves a part of the Purgatory industry, since their grateful inmates were expected to pass their time praying for the welfare of the souls of their benefactors). Indulgences were as ubiquitous as the modern lottery ticket, and indeed the earliest dated piece of English printing is a template indulgence from 1476.[11] That same year, unknown to the printer in Westminster, a very considerable extension of the system's potential had occurred when the theologian Raimund Peraudi argued that indulgences were available to help souls of people already dead and presumed to be in Purgatory, as well as living people who sought and received an indulgence; a papal bull followed to implement this suggestion. With that the system was complete, and ready to have its disastrous effect on Martin Luther's volcanic temper (see pp. 608–10).

Perhaps significantly for the Reformation, the development of an obsession with Purgatory was not uniform within Europe. It seems to have been the north rather than the Mediterranean area, perhaps most intensively the Atlantic fringe from Galicia on the Spanish Atlantic seaboard round as far as Denmark and north Germany, which became most concerned with prayer as a ticket out of Purgatory. Dante Alighieri's detailed descriptions of Purgatory in his fourteenth-century masterwork the *Divina Commedia* might suggest that southerners were indeed concerned with Purgatory, but his Italian readers do not seem to have transformed their delight in his great poem into practical action or hard cash. This action can be monitored through the contents of late medieval wills – one of the rare ways in which we meet thousands of individuals facing death across the centuries. In the north, will-makers put big investment into such components of the Purgatory industry as Masses for the dead. In Germany there was a phenomenal surge in endowment of Masses from around 1450, with no signs of slackening until the whole system imploded under the impact of Luther's message in the 1520s.[12] Samplings from Spain and Italy do not reveal the same concern. Several studies of localities in southern Europe suggest that such activity was imported by reforming 'Counter-Reformation' Catholic clergy in the late sixteenth century, and only then created a piety reminiscent of that which the Protestants were destroying in much of northern Europe. A similar process of transfer southwards occurred at the same time with the devotion of the rosary, originally German.[13]

Another important symptom of a north–south difference on salvation occurs in the many books published to provide clergy with models for sermons about penitence. These books were widely bought throughout Europe in the fifteenth century, because the faithful particularly demanded sermons during the penitential season of Lent, and expected their clergy to urge them to use the confessional properly at that time. However, different books sold well in northern and in southern Europe, and contrast in emphasis in what they say about penance. In the north, the preacher throws the spotlight on the penitents themselves, on the continual need for penance in their everyday lives and on the importance of true contrition and satisfaction when they come to confession; the priest in confession is cast in the role of judge, assessing the sincerity of all this busy work. In the south, the sermons pay more attention to the role of the priest, who is seen as doctor or mediator of grace in absolution of sin; the preacher is not so concerned to urge the layperson on to activity.[14]

The significance of this contrast is that the Purgatory-centred faith of the north encouraged an attitude to salvation in which the sinner, lay or clerical, piled up reparations for sin; action was added to action in order to merit years off Purgatory. It was possible to do something about one's salvation: that was precisely the doctrine which Martin Luther was to make his particular target after 1517. So the difference between attitudes to salvation in northern and southern Europe may explain why Luther's first attack on some of the more outrageous outcrops of the soul-prayer industry had so much more effect in the north than in the south. He was telling northern Europeans that some of the devotions which most deeply satisfied them, and convinced them that they were investing in an easier passage to salvation, were nothing but clerical confidence tricks. This message was of much less interest or resonance in the Mediterranean lands, which had not paid so much attention to the Purgatory industry.

PAPAL MONARCHY CHALLENGED (1300–1500)

Martin Luther's rebellion against late medieval views on salvation was also a rebellion against papal authority, but he was by no means the first to question the assumptions of papal monarchy. He could borrow virtually all his language of condemnation from the poison created by 'Imperialists', apologists for the Holy Roman Emperor in thirteenth-century conflicts with the papacy, and by similar abuse created during the clash between certain popes and the Spiritual wing of the Franciscans (see pp. 410–11). It was imperial spokesmen who first regularly termed the pope 'Antichrist', that enemy of Christ constructed out of various apocalyptic passages in the Bible – papal spokesmen were rather less successful in fastening the same image on the emperor. The Franciscan Spirituals elaborated talk of the Antichrist, particularly to condemn Pope Boniface VIII (Pope 1294–1303). In order to become pope, Boniface had summarily displaced and brutally imprisoned a disastrously unworldly hermit-partisan of their movement who had been unwisely elected pope as Celestine V.[15]

Boniface went on to claim jurisdiction for the papacy throughout the world in a bull of 1302, *Unam Sanctam* ('One Holy [Church]'). This was a culminating moment in the universal pretensions of the papacy, but the Pope's aspirations were curtailed by his imprisonment and humiliation at the hands of King Philip the Fair of France. A French successor-pope then chose to live in the city of Avignon, a small papal enclave in southern France. There were many good reasons why Pope Clement V should choose Avignon in 1309: it saved him encountering the constant infighting in Rome, and since the papal court was now a bureaucratic centre affecting all Europe, it made sense to find a more accessible place from which it could operate. Nevertheless, the move brought the papacy closely under French influence, and it caused great indignation in Italy, where the great poet Petrarch described it as a 'Babylonian captivity'. It showed how far the pope had moved from the intimate association with the body of St Peter which had brought him his power in the Church.

Pope John XXII made further vocal enemies when after first crushing the Spiritual Franciscans, he further infuriated the 'Conventual' wing of the order which had made careful arrangements to avoid holding property while still establishing a regular life in convents. In 1321 John reversed earlier papal pronouncements supporting Franciscan poverty, and repudiated previous papal trusteeship of their goods, restoring ownership to the Franciscans themselves, a far from welcome gift. Pope John's canonization of Francis the following year by no means mollified the Franciscans: new identifications of the Pope with Antichrist outdid all previous efforts in shrillness, and some Franciscans accused John of heresy for repudiating the pronouncements of his predecessors. That lent an urgent topicality to earlier rather theoretical discussions about how to deal with a pope who was a heretic. One of the most distinguished of Franciscan philosopher-theologians, the Englishman William of Ockham, was among those leading the campaign. He had no hesitation in declaring Pope John a heretic to whom no obedience was due: 'Our faith is not formed by the wisdom of the Pope. For no one is bound to believe the Pope in matters which are of the faith, unless he can demonstrate the reasonableness of what he says by the rule of faith.'[16] Ockham survived John XXII's condemnation for this opinion, and his nominalist approach to philosophy flourished, becoming one of the most influential modes of philosophical and theological argument in late medieval Europe.

Ockham was naturally supported in his attacks by Imperialists, and they had their own powerful spokesman in a former rector of the University of Paris, Marsilius or Marsiglio of Padua, principally presented in his *Defensor Pacis* ('Defender of Peace') of 1324. What was so effective about Marsilius's polemic on papal jurisdiction was that it was a careful dialogue with Thomas Aquinas, and through him with Aristotle, punctiliously backed up at every stage by biblical quotation. Since Thomas had so effectively shown that Aristotle could be reconciled with Christian doctrine, if it appeared that Aristotle's teaching on political arrangements clashed with current Christian understandings, then the fault must lie with mistaken Christian teachers, not with the great philosopher. And the chief Christian teacher was of course the Holy Father in Rome, who could further be shown to have caused much of the political troubles of Christendom in his own time. Protestant monarchs and their publicists much relished Marsiglio's arguments two centuries later; in the 1530s Marsiglio was to be translated (and judiciously tweaked) to support Henry VIII's break with Rome, on the initiative of his unusually well-educated minister Thomas Cromwell.[17]

Although Gregory XI a generation after John XXII tried to cure the wars in his Italian possessions by moving back to Rome in 1377, the situation which emerged from the political wrangles of the late fourteenth century was still worse: from 1378 there were two rival popes, both lawfully elected by the College of Cardinals.[18] An effort to solve the situation at the Council of Pisa in 1409 only resulted in a third candidate emerging: in 1414 one of them, John XXIII, took action in conjunction with the Holy Roman Emperor Sigismund to call a council safely outside Italy across the Alps at Konstanz. The council finally ended four decades of schism when, in 1417, it recognized the election of a new pope acknowledged by all factions, Martin V. In the midst of the complex wrangles which produced this result, the council produced a decree, 'Sacrosancta', proclaiming itself to hold its authority 'immediately from Christ; everyone, of every rank and condition, including the Pope himself, is bound to obey it in matters concerning the faith, the abolition of the schism, and the Reformation of the Church of God in its head and its members'.[19]

There could be no clearer statement that papal primacy was to be put firmly in its place in favour of a general council, but Konstanz added a further idea in its decree of 1417, ordering that a council should henceforth meet every ten years. If this took effect, a council was to become an essential and permanent component of continued reform and reconstruction in the Church. The next few years saw increasing tension between those wishing to develop this conciliar mechanism and successive popes seeking to build on the papacy's newly restored integrity. The eighteen-year session of a council at Basel from 1431 helped to discredit the conciliar option because despite much constructive work, including setting up its own legal processes to rival Rome's, it culminated in a fresh schism. In 1460 a former conciliarist sympathizer, now Pope Pius II, formally forbade appeals from a decision of the papacy to a general council, in a bull entitled Execrabilis. Pius II's change of heart was understandable: seven years before, Constantinople had fallen to the Ottoman Turks. For a pope contemplating this disaster and trying to summon fresh crusades to defend what remained of Christian Europe, now was no time to risk the future of the West by collective leadership which might be divided and uncertain.

Moreover, there was much that was incoherent or unresolved in the bundle of ideas carrying the conciliarist label. Conciliarists never achieved consensus as to how to define the Church or account for the authority of a council. Was it a representation of all the people of God, in which case its authority rose up or ascended from the whole body of the faithful? Or was it an assembly of God's ordained representatives, the clergy, in which case its power descended from God through the Church's hierarchy? Who precisely among the clergy were to be represented? Konstanz had been an assembly of bishops and cardinals; Basel widened its membership so that lower clergy were also given delegates, even with a voting majority over the bishops. Conciliarists tended to be clergy and were naturally clericalist in their outlook; this was not a movement which viewed lay participation with much sympathy. And if conciliarists were drastically limiting the pope's power, how did that affect the centuries-long disputes between the pope and secular rulers? It was unlikely that Philip the Fair's successors as kings of France were going to accept a new rival for power in an effective and permanent General Council of the Church, at least not without a good deal of careful explanation from sure-footed theologians that their own power was not affected by the special sacred status of the council.

When the French theologian Jean Gerson, one of the most prominent activists in the Council of Konstanz, consequently struggled to find a way of reconciling conciliarism with the traditional claims of the French monarchy, he developed a view of the Church's history later of great importance to Reformation leaders who sought to achieve the same balance between Church and secular commonwealth against more radical Christian thinkers. Gerson saw a threefold development in the Church: a first primitive heroic era while it was still unacknowledged and often persecuted by the Roman Empire; a second period after the Emperor Constantine I had allied with it, when Church leaders had justifiably and responsibly accepted power and wealth; but then a third era of decay after the time of Gregory VII, when this process had been taken to excess, so that it must now be curbed. Gerson was not a revolutionary, but in his meditations on the Church he had hit on that perpetually subversive anonymous writer Dionysius the Areopagite. One of the aspects of Dionysius's picture of a heavenly hierarchy which especially appealed to Gerson was an insistence on the highest standards possible for the clerical order, clergy's imitation of the order of Heaven itself. This Dionysian emphasis resonated with many reform-minded clergy; often it produced a clericalism so high as to seem almost anti-clerical.[20]

Gerson was not seeking to destroy hierarchical Church structures, simply to recall them to purity, but he did not see a hierarchy as neces-sarily culminating in a papal monarchy. He was also a strong defender of parish clergy against the pretensions of monks and friars, pointing out that there had been no monastic vows in the Church in the time of Christ, Mary and the Apostles.[21] Sixteenth-century Reformers and the princes who supported them chose what they wanted from these various emphases in his writings. They took note of what Gerson had said about history, hierarchy, monks and friars, just as they took notice of Marsiglio's views on authority in the Church. For the problem which conciliarism had originally raised – principally, how to deal with a pope who cannot lead the Church as God wishes – would not go away. After 1520, Martin Luther was forced to give the drastic answer, going way beyond Ockham and the fourteenth-century Franciscans, that if the pope turned out to be Antichrist, then one must walk out of the pope's false Church and recreate the true body of Christ. Even though in political terms conciliarism faced eclipse from the mid-fifteenth century, plenty of leading churchmen and academics (particularly canon lawyers) continued to believe that conciliar action to solve the Church's problems would be preferable to the rapid rebuilding of centralized papal power now taking place.

Meanwhile, the papacy consolidated its recovery. For a while the rival council that in 1438 the Pope had called to Ferrara and Florence seemed to have achieved spectacular results in reunifying Christian Churches, both East and West, under papal leadership (see pp. 492–3). From 1446 popes were once more permanently based in Rome, never again willingly to desert this symbol of their supremacy in the Church. Soon after, in 1460, came a remarkable piece of accidental good fortune for the Pope when large deposits of alum were discovered at Tolfa, in the papal territories north-west of Rome. This mineral was highly valuable because of its use in dyes, and before that it could only be imported at great expense from the Middle East. The new source of income (which the popes were careful to ensure became a monopoly supply of alum in Europe) began benefiting the papacy just when Pius II reasserted its central power with *Execrabilis*. Various practical expressions of this power followed, taking their cue from a grant made by Pope Nicholas V in 1455 to the Portuguese monarchy of the right to rule in certain regions of Africa.[22] Now that popes were back in Italy, it was unsurprising that they took a particular interest in Italian politics like the other Italian princes around them, and it was no fault of theirs that suddenly in the 1490s Italy became the cockpit of war and the obsessive concern of the great dynastic powers of Europe. The trigger was the ambition of the Valois dynasty of France, when in 1494–5 Charles VIII intervened in the quarrels of Italian princes with a major military invasion; this gained France little, but threw the various major states of Italy into chaos, war and misery for more than half a century.

Amid this suddenly unbalanced high politics, it was a natural protective strategy for the papacy stranded in the middle to redouble its self-assertion, a mood which in any case came naturally to the successive popes Alexander VI (1492–1503) and Julius II (1503–13), despite their mutual detestation. Alexander followed the example of Nicholas V with an adjudication in 1493–4 between the claims of the two European powers which were now exploring and making conquests overseas, Portugal and Spain; he divided the map of the world beyond Europe between them, commissioning them to preach the Gospel to the non-Christians whom they encountered, in an action which had all the ambition of the twelfth-century papacy. Likewise, fifteenth-century popes began to restore the architectural splendour of their sadly ramshackle city; display was an essential aspect of power for secular rulers, and surely it was all the more important for Christ's representative on earth. The most important – and, as we shall see, the most fateful – project was the demolition of the monumental basilica of St Peter built by the Emperor Constantine, so that it could be replaced with something even more spectacular. This was a particular enthusiasm of Julius II, one of the most discriminating but also one of the most extravagant patrons of art and architecture in the papacy's history (see Plate 26).

The two popes who between them occupied St Peter's throne for two decades had a very selective understanding of what might glorify the papacy. Alexander VI, from the Valencian noble family of Borja (Borgia), shielded his vulnerability as an outsider against his many Italian enemies by ruthlessly exploiting the Church's most profitable offices to promote his relatives, including his own children by his several mistresses. It was a scandalous flouting of the clerical celibacy imposed by the twelfth-century Reformation, even if Lucrezia and Cesare, the Pope's most notorious children, had not provided extreme examples of aristocratic self-indulgence. Julius II relished being his own general when he plunged into the Italian wars which proliferated after the French invasion, and he was especially proud when in 1506 he recaptured Bologna, second city of the Papal States after Rome, lost to the papacy seventy years before.[23] Nor was Julius a pioneer in this. He merely improved on the previous practice of the Papal States, where for a century or more cardinals had been the military commanders most trusted alike by the pope and by their mercenary soldiers. One of the most effective generals of the early fifteenth century had been a cardinal, Giovanni Vitelleschi; his spiritual duties as Archbishop of Florence, still less his titular status as Patriarch of Alexandria, do not seem to have curbed his streak of sadism. A recent study describes him as 'a master of sackings, massacres and summary executions', and his own death by summary execution in 1440 had reputedly forestalled his seizure of the papal fortress in Rome, Castel Sant'Angelo, with a view to the papal throne itself.[24]

NOMINALISTS, LOLLARDS AND HUSSITES (1300–1500)

A centralized papacy, particularly one which recruited such dubious assistants, could not stop people thinking new thoughts. Two movements, the Lollards and the Hussites, rose to challenge the Church authorities. Another potential challenge was from the nominalism espoused by William of Ockham. The Franciscan Ockham denied the assumptions embodied in the Dominican Thomas Aquinas's adaptation of Greek philosophy to Christianity, centring on the word *nomen*. At its simplest this is the ordinary Latin word for 'name', but in the philosophical terminology of the time it signified the universal concept of a particular phenomenon: the word 'tree', for instance, is the *nomen* which unites our perception of every individual tree and points to the universal concept of a tree. Ockham and his fourteenth-century nominalist successors denied that there was any such individual reality behind a *nomen*. For them, it was simply a word to organize our thinking about similar phenomena – thus individual examples of objects which we decide to label trees. If this was accepted, it became impossible to construct overall systems of thought or explanation by the use of reason. This denied the value of Aquinas's work, with its majestic system of relationships throughout the cosmos: it implied that the line of analytical thought derived from Aristotle was pointless.

To turn from trees to the problem of discussing one of the chief issues of the Christian faith: what happens when bread and wine are consecrated in the Eucharist? If they become the body and blood of Christ, as virtually all medieval Western Christians agreed was the case, how can this be explained? As we have seen, those theologians or philosophers like Aquinas who drew on the vocabulary provided by Aristotle, could do so in terms of 'substance' and 'accidents' (see pp. 405–6). Ockham and nominalist philosophers or theologians denied the usefulness of this language of substance and accidents, so they had no way of constructing such an explanation. The doctrine, and indeed any other doctrine of ultimate divine truths, could only be treated as a matter of faith, relying on the authority of the Church. And what would happen if one felt that the authority of the Church was at fault, as many nominalist-trained clergy were to do in the sixteenth century? As a result, nominalism was a corrosive doctrine for the accepted principles of medieval Western Christianity; while still glorying in the disputes of scholastic debates, nominalist academic debaters disrupted many of the given principles within those debates, and split apart the concerns of philosophy and theology. Still nominalism came to dominate the universities of northern Europe during the fifteenth century, wherever the Dominicans could not defend the standing of their hero Aquinas. Many Protestant Reformers gained their university education in a nominalist tradition.

Yet nominalism should not simply be seen as a high road to Protestantism, because in one vital respect, its soteriology (view of salvation), it provided a thoroughgoing explanation of how human beings could have a role in their own salvation, despite Augustine's pessimism about human capacity. The school of nominalist theology known as the *via moderna* ('present-day/modern system') squared this circle by fusing medieval economic theory with the language of 'contract', which had so appealed to Francis of Assisi in thinking of a merciful God's relationship with his people (see pp. 416–17). Human virtues may be worthless because of Adam's fall, but they can be treated like a technically worthless or token coinage issued by monarchs in a time of emergency: after all, there could be no greater emergency for humanity than Adam and Eve's sin in Eden. Such temporary coins, unlike the normal silver coinage of medieval Europe, possess no value other than what the ruler decrees them to bear. The ruler has entered an agreement, a contract or covenant, with his people to sustain this fiction for the general good. So God in his infinite mercy ascribes value to human worth, and makes an agreement with humanity to abide by the consequences and let it do its best towards its salvation. In a famous phrase of the fifteeenth-century nominalist theologian Gabriel Biel, he allows a human being 'to do that which is in oneself' (*facere quod in se est*). The system avoids troubled scrutiny of Augustine's view of humanity's utterly fallen state, as long as one accepts its principles.

When nominalism removed the human relationship with God from the sphere of reason, it came close to the mysticism which flourished from the thirteenth century. This also spoke of the unknowability of God, and it broadened into a style of personal piety known as 'present-day/modern devotion', *Devotio Moderna*. In Gabriel Biel, indeed, the two streams of nominalism and the *Devotio* flowed together. The *Devotio* became the dominant outlet for pious expression in the fifteenth-century West: it was an intense and creatively imaginative mode of reaching out to God. It also tended to introspection, aided by that crucial contemporary technological advance in the spread of texts, printing. Printed texts made far more easily available to an increasingly literate public the writings of the mystics, or works which meditated as John de Caulibus had done (see pp. 417–18) on aspects of the life of Jesus. For someone who really delighted in reading, religion might retreat out of the sphere of public ritual into the world of the mind and the imagination. Reading privileges sight among the other human senses, and it further privileges reading text among other uses of the eye; it relies not at all on gesture, which is so important a part of communicating in liturgy or in preaching.

So without any hint of doctrinal deviation, a new style of piety arose in that increasingly large section of society which valued book-learning for both profit and pleasure; the Netherlands, which had a level of urban life more concentrated than in any other part of Europe and high levels of literacy, were particularly prominent in this development. Even if such people were in the crowd at the parish Mass, they were likely be absorbed in their layfolk's companion to the Mass, or a Book of Hours – books commonly known as primers. These primers had already been mass-produced in the days of manuscript book production, but printing made them far cheaper and more widely available, and there quickly developed an eager market for primers in the major European languages.

The wealthier folk in such congregations increasingly built themselves an enclosed private pew in their church to cut themselves off from the distractions provided by their fellow worshippers.[25]

One should not overemphasize this exclusive characteristic of the *Devotio*. It also had the capacity to offer laity as well as clergy, women as well as men, the chance of achieving the heights and depths of religious experience in their everyday lives and occupations, just as if they had set out on pilgrimage. The earliest great name in the movement, the fourteenth-century Dutch theologian Geert Groote, was never ordained beyond the order of deacon; after spending some time in a Carthusian monastery near Arnhem, he went on to conduct a roving ministry of preaching in the Netherlands and to found his own informal community of friends in his native Deventer. After Groote's death in 1384, this group did take on the character of a formal religious order, the Brethren of the Common Life, which spread widely through central Europe and enrolled clergy of the calibre of the mystical writer Thomas à Kempis, the philosopher-theologian Gabriel Biel and the future Pope Adrian VI.

Despite this, the *Devotio Moderna* was never a purely clerical movement. Even the formally organized Brethren discouraged members from becoming ordained clergy, and they put their houses of Sisters and some of their own communities under the control of local urban corporations rather than the Church authorities.[26] Notably, married couples (and of course their children) might be involved on an equal basis in a lifestyle inspired by the *Devotio*. Its promise was that serious-minded laity could aspire to the high personal standards which had previously been thought more easily attainable by the clergy: a programme of practical action and organization of one's thoughts and life which was summed up in the title of Kempis's famous devotional treatise *The Imitation of Christ*. The idea of imitating Christ was not much older in the Western tradition of Christianity than the twelfth century; it sat uneasily with Augustinian assumptions about fallen humanity. It was also a solvent of that assumption which had developed particularly in the West, that clergy and religious had a better chance of getting to Heaven than laity.

Those same thoughts – the comparability of layfolk and clergy, and the calling of all to the highest standards – were behind the two movements of Church reform which sprang like nominalism from universities, but which were forced out by official opposition and repression. John Wyclif, an Oxford philosopher, was the reverse of a nominalist: in the manner of philosophers like Aquinas, he championed the idea that there were indeed universal, indestructible realities, greater than individual phenomena. Wyclif's career in controversy was comparatively brief, no more than a decade or so. In the mid-1370s, well into his career, having returned from an unproductive royal mission to Bruges to argue the case for a remission of England's taxation to the pope, he began turning his philosophical assumptions into an attack on the contemporary institutions of the Church: not merely their everyday faults, but their whole foundation. Enemies said that this new departure arose because Wyclif was angry at the lack of promotion in the Church, while his fellow delegates were well rewarded. That is not impossible; Wyclif would not be the first or the last to be jolted into genuinely principled indignation by mundane disappointments.

Wyclif contrasted the universal reality of the invisible true Church with the false Church which was only too visible in the everyday world. He maintained that the true Church was made up solely of those who were saved, not just in the next world, but here and now. There were some people, probably most, who were eternally damned and who therefore never formed part of the true Church. No one could know who was damned or who was saved, and therefore the visible Church, that presided over by popes and bishops, could not possibly be the same as the true Church, since it claimed a universal authority in the world. Moreover, since all authority to rule or the right to own property (*dominium*) was in the hands of God, only those in a state of grace could enjoy them. Wyclif argued that it was more likely that rulers chosen by God like kings or princes were in this happy condition than was the pope, and therefore *dominium* should be seen as being entrusted to them. Churchmen who were critical of the Church had discussed *dominium* before, particularly in the controversies around papal authority at the beginning of the fourteenth century, and they had pointed out that it was ultimately still in the power of God, but rarely with this radical conclusion.[27]

Wyclif's arguments were decidedly convenient for the English prince and noblemen who acted as his patrons and protectors, but they had other implications for the whole people of God. In place of the Church's authority, Wyclif urged people to turn to the Bible, reading and understanding it, for it was the only source of divine truth. Readers would see that the Mass, on which so much of the Church's power was based, was a distortion of the Eucharist which Christ had instituted. Wyclif deeply loathed not merely the eucharistic doctrine of transubstantiation which was now standard within the Western Church, but the whole notion of divine bodily presence in bread and wine. He regarded the doctrine as a clerical deception developed during the Church's eleventh-century usurpation of worldly power – so his philosophical realism had led him in a completely different direction from Aquinas's Aristotelian realist arguments.[28] He plunged the University of Oxford into bitter divisions; although political circumstances saved him from what ought to have been inevitable condemnation and death for heresy, he retreated to his country rectory, his literary attacks on the Church and his revisions of his earlier work becoming ever more extreme. Several decades elapsed after his death in 1384 before the Church authorities sent a commission to his Leicestershire grave to dig up his bones and burn them for heresy.

Wyclif's followers, first Oxford academics, then a wider circle of clergy and laypeople influenced by the first university enthusiasts, were given the contemptuous nickname of 'Lollards': that is, mumblers who talked nonsense.[29] They became mixed up with the losing side in early-fifteenth-century English politics, and now Crown and Church could combine in purging Lollard influence from the universities and among politically significant people. With just one permanent political backer, the Lollard story might have been very different, and more like that of the movement started a century later by another university lecturer, Martin Luther. Instead, Lollardy's repression included one feature unique to England. Wyclif's Oxford admirers had followed his teaching on the unchallengeable authority of the Bible by producing the first complete translation of the Vulgate into English, so that all might have a chance to read it and understand it for themselves. In 1407 all existing versions of the Bible in English were officially banned by the English Church hierarchy, and no replacement was sanctioned until Henry VIII's Reformation in the 1530s. In the intervening period, only the most obviously ultra-respectable could get away with open possession of a vernacular Bible, and indeed, their respectability seems itself to have made their copy of the text respectable.[30]

No other part of Europe went to such lengths, even though that great activist and reformer Jean Gerson did propose a general ban on Bible translations to the Council of Konstanz; he was worried that the laity would spend too much time reading for themselves and not listen to the clergy's increasingly generous supply of preaching. In most of Europe, when printing technology arrived in the early fifteenth century, the supply of vernacular Bibles hugely increased: the printers sensed a ready market and hastened to supply it in languages which would command large sales. Between 1466 and 1522 there were twenty-two editions of the Bible in High or Low German; the Bible reached Italian in 1471, Dutch in 1477, Spanish in 1478, Czech around the same time and Catalan in 1492. In 1473–4 French publishers opened up a market in abridged Bibles, concentrating on the exciting stories and leaving out the more knotty doctrinal passages, and this remained a profitable enterprise until the mid-sixteenth century. Bernard Cottret, Calvin's biographer, has suggested that this huge increase in Bibles created the Reformation rather than being created by it.[31]

The suppression of Lollardy by no means ended talk of reforming the Church in England. Since at least the eleventh century, it had been one of the best-regulated parts of the Western Church, and accordingly had bred many clergy with ultra-rigorous standards, who were not going to cease lamenting clerical faults just because Wyclif had been part of the stream of lamentation. Yet to do so brought new risks: the English Church authorities were so traumatized by the Wyclif episode that they were liable to regard any criticism as heretical. Even a well-meaning and conscientious Bishop of Chichester, Reginald Pecock, was accused of heresy in 1457–8. He was forced to resign and recant because he chose to defend the Church against Lollardy by privileging reason over the authority of scripture and the Fathers of the early Church; moreover, contrary to Gerson, he questioned the value of preaching without the laity doing their own reading to reinforce the message from the pulpit.[32]

English Lollardy survived through personal networks, often involving quite prosperous people but rarely gentry or clergy, who kept in touch over wide areas, treasuring their manuscripts of vernacular Bibles and increasingly tattered copies of Wyclifite tracts right down to the six-teenth-century Reformation. Significantly they did not produce much fresh literature after the first decades of the fifteenth century, apparently living off past achievements. Their rebellion against the Church was very qualified, for many of them remained involved in its life alongside their clandestine religious activities, rather as early Methodists were half inside, half outside the official English Church in the eighteenth century. It is understandable that Lollards did not gain access to the first English printing presses, which were to prove so important to Protestantism, but it is less easy to understand why they do not seem to have exploited those other great populist weapons of the sixteenth-century Reform-ation, hymns and songs; their meetings seem to have been dominated by readings from their literature and by sermons. This suggests that their dissent was as much intended to complement public religion as to challenge it, but that did not stop flurries of ecclesiastical investigations and burnings at the stake at intervals into the 1520s.[33]

Linked with this English movement of dissent was that of the Hussites, whose development in the kingdom of Bohemia in central Europe was very different. The unanticipated connection between England and far-away Prague, two parts of Europe with no natural links, arose through the marriage in 1382 of the Holy Roman Emperor Charles IV's daughter Anne of Bohemia to the English King Richard II. The Emperor Charles, also King of Bohemia, had made Prague his capital, lavishing money on it to create one of the most spectacular ensembles of public buildings in central Europe, providing Prague not merely with the beginnings of a great cathedral but with a new university. Such a lively city, owing its beauty to Charles's determination to make his capital a new Jerusalem for the Last Days of the world, was a natural breeding ground for urgent advocacy of Church reform even before the dean of the university's Philosophical Faculty, the priest Jan Hus, became fired by Wyclif's reforming message. Hus preached a series of increasingly outspoken sermons in Prague, and his attacks on the Church were like Wyclif's, easy to link to contemporary politics: the Czech nobility had come to resent what they saw as the Church authorities' interference in their affairs. Hus's movement became an assertion of Czech identity against German-speakers in the Bohemian Church and commonwealth, and unlike Lollardy it remained supported in all sections of society, from the university to the village.

In 1412, by now rector of the university, Hus was excommunicated by one of the three claimants to the papacy and appealed to a coming general council. Amid this gathering crisis Hus and his followers made a particularly provocative gesture: in 1414 they began offering consecrated wine as well as bread to the laity in their Eucharists, for the first time in centuries. This restoration of the elements 'in both kinds' became central to the movement which now developed in Bohemia; the eucharistic chalice containing the wine was to become a cherished symbol of the 'Hussite' movement, which against the general practice of the time, although in harmony with a demand of Jean Gerson and certain other theologians, came to insist on frequent communion for the laity, even for infants. The Hussites' eucharistic devotion offered a great contrast both to Wyclif's outlook and to the text-based gatherings of the later Lollards, although the original links between the movements meant that a significant number of English Wyclifite manuscripts have survived into the modern Czech Republic. Yet soon Hus himself was dead, betrayed at the Council of Konstanz in 1415 when the assembled clerics prevailed on the Holy Roman Emperor Sigismund to set aside an imperial promise of safe conduct to the Prague Reformer. After being imprisoned in vile conditions, Hus was burned at the stake. It was a powerful symbol that the institutional Church was no longer capable of dealing constructively with a movement of reform.

Hus's death turned him into a Czech martyr: an explosion of fury in Prague established what was in effect a separate royal Bohemian Church, at first supported by the nobility. Pressure from both emperor and pope resulted in the abandonment of much of this experiment, which caused further anger in the city. Once more the Eucharist became a symbol of the revolution: a mob was led by the insurrectionary preacher Jan Želivský bearing the eucharistic monstrance from his parish church to the city hall, where the crowd hurled thirteen Catholic loyalists from an upper window to their deaths, the first 'Defenestration' of Prague.[34] The following insurrection featured violent destruction of symbols of traditional religion: the first large-scale wrecking of monasteries and church art by Christians in the history of Christian Europe, as thoroughgoing as anything the continent was to see from the 1520s to the 1560s. The period between the first and the second (rather less bloodthirsty) Prague Defenestration a year short of two centuries later (see p. 646) was one of continuous if intermittent religious warfare focused on Bohemia, all springing out of the martyrdom of Hus, although merging with the wider conflict of the Reformation. For four centuries and more, Prague's half-finished Cathedral of St Vitus, whose rebuilding the Emperor Charles IV had begun in the decades before the Hussite crisis erupted, was a permanent memorial to that troubled time. Its lavish eastern wing was the equal of any earlier French cathedral, but it petered out in the huge empty void windows of its half-built transepts, a bathetically unfinished spire, and an incoherent muddle where the nave should be (see Plate 11).

But after decades of vicious civil war and the defeat of successive outside attempts to destroy the revolution, an independent Hussite Church structure still survived, grudgingly and incompletely recognized by Rome. After all the destruction of the previous decades, it was a surprisingly traditionalist body, still cherishing images, processions and a cult of Mary, but it was proud of two points of difference from the pope's Church: its use in worship of Czech, the language of the people, rather than Latin, and its continuing insistence on reception in both kinds or species (*sub utraque specie*). So important was the latter to the mainstream Hussite Bohemian Church that it took the name 'Utraquist'. From 1471 the Utraquist Church had no archbishop of its own, and in a curious compromise with the rest of the Catholic world, it sent prospective priests off to Venice for ordination by bishops in that independent-minded republic. In default of a native episcopate, effective power in the Church was firmly in the hands of noblemen and the leaders of the major towns and cities. It was an extreme example of a transfer which was quietly happening in large areas of Europe, and which became a major feature of the official 'magisterial' Reformations in the following century: a slow decentralization of the Church from below, inexorably working against the late medieval papacy's attempts to reassert its authority.[35]

Formally separate after 1457 from the Utraquists were remnants of the more radical Hussites, the Union of Bohemian Brethren (*Unitas Fratrum*). What survived of their religious radicalism had major social implications, for, inspired by the south Bohemian writer Petr Chelcický and in the name of New Testament Christianity, they condemned all types of violence, including political repression, capital punishment, service in war or the swearing of oaths to earthly authorities. They rejected the idea of a separate priesthood, as well as the belief (still so dear to the Utraquists) that the Eucharist was a miracle in which bread and wine became the body and blood of Jesus. All these doctrines were to re-emerge in the sixteenth-century Reformation. After yet further upheaval in Bohemia in 1547, much of the group took refuge in the province of Moravia, and they came to be known as the Moravian Brethren. It was a curious turn of history that successors of these Moravians, whose first hero Hus had taken inspiration from the writings of one great English Christian, eventually after three centuries had a major influence on another Englishman who sparked great religious change: John Wesley (see pp. 749–50).

So, between the Utraquist Church and the *Unitas Fratrum*, Bohemia became the first part of Latin Europe to slip out of its medieval papal obedience. Only a few German-speaking areas and a few royal free cities within the Bohemian kingdom retained their papal loyalty through the fifteenth century. These lonely outposts of obedience to Rome in Bohemia are worth noting, because they represented the only part of medieval Europe to which the description 'Roman Catholic' can be applied with any meaning. It may at first sight seem surprising that this term familiar in the anglophone world makes no sense before the Reformation, but it is clearly redundant when applied to an age when everyone outside Bohemia consciously or unconsciously formed part of the same Catholic Church structure, tied in so many complex ways to the heart and head of the whole organization in Rome. Soon that was to change. By 1500, the failings of successive popes in their pretensions to be leaders of the universal Church compromised their defeat of the conciliarists in the fifteenth century, and did nothing to end continuing criticism of papal primacy. That made the papal machine all the more sensitive to any new challenge to its authority, or to any attempt to resurrect language and ideas which had been used against it before, as Luther discovered in the years after 1517. Even before Luther, challenges were being posed by some of the best minds in Europe.

OLD WORLDS BRING NEW: HUMANISM (1300–1500)

From the fourteenth century, there developed in Italy a new way of looking at the world which has come to be called humanism. Humanism can seem a difficult phenomenon to pin down and define, not least because no one used the word at the time. Early-nineteenth-century historians newly coined it from words actually in use in the late fifteenth century, when it became common to talk about the liberal/non-theological arts subjects in a university curriculum as '*humanae litterae*' (literature human rather than divine in focus), while a scholar with a particular enthusiasm for these subjects was called a '*humanista*'.[36] A further complication is that 'humanist' has come to be used in modern times for someone who rejects the claims of revealed religion. This was not a feature of the movement we are considering. The vast majority of humanists were patently sincere Christians who wished to apply their enthusiasm to the exploration and proclamation of their faith. They were trying to restore a Christian perfection to humanity.

A phrase now frequently used as a synonym for humanism, 'the New Learning', is best avoided, because although it was indeed used in the sixteenth century, it described something different: it was an abusive Catholic term for Protestant or evangelical theology, and that is by no means the same as humanism.[37] By contrast, a term usefully associated with humanism is 'Renaissance': something new was happening in Europe between the fourteenth and sixteenth centuries, although it was seen as a rediscovery of something very old. The fourteenth-century

Italian humanist poet Petrarch so admired the poetic achievements of his older contemporary Dante Alighieri that he proclaimed that they represented a 'rebirth' ('*renascita*') of poetry as good as anything which had been written in ancient Rome. Nineteenth-century scholars then used this word in its French form (*Renaissance*) to describe the cultural phenomenon which the humanists represented.

There were good reasons for humanism and the Renaissance to take their origins from fourteenth-century Italy. More spectacularly than anywhere else in western Europe, the Italian peninsula had the advantage of 'the encyclopaedia of antiquity buried beneath it': the physical legacy of art and architecture from the heart of the Roman Empire which might be seen as mocking the achievement of medieval Italians.[38] Besides this, Italy had its special political conditions: it exhibited greater contrasts in forms of government than elsewhere in Europe, and experienced ruinous confrontations between popes and Holy Roman Emperors played out in the peninsula between the twelfth and fifteenth centuries, the factional warfare of papal 'Guelphs' versus imperial 'Ghibellines'. Citizens of the great cities and the principalities of Italy, impelled by circumstances to consider the nature of government, looked for diverse precedents in the most impressive and successful commonwealths in the history books, the cities of Classical Greece and republican or imperial Rome.[39]

The rediscovery of texts had galvanized intellectual life in ninth- and in twelfth-century Europe to create two earlier Renaissances. But now the impact was far more widely spread, because the technology of printing on paper opened up rapid possibilities of distributing copies of the texts, and gave much greater incentives for the spread of literacy associated with these innovations. This meant that the new haul of rediscovered ancient manuscripts, often lying neglected in cathedral or monastery libraries since earlier bursts of enthusiasm for the past, had a much greater impact than before, once they had been brought back into scholarly consciousness. Moreover, many more Greek manuscripts re-emerged from this latest treasure hunt. Paradoxically, the Ottoman conquests which so terrorized Europe tipped the balance in the supply of manuscripts, bringing Greek culture west. Medieval western Europe had access to remarkably little Greek literature; the text of even such a central work of literature as Homer's epics was hardly known until the fifteenth century. Few scholars had any more than the vaguest knowledge of the Greek language. If they knew a learned language other than Latin, it was likely to be Hebrew, for the good reason that while there were virtually no Greeks in the west, there were plenty of argumentative and

ingenious Jewish rabbis with an awkward ability to question Christianity, forcing refutations with reference to their own Hebrew literature.
Now, however, Western humanists needed Greek if they were to make
use of the texts suddenly available.

Greek manuscripts came in the baggage of scholars fleeing from the
wreckage of Christian commonwealths in the east, or were snapped up
by Western entrepreneurs profiting from the catastrophe. Especially
significant was the presence of the great Greek philosopher Georgios
Gemistos Plethon at the negotiations for reunion at the Council of
Florence at the turn of the 1430s and 1440s (see pp. 492–3), because
he was a charismatic exponent of Plato. While the Greek Church establishment posthumously repudiated Gemistos after the fall of Constantinople (see pp. 495–6), the Medici rulers of Florence celebrated his
scholarship, and commissioned the equally gifted Marsilio Ficino to
translate Plato into Latin. Plato's reappearance was especially significant,
because twelfth- and thirteenth-century Western scholasticism had been
shaped by the rediscovery of his very different pupil Aristotle. Now
Plato's attitude to the ultimate problems of philosophy, his sense that
the greatest reality lay beyond visible and quantifiable reality, disposed
humanists to disrespect the whole style of scholastic learning, its careful
distinctions and definitions. Indeed, Ficino saw Plato as having been
providentially provided by God to illuminate the Christian message, first
through Origen but now once more in his own city, and he viewed
contemporary exponents of Aristotle as 'wholly destructive of religion'.[40]

Ficino's insight that Plato's writings had profoundly affected early
Christian thought was one of humanism's legacies to our understanding
of Christianity, long after his apocalyptic excitement had faded. One of
the most important and distinctive features of Western Christian culture
is its capacity to stand back from societies, both its own and others, and
its yearning to understand past cultures in their own terms. In 1440 a
group of humanist friends, headed by the architect and writer on art
theory Leon Battista Alberti and encouraged by the local lord Cardinal
Prospero Colonna, attempted the first major conscious venture in a
scholarly exploration which had virtually no precedent in the ancient
world, certainly none among its respected intellectual disciplines: archaeology. In the presence of an excited crowd and virtually all the leading
men of the papal court, they tried to raise from the depths of Lake Nemi
one of two giant Roman ships lying below: pleasure-craft commissioned
by the Emperor Caligula, if they had but known. Their efforts succeeded
in tearing the hulk apart but, undeterred by their own destructiveness,

they analysed the fragments they retrieved and taught themselves about lost techniques of Roman shipbuilding. The Pope reapplied some of their findings to roof construction in the churches of Rome. These pioneer archaeologists had learned almost for the first time how artefacts from the past might be witnesses to its strangeness, its difference, as well as how the present might gain from the discovery. They could apply the same thought to written texts.[41]

Alongside their exhilarating rediscovery of Greek, humanists gained new perspectives on Latin language and culture. They developed great enthusiasm for the first-century-BCE politician-turned-philosopher Marcus Tullius Cicero ('Tully' to his English-speaking admirers). Civic humanists appreciated Cicero's detailed discussion of government, disregarding the inconvenient fact that he had been a very unsuccessful politician, and when in 1421 Cicero's treatise on oratory was rediscovered in the cathedral library at Lodi in northern Italy, the new book sealed his reputation as the ideal model for powerful and persuasive Latin prose. It became the ambition of every cultivated young scholar to write just like Cicero, given inevitable adjustments like newly coined words for printing, gunpowder and cannon-fire.[42] This humanist literary style was very different from the Latin which scholastic philosophers and theologians had spoken and written over the previous few centuries; one can tell a humanist prose composition from a scholastic text merely by seeing how the sentences are constructed and the sort of vocabulary used.

The contrast became even more obvious when humanist manuscript writers painstakingly mimicked the 'Roman' characteristics of what they took to be ancient script – in fact, it was the minuscule used by Carolingian copyists of older manuscripts in that earlier 'Renaissance' (see pp. 352–3). Some southern European printers then imitated their script, producing a typeface similar to what you are reading here, and completely unlike the Gothic type which other printers used in imitation of medieval manuscript 'bookhand'. A further imitation of a cursive, more rapidly written script which humanists developed from minuscule produced an 'italic' form of the new typefaces. This tribute to a slightly misunderstood past was paralleled in the Renaissance's architectural and artistic revolution, which began in Italy in the fifteenth century and gradually spread northwards over the next two centuries. The visual forms of ancient buildings, sculpture, paintings and gardens were more and more accurately imitated as part of the effort to bring back to life the lost world of Greece and Rome – even for Christian church buildings

– at a time when Orthodox Church art was turning away from such experiments in naturalism, and single-mindedly developing a contrasting ancient artistic and architectural tradition deriving from Hagia Sophia in Constantinople (see pp. 495–6).

Among the flood of new and strange material from the ancient world, which might or might not be valuable if put to use, was a set of writings about religion and philosophy purporting to have been written by a divine figure from ancient Egypt, Hermes Trismegistus. In fact they had been compiled in the first to third centuries CE, at much the same time as early Christianity was emerging. Some were then codified in Greek in a work now known as the *Corpus Hermeticum*, and others later trans-lated into Latin and Arabic. Some dealt with forms of magic, medicine or astrology to sort out the problems of everyday life; some appealed to the same fascination with secret wisdom about the cosmos and the nature of knowledge which had created gnostic Christianity and later Manichaeism (see pp. 123–4 and 170–71). So this 'hermetic' literature chimed in with many traditional Christian preoccupations, and it became newly accessible after the 1480s when the Medici in Florence commissioned Marsilio Ficino to translate into Latin the available sec-tions of the *Corpus Hermeticum*.[43] Humanists savoured the cheery pros-pect that with more investigation, hard work and possibly supernatural aid, more ancient wisdom might be more fully recovered.

Equally exciting were the possibilities opened up by the increasing attention that Christian scholars paid to Cabbala, the body of Jewish literature which had started out as commentary on the Tanakh, but which by the medieval period had created its own intricate network of theological speculation, drawing on sub-Platonic mysticism like the gnostics or the hermeticists. Many humanists were gratified to find reinforcement for their own sense of infinite possibilities in humankind; Cabbala embraced a vision of humanity as potentially divine and indwelt by divine spirit. It was the hope of Ficino, or of Giovanni Pico della Mirandola, the aristocratic translator of Cabbala, that cabbalistic and hermetic ideas together might complete God's purpose in the Christian message by broadening and enriching it. These themes were to play a great part in intellectual life and discussion throughout the sixteenth and seventeenth centuries, while also attracting derision and hostility from many theologians in both Catholic and Protestant camps. We will find that, in the end, they helped to bring the Reformation era to a close (see pp. 773–6).

How might one establish authenticity amid this intoxicating but unsorted flow of information? One criterion must be to assess a text in every respect: its content, date, origins, motives, even its appearance. So much depended on texts being accurate. This meant developing ways of telling a good text from a corrupt text: looking at the way in which it was written and whether it sounded like texts reliably datable to the same historical period. Historical authenticity gained a new importance: it now became the chief criterion for authority. The attitude which had once led holy men cheerfully to forge supposedly historical documents on a huge scale (see pp. 351–2) would no longer do. A 'source' (*fons*) for authority now outweighed the unchallenged reputation of an *auctoritas*, a voice of authority from the past. *Ad fontes*, back to the sources, was the battle-cry of the humanists, and Protestants took it over from them. An individual, equipped with the right intellectual skills, could outface even the greatest and most long-lasting authority in medieval Europe, the Church.

A particularly notorious example of a revered text demolished was the Donation of Constantine, that venerable forgery claiming to grant the fourth-century Pope Sylvester I sweeping powers throughout the Christian world. Unsurprisingly, one can still enjoy the Donation legend in the art of churches in Rome. There are, for instance, admirable but mendacious frescoes of the whole story decorating a chapel of St Sylvester in the centre of Rome beside the Church of Santi Quattro Coronati ('the Four Holy Crowned Ones'); these had been commissioned by a thirteenth-century pope whose quarrel with the Holy Roman Emperor had become especially fierce. Equally interesting, since it incidentally provides a reliable view of the interior of Old St Peter's Basilica, is the early-sixteenth-century representation of the moment of the Donation painted by Raphael and his assistants in the Vatican itself (see Plate 26). By the time that Julius II, that most imperious of popes, commissioned this egregious work of fiction, in the years immediately preceding Martin Luther's challenge to papal authority, the Donation had long been discredited. Scepticism about it was pioneered by a Dominican scholar in the late 1380s, and fifty years later swelled into a chorus, significantly from different scholars working independently: the future German Cardinal Nicholas of Cusa in 1432–3, the Italian Lorenzo Valla in 1440 and the English bishop Reginald Pecock in 1450.[44] All concluded that the phraseology and vocabulary of the Donation were radically wrong for a fourth-century document, instantly demolishing a prop of papal authority.

Far from being 'New Learning', humanism represented a refocusing of old learning. It brought a new respect for sections of traditional scholarship of secondary importance in medieval universities: the non-theological parts of their arts curriculum, especially poetry, oratory and rhetoric. Humanists were lovers and connoisseurs of words. They saw them as containing power which, if used actively, could change human society for the better, and they were particularly concerned therefore to find the 'true' or original meaning of words. The words which inspired such excitement were found in ancient texts from long-vanished societies with the same belief in the transforming power of poetry, oratory and rhetoric: ancient Greece and Rome. Part of the project of transforming the world must be to get as clear as possible a picture of these ancient societies, and that meant getting the best possible version of the texts which were the main records of how those societies had thought and operated. Hence another possible definition of a humanist: he or she was an editor of texts – or an even cruder but still serviceable definition would be to say that it was someone who realized that there was more to life than the Middle Ages. And crucially for the future of Christianity, a humanist was someone whose cultural roots were in Western Latin culture, and who knew little of the Christianities of either the Chalcedonian or non-Chalcedonian East.

Eventually the central document of the Christian Church, its ultimate *fons*, the Bible, must come under humanist scrutiny. Now the humanists' preoccupation with words was very relevant, because the Bible's words were translations at various different levels. Christians saw them as interpretations of the mind of God to humanity, but beyond this ultimate translation from the perfect to the imperfect, readers experienced the biblical texts at different removes from their original human writers. Medieval Western Christianity knew the Bible almost exclusively through the Vulgate, the fourth-century Latin translation made by Jerome (see pp. 294–6). Humanist excavation now went behind the Vulgate text to the Tanakh and its principal Greek translation, the Septuagint. Jerome had done his considerable best to re-examine the Hebrew text behind the Septuagint; nevertheless, faults remained. Some of his mistranslations in the Old Testament were more comic than important. One of the most curious was at Exodus 34, where the Hebrew describes Moses's face as shining when he came down from Mount Sinai with the tablets of the Ten Commandments. Jerome, mistaking particles of Hebrew, had turned this into a description of Moses wearing a pair of horns – and so the Lawgiver is frequently depicted in Christian art, long after humanists had gleefully removed the horns from the text of

Exodus. They are sported by Michelangelo's great sculpted Moses now in the Roman church of San Pietro in Vincoli ('Saint Peter in Chains'), yet another commission for Pope Julius II. One finds them frequently in the paintings of Moses and Aaron flanking the Commandment boards in English parish churches, dating as late as the nineteenth century.[45]

Examining the New Testament had more profound consequences. In translating the Greek, Jerome had chosen certain Latin words which formed rather shaky foundations for very considerable theological constructions by the later Western Church, like the doctrine of Purgatory, as the prince of humanists Desiderius Erasmus was to demonstrate (see p. 96). It was not simply that Jerome gave misleading impressions of the Greek text. The mere fact that for a thousand years the Latin Church had based its authority on a translation was significant, when scholars heard for the first time the unmediated urgency of the angular street-Greek poured out by Jesus's post-Resurrection convert Paul of Tarsus, as he wrestled with the problem of how Jesus represented God. The shock of the familiar experienced in an unfamiliar form was bound to suggest to the most sensitive minds in Latin Christianity that the Western Church was not so authoritative an interpreter of scripture as it claimed. If there is any one explanation why the Latin West experienced a Reformation and the Greek-speaking lands to the east did not, it lies in this experience of listening to a new voice in the New Testament text.

Humanist scholarship had general consequences for the way in which the Bible was experienced in the Western Church, and moved it still further from the common tradition which had united Catholicism and Orthodoxy, just at the time when political circumstances were doing the same thing. Increasingly, the Bible would be perceived as a single text and read as other texts might be – or perhaps, more accurately, as a library of self-contained continuous texts, each of which might be read in a different way. Previously, congregations in the West as in the East would have experienced the Bible primarily as performance: countless fragments of it rearranged mosaic-like in the liturgy, mediated through the words of a preacher or experienced in declaimed paraphrase in the Bible plays, which perhaps reached their apogee in the English vernacular dramas, staged in open-air processional stations by urban gilds or 'mysteries'. This public performance of the Bible had depended in turn on a clergy who knew the Bible as an intricately layered set of allegorical meanings, because they used it as the basis for contemplation. One word might point beyond itself, so that at the very simplest level the boy Isaac who was to be sacrificed was God the Son, and his father Abraham who was to sacrifice him was God the Father. 'Pray for the peace of Jerusalem,' sang the psalmist: Jerusalem had been replaced by Rome, so the psalmist was actually asking for peace for the pope. Since the ninth century, when a group of Frankish scholars had created the commentary known as the *Glossa Ordinaria*, the Church had provided an increasingly rich databank of such allegories. Now the humanist perception of the Bible as a text written and then to be read like any other book began to place a question against a great deal of this venerable tradition.

It is perfectly possible that the Western Church could have survived these shocks intact. The Reformations which actually took place were not what the humanists sought; they had no intention of overthrowing the old ecclesiastical system. Bishops and cardinals hastened to be the patrons of humanists, and they were prominent in widening university curricula by founding colleges whose statutes specifically promoted humanist studies, with the particular aim of creating a pool of experts in Greek and Hebrew to aid biblical scholarship. Not surprisingly some humanists, excited at the novelty of what they were doing, sounded what might seem a call to revolution when they trumpeted their achievement at the expense of older scholarship. This was adolescent self-assertion from a new type of intellectual discipline previously subordinate to theology in the universities, and (as usual with adolescent self-assertion) it annoyed older professionals who had good reason to be proud of their traditional learning and resented non-professionals giving themselves airs. So university theologians attacked Lorenzo Valla for his presumption in undertaking textual criticism of the Bible. They likened it to 'putting one's sickle into another man's crop', and it became a common charge against humanists.[46]

Many humanists chose not to enter the traditional university system. They produced their scholarly editions in close cooperation with printers, who were inclined to set up workshops in big commercial centres, rather than in university towns. Many humanists also saw the value of entering the service of powerful and wealthy people who would pay for their skills as wordsmiths, employing them to produce official documents in sophisticated Ciceronian Latin to maintain courtly prestige among other powerful people. Humanist scholars could therefore easily portray themselves as practically minded men of ideas, closely involved with ordinary life and government, in contrast to isolated ivory-tower academics who wasted their time arguing about how many angels could dance on the head of a pin (this famous caricature of scholasticism was invented by humanists). A less cynical way of looking at this stand-off would be to see it as a dispute about the best road to discovering truth: was it best done through the persuasive skills of rhetoric, which the humanists valued, or through formal analysis and enquiry in argument, the refinement of dialectic which scholastic theologians had perfected?

It would be misleading to see humanism as the only path to Church reform. Many professional theologians whose primary loyalty was to scholasticism felt as dissatisfied as the humanists with the nominalist scholasticism which had dominated university theology faculties over the previous century and a half. The Italian Dominican Tommaso de Vio (usually known as Cajetan, *Gaetano*, from his Italian home town Gaeta) returned to the philosophical and theological achievement of his own order's most celebrated product, Thomas Aquinas, determined to restore Thomism to its central place in the Church. Between 1507 and 1522 Cajetan published a commentary on the *Summa Theologiae*, Thomas's greatest work, which he was reputed to be able to recite by heart. He did not confine himself to expository scholarship, and won both enemies and, in 1517, a cardinal's hat for his consistent support of papal authority, which he was determined to see used for the renewal of the Church. One of his characteristic achievements was to stop Pope Julius II establishing a new feast of the sufferings of Mary, the Mother of God. Commissioned to investigate the possibility, de Vio reported back in 1506 that popular devotion to her swooning away out of grief at Christ's death on the Cross was an unscriptural idea. He craggily commented that in any case swooning was a 'morbid state' which irreverently implied that Mary had suffered some bodily defect: the Queen of Heaven could suffer only mental anguish on behalf of her son. No more was heard of the proposed feast, and Cajetan's intervention began a long process of official restraint on the physical exuberance of Western piety, a restraint which as well as being a feature of the Protestant Reformation affected the Counter-Reformation Church also.[47]

Cajetan's volumes sparked a major revival of interest in Aquinas's thought, and in the Reformation turmoil, for all Thomas's emphasis on the mystery of God, Thomism came to seem the perfect weapon for the pope against Protestantism's radical pessimism about the human mind's capacity to approach the divine. The Society of Jesus (see pp. 665–7) obliged its members to follow Aquinas in theological matters. After all, Thomism fought Protestantism on its own ground, in a shared reverence for Augustine, whose thought had from 1490 been made more widely available to humanists and scholastics alike, through the first scholarly printed edition of all his known works, a formidable task undertaken by the Basel printer Johann Amerbach. No one could have predicted that Augustine would spark a religious revolution. With this new resource, there was a general move among theologians over the next century, whether traditionalist in their scholasticism, humanist or Protestant, to listen afresh to the Bishop of Hippo.[48] The problem was what to take from the breadth of Augustine's discussion of the Christian faith. As the twentieth-century Princeton historian of theology B. B. Warfield famously observed, 'The Reformation, inwardly considered, was just the ultimate triumph of Augustine's doctrine of grace over Augustine's doctrine of the Church.'[49] Western Christians would have to decide for themselves which aspect of Augustine's thought mattered more: his emphasis on obedience to the Catholic Church or the discussion of salvation which lay behind the rebellion by Martin Luther and other theologians in his generation. From one perspective, a century or more of turmoil in the Western Church from 1517 was a debate in the mind of the long-dead Augustine.

REFORMING THE CHURCH IN THE LAST DAYS (1500)

European-wide yearning for renewing the Church long predated Martin Luther's turbulent public career. At the end of the fifteenth century, it was easy to believe that God had some new and decisive purpose for his creation. We have already seen that Orthodox Christians and Muslims were convinced that 1492–3 would witness the end of the world (see pp. 523–4), and even when that milestone passed without apparent incident, the obvious fact remained that 1500 marked a millennium and a half since the presumed date of Christ's birth. To east and south, the Ottoman Turks and other Islamic rulers continued to press in on Christian Europe, relentlessly conquering new territories in the Balkans and terrorizing large swathes of the Mediterranean coast with their piracy.[50] Only in the west in Iberia was there Christian success – but this was a spectacular exception, leading to the greatest upheaval of culture and population in the peninsula since the first eruption of Islam, with profound consequences for all Europe. The year 1492 did prove to have a special significance, but not in the way anticipated in Moscow or Constantinople. Centuries of gradual Christian reclamations from the Moors culminated in the capture of the Islamic kingdom of Granada, in the extreme south of the peninsula; the news was celebrated all over Christian Europe. The victorious troops were in the service of two monarchs who had joined in marriage in 1474: Fernando, ruler of eastern Spanish kingdoms, Aragon and Valencia and the principality of Catalonia, and Isabel of Castile, the much larger though mostly much more thinly populated kingdom which ran from north to south through Iberia. Mindful of the symbolism of their victory, they chose their future burial place at the heart of their new conquest on the site of Granada's main mosque, in a splendid chapel which they commissioned alongside a brand-new cathedral (see Plate 57).

Aragon and Castile, precariously united by the joint accession of Fernando and Isabel when they married, remained separate political entities, and there was no reason for them to remain linked when Isabel died. However, the death of her successor, Philip of Burgundy, after only two years resulted in a second union of the crowns under her widower, Fernando; henceforth they were never again divided, and Aragon and Castile could be regarded for external purposes as a single Spanish monarchy. To the west, the kingdom of Portugal, at the remote edge of Europe on the Atlantic seaboard, had won its struggles against the Muslims long before; it had also secured its independence against Castile, and kept that independence until 1580. First Portugal and then the Spanish monarchs launched expeditions across the seas westwards and southwards, which from the fifteenth to the seventeenth centuries turned Christianity into the first worldwide religion, a story which we will trace in Chapter 19.

Constant medieval warfare against Islam (and the Judaism which it sheltered) gave Spanish Catholicism a militant edge and an intensity of devotional practice not found elsewhere in western Europe. Even after the sequence of medieval reconquest (*Reconquista*) had been largely completed, Iberian Christian culture showed a frequently obsessive suspicion of former members of the rival cultures. In 1391, a particularly vicious wave of anti-Jewish preaching provoked the massacre of around a third of the Jews in Christian Spain, and forced the conversion of another third. Such Jewish converts ('New Christians' or *conversos*: former Muslims were known as *Moriscos*) remained a perennial object of worry, to be scrutinized for doubtful loyalty in any time of heightened tension, despite their theoretical shared membership of the Body of Christ. Even when they were long-established Christians and had rejected all connection with Judaism, 'Old Christians' found a new reason for hating them: they were now eligible rivals for positions of power in Church and commonwealth. In return 'New Christians' were furious that their genuinely held faith and loyalty to the Crown should be questioned, and their fury occasionally erupted into violence.[51]

Such tensions remained particularly lively in Castile, the area still on the front line against Islam. Isabel's hold on the Castilian throne had initially been shaky, and her early political calculations established strategies through what became a long reign: first a new assault on Judaism, and later, after Granada's fall in 1492, a parallel assault on Islam.[52] The agent of her campaign was a newly constituted version of an inquisition, a body not previously present in Castile. Although it imitated the many local inquisitions which had investigated heresy in Europe since the thirteenth century (see pp. 407–8), now it was organized by the monarchy, and after complicated royal haggling with Pope Sixtus IV between 1478 and 1480 to create its legal framework, it settled down to work against 'Judaizers' in the kingdom of Castile, burning alive around seven hundred between 1481 and 1488. In the middle of this came another momentous development: Pope Sixtus finally yielded to royal pressure in 1483 and appointed the Dominican friar Tomás de Torquemada as Inquisitor-General of all Fernando and Isabel's peninsular dominions.

When Granada fell, Isabel gave Jews in Castile the choice of expulsion or conversion to Christianity. The excuse was yet another blood-libel accusation, this time from Toledo in 1490, that Jews had murdered a Christian boy, who has become known to his devotees as the Holy Child of La Guardia and was later attributed the significant name Cristóbal – Christ-bearer. Perhaps 70,000 to 100,000 Jews chose to become refugees abroad rather than abandon their faith, forming a European-wide dispersal which has been called Sephardic Judaism (since the Jews had applied the Hebrew word *Sefarad* to Spain). Yet more Jews chose to convert rather than leave their homes, and the authorities were determined that their conversion should not be a token one.[53] By contrast, at first there was an official agreement to allow the continued practice of Islam in Granada, but harassment by the Church authorities led to rebellion. In 1500 this provided the excuse for Isabel to insist on conversion of all Granada's Muslims to Christianity; she extended this requirement throughout Castile two years later. For the time being, King Fernando stood faithful to his coronation oath to preserve the liberties of his remaining Islamic subjects (*mudéjars*), but the attitudes fostered by Isabel in Castile set patterns for the future. Her expulsions of Jews were imitated in Portugal, when in 1497 King Manoel (who was hoping

to marry her daughter) ordered mass conversion of the Jewish population, many of whom had only just fled from Spain.[54]

So Latin Christianity, in an especially self-conscious version of its
traditional form, became the symbol of identity for Iberia's kingdoms,
and Protestantism would stand little chance of making any headway
there against the project of building a monolithic Catholic Christian
culture. Indeed it is possible to talk of an Iberian Reformation before
the Reformation: well in advance of the general Protestant Reformation in Europe, Spain tackled many of the structural abuses – clerical
immorality, monastic self-indulgence – which elsewhere gave Protestant
Reformers much ammunition against the old Church. This Reformation
was promoted by the monarchy, which increasingly excluded any real
possibility of interference in the Church from the pope. A series of papal
concessions allowed the Crown to appoint bishops, and by 1600 a third
or more of the yearly income of the Castilian Church disappeared into
the royal treasury.[55] The pope tolerated being thus kept at arm's length
partly because he had little choice, but partly because Spanish royal
power was consistently exercised to create a 'purified' and strong Latin
Christianity free from heresy or non-Christian deviation, and indeed to
spread it throughout the Spanish Empire overseas. Such a satisfactory
deal for the Iberian monarchies meant that they had no reason to
sympathize with any other challenge to papal authority.

The first chief agent of the royal programme in the Church was
Francisco Ximénes de Cisneros, a Castilian who gave up a distinguished
career in Church administration to join one of the most rigorous
religious orders, the Observant Franciscans, within which he sought to
escape the world as a hermit. Yet when the fame of his single-minded
spiritual activism forced him, against his better judgement, to become
confessor to Queen Isabel in 1492, he found himself in Castile's highest
offices in Church and commonwealth, Archbishop of Toledo (Spain's
primatial see) and eventually, from 1516, regent of the kingdom during
the minority of Charles Habsburg. In his austere, focused piety and his
determination to proclaim his vision of Christian faith to the peoples of
the Spanish kingdoms, he was much more like Luther, Zwingli or Calvin
than his Spanish contemporary Pope Alexander VI, yet many of his
reforms anticipated what the Council of Trent was to decree many
decades later. He used his unequalled opportunities for action in ways
which do not now seem entirely consistent, but which sum up the main
themes of the Spanish religious revolution. An advocate of apostolic
poverty who was also the premier statesman in Spain, he spent money

lavishly as a major patron of the most advanced scholarship of his day: he founded the University of Alcalá out of his own resources, and funded the printing of a great number of books particularly aimed at introducing the writings of his favourite mystics to a literate public. At the same time, he was responsible for burning thousands of non-Christian books and manuscripts, and he became Inquisitor-General in 1507, the same year that he was made cardinal.

In the aftermath of the fall of Granada the Inquisition became central to the programme of eliminating the rival civilizations of the peninsula. It was not going to let up on the *converso* population just because *conversos* claimed to be Christian. This illogicality was aided by a sinister feature of the supposed martyrdom of the 'Holy Child of La Guardia' in 1490: the alleged perpetrators had been a mixed group of professed Jews and New Christians.[56] The Inquisition not only sought out evidence of continued secret practice of Islam or Judaism, but reinforced an existing tendency in Spanish society to regard heresy and deviation as hereditary. So it became increasingly necessary for loyal Spanish Catholics to prove their *limpieza de sangre* (purity of blood), free of all *mudéjar* or Jewish taint. Evidence of *converso* descent ended one's chances of receiving major promotion in the Church, such as a canonry in the chapter of Spain's premier cathedral, Toledo. The main religious orders started insisting on *limpieza de sangre*, starting in 1486 with the influential native order much patronized by the nobility, the Jeronimites, closely followed by the Franciscans and Dominicans, as well as the secular clergy – in the end the Inquisition even required this assurance for its 'familiars', its network of spies and helpers. The authorities in Rome never liked the custom and did their best without much success to dismantle it, and there were ironies in this ideological use of genealogy: few of the higher Spanish nobility could claim such purity of blood, and they found themselves excluded from high office in the Church in favour of social inferiors who could prove their lack of taint.[57]

The Inquisition's work was justified in the eyes of the reliably Catholic population, and led to a steady stream of spontaneously volunteered information, because there were real continuing challenges to Christian Spain, both internal and external. The general perception of Spain in the rest of Europe was that it remained an exotic place, full of Moors and Jews: a mortifying image for hypersensitive Catholic Spaniards (and so for the many in Europe who came to loathe Spanish power, also a useful theme with which to annoy them). Rebellions from the Morisco

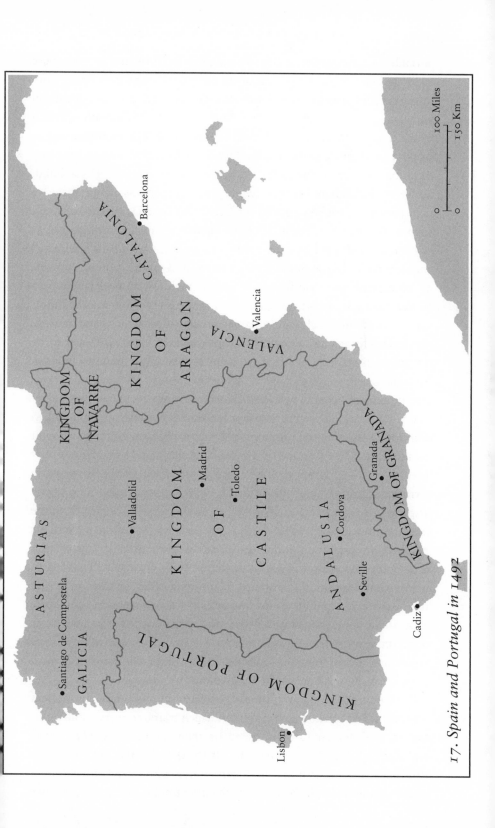

17. *Spain and Portugal in 1492*

population continued well into the sixteenth century, and in 1609 there was finally a general expulsion order against 300,000 Moriscos, more than a century after Granada had fallen, the largest population expulsion anywhere in early modern Europe. After 1492, the Christianity of much of the newly converted Jewish population was at best confused and at worst a cloak for their older faith. One of them described their unhappy situation as floating aimlessly 'like a cork on the water'.[58] Disoriented, leaderless and caught between two conflicting religions, *conversos* were easy prey for prophets proclaiming that the Last Days were coming. Such uncontrolled religious energy spilled over into the population at large, itself disturbed by the sudden change in the peninsula's religious balance; around 1500 Spain was in a ferment of expectation of a universal monarchy, and avid for any dramatic manifestation of God's plan for the future. By the second quarter of the sixteenth century, the Inquisition was making it clear that sudden conversions, sightings of messengers from Heaven or reports of statues that bled were no longer to be treated with respect, and it was bringing a new discipline to Spanish religion.[59]

The Spanish version of Catholicism thus presents a complex set of features. It fostered deep personal yearnings for closeness to God, linked to mystical spirituality in Judaism and Islam and later bearing rich fruit in the mystical experience of Teresa of Ávila and John of the Cross (see pp. 673–5). Alongside official and unofficial moves to remove corruption from Church institutions, churchmen revealed a paranoid suspicion of any rival culture, which found increasing support from the secular authorities. After official Spain decisively rejected the peninsula's multicultural past, it is not unfair to see subsequent Spanish Christianity as a major exponent and practitioner of ethnic cleansing. That led to major complications, for instance in the renewal of Spanish monastic life: Ximénes, as an Observant Franciscan, was energetic in promoting reform, but some monks and friars most enthusiastic for change came from *converso* circles, and their tendency to draw their spiritual intensity from the defeated religious cultures in the peninsula provoked much suspicion from Ximénes in the Inquisition.

The independent forces in Spanish Christianity produced a movement of mystical and spiritual enthusiasm in which friars, *conversos* and pious women (*beatas*) came to be styled by their admirers as *alumbrados* ('enlightened ones'). It is now difficult to recover what the movement believed, if indeed it should be regarded as a movement rather than a label by a paranoid Inquisition, for the *alumbrados* never had a chance to express themselves publicly in complete freedom, and their fate was sealed when some of them began taking an interest in a new import of northern European spirituality, the writings of Martin Luther. The *alumbrados* were formally condemned in September 1525, scattered, cowed or executed. Quite apart from their legacy in later-sixteenth-century Spanish mysticism, as the *alumbrados* were dispersed, they had far wider impact first through the *Spirituali* of Italy and then throughout Europe, as we will discover (see pp. 655–62 and 778–9).

Contemporary events in Italy made it equally easy for Italians to see the Last Days arriving. Two years after Granada had fallen, French armies invaded the Italian peninsula, sparking warfare and miseries of half a century's duration. A terrifying and hitherto unknown disease also broke out. Although apparently as fatal as the plague, it played with its victims for months or years, destroying their looks, their flesh and sometimes their minds. Equally seriously, it brought public shame, because very quickly people realized that it was associated with sexual activity. Naturally the Italians in their double affliction called the new scourge the French pox, a name which soon caught all Europe's imagination, much to French annoyance; France's attempt to relabel the pox as the Neapolitan disease was not an especially successful ploy. The title of a poem about the pox published in 1531 by an Italian doctor, Girolamo Fracastoro, has given the modern descendant of this disease the name syphilis.[60]

These disasters gave public credibility to the message of a charismatic Dominican friar, Girolamo Savonarola. First brought by his order to Florence in 1482, from the early 1490s Savonarola began to preach in the Church of San Marco about the Last Days, and his preaching was soon accompanied by visions and announcements of direct communications from God. The Medici family's grip on the former republic was faltering, and the extraordinary flowering of art and culture which they had fostered in Florence seemed mocked by the growing misery of the situation throughout Italy: perfect conditions in which Savonarola could thunder apocalyptically about the dangers of rampant sexuality, especially sodomy, and demand radical political and moral reform in the name of God. To the existing Florentine secular republican resentments against tyranny was added the dangerously potent idea that divine action would bring a total transformation in existing society: it was to be a theme of militant religious radicalism in Europe over the next two centuries. Accordingly the Medici, humiliated in battle by King Charles of France in 1494, were expelled and a rigorously regulated republic proclaimed, in which Savonarola's reorganization of society could begin. The message of his oratory was that his audience could rule supreme, or, if they remained stubborn, they would lose everything:

I gave you an apple, as a mother does when she gives an apple to her son when he cries in order to comfort him; but then when he continues to cry further and she cannot soothe him, she takes the apple away and gives it to another son ... If you do not want to repent and be converted to God, He will take the apple from you and give it to another ... do these four things that I have told you, and I promise you that you will be richer than ever, more glorious than ever, more powerful than ever.[61]

This was the first republic in human history where those in charge narrowly defined the concept of 'republic' as necessarily involving rule by the whole people – Savonarola's Florence has not often been awarded the credit for this innovation. That legacy of a particular and rather frightening Christian vision of reform has become one of the most important political ideas of the modern world.[62] Savonarola was self-consciously traditional in religion, but for the moment he was able to defy Pope Alexander VI's order to cease preaching, and he scorned the excommunication from what he called in 1495 and at other times the 'Babylon of Rome'. Alas for him, the continuing political and economic miseries of the city did not suggest any imminent intervention by an approving God, and his enemies were able to overwhelm the political faction supporting him. In 1498 the friar's power collapsed: he was tortured and burned at the stake with his chief lieutenants. He left many admirers. Throughout Europe, pious humanists valued the deep spirituality of his writings and overlooked the grim chaos into which his republic had descended. Far away in the kingdom of that aspiring Medici Henry VIII, Savonarola's meditations composed in prison after his torture continued to be much read, and two were incorporated in an officially approved English primer in 1534. Archbishop Thomas Cranmer quoted the friar unacknowledged in his final dramatic sermon before himself being burned at the stake in 1556, and half a century later, by ecumenical contrast, the English Catholic composer William Byrd created a choral setting of a Savonarolan prison meditation; many other composers across Europe had previously done the same.[63]

In Savonarola's own land his legacy remained alarming to those in power. A group known as the Piagnoni sprang up in Florence to preserve his memory; their organization might be seen as a particularly potent example of an Italian devotional gild or confraternity, emphasizing mystical meditation and missionary work, and promoting such *Devotio Moderna* classics as the *Imitation of Christ*. Although the Dominican Order throughout Italy was very wary of stepping out of line after the Savonarola debacle, friars continued to be prominent among the Piagnoni, and in later years the sizeable group of considerable scholars who were adherents were firm against Luther, while still continuing to advocate reform in the Church. The Piagnoni nursed the same combination of political and theological republicanism which had shaped the Savonarolan years, but after they succeeded in overthrowing the Medici afresh in 1527–30, their rule became a sadistic tyranny which did much finally to kill off Florentine republicanism and ensure the future of the Medici in power.[64] Even after that, as the Society of Jesus, a new Catholic renewal movement, developed in the 1540s, its founder Ignatius Loyola still felt constrained to ban members of the Society from reading Savonarola's writings, despite seeing a lot of good in them, simply because the friar's fate still stimulated unseemly disagreement between supporters and detractors. As late as 1585, the Medici Grand Duke had to forbid Florentine monks, friars and nuns even to utter his name.[65]

The Piagnoni movement was only one symptom of the chronic neurosis and apocalyptic expectations which disturbed the Italian peninsula for decades after Savonarola was ashes. As in Spain, the mood affected high and low, powerful and destitute; female 'living saints' got a respectful hearing when they turned up to proclaim their message of imminent judgement in Italian princely courts. Through the sixteenth century and beyond, prophecies, accounts of monstrous births and wondrous signs became sure-fire money-spinners for the printing presses, as so often since in troubled times (see Plate 12). One text caused a sensation even though it remained in manuscript: the *Apocalypsis Nova* ('New Account of the Last Days'). Announced in 1502, it claimed to have been written some time before by a Portuguese Franciscan, Amadeus Menezes da Silva, and certainly it built on earlier monastic or Franciscan literature in the style of Joachim of Fiore (see pp. 410–11). This 'Amadeist' manuscript, which still has its devotees, especially in the wilder corners of the Internet, predicted the coming of an Angelic Pastor or Pope, righting the world's ill and heralded by Spiritual Men. A crucial task was correctly to identify these important characters. Plenty of candidates were lined up or fearlessly stepped forward: Popes Julius II, Leo X and Clement VII had their advocates, while Cardinal Mercurino di Gattinara saw his young master, Charles V, as one of the heralds, the Last World Emperor – an insight which had not hindered him winning high office as Imperial Chancellor, under a youth who needed some means of understanding his staggering accumulation of thrones and territories.[66]

There were plenty who in due course transferred the identification on to Martin Luther and the early Protestant Reformers. For over three decades from the 1490s, much of Europe was in high excitement about the future, ranging in expression from decorous humanist editing of hermetic and cabbalistic texts to prophecies from wild-eyed women in Spanish or Italian villages and angry sermons of respected clergy. When a would-be reforming council was convened by the Pope (with initial great hopes and widespread goodwill) to the Lateran Palace in 1512–17, one of its many ineffective provisions was to forbid preaching on apocalyptic subjects. A literary fashion emerged for imagining ideal societies and how they might work. The English humanist Thomas More invented a word to describe them all in the title of his enigmatic and straight-faced description of such a place: *Utopia* – in cod-Greek, that means 'nowhere'.

ERASMUS: NEW BEGINNINGS?

One man seemed to offer the possibility of a reasonable, moderate outcome to Europe's excitements and fears in the early 1500s: Desiderius Erasmus. His life and achievements combine so many themes of European renewal. The supreme humanist scholar came from the Netherlands, home of the *Devotio Moderna*. He became a friend not merely to princes and bishops, but to any clever, wealthy or attractive well-educated European who shared his passion for ideas. All Europe wanted Erasmus as its property: Cardinal Ximénes made vain overtures to get him to Spain, and the cultivated humanist Bishop of Cracow Pietr Tomicki had just as little success with his invitation to Poland – in a curious superstition, Erasmus would never travel very far east of the Rhine, although he was frequently prepared to risk the English Channel. Instead, people came to Erasmus as devotees. He constructed a salon of the imagination, embracing the entire continent in a constant flow of letters to hundreds of correspondents, some of whom he never met face to face. Erasmus should be declared the patron saint of networkers, as well as of freelance writers.

It is interesting that we habitually refer to Erasmus as 'of Rotterdam': in reality, he was indifferent to where he lived, as long as he had a good fire, a good dinner, a pile of amusing correspondence and a handsome research grant. Erasmus himself created this misleading use of the place name, and he also added the 'Desiderius' as a supposed Greek synonym for 'Erasmus'. His crafting of his name is only one aspect of the great humanist's careful construction of his own image: he perfectly exemplified the humanist theme of building new possibilities, for he invented himself out of his own imaginative resources. He needed to do this because when he was born as Herasmus Gerritszoon in a small Dutch town (either Rotterdam or Gouda), he was that ultimate non-person in medieval Catholic Europe, the son of a priest. His family put him on the customary road to self-construction by preparing him for office in the Church. After a *Devotio Moderna*-inspired education, the young man was persuaded to enter a local Augustinian monastery at Steyn, but he did so with great reluctance. He hated monastic life and became additionally miserable when he fell in love with Servatius Rogerus, a fellow monk – but then he identified an escape route: his passion and talent for humanist scholarship.[67]

The Bishop of Cambrai, conveniently far to the south of Steyn, needed a secretary to give his correspondence the fashionable humanist polish appropriate to an important Church dignitary, and Erasmus persuaded his superiors to let him take the post, which he held just long enough to make sure that Steyn was well behind him and that there would be no serious recriminations when he moved on. Erasmus never returned to monastic life (the authorities in Rome eventually regularized this unilateral declaration of independence in 1517, after he had become a celebrity). Although he had been ordained priest in 1492, he never took conventional opportunities for high office in Church or university, which someone of his talent could have had for the asking. Instead, he virtually created a new category of career: the roving international man of letters who lived off the proceeds of his writings and money provided by admirers. He wrote the first best-seller in the history of printing after a stroke of bad luck: desperate for cash after English customs officials confiscated the sterling money in his luggage, he compiled a collection of proverbs with detailed commentary about their use in the classics and in scripture. This work, the *Adagia* or *Adages* (1500), offered the browsing reader the perfect short cut to being a well-educated humanist; Erasmus greatly expanded his money-spinner in successive editions.

At much the same time, Erasmus changed direction in his scholarly enthusiasms, with momentous consequences for the history of European religion: he moved from a preoccupation with secular literature to apply his humanist learning to Christian texts. On one of his visits to England,

his admiration for his friend John Colet's biblical learning nerved him
to the painful task of acquiring the specialist skill of Greek; Greek would
open up to him the writings of then little-known early Fathers of the
Church, together with the ultimate source of Christian wisdom, the New
Testament. He produced new critical editions of a range of key early
Christian texts, the centrepiece of which was his 1516 edition of the
Greek New Testament, accompanied by an expanding range of commentaries on the biblical text. The effect of his superbly presented editions
was much enhanced by his collaboration from 1516 with one of the
most brilliant and artistically sensitive publishers of his day, Johann
Froben of Basel.

Erasmus's New Testament was an inspiration to many future
Reformers, because he provided not only the Greek original but also an
easy way of puzzling out what this difficult text might mean with the
aid of a parallel new Latin translation, tacitly designed to supersede
the Vulgate and the commentary which Jerome had created around it.
Erasmus hugely admired Jerome's industry and energy, but his work of
retranslation and commentary amounted to a thoroughgoing onslaught
on what Jerome had achieved a millennium before. To attack Jerome
was to attack the structure of understanding the Bible which the Western
Church took for granted. Most notorious was Erasmus's retranslation
of Gospel passages (especially Matthew 3.2) where John the Baptist is
presented in the Greek as crying out to his listeners in the wilderness,
'*metanoeite*'. Jerome had translated this as *poenitentiam agite*, 'do
penance', and the medieval Church had pointed to the Baptist's cry as
biblical support for its theology of the sacrament of penance. Erasmus
said that John had told his listeners to come to their senses, or repent,
and he translated the command into Latin as *resipiscite*. Indeed, throughout the Bible, it was very difficult to find any direct reference to Purgatory, as Orthodox theologians had been pointing out to Westerners since
the thirteenth century.

Much thus turned on one word. In Erasmus's view, bad theology
stemmed from faulty grammar, or faulty reading of the Bible. The
characteristic medieval way of making sense of the frequently puzzling
or apparently irrelevant contents of the Bible was to allegorize them in
the manner pioneered by Origen (see pp. 151–2). Commentators found
justification for their allegorizing by quoting a biblical text, John 6.63:
'The Spirit gives life, but the flesh is of no use' – allegory was the spiritual
meaning, the literal meaning the fleshly. This text became a favourite of
Erasmus too, but he was irritated that it should be used as a support for

allegory. Readers of the Bible were right to note allegory in its text, but they should do so with caution and common sense. This principle was particularly significant in the cult of Mary, the Mother of God; it had been a natural impulse for commentators to try to expand the rather slim biblical database about her through the use of allegory. Erasmus came to deplore the redirection on to Mary of Old Testament texts. Protestant Bible commentaries rammed home this message later, and drew gratefully on Erasmus's other redefinitions of biblical terms in order to cut down to size Mary, her cult and her ability along with the lesser saints to intercede with her Son to the Father.[68] More generally, they followed Erasmus in his cautious attitude to the use of allegorical interpretation of the Bible, which they came to consider prone to Catholic misuse.

Erasmus faced up more honestly than most theologians to one problem which later proved as troublesome to Protestants as to Catholics, and whose solution was unavoidably dependent on the exploitation of allegorical reading of the Bible, whether humanists and Protestants liked it or not. This was the universally held belief in Mary's perpetual virginity – that she had remained a virgin all her life. Much of the traditional case for this belief, which has no direct justification in scripture, was based on allegorical use of Ezekiel 44.2, which talks about the shutting of a gate which only the Lord could enter. This was then bolstered by the forced Greek and Latin reading of Isaiah's original Hebrew prophecy that a young woman would conceive a son, Immanuel (Isaiah 7.14; see p. 81). Erasmus could not read these texts as Jerome had done. In response to shocked complaints about his comments, he set out a precise position: 'We believe in the perpetual virginity of Mary, although it is not expounded in the sacred books.'

In other words, Erasmus acknowledged the ancient claim that there were matters of some importance which had to be taken on faith, because the Church said that they were true, rather than because they were found in the Bible. Erasmus had begun to discover a problem which became one of the major issues of the Reformation and which faced all those who called for Christianity to go back 'ad fontes'. Did the Bible contain all sacred truth? Or was there a tradition which the Church guarded, independent of it? The issue of scripture versus tradition became a vital area of debate in the Reformation, which had no straightforward outcome for either side, whatever they might claim. Protestants were to find to their dismay that rather basic matters, like the justification for universal infant baptism, could only be resolved by appeal to tradition, rather than to any clear authority in the Bible.[69]

In a monumental set of dialogues or *Colloquies* intended to charm students into learning to speak elegant Latin, Erasmus made light comedy laced with biting criticism out of his pilgrimage journeys to the English shrines of Our Lady at Walsingham and Canterbury's Thomas Becket. So Menedemus and Ogygius snigger over Ogygius's visit to Norfolk's Marian cult centre, playing around with the fact that the shrine was guarded by a priory which was a community of Augustinian Canons Regular (see p. 392):

Og. She has the greatest fame throughout England, and you would not readily find anyone in that island who hoped for prosperity unless he greeted her annually with a small gift according to his means.

Men. Where does she live?

Og. By the north-west [*sic*] coast of England, only about three miles from the sea. The village has scarcely any means of support apart from the tourist trade. There's a college of canons, to whom, however, the Latin title of regulars is added: an order midway between monks and the canons called secular.

Men. You tell me of amphibians, such as the beaver.

Og. Yes, and the crocodile. But details aside, I'll try to satisfy you in a few words. In unfavourable matters, they're canons; in favourable ones, monks.

Men. So far you're telling me a riddle.

Og. But I'll add a precise demonstration. If the Roman pontiff assailed all monks with a thunderbolt, then they'd be canons, not monks. Yet if he permitted all monks to take wives, then they'd be monks.

In reflecting on Becket's shrine, Eusebius observes to his friend Timothy:

it's robbery to lavish upon those who will make bad use of it that which was owed to the immediate needs of our neighbour. Hence those who build or adorn monasteries or churches at excessive cost, when meanwhile so many of Christ's living temples are in danger of starvation, shiver in their nakedness, and are tormented by want of the necessities of life, seem to me almost guilty of a capital crime. When I was in Britain I saw Saint Thomas's tomb, laden with innumerable precious jewels in addition to other incredible riches. I'd rather have this superfluous wealth spent on the poor than kept for the use of officials who will plunder it all sooner or later. I'd decorate the tomb with branches and flowers; this, I think, would be more pleasing to the saint.[70]

Such thrusts by Erasmus proved handy for officials who only a decade or two later did indeed zestfully plunder the wealth of shrines, in various Reformations enacted throughout Europe. Erasmus's moral indignation concealed a very personal agenda in his religion. When he published his New Testament, he wrote movingly and sincerely in his Prologue about his wish to see the countryman chant the Bible at his plough, the weaver at his loom, the traveller on his journey – even women should read the text. His zeal for Church reform was the opposite of the high clericalism of the likes of Jean Gerson, so enthusiastic for Dionysius the Areopagite. Erasmus wanted to end the excesses of clerical privilege, particularly the clergy's pretensions to special knowledge, and he was always ready to show contempt both for incompetent and unlearned clergy and for what he saw as the pompous obscurity of professional theologians. But lay piety was to be reconstructed on Erasmus's own terms. After Steyn, he had grimly disciplined himself never again to lose control of his emotions: his passions were to remain as abstractions of the intellect.

Erasmus was profoundly repelled by the everyday reality of layfolk grasping at the sacred, the physicality and tactility of late medieval popular piety. For him this was fleshly religion, ignoring the inner work of the Spirit which comes to the faithful through the mind and through pure use of the emotions: 'The Spirit gives life, but the flesh is of no use'! He bequeathed this austerity to much of Protestantism when it reconstructed worship in the Reformation. Erasmus would have applauded C. S. Lewis, the no-nonsense Anglican Oxford don of the twentieth century, when Lewis entitled an introductory devotional work *Mere Christianity*. His own planed-down, whitewashed version of medieval Western faith was set out in 1504 in his best-selling *Enchiridion Militis Christiani*: the 'Dagger for a Christian Soldier', a dagger in the sense of an all-purpose tool, the spiritual equivalent of the modern Swiss Army knife. This sets out his vision of a purified, Christ-centred faith: it could appeal to readers who had previously devoured *Devotio Moderna* literature. Outward ceremonies and ritual mattered much less than quiet, austere devotion springing from inner contemplation. But contemplative ecstatic mysticism was equally not for Erasmus, and he never went down the humanist road which delighted in cabbalism or any of the ancient magical variants on the thought of Plato.

Erasmus later borrowed a phrase from the Dutch humanist abbot Rudolf Agricola to describe his vision of a cerebral, disciplined, biblically based Christianity, echoing in humanist style with the timbre of classical philosophers: *philosophia Christi*, the learned wisdom of Christ.[71] It was not surprising that a man with so little time for the everyday life and public liturgy of the Church showed no deep affection for its institutions. Of course he said respectful things about both liturgy and Church, and on one occasion he even composed a rather moving liturgy for a Marian Mass, but one should never place too much faith in individual writings of Erasmus, who wrote a great deal for effect, for money and to curry favour. The Church as a visible institution was chiefly important to him as one of his main sources of cash, as he sought a spectrum of patrons to sustain the writing and research which were his real concern.[72] By contrast, Erasmus was enthusiastic for godly princes substituting for what he saw as the official Church's failures. With typical humanist optimism, he believed that he could improve the world with the help of the leaders of commonwealths (as long they read and paid for his books), and that he could make his own agenda of universal education and social improvement into theirs. He might even persuade them to abandon war, which threatened his programme for a sweetly reasonable and decently educated pan-European society. One of the most important sections of his *Adages*, a particularly sustained and impressive pioneering advocacy of pacifism, springs out of the proverb *Dulce bellum inexpertis* ('war is sweet to those who have not experienced it').

By his last years Erasmus realized that princes like Henry VIII and François I had deceived him in their elaborate negotiations for universal peace, but his belief in the potential of princely power for good remained undimmed. In a letter to his friend Abbot Paul Volz, antiquary and future Lutheran preacher, written to preface the 1518 edition of the *Enchiridion*, Erasmus asked the rhetorical question, 'What is the state ['*civitas*'] but a great monastery?'[73] This had important implications. First, it denied that there was anything distinctive or useful about monasteries: if the city-state or commonwealth (that is, the whole of society) was to become a monastery, then the monastic vocation which Erasmus himself loathed and had escaped was put firmly in its place, and perhaps his own personal guilt at his flight was exorcized. Second, in Erasmus's ideal society everyone was to be an active citizen of a '*civitas*' as in ancient Greek city-states, and everyone had a duty to behave as purely as monks were supposed to do under a monastic rule. Third, the person to make sure that they did so was the prince. This message much appealed to secular rulers, and fitted in with the existing late medieval trend towards princes and commonwealths taking power in matters of religion and morality out of the hands of churchmen. Catholic and Protestant alike developed this theme of Erasmian humanism, so that the sixteenth and seventeenth centuries became an age which historians have termed 'the Reformation of Manners', when governments began to regulate public morality and tried to organize every individual in society in an unprecedented fashion – on both sides of the Reformation chasm. That was one of the most long-lasting consequences of Erasmus's writings and in that respect sixteenth-century Europe is his Europe.

Yet his legacy was much wider. Beyond the appreciation of scholars, cultivated people showed their cultivation by enjoying his prose. The people of the Netherlands were proud of his birth there and they did not forget his pleas for tolerance. Significantly, the Roman Inquisition at one stage tried to ban all his writings, and religious radicals of whom mainstream Protestants disapproved found much varied inspiration in what he had written. One important matter to interest radicals was that Desiderius Erasmus did not share in Western theologians' general stampede to praise Augustine of Hippo. He had too much respect for creativity and dignity in human beings to accept Augustine's premise that the human mind had been utterly corrupted in the fall of Adam and Eve. Even before he turned towards theology as his main preoccupation, he began around 1489 drafting a work called the *Antibarbari*, eventually published in 1520. One of the aims of this was to defend humanist learning against scholastics, but it had a more general underlying purpose: Erasmus was protesting against the whole perspective on knowledge which sees the only real truth as what is revealed by divine grace, rather than what is available through the reasoning faculties of the human mind and through the acquisition of education. He was expressing his distrust of mysticism, such as that of the *Devotio Moderna* so strong in his native Netherlands, and he deplored the rejection of the created world which often accompanied it; his detestation of the monastic life was related to this feeling.[74]

So Augustinian pessimism was not for Erasmus. Instead he preferred that other giant of the early Church's theology, the great counterpoint to Augustine across the centuries, Origen. Origen's works first became readily available to Latin-speakers in a good scholarly edition in 1512, but Erasmus's esteem for Origen is already evident in the *Enchiridion*. One major reason was Origen's distinctive view of humanity (in jargon terms, his 'anthropology'), which the Alexandrian had built on a passing phrase in Paul's letter to the Thessalonian Church: a human being was made up of three parts, flesh, spirit and soul.[75] Although Paul had not been very helpful in explaining the difference between spirit and soul, Origen and now Erasmus drew their own inferences from the passage. Of the three components of humanity, Origen had said, only the flesh had been thoroughly corrupted, and the highest part, the spirit, was still intact. No wonder Erasmus made so much of the Spirit in his theology.

Here was a splendid basis for humanist optimism in the face of Augustine.[76]

Naturally, with his usual instinct for self-preservation, Erasmus made disapproving noises in his writings about the officially condemned side of Origen's thought – the amount of Platonizing heresy which he had produced – and he also covered his tracks thoroughly against charges of Pelagianism, a word which Augustine had established as one of the ultimate put-downs in Christian vocabulary. However, when Erasmus wrote his interpretations of Paul's Epistle to the Romans, the crucial part of the Bible on which Augustine had constructed his bleak view of humanity, he frequently turned both to Origen and to Jerome's analysis of them, but he was notably more reticent about his attitude to what Augustine had said. Likewise, Erasmus's fierce belief in pacifism, consistently one of the emphatic and radical elements in his thinking, was opposed to the discussion of the legitimacy of war which Augustine had pioneered and which Aquinas had then developed into a theory of 'just war'. Occasionally he could be remarkably bold, as in his studied comment in a long letter to the celebrated theologian of Ingolstadt Johann Eck: 'a single page of Origen teaches me more Christian philosophy than ten of Augustine'.[77]

Erasmus's discreet fascination with Origen and equally discreet coldness towards Augustine was a pointer to a possible new direction for Western Christianity in the early sixteenth century. It was a direction rejected alike by mainstream Protestantism and those who remained loyal to the pope, but it did inspire many of the more adventurous minds of the period, radicals who refused to be absorbed into hardening theological categories – many of whom no doubt first encountered the unfamiliar name of Origen through the pages of Erasmus's *Enchiridion*. Pacifist radicals also honoured his pacifism, while others noted certain discreet indications that he might not have been entirely convinced of the adequacy of the views of God, Christ, salvation and Trinity which the Council of Chalcedon summed up back in 451. Erasmus had rightly (but at the time unsuccessfully) poured scorn on the so-called 'Johannine comma', the suspect text in I John 5.7–8 which is the only explicit mention in the Bible of the Trinity in something like its developed form.[78] Erasmus had also noted that the term 'God' is rarely used for Christ in the biblical text, being normally reserved for the Father alone. When editing the fourth-century theologian Hilary of Poitiers he acutely picked up the same phenomenon in Hilary, besides Hilary's total silence on the divine status of the Spirit. And it was hard to miss one very individual strand running through so much of Erasmus's writing: he brought an ironic smile to the contemplation of the divine and the sacred, and he discerned an ironic smile on the face of the divinity. That sense of irony has not left Western theology since.[79]

Erasmus did not end his life feeling that his career was a success. His pan-European humanist project seemed at its most convincing and his reputation at its highest peak in a brief period after 1517, that same year which saw the beginning of Martin Luther's rebellion. When Erasmus died on a visit to Basel in 1536, his chaste red marble monument was placed in the former cathedral, from where the prince-bishop had already fled and where Reformers had smashed sacred furniture and images of the saints, much to the elderly scholar's alarm and misery. For a decade and more before his death, Erasmus unhappily shifted his centre of operations (he never really looked for a home) round a circuit of western Europe, successively from Louvain to Basel to a house overlooking the cathedral in Freiburg im Breisgau. He had taken one principled stand against Luther, and thus had signalled that he would not abandon the old Church (see pp. 613–14), but he still desperately tried to avoid decisively taking sides in the storm which was now tearing apart the world of elegantly phrased letters, high-minded reform projects and charming Latin-speaking friends which he had patiently extended across the face of Europe. As a result, increasing numbers on either side of the new divide regarded him as a time-serving coward who lacked courage to take sides now that everyone was expected to do so. What had gone wrong? What had happened to the humanist project for changing the world through the power of a perfectly balanced Ciceronian sentence?

17

A House Divided
(1517–1660)

A DOOR IN WITTENBERG

Two incidents stick in the popular consciousness from Martin Luther's career: first, that he nailed some theses to a door in Wittenberg, and second, that he came through a spiritual crisis to new faith while sitting on a latrine – his 'Tower Experience' or *Turmerlebnis*. The first incident probably did happen, and maybe on 31 October 1517, although the original door is not there to enlighten us, having been burned by French troops in 1760.[1] Its replacement is a nineteenth-century confection, part of a lavish and romantic Gothic Revival reconstruction of the dynastic chapel of the Wettin family, beside their former palace. This 'Castle Church' now rather uncomfortably tries to kill three birds with one stone: to celebrate the medieval Holy Roman Empire, the Protestant Reformers whose work helped to tear the empire apart, and the nineteenth-century Hohenzollern dynasty who paid for the new work, and who were concurrently busy constructing a new German Empire (see pp. 837–8). Since the Hohenzollern were ancient and bitter rivals of the Wettin, the rebuilding had a certain piquancy. In an additional level of irony, a distinctly unreformed or under-reformed Hohenzollern prelate had triggered Luther's protest in the first place, as we will see.

The reconstructed door is a focus for Lutheran pilgrimage on Reformation Day, 31 October, the only day of the year on which the place now enterprisingly styling itself 'Lutherstadt Wittenberg' is crowded with visitors. Luther is about the one flourishing industry left in this small east German town in Saxony. By contrast, Luther's basement latrine in Wittenberg has not as yet developed much of a following after its recent rediscovery by archaeologists (the tower above it in his former monastery and family home having inexplicably been demolished by thoughtless Lutherans in 1840). Its continuing neglect is just as well, as its role in the Reformation story is myth, and based on a misunderstanding of the grammar in Luther's Latin reminiscence of his *Turmerlebnis*. We can still enjoy these and less dubious souvenirs of Wittenberg's glory years in the Reformation because the town was one of the few in Germany to be spared bombing in the Second World War. That exemption was a tribute to the worldwide impact of a monk-lecturer's spiritual turmoil in what in 1517 was one of Europe's newest universities.

The university owed its existence to the then head of the Wettin dynasty, Friedrich of Saxony, a strong-minded and creative ruler, by hereditary right one of seven electors, who chose a new Holy Roman Emperor when required (the imperial title had never become hereditary). That honour gave Friedrich a good deal of influence on the Habsburg dynasty, who since the early fifteenth century had normally provided one of their number as the next emperor, but who could never be certain that the electors would allow this to continue. Without the Elector Friedrich's support (puzzling in its consistency – he did not know Martin Luther well and never approved of his religious revolution), it is likely that Luther would have suffered the fate of Jan Hus a century before, burned by the authority of the Church. The Wettin were hugely wealthy from the profits of mining, particularly mining for silver, and one of the justifications for Friedrich's later nickname 'the Wise' was the constructive uses to which he had put his generous inheritance, especially the improvement of the little market town at the gates of his palace in Wittenberg. Some of his spending was what was expected of a medieval prince, like the beautiful music which he sponsored in the Castle Church, or the large collection of holy relics which he also assembled there, all lovingly listed for pious visitors in a printed catalogue. The foundation of the university was less conventional. The first in Germany to be founded without the blessing of the Church authorities, it brashly boasted against its older rivals that it could provide students with an up-to-date immersion in humanist learning.[2]

The lecturer who arrived in 1511, nine years after Friedrich had founded the university, came from the sort of family who provided most of the Western Church's most effective clergy: not especially rich or endowed with long pedigrees, but hard-working and high-achieving. Martin Luther's father made his money in the mining industry, and with a miner for a father, Luther was prone in later years to emphasize his credentials as a man of the people. In fact his mother's family boasted more than one successful graduate. It was only natural for Hans Luther to direct his son towards graduate study to become a lawyer, but Martin struck out in his own direction into the religious life, after an incident which, if he had become a saint of the Catholic Church, would have been the perfect opening for hagiography in a traditional mould. Caught in a thunderstorm in 1505, the young man was so terrified that he vowed to St Anne, the mother of Mary, that he would enter monastic life if he survived. When the storm was over, he kept his vow to that apocryphal lady (a useful ally against any parental opposition, since she was the patron saint of his father's mining industry, as well as being maternal grandmother of God). Martin Luther moved only a little way down the road from his college in Erfurt to the house of the strict monastic Order of Augustinian Eremites; it was they who sent him to Wittenberg.

Perhaps it was his order's devotion to Augustine that directed Luther to his fresh perception of Augustine's views on salvation and grace, but he was hardly alone around the turn of the century in returning to Augustine's grand narrative of human helplessness remedied by divine mercy. Luther was not a conventional humanist.[3] There was little in his theology as it developed which suggested the optimism and sense of boundless possibility which characterized so much humanist learning. Yet as he worked out a theology of salvation which echoed Augustine's exposition of Paul, humanist techniques of scholarship constantly prompted him to challenge scholasticism. Increasingly openly, he despised the scholastic tradition both Thomist and nominalist: he loathed the presence of Aristotle in scholastic theological discussion, and he came to despise the nominalist idea of a salvation contract between God and humanity which Gabriel Biel had pioneered (see pp. 565–6). In 1513 he began lecturing on the Psalter, a natural choice for a monk who structured his daily life around the chanting of the psalms. To help his students, he had a batch of psalters printed with the text broadly spaced surrounded by wide blank margins, so that they could make their notes around the text as he spoke. Absent was all the medieval commentary, that ready-made lens through which students would have been expected to view the Bible, forcing them to look afresh at the text itself.[4]

In 1515 Luther moved to lecturing on Paul's letter to the Romans, so central a text for Augustine's message about salvation. It is worth noting that this took place before Erasmus had published his edition of the New Testament, and so it owed nothing to that monument to humanist learning. Luther discovered good news there for himself: an 'evangelical' message, direct as he saw it in the *evangelium*. His own manuscript notes survive from these two lecture courses and in them themes appear which later coalesced behind his proclamation of justification by faith:

his presentation of the psalms as a meditation on the message and significance of Jesus Christ, his affirmation that all righteousness comes from God, his pointers to the revelation in the words of scripture, a revelation dwarfing any truths provided by human reason. When Luther turned to Romans, at the heart of his presentation of the message of salvation was the doctrine of predestination: 'whoever hates sin is already outside sin and belongs to the elect'. How could we get to this state without help from outside ourselves? A terrifying image in his notes underlines the plight of human beings after the Fall in the Garden of Eden: so trapped in sin that both body and spirit are twisted up claustrophobically without any escape from their agony – *incurvatus in se* – 'turned in on themselves'.[5]

Whenever the *Turmerlebnis* occurred (in fact almost certainly after 1517), Luther remembered or reinterpreted this moment of agony resolved as a turning point forcing on him the realization that faith was central to salvation.[6] Predictably the trigger was a text from Romans, 1.17, itself sheltering a Tanakh quotation from Habbakuk 2.4: 'the righteousness of God is revealed through faith for faith, as it is written "he who through faith is righteous shall live"'. In this sentence, the words 'righteousness/righteous' were in the Vulgate's Latin '*justitia/ justus*': hence the word justification.[7] In Latin that literally means making someone righteous, but in Luther's understanding – in a literally crucial difference – it rather meant declaring someone to be righteous. To use the technical language of theologians, God through his grace 'imputes' the merits of the crucified and risen Christ to a fallen human being who remains without inherent merit, and who without this 'imputation' would not be 'made' righteous at all. That is the essential contrast with the *via moderna* notion of a covenant in which a merciful God allows human merit 'to do that which is in oneself'. Since the word *justitia* is linked so closely with faith, as in Romans 1.17, we see how Luther constructed his evangelical notion of justification by faith from Paul's closely woven text. That was the core of his liberating good news, his Gospel.

Later Luther told this story of a theological revolution as autobiography, portraying his years in the Wittenberg Augustinian monastery as tortured and unprofitable. Partly this was hindsight, given all that happened afterwards, and partly it can be accounted for by his generous efforts in later years to cheer up a long-term house guest, Jerome Weller, who suffered repeated bouts of depression, and who needed to hear about someone else who had successfully endured similar troubles.[8]

Luther also freely admitted that he had been a good and conscientious monk, one of the best products of the healthiest parts of the monastic system. Indeed, that was the trouble. After all his frequent anxious visits to the confessional to seek forgiveness for his (in worldly terms trivial) sins, he still felt a righteous God's fury against his sinfulness. Reminiscing later, he said that he had come to hate this God who had given laws in the Old Testament which could not be kept and which thus held human-kind back from salvation. The opposition of Law and Gospel, an opposition set up by God himself, remained a fundamental theme of his theology.

Luther needed to reconstruct his own story in the light of later events because the drastic implications of his personal struggle only gradually became clear. They developed into the rediscovery of good news which has come to be called the Protestant Reformation, but which called itself, to begin with, an 'evangelical' movement. That remains the official self-description of the Lutheran Churches, in a use of this word which has separate connotations for English-speakers with their own historical references to an anglophone Christian history. What happened in the years after Luther's first lectures on Romans was a turnabout in the whole Western Christian scheme of salvation (soteriology) which had constructed that great theological success story, the doctrine of Purga-tory, with all its attendant structures of intercessory prayer for the dead – chantries, gilds, hospitals – that comforting sense that through divine mercy we humans can busy ourselves doing something to alter and improve our prospects after death. In the end, for Luther and all who came to accept his new message, the problem was that it was not divine mercy upholding this system, but a lie told by clergymen. Yet to begin with, Luther did not see this; nor did he object to Purgatory. In fact he continued to accept Purgatory's existence until around 1530, when he finally realized that his soteriological revolution had abolished it (his change of mind demanded a certain amount of re-editing of some of his earlier writings).[9] Instead, he seized on a lesser problem within the system: the sale of indulgences.

Indulgences, the Western Church's grants remitting penitential pun-ishments, could be seen as a practical demonstration that God loved sinners, and that God's love was channelled through the power of the Church. Yet many loyal church people and theologians had seen the commercialization of the system as vulgar and needing reform, whatever they thought of the principles behind it. Now Luther was provoked to confrontation with the Church hierarchy by a particularly reprehensible campaign, backed by Pope Leo X himself. It raised funds from the German faithful to finish rebuilding St Peter's Basilica in Rome, in a deal which also looked after the financial needs of the great Hohenzollern prelate Albrecht, Archbishop of Magdeburg. The preaching campaign for the indulgence was headed by an extrovert Dominican, Johann Tetzel, who was capable of urging his hearers, 'Won't you part with even a farthing to buy this letter? It won't bring you money but rather a divine and immortal soul, whole and secure in the Kingdom of Heaven.'[10] The squalid implications of this, an insult to the Apostle Paul's view of grace and salvation, led Luther to announce (probably with a notice on the Castle Church door) that he proposed a university disputation on ninety-five theses, taking a decidedly negative view of indulgences. He enclosed these theses in a letter of 31 October 1517 to that same Albrecht, who happened to be his own archbishop.

Luther's protest was quickly turned into an act of rebellion because powerful churchmen gave a heavy-handed response. He wanted to talk about grace; his opponents wanted to talk about authority. That chasm of purposes explains how an argument about a side alley of medieval soteriology escalated into the division of Europe. His own order was broadly sympathetic to his arguments, but throughout 1518 Luther's opponents relentlessly called him to be obedient to Rome, and the incendiary idea of conciliarism (see pp. 560–63) constantly hovered around their diatribes. A veteran Dominican papal theologian, Silvestro Mazzolini of Prierio (sometimes known as 'Prierias'), was commissioned to write against the ninety-five theses. He saw a familiar conciliarist enemy in Luther, and he discussed the infallibility of Church authority at such length that it made Luther much more inclined to wonder whether the Church might be fallible. Luther's meetings with Cardinal Cajetan, one of the most admirable and irreproachable of senior churchmen (see p. 583), became a fiasco for the same reason. Each confrontation made him seem more of a rebel, a reincarnation of the executed rebel Jan Hus.

Cajetan's meeting with Luther need not have ended as it did. Cajetan's immersion in the writings of Thomas Aquinas led him, like other Thomist Dominicans, to emphasize the role of predestination in salvation, an emphasis which Aquinas shared with both Augustine and the Augustinian monk of Wittenberg.[11] Moreover, soon after Luther's first protest in 1517, Cajetan had decided to examine the question of indulgences for himself, and his conclusions (published later at great length) were typical of his brusquely independent thinking. While defending the existence of indulgences, he took a realistic view of their historical origins, and downplayed both the theology of merit and the proposition that the Church could control the measuring out of lengths of penance in Purgatory.[12] Yet in 1518 this meeting of Dominican and Augustinian reformers degenerated into an angry confrontation, in which Cajetan demanded unquestioning obedience to the Pope from Luther, while Luther would not withdraw what he had said about grace. In the terms of B. B. Warfield's characterization of the Reformation as Augustine's doctrine of Grace triumphing over Augustine's doctrine of the Church (see p. 584), Cajetan prioritized Augustine on the Church over Augustine on grace. His Thomist successors in the Catholic Church continued to do so, in the Counter-Reformation (see Chapter 18), a version of Church reform which sought the destruction of the project for Christendom which Luther and his admirers now developed.

Finally in 1520 Luther found himself excommunicated, cut off by the Pope from the fellowship of the whole Church. He publicly burned the bull of excommunication in Wittenberg, cheered on by the students and townsfolk, to whom he had become a hero. Luther was beginning to see himself as chosen by God precisely for a heroic role: to deliver the Church from a satanic error. He had accepted his total sinfulness. This gave him a paradoxical sense of his own rightness, and if the Pope was telling him that he was wrong in proclaiming God's cause, that must mean that the Pope was God's enemy. What was worse, the Church had taken God's sacraments and turned them into part of an elaborate confidence trick on God's people. Luther proclaimed his message to all the victims of the cheat: not just to scholars in Latin but to all laypeople, powerful and humble, in German. Three great treatises in 1520, the *Address to the Christian Nobility of the German Nation*, *The Babylonian Captivity of the Church* and *The Freedom of a Christian*, stood out amid the increasing flood of Luther's polemic from the Wittenberg printing presses.

The first of these three drew on the ancient tensions between pope and emperor to proclaim that the pope was the enemy not just of the empire but of all Christendom. As imperialist spokesmen had long maintained (see p. 558), he was Antichrist, but furthermore, so was the whole apparatus of his Church. The *Babylonian Captivity* addressed itself in Latin to those inside that apparatus, seeking to convince clergy that the sacraments which they administered had been perverted from their biblical forms. Above all, God's Eucharist had been turned to a Mass which falsely claimed to be a repetition of Christ's sacrifice once

offered on the Cross. Luther performed something of a balancing act
when he spoke of the Mass: he kept a passionate sense of the presence
of the Lord's body and blood in the eucharistic bread and wine, but he
scorned the scholastic and non-biblical explanation of this miraculous
transformation which the Church had provided in the doctrine of transubstantiation. The third book explored the problem of its title: how
could utterly fallen humanity, enslaved to sin, claim any liberty? Luther,
never afraid of paradox, boldly gave an answer answerless: 'A Christian
is a perfectly free lord of all, subject to none. A Christian is a perfectly
dutiful servant of all, subject to all.'[13] The paradox was solved by the
utterly undeserved death of Christ, which gave back freedom to those
whom God had chosen from amid an utterly undeserving humanity.

What would the powers of this world make of Luther's call to liberty?
Now that that Church authorities had responded, it was for the civil
commonwealth to pronounce, in the person of its most exalted representative, the Holy Roman Emperor. Charles V, elected in summer 1519
to the huge relief of the Habsburg family, was then not out of his teens,
but he ruled the largest empire that the Christian West had ever known.
A serious-minded young man whose sense of destiny as Christendom's
leader was not diminished by his advisers (see pp. 593–4), he was
anxious not to jeopardize the unity of the dominion entrusted to him,
but also anxious to do what God wanted. Eventually setting aside papal
protests, he heeded Friedrich the Wise and gave Luther a formal hearing
within the boundaries of the empire at the first available meeting of the
Diet, the regular imperial assembly, at Worms in April 1521. Luther
arrived after a triumphal tour across Germany. Facing the Emperor, he
acknowledged a long list of books as his own. Ordered to say yes or no
to the question 'Will you then recant?' he asked for a day's grace to
answer. Would he return to being the best monk in Germany, or go
forward into an unformed future, guided only by what he had found in
the Bible?

Luther's answer next day was no single word, but a careful and
dignified speech. His books were of various sorts, some of which were
indeed 'polemic against the papacy' which reflected 'the experience and
the complaint of all men': 'if then, I revoke these books, all I shall
achieve is to add strength to tyranny, and open not the windows but the
doors to this monstrous godlessness, for a wider and freer range than it
has ever dared before'. He spelled out to the Emperor that without a
conviction from 'scripture or plain reason (for I believe neither in Pope
nor councils alone)', he could recant nothing. It was such a momentous

culmination that not long after his death, Georg Rörer, the first editor of his collected works, felt compelled to construct two tiny summary sentences in German which have become the most memorable thing Luther never said: 'Here I stand; I can do no other'.[14] This can stand for the motto of all Protestants: ultimately, perhaps, of all modern Western civilization.

To his great credit, Charles ignored the Emperor Sigismund's treachery to Hus in 1415 (see pp. 571–2) and honoured Luther's safe conduct from the Diet. Still Luther was in peril, and the best solution was for him to vanish; the Elector Friedrich duly arranged that. Luther occupied those months in the Wartburg, a Wettin stronghold on the wooded massif high above Eisenach, familiar to him from his childhood, by beginning a translation of the Bible into German. It would present his own spin on the text, to make sure that his liberating message got across, but it was an astonishing achievement at a time of great personal stress and amid a welter of polemical writing.[15] Although time only allowed the completion of the New Testament, and the complete Old Testament followed later, his text has shaped the German language. Luther was a connoisseur of the vernacular, like his English contemporary Thomas Cranmer, whose speech has haunted formal English to the present day (see pp. 630–32), but Luther had a different gift. Cranmer's meticulously calculated liturgical prose presented a public, ceremonial face of the Reformation in restrained dignity, even sobriety, whereas Luther's talent was for seizing the emotion with sudden, urgent phrases. His hymns, first published in Wittenberg and Strassburg in 1524, reveal his genius perhaps even more than his Bible, because they transcend the notorious and already then well-established tendency of German to pile syllable on syllable in conglomerations of compound notions.

Singers of Luther's hymns can revel in strong words of one or two syllables, like his famous '*Ein' feste Burg ist unser Gott, Ein gute Wehr und Waffen*'. Almost certainly Luther also wrote its tune, which has become the universal anthem of Lutheranism. The words still provide a glimpse of how his genius seized on the fears of ordinary folk in a world full of evils and terrors, and helped his congregations roar away these terrors in song. Americans will probably know it in English translation as 'A mighty fortress is our God', but British hymn-singers will be more familiar with the vastly superior translation made by the Victorian historical writer Thomas Carlyle, who had a feel for craggy men of action like Luther, and captured far better the breezy directness of his German:

A safe stronghold our God is still,
A trusty shield and weapon;
He'll help us clear from all the ill
That hath us now o'ertaken.
The ancient prince of hell
Hath risen with purpose fell;
Strong mail of craft and power
He weareth in this hour;
On earth is not his fellow.

And were this world all devils o'er,
And watching to devour us,
We lay it not to heart so sore;
Not they can overpower us.
And let the prince of ill
Look grim as e'er he will,
He harms us not a whit;
For why? – his doom is writ;
A word shall quickly slay him.

Inevitably in the storm now spreading throughout the continent, Erasmus was urged to confront Luther, and he needed to do so in order to refute the charge that his own delicate sarcasm at the Church's expense had spawned this monstrous rebel. Erasmus chose his question carefully. The choice reflected his own distaste for the Augustinian theology which meant so much to Luther: has humanity retained free will to respond to God's offer of grace? He set out his attack in September 1524: *A Diatribe on Free Will*. Fully aware that he must play by Augustinian rules, Erasmus emphasized that the initiative in grace was with God. After that, however, he sought to avoid a dogmatic single formula on grace; for him this was Luther's chief fault. His attack was as much on Luther's way of doing theology as on the resulting theology: Luther was exposing controversial questions to public excitement when there was no need to do so. Erasmus preferred to seek consensus, put forward an opinion which seemed most probable – that process is actually the technical meaning of the word *diatribe*. Erasmus was a humanist pleading for people to be reasonable – and also saying bluntly that unreasonable people should not be brought into technical discussions of theology. Moreover, he believed that human beings could indeed be reasonable, because when Adam and Eve fell in the Garden of Eden, their God-given capacity to reason had not been fully corrupted, only damaged.

Luther by contrast was a prophet proclaiming an inescapable message to all fallen humanity. In his response, uncompromisingly entitled *On the Slavery of the Will* (*De servo arbitrio*, published in December 1525), Luther set out a pitiless message that human beings could expect nothing but condemnation, and had nothing to offer God to merit salvation:

> If we believe that Christ redeemed men by his blood, we are forced to confess that all of man was lost; otherwise, we make Christ either wholly superfluous, or else the redeemer of the least valuable part of man only; which is blasphemy, and sacrilege.[16]

This parting blow in his book was the very heart of the Reformation's reassertion of Augustine, proclaiming that the humanist project of reasonable reform was redundant. It was not surprising that Erasmus went on fighting, in two bulky and bitter volumes published in 1526 and 1527, in which he showed how Luther had forced him back to reaffirm his loyalty to the imperfect structures of the old Church: 'Therefore I will put up with this Church until I see a better one; and it will have to put up with me, until I become better.'[17] Wearily he was confronting not only Luther, but also his own humanist sympathizers like Luther's brilliant young university colleague Philipp Melanchthon, who had likewise determined to favour Augustine's doctrine of grace over Augustine's doctrine of the Church.[18]

THE FARMERS' WAR AND ZWINGLI

What degree of change was Luther proclaiming, and what needed changing? Many ordinary people, especially those defending their livelihoods against new exactions by their lords and by governments, saw Luther's defiance of authority as a sign that all authority was collapsing in God's final judgement on human sin. The Last Days had arrived, and everyone had a duty to hurry along God's plan, which included overthrowing God's enemies in high places. In 1525 large areas of central Europe were convulsed by revolts against princes and Church leaders: the *Bauernkrieg*, often misleadingly translated into English as the 'Peasants' War', but better rendered the 'Farmers' War' to get a sense of the sort of prosperous people – not so different from Luther's family – who in their righteous anger and excitement led the crowds. The revolts were brutally crushed – and Luther, terrified by the disorder, applauded the rulers' brutality. Another text from Paul lit up for him: Romans 13.1, 'Let everyone obey the superior powers, for there is no authority except from God'. This has been described as the most important text of the Reformation. Many humanist scholars now drew back from the Reformation in fright; others committed themselves to an ordered, modulated programme of change. For many of the cowed, resentful rebels, the Reformers' message of liberation now seemed as big a sham and betrayal as the pope's old offer of salvation. Luther and his supporters would have to find some other means for pursuing their revolution than their first idealistic appeal to the good sense of all God's people.

What they did was to woo the 'magistrates': the term which sixteenth-century Europe used to describe all its temporal leaders outside the Church hierarchy. These magistrates were indeed the superior powers referred to in Romans 13.1, just as the Roman emperor had been when Paul was writing. The leaders of the Church, the bishops, for the most part did not defect from the old organization, particularly those who were 'prince-bishops' of the Holy Roman Empire, temporal rulers as well as heads of their dioceses. Other magistrates might well be interested in a reformation which stressed theologies of obedience and good order, and also offered the chance to put the Church's wealth to new purposes. The first prince to come over was a major coup from a rather surprising quarter: the current Grand Master of the Teutonic Order, Albrecht of Brandenburg-Ansbach, a Hohenzollern and cousin of Cardinal Albrecht of Mainz. The Teutonic Order had met increasing reverses in its long struggle with Poland-Lithuania (see pp. 516–17), and demoralized by major defeats in 1519–21, many of the Grand Master's knights had turned to evangelical religion, quitting the order. To save himself from ruin, he begged another cousin, King Sigismund I of Poland, to remodel the order's Polish territories in east Prussia into a secular fief of the Polish kingdom, with the Grand Master himself as its first hereditary duke; he did his first act of fealty to a gratified Sigismund in Cracow in April 1525. Naturally such a radical step as secularizing the territory of a religious order needed a formal act of rebellion against the old Church, and Albrecht of newly 'ducal' Prussia, who had already sounded out Luther in a face-to-face meeting in Wittenberg in late 1523, institutionalized this during summer 1525, creating the first evangelical princely Church in Europe.[19]

Before Albrecht of Prussia, the initiatives in backing evangelical religious change had come from the self-confident towns and cities of the Holy Roman Empire, who enjoyed varying degrees of autonomy from emperor or princes. The first in the empire proper had been the Free City of Nuremberg, a great prize because the central legal and administrative institutions of the empire were sited there; the Nuremberg authorities allowed evangelical preaching in 1521. But a move of even greater significance came from a wealthy city in Switzerland, whose ties to the empire had been nominal since a victory of combined Swiss armies over Habsburg forces in 1499. Amid various cantons and free jurisdictions which made up the Swiss Confederacy, Zürich became home to another variety of evangelical Reformation which had little more than an indirect debt to Luther, and whose chief reformer, Huldrych Zwingli, created a rebellion against Rome with very different priorities. Certainly at the heart of it was a proclamation of the freedom of a Christian to receive salvation by faith through grace, and although Zwingli would never acknowledge his indebtedness to Luther on this point, it has always seemed rather more than coincidence that the Swiss Reformer should stumble independently on the same notion during the same European-wide crisis.

While Luther was a university lecturer who never formally had pastoral responsibilities for any congregation, Zwingli was a parish priest who, as an army chaplain, had seen the most extreme of pastoral experiences – that traumatic episode left him with a long-term commitment to Erasmus's arguments against war (contradicted at the last, as we will see). Parish ministry mattered to him deeply. A charismatic preacher at Zürich's chief collegiate church, the Grossmünster, he won a firm basis of support in the Zürich city council, which pioneered a Reformation steered by clerical minister and magistrate in close union. In Lent 1522, he publicly defended friends who had in his presence ostentatiously eaten a large sausage, thus defying Western Church discipline which laid down strict seasons and conditions for abstinence in food. Later that year, he and his clerical associates made an even more profound breach with half a millennium of Church authority than the inappropriate sausage by getting married. It took Martin Luther three years to follow suit.

Now not Rome but Zürich city council would decide Church law, using as their reference point the true sacred law laid down in scripture. From the early 1520s, Zwingli's Church was the city of Zürich, and the magistrates of Zürich could hold disputations to decide the nature of the Eucharist, just as they might make directions for navigation on Lake Zürich or make arrangements for sewage disposal. With their backing, Zwingli's clerical team, untrammelled by any major monastery,

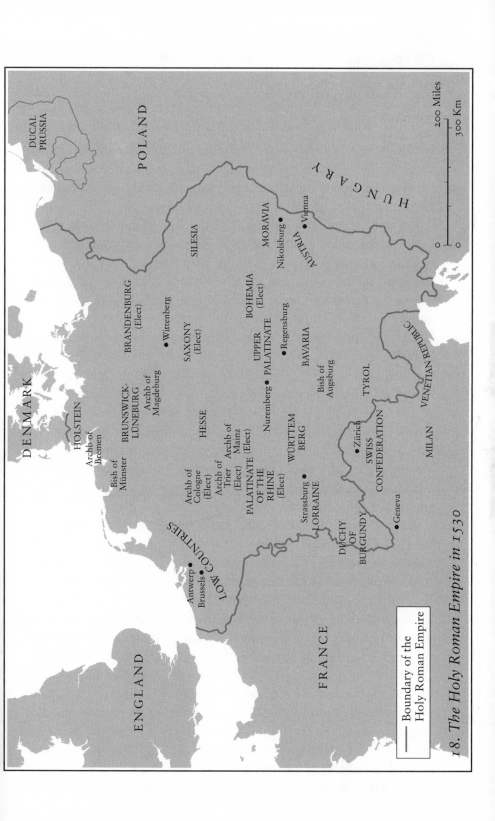

18. *The Holy Roman Empire in 1530*

DENMARK

ENGLAND

DUCAL PRUSSIA

POLAND

HOLSTEIN

Archb of Bremen

Bish of Münster

BRUNSWICK-LÜNEBURG

Archb of Magdeburg

BRANDENBURG (Elect)

• Wittenberg

SILESIA

SAXONY (Elect)

HESSE

Archb of Cologne (Elect)

Archb of Mainz (Elect)

Archb of Trier (Elect)

PALATINATE OF THE RHINE (Elect)

Nuremberg •

UPPER PALATINATE

BOHEMIA (Elect)

MORAVIA

• Nikolsburg

Regensburg •

BAVARIA

Bish of Augsburg

AUSTRIA

• Vienna

HUNGARY

LOW COUNTRIES

Antwerp •
Brussels •

Strassburg •

LORRAINE

WÜRTTEM-BERG

• Zürich

SWISS CONFEDERATION

TYROL

VENETIAN REPUBLIC

DUCHY OF BURGUNDY

• Geneva

MILAN

FRANCE

—— Boundary of the Holy Roman Empire

0   200 Miles

0   300 Km

university theology faculty or local bishop, forged a distinctive pattern of evangelical belief with a great worldwide future. By the end of the sixteenth century, this Protestantism would be called Reformed, which crudely speaking meant all varieties of consciously non-Lutheran Protestantism. Often Reformed Protestantism has been called 'Calvinism', but the very fact that we are beginning to discuss it in relation to an earlier set of Reformers than John Calvin immediately reveals the problems inherent in that label, and suggests that it should be used sparingly.

The term 'Calvinist' began life, like so many religious labels, as an insult, and during the sixteenth and seventeenth centuries, it persisted more among those abusing Reformed Protestants than among the Reformed themselves. There has never been any imposed uniformity among the Reformed family. Reformed Protestantism from the beginning differed from Luther's Reformation – much to his fury – in several key respects, principally its attitude to images, to law and to the Eucharist. The seeds of division were actually sown even before there was much contact between Wittenberg and Zürich, since, from 1521 onwards, Luther's independently minded colleague in Wittenberg University Andreas Bodenstein of Karlstadt had already started to push the logic of what Luther had said, in regard to these same questions. As Luther immediately failed to find common ground with Karlstadt, and eventually got him expelled from Wittenberg, it was not surprising that he failed to reach agreement with the reformers of the faraway Swiss city when he found that they were making similar statements.

It was Zwingli's friend Leo Jud, pastor of St Peter's across the river from the Grossmünster, who in a sermon of 1523 pointed out quite rightly that the Bible ordered the destruction of images in no less prominent a setting than the Ten Commandments. Jud (as that nickname 'Jew' indicated) was a distinguished Hebrew scholar: he noticed the significant oddity, forgotten by most of the Western Church, that there were two contrasting ways of numbering the Commandments, and that the system to which Augustine of Hippo had long ago given his authority conveniently downplayed the command against images. So Jud was reopening the question of images which had nearly brought the Byzantine Empire to ruin in the eighth and ninth centuries (see pp. 442–53), and which had been only briefly and partially reopened by John Wyclif and the avengers of Jan Hus a century before – Wyclif had noted that same numbering anomaly in the Ten Commandments. Now Zürichers started pulling down images from churches and from the roadside. This frequently involved disorder, and disorder has never enthused Swiss society. The city council took action: in October 1523 it arranged a further disputation, leading to the first official statement of doctrine produced anywhere in the Reformation. First, images were systematically removed from churches in June 1524 and then, in April 1525, the traditional form of the Mass itself was banned in the city. Until that latter moment, astonishingly, Zürich still remained in communion with its traditional ally the Pope, who had let politics blind him to the seriousness of what was happening there, and who never made any official condemnation of the man who was steering events in the city.

On the matter both of images and of the Eucharist, Luther was less inhibited than the Pope, and strongly and publicly disagreed with Zürich. Thanks to Karlstadt he had already faced image-smashing in Wittenberg in 1522, when he was alarmed enough by the disorder to hurry back from the Wartburg to preach against it, standing in the pulpit pointedly dressed in a brand-new monk's habit of his Augustinian Order.[20] After that bruising episode, Luther decided that the problem of sacred art was no problem at all. Once the most obviously absurd images had been removed in orderly fashion, destroying sacred art was actually a form of idolatry: it suggested that images had some power, and in fact they had none. What could be wrong with beautiful pictures of God's mother or of Christ hanging on the Cross? Luther used a battery of biblical arguments to offset the Ten Commandments; as early as 1520, when preparing teaching material on the Commandments, he showed his characteristic ability to play fast and loose with scripture by omitting all reference to the Commandment prohibiting images. He was certainly not going to adopt the 'Zürich' renumbering: the result, bizarrely, is that the Churches of western Europe still number the Ten Commandments differently, and the split is not between Roman Catholics and Prot-estants, but between on the one hand Roman Catholics and Lutherans, and on the other all the rest – including the Anglican Communion. Luther produced a formula to convey the usefulness of images: '*zum Ansehen, zum Zeugnis, zum Gedächtnis, zum Zeichen*' ('for recognition, for witness, for commemoration, for a sign'). After 1525, he rarely felt the need to enlarge on these points.[21]

Great principles were at stake. Zwingli did not share Luther's negative conception of law, and because he so strongly identified Church and city in Zürich, he found the image of Zürich as Israel compelling. Israel needed law; law forbade idols. Where Luther had contrasted law (bad) and Gospel (good), Zürich now contrasted law (good) and idolatry (bad). Despite being a talented and enthusiastic musician, Zwingli even banned music in church, because its ability to seduce the senses was likely to prove a form of idolatry and an obstacle to worshipping God. Turned into a point of principle by Zwingli's successor Heinrich Bullinger, this ban lasted until 1598, when bored and frustrated Zürich congregations rose in rebellion against their ministers and successfully demanded the satisfaction of singing hymns or psalms in their services, since by then all other Reformed Churches allowed sacred music. The printers of Zürich had in fact been happily printing hymnals for those other churches for the previous fifty years.[22]

Equally profound was the two men's disagreement about the Eucharist. Zwingli, a thoroughgoing humanist in his education and a deep admirer of Erasmus, emphasized the spirit against the flesh. A favourite biblical proof-text with him was Erasmus's watchword, John 6.63: 'The Spirit gives life, but the flesh is of no use' (see pp. 596–9). Luther, he thought, was being crudely literal-minded to flourish Christ's statement at the Last Supper, 'This is my body . . . this is my blood', as meaning that bread and wine in some sense became the body and blood of Christ. When Luther had jettisoned the idea of the Mass as sacrifice and the doctrine of transubstantiation, why could the obstinate Wittenberger not see that it was illogical to maintain any notion of physical presence in eucharistic bread and wine? Jesus Christ could hardly be on the communion table when Christians know that he is sitting at the right hand of God (this argument pioneered by Karlstadt may seem crass now, but it became a firm favourite with Reformed Christians). In any case, what was a sacrament? Zwingli, as a good humanist, considered the origins of the Latin word *sacramentum*, and discovered that the Latin Church had borrowed it from everyday life in the Roman army, where it had meant a soldier's oath. That struck a strong chord in Switzerland, where regular swearing of oaths was the foundational to a society whose strength came from mutual interdependence and local loyalty. It also resonated with that ancient Hebrew idea which has repeatedly sounded anew for Christians: covenant.

So the sacrament of Eucharist was not a magical talisman of Christ's body. It was a community pledge, expressing the believer's faith (and after all, had not Luther said a great deal about faith?). The Eucharist could indeed be a sacrifice, but one of faith and thankfulness by a Christian to God, a way of remembering what Jesus had done for humanity on the Cross, and all the Gospel promises which followed on from it in scripture. And what was true for the Eucharist must be true for the other biblical sacrament, baptism. This was a welcome for children into the Lord's family the Church; it did not involve magical washing away of sin. For Zwingli, therefore, the sacraments shifted in meaning from something which God did for humanity, to something which humanity did for God. Moreover, he saw sacraments as intimately linked with the shared life of a proud city. The Eucharist was the community meeting in love, baptism was the community extending a welcome. This nobly coherent vision of a better Israel, faithful to God's covenant, was a reformed version of Erasmus's ideal of how the world might be changed. It was utterly different from the raw paradoxes about the human condition, the searing, painful, often contradictory insights which constituted Luther's Gospel message.

Therefore the two could never agree on the Eucharist, even when in 1529 their frustrated princely supporter Philipp, Landgrave of Hesse, brought them face to face at Marburg to heal the breach. Such was the bitterness that in 1530 Luther told his followers that they should get married and have their children baptized in Catholic churches rather than among Zwinglians, as Zwingli was far more in error than the Pope.[23] This was all the more remarkable because Luther, as much as Zwingli, found that he was reliant on German princes for help in two directions: first, against ordinary people who did not want to be reformed and who needed orders from princes to move them along; second, against the Holy Roman Emperor Charles V, who had outlawed him after Worms, and who now wished to destroy him and his whole programme. In fact from princely support came a new label for the movement, when a group of the princes supporting Luther made a protest against the decisions of the Imperial Diet at Speyer in 1529. They were accordingly nicknamed Protestants, the first time this word had been thus used; the nickname stuck. At the next imperial Diet, at Augsburg in 1530, the party of Luther's supporters presented a statement of doctrine to Charles V, drafted by Philipp Melanchthon, which in its studied moderation was intended to win the Emperor's assent. It failed in that purpose, but the group who were increasingly being styled 'Lutheran' retained this 'Augsburg Confession' as their flagship statement of faith.

REFORMATIONS RADICAL AND MAGISTERIAL: ANABAPTISTS AND HENRY VIII

So the period after 1525 was one in which the dark memory of the Farmers' War ended any chance of a united continent-wide popular revolution. Instead a 'magisterial' Reformation was created: these were the Protestant movements led by the *magistri*, the theologically educated masters, and magistrates of all descriptions – kings, princes, city councils. The description 'magisterial Reformation' is worth using, and I will frequently use it in this narrative, because there were nevertheless still many radical Christians, who proposed their own versions of religious revolution, and whose radical Reformations remained very different in character and belief from magisterial Protestantism. In Switzerland, some were inspired by their realization that Zwingli was much more systematic and logical in his rejection of the past than Luther. They took up Zwingli's thinking on Eucharist and baptism. If Zwingli said that the sacraments were pledges of faith by Christian believers who had already received God's gift of saving faith, surely Christian baptism ought to be a conscious act of faith by the person baptized – 'believers' baptism'. Clearly babies could not make such an act, so baptism ought to be reserved for adults. After all, the New Testament contained not a single explicit example of infant baptism. Historically, this was correct, but the argument against infant baptism had hardly ever been made before in Christian history, and it came as an unpleasant shock to magisterial Reformers. Because the radicals sought to give a new and genuine baptism to those who had been baptized as infants, their enemies called them in cod-Greek 'rebaptizers' or Anabaptists. Clearly no proponent of believers' baptism would see what they were doing as rebaptizing; their self-image would better be expressed in the neutral term which German uses for them, *Taüfer* (baptizers).

Zwingli was appalled at this logical deduction from his own theology, because it contradicted another axiom of his thought, that the Church of Zürich embraced the whole city of Zürich. To opt in to baptism as an adult was to split the wholeness of the community, into believers and non-believers. That would end the assumption which both he and Luther held as dear as the Pope, that all society should be part of the Church in Christendom. So from 1526 Zürich, embittered by the recent Farmers'

War, persecuted Anabaptists to the extent of drowning four of them in the River Limmat, just at the time when the old Church began persecuting champions of the magisterial Reformation. The Anabaptists were harried out of ordinary society. Their one alliance with a magistrate, when Count Leonhard von Liechtenstein allowed them to take over the Moravian town of Nikolsburg and form an established Church professing believers' baptism, ended abruptly in 1527 on the orders of the Count's Habsburg overlords; the Habsburgs burned at the stake the would-be Zwingli of Nikolsburg, a former senior academic called Balthasar Hubmaier. Accordingly, radicals began stressing their difference from ordinary society.

When they turned to the Bible for guidance, such people noticed quite correctly that early Christians had separated themselves from the world around. The Book of Acts talked of Christians holding all goods in common (see pp. 119–20). 'Do not swear at all,' said Jesus Christ (Matthew 5.34). 'Commit no murder,' said the Ten Commandments. So radicals looked for the rare corners of Europe where they had a chance to create their own little worlds, in which goods could be held in common, where no one would force them to swear the oaths which governments and magistrates required, or take up the sword when rulers ordered them to. They took a selective view of the demand for obedience in Romans 13.1, infuriating and frightening the superior powers. Many looked back to the nearest thing that 'Anabaptists' ever had to a common confessional statement: articles drawn up in 1527 at the Swiss town of Schleitheim, which were insistent on 'separation from the Abomination'. Their principal author was a former Benedictine monk, Michael Sattler, and it is tempting to see the communal institutions of radicals as a new effort to return to the early Benedictine ideal. Yet one feature was far from Benedictine: it returned radicals to a still earlier Christianity, which had suffered from official persecution. 'True believing Christians are sheep among wolves, sheep for the slaughter. They must be baptized in anguish and tribulation, persecution, suffering, and death, tried in fire, and must reach the fatherland of eternal rest not by slaying the physical but the spiritual,' wrote the young Zürich patrician Conrad Grebel to Thomas Müntzer, a year before Müntzer, a leader in the 1525 revolts, was cut down by the vengeful soldiers of princes.[24]

More frightening still for Christendom was that, even after the defeats of 1525, some radicals continued to believe that they needed force to usher in the Last Days. They heard Jesus say, 'I have come not to bring peace, but a sword' (Matthew 10.34), and they wanted to help God fulfil his political programme in the Book of Revelation. So in the early 1530s, groups from the Low Countries began joining with other radicals in converging on the western German city of Münster. They arrived in thousands; they took over Münster's civic Reformation, which had begun in conventionally Lutheran mode, and their charismatic leaders proclaimed the new Jerusalem. A joint force of Lutherans and Catholics besieged them. Under pressure, with the city running short of food, the radicals' revolution turned to nightmare. Their final leader, a young Dutchman, Jan Beuckelszoon ('John of Leyden'), lived as their king in insane luxury, surrounded by his harem, as his followers starved and died defending him. In the end, the besiegers breached the defences in 1535 and Münster Anabaptists were sadistically suppressed. Radicalism thereafter turned from militancy to quiet escapes from ordinary society, tolerated by some rulers who recognized that such gathered communities were actually industrious and honest-dealing. Yet Münster remained as a constant dark memory: peaceable, inoffensive Anabaptists were burned and harried because of what John of Leyden had done.[25]

The challenge of radicalism to Western Christianity was in fact more long term and subtle than this.[26] Perhaps basic to all of it was a newly negative view of the Emperor Constantine I – 'the Great', as he had so long been called. It was a general conviction among radicals that over the previous millennium the Church had made a grave error in entering into alliance with the powerful, after a decisive wrong turn in Constantine's alliance with Christianity. Radicals noted that a very great deal of the Church's doctrine had been formulated by agreements of councils in that tainted period after Constantine's seizing of the doctrinal reins at Nicaea in 325 (see pp. 214–15), and if that was so, all such doctrine was ripe for reassessment. If one looked at the Bible with fresh eyes, where were some of the central doctrines of traditional Christianity which the Church said were there, such as the Trinity? Obstinately, many Bible readers continued to fail to find infant baptism mentioned in its pages. Some went further and came to the conviction that the Bible was not the ultimate guide to divine truth: they called it a 'paper Pope', and affirmed that God spoke to the individual as he (or even she) pleased through 'inner light'. If so, it was unlikely that there was any one normative perception of truth, un-Christian to coerce any beliefs and even undesirable that there should be one single Church. The radicals in the Reformation may posthumously claim success, for something of all these notions can now be found in Churches which are the heirs of the magisterial Reformation, and even within the Church of Rome.

The magisterial Reformers went on battling for the minds of rulers, partly because they were appalled by hearing any selection of such beliefs. They succeeded in much of Germany and Scandinavia; they failed in Jagiellon Poland, Valois France and the Habsburg lands. Yet through much of central Europe, nobility were receptive where monarchs were not, sensing the advantages of challenging the religion of their overlords. In 1525 the Estates in Upper Austria backed the Habsburg King Ferdinand's suppression of the Farmers' War, but their price for further cooperation in suppressing Anabaptists was to force him to tolerate evangelical activists and preachers in the mould of Luther. From the mid-sixteenth century, the overwhelming majority of the Lower Austrian nobility, and of the inhabitants in the Habsburg capital Vienna, were avowed Lutherans, despite all Habsburg efforts to obstruct this growth, and Lutheranism quietly consolidated itself elsewhere.[27] In central Europe, a defining catastrophe for traditional authority was the Ottoman victory at Mohács in 1526, when the Holy Roman Emperor's twenty-year-old brother-in-law, King Louis II of Hungary and Bohemia, was killed, along with a large proportion of his nobility, five bishops, two archbishops and sixteen thousand of his soldiers; the Turks occupied a wide sweep of the former kingdom. Quite apart from the shattering of a ruling elite, the blow to the old religion's prestige was severe; the situation was wide open for many varieties of religious reform, and individual noblemen took up the cause of Reform as they pleased.

The early Reformation gained a curious sort of victory in England, where the murderously opinionated monarch Henry VIII found an alliance with Reformers useful during his eccentric marital adventures. Determined to rid himself of his tiresomely loyal first wife, Catherine of Aragon, in order to secure a legitimate male heir, he found himself frustrated by the Pope's refusal to accept his contention on theological grounds that the marriage had never actually taken place. Henry demanded that it should be recognized as null so that he would be free to marry whomever he wished – by the late 1520s that meant a spirited young lady at Court, Anne Boleyn. Pope Clement VII was under pressure from Queen Catherine's nephew, the Holy Roman Emperor Charles V, who was rather nearer to hand than the King of England, and who in 1527 had demonstrated what that might mean when his soldiers (mostly Lutheran sympathizers) rampaged through Rome itself uncontrolled for weeks on end, bringing horror and chaos within earshot of the terrified Pope taking refuge in Castel Sant'Angelo.

Henry, increasingly convinced that the Pope was God's enemy as well as England's in denying him his annulment, conceived the idea of repudiating papal jurisdiction. He was the first king in Europe to do so, and in order to underpin this revolutionary measure with wide political consent, he used the organizing skills of a newly recruited royal minister, Thomas Cromwell, to secure legislation in his Parliament enacting a break with Rome. His new wife, Anne Boleyn, was a none-too-discreet sympathizer with evangelical Reformation, and was able to encourage evangelicals at Court.[28] Among them was Cromwell, who was working closely with another new recruit, the Archbishop of Canterbury Thomas Cranmer, appointed in 1533 to formalize Henry's annulment and new marriage. Between them, from 1534 Cromwell and Cranmer discreetly encouraged a piecemeal dismantling of the old Church, not always in harmony with the King's wishes; in 1540, Cromwell was disgraced and executed, partly because of this, and partly because of his disastrous recruitment of yet a fourth royal wife who turned out unacceptable.[29] By then, Henry was twice a widower. Queen Anne had failed to provide the much-sought male heir. Henry could not foresee that the birth of her daughter, Elizabeth, in 1533 had furnished a worthy successor to the throne, and in default of any boys, Anne preceded Cromwell to the scaffold, beheaded in 1536 on absurd charges of adultery and incest. Her replacement, Jane Seymour, suited the king well, and provided the vital male heir, Prince Edward, but she died of post-partum infection. Through all these crises and more, Cranmer's survival skills were sorely tested.

One of King Henry's most celebrated executions was done by proxy, the victim dying on the command of the Emperor Charles V. He was William Tyndale, one of the geniuses of the English Reformation; after Henry's agents secured his kidnap while he was in exile in Antwerp, he was strangled at the stake before his corpse was burned near Brussels. He bequeathed the English nothing less than the first translation of the New Testament and Pentateuch in their own language since the by then archaic version of the Lollards 150 years before. Tyndale, an Oxford scholar from Gloucestershire, made the English Bible his life's work, had to flee his native land to continue his labours on it and lost his life because of it. He brought not just evangelical fervour and an exceptional skill in Greek and Hebrew to his task, but an exceptional ear for languages, perhaps borne of his childhood spent in English western borderlands, where the sound of Welsh was almost as familiar as English. He understood that English might actually be closer than Latin to Hebrew in its rhythms and driving narrative force, and the results coruscate with life and energy –

here is the moment at which Adam and Eve fell from obedience to God, that greatest tragedy of humankind in the Christian story:

And the woman saw that it was a good tree to eat of and lusty unto the eyes and a pleasant tree for to make wise. And took of the fruit of it and ate, and gave unto her husband also with her, and he ate. And the eyes of both of them were opened, that they understood how that they were naked.[30]

Or we can sample of Tyndale's own vigorous words introducing his translation of Deuteronomy (it is noticeable that when he started translating the Books of the Law in the Tanakh, he abandoned his previous practice of filching the individual prefaces of books from Martin Luther's Bible to translate or paraphrase in his English prefaces, and instead expressed his own thoughts):

This is a book worthy to be read in day and night and never to be out of hands. For it is the most excellent of all the books of Moses. It is easy also and light and a very pure gospel that is to wete, a preaching of faith and love: deducing the love to God out of faith, and the love of a man's neighbour out of the love of God.

The New Testament which Tyndale prepared first had an immediate impact when clandestine copies arrived in England in 1526–7: nothing else was so important in creating a popular English Reformation which was independent of King Henry's whims. By the time of Tyndale's martyrdom in 1536, perhaps sixteen thousand copies of his translation had passed into a country of no more than two and a half million people, with a very poorly developed market for books.[31] And in one of the religious ironies with which Henry's reign was replete, the King came to authorize the translation made by the man whose murder he had in effect arranged. Only a year after Tyndale's death Thomas Cromwell secured a royal order for every parish in England to buy a complete Bible, most of whose text was in fact Tyndale's translation (Henry VIII never seems to have realized this). It is the ancestor of all Bibles in the English language, especially the 'Authorized' or 'King James' version of 1611 (see pp. 649–50); Tyndale's biographer David Daniell has bluntly pointed out that 'Nine-tenths of the Authorized Version's New Testament is Tyndale's.'[32]

By the time King Henry died in 1547, England's traditional religion was under severe attack. The Bible was now available to Henry's subjects in a complete version created by English evangelicals building on Tyndale's achievement, although with a characteristically unpredictable swing of policy in 1543, the King sought to ban his less well-educated subjects from reading it, deeply troubled at the possibility that they might have radical thoughts as a result of irresponsible thumbing through its pages. Despite this major setback for evangelicals, a terrible blow had been delivered to the old faith by the closure of all monasteries, nunneries and friaries in England and Wales (1532–40). This was the swiftest and most thoroughgoing such campaign in Europe, against one of the continent's best-administered groupings of religious communities, whose place in English life stretched back for a thousand years. The dissolution had been masterminded by Thomas Cromwell during his years of power, but even after Cromwell's execution, the King and his advisers extended the attack on traditional centres of intercession for the dead by a systematic dissolution of chantry foundations, although they did not give ideological reasons for what they were doing, simply announcing that King Henry needed the money.[33] The way lay open in 1547 to a more coherently ideological Reformation for England, presided over enthusiastically by Henry's young son, Edward VI.[34]

Magisterial Reformations in the city-states of mainland Europe took their cue from Zürich. They also took note of the disaster which rewarded Zwingli's ambitious aim of steering the city into becoming a militant new Israel, leading a Reformation through Switzerland and perhaps even further. The Catholic cantons of Switzerland defeated Zürich's armies on its border at Kappel in 1531, and among those who died there was Zwingli himself, cut down in full armour on the hillside battlefield, in a drastic consequence of abandoning his pacifist principles (Luther showed rather distasteful *Schadenfreude* about this). Zürich never again took up such an aggressive programme, but the young cleric hastily chosen to take over leadership from Zwingli, Heinrich Bullinger, proved a most effective and wise ecclesiastical statesman over more than four decades. One of the Reformation's most prolific letter-writers in the face of formidable competition for that title, he revealed a talent for sustaining friendships and intervening helpfully in the troubles of Reformed Churches right across the continent. He was one of the sixteenth century's most successful communicators, both through his collected and systematized sermons, the *Decades*, and because of his sensible little book on marriage, which had the advantage of forming the perfect wedding gift in serious-minded households throughout Protestant Europe.[35]

STRASSBURG, ENGLAND AND GENEVA (1540–60)

One of the most apparently promising solutions to the relationship of Church and temporal power in the first three decades of the Reformation was developed in the city-state of Strasbourg (then the overwhelmingly German-speaking Strassburg), led by a former Dominican friar, Martin Bucer. Until the middle of the century, it looked as if Strassburg would become the centre of the future Reformation, for Bucer was a self-proclaimed (though fatally verbose) broker of consensus amid the Reformers' disagreements, and the city lay at the heart of European trade and culture. It attracted a good many radical enthusiasts, but thanks to Bucer's unwearying powers of argument and obvious concern for the purity of the Church, it was rather better at persuading radicals back into the mainstream than most Protestant states and generally more humane in its reaction to them.[36] Nevertheless, Strassburg was soon to fall away from European leadership because of military defeat, and then there would be other contenders: first England, followed by Geneva.

Prospects for a civilized religious settlement and the reunion of the Western Church were high around 1541–2, but they ended in disappointment. This was the time when Hermann von Wied, Archbishop of Cologne, the only prince-bishop in Germany to try meeting the Reformation halfway, was attempting to lead his archdiocese in a Reformation whose planning involved not just his own clergy but also Martin Bucer. In the next few years, however, he failed, defeated by fierce opposition from traditionalists in his own Cathedral Chapter and by firm intervention from Charles V which eventually saw him ejected from his see. If von Wied's plans had worked, Cologne might have been an example to other Catholic prelates of how to find a middle path of change within the old structures.[37] With the failure of discussions between Protestants and Catholics around the imperial Diet at Regensburg in 1541 (see pp. 662–3), the time for humanist moderation was evidently past; against this background, in 1545 a council of the Western Church convened by the Pope at last began meeting at Trent, in a mood of aggressive confidence, to take new initiatives in the papal Church. By the late 1540s, it looked as if the Reformation's opponents were triumphing. Luther died in 1546, by which point Zwingli was long dead.

The Holy Roman Emperor confronted the military alliance formed by his Lutheran princes, the 'Schmalkaldic League', and in 1547 roundly defeated them (see Plate 55): as part of his victory, he ended the independent career of the Reformation in Strassburg, which had with uncharacteristic rashness committed itself to the Schmalkaldic alliance.[38]

Martin Bucer hastily left Strassburg for England, where the group of politicians ruling in the name of Henry VIII's young son, Edward VI, after Henry's death in 1547 now had the chance to propel England into the leadership of the Reformation throughout Europe. Archbishop Cranmer, one of their number and now a hardened political operator, led a thoroughgoing destruction of the traditional devotional world in England. His Reformation owed most to the example of Strassburg and the Swiss, though in his vernacular liturgy for the English Church, the *Book of Common Prayer* of 1549, revised in more uncompromisingly Reformed style in 1552, Cranmer was ready to draw on any useful precedent. Those included the more conservative Lutheran forms of worship recently devised in Germany (he had married a German theologian's niece in the conservatively Lutheran city of Nuremberg when on embassy there for Henry VIII in 1532).[39] Consequently the English Prayer Book, only lightly revised in 1559 and finally given a slightly more Catholic-leaning makeover in 1662, has remained an extraordinarily flexible vehicle for a form of Western Christianity which, in its development as 'Anglicanism', has sometimes looked with some distaste on its Reformation inheritance from the Cranmer years.

One incomparable aspect of the book is the language in which it was written, which even those who distrust its theological content can unreservedly admire. The processes of the Prayer Book's original construction will probably always remain obscure, but it is evident that a single powerful voice lies behind its phrasing and that can only be Cranmer's. The unity of the book, and the subtle way in which it draws on and transforms an astonishing variety of earlier texts in Latin, German and English, indicate that Cranmer was very much more than simply the chairman of a drafting committee. His particular literary genius was narrowly for formal prose, without the range of conversational or dramatic tones of which Tyndale was capable, but prose which can be spoken generation on generation without seeming trite or tired – words now worn as smooth and strong as a pebble on a beach. The Archbishop bequeathed first England and then the whole world a liturgical drama which he wished to be enacted by all those present in an act of worship; and so it has proved. The words of his Prayer Book have been recited by English-speakers far more frequently than the speeches and soliloquies of Shakespeare. Fragments remain even with the unchurched: 'for richer, for poorer, in sickness and in health, to love and to cherish, till death us do part', or from another resonant moment in human experience, 'earth to earth, ashes to ashes, dust to dust'.[40] Cranmer's words are the common inheritance of all those who use English, that language which in his age was so marginal to European cultural life, yet is now so universal.

Besides its prose, Cranmer's Prayer Book has left one liturgical legacy to all Western Christendom: an evening service or 'office' called Evensong. Evensong is the part of the Prayer Book now most regularly performed in Anglicanism, and so it is there that Cranmer's superbly dignified prose is still most frequently appreciated in its proper context. Cranmer had a particular aptitude for creating the short prayers known as 'collects', of which he wrote a set for the changing weeks of his new English liturgical year (considerably simplified from the pre-Reformation yearly kalendar of holy days). These small jewels of prayers are rarely simply his own work, but their expression and the delicately precise choice of language are his. One of the briefest of all, second of the Evensong collects used throughout the year, is also one of the most memorable. It was a translation of an existing eighth-century collect from the Latin West, but Cranmer tweaked the text in his own way. Taking its controlling metaphor from the setting of the service in the fading evening light, the collect is a perfectly balanced threefold structure: a petition of two thoughts is followed by an appeal to the Trinitarian relationship of Father and Son. Cranmer has characteristically added a pairing of words, 'perils and dangers', in place of the Latin *insidias* for 'snares' – and crucially, at the end, he has enriched the Trinitarian idea with the word 'love':

Lighten our darkness, we beseech thee, O Lord; and by thy great mercy defend us from all perils and dangers of this night; for the love of thy only Son, our Saviour Jesus Christ.

Amen.[41]

Anglican Evensong has proved such a dignified and compelling approach to the divine that it has brought spiritual consolation way beyond the borders of the Anglican Communion, to Protestant and Roman Catholic alike. There is some paradox in its use today, because Cranmer did little to hide his contempt for both cathedrals and elaborate church music, yet nowadays Evensong is most characteristically encountered sung by the choirs of Anglican cathedrals, and draws on a rich five-centuries-old inheritance of specially composed anthems and settings. It is possible that Cranmer's quiet sense of humour might make him appreciate this strange outcrop of his attempt to provide England with a decently Reformed vehicle for the worship of God.

Yet this English experimentation abruptly ended when Edward, after a healthy and assertive childhood in which he bade fair to be as over-life-size as his formidable father, died young in 1553.[42] With dramatic speed, England rejected Edward's chosen Protestant successor, his cousin Jane Grey. Against the expectations of English politicians and foreign ambassadors alike, widespread popular fury challenged the deal done in Westminster, more decisively than at any other moment in the Tudor age. Armed demonstrations across south-eastern England forced the kingdom's leaders to accept the claim to the throne made by the dead king's Catholic half-sister, the Lady Mary.[43] Although Mary's status as King Henry's daughter probably mattered to the kingdom more than her religion, once she had thrust aside Queen Jane, she embarked on as great an experiment as that of Edward, but in mirror-image. She returned an entire kingdom to Roman obedience and the possibility of innovations in Catholic reform. In the process she burned at the stake some of the leading English Protestant reformers, Thomas Cranmer included. She also overcame the objections of English politicians to her marriage plans to King Philip II of Spain, which promised to bind the future of her kingdom to the most powerful Catholic monarchy in Europe (see pp. 671–5). The hopes for asserting God's word seemed doomed through most of Europe. The Last Days had not arrived; many had rejected the message. What could be done?

The man who led Protestantism out of stagnation in the 1550s was an exiled French humanist legal scholar who had wandered Italy and Switzerland and ended up by accident in 1536 on the margins of the Swiss Confederation in the city of Geneva: John Calvin.[44] He probably never liked Geneva very much, but he felt that God had sent him there for a purpose, and so he resigned himself to a dour struggle to stay there and lead God's work in the city. After one false start, he was thrown out of Geneva, but that gave him the chance to go to Bucer's Strassburg and see how a Reformation might be put into practice. When the Genevans faced chaos and in desperation called him back, he was ready to build a better Strassburg in Geneva. In a set of *Ecclesiastical Ordinances* which the city authorities ordered Calvin to draft in 1541, he put into practice a scheme to restructure the Church which Bucer had envisaged for Strassburg: a fourfold order, rather than the threefold traditional order of bishop, priest and deacon.[45]

Bucer had asserted that the New Testament described four functions of ministry, pastors, doctors, elders and deacons. Pastors carried out the general ministry of care of the laity exercised by medieval parish priests and bishops; doctors were responsible for teaching at all levels, up to the most searching scholarly investigations of the Bible. Together, pastors and senior doctors who were obviously close to them in ministry (notably Calvin himself) formed a Company of Pastors. Elders bore the disciplinary work of the Church, leading it alongside the pastors in a Church court called a consistory. It was government by committee; in other contexts, the committees were called presbyteries, so the system is generally labelled presbyterian. Calvin was not particularly worried about the forms that this fourfold system might take, as long as all its functions were properly carried out, but the next generation of 'Calvinists' tended to be more doctrinaire about forms than he was, and tried to copy exactly what had been done in Geneva – developing, for instance, a hostility to the office of bishop which Calvin himself never exhibited, and which other Reformed Churches, such as those of Zürich, Hungary/Transylvania and England/Ireland, did not share (see Plate 14).

It took Calvin years to secure the stability of his Reformation, but the Genevans never dared lose face by throwing him out a second time, and they were also shrewdly aware that he was good for business. He attracted talented foreign exiles to the city (and did his best to ensure that poor exiles were not a burden on city finances), while his writings and those of his friends sold dynamically through much of Europe and were the making of the city's new printing industry.[46] In the end, one event which we might regard as tragic made Calvin's name on a European-wide scale. In 1553 he was faced with the arrival in Geneva of a prominent radical intellectual, an exile like himself, Michael Servetus from Spain, on his way to join secret sympathizers in Italy, and appearing with baffling rashness in public in Calvin's city. Servetus, with the Islamic and Jewish heritage of his country in mind, denied that the conventional notion of the Trinity could be found in the Bible; he had already been condemned by a Catholic inquisition as a heretic, with Calvin's connivance. Calvin saw his duty as clear: Servetus must die. So the Genevan city authorities burned Servetus at the stake, though Calvin wanted a more merciful death, such as beheading. Thus Calvin established that Protestants were as determined as Catholics to represent the mainstream traditional Christianity which had culminated in the Council of Chalcedon in 451.[47]

Consistently with this, from 1536 Calvin published and repeatedly rewrote a textbook of doctrine, the *Institution of the Christian Religion* – commonly known as the *Institutes*.[48] This was designed to lay claim to Catholic Christianity for the Reformation: since the Pope obstructed the Reformation, he was Antichrist, and Protestants were the true Catholics. In greatly expanded later editions and the complete rearrangement which Calvin made in 1559 not long before his death, virtually all the original text is still there. The opening sentence was never displaced, though Calvin enlarged its scope from a reference simply to 'sacred [i.e. Christian] doctrine' to all human knowledge; so in the 1559 version it reads, 'Nearly all the wisdom we possess, that is to say, true and sound wisdom, consists of two parts: the knowledge of God and of ourselves'.[49] From this premise, Calvin leaps to another assumption fundamental to his book from 1536 onwards: scrutinizing ourselves honestly after contemplating God is bound to shame us. None of our capacities can lift us from this abyss in our fallen state, only an act of free grace from God. This is Augustine restated, the Luther of the *Slavery of the Will*.

For Calvin this 'double knowledge' (*duplex cognitio*) lay at the heart of Catholic Christianity, and it became his life's work to recall his beloved France to a real version of the Catholic Church. Over time, he came to explain the failures of the Reformation by reference to a doctrine which Luther had also held, but which many of his fellow Lutherans followed Melanchthon in finding difficult and downplayed: God's plan of predestination. After reading Bucer's commentary on Romans of 1536, Calvin discussed this in increasing intricacy in the *Institutes'* enlargements. If salvation was entirely in God's hands, as Luther said, and human works were of no avail, then logically God took decisions on individual salvation without reference to an individual's life-story. God decided to save some and logically also to consign others to damnation. Predestination was thus double. Evidently those who did not listen to and act on the Word were among the damned; that lessened the sense of disappointment that not all heeded the Reformation message. The good news was that the elect of God could not lose their salvation. The doctrine of election became ever more important, and ever more comforting and empowering, to Calvin's followers.

But there was much more to Calvin than expounding predestination. He never received ordination from either old or new Church, but his self-image was as teacher (*Doctor*), and he relentlessly preached and wrote biblical commentary around the ever-growing *Institutes*. Central to his vision of a renewed Catholic Church based on the achievement of the early centuries was the Council of Chalcedon's careful crafting of the 'Chalcedonian Definition'. Christ was one person in two natures inextricably linked – God the Son and so fully part of the Divine Trinity, while at the same time Jesus the human being, born in Palestine. Chalcedon had a particular significance for magisterial Protestants, who saw it as the last general council of the Church to make reliable decisions about doctrine in accordance with the core doctrines proclaimed in scripture – they were all the more inclined to respect the early councils because radicals rejected that legacy (see p. 624). The careful balance of statements within the Chalcedonian Definition, with its emphasis on the indivisibility of the two natures of Christ, gave Calvin a model for a general principle which became very important to him: distinction but not separation (*distinctio sed non separatio*).

This was the perfect model to be used by this theologian so consciously striving for a newly purified and balanced Catholicism for the Western Church. It can be seen, for instance, in Calvin's discussion of the Church – both visible and invisible – or of election – both general for the Church (as it had been for the Children of Israel) and particular for elect individuals (such as great Patriarchs like Abraham). Above all, it structures what Calvin says about the Eucharist. He made a firm distinction between 'reality' and 'sign' which nevertheless would not separate them completely. The old Church betrayed this principle by confusing reality and sign, attributing to the signs of bread and wine worship which was only due to the reality behind them. Luther, Calvin felt, had also wrongly attributed to the signs what was only true of the reality: in particular when Luther asserted that the physical body and blood of Christ were capable of being everywhere (*ubique*) wherever the Eucharist was being celebrated in the world – a Lutheran doctrine called ubiquity, which Calvin devoted a substantial section in the final version of the *Institutes* to ridiculing. He thought on the other hand that Zwingli had separated sign and reality too much, and emphasized that 'in the sacraments the reality is given to us along with the sign'.[50] In the Eucharist, God does not come down to us to sit on a table; but through the sign of the breaking of bread and taking of wine, he draws us up to join him in Heaven. It is the idea proclaimed in the ancient exhortation of the Latin Mass, 'Lift up your hearts' (*Sursum corda*).[51]

Calvin devoted much effort to seeking the middle ground among Protestants, as part of his plan to replace papal Catholicism by something that he saw as being more authentically Catholic. He was saddened by the division between the Swiss and Lutheran loyalists over the

Eucharist, which seemed particularly lunatic at the time of Protestant defeats by Charles V in the Schmalkaldic Wars. Working with Heinrich Bullinger, he forged a statement in 1549 which has become known as the *Consensus Tigurinus* ('Zürich Agreement').[52] With its commitment to creating forms of words which could be understood slightly differently by different people, it represented a rare moment of statesmanship in the sixteenth-century religious divides, and as such, it failed to satisfy Lutherans fiercely guarding Luther's theological legacy: they stuck as strongly as the Pope himself to the proposition that body and blood of Christ were present in the eucharistic bread and wine. As a result, the mid-century attempt to unite Protestantism against the Roman menace only resulted in a deeper divide among Protestants.

Self-conscious Lutherans increasingly directed Protestantism in Germany and Scandinavia and most German-speaking communities in eastern Europe (see Plate 55). After many internal disputes about who was being most true to Luther's legacy, they sealed the boundaries of Lutheran identity by a Formula of Concord in 1577, confirmed by a Book of Concord in 1580. Its version of Luther's own beliefs was selective, and not unconnected to the unspoken thought about certain key points of theology that if Calvin was for them, developed Lutheranism should be against them, regardless of whether Luther might have concurred with Calvin.[53] One carved plaque from a house in Wittenberg, now ruefully exhibited in the museum of Luther's home, bluntly (and indeed ungrammatically) proclaims: GOTTES WORT UND LUTHERS SCHRIFT / IST DAS BABST UND CALVINI GIFT – 'The Word of God and Luther's writing are poison for the Pope and Calvin'. The hatred was not on the whole symmetrical: as time went on, the Reformed sponsored a number of efforts at reunion, galvanized by the increasing effectiveness of Counter-Reformation Catholicism, but the habitual response among Lutherans was offensive and verbose rejection.[54]

Elsewhere, the powerful prose and driving intellectual energy of Calvin's *Institutes* inspired a variety of Churches who felt that Luther's Reformation had not gone far enough. Other major theologians lined up with Calvin against dogmatic Lutheranism, often regretting the division, but seeing little other option: such figures as the exiled Polish bishop Jan Łaski (Johannes à Lasco to Latin-speakers trying to get their tongue round Polish consonants), the one-time star preacher of Italy Peter Martyr Vermigli (see pp. 658–62), or the charismatic wandering Scot John Knox. More cautiously, the older established Swiss Protestant Churches made common cause with Calvin. In the Palatinate, an important principality of the empire whose Elector-Prince Friedrich III came to sympathize with the Reformed cause, an international team of Reformed scholars drew up a catechism (a statement of doctrine for teaching purposes) like the *Consensus Tigurinus*, designed to unite as many Protestants as possible. Known as the Heidelberg Catechism, since Heidelberg was the Elector Palatine's capital and home to the university where it was created, it had wide influence from its publication in 1563.[55] Three years later, in 1566, Bullinger drew up a statement, the 'Second Helvetic Confession', with the same agenda of unity, which also won widespread acceptance. Reformed Christianity saved the Reformation from its mid-century phase of hesitation and disappointment. Lutheranism tended to remain frozen in German-speaking and Scandinavian cultures; Reformed Christianity spread through a remarkable variety of language groups and communities, partly because so many of its leading figures had the same experience as Calvin, finding themselves forced to leave their native lands and to proclaim their message in new and alien settings.

REFORMED PROTESTANTS, CONFESSIONALIZATION AND TOLERATION (1560–1660)

During the 1560s Reformed Christianity brought militancy and a rebellious spirit to the magisterial Reformation. Like Luther, Calvin was a theologian of Romans 13.1 – of obedience. Yet as he built his Church in Geneva, he was much more careful than Luther or Zwingli to keep Church structures separate from the existing city authorities. He had a clear vision of God's people making decisions for themselves: his Church had a mind of its own over and against temporal power, just as much as the old Church of the Pope. In Geneva this was not a problem, after Calvin had clawed his way to political dominance, because Church and temporal power were in general agreement, but elsewhere people might take up Calvin's blueprint for Church structures and ignore what the magistrate wanted or ordered. To Calvin's alarm, he found that in the Netherlands, Scotland and France, he had sponsored movements of revolution, people inspired by the thought that they were the elect army of God whose duty was to take on Antichrist.

Very often revolutionary Reformed leaders were actually noblemen rebelling against their monarchs; rather than humble enthusiasts like the

Anabaptists, they were themselves magistrates with power granted by God, just like kings or princes. That made their rebellion all the more effective, as Lutheran princes had earlier found in the 1520s, when the Holy Roman Emperor had tried to force them back into the Catholic mould. Noblemen could harness traditional loyalties alongside the destructive enthusiasm of Protestant mobs who wanted physically to smash the old Church. Crowds determined to fight the Antichrist shattered stained-glass windows and hurled down statues, roaring out the psalms of David in easy-to-remember rhymes set to popular song tunes, in a fashion popularized in Geneva – when they were taken up in England's rather more decorous religious revolution, they were called 'Geneva psalms'. Music was the secret weapon of popular reformation. Singing or even humming or whistling the telltale tunes spread where preaching dared not go, and where books might be incriminating. The political effect was startling.

In Calvin's lifetime, Reformed Protestants began challenging the French monarchy, and it took fifty years of warfare and royal treachery for the monarchy to bring them to heel. In France they gained the nickname 'Huguenots', a name whose origins have defied all efforts at definitive explanation.[56] Reformed activists in Scotland humiliated and then dethroned the Catholic Mary Queen of Scots, meanwhile setting up a Church ('Kirk' in Scots) which marginalized its bishops and followed the Church government of Geneva in a presbyterian system (see Plate 14). It became the example *par excellence* of a Church exercising discipline within society like the Genevan Consistory, but its very public discipline, complete with penitents sitting on a special bench before the gaze of the whole congregation in crowded churches Sunday by Sunday, gave the congregation a significant say both in choosing elders who maintained the system and in monitoring the sincerity of those who did public penance. In modern societies, these 'Calvinist' systems have a dark and oppressive reputation, but we forget that they worked because people wanted them to work. Rates of reoffending were low. Reformed discipline provided structures for controlling a frighteningly violent and arbitrary world, and involved the whole community in doing so.[57]

Other Reformed activists were vital to the successful revolution which threw off Catholic Spanish rule in the northern Netherlands, and set up an established Reformed Church there, likewise presbyterian in government (see Plate 17). In eastern Europe, the militant self-confidence of the Reformed Prince and nobility of Transylvania intimidated and bewildered the Turks after earlier Ottoman victories in Hungary. The Church in England was deeply affected by Reformed piety, despite the hostility of a Protestant monarch, Queen Elizabeth, who was nearly as self-willed in her theological outlook as her father, King Henry. When her half-sister Mary's death in 1558 delivered the realm into Elizabeth's hands, her new religious settlement of 1559 restored a fossilized version of Edward VI's half-finished religious revolution as the Church of England. Many of Elizabeth's activist Reformed Protestant subjects could see no reason why it should remain fossilized or half-finished, and kept up pressure on her for more change. Increasingly those who were prepared to conform to the Queen's wishes named the discontented, in no friendly spirit, 'Puritans'.[58]

The result by 1570 was a Europe in which the divisions were increasingly clear. A series of separate political crises shifted the balance in favour of Protestants in the north and Catholics in the south. The contrasting stories in north and south after 1570 can be symbolized by the fortunes of two Catholic navies, one victorious, another destroyed. In 1571, a fleet recruited overwhelmingly from the Catholic world and commanded for the King of Spain by Don John of Austria, an illegitimate son of Charles V, crushingly defeated the Turkish fleet at Lepanto (the Gulf of Corinth or Nafpaktos); this was one of the most decisive checks on Islamic expansion into western Europe. Far to the north, in 1588, the other Spanish Armada was outmanoeuvred in the English Channel by Queen Elizabeth's naval commanders, and then scattered by the storms of the North Sea and the Atlantic, never to achieve a Roman Catholic conquest of Protestant England. As a result of this north–south divide, people were forced to make decisions, or at least their rulers forced decisions on them. Which checklist of doctrine should they sign up to?

Historians have given an unlovely but perhaps necessary label to this process: confessionalization – creating fixed identities and systems of belief for separate Churches which had previously been more fluid in their self-understanding, and which had not even sought separate identities for themselves.[59] Confessionalization represents the defeat of efforts to rebuild the unified Latin Church. In western Europe, it was difficult to escape this impulse to tidy and to build boundaries. One small part of Switzerland, the Grisons or Graubünden, quickly took advantage of the freedom bestowed by their Alpine remoteness and poverty: in 1526, as the Reformation began dividing Europe, they came to a deal in their chief town of Ilanz, by which each village could choose to maintain either a Catholic or a Reformed church. Despite much bickering, this arrangement persisted for more than a century, by which time some imaginative thinkers elsewhere in western Europe were just beginning to glimpse the sense in the idea.[60] Another important area for religious pluralism, in this instance emphatically against the wishes of its established Protestant Church, was the northern Netherlands. Having thrown off one clerical tyranny and jealously guarding a host of local autonomies, the secular rulers (the 'regents') of this new republic were not going to allow their Reformed clergy to establish a real monopoly of religious practice. Dutch people were free to ignore the life of their parish churches, as long as they did not cause trouble; even, in the end, Roman Catholics.

Otherwise, it was in eastern Europe that the most practical and official arrangements were made for religious coexistence – and indeed, the east outdid the Graubünden, most spectacularly in the principality of Transylvania which emerged from the wreck of the old Hungarian kingdom. Transylvanian princes, battling to survive against both Habsburgs and Ottomans, were anxious to conciliate as many Hungarian nobility as possible. Yet the nobility were backing a great variety of religious belief, few of them from the discredited old Church, and ranging from card-carrying Lutheranism to a startlingly open denial of the Trinity – the latter encouraged by a diaspora of Italian radical thinkers fleeing the increasingly thorough purges of the Roman Inquisition (see pp. 662–4). The religious spectrum was exemplified in the spiritual journey of the charismatic Hungarian Church leader Ferenc Dávid from Lutheranism to anti-Trinitarianism; he much impressed one prince, János Zsigmond Zápolyai.

Accordingly, but extraordinarily by the standards of the time, the Transylvanian Diet decided that it was impossible to reconcile the various factions and instead it would recognize their legal existence. In 1568 it met in the chief church of the town of Torda (a building which now, in its Catholic reinvention, does not commemorate this momentous occasion) and declared:

ministers should everywhere preach and proclaim [the Gospel] according to their understanding of it, and if their community is willing to accept this, good; if not, however, no one should be compelled by force if their spirit is not at peace, but a minister retained whose teaching is pleasing to the community . . . no one is permitted to threaten to imprison or banish anyone because of their teaching, because faith is a gift from God.[61]

This was the first time that radical Christian communities had been officially recognized in sixteenth-century Europe (albeit more by silence than by explicit permission), with the brief and ill-fated exception of little Nikolsburg. Subsequent Transylvanian princes withdrew from their flirtation with the anti-Trinitarians. With the majority of their Magyar nobility, they committed themselves to the Reformed faith, which led them into occasional harassment and occasional persecution of indiscreet anti-Trinitarians; but still they adhered to the general principles of Torda.

The Reformed faith of Transylvania's princes eventually led them into overenthusiasm for the role of their principality in God's purposes. In the mid-seventeenth century the talented and ambitious Prince György II Rákóczi was encouraged by the preaching of his Reformed ministers to see himself as King David of Israel, poised to be God's champion against all God's enemies. Unfortunately God showed no apparent favour to Prince György's increasingly unrealistic campaigns to win the Polish throne and his defiance of his Ottoman overlords, and after his death from battle-wounds in 1660, the principality faced ruin. It was a telling symbol of changed times that by the late seventeenth century the Rákóczi family, now no longer the princely dynasty, converted to Catholicism. Yet even when the Catholic Habsburgs acquired the territory and did their best to chip away at its religious liberties, the Torda agreement obstinately left its mark on Transylvania's religious landscape. In a country where the medieval parish network is about as dense as in many parts of western Europe, it is an exhilarating experience to travel from village to village and find the ancient parish churches of Transylvania still exhibiting here a rich German Lutheran interior, there assertive Baroque Catholicism, now a whitewashed Reformed preaching house, bright with colour from cheerfully decorated lace hangings, or finally the exotic sight of a place of worship from the Middle Ages which is home to a Unitarian parish – distinguished in appearance from the Reformed church in the next village largely by the proud motto on the wall in Magyar, 'God is one!'

Transylvania's initiative was soon followed by Poland-Lithuania, albeit with very different end results. Even in 1600, the identification of Catholicism with Polish identity, which in the twentieth century survived Hitler and Stalin, produced a Polish pope and crippled the power of Soviet Communism, still remained remote, while at the beginning of the 1560s it would have been impossible to say whether the religious future of Poland-Lithuania lay with Roman Catholics, Lutherans or the Reformed – maybe even the Jews. Lutherans, mostly German-speakers in the towns and cities, were vital to Poland-Lithuania's economic life. The Reformed not only boasted one of the most statesmanlike of European Protestant leaders, Johannes à Lasco, but also commanded the allegiance of some of Poland-Lithuania's greatest families, in particular the Radziwiłłs, who lived like kings and controlled the main armed forces of the Grand Principality of Lithuania. Perhaps a fifth of the nobility became Reformed, and in the Polish Senate in the 1560s and 1570s an absolute majority of the non-clerical members were Reformed sympathizers or adherents.[62]

Anti-Trinitarian radicals in their own 'Minor' or Arian Church enjoyed a more open life than any similar group in Europe except for their near allies in Transylvania. Their strength was particularly in the east of the Duchy of Lithuania, and they may have connections with various pre-existing Orthodox dissident groups, notably the so-called 'Judaizers', who also expressed doubts about the Trinity and rejected icons (see p. 527). However, these existing Orthodox roots were soon enriched by exiles from southern Europe, to the extent that the anti-Trinitarians became known as 'Socinians' after two further Italian radicals, Lelio Francesco Sozini (Socinus), whose nephew Fausto Paolo Sozzini [sic] brought his teachings to Poland. Remarkably swiftly, in 1569 the anti-Trinitarians were even able to open their own institution of higher education in Poland, the Raków Academy, complete with printing press: the Catechism of Raków produced in 1609 became in its Latin version an internationally known statement of anti-Trinitarian belief.

The academy was at the heart of another effort to provide an alternative to the normal organization of society: like the communitarian Hutterites enjoying an oasis of freedom in Moravia, the community held property in common, embraced strict pacifist principles and observed no distinctions of rank. Unlike the Hutterites, Raków was not suspicious of independent thinking or advanced learning. It represented the most thoroughgoing challenge so far to sixteenth-century Europe's hierarchical assumptions, yet there was much else in the fertile variety of Polish radical Christianity. Anti-Trinitarians also argued in their Church gatherings as to whether or not Christian believers were justified in possessing serfs, for the very practical reason that patrons of anti-Trinitarian congregations there were normally serf-owning noblemen. This was a very different version of radical Christianity from that of the unassuming Hutterite craftsmen of central Europe.[63] In what was then Lithuania (now Belarus), Simon Budny, a long-lived scholar with a tendency to change his mind which disconcerted even the anti-Trinitarians, published his first version of the Polish Bible in 1572. In its preparation, several rabbis of the Karaites, a branch of Judaism which like Protestantism respected only what it saw as the literal meaning of scripture, amicably cooperated with this Protestant Christian who emphasized his admiration for the Tanakh.[64]

Amid the competitive religious market which was Poland-Lithuania in the mid-sixteenth century, its leaders launched political changes with profound implications for the future of the region. First came the restructuring of their polity in the Union of Lublin of 1569 (see p. 533) and then an opportunity to enshrine religious pluralism in the constitution of the commonwealth. King Sigismund Augustus died in 1572: after a tragically tumultuous marital history, he was the last of the Jagiellon male line. Now the provisions in the constitutional settlement of the Union of Lublin came into operation: the election of a new monarch was in the hands of the noblemen of the commonwealth. A majority was determined to keep the Habsburgs from adding to their collection of European thrones, and the obvious alternative candidate would come from the Habsburgs' chief dynastic rivals in Europe, the Valois dynasty of France. Accordingly, negotiations began with the younger brother of King Charles IX, Henri, Duke of Anjou. A major complicating factor, however, was the arrival in early autumn 1572 of shocking news from France; in the St Bartholomew's Day Massacre, Catholics had turned murderously on Huguenots and the butchery had spread right across France (see p. 676). It was not surprising that Protestant Polish nobility were determined that Henri would not take their throne without a guarantee that there would be no repetition of these atrocities in the commonwealth.

The result was a meeting of the *Sejm* (Diet or Assembly) in Warsaw in 1573, at which a clause on religious freedom was unanimously approved in the agreement ('Confederation') proposed with the new king. It was couched as a declaration of the nobility's intent, which Henri would have to recognize to gain his throne:

Since there is in our Commonwealth (*Respublica*) no little disagreement on the subject of religion, in order to prevent any such hurtful strife from beginning among our people on this account as we plainly see in other realms, we mutually promise for ourselves and our successors forever ... that we who differ with regard to religion will keep the peace with one another, and will not for a different faith or a change of churches shed blood nor punish one another by confiscation of property, infamy, imprisonment or banishment, and will not in any way assist any magistrate or officer in such an act.[65]

The young King Henri agreed, despite misgivings from his French advisers and furious protests from the Polish bishops (only one of whom signed the Confederation). While the Polish-Lithuanian Commonwealth endured, the Confederation remained a cornerstone of its political and religious life. The agreement of 1573 gave credibility to the proud Polish claim (almost but not quite true) to be a land without execution of heretics: a 'State without Stakes'.[66] Europe entered the seventeenth century with the constitutionally governed realms on its eastern flank, from the Baltic to the Black Sea, showing other Europeans how they might make the best of the schisms in Western Christianity. Subsequent history of the region sadly betrayed that early promise and held back the achievement of a wider toleration. New initiatives had to appear elsewhere, and they only came in the wake of vicious religious warfare which blighted much of Europe and its British archipelago into the eighteenth century.

REFORMATION CRISES: THE THIRTY YEARS WAR AND BRITAIN

A remaining problem of the Reformation was the boundary between its Protestant and Catholic halves of western and central Europe, since Catholic Habsburg power straddled north and south. Charles V had not been able to sustain his early success in the Schmalkaldic Wars, and the Peace of Augsburg between the Habsburgs and Protestants in 1555 established for the first time a reluctant recognition by a Catholic monarch of a legal existence for Protestants. From then on, within the patchwork of jurisdictions which the Holy Roman Empire had become, each ruler could decide on which side of the Reformation divide his territory and subjects were to fall: the principle of *cuius regio, eius religio*. The arbitrariness of this solution was mitigated by the extreme complication of imperial territorial boundaries, which meant that subjects who disagreed with their ruler might only have to relocate by a mile or two, but there was also a major limitation.

The 1555 settlement reflected the realities of the Schmalkaldic Wars: the bulk of Protestants fighting the Catholics had been Lutherans, and the only two permissible religions of the empire were papal Catholicism and Lutheranism. Only four years after Augsburg came a twist of genealogical fate which brought the accession of a serious-minded

new monarch in the Palatinate who adhered to neither of these confessions. As the Elector Palatine Friedrich III, he championed a non-
Lutheran and increasingly confessionally Reformed Church in the
Palatinate (that Church which created the Heidelberg Catechism of
1563: see p. 637). Although Friedrich's successors wavered between
Lutheranism and the Reformed, other German princes followed his
example in turning away from increasingly dogmatic Lutheranism
towards the creation of Reformed Church polities, reorganized from
Lutheran Churches in a 'Second Reformation'.

To their sorrow and puzzlement, these rulers found that their Lutheran
subjects were not pleased. When in 1614 the unfortunate Elector Johann
Sigismund of Brandenburg tried to defend his Reformed preachers
against popular hatred, a cry was heard in the Berlin crowd: 'You
damn black Calvinist, you have stolen our pictures and destroyed our
crucifixes; now we will get even with you and your Calvinist priests!'[67]
The Reformed were confronting Lutheran Churches which, amid an
enormous diversity of traditional practice, seemed to have become the
shelter for traditional religion as it had been before the Reformation
upheavals. The Lutheran Mass (still so called) continued to be conducted
partly in Latin, by clergy in vestments, who even elevated the consecrated
bread in the service in traditional style. Luther in popular memory had
become a saint, his picture capable of saving houses from burning down,
if it was fixed to the parlour wall. Right into the nineteenth century,
Danish Lutheran visitation teams were alarmed to find rural parishes
where the faithful delighted in pilgrimages, holy wells, festivals and
intercession to saints from centuries before, and Denmark was not
unique around the Baltic.[68] By the end of the sixteenth century the
Reformed grouping in central Europe could not be ignored, but still they
had no place in the 1555 Augsburg agreement, which strictly recognized
only those who adhered to the Augsburg Confession. The situation was
not made any easier by the fact that there was no agreement as to
whether this meant solely the original 'unvaried' Augsburg version of
1530, or included a *Variata* revision which Melanchthon had undertaken in 1540, hoping (to Luther's distinct annoyance) to accommodate
the theology of those who did not take the Lutheran line on the
Eucharist.

This instability was the background to the eventual outbreak of continent-wide war, and the flashpoint was the kingdom of Bohemia, which
for a century had been ruled by the Habsburg dynasty. The Bohemians
had stonily preserved their established Hussite or 'Utraquist' Church,

product of their fifteenth-century risings against the Holy Roman Emperors (see pp. 571–4), against any Habsburg or Catholic encroachment. In 1618, provoked by increasing Habsburg self-assertion, they began their defiance of the dynasty by imitating their ancestors in a second 'Defenestration' of imperial representatives in Prague (see p. 572), although this time a providentially placed heap of straw broke the victims' fall. They then looked around Europe for a champion to defend their independence and their Utraquist inheritance: since Utraquism was an exclusively Bohemian movement, a monarch to supplant the Habsburgs would have to be recruited from among the Protestants of the sixteenth-century Reformation. In 1619 the Bohemian nobility elected as the next king of Bohemia, in preference to the Catholic Habsburg claimant, the Elector Palatine, Friedrich V. He was an idealistic and charismatic ruler, firmly Reformed in his confessional allegiance, and he had already generated febrile excitement across the continent as a possible leader for all Europe against the popish menace. As the Bohemian electors were choosing Friedrich, the militantly Calvinist Prince Gábor Bethlen of Transylvania made his own bid to attack God's enemies (and acquire the Hungarian throne) by routing Habsburg armies in Hungary and taking over the Habsburgs' territories there. The Ottoman sultan joined in the fray by offering his support to the Transylvanians.

The Habsburgs reacted quickly to this hammer-blow to their power, and their reconquest of Bohemia proved unexpectedly easy. Friedrich's Reformed faith put him quickly at odds with his Bohemian sponsors; the conservative Utraquists were outraged by the iconoclasm which his Reformed preachers encouraged in Prague, and a rout by Habsburg forces at the Battle of White Mountain in 1620 sealed Friedrich's fate. Immediately the Habsburg Emperor Ferdinand began dismantling a century of safeguards for Protestantism and two centuries of established status for the Utraquist Church, which is the only Church since the disappearance of the Arians totally to have vanished from European Christianity. Sustained attacks on Protestant privileges followed in Austria as well; it was the beginning of a successful effort to install the most flamboyant variety of Counter-Reformation Catholicism as an almost monopoly religion in the Habsburg heartlands, a remarkable achievement considering that in 1619 around 90 per cent of the population of Bohemia were not Catholic.

While Friedrich fled from his briefly held second throne into lifelong exile, European powers both Protestant and Catholic were deeply worried by the Habsburg triumph. Not only Protestants were alarmed at the intransigent terms of Ferdinand's Edict of Restitution in 1629, which restored lands to the old Church lost even before the Peace of Augsburg, and virtually outlawed Reformed Christianity in the empire: the alarm was enough to provoke many more to take up arms. Catholic France and Lutheran Sweden both intervened in wars which proved so destructive and prolonged that it was only in 1648 that the exhausted powers were able to agree on the Treaty of Westphalia to end the Thirty Years War. The boundaries between Catholic and Protestant territory chosen represented some rough parity of misfortune in terms of the territories which Catholics and Protestants had held at the stage that warfare had reached in the year 1624. Those religious boundaries still survive in European society at the present day.

At the end of it all, Western Christianity would have to face new realities. On the outbreak of war, many believed strongly in the sacred reality and God-given destiny of the Holy Roman Empire: these were principles which for a serious-minded prince like the Lutheran Elector Johann Georg of Saxony even now outweighed his suspicion of the Catholic Emperor Ferdinand, and made him support the Emperor against fellow Protestants during the war. After 1648, there was no prospect that this foundational institution of medieval Western Christendom would ever become a coherent, bureaucratic and centralized state, not even on the open model of the Polish-Lithuanian Commonwealth (itself now in deep crisis: see pp. 536–9). Imperial institutions continued to operate, and provided a framework for German life, but Christian rulers would have to devise other ways of understanding how and why they ruled. Having seen the results of religious war through the years of the Reformation up to 1648, fewer of these rulers would be inclined to embark on crusades for the faith, especially against fellow Christians. Crusades simply had not worked.

Alongside this struggle in mainland Europe was a conflict which took place over more than twenty years from 1638 in the Atlantic Isles, the three British kingdoms of Ireland, Scotland and England ruled over by the Stuart dynasty. Once more, the main issue was religion.[69] When dynastic quirks delivered Ireland and England into the impatient hands of James VI of Scotland in 1603 on the death of the unmarried Queen Elizabeth, he found himself presiding in his two new kingdoms over established Churches which were something of a puzzle. Were they part of the Reformed world? James was himself a devout Reformed Protestant who had done his best to cope with (and curb) a Reformed Church of Scotland convinced that it had the God-given right to tell him

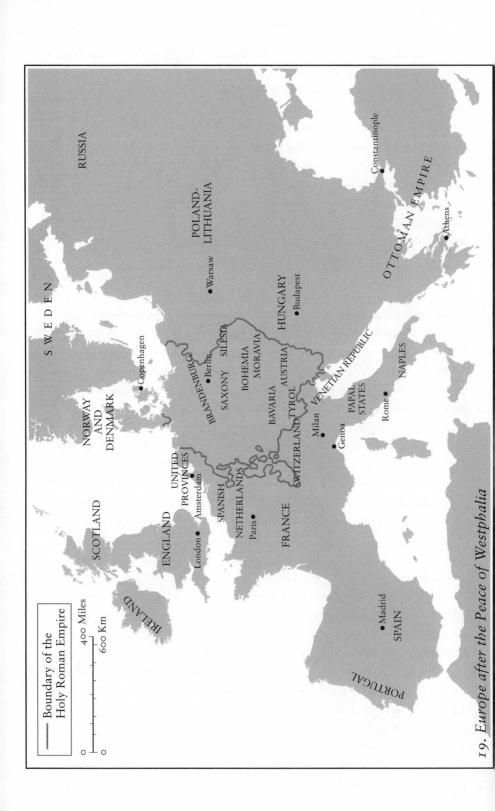

19. Europe after the Peace of Westphalia

Boundary of the
Holy Roman Empire

0 ⊢ 400 Miles

0 ⊢ 600 Km

what to do. He had been inclined to disparage the Church of England, aiming to please his Scottish clergy, and perhaps at that stage genuinely disapproving of an institution which he had never personally experienced; in 1590 he sneered that the English communion service of Cranmer's *Book of Common Prayer* was 'an evil said masse in English, wanting nothing but the liftings' (that is, the Catholic and Lutheran elevation of the consecrated host). He may also, in another sneer from 1598, have invented the word 'Anglican'.[70]

Experience of the real thing changed his mind: as James I of England, he found himself enthusiastic for the Church of England. Its confessional statement, the Thirty-Nine Articles of 1563, placed it firmly in the Reformed camp in terms of doctrine, but its liturgy, devised mainly by Cranmer half a century before, was more elaborate than any other in the Reformed world. For reasons locked up in the mind of the late Queen Elizabeth, it had retained not only bishops (Scotland had bishops too, after a fashion), but fully functioning cathedrals, with a positively medieval apparatus of worship: deans, canons, paid choirs and organists, a large ancillary staff, and an inclination to use the English Prayer Book in a ceremonial style. The survival of cathedrals had given rise to an initially small group of English clergy and some lay sympathizers who had a very un-Reformed attitude to the Church, a style which in its later forms has come to be called 'High Church'.

These High Churchmen did not exactly despise preaching (indeed, one of their most influential members, Lancelot Andrewes, was a famous preacher), but they emphasized the solemn performance of public liturgy and the offering of beautiful music in settings of restrained beauty as the most fitting approaches to God in worship. They spoke much of the value of the sacraments: indeed, another useful label for them might be 'sacramentalist'. To emphasize the sacraments placed more importance on the special quality and role of the clergy who performed the sacraments, so sacramentalists were also more clerical in their outlook than was common among English Protestants. They mostly held little respect for the Reformed scheme of salvation which stressed predestination, and in allusion to followers of a Dutch academic, Jacobus Arminius, who were also challenging predestination in the Dutch Reformed Church, during the 1610s their enemies took to calling them 'Arminians'.[71] Some of them, first in private but then provocatively in public, began saying that many aspects of the Reformation were regrettable. That might suggest a more radical conclusion that much in the Reformation should be reversed.

Arminians defined all who disagreed with them, all the way up to bishops and noblemen, as 'Puritans', the implication being that such people were disloyal to the English Church (actually a version of the Church which existed beyond the cathedrals largely in the sacramentalists' own imaginations). Notably for James, the Arminians were a good deal more respectful to monarchs than the ministers of the Scottish Kirk. The King favoured leading spokesmen of this group, but he judiciously balanced them with more conventional Reformed clergy. In one of the most statesmanlike actions in the career of a man who much esteemed himself as an international Reformed Protestant statesman, he persuaded both sides to cooperate in a new venture of biblical translation, an 'Authorized Version' which was issued in 1611 and which remains his happiest lasting achievement.[72] Basing itself on the hierarchy of translations back to the time of William Tyndale ninety years before, even taking notice of the Roman Catholic 'Douai' version, which had scored some palpable hits against previous Protestant English translations, it has remained vital for anglophone culture worldwide: the 'King James' version beloved of conservative Christians professing their faith in Churches of whose nature the original King James would profoundly disapprove.[73]

By contrast with James, his son Charles I, discreetly encouraged by Andrewes (now a powerful bishop), was not noted for judiciousness when he came to the throne in 1625. He was authoritarian by nature, and his reaction to opposition was to become not merely more authoritarian, but distinctly devious in his attempts to get his way. The new king had a soulmate in one particularly busy, conscientious and tidy-minded sacramentalist who was a former Oxford academic, William Laud, to the extent that in 1633 Charles promoted Laud to be Archbishop of Canterbury. Archbishop Laud used his talents to disastrous effect. He vigorously promoted his sympathizers in the Church. Taking a lead from more cautious and tactful moves by the late King James, he increasingly cast himself as a patriarch for an archipelago-wide British Church.[74] He made matters worse by genuinely believing that anyone in the Church who disagreed with him was part of a single 'Puritan' conspiracy; his high-handed reactions against this imaginary network infuriated enough Protestants in England for the label 'Puritan' to be worn for the first time as a badge of pride, rather than an insult to be repudiated with indignation.[75] Many of these angry people sailed for the hitherto languishing English colonies in North America, rather than stay in an increasingly tainted English Church, with hugely significant results for the future of Protestant Christianity worldwide (see Chapter 20).

Laud's interference in the affairs of the Church of Ireland, aided by Charles's high-handed Lord Deputy in Ireland, Thomas Wentworth, Lord Strafford, likewise angered the Irish primate, James Ussher, Archbishop of Armagh. Ussher was a rare figure as a member of an old Irish family which had become firmly Protestant, for the established Church had failed to carry more than a minority of the people of Ireland with it away from Catholicism. He is now unfairly remembered only for the misguided humanist historical precision of his calculation that God created the world on the night preceding 23 October 4004 BCE, but he was a formidable scholar who wanted to defend the independence of his Protestant Church. Ussher knew the Irish Church's weakness was the result of a badly funded and badly administered Reformation, in a country in which English colonial interference produced a state of permanent crisis, but nevertheless he saw it as a potential vehicle of proper Reformation in Ireland. He was very consciously part of an international Reformed Protestant world, but in his discreet efforts to maintain his position against Archbishop Laud, Ussher might also be seen as the first senior churchman to have a vision of episcopally governed sister Churches which might cooperate in a common identity across national boundaries, without any single leader to tell them what to do. Without knowing the later phrase, he was envisioning the worldwide Anglican Communion.[76]

That was for the future. In the short term, Charles and Laud alienated leaders in the three kingdoms to such an extent that rebellions broke out, first in Scotland in 1638 against a typically heavy-handed royal attempt to introduce a version of the English Prayer Book without consultation; then in 1641 in Ireland, where Catholics determined to throw off English rule saw their chance in the Protestant disarray. Finally in 1642 came civil war in England, between forces led by a majority of the English Parliament in Westminster and supporters of the King, who felt that such opposition was a fight against God's anointed, whatever Charles's faults. In England the trigger for war was stark disagreement as to whether Charles could be trusted to lead armies against Irish Catholics, after his support for the deeply unpopular ecclesiastical policies of Laud and his friends, and his blatant attempts to double-cross his opponents. Although some Catholics fought for Charles, and the majority of Irish Catholics eventually tactically allied with him against the Westminster Parliament, the wars and civil wars of England and

Scotland up to 1660 were overwhelmingly fought by Protestants against Protestants, to decide the future shape of British religion.[77]

In the course of the war, episcopacy in Scotland and England was abolished, along with the *Book of Common Prayer*. The question was now whether a strict version of Scottish presbyterianism would be set up in England, or some looser system of Church government. Calvinist theories of resistance to tyranny reached the ultimate conclusion when, after Charles's defeat by Westminster's armies, a radical group among the victorious Puritans forced the King's trial and then his beheading in 1649: this was no arbitrary lynching, but an attempt to punish the King for his crimes against his people, in the name of a Protestant God. In Cromwell's eyes, Charles deserved the name which the furious prophet Shimei had bestowed on King David at a particularly low moment in that charismatic but murderous and usurping monarch's career: 'you man of blood, you worthless fellow'.[78] The Old Testament had in that moment revealed its not infrequent low opinion of kings, and English Puritans hearkened: Charles deserved to die. They created an English Republic, or 'Commonwealth', though angry Royalists looking back after the Commonwealth's destruction were inclined among more abusive names to style it the Interregnum, period between two reigns. The Republic's armies were so successful that, in the decade after 1650, they united the Atlantic archipelago in a single political unit for the first time in its history. Having defeated the Scots, the regime was not inclined to set up presbyterianism in England, and was content for the English Church to become little more than a nationwide federation of Protestant parishes.

Nevertheless in the end the victorious Puritans were defeated and thrust aside because they were as tidy-minded as poor Archbishop Laud (executed for his High Church tidy-mindedness in 1645, even though he had been a helpless prisoner of the Westminster Parliament for the previous four years). The successive Puritan regimes were too straitlaced for the people of England and they could find no popular political substitute for the monarchy. The de facto ruler through most of the 1650s, Oliver Cromwell, former military commander turned reluctant dictator in the name of godly Reformation (and a distant cousin of Henry VIII's minister Thomas Cromwell), eventually authorized the abolition of Christmas and tore down the maypoles around which the English had danced on their spring holidays. Worse still for the population was one respect in which the regime was not tidy-minded: it tolerated with different degrees of reluctance a variety of radical sects who were widely seen as offending against all convention. There were English Baptists, who took up the principle of adult or believers' baptism like the Anabaptists of mainland Europe in the previous century; Baptists had been a tiny group before the civil wars began, but their numbers swelled in the Parliamentary army and in the country at large in its aftermath, causing huge offence to the vast majority who took it for granted that a Christian society depended on all its members being baptized in infancy.

Most shocking were those whom scandalized respectable folk called 'Ranters': they were a group like some of the sixteenth-century radicals of mainland Europe who believed that God had sent them a particular revelation, an 'inner light', surpassing that in the printed pages of the Bible. Yet they shared and drew extreme conclusions from Martin Luther's central scriptural affirmation that God's free grace was the only source of salvation. That freed all the saved from any law, human or divine, or (if God were truly to be glorified) from good behaviour at all. This was the 'antinomian' conclusion (*nomos* is a Greek word for 'law' – hence antinomianism is 'against law') which had haunted the respectable magisterial Reformation from its earliest days. God-given antinomian freedom might be expressed by such gestures as ecstatic blasphemy, joyous tobacco-smoking and running naked down the street. Such tales lost nothing in the telling, especially in the burgeoning sensationalist journalism of those years.[79] More closely associated with the Ranters than they liked to admit in later years were the 'Friends', whom their enemies called Quakers. Their conviction of their special role in God's purposes and of their 'inner light' led them to disrupt public worship and refuse to doff their hats to social superiors, among many signs of contempt for the norms of ordinary society.

The bulk of the English people applauded the beating up of Quakers – and the bulk of the English people also refused to open their shops on Christmas Day, as the regime demanded. Cromwell's morose authority postponed any greater reversal until his death in 1658, but after two years of increasing disorder, maypoles, Christmas and King Charles II were all summoned back from exile.[80] The Church of England which Charles restored, episcopal and ceremonial, complete with expensively refurbished cathedrals, had gained new martyrs for its cause, for the first time since the reign of Queen Mary Tudor. Newly aggressive against Puritanism after their sufferings, the clergy who dominated it were much more obviously out of step with the continent-wide Reformed ethos than they had been before the war, and the Church Settlement of 1662, with a revamped version of Cranmer's *Book of Common Prayer*, excluded many Protestants who before the civil wars would have found a home within the national Church; now they were labelled Dissenters, whether they liked it or not.

So, in the twenty-year civil wars of the Atlantic Isles, a new identity was born for the Churches of England and Ireland, which was occasionally at the time called Anglican, a term which came to be much more widely used in the nineteenth century. Alongside Anglicanism was a strong and irrepressible Protestant Dissent.[81] Anglicanism is a religious outlook which has kept its distance from the rest of the Reformation, but also from Rome, and is prepared to live with the ambiguous consequences. It took time for this conscious middle ground to develop; those in charge in the Church to begin with after 1660 tended to remember their sufferings and emphasize what made their new Church exclusive in its identity. Those who regretted that outlook, while also deploring the extremes of 'Puritanism' which were its mirror-opposite, were soon abusively known as 'Latitudinarians'; and their hour had not come.[82] Between Anglicanism and Dissent, in concert with the allied but contrasting story of Scottish Protestantism, anglophone Protestantism gained a religious profile which has reproduced its peculiarity across the world, as we will discover in tracing the fortunes of British imperial adventures in Chapters 19 and 20.

In tracing the fortunes of Protestantism, we have been neglecting half a Reformation: that which remained loyal to Rome. There is still much argument about what to call this other movement: 'Counter-Reformation' has long been popular, but narrowly ties it to a reaction to the Protestant Reformation, particularly that within the Holy Roman Empire, about which the expression (in German, *Gegenreformation*) was first used. One distinguished modern scholar of the subject has suggested a broader usage, 'Early Modern Catholicism', but that seems too wide and shapeless.[83] Probably the best formulation, which suggests the internal dynamism of what happened, is 'Catholic Reformation'. That is a reminder that if Luther was the heir of the reformist neuroses of 1500, so were popes, and that it was also popes who oversaw an expansion of Western Christianity over two centuries from 1500 which took it to every continent of the world except Australasia – at a time when Protestantism was hardly looking beyond European horizons. It is to that remarkable transformation in the fortunes of the Latin Western Church, and the formation of world Christianity, that we now turn.

18

Rome's Renewal
(1500–1700)

CROSS-CURRENTS IN SPAIN AND ITALY: VALDESIANS AND JESUITS (1500–1540)

As the fifteenth century came to a close, two brothers were born in the Spanish city of Cuenca – they may have been twins. Alfonso and Juan de Valdés became respectively an emperor's servant and a heretic. Alfonso was in his early thirties at his death in 1532, but already he was in the inner counsels of the most powerful Christian ruler of the century, the Holy Roman Emperor Charles V, through service to the apocalyptically minded Imperial Chancellor Cardinal Gattinara (see pp. 593–4). Alfonso wrote Erasmian-style dialogues on Church reform and (like Gattinara) promoted his master's destiny in God's plan; when he met Philipp Melanchthon at the Imperial Diet discussing the Augsburg Confession in 1530 (see p. 621), he was pleased to find much in common with the Wittenberg humanist. Juan had time to develop further than his brother: he became much more of a heretic than Melanchthon. These two independently minded Spaniards, alert to the crisis in the Church and themselves players in it, are testimony that there was nothing monolithic about Spanish Catholicism in their generation. They came from an 'Old Christian' gentry family on their father's side, but the Spanish Inquisition had burned their mother's brother in 1491 for secret Jewish practices, and their mixture of *alumbrado* sympathies and refined Erasmian culture was liable to arouse equal paranoia in a new generation of inquisitors. The year before Alfonso befriended Melanchthon at Augsburg, Juan had judged that a voyage to Italy might enhance his likelihood of avoiding a fiery death, and he never returned to Spain. Instead, he had a remarkable if diffused effect on Western Christianity, not just in

Italy but beyond. His story sheds an unexpected light on the Catholic Reformation.[1]

The land which Juan de Valdés now made his home was by then renewing Catholicism in its own fashion. Gilds, more commonly known here as brotherhoods or confraternities, flourished in Italy as they had done for centuries. Their popularity has been seen as the chief reason why Italians had so little investment in the anti-clerical rhetoric common in northern Europe, but they also threw up some surprising variants beyond the Church hierarchy's control, under the stress of shocks to society like the Black Death or the French invasions of the 1490s: the flagellant movement (see pp. 400–401) and the Florentine *Piagnoni*, who revered Savonarola's memory (see pp. 592–3). Now their capacity for renewal and self-propagation produced more surprising offshoots. In 1497 Ettore Vernazza, a layman from Genoa, founded a confraternity which he called the Oratory of Divine Love. He was much influenced by his spiritual contacts with an aristocratic mystic, Caterina Adorno: she was preoccupied both with reverence for the Eucharist and with comforting and helping the sick, particularly victims of that new and especially terrifying and shaming disease syphilis, which appeared for the first time alongside French armies in the 1490s (see p. 563). The Oratory reflected these twin concerns: clergy and laity combined communal devotions and care for the sick, including the administration of a syphilis hospice. Not unconnected with this latter work was provision for gentlefolk in financial or other distress, a distinctively Italian charitable concern which became a prominent feature in various parallel foundations in other cities.[2]

Several leaders prominent in the Italian Church's later recovery of nerve against the Reformation learned pious activism in oratories, and some extended this into the renewal of various religious orders. One founding member of an Oratory of Divine Love in Rome between 1514 and 1517 was a nobleman of Naples, Giovanni (Gian) Pietro Carafa. Carafa turned away in self-disgust from a comfortable Church career as a papal official financed by multiple benefices, and in 1524 he joined with Gaetano da Thiene, a nobly born priest from Vicenza and fellow member of the Roman Oratory, to found a congregation of clergy under special vows, or 'clerks regular', in an echo of the 'Canons Regular' of long-standing Augustinian usage (see p. 392). Their austere life was intended to provide a shaming example of vocation to less conscientious priests. Carafa was at that time Bishop of Chieti or 'Theate', hence the new order was called the Theatines.[3] In northern Europe, such commitment among serious-minded articulate clergy was rapidly being diverted into new forms of Protestant clerical ministry: the difference in this Mediterranean initiative by a former papal diplomat was its complete loyalty to the papacy. That loyalty, which fatefully shaped Carafa's entire career, was twinned with his talent for hatred, the diverse if not contradictory objects of which included Spaniards (loathed automatically by all patriotic Neapolitans as their colonial power) but extended also to Erasmus, Protestants and Jews.

A different form of loyalty to Rome was shown by another member of the Roman Oratory, Gasparo Contarini, a Venetian nobleman and diplomat, who helped to set up a similar group in Venice. Around 1511 he experienced the sort of spiritual crisis that a few years later overtook Luther, and it had a similar result. When Lutherans began preaching Luther's message of free justification by faith, Contarini recognized what they were saying, and he devoted his distinguished later career in the Church to an effort (ultimately vain) to bring the opposed sides together. In the 1530s he became acquainted with Juan de Valdés, and introduced him to a cultured English émigré, Reginald Pole. Pole was born with a rather better hereditary claim to the throne of England than King Henry VIII; after some hesitation (a feature of his whole career), he bit the royal hand that was feeding him in his expensive Italian education and sided with the King's wronged wife Catherine of Aragon, leading to permanent exile in Italy. Pole's enforced leisure, exalted birth and reasonably comfortable income combined with a strong sense of duty and a thoughtful, introspective piety to make him a major player in Italian theological ferment. Like Contarini, he emphasized the central role of grace by faith in the Christian life, and he was not blind to the fact that Martin Luther had proclaimed the same message.

The oratories did not simply foster elite or clerical spirituality. One of their founding inspirations had been a woman, and now a relatively humble and not especially educated woman, Angela Merici, companion to a widowed noblewoman in Brescia, made it her goal to encourage single women to embrace a religious life while living in their own homes, rather like the early beguines in northern Europe. She laid down no specific tasks for her association, but she was insistent that only virgin women – not even widows – could join. To underline her intention, she took as her symbolic patron a supposed fourth-century martyr, St Ursula. The point was that Ursula, in the course of what appears to have been a scribal error in a medieval manuscript, had acquired eleven thousand virgin companions, all massacred by an industrious army of Huns near

Cologne. In a true miracle, these fictional ladies now became reality in Italy and far beyond: a host of enthusiastic Ursulines, thirsting to help a rather startled and intimidated male-run Church.

The Ursulines considered their options and began concentrating on working among the poor and teaching children in settings which men either did not want to or could not enter. In 1544 Pope Paul III supplied a Rule which moulded them into something more like a traditional religious order, but still its model was the free-form adaptability of the Augustinians (see p. 392), and crucially it did not provide for central direction. From the 1560s Carlo Borromeo, Archbishop of Milan, a great believer in central control so long as he was at the centre, sought to discipline the Ursulines under his jurisdiction by forming them into an order of nuns, but even then, Merici's original vision of individuality survived and inspired new Ursuline initiatives. Under the cloak of Ursuline identity, a number of strong-minded women pressed their own vision of vocation in the Church and seized varied opportunities offered to them, with a judiciously deaf ear to alternative plans laid down by the hierarchy. It was a recurrent pattern in the Catholic Reformation.[4]

Juan de Valdés eventually settled in Naples, Spanish-governed but happily free from the Spanish Inquisition, where from his arrival in 1535 he developed a circle of friends, wealthy or talented or both, who shared his passion for humanist learning and for promoting a vital, engaged Christian faith. They included two powerful preachers, leading figures in their respective religious orders, Bernardino Ochino from a newly founded Franciscan reformed order named the Capuchins, and Piermartire Vermigli ('Peter Martyr' in his later north European career), an Augustinian who became Abbot of San Pietro ad Aram in Naples. Both men set off on individual paths. Brooding on the message of his order's patron, Augustine of Hippo, Vermigli went further than Contarini and developed a predestinarian theology of salvation as thoroughgoing as Luther, Bucer or Calvin. Ochino's followers whitewashed over the frescoes in the Neapolitan church in which they met, not a conventional action for Italian Catholics.[5] Among Valdés's other admirers were talented members of some of Italy's premier noble families, such as the two poets, artistic patrons and lay theologians Vittoria Colonna and her cousin by marriage Giulia Gonzaga. Gonzaga was a celebrated beauty who, in her widowhood, retired to a Neapolitan convent to become part of the Valdés circle in Naples – indeed, provided the equivalent of a salon for it. The Colonna, an ancient dynasty in Rome, had produced two popes and claimed others as ancient family members – one relative

had been Cardinal Prospero Colonna, who in the fifteenth century pioneered investigative archaeology (see pp. 576–7). With such support,
Valdés had a ready entry to courts and noble palaces all over Italy.

Divergent preoccupations naturally emerged from such a group, yet
central was a renewed emphasis on the grace which God sent through
faith, together with a consistent urge to reveal the Holy Spirit as the
force conveying this grace. Associates of the movement were indeed
soon characterized as *Spirituali*, and it is equally possible to acknowledge
the leading role of Valdés in their thought and call them Valdesians.
They brooded much (like Luther far away in Wittenberg) on the Cross
and Passion of Christ, themes which dominated the later art and poetry
of Michelangelo, who was a close friend of Vittoria Colonna. Valdés
produced two of their key texts: one the so-called *Alphabet*, the other
yet another specimen of a *Catechism* (they were now proliferating, as
Europe argued about what sort of Christianity to teach the uninstructed).
Valdés was an assiduous commentator on and translator of the Bible.
There is evidence that he read Luther with interest. However, he parted
company with north European evangelicals in his belief that the Spirit
progressively offered its light to Christians: he believed that some
favoured children of God would be led to ever deeper union with Christ,
and the scriptures might not be the only or chief illumination on the
way. He was notably reticent in what he said about the Trinity, perhaps
because he regarded it as one of the deeper mysteries of the faith for
initiates, but perhaps for more dangerous reasons. He also had little to
say about the sacraments or the institutional Church – an Erasmian
indifference, perhaps, but one has to remember his Jewish *converso*
ancestry and weigh up these silences.

Among the Valdesians, Vittoria Colonna became the subject of discreet pressure from Reginald Pole, who urged this prominent patron of
the *Spirituali* more fully to acknowledge that the institutional structures
of the Church were of vital importance in the Christian life. Pole's
insistence on loyalty to the visible Church did seem more plausible from
the mid-1530s, because now the papal machine seemed at last to be
harnessing its potential resources. Poor Pope Clement VII, overwhelmed
by multiple catastrophes which had included Martin Luther, died in
1534. His successor, Cardinal Alessandro Farnese, came from the same
northern Italian aristocratic circle as Clement, and devoted much of his
fifteen years as Pope Paul III to indulging his scandalously greedy children and family, just like his notorious predecessor and former patron
Alexander VI, the Borgia pope. Paul was nevertheless also a perceptive

and intelligent Renaissance prince anxious to capitalize on all his assets.

While he made two of his teenage grandsons cardinals in 1535, the Pope additionally bestowed cardinals' hats on respected promoters of reform: Pole, Contarini, Carafa, Jacopo Sadoleto and the imprisoned English bishop John Fisher. Fisher's pleasure in this honour may have been qualified by the effect of the news on an infuriated Henry VIII, who immediately had him beheaded. The Pope even appointed Contarini, Pole, Carafa and other reformers to a commission to consider faults in the Church, and although this commission, *De emendanda ecclesia*, confined itself in its report of 1537 to recommending an administrative shake-up, its frankly expressed picture of corruption and misused resources immediately proved a mine of congenial information for Protestant polemicists. Paul then began making plans for a general council of the Church, much to the alarm of northern European rulers who had broken with papal obedience. The Emperor Charles V was also extremely suspicious, and his obstruction was one of the main forces postponing the council meeting for nearly a decade.

Carafa was happy to cooperate with Pole and Contarini in the commission *De emendanda*, but their friendly personal relations were increasingly strained by Carafa's mistrust of their religious agenda and by his conviction that any concession to Protestants was a blasphemous betrayal of the Church. Senior clerics sympathetic to Carafa's bleakly rigorist and authoritarian style of Catholic reform have often been described as the *Zelanti* ('the zealous ones'). In the confused and developing situation, relationships never amounted so crudely to two team line-ups, *Spirituali* and *Zelanti*, but the descriptions still have some value in identifying two polarities while clergy and theologians argued about the best way to save the Church. As we observe the answers emerging, some curious cross-currents will become apparent, notably in the development of one of the greatest forces for revival in the Roman Church, the Society of Jesus. Like Valdesianism, it was a movement which sprang from the Iberian peninsula. It was founded by a Basque gentleman who had been a courtier of Charles V and who, like Valdés, had to take refuge from the Spanish Inquisition. Iñigo López de Loyola (see Plate 15) has become known to history as Ignatius after making the most of a scribal error over his Christian name when he matriculated in the University of Paris.[6]

Like Luther and Contarini, Iñigo had a crisis of faith, but his crisis, triggered by devotional reading during prolonged convalescence from a severe war wound, led in the opposite direction to Luther: not to rebellion against the Church, but to a courtier's obedience. In medieval knightly style, in 1522 he spent a vigil night in dedication to his lady before departing on crusade to the Holy Land – the lady was God's Mother, in the shape of the pilgrimage statue of the Black Madonna at Monserrat. In fact his departure for Jerusalem was to be much postponed, and Jerusalem proved not to be the goal of his life that he hoped. Amid many painful and poverty-stricken false starts, Loyola began to note down his changing spiritual experiences. This was raw material for a systematically organized guide to prayer, self-examination and surrender to divine power. He soon began using the system with other people. It was to reach a papally approved final form in print in 1548 as the *Spiritual Exercises*, one of the most influential books in Western Christianity, even though Ignatius did not design it for reading any more than one might a technical manual of engineering or computing. It is there to be used by clerical spiritual directors guiding others as Ignatius did himself, to be adapted at whatever level might be appropriate for those who sought to benefit from it, in what came to be known as 'making the *Exercises*'.

It was the Spanish Inquisition's unfavourable interest in this devotional activity which led to Loyola's hasty exit from Spain for the University of Paris in 1528, a year before Valdés's own flight. Around the exiled Spaniard gathered a group of talented young men who were inspired by his vision for a new mission to the Holy Land. To their severe disappointment, the international situation in 1537 made it impossible for them to take ship, but the friends resolved to look positively on their setback and create yet another variant on the gild/confraternity/oratory model: not a religious order, but what they called a *Compagnia* or Society of Jesus. Soon the Society's members were known informally as Jesuits: a weapon to be placed in the pope's hand as a gift to the Church. Ignatius never lost his courtly skills, particularly with pious noble ladies of exceptional political power, and his pastorally sensitive intervention in a papal family crisis was the main spur to secure the Society Pope Paul III's generous Bull of Foundation in 1540. It was an astonishingly quick promotion for such an unformed organization, whose purposes were at that stage unclear.[7]

The early history of the Jesuits has been interestingly obscured in light of their extraordinary later success and institutionalization. The reasons for that obscurity are enmeshed in the turbulent politics of the 1540s which decided the future direction of the Catholic Reformation. Before this outcome, the Jesuits were part of that multiform movement of spiritual energy, the *Spirituali*, and like much else in *Spirituale* activity, their work could easily have been destroyed.[8] That they and their work were not is a tribute to the inspired political talents of both Ignatius and his successors. A curious feature of Ignatius's voluminous surviving correspondence is that almost all of it concerns matters of business. One has difficulty gauging from it what spiritual qualities singled out the writer to be a saint – this author of that key text of Catholic spirituality, the *Exercises*. The silence indicates a huge missing body of letters. Evidently an efficiently comprehensive hand, probably in the 1560s, refashioned the early years of the Society by deleting large portions of the story.[9]

REGENSBURG AND TRENT, A CONTEST RESOLVED (1541–59)

There was good reason for this prudence. In the early 1540s the *Spirituali* might seem to be shaping the future of reform in the Church; yet against Cardinal Contarini's energetic efforts to find common ground with Protestants, particularly on justification by faith, was ranged the hostility of Cardinal Carafa to any such concession. Carafa's suspicion of the newly formed Jesuits was equally heartfelt, for he detested Ignatius Loyola. The dislike may have been personal, but in the Neapolitan Carafa's mind the crucial factor was that Loyola came from Spain. *Spirituali* and Jesuits now faced a crisis. Contarini's peace-making efforts gained warm backing from the Holy Roman Emperor, but the Cardinal failed to clinch an ambitious scheme of reconciliation proposed in discussions with Protestant leaders (a 'colloquy') around the Imperial Diet at Regensburg (Ratisbon) in 1541. Within a year Contarini died a bitterly disappointed man under house arrest. After that, some of the more exposed leaders of the *Spirituali* fled north to shelter with Protestants. Valdés avoided the emergency, having died in 1541, but Ochino and Vermigli led the stampede, their departure causing a huge sensation – Ochino was by then General of the Capuchin Order. Prominent among other defectors were wealthy merchants, more able to relocate their assets than either humble adherents or members of the nobility; soon they and the intellectuals they financed were bringing a remarkable variety of religious views and free-thinking to the Reformed lands of eastern and northern Europe, with momentous long-term consequences (see pp. 640–42 and 778–9).

Gian Pietro Carafa's hour had come. The conciliators had not merely failed to land a result from the Regensburg Colloquy (an enterprise which he had consistently denounced), but many of their brightest stars were revealed as traitors to the Church, and tainted all their associates who stayed. Now Carafa could persuade the Pope to set up a Roman Inquisition, modelled on the Spanish Inquisition founded seventy years before, with Carafa himself as one of the Inquisitors-General. One of its functions (a function which remains to the present day in the Roman Inquisition's rather more bland guise as the Vatican's Congregation for the Doctrine of the Faith) was to determine what the norm for theology was within the Catholic Church. It usurped this role from the Sorbonne in Paris, a venerable academic institution, but inconveniently beyond the pope's control. There was much less incentive now for remaining *Spirituali* to feel any commitment to the traditional Church. Cardinal Pole, who always tried to avoid closing options or drawing clear boundaries, did what he could to protect his dependants, who included some of Valdés's former admirers, and to keep them faithful to the Church. His friend Cardinal Giovanni Morone held the Inquisition at bay in his religiously turbulent diocese of Modena by an extensive campaign of swearing leading citizens to a Formulary of Faith which Contarini had designed to persuade truculent evangelicals back into the fold.

Some persisted within the Church. The most influential work of Italian spirituality in these years, the *Beneficio di Cristo*, was published in 1543 under Pole's patronage and apparently sold in tens of thousands before being translated into other European languages. Originally written by a Benedictine monk, Benedetto da Mantova, drawing on Benedictine devotional themes, it was revised by Benedetto's friend Marcantonio Flaminio, a protégé of Valdés and Pole, to heighten its presentation of the spiritual and mystical aspects of Valdesian theology, and it also silently incorporated substantial quotations from the 1539 edition of John Calvin's *Institutes*! The text emphasized justification by faith alone and celebrated the benefits of suffering for the faith, yet Cardinal Morone loved it for its eloquence on the benefits of the Eucharist. The new Roman Inquisition's opinion of it (and therefore Carafa's) can be gauged by the fact that of all the thousands of copies printed in Italian, none was seen again from the sixteenth century down to 1843, when a stray turned up in the University Library in Cambridge, England. That disappearance, proof of the Inquisition's energy when it felt the need, is an eloquent symbol of the exclusion of the *Spirituali* from the future of the Catholic Church.[10]

Only now did a council of the Church meet, in a compromise location to satisfy the mutual distrust of Pope and Emperor. It took place south of the Alps, but in a prince-bishopric which was imperial territory, at Trent in the Tyrol. The episcopal host and chairman from 1545, Cristoforo Madruzzo, was a *Spirituale* sympathizer and old friend of Reginald Pole, and Pole was one of the Pope's three legates – but soon it became clear that other forces, among whom Carafa was an *éminence grise*, were directing the agenda. The council's decrees rained down to shut out compromise. First was a decree on authority, which emphasized the importance of seeing the Bible in a context of tradition, some of which was unwritten and therefore needed to be exclusively expounded by an authoritative Church. Then came a decree on justification which achieved the remarkable feat of using Augustine's language and concepts to exclude Luther's theology of salvation, particularly his assertion that sinful humanity cannot please God by any fulfilment of divine law. Before that decree was passed in January 1547, Pole had left the council, his plea of illness all too real in terms of mental anguish.

The last chance for the now dispirited *Spirituali* came on Pope Paul III's death in 1549. There was a distinct possibility that Pole might become pope – the dying pontiff had been one of those recommending him – but Carafa's dramatic intervention with charges of heresy against the Englishman turned a series of close votes away from him and a safe papal civil servant was elected as Julius III. Pole was not the sort of man to put up a fight. Even though in private correspondence with trusted friends in the 1550s he was prepared to declare the Roman Inquisition satanic in its operations, he was always inclined to leave the Holy Spirit to do the political manoeuvring. One might regard that instinct as admirably unworldly. It could also be seen as unrealistic, egotistically idealistic, or even springing from an apocalyptic certainty that God's purposes were about to be summed up in the Last Days, with Pole as his agent.[11] The Holy Spirit did not oblige, and with Pole's defeat there died the last chance of a peaceful settlement of religion in Western Christendom of which his hero Erasmus might have approved.

One sign of radical change and of the quashing of alternative futures in that decade after 1545 was a literally spectacular volte-face from the best-informed family in Italy, the Florentine Medici. Throughout the 1540s, Duke Cosimo de' Medici continued to extend patronage and protection to disciples of Juan de Valdés, not least because Cosimo hated both Paul III (who was not above sheltering admirers of the unmentionable Savonarola) and Cardinal Carafa, who became Pope Paul IV in 1555. Apart from his fear of the family ambitions of a Farnese pope, Cosimo shared the determination of his own patron, Charles V, to seek ways of conciliating Protestants in the fashion of the Regensburg Colloquy. He prolonged his policy dangerously late. For a decade from 1545, the Medici were paying for a new scheme of fresco decoration for the choir and family chapels in their ancestral parish church of San Lorenzo, one of Florence's oldest and most famous churches. Their frescoes were an open declaration of support for evangelical reform in the Catholic Church.

It is unlikely that the artist, Jacopo da Pontormo, himself dreamt up the iconography of this highly sensitive project, startling in what it did not depict: any emblem of Purgatory, sacraments, institutional Church or Trinity. What it did draw on were themes from the *Catechism* of Valdés, already prohibited in 1549 by the authorities in Venice, later also by the Roman Inquisition – images which clearly pointed those with eyes to see to the doctrine of justification by faith. Like Valdés's tract, Pontormo's paintings approached this incendiary theme through well-known Old Testament stories such as Noah building his ark, or Abraham about to sacrifice his son Isaac. With Pontormo dead in 1556 and Paul IV's death in 1559 bringing a pope much more congenial to the Medici, silence descended on the conundrum of why Pontormo had painted what he had painted. Medici publicists, led by the art historian Giorgio Vasari, attributed the fresco design to the artist's mental instability, and while the Medici became devout patrons of the Counter-Reformation (gaining an augmented title of Grand Duke from Pope Pius V), the unfortunate Pontormo has gone down in art history as a lunatic. Although his frescoes survived much criticism and perplexity up to 1738, now we only have some of his original cartoons and a few rough sketches.[12]

It is worth focusing on this episode, because it illuminates the murky and uncertain background to the early development of the Jesuits. It is no coincidence that they remained aloof from the work of the Inquisitions, conscious of the harassment which their founder had suffered in Spain; indeed no Jesuit has ever sat on an inquisitorial tribunal, leaving that duty to the various orders of friars. Ignatius and his successors played their hand through those turbulent and dangerous years with consummate skill and remarkable creativity. They more or less sleepwalked into one of their future chief occupations, secondary and higher education. They quickly set up 'colleges' in certain university towns, originally just intended as lodging places for student members of the Society. Unfortunately, potential lay benefactors were not excited by the inward-looking reference of such projects, which was an incentive for the Society to think about expanding the colleges' roles. By the 1550s, city authorities across Europe were scrabbling to secure de luxe school facilities like the first Jesuit experiments in Spain and Sicily.

Although Jesuit education was proudly proclaimed as free of charge (the Society put a huge and increasingly professional effort into fund-raising to ensure this), their limited manpower was concentrated on secondary education. It was very difficult for children of the poor to get the necessary primary grounding to enter schools at such an advanced level; so without any single policy decision, a Jesuit educational mission emerged to secure the next generation of merchants, gentry and nobility – in other words, the people who mattered in converting Europe back to Catholic obedience. In time, Jesuits allied with another unconventional religious organization, the Ursulines, and steered Ursuline energies towards parallel female education, which was obviously problematic for males to undertake. It was a fruitful cooperation, which did not end the Ursulines' ability to mark out for themselves new initiatives in charitable and educational work.[13]

The Jesuits created a highly unusual form of the religious life: while keeping tight central control through their Superior-General, they had no regular decision-making community gatherings corporately 'in chapter', or a daily round of communal worship, gathering 'in choir' in church. Moreover they refused to require a distinct dress or habit for members, nor were they even necessarily ordained, despite the fact that their core tasks, preaching and hearing confessions, were the same as the orders of friars. It was not surprising that the Society soon attracted resentment from friars for what could be regarded as wilful selectivity from past disciplines – Jesuits did not always help themselves by their patronizing attitude to other organizations, an unfortunate side effect of the fact that they were very well trained and mostly very clever. Whatever their faults, their non-clerical style (given that laymen were among their numbers) did address the excessive pretensions of clergy which had provoked much of the passion behind the Protestant revolution. They did not wish to become an enclosed monastic order because Ignatius passionately wanted to affirm the value of the world, and believed that it was possible to lead a fully spiritual life within it. He had after all seen more of the world than most Europeans, in wanderings as far as London and Jerusalem.

During the 1540s, Ignatius delicately finessed the Society's constitution so that it was clearly understood that the Superior-General and
not the pope was responsible for directing Jesuit mission policy.[14] Jesuits
were very determined to keep their own identity. They resisted amalgamation with Carafa's Theatines, even though in many ways they
resembled that organization. When Carafa became Pope Paul IV on the
death of Marcellus III in 1555, he was intent on settling many old scores,
especially against remnants of the *Spirituali* like the Society of Jesus. He
began remodelling it into a conventional religious order, but fortunately
for the Jesuits, the pontificate of this choleric and vindictive old man
proved brief. In the wake of that trauma came a quiet reshaping of the
Society for the service of the Church. Central was a new stress on a
mission which seemed urgent after the Peace of Augsburg had recognized
the existence of Lutheranism in 1555 (see p. 644). In a revised statement
of purpose in 1550, the Society had added to 'propagation of the faith'
the idea of 'defence' – that is, confronting Protestants. The programme
this implied was accelerated after Ignatius Loyola's assistant Jerónimo
Nadal visited Germany in 1555. Protestantism's dominance there profoundly shocked him, and convinced him that the Society must devote
itself to reversing the situation. This represented a major change in
direction: Nadal, prominent in Jesuit rebranding, now deliberately promoted the idea that the Society had been founded to combat the
Reformation.[15]

COUNTER-REFORMATIONS AFTER
TRENT: ENGLAND, SPAIN AND
THE MYSTICS

The Jesuits thus moved into an era which can truly be styled 'Counter-
Reformation', the aftermath of the Council of Trent's final session.
Paul IV had refused to summon the council, disinclined to share decision-
making with others, so Trent was not convened between 1552 and 1562,
by which time Pope Paul had been safely dead for three years. By the
end of 1563 it had completed its work, producing a coherent programme
for a Catholicism conveniently labelled 'Tridentine', from the Latin
name for Trent. The work was sealed with a uniform catechism of the
Catholic faith, and a uniform liturgy: this uniformity of worship had no

precedent in the history of the Western or indeed any other branch of Christianity, with the recent but significant exceptions of England and some Lutheran Churches. Naturally the Tridentine liturgy remained in Latin and not, like Protestant worship, in vernacular languages, but here there was a major complication, in the shape of the Greek, Eastern or Armenian Churches affiliated to Rome, all of which had long enjoyed their worship in their own various languages. So with a brevity and restraint which did not reflect any concern for Protestants, but rather a consciousness of that other expanding field of papal concern on the frontier with Orthodoxy, the Council had commended Latin mainly by deploring the assertion that liturgy should always be in the vernacular. The equally muted tone in the council's commendation of obligatory celibacy for the clergy is likely to have had the same diplomatic motivation in regard to the Eastern Churches, with their tradition of married clergy. Greater flexibility and imagination in implementing the celibacy requirement would greatly have helped the Church's world mission in societies where an insistence on celibacy was countercultural and baffling.[16]

Everything nearly collapsed over one issue: where ultimate authority lay in the Church. This began with attempts to compel bishops to reside in their dioceses, and by a general and rather necessary debate about the nature of ordination – had the office of bishop been constituted by Christ or by the Church in its early development? If the latter, it implied that the authority of bishops came from the pope, successor of Peter, chosen by Christ to be the rock on which he built his Church (Matthew 16.18), rather than that every bishop was a direct representative of Christ's authority. Prince-bishops in the empire were only the most prominent members of the episcopate to feel unenthusiastic about an exclusive affirmation of the pope's position. The issue was too explosive to resolve, and it took some masterly drafting to create a formula which would not definitively place exclusive divine authority in either the papacy or the general body of the episcopate. In practice, many centralizing reforms later in the century put the advantage in the hands of the papacy, particularly because these reforms gave the pope and his officials prime responsibility for interpreting what the decrees and canons of Trent actually meant. In the very different situation of the nineteenth century, the first Vatican Council of 1870 formally made the resolution in favour of papal primacy which had been impossible in the 1560s (see pp. 824–5).

Trent bequeathed the Church a programme which had first been tried out in the kingdom of England in the reign of Queen Mary, after her unexpected accession in 1553 (see p. 632). Mary's reign has not often been seen as a Tridentine experiment, partly because it hardly had time to get going in the five years of life left to her, so it has been treated by Protestant English historiography as a sterile interlude in a smoothly developing Protestant Reformation. Mary deserves pity for the disappointment of her passionate hopes for a son who would carry on her work, making her believe in pregnancies long after it was sadly obvious to all those around her that they did not exist. She did not improve her historical legacy by sponsoring the burning of Protestants as heretics, a campaign whose intensity was, in comparison with other parts of Europe, a decade or two out of date. It only bred a celebration of martyrs to which English Protestantism rallied for centuries. At the same time the Queen was not helped by Pope Paul IV, who after his accession, among his many efforts to settle old scores, tried to bring down his old adversary Cardinal Pole, as a pestilential survivor of the *Spirituali*. Pole was now back in his native land, having succeeded the executed Thomas Cranmer as Archbishop of Canterbury. Julius III had very sensibly chosen Pole as papal legate (representative) to the newly Catholic England, but now Paul summoned the Cardinal Archbishop to Rome to face charges of heresy. Pope Paul also declared war on Mary's husband, King Philip II of Spain. Poor Mary, devout daughter of the Church, found herself in the crazy position of defying the Pope and forbidding Pole to leave her realm for what would almost certainly have been a heretic's death in Rome. The equally Catholic King of Poland had a similar experience of Paul's paranoia.[17]

Yet if we look past the ghastly mistake of the burnings and the dismal relations with the papacy, creative re-examination reveals Mary's Church as a forerunner of much which happened in the Tridentine world, led after all by an archbishop who had devoted his career to meditating on Church reform.[18] England undertook a remarkably efficient operation to discipline clergy who had married in King Edward VI's reign, in no more than a couple of years separating them from their wives and successfully redeploying most of them in new parishes; Rome spent the next half-century trying to secure such uniform clerical celibacy in central Europe. In the synod of the English Church which he was able to summon as papal legate, Pole sorted out decades of deteriorating Church finance and pioneered new eucharistic devotions; his bishops encouraged preaching and published official sermons to match those of Protestants, and crucially set out to implement a programme of clergy training schools, seminaries, for each diocese: the first time that the Catholic Church had seriously addressed the problem of equipping a parish clergy to equal the developing articulacy of Protestant ministers.

In the five years of Mary's reign, the Jesuits did not begin work in England. For the time being they left the task to distinguished Spanish Dominicans imported by King Philip, since they had much else to do and currently had no trained English members for the Society – but an English version of Ignatius's *Exercises* went on sale, and Jesuits actually arrived in 1558 poised for action, only to be pre-empted by Mary's death.[19] English Catholicism now faced a disaster, since Philip could only have succeeded to the English throne if Mary had borne him an heir, under the stringent terms of the marriage deal of 1554, negotiated by English politicians whose suspicion of Habsburg acquisitiveness had outweighed their Catholic sentiment. Instead, the new queen, last of the Tudors, was Protestant Elizabeth, who did not expend great energy in responding to some rather unconvincing courting from her half-sister's widower. Now the Jesuits were banned from the realm, together with all other Catholic clergy trained abroad, facing execution if they arrived in England and were captured, yet Catholics still felt an urgent need to sustain the minority who wanted to remain loyal to Rome. In the face of often savage though inconsistent repression (and also amid some bitter internal disagreements about future strategy), Jesuit and non-Jesuit clergy alike patiently and heroically built up a community of Catholics, led by gentry families scattered throughout England and Wales. It survived Elizabeth's death in 1603 and persisted through seventeenth-century persecutions and eighteenth-century marginalization, embodied in a formidable set of discriminatory legislation, into modern times.[20]

In Elizabethan Ireland, Franciscan friars led a parallel mission which was able to enjoy far wider success, partly because the Protestant Reformation there quickly became fatally identified with Westminster's exploitation of the island and made little effort to express itself in the Gaelic language then spoken by the majority of the population. Ireland became the only country in Reformation Europe where, over a century, a monarchy with a consistent religious agenda failed to impose it on its subjects: an extraordinary failure on the part of the Tudors and Stuarts. Yet there is irony in that exceptional story. It was Catholic Queen Mary who implemented a policy of planting settlements of English incomers in Leix and Offaly, counties which were officially known until the revolution of 1918–22 as King's and Queen's Counties, a commemor-

ation of both Mary and her husband, Philip of Spain, already the proprietor of the spectacularly successful Spanish colonies in Central and
South America. If the English monarchy had remained Catholic, perhaps
Ireland would have become as Protestant as the Dutch Republic in
reaction to this alien colonial occupation; but as it was, Mary's early
death and Protestant Elizabeth's accession made it increasingly easy for
both the Gaelic- and English-speaking Irish to identify Catholicism as a
symbol of Irish difference from the English.

With England lost, and most of northern Europe in Protestant hands,
Tridentine Catholicism looked to Habsburg power. Charles V on his
abdication as emperor in 1556, exhausted by the effort of governing his
vast empire, had divided his family inheritance: his younger brother
Ferdinand had been elected Holy Roman Emperor and took the other
Habsburg territories of central Europe, while Charles's son Philip had
received Spain and all its overseas dominions. Although both branches of
the family were determined to uphold papal Catholicism, their priorities
differed, and the Austrian Habsburgs were themselves divided. Ferdinand I was mindful of the Habsburgs' recent defeat at the hands of
Lutheran princes of the empire which had forced him to sign the Peace
of Augsburg (his brother Charles could not bring himself to do this). He
was ruler over three powerful varieties of Western Christianity: Roman
Catholicism, Lutheranism, Bohemian Utraquist Hussitism. Both Ferdinand and his son Maximilian II sought accommodations with Lutherans,
wheedled a reluctant pope into allowing Catholic laity into receiving the
Eucharist Hussite-style in both bread and wine, and maintained a Court
in Vienna sheltering a remarkable variety of religious belief. Maximilian's younger brother Archduke Ferdinand felt very differently, and
he implemented an aggressive Catholic agenda in the various family
dominions which he administered in the course of a long life. A further
brother, Karl, joined the Archduke Ferdinand in his intransigence, and
entered a marriage alliance with the one prominent imperial princely
family who had remained Catholic, the Wittelsbach Dukes of Bavaria.[21]
In concert they encouraged the Jesuits to set up institutions in towns
and cities under their control, and they also made sure that important
bishoprics of the empire did not slide into the hands of Lutherans in the
manner pioneered by the Hohenzollern Grand Master of the Teutonic
Order (see p. 615).

King Philip II of Spain, freed by bereavement from his unexciting and
ultimately embarrassing marriage to Queen Mary of England, returned
to Spain in 1559 to sort out a rising tide of turbulence and financial

chaos; in tackling this, he saw the Spanish Inquisition as a chief ally. Ruling from a monumental but bleak new monastery-palace, the Escorial, which also incorporated his future tomb, Philip brought his temperamental workaholism to the task of being a world ruler as significant in God's plan as his father before him – the Escorial's grid-pattern plan was based on Solomon's Temple in Jerusalem, although it is not surprising that visitors commonly supposed it to have been based on the gridiron which legend said had been the instrument of torture and death for the palace's patron saint, Lawrence.[22] Philip and his government committed themselves to the proposition that there was only one way to be a Spaniard: a traditionalist Catholic, untainted by unsupervised contact with alien thought, now Protestant as well as Islamic or Jewish. The King was readily persuaded to back the Spanish Inquisition's busy efforts to achieve this end.

Some unlikely figures became victims of the Inquisition's implementation of the policy. The Society of Jesus was still as much an object of suspicion as the young Iñigo de Loyola, and the nobleman who had pioneered Jesuit general education projects, no less a figure than Francisco de Borja, Duke of Gandía, former Viceroy of Catalonia now turned Jesuit, was hounded out of the country before becoming an outstanding Superior-General for the Society.[23] The Inquisition even ruined the career of Bartolomé Carranza, Archbishop of Spain's primatial see of Toledo, and a distinguished Dominican theologian. He had been an important assistant to Cardinal Pole in the English Marian experiment, but he had made the mistake of learning too much about Protestant heresy during his conscientious efforts to refute it. As a result Carranza spent nearly seventeen years in prison deprived even of attendance at Mass, and although briefly rehabilitated, he died a broken man when he might have been an ideal Counter-Reformation leader for Spain. Moreover, Carranza's arrest had been triggered by the Inquisition's alarm at the content of the Catechism which he had drafted for use in Marian England, and which was eventually to appear as a banned book in the Indexes issued by both the Roman and Spanish Inquisitions. Carranza's Catechism was nevertheless taken up to form the basis for the Tridentine Catechism authorized by the Pope after the Council of Trent, a final touch of black comedy in this dismal affair.[24]

Also troubled by Spanish officialdom were two religious later to become among the most famous personalities in the history of Christian mysticism, Teresa of Ávila and Juan de Yepes (John of the Cross). In the Inquisition's terms, both were automatically suspect by the fact that their families were *conversos*, and they might be seen as emerging from that maelstrom of religious energy released by the religious realignment of Spain in the 1490s (see pp. 584–91). They both joined the Carmelite Order (and their close personal relationship also attracted official worries); Teresa sought to bring the Carmelites to realize more intensely the significance of their origins in the wilderness by a refoundation of the order in which the men and women of the Reform would walk barefoot (Discalced). She struggled to persuade the Church authorities to make a leap of imagination, to allow the women who joined her to engage in a Carmelite balance of contemplation and activism. The journeyings of the soul characteristic of the mystic in every century would be paralleled by journeyings through the physical world, as and when necessary. Through many troubles and setbacks, Teresa developed what one of her admirers has called 'a gift for making men give her the orders she wanted to obey'.[25]

Teresa is often remembered now in the dramatic and highly sexualized statue of her ecstasy which Gianlorenzo Bernini sculpted for the Church of Our Lady of Victory in Rome. She would not have been pleased by this, because (according to one of her nuns) in a typically precise and much more decorous piece of self-fashioning, she made sure that she breathed her last posed as the penitent Mary Magdalene was commonly seen in paintings.[26] She spoke plainly, and told her ascetics to do the same:

Let them also be careful in the way they speak. Let it be with simplicity, straight-forwardness, and devotion. Let them use the style of hermits and people who have chosen a secluded life. They should not use the new-fangled words and affectations – I think that is what they call them – that are popular in worldly circles, where there are always new fashions. They should take more pride in being coarse than fastidious in these matters.[27]

Teresa certainly spoke of her meetings with the divine in the passionate and intimate terms that mystics (mostly but not exclusively female) had employed for centuries. She spoke of the piercing of her heart, of her mystical marriage with the divine, although she managed to avoid quite the degree of physical relish exhibited by Agnes Blannbekin (see p. 421). She was very conscious of the tightrope which any woman walked in the Spain of her time when putting herself forward to speak on spiritual matters, but she still grittily insisted that women had something distinc-tive to say, and that it was their Saviour who made them say it: 'Lord of my soul, you did not hate women when You walked in the world;

rather you favored them always with much pity and found in them as much love and more faith than in men.'[28]

For both Teresa and Juan, the erotic biblical poem the Song of Songs became a key text for the divine revelation. Juan was not afraid of repeatedly picturing himself as the lover, and frequently the bride, of Christ, appropriating for himself the image which is more conventionally given to the institution of the Church or the female soul, and as a result, expressing himself in ways which now sound startlingly homoerotic:

> Oh, night that joined Beloved with lover. Lover transformed in the Beloved!
> Upon my flowery breast, Kept wholly for himself alone, There he stayed
>   sleeping, and I caressed him, And the fanning of the cedars made a
>   breeze.
> The breeze blew from the turret. As I parted his locks; With his gentle hand,
>   he wounded my neck. And caused all my senses to be suspended.
> I remained, lost in oblivion; My face I reclined on the Beloved. All ceased,
>   and I abandoned myself, Leaving my cares forgotten among the lilies.[29]

Juan found that even the ancient technical language of theology, the Chalcedonian Definition of 451, could be fired with his own sense of what the Song of Songs might mean:

After the soul has been for some time the betrothed of the Son of God in gentle and complete love, God calls her and places her in his flowering garden to consummate this most joyful state of marriage with Him. The union wrought between the two natures and the communication of the divine to the human in this state is such that even though neither change their being, both appear to be God.[30]

He spoke not only of love in such very physical modes, but also searingly explored the ultimate loneliness of humanity – the loneliness and sense of rejection and debasement to which he himself had sunk during nine months' close solitary confinement in 1577–8 at the hands of the leadership of his own Carmelite Order, from which imprisonment he had to effect a dramatic escape. His incomplete meditation *Dark Night of the Soul* was the culmination of the treatise which he called *The Ascent of Mount Carmel*. The *Ascent* described this 'dark night' as the third stage of the soul's experience after its early sensuality and subsequent purification, 'a more obscure and dark and terrible purgation'.[31] The treatise presents itself as an exposition of the eight-stanza love poem, whose later stanzas have already been quoted. It breaks off before no more than a few lines have been subjected to John's intense scrutiny: in its detailed and patient explanation of the myriad meanings which they present to the reader, it reveals how far the mystic might travel beyond the deep sensuality of the poetry, which has the power to astonish the modern secular reader. This journey in the poem is what Juan describes as

purgative contemplation, which causes passively in the soul the negation of itself and of all things referred to above. And this going forth it says here that it was able to accomplish in the strength and ardour which love for its Spouse gave it for that purpose in the dark contemplation aforementioned. Here it extols the great happiness which it found in journeying to God through this night with such signal success that none of the three enemies, which are world, devil and flesh (who are they that ever impede this road), could hinder it.[32]

After all the conflicts which Teresa and Juan experienced and to some extent initiated, the Discalced Carmelites were left flourishing, backed at the highest levels of Spanish society. The order was determined not merely that Rome should recognize its foundress as a saint (achieved in 1612, only thirty years after her death) but, in a much more ambitious project, that she should replace Santiago himself as the patron saint of Spain. This was both a devotional act and a political self-assertion against all the forces of the Church which had made life so difficult for Teresa and Juan: luckily for the Carmelites, it had the backing of the Spanish monarchy. In 1618 King Philip III, strongly seconded by the Castilian assembly, the Cortes, persuaded the Pope to designate Teresa co-patron of Spain, though opposition was by no means at an end, and became much entangled in Spanish high politics.[33] John of the Cross had to wait until 1726 before he was finally officially declared to be a saint of the Church.

TRENT DELAYED: FRANCE AND POLAND-LITHUANIA

In the early sixteenth century, the Habsburgs had been balanced by the 'Most Christian King' of France, and the Valois dynasty which looked back to Clovis's conversion remained consistently loyal to Rome all through the Reformation years. Circumstances nevertheless conspired long to prevent the French Church implementing the major decisions made at the Council of Trent on such vital matters as uniformity of worship, doctrinal instruction and clergy training and discipline. In a ghastly irony, the Valois monarchy was crippled when, in 1559, Henri II died in agony after an accident in a tournament which was celebrating the end of more than half a century of Valois war with the Habsburgs, through a treaty signed on their mutual frontier at Cateau-Cambrésis. His death left the realm in the hands of his wife as regent for her young sons. Queen Catherine de' Medici's real talents for government were not equal to the dire religious crisis which then engulfed France and led to four decades of frequently atrocious civil war between Catholics and Protestants (see Plate 54). A very substantial community of Huguenots, led by powerful noblemen, proved impossible to defeat, even though they were still a minority across the realm.

The Massacre of Saint Bartholomew's Day in 1572 was the worst incident, and illustrated just how deep the passions in France now ran. It was sparked by an event intended to heal the kingdom's wounds: the marriage of the King of France's sister Marguerite to Henri, King of Navarre, now the head of the Huguenot party in France. An assassination attempt on the Protestant leader, Gaspard de Coligny, a provocatively self-invited guest at the wedding, spurred Huguenots to fury, and their reaction in turn frightened Catherine and her royal son to allow counter-attacks by their own troops. Catholic crowds took the hint, and around five thousand Protestants were murdered and many more terrorized throughout the realm.[34] St Bartholomew's Day long remained for Protestants across Europe a symbol of Catholic savagery and duplicity, but at the time many French Catholics were also shocked by the extremism displayed by their co-religionists. French Catholics bitterly disagreed among themselves as to how far – if at all – concessions should be made to the Huguenots, and the talented but unstable Henri III found it impossible to impose any sort of statesmanlike settlement. In 1589 he was stabbed to death by a Catholic extremist, and since he was the last of the Valois line, his heir was that same Henri of Navarre, who in the end was able to unite moderate ('politique') Catholics behind him against the ultra-Catholic Ligue (League), after his adroit conversion from Protestantism to Catholicism.

When negotiating with moderate Ligueurs in 1593, Navarre, now Henri IV of France, is often said to have mused, 'Paris is worth a Mass.' Although this famous quotation is even more insecurely founded than Martin Luther's precisely contradictory sentiment, 'Here I stand, I can do no other', it should not be jettisoned from history, for it likewise encapsulates a vital moment in the Reformation. In its weary rejection of rigid religious principle, the phrase echoes what many of Europe's politicians and rulers felt after seventy years of religious warfare across Europe.[35] Taking advantage of France's war-weariness, in 1598 Henri brokered a settlement, the Edict of Nantes, a version of schemes which Henri III had never been able to enforce in the face of bitter opposition from the Ligue.[36] Now Huguenots had not universal toleration but a guaranteed privileged corporate status within the realm, with their own churches and fortified places. Henri IV's much more sincerely Catholic successors spent the next nine decades whittling away these privileges, but during that time, France represented western Europe's most large-scale example of religious pluralism, despite a major upsurge of French Catholic renewal and rebuilding. In the end they created one of Europe's most impressive Counter-Reformations.

This belated Counter-Reformation in France was linked to another delayed Catholic Reformation far away in Poland-Lithuania, through the peculiar circumstance that for a few months in 1574 they shared a common monarch, Henri, Duke of Anjou. We have met Henri in Poland, as the distinctly unwilling agent in 1573 of the Polish-Lithuanian Commonwealth's remarkable enactment of religious toleration, the Confederation of Warsaw (see pp. 643–4). The hopes which all sides placed in that agreement for a golden future under their imported French king were not to be fulfilled, for Henri did not prolong his stay in his new kingdom. He was dismayed not only by a seemingly boundless and unfamiliar realm, but by intimidating excitement from his middle-aged prospective bride (last of the previous Jagiellon dynasty), and by his dawning consciousness that the Polish nobility were even less deferential than their French counterparts. Then only a few months after his coronation in Cracow, he received astonishing news: his brother Charles IX of France was dead and consequently he had become King of France, as Henri III. Henri's secret flight across Europe and back to Paris in June 1574 was a bitter blow to his subjects in the Commonwealth, and they swiftly disabused him of any illusion that he could rule the Commonwealth in addition to France (it might have been better for Henri if he had stayed). After two years of political chaos, a replacement candidate emerged who could once more block the Habsburgs: István Báthori, the current Prince of Transylvania, better known when King of Poland as Stefan Bathory.[37]

Bathory proved to be an excellent choice in his exceptional wisdom and military capacity. He was a devout Catholic, but was not going to jeopardize his chances of the Polish throne by objecting to the toleration clause in the Confederation of Warsaw, which in any case had been anticipated eight years earlier in the declaration of his native Transylvania at Torda. Yet it was from Bathory's reign that the demoralized and divided Catholic Church in the Commonwealth began consolidating its position which eventually produced one of the very few successes for Catholic recovery in northern Europe. Against the great variety of Protestant activity in Poland-Lithuania, Roman Catholicism already had some advantages. It never lost control of the Church hierarchy or the landed endowments of the old Church – in any case rather more modest than further west in Europe, and therefore perhaps less vulnerable to secular greed.

Crucially, the Polish monarchy never finally broke with Catholicism, and that, combined with unbroken adherence from most of the lower orders in the countryside, proved decisive over a century and a half. Already before Stefan Bathory's reign, in 1564, the Society of Jesus had established a foothold in Poland. Now King Stefan was responsible for founding three major Jesuit colleges in the far north-east of the commonwealth at Polotsk, Riga and Dorpat, deliberately chosen as cities where the Reformed Churches were at their strongest. From the late 1570s there was a Jesuit-run academy (university college) in Vilnius, chief city of Lithuania, and by the early seventeenth century, every important town (more than two dozen scattered throughout the Commonwealth) had a Jesuit school. Lutheran, Reformed and anti-Trinitarian schools could not compete with such large-scale educational enterprise. The steady work of the Society of Jesus in providing schools and colleges attracted members of the gentry and nobility, even Protestants, to send their children for a good education, and that schooling remorselessly thinned the ranks of the Protestant elite.

Sometimes the story of the Polish Counter-Reformation has indeed been presented as a one-man-band achievement by the Jesuits. This is dangerously oversimplified. In reality, many Polish-Lithuanian Catholics deeply distrusted the Society, which they saw as too inclined to uphold the monarchy or even advocate increases in royal power, and so threaten the liberties of noblemen in the Commonwealth. Poland, after all, from the time of the Council of Florence, had been one of the strongholds of conciliarism (see pp. 560–63), and at the end of the sixteenth century that tradition remained strong in the face of the Jesuits' Tridentine papalism. Yet in a strange paradox only recently perceived by historians, this level of Catholic distrust of the Jesuits, which one might think would have encouraged defections to Protestantism, equally benefited

Catholicism in Poland-Lithuania. The Polish Dominicans, long-established in the venerable University of Cracow and in major towns of the Commonwealth, hated the Jesuits, rightly suspecting them of wanting to take over existing Dominican educational institutions, and they frequently obstructed Jesuit work, earning themselves sad and angry royal rebukes. The Dominicans' consistent and open hostility to the Jesuits demonstrated that it was perfectly possible to be a good Catholic and still detest the Society of Jesus: one did not have to go over to the Protestant side.[38]

Equally significant was King Sigismund III's triumphant Catholic diplomacy which led to the creation of the Greek Catholic Church in the Commonwealth through the Union of Brest in 1596 (see pp. 534–6). The existence of the Greek Catholic Church, whatever its subsequent troubles in relation to Russian Orthodoxy, meant that there was yet a third possible identity for those Poles and Lithuanians who wished to keep their allegiance to the Holy See in Rome. Ultimately they had the choice of placing their faith in the Society of Jesus, applauding cussed Dominican harassment of the Society, or exercising their religion in churches of Orthodox tradition, adorned with icons, whose clergy wore beards and had wives and families. All these options represented Catholicism. Accordingly, the Catholic Church increasingly flourished in its diversity, while a long slow decay affected the divided ranks of the Protestants in the Commonwealth. Polish constitutional toleration was undermined by the monarchy's steadily more confessional Catholicism and by the circumstance that further dynastic problems, which gave the kings of Sweden a claim to the Polish throne, ranged Lutheran Sweden against Poland in war. It was easy in that traumatic era to see Protestantism as an enemy of the Commonwealth's independence. The Socinians were expelled en masse from the Commonwealth in 1660, although in their dispersal they were to have a remarkable effect on western Europe and the Christian story generally (see pp. 778–9). This sign of a new intolerance in Poland-Lithuania came amid the growing stream of conversions back to Catholicism among its Protestant elites.

Thus the future of Poland, once such a fertile seminary of Protestant experiment, proved against all the odds to be bound into that of the Catholic Church. When the political institutions of Poland-Lithuania were wrecked and then utterly destroyed by the selfish acquisitiveness of eighteenth-century monarchs in Prussia, Russia and Austria, the Catholic Church was all the Poles and Lithuanians had left to carry forward the identity of their once-mighty commonwealth. One extraordinary twentieth-century product of the alliance between Polish national identity and an increasingly monolithic Catholic Church was the career of Karol Wojtyła, who as Pope John Paul II might be seen as a belated embodiment of the Counter-Reformation (see pp. 994–1000). Yet beyond his quarter-century papacy, the consequences of destroying the old Polish-Lithuanian Commonwealth, and of the painful rebuilding of national identities in eastern Europe aided by the Catholic and Greek Catholic Churches, are still unfolding in the politics of our own age.

LIVES SEPARATED: SAINTS, SPLENDOUR, SEX AND WITCHES

The Reformation and Catholic Reformation dividing Latin Christendom, previously remarkably united across a whole continent, produced a rift in the rhythms of life to a degree without parallel in Christian history. The shape of the year became experienced in very different ways in Protestant and Catholic regions. Protestant societies which had rejected the power of the saints observed few or no saints' days, so holidays ceased to be the 'holy days' of the saints and some (usually not many) were reinvented as Protestant feasts. In England, yearly November bonfires and celebrations reminded the English of their new Protestant heritage in defeating the Spanish Armada (1588), foiling a Roman Catholic who tried to blow up the king and Parliament (1605) and eventually ejecting a Roman Catholic king who appeared to threaten the whole Protestant settlement of the British Isles (1688). By contrast, the Europe loyal to Rome discovered new saints and festivals to emphasize that loyalty. A happy coincidence helped: in 1578 a large number of Christian catacombs (see p. 160), almost unknown for centuries, were rediscovered beneath the soil of Rome and seemed to be full of the bones of early Christian martyrs. The bones were exported all over the Catholic world, a great morale-booster against Protestants in underlining the glorious history of suffering in the Roman Church, and they were joined in their fruitful travels by countless fragments of Ursula's eleven thousand virgins from Cologne. The Jesuits were chief brokers in this sacred commerce.[39]

The greatest separation came in the way in which Protestants and Catholics approached their God in church. In most Reformed Churches, it quickly became the norm to lock church buildings between services to discourage superstitious devotions by individuals who did not have the benefit of community instruction from the pulpit (and those who tried were often punished). This went hand in hand with the drastic slimming down of the Protestant ministry in the interests of greater professionalism in preaching: churches were there for sermons and the occasional community Eucharist. Their most prominent piece of furniture was not an altar but a pulpit. With varying degrees of thoroughness, Lutheran church interiors tended to be remoulded in this pattern, as were parish churches in the Church of England, increasingly ambiguous in its Reformed identity though it was.[40] By contrast, Catholic churches continued as in the pre-Reformation past to be open and available for private devotions between the frequent communal liturgical acts. As before, there would be plenty of clergy for laypeople to encounter on the premises. Priest-confessors would commonly be available to relieve afflicted consciences, increasingly using a new piece of liturgical furniture, an enclosed double box with a communicating grille hiding the identity of priest and penitent, which was pioneered by Archbishop Carlo Borromeo for his archdiocese of Milan, as part of his intensification of confessional discipline for the faithful.[41]

Borromeo's penchant for order was paired in Counter-Reformation Catholicism with a carefully regulated enthusiasm for the extrovert. Counter-Reformation clergy and their architects, anxious to harness and concentrate the devotional enthusiasm of its people, swept away the screens of medieval churches which obstructed congregations' view of the high altar in church. They placed the tabernacle of the reserved eucharistic Sacrament on the altar itself, where previously the tabernacle had often been separate from it. So the high altar became overwhelmingly the visual focus of a Counter-Reformation church, just as the single altar had been in the early basilicas, though the Western Church's medieval host of side altars remained undisturbed. After some initial gestures towards remedying late medieval excesses in architecture and music by greater austerity, Catholics realized that splendour was one of their chief assets. Worship in Catholic churches became ever more expressive of the power and magnificence of the Church, as a backdrop to feast and fast.

The city of Rome, enhanced by its newly discovered martyrs and receiving crowds of pilgrims to its ancient holy places, was the greatest of all these Catholic theatre sets. It now became ever more stately after centuries of decay, through a huge investment in building. This was led by the papacy and aided by the wealth of the cardinals resident in the city, who paid particular attention to the various parish churches of which they were theoretically the parish priests, together with palaces to provide a suitable backdrop for their own lives of splendour. The centrepiece of Rome was not its cathedral of St John Lateran, grand though that was, but the triumphant (not to say triumphalist) completion of the new St Peter's Basilica. Between 1602 and 1615, this was hugely extended by Carlo Maderno, westwards from the earlier centrally domed building designed by Donato Bramante and Michelangelo and slowly completed over the previous hundred years. Maderno's least happy achievement is the basilica's western façade, which partly thanks to problems with its foundations that became apparent during its construction, fails to soar or inspire. Yet the resulting architectural bathos was redeemed within half a century by being fronted with one of the most extraordinary public spaces not just of the Counter-Reformation, but of all Christian architecture.

This oval colonnaded piazza was designed by Gianlorenzo Bernini, Baroque architect of genius as well as inspired sculptor. Bernini had already provided the chief coup de théâtre of the basilica's interior, the monumental bronze canopy or baldachino over the high altar and tomb of St Peter. His piazza, which he artfully extended at either end by smaller funnel-shaped piazze, so that it could lead up to the basilica and still fit round older buildings impossible to pull down, brilliantly performs two functions. It provides a breathtaking pathway to the basilica from the River Tiber (an effect helpfully enhanced by Mussolini's modern demolitions), but it is also a space capable of holding thousands of pilgrims, ready for their glimpse of the pope if he chooses to appear at one of the windows of the Vatican Palace, which rather untidily looms above the south colonnade. Over the last century, the technology of amplification has made this piazza an especially effective dramatic backdrop for the pope when he communicates from his palace with a constantly changing multitude of the faithful from all over the world, week by week eager to pray with him or cheer to the skies his greetings and devotional and ethical pronouncements. No other modern Christian leader enjoys a setting so ready-made for dominating his flock, although some contemporary Pentecostals and televangelists have done their best. The combination of microphone and Baroque architectural magnificence offers formidable obstacles to overcome, should any future pope wish to depart from the monarchical style to which the Bishops of Rome have become accustomed.

Jesuits, who had initially been discouraged by Ignatius even from celebrating sung High Masses in their churches because of his fears of excessive elaboration, enthusiastically adopted the new extrovert strategy of the Church in tackling the problem of formalization of religious practice and indifference. Taking their cue from an order of priests known as Barnabites, who had been another product of the Italian renewal movements of the 1530s, the Society began drawing on every device of dramatic sensation to capture the imaginations of people who had a fixed idea of what the Church represented, and apparently thought little about it. They staged spectacular devotional missions, seizing the churches and streets of a particular community and its locality for days or even weeks on end. The Jesuits became actors and showmen: their visit must be a heart-stopping special occasion, bringing God's circus to town. This was carnival, but the carnival employed that ultimate carnivalesque reversal of human hierarchies, in which all humanity is laid low in death, as Jesuit preachers pitilessly reminded their enthralled audiences from pulpit or market cross. The Church offered the remedy: its contact with the divine, summed up in the consecrated Host exhibited amid a blaze of candles, promised hope and salvation. Although the means of salvation differed, the histrionics and the saving of the desperate from despair were not dissimilar in their message from themes prominent in the revivals which Protestants began to foment a century later (see chapter 20).[42]

Time itself was divided by the Reformation. An energetic and intellectually curious pope, Gregory XIII, took it upon himself, with the new-found papal confidence of the Counter-Reformation, to reform the deficiencies of the existing Julian calendar, from 15 October 1582. He was much concerned for unity with the Eastern Churches, that process which indeed did produce the Union of Brest under his one of his successors fourteen years later. So to emphasize the temporal as well as ecclesiastical role of the papacy as focus for world unity, Gregory decided to model himself on Constantine the Great. According to Eusebius, Constantine had been commanded by God to convene the Council of Nicaea in order to fix a universally reliable date for Easter in the face of the Julian calendar's inaccuracy. Unsurprisingly, Protestants took the papacy's overdue scientific correction as a sinister plot. They took a long time to accept it, at different dates in different parts of Europe, to the despair of later historians trying to work out relative dates in documents. In England, the delay extended to 1752, over 150 years after the more Protestant but also more logical Scots had accepted (without obvious public gratitude) that the Pope was right.[43]

Having made the correct scientific decision over the calendar, Rome made a disastrous miscalculation in its treatment of the great Italian astronomer and mathematician Galileo Galilei. Galileo was condemned by the Roman Inquisition in 1633 for providing empirical evidence for the radical revision of cosmology proposed by the long-dead Polish cleric Nicolaus Copernicus. In 1616 the Church had belatedly declared Copernicus to be in error; the Roman authorities then forced Galileo to deny that the earth moved round the sun and not the other way round, because his observations challenged the Church's authority as the source of truth. There were good theological reasons why they should reject heliocentric theory: the Bible presents creation in moral terms, and depicts a cosmic drama of sin and redemption centred on God's relationship with humankind. It was not unreasonable to assume that in his creation, he would have made the planet earth, the stage for that drama, the centre of his universe, rather than a morally neutral fiery disc.

Yet Galileo's observations represented reality. Obstinately he turned his humiliation by the Roman authorities to positive use: after they had forced him in 1633 to abject recantation for the boisterous boldness of his astronomical discussions in the *Discorsi*, he set to work in house arrest secretly producing a new version, calmly discussing the physics of motion. This last work before his death was perhaps his greatest contribution to Western thought: an enterprise of truly rational investigation of empirical evidence, ignoring the pressure from powerful traditional authority. It anticipated the detached investigation of phenomena which has become one of the hallmarks of Europe's Enlightenment culture. Were it not for the papacy's defensiveness after Luther's rebellion, it is unlikely that the Catholic Church would have made such a major mistake. Galileo's trial also happened during the Thirty Years War, a destructive battle for the soul of central Europe between Catholic and Protestant, and a time when the Pope was feeling unusually vulnerable. Protestants should not be too quick to sneer at Pope Urban VIII, because much Protestant scholarship showed itself just as suspicious of the new science of observation.[44]

For there was much to unite the Church of Rome and the magisterial Reformations, both Lutheran and Reformed. Both sides based their beliefs on the pronouncements of the Bible, however much they disagreed on what the Bible meant. Those who appeared to challenge that authority, like radical Christians or Galileo, could expect to find themselves regarded as enemies of God. Both sides remained suspicious and contemptuous of other religions, although Protestants generally were more inclined to tolerate Jews because they found Jewish biblical scholarship a useful tool against Catholics. The Reformed in particular, thanks to their various political troubles, came to have the same experience of exile and loss as they saw in the history and present experience of the Jewish people.[45] Such impulses notwithstanding, there was still a powerful hankering for a restoration of a lost Christendom which would be characterized by a single God-given order on both sides of the Reformation. Europe became a newly intensively regulated society, as Catholics and Protestants vied with each other to show just how moral a society they could create. More than a century ago, the sociologist Max Weber wrote at length to argue for a fundamental difference between the two religious groupings, which resulted in Reformed Protestants becoming identified with self-discipline and a 'spirit of capitalism', and Protestants associated with a highly regulated 'work ethic' rarely possessed by Catholics. The notion still holds some sway in popular consciousness, but detailed acquaintance with the story of Reformation and Counter-Reformation makes it dissolve into qualification and contradiction; it is an idea best avoided. Discipline and the urge to order people's lives were ecumenical qualities.[46]

One motive for this had little to do with the Reformation and much to do with that newly rampant sexually transmitted disease syphilis, which generated much anxiety about social habits. Also echoing in the minds of rulers was Erasmus's rhetorical question, 'What is the state but a great monastery?' (see p. 600). When Protestants closed the old monasteries en masse, that question became all the more pressing – including subsidiary problems, such as how Protestant societies would relieve the poor or disabled if there were no religious houses or confraternities dependent on the soul-prayer industry to do the job. Protestants had another new reason for unease and social regulation, because they were shifting the moral emphasis in sexuality. When they closed celibate communities and proclaimed that clergy were no different from other men and should make a practical demonstration of a theological point by getting married, they were prioritizing heterosexual marriage over celibacy: indeed, casting a large question mark against the motives for compulsory celibacy. Protestant ministers were soon in the habit of growing substantial beards to back up their theology.[47]

Both sides of the religious divide energetically shut down the brothels which the medieval Church had licensed as a safety valve for society (though brothels had a way of discreetly reopening). Both sides stepped up the pressures to suppress male homosexuality, the celibate Catholic clergy especially terrified of anything which might justify Protestant slurs on their sexual inclinations. In self-defence, Catholics could point to a long tradition of discussion and celebration of the family, but Protestants could point to an innovation which was distinctly theirs in Western Christendom, and which overall proved a real success: their re-establishment of the clerical family. The parsonage was a new model for Europe's family life. It was perhaps not the most comfortable place to live, on a modest income and under constant public gaze, but children grew up there surrounded by books and earnest conversation, inheriting the assumption that life was to be lived strenuously for the benefit of an entire community – not least in telling that community what to do, whether the advice was welcome or not. It was not surprising that clerical and academic dynasties quickly grew up in Protestant Europe, and that thoughtful and often troubled, rather self-conscious parsonage children took their place in a wider service. Such personalities as John and Charles Wesley, Gilbert and William Tennent, a trio of Brontë novelists, Friedrich Nietzsche, Carl Jung, Karl Barth and Martin Luther King Jr took their restlessness and driven sense of duty into very varied rebuildings of Western society and consciousness, not all of which their parents might have applauded.

One of the aspects of Reformation in which there are the most puzzling connections between Catholic and Protestant is in the treatment of witches. Both sides, with honourable exceptions such as Martin Luther and the Spanish Inquisition (an unpredictable combination), moved from the general medieval belief in witches to a new pursuit, persecution and execution of people thought to be witches. Encouraged by the precedent of medieval scholarly analysis dating back to the fourteenth century (see p. 420), they considered these unfortunates to be agents of the Devil. It is remarkable how seriously Protestants fearful of witch-craft took a misogynistic and rambling textbook on witchcraft written by two pre-Reformation Dominicans, one of whom, Jacobus Sprenger, had also been instrumental in promoting the Marian devotion of the Rosary: this was the egregious *Malleus Maleficarum* ('Hammer of Witches'), first published in Strassburg in 1487.[48] Maybe forty or fifty thousand people died in Europe and colonial North America on witch-craft charges between 1400 and 1800, most noticeably from around 1560, at just about the time when large-scale execution of heretics was coming to an end. The activity had curiously different peaks and troughs in different parts of Europe, and the common stereotype of the witch as a gnarled old woman does not reflect the reality in England that accused were characteristically prosperous or significant figures in their community, though commonly not the most peaceable. If they were indeed elderly women, there was often a long history of accusations against them, but also a sudden lack of male protection when their husbands died.[49]

A high incidence of witchcraft prosecutions was often found in western European regions, both Protestant and Catholic, which evolved effective systems of court discipline which people living under them would have difficulty in challenging. Individual personalities might then make all the difference. Some of the worst persecutions took place in the Archbishopric of Cologne after it was secured for the Bavarian Wittelsbach family. Ferdinand, Archbishop of Cologne from 1612, was a typical product of the radical Counter-Reformation self-discipline which characterized both his own Wittelsbach dynasty and the more militant Habsburgs in alliance with them (see p. 671). It has been plausibly suggested that these devoutly Catholic rulers were fighting more than the Protestantism which certainly obsessed them: their Jesuit mentors gave them a preoccupation with sin and judgement, now strengthened for the clergy among them by the new demands of a clerical celibacy much more conscientiously maintained than in the pre-Reformation Church. As Habsburgs, Wittelsbachs and an array of conscientious Counter-Reformation bishops struggled with their own temptations, witches became symbols of the general temptations which Satan used to torment society.

Among Protestants it took one independent-minded Dutch Reformed minister, Balthazar Bekker, to excoriate witch-hunting in an influential book, *Bewitched World* (1691); this finally shamed many Protestant authorities in Germany into giving up witch trials. The Dutch Reformed Church did not thank him. Their colleagues in the mid-seventeenth-century Church of Scotland had distinguished themselves by one of the most statistically intense persecutions in Europe, which was not unconnected to the Scottish clergy's constant struggle to assert their authority in the kingdom against secular authority. The Scots Kirk had the distinction of inventing that form of torture still popular in the contemporary world, sleep deprivation, in order to extract confessions.[50] The pattern in eastern Europe was different again: the paranoia started later, lasted longer and in fact climaxed in the eighteenth century. By then half of those charged with witchcraft in now strongly Catholic Poland ended up being burned, whereas the proportion had been around 4 per cent in the sixteenth century. The 'State without Stakes' was increasingly belying its reputation, in parallel to the decline in its toler-ance of religious diversity. The executions ended only with a Polish royal decree in 1776, by which time perhaps around a thousand people had died, a similar figure to that in Hungary and Transylvania through the same period. The eastern persecutions were being fuelled by new crises and social tensions in the lands where Habsburg, Romanov and Hohen-zollern were remaking the map and disposing of ancient political rivals.

By the end of the seventeenth century, despite losses to Russian Ortho-doxy in the east, far more of the religious life of Europe was under Catholic obedience than in 1600. There had been a number of political milestones on that journey: the Union of Brest in 1596, which had seemed to absorb most of the Orthodox of eastern Europe into the Catholic Church; the Battle of White Mountain, which had crushed Bohemian Utraquism in 1620; the Treaty of Westphalia, which restricted Protestant recovery of territory in 1648; the Revocation of the Edict of Nantes in 1685, which repudiated Henri IV's generous vision of two Christian confessions coexisting in a single kingdom. The story was partly of war, high diplomacy, official persecution and coercion; but it was also the result of much patient missionary work, preaching, rebuild-ing of a devotional life part traditional and part as innovative as anything Protestants did. And those Jesuits, friars or secular priests who laboured in the forests and plains of eastern Europe, or tried to spark fresh vigour into Church life in secretive villages down the heel of Italy, were encouraged to do so because they knew that they were part of a still wider mission. Not for nothing did the Jesuits refer to the remote parts of Europe in which they laboured as the 'Indies' – because the Society had also reached Indies overseas, both India and lands newly named and hitherto unknown to Europeans. The missionary goal was to make a reality of Pope Gregory VII's ancient vision: to see the world turning in obedience to the Church ruled over by Christ's Vicar on earth.

19
A Worldwide Faith
(1500–1800)

IBERIAN EMPIRES: THE WESTERN
CHURCH EXPORTED

The distinctive Christianity of Spain and Portugal in the Iberian peninsula, which during the fifteenth century had destroyed the last non-
Christian societies in western Europe, simultaneously began to extend
Western Christendom beyond its historic frontiers across the sea. Their
successes were in sharp contrast to Christian defeats and contraction in
the East. The Portuguese took the lead: their seafaring expertise was
forced on them by their exposed position on the Atlantic seaboard and
by their homeland's agricultural poverty, but they also had a tradition
of successful crusading against Islam. They began in North Africa,
capturing the Moroccan commercial centre of Ceuta in 1415, and went
on to contest for dominance in African trade, seeing their efforts as a
fight for Christianity as well as a quest for wealth. Portuguese ships soon
became more ambitious, fuelled in their adventures by the optimistic
myth of 'Prester John', an unbeatable ally against Islam (see pp. 284–5),
and although he never fulfilled European hopes, the galvanizing effect
was enough. The Portuguese eventually rounded the Cape of Good
Hope, reaching India by 1498 and sailing around the Chinese coast by
1513. In 1500 they made their first landing on the east coast of what
later became their colony of Brazil.

Once abroad, the Portuguese turned their crusading ethos to religious
intolerance as extreme as anywhere in western Europe. Having established a secure Indian base in Goa in 1510, they massacred six thousand
Muslims, and by mid-century they had also forbidden the practice of
Hinduism in Portuguese royal dominions; for good measure they
despised and severely harassed the heretical 'Nestorian' Dyophysite
Christians of India.[1] If later Christian missions based on the worldwide

Portuguese Empire showed a certain humility and caution in their operations, it was largely because the Portuguese never overcame their poverty. Their empire, run on a shoestring, consisted of a motley collection
of fortified but under-garrisoned coastal trading posts. The historian
Garrett Mattingly once unkindly but accurately commented that by the
mid-sixteenth century the King of Portugal had become the proprietor of
'a bankrupt wholesale grocery business'.[2] Consequently the Portuguese
usually lacked the military power to impose Christianity over widespread territories or on their African or Asian neighbours, with significant consequences for missionary strategy (see pp. 704–9).

The frayed texture of Portuguese empire-building contrasted with
spectacular parallel achievements under the Spanish monarchy. In 1492,
the same year that the Muslim kingdom of Granada fell, the adventurer
Christopher Columbus rewarded Fernando and Isabel's trust by making
landfall across the Atlantic on islands in the Caribbean. His achievement
caused tension with the Portuguese, which prompted Pope Alexander VI
(a former subject of King Fernando) to partition the map of the world
vertically between the two powers in 1493, intending the Spaniards to
enjoy the fruits of their new discoveries westwards. As the King of
Portugal remained aggrieved at the result, the kingdoms revised this
agreement in 1494 with the Treaty of Tordesillas. Uncertain conditions
of mapmaking meant that the revised line was still not as clear a division
through Atlantic waters as intended, and the Portuguese were later
able successfully to appeal to the geographical bounds established at
Tordesillas when they established their transatlantic colony of Brazil.
Nevertheless, the bulk of westward activity was Spanish (technically
their new dominions became part of the kingdom of Castile), while the
Portuguese put most of their efforts into Africa and Asia. Over the next
three decades the Spaniards realized that their westward discoveries
promised not merely Columbus's scattering of islands, but a whole
continent.

An important part of this militantly Latin Christian enterprise was
the promotion of its faith among peoples now encountered, although
Ferdinand and Isabel had originally envisaged evangelizing Asia (hence
the Spanish named the native peoples 'Indios', in allusion to Columbus's
ever more desperately messianic belief that God had sailed him to Asia).
Pope Julius II further granted the Spanish monarchy a *Patronato*, exclusive rights to preach the Gospel in its new territories: a major step in a
gradual papal abdication of real authority within Spanish dominions.
He granted the Portuguese a similar right in their empire, the *Padroado*,

and his successors rapidly regretted both concessions, without being able to withdraw them. Now good intentions clashed with naked greed and brutality.

There had in fact been a precedent both well intentioned and ultimately unhappy. The earliest Western conquests and missionary work outside continental Europe were in the Canary Islands off the west coast of Africa, while successive Iberian powers fought for mastery there up to a Castilian conquest in the 1480s – the Canaries were the first place in which medieval Europeans encountered the Stone Age. Even before the Castilian conquest, there were missionary friars in the Canaries, first Aragonese Catalans and Majorcans, latterly Franciscans from Castile's southernmost province, Andalusia; their behaviour contrasted with that of later Portuguese in Africa. They spoke out strongly against enslaving native people who had converted to Christianity, and sometimes made a leap of imagination to oppose enslaving those who had not converted. They also persuaded the authorities in Rome to allow ordination of natives. But in any case, in a sad anticipation of what was to happen elsewhere in Iberian conquests, by the sixteenth century most of the indigenous people were dead from European diseases, and some had been deported to Spain as troublemakers.[3]

Franciscan attitudes in the Canaries offered possible precedents for what Europe now came to call 'the New World', or, through a somewhat tangled chain of circumstances, 'America'.[4] One problem with improving on the Canary Islands model was the contrasting and appalling record of military adventurers who undertook Spain's forward movement in America: notably Hernán Cortés against the Aztecs in Central America and Francisco Pizarro against the Inkas of Peru. Many who took part in these unsavoury and unprovoked feats of treachery, theft and genocide saw themselves as agents of the crusade begun back home with the *Reconquista*, the destruction of Spanish Islam and Judaism. Crusading rhetoric there was in plenty, but there was something else. It has been well said that the Spanish Empire is unequalled in history among similar great territorial enterprises for its insistent questioning of its own rights to conquer and colonize.[5] From 1500 there were Franciscans in America, and within a decade Dominicans had also arrived. Very soon the Dominicans began protesting against the vicious treatment of the natives. The authorities at home did go some way to responding to such appeals to conscience. As early as 1500 Fernando and Isabel formally forbade enslavement of their subjects in America and the Canaries. The Laws of Burgos tried in 1512 to lay down guidelines for relations, and even created a set of 'rules of engagement' for further conquests: newly contacted peoples were to be publicly read (in Spanish) a so-called Requirement, formally explaining the bulls of Alexander VI which granted Spain overlordship of their territory. If they cooperated and agreed that Christianity could freely be taught among them, then no force would be used against them.

Alas, the atrocious exploits of Cortés and Pizarro postdated the Laws of Burgos. The friars' fury at the injustice continued. Their most eloquent spokesman was a former colonial official and plantation owner, Bartolomé de las Casas, galvanized out of making money by hearing a Dominican sermon about the wickedness of what he and his fellow colonists were doing. The shock turned him to ordination, and he made it his especial task for half a century from 1514 to defend the natives – he became a Dominican himself in 1522. He won sympathy from the aged Cardinal Ximénes; later his insistence that native Americans were as rational beings as Spaniards, rather than inferior versions of humanity naturally fitted for slavery, sufficiently impressed the Emperor Charles V that debates were staged at the imperial Spanish capital at Valladolid on the morality of colonization (with inconclusive results).

Las Casas insisted that Augustine of Hippo's gloss on the biblical text 'Compel them to come in' (see p. 304) was simply wrong: Jesus had not intended conversion to his 'joyful tidings' to be a matter of 'arms and bombardments' but of 'reason and human persuasion'.[6] His writings about Spanish barbarity in America were so angry and eloquent that ironically they became part of the general Protestant stereotype of Spaniards as a naturally cruel race. At one stage he suggested a fateful remedy for the exploitation of native labour: African slaves should be imported to replace natives on plantations, radically extending the slave trade which the Portuguese had pioneered in the previous century. Las Casas eventually realized his mistake, but it was too late.[7] Here idealism trying to end one injustice blundered unhappily into colluding with a genocidal crime of three centuries' duration, whose consequences are still built into the politics of both Americas.

Rather more equivocally expressed, but equally important for Latin Europe's future relations with other world civilizations, was the work of a Dominican who never saw the 'New World'. Francisco de Vitoria, for the last two decades of his life highly influential as the leading theologian in Salamanca University, built on earlier Dominican thought to consider what was happening in America in the light of 'just war' theory. Conventional Christian legal wisdom saw nothing wrong in enslaving non-Christians captured in a just war, but there seemed to Vitoria little that was just in the idea of a crusade, particularly in its exploitation in America. War was only justified as a response to inflicted wrong, and the various peoples of America had offered no wrong to Spaniards before the Spaniards decided to move in on their territory. The Aztec practice of human sacrifice did offer a different justification for Spanish action in Central America, since it was a clear offence against universal natural law. There were other possible interpretations of wrong: resistance to preaching the Gospel, for instance, once the intention to do so had been proclaimed in the Requirement. Vitoria also considered authority within commonwealths. He discussed it in terms of sovereignty, a ruler's untrammelled power within the boundaries of a commonwealth or state. Such sovereign commonwealths need not be Christian: Aztecs or Ottomans were as sovereign as Fernando and Isabel. If so, Pope Alexander had no right to grant sovereignty in America to Spaniards in 1493, at the same time as he perfectly legitimately granted them exclusive rights to preach the Gospel. Such reasoning (coming from an Iberian Catholic tradition which had already put the pope firmly in his place) was a clear denial of that idea of universal papal monarchy which had originally fuelled Western Christendom's unity in the twelfth century.

Vitoria's discussions had a wider application. He was pioneering the concept of a system of international law, based on the older idea of *ius gentium* ('the law of peoples/nations'), the legal principles applicable to humans everywhere. His assertions heralded the end of belief in the crusade as a means of extending Western Christendom, just when Europe began a wider mission to spread its particular brand of Christianity throughout the world. The question would soon arise as to whether Western Christianity was completely identical with authentic Christianity, but there was more to the development of international law than this. Western European political thought was to develop a relativistic concept of dealing with other cultures and other political units – eventually without reference to their religious beliefs or any sense that one religion was superior to another. Vitoria would have profoundly disapproved of this development, but it emerged as a consequence of Iberian worldwide adventures.

Christian mission nevertheless proceeded backed by military force: first in Central America including modern-day Mexico, which remained the flagship Spanish territory and was therefore styled New Spain, and later in South America. In large part because of the friars' scruples, there

20. *The Iberian worldwide empires in 1600*

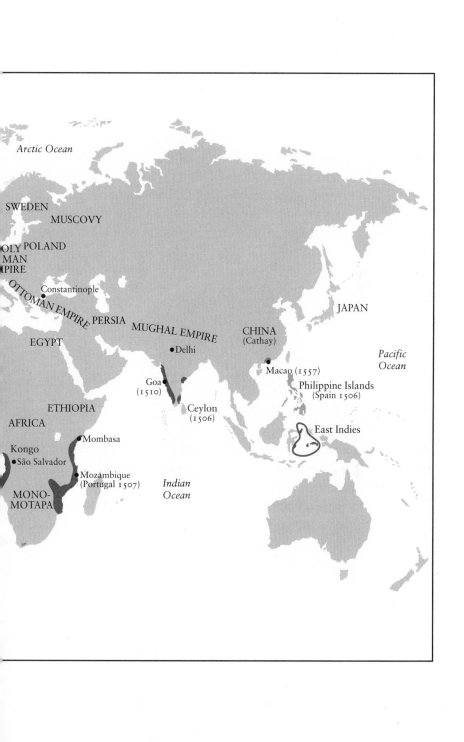

Arctic Ocean

SWEDEN

MUSCOVY

OLY POLAND
MAN
PIRE

OTTOMAN EMPIRE

Constantinople

PERSIA MUGHAL EMPIRE

EGYPT

Delhi

CHINA
(Cathay)

JAPAN

Pacific
Ocean

Macao (1557)

Goa
(1510)

Philippine Islands
(Spain 1506)

Ceylon
(1506)

ETHIOPIA

AFRICA

East Indies

Mombasa

Kongo

São Salvador

Mozambique
(Portugal 1507)

Indian
Ocean

MONO-
MOTAPA

was no systematic intention to obliterate pre-Christian structures in government and society: a number of peoples allied with the Spaniards against their neighbours, or came to a deal with the newcomers, and preserved autonomous forms of government. Much destruction resulted not from Spanish arms but from a much more devastating weapon which Westerners did not even realize they possessed, the diseases they were carrying. No major native American kingdom succumbed to the Spaniards before disease took hold, but once it had, the effect was crippling, and maybe half the population of the Americas died in the first wave of epidemics. That in itself was a powerful argument to bewildered and terrified people that their gods were useless and that the God of the conquerors had won. It has been estimated that by 1550 around ten million people had been baptized as Christians in the Americas. Another informed and sobering estimate is that by 1800 indigenous populations in the western hemisphere were a tenth of what they had been three centuries before.[8]

COUNTER-REFORMATION IN A NEW WORLD

The Council of Trent said nothing in its official statements about the world mission of the renewed Catholic Church, but this mission became one of the most distinctive features of southern European Catholicism, a project of taking Christianity to every continent, which made Roman Catholicism Western Christianity's largest grouping, and the Spanish and Portuguese languages the chief modern rivals to English as the mode of Western communication. Trent's silence seems all the more surprising since Catholic world mission had been in operation for over half a century when the council met – this was not like the council's silence on the menace of militant Calvinism, which had only emerged as a real threat just before its last session. Committees are even more prone than individuals to miss the point in the business in front of them, but it is worth observing that there was little that Rome could do about mission – at the beginning of the century, the papacy had signed away control of Catholic activity. Ignatius Loyola was characteristically more far-sighted: it was no coincidence that Portugal was one of the first kingdoms on which he concentrated the efforts of his infant Society, founding as early as 1540 a headquarters in Lisbon and only two years later a Jesuit college for missionary training, set up with royal encouragement in the university town of Coimbra. A new world mission based on Portugal would more than compensate for his abortive plans for the Holy Land.

While the Jesuits rapidly began following up their initial advantage in Portuguese territories in Africa, Asia and Brazil, they were comparatively late into the Spanish Empire, since the Spanish Inquisition for a couple of decades after the Society's foundation remained suspicious of an organization whose leader had twice briefly spent time in their prison cells. The Society only began arriving in the 1560s and 1570s, after more than half a century in which Franciscan and Dominican missions had been forced to think out a new theology of mission. Western Catholicism had limited experience to draw on; the last great ventures had been by the friars in Central Asia during the thirteenth and early fourteenth centuries (see pp. 272–5). Apart from that not very fruitful precedent and small beginnings in the Canaries, only the officially sponsored changes of religion in medieval Lithuania and Spain provided any reference point.

America presented a complex weave of powers and hierarchies which the missionaries needed to navigate with care. The Spaniards were very ready to distinguish between tribal societies and the sophistication of city-based cultures with recognizable aristocracies like their own. In such urban settings, they might very willingly strike marriage alliances with members of the local elites, in a notable contrast with the attitudes of Protestant English colonists in North America. Maybe Spaniards were simply more secure in their own culture than Tudor and Stuart Englishmen, who were products of one of Europe's more marginal and second-rank monarchies, and conscious that they had failed badly in their effort at cultural assimilation in their neighbouring island of Ireland.[9] The nephew of Ignatius Loyola, Martín García de Loyola, symbolizes the complexity in Spanish America. He led the expedition which in 1572 seized the last independent Inka ruler in Peru, Tupac Amaru, and executed him in the Inka capital, Cuzco, but Loyola also eventually married Beatriz, Tupac's great-niece. Their politically motivated nuptials were proudly commemorated (and idealized away from a murky reality) in a portrait which is still one of the most remarkable features of the Jesuit Church in Cuzco (see Plate 59). In it there stand beside the Spanish newcomers the Inka grandees in their traditional finery, but also duly equipped with the blazons of European heraldry.[10]

As Christianity took shape in the new setting, it was hardly surprising that even those most concerned to protect the native 'Indio' populations

brought with them the exclusive attitudes of their Christian monopoly
culture when dealing with the religions that they found. Sometimes one
encounters echoes of Spain's non-Christian past, some presumably the
result of craftsmen bringing their own style from Europe: for instance,
the intricate Moorish abstract designs decorating the ceilings of the
Franciscan church at Tlaxcala in New Spain (modern-day Mexico),
which was built in the 1530s for a people who had done well out of a
military alliance with the Spaniards against the Aztecs. More common
was a conscious appropriation of important pre-Christian sacred sites,
neutralizing or converting them by building major churches. The model
was actually the missionary practice of Augustine of Canterbury's mission to the Anglo-Saxons back around 600 CE, with Pope Gregory's
famous advice to Augustine's team of clergy to do precisely this – there
were plenty of good libraries in Spanish America's rapidly developed
network of colleges and universities where Bede's *Ecclesiastical History*
might be consulted.[11] Not far from Tlaxcala in the highlands of New
Spain is the sacred city of Cholula, whose princes made a treaty with
the Spaniards after fierce resistance. It boasts amid its pre-Conquest
pyramids a formidable array of churches, and the former chief temple,
the largest man-made pyramid in the world, is now crowned by the
Church of Our Lady of Succour: one place of sacrifice transformed into
another. One Dominican, Diego Durán, even envisaged turning the
great stone basin supposedly previously used for human sacrifice in
Tenochtitlán (Mexico City) into a font: 'I think it good that . . . what
used to be a container of human blood, sacrificed to the devil, may now
be the container of the Holy Spirit. There the souls of Christians will be
cleansed, and there they will receive the waters of baptism.'[12]

The most remarkable church in Cholula is the *Capilla Real*, built in
the 1540s for the far-off Emperor Charles V as his symbolic Chapel
Royal, but also as a gift to the defeated nobility of the region. This
presents a complicated message about past and present. It is unlike any
Christian church building in Europe, for inside and out it is a deliberate
replica of the Grand Mosque of Cordoba, without obvious orientation
or liturgical focus, and with the same forest of arches inside and vast
courtyard outside. Back home, Spanish Catholics had crushed Islam and
turned mosques into churches. Now in New Spain they had crushed
other false gods and conquered the native princes. So, here in Cholula,
they celebrated a new victory in the same way by building the princes a
church which looked like a mosque. Significantly, Cortés in his forays
through the region habitually referred to the native temples he encoun-

tered as 'mosques'.[13] While this building of the *capilla* at Cholula had a few companions in New Spain, there were many more parallels for its great square courtyard, with open corner chapels for devotional stations in processions (*capillas posas*), partly because of the courtyard's utility for an open-air worship which presented Latin liturgy in a setting where many in the crowd might not have been baptized. Such courtyards have no exact precedent in Christian Spain, but they recall another Islamic building known to Spanish pilgrims, the Al-Aqsa Mosque in Jerusalem. At the time that structure was widely considered to be the Palace of Solomon, and so a second message of the *Capilla Real* and its courtyard may be that a New Jerusalem could be found in Cholula for a new Christian people – just at the moment in the 1540s when so many souls were being lost to Protestantism in Europe.[14]

The Spanish mission in America soon became not so much crusade as apocalypse. Franciscans coming from Iberia were particularly prone to the millenarian enthusiasm which gripped southern Europe around 1500, and which the Franciscan Order had so long fostered. They believed that they were living in the End Times and so their task of bringing good news to new peoples was desperately urgent (Chancellor Gattinara was not the only cleric to identify Charles V with the Emperor of the Last Days). In much of New Spain, an entirely new pattern of settlements of villages and towns was laid out on a grid plan – again, the ideal plan of a perfect Jerusalem – each centring on a church. This redrew the map of Central America, in a fashion which had no precedent in the architecture of old Europe and which, in its social engineering, made it impossible to separate out religious from secular concerns.[15] Nothing could be further from the clergy's minds than any need for Christianity to develop a long-term strategy of coexistence with other world faiths; there was no more room for rival religions in the 'New World' than back in Spain. When clergy noticed curious analogies in Aztec religion with Christian practice – an apparent sign of the cross, or belief in the virgin birth of a God – such similarities did not inspire them to inter-faith dialogue. These devices mocked and deceived God's Church in Satan's struggle against God's imminent Second Coming.[16] Apocalyptic fervour merged with Dominican concerns for legalities. Since Dominicans like Vitoria denied that the pope had the right to grant temporal rights of conquest in the New World in 1493, they were driven to stress the rationale of what he had done in terms of bringing the good news of Christianity and banishing Satan. Yet sometimes their very anxiety to destroy the demonic quality of the religion they found affected their message: anxious to banish the worship of the sun, priests appropriated sun imagery to the Christian Eucharist. One result seems to have been a notable stylistic innovation affecting the entire Tridentine Catholic world: eucharistic monstrances (vessels for displaying the consecrated wafer) which place their Host-container at the centre of a golden sunburst. Some of the earliest surviving examples were manufactured in the Spanish New World and imported back to Europe, and they were common in the Americas before they were in the Old World. They remain one of the most recognizable symbols of Tridentine Catholicism.[17]

Clerical attitudes to indigenous cults hardened from the 1530s. In 1541 and 1546, major uprisings among the Maya of Yucatan were directed against all things Spanish, including Catholicism; they involved savage revenge attacks on the Spanish settler population and were naturally suppressed with equal cruelty. In 1562, Franciscan missionaries in Yucatan discovered that some of their converts were continuing secretly to practise pre-Conquest religious rites. It was bad enough to find that people had been burying figures of the old gods next to crosses so that they could go on publicly worshipping them undetected, but those questioned reported cases of human sacrifice, some including crucifixions, staged with satirical blasphemy during the Christian solemnities of Holy Week. The Franciscan provincial Diego de Landa set up a local Inquisition which unleashed a campaign of interrogation and torture on the Indio population. A newly appointed bishop, horrified at zeal gone wild, abruptly stripped de Landa of his authority, and put a stop to the atrocities, but the Maya had already paid a terrible price.[18]

The effect of such disappointments was that Spanish clergy radically limited their trust in the natives. Indigenous people might become assistants in the liturgy, but never principals – catechists, sacristans, cantors and instrumentalists, not priests. At first, native men were not even allowed to enter religious orders. A problem arose which has remained constant for the Catholic Church entering new cultures (see p. 884): compulsory celibacy for the priesthood, restated with renewed vigour in the Counter-Reformation, was an alien idea in most cultures. Only in the eighteenth century did significant numbers of indigenous men become priests, at a time when consciously non-Christian religious practice in peoples under Spanish control had long ceased.[19] There were even serious debates throughout the sixteenth century as to whether natives should be banned from receiving the eucharistic Host when they came to Mass – after all, European laity only did so once a year, while these people were barely fit to be considered full Christians.[20] In South

America, first under Portuguese rule in Brazil and then in the south-eastern Spanish territories, Jesuits treated their hunter-gatherer converts almost as children, organizing them into large settlements to protect them against the greed and exploitation of the other colonists, but always in a benevolent European-led dictatorship of estates, the 'Reductions'. When the Jesuits were forcibly expelled from the Americas in 1767, they left their natives without any experience of leadership, and the carefully structured communities in the Reductions quickly collapsed. Only in Bolivia did priests of supposedly pure Spanish blood (Creoles) manage to carry on similar work after the Jesuits had left.[21]

Within this framework, the Church did achieve a remarkable degree of synthesis between Christianity and what it allowed to survive from native culture. Naturally friars and Jesuits worked with the languages which they found, particularly since they were reluctant to open natives up to unhealthy influences from colonists by teaching them Spanish. They had utterly different priorities from the Protestant Reformation's insistence on the vernacular. Protestants would demand vernacular Bibles, but for Tridentine Catholics, not even vernacular preaching mattered as much as safeguarding the confidentiality of sacramental confession: if a priest heard a penitent's confession through an interpreter, many felt that it made a mockery of the sacrament. As missionaries developed their vernacular work, they tended to privilege certain languages in order to simplify their task, choosing for instance in New Spain the former official lingua franca of Náhuatl. Sometimes they imported into these languages some Latin theological terms, such as the Latin *anima* for soul, to avoid further conscious or unconscious local syncretism with pre-Christian concepts – there were just too many possible conceptions of 'soul' in Náhuatl to risk using any native words. Nevertheless, priests recognized that too much borrowing like this might cause pastoral problems, so one early-seventeenth-century guide for priest-confessors suggested that they talk to their penitents about Hell using a choice of Náhuatl words: *Mictlan* (Place of the Dead), or more picturesquely *Atlecalocan* (Place without a Chimney) or *Apochquia-huayocan* (Place without a Smoke Vent).[22]

Above all, missionaries realized that after the traumas of the conquest and epidemics, they must show that there was joy and celebration in the new religion. Frequently they turned their catechisms into song, just as the Jesuit Francis Xavier in India turned the creed into poetry for recital, and out of these initiatives sprang a vibrant indigenous tradition of music in church; many clergy also encouraged the Indios to dance, even inside the church buildings.[23] In the multitude of new churches, the extrovert art and architecture of the developed Counter-Reformation gleefully fused with native artistic traditions to create some of the most sumptuous monuments of the Catholic world (see Plate 60). Catholic festival days were soon assimilated as community celebrations. In Peru, where the pre-Conquest aristocracy survived, Inka nobles might send their daughters to convent school to receive a good Spanish education from Creole nuns, but then on Corpus Christi day or the like, the nobles joined the eucharistic procession proudly wearing Andean costume and insignia, to emphasize their continuing privileged position within indigenous society.[24] The long-term success of Spanish evangelism in the Americas was to make the Catholic Church both essential in native culture and a tie binding the indigenous peoples to the cultures of southern Europe. Beyond the sacramental life of the Church, a great deal of this activity was sustained by catechists, native or mixed-race laymen without any right to preside over sacraments, but devoted to repeating in their own communities what they had learned of the faith from clergy, interpreting, visiting, leading prayer. This was something new: there was little known precedent for the importance of catechists in the medieval European Church, even in its early medieval missions.

In Mexico, the resulting vernacular culture is symbolized by the centrality to national identity of the Virgin of Guadalupe. This apparition of Our Lady is supposed to have been experienced by an Aztec lay convert with the Spanish name Juan Diego. As Diego was affirming his experience to his bishop, her image became miraculously apparent in the cloak he was wearing; the cloak and its painted image remain an object of veneration at the shrine of Guadalupe Hidalgo, now engulfed by the vast sprawl of Mexico City, but a quiet hillside in the country when these events are said to have taken place in 1531. The Guadalupe tradition in written form cannot be traced earlier than the work of Fr Miguel Sánchez in 1648; that hardly matters to the impact of Our Lady's appearance. It perfectly united old and new Latin American cultures in affirmation of divine motherhood – the very place name Guadalupe comes from Arabic Spain and a Marian shrine there, yet it was to a native that the sign of divine favour had been given, and the name sounds conveniently like the Náhuatl attribute of a goddess, *Cuatlaxopeuh* – she who trod the serpent underfoot. A recent study of the 'miracle' highlights the narrative achievement of the Creole priest Sánchez, who drew on both Augustine of Hippo and John of Damascus in meditating on the Guadalupe miracle. It is an extraordinary tribute to Augustine, the source of Luther's and Calvin's Reformations, that he should also fire the imagination of this Mexican priest.[25]

COUNTER-REFORMATION IN ASIA: EMPIRES UNCONQUERED

Whereas in Iberian America, Christianity could rely on official backing from colonial governments (subject to the myriad other concerns of colonial administrators), this was not so in Asia or Africa; nor did Europeans have disease on their side to weaken the great Asian empires they encountered, thanks to the centuries of continuous contact between Asia and Europe. Here the Portuguese were the main European Catholic power, and even after Philip II of Spain gained the Portuguese throne in 1580, Portuguese weakness meant that there was little or no military backing for Christianity, particularly against far stronger native empires in India and China. Only in the small enclaves where the Portuguese authorities were able to exercise real control, such as their Indian fortress headquarters at Goa, could they emulate the Spaniards' creation of a monochrome Christian culture – if monochrome is the right word for the heady Counter-Reformation Baroque of the colonial churches of Goa, which include the largest Catholic cathedral so far built in Asia. Portuguese religious rhetoric tended to ignore political realities, and Portuguese Church authorities often made things more difficult for non-Portuguese European missionaries by insisting on the paramountcy of their own culture and ecclesiastical jurisdiction as granted in the *Padroado*: the Archbishop of Goa became primate of all Catholic churches around the Pacific Ocean.

So once outside these uncomfortable pockets of European rule, Catholicism in Asia had to make its way on its merits, often where earlier Eastern Christian missions had already known success followed by gradual decline and contraction (see Chapter 8). Only in the Philippine Islands, a Spanish colony named after King Philip II, did Christianity eventually secure a substantial foothold among a large population in Asia – but the reason for this exception proved the rule. There, as in America, the Augustinian friars leading the Church's mission could rely on backing from colonial authorities with substantial military force. In fact, in a link-up at first sight bizarre, but highlighting the Philippine analogy with Spanish American experience, the bishopric of Manila in the Philippines was first ranked as part of the archdiocese in New Spain, thousands of miles across the Pacific, since most links with the home government in Madrid were via America.

Presenting the Christian message without military backing posed considerable problems for a missionary priest. Nearly always a Jesuit or a friar, he faced Asian peoples with age-old and subtle cultures, full of self-confidence and likely to be profoundly sceptical that Westerners could teach them anything of value. Muslim rulers and Hindu elites in India could contemplate with sarcastic interest the normally dire relations between the Christian newcomers and the ancient Dyophysite 'Mar Thoma' Church in India which derived from Syria. The Portuguese contempt for Christians they regarded as schismatics or heretics, and the schisms and disputes which Portuguese interference provoked in these Churches, were not impressive demonstrations of Christian brotherly love, as Catholic Christians burned venerable Christian libraries and occasionally people too for Dyophysite heresy. Catholic clergy did not at first appreciate a perennial obstacle in India: Hindu converts to Christianity automatically lost caste. It was not surprising that the missionaries' main success was with peoples lowest in the caste system (though it must also be said that the Mar Thoma Christians, who had over the centuries established themselves with higher-caste status, showed no signs of ever having reached out to such people).

One story of Christian success should be better known, because it is particularly significant for the future success of Christian mission in Asia and Africa. João de Cruz was a Hindu merchant who converted to Christianity and acquired his new Portuguese name in Lisbon in 1513. His efforts to restore his shaky finances led him to trade on the Fisher Coast of south India, where he was touched by the misfortunes of the pearl fishers (Paravas or Bharathas), once a privileged caste but now poverty-stricken and facing extermination by local rulers and their Arab merchant allies after they had rebelled. He advised the Paravas that their one hope of deliverance was to seek Portuguese protection – that would necessarily mean adopting Christianity. Twenty thousand Paravas are said to have been baptized as a result.[26] Because the Paravas customarily moved over wide areas with the changing seasons, they spread their enthusiasm for their new faith across the Gulf of Mannar to Ceylon (Sri Lanka). Even when the Protestant Dutch captured Ceylon in 1658 and, with their own religious prejudices from Reformation Europe, systematically repressed Catholic practice where they exercised power, the local Catholicism persisted in secret. By the mid-eighteenth century the Dutch were baffled and furious to find that there were more Catholics than members of the Dutch Reformed Church in Ceylon, despite all its official favour, and when Dutch rule ended, the Reformed Church there collapsed, unlike Catholicism.[27] The initiative by an insider to the subcontinent showed how an indigenous foundation might survive when Christian missions begun and run by Europeans might rise and fall in step with the ability of Europeans to sustain them.

The Jesuits began building up their strength after Ignatius Loyola's early companion in the Society Francis Xavier embarked on a prodigious decade of Asian mission in 1542. Now a new attitude emerged among the Jesuits, very different from Iberian missions in the Americas: other world faiths might have something of value and reflect God's purpose, and it was worth making an effort to understand Indian culture, language and literature. This was a far cry from Jesuit attitudes to Protestantism back in Europe: heresy was a greater danger than other faiths. This proposition was also attested by the fact that that same Francis Xavier was also responsible for recommending the introduction of the Portuguese royal Inquisition to Goa, with an eye on Mar Thoma Christians, though one of its first victims, in classic Iberian fashion, was a Jewish 'New Christian' from Portugal.[28]

The boldest experiment in India was made by an Italian Jesuit, Robert de Nobili (1577–1656). He took the unprecedented step of living in southern India as if he were a high-caste Indian, adopting dress appropriate to an Indian holy man. Becoming fluent in the appropriate languages, he also took particular care to point out to those to whom he preached that he was not a *Parangi* (a Portuguese). Higher-caste Hindus still tended to ignore him, but his strategy did produce results in establishing his guru status among lower-caste people. The Portuguese authorities fiercely opposed de Nobili, but finally lost their case against him in Rome in 1623; his reports back to Europe in the course of these disputes are among the earliest careful western European accounts of Hinduism and Buddhism. Whatever success the Church had in the Tamil country of south India was entirely thanks to Nobili and his Italian successors, but their work suffered during the eighteenth century both from severe Muslim persecution and, as in South America, from the general suppression of the Society of Jesus.[29]

Nobili was actually adopting a precedent of his Society from another vast mission field, China. Here, in the face of one of the world's most powerful empires, Portugal had even less influence than in India.[30] The Chinese were not especially interested in large-scale contacts with foreign countries, not even for trade, and with their military might they were certainly not prepared to let the Portuguese in their small trading enclave at Macau adopt the ruthless proselytizing methods of Goa. The Jesuits quickly decided that missionaries must adapt themselves to Chinese customs. This involved much rapid self-education. Their first great missionary, the Italian Matteo Ricci, on his arrival in 1582, adopted the dress of a Buddhist monk (*bonze*), without realizing that *bonzes* were despised by the people who mattered.[31] When his mistake was pointed out, he and his fellow Jesuits began dressing as Confucian scholars, complete with long beards (see Plate 46); they were determined to show that their learning was worthy of respect in a culture with a deep reverence for scholarship (an ethos of which naturally they greatly approved). In this they had the advantage of the network of colleges and educational experience built up back in Europe in the previous decades. One Portuguese member of the Society in 1647 used a metaphor for a Jesuit college drawn from a more militant mission field: it was 'a Trojan horse filled with soldiers from heaven, which every year produces *conquistadors* of souls'. He also commented whimsically that the Jesuits' long training was reminiscent of the naturalist Pliny's assertion that baby elephants were carried in their mother's womb for two years. The purpose of such long gestation both for elephants and for Jesuits was that they would be prepared for battle and strike fear into other creatures.[32] The Chinese upper class was indeed impressed by the Jesuits' knowledge of mathematics, astronomy and geography, and the Society gained an honoured place at the emperor's court through its specialist use of these skills, even taking charge of reforming the imperial calendar – but not gaining many converts.

The Jesuit emphasis on their honoured place at Court was always something of a diversion from the real reasons for the growth of adherents, who were very different in their social profile from the exalted figures around the emperor. At the peak of the Chinese mission's success at the end of the seventeenth century, it was serving perhaps around a quarter of a million people – an extraordinary achievement, even though still, as in India, a tiny proportion of the whole population.[33] Yet at that time there were only seventy-five priests to serve this number, labouring under enormous difficulties with language: how, for instance, to solve that problem already encountered in America, to hear confessions in such circumstances? What the Jesuits did very effectively in this situation was to inspire a local leadership which was not clerical, both catechists in the classic American mould and a particular Chinese phenomenon (perhaps inspired by the Ursulines), 'Chinese virgins': laywomen conse-crated to singleness but still living with their families, teaching women and children. This preserved the mission into the nineteenth century despite worsening clerical shortages, which became acute when the emperor expelled foreign clergy in 1724. If the trend in Counter-Reformation Europe was for the clergy to take more control of the lives of the laity, circumstances in China consistently promoted lay activism – and the same was to prove true of Chinese Catholicism's daughter-mission to Korea in the eighteenth century (see pp. 899–902).[34]

As elsewhere in Asia and Africa, Portuguese suspicion of non-Portuguese clergy complicated the spread of Catholicism in China, and more serious problems emerged. When Dominicans and Franciscans arrived in China from the Philippines in the 1630s, they launched bitter attacks on their Jesuit rivals, and raised major matters of missionary policy. The friars, with a background in America assuming total confron-tation with previous religions, violently disagreed with the Jesuits in their attitude to the Chinese way of life, particularly traditional rites in honour of Confucius and the family; they even publicly asserted that deceased emperors were burning in Hell. The French, including many French Jesuits of 'Jansenist' sympathies (see pp. 797–9), weighed in against the policy of flexibility when they became a significant presence in the 1690s. Complaints about the 'Chinese rites' were taken as far as Rome itself, and after a long struggle successive popes condemned the rites in 1704 and 1715. This was a deeply significant setback for Western Christianity's first major effort to understand and accommodate itself to another culture, and it was not surprising that the Yongzheng Emperor reacted so angrily in 1724.[35]

Christian work in Japan was the most extreme story, as the most spectacular success of any mission launched from Portuguese bases in Asia or Africa ended in almost total destruction.[36] Francis Xavier and his fellow Jesuits arrived as early as 1549, only seven years after the first Portuguese visit to Japan, and Jesuits continued to dominate the Japanese mission. They quickly achieved results: by the end of the century there were perhaps as many as 300,000 Christian converts in Japan, aided by a determined and imaginative effort to meet Japan on its own terms. From the beginning, the Jesuits took Japanese culture seriously: 'these Japanese are more ready to be implanted with our holy faith than all the nations of the world,' Xavier affirmed, and he recommended bringing members of the Society from the Low Countries and Germany since they were used to a cold climate and would work more efficiently in it.[37]

The Italian Jesuit Alessandro Valignano envisaged the formation of a native clergy, and a Portuguese, Gaspar Coelho, was active in recruiting some seventy novices by 1590, concentrating especially on the sons of noblemen and samurai who would command respect in Japanese society (his colleagues felt more cautious and restrained his initiative).[38]

In counterpoint to this success was a fatal entanglement with politics, both Portuguese trading policy and the internal concerns of Japan. The Portuguese trade was led by their so-called 'Great Ship' trading in bullion and luxury goods annually; the Jesuits not only invested in this to support what had proved to be an extremely expensive mission, but also encouraged the ship to travel to as many Japanese ports as possible to excite interest in Christianity. The missionaries and merchants were lucky enough to arrive at a time when Japan was split between rival feudal lords. Many lords saw Christianity as a useful way of attracting Portuguese trade and also of furthering their own political aims, particularly the powerful Tokugawa family, who initially encouraged the missionaries. By 1600 the Tokugawa had eliminated all their rivals in politics, and now saw Christianity not as a convenience but as a nuisance, even a threat. They had some justification: the Philippines fell under Spanish royal control with such comparative ease because missionary activity by Augustinian friars had preceded the arrival of King Philip's ships and soldiers.

Matters were made worse when Franciscan friars arrived in Japan to establish a missionary presence in 1593. Anticipating the controversies with Jesuits that were to arise in the Chinese Empire, they adopted an aggressively negative attitude towards Japanese culture, which led to a number of them suffering death by crucifixion. In the early seventeenth century the Tokugawa expelled Europeans from Japan except for one rigorously policed trading post.[39] They then launched one of the most savage persecutions in Christian history, and their repression of Japanese Christians was not without some military assistance from the Protestant Dutch, who were doing their best to wreck Portuguese power in eastern Asia, and had few regrets about campaigns against popish Jesuits and friars. The Church in Japan, despite the heroism of its native faithful, was reduced to a tiny and half-instructed remnant. It struggled to maintain even a secret existence for more than two centuries until Europeans used military force to secure free access to the country after the 1850s, and rediscovered it with astonishment. They had then to abolish the official imposition of 'Christ-stepping', a test of rejection of Christianity in which those suspected of Christian allegiance were forced to walk on pictures of Christ or the Virgin. The Japanese persecution is a standing argument against the old idea that the blood of the martyrs is the seed of the Church.[40]

COUNTER-REFORMATION IN AFRICA: THE BLIGHT OF THE SLAVE TRADE

Christian mission in Africa was likewise based on Portuguese trading posts and contacts with local powers, and, as in Japan, it achieved some success among local elites. There were even efforts to create an indigenous clergy, spurred by a chronic shortage of clerical manpower: the climate and disease ecology proved lethal to most European missionary clergy, in an exact reversal of the American situation. An early attempt at what might now be called indigenization occurred in one of the first forts which the Portuguese built on the West African coast, Fort St George of Elmina, in what is now Ghana. A wooden statue of St Francis was so affected by the humid heat that his face and hands turned black: the Governor announced a miracle, in which the saint had proclaimed himself patron of the local population by identifying with them.[41]

Yet Francis's favour could not counterweigh the disastrous flaw in European Christian mission in Africa, its association with the Portuguese slave trade. Millions were rounded up in the African interior by local rulers and shipped out through the Portuguese forts across the Atlantic to sustain the economy of American plantations; they introduced a third element to the racial kaleidoscope of the Iberian American empires. Portuguese Brazil accounted for the largest number – perhaps 3.5 million people over three centuries – but from the late sixteenth century the Portuguese were (unwillingly) sharing this trade with the English and Dutch, and hundreds of thousands of slaves were taken to new plantations in Protestant colonies in North America.[42] The Spaniards were not actively involved in the shipping trade, but their plantation colonies could not have survived without it.

Depressingly, as we have noted in discussing the polemic of Bartolomé de las Casas (see p. 692), the expedient of importing African slaves was in part meant to protect the native American population from exploitation. Not many clergy comprehended the moral disaster. One Franciscan based in the University of Mexico City, Bartolomé de

Albornoz, in a book on contract law published in 1571, had the clear-sightedness to condemn the common argument that Africans were being saved from pagan darkness by their removal to America, remarking sarcastically, 'I do not believe that it can be demonstrated that according to the law of Christ the liberty of the soul can be purchased by the servitude of the body.'[43] His words found few echoes: such missionary concern as there was was mostly limited to souls. In early-seventeenth-century Cartagena in what is now Colombia, one of only two entry points for slaves in the Spanish dominions, two maverick Jesuits, Alonso de Sandoval and Pedro Claver, spent years amid terrible conditions ministering to and baptizing those West African slaves who had managed to survive the Atlantic crossing and were newly arrived in the docks. A telling detail of the Jesuits' ministry was to make sure that their baptismal ceremony included plenty of cool drinkable water; the desperate and grateful slave would be more receptive to the Christian message.

In its context, this pastoral work was bravely countercultural, arousing real disapproval among the settler population, but the Jesuits' efforts to instil first a sense of sin (particularly sexual sin) and then repentance in their wretched penitents now seem oddly placed amid one of the greatest communal sins perpetrated by Western Christian culture.[44] Attempts to adjust the system and improve on their work by transferring baptism across the Atlantic do not impress. The city of Loanda in what is now Angola was the main departure point for enslaved people from the south-west, and the clergy's main role in the city became to baptize them before departure; right up to the 1870s, forty years after the British had declared slavery abolished in their dominions and the Portuguese had officially followed suit, the Portuguese Bishop of Loanda was accustomed to being enthroned in a marble chair at the dockside, presiding over the rite before captives were dispatched across the Atlantic.[45] It was hardly surprising that popular mission was hampered in Africa or that the native population despised Christianity.

The most promising initiative for Catholic Christianity came under local patronage rather than at the command of Portuguese guns: in the Central African Atlantic kingdom of Kongo. Here the ruler Mvemba Nzinga became a fervent Christian and adopted the Portuguese title of Afonso I. He welcomed Iberian priests, saw to it that one of his sons was consecrated in Portugal in 1518 as a bishop, opened schools to teach the Portuguese language, and created a stately inland cathedral city, São Salvador, as his capital; he has been called 'one of the greatest lay Christians in African Church history'.[46] His successors continued officially Catholic into the eighteenth century, and together with their nobility they created a genuinely indigenous Church (see Plate 16). Its government was always problematic. The kings of Kongo were constantly at odds with the Portuguese, who tried to impose *Padroado* rights in appointing bishops: this inhibited the arrival of non-Portuguese European clergy, severely limited the creation of a native clergy, and drew attention to official Christianity's entanglement with the slave trade. The Italian Capuchin Franciscan missionaries whom the Kongo monarchy welcomed in during the seventeenth century (at a moment when the Portuguese were distracted by war with the Dutch) did their best in protest; in 1686 they secured from the Roman Inquisition an unprecedented general condemnation of the slave trade, long predating any such Protestant official action or statement.[47]

Yet despite this striking symbolic pronouncement, the papacy continued to employ slaves in its Mediterranean galleys up to the French Revolution, some of them market-purchased. While Capuchin anger was ignored, the slave trade continued to subvert Central African society. When the Kongo descended into political chaos in the seventeenth century, the official structures of the Catholic Church were also crippled.[48] As in Iberian America and China, what Church life survived continued to depend on local catechists, who with their knowledge of Portuguese could communicate with such European clergy as remained, but who could also perpetuate what they knew of Christian belief and practice to their own people, albeit necessarily in a non-sacramental form. This pattern was to flourish once more in nineteenth- and twentieth-century Africa, and it sustained what remained of Africa's first indigenous Catholicism, in a variety of creative popular syntheses of Christianity with local religions. Two successive prophetesses arose around 1700, and significantly a major element in their visions was the demand from Heaven that the ruined capital São Salvador should be rebuilt. The second of them, Dona Beatriz Kimpa Vita, who had taken on herself the character of the Capuchins' much-loved saint Antony of Padua, was burned at the stake in 1706 by one of the kings of the now-fragmented Kongo, but she had indicated a future strength in African Christianity: independent Churches which would build what they wanted out of European Christian teaching (see pp. 887–8).[49]

Ethiopia's ancient Miaphysite Christian culture proved not to be headed by Prester John, Europe's hoped-for ally against Islam. Events indeed entirely reversed expectations, for in the 1540s a Portuguese expeditionary force at very great cost in lives helped the Ethiopian kingdom defeat an Islamic holy war under the charismatic Muslim emir Ahmed Granj, which had nearly annihilated both it and its Church. Latin Christianity could therefore initially count on Ethiopian goodwill; indeed, one of the first authentic African voices to be heard in Western literature is that of an Ethiopian ambassador to Portugal, whose account of his homeland's Church was printed in 1540 within a widely popular Latin description of Ethiopia by a Portuguese, Damião de Goís.[50] Yet the Jesuits thereafter dissipated the advantage, despite zestful and heroic wanderings which may have led them to be the first Europeans to see the source of the Blue Nile, a century and a half before the Scotsman James Bruce.[51]

Contemporary Catholic battles with Protestants created a blind spot in the missionaries. Just as with the Dyophysite Christians of India, the Society was much less prepared to make allowances for local custom in fellow Christians than it was for other world faiths such as Hinduism, Shintoism or Confucianism. Ethiopian public immersion baptisms in which both priest and candidates were entirely naked were something of a shock. There was also a fatal reminiscence of Iberia's cultural wars: Jesuits violently criticized the Ethiopian Orthodox Church for what they saw as Judaizing deviations – celebration of the Sabbath, male circumcision and avoidance of pork. Eventually the Ethiopians were infuriated into retaliation: brutal expulsion of the Jesuits, including some executions, followed in the 1630s, together with an emphatic reassertion (and perhaps a little invention) of authentic Ethiopian custom and theology. The missionaries left behind them some evocatively Mediterranean church ruins and a paradoxically large amount of new iconographic themes in Ethiopian art: Christ with his crown of thorns, European-style compositions of the Virgin and Child, and even motifs deriving from engravings by Albrecht Dürer. The Ethiopians clearly enjoyed the Jesuits' pictures more than their theological instruction.[52]

So Africans made their choices when confronted with Western Christianity. They still made choices when choice had apparently been taken away from them, in the vast diaspora throughout the Spanish and Portuguese (and latterly French) plantation cultures in America. They brought to America a mass of memories of religious belief and practice. Particularly in the sixteenth and seventeenth centuries, slave masters made an effort to split up groups related to each other, but that became less easy in the eighteenth and nineteenth centuries, as restrictions began to bear down on the slave trade and more coherent groups survived from particular areas of Africa in a new setting. Given endemic warfare in Benin and Nigeria, which sent great numbers of captives to the slave markets of the coast, West African religions dominated. So much of it was difficult to sustain, tied as it was to place and group identity, both now lost. So ancestor cults were replaced, and familiar deities given new honour by drawing on the Catholicism which surrounded the people imported to the colonial world. The Catholic Church allowed slaves confraternities and, as everywhere else in Catholic societies, confraternities proved to have a life which it was not necessarily easy for officialdom to control. Out of this subculture of Catholicism constructively melded in syncretist fashion with memories of other spiritualities came a variety of new religion with various identities: among much overlap were the *Vodou* (voodoo) of French Haiti, the *Candomblé* of Portuguese Brazil, the *Santería* of Spanish Cuba. In turn the syntheses in America fertilized and reinvigorated African religion back in Africa: part of a continuous traffic across the Atlantic.[53]

That name *Santería* is itself instructive because, as with so many other Christian labels, it began as an insult or term of condescension – an English coinage equivalent to this Spanish word might well be 'saintery' – but it is now a label of pride for a form of religion constructed, like so much Iberian-African syncretism, with practical good sense. *Santería* is probably the variety of these syncretist religions closest to Catholicism, so that in Cuban Catholicism it is difficult to separate much Catholic practice in the parish churches from *Santería*, and it is really impossible to put statistics on the number of its practitioners, so all-pervasive is its influence. The great advantage of the panoply of saints which the enslaved might encounter in their confraternities was that the saints could stand in for the hierarchy of divinities who in West Africa were offered devotion in the place of the supreme creator god Olurun (who was himself too powerful to be concerned with the affairs of feeble humans). Below the creator god were also *orishas*, subordinate divinities in African religion connected with the whole range of human activities. Every person born might have a connection to an *orisha*, and it was also perfectly acceptable in Catholic practice for everyone to choose a personal patron saint; it was only natural to look for compatible attributes between sacred figures from the two worlds. The Virgin Mary could hardly be ignored in Catholicism and in the interiors of churches, and it was not a problem to identify her omnipresent image with the Taino goddess Atabey or the Yoruba *orishas* Oshun and Yemaya. In Cuba, Mary has never had any competitor as the national patron saint.[54]

Without such doubling, it would be difficult to account for the popularity of St Barbara among the altars and paintings of Cuban churches. Traditionally, Barbara had a particular concern for thunder, and latterly for gunpowder. She could thus stand in for the *orisha* Shangô; he duplicated her powers over thunder, and despite being male and a notorious womanizer, he had conveniently once escaped from the wrath of his cuckolded brother Ogun disguised as Ogun's wife Oya (one can imagine the humour of the situation appealing to devotees as they lit their candles under the approving eyes of some missionary priest). In other settings, less riskily, Barbara could be identified directly with Oya.[55] Equally surprising is to find St Patrick so prominent in many Vodou shrines (see Plate 61), until one remembers that he too had been a slave who had twice crossed the sea, the second time to freedom, and that he had particular power over snakes, like the *loa* (Haitian equivalent of *orisha*) Dambala Wèdo. And so the evangelist and patron saint of Ireland, that land so ruined and distorted by English colonial rule, found new hospitality among other peoples whose lives had been stolen by colonial regimes.[56] After such fertile and sophisticated amalgamations of symbolism, it is not surprising to find the Fon/Yoruba deity Ogou, a warrior with a strong sense of justice, joining identities with the warrior St James of Compostela (complete with Moorish corpses), and both of them in Haiti absorbing the identities of the island's heroes of liberation such as Jean-Jacques Dessalines, Toussaint L'Ouverture or Henri Christophe. When it was forbidden to speak of Dessalines in nineteenth-century Haiti, it was always possible triumphantly to process around the town with an image of the original St-Jacques.[57]

Again and again, missionary Jesuits and friars proved their heroic commitment to spreading their Christian message throughout the world. The prolonged sufferings and ghastly deaths of Jesuit missionaries at the hands of hostile First Nations on the borders of the French colonies in Canada in the early seventeenth century rank high in the history of Christian suffering. Even the hazards of travel were a martyrdom in themselves: of 376 Jesuits who set out for China between 1581 and 1712, 127 died at sea.[58] The perpetual trouble everywhere was European reluctance to accept on equal terms the peoples whom they encountered, even when Europeans distinguished between what they saw as varied levels of culture. Such attitudes meant that the missionaries were always loath to ordain native priests on a large scale or with equal authority to themselves. In Kongo, many clergy (generally from elite backgrounds) were so infuriated at being patronized or marginalized by European colleagues that they became a major force in articulating local hatred of the Portuguese. As in America, that old problem of compulsory clerical celibacy gnawed away at the credibility of the Church.

In step with increasing weakness in the Spanish and Portuguese empires, it was not surprising that when a Church infrastructure which remained overwhelmingly European fell into decay in any area of the world Christianity itself began to fade. It had been a remarkable achievement for comparatively ill-endowed Iberian kingdoms to put together world empires, but they faced mounting problems and increasing interference from other European powers, first the Protestant United Provinces of the Netherlands, and later Britain and France. The Catholic French to some extent filled the gap as the settlement of the Edict of Nantes began to enable the kingdom to recover its leading place in European life; during the seventeenth century, France assumed the role of patron of Christianity in the Ottoman Empire, and sponsored mission in the far north of America. In 1658, two French missionary bishops created a society of secular priests, the Missions Etrangères de Paris, with a brief to work in the Far East, in Vietnam and later, where it was allowed, in the Chinese Empire – at first, as we have seen, being as much sources of disruption there as of growth (see p. 707). But as the power of Louis XIV met reverses at the hands of Protestant armies in Europe (see pp. 735–6), the initiative shifted from the Catholic south to Protestant central Europe and the British Isles. The final blow to nearly three centuries of Catholic world mission came in 1773 when the Catholic powers in concert forced the Pope to suppress the whole organization of the Society of Jesus; that was followed by the trauma of the French Revolution. It was now the turn of Protestant Churches to find a call to world mission.

20

Protestant Awakenings
(1600–1800)

PROTESTANTS AND AMERICAN
COLONIZATION

When the Western Church divided after 1517, Protestants might have envied Spanish Atlantic conquests, but they had too many preoccupations to follow friars and Jesuits into overseas mission. They were fighting for their existence against Catholics, and bickering among themselves in their efforts to establish what Protestantism actually was. When they did found colonies in the seventeenth century, it was mainly for their own religious self-expression, which in English North America was especially varied. The principal thrust of Protestant missionary work lagged behind the urge of Protestant states to colonize and did not appear until the eighteenth century. What beginnings of colonization there were in the sixteenth century all ended in failure. The English and Americans remember and mourn abortive efforts in what later became Virginia, sponsored by Queen Elizabeth's Protestant courtier Walter Raleigh in the 1580s, but they tend to forget that it was actually France that pioneered efforts at settlement to rival Spain and Portugal.

In 1555, the French set up a fortress near what is now Rio de Janeiro in Brazil, with the clear intention of supplanting the Iberians in a huge area of South America. Five years later, just as they began withdrawing from the continent as part of their peace deal with the Habsburgs at Cateau-Cambrésis (see p. 676), they rashly tried a similar project in Florida, which lasted another five years before the Spaniards eliminated it and massacred its garrison. In both cases, Protestants were involved, although their role was exaggerated by Huguenot historians after the event, seeking out Protestant sufferings to add to their quota of persecutions back home. It was understandable that Protestants who found their position at home problematic should become involved in these new ventures, but the increasing fragility of French royal power from the 1560s ended any further French initiatives in America. Renewed French activity had to wait for the reconciliation achieved by Henri IV in 1598, and once more, although Huguenots became involved in the first successful American settlements in 1604, safely far to the north of New Spain, Louis XIII and his ministers quickly eliminated their influence. New France, the basis of the future Quebec and Canada, became much more monochrome in its Catholic religion than the home country – the opposite story to the English colonies, which took their shaky beginnings three years later.[1]

Like the French, the English had long fished in Atlantic waters and visited North American shores. Southern Europeans found these less enticing, particularly since the cold increased as the coastline stretched further north, and it was thus natural for northerners to take more interest in them. The English were to some extent distracted from America by their own more accessible Atlantic New World in Ireland: here they could plant true religion and steal land from people whom they were often inclined to regard in much the same light as the Spaniards did the native peoples of America. Both in Ireland and in America, the first English initiatives certainly employed Protestant rhetoric, presenting English colonists as fighting against miscellaneous forces of Antichrist, either papists or satanic non-Christian religions, but theirs was a rather political Protestantism. One intriguing possible way forward involved the Muslim ruler of Morocco, Ahmad al-Mansur, who in 1603 proposed to his ally Queen Elizabeth of England a follow-up to the successful Anglo-Moroccan raid on Cadiz in 1596. They should jointly attack the Spaniards in their American colonies and set up their own, in which, given the hot climate, Moroccans would be more suitable settlers than the English. Although nothing came of the scheme, it is one reminder among many that Protestants might hate idolatrous Spanish Catholics more than they did iconophobic Muslims. It also suggests an interesting alternative history for the United States of America.[2]

The first English efforts across the Atlantic were as short-lived as the French, but England had enough political stability and will to try again. After much loss of life and capital, an English settlement established a precarious but continuous existence from 1607, without Islamic help; it borrowed the name Virginia (after the lately deceased 'Virgin Queen' Elizabeth) from the earlier unsuccessful efforts at colonization. The Virginian settlers brought a clergyman with them and quickly made public provision for a parish ministry. So this was an official Church which identified itself with the established Church back home, although it continued more along the lines of the undemonstratively Protestant Church of James I than the growing sacramentalism promoted by William Laud (see pp. 647–51). Even after Charles I's execution in 1649, the colony stayed fiercely loyal to Cranmer's Prayer Book and episcopally ordained clergy, which made its relations with Oliver Cromwell's regimes difficult – it was one of two places in the world, the other being the rather similar colony on the Caribbean island of Barbados, where Anglicanism survived through the 1650s as an established Church.[3] Yet after 1660, the Virginian colonists' theoretical love of bishops was not ardent enough to lend much support to proposals to establish a bishop on their side of the Atlantic, let alone any system of English-style church courts. They made sure that their parishes were run by powerful 'vestries' of laypeople rather than clergymen.

Virginian Anglicanism was thus made safe for gentry who appreciated a decent and edifying but not overdramatic performance of the Prayer Book, and the colony continued much more reminiscent of the hierarchical countryside of Old England than any of the other more northern English ventures. These northern colonies saw the early Stuart Church of England as too flawed to be truly God's Church. America was often not the first choice of these settlers when they looked for somewhere to build a purer community. Some migrated to the Protestant United Provinces of the Netherlands, as discontented English godly folk had done since the middle of Elizabeth's reign, but however godly the atmosphere in this properly reformed Church setting, there was little land to spare, and rather too many Dutch people. Ireland offered better possibilities, but by the late 1620s Charles I had an unfriendly eye on potentially subversive settlers from England; when in 1632 his aggressive Lord Deputy, the Earl of Strafford, arrived to lead the government in Dublin, he even made major concessions to Irish Roman Catholics. So the best alternative was in the new lands of America.

The godly ventured far to the north of Virginia, in an area of forests and deep sea inlets soon named New England. The first colony in this northern region, Plymouth in what later became part of Massachusetts, was founded in 1620, by separatists who made no bones about their wish to isolate themselves completely from corrupt English religion. This group, since the nineteenth century commonly given the celebratory title the 'Pilgrim Fathers', had first migrated as a single congregation to the Netherlands, but now sought a less restricting place, to become a 'civill body politick, for our better ordering & preservation'.[4] For all its

35. The organ (1735–8) in the medieval Grote Kerk of St Bavo, Haarlem, Netherlands, is a magnificent symbol of the Dutch governing elite's fine disregard for their Reformed ministers' suspicion of pipe organs. Handel, Mozart and Mendelssohn were among the great musicians who made the pilgrimage to play this instrument. Organ music has dominated the Western Christian musical tradition from the medieval period.

36. The autograph MS of the brooding string and woodwind opening of the *St John Passion* (1724) by Johann Sebastian Bach (1685–1750), one of the first works he wrote for his often unappreciative Lutheran congregation at the wealthy church of St Thomas, Leipzig.

37. George Whitefield (1714–60) was a histrionic genius, whose extreme strabismus may only have enhanced his electrifying sermons. His Evangelical open-air preaching took him across the Atlantic, and he died in Massachusetts, but John Collett (c. 1725–80) portrays him here addressing an emotional crowd outside London, dressed, as was his custom and right, in the gown and preaching bands of a Church of England clergyman.

38. In John Wesley's 'New Room' in the Horsefair, Bristol, England (1739), Methodism's earliest purpose-built chapel, we see the building from the preacher's point of view; Wesley occupied this pulpit countless times, appearing in it in gown and bands directly down from the preachers' lodgings built above the chapel.

39. In an early nineteenth-century engraving, the newly discovered early Christian martyr Saint Napoleon expires in a remarkably similar pose to George Washington, and with an equally remarkable resemblance to the first Emperor of the French. Nothing could symbolize better the peculiar rapprochement with traditional Catholicism attempted by Napoleon after the devastation of the Revolution and cemented in the Concordat of 1801.

40. George Washington lies on his deathbed surrounded by a panoply of Christian symbolism ready to guarantee his place in heaven; a posthumous remoulding of him from the early nineteenth century. Washington's personal beliefs were barely Christian, but this aspect of the national hero would not do for a Republic so profoundly affected by Evangelical Awakenings.

41. Open-air baptism in a late nineteenth-century African-American congregation at Work House Pond, Fayette County, Kentucky. Black Americans made Evangelical Protestantism their own.

SUBJECTS:

i.) GEOLOGY, (ii.) PHYSICAL GEOGRAPHY, (iii.) ETHNOLOGY
(iv.) PHILOLOGY, (v.) THE PLURALITY of WORLDS;
The Atmosphere, Water, Light, Heat, Sound, &c.

THEOLOGY IN SCIENCE;

OR,

THE TESTIMONY OF SCIENCE

TO THE

WISDOM AND GOODNESS OF GOD.

(A BOOK ESPECIALLY SUITABLE FOR SUNDAYS BOTH IN SCHOOLS
AND PRIVATE FAMILIES.)

BY

THE REV. DR. BREWER,

Trinity Hall, Cambridge;

Author of "Guide to Science," "Evidences of Christianity,"
"History of France, brought down to the present time," &c., &c.

SEVENTH EDITION.

LONDON: JARROLD AND SONS,
3, PATERNOSTER BUILDINGS.

42/43. The Rev. Dr Ebenezer Cobham Brewer (1810–97) was an energetic educator whose little textbook cheerfully reassuring England's schoolchildren that modern science held no threat to Christianity sold in its tens of thousands.

44. The crowds of sick and pilgrims at Our Lady's Fountain in Lourdes, *c.* 1890: a woodcut after a painting by Jose Ramon Garnelo y Alda (1866–1940), one of the most popular Spanish artists of his day.

45. The statue of the adventurously free-thinking Dominican philosopher-friar Giordano Bruno in the Campo dei Fiori in Rome was erected in 1889 on the site where he had been burned for heresy by the Romans in 1600. Intended on the centenary of the French Revolution by its Freemason and anticlerical Liberal sponsors as a provocation to the Roman Catholic Church, it is still a rallying-point for ceremonies celebrating intellectual freedom.

46. Members of the Society of Jesus in its Chinese mission, c. 1900. Like Matteo Ricci, the sixteenth-century Jesuit missionary pioneer in China, they sport long beards, to proclaim their status as scholars alongside the Chinese Mandarin elite.

47. The Lutheran/Reformed cathedral in Berlin, symbol of the nexus between Protestantism and the Second Reich, was rebuilt under patronage from Kaiser Wilhelm II by 1905. The East German government restored the shell wrecked in Second World War bombing against the wishes of the Lutheran Church, using church taxes from the non-Communist West. The DDR feared that demolishing it would destabilize the neighbouring Palace of the People, newly built on the site of the Hohenzollerns' castle.

48. The pulpit in the Martin Luther Memorial Church in Mariendorf, Berlin: a propaganda project of Nationalist Lutherans funded after 1933 by the Third Reich. Symbolizing Adolf Hitler's New World Order, a German soldier, a mother and the church's architect are among those processing behind the Saviour. All swastikas have not surprisingly been removed from the building, but the pulpit survives intact.

. Anglo-Catholics on the march: in the era
ich saw their confidence in their future
its height, one of the most forthright
ampions of the movement, the Anglican
shop of Zanzibar, Frank Weston, is led in
lemn procession to High Mass for the 1920
iglo-Catholic Congress in London. During
proceedings the Congress sent a greetings
egram to the Pope, to the fury of other
iglicans.

50. In the late 1920s Aimee Semple
Macpherson, Pentecostalist pioneer of the
International Church of the Foursquare
Gospel in Los Angeles, gleefully embraces
modern communications in the shape of a
wireless-set, preparatory to taking to the
skies for another evangelistic campaign.

. The Turkish army's near-total destruction of the great Greek city of Smyrna by fire in
ptember 1922, and the expulsion of its Christian population, symbolized the sudden end of
eek culture throughout Asia Minor after three thousand years.

52. A Prince of the Church, Anglican style: Robert Runcie, 102nd Archbishop of Canterbury, umpires the episcopal cricket match between Australia and the Rest of the World, which enlivened the Lambeth Conference of Anglican Bishops, 1988. Subsequent Anglican episcopal contests have been less easy to regulate.

53. Pope John Paul II, first Pope of the modern globalized age, travelled the world to an extent unprecedented among his predecessors. On his visit to Brazil in 1980 he seemed more sympathetic to the cultural situation of indigenous peoples than to the propositions of liberation theologians.

subsequent fame in American mythology, the settlement remained small and poor, for not many wished to join the Pilgrims; they made their brave voyage in the years before the group around William Laud achieved power in England. Notably, for all their intense practice of piety, there was no clergyman among them for the first nine years of Plymouth's existence; the sacrament of the Eucharist was not among their devotional priorities.

The impulse during the 1630s was different: the 'Arminian' innovations of Charles I's regime encouraged many gentry, clergy and ordinary people who had no inclination to separatism to risk the long Atlantic voyage. Up to the 1630s there were fewer English in North America than in North Africa, with its thousands of English slaves, Muslim converts, traders and adventurers. Now that quickly changed. In that decade perhaps as many as twenty thousand emigrated to the New World – rather more than the entire contemporary population of Norwich, early Stuart England's largest city after London.[5] Some colonists established themselves far to the south in islands in the Caribbean, financed by Puritan grandees who saw these as useful bases for harassing the Spanish colonies, in the manner of the great Elizabethan Protestant captains like Francis Drake. Most did not: they followed the earlier separatists to New England and in 1630 founded a new colony of Massachusetts, taking under their wing an ailing earlier venture in that region sponsored by the prominent Puritan minister of Dorchester John White.[6] The New England leadership of the Massachusetts Bay Company was generally less socially prominent than in the Virginian and Caribbean enterprises – ministers and minor gentry – and those in charge now proposed to migrate to the colony themselves rather than stay in England. This was a measure of their commitment to starting England afresh overseas. From the beginning, they were a 'Commonwealth', whose government lay in the hands of the godly adult males who were the investors and colonists.

The first governor chosen by the investors, John Winthrop, was like his Puritan contemporary Oliver Cromwell an East Anglian gentleman of no great local standing who had survived financial and family crisis in the late 1620s. Winthrop's family had a tradition of cosmopolitan Protestantism stretching back to the 1540s. Rejected in his attempt to secure election to Parliament to promote the godly cause, he devoted his talent for leadership, previously confined in the roles of justice of the peace and minor royal official, to a grander enterprise.[7] His associates included a number of university-trained ministers ejected from or not prepared to serve in Laud's Church, and as early as 1636 they founded a university college in Massachusetts to train up new clergy. Significantly, they placed the new college (soon named Harvard after an early benefactor) in a town named Cambridge – back in England over the previous century, Cambridge had been a much firmer centre of Reformation than Oxford. Equally significantly, they took care to furnish Cambridge with a printing press; the third book printed was a new version of the Genevan-style metrical psalms already so familiar in the parish churches of England. They ignored the other component of English worship, Cranmer's Prayer Book, which the Laudians had now tainted irredeemably by their ceremonial adaptations of it.

The rhetoric of this emigration sprang out of Puritan and Reformed themes which had sounded from English pulpits since the 1560s. Naturally, the idea of covenant, first proclaimed in Zwingli's and Bullinger's Zürich (see pp. 620–21), was prominent. A highly influential book, *Seven Treatises called the practice of Christianity*, by one of East Anglia's principal Puritan ministers, Richard Rogers, was published in 1603; by the time the Massachusetts venture was launched, it had gone through eight editions. One of its highlights was a description of how, twenty years before, Rogers had made a solemn agreement – covenanted – with those of his people in his Essex parish of Wethersfield who were prepared to separate out from the temptations of the world. Their covenant had endured ever since. This was a potent image, and the communities set up in New England were prompt to covenant for their future.[8] They were a chosen people, making a treaty with God and with each other. Other words besides 'covenant' also inspired people as they leafed through their Bibles in meditation on the cramped and stinking ships of the Atlantic voyage or amid the deep snow of a New England winter. They found themselves in a wilderness, like the Children of Israel, but was this any worse a wilderness than the Church of England under Laud's leadership? Might they rather be re-entering an Edenic garden, as their home communities had once been, to tend and bring to order and peace? So they named their new settlements Boston, Dedham, Ipswich, Braintree, to begin cultivating and replicating these gardens of godly England which they had lost to the weeds and pollution of Charles I's religion.

Although the New England settlers made their commonwealth much less like Old England than Virginia was intended to be, it is important to re-emphasize that the vast majority were not separatists but Puritans. They wanted a truer form of the established Church, which somehow (perhaps uncomfortably and untidily, like Rogers's Wethersfield) would also have the characteristics of a Church of the elect. The New England venture was more than wilderness or garden: it was (in the words of Governor Winthrop as his party prepared to sail out from Southampton) 'a city upon a hill'. This quotation from Matthew 5.14 has become a famous phrase in American self-identity, but Winthrop did not intend to confer a special destiny on the new colony. He meant that like every other venture of the godly, and as in the quotation's context in Matthew's Gospel, Massachusetts was to be visible for all the world to learn from it. At such a moment of crisis, with England's Protestant Church in disarray, those leaving Southampton should be conscious that the eyes of many in England, and perhaps as far away as Transylvania, were upon them.[9]

The form assumed by the Church of Massachusetts was therefore the paradox of an established Reformed Church with an all-embracing system of parishes like England, but run by local assemblies of the self-selected godly – a form of Church government which was 'Congregational', a Latin-derived word first given currency by John Cotton, one of the Church's early ministers. The early foundation of Harvard College meant that Massachusetts was unique among the North American colonies in never being short of ministers to serve its parishes, and that made establishing a single dominant Church all the easier. The clergy ministered to a federation of parishes made up of laity who were devotees of the Religion of the Book, possibly the most literate society then existing in the world. They felt as keenly as any godly congregations in the worldwide Reformed Protestant family that they must fulfil the hopes of a century of Reformation; they kept in close touch with like-minded congregations in England throughout the century and beyond, and were very conscious of their international heritage.[10]

Technically this was not a theocracy, a state run by the Church, but the Church's government functioned side by side with secular government, as in Geneva. The elect were in charge of the Commonwealth; they were nevertheless still a minority of the population, particularly as children were born and grew up without having experienced the excitement of committing to emigration and a new life. Winthrop and his fellows were in any case conscious that not all who had crowded the Atlantic migration boats were pure in heart or sought godliness, and that some might have murkier reasons for fleeing England than objections to Laud's sacramental theology. Such people should not be allowed to pollute the purified Church and should be excluded from government.

In 1631, the franchise for the colony's assembly was limited to Church members. Still it was compulsory for everyone to go to their parish church (known in New England simply as a 'meeting house'), and the Massachusetts government tried to stop people settling beyond a certain distance from the meeting houses so that they could be properly supervised.

In the Interregnum after 1649, government back home in England came to look pleasingly more like the Massachusetts model, and many New Englanders returned across the Atlantic to help out the new regime. However, the return of Charles II in 1660 threatened to bring everything to ruin on both sides of the ocean; the flow back to England abruptly dried up.[11] As the leadership argued about how to preserve the delicate balance of their polity, they evolved a compromise which ingeniously built on their favourite notion of covenant. In 1662, after every congregation had voted on the issue, they agreed on establishing a 'Half-Way Covenant'. Some could remain members of the Church by virtue of their baptism only, but the fully committed would have to offer proof of repentance and lively faith to gain the full Church membership which allowed them to receive communion at the Lord's Table.

Thus godliness, a wide franchise in the Massachusetts Assembly and an established Church could all be preserved. New England's Congregationalism faced many challenges: the arguments around the 'Half-Way Covenant' proved very disruptive of the ministers' authority as rival clergy lobbied the congregations against their opponents. After royal intervention in the 1680s there was the extra annoyance of governors appointed by the Crown who were rarely sympathetic to the Congregationalist ministry, and who even encouraged the indignity of an Anglican church built in the middle of Boston (worse still, in 1714 it acquired that engine of popery, a pipe organ, the first in New England).[12] Nevertheless the Congregational establishment continued to rally its support in the legislature in the name of independence from outside interference. It retained its dominant position until challenged by the disruptive religious enthusiasms released in the eighteenth-century 'Great Awakening' (see pp. 755–65).

The Commonwealth of Massachusetts, self-consciously a protest against King Charles's Church, in turn experienced religious dissent. As early as 1635 an independent-minded Boston woman called Anne Hutchinson horrified the leadership by challenging the whole framework of Puritan piety established by covenant theology. An exponent of one version of antinomianism, that recurrent Protestant neurosis (see pp. 652–3), she criticized the way that Puritan theology constantly forced the elect to prove to themselves that they were growing in holiness. Worse still, she asserted her authority by holding her own devotional meetings and claiming special revelations of the Holy Spirit. The ministers of Massachusetts were split as to whether her charisma was from God or from the Devil, and all sorts of personal clashes became mixed up in the dispute.[13] After two years' tense confrontation, Hutchinson was banished, and travelled south to join a scattered set of coastal communities called Rhode Island. This had been set up by Roger Williams, a strict separatist minister, who had himself fled Massachusetts to escape arrest for his religious views in 1636; it soon became a haven for an intimidating variety of the discontented, and the fastidious godly of Boston looked on it as the 'latrina of New England'. As Williams struggled to create order out of chaos, any thoughts of a single Church of God quickly disappeared. He came to embrace complete religious toleration, even including Jews and 'Turks' in his envisaged freedom (Rhode Island was then likely to be short of Turks, but it was a striking rhetorical gesture). Calvinist that he still was, Williams believed that all the non-elect would go to Hell, but it was not his responsibility to make matters worse for them in this life. In 1647, his Rhode Island towns proclaimed that 'all men may walk as their consciences persuade them, every one in the name of his God'.[14]

Massachusetts still begged to differ. Its leaders were responsible in 1651 for whipping a Baptist who had organized private worship, and worse was to come.[15] Quakers arrived in 1657, determined to spread their ecstatic message of freedom and inner light, apparently spoiling for martyrdom, and raising bitter memories of Anne Hutchinson as they encouraged women to preach. The Friends' wilful separation from secular life aroused even greater fears than in England; after all, the Commonwealth was still no more than a quarter-century old, and bound together socially as well as in religion by its covenants. Quakers were publicly flogged and had their ears cropped; then, between 1659 and 1661, four were hanged for missionary activities – one of the victims was a woman, Mary Dyer, who had deliberately returned from banishment to see her previous sentence fulfilled. This caused a sharp reaction of protest both in New England and in the home country. Charles II ordered the executions to stop, even though his government had little time for Quakers and was itself imprisoning them; it was ironical that a royal regime so like the one from which the Puritan settlers had fled should now restrain their zeal for persecution. The executions exercised many New Englanders as to whether even the religiously obnoxious ought so to be treated. Pointedly, Rhode Island respected the Quaker commitment to pacifism by exempting them from military service. This unprecedented concession survived even the dire crisis of native all-out war in 1676, while still allowing Quakers a say in the government of the colony, which included decisions about war.[16]

Roger Williams was one of the few early colonists to think of making an effort to spread Christianity among the Native American population, taking the trouble to learn and analyse their languages and publish a guide to them. However, he too came to let this part of his ministry lapse, and the work awaited the personal decision of one New England minister, John Eliot, before it was taken up again. The early English Protestant neglect of evangelizing among indigenous peoples makes a curious contrast with the precocious Spanish attention to converting native peoples in South and Central America, or French efforts to the north in New France. It cannot simply be accounted for by the early difficulties of the colonies in surviving at all, or the tensions and cultural incomprehensions between the two societies. Elizabethan writers who published propaganda for founding colonies, principally George Peckham, Thomas Harriot and Richard Hakluyt the younger, had stressed the importance of bringing Christianity to the peoples of America.[17] This makes it all the more surprising that actual colonists were so slow to take up the work, and undermines the message of the noble image on the first seal of the Massachusetts Bay Company: a Native American pleading, in the words of Paul's missionary vision (Acts 16.9), 'Come over and help us.'

The explanations are probably theological rather than the result of inertia or straightforward racism, both of which Iberian colonists had also exhibited in generous measure. The considerations of natural law which troubled Spanish consciences through the Thomism of Las Casas or Vitoria cut little ice with Reformed theologians, who would be more inclined to seek the will of God embodied in specific commands – one of which, the stark order to Adam to 'fill the earth and subdue it', was another echo of Eden. Puritan covenant theology may have inhibited the idea of mission: believers in covenant theology might well feel that natives should prove their status as part of God's elect by spontaneously showing an interest in and making an effort to imitate the Christian beliefs of their neighbours, without any artificial effort on the colonists' part. Roger Williams and John Cotton were also affected by their longing for the imminent arrival of the Last Days, because they both shared

Oliver Cromwell's biblically based belief that this event must be heralded by the conversion of the Jews (see pp. 773–4). Logically, therefore, that should happen first, and any conversion of new Gentile peoples would form a later stage of God's plan.[18] Like their counterparts to the south, North American natives died in horrific numbers from European diseases; equally, that suggested to some commentators that their bodies had been created inferior to Europeans by God, for reasons wrapped up in his inscrutable will, and their idleness when introduced to European farming suggested a connection to the failed farmer and first murderer Cain.[19]

It took Eliot's generous imagination to overcome such theological or psychological barriers. Beginning work in 1646, by 1663 he had produced the first Bible of any language to be printed in America, in a dialect of the Native American Algonquin language now extinct, and composed a catechism in the main local language. His intensive work produced thousands of Indian converts, organized in 'prayer towns' next to English-cultivated territory, governed by the natives themselves, but imitating as far as possible English models of life. Few settlers displayed Eliot's spirit of openness. As the colonies expanded in numbers and territorial ambitions through the century, such settlements were generally destroyed by warfare and colonial betrayal: a beginning of a long-drawn-out and wretched story of suffering for the indigenous people of North America at the hands of Protestant Christians. English Anglicans formed a missionary society in 1701, the Society for the Propagation of the Gospel, but it was at first largely intended to rally to the established Church white settlers in America (and their slaves), despite a good deal of rhetoric presented to early subscribers.[20]

Slavery formed another problem for and a blot on English-speaking Christian mission. As the southern colonies and English islands in the Caribbean developed a plantation economy, particularly for tobacco and sugar (cotton came much later), they became deeply enmeshed in the system of importing African slaves which had already sustained the Iberian colonies for more than a century. The first record of enslaved people in Virginia is as early as 1619.[21] It was ironic that in the 1640s and 1650s, as the English on both sides of the Atlantic were talking in unprecedented ways about their own freedom and rights to choose, especially in religion, slaves were being shipped into the English colonies in hundreds, then thousands. Christianity did not seem to alter this for Protestants any more than it had for Catholics. An act of the Virginia Assembly in 1667 spelled out that 'the conferring of baptisme doth not

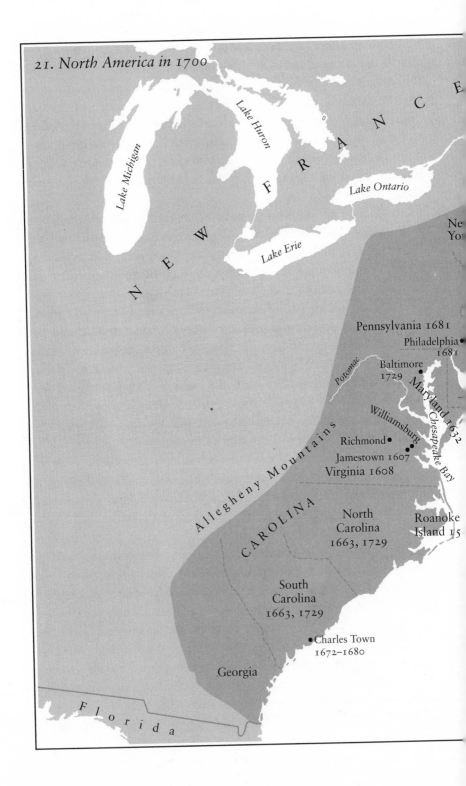

21. *North America in 1700*

NEW FRANCE

Lake Michigan

Lake Huron

Lake Ontario

Lake Erie

N E W   F R A N C E

Ne
Yo

Pennsylvania 1681

Philadelphia
1681

Potomac

Baltimore
1729

Maryland 1632

Williamsburg

Chesapeake Bay

Richmond

Jamestown 1607

Virginia 1608

Allegheny Mountains

CAROLINA

North
Carolina
1663, 1729

Roanoke
Island 15

South
Carolina
1663, 1729

Charles Town
1672–1680

Georgia

Florida

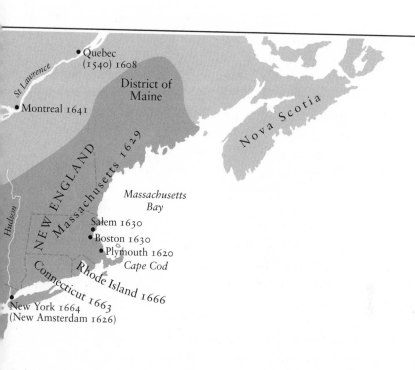

St Lawrence

• Quebec
(1540) 1608

• Montreal 1641

District of
Maine

Nova Scotia

NEW ENGLAND

Massachusetts 1629

*Massachusetts
Bay*

Hudson

Salem 1630
• Boston 1630
• Plymouth 1620
Cape Cod

Connecticut 1663
Rhode Island 1666

• New York 1664
(New Amsterdam 1626)

—*Delaware Bay*
—Delaware
(England 1608)

A t l a n t i c   O c e a n

○ 125   250 Miles
├──────┼──────┤
○ 200   400 Km

Extent of British territory about 1748

alter the condition of the person as to his bondage or Freedome', which was only to restate the policy already adopted by the Portuguese in their slave trade, and to look back to the position of English serfs, formally enshrined in English common law (as it still is).[22] It was a different position from that of the Reformed Protestant Dutch in their seventeenth-century colonial venture in the southern Cape of Africa – there, slaves who were baptized could not be sold again, and the Dutch were therefore careful to keep those baptized to a minimum.[23]

The double standard seemed to be ever more entrenched. The great exponent of toleration and liberty John Locke, in his *Two Treatises of Government*, resoundingly declared to Englishmen that 'Slavery is so vile and miserable an Estate of Man . . . that 'tis hardly to be conceived, that an Englishman, much less a Gentleman, should plead for 't'. But that is precisely what Locke himself had done when (as one of the first hereditary peers created in English North America) he helped first to draft and then to revise a constitution for a vast new English colony in the south called Carolina, at much the same time in the 1680s as he was writing *Two Treatises*. Blacks were different.[24] Slave numbers rocketed at the end of the seventeenth century: blacks outnumbered whites in South Carolina by the 1710s, and in Virginia the proportion of blacks to whites shot up from less than 10 per cent in 1680 to about a third in 1740. This is the context for the remarkable liturgical innovation of one South Carolina Anglican clergyman, Francis Le Jau, who added to the baptism service a requirement that slaves being baptized should repeat an oath 'that you do not ask for the holy baptism out of any design to free yourself from the Duty and Obedience you owe to your Master while you live'. This reflected a clerical dilemma in a Church so dominated by the laity: when masters were putting up much resistance to converting slaves, was it better to let souls perish or to accept the norms of the society in which the Church found itself?[25]

As early as the mid-seventeenth century, Virginia in the south and New England in the north had created two contrasting forms of English-speaking colony. Both were firmly committed to their different patterns of established Churches, just as in Europe, though Rhode Island remained as a thorn in the side of the New England establishments and was a model for their gradual loosening of official restrictions on other Protestant congregations. Between the two regions, a variety of 'Middle Colonies' was set up, not all initially English. Swedish Lutherans settled on the Delaware River, and the Protestant Dutch seized a spectacular natural harbour in the Hudson estuary which they named New Netherland and which quickly emerged as the focus for European shipping along the North American coast. An English flotilla annexed this tempting prize during the Anglo-Dutch Wars in 1664, and its capital New Amsterdam on the Manhattan peninsula became New York, only briefly retaken by the Dutch in 1673.

Once more the aim of the Swedes and Dutch had been to reproduce the national Churches back home, but even before 1664 the religious cosmopolitanism of the northern Netherlands had already been reproduced in New Amsterdam, whether the Dutch Reformed Church liked it or not. That included pragmatic Dutch toleration of a wealthy Jewish community, since there were a significant number of Jewish shareholders in the Dutch West India Company, the colony's proprietor. English rule was the coup de grâce to any thoughts of a Dutch Reformed monopoly. It was New York that first experienced the bewildering diversity of settlers which, during the eighteenth century, swelled into a flood, and made any effort to reproduce old Europe's compartmentalized and discrete confessional Churches seem ludicrous. Rather than the colonies of north and south which had been English from the beginning, this Dutch settlement pointed to the future diverse religious pattern of North America.[26]

Further religious experiments intersected with the crises of mid-seventeenth-century England in different ways from New England and Virginia. In 1632 Roman Catholic aristocrats friendly with Charles I sponsored a colony in a region known as the Chesapeake north of Virginia, and named it Maryland after the King's Catholic wife, Henrietta Maria. In fact the Royalists' defeat in the English civil wars meant that Catholics did not take the leading role in Maryland. Feeling that their already tenuous position was under threat, in 1649 they seized on a brief moment of local strength and sought to create a unique freedom to practise their religion by outmanoeuvring their Protestant opponents in a huge concession. They guaranteed complete toleration for all those who believed in Jesus Christ. They ordered fines and whipping for anyone using the normal religious insults of seventeenth-century England, elaborately specified in a list: 'heretic, schismatic, idolator, Puritan, Independent, Presbyterian, Popish priest, Jesuit, Jesuited Papist, Lutheran, Calvinist, Anabaptist, Brownist, Antinomian, Barrowist, Roundhead, Separatist'.[27] This was an extraordinary effort to blot out the bitterness of the Reformation; it approached Rhode Island's universal toleration by a very different route. Maryland showed the limitations of its vision by still ordering property confiscation and execution for anyone denying the Trinity, and Anglicans seized control of the colony in the 1690s, doing their best to restrict Roman Catholic rights – an ironical outcome of the 'Glorious Revolution', which is seen in English history as a milestone in the development of public religious toleration (see pp. 733–6). Nevertheless, amid the steadily encroaching diversity of the whole colonial seaboard, the Maryland example was not forgotten.

A new chance for the hard-pressed Quakers came when one of their number, William Penn, became interested in founding a refuge for them. He was the son of an English admiral, and friendly with the Catholic and nautically minded heir to the throne, the future James II. Drawing on these useful connections, he got a royal charter in 1682 for a colony to be called Pennsylvania, in territories lying between Maryland and New England. His plan was bold and imaginative: going further than the Catholic elite of Maryland, he renounced the use of coercion in religion, and granted free exercise of religion and political participation to all monotheists of whatever views taking shelter in his colony. He also tried to maintain friendly relations with Native Americans. Soon Pennsylvania came to have a rich mix not simply of English Protestants, but also Scotch-Irish Presbyterians, Lutherans and the descendants of radical Reformation groups of mainland Europe who were fleeing from Roman Catholic intolerance in central Europe (see p. 647). Among the latter, the Old Order Amish from Switzerland have done their best ever since to freeze their communal way of life as it was when they first arrived in the early eighteenth century.[28]

All this diversity proved destructive for Penn's original vision of a community run according to the ideals of the Friends. Under pressure from the English government, Pennsylvania's assembly even disenfranchised Catholics, Jews and non-believers in 1705.[29] Soon good relations with the native population were also badly compromised. Pennsylvania nevertheless fostered a consistent hatred of slavery among Friends, a development of great future significance for all Christians (see p. 869). It set another notable example: no one religious group could automatically claim exclusive status, unlike nearly all other colonies where a particular Church continued to claim official advantages even if it was a minority. This was the first colony to evolve the characteristic pattern of religion of the modern United States of America: a pattern of religious denominations, none claiming the exclusive status of Church, but making up slices in a Protestant 'cake' which together adds up to a Church. Anglicanism did manage to strengthen its position in the southern English

American colonies after Charles II's restoration (even in cosmopolitan New York), gaining established status in six out of the eventual thirteen. However, the origins of so many colonies in religious protest against the Church of England back home guaranteed that Anglicanism would never fully replicate its full English privileges in North America.

Established churches might have been able to resist the growing pluralism better if they had more effectively set up their structures of government, but virtually everywhere except Massachusetts, the colonies suffered a shortage of clergy in the first formative century, and lay leaders of local religion were generally less inclined to take an exclusive view of what true religion might be than professionally trained clerics. In this they were aided by a strong consideration swaying many promoters of colonies: religious coercion discouraged settlement and was therefore economically bad for struggling colonial ventures. Reformation Europe had known religious toleration; now religious liberty was developing. Toleration is a grudging concession granted by one body from a position of strength; liberty provides a situation in which all religious groups compete on an equal basis. We have already seen precedents: first in the 1520s the pragmatism of the Graubünden in Switzerland, then the Hungarians and Transylvanians in the Declaration of Torda, soon followed by the Polish-Lithuanian Commonwealth's Confederation of Warsaw (see pp. 639–43). Just as the increasing confessional rigidity of old Europe was turning from these sixteenth-century ideals, a new European enterprise was taking up the challenge.

THE FIGHT FOR PROTESTANT SURVIVAL (1660–1800)

The growing success and stability of these new transatlantic Protestant polities (gained at the price for Native American societies of increasing disruption and exile westwards) contrasted with a long-drawn-out crisis for Protestants in late-seventeenth-century Europe. The Habsburgs began systematically dismantling a century and more of Protestant life in central Europe from Bohemia to Hungary, Catholic advance in the Polish-Lithuanian Commonwealth continued apace, and France re-emerged under Louis XIV (reigned 1643–1715) as a major European power with an aggressively Catholic agenda. The Stuart dynasty restored in Britain in 1660 was from its return a client of Louis, seeking his financial support against its stridently but selectively loyal and inconveniently Anglican English Parliaments. Charles II and James II became pawns in Louis's plans, which included improving, or better still reversing, the marginal position of Catholics in the Atlantic Isles.[30]

Louis XIV died an exhausted and defeated old man, but in his prime he directed an army of 400,000, supported by a taxable population of twenty million; he had increased the size of that army fivefold in four decades.[31] Beyond his own borders, he spurred on the Duke of Savoy in murderous campaigns against Savoy's Protestant minority, and in 1685 he overturned his grandfather Henri IV's religious settlement for France by revoking the Edict of Nantes – 150,000 Protestants are estimated to have fled France as a result, the largest displacement of Christians in early modern Europe.[32] Louis conquered largely Protestant lands of the Holy Roman Empire in Alsace, making a Catholic Strasbourg out of Lutheran Strassburg, which long before in Martin Bucer's time had been the prime candidate to lead the Protestant world (see pp. 629–30). In his military campaigns of 1672, Louis nearly succeeded where the Spanish monarchy had failed, in overwhelming the United Provinces of the Netherlands – and in that ambitious venture lay the seeds of his own failure. For the outrage of France's invasion provoked Prince Willem of Orange, appointed Stadhouder (the word which in French would be 'Lieutenant') by most provinces in the Netherlands, to take up arms against the Catholic Leviathan. His ancestor Willem 'the Silent', eventually murdered by a Catholic fanatic, had done the same a century before, but Prince Willem would more than avenge his fate.

Willem made it his life's work to humble French Catholic power across Europe. His success exacted dynastic revenge not simply for Willem the Silent but for the disaster suffered by his great-uncle by marriage, the Elector Palatine Friedrich, back in 1618–19 (see pp. 646–7). As a by-blow in the course of his relentless campaigns against Louis, Willem gained the three thrones of Britain in 1688 – but what a by-blow this proved! It was the culmination of a decade of political turmoil in the Atlantic Isles, and was provoked by the extraordinary stupidity of King James II, a sincere but inept convert to Roman Catholicism. While James was still Duke of York and heir to the throne, his wily brother King Charles II had saved him between 1679 and 1681 from a real prospect of being excluded from the succession in favour of James's daughters, Mary and Anne, by his first wife, Anne Hyde; unlike their father, both ladies had remained firm in their loyalty to the Church of England.

The King's strategy to save James from exclusion had been to strangle opposition from the 'Whig' group, which was promoting exclusion, through a royal alliance across the whole Atlantic archipelago with a rival political grouping within the Protestant establishment. They were christened 'Tories' by the more radical Protestant enemies, an insulting reference to Irish Catholic bandits (similarly the Whigs were nicknamed after Protestant Scots cattle thieves). Tories were Protestants who championed government by bishops in the established Protestant Churches of the three kingdoms, and they trumpeted their belief in the divine right of kings as well as bishops, in return for royal support in oppressing rival Protestants and (in Ireland) riding out resentment from dispossessed Catholics. King Charles died in 1685, leaving his brother in the best possible position, but King James II failed to see that Charles had bought success by becoming prisoner to a political party.[33]

When James's antics in promoting the interests of his fellow Catholics made Tories snarl, he promptly abandoned the Tories and tried to outflank them, courting Protestant Dissenters by offering the same emancipation he was promoting for Catholics.[34] Dissenters were torn between pleasure at the end of their persecution and a very real fear of international Catholicism. James might have got away with his plans if the succession had remained with his Protestant daughters, but he now had a second wife, the Catholic Italian Mary of Modena. Their fatal mistake was to provide a half-brother for the Princesses Mary and Anne, James Francis: 'Francis', with its multiple Catholic resonances, was not a clever name to give a prospective English king. From that moment in 1688, James II was doomed, because the boy was bound to be brought up a Catholic. Grimly observing was Mary's husband, Stadhouder Willem, whose wife stood to lose her future thrones through this new arrival.

It only needed an invitation from a few English notables for Willem to launch naval and military intervention against his father-in-law, who fled the country in a state of nervous collapse, and the throne was declared vacant. 'Dutch William' was as much a conqueror as his Norman namesake, though the fact that virtually no one in England lifted a finger to stop his invasion has mitigated the embarrassment for the English national myth of a scepter'd isle perpetually preserved from invasion since 1066 (a rhetoric often still employed by those hostile to the United Kingdom's membership of the European Union). At least the Dutch were Protestant, and good at gardening. Indeed, to minimize the impropriety of William's landing of his forces at Torbay in Devon, November 1688 gained its own mythological status, as a 'Glorious

Revolution' which saved the Protestant state at the cost of very little English blood, though more in Scotland, and still more in Ireland.

In the very last days of 1688, William summoned members of the English House of Lords and House of Commons to what they slightly awkwardly termed a 'Convention'. Acting as if it were Parliament, the Convention contrived an ingenious if unorthodox replacement for its missing monarch by recognizing a team, William (III) and Mary (II) – but it was nervously aware that the kingdom of Scotland might make a different choice, while the Catholic Irish mostly rallied behind King James and suffered three years of bloody warfare before being forced to change their minds. A trio of national 'Revolutions' now produced a contrasting trio of religious settlements. The episcopally structured Church of England, which did represent the overwhelming majority of English people, grudgingly agreed henceforth to tolerate Protestant Dissenting groups, albeit on rather less generous terms than James had offered. The English bishops turned uncomfortably aside while in 1690 Presbyterian activists were sweeping away episcopal government in the Church of Scotland, against the wishes of many Scots.[35] English bishops' compensation was to see the Protestant Episcopal Church of Ireland confirmed in privilege and power, despite its ludicrously small proportion of adherents among a sea of Irish Catholics. In each kingdom, the deciding factor was who would best support the fragile new monarchy.

Tory High Churchpeople agonized about this untidy solution. Some left the Church of England, insistent that their duty to God meant that they could not break their oath to King James, however obnoxious he had proved. Among these 'Non-Jurors' was the then Archbishop of Canterbury, William Sancroft (times had changed; at least he was not beheaded like Laud). Altogether, the Non-Jurors were a distinguished and conscientious grouping who were now free to think new thoughts about why they were still Anglicans when not part of an established Church. The long-term consequences of those musings were considerable (see pp. 840–41), even though the Non-Juring Church itself eventually faded away along with the Stuarts' chances of retaking the throne. It was not surprising that the leadership of the Church now shifted to those whom their more partisan colleagues had already angrily christened 'Latitudinarians' (see p. 654): those willing to allow a wide latitude of religious belief within a broadly tolerant Church, and to accommodate their allegiance to the new political realities. The triumphant Whigs also needed to justify the change of regime which now brought them to power in the state alongside Latitudinarians in the Church. The most clear-sighted Whig spokesman, although not at the time the most popular precisely because of his clear-sightedness, was John Locke.

Locke had first plunged into political controversy in order to formulate a Whig case for James, Duke of York's exclusion from the succession in 1679–81, and his arguments could equally well justify the 1688 revolution. He appealed to the Bible to demolish the idea that it provided a case for the divine right of kings. If seventeenth-century divine-right theorists like the Englishman Sir Robert Filmer turned to Genesis and claimed a hereditary succession from Adam, granted by God, to justify the divine character of royal succession in their own day, Locke denied that the idea of hereditary succession could be found in Genesis, and he used its stories to construct a different myth. Although Adam's fall had brought about the punishment that humans would have to labour in order to survive, this burden had engendered a natural right in all people to labour and to possess the land for labour. This preceded any authority to govern, which resulted from contracts freely made by humans in order to live more easily with each other. So the Bible provided the basis of Locke's distinctive ideology of a social contract, and justified his scheme of rights and duties. Locke's programme was not immediately attractive to the new Whig establishment, which did not want to endanger its fragile alliance with Anglican Tories, and which was therefore inclined to prefer providentialist arguments to defend King William's rule: Whigs saw him as God's agent in defending the English Church.[36] Nevertheless, over the next century, Locke's language of rights and contract fermented in the political arguments of the anglophone world and then spread into Europe generally, decisively undermining the concept of sacred monarchy.

After William III's death in 1702, English-led armies continued to fight the French under his British successor and sister-in-law, Queen Anne, decisively blocking Louis's seemingly inexorable advance. Before John Churchill's victory at Blenheim in 1704, English armies had not won a major victory since Flodden in 1513, or in mainland Europe since Agincourt a century before that. Churchill gained his title of Duke of Marlborough, and the money to build Blenheim Palace, one of Europe's most splendid houses, thanks to the gratitude of British monarch and Parliament; his brilliant command of the armies had, in four major battles, permanently halted the Catholic tide from washing away all surviving Protestant power. It was not surprising that the people of northern Europe were still virulently anti-Catholic in 1700. They continued to read their sixteenth-century martyrologies – especially for the

English the luridly detailed and luridly illustrated folios of John Foxe's *Book of Martyrs* – but Protestants had no need merely to recycle passions from the days of Reformation sufferings: the Catholic menace was a living reality.[37] So there was no possibility of England countenancing a Catholic Stuart succession when Queen Anne died with no surviving children in 1714. The thrones of Ireland and Great Britain (from 1707 there had been a United Kingdom of England and Scotland) went to another descendant of the Elector Palatine Friedrich, the Elector Georg of Hanover. Now he was King George I of Great Britain and Ireland. His new British subjects never felt much affection for him as a person – charm was not his strong suit – but overwhelming numbers of them in England deeply valued him as a saviour of the Protestant Glorious Revolution and a bulwark against the return of the Stuarts.

The outworkings of the Reformation thus pulled England back into an intimate territorial involvement in the affairs of mainland Europe, from which the French had previously expelled it when they captured the last medieval English mainland enclave of Calais in 1558. From 1688 to 1702, and again from 1714 until 1832, when different laws of succession severed the thrones of Britain and Hanover, the British Isles were part of a joint European and vigorously Protestant state enterprise spanning the North Sea, while the British also built up a seaborne empire, first in North America and then in India. Initial British interests in Asia, to begin with in fierce competition with their Protestant co-religionists the Dutch, were not to acquire territory but, like the Portuguese before them, to create small bases which would stabilize their trade in cottons and a swelling volume of other consumer goods.

The momentum of British prosperity sustained their enterprise where the penurious Portuguese had failed, and their markets seemed limitless; the Dutch proved unable to sustain the same momentum in political organization and financial resources, and so the United Provinces fell behind the United Kingdom in power and world reach. In the British Isles, the pace of manufacturing quickened until, with the aid of a new technology harnessing the power of steam for production, Britain developed Europe's first industrial revolution, resulting in huge wealth for some, and a great deal of modest prosperity and spending power for many – not to mention other equally profound changes, as we will see (see pp. 787–91). This was the basis for a British world empire, based improbably on a comparatively minor archipelago of Atlantic islands. Its self-image was based on a narrative of heroic struggle against popery and arbitrary tyranny (represented generally by the French), in which

Protestant English and Protestant Scots had buried their differences in the Glorious Revolution of 1688, creating a common new home for their two peoples: Great Britain. A leading historian of this period has subtitled her study of it with an appropriate play on words, speaking of the process as 'forging' a nation. British adventures across the world became, for the next century and more, an overwhelmingly Protestant story.[38]

In the eighteenth century, European politicians and generals began to realize that the Mughal Empire in India, which had seemed so formidable to Catholic European powers in the sixteenth and seventeenth centuries, was beginning to fail. By contrast, their own governmental and military organizations were growing ever more efficient and effectively financed, tested by the century of European confessional wars from 1618 onwards. India was only the centrepiece: everywhere, Spanish and Portuguese power was looking far more vulnerable. In the mid-eighteenth century, Great Britain and France contended for supremacy: a 'Seven Years War' drew in all the major European powers, the first war to be fought in continents circling the globe. American 'Indians' were enlisted on the borders of New France and the thirteen English American colonies; Africans were swept in; in armies of the Indian subcontinent, Muslims and Hindus found themselves fighting European quarrels, the beginning of two centuries during which the Christian West was to be the dominant force in world power struggles.

When the British fought the French to a standstill and concluded a peace treaty in Paris in 1763, they found themselves in charge of a land empire which needed defending across the world, and their armies were now carried by a navy with a near-universal range. Their victory was sealed in 1799, when British armies defeated Tipu Sultan, the last Indian ruler capable of seriously challenging them; in Tipu's defeat, they dashed the hopes of his French allies, now revolutionary Republicans spoiling to reverse the French monarchy's humiliation of 1763.[39] The large British gains in India had been equalled in 1763 by Britain's acquisition of France's Northern American territories to the north and west of their own thirteen colonies. It was tempting to see Protestantism as the Christianity of the future.

PIETISM AND THE MORAVIANS

There was a force behind this expansion greater than British imperial power: the Protestant religious movements underpinning it were international. What is remarkable about these stories is their interconnection across Europe and the world, and the fact that they took both their immediate and their long-term origins from Protestant Germany.[40] King George I came to England in 1714 from a Lutheran northern Europe very conscious of its own providential survival in the Thirty Years War, yet still not at ease. Battered by the armies of Louis XIV, it then suffered several further decades of calamities from the 1690s: a run of terrible weather producing famine, which nurtured epidemics, and from 1700 the Great Northern War, which, over twenty years, broke Swedish aspirations to great-power status in the Baltic and consolidated the imperial power of Peter the Great's Russia (see pp. 541–4). Such catastrophes placed a heavy pastoral burden on Lutheran clergy in Scandinavia and Germany, and made them look for Protestant spiritual resources beyond their own tradition. Although they would have not wished to admit it, they were also trying to find a substitute for something which the Reformation had destroyed: monastic life and spirituality. With certain formal exceptions in Germany, which owed a rather accidental survival to their convenience for the German nobility, all monasteries, nunneries and friaries had disappeared from Protestant Europe, and all devotional life devolved to the parishes. Even there, parish gilds and confraternities had largely been dissolved or had concentrated on commercial purposes to avoid any hint of popish superstition.[41] With the religious houses and gilds there had disappeared a host of Christian ministries and activities, from charitable work to itinerant preaching to contemplation, which the Reformation had done its best to replace, but with incomplete success. Now in compensation came a renewal of German and Scandinavian Protestantism, which has come to be known as Pietism.

Pietists liked to emphasize the novelty of what they were doing, and certainly they were impatient with conservative ('Orthodox') Lutheran civil authorities and clergy who obstructed them, but there was little in their activities that was actually new or without precedent in Lutheran life. What they initially sought was an enriched use of the existing parish system, pulling parish life out of a mass of surviving pre-Reformation habits of worship to a more heartfelt expression of Christian faith, which would be more robust in the face of Counter-Reformation Catholicism. Many deplored the divisions within Protestantism, which could plausibly be considered as contributing to the disasters of the seventeenth century. Lutherans ashamed of such schism paid more attention to their Reformed neighbours in the Netherlands and Germany, and they were impressed by the intense and personal piety they encountered, itself owing much to the preaching and writing of English Puritans who had become dissatisfied with or had been ejected from the Church of England. In many areas of Germany, particularly large cities, Lutherans were also confronted with an influx of French Huguenot refugees whose plight was directly the result of their steadfastness in Reformed religion back home.

From its earliest days, Pietism was intimately bound up with education. Thoughtful scholars and students – backbone of the parish clergy – were frustrated with the collection of northern universities which served the Protestant Churches. Protestantism in both its Lutheran and its Reformed identities had rather quickly channelled its early bursts of energy into forms which could be taught to prospective ministers in the theology faculties of existing universities. Often these universities shaped their curriculum using the medieval scholastic methods which Martin Luther himself had come to scorn, and Pietists scorned them too. They did their best to recapture the initial excitement and urgency of the Reformation, the sense of personal and public conflict which had so galvanized popular Protestant enthusiasm in the 1520s and again in the 1560s. Yet these were orderly folk: they found themselves trying to cope with the strains of a Protestant European society which was in the middle of rapid change, and they sought ways of channelling and disciplining the enthusiasm which they themselves were inciting. It was a difficult balancing act, which bequeathed enduring tensions.

Crucial to Pietist formation were two Lutheran pastors, Philipp Jakob Spener and his younger contemporary August Hermann Francke. Spener, who left his native Alsace before its takeover by Louis XIV, and became successively pastor in Frankfurt am Main and the Hohenzollern capital Berlin, was alarmed by the rapid growth of such population centres and the strains that this placed on the parish clergy. His solution was to seek out the most energetic and serious layfolk in the parishes and treat them as partners in ministry, gathering people outside service-time to meet for Bible-reading, prayer and hymn-singing in what he called *collegia pietatis*. Under his influence, in 1694 the Hohenzollern Elector Friedrich of Brandenburg founded a new university for his territories in the city of Halle, which was to prove a major source for disseminating a new spirit in Lutheranism. Spener's genius, and that of the other leaders of the movement, was for detailed organization, plus strategic alliances with sympathetic rulers and nobility, and although Spener met opposition which eventually crushed his spirit, Francke consolidated his work in spectacular fashion. Pietism, with its varied Protestant roots and openness to crossing the Lutheran–Reformed divide, was always going to get a sympathetic hearing from the monarchs of the house of Hohenzollern, whose leading representatives in Branden-burg were Reformed princes stranded uncomfortably in a landscape of Lutherans.

From 1695, Francke created at Halle an extraordinary complex of orphanage, medical clinic, schools for both poor children and young noblemen and a teacher-training college, complete with printing press, library and even a museum to demonstrate to the pupils the wonders of God's creation. The work was paid for by an enterprise useful in itself: the first commercial production in Europe of standardized medical rem-edies, complete with multilingual advertising brochures.[42] All this was eventually housed in monumental buildings which have survived the twentieth-century disasters of Germany remarkably intact and available for their original functions. Franke's principle was that everyone, what-ever their position in life, should come out of childhood education able to read the Bible and to take pride in at least one special skill. This was to link the profession of Christianity to personal self-confidence and practical achievement, in a fashion which had no exact precedent, and which has become characteristic of modern Evangelicalism.

Halle set patterns in the Protestant world for institutions created by private initiative, as Jesuits had done for Catholics a century and more before. The work of Halle extended throughout northern Europe and deep into Russia, as Francke sent out his pupils into government service or clerical ministry, printed innumerable devotional tracts and kept up a correspondence with a vast diaspora of the like-minded – around five thousand of them.[43] In 1690–91, he wrote an autobiography which, although looking back to patterns set by Augustine and Luther as they described their conversion experiences, laid out the whole first thirty years of his life in terms of progressive and not instantaneous conversion: a continuous spiritual struggle marked by dramatic high points. It was hugely influential. Countless Evangelicals thereafter tried to shape their lives in the same way, and many of them turned their efforts into books.[44] All this busy activity had an urgent purpose: it was a preparation for the End Times, which would be heralded by the conversion of the Jews. Like Spener before him, Francke was very aware of the decades of excited speculation about the return of the Messiah which had agitated contemporary Judaism, along with the appearance of several Jewish candidates for the post. That was one of the reasons that Francke's eyes turned so much towards eastern Europe, with its vast spread of Jewish communities. Despite the enthusiasm which he inspired in others for the cause of conversion, leading to the foundation in Halle of the first Protestant institution for Jewish mission, this effort proved one of the real failures of the Pietist movement (apart from the non-appearance of the Last Days).[45]

Ringing through these varied institutions, sounding through the little groups of layfolk and the churches where Pietist pastors managed to overcome the disapproval of more conventional Lutherans, was a new burst of hymnody. Here was the solvent of the tensions within the movement caused by its challenge to Lutheran tradition and its adventurous reaching out to the Reformed; here was cheer for the anxious faithful, mindful of the fragility of the war-damaged society round them. It was a warm renewal of a tradition which had distinguished precedents in the hymns of Luther and his successors in the Lutheran tradition. One of those best known in the English-speaking world as well as in Germany, thanks to its translation by Frances Cox, a Victorian enthusiast for German hymnody, was written in 1675 by Johann Jakob Schütz, a young lawyer who was an eager associate of Spener in the activities of his *collegia pietatis* in Frankfurt, but whose search for a religion of the heart led him on further to plan colonizing schemes in William Penn's Pennsylvania, and propelled him into an excitement about the Last Days exceptional even among Pietists. Schütz begins his hymn with an evocation of the power of God which is classically Lutheran but has its own intensity. Since Pietism was so much the voice of eighteenth-century Germany in anguish and in joy, it is worth viewing Schütz's German text along with Miss Cox's English. The words 'God' and 'Good' ring through the original like a mantra, although the English turns them all into 'God':

> *Sei Lob und Ehr' dem höchsten Gut,*
> *Dem Vater aller Güte,*
> *Dem Gott, der alle Wunder tut,*
> *Dem Gott, der mein Gemüte*
> *Mit seinem reichen Trost erfüllt,*

> *Dem Gott, der allen Jammer stillt.*
> *Gebt unserm Gott die Ehre!*

> Sing praise to God who reigns above,
> the God of all creation,
> the God of power, the God of love,
> the God of our salvation;
> with healing balm my soul he fills,
> and every faithless murmur stills:
> to God all praise and glory.

As the hymn progresses, its mood changes to speak of trouble and sorrow, but then Schütz brings back his same God as intimate, even maternal, a personal, private comfort to those crowding in from the streets of the city:

> *Der Herr ist noch und nimmer nicht*
> *Von seinem Volk geschieden,*
> *Er bleibet ihre Zuversicht,*
> *Ihr Segen, Heil und Frieden.*
> *Mit Mutterhänden leitet er*
> *Die Seinen stetig hin und her.*
> *Gebt unserm Gott die Ehre!*

> The Lord is never far away,
> but through all grief distressing,
> an ever present help and stay,
> our peace and joy and blessing.
> As with a mother's tender hand,
> God gently leads the chosen band:
> To God all praise and glory.

And all ends again in praise: '*Gebt unserm Gott die Ehre!*' – 'Give our God the honour!'

Pietists who loved such hymns were generally not sympathetic to the continuing splendour and musical elaboration of well-financed Lutheran liturgy. Their preference for informality and the extrovert expression of emotion in worship contributed to a gradual abandoning of the continuing use of Latin in the Lutheran Mass and the jettisoning of much traditional ceremony in German and Scandinavian Lutheran worship. It was predictable, therefore, that Lutheranism's greatest musician, Johann Sebastian Bach, experienced a complicated relationship with the Pietist movement which spanned his career. Undoubtedly influenced in his own passionate Christian commitment by Pietist themes and by Pietist books in his own extensive library, Bach was a man whose strenuous temperament was certainly conducive to spiritual struggle. Yet he eventually felt compelled to leave his post directing church music in the city of Mühlhausen, uneasy with the restrictions that its Pietist pastor placed on him (although also with an eye on a better-paid job at a ducal court).[46] Later, based at the richly endowed parish church of St Thomas in Leipzig for the last quarter-century of his life, Bach found a conservative Latin-based liturgy which he was very ready not to supplant but to enhance, with an innovative outpouring of musical composition for organ, choir and orchestra. His cantatas – orchestral and choral commentaries in German on the preaching and liturgical themes set for the day, incorporating some of the great German hymns of the Reformation – are one of Lutheranism's greatest creative contributions to the Western cultural tradition. It is questionable whether many contemporary Pietists would have been enthusiastic for them.

Bach was never an easy man to employ or to live with, and the St Thomas congregation did not altogether appreciate what they were being offered in his barrage of musical composition – which in the end included five complete yearly cycles of cantatas (see Plate 36). When his *St Matthew Passion* was performed for the first time, influential members of the congregation became steadily more bewildered by the way that the music branched out from the chorales that they knew, and one elderly widow cried, 'God help us! 'tis surely an opera-comedy!'[47] In one sense, she was right: Bach had poured his choral creativity into his cantatas and, mysteriously, was the only major composer of his time never to write an opera. In later years he concentrated more and more of his talent on solo works for keyboard and other instruments, which had little to do with his official church duties, and that may reflect his growing impatience at the quarrels in which he had become involved at St Thomas's. His monumental late work, the Latin Mass in B minor, escapes beyond the requirements of Lutheran liturgy, for which its first components, written in 1733 for the Elector of Saxony, had still been appropriate. Taking its cue from the Elector's own conversion to Catholicism in defiance of his affronted subjects in the heartland of the Reformation, the Mass transcends the battles of the previous two centuries, to reunite the divided Western Latin Church in music. No Protestant had previously written anything like it.[48]

While Lutheranism was largely able to contain the Pietist movement, the Pietists engendered one distinctive offshoot which, although never very large-scale, had a rapid and significant effect on Protestantism worldwide. This was the Moravian Church, a radical restructuring of some of the last remnants from the pre-Reformation movement of dissent in the kingdom of Bohemia, the *Unitas Fratrum* (see p. 573). From 1722, a handful of these refugees from Moravia in Bohemia, victims of the inexorable Habsburg recatholicization of central Europe, were given shelter to the north of the Habsburg frontiers by a Lutheran nobleman, a Pietist with the strongest credentials as a former student of Francke at Halle and a godson of Spener. Count Nikolaus Ludwig von Zinzendorf used his estate in the hills of southernmost Saxony to build a showcase village for a growing collection of protégés. He named it Herrnhut, a place for craftwork and farming, the first of a network of communities which eventually spread as far as Russia, Great Britain and across the Atlantic.

Zinzendorf was a charismatic and passionate man. Proudly conscious of his family's Lutheran heritage stretching back to the Reformation, he found that the only way he could remould the Lutheran Church was by leaving it; he arranged for bishops of the *Unitas Fratrum* to consecrate him as bishop for his Herrnhut community. There was a certain convenience for Zinzendorf in the fact that very few of the people who gathered at Herrnhut were genuinely from Moravia. That meant that he could forge a unifying myth out of the Moravian past, to create an identity for a new community which was in reality a very disparate group, drawn from radically different and contending Churches – Lutherans, Reformed, Anabaptists. Most were Pietists who had found their own religious environments increasingly difficult and had now made the momentous choice to start a new life, uprooting themselves from a familiar homeland. It was not surprising that their emotions ran high in those pioneering decades.

Zinzendorf never lost his commitment to an ecumenical benevolence towards all Churches, symbolized by his inheritance of the Moravians' continuing government by bishops in succession from the united Western Church – an episcopal succession which was recognized by the British Parliament in 1749, in an ecumenical gesture without parallel at the time. The Count's authoritarian temperament and Pietist compulsion to organize demanded a new congregation as highly structured and centred round worship as the most rigorous monastic order, while it also moulded the whole family lives of men, women and children. Zinzendorf's communities worshipped as frequently as monks – seven times a day on weekdays, longer on Sundays – and their worship was full of song: sermons might be sung, they wrote a whole new crop of hymns, enjoyed a daily hour of singing with the congregation as full choir, and moreover had no Puritan fear of musical instruments. The Count had a special liking for trombones and recommended them as a way of cheering up funerals.[49] The Moravians much valued cheerfulness. It was Zinzendorf's chief quarrel with Francke that he had seemed to make the Christian life too much of a grim struggle.[50]

Stressing emotion against reason as the best means of reaching out to Christ, Zinzendorf set aside all previous Christian doctrinal requirements, with the sole exception of his own Lutheran inheritance, the Augsburg Confession of 1530. What he added was an idiosyncratic and intense communal piety, in which he placed extreme stress on his own selection from very traditional themes. He took up the language of mystical marriage familiar to many medieval spiritual writers, and made this one of the principal themes of Moravian worship, the eroticism of the vocabulary forming a sometimes unstable combination with a rigorously policed set of everyday relations between the sexes. He spoke of the Holy Spirit as Mother, as Syrian Christians had done long before (see pp. 182–3). He almost fetishized Luther's emphasis on Christ's sufferings for humankind, producing an obsession with Christ's blood and wounds – 'so moist, so gory', as Zinzendorf's *Litany of the Wounds* described them, with a relish which may have little appeal now.

In 1749, after the Count himself had encouraged emotions in some Moravian communities to boil too high, in what was later euphemistically termed the 'Sifting Time', he now felt compelled to rein them in. He banned his people from celebrating Christ's 'little side-hole' (*Seitenhölchen*). This was the toe-curling designation which he and they had given to the spear wound suffered by Christ on the Cross, a wound which represented for Zinzendorf 'the Mother of our souls, as the earth is the mother of the body'. The Count's embarrassment at the consequences of his devotional imagery led to a not untypical outburst which, in his struggle to regain control, blended his usual mystical language (much of it baffling to outsiders) with a choleric threat to bring the whole Moravian edifice crashing down. Having signed off a long and testy letter from London 'Your brother, Ludwig', he continued menacingly in a postscript:

If you do not follow me, I will not only lay down my office completely in all *Gemeinen* [Moravian communities] and at the same time make a new departure to the heart of Jesus, but I also want to assure you in advance that the Elder-Office of the Savior will also cease. I know behind what I stand, and I cannot help myself.[51]

The crisis passed, and as Moravians travelled to missionary work in new settings, their bloodthirsty language struck unexpected chords with some of the peoples they met, particularly indigenous peoples in North America, and that brought Moravian missions great success. For one of the most significant characteristics of this ebullient yet tightly structured movement was its hunger to undertake missions overseas to non-Christians. People who had already exiled themselves once to join the Moravian family zestfully threw themselves into fresh exile to spread the excitement which they had experienced in their own new lives. This was the first Protestant Church to commit itself to the task with such consistency, just at the moment when Protestant powers were creating overseas empires which might aid the work. Pietist Lutheranism did offer one outstanding precedent. In 1706, when Count Zinzendorf was still only six years old, August Francke had encouraged a former student of Halle, Bartholomaeus Ziegenbalg, to travel to India and begin mission among Hindus.

Ziegenbalg was the first Protestant missionary in the subcontinent. He took advantage of the kingdom of Denmark's modest but significant foothold at Tranquebar, the only European outpost in Asia offering a potential direct bridgehead for Pietism, to provide a base for his mission. He adopted strategies which were often subsequently ignored: like the Jesuit de Nobili before him (see p. 705), he showed a deep respect for Hindu traditions and tried to avoid presenting Christianity in woodenly Western terms. His resolution to discuss his faith thoughtfully with Muslims and Hindus took precedence for him over seeking rapid conversions. Ziegenbalg's work aroused the interest of Anglicans: it helped that Queen Anne of England's husband, Prince George, was Danish, and that the Prince's chaplain was a friend of Francke's. In a gesture of ecumenical cooperation rare at the time and not consistently shown later, the Anglican educational Society for Promoting Christian Knowledge sent Ziegenbalg a printer and press to make it possible to publish a pioneering translation of the Bible into Tamil. Alas for his gradualist strategy, he was beset by political troubles in India, and his fragile constitution led to an early death.[52]

Zinzendorf had his own close connections with the Danish Court, and from the 1730s he made something permanent of Ziegenbalg's interrupted work. Yet there was a difference from nearly all previous Western missions: the first Moravian missionaries whom he sent out were laypeople, often quite humble and uneducated folk, who tried to earn their livings by their craft skills on mission (see Plate 62). The Count himself personally joined his followers on an extraordinary series of journeys worldwide – to North America and the Caribbean, as well as travels through Europe from France to Britain to Scandinavia. These adventures came close to bankrupting him, and the work had to be rescued by others, but it continued. Moravian missionary work among slaves in the British West Indies and in America proved acceptable to slave owners, as they found that the Moravians taught their converts obedience and made them more hard-working. Moravians sought to improve the welfare of slaves rather than give institutional support to the growing British calls for the abolition of the trade and the institution (see pp. 870–71). Ostentatiously abstaining from involvement in politics, they still managed, in an astute balancing act, to preserve the esteem of British abolitionists. More generally, the Moravians showed other Protestant Churches that missions could be successful and that the initiative was worth imitating. Moravian numerical strength now lies outside their European homeland, thanks to their missionary work worldwide.[53]

THE EVANGELICAL REVIVAL: METHODISM

In parallel with the Pietist movement in Germany and enjoying many links with it was a renewal of English-speaking Protestantism which came to be described as the Evangelical Revival.[54] In the background were similar concerns to those which had galvanized the Pietists to action: devout English Protestants were unnerved by the changing character of the society in which they found themselves. England's prosperity and increasingly secular preoccupations (see pp. 787–91) were matched by a failure of its ecclesiastical courts, the disciplinary structure which the Church of England had inherited from the pre-Reformation Church. These had been effective enough up to the outbreak of the first English civil war in 1642, but they had never regained their authority when the restored episcopal establishment failed to include all English Protestants after 1662. The courts' decay was all the more pronounced after 1688. This collapse in ecclesiastical discipline was much more radical than in Lutheran countries, where the growth of Pietism had been impelled by different disruptions of society (see p. 738), but the resulting anxiety was similar. The English Parliament passed in 1697–8 an 'Act for the effectual suppressing of blasphemy and profaneness', by which it principally meant systematic anti-Trinitarian belief. The Act was an admission by the legislators that it was now possible to see 'Socinianism' as a serious threat to the Church, and that the Church was not capable of taking its own action against the threat. Earlier in 1697, the Scots had executed a rashly garrulous sceptic named Thomas Aikenhead as a blasphemer, an assertive piece of practical Christianity which was widely criticized even in Scotland and not there-after repeated. The English Act of Parliament did not stem the tide of theological change.[55]

One first reaction to the new situation in England was the channelling of Christian activism into voluntary societies. Some were like Spener's *collegia pietatis*, devotional groups within individual parishes, but many of these ran into problems through worries that they might be 'Jacobite' front organizations for those seeking a restoration of the exiled King James or his heirs.[56] It was politically safer to concentrate on voluntary organizations with specific practical focuses on obvious needs, two of which organizations we have already met in passing: the Society for Promoting Christian Knowledge, founded in 1698, and the Society for the Propagation of the Gospel, founded in 1701 (see pp. 746 and 725). A third element was Societies for the Reformation of Manners, voluntary organizations set up from the 1690s in London and other provincial towns to enforce public morality. They involved a not altogether stable coalition of all those who mourned the collapse of social discipline, and who together sought to recruit paid informers to search out varieties of human sin for public prosecution. This plan for a Protestant subscribers' version of the Spanish Inquisition found few recruits to do the informing: England had been heartily sickened by the efforts of Puritans in Oliver Cromwell's time to improve on the discipline exercised by courts of the pre-war episcopal Church. By the 1730s the work of the Societies for the Reformation of Manners had collapsed, aided by their internal doctrinal squabbles.[57] One might say that the Evangelical Revival was an answer to this failure; it was in the decade of the Societies' collapse that the new movement began gaining momentum.

Like the Pietists and Moravians, English Evangelicals sought to create a religion of the heart and of direct personal relationship with Jesus

Christ, in consciousness of his suffering on the Cross – his atonement to his Father for human sin. Once more, it was the message of Augustine, filtered through Luther. The impulse in part found a home in the Church of England, but it also revitalized existing English Dissenting denominations from the mid-seventeenth century, and it produced a new religious body which by accident rather than design found itself outside the established Church: Methodism. The leader in what became a world-wide movement was John Wesley, a man who made sure that his career was as well documented as any Pietist might desire, assuring that his own version of his story would get first hearing.[58] He was an Anglican clergyman, as was his father. His mother's father had likewise been a clergyman, ejected from the national Church after Charles II's restoration as a Dissenter, but both John's parents were strong Tories. Indeed his mother was for some time a Non-Juror (see p. 734), and Samuel and Susanna Wesley's disagreements over the royal succession had disrupted the marital bed – John's conception was actually the sign of their ideological reunion.[59] High Churchpeople were increasingly left aside after James's flight, as subsequent regimes harboured often justified suspicions about their loyalty. The Church which Wesley knew as a young man was dominated by the very different religious style of the 'Latitudinarians'.

The young Wesley, already out of step with the establishment of his Church, followed the family profession of ministry to ordination and a Fellowship of an Oxford college, in a university itself still an obstinate stronghold of the embattled High Church party. Here he gathered a group of friends to share a devotional life and carry out works of charity rather in the style of a Counter-Reformation confraternity (see p. 656); their ordered lifestyle earned them the initially mocking title of 'Methodists'. Now wider influences came to bear on Wesley's religious outlook. He and his brother Charles set off in 1735 for the newly founded English American colony of Georgia to work among the settlers on behalf of the Society for the Propagation of the Gospel (itself dominated by High Churchmen). This ended in an ignominious voyage home, mainly thanks to John's pastoral clumsiness, but while heading out he had been much impressed by the piety and cheerful courage of a group of Moravians, apparently unmoved by storms which terrified everyone else on board.

On John Wesley's return from Georgia, his self-confidence severely damaged, he was much comforted by Moravians, and that led to an important moment for him – characteristically ambiguous in its setting between his High Church past and something which he found both old and new. One night in 1738, having attended Evensong at St Paul's Cathedral in London, he went on 'very unwillingly' to a Moravian prayer meeting nearby in Aldersgate. While the solemn music of Evensong still rang in his memory, he was listening to a reading from Martin Luther's restatement of Paul's message to the Romans – justification by faith alone. In a phrase now famous, he felt his 'heart strangely warmed' – less frequently remembered, though characteristic of the man, is the fact that this led him immediately to pray in a somewhat passive-aggressive manner 'for those who had in a more especial manner despitefully used me and persecuted me'.[60] The Reformation came alive for him. With a conviction that he must not simply seek personal holiness but spread a message of salvation as far as he could, Wesley embarked on a lifetime's mission throughout the British Isles. He learned much from the Moravians, even though he eventually broke with them – not least, the importance of travel. His restless journeyings were eventually to wreck a marriage already ill-chosen when he entered it in 1751, and were also to prove a welcome escape from that mistake.[61]

Wesley's mission was set amid rapid economic transformation in Britain, and a great shift in population to new manufacturing centres much accelerated during the course of his long ministry as the industrial revolution gained momentum. Such places were a problem for the established Church, whose ancient distribution of parishes was very difficult to amend and expand. How could the new populations receive the pastoral care they deserved and hear of the good news he had received? Wesley's answer was unconventional for a High Church Anglican: in 1739 he followed his friend and fellow clergyman George Whitefield (at first rather nervously) in preaching in the open air, as revivalist Jesuits did in Catholic Europe. He was astonished at the dramatic result. Crowds unused to such direct personal address or much consideration from educated clergymen were gripped by mass emotion and a sense of their own sin and its release. They laughed, they wept, they rolled on the ground. Something must be done with them.

Wesley relished organizing people. He sent out travelling ('itinerant') preachers to build up societies from among the excited crowds, who found peace and personal dignity in the Christian message, and took on the Oxford nickname of 'Methodists'. Soon they learned to sing the hymns written by John's gifted brother Charles – around nine thousand in all. They featured much reference to divine wounds and blood (although not in the same soaking quantities that Moravians enjoyed) and through them ran a characteristic Wesley theme, that life could be totally transformed by this acceptance of Christ's sufferings: all for 'me'. That is a characteristic Evangelical emphasis on Jesus's direct address to the individual, the Saviour's gaze turned lovingly on the poorest wretch.[62]

Methodists can still thrill the listener when they return to this heritage, sung to one of their vigorous early hymn tunes, many of which delight in repeating the words in glorious tumbles of competing melody, before the satisfyingly harmonious resolution. These so-called 'fuguing tunes' require a certain skill to sing, and Methodists appreciated skill.[63] Over time, their music became one of the distinguishing marks of the culture of the 'chapel', an all-embracing society which was a safe and wholesome setting for ordered family life. The English now prefer to sing one such fuguing tune from Kent called 'Cranbrook' to a nonsense verse, 'Ilkla Moor Batat', said to have been made up by a Yorkshire chapel choir out on a country jaunt, but 'Cranbrook' will be found to make a fine sound of Charles Wesley's original words. Effectively it is the universal anthem of Methodism:

Oh, for a thousand tongues to sing
My great Redeemer's praise,
The glories of my God and King,
The triumphs of His grace!

Jesus! – the name that charms our fears,
That bids our sorrows cease;
'Tis music in the sinner's ears,
'Tis life and health and peace.

He breaks the power of cancelled sin,
He sets the prisoner free;
His blood can make the foulest clean;
His blood avails for me.[64]

Methodist hymns were an element in the gradual separation of Wesley's movement from the Church of England. The irregular and noisy activity of the Methodists deeply worried the Church authorities and infuriated many parish clergy. Faced with much hostility, Wesley had no choice in some places but to continue with open-air preaching, or even to forget his Anglican principles and accept the hospitality of Dissenting congregations. He built headquarters in London and Bristol in 1739; soon his societies were putting up other preaching houses ('chapels') for themselves all over the country (see Plate 38). This posed questions of identity – much as Wesley tried to avoid the issue by labelling his movement not a Church but a 'Connexion', and in mid-career (1758) writing a pamphlet entitled *Reasons against a separation from the Church of England*. Was he simply founding yet another new society to bring fresh life to Anglicanism? What about his congregations in Presbyterian Scotland, if this was so? The only legal way in either England or Scotland to sustain his preaching houses was to declare them to be Dissenting chapels and get them registered as the law demanded; reluctantly in 1787 he had to advise his societies that this must be done.

By then other circumstances had made this inevitable. Wesley's preachers had begun successful work in the British American colonies, but when revolution broke out in 1776, they were seriously affected. Many Anglican clergy withdrew and there was virtually no one left to whom Wesley's American followers could go to receive Holy Communion. Wesley, High Church sacramentalist that he was – both John and Charles were prepared to use the language of 'real presence' in talking about the Eucharist – saw this as a desperate situation. There was still no Anglican bishop in America to ordain new clergy and Wesley could not persuade any English bishop to do so. Accordingly he searched for precedents to help out, and more or less found what he wanted in the early history of the Church in Alexandria, where priests as well as bishops had been involved in ordinations. So, on the basis of being a 'Presbyter of the Church of England', he took it on himself to revive the practice. His brother Charles, also an Anglican clergyman, deplored the move, but John obstinately refused to recognize that he had done anything decisive, even when he went on to ordain men for areas within the British Isles and elsewhere where he thought an emergency justified the action. With further inconsistency, he was furious when the leaders of the American Methodists called themselves bishops – a tradition which has remained within the American tradition of Methodism. And even towards the end of his life he repeated (as did Charles, with rather less complication) that he lived and died a member of the Church of England.[65]

So Wesley in his latter days was an Anglican in the fashion that the elderly Zinzendorf was a Lutheran; he was, and was not. Born in a different time and place, Wesley might have founded a religious order or a flexibly structured society which could find a home in the Church as the Jesuits had done (and even they had experienced early difficulty), but the English Reformation had set its face against monasticism. Wesley's deliberate avoidance of the full consequences of his actions meant that he left a host of problems for his preachers and societies. On his death in 1791, they grappled with issues of identity and Church government which his immense personal prestige had postponed. The resulting quarrels were often bitter, and although British Methodism continued growing in numbers and influence, it was characterized for almost a century by constant internal schisms away from the original 'Wesleyan Connexion' – in fact, worldwide, Methodism has been extraordinarily fertile in creating new religious identities, as we will discover. Methodists still all sang Charles Wesley's hymns and shared a common ethos, practising a 'religion of the heart' which treasured Wesley's optimistic affirmation of the possibility of Christian perfection. Here once more was a typical Wesley contradiction. While John Wesley loved Luther's exposition of Christ's sacrifice for sin in his Passion and the need for the gift of free grace for salvation, his High Churchmanship led him to reject predestination and to affirm humanity's universal potential for acceptance by God. He wanted to challenge his converts to do their best in an active Christian life, and he commended the challenge to Reformed views of salvation offered by the sixteenth-century renegade Dutch Reformed minister Jacobus Arminius (see p. 649). He even called the house journal of his Methodists the *Arminian Magazine* to ram home the point; and it was a point with which most Church of England clergy would then have agreed. Wesley's distinctive soteriology was to have great long-term resonances.

By no means all the leading figures of the Evangelical Revival were swept into Wesley's Connexion or its offshoots. His early associate George Whitefield deeply disagreed with Wesley's rejection of Calvinist predestination, and he founded his own association of Calvinist congregations. Whitefield lacked Wesley's organizational talent; his genius lay in oratory (see Plate 37). His cenotaph in Old South Presbyterian Church, in Newburyport, Massachusetts, says with an idiom which may mislead modern ears but is intended as a compliment to a preacher of the post-Apostolic age, 'no other uninspired man ever preached to so large assemblies'. Many Evangelical clergy nevertheless managed to avoid the separation from the Church of England forced on the followers of Whitefield and Wesley. While Wesley famously wrote 'I look upon all the world as my parish', they were prepared to work within the existing parish structure of the Church of England.[66] Through their energies, certain areas and parishes became strongholds of Evangelical practice. As a result, by the end of the eighteenth century, there was a recognizable Evangelical party among English clergy and gentry – still divided by those inclined to Calvinism and those like Wesley inclined to Arminianism.

Such Evangelicals and their Methodist and Dissenting allies or rivals began a long process of remoulding British social attitudes away from the extrovert consumerism of the eighteenth century, in an effort to make people exercise a self-discipline in their daily lives which would police itself, in the absence of any possibility of the national Church now doing so. Congregations were encouraged to better themselves materially as well as spiritually, a broad hint being given in one of Charles Wesley's best-loved hymns:

> And can it be that I should gain
> an interest in the Saviour's blood!
> Died he for me? who caused his pain!
> For me? who him to death pursued?
> Amazing love! How can it be
> that thou, my God, shouldst die for me?
> Amazing love! How can it be
> that thou, my God, shouldst die for me?

Here Wesley's fertile imagination has sought his controlling metaphor in the language of a vigorously commercial society: sinners 'gain an interest' in the Saviour's blood, just as they might gain an 'interest', a commercial stake, in a little shop, a busy workshop – perhaps even, if they did well enough, a factory or a bank. Such would be the aspiration of many of the struggling, financially vulnerable people who sang Wesley's hymn, turning their sense of joy and relief at their salvation to making a more decent life for themselves and their families. Hard work was allied with strict morality; if ever there was anything resembling the 'Protestant work ethic', it came out of Methodism and the Evangelical Revival rather than the sixteenth-century Reformation.[67] One of the most remarkable English Evangelical activists in education and charity among the poor both nationwide and in her native West Country, Hannah More, has appropriately been styled by her recent biographer 'the first Victorian'. Even though she died when the future Queen Victoria was only fourteen, More anticipated and set patterns for the moral seriousness which was the preferred public self-image of most nineteenth-century Britons.[68] The effect did not wear off until the 1960s (see pp. 985–901).

Evangelicals were by nature activists, and they began to follow the Moravians abroad. In doing so, they did much to influence the behaviour of two great international institutions created by a century of warfare and imperial expansion, the British army and navy. Many of John Wesley's travelling preachers were former soldiers, ideally suited to the rigorous life he required of them. Worldwide in range and a solvent of local difference among their recruits, the British armed forces have often been injudiciously ignored as agents in the spread of Evangelical revival, probably because of traditional unflattering stereotypes about military behaviour. We need to see the army as like other institutions and communities in flux in the eighteenth and nineteenth centuries, where uprooted individuals sought identity and frameworks for their lives amid confusion and danger: Evangelical principles were as likely to appeal to soldiers as to anyone else, perhaps more in view of their confrontations with violence and death. Moreover, the British army's and navy's steady embrace of a non-partisan patriotism chimed well with a general tendency in British Evangelicalism to keep away from politics unless absolutely necessary, while tending to patriotic conservatism.[69]

THE GREAT AWAKENINGS AND THE AMERICAN REVOLUTION

American Evangelicalism had its own preoccupations, which from the early eighteenth century produced its distinctive style of Protestant revival, soon christened 'Great Awakenings'. These emerged at a time when the leaderships of many American Churches were feeling that the dreams of the first colonists had been betrayed; the Church establishments in several colonies represented only a minority of the population, and many people had no Church contacts at all. Just as in Old England, systems of Church discipline, once so important in New England's sense of its identity, were now impossible to enforce. The tensions in trying to maintain them against such frightening phenomena as premarital sex and Quakers produced one embarrassing high-profile excess in 1692 at Salem, Massachusetts. A short-lived and belated repetition of Protestant English paranoia about witches led to around 150 prosecutions and nineteen executions, and then in short order to the discrediting of the old ethos. A similar witchcraft case in Connecticut in the same year was dropped after widespread and powerfully expressed disquiet from clergy and laity alike, and indeed one of the judges in the Salem trials, Samuel Sewall, subsequently repented and five years later publicly asked fellow members of his Boston congregation for forgiveness for what he had done.[70]

Before Wesley's movement reached across the Atlantic, the Awakenings in the northern colonies were more purely Reformed, associated with Churches which sprang from Scottish or Dutch roots rather than from those of English origin. Scots had begun emigrating from their kingdom in the early seventeenth century, though their first destination had been not America but Ireland. King James VI and I, after succeeding to the English throne, encouraged them to settle there in order to counter Catholic militancy, sending them to the most troublesome part of Gaelic Ireland, Ulster. Those immigrants may not have been especially convinced Protestants to begin with, but they had every incentive to discover their Protestantism in the face of a resentful Catholic population whom they were seeking to supplant. Anxious, rootless, looking for identity in a strange land, they turned with fervour not so much to the feeble existing Protestant parish system of the Church of Ireland but to ministers of their own, who brought with them the vigorously developing popular life of the Scottish Kirk, centred on massive open-air occasional celebrations of the Eucharist, preceded by long periods of catechism and sermonizing. So large were the gatherings that often no church building could hold them and they turned into open-air 'Holy Fairs', occasions of mass celebration and socializing within a framework of emotional worship: a shared experience of ecstatic renewal, or 'revival'.[71]

From the beginning, such popular excitement was associated with those who wished to emphasize the distinctiveness of Scottish religion in the face of Stuart attempts to conform it to English practice, and Britain's conflicts in the seventeenth century crystallized the movement's identification with the Presbyterians who seized power in Scotland in 1691 (see p. 734). 'Holy Fairs' continued to break out into revival in the motherland and in Ulster through the eighteenth century. In both settings, Scottish identity struggled to assert itself against an English and Anglican state which, after the Union of England and Scotland in 1707, held increasing political power over Scots. In particular, Ulstermen who cherished their Presbyterianism were discontented at the increasingly unchallengeable established status of the episcopally governed Church of Ireland (they were also fairly accomplished at quarrelling with each other), and the discontented looked across the Atlantic. Scots also emigrated to North America, in default of their own colonies: the English had played a part in helping to stifle an ill-conceived independent Scots colonial enterprise in Central America. There these immigrants from

Ulster and Scotland set up their own Presbyterian Churches, and the 'Holy Fairs' proved no less appropriate to the American frontier than they had been to the frontiers of Ulster. By the 1720s their network of Churches ('Scotch-Irish' in American usage) was flourishing, especially in the Middle Colonies, where religious patterns were so much more open than further south or north. They came into increasing conflict with the older English established Churches. The tensions of a new element in the American religious mix were about to burst into creative energy.

One of the earliest public stirrings in the 1720s sprang from the dissatisfaction felt by a newly arrived minister from north-west Germany, Theodorus Frelinghuysen, with what he saw as the formality of the Dutch Reformed Church in New Jersey. In his German homeland, a borderland between Lutheranism and the Reformed, he had been spiritually formed by Pietism. In his own Church in New Jersey he probably did more to stir up trouble than to bring new life, but he helped to create a lasting pattern: an appeal to the need for personal conversion and 'revival' in the Church, and a tension between those who advocated revival and those who did not find this a useful or appropriate way of expressing their Christian commitment. During the 1730s a similar excitement (and similar backlash) appeared in the anglophone Presbyterian Churches, led by a family of ministers who classically were Scots immigrants from Ulster, William Tennent and his sons Gilbert and William.

Gilbert Tennent's often uncomfortable ministry looked back to the enthusiasms of Ulster, and when he met Frelinghuysen in America, he was delighted to find that model confirmed. Soon he was roving beyond his own congregation in New Brunswick, New Jersey, to take the message further. From 1739 he found a like-minded Calvinist colleague in the electrifying English preacher George Whitefield, but their style developed very differently. Whitefield's ministry in North America was consistently marked by its combative spirit, often towards fellow Calvinists whom he felt were obstructing revival, but Tennent was jolted out of his tendency to similar confrontation by an abrasive meeting in 1741 with no less a representative of German Pietism than Count Nikolaus von Zinzendorf, in the course of one of the Count's tours of America for the Moravians, his most far-flung journey from Herrnhut. Alarmed both by Zinzendorf's theology and his aggressive personality, Tennent spent the latter half of his career mending fences with those in his own Church whom his extrovert and emotional preaching had alienated. The encounter and its effect on Tennent are a significant symbol of a constant tension within modern Evangelicalism, not merely between Calvinists and Arminians as in the case of Wesley and Whitefield, but between institutional loyalties and individual initiatives – often also between considerable rival egos.[72]

In the northern colonies, Awakenings were led in the Congregational Church by Jonathan Edwards. Edwards combined an academic rigour which came from his deep interest in philosophy with an uncompromising attachment to Calvinism, reinforced by an experience of conversion in 1727. He insisted that we must worship God with the whole person, mind and emotion, and from the greatest philosopher to the smallest child we must love God in simplicity. In a sermon of 1738, he ended by assuring his listeners, 'if ever you arrive at heaven, faith and love must be the wings which must carry you there'.[73] There are echoes here of words which Edwards would have known from one of Protestant England's earliest hymn writers, his fellow Congregationalist Isaac Watts, who thirty years before had prayed:

> Give me the wings of faith to rise
> within the veil, and see
> the saints above, how great their joys
> how bright their glories be.

Edwards was a champion of the composition of new hymns over the traditional Puritan singing of metrical psalms, and they became a major feature of the revival meetings of the Great Awakenings. As so often, a new religious movement which had little actually new in its beliefs (Edwards prided himself in his traditional Reformed theology) took a novel face through its use of music.[74]

In 1734, at much the same time that Gilbert Tennent's revival ministry began stretching beyond a single congregation, Edwards's people in Northampton, Massachusetts, experienced the exhilaration and disruption of revival, to the astonishment of New England – not least because it was reported that the folk of Northampton had no time to be ill while the 'awakening' was seizing the town.[75] Edwards continued to puzzle over the phenomenon and, unusually among his fellow revivalists, he tried to analyse it in a major study of the psychology of religion, *A Treatise concerning religious affections* (1746). He was hospitable to George Whitefield, while doing his best to deal with the emotional havoc caused in congregations in the wake of Whitefield's visits, and he agonized about how far to restrict the communion table to the demonstrably regenerate, remembering the Half-Way Covenant of his forebears. His ministry, largely as a consequence of his agonizing, was never free of quarrels. But he remains among the most celebrated of the powerful personalities who rallied crowds to the themes of the Awakening.

An important consequence of Edwards's teaching was that his great intellectual reputation lent respectability to a seductive conception of the Last Days, known in the jargon of theologians as 'post-millennialism'. This proposition was a development of that traditionally exciting idea, dating right back to Justin Martyr and Irenaeus in the second century CE, that human history would culminate in a thousand-year rule of the saints. Edwards believed that this millennium would take place before the Second Coming of Christ – hence the Second Coming would be 'post-millennial'. So the millennium would indeed be part of history, unfolding out of present-day human experience, and open to the reconstruction of a perfect human society, for which it was possible to make practical plans. Edwards was among those suggesting that America might be the place where the golden age of the millennium was scheduled to begin, in untamed wildernesses unsullied by ancient European sins. It was an exhilarating idea which bound those in its grip to begin activist efforts to improve society in a great variety of ways, and it suggested a special destiny for the thirteen colonies. Despite Isaac Watts's dry comment on his fellow Congregationalist's excitement, 'I think his reasonings on America want force', the mood has never fully left America.[76]

The Great Awakenings thus shaped the future of American religion. They destroyed the territorial communality which was still the assumption of most religious practice back in Europe. Religious practice, like conversion, became a matter of choice. Charismatic ministers who lacked the scruples of Gilbert Tennent or Jonathan Edwards ignored traditional boundaries in setting out to win souls – but in turn, if they were successful in setting up a new congregation which hearkened to their message, they found themselves prisoners or servants of their enthusiasts who were their means of support. Freelance preachers are not unnaturally often much concerned with financial survival, which can be an unhealthy preoccupation. Priorities in worship changed in the Awakenings. Renewal was experienced as renewal of enthusiasm rather than performance of an unchanging liturgy; Protestant Churches which did not adapt, and which based themselves on traditional European models, suffered. The Anglicans, strongly linked to the Church of

England, which was struggling at the same time with the Methodist and Evangelical Revivals, were even more resistant than the Congregationalist Churches of New England to the style of the Awakenings. They did little missionizing on the ever-expanding frontiers, and they lost out as a result. In 1700, they served roughly a quarter of the colonial population; in 1775, even after rapid population growth, roughly a ninth.[77]

Coalescing out of the welter of new gatherings came new denominations. In the south, a Church called the Separate Baptists was virtually created by the Awakenings, and the Methodists, after suffering setbacks for their British loyalism during the Revolution, soon took off once more; so two of the most influential strands within American Protestantism owe their prominence to the first Awakenings period. The sense of common American heritage among different Protestant denominations was much strengthened by this experience. That would have a considerable effect on politics. Moreover, the Awakenings enjoyed huge success among enslaved people. In 1762, one Anglican missionary calculated sadly that of around 46,000 enslaved in South Carolina, only five hundred were Christians.[78] That reflected the fact that many plantation owners were reluctant to allow their human property Christianity, but it is possible that he really meant that only five hundred were Anglicans, because he was writing amid the religious fervour of the Awakenings sweeping through the colonies. These eventually made spectacular breaches in the earlier barriers to evangelization of the enslaved, and fostered an African-American Christian culture which expresses itself in the fervency of extrovert Evangelical Protestantism rather than in the cooler tones of Anglicanism.

Why did the Awakenings succeed so mightily with enslaved Africans where the Anglicans failed? Central to the answer must be the Evangelical demand for a personal choice: that gave dignity to people who had never been offered a choice in their lives, just as the confraternities and saints' devotion of the Catholic Church provided the opportunity to make religious choices (see pp. 712–14). Related was Methodism's insistence on complete personal transformation or regeneration, an attractive theme in lives which offered little other hope of dramatic change. Moravians brought song and uninhibited celebration of God's blood and wounds to people who knew much of both. Moravians also insisted that God was pleased by cheerfulness, a congenial thought in a culture which remembered better than Europeans how to celebrate. And at the centre was the library of books which was the Bible, in which readers could suddenly find themselves walking into a particular book and recognizing their own life. Where Catholic enslaved peoples in the Caribbean or Iberian America had saints, Protestant American enslaved people had texts which gave them stories and songs. They sang about the biblical stories which made them laugh and cry, in some of the most compelling vocal music ever created by Christians, 'Negro Spirituals': a fusion of the Evangelical hymn tradition of the Awakenings with celebratory rhythms and repetitions remembered from days of African freedom.

What might the Bible-readers choose? For people made slaves, the Bible contained the experience of Israel's exile and desolation, in the prophets and psalms. A captive people escaped and entered a promised land (and the deliverer Moses, like St Patrick, brooked no nonsense from snakes). The Saviour was a poor man, whipped and executed, who died for all and rose again. There were thrones for the downtrodden people at the end of time. In other words, there was justice. It was irrelevant that many of these themes had inspired the English to cross the Atlantic a century before, only to become the colonial people who oppressed the African-American; this was a discovery anew, forged painfully out of the acquisition of literacy by a minority of privileged or freed people. How could they not accept such a vulnerable, all-powerful Saviour? They sang of him:

> Poor little Jesus boy
> Made him to be born in a manger
> World treated him so mean
> Treat me mean, too.[79]

The results were spectacular, but posed new questions. By 1800, around a fifth of all American Methodists were enslaved people – and enslaved they were still, despite being Methodists. In this aftermath of the Revolution which had talked much of life, liberty and human happiness, African-Americans whether free or bonded found little welcome in white Churches and at best would be directed to a segregated seat. So they frequently made a further choice – to create their own Churches (see Plate 41). From 1790 there was an African Methodist Episcopal Union; there followed Black Baptist Unions, taking their known origin from a congregation of Baptists no more than eight strong in the 1770s.[80] Congregations demanded their share in Christian decency – and how could Evangelical Protestants deny them that? Clothing and the dignity it conveyed, indeed, would become a major theme in

Evangelical mission worldwide. Plantation slaves had frequently been kept naked for work – fuelling white fantasies about their innate lasciviousness.[81] Now members of black congregations were known to walk more than fourteen miles to church, dressed in their special Sunday clothes but barefoot, carrying their clean shoes with them, which they put on when they reached their church buildings. Such independent Churches naturally wanted their own clergy – white clergy would not minister to them in such settings. In a land which restricted any blacks to the manual work for which they had been imported, suddenly there was a profession open to them, and it was difficult for white Evangelicals to deny the clerical character of such ministers who used the same charged language of conversion, and won souls for Christ just as they did.[82]

So a racial revolution, shaped by Evangelical Christianity, took shape quietly alongside a different revolutionary uprising by whites against whites. In the 1770s a gradual poisoning of relations between the British mother-country and the thirteen colonies became a political crisis, which ended in a colony-wide Declaration of Independence in 1776. The relationship of the Awakenings to this great fracture in anglophone power is not straightforward. One element in it was paradoxically the British victory in the Seven Years War, which in 1763 delivered New France (Canada) into British control. This forced the British government to face the problem of how a Protestant power might govern an overwhelmingly Catholic territory. One precedent was Protestant 'Ascendancy' government in Ireland, but already the punitive policies against Irish Catholics produced by two centuries of warfare after the Reformation were beginning to be modified; and the political situation in Canada, where there was no loyalist Protestant aristocracy with whom to ally, was very different. The British answer, embodied in the Quebec Act of 1774, imitated the success of a small-scale previous experiment in the Catholic Spanish island of Menorca, a British-ruled strategic base in the Mediterranean: it was a pragmatic alliance with the local French elite, and therefore inevitably with the Catholic Church. Protestants in the thirteen colonies were furious at this arbitrary outflanking of their culture and shared British values. A Continental Congress summoned to Philadelphia in 1774, amid statements on many commercial and taxation grievances, recorded its 'astonishment that a British Parliament should ever consent to establish in that country a Religion, that has deluged your island in blood and dispersed impiety, bigotry, persecution, murder, and rebellion through every part of the world'.[83]

When anger turned to open war, American Evangelicals were divided. Scotch-Irish clergy, with their own traditions of warfare against Westminster, were influential in articulating opposition to British misgovernment; Princeton University, forcing house for leaders of the Presbyterian Awakening, was a ready source of morale-boosting sermons and literature, and its Scottish President, John Witherspoon, was a leading figure in the Continental Congress through the revolutionary years.[84] Yet Baptists gave no single opinion on the Revolution, mindful of the angry reaction which they had provoked in that same Continental Congress when they had complained about New England's compulsory levies for the established Congregational Church. The irony of the revolutionary slogan 'no taxation without representation' was not lost on Baptists.[85] Quakers were harassed by the revolutionaries for their pacifism and, in ugly incidents echoed recently amid the American outburst of flag displays after the 9/11 attacks of 2001, they had their houses trashed for not displaying candles after the British defeat in 1783.[86] Methodists, taking their cue from John Wesley's emphatic Tory loyalism, opposed the Revolution; so, unsurprisingly, did many Anglicans. When, in 1775, the Rev. Samuel Andrews of Wallingford, Connecticut, received Congress's order to lead his Anglican congregation in observing a day of fast, he obeyed it with aggressive wit by choosing his sermon text from Amos 5.21: 'I hate, I despise your feast days.'[87] It was not surprising that Andrews was among those loyalists who could find no place in the new Republic, and who trooped north (often suffering great hardship) to take refuge in the remaining British territories of Canada.

Nevertheless, because the revolutionary leadership sprang from the social establishment in several colonies, it included many who were Anglicans by denominational loyalty, no less than two-thirds of the signatories of the Declaration of Independence.[88] Elite education tended to lead these Founding Fathers not to the Awakenings but to the Enlightenment and Deism (see pp. 786–7): cool versions of Christianity, or virtually no Christianity at all. The polymath Benjamin Franklin seldom went to church, and when he did, it was to enjoy the Anglican *Book of Common Prayer* decorously performed in Christ Church, Philadelphia; he made it a point of principle not to spend energy affirming the divinity of Christ. Thomas Jefferson was rather more concerned than Franklin to be seen at church on key political occasions, but he deplored religious controversy, deeply distrusted organized religion and spoke of the Trinity as 'abracadabra . . . hocus-pocus . . . a deliria of crazy imaginations, as foreign to Christianity as is that of Mahomet'.[89] In the face of such low-temperature religion, many on the present-day American religious right, anxious to appropriate the Revolution for their own version of modern American patriotism, have sought comfort in the ultimate Founding Father, George Washington, but here too there is much to doubt. Washington never received Holy Communion, and was inclined in discourse to refer to providence or destiny rather than to God. In the nineteenth century, patriotic and pious artists often spiced up Washington's deathbed with religion, giving him on occasion an almost Christ-like ascension into Heaven accompanied by a heavenly choir (see Plate 40), but the reality of the scene in 1799 did not include prayers or the presence of Christian clergy.[90]

What this revolutionary elite achieved amid a sea of competing Christianities, many of which were highly uncongenial to them, was to make religion a private affair in the eyes of the new American federal government. The constitution which they created made no mention of God or Christianity (apart from the date by 'the Year of our Lord'). That was without precedent in Christian polities of that time, and with equal disregard for tradition (after some debate), the Great Seal of the United States of America bore no Christian symbol but rather the Eye of Providence, which if it recalled anything recalled Freemasonry (see pp. 771–2).[91] The motto 'In God We Trust' only first appeared on an American coin amid civil war in 1864, a very different era, and it was 1957 before it featured on any paper currency of the United States. Famously, Thomas Jefferson wrote as president to the Baptists of Danbury, Connecticut, in 1802 that the First Amendment to the American Federal Constitution had created a 'wall of separation between Church and State'. There was no one more shrewdly aware than Jefferson of the complexities of American politics, and he was speaking exclusively of the federal 'State', not of the constitutions of individual states.

Nevertheless one by one, those state Church establishments were dismantled; Massachusetts Congregationalism, almost the first establishment to be created, was the last to go, in 1833.[92] Those Anglicans who had not fled north to Canada quickly saw sense and formed themselves into an episcopally led denomination suitable for a republic, the Protestant Episcopal Church of the United States of America; but their future was as a relatively small body with a disproportionate number of the wealthy and influential, their restrained and European ethos of devotion rather countercultural amid American Protestantism. Thus though the first lasting American English-speaking colony was Anglican Virginia, the rhetoric of covenant, chosenness, of wilderness triumphantly converted to garden, has descended in American political and religious consciousness from Governor Winthrop's expedition to New England. Since Winthrop's would-be monolithic Congregational Church establishment has also long gone, American Protestantism in its exuberant variety has adroitly grafted on to its memories of Massachusetts the obstinate individualism and separatism of the Plymouth Pilgrim Fathers – an ethos which Winthrop and his covenanting congregations deplored. All of this is served up with a powerful dose of extrovert revivalist fervour ultimately deriving from the Scottish Reformation.

The consequences of the British upheavals between the 1620s and 1660s were thus wholly out of scale with what could have been expected in the seventeenth century from a marginal, second-rank European power. Because Protestant anglophone culture has until the present century remained hegemonic in the USA, the American varieties of British Protestantism are the most characteristic forms of Protestant Christianity today – together with their offshoots, the most dynamic forms of Christianity worldwide. American Roman Catholicism too has largely left the Counter-Reformation behind, and in much of its behaviour and attitudes, it has been enrolled as a subset of the American Protestant religious scene. This is a Christianity shaped by a very different historical experience from western Europe, and similarities in language and confessional background may mislead us into missing the deep contrasts. In the next century, American and European Protestants went into partnership with the aim of creating a new Protestant empire of the mind across Asia and Africa; but when they set out to bring the Gospel to new lands, they did so from countries increasingly in disagreement about the nature and content of that Gospel and the God which it proclaimed. When the literary executor of C. S. Lewis, the British novelist, literary scholar and Christian apologist, gathered together a set of Lewis's popular apologetic essays, he gave the little book and one of its chapters a title from Lewis's metaphor of God standing in the accused's box in an English courtroom – 'God in the Dock'.[93] To see how God arrived there, we need to venture into a meeting with the Enlightenment, that transforming force of Western culture which took shape alongside the Reformation itself.

PART VII

God in the Dock
(1492–present)

21

Enlightenment: Ally or Enemy?
(1492–1815)

NATURAL AND UNNATURAL
PHILOSOPHY (1492–1700)

In 1926 Max Ernst, Surrealist German artist, lapsed Catholic and hag-ridden veteran of the First World War, created a startling image of the Christ Child (see Plate 65). It may be read merely as a piece of smart modernist irreverence: Ernst painted the Virgin Mary delivering young Jesus a good slapping over her knee, with the naked Child's halo fallen ignominiously to the ground. Yet, as with so much of Western culture over the last three centuries, Ernst's risky creation is resonant with echoes of ancient Christian themes. Quickly apparent is its reversal of one of the commonest clichés of Western medieval art. Many a de-votional painting in the churches of medieval Europe had portrayed the donors directing their gaze to the Virgin and Child; now, in 1926, Ernst and his friends the writers André Breton and Paul Éluard turned their cold and casual glances on the scene almost covertly from a window.

Ernst would have known that he and his Surrealist friends were viewing another persistent motif from the medieval Age of Faith: the delinquent boy Jesus. It originated in apocryphal 'Gospels' from the first few centuries of Christian history which tried to improve on the scanty amount of information in the Bible about Jesus's childhood, and the stories descended into medieval poetry. Our Lord's apocryphal child-hood misdemeanours could be extremely disagreeable, up to and includ-ing the murder of his playmates, albeit followed by his shamefaced restoration of the victims to life.[1] Unsurprisingly, Our Lady considered it her parental duty to punish him, and she can be found doing precisely that, carved in wood and stone. There do not appear to be any extant examples of these spankings in stained glass; although glass was a favourite setting for visual images of the Mother of God (see Plate 30), it was more consistently elevated than sculpture in its doctrinal content, probably because it was more consistently visible. Christian music too took up the theme: a ballad probably seventeenth century in date, since it was sung in both old England and the American Appalachian Mountains, is entitled 'The Bitter Withy Tree'. It sings of the Christ Child cursing the tree from which his Mother has fashioned a cane with which to beat him for his brutal arrogance:

> Then he says to his Mother, 'Oh, the withy! Oh, the withy!
> The bitter withy that causes me to smart, to smart,
> Oh, the withy, it shall be the very first tree
> That perishes to the heart!'

Behind the story of European Enlightenment, which is sometimes told as a fairy-tale progression from Christian (and clerical) short-sightedness to a secularized clarity of vision, there lies a more interestingly complex narrative in which religion and doubt, blasphemy and devotion remained in dialogue, as they had done throughout Christian history. Western Christianity has faced the problem of Enlightenment more directly and perhaps more honestly than its devotional cousins among the Orthodox and non-Chalcedonians, and those who follow Western paths have often found the journey taxing and distressing. Yet there remains a Christianity which can claim to be a child of the Enlightenment, while still asserting its birthright in the past, rather as Ernst's picture can only be read within the Christian tradition which it might seem to be mocking. We may begin to see how this tangle developed if we return to the Reformation and Counter-Reformation.

Amid the theological storms which fractured the Western Latin Church are repeated glimpses of other eddies of ideas which disrupted the assumptions of medieval Europeans about the world around them. Humanist scholarship was a vital force in these currents, because it opened up much new non-Christian literature surviving from the ancient world, innocent of Christian theological preoccupations. Renaissance humanists and the Protestant Reformers both tried to break away from old thinking, but they might have radically different goals. Luther and Zwingli saw many humanist concerns as no more relevant than any excess of scholasticism to humanity's absolute need for salvation by external grace. Accordingly the archetypal humanist scholar and activist Zwingli supported the primarily scholastically trained lecturer Luther rather than his former humanist hero Erasmus in the clash over human free will in 1524 (see pp. 613–14). Rival Churches commandeered humanist scholarship for their own purposes in theological warfare. They deployed skills like philology and historical criticism, but rarely valued objectivity; they drew on creative humanist discussion of schooling, the more efficiently to drum uniformity into young minds. The suppression of humanist doubt proved temporary, yet confessionally engaged scholars kept on trying.

Faced with the change of atmosphere in the 1520s, some humanists withdrew into an interior exile, ceasing to publish, or moving to fields of enquiry such as Classical history which could not easily be drawn into theological controversy. Distinguished scholars like Maarten van Dorp, Beatus Rhenanus and Willibald Pirckheimer thus earned themselves a quiet life, but with the consequence that their names are now known only to specialists in intellectual history.[2] Nevertheless, their silence on matters of religious controversy reminded the literary public that there might be ways of approaching the sacred which did not dance to agendas set by Martin Luther or the pope. Just such an alternative perspective came from various forms of esoteric ancient literature beyond scripture: the hermetic books, Neoplatonic writings and Jewish Cabbala (see pp. 577–9).

One of the most independent-minded (or eccentric) scholars of the sixteenth century, the German polymath Paracelsus, gloried in the Cabbala and became an all-purpose symbol for wide-ranging 'Paracelsian' investigation which riskily combined irreverence with a sense of magical possibilities. He particularly excited less conventional Protestants, especially Protestant doctors, who valued the Reformation as a liberation from centuries of falsehood.[3] Yet many mainstream Reformed Protestants shared Paracelsus's enthusiasm for the esoteric. Their Reformed theology was dependent on themes of the Tanakh, such as the motif of covenant, and it was logical to welcome apparent new shafts of light from Hebrew wisdom. These might aid that common Reformation preoccupation, the timing of the Last Days, or illuminate some of the theological problems which caused so many murderous arguments in the Reformation.

Perhaps the most surprising outcrop of Reformed Protestant interest in the esoteric was the phenomenon of Freemasonry. Although this very varied worldwide movement now boasts mythology tracing its origins to antiquity, Masonic practice actually began in late-sixteenth-century Scotland as an outcrop of Reformed Christianity. The new conditions of comparative peace brought by that shrewd monarch James VI produced a surge of domestic building, as the Scottish nobility and gentry rehoused themselves in greater comfort amid spectacular outward display. Patrons naturally took an interest in their projects, especially the theories behind the new Classical architectural styles being used: they were educated men seized with enthusiasm for Renaissance rediscoveries of Classical wisdom. At the centre of this activity was the royal Master of Works, William Schaw, actually a crypto-Catholic. From the 1590s, various Scottish notables in contact with Schaw joined the trade 'lodges' of masons and builders, which clearly replaced in their esteem the devotional gilds which the Scottish Reformers had destroyed only a few decades before.

Soon lodges were adding dignity to their socializing with the aid of esoteric literature: late-medieval masons had already constructed proud histories for themselves out of such material and their own craft traditions. The Church of Scotland, in interesting contrast to its growing paranoia about witchcraft (see p. 687), showed no signs of alarm at the new departure; many of its clergy were caught up in the same intellectual fashions. The impressive ancient history manufactured by Scottish Freemasons gradually travelled throughout Europe and eventually beyond, as Masonic lodges spread as congenial settings for male camaraderie with a habit of secrecy calculated to put them beyond the reach of the Church authorities. Part of Freemasonry's continuing Reformed inheritance was a general hostility to the institution of the Catholic Church. This was inclined to linger even when Masons spread beyond Reformed societies and into the Catholic world, forming a major focus for anticlericalism wherever the Catholic Church was strong (see pp. 821–2).[4]

So a heady mixture of Paracelsianism, hermeticism and Cabbala bred an optimism in Protestant Europe which sat curiously alongside the pessimism about human capability built into the thought of Augustine of Hippo. The ancient esoteric books became more rather than less important through the seventeenth century, particularly in universities in central Europe. Here ecumenically minded scholars were trying to find theological ways of bridging the gulf between Lutheran and Reformed theology – while also exploring many other fields of knowledge, often with the agenda of extending the bounds of human wisdom in preparation for the Last Days. The discipline which is the ancestor of modern specializations like astronomy, biology, physics and chemistry was then called natural philosophy. It demarcated itself from theology's concentration on the world beyond by exploring evidence from nature, the visible created world. We define this exploration as 'science', and the story of natural philosophy in the sixteenth and seventeenth centuries has in the past often been called a 'Scientific Revolution'. In the modern West, that term has commonly been yoked to the thought that 'science' is a rational mode of enquiry, waging an ideological battle with an irrational foe, Christianity.

'Science' is a very imprecise word, and in the era of the Reformation and Renaissance it simply meant knowledge – from any quarter. Natural philosophy was as much an examination of God's creation as theology, and exhibited no sense of clash of purpose or intention with religion. Evidence from the created world might have its own mysterious or magical dimension when seen through the eyes of a Paracelsian or Neoplatonist, and so it might link directly with religious and even political concerns. One example was the curious episode of the 'Rosicrucians'. Unlike the Freemasons, the Rosicrucians never existed. The texts which described this ancient and benevolent secret society of philosophers of the 'Rosy Cross' were principally written between 1614 and 1616 by a Lutheran pastor, Johann Valentin Andreae, who had spent perhaps too much time poring over hermetic wisdom and Paracelsianism. Over the next decade Andreae's fantasy was presented as documentary reality. It sparked febrile excitement and expectation right across Europe, and became intimately entwined in the politics of the Elector Palatine Friedrich's attempted Reformed Protestant crusade against the Habsburgs which led to the Thirty Years War (see p. 646).[5]

Protestant hopes for a coming apocalypse, disappointed in Friedrich's downfall, persisted. The renowned Reformed Protestant scholar Johann Heinrich Alsted proclaimed calculations of the divinely ordained End Times, eventually choosing 1694 as the crucial date; significantly much of his theorizing was drawn not from the Bible but from hermetic literature.[6] The possibilities offered by the apocalypse were constructively developed by two of Europe's most restlessly creative Protestant scholars, Alsted's pupil the much-exiled Czech Johannes Comenius and the equally much-travelled Scots minister John Dury. They saw in England's Republic in the 1650s a new flowering of scholarship and radical extension of human knowledge in the many different fields of natural philosophy. Both men believed that Classical esoteric literature was not a series of ancient dead ends, but an entry into knowledge long forgotten. They hoped that the Protestant confusions so obvious both in Oliver Cromwell's England and in the Netherlands might be exploited positively to lead a newly reunited and tolerant Church for all Europe, to welcome back the Saviour.[7] Their enthusiasms included the readmission of the Jews to England after their expulsion back in 1290: this would hasten the Last Days, provided of course the Jews dutifully converted. The scheme succeeded in 1656, thanks to the sympathy of that conflicted seeker of the Last Days Lord Protector Cromwell, who rather characteristically disguised the revolutionary nature of what he was allowing by conniving at a very technical decision in the English law courts about property rights.[8]

The efforts of the Interregnum optimists did not have the result they expected. Alsted's apocalyptic calculations helped inflame the disastrous political ambitions of Reformed Transylvania (see p. 641), and the only second coming at the end of the 1650s was the return of the Stuart dynasty to its Atlantic kingdoms from exile. Yet there were significant and practical consequences: not only the readmission of the Jews (which Charles II, probably primed with Jewish cash from Amsterdam, did not challenge), but also the foundation with Charles's patronage of England's premier forum for a continuing gentlemanly discussion of natural philosophy. This 'Royal Society' was a regrouping of several of the most prominent speculative thinkers who had flourished under the Interregnum regime. Sir Isaac Newton, one of the most prominent early members of the Society, illustrates the contemporary blend of fascination with a mysterious past, innovative observation and abstract thinking; he wrote as much about the Book of Revelation as about 'the Book of Nature' which revealed the theory of gravity. In fact, in Newton's eyes, all his enterprises were part of a common task of Reformation, which in the case of his religious investigations led him to a discreet dismissal of doctrines like the Trinity. Newton's task was to recover a lost rationality: 'the first religion was the most rational of all others till the nations corrupted it. For there is no way ['without revelation', he inserted in his manuscript in an afterthought] to come to the knowledge of a Deity but by the frame of nature.'[9]

Another variant of rationality was to be found in Francis Bacon, the philosopher and eventually disgraced politician who died a couple of decades before Newton was born. Bacon's writings were a great inspiration to the natural philosophers of Europe, and the Royal Society could be seen as a fulfilment of his posthumously published work *New Atlantis*, which had portrayed a 'Foundation' of philosophers devoted to improving human society through practical ('empirical') experiment and observation – the Royal Society borrowed his term for its members, 'Fellows'. Bacon did set his project of extending human knowledge in a theological context: in his first manifesto for his 'Great Instauration' (that is, restoration) of natural philosophy, *Temporis partis masculus* (1603), he presented what he was doing as the 'instauration' of human-kind's dominion over creation lost in Adam's fall: a restoration of the image of God in humanity.[10] That much appealed to the likes of Alsted and Comenius, but Bacon coupled this programme with contempt for both Neoplatonism and Aristotelian scholasticism, and he quickly became brutally sceptical about the Rosicrucian rivals of his Foundation. Indeed, he failed to see the importance of many of the discoveries of his time precisely because they employed what he regarded as obsolete methodologies. And he provided a convenient escape route for the increasing number of scholars who wished to ignore the constraints of Christian teaching in investigating the problems of nature and humanity: knowledge of God could only come from divine revelation, and so his own enquiries could be neatly separated from theology as representing a different sort of truth: 'God never wrought miracle to convince Atheisme, because his Ordinary Works convince it.'[11] What did that say about biblical miracles?

It was perfectly possible for natural philosophers to share Bacon's priority for empirical research by drawing on Reformed Protestantism – he was himself a Reformed Protestant, son of Sir Nicholas Bacon, one of the architects of Elizabeth I's 1559 religious settlement (see p. 639). Humankind's capacity for abstract, speculative thought had been impaired in the Fall, so what was left was patient observation of the Book of Nature. Yet some areas of natural philosophy which also valued practical observation had long revealed tensions with theology. One was medicine, where for centuries doctors had been inclined to see the evidence of their eyes as more important than what the textbooks told them. That shocked theologians, who were inclined to take very seriously what the great Classical authorities Aristotle or Galen said about the human body, and who then constructed theological conclusions out of it – such as the proposition that women were physically and probably therefore in other ways inferior versions of men.[12] Ironically, humanist doctors were generally more conservative in medicine than doctors with a medieval scholastic training, simply because they placed a new value on the ancient texts: a problem arose for humanists, for instance, when they tried to understand syphilis, a new disease unknown to the ancients.[13]

A more difficult frontier between natural philosophy and theology was astrology and astronomy. Natural philosophers concerning themselves with the planets and the stars made statements about the heavens which

might seem to be the business of theological faculties, particularly since
the Bible makes certain confident pronouncements on the make-up of
the visible heavens. The divisions were unpredictable: Philipp Melanchthon and John Calvin flatly disagreed about the value of astrology,
which meant that sixteenth-century Lutheran ministers lined up on
confessional grounds behind Melanchthon against Calvin, and proclaimed astrology as a respectable and valuable guide to God's purposes.[14] At least astrology was a scholarly pursuit with a long history.
Much more problematic was the body of opinion growing from the
early-sixteenth-century work of Copernicus that the Bible contained a
mistake about the physical universe: its assumption (on the few occasions
that it addressed the question) that the sun revolved around the earth.
We have already noted the unfortunate clash which this produced
between the Catholic authorities in Rome and the scientific work of
Galileo Galilei (see p. 684).

   Although many Protestants might rage against Copernicans, they did
not take action against them as the Roman Inquisition had done in the
Galileo case; moreover his treatment did seem all of a piece with the
efforts of Europe's various Inquisitions to ban so much of the creative
literature of the previous centuries through their Indexes. There was no
doubt that natural philosophy had more room to manoeuvre amid the
complexities and divisions of the Protestant world. By the end of the
seventeenth century, it was gaining new strength and confidence in
Protestant northern Europe. Despite the intentions of most of its practitioners, when its privileging of reason was united with Baconian insistence on observation, the alliance of natural philosophy with the wisdom
of an esoteric past was gradually abandoned, calling into question mainstream Christian authority. Other forces besides the empiricism of
Francis Bacon converged on this development.

JUDAISM, SCEPTICISM AND
DEISM (1492–1700)

Doubt is fundamental to religion. One human being sees holiness in
someone, something, somewhere: where is the proof for others? The
Old Testament is shot through with doubt, although in its stories
doubters often feel God's wrath, as when Adam and Eve doubted the
reasons which God gave for not eating from the Tree of the Knowledge

of Good and Evil. Jesus Christ could be kinder to doubters – for instance, to his own disciple Thomas, who doubted the Resurrection until Christ challenged him to touch and be sure. And human beings have commonly liked a good laugh at what they hold most dear. But a distinctive feature of modern Western culture, and through it any Christianity exposed to the spread of Western culture, has come to be an inclination to doubt any proposition from the religious past, and to reject the assumption that there is a special privilege for one sort of religious truth. How may we account for this extraordinary development?

The greatest question mark set against Reformation and Counter-Reformation Christianity was posed by the continuing existence of Judaism, a separate and much disadvantaged religion within the bounds of Christendom. The 1490s had brought the greatest single disaster for the Jewish people since the destruction of Jerusalem back in 70 CE, their official expulsion from the Iberian peninsula and the creation of a 'Sephardic' diaspora (see pp. 585–91). The Portuguese were never as single-minded as the Spaniards either in expulsions or in efforts to achieve proper conversions, although after a serious '*converso*' rebellion, the Portuguese monarchy did set up its own imitation of the Spanish Inquisition in 1536. In consequence, a cosmopolitan crypto-Jewish community developed, adopting Portuguese customs and language while travelling, and settling in western Europe wherever it seemed safe. Portuguese Sephardic Jews prospered, usually through trade, but also through practising that usefully marginal profession medicine and sometimes teaching in the less rigidly exclusive or more unwary universities and colleges – the municipal Collège de Guyenne in the great French port of Bordeaux proved particularly significant in mid-century.[15] The Portuguese monarchy, always on the lookout for ways of stretching its straitened resources, could see the usefulness of this talented and mobile community, and it was inclined to look the other way if some seemed less than whole-hearted in their Christianity – much to the displeasure of its own Inquisition.

As the Reformation developed, Jews viewed it with sarcastic interest, not unreasonably seeing these bitter intra-Christian disputes as evidence of God's anger with the persecutors of the Jewish people.[16] They soon found that their fortunes were as varied in Protestant as in Catholic lands, but their long experience of surviving amid Christian prejudice soon alerted them to where the danger was least. In the Polish-Lithuanian Commonwealth, traditionally multicultural and from 1573 committed to a considerable degree of religious toleration (see pp. 643–4), there

was a great flourishing of Jewish society, whose language Yiddish, effectively a dialect of German, marked its closeness to the German elites of
eastern European urban communities. In central Europe, Prague proved
a cultural melting pot for various strands of European Jewry of Iberian,
eastern and Ottoman origins – thanks more to the Habsburgs than to
their Bohemian subjects, whose celebrated enthusiasm for religious
liberty did not extend that far.[17]

Above all, there was the port city of Amsterdam in the Reformed
Protestant United Provinces of the Netherlands. As Amsterdam rose to
commercial greatness after the War of Independence from the Spaniards,
it became a major haven for Judaism, especially the Sephardic community looking for a new secure home to replace the lost glories of
Iberia. The tolerance maintained by the 'regents' of the Netherlands in
general and Amsterdam in particular (against the wishes of most of
their Reformed clergy) allowed some remarkable cross-fertilization. In
Amsterdam, most cosmopolitan of urban settings, stately synagogues
were by the late seventeenth century a tourist attraction and an object
of astonishment all over Europe – they looked remarkably like the most
splendid of the Protestant churches being rebuilt at the same time by
Sir Christopher Wren after the Great Fire of London. Around them
developed a Jewish culture which acted as a solvent on the certainties
which the Reformation and Counter-Reformation sought to establish.

The events of the 1490s in Spain and Portugal left a deep mark
on sixteenth-century Christian upheavals. We have seen the result: a
peculiarly intolerant official form of Iberian Christianity obsessed with
conformity to a Catholic norm, alongside a different type of Christian
religious expression with a rich and varied future. The excitements
released by the destruction of Muslim and Jewish civilization in Spain fed
into Spanish Christian mysticism: not only elements like the Carmelite
spirituality of Teresa of Ávila and John of the Cross which managed to
hang on inside the official Church, but also the amorphous movement
labelled *alumbrado* (see pp. 590–91.) From Spain, via the mystical
theologian Juan de Valdés, the *alumbrado* style of Christianity influenced the *Spirituale* movement in Italy, which produced such unexpected
outcrops as Ignatius Loyola's Society of Jesus. When the *Spirituali* were
dispersed in the 1540s, Italians spread all over Protestant Europe in their
own diaspora (see pp. 662–4). Many proved remarkably independent-
minded once released to think for themselves, especially on the Trinity
– again, Spanish crypto-Judaism was an influence here – and the result
was the 'Socinianism' of eastern Europe (see pp. 642–3). Catholic Spain,

through the unlikely agency of John Calvin, produced the classic martyr for radical religion, Michael Servetus, whose project for reconstructing Christianity was inspired by his consciousness of what had happened to religion in his Iberian homeland. All these stirrings were challenges to Christian orthodoxy, and now they met new forces of doubt among the Sephardic Jews of Amsterdam.[18]

At the time, doubt was generally given the blanket label atheism, just as a whole variety of sexual practices of which society pretended to disapprove were given the blanket label sodomy.[19] Specific examples of doubt are generally hidden from us throughout the Reformation and Counter-Reformation, since it was suicidal for anyone to proclaim doubt or unbelief, and the kindly instinct of priests and pastors was no doubt normally to still doubts in their flocks rather than risk their parishioners' lives by exposing them. Educated and powerful people in the sixteenth century of course did speak seriously of doubt, but rather like medieval discussion of toleration, such talk had to be understood as theory only, if it was to be considered respectable. The best way (as with sodomy) was to shelter behind interest in Classical literature. The scrupulously dispassionate Latin poet Lucretius and the Greek satirist of philosophy and religion Lucian were widely read, while the sceptic Sextus Empiricus was rediscovered in the sixteenth century, giving his name to 'empiricism'.

Though Christian leaders regularly expressed their deep disapproval of such 'atheistic' writings, it was difficult to burn someone simply for reading a Classical author. Then gradually in the seventeenth century doubts melded into that systematic and self-confident confrontation with religious tradition which has become part of Western culture and has deeply affected the practice of Christianity itself. At least one impulse provoking this seismic shift had come – with poetic justice – from the Iberian Inquisitions, which demanded a profound and complete conversion from people, many of whom held a deep faith already. Among many possible outcomes of this shattering experience, one effect for some was to breed scepticism about all religious patterns.[20] The same was true in the Netherlands, another region riven by an intense effort to eliminate one set of religious beliefs in favour of another: first Catholics persecuted Protestants and then victorious Protestants harried Catholics (see Plate 17).

Plenty of the Dutch, those whom the Reformed contemptuously called 'Libertines', were weary of all strident forms of religion by the end of the sixteenth century, and they remembered with pride the fact that the great Dutchman Erasmus had talked much of tolerance and thoughtfulness.[21] They were joined in the 1620s by some of the most conscientious of Dutch Reformed clergy and people, the followers of Jacobus Arminius, expelled from the Church and further victimized as a result of the major Church synod at Dordt (Dordrecht) in 1618–19. This had been such an important event that it attracted delegates from overseas Reformed Churches like England. It was the nearest approximation that the Reformed Churches ever achieved to a general council, and although it produced a firm and lasting shape to Reformed orthodoxy, it did as much to alienate dissenters and force them to make decisions about their religious future outside the mainstream. Some, the 'Collegiants', produced their own brand of rational religion which dispensed with any need for clergy.[22]

When Sephardic Jews arrived in this argumentative land and regrouped in Amsterdam, they had many possible identities to adopt. Some who had been almost completely cut off from their old religion now painstakingly reconstructed their ancient belief with new devotion and orthodoxy. Others emerged from their experience still conscious of their heritage, but prepared to take very new directions. In the Netherlands they met Christians – Libertines, Arminians, Collegiants, Socinians quitting an increasingly inhospitable Poland – who were ready to do the same thing.[23] At the centre of this fusion of ideas was Baruch or Benedict de Spinoza. Son of a Portuguese-Jewish merchant in Amsterdam, and so more or less ineligible for a normal university education, he quietly taught himself amid all the intellectual opportunities that the city had to offer – and in his teenage years, those included contact with the great mathematician and natural philosopher René Descartes.

In 1656, aged twenty-three, Spinoza was sensationally expelled from the Amsterdam Portuguese synagogue, accompanied by public curses. To incur such an extreme penalty, it is likely that he had already questioned some of the basic principles of all the great Semitic religions: the prospect of immortality for human beings and the intervention of God in human affairs.[24] In Spinoza's remaining two decades of life, he produced two revolutionary treatises. The *Tractatus Theologico-Politicus* (1670), a prototype of which may have been the cause of his expulsion, demanded that the Bible be treated as critically as any other text, particularly in its description of miracles; sacred texts are human artefacts, venerable religious institutions 'relics of man's ancient bondage'. The whole argument of the work was designed to promote human freedom:

the supreme mystery of despotism, its prop and stay, is to keep men in a state of deception, and with the specious title of religion to cloak the fear by which they must be held in check, so that they will fight for their servitude as if for salvation, and count it no shame, but the highest honour, to spend their blood and their lives for the glorification of one man.[25]

Spinoza's *Ethics* (1677) saw God as undifferentiated from the force of nature or the state of the universe. Naturally such a God is neither good nor evil, but simply and universally God, unconstrained by any moral system which human beings might recognize or create. Calvin might have assented to the latter proposition, but emphatically not the former. There could be nothing further from the spirit of vast separation between Creator and created expressed in Calvin's 'double knowledge' of God and the human self (see p. 634) than Spinoza's proposition that 'the human mind, insofar as it perceives things truly, is part of the infinite intellect of God, and thus it is as inevitable that the clear and distinct ideas of the mind are true as that God's ideas are true'.[26] Soon Spinoza was regarded as the standard-bearer for unbelief, even though pervading his carefully worded writings there is a clear notion of a divine spirit inhabiting the world, and a profound sense of wonder and reverence for mystery. It was too much for the authorities in the Dutch Republic: they banned the *Tractatus* in 1674, and more predictably the Roman Inquisition followed suit in 1679, after the work had widely circulated in French translation.

'Atheist' was an easily hurled term of abuse in Spinoza's day, generally pointed with gloomy relish at someone whose sordidly self-indulgent lifestyle satisfyingly demonstrated the results of denying conventional divinity. Spinoza inconsiderately upset such rhetorical symmetry by living in serene simplicity, his only vice a very Dutch addiction to tobacco, which along with the lens-grinding by which he made his frugal living probably brought his early death at forty-four. He lived with all the contemplative austerity of a St Jerome, but was cheerfully ready to discuss sermons of the day, or to receive a stream of philosopher-tourists.[27] Within a few years of his death, Pierre Bayle, son of a French Huguenot pastor but in permanent exile in the Dutch Republic after the Revocation of the Edict of Nantes, was openly saying the previously unsayable, the conclusion to which Spinoza's writings inexorably led: it was probable that 'a society of Atheists wou'd observe all Civil and Moral Dutys, as other Societys do, provided Crimes were severely punish'd, and Honor and Infamy annex'd to certain Points'. Bayle tartly observed that morality in Christian societies seemed as prone to fashion and local custom as in those of any other faith. This was a radical attack on any assumption that Christian ethics were necessarily a product of Christian doctrine. It is perhaps the most challenging proposition that the Enlightenment has presented to the Christian Church.[28]

So around Spinoza other voices began to be raised also challenging the ancient wisdom of religion and suggesting that the Bible was not quite what it seemed: a point which Erasmus had made much more discreetly in the previous century. Few of them had the dour talent of the Englishman Thomas Hobbes, but many were excited by Hobbes's sledgehammer demolition of the sacred authority of clergy in the interests of civil power, and by the boldness of his theological revisions: Hobbes denied that it was possible for a God to exist without material substance, delicately ridiculed the Trinity out of existence and gave broad hints to his readers that they should take no Christian doctrine on trust.[29] When other anti-Trinitarians followed Hobbes, their main weapon against Christian orthodoxy was the biblical text itself, which, as was rapidly becoming apparent, was full of variant readings between manuscripts – by 1707 one distinguished mainstream English biblical scholar, John Mill, reckoned these to be around thirty thousand in number. Some of these variant readings could plausibly be considered as later interpolations in the interests of Trinitarian belief.

Important in this questioning were the early Quakers. Since Quakers drew divine authority from the light of the Spirit within them, they were inclined to demonstrate this by denigrating the authority of the Bible. Already Martin Luther had moved the boundaries of the biblical texts by creating the category of Apocrypha, which he had cordoned off from the Old Testament, even though Jews and the pre-Reformation Christian Church had made no such distinction. Now Quakers noted scholars' increasing rediscovery of manuscripts containing inter-testamental literature or Christian apocrypha, much of which looked remarkably like the Bible. The gifted Hebrew scholar and Quaker Samuel Fisher, who may have used the young Spinoza to translate tracts into Hebrew, and who certainly got to know the Amsterdam synagogues in his efforts to convert Dutch Jews, gleefully pointed out in 1660 that Paul's Epistle to the Laodiceans (which Paul had demanded be read in community worship, and so should be considered canonical), appeared to have gone missing altogether – or rather did exist, in a text extant but not acknowledged by the Church. He also drew attention to Jesus Christ's supposed correspondence with King Abgar of Edessa (see pp. 180–81)

– why were these texts outside the Bible, when a trivial letter of Paul's to Philemon was in?[30]

Europe's encounter with the Americas, so highly populated with other humans, had long posed doubts about humanity's single descent from the dwellers in Eden. More ambitiously still, others who accepted Copernican cosmology suggested that there were other inhabited worlds. A major contribution to that question in the years when Spinoza was reaching his moment of crisis with the Amsterdam synagogue was made by Isaac La Peyrère, a French Huguenot but with a name which reveals underneath its French guise a further descendant of the Iberian diaspora. His publication in Amsterdam and elsewhere of *Prae-Adamitae* ('Men before Adam') was one of the publishing sensations of 1655: reputedly it even became light reading for the Pope and his cardinals. La Peyrère was one of the most fervent apocalypticists of his day, and he urged Jews and Christians to reunite to bring on the Last Days, but his book, as its title indicated, threw the Creation story into the melting pot by arguing that there had been races of humans earlier than Adam and Eve, who were the ancestors of the Jews only.

La Peyrère's argument in fact gave a particular privilege to the Jewish race, but it also wiped out the Western Christian doctrine of original sin: if the Gentiles were descended from the race before Adam, presumably they could not be participants in Adam's Fall. La Peyrère was imprisoned, embraced Catholicism and died in a French monastery, but at least he did not suffer the fate of Jacob Palaeologos, a Greek exile in Prague who a century before had made the same argument about Adam, and had been executed in Rome in 1585. *Prae-Adamitae* went on selling, and did so because its author was increasingly not alone in his questions. If there were other worlds, not merely original sin seemed a dubious doctrine; how could the Church proclaim the uniqueness of biblical revelation?[31]

Around 1680 there followed yet another work from the Netherlands. The anonymous *Treatise of the three impostors* was too shocking to put in print until 1719, but it had circulated widely throughout Europe in manuscript, often with a false attribution to Spinoza to give it authority. Written in French, probably by renegade Huguenots in exile from France, it was a crude attempt to popularize an anti-religious version of the message of Spinoza's *Tractatus*, married with ideas freely adapted from Hobbes and other sceptical writers. Its 'three impostors' were Moses, Jesus Christ and Muhammad, and in its condemnation of all three Semitic faiths, it proclaimed that 'there are no such things in Nature as either God or Devil or Soul or Heaven or Hell ... [T]heologians ... are all of them except for some few ignorant dunces ... people of villainous principles, who maliciously abuse and impose on the credulous populace'.[32]

Behind the stories of doubters from Spinoza and La Peyrère to Bayle and the *Treatise of the three impostors* were two imperilled and highly articulate communities, producing radical spirits who contributed to the reassessment of religion: Jews and Huguenots. The Huguenots were part of the international Reformed Protestant bloc which, like Jews at the same time, embraced high hopes of apocalypse and divine consummation, only to have them dashed in the political disappointments of the mid-seventeenth century which ranged from England to Transylvania. After Louis XIV revoked the Edict of Nantes in 1685, the Huguenots had their own catastrophe to ponder as they followed the Jews into continent-wide exile. Even before that, Huguenots had been among the first to make a consistent return to Erasmus's project of historical criticism of the biblical text, particularly at Saumur's Royal Academy for Protestant theology, before Louis XIV closed it (Louis did not close Saumur's pioneering Academy for cavalry instruction, which formed part of the same foundation). The first major controversy was provoked in the early seventeenth century by the Saumur scholar Louis Cappel's demonstration that the elaborate Hebrew system of vowel pointing and accenting in the text of the Tanakh was not as ancient as it claimed to be. Many regarded this comparatively minor philological correction as a dangerous attack on the integrity and divine inspiration of scripture; but Cappel was clearly right in his conclusions, and by the end of the century they were accepted wisdom among Protestants.

This was a basis for much more searching scholarly investigation of both Old and New Testaments, which has continued ever since. Saumur led the way, but the systematic application of critical principles to textual scholarship in general was actually a product of the Counter-Reformation in the same kingdom. A seventeenth-century Congregation of reformed French Benedictine monasteries dedicated to St Maur (a disciple of St Benedict credited with introducing his Rule to France) developed the ancient Benedictine commitment to scholarship in a specialized direction: Church history. Generally they eschewed the delicate business of scrutinizing the Bible itself, but they established, on a scale so comprehensive as to be impossible to ignore, the requirement to scrutinize historical texts without sentiment or regard for their sacred character. All texts were there as part of the range of historical evidence, not simply the familiar material of narrative historical sources such as chronicles, but official and legal documents.

Even if the Maurists did not follow the logic of this through into biblical scholarship, others would. The Pope might laugh at La Peyrère, but the questions about the Bible troubled Catholics as well as Protestants. One Jesuit working in China, Martino Martini, was driven by his fascination with Chinese civilization and its historical writing to point to the shakiness of biblical chronology, in a work published three years after La Peyrère's best-seller.[33] Protestants were nevertheless more seriously affected than Catholics, because of their general rejection of allegory in interpreting the Bible unless absolutely necessary (see pp. 596–7). They were left with the literal sense of the biblical text, if sense there was (try some of the visions of Ezekiel), and scholarship proved alarming for literalists then as now. La Peyrère had been joined by Hobbes and Spinoza in pointing out a conclusion now obvious to the historically minded, but which with enough willpower can be avoided for centuries, that Moses could not have written the entire Pentateuch.

As a result of this new scrutiny of the Bible, there was a growing feeling among some Western Christians that not merely other Christianities or even Judaism, but other world religions, might provide insight into truth – a conclusion opposed to the scabrous abuse in the *Treatise of the three impostors*.[34] This new spirit of reverent openness directly related to the worldwide reach of Western power and trade by 1700. Islam seemed much less threatening politically as the Ottoman, Iranian and Moghul empires fell into decay. Now educated Europeans had a much better chance of understanding this other monotheism. Thanks to André du Ryer, a French diplomat who spent much of his career in Alexandria, they had access to a Turkish grammar in Latin and French translations of Turkish and Persian literary texts, something almost unprecedented in the West – but above all, du Ryer's reliable translation (1647) of the Qur'an into French, which was rapidly taking over from Latin as the international language of scholarship. That translation was the source of all Europe's vernacular translations of the Qur'an. English came first in 1649, not without incident in a turbulent year for England, the translation meeting a storm of abuse from all sides. Parliament briefly imprisoned the English printer, while one High Church pamphleteer ascribed the work to the Devil – rather paradoxically, since the principal translator appears to have been a former protégé of Archbishop Laud, and elsewhere denounced Copernicus, Spinoza and Descartes.[35] The

Jesuits had already stimulated Western curiosity about China; Franco-British rivalry in India aroused equal interest in the cultures and religions of the subcontinent. Sir Isaac Newton was among those who concluded from these various stirrings that all the world's cultures sprang from a single civilization informed by knowledge of the divine, but scattered in Noah's Flood.[36]

Between 1640 and 1700 a growing divide opened up between scepticism or openness on biblical matters among an educated and privileged minority, which parted with the passions of the Reformation, and continuing untroubled if miscellaneous beliefs among the multitude. In place of the idea which runs through the Tanakh and New Testament of a God intimately involved with his creation and providentially repeatedly intervening in it, there was the concept of a God who had certainly created the world and set up its laws in structures understandable by human reason, but who after that allowed it to go its own way, precisely because reason was one of his chief gifts to humanity, and order a gift to his creation. This was the approach to divinity known as deism. Deist Christians have been much sneered at by later generations who like religion to be full of urgent propositions granted by revelation. It is worth reaching beyond such criticism to hear the voice of one English deist of the early eighteenth century, Joseph Addison. He was son of an Anglican cathedral dean, a poet, playwright and an undistinguished politician whose serenity was capable of rising above the disappointments of his life: for that considerable virtue he was widely loved. Taking inspiration from Psalm 19, Addison thus expressed his calm confidence in the benevolence of the Creator God:

> The spacious firmament on high,
> With all the blue ethereal sky,
> And spangled heavens, a shining frame
> Their great Original proclaim.
> Th'unwearied sun, from day to day,
> Does his Creator's powers display,
> And publishes to every land
> The work of an Almighty Hand.
>
> Soon as the evening shades prevail
> The moon takes up the wondrous tale,
> And nightly to the listening earth
> Repeats the story of her birth;

While all the stars that round her burn
And all the planets in their turn,
Confirm the tidings as they roll,
And spread the truth from pole to pole.

What though in solemn silence all
Move round the dark terrestrial ball?
What though no real voice nor sound
Amid the radiant orbs be found?
In reason's ear they all rejoice,
And utter forth a glorious voice,
Forever singing as they shine,
'The hand that made us is divine.'[37]

It was tempting even for clergy in established Churches to sit easily to confessional statements which they had inherited from the deplorably violent age of the Reformation, and see the reasonableness of deism as both congenial and morally superior to what had gone before. It was the same mood which after 1660 had produced the 'Latitudinarian' outlook in the Church of England (see pp. 653–4). Ranged against the rationalists or deists were the anxious voices of other members of the same intellectual elite, who were promoting the view of an intensely personal, interventionist God in the various Protestant Evangelical Awakenings, from Pietism in Germany to Jonathan Edwards on the eastern American seaboard. We cannot understand the rise of Evangelicalism without seeing it against the background of seventeenth- and eighteenth-century Christian and post-Christian rationalism – but also in the context of other profound changes in European society of which the Evangelicals were uncomfortably aware.

SOCIAL WATERSHEDS IN THE NETHERLANDS AND ENGLAND (1650–1750)

If Judaism and Reformed Protestantism were one fundamental pairing behind the creation of a new spirit in Christian religion and metaphysics, the other came through those sometimes uncomfortably yoked Protestant states, the Netherlands and England. The chief settings in which the millenarian, messianic or apocalyptic excitements of Reformed Protestantism and Judaism united, they pioneered the future in another and very different respect: towards the end of the seventeenth century, both societies began a long process of moving Christian doctrine and practice from the central place in European everyday life which it had enjoyed for more than a millennium, and placing it among a range of personal choices. The background to this was a conjunction of political, social and economic peculiarities in the two countries flanking the North Sea. Quite apart from their crabwise and often reluctant embrace of religious toleration for a wide variety of religious dissidence, both countries achieved a wider distribution of prosperity than any other part of seventeenth-century Europe. By improving their farming techniques and breeding new money through an exceptional range of manufactures and commercial enterprises, they were the first regions to escape famine, the constant danger of mass starvation following harvest failure.[38]

This had momentous consequences. An increasingly general distribution of surplus wealth opened up for the Dutch and the English. By 1700 these two nations were establishing their dominance in an ever-growing trade with Asia. Merchants shipped home a range of goods which had the especial attraction that the cheaper end of the market could successfully imitate luxury items: principally textiles and pottery – even that unprecedented household amenity, wallpaper. Manufactures at home sustained this trade and added to the abundance of goods now available. Ordinary people in these late-seventeenth-century societies revelled in the unfamiliar sensation of possessing more and more objects which they did not strictly need, and just as much, they enjoyed access to a degree of leisure, now that the provision of food was not a constant anxiety. Such leisure, consumer durables and spare money might look trivial by modern standards of prosperity, but previously these commodities were restricted to a tiny privileged elite. Now choice was becoming democratized in society, long before democracy had customarily been extended into politics.[39] Christianity must now face the consequences in many different ways.

Take one significant shift in seventeenth-century Europe: a proportion of public Christian devotional music was being turned into a personal leisure activity. Without doubt throughout Christian history, there had been a very considerable element of pure aesthetic satisfaction in listening to sacred music, but listening had always been done in the context of worship. During the seventeenth century, the Dutch developed the concept of the organ recital: a use of church buildings without specific devotional reference which was to spread throughout the Western Christian world. These recitals were detached from church services, for the very good reason that major Dutch parish churches had magnificent pipe organs of which their clergy disapproved, but which were protected from clerical wrath and maintained by the civic authorities – organs were in fact one of the symptoms of the Dutch regents' consistent aim to keep the clergy from tyrannizing them (see Plate 35). Dutch and north German composers led by the great Jan Pieterszoon Sweelinck wrote intricate compositions to show off the splendours of these organs, which might take as the theme of their ingenious variations the metrical psalm tunes of the Reformed Church, but which were by their nature unlikely to form part of worship.

A musical, social and religious straw in the wind beyond this was the changing fortunes of the oratorio. As its name implied, this was originally an Italian and therefore Catholic musical form suitable for staging by an 'oratory' or confraternity: a choral and orchestral work on a sacred subject. By 1700 in Protestant Europe oratorio performances were moving out of churches into secular public buildings, and sometimes acquiring secular subjects to match; that was not such a common phenomenon in the Catholic south, and it brought the oratorio close to another new choral musical form, the opera, which it had originally been designed to supplant during the solemnity of the Catholic Lent. The English got the best of both worlds with their acquisition in 1712 of a Protestant composer of opera and oratorio from Halle, Georg Frideric Händel. Domesticated as George Frederick Handel, he gave them in 1742 an oratorio on the birth, life, death, resurrection and second coming of Christ, *Messiah*, which became a national trophy of musical culture even for the unmusical – it was given an agreeable moral edge by being a frequently performed work at charity concerts.[40] But the *Messiah* was first performed in a Dublin public concert hall, a building which was itself an innovation – not in either of Dublin's Protestant cathedrals, even though the two cathedral choirs combined to sing it. This was an unmistakable transition of sacred music from worship to leisure, and it began a process by which the performance of or experience of music became for many Europeans the basis of an alternative spirituality to the text-based propositions of their Christian faith.

There are other hints that even public institutions in Protestant nations were beginning to accept society's gradual shift from its construction around Christian revelation and biblical story, even within its worship.

The clergy's sermons on state occasions in Anglican England, Lutheran Sweden and the Reformed Netherlands can be shown to have changed emphasis in their themes after the 1740s, with England being the most precocious, but even the very confessionally uniform Sweden following suit in due course. There was less construction of the nation as chosen like the kingdom of Israel, following God's judgement and fearing the collective sin of its people: instead, much more celebration of the nation's honour, its ability to generate prosperity and liberty and therefore personal happiness. These were still rewards from God for society's good behaviour, but the reward was seen more as a matter of logical consequence than of direct divine intervention. Rome as much as Israel now shaped the preachers' rhetoric as they tried to describe the nation's glories to itself. For such a major turnaround on occasions when kings and clergy were at their most self-conscious as representatives of wider society, more general changes in society must have emerged over many previous decades. These new emphases reflected the influence of deism, that view of God which envisaged a separation between creator God and creation.[41]

While Western Europe's spirituality was showing signs of becoming detached from its liturgy, divinity parted company with revelation, and patterns of society were being shaped by other sources besides Christianity's sacred book, Western discourse on philosophy came to be dominated by a philosopher whose assumptions likewise radically detached the spiritual from the material. René Descartes was a devout French Catholic who from 1628 had found that the Protestant but pluralist northern Netherlands were the refuge best enabling him to express himself without inhibition and to strip away philosophical assumptions which he found constricting. He was the decisive influence in encouraging his contemporaries and successors to think of a human being as dual in nature: material and immaterial. The problem which has haunted Cartesian views of personality thereafter has been to show how in any sense the two natures might be united. The Oxford philosopher Gilbert Ryle in 1949 satirically characterized this approach to consciousness as the 'ghost in the machine': a spirit lurking in a contraption of material components, which together somehow interact to spring from consciousness to motivation to action.[42]

As Ryle pointed out, Descartes would have been aware of the long history of Christian arguments about the soul; equally, when he created his own dualism for humanity, the Jesuits had schooled him in understanding the orthodox concept of the dual nature or natures of Christ, divine and human. While Chalcedonian Christianity had sought to settle that difficulty by insistent formulae of balance, Cartesian dualism, combined with Thomas Hobbes's relentless materialism and Isaac Newton's demonstration of the mechanical operation of the universe, has tended to resolve the difficulty by privileging the material over the spiritual – after all, material substance seems a good deal easier to encounter, register or measure than spirit. The eternal problem for Cartesian views of consciousness, or for the Baconian empiricism which allied itself with Cartesianism, was to account for the criteria by which the mind registers or measures these material encounters. John Locke, considering problems of consciousness, had written that since the human mind 'hath no other immediate Object but its own *Ideas* . . . it is evident, that our Knowledge is only conversant about them'.[43] What, then, is the source of those ideas? The problem has not ceased to trouble the heirs of Descartes.

GENDER ROLES IN THE ENLIGHTENMENT

It was that genial eighteenth-century sceptic David Hume, uncommonly sharp in seeing how philosophy and economics interacted, who observed of the consumer revolution around him that 'a commerce with strangers . . . rouses men from their indolence; and . . . raises in them a desire of a more splendid way of life than what their ancestors enjoyed'.[44] Varied possessions stimulate the imagination because they stimulate choice. Equally, leisure stimulates the imagination and provides the chance to make very profound choices: to reflect on personal identity beyond prescriptions laid down by others. That is a practical application of Locke's principle about the human mind, with all its attendant complications. In that most personal of realms, human sexuality, the late seventeenth century witnessed great shifts in the way in which masculinity and femininity were understood, and much remains mysterious about the reasons for this change. Gender roles became more rigidly divided. Most choices still favoured men: so where once women had been regarded as uncontrollable and lustful like fallen Eve, now they were increasingly regarded as naturally frail and passive, in need of male protection.[45] Most surprising of all was a new phenomenon in both Amsterdam and London: from the 1690s, both hosted a male homosexual public subculture, braving official hostility and developing a social network of bars and clubs. 'Lesbians' were so named in the early eighteenth century, a century and more before the invention of the word 'homosexual', but the activities of women did not excite so much public emotion as those of men, and it was the new visibility of gay men which provoked periodic purges and moral panics in both cities – no wonder the Societies for the Reformation of Manners were such urgent causes.[46]

None of these developments owed much to existing Christian ethical teaching: Christianity was going to have to engage in new thinking for a new society which constructed its own priorities with an increasing lack of respect for Christian tradition. Even patterns of churchgoing were affected. It was in Dutch and anglophone Protestantism during the seventeenth century that there developed one of the distinctive features of modern Western religion: Christianity was becoming an activity in which more women than men participated. The spectacular growth of female religious communities like the Ursulines in Counter-Reformation Catholicism was one symptom, but in Protestantism there was a different and more fundamental phenomenon: in various settings, church attendance was becoming skewed, and congregations were beginning to contain more women than men.

Once again, this was a matter of personal choice, and hence first perceptible where voluntary religion was possible. Studies of the far north of the United Provinces in the early seventeenth century, the province of Friesland, where so many people had opted to join radical groups like the Mennonites (see pp. 919–20), already show an imbalance in membership between men and women, even for the official Church.[47] In the English civil wars of the 1640s, when the coercive structures of the established Church collapsed, membership lists of the growing number of voluntary churches – Independents, Baptists, Quakers and the like – often reveal women outnumbering men by two to one.[48] At much the same time on the other side of the Atlantic, the authorities in the established Congregational Church of Massachusetts also began to notice the phenomenon of gender-skewed church attendance.

It is likely that a disproportionate number of women joined the English voluntary congregations because they had more room to assert themselves than in the established Church. This assertion was at its greatest among new radical groups such as the early Quakers: in the 1650s, Quaker women could enjoy prophetic roles reminiscent of those in the early days of some radical groups in the 1520s and 1530s, and just as in sixteenth-century radicalism, the male leadership of the Quakers over subsequent decades steadily moved to restrict women's activism.[49] By the early eighteenth century, the appeal of the Quakers to women may have changed because the ethos of the Quakers changed: the quiet waiting on the Lord which now characterized the worship of the Friends resonated with a traditional and predominantly female form of spirituality. The *collegia pietatis* of Pietism (see pp. 739–40) developed a spirituality which likewise emphasized an inner encounter with the divine, although in this case the devotional group took its place alongside Lutheran public worship. It is interesting that these Pietists were among the few people to take an interest in the writings of women activists from the earliest days of the Lutheran Reformation, like those of an outspoken noblewoman of the 1520s and 1530s then otherwise long forgotten, Argula von Grumbach.[50]

The phenomenon of gender-skewed congregations was already noticed in the late seventeenth century, and it contributed to new Christian reflections on gender. The English clergyman and ethical writer Richard Allestree and the leading Massachusetts minister Cotton Mather agreed in finding women more spiritual than men, who were slaves to passions: 'Devotion is a tender Plant', said Allestree, 'that . . . requires a supple gentle soil; and therefore the feminine softness and plyableness is very apt and proper for it . . . I know there are many Ladies whose Examples are reproaches to the other Sex, that help to fill our Congregations, when Gentlemen desert them'. That Protestant Oxford don even regretted the Reformation's abolition of nunneries. Mather felt that women had a greater moral seriousness than men because of their constant consciousness of death in childbirth.[51] Whether he was right or not, such notions were a striking turnaround from traditional medical talk of humours and a continuous spectrum of gender, or of Augustine of Hippo's disparaging theological comments on women's uncontrolled natures.[52] As women apparently showed themselves more devout than their menfolk (and perhaps more gratifyingly appreciative of the clergy's efforts), the ancient Christian stereotype of women as naturally more disordered than men and more open to Satan's temptations began to look steadily less convincing. That probably contributed to the growing elite distaste for hunting down witches.

Women alert to the change in atmosphere began seeking their own reconstructed place in the Church. Mary Astell was a celibate High Church Anglican Tory with a lively interest in contemporary philosophy, and her Toryism made her a clear-eyed critic of the limitations of Whig proponents of a renewed Christianity like John Locke, who seemed to talk much of freedom for men, but not for half the human race (or indeed more than half, given Locke's attitude to enslaved Africans). During the 1690s she began publishing her own vision, which amounted to a new Christian feminism: 'That the Custom of the World has put Women, generally speaking, into a State of Subjection, is not denied; but the Right can no more be prov'd from the Fact, than the Predominancy of Vice can justify it.' She was indignant that girls were deprived of decent education in favour of boys, and seized on what Allestree and other sympathetic commentators were saying, making their arguments her own, with a certain added sarcasm: 'One wou'd . . . almost think, that the wise disposer of all things, foreseeing how unjustly Women are denied opportunities of improvement from *without*, has therefore by way of compensation endow'd them with greater propensions to Vertue, and a natural goodness of Temper *within*.'[53] Much of this feminism would be absorbed into the Evangelical movements, which benefited from its activist enthusiasm and provided its chief outlet in Western culture right into the twentieth century (see pp. 828–30); but Evangelical Protestantism was ultimately not able to set boundaries to the feminism of Western culture, as will become apparent.

ENLIGHTENMENT IN THE EIGHTEENTH CENTURY

The history of the Enlightenment, a story usually associated with the eighteenth century, therefore saw virtually all its elements in place by 1700. Many of its assumptions derived from the Old and New Testaments and the two religions which had created this literature, Judaism and Christianity. Seventeenth- and eighteenth-century Europe produced two apparently contrary but actually deeply entangled movements, both of which were destined to affect a world far beyond their original settings in countries around the North Sea. The Enlightenment bred an open scepticism as to whether there can be definitive truths in specially privileged writings exempt from detached analysis, or whether any one religion has the last word against any other; in its optimism, commitment to progress and steadily more material, secularizing character, it represented a revulsion against Augustine of Hippo's proclamation of original sin. Yet beside the Enlightenment, the series of Protestant awakenings drew their inspiration from that same Augustine and from his interpretation in the Reformation. The mainstream Reformers had not merely proclaimed original sin as the key problem for humanity, capable of being solved only by a gracious God, but in their proclamation, they affirmed the authority and transcendence of the biblical text and jettisoned a whole raft of creative allegorical ways in which its meaning might be extended. It is possible to read the Protestant awakenings as a shocked reaction to the social and intellectual innovations of the early Enlightenment.

The two movements might therefore seem to be radically opposed. The reality was more complicated, for they constantly interacted and tangled. Key figures of the Evangelical awakenings respected the impulse to rationality which informed Enlightenment thought, and were fascinated by the intellectual ferment and the extensions of knowledge around them. Jonathan Edwards saw the Enlightenment philosophy's use of reason as an essential ally in reaffirming the Reformation message of the bondage of the human will. John Wesley, an intellectual omnivore himself, was determined as much as the Halle Pietists to introduce his flocks to the excitement of knowledge and the achievements of natural philosophy. To do so he published voluminously: one of the attractions of Methodism was its encouragement of self-education and self-improvement among its flocks (see p. 754). Among Wesley's best-selling books was his steadily extended handbook of practical medicine, *Primitive Physick*, based on both wide amateur reading and much personal observation. Having deplored the way in which in the history of medicine, 'Men of Learning began to set Experience aside, to build Physick upon Hypotheses', he reversed the process with Baconian empirical brio in favour of remedies which could be proved to work, although he coupled with experiment 'that Old, Unfashionable Medicine, Prayer'.[54]

Indeed, the Enlightenment in northern Europe was generally led not by those who hated Christianity but by Christians troubled by the formulations of traditional Christianity. In some measure, in its attempts to improve the human condition, the Enlightenment was a project for the reconstruction of the Christian religion, and it was in dialogue with the other projects for human improvement contained in Evangelicalism. The great exception was the Scottish philosopher David Hume, whose consideration of morality led him to the conclusion that it was entirely based on human feeling or 'moral sentiment', and that human experience could not move beyond knowledge of itself to provide real

answers to such problems as the creation of all things. He therefore
found revealed religion incredible in a literal sense, and, as Bayle had
done before him, he radically separated morality from the practice of
organized religion. The problem for pious Christians who knew Hume
in his everyday life in Edinburgh was that he was a thoroughly likeable
man; abuse of him generally came from those who had not met him. Dr
Johnson's celebratory biographer James Boswell, a devout member of
the Kirk who tried to frighten Hume with the fear of death, was baffled
by his cheerful indifference to the prospect: 'I could not but be assailed
by momentary doubts,' Boswell admitted, 'while I had actually before
me a man of such strong abilities and extensive inquiry dying in the
persuasion of being annihilated.'[55] In the end, some thoughtful Christian
critics even felt that Hume might have done good 'by purging our
religion of all the absurdities it contains ... thereby enabling it to
triumph over all opposition'.[56]

Catholic Europe was not immune to the excitement of the Enlightenment.[57] By the mid-eighteenth century the Jesuits were running the
largest single directed system of education that the world had ever
known, an intellectual network unique at the time in its cultivation of
scientific and cultural investigations, and inevitably their research culture formed an important component of the Enlightenment. Even when
they were suppressed in 1773 (see pp. 804–5), the impulse to reform
continued. Pius VI, whose predecessor had been forced into that humiliating betrayal of the Jesuits, pushed forward an ambitious programme
of building in Rome after his election in 1775, putting finishing touches
to St Peter's Basilica, the church which had helped to spark the Reformation, just in time for the equally severe challenge to the Church sparked
by the French Revolution). He promoted the past vglories of the Vatican
in an age which had otherwise seen a brutal diminution in power for
the papacy, by founding a papal museum, but he also followed his fellow
monarchs elsewhere in Europe by permitting the suppression of small
monasteries when a terrible earthquake hit southern Italy in 1783. The
intention was to help the poor; in the fashion of many such suppressions,
the proceeds ended up at the mercy of landed interests who had a good
less concern for the poor than their clerical predecessors.[58]

It was the Catholic world rather than the Protestant which produced
a form of Enlightenment consciously setting itself against Christianity,
proclaiming itself the enemy of mystery and the emancipator of humankind from the chains of revealed religion. Much of this was focused on
France and started as being anti-Catholic rather than anti-Christian; to

see why requires understanding the peculiar situation of the Catholic Church in France. The French Church had won a long-drawn-out victory against Protestantism, culminating in Louis XIV's great betrayal of trust in revoking the Edict of Nantes in 1685. It showed every sign of life and success; its monasteries great and small were being rebuilt to look like imposing modern châteaux. Its greater churches resounded to splendid brand-new organs, tailor-made for the distinctive style of French organ and choral music, their splendid cases major features of lavishly re-designed church interiors, from which medieval furnishings had been banished in favour of opening up sweeping vistas highlighting the drama of the Counter-Reformation High Mass.[59]

Beyond this liturgical magnificence, the Church in France was bitterly divided by disputes looking back to the Reformation years. Throughout the civil wars of the sixteenth century, a great polarity remained among French Catholics. On one extreme were those prepared to compromise with Protestants for the sake of preserving France in its sacred trust of being the Catholic Church for French people: a 'Gallican' version of Catholicism, sneeringly styled *'politique'* by its enemies. On the other were those anxious to cement France in its commitment to Counter-Reformation, and to an allegiance to the papacy which might run counter to the priorities of the monarchy. Running through this was yet another theological dispute which involved the ways in which that multifaceted theologian Augustine of Hippo might be used to explore the problems which agitated Western Christianity through the Reformation. Although Protestants from Martin Luther onwards took up Augustine's theology of God's grace, some theologians who stayed loyal to Rome were also compelled by his pessimistic account of the human condition unaided by grace.

A new Augustinianism surfaced in the University of Leuven in the Spanish Netherlands, in particular in the thought of Cornelius Jansen (1585–1638), who as an exile from the Protestant northern provinces of the Netherlands had particular reason to be conscious of the power in Reformed accounts of salvation based on Augustine. Jansen, who became Bishop of Ypres, clashed bitterly with Jesuit theologians attempting their own finessing of Augustine's thought in order to defend human free will. Jansen ensured that his exposition of a predestinarian theology as thoroughgoing as anything that Calvin wrote was published by his executors when he was safely dead; it was a treatise aggressively titled *Augustinus*. A condemnation of *Augustinus* secured from the Pope by the Jesuits in 1641 did not stop leading French theologians reading it with fascination. 'Jansenist' theology became a rallying point for those who had diverse grievances against the Jesuits: these ranged from their encouragement of Catholic extremism during the civil wars of the previous century, through their scandalous love of theatre and dance as an educational tool, to their shocking tolerance of aspects of Chinese and Indian religion (see pp. 705–7). Jansenism was a call to seriousness.

From the mid-seventeenth century, therefore, disputes about Jansenism turned into a struggle for the soul of the French Church, now vigorously resurgent against a steadily more beleaguered Reformed Protestantism. Jansenism was championed in Paris by an austere and much-respected community of nuns who originated among the newly reformed Cistercian houses, and who then secured their own autonomy, exporting the name of their original rural monastery of Port-Royal when they opened two new establishments around the city. The struggle between Jansenist supporters of Port-Royal and the Jesuits became entangled with the politics of the French Court, and among the several strands of conflict in this situation was a contrasting vision of the future of the whole Catholic Church, which reopened old questions agitated by Conciliarists before the storm of the Reformation stilled their voices. Was Catholicism to be directed by the wisdom of the pope in Rome, or was its theology to be constructed from the creative arguments of the wider Church, such as theologians in the Sorbonne? Where did authority lie to make decisions in such controversies, with a papal monarch, or with a collegiate decision by the bishops of the Church?

Louis XIV, influenced by his devout mistress Madame de Maintenon, eventually sided with the papalists against the Jansenists. Debates did not end with the persecution of the Port-Royal community, which culminated in an official order for the destruction and deliberate profanation of its chief house in 1710; a new papal condemnation of the whole movement in the bull *Unigenitus* followed in 1713. Louis' initiative in obtaining this from the Pope was his most disastrous legacy to the French Church, because the Jansenists would not go away. From 1727 crowds began gathering at the cemetery of St-Médard in Paris, where miracles had been reported at the grave of a Jansenist deacon. After six years, with thousands of people gathering, and frequent scenes of people rolling in convulsions and fanatically prophesying national disaster, the cemetery was closed. What was worse still was that these phenomena had previously been more associated with desperate groups of French Protestants, who had only been crushed in armed rebellion a couple of decades before; now leading lawyers were seen in the crowds, linking their protest to their resistance to centralizing royal policies.[60] Around Jansenism gathered all sorts of dissident strains in both Church and State. When the Society of Jesus came under attack, it was not unbelievers of the Enlightenment but a surviving network of Jansenists who contrived its destruction in France, and the degree of viciousness inflicted on the dispersed Jesuits was extraordinary, considering that both sides professed loyalty to the Catholic Church.[61]

The line connecting the Jansenists to the French Enlightenment is not straightforward, because their theology could be seen as deeply opposed to reasonable religion, of which a prime example was the theology and philosophy taught in the network of educational institutions maintained by the Jesuits. The wild scenes at St-Médard are remarkably reminiscent of the crowd phenomena in the revivals which were about to sweep through Protestantism in Britain and North America, as well as of those associated with recent 'prophets' among the repressed Huguenot communities of southern France; yet it is significant that Jansenist lawyers who trooped to the cemetery linked their oppositionist politics to their religious enthusiasm. The Jansenist disputes created continuing bitterness and schism in a Church which was also fighting on other fronts. The French Church was an unstable mixture of triumphalism and disarray. It aspired to a stricter Counter-Reformation control of society than any other part of the Catholic Church in Europe, fitfully backed by coercion from the monarchy and yet encouraged by Jansenist campaigns for purity and austerity in everyday life. Its confrontation with the secular stage, for instance, reached levels equalling that of English Puritans in the 1650s, and tipped over into the tragically absurd. In the 1690s, the Archbishop of Paris banned his clergy from presiding over the weddings of anyone connected with the theatre, and actors remained banned from receiving the last rites, which meant that they could not be buried in consecrated ground.[62]

It was not surprising that when reaction came, it was in the name of a wider freedom of life. Attacks on the Church establishment came from angry Jansenists, lawyers and repressed Protestants as well as Freemasons and actors who wanted a wife; soon scepticism or hatred of the Church moved on to become what we would define as atheism. The battle had its self-appointed generals in a group of intellectuals who all knew each other (though were not all necessarily friends) and who had no hesitation in styling themselves *philosophes*: a label which would have done them no favours in an anglophone society, but which has continued to command respect in France. Two of them, Voltaire and Rousseau, were to achieve a secular form of sainting in the new France of the Revolution, when the former showpiece city church, Ste-Geneviève, rebuilt at the expense of France's penultimate monarch in the old regime, was transformed into the 'Pantheon', a giant holding pen for the corpses of the specially honoured heroes of a self-consciously renewed and secularized society. There they still lie in great solemnity, their bones brought to the former church in the 1790s amid a welter of non-Christian pageantry.

The most famous publicist for the French Enlightenment was the writer François-Marie Arouet, usually known by his pen name, Voltaire. Not an especially profound writer, without any formal university training, but equipped with charm, immensely quick wit and a genius for making money which gave him the chance to live independently and write what he wanted, he was perhaps the most famous man in Europe when he died in 1778: the Erasmus of his age, read with delight in multiple translations, and master of the usefully calculated relationship, especially with monarchs. His effect on the reputation of the Catholic Church was even more immediately disruptive than Erasmus's: he set himself up as a lifelong campaigner against it. He much admired England, where he had spent a couple of years when he needed to escape from French officialdom after two spells of imprisonment in the Bastille. If the philosophy of Locke and the mechanical universe of Newton had banished mystery from human affairs, Voltaire saw Catholicism as a self-interested conspirator to perpetuate that mystery.[63]

Voltaire's was an elitist view of Enlightenment: he added an aristocratic 'de' prefix to his pseudonym, and loved the life of the great seigneur that he had created for himself out of harm's way at Ferney in the Swiss Confederation. From that safe refuge just beyond the French border, he spoke out against injustices perpetrated by French Catholic authorities against Huguenots and those accused of blasphemy, but it was the Church's capacity to interfere with the minds of the intelligent that he chiefly detested; religion could be left to the 'rabble' (canaille), a favourite word of his. His Jesuit education had left him with an intimate knowledge of the Bible, which he was almost obsessively ready to employ, far more than most of his philosophe contemporaries. It has been calculated that around 13 per cent of his letters contain biblical quotations, but most of them are there in order to structure a joke. Jesus he often referred to with a sneer as 'the hanged man', or elsewhere 'the first theist'.[64] Towards the end of his life, he famously said, 'If God did not exist it would be necessary to invent him': significantly, this was in a poem addressed to his far less talented predecessors, the anonymous authors of *Treatise of the three impostors*. Couched as an attack on them, its snarls at organized religion were as thoroughgoing as theirs, but, with his usual oblique wit, Voltaire seemed to be saying that even an imagined God might preserve the morality of society when the 'coarse atheism' of the *Treatise* would not. The effect of his attacks on organized religion was to deny any meaningful place to God in human affairs.

Voltaire, with characteristic prudence, kept his distance from and wrote little in the most substantial as well as the most risky enterprise of the French Enlightenment, the *Encyclopédie*. Its editor and major contributor was Denis Diderot, a former seminarian turned unmemorable novelist, whose atheism was much more thoroughgoing than that glimpsed in Voltaire's carefully modulated sarcasm. Diderot's view of knowledge was severely material: the world was a collection of molecules, and knowledge was that available to the senses, which might structure morality – why should a blind person have any shame in being publicly naked? His project, the most significant product of the contemporary fashion for encyclopedias, was a vast compendium of knowledge, arranged now in no hierarchy of being but in the fashionable alphabetical style (a rather tricky business if one was to be consistent over an enterprise which eventually ran to twenty-eight volumes). Alphabetic order was the eighteenth century's levelling riposte to the systems and classifications of Aristotle and Thomas Aquinas, and the insistence on subverting contemporary hierarchy was all-pervasive. Even within a single article, the subject matter might begin with discussion of a rare and monstrous bird, and end with discussion of a duke.

The overall tone of the *Encyclopédie* was deist, and despite official French censorship the assumptions behind it were those of natural religion; in the Baconian manner, hard facts were hard facts. No Jesuit wrote in the *Encyclopédie*, and Jansenists were offended by its tone. Religious articles were dealt with largely by an apparently pedantic and ultra-conservative cleric, neither Jesuit nor Jansenist, who was Royal Professor of Theology in Paris's Collège de Navarre, the Abbé Edmé-François Mallet. His work was so crassly unimaginative – for instance, in its solemn discussion of the precise location of Hell or the problems associated with Noah's Ark – that some have considered that it was intended to make religion look ridiculous. Even the cross-references of the *Encyclopédie* (an innovative way of making novel links between subjects) appeared subversive – in the reference to *Anthropophages* (cannibals) was the straight-faced instruction to 'see Eucharist, Communion'.[65]

If God departed from our consciousness, or had become impersonal or a mere abstraction, the world would be a cold and empty place. Diderot's close friend and contributor to the *Encyclopédie* Jean-Jacques Rousseau tried to remedy this by devising a 'natural' religion, based on the Christian Gospels, that sought to avoid what he saw as the unhealthy dogmatism disfiguring traditional Christian belief. Like so many of these intellectual systems formed in admiring consciousness of Francis Bacon's proposals for 'instauration', Rousseau's was based on an optimistic view of humankind's potential. A century before, Thomas Hobbes had seen the state of nature as a state of brutality, but Rousseau believed that we are born good, and it is the fault of social institutions that we are pushed towards vice and selfishness. Even the structure of traditional knowledge in arts and sciences is part of the distortion which stops people from knowing their true liberty. So although Rousseau looked to a past golden age, like traditional Christianity, his Fall was merely a wrong turning, a mistake, rather than a catastrophe which humankind had brought upon itself. The force of love and the right ordering of human affairs would put right the mistakes of the past.

Much of this Rousseau expressed in what are avowedly romantic novels. When the chance came in 1789 to change the world, many looked to a future where love would dissolve traditional corruption and constraints on human potential. Events did not quite turn out that way. The reason why is hinted at in the expansive paradox contained in Rousseau's doctrine of a 'General Will', the consent of the generality of society, whose urge to seek equality is irresistible and the embodiment of right: 'whoever refuses to obey the general will shall be constrained to do so by the whole body, which means nothing other than that he shall be forced to be free ... for this is the condition which, by giving each citizen to the nation, secures him against all personal dependence'.[66] Rousseau's own personal life had already suggested the shortcomings of his love ethic: he consigned his five children to a foundling hospital, and his visit to Britain to stay with David Hume turned into a saga of exploitation of Hume's hospitality and friendship, which in turn provoked an unwonted deviousness in that normally serene philosopher.[67]

Alongside the gleeful and publicity-seeking assaults on the Church and Christianity from *philosophes* came a more profound challenge from an academic far to the north in the University of Königsberg, Immanuel Kant. He was a total contrast to Rousseau: no whiff of scandal came out of a very private single life, and no open deviation from the Lutheran Pietism of his parents. Yet he shaped the way that the West did its thinking through the nineteenth and twentieth centuries, and the effect of his work was to reduce still further the place that a historical Christian faith and its institutions might have in the concerns of Western culture. It was he who in a short essay of 1784 gave the most celebrated answer to a question about this new movement posed by one of his Berlin contemporaries, 'What is Enlightenment?': 'Enlightenment is mankind's exit from its self-incurred immaturity'.[68]

Determined to use the mechanist method of Newton to rebuild philosophy, analysing observed phenomena in order to create clarity of definition, Kant argued like Descartes from the existence of individual consciousness rather than from the givenness of a God found in revelation. He developed the questions about human consciousness posed by David Hume; he denied that it was possible to prove the existence of the self even by Descartes' formulation 'I think, therefore I am.' He could say that the mind orders everything which it experiences, and that somehow it has a set of rules by which it can judge those experiences. These rules enable the mind to order the information which it receives about space and time within the universe. Yet the rules themselves come before any experience of space and time, and it is impossible to prove that these rules are true. All that can be said is that they are absolutely necessary to ordering what we perceive and giving it a quality we can label objectivity.

Kant was therefore reversing the priorities of previous philosophies, in what he saw as a revolution equal to that of Copernicus. Philosophy had worked on the premise that each individual mind gives a picture of structures in a real world which lies outside that mind. Now Kant maintained that the mind orders the world by the way in which it interprets experience. There are vital 'Ideas' which are beyond the possibility of experience, and therefore beyond any traditional proof derived by reasoning: Kant called these God, Freedom and Immortality. Although these are not accessible through reason, they can be reached by the conscience within the individual, a conscience which forces us to regulate our affairs according to its dictates. This is a new sort of faith to meet the battle between faith and reason: in a famous phrase, Kant said, 'I had to deny knowledge in order to make room for faith'.[69]

Thus there is a God in Kant's system: the ultimate goal to which (rather than to whom) the individual turns, hoping to meet this goal in an immortality which stretches out beyond our imperfect world. Yet this is a God whose existence cannot be proved; who needs no revelation in Bethlehem or on the Cross, no Bible, but the inner conscience calling us towards a distant image. Kant's removal of knowledge in the interests of faith is a solvent of Christian dogma, though it would present no problem for many Christian mystics throughout the history of the Church, who have ended up saying much the same thing. It may be that Kant would have known the writings of one of the more difficult characters of the Reformation, Andreas Osiander, distrusted by most of his fellow Lutherans and attacked by Calvin for his attempt to create a mystical theology within a Protestant framework; Kant's own University of Königsberg in its early years had provided the final refuge for that prickly but determinedly original Protestant pioneer. Yet Kant discarded the religion of revelation which had still underpinned Osiander's mystical version of Lutheranism.[70]

Kant was an optimist whose optimism was not even completely dimmed by the violence which followed the French Revolution, and he had seen the century embodied in the ruler of Königsberg, King Friedrich 'the Great' of Prussia. He was not the only philosopher of the Enlightenment to have high hopes of a generation of monarchs in central and eastern Europe who took sufficient interest in the ideas of change promoted by their contemporaries to gain the name 'Enlightened Despots': besides Friedrich, the Empresses Elizabeth and Catherine the Great of Russia, the Emperor Leopold of Austria, and a host of lesser rulers in their shadow. Even while they flattered *philosophes* into thinking that Enlightenment ideas were shaping government policy, their main concerns could be called enlightened self-interest: increasing their own power and grabbing territory, for which purpose huge standing armies were necessary. Medieval tradition, ancient local privileges and inherited intricacies of government were an obstacle to their plans, making their countries inefficient producers of taxes to pay for their armies. Medieval institutions were left alone if they did not get in the way; there was no change for change's sake. If benefiting the people at large clashed with the interests of government, that would be a reform too far, though if both could be accommodated, that was eminently desirable. But rival powers must be crushed, ecclesiastical powers included.

Accordingly, Catholic monarchs beginning with King José I of Portugal in 1759 brought mounting pressure on successive popes to dissolve the whole Society of Jesus, because they resented its vision of priorities wider than their own, including its loyalty to the papacy. After individual suppressions in various empires, they finally bullied the Pope into complete suppression in 1773. The dismantling of the Society led to the disintegration of the unrivalled Jesuit network of schools and colleges.[71] Such a wanton act of cultural vandalism was a sign that the religious outlook of such monarchs had shifted far from the confessional warfare of the Reformation; more evidence was the cynical process which, between 1772 and 1795, witnessed Catholic, Protestant and Orthodox great powers, respectively Austria, Prussia and Russia, amicably dividing up the diminished remnant of the once-great Commonwealth of Poland-Lithuania, and exiling its Catholic monarch to St Petersburg. More creditably, and with considerable irony, the Society of Jesus could maintain a covert existence only beyond the boundaries of Catholic Europe, through the connivance of Protestant Prussia and Orthodox Russia, whose respective monarchs Friedrich and Catherine, neither high-temperature Christians, were alarmed at the likely destruction of educational institutions in their Catholic lands.[72] Equally, the repression of religious minorities had gone out of fashion in these countries: when the Prince-Bishop of Salzburg sent his Protestant subjects packing in 1731, he incurred widespread disapproval from other rulers, including Catholics, and by the end of the century, edicts of toleration began the restoration of a public life to formerly persecuted groups from Ireland and Britain to France, Austria and Russia.

Eighteenth-century Europe thus presented curious contrasts between government-sponsored change and vigorous survival from the past. While the Catholic Church was under attack even from Catholic monarchs, it was also full of life and energy. The monasteries of central Europe plunged into rebuilding schemes with the same panache as their French counterparts, the bishops still patiently worked away at the huge task of carrying out the reforms mapped out two centuries before at the Council of Trent. One symptom of what resources this Church might discover that it commanded was the fate of Joseph II of Austria's attempts to impose his own vision of reform on the Catholic Church in Habsburg lands. Briskly contemptuous of the contemplative life, the Holy Roman Emperor dissolved a large proportion of the monasteries in his territories, creating a Religious Fund under the monarch's control for other Church purposes, such as the endowment of parishes. He would have preferred a complete confiscation, which would decisively have placed the Church in the hands of the Crown – but even his modified plan provoked disaster for him. The people's reaction in the Austrian Netherlands (modern Belgium) was to rise in revolt in 1789, forcing the dying emperor humiliatingly to abandon much of his scheme from the Netherlands to Hungary. It was a curious Catholic counter-point to what was happening in France at the same time, and a harbinger of the Catholic resurgence of the nineteenth century (see pp. 817–27).[73]

What is striking about Christian Europe at this period, Catholic, Protestant or Orthodox, is the withering of autonomous Church govern-ment in the face of State onslaught: the decay of the Oecumenical Patriarchate in Constantinople, the shackling of the Russian Orthodox Church to the imperial government, the growing impotence of the pope witnessed in the destruction of the Jesuits, but also, in the Protestant world, the effective silencing of the Church of England's deliberative bodies. The Hanoverian monarchs did not allow Convocations of Canterbury and York to meet to transact business, and for nearly a century and a half after 1717, English bishops lacked any forum for concerted action. John Wesley's authoritarian answer, his tightly con-trolled organization of Methodism, also faced rapid disintegration after his death. At the end of the century, an unexpected convulsion of society appeared to accelerate this process, threatening complete dismember-ment in the Catholic Church. In fact new power relationships and a new debate about authority in Western Christianity emerged, the conse-quences of which are still being worked out today. From 1789 events moved so quickly that, already in the 1790s, the French were talking about the 'ancien régime', the former state of things, looking back to this society so confusingly tangled between medieval survival and Enlightenment, and seeing something remote and discredited.

THE FRENCH REVOLUTION
(1789–1815)

Few in 1789 could have predicted that France would be the seat of revolution. It was western Europe's greatest power, its language spoken by elites everywhere. After the crushing of the Huguenot uprisings in the first decade of the century, it was generally a less violent or excitable country than its otherwise not dissimilar rival Great Britain.[74] Its weak-ness, however, in another contrast with Britain, was government finance. France had never established a proper national banking and credit system, and thanks to the centralizing impulse of its monarchy, failed to maintain a national representative body which could cooperate in raising revenue. This was disastrous even when France was victorious in war, as happened when the French supported Britain's former North American colonies in their War of Independence after 1776. Within four years of the Treaty of Paris recognizing the United States (1783), the French government faced bankruptcy, and it had no effective means of cutting through France's archaic revenue system. A run of terrible harvests and consequent famine inflamed the political temperature still further. An assembly of notables called in 1787 refused to help solve the financial crisis; so did an assembly of the clergy, who had jealously guarded their ancient right to tax themselves. However, the clergy raised the whole level of the argument by pointing out that their privileges survived from a time when all taxation had been levied with the consent of the feudal estates of the realm meeting as the States General. The clergy, or at least an idealized image of the good and conscientious *curé* (parish priest), became hugely popular nationwide – for the moment.[75]

The idea of reviving this representative institution therefore met with great enthusiasm, and if Louis XVI and his successive ministers had been more adroit in using it, they might have carried out substantial reform without disaster. Unfortunately the King was not a decisive man. Having assembled the States General in 1789 after more than a century and a half in abeyance, he could not make his mind up on vital procedural matters. In an atmosphere of expectation and with a torrent of suspicions and grievances already released by the summoning of the delegates, he lost the initiative. On 17 June 1789 the 'Third Estate', those delegates neither clergy nor noblemen, declared themselves a National Assembly; they were soon joined by dissident clergy and noblemen from the First and Second Estates. Further clumsy moves from the King increasingly destabilized the situation; rural France fell into turmoil. On 26 August 1789 the Assembly passed a Declaration of the Rights of Man, owing much to the American Declaration of Independence thirteen years before. It is worth noting what a break with the past this was, a high point of Enlightenment optimism: it was a declaration of rights, not accompanied by a declaration of duties. It took half a decade of mounting atrocity in war and revolution before duties were officially formulated.

It was still likely that France would develop a monarchy under a constitution, a tidier version of the British system, but the religious question pushed events a stage further. The National Assembly was as determined to reform the Church as everything else. Its plan was to create a national Church like that in England, but Catholic in doctrine and without the faults evident in the English Church. Gallican Catholics in France had long sought such arrangements, and indeed since the fifteenth century the monarchy had episodically done much to encourage such an outcome. Yet what was proposed took the most extreme form – it would be a national Church indeed, because bishops would be elected by the entire male population, including the newly emancipated Protestants and Jews.[76] Church lands were confiscated, and the rural labouring classes watched in growing anger as wealthy merchants, office-holders and former officials flush with compensation for lost jobs all used their cash to build up new landholdings.

The 'Civil Constitution of the Clergy', passed by the Assembly in 1790, left the Pope with no power, merely a formal respect. The fact that its passage paid no attention to what the Pope might think horrified many clergy who had gone along with reform so far. Recklessly the Assembly forced all clergy to take an oath of obedience to the Civil Constitution in January 1791. About half refused – and in the country-side that was particularly serious, because parish priests refusing were liable to carry their congregations with them. So now large sections of the population were cast as opponents of the Assembly: a fatal moment for the Revolution and the Church. Resistance was much strengthened when the Pope officially condemned the Civil Constitution that spring.[77] The King, a devout Catholic, was increasingly identified with this opposition, and when he failed in an attempt to flee the country later that year, he was deprived of all power.

It was more or less inevitable as events swept on that the Assembly should declare war on the traditional great powers of Europe, beginning in 1792 with the bulwark of the old system, the King's brother-in-law the Holy Roman Emperor. The Pope was one of those enemies: the lynching of a tactless Jacobin envoy in Rome, Nicolas Jean Hugon de Basseville, only cemented that impression in the minds of the government in Paris. War had a terrible effect on the Revolution. In 1792, spurred by provincial rebellions in the name of Catholic Christianity and the King, the State had begun large-scale executions of its aristocratic and clerical enemies in Paris. The numbers were at first small scale by modern standards of State terror, but they were horrifying at the time, particularly since they included nearly all available members of the French royal family, the King and Queen among them – the King died a week after de Basseville. At Nantes there were mass drownings of prisoners, beginning with priests, and the massacres in the Catholic Vendée set standards for later European atrocities in dehumanizing victims in order to make mass slaughter easy and virtuous. Europe's first single-party dictatorship in the name of the people had emerged. The awful tidy-mindedness of Enlightenment thought bred an insistence on everyone being liberated in ways defined by Revolutionaries – forcing them to be free, in a ghastly echo of Rousseau.

What was new about this regime – contrasting, for instance, with the austere enthusiasm of Savonarola's Republic of Florence or the nightmare popular kingdom of the Anabaptists besieged in Münster (see pp. 591–3 and 623–4) – was that the Jacobins, most extreme Revolutionaries of the French Republic, radicalized the snickering scepticism of French *philosophes* about the whole Christian message. They came to regard any form of Christian faith as a relic of the *ancien régime* which they were destroying, though they had to acknowledge that the people on whom they were imposing liberty, equality and fraternity craved for some sort of religion. The Revolution which had begun with a sincere effort to improve the Church now sought to replace it with a synthetic religion, constructed out of classical symbolism mixed up with the eighteenth century's celebration of human reason: the Christian calendar of years and months was abolished, religious houses closed, churches desecrated.

Much of the violence against the Church exploded out of popular feeling, striking out at anything which spoke of past authority, but much de-Christianization was imposed by government decree, and it was particularly hard to create new public ceremonies for a manufactured religion that did not seem ludicrous. An opera singer posed as the Goddess of Liberty (or Reason – her sponsors changed their minds) on a stage in Notre-Dame de Paris. She had novelty value but no staying power. When the coldly anti-Christian revolutionary leader Maximilien Robespierre tried to redesign and calm down the revolutionary liturgy, his efforts turned into a trigger for his own sudden march to the guillotine.[78] Although the campaign of active de-Christianization petered out by the end of the 1790s, the Revolution had served long-term notice that the institutional Church and perhaps Christianity itself would be seen as an enemy of the new world. The Constitutional Church was wrecked; this ally of the Revolution was caught miserably between the de-Christianizers and those fighting the Revolution.

As wars with all France's neighbours dragged on, the French people became increasingly disillusioned with their masters: the Church had been shattered apparently to no purpose, and, since before the Revolution it had a virtual monopoly on caring for the poor and helpless, the weakest suffered most by the destruction of Church institutions. The most successful of the Revolution's generals, the Corsican Napoleon Bonaparte, gained more and more popular support, in contrast to the revolutionary government's waning popularity. It would have taken a man with no ambition to resist this temptation, and Napoleon did not. He staged a coup d'état in 1799, and successive plebiscites, only partially rigged, gave overwhelming majorities to his assumption first of the Republican title of First Consul and then of Emperor of the French. Right up to the final collapse of his extraordinary conquests in 1813–14, Napoleon continued to enjoy widespread support throughout France.

An astute politician as well as a brilliant general, Napoleon attached great importance to religion – not because he cared about it personally, but because he saw that other people cared about it a great deal. The Republic had made a gross error in attacking the Church. Now, if he was to unite France, he would have to come to an understanding with this institution which so controlled human emotions. He would benefit not only in France but throughout the large areas of Catholic Europe that came to be under French rule. If Napoleon was to clinch an agreement to cover all these territories, he would have to approach the Pope. Accordingly, in 1801, he and Pope Pius VII reached an agreement or Concordat, the model for many similar deals between the papacy and a variety of governments throughout the world during the nineteenth and twentieth centuries. Napoleon said that its negotiation was the most difficult task of his life.[79]

This Concordat was important not simply for its extensive reorganization of the French Church in partnership with the State, but for its effect on the pope's position. The marginalization of the pope begun by 'Enlightened Despots' had seemed to be complete when revolutionary French armies arrested Pius VI and watched him die in French exile in 1799. Now the new pope was negotiating terms for the whole French Church, once so proud of its independence. The new structure of appointments and hierarchy among the clergy gave the pope much more power, a move which many lower clergy welcomed since it was likely to curb the powers of their immediate superiors the bishops. The Pope's new position was most effectively symbolized when in 1804 he agreed to be present at the coronation ceremony for Napoleon as Emperor in Notre-Dame Cathedral in Paris: a curious reconciliation of the traditional Church with the new people's State, as Napoleon placed on his own head the crown which the people's armies had won for him. Nor was the Pope's usefulness over then: Napoleon prevailed on his new ally to discover a new saint of the Church, an ancient Roman martyr called with providential coincidence Napoleon, whose feast day on the Emperor's birthday, 15 August, usefully fell on that popular holy day of the Church, the Feast of the Assumption of Our Lady (see Plate 39). Even after the Emperor's fall, the Feast of St Napoleon remained a rallying point for Bonapartists throughout the nineteenth century, a sore annoyance to those French Catholics who detested the Emperor's memory and wanted to concentrate on celebrating God's Mother.[80]

Napoleon had a genius for the public gesture. In 481 King Childeric, father of Clovis, the first Christian king of what became France, had been buried in what is now the city of Tournai. Childeric's richly furnished grave was rediscovered beside a Roman fort in 1653, becoming the subject of Europe's first detailed archaeological report. Among the many precious objects recovered were hundreds of little gold-and-garnet bees (some think that they were actually badly drawn eagles); they had probably decorated a rich cloak or horse-covering. Most of them disappeared in a burglary in the nineteenth century, but before that the bees caught Napoleon's imagination, and he adopted them as his dynastic emblem because he could thus identify himself with a French monarch who predated but had literally fathered the ancient Christian monarchy so recently destroyed by the French Revolution. The Bonapartes' bees could thus upstage the old French royal family's symbol of the fleur-de-lys; it was an adroit attempt to remould traditional Christendom, rather like the Concordat itself. Napoleon had grasped a truth which had eluded the Revolutionaries whose commitment to the Enlightenment spurred them to abolish the past: tradition and history had their own authority, which could become the ally of change, and at the heart of that tradition in western Europe was Christianity.[81]

Popular enthusiasm greeted Pius VII on his visit to Paris in 1804. That surprised everyone, but it was all of a piece with the fierce resistance to the Revolution in parts of France, and with the fury which had confronted the Emperor Joseph II's attempted monastic confiscations in the Austrian Netherlands. This was the beginning of a new era of popular Catholic activism, increasingly directed towards a charismatic papacy. The popular mood was only strengthened when Napoleon seized papal territories in Italy in 1809, and the Emperor effectively imprisoned Pius for four years. The papacy's sufferings at the hands of the Revolution transformed the Pope from ineffectual Italian prince to a confessor for the Faith, pitied throughout Europe. Significantly, even in Protestant England, centuries of anti-papal prejudice were weakened by sympathy for the enemy of England's enemy. Already refugee Catholic priests and monks had been welcomed to England as victims of the Revolution, something inconceivable before 1789.

A further catastrophe for the Church indirectly benefited the Pope. In 1803 all the ecclesiastical territories in the Holy Roman Empire ruled by prince-bishops and abbots were turned over to secular governance, and huge amounts of Church property confiscated; henceforth more than half of German Catholics were under the rule of Protestants.[82] Often these prelates, secure in their ancient privileges, had shown scant respect for His Holiness. Now they were gone, and in 1806 the Pope also saw the end of that traditional counterweight to papal power, the Holy Roman Empire itself, when the Emperor Francis II remodelled himself as the Emperor Francis I of Austria. Without much public fuss, in 1814 the Pope reconstituted the Society of Jesus. The future of the Catholic Church was veering towards monarchy, as a result of the revolution which had aimed to overthrow all monarchs. This was one of the many paradoxes of the century between the downfall of Napoleon in 1815 and the outbreak of the First World War, the last century in which the fabric of Christendom might be said to be intact. Although that period was to bring further revolutions in both Western politics and consciousness, Christianity worldwide is still trying to make what it can of the Enlightenment, and of the French Revolution which was its unexpectedly violent experiment.

AFTERMATH OF REVOLUTION: A EUROPE OF NATION-STATES

In 1815 a combination of the Revolution's victorious enemies among the great powers of Europe confirmed the restoration of the senior surviving Bourbon as King Louis XVIII of France. Yet it is never possible to recreate the past. In two significant respects, the victorious allies did not try when they met at the Congress of Vienna to remap Europe. Since the Habsburgs no longer wanted their recently renounced title of Holy Roman Emperor, it was not revived, and neither were any of the ecclesiastical territories within the empire – the only clergyman to regain his temporal jurisdictions (with a few subtractions) was the Pope in Italy. However effective governors the imperial clergy had been – and generally their record had been good – the Enlightenment had destroyed their credibility in government. Thus ended one component of Christendom which had been in place for a thousand years. For a century afterwards, Europe avoided a repetition of universal war, but when it came in 1914, it was to damage the concept of Christendom irreparably. During that hundred years, Western Christianity experienced both renewal and challenges to its faith and practice as fundamental as anything that happened in the 1790s.

Throughout Europe, the rhetoric of revolution and the traumas of war left in their wake new possibilities, particularly the possibility of ordinary people having a say in shaping their own destinies. As the industrial revolution based on steam power spread from its original base in Britain through economically suitable enclaves as far away as Russia, large populations were drawn to new manufacturing communities, which might grow as large as any traditional city. More and more people had the experience of building up their own lives without traditional resources of family or custom, though often amidst demoralizing poverty and lack of alternatives. It was a pattern which was to spread through the rest of the world and continues now. The movements of peoples, their conversations and the spread of ideas became all the easier because (beginning in the 1830s in Britain) the map of Europe was covered with a network of steam railways, the most spectacular leap in the speed of transport since humankind had first mastered horse-riding. There were far greater sudden lurches of speed to come. During the nineteenth century, first the electric telegraph and then the telephone made communication instant over long distances, at least for those who could pay for it. Now the history of Christianities, previously fairly easy to distinguish as three separate stories of non-Chalcedonians and Western and Eastern Chalcedonians, began to merge and interact far more closely.

The established Churches of Europe, and Churches throughout the world which sprang out of them, had to adjust to these new realities, to compete with new messages which the revolutionary years spread from the elegant tracts of *philosophes* into a much wider public domain. So much could not be unsaid: the French Revolution's slogan of 'liberty, equality, fraternity' could not be forgotten. The French National Assembly had created a citizen army, whose soldiers were the State, and who therefore had a right to a direct say in it (some voices suggested that their wives might have the same rights). That implied a new type of politics, different from the traditional view of political representation which survived, for instance, in early-nineteenth-century British parliamentary life, where privilege, wealth or the possession of property was still the main qualification for having a voice in the kingdom's affairs. The French Revolution had overtaken a dynastic kingdom which had seemed as powerful as Britain, and with a far more coherent and ancient ideology of sacred monarchy. As a substitute, it had decreed into existence a nation-state, whose project was to replace a patchwork of jurisdictions, dialects and loyalties by a centralized government, a single French language to be spoken by all, and a shared sense throughout the population that this was the only way to live – the ideology known as nationalism.[83]

This idea of a nation became the chief motor of politics in nineteenth-century Europe: varied struggles to create nations, where often no comparable political unit, common culture or mass consciousness had ever previously existed – and equally, varied struggles by surviving traditional governments to resist this process. For many in the nineteenth century, nationalism became an emotional replacement for the Christian religion. It might imitate the French example, but many of the lands which the French revolutionary armies had overrun in the 1790s gained a full sense of national unity through their resentment at this violation. On that basis, Belgium, Italy and Germany all built up national identities during the nineteenth century, in the process also overturning ancient political structures. Their rhetoric of national resistance in turn provided a model for the twentieth-century struggles of non-European colonial peoples against the rule of those same nation-states.

Alongside nationalism was an economic revolution, which brought the struggle of a new elite against an old. The industrial revolutions were as important as the French Revolution in challenging aristocracies whose wealth and power were based mainly on land and agriculture. Even in pre-industrial France, the main impulse to overthrow the *ancien régime* had come from groups outside the landed class: lawyers, journalists, businesspeople, urban workers with specialist skills – what is clumsily but unavoidably called the middle class. In the more decorous politics of Britain as much as in mainland Europe, middle-class groups now sought to legislate into being political institutions to give themselves voices in national affairs appropriate to their wealth and talent, at least to share power with the landed aristocracy. They aimed to create structures designed to reward ability and personal achievement rather than birth, and to gain the right to express their political and religious opinions as they wished. This was the politics of liberalism.

Liberals looked to the Revolution's rhetoric of liberty and equality. It was not enough. The early nineteenth century was chastened by the memory of what had happened when Enlightenment ideals were put into practice, and that led to a general shift in mood among western Europeans towards what was styled romanticism. People who cared about the restructuring of Europe in the wake of events from 1789 to 1815 respected the rationalism of the Enlightenment less than a new expression of emotion and a search for individual fulfilment. Romanticism became a major colouring for political movements in Europe, whether looking to the past or to the future. In a chastened age after Napoleon's fall, it provided multiple opportunities for Europeans to posture. Fraternity, the third element of the revolutionary trinity, became the watchword of groups who envisaged a brotherhood of all oppressed people against both old and new oppression, confronting both Europe's surviving monarchical pattern and the newly wealthy elites of the industrial revolution. Quite suddenly in the 1830s, radical politics in Britain and France acquired a new word: 'socialism'.

'Socialists' asserted that without the distortions of inequality or poverty, people would naturally behave to one another as brothers (once more, sisters were not then greatly considered). This was a restatement of Enlightenment optimism, but socialists often sought to co-opt the love ethic of Jesus Christ and occasionally even of his Church, though generally in the face of deep lack of sympathy from Church hierarchies.[84] Robert Owen, one of the chief personalities in the movement, who from 1816 turned theory into remarkably productive practice in his New Lanark cotton mills in Scotland, detested established Churches, but he certainly did not lack religious seriousness, which included his own fervent belief in an age of human perfection to come.[85] Sometimes those who admired Owen's commitment to social engineering rejected the industrial society which he had embraced, channelling their efforts into setting up new agriculturally based communities which would not be tainted by industrial misery. The favoured destination was North America, where Owen's export of his proto-socialism had been defeated by the sturdy individualism of the people of Indiana. In America, there was available land (discounting the Native American population) and, among immigrants, none of the social inequalities of Europe. Such efforts usually ended in failure, like Owen's own ill-starred venture across the Atlantic, and could easily be dismissed as romantic and backward-looking. Not surprisingly, the hard-pressed governments of early-nineteenth-century Europe felt that such groups were less of a threat to their survival than the more radical forms of liberalism.

This was a mistake: a new generation of theorists transformed socialism. In France, Louis Blanc presented a vision of a national state run by the people to implement socialist policies, and he became a member of the brief and fragile revolutionary 'Second Republic' regime of 1848, which almost gave him a chance to see what the reality might be. In the 1840s Friedrich Engels used his personal connections with English industry to construct an accurate description of the social injustice of contemporary English society, going on to identify both cause and solution in class conflict. His friend Karl Marx applied to socialist ideas and rhetoric a newly rigorous system and a philosophy of both the past and the future. The latter, a vision of the inevitable consummation in what he termed the dictatorship of the proletariat, was no less a prophetic and apocalyptic vision than anything that Christianity had produced in its two millennia.

Yet while Marx prophesied in the Judaeo-Christian tradition, what was distinctive about this new phase of socialism was its commitment to materialism and rejection of religions of revelation. This echoed one of the greatest influences on Marx: the rejection of religious consciousness in the writings of Ludwig Feuerbach (see p. 833). As early as 1844, Marx was writing of the need to abolish religion, since it was a distraction from the task of freeing workers from their burdens. When he and Engels took over a socialist organization called the League of the Just in 1847, they changed its name to the League of Communists and its slogan from 'All men are Brothers' to 'Proletarians of all Countries – Unite!'[86] Henceforth, the growing proportion of socialists looking to Marx's prophetic scheme of the future regarded Christianity as an obstacle rather than an ally in their confrontation alike with liberalism, nationalism and the remains of the *ancien régime*. Christians must now decide who were their enemies indeed.

22

Europe Re-enchanted or Disenchanted? (1815–1914)

CATHOLICISM ASCENDANT: MARY'S TRIUMPH AND THE CHALLENGE OF LIBERALISM

The European Churches had many different responses to the traumas of the revolutionary wars and the eventual defeat of Napoleon. Up to the great convulsions after the First World War, virtually everywhere in Europe still had an established Church whose establishment owed itself to an equally long-established monarchy. As a result, anyone opposing or seeking to curb the power of such monarchies was liable to regard the Church as an enemy. Yet complications arose in countries of multiple religions, and, wherever a grouping with a common culture and language ruled by an external power adhered for the most part to one Church, that Church was likely to become the focus for nationalist self-assertion. The situation was still more complex where both sides owed allegiance to Roman Catholicism.

One underlying structural consideration was that in Western Churches, whether Catholic or Protestant, a large proportion of the clerical leadership had always been drawn from the able rather than the well born, unusually among the institutions of traditional society. Now that prince-bishops, abbacies and cathedral chapters stuffed with aristocratic dimwits had been swept away from the Catholic Church in the former Holy Roman Empire, this became even more obviously the case. In the long term, such a shift in clerical leadership, in parallel with the growing professionalization of secular government and bureaucracy in Europe, was going to produce a predisposition to liberalism in Western Christianity, but in Roman Catholicism its immediate effect was to strengthen the growing concentration of power and emotional loyalty in the papacy, as clergy turned from their traditional aristocratic leaders to the ultimate patron in Rome.

The movement embodying this mood had long borne the name of ultramontanism, deriving its image of 'looking beyond the mountains' from the perspective of people in northern Europe, caught up in papacy's great medieval conflicts with the Holy Roman Empire. 'Ultramontanes' were thus those who looked across the Alps to Italy, reverencing the pope's authority. It contrasted with those localist moods in Catholicism such as Gallicanism in France, which had not sought leadership across the Alps in Rome, and which looked first to their own resources. Ultramontanism is often seen as a conservative force in the Church, but after 1815 it represented innovation and the prospect of Church reconstruction and revival, albeit of a particular type. The papacy was now Europe's last elective monarchy. As such, the pope was a symbol of the old world, but he also embodied a form of centralizing Catholicism so old as to seem new: ultramontanism revived the ambitions of Gregory VII and Innocent III centuries before. Papal power continued to sit uneasily alongside that of Europe's royal dynasties. These monarchs sought to maintain their inherited positions with the aid of the Church. They generally negotiated concordats with Rome in the style of Napoleon, giving them many opportunities to interfere in Church affairs in their realms, including extensive powers of appointment to bishoprics – far more, indeed, for the time being than the pope himself.[1] The Austrian emperor, after all the varied religious commitments of the Habsburg dynasty, still identified himself as the leader among Catholic monarchs, and as late as 1903, Francis Joseph, Emperor-King of Catholic Austria-Hungary, vetoed a likely candidate for the papacy in a papal election.[2]

Francis Joseph was expressing a tradition of dispersed power in the Western Church which now had much to contradict it. Ultramontanism built up its new emotional power in alliance with a startling revival in popular Catholic practice; this was heralded in the eighteenth-century popular resistance to the efforts of monarchs and revolutionaries alike to interfere in the everyday lives of Catholics. New pilgrimage cults and religious orders mushroomed to reverse earlier destruction, but just as in late-sixteenth-century Catholic Europe, this was no mere restoration of the past. Against a French Revolution which represented more than two decades of male nationalist violence, the Church found itself managing an international uprising of women – what has been termed with a pleasing overturning of modern sociological assumptions 'ultramontane feminism'.[3] It followed the trend first perceptible among both Protestants

and Catholics in seventeenth-century Europe (see pp. 791–4) that
women were becoming more active than men in devotional practice. As
far afield as Mexico, while men began to drift away from the sacramental
life of the Church, lay women's associations played an ever growing
part in running parish affairs.[4]

Everywhere, a maelstrom of nuns descended on the Church. In the
land which became Belgium, for instance, the proportion of women
religious to men reversed from 1780 to 1860, from 40:60 to 60:40, and
at the end of this process, in a development to horrify any bishop
from the Council of Trent, only 10 per cent of Belgian nuns were in
contemplative orders: the vast majority were involved in teaching, health
care and help for the poor.[5] Even would-be female contemplatives could
be distinctively active when it suited them. The world-denying and
savagely self-punishing teenager Thérèse Martin of Lisieux in Normandy, overexcited by her pilgrimage to Rome in 1887, seized on a
routine papal audience to beg no less a figure than Pope Leo XIII for
permission for immediate entrance to the Carmelite Order despite her
age. The hapless pontiff was understandably alarmed, particularly when
she clung to his knees and had to be removed by ecclesiastical bouncers.
She got her way in the end, to the point of canonization half a century
after her early death from tuberculosis.[6]

The most assertive woman of all was the Mother of God. The nineteenth century proved one of the most prolific periods for Mary's activity
in the history of the Western Church since the twelfth century. She seems
to have made more appearances all over Europe and Latin America than
in any century before or since: generally to women without money,
education or power and in remote locations, and often in association
with the political upheavals or economic crises which repeatedly hit a
society in the middle of dramatic transformations.[7] Our Lady conveyed
a rich variety of messages and opinions. In Paris in 1830 she manifested
herself three times to Catherine Labouré, a newly professed young nun.
The first occasion was in July, at the height of the political upheavals
which less than a fortnight later swept away the Bourbon monarchy and
replaced it by the Orleanist Louis Philippe. Mary gave the nun the
pattern for a medal to be struck with her image: within twelve years, a
hundred million copies of the medal were providing more comfort to the
faithful than a French Orleanist monarchy which many of them regarded
as a distressing usurpation and compromise with the Revolution.[8]

When Our Lady appeared again at Marpingen in Germany to three
village girls in 1876, she made a political point as she had already done

frequently in France. Although she never brought the good folk of Marpingen anything like her earlier success at Lourdes (see p. 824), she strengthened the morale of ordinary German Catholics caught up in the so-called *Kulturkampf*, a fierce confrontation with the Protestant state apparatus of the new German Empire, and so she contributed to the *Kulturkampf*'s failure to intimidate Catholicism in Germany. She did so without any help from the diocesan hierarchy of the Rhineland, who, if they had not been under such government pressure, would have done their best to bring her cult to a swift end.[9] Mary had technology on her side: the steady speeding up of communications and the sudden availability of cheap print, two of the motors of social change generally, were of great benefit, spreading the news of her growing loquacity at an unprecedented pace. As her shrines old and new flourished, much of their prosperity was dependent on the steam train. Protestants went on trains to the seaside, Catholics to light a candle in a holy place; devout pilgrimage had never been easier or more enjoyable.

Many of Mary's appearances were surrounded by fierce controversies, as were parallel events such as twenty or so cases of the appearance of stigmata (despite the experience having been pioneered by a man, Francis of Assisi, nearly all those bearing stigmata in modern times have been women).[10] Such wonders pitted Catholics against Catholics, with a regular pattern of sceptical clerical men versus heroically insistent women who went on to find clerical and lay support for their experiences. They continued into twentieth-century crises for Catholic communities across Europe. Mary's manifestations to three children in Fátima in Portugal 1917 were classics of the genre, during a world war and seven years after the overthrow of Portugal's monarchy. Similar were her appearances in the strongly Catholic Croat town of Medjugorje in 1981, as the Yugoslav Federation began to lose the political will to survive on the eve of catastrophic inter-confessional violence in the region. During the Yugoslav war that followed, Mary's Catholic partisans in Herzegovina became virulent anti-Muslim nationalists, who also bizarrely threatened to blow up the Catholic cathedral in Mostar if the bishop there did not abandon his scepticism about the heavenly visions.[11]

For people caught up in this exhilarating outburst of religious energy, Catholic ultramontanism represented a unifying ideology against the onslaughts of the Enlightenment, and the pope came to symbolize the sufferings and eventual triumph of the whole Church in the revolutionary era. The French arch-polemicist Joseph de Maistre was a prophet of absolute monarchy in Church and State, and a fanatical opponent of everything that the French Revolution represented: in 1819 he spelled out that 'Christianity rests wholly on the Sovereign Pontiff' and 'all sovereignty is infallible in nature'.[12] The confrontational style of such ultramontane rhetoric was sharpened by the papacy's anger at the direct challenge to its temporal rule in central Italy. Nationalists and liberals sought to unite the peninsula for the first time since the disappearance of the Roman Empire. The charismatic, creative (and often naive and self-assertive) Pope Pius IX opened his pontificate in 1846 with startling measures of modernization, such as plans for a railway system in the Papal States. It was easy to see such gestures as liberalism: a possibility intoxicating in its unexpected emergence from the Vatican. It seemed as if the Pope himself might lead Rome into the leadership of a liberal reconstruction of all Europe, but the nationalist revolutions of 1848 revealed his confusion, which readily tipped into his horrified opposition to Italian unification, not least because it would involve an end to the Papal States.

By 1864, after a series of humiliating losses of territory to a new Italian monarchical state based on the once devoutly papalist House of Savoy, Pius reacted in frustration by issuing an encyclical letter to which was attached a *Syllabus of Errors*, hastily gathered from a series of recent papal pronouncements. Some were uncontroversial, but they included a series of peevish statements which among other things condemned socialism and the principle that non-Catholics should be given freedom of religion in a Catholic state. They culminated in the proposition that it was wrong to believe that the Pope 'can and ought to reconcile himself with progress, liberalism and modern civilization'.[13] There were many in Catholic Europe to applaud the Pope: those with memories of the atrocities inspired by that parent of liberalism and modern civilization, the French Revolution, and those still witnessing Spanish, Portuguese, Italian or Latin American anticlerical liberals – even Swiss liberals – continuing to close convents and seize schools from the Catholic Church. In Spain, between 1829 and 1834, liberals forced the King to disband that faithful guardian of Spanish Catholic identity, the Spanish Inquisition. What did that say about the Spanish patriotism of liberals?

Catholics could also readily link such destructive fruits of liberalism to that curious offspring of the Scottish Reformation, Freemasonry (see pp. 771–2). By the eighteenth century, Freemasonry had become the adopted son of the Enlightenment, just as so many eighteenth-century Protestant Scots had done more generally; long before the French

Revolution, Freemasonry's leading figures came to sound more like Voltaire than John Dury or Johann Heinrich Alsted. Now especially in Catholic countries in southern Europe, Central and South America and the Caribbean, in the absence of any popular Protestant alternative to the Catholic Church, the Masonic Lodge became a rallying point for all who loathed ecclesiastical power. Here Freemasonry often did indeed become the chief force within liberal politics: a rival to that other closed male caste, the Catholic clergy, complete with Masons' own engrossing (though a good deal less public) ritual life. A remnant of this survived to our own age in that time-warped and embattled island, Fidel Castro's Cuba. A promenade around the cheerfully shabby towns and villages of Cuba at the turn of the second and third millennia would reveal an unexpected (and interestingly little-remarked) feature of this determinedly anti-Catholic state with its opportunistic version of Communism. Alongside the local Communist Party headquarters, one of the best-kept buildings on the street was the hall of the local Masonic Lodge, complete outside with its proudly displayed bust of the great nineteenth-century liberal hero and liberator José Martí. President Castro was as much heir to the nineteenth century's anticlerical liberalism as he was to Marx.[14]

Yet in 1864 'liberalism' had a different and less negative sound for Catholics elsewhere. Even in France, tormented by the rift between those venerating and those execrating the Revolution, several influential bishops were privately appalled at the *Syllabus*'s potential effects. One of their number not ashamed of joining the word 'liberal' to 'Catholic', Félix Dupanloup, Bishop of Orléans, wrote a best-selling pamphlet defending the *Syllabus* by the backhanded method of explaining away its intemperate propositions.[15] Likewise in the British Empire, Catholicism owed its opportunities for expansion to liberal principles. The precedent came in the historic decision of the British Crown in 1774 to secure its newly won Canadian dominions by allying with the Catholic elite of New France. This effectively prevented French Canadian Catholics from abetting France's aid to the Protestant revolutionaries of the United States. Their decision was vindicated by the anticlerical horrors perpetrated by French revolutionaries a decade later – indeed, the Catholic Church in Quebec became well aware that it enjoyed much less interference under the British than from the previous royal French government.[16] Then Britain and Ireland witnessed a gradual dismantling of public disabilities for Catholics (not yet completed in the early twenty-first century, with a repeal of the legislation of 1701 forbidding Catholics to succeed to the British throne still pending). Without such new freedoms, the authorities in Rome could not have launched a comprehensive reform of the startlingly pre-Tridentine and lay-dominated Catholic Church in Ireland, to bring it into line with the well-regulated devotional revolution in the rest of Catholic Europe.[17]

Not only Catholics subject to the British Crown benefited from the rearrangement of the modern world. In the Protestant republic which was the United States of America, Enlightenment was the benevolent force in separating Church and State, allowing the Catholic hierarchy complete institutional freedom and the chance to exercise pastoral care for a growing flood of Catholic immigrants, protected by the Constitution in the face of widespread Protestant popular hostility (which was nevertheless often paradoxically couched in the language of liberalism and resistance to Catholic priestcraft). In Lutheran northern Europe, the new constitutional arrangements for state boundaries which so favoured Protestant monarchies were mitigated by a liberal idea of *Parität* – fair play between Catholics and Protestants – which was especially important in the former Holy Roman Empire in protecting Catholic subjects against their newly acquired Protestant princes.[18] In the southern Netherlands, a revolution of unmistakably liberal character in 1830 against the lump-ishly discriminatory rule of a Protestant Dutch monarchy created a new state, Belgium, whose cement across linguistic divisions between French- and Flemish-speakers was its flamboyant Catholicism. Despite having to accept a German Lutheran monarch, the Belgian Catholic Church enjoyed a freedom without parallel in any Catholic country in Europe; the closest analogy was British Quebec. This was specifically thanks to the adventurous liberalism of the new Belgian Constitution: now liberals could conveniently defend their freedoms against any royal attempts at encroachment by judicious deployment of fervent loyalty to the pope and appeals for his support.[19] The Belgians were more fortunate in their access to Rome than the Catholic Poles and Lithuanians, whose repeated national risings against the Russian tsar in 1830, 1848 and 1863 met with a cold lack of support (and indeed initially even rebuke) from the Vatican, which shocked educated opinion in Europe, including French ultramontanes.[20]

In such varied settings, the *Syllabus* was a poisonous mistake, yet Pope Pius never admitted as much. His delighted response to the fervency of popular Catholicism, which even after his repudiation of the revolutionary fervour of 1848–9 included a rising tide of devotion to his own genial person, was to affirm more and more previously left indeterminate. In reaction to the dramatic revival of Marian cults, in 1854 he used his authority to promulgate that doctrine first formulated by English monks in the early twelfth century that Mary had been conceived without the spot of sin (see pp. 393–4). It was the final defeat of centuries of Catholic rearguard action against the notion of the Immaculate Conception, which had long been led by the Dominicans, following the opinions of their greatest theologian Thomas Aquinas. So great was the tide of opinion that even the Dominicans countenanced the foundation in 1860 of an Order of Dominican Nuns of the Immaculate Conception, in devoutly Marian Poland.

Our Lady showed her approval of the Pope's action by appearing at Lourdes in the French Pyrenees only four years after the Definition, announcing to a peasant girl, Bernadette Soubirous, with a fine disregard for logical categories, 'I am the Immaculate Conception.'[21] Over the next few months she proceeded to produce alarming enthusiasm in other visionaries in Lourdes; large numbers of village women and girls had visions, saw ghostly lights and had to be restrained from throwing themselves into the river or from dizzy rocky heights. In time-honoured folkloric fashion, Our Lady was not above giving salutary frights to local sceptics – such as the state officials who unsympathetically interrogated Bernadette, and then found themselves troubled by poltergeist-like phenomena and specifically directed storms, or the drunkard who had defecated in the Grotto and was then terrified by a night of acute diarrhoea. These two aspects of the events of 1858, zestfully narrated by locals at the time, have subsequently been edited out of the shrine's official narratives; Our Lady of Lourdes has become a much better-behaved Virgin.[22] Lourdes has become perhaps the most visited of all Christian shrines, Christianity's answer to Mecca (see Plate 44). It has also served as a riposte to those Catholics who had questioned the wisdom of defining the Immaculate Conception.

The most radical of Pius's achievements was to go where the Council of Trent had feared to proceed and produce a new definition of papal authority. The setting for this was a further council of the Church, in which seven hundred bishops from all over the world, including more than a hundred from across the Atlantic, arrived at the Vatican in December 1869, and occupied themselves in discussion for the next ten months. The council was paradoxical in its chief work, which was a thoroughgoing denial of the principles of conciliarism. Pope Pius was once more influenced by the political events around him: the Italian army was surrounding his last territory, the city of Rome. When external political crises resulted in the hasty withdrawal of French protective troops, it poured through the city defences, halting only at the locked gates of the Vatican. Soon afterwards, the bishops of the Vatican Council dispersed after a hasty adjournment. Some had gone already, before the moment in July 1870 when the vast majority, with varying degrees of enthusiasm, backed a decree, *Pastor aeternus* ('The Eternal Shepherd'). This decisively exalted papal power at their expense, just at the moment when the pope's temporal power was about to disappear for ever. Only two bishops voted against the decree, though fifty-seven (including nearly all the bishops from 'Uniate' or Greek Catholic Churches) left to avoid the pain of voting against a frail and personally highly popular and respected old man in his hour of misfortune.

Now, with careful limitations, agreed after much charged episcopal debate in bad Latin in the echoing acoustic of St Peter's Basilica, the pope had been declared 'possessed of that infallibility with which the divine Redeemer willed that his Church should be endowed for defining doctrine regarding faith and morals'.[23] Only on one subsequent occasion, once more a Marian declaration in 1950, on the subject of Mary's bodily assumption into Heaven, has the pope used this infallible authority. Yet even to recognize it was a triumph for ultramontanism. When Joseph de Maistre had proclaimed the infallible sovereignty of the papacy in 1819, the Vatican had been nervous, and liberal Catholics had been furious. Now such statements were guiding principles for the Roman Church. It is extraordinary that the conciliarist tradition, which flourished in the fourteenth- and fifteenth-century Western Church and which still had weighty advocates in the eighteenth century, should crash in ruin at the time when Europe's temporal powers were all yielding to the logic of constitutionalism. That was a mark of how much the ultramontanes decided that the principles of liberalism were potentially subversive of their whole project.[24]

At least in its rhetoric, then, the late-nineteenth-century Catholic hierarchy set itself up against liberalism, whatever local accommodations it might make to circumstance. Perhaps that was inevitable when liberalism and nationalism humiliated the pope in his own city. Anti-clericals in the new Italian regime sponsored the erection of a statue of the sixteenth-century free-thinking Dominican maverick Giordano Bruno, placed in the Roman square where the Church had burned him alive – Pope Leo XIII was so upset that he threatened to leave Rome for good (see Plate 45). They also built a massive and leeringly visible monument to Vittorio Emanuele II, first king of Italy, and with exquisite wit adorned the King's tomb in the Pantheon with bronze ornaments cast from cannon which had formerly defended the pope's Castel Sant'Angelo. Meanwhile, year on year, the steam trains to the Eternal City carried crowds of devout Catholics like the young Thérèse of Lisieux. They savoured the sufferings of early Christians in ill-ventilated visits to the newly exposed catacombs, and they returned from these archaeological outings to show their vocal support for the suffering papal 'Peter in Chains', often provoking riots with angry Italian nationalists which anticipated the aftermath of international football matches in more recent decades.[25]

Such confrontations were a stark symbol of a new battle for popular allegiance throughout Catholic Europe. In this, Catholicism might outflank liberalism by proclaiming its commitment to social reform, just as increasing numbers of ordinary Europeans were looking beyond liberalism to socialism, voting for socialist parties in European parliaments. In England, the ultramontane Cardinal-Archbishop of Westminster, Henry Manning, was a key mediator in ending a bitter industrial dispute in London Docks in 1889, a turning point in the recognition of the rights of trade unions in Britain. It was the first occasion on which a Catholic priest had been able to play such a role in the society of Protestant Britain since the Reformation, and it was more than most Anglican bishops seemed able to do at the time.[26] Manning's achievement was important in the background to the encyclical of 1891, *Rerum novarum*, in which Pope Leo XIII restated the Catholic Church's commitment to social justice for the poor, even to the extent that it would promote trade unions with a Catholic base. Its tone was passionate and direct, with a passion whose direction was very different from that of Pius IX's *Syllabus of Errors*:

some opportune remedy must be found quickly for the misery and wretchedness pressing so unjustly on the majority of the working class: for the ancient workingmen's guilds were abolished in the last century, and no other protective organization took their place. Public institutions and the laws set aside the ancient religion. Hence, by degrees it has come to pass that working men have been surrendered, isolated and helpless, to the hardheartedness of employers and the greed of unchecked competition.

True to the scholastic Thomism which was now the approved theological style of the Church, there was a pervasive medievalism in Leo's encyclical. It urged the forming of corporations like the gilds of the Middle Ages, which would repudiate class conflict and ground society in organic cooperation between interest groups. Despite its fairly shallow social analysis and inbuilt political caution, the document provided a convenient shield against the hostility of later popes for Catholics who wished to take part in the enterprise of social reform with liberal groups, or even to find common ground with socialism.

Pope Leo's realism also led him to seek an understanding with French Republican leaders, when it became apparent in the 1880s that any form of monarchy in France, Bourbon, Orleanist or Bonapartist, was unlikely to overturn the Third Republic. His successors proved less capable of maintaining good relations. Many Republican politicians were still mentally fighting the battles of the 1790s against the Catholic Church. It was easy to see why they should, when from the mid-1890s so many in the Church irrationally supported the harsh imprisonment of a Jewish army officer, Alfred Dreyfus, long after it was clear that he was innocent of the betrayal of military secrets of which he was accused. The sheer nastiness of the 'Anti-Dreyfusards' did not present French Catholicism in a good light, particularly their hatred of 'deicidal' Jews, whom they saw as staging a conspiracy along with the Freemasons against Christian society. Their paranoia was matched by anticlerical fears that the Catholic Church was sponsoring conspiracy against the Republic, led by Jesuits and the anti-Dreyfusard promoters of the Lourdes shrine, the Assumptionist Order of Augustinians.[27] After tense confrontations, Napoleon's Concordat was abrogated in 1906. For a hundred years from the mid-nineteenth century, every village in France was liable to become a battleground between church and school, pitting the power of the *curé* against the state-paid schoolmaster to win the minds of the next generation. The fault line in French politics between Church and Revolution persisted into the 1960s, anachronistically shaping the structure of political parties, and absorbing political energies which could have been spent on more pressing social and political problems.[28]

PROTESTANTISM: BIBLES AND 'FIRST-WAVE' FEMINISM

Protestantism benefited as much as Catholicism from all the new resources of transport and communication at the disposal of organized religion, and showed a similar institutional and devotional vigour. Cheap print was naturally of huge importance to a Bible-based religion. The sheer numbers of Bibles produced was staggering: between 1808 and 1901 one Protestant anglophone agency alone, the British and Foreign Bible Society, produced more than 46 million complete Bibles and nearly three times as many New Testaments and sections of the Bible. Moreover, the advance of printing technology tempted Protestants away from their long-standing suspicion of the sacred visual image. Bibles became prodigal with illustrations, particularly scenes set in the newly accessible Holy Land, and the 'Family Bible' (naturally, the 'King James' version for English-speakers) became a symbol of domestic success. It was hawked by salesmen from door to door in the way that encyclopedias would be in the twentieth century, boasting an impressively decorated pseudo-leather cover, opened ceremoniously for children with clean fingers carefully to leaf through its pictures of an idealized ancient Middle East, and linger over its proud entries of family births, marriages and deaths on a handsomely illuminated template page. Certain other pictures gained a special resonance for Protestant Christians. One of the greatest successes was achieved by William Holman Hunt, an English 'Pre-Raphaelite' artist and a strenuously if unconventionally devout Anglican, who in 1853 created an endearingly intimate image of the Saviour bearing a lighted lamp, bringing warmth and light to a neglected and melancholy doorway: 'the Light of the World'. The critics sneered at it, but its triumphant tour of the British Empire on exhibition in 1905 confirmed it as a global rival to any of the classic icons of Orthodox or Latin Christianity.[29]

Likewise, Christian feminism became as vital a feature of Protestantism worldwide as in Catholicism. Little of it was expressed in terms of vocations to the religious life. That was a difficult concept for Protestants after the Reformation's monastic dissolutions, although from 1845 onwards a significant number of strong-minded women intimidated or nonplussed male leaders in the Anglican Communion by founding nunneries which exalted episcopal authority while defying actual bishops, persisting with charitable work or the contemplative life in the face of all discouragement.[30] Otherwise, visionary Protestant women lacked the opportunities which Marian devotion offered their Catholic counterparts to find a place within existing Church structures. Since Mary was not available to them as a mediator for their messages, they tended to don the mantle of Old Testament prophets, and some of them found themselves excluded from existing Churches as a result.

The earliest and most famous of these prophetesses was Joanna Southcott, a gentlewoman from Devon, who passed through Methodist enthusiasm to something more individual. Her first vision in middle age in 1792 led to a large-scale apocalyptic movement which remained resolutely female in its leadership during her lifetime, despite frequently manipulative interventions from maverick men. It challenged the male Church establishment by treasuring a box of Joanna's prophecies which could only be opened in the presence of twenty-four Anglican bishops; this cousin of the hidden last prophecy of Our Lady of Fátima may still be waiting in Bedford, England.[31] Of greater long-term significance were the experiences of two charismatic Scottish sisters from Clydeside, Isabella and Mary Campbell. Isabella built up a reputation as a person of exceptional holiness, and after her early death, crowds were drawn to her home by an enthusiastic memoir of her published by her parish minister. Amid this excitement, Mary began making pronouncements in an unknown language, inspiring others in her neighbourhood to do likewise, and also undergoing a miraculous cure from apparently terminal ill health. Reports of these Scottish displays of 'gifts of the Spirit' deeply interested an influential group of Evangelical friends in their regular meetings in the elegant rural seclusion of Albury in Surrey. One of the Albury regulars, Edward Irving, a well-known and extrovert minister of the Church of Scotland, was inspired to begin a spiritual journey into prophecy which had consequences for the Christian Church worldwide. The Campbells and their impact on Irving had unknowingly provided the first glimmers of the modern Pentecostal movement (see pp. 910–14).[32]

More commonly women's activity followed the logic of the earlier English Protestant feminists like Mary Astell (see pp. 793–4). That was easier in those Churches not burdened with established status and with a strong ethos of congregational decision-making. In one case which attracted a great deal of interest, a congregation of Seventh Day Baptists in London was reduced by death and its choosiness about membership to seven women without a minister. After much conflict with the congregation's male trustees and repeated assertions that leadership functions were reserved by divine resolution to men, male Baptist ministers reviewed the dispute in 1831. They looked at the congregational logic of Baptist theology on the nature of the Church, and decided nineteen to eleven (in the face of warnings that they would be laughed at) that women were perfectly capable of forming a Church and calling a (male) minister.[33] In 1853 a Congregational Church in South Butler, New York, extended the same logic in ordaining Antoinette Brown as minister, the first woman outside the countercultural Quakers to hold such an office in modern Christianity.

Evangelical Protestantism, influenced by the optimistic social activism of post-millennialism (see p. 759), was particularly hospitable to this 'first-wave' feminism. Women offered themselves for missionary work overseas, a huge asset in cultures where men could not communicate face to face with the opposite sex. At home women involved themselves in a great range of causes envisaging radical change in social behaviour, especially the abolition of slavery, and a war on that male-dominated subversion of quiet family evenings and secure finance, indulgence in alcohol. They were active in matters where men might easily be compromised if they showed excessive interest, most obviously the welfare of millions of poverty-stricken young women forced into prostitution. The English Evangelical Josephine Butler, daughter of a liberal-minded Whig MP, took his hatred of slavery to the streets of Britain. She told the story of hearing a woman's cry from the window of her comfortable Oxford home: 'a woman aspiring to heaven and dragged back to hell – and my heart was pierced with pain. I longed to leap from the window, and flee with her to some place of refuge.' Instead she concentrated on rather more systematic and effective campaigns against male indifference to the humiliation of women who ended up selling their bodies. She aroused horror that such a well-brought-up married lady could talk on public platforms about venereal disease. 'That dreadful woman, Mrs Butler' was the comment of one leading Oxford High Churchman, Canon Henry Liddon.[34]

A PROTESTANT ENLIGHTENMENT: SCHLEIERMACHER, HEGEL AND THEIR HEIRS

Despite their often curiously overlapping trajectories, the two halves of Western Christianity diverged significantly in at least one respect. The relationship of Protestantism to the Enlightenment was much more ambiguous and less confrontational than that of Rome: it embraced a theological and scholarly project to make sense of the new intellectual landscape rather than condemn it. At the heart of northern Europe was Berlin, capital of a Prussian Hohenzollern monarchy which had led Germany's successful resistance to Napoleon. One important element in the national renewal which the Hohenzollern took as their sacred duty was the creation in 1810 of a new university, a project conceived at the lowest point in their campaigns against the Emperor of the French. Steeped in the Pietist tradition, King Friedrich Wilhelm III of Prussia was aware not only of the grievous damage done to European education by the dispersal of the Jesuits and the Revolutionaries' closure of a clutch of great Catholic universities, but also of the general decay in the Protestant university system. There were certainly doubts as to whether such a medieval and pre-Enlightenment word as 'university' should be used for the sort of institution the King envisaged, but Wilhelm von Humboldt, his chosen head of a new department significantly yoking 'Ecclesiastical Affairs and Public Education', persuaded the King that it would be appropriate for an institution designed to perpetuate Protestant culture, of which the King's great-uncle Friedrich the Great had been such a distinguished patron.[35]

Berlin's university was intended to set new standards for both teaching and research, and from its foundation it triumphantly succeeded, proving the model for similar institutions throughout the world – even as far afield as that creatively selective borrower of Protestant values, post-1868 Japan. The Berlin model committed Prussian Protestantism and all those who admired it to a conscientious exploration of how Christianity might make the methods of the Enlightenment its own. The Hohenzollern, Reformed Protestant rulers presiding over a Lutheran kingdom, were not inclined to make specifically confessional instruction a priority. They had some initial hesitation in including theology in the new institution's brief at all, but doubts were overcome by the advocacy of a brilliant migrant from the University of Halle, Friedrich Schleiermacher. He recognized that theology could no longer claim its place as the senior discipline in a university, but he vigorously defended a dual role for it: as a practical discipline for improving general pastoral care in a Christian society, and equally as a general branch of scholarship, with as much potential as any hard science for research and analysis. This became the basis for a liberal Protestant discipline of theology, increasingly eschewing particular confessional allegiance. It is an ideal which (for all its problems) has survived in the Western world, increasingly including the Catholic university world, until the present day.[36]

Such a theological project, explicitly embracing the Enlightenment, looked back to Immanuel Kant and sought to enrol him in the project of Protestant renewal. For Schleiermacher, Kant's notion of individual conscience shaped not just knowledge of the paths of morality which humans must follow in order to be true to themselves, but more specifically religious consciousness. Schleiermacher was seized by the Romanticism of early nineteenth-century Europe, and melded it with the religion of the heart so instilled in him from his experience of Moravians in childhood and student days. For a while in his youth, he had lost that faith altogether; he cultivated his doubts in his philosophy studies in Halle, which in his time had turned far from the university's original Pietism towards an austere Enlightenment rationalism. When faith returned, he rebelled against rationalism, and saw feeling and emotion as the senior partners of reason. Travelling in the same direction towards the divine, they could leap beyond reason to perceive the infinite.

On Schleiermacher's deathbed, his wife heard him say, 'I must think the deepest speculative thoughts, and they are to me completely at one with the most intimate religious sensations.'[37] So humans should not merely perceive what must be done in some abstract form, but should make a conscious effort of will to seek the source of all that was holy and dependable: a loving God. Schleiermacher summed up the conviction which had emerged out of Western Christianity since the seventeenth century, that other great world faiths might also perceive this God; such consciousness of God lay at the foundation of all religions, and was the fruit of revelation. The unique gift of Christianity was the person of Jesus, who revealed his own divinity by representing the most perfect consciousness of God that there could be. The questions which scholarship increasingly posed about the biblical text were unimportant beside Schleiermacher's conviction that 'to ascribe to Christ an absolutely powerful consciousness of God and to attribute to him an existence of God in him are entirely one and the same thing'.[38]

Schleiermacher's colleague in the University of Berlin, Georg Wilhelm Friedrich Hegel, was never his soulmate, and followed a very different path away from Kant. Hegel was not seized by the personal emotion which made Schleiermacher return to his Pietist inheritance, and sought instead to build a system of knowledge and of being which would dwarf the achievements of Aristotle and go beyond the scepticism of Kant. Like Kant, Hegel took human consciousness as his starting point, but he denied that anything was beyond the mind's capacity to know, and he constantly emphasized the role of human history, properly understood (and therefore of course properly researched by scholars), as the stage for the drama of reflection. All things are in a state of progress, or becoming, within history: a process achieved by the dialectic principle. A *thesis* is followed or met by an *antithesis*, and the encounter in turn produces a *synthesis* which reaches a higher level than either. Such syntheses at their higher resolutions can only be understood by a philosophical elite, so all religions are a mediation of higher truths to those less able to perceive them. That follows from the relationship of God to creation, the one bound to the other without separation: 'Without the world God is not God.'[39] Human consciousness is a progress towards absolute knowledge of the Absolute, the Spirit which alone is reality.

For Hegel, there was no problem in identifying this Spirit with the transcendent God whom Luther and the magisterial Reformers had described, yet his God as essence or reality seems as far from the wholly other God of Platonism as it is from the passionate and personal God of Judaism. Not all his disciples, amid his varied and profound influences on European thought, would be able to find any God at all. Among them was Ludwig Feuerbach, whose reading of Hegel led him along with a number of self-styled 'Young Hegelians' to the conclusion that Christianity must be superseded because it represented a form of 'false consciousness'. Humanity's sense of its intimacy with God arose from the fact that humanity itself had created God in its own image: 'the object of any subject is nothing else than the subject's own nature taken objectively. Such are a man's thoughts and dispositions, such is his God; so much worth as a man has, so much and no more has his God.'[40] That which was called divine revelation only revealed humanity to itself. It was this proposition which lay behind the radical rejection of the Christian Church by Marx and his admirers, though not all Marxists have found it impossible to hold together Marxism and Christianity.

The strangest reaction to the progress of Protestant philosophy from Kant to Hegel, yet perhaps one of the most significant in the long term for Western Christianity, came from a Danish Lutheran, Søren Kierkegaard. He was never short of money thanks to his father's prosperity in business and his own earnings from writing (matched by his ability to spend them on himself), so he hardly bothered having a life, outside his publication of thirty books and a heap of writings still in manuscript at his death. Famously he broke off his one engagement, and much (probably too much) has been made of that in interpreting the discussion of tragedy and meaninglessness which runs through his works. Retreating from much practical engagement with the world – though he would regularly and cheerfully venture from his desk for a 'people bath' in the streets or the theatre – he plunged himself in his solitariness into an engagement with human experience in turns savage and apparently frivolous, shape-shifting in his writings under a variety of pseudonyms, and mocking the good-mannered Christianity which Lutheranism in Copenhagen had constructed out of good education, everyday virtue and measured interpretation of Hegel. He looked behind his father's respectability to see the poverty-stricken boy who had cursed God, married his house-keeper (Søren's mother) because of her pregnancy, and had never lost his sense of horror and despair at his own sins.[41]

In reflecting on such anguish lying behind the decorous façade of city life, Kierkegaard explored the inner consciousness of the individual, and he condemned Hegel's dialectic path to the Absolute as a betrayal of the individual. Sin was not an aspect of some impersonal Hegelian process; it was a dark half of human existence, a stark alternative to a road which led to the broken, powerless Christ. Faced with such a choice, there could be no middle ground – so Kierkegaard offensively expressed loathing and contempt for the most respected clergy of his Church, whom he saw as tainted by just such a compromise. The Church had ceased to be other. Amid obsessive diatribes against the criminal respectability of the unfortunate (and fortunately deceased) Bishop Mynster, he declared:

Original Christianity relates itself so militantly to this world that its view is: not to want to slip happily and comfortably through this world but to take care to collide in dead earnest with this world ... Thus there is a world of difference, a heaven of difference between the Mynsterian life-view (which actually is Epicurean, one of the enjoyment of life, zest for life, belonging to this world) and the Christian view, which is one of suffering, of enthusiasm for death, belonging to another world.[42]

This torrent of words was a declaration of war on the notion of Christendom, but it was also a declaration of war on all intellectual systems, dogmatic or otherwise: 'no generation has learned from another how to love, no generation can begin other than at the beginning, the task of no later generation is shorter than its predecessor's'.[43]

Kierkegaard's vehemence was mixed with laughter, his destruction of contemporary religion and philosophy based on a mockery of complacency and a constant sly questioning which he had discovered in Socrates. Kierkegaard's contemporaries did not put him on trial or kill him for his Socratic fun, but they found him baffling, just as Athenians long ago had puzzled over Socrates. How could the bitterness he displayed towards contemporary Christianity emerge from such a playful eccentric? It is not surprising that Kierkegaard did not have a speedy impact in the nineteenth century – particularly since he was writing in one of Europe's more narrowly distributed languages. Amid the blows which the twentieth century has delivered to humanity's self-esteem,

Kierkegaard's steady concentration on the sufferings and loneliness of a God-Man on the Cross addresses the perplexities of Western Christianity, while not necessarily providing any answers beyond serene resignation and an appreciation of the laughter which may emerge from pain.

Kierkegaard was only too correct that Christendom still dominated the vision of official northern European Protestantism. Both Schleiermacher and Hegel, deeply affected by the memory of French invasion and eventual German victory, enthusiastically identified themselves with the Prussian state's project of national renewal, and they looked beyond Prussia, not only to the creation of a true German unity but to something more. Hegel's view of progress encompassed the attainment of world peace, but it entailed the emergence of a superior state which would overcome all others in political organization and cultural dominance as part of its recognition of the God of history. That state might well be planned in the University of Berlin. Kant had also sketched out a vision of world peace, without that alarming corollary – but now after Napoleon's defeat, it was characteristic of liberal German Protestantism also to be nationalist; and then after the failure of parliamentary efforts at reunion in 1848–9, also largely monarchist. Hohenzollern Prussia triumphed between 1867 and 1870 over first the Austrian and then the French emperor. A Second Empire (*Reich*) was proclaimed in 1871, self-consciously an heir to the old Holy Roman Empire, and so a Protestant alternative to that still-existing Catholic empire of the Habsburgs. German academics, theologians included, gave it their allegiance with extraordinary fervour.

The great historian Leopold von Ranke, historiographer to the Prussian Court and giant among the professors of the University of Berlin for half a century, saw the new German Emperor as 'immediate to God' (*unmittelbar zu Gott*). This was a fusion of nationalism and divine right theory in which liberty and equality took a distinctly subordinate place to monarchy and a new imperial Court.[44] An essential underpinning of this vision was a sense of the divine right of Protestantism. From early in his career, Ranke also included in his vision of the future a sense of the unity of the 'Teutonic' nations of northern Europe, in which one essential element was the Reformation. He was not alone in this. Protestant nations of northern Europe, several of them precociously industrialized, and mindful of the rapid imperial expansion of Britain and the United States in contrast to the fading of Spain and Portugal, could be forgiven for seeing their prosperity and growing power as God's will against a decaying world Catholicism. Towards the end of the century, one best-selling British Evangelical rant culminated in a typical paean of praise in that vein to God's chosen nations: 'When we contrast Popish countries with Protestant lands, can we doubt any longer which religion most promotes *National Prosperity?*'[45] It was a vulgar expression of the mood which prompted Max Weber to create the thesis embodied in *The Protestant Ethic and the Spirit of Capitalism*.

All through the nineteenth century, Evangelicals kept up the transcontinental links sustained since the first days of Pietism, which were now encouraged by the continuing family ties of the British monarchy to German royal houses. The Prussian monarchy was central to this. King Friedrich Wilhelm III's rather shapeless religious energies led him to press, against much opposition, for a union of his Lutheran and Reformed Churches, complicated by his eccentric amateur interest in the High Church aspects of Anglicanism, which produced some bizarre liturgical experiments and even more ill-will.[46] More problematic still was the project which Friedrich Wilhelm's son, successor and namesake sponsored in 1841 for a joint Anglo-Prussian bishopric in Jerusalem. There could have been no better symbol of the worldwide aspirations of northern European Protestants, but the Prussian enthusiasts had totally misunderstood the delicate political situation in the contemporary Church of England. Despite the fact that the plan provided for the bishop in Jerusalem always to be in Anglican orders, English High Churchmen were outraged (see pp. 841–2). The joint venture eventually lapsed; a conventionally conceived Anglican bishopric remains in Jerusalem, today making its own sterling contribution to ecumenical and inter-faith endeavours in that troubled region.[47]

More long-lasting, and of genuinely worldwide significance, was another segment of the same enterprise which shared its focus on Palestine: an Evangelical Alliance linking British and German Evangelical Protestants, founded in 1846. One of the Alliance's concerns was to return Jews to Palestine and convert them there. This was an unprecedentedly practical attempt to hasten on the Last Days, that recurrent Protestant preoccupation. Most supporters of the Jerusalem bishopric project had viewed that enterprise in the same light, much excited by the fact that the first man chosen as bishop, Michael Solomon Alexander, was an English convert from Judaism and former rabbi. Alexander had demonstrated in his own person that the conversion of the Jewish people was imminent – an essential preparation for the End Times. The Evangelical Alliance found many other battles to fight as new threats to the Evangelical world view repeatedly emerged, but its first close association with Jerusalem projects was a precocious sign that international Evangelical Protestantism was going to link itself to the fate of the land of Palestine, even before many Jews began to share that concern (see pp. 992–3).[48]

It was with this triumphalist Protestant ideology in the background that the architect of the Second Reich, the Imperial Chancellor Otto von Bismarck, launched in 1871 what one of his severest Protestant critics, Rudolf Virchow, Berlin's independent-minded Professor of Pathology, usefully christened the *Kulturkampf* – the clash of cultures. What cultures were these? Liberalism and Protestant Germany in alliance against international and conservative Roman Catholicism. Bismarck was hoping to yoke the new power of the Protestant imperial state to the horror of liberals at Pope Pius IX's various dogmatic statements leading up to the declaration of infallibility – he could also draw on German nationalist contempt for and fear of Polish Catholics, whose dismembered nation lay partly within the Reich. The Chancellor was attempting nothing less than a permanent shift in the balance of power within the new empire, to eliminate Catholicism as a significant political force in northern Europe. He did not succeed: by 1887 he was forced to abandon the policy, having achieved little permanent beyond some enhanced government interference in Catholic education and clergy appointments. Partly Bismarck was defeated by the past: the religious geography which the Peace of Westphalia bequeathed Germany in 1648 (see pp. 647–8) was more powerful than the pattern of governments established after the end of the Holy Roman Empire in 1806, and popular Catholic support for suffering clergy was too strong for a state whose liberal instincts forbade the extreme violence which would have been necessary to make a success of its authoritarian policies. Moreover, the tangle of jurisdictions on which the new German Empire was constructed made it impossible to achieve even limited consistency in containing Catholic resistance.[49]

There was a new and more profound reason for the imperial government's half-hearted repression. A large proportion of the non-Catholic population of the empire had no real connection with Christian practice and Christian obsessions, and was itself hostile to the Bismarckian Reich. Already in eighteenth-century German cities, a significant number of people had ceased to go to church. Later patterns were complex, and it was not merely in urban areas that religious observance had ebbed, as statistics of those making their communion at Eucharists in State Churches demonstrated. In 1910, a classically high level of 140 yearly communions per hundred Church members was recorded in the country-side of Hesse-Kassel, but at the other extreme the equally rural district of Jever in north-west Germany registered seven communions per hundred members, which was much the same as the most extreme example of urban abstention, six per hundred, in the north German port of Kiel. By then one factor had become clear: a great many working-class people turned away from Protestant churches which had identified themselves with the conservative imperial system, and instead embraced a socialism which had begun providing them with a whole alternative subculture for leisure activities and welfare, paralleling what the Church could provide. The German Social Democratic Party was Europe's first mass socialist party, and it was as much the subject of government repression as the Catholic Church. German Protestantism was thus caught between Catholics and socialists. In 1869 around 1 per cent of the working class had attended church in Berlin's Protestant parishes, and that figure had halved by the outbreak of war in 1914.[50]

BRITISH PROTESTANTISM AND THE OXFORD MOVEMENT

Patterns were different in northern Europe's other major Protestant monarchy, Great Britain. Here, ecclesiastical complexity dated back to the seventeenth-century disruptions of British Protestantism (see pp. 647–54). While after 1801 the two established Protestant Churches of Scotland and of England/Ireland still suffered mutual tensions through their differing confessional commitments and ecclesiastical systems, the separated non-established Protestant denominations – Dissenters and Methodists – were increasingly powerful and vocal in England and Wales. They formed a distinct Protestant mode of life, 'Chapel' as opposed to 'Church'. In Ireland, a Roman Catholic majority chafed for lack of a voice in state affairs alongside the minority Protestant Irish establishment. Anglican clergy, not much interested in the existence of the established Presbyterian Church of Scotland, tended to regard their Church as synonymous with national identity, although Anglican Evangelicals tended to be less dismissive of their fellow Protestants than were Tory High Church Anglicans.[51] The national Anglican fiction beloved of Tories was in fact proving increasingly difficult to sustain: English Protestantism was much more riven than Protestantism in any other part of Europe, apart from the kingdom of the Netherlands. Paradoxically, in the long term this meant that levels of churchgoing remained higher in Britain's cities than in Germany; England's tradition of vigorous dissent meant that hostility to the established Church did not turn into general anticlericalism or hostility to Christianity, but was channelled into alternative Christian practice. British socialism notoriously owes more to Methodism than to Marx – indeed, in the twentieth century it came to owe more to the Mass than to Marx, as newly enfranchised working-class Catholics turned their votes to the Labour Party.[52]

British governments actually increased their support for the Church of England in the aftermath of the American Revolution and in nervous reaction to the French Revolution. In 1818 Parliament voted funds for a large number of new (and remarkably joyless) urban churches, and for around forty years from the late 1780s it was also official policy to finance Anglican establishments in British colonial possessions. Quite abruptly that changed.[53] In 1828 the Tory government abolished restrictions on Protestant Dissenters holding public office in England and Wales, but worse was to come for conservative Anglicans. Protestant traditionalists of all complexions were outraged by Parliament's passage of Catholic Emancipation the following year; now, among other reliefs of their legal disabilities, Catholics could be elected as members of the British Parliament, and so the monopoly of members of the Established Churches on government was broken. Renegade Tory sponsors of emancipation, led by the Prime Minister, the Duke of Wellington (veteran of far trickier campaigns in the Napoleonic Wars), performed this volte-face against their natural instincts because they were desperate to solve problems posed by Catholic discontent in Ireland. Their Whig successors in government, not inhibited like the Tories by much nostalgia for Anglican monopoly, went further. In 1833 they proposed remedies for some of the greater absurdities in the government of the Protestant Church of Ireland, which perpetuated a ghostly institutional structure inherited from the pre-Reformation Irish Church while serving only a fraction of the modern population.

It was a sign of a serious identity crisis in British Anglicanism that an Oxford sermon of 1833 protesting against this eminently sensible measure became a national sensation. A local High Church clergyman, John Keble, had been invited to give this customary sermon for the opening of the Oxford Assizes, the biannual session of the judges from Westminster. He seized the chance to alarm the assize judges and a large audience of university and local worthies with an attack on 'National

Apostasy'. Keble saw the suppression of a crop of Irish Anglican bishop-rics as a deliberate attack on the Church by the State, breaking the unity they had formerly enjoyed. The Whig government's disregard for Irish bishops was no less than 'enmity to Him who gave them their com-mission at first'.[54] Clearly many of Keble's fellow clergy agreed. Keble was enthusiastically supported by the vicar of the University Church, John Henry Newman, who had jettisoned the Evangelicalism in which he had been raised and was now embracing Anglican High Church-manship with the zeal of a convert, to the point of rapidly rethinking its nature, in ways which only gradually became apparent. Newman was himself a preacher of unusual charisma, whose sermons packed his stately church with young admirers. The power of his oratory can still be felt through the very considerable quantities of resonant prose which he produced in his long life.[55]

Throughout the rest of the 1830s, Keble, Newman and a number of friends mostly associated with Oxford University put forward a new vision of the Church of England in a series of *Tracts for the Times* (hence the activity they inspired has been called either the Oxford Movement or Tractarianism). Their project was to minimize the Church of Eng-land's debt to the Reformation which had actually created it as a State Church; to restore a sense of Catholicity to it and to its worldwide offshoots, emphasizing its apostolic succession of bishops across the Reformation divide, its distinctive spirituality and the sacramental beauty of its liturgy. It was thanks to the Tractarians in the 1830s that the word 'Anglican', that casual and unflattering coinage of King James VI (see p. 648), gained its first real currency. 'Anglicanism' had a pleasing echo of that French variant on Catholic identity, 'Gallicanism', and thus suggested a Church which combined a truly Catholic character with a national focus, and which might – just might – acknowledge the primacy of a properly ordered papacy. Tractarians also tried out a new coinage, calling themselves 'Anglo-Catholics'.

Much of what the Tractarians were saying amounted to a restatement of the rebranding of the Church of England attempted by Archbishop Laud and his associates in the early seventeenth century (see pp. 649–50), but there were other important elements. If the State was apparently no longer going to support the Church of England, then the Church would have to look to its own devices – and the only English precedent for that was to be found in that group of High Church refuseniks who, in impressively perverse loyalty to an ungrateful James II, had formed the 'Non-Juring' Church in 1689. Freed from the imperatives to discretion which establishment brings, and including in their ranks some formidable intellects, the Non-Jurors had ranged freely in their thoughts about the shape of an authentically Catholic Church of England, possessing an episcopate continuous with the Church of the Apostles, uncorrupted by Roman error and unshackled from the State. A large dose of their radical conclusions in both liturgy and ecclesiology (that is, their theology of the nature of the Church), together with their interest in Eastern Orthodoxy and their frequent open rudeness about the Reformation, now enriched the spiritual explorations of the Tractarians. That separated them from older High Churchmen, who had not shown much sympathy with the eventually expiring Non-Juring Church.[56]

Tractarianism was thus a movement with a good many opinions, as well as a good opinion of itself – perhaps not surprisingly, given the large number of young and single Oxford dons among its leadership.[57] The Tractarians' problem was that this good opinion was not shared by the bishops whose government in the Church they theoretically exalted. In 1841 Newman produced the ninetieth of their tracts, arguing, with more ingenuity than was sensible, that England's Reformed Protestant doctrinal statement, the Thirty-Nine Articles of 1563, was not directed against the doctrines which made the Church of Rome distinct from those of the Church of England. He seemed genuinely surprised at the uproar which followed, including his own bishop's urgent requirement that the tract should be withdrawn.[58] Later in the year came the hammer blow (as far as Newman and his sympathizers were concerned) of the project for the Anglo-Prussian bishopric of Jerusalem. Their fears for the Catholic integrity of the English Church were blended with a refined disdain for Michael Solomon Alexander, the first bishop appointed under the scheme, and for the fact that Evangelicals celebrated his Jewish ancestry. In retrospect, Newman reflected with not untypical feline sarcasm about the Jerusalem bishopric, 'I never heard of any good or harm it has ever done, except what it has done for me; which many think a great misfortune, and I one of the greatest of mercies. It brought me on to the beginning of the end.'[59]

What Newman meant was that he could no longer escape the instability of the view of Anglicanism which he had constructed for himself. Behind Laud and the Non-Jurors loomed the far simpler identity of the Roman Catholic Church, towards which Newman was swept by a tide of doubt, which had gathered strength in him for some years as he contemplated the history of the early Church. Lutheranism and Calvinism were heresies, and he denounced them bluntly in a letter of protest about the Jerusalem bishopric, solemnly sent to his bishop and the Archbishop of Canterbury; but two years before that, he had already privately come to see the Church of England as nothing better than the Monophysites of the fifth century: no Church at all.[60] His piecemeal withdrawal from Anglicanism was completed in 1845, to general dismay (except among those on all sides who saw it with gloomy relish as the natural result of Tractarianism). A further crisis for many High Churchmen was provoked by a legal judgement from the Privy Council in a case between two exceptionally obstreperous clergy, whose theological clash paralleled their combative personalities: the Evangelical Rev. George Cornelius Gorham and Henry Phillpotts, Bishop of Exeter, one of very few High Churchmen then on the episcopal bench. Phillpotts had refused to accept Gorham's promotion to a new parish because he thought Gorham 'Calvinist' in his theology of baptism. Gorham appealed to the Archbishop of Canterbury's highest court, the Court of Arches, which found in favour of the bishop. Gorham then appealed to the Privy Council, which with some hesitation, unsure of its ground in a matter of some theological intricacy, found in his favour.[61]

There was widespread High Church outrage that a secular court should thus interfere in a strictly ecclesiastical dispute. As a result, Newman was followed to Rome by several like-minded clergy and prominent laity, including the man whom many had regarded as his replacement in leadership of the Oxford Movement, Archdeacon Henry Manning, whose talents were such that he was to end his career as a distinguished Cardinal-Archishop of Westminster.[62] This journey, virtually unknown among Laudians and Non-Jurors, has been a recurrent pattern among Anglo-Catholics ever since; yet by no means all followed suit. Newman's background in intense Evangelical religiosity meant that his years as a Tractarian were a staging post on an unstable lurch away from his roots, but the existing High Church party, much caricatured by callow Tractarians as 'High and Dry', was not so easily tipped towards Rome, and beyond the shores of Britain there were other sources of strength.

In the Episcopal Church of the United States of America, High Churchmen had already with a good deal less fuss faced up to the reality of being a disestablished Church whose very existence was centred on a sacramental life and episcopal government. In John Henry Hobart, Bishop of New York from 1811, they had what one of the doyens of American Church history has called 'perhaps the greatest religious leader the American Episcopal Church ever produced'.[63] Hobart had a dramatic preaching style worthy of the Methodists, and he was the inspiration in founding in New York the General Theological Seminary, the first Anglican equivalent of the Catholic Tridentine seminary. This was a vital springboard for the world mission which the Episcopal Church launched alongside its English counterpart. Yet what was especially significant about Hobart, besides his exceptional practical abilities, was the reasoning behind his vigorous defence of episcopacy. He saw it as the surest foundation for proper continuity with the earliest Christians: those who had struggled for their faith in a hostile empire before Constantine had favoured the Church. This was an example for the Episcopal Church in his own day, its established status gone, coming to terms with its role as a minority in the new republic. For Hobart, his Episcopal Church had a very different destiny from that of the United Church of England and Ireland as by Law Established.[64]

What the Americans first experienced and both the Church of England and the Presbyterian Church of Scotland then had to face up to was the discovery that a Church needs to make decisions for itself, whether or not it clings in some form to establishment – something obvious to European Protestant Radicals and English Dissenters from their earliest sixteenth-century stirrings. In that respect, the Oxford Movement could integrate successfully in an initially hostile Church, because it offered a positive answer to a problem more widely felt. With its insistence on the continuity in succession of bishops right back to the Apostles, and the role of the bishop as guardian of the sacraments, it provided a coherent view of what a bishop was and what he should do (although High Churchpeople's view of episcopacy tended to become more nuanced if a bishop forbade them to do what they wanted). Even those who were not High Churchpeople approved of the Church gradually gaining a forum for its own debate, first in the revival of the Convocations of Canterbury and York in 1852 and 1861, and then in the creation of a series of Church assemblies which paid steadily more attention to the opinions of laypeople.

It was also clear that the High Church commitment to liturgy and episcopal government gave coherence to the worldwide and hitherto unlabelled Church which was emerging from British imperial conquest and American Revolution. In fact it was in New Zealand, under the guidance of a notable High Churchman who later returned to an English diocese, Bishop George Selwyn, that the first Anglican experiments in lay participation in Church government took place, furnishing precedents to the Church of England.[65] The term which Tractarians had revived for

their own party purposes, 'Anglicanism', was now conveniently appropriated to describe a new beast with a reach across the globe: 'the
Anglican Communion'. Its bishops worldwide first met after an informal
invitation to Lambeth Palace in 1867, hoping to solve the problem of
the South African bishop John William Colenso, who had made the
mistake of challenging the comfortable consensus of the English Church
on interpreting the Bible.[66]

The mood of ecclesiastical self-assertion encompassed the other established Church in the British Isles, in Scotland, and there it had far more
catastrophic effects than the Tractarians achieved in England. Devout
members of the Church of Scotland who valued their Reformed heritage,
and the theology of Presbyterian Church order within it, had grown
increasingly outraged that, thanks to past compromises with the English
government, parish congregations could not choose their own ministers,
and were forced to accept the decisions of patrons who treated that right
as a piece of property. Evangelicals found this particularly offensive. In
protest at the lack of reform of this scandal after years of agitation, in
1843 no fewer than a third of the parish ministers walked out of the
Church of Scotland and took most of their congregations with them.
Providing one of the most remarkable demonstrations of Protestant
energy in nineteenth-century Europe, they founded a complete alternative 'Free Church of Scotland' – not a dissenting Church, but an essay
at an alternative established Church in waiting. They covered Scotland
with a network of new parish churches, clergy houses and organizations
alongside the old ones – a tribute not merely to Scotland's continuing
consciousness of its Reformation principles, but to the large amount of
surplus wealth which its industrial revolution had generated. The schism
was not healed until a reuniting of most of the parties concerned in
1929, by which time the problem of patronage had long been solved in
the old established Church. Now it seems incredible that such an issue
could have so dominated a major national Church and split it down the
middle. Christian preoccupations move on.

In England, the Oxford Movement had aesthetic and emotional
advantages to sustain it. The Church of England commanded a heritage
of thousands of beautiful medieval church buildings inherited from the
pre-Reformation Church, over three centuries much altered in cheerfully
miscellaneous ways to adapt them to Protestant use. In a society still
saturated with Romantic love of the medieval, the impulse to restore
their architectural beauty could combine with a High Church desire to
develop a liturgy drawing on the buildings' medieval functions. That

endeavour might not lead straight to Rome, but to an enhanced dignity and solemnity in Anglican worship, which even those not styling themselves Anglo-Catholics might savour in moderate measure.

And after initial wide public disapproval – even riots against the 'Popery' of Anglo-Catholic liturgy – there came the realization that High Church clergy genuinely did care for the Church's mission to save souls. One of the most important ways in which the movement gained respect in the Church from the 1860s was to launch public missions, especially in settings of urban squalor: Anglo-Catholics took as their model not the emotionalism of Methodist or Evangelical mission but, appropriately, the dramatic missions conducted by various religious orders in Roman Catholic Europe on the classic Jesuit model (see pp. 682–3). Their strategy proved successful. The urban poor may not have been that impressed by Catholic ritual, but what they did appreciate was being taken seriously, and being shown love and consideration by well-educated Christian gentlemen. Many inner-city strongholds of Anglo-Catholic practice were established as a result, and remain even when their settings are now socially very different: in London, for instance, St Alban's Holborn or St Mary's Somers Town.[67]

As a result of these early Victorian excitements, the Church of England, and the Anglican world generally, developed two self-conscious groupings of Anglo-Catholicism and Evangelicalism, plus a 'Broad Church' middle ground whose adherents were more than a little impatient with the extremes (see Plate 63). The fact that the nineteenth-century Church of England never managed to provide any centrally planned system of clergy training, in the fashion of Roman Catholic seminaries, afforded each of the three 'parties' the chance to found their own theological colleges. These colleges proved the most effective agent possible in perpetuating the party spirit, which in Anglican circles can sometimes resemble the passions others devote to competitive team sports. The contrast with British Methodism, which from the earliest days of its clergy training planned its provision centrally, is instructive; Methodists are still much less inclined to fall into party camps.

Not even the rather hasty condemnation of Anglican clerical orders by Leo XIII in a bull, *Apostolicae Curae*, in 1896 could discourage High Church Anglicans from continuing to puzzle away at the conundrum of Catholic Anglicanism – much as their Evangelical fellow Anglicans might disapprove of their even trying. They developed a spectrum of solutions, stretching between a moderate style which became known as 'Central' Churchmanship and an extreme Anglo-Catholicism which delighted in being more Roman than the pope.[68] That spectrum has been one of the most fruitful products of that always tense structure, the Anglican Communion. It demands that its adherents use their brains to understand what Anglicanism might be, as well as their aesthetic sense to appreciate how it might reach out to the beauty of divine presence. It encourages a strong sense of paradox and uncertainty, of which Kierkegaard might well have grudgingly approved. It is one of the engaging features of the Oxford Movement and its offshoots, so apparently backward-looking and medievalizing in both their origins and some of their later posturing, that they have found it much easier to cope with the Enlightenment than has Anglican Evangelicalism.

Moreover, there is an often camp mischief about High Church Anglicanism. Many Anglo-Catholic clergy and laity have relished shocking bishops by their extravagant borrowings from Roman Catholic ritual. Since Anglo-Catholicism also borrowed from Rome an emphasis on clerical celibacy new to the Anglican tradition, celibate vocation to the priesthood created Victorian England's only profession which did not raise an eyebrow at lifelong abstention from marriage. That frequently aroused the fears of the Victorian paterfamilias, paralleling the neurosis of the Catholic layman since the High Middle Ages that his wife or daughter would be seduced in the confessional by lustful celibate priests. The worries were generally groundless, partly because the unprecedented singleness of many Anglo-Catholic clergy had a rather different dimension. From its earliest phases in its eponymous university, the Oxford Movement came to host a male homosexual subculture which even the sexual liberation movements from the 1970s did not entirely absorb or supplant.[69]

ORTHODOXY: RUSSIA AND OTTOMAN DECAY

While the nineteenth century saw victory for new centripetal forces in Roman Catholicism, Orthodoxy's renewal took place against the background of two very different experiences: in Russia, within an already monolithic Russian Church, and to the south, amid much institutional fragmentation caused by the decline of the Ottoman Empire. From the time of the Russo-Turkish War of 1768–74, the victorious Russian tsars claimed to be protectors of all Orthodox Christians under the sultan's rule, and Catherine the Great extended Russian control over the kingdom of Georgia in the 1780s, taking care to leave intact its ancient independent Church, while bringing it under her control with a seat on the Holy Synod. As the Ottoman Empire further decayed, an exhilarating prospect emerged that an Orthodox tsar might ultimately take the sultan's place and outdo the sway which Byzantine emperors once enjoyed in Orthodoxy; or that an assortment of Christian monarchs would once more rule Orthodox lands still under Ottoman control.

Both these alternatives nevertheless pointed to a steep decline in the power which the Oecumenical Patriarch exercised among the various nationalities constituting Orthodoxy. He had long been so identified with the privilege and influence enjoyed by his Greek entourage in their Phanar enclave in Constantinople that the institutions of the patriarchate were often known, without any sense of compliment, as 'the Phanar'. The Phanar's decline proceeded in step with the decay of the Ottoman Empire which had so promoted the patriarch after the seizure of the city (see pp. 497–8). Given this ongoing home-grown crisis, the memories of 1789 which so agitated the Western Church were only one competitor for Orthodox attention. It was difficult for the embattled Greek Orthodox to look past their ancient grievances against Catholic aggression from 1204 onwards. So when Napoleon invaded Ottoman Egypt in 1798, intent on pursuing the British to India, but also proclaiming the rhetoric of liberty, equality and fraternity, the Orthodox Patriarch of Jerusalem published a book in Constantinople which argued that God had created the Ottoman Empire to defend his Church from Latin heresy, let alone French Revolutionaries, so God required loyalty to the sultan from all good Christians.[70]

Equally, the Russian tsar continued to expect God to deliver him the loyalty of his subjects. In Russia, the shackling of Church institutions to the tsar's centralizing bureaucracy (see pp. 542–3) caused many thoughtful Orthodox discomfort, but few had any objection to the steady expansion of Orthodox culture which accompanied the tsar's conquests south, east and west from the eighteenth century. Given Russia's absorption of much of the old Polish-Lithuanian Commonwealth and its moves eastwards, Russian Orthodoxy was always also going to be conscious of both its European and its Asian neighbours. During the early nineteenth century, its armies had marched to Paris, as well as in striking distance of Constantinople and Teheran. In central Asia, the Tsaritsa Catherine and her successors controlled Islam by a policy straightforwardly borrowed from their existing control of official

Orthodox Christianity: a central 'Muhammadan Assembly' of mullahs, and even a system of parishes. In the 1820s and 1830s they issued regulations for Muslim burials in the interests of bureaucratic record-keeping which bore all the cavalier disregard for ritual propriety that Peter the Great had shown to the Christian institution of sacramental confession.[71]

The tsars who succeeded Catherine the Great parted with her fascination for Enlightenment values, but they did not find it a problem to combine Tsar Peter's bureaucratic shackling of the Church with their intense commitment to a role as Christian absolute ruler. Tsar Alexander I (reigned 1801–25) was in thrall to a mysticism which once made him entertain the great Austrian politician Prince Metternich at a table laid for four: the other guest present was a noblewoman from the Baltic who had taken up a career as a prophetess, and the absentee was Jesus Christ. Tsar Alexander was fascinated by pronouncements from the Baroness Juliane von Krüdener which seemed to be an accurate prediction of his own pivotal role in defeating the Emperor Napoleon; he was less impressed by her advocacy of Greek revolutionary independence, which triggered an irreparable breach between them.[72] For Alexander, religion was a necessary component of absolute power. That led him in 1815 to conclude a so-called 'Holy Alliance' with the Catholic Emperor of Austria and the Protestant King Friedrich William III of Prussia – the British government kept its distance from any public commitment to this unprecedented exploration of ecumenical despotism. The alliance formally died with Tsar Alexander, but his successor, Nicholas I, possessing not a mystical bone in his body, nevertheless saw the usefulness of the principles that his elder brother had established. Russian identity was to be founded on a triangle of Orthodoxy, autocracy, nationality. Whatever the personal religious quirks of Nicholas's successors, that threefold foundation remained up to 1917. It was liable to stigmatize any subject of the tsar not included within it, particularly in European Russia, where alternative religious identities might be identified with nationalist dissidence.

Jews and Greek Catholics suffered the worst from this attitude, the latter losing the legal existence and property of their Church to the Orthodox Church in 1839, and the former undergoing repeated bouts of murderous persecution, tolerated and often encouraged by the tsarist government. One of the most pernicious offshoots of official Russian anti-Semitism was a work of propaganda published in 1903, the brain-child of an agent of the tsarist secret police based in France, Matvei

Golovinskii: *The Protocols of the Elders of Zion*. This picture of an imaginary worldwide Jewish conspiracy has sustained a malign life among the worst sort of conspiracy theorists down to the present. It was one of three books found in the room of the last tsarina in Ekaterinburg, just after her murder by the Bolsheviks in 1918.[73] Beyond Jews and Greek Catholics, a host of Old Believers and sects of undoubtedly foreign inspiration provoked constant official suspicion and fitful harassment; in turn, they built up a head of anger against the regime, which fed into its eventual collapse.[74] The autocracy was increasingly despised even by some of the best and most conscientious Orthodox laypeople and clergy. A deeply symbolic issue after 1896 was temperance, that preoccupation alike of Eastern and Western nineteenth-century Christian reformers. The Orthodox Church was at the forefront of a powerful temperance movement throughout the empire, yet it was well aware that the state made polite noises in support of such efforts while squeezing maximum profits out of a newly proclaimed imperial monopoly on the sale of alcohol.[75]

At many different levels, despite the moral and political damage wrought by the tsars' jealousy of its power, the Russian Church did its best to guide its flock through the social revolution percolating the vast expanses of the empire from the West. An incentive for enthusiastic pastoral care was the extraordinarily high level of churchgoing, which contrasted with the perceptible declines in the West: in 1900, 87 per cent of male and 91 per cent of female believers were recorded at confession and communion, marginally higher figures than in 1797.[76] It was Filaret, the Metropolitan of Moscow, a churchman whose liberal reputation led to his complete exclusion from meetings of the Holy Synod between 1836 and 1855, who drafted one of the most idealistic reforming measures of the century to originate with a tsar, Alexander II's decree freeing the serfs of Russia in 1861.[77] As social misery exceeded the capacity of traditional monastic charity, Orthodoxy creatively revived an institution which had served it well in the Polish-Lithuanian Commonwealth during the crisis years around the Union of Brest (see p. 538): confraternities which would organize charity in the worst areas of deprivation in Russian cities.

The secular clergy of nineteenth-century Russia, in contrast to its monks, have traditionally had a bad press, but that is at least in part because they have most commonly been viewed through the eyes of Russian novelists and writers who had little sympathy for the realities of life in the thousands of rural parishes through the empire. It is possible to tell a different story from the autobiographies of sons of the clergy. Even if they were idealizing their backgrounds, their accounts reveal a world of high-minded austerity, pride in vocation, admiration for learning and concern for parishioners which is remarkably reminiscent of the standards aspired to in the Western Protestant manse.[78] There was another similarity to the West: amid a welter of initiatives for social welfare, education, mission at home and in the furthest corners of the empire, Orthodoxy experienced that new phenomenon, the general rise of women's activism in Christian practice. Here it was seen most clearly in monasticism, now undergoing a major revival after Catherine the Great's Enlightenment-inspired government had sorely restricted it. While the number of male religious slightly more than doubled between 1850 and 1912 to just over 21,000, the number of women in monastic life had risen astonishingly from 8,533 to 70,453.[79]

The problem for an institution which was inextricably part of the everyday life of a great imperial society was how to minister to a society in sharp debate about its identity. Alexander II was an autocrat who in 1861 had borrowed the great principle of 1789, to give the bulk of his subjects their personal freedom: was he the only person in Russia entitled to have liberal ideals? The spread of higher education created a caste of articulate and ambitious young men with little precedent for their position in Russian society; they were as awkwardly placed as the surplus of seminary-educated clergy children. In their attempts to find a role for themselves, many were completely alienated from the Church, while others turned their aspirations on to its identity: at one end of a polarity, absorbed by Slavophile insistence on the self-sufficiency of Russian identity and by a fierce hatred of everything defined as opposing it; at the other, possessed by a revolutionary nihilism which (encouraged by sporadically savage official reprisals) turned to crime or political assassination, as a symbol that there was nothing worthwhile or sacred in contemporary society. The first successful suicide bombers in human history were anarchists responsible for the murder of Alexander II in 1881.[80]

The Church shared in this self-examination. How far could it look beyond itself for its spiritual resources? The problem was not new: in the perceptive words of one Orthodox priestly theologian born in post-1917 exile, 'if there is a feature of "Russian" Orthodoxy which can be seen as a contrast to the Byzantine perception of Christianity, it is the nervous concern of the Russians in preserving the *very letter* of the tradition received "from the Greeks"'.[81] It is an irony that this yearning to be faithful to a tradition beyond Russia led many churchmen to play a prominent role in the Slavophile movement. Slavophilism was itself a modern invention influenced by external forces: Aleksei Khomiakov, a nobleman who was one of its first exponents and also one of Russian Orthodoxy's first ever lay theologians, was profoundly learned in Western history and culture and much influenced by German Romanticism. He also defiantly grew his beard when it was frowned on in upper-class society, and urged his fellow Slavs to keep their distinctive clothing rather than adopt Western fashions. Key to his thought was a concept which has become central to modern Russian Orthodox think-ing, *Sobornost'*, the proposition that freedom is inseparable from unity, communion or community. In Khomiakov's view, the concept contained a critique of both halves of Western Christianity, as Catholicism pre-sented unity without freedom and Protestantism freedom without unity. It was within a pan-Slav community that the Orthodox Church would carry out the divine commission entrusted to it, but (in ways which Khomiakov did not clearly specify) its historic destiny was also to bring the whole world under its 'roof'.[82]

For others in the Church, there was less inhibition about looking to Western liberalism or socialism. In St Petersburg, that most cosmopoli-tan of Russian cities, where the main streets were hospitable to an extraordinary spectrum of churches representing the variety of European Christianity, many Orthodox parish clergy spoke of social progress and questioned tsarist autocracy, in a fashion which had more in common than might be expected with the reformist mood of American Evangelical Protestantism. The ultimate fruit of this was the large part played by clergy in the reformist upheavals of 1905. It was then that Fr Georgii Gapon, a popular and charismatic (one might say headstrong) young St Petersburg parish priest, led a mass demonstration of unarmed workers in the city, demanding political and social reforms. The reaction of the government was to shoot them down, a piece of brutal stupidity which turned demonstrations into attempted revolution. The outburst of popular fury nearly destroyed the regime twelve years before its eventual fall, and left a lasting legacy of mistrust and contempt for imperial rule. It was remarkable how much support Fr Gapon had received from the Church authorities during his outspoken campaigns, but the bloody end to the events of 1905 left the Church bitterly divided as to how to proceed in an atmosphere of repression and censorship. A radical wing among its clergy, the Renovationists, would continue to seek ways of reconciling Christianity with the increasingly militant stance of angry workers in Russian cities.[83]

The dynamism and questioning of Russian Orthodoxy were paralleled by those experienced by Churches seeking to escape four centuries of second-class status under Ottoman rule. Serbia and Greece were the first two regions to seize their freedom, and their different trajectories away from Constantinople were to cast long shadows into modern European politics. Serbia had little external help in its successful fight between 1815 and 1817 for independence, which was only acknowledged and given international recognition in 1878. Successive native dynasties were closely associated with the creation of a Serbian Orthodox Church which was autocephalous (independent of the Oecumenical Patriarch). That new establishment followed historic precedents, and so the patriarch could regard it as a restoration of former independence; a deal was carefully negotiated with Constantinople. The Orthodox Church had been vital to the survival of a Serb consciousness over the centuries of occupation. Now it had little hesitation in identifying with an expansionist Serbian nationalism, fuelled by a view of history shot through with consciousness of heroic suffering, and inclined to look for support to Russia, which was formal guarantor of Serbian independence from 1830.

By contrast, when an independent state took shape in the Greek peninsula, the fascination of Western Europeans with the Classical past complicated Greece's assertion of Orthodox values with a strong dose of Western liberalism. Greeks had in any case long enjoyed more commercial and travel contacts with the West than most other Orthodox, and it was noticeable that it was in Greece that Orthodoxy was faced with one of its own who had turned to expounding Enlightenment ideas in his own language. Christodoulos Pamblekis had been excommunicated in 1793: perhaps a resonant year even for churchmen far from Paris.[84] The Church hierarchy was initially hostile to the Greek nationalist uprising because of the rebels' Western liberal rhetoric. The hostility was ended by the savagery of Ottoman reprisals for Greek massacres of Turks in the peninsula in the 1820s, when thousands of clergy were killed, beginning with the Oecumenical Patriarch himself, hanged from his own palace gateway in the Phanar district. Ottoman violence outraged all Christian Europe, and military intervention by Britain, France and Russia eventually forced the Sultan to recognize an independent Greek state.[85]

The first head of what was planned as a republic, Ioannis Kapodistrias, was devoutly Orthodox, and he succeeded in winning over the new Oecumenical Patriarch, who recognized his innovative state in 1830.

Chaos descended after Kapodistrias's assassination the following year. The three European great powers then adopted an expedient employed in the newly independent Belgium. In 1833 they imported a German prince to be monarch (there would be other such royal implants in newly independent Orthodox nations later in the century, with varying fortunes). Otto of Bavaria was a Catholic with Lutheran advisers, and his regime infuriated the Oecumenical Patriarch by unilaterally creating an unprecedented autocephalous state Church, with Otto as head. There was no historical precedent for this independent Church in Greece, unlike the Serbian situation. It was not until 1850 that the patriarch gave recognition to this miniature version of Peter the Great's ecclesiastical system in Russia (which, as we have seen, had itself derived from Lutheran models).

One reason that the Greek bishops eventually found this arrangement acceptable was that, although the monarchy might seem an alien graft, it backed the aspiration of the initially small-scale territorial state to expand and encompass Greeks scattered through the southern Balkans and Anatolia. The Greek State Church's new-found freedom and privilege were exhilarating after four centuries of humiliation, and not surprisingly it became vigorously nationalist. That brought its own tensions with other Orthodox national groupings, Serbs, Bulgarians and Romanians, who had long resented the Greek domination of the patriarchate in Constantinople. Although the Ottoman Empire's decay did lead to enlargement of the kingdom of Greece in later wars, the ambition of Greeks for even greater gains was a catastrophe in the making for all Eastern Christians.

A different situation shaped first independent Church and then monarchy in Bulgaria. The delays in political independence, which the Bulgars did not formally achieve in full until 1909, threw all the greater attention on the status of their Church. That was tangled up with long-standing hostility between Greeks and Bulgarian-speakers, who resented the continuing favour shown to Greeks by the Oecumenical Patriarch. Matters came to a head in 1860 when one leading bishop announced the creation of an independent Bulgarian Church. The Ottoman authorities were only too happy to encourage Christian divisions: ten years later they formally recognized a Bulgarian exarch (a bishop whose authority over other bishops was similar to that of the six ancient patriarchates). It took until 1961 for the Oecumenical Patriarch to recognize the exarch's successors. The struggle between the exarchate and the Phanar was unusually bitter, and it produced a notable assertion of principle from the Oecumenical Patriarch. Faced with a situation where congregations and whole dioceses were declaring for the exarch on the basis of their common Bulgarian language and culture, in 1872 the Patriarch led a synod in Constantinople that condemned this as 'ethnophyletism', declaring it a heresy. The argument ran that there was no justification for an independent Church in Bulgaria, since it was still a territory under Ottoman suzerainty and with no other sovereign, unlike the Churches in the independent states of Serbia and Greece.

The denunciation of 'ethnophyletism' was a commitment to a vision of Orthodoxy which affirmed that it must never simply be an expression of nationalism or even of a single national culture. Despite the fact that from its first expansion into the Balkans, Orthodoxy has often become precisely such particular expressions, the affirmation of 1872 is likely to prove of great importance to Orthodoxy in the future. In practical and immediate terms, it did not prevent either the continuing de facto independence of the Bulgarian exarchate or the eventual development of a kingdom of Bulgaria which reflected the exarchate's boundaries. This was an unusually intimate melding of nationalism with the Church, which was treated by the monarchy rather in the fashion of Tsar Peter the Great and his successors in Russia (indeed, from 1908 until 1944, the monarchs of Bulgaria also styled themselves tsars). Ultimately this led to a routine politicization of Bulgarian Church leadership which antagonized many laypeople, and that has been seen as one of the reasons for the eventual weakening of Bulgarian Orthodox practice in the twentieth century. Despite the Church's crucial role in creating modern Bulgaria, the post-Communist republic now has one of the lowest rates of participation in Church life of any Orthodox country in Eastern Europe.[86]

As the Ottoman authorities suffered humiliating losses of territory to new Christian polities which justified independence precisely by their Christian identity, it was not surprising that sultans were increasingly inclined to see their remaining Christian subjects as a threat to their survival, and emphasize their authority with reference to their Muslim identity. Since their sixteenth-century conquest of Egypt with its Abbasid caliphate, Ottoman sultans had asserted their claim to be caliph, but it was only in the reign of Abdul Hamid II at the end of the nineteenth century that a sultan (in turns reformist and arbitrarily violent) chose to emphasize his role as protector of all Muslims. This was a desperate grab for enhanced spiritual authority by a monarchy losing control, rather like the pope's claim of infallibility at the moment of the loss of the Papal States.[87] By the end of the nineteenth century, the sultan presided over an empire still multinational and multi-confessional, but in which the traditional mesh of understandings between faith groups was being much eroded, and much more was being said about the Islamic character of Ottoman rule.

Earlier in the century, the Ottoman rulers' pursuit of *Tanzimat* ('reorganization') brought modernizing reforms in edicts of 1839 and 1856 which dismantled the *millet* system of separate religious communities. This provoked a good deal of resentment from Muslims, who now saw former second-class status groups claim equality with themselves – and more than that, gain favour and economic preference from a variety of Christian European powers who were interesting themselves in the affairs of the Middle East. These were developments fraught with danger for Christian minorities. There was little inter-communal trouble in the Arab portions of the empire, where after one bad outburst of violence in 1860 in Lebanon and Syria, Muslims, Christians and Jews tended to develop a sense of common Arab identity under Ottoman auspices. The problem was further north, where Russian imperial religious intolerance sent hundreds of thousands of Muslims fleeing for refuge over the Russo-Ottoman border into Ottoman territories, decade on decade. There seemed good reason to distrust and envy Christians.[88] In 1843 came a grim precedent: a series of massacres of Dyophysite Christian mountain communities by Kurds in what is now Iranian Azerbaijan, provoked by anger at Western missionary activity and Russian military advances. Equally ghastly were a series of massacres of Armenians in the Caucasus and further south during the 1890s, which included the burning alive in 1895 of several thousand Armenians in their cathedral in Urfa – once that venerable Christian centre, Edessa.[89] All this heralded even worse times to come, whose lasting effects threaten Christianity's ability to survive in the lands of its origin.

MASTERS OF SUSPICION: GEOLOGY, BIBLICAL CRITICISM AND ATHEISM

While in Ottoman lands Christianity found itself under one form of attack, developments that had started with the Enlightenment led to another, asking whether the Christian picture of God was believable. During the eighteenth century, the Newtonian system of mechanics and the deism associated with it seemed to safeguard the place of God as creator, and little in scientific discoveries seemed to suggest a denial of the biblical idea of a benevolent maker of the universe. Indeed, the mood of intelligent Christians was symbolized by the immense popularity in England of an apologetic book by the Cambridge mathematician and theologian William Paley, his *View of the Evidences of Christianity* (1794). This was the work which made much of 'God the watchmaker', an image whose antecedents could already be found in pre-Christian philosophy: its argument for God's existence was based on the evidences for design in creation. The intricate structure of a watch could never have come about by chance, and neither could the intricacy or even adaptation and change in nature.[90]

Against this background, there developed an enthusiasm for a systematic physical exploration of the landscape, described by a new word-coinage, 'geology'. This made it clear that traditional estimates of the date of biblical creation such as Ussher's 4004 BCE bore no relation to the reality of the huge epochs of the earth's existence. From the late eighteenth century, investigations in France laid down the way to proceed. The pioneer zoologist Georges Cuvier patiently mapped out the strata of the Paris river-basin even as the French Revolution raged about him; he showed that there could be a history of rocks and extinct creatures, just as there was a history of human empires.[91] When English scholars added their contributions to this work, many of them were devout and orthodox Anglican clergy, led by the cheerfully learned and multifariously curious William Buckland, who kept a hyena at home as much for the enjoyment of its company as for research, and announced his intention of eating his way through the whole range of created animals. Geological work offered no problem to faith for such scholars; for them, creation stories in Genesis merely spoke figuratively of the time-spans involved in God's plan. When Buckland recognized extinct fossil species, apparently changing in regular fashion over time, this was an additional proof of God's providence: all earthly things have a tendency to decay, given the fallenness of creation, but God had provided for their replacement by creating new species. 'Erratic' rocks traceable to some rockbed large distances away after age-old glacial movements in ice ages seemed satisfying proof of the Flood's universal reach.

This picture was abruptly made less comforting by the work of Charles Darwin, once a prospective clergyman, who in 1835 turned from an early and not especially fruitful interest in geology to observing natural phenomena on the remote Pacific islands of the Galapagos, during a voyage which was actually launched with the main purpose of expanding Christian missionary work. He noted the remarkable differences in animal and plant species here from anywhere else, and indeed from island to island, and at first he marvelled at the insight which this gave into what God's creation had originally been like. But in 1837, reflecting on what he had seen, a wholly new idea came to him: perhaps these new species were not relics of Eden, but instead the end product of an immensely long chain of development in isolation from the rest of the world. Over the next two years, he worked from this perception to produce a theory of evolution which totally contradicted the world view of Paley (previously among his most treasured authorities). The only way in which Darwin's data made sense was to suppose that species battled for survival, and that evolution came when one slight adaptation of a species proved more successful than another in the battle: a process which he named 'natural selection'. There was nothing benevolent about the providence which watched over the process. Reason was served her notice as the handmaid of Christian revelation.

Darwin was by no means the first to popularize evolution. In 1844 the Scottish publisher and amateur geologist Robert Chambers presented the idea in his anonymously published *Vestiges of the Natural History of Creation*, in many ways an eccentric and credulous book, despite the elegance of Chambers's literary style, but hugely popular. Chambers was himself an interesting product of evolution, since he possessed twin sets of six fingers and six toes. It was easier to rebut him than Darwin, who in contrast to the apparent atheism of Chambers's work (Chambers was in reality a deist) ended *On the Origin of Species* in 1859 with a lyrical reference to the 'grandeur' breathed into life by the Creator 'from so simple a beginning'.[92] Between that much-revised work and his later major book *The Descent of Man* in 1871, Darwin retreated from his insistence on natural selection; subsequent work on genetics stemming from the observations of the Austrian monk Gregor Mendel shows that he should have stuck to his earlier insight. Yet he remained unmoved in his central contention that humankind was not a special creation of God, but part of the chain of evolution. His family in its various ramifications had been at the heart of William Wilberforce's and Thomas Clarkson's fight against slavery since the 1780s (see pp. 870–73), and Darwin was no exception to that general enthusiasm, even if he left behind the Evangelical Christianity which had inspired so many of his relatives. He saw his experimental demonstrations of the essential unity of all life as affirmations of the unity of all humankind across racial divides. Whatever uses so-called 'scientific' racists have made of the theory of evolution are perpetrated in the face of Darwin's ringing affirmations in *The Descent of Man*:

all the races agree in so many unimportant details of structure and in so many mental peculiarities, that these can be accounted for only through inheritance from a common progenitor; and a progenitor thus characterized would probably have deserved to rank as man.[93]

There has been no intellectually serious scientific challenge to Darwin's general propositions since his time. The modern conservative Christian (and Islamic) fashion for Creationism is no more than a set of circular logical arguments, and Creationist 'science' has been unique among modern aspirations to scientific systems in producing no original discoveries at all. From the 1860s, the idea of evolution gained wide acceptance among the educated public of the Western world, which was still overwhelmingly Christian in outlook and belief. Darwinian theory fitted the Hegelian scheme of an evolutionary universe, and far from seeming unremittingly bleak, it chimed in with the optimism about the possibility of human progress which was widespread in the vigorous and expansive society of the industrial revolutions. Many Protestant theologians began constructing a new natural theology which saw evolution as a gradual unfolding of God's providential plan (see Plates 42 and 43). James McCosh, an Ulsterman appointed president of that powerhouse of Reformed Protestantism, Princeton University, in 1868, did not allow his enthusiasm for the revivalist movements of Ulster and America to chill his friendly reception of Darwin's work.[94] Equally, by the end of the nineteenth century, the Anglican Communion was headed by an Archbishop of Canterbury, Frederick Temple, who in earlier years had presented a series of lectures in Oxford on the relation between religion and science which depended on the assumption that evolution was basic truth.[95]

More fundamentally challenging to the authority of the Christian Churches than the discoveries of nineteenth-century science was the reassessment of the Christian Bible, which now spread beyond the various scepticisms of earlier radical Christianity and the Enlightenment into the mainstream of the Western Church. French Maurist monks and French Huguenots between them had provided the scholarly tools in the seventeenth century when they edited medieval and ancient texts with scrupulous concern for forgery and contextual dating. German biblical scholars followed them with increasing tenacity over the next hundred years, and the impulse to stand back from the Bible and scrutinize it afresh was much encouraged by Hegel's evolutionary approach to human affairs. Since Hegel saw the Christian God as an image of Absolute Spirit, the stories about God in the Bible must also be images of greater truths which lay behind them. The biblical narratives could be described as myths, and that put them in the same league as the myths of other world religions.

This attitude was given wide publicity by a young Lutheran pastor and lecturer at the University of Tübingen, David Friedrich Strauss. Before Strauss, most critical reassessment of the biblical text had concentrated on the Old Testament. Strauss, enthusiastic for Hegel's symbolic approach to Christianity, wanted to apply his analytical skills to the New Testament as well. In 1835 he published the result, usually known by its shortened German title *Leben Jesu*, or in the English translation made by the freethinking novelist Marian Evans or 'George Eliot', *The Life of Jesus Critically Examined*. The Jesus Strauss portrayed was a great Jewish teacher whose followers had retold the story of his life in the best way they knew by borrowing themes from Old Testament stories and fitting their hero's life into them. No conscious deception was involved, but the New Testament narratives were works of theological symbolism rather than historic fact. Much of my own survey of the life of Jesus (see Chapter 3) has drawn on these insights, which have become fundamental to Western biblical scholarship, but at the time the public shock was profound. Strauss's job in Tübingen came to an end; when he was proposed for a chair in Zürich, there were riots on the streets, and it was impossible to appoint him. We should not feel too sorry for him, since he was paid his professorial salary for the rest of his life, but he gradually moved further and further from Christianity in his disillusionment. For many, he had destroyed faith. Friedrich Engels started on his journey away from Lutheran Christianity through his enthusiasm for the Hegelianism of the *Leben Jesu*.

Much else followed from that scrutiny; Tübingen's transforming role in biblical scholarship did not stop with Strauss. Ferdinand Christian Baur took the treatment of the Bible as a historical document to the point where he argued that the whole New Testament was a product of violent conflicts between the continuing commitment to Judaism of Peter and the older disciples against the Gentile mission strategy of Paul. The search had begun for a 'historical Jesus', a figure in whom the Church could believe despite the huge gap separating thought-forms and assumptions of the first Christians from those of the nineteenth century. In 1906 the theologian and medical missionary Albert Schweitzer, son of a Lutheran pastor in Alsace, wrote *The Quest of the Historical Jesus*, which argued that this preoccupation of liberal scholarship was misguided. The historical Christ Schweitzer saw in the Gospels was a man who believed that the end of the world was coming immediately, and had gone on to offer up his life in Jerusalem, to hasten on the time of tribulation. His career had therefore been built round a mistake. If there was a historical Jesus to be found in the Gospels, he was a figure of failure and tragedy who could only speak of failure and tragedy to the modern world.[96] Kierkegaard had reached this vision by another route: it was a faith infinitely remote both from the old Christianity of dogmatic systems and from the rationalizing Christianity of the nineteenth-century liberals.

Alongside this textual investigation was a virtually new science, archaeology, which explored the lands in the Middle East where the Bible stories were actually set. Christians enthusiastically promoted this, believing that it would confirm biblical truths; they set up funds for such exploration. The results were in fact equivocal: ancient Israel seemed much less important or even visible than in its own accounts in the Old Testament, and many works of literature from other cultures were revealed, which indicated that biblical writers had borrowed plenty of their ideas and even texts from elsewhere.[97] Yet the first golden age of these sciences of history and archaeology in the new universities failed to daunt liberal Protestants any more than they were unnerved by Darwin. One of the greatest of them, Adolf von Harnack – like von Ranke, ennobled by the Reich for his contribution to scholarship – was gleeful in his conviction that the work of the Reformation was thus completed: 'Cardinal Manning once made the frivolous remark "One must overcome history with dogma." We say just the opposite. Dogma must be purified by history. As Protestants we are confident that by doing this we do not break down but build up.'[98]

Nevertheless, for many sensitive people, science and history between them had irretrievably shaken the basis of revealed religion. Hegel had pictured the world of being and ideas as a continuous struggle; now the struggle, mindless, amoral and utterly selfish, extended to the natural world. In an age deeply concerned to live by moral principles, it was unnerving to suppose that the Creator did not share that concern. Evolution turns some of the human characteristics which seem most divine – moral fastidiousness, love – into products of self-interested evolution. It robs the world of moral or benevolent purpose, and even if God is taken as a first cause as the *Origin* still proclaimed, it is difficult to summon up enthusiasm for worshipping an axiom in physics.[99] If evolution suggested that humanity partakes of the world's general selfishness and amorality, then a subsequent Western thinker, Sigmund Freud, who published his first work on psychoanalysis thirteen years after Darwin's death, and who remained fascinated by the myths of his ancestral Judaism and their development in Christianity, completed this picture of the amoral basis of human motivation beyond consciousness or public profession. The sexual drive was the most important force lying behind human behaviour.[100]

Darwin himself, whose first publication was actually a defence of Christian missions co-written during his Galapagos adventure, lost any sense of a purpose in the universe, though he did so without public drama.[101] 'I never gave up Christianity till I was forty years of age . . . It is not supported by evidence,' he responded to uncourteously persistent questioning a few months before his death in 1882. Still he was given a funeral in Westminster Abbey, with a grave near that unconventional Christian, Sir Isaac Newton, and with two dukes and an earl among those bearing his coffin.[102] An article in *The Times* of London in 1864 had spoken of the conflict between science and religion, and the idea of this conflict became one of the clichés of Western public discourse. Marx clearly believed in it, for in admiration he sent Darwin a signed copy of *Das Kapital* (it remained uncut in Darwin's library).[103] Many, like Darwin, identified themselves as not prepared definitely to pronounce on matters of divinity. They called themselves 'agnostics', yet another of those newly minted words which were signs of nineteenth-century struggles to describe phenomena with no precedent, in this case a coinage of 1869 from Darwin's extrovert and aggressive friend Thomas Huxley. A few were driven by nineteenth-century seriousness to reject God in an almost religious fashion, giving that ancient insult 'atheist' a new resonance, and borrowing the word 'humanist' from its previous incarnation as an attitude to a branch of learning. They founded atheist or humanist associations with the sort of improving activism which one might expect from contemporary Protestant Free Churches: Sunday Schools, lectures, social activities, even hymn books. Perhaps their beliefs were the ultimate form of Protestant dissent.

Some who felt that science had won the struggle with Christianity were driven to explore the great religions of eastern Asia. A curious construct of religious belief newly named 'Theosophy' (from its emphasis on the search for divine wisdom) gained an enthusiastic anglophone middle-class following during the 1890s; it was one of the earliest expressions of that major component of modern Western religion, 'New Age' spirituality. One of the most dramatic of the many dramatic conversion experiences of the nineteenth century was that of the former Anglican country parson's wife Mrs Annie Besant, who after years as president of the National Secular Society, horrified her fellow secularists by her transfer in 1889 to Theosophy. Soon she was once more exercising her lifelong gift for leadership by presidency of the Theosophical Society, sharing her new ministry with an even more exotic exponent of the New Age, Madame Blavatsky.[104] It is no coincidence that several eminent late-nineteenth-century researchers in physics and chemistry were affected by the allied craze for spiritualism. This was a movement imported from the United States, which seemed able to restore the connection between the material and the spiritual in 'seances' which closely resembled the method of the scientific experiment. Darwin despised spiritualism, which he considered no more evidence-based than conventional Christianity, and he left in disgust the one seance he was persuaded to attend (perceptively, since the medium was later revealed as a fraud). His fellow explorer in evolutionary theory, Alfred Russel Wallace, by contrast enthusiastically went into print to celebrate the movement, undaunted by such disappointments.[105]

Roman Catholicism had a predictably more combative relationship than mainstream Protestantism with developments in scientific and historical study. The pattern was set in the career of Joseph Ernest Renan, a Breton destined for the priesthood, who found that the combination of his reading in German biblical scholarship and his contempt for the superficial religion he met with in Paris drove him beyond Christian faith. In 1863 Renan produced a *Life of Jesus* which utterly denied that this Jewish teacher had any divine character. It was with that in mind, against a background of bruising conflicts with liberal Protestantism in Germany and aggressive secularity in France, that the mood in Rome turned decisively against adventurous scholarly enquiry. Leo XIII initiated a drive against 'Modernism' in the Church, which intensified under his successor, Pius X, and destroyed any chance of Roman Catholicism taking a positive attitude to new ideas in biblical and theological scholarship until well into the twentieth century.

The same defensive mood affected Protestant Christians most antagonistic to papal Catholicism. Not all Evangelicals were as sanguine about Darwin as President McCosh of Princeton. From the 1870s a series of Evangelical conferences, among the most prominent of which were those held at Niagara-on-the-Lake in Ontario, reinforced a mood of resistance to Darwinist biology and the Tübingen approach to the Bible. The movement was given an international dimension by Ira Sankey and Dwight L. Moody, who adapted the old American revivalist style to nineteenth-century theatre entertainment: Sankey sang sacred songs, many freshly composed, and Moody was a preacher of extrovert charisma. Their extensive travels had an impact throughout the anglophone world; those involved were much influenced by the growing Evangelical enthusiasm for a 'dispensationalist' view of God's purposes in history (see pp. 911–12). From dispensationalism grew another 'ism': 'Fundamentalism' was a name derived from twelve volumes of essays issued in the USA by a combination of British and American conservative writers between 1910 and 1915, entitled *The Fundamentals*. Central to these essays was an emphasis on five main points: the impossibility of the biblical text being mistaken in its literal meaning ('verbal inerrancy'), the divinity of Jesus Christ, the Virgin Birth, the idea that Jesus died on the Cross in the place of sinners (an atonement theory technically known as penal substitution) and the proposition that Christ was physically resurrected to return again in flesh. Fundamentalists created organizations to promote this case: in 1919 the World's Christian Fundamentals Organization was founded, expanding through its use of mass rallies from a mainly Baptist base to affect most Protestant Churches. Fundamentalism is a distinctively Protestant idea, because it centres on the Reformation way of reading the Bible. Reformation Protestantism turned its back on most of the ancient symbolic, poetic or allegorical ways of looking at the biblical text, and read it in a literal way. As part of that literal reading, concentrating on a line of thought on salvation pursued by St Paul, came the penal substitution theory, and Fundamentalists rightly concluded that these were the aspects of Christianity most vulnerable to attack from nineteenth-century intellectual developments. Fundamentalists were nevertheless to find in the twentieth century and beyond that many new battles grew out of their five principles.

By 1914, then, Western Christianity was caught between two extremes of proclamation: stark and selective affirmations of traditional beliefs and, at the other end of the spectrum, a denial of any authority or reality behind Christian truth-claims. Beyond the materialism of Feuerbach and Marx was a vigorous hostility to Christianity developed by the son of a Lutheran pastor, Friedrich Nietzsche. His experience of revelation in

August 1881 was the exhilarating discovery that to be conscious of the lack of divine purpose or providence is to find freedom.[106] Through this, we can truly affirm our being, and for this internal freedom to find fulfilment, it is necessary for the external God to 'die', since there is no cosmic order to regulate our lives. It is seldom appreciated that Nietzsche's emphasis on the death of God was not original: he was standing in the logic of the Lutheran tradition which had moulded him, and so of Augustine and Paul beyond. Before Nietzsche, Hegel had emphasized that the death of God himself in Jesus was an inescapable aspect of the humanity within God. He had backed his affirmation by citing the cry 'God himself is dead', in a hymn of seventeenth-century Lutheranism by another Lutheran pastor's son, so classic as to have been harmonized by J. S. Bach and made the subject of an organ prelude by Brahms: O Traurigkeit, O Herzeleid ('Oh darkest woe! Ye tears, forth flow!').[107] Nietzsche simply reversed the logic of the tradition from Paul to Augustine to Luther. He saw Christ as an example to be avoided, because Christ denied the world. God was not merely in the dock, but condemned and executed. This would lead to another death, as Darwinian biology had already indicated for Nietzsche: 'morality will gradually *perish* now: that great spectacle in a hundred acts that is reserved for Europe's next two centuries, the most terrible, most questionable, and perhaps also most hopeful of all spectacles'.[108]

The philosopher Paul Ricoeur has described Nietzsche as the central figure in a trilogy of what he usefully terms 'the masters of suspicion', the predecessor being Karl Marx and the successor Sigmund Freud: those who gathered together the two previous centuries of questions posed to Christian authority, and persuaded much of the Western world that there was no authority there at all. Behind all three lies Ludwig Feuerbach, who first voiced the idea that God might be part of humanity's creation, rather than vice versa.[109] There is thus a deep contradiction in the period. The nineteenth century has usually been seen as principally the time of these 'masters of suspicion' in Europe: a century of disenchantment with Christianity and the supernatural in an age of science, a period of ebbing of European faith. Yet it was crowded with visionaries both Catholic and Protestant, full of excitement about the End Times, noisy with the sound of building for new churches and monasteries and the voices of furious quarrels about the best way forward for Christian renewal. It saw the beginning of a move towards virtual extinction for ancient non-Chalcedonian Christian Churches in their homelands, and the posing of profound questions for the authority of Western

Christianity. Yet as we will discover, it was also the period in which the Christian faith triumphantly spread its reach into every continent with a vigour never before witnessed and in which Christian governments came to support one of the most profound changes in Christian morality since the Crusades first sanctified full-scale warfare in the name of Christ.

23

To Make the World Protestant
(1700–1914)

SLAVERY AND ITS ABOLITION:
A NEW CHRISTIAN TABOO

In the United States of America, alongside 'The Star-Spangled Banner', given Congress's blessing in the twentieth century, there is a rather older unofficial national anthem:

> Amazing grace, how sweet the sound
> That sav'd a wretch like me!
> I once was lost, but now am found,
> Was blind, but now I see.
>
> 'Twas grace that taught my heart to fear,
> And grace my fears reliev'd;
> How precious did that grace appear,
> The hour I first believ'd!

A haunting melismatic tune, an anonymous product of the popular hymnody of the eastern American seaboard, has fixed these words as emblematic of American Protestantism, beloved alike among black, white and Native American congregations. Yet they come from a different world which has never had quite the same affection for them – a remote and scattered parish in Buckinghamshire, west of London, where they were penned by a former slave trader turned parson of Olney.[1] At many levels, 'Amazing Grace' is a fitting anthem to commemorate a century of Anglo-American Protestant expansion, whose prosperity had been founded on slave-owning and slave-trading. That same Protestant society then led the world away from slavery.

In that hour when John Newton 'first believ'd', he saw no incongruity between his newly awakened faith and his trade of shipping fellow human beings from West Africa to America. In fact he saw the slave trade as having helped him reshape his life after a chaotic youth, and in his autobiography, written in mid-life, he observed with no condemnation of his former career that he had been 'upon the whole, satisfied with it, as the appointment Providence had marked out for me'.[2] The trade taught him discipline, and formed the setting for his Evangelical Calvinist conversion in 1747, after which happy experience he continued to pass on his new-found discipline to his unruly charges by applying thumbscrews to them when necessary. A stroke, not any qualm of conscience about slavery, ended his career at sea in 1754. It took three decades for him publicly to express revulsion for his old business and make common cause with those now seeking to abolish it, grown from a group of eccentrics to a national movement. 'I am bound in conscience,' the old man said bravely in 1788, 'to take shame to myself by a public confession, which, however sincere, comes too late to prevent or repair the misery and mischief to which I have, formally been an accessory.'[3] Newton's belated change of heart was part of a new departure in Christianity: a conviction which over two centuries has now become well-nigh universal among Christians that slavery in all circumstances is against the will of God.

There had of course long been a widespread opinion that slavery was not a desirable condition – particularly for oneself. Frequently Christians had felt that being a Christian and being a slave were not compatible, so that it was an act of Christian charity to free slaves. But that is very different from condemning the whole institution – hardly surprisingly, since the Christian Bible, both Tanakh and New Testament, unmistakably takes the condition of slavery for granted.[4] Quite apart from its general connivance with slavery's existence, the Bible contributed a useful prop to the institution, in the story of the drunkenness of Noah. A drunken and naked Noah was humiliated when his son Ham saw him in this state, and subsequently Noah cursed Canaan, son of Ham, and all his descendants to slavery at the hands of Ham's elder brothers, Shem and Japheth.[5] Apart from its popularity among medieval Western preachers, who saw in the story a pleasingly ingenious allegory of Christ's Passion and human redemption (Michelangelo uses it thus on the Sistine Chapel ceiling), this story was regularly trotted out by slave traders both Christian and Muslim to justify enslaving Africans, children of Ham.[6] It is in early Muslim sources that the Bible's listing of many black races among Ham's descendants was first extended into an aspect of Noah's curse – the first Muslims were familiar with black slaves from across the Red Sea. This interpretation ignored the fact that the Bible indicated that the curse was actually pronounced on Canaan and not his voyeur father (a baffling shift which Genesis does not explain), and further that Canaanites were not actually among the black races of the ancient world.[7]

The link between blackness and slavery reached the Christian West late, and it was ironically via Judaism. Just when the Portuguese were beginning to take their share of the African slave trade, in the late fifteenth century, a celebrated Portuguese Jewish philosopher, Isaac ben Abravanel, suggested that Caanan's descendants were black, while those of his uncles were white, and so all black people were liable to be enslaved. Genesis 9 gives no support to this belief; nevertheless Abravanel's innovative exercise in biblical hermeneutics now proved extremely convenient for the same Iberian Christians who persecuted his own people, and later for Christian slavers everywhere.[8] Other Christians followed a different line in biblical interpretation not found in any Western Bible, but traceable right back to a reading in the Syriac *Peshitta* version of the story of Cain in Genesis 4.1–16: according to this Syriac take on the biblical text, black people actually descended from Cain because when God had punished Cain for killing his brother Abel, the 'mark' he gave the murderer was to blacken his skin. It was reasonable to suppose that this applied to all Cain's descendants.[9] Neither biblical approach was calculated to raise the status of people defined as black.

It took original minds to kick against the authority of sacred scripture. What was needed was a prior conviction in one's conscience of the wrongness of slavery, which one might then decide to justify by a purposeful re-examination of the biblical text – it was an early form of the modern critical reconsideration of biblical intention and meaning.[10] It was possible for people in the Puritan tradition to do so: that independent-minded Massachusetts judge Samuel Sewall, who had recently had the courage to make a public apology for his part in the Salem witch trials (see pp. 755–6), was one of the first. In 1700 he wrote a pamphlet highlighting a comment in Mosaic Law which had not been much considered before: 'He that stealeth a man and selleth him, or if he be found in his hand, he shall surely be put to death' (Exodus 21.16). Coolly Sewall's pamphlet then demolished the standard Christian wisdom of his day on slavery, argument by argument.[11] Back in Europe, it was possible for the Enlightenment to motivate people to argue for abolition, as part of the general Enlightenment urge to question ancient certainties. The *Encylopédie*'s entry on 'Commerce' furiously attacked the slave trade, while in his *De l'Esprit des Lois* (1748) one of the most respected authors of the French Enlightenment, the Baron de Montesquieu, himself an inhabitant of the great slaving port of Bordeaux, like Sewall pitilessly dissected the various arguments justifying slavery, biblical and Classical, and showed their inadequacy.[12]

By contrast, other intellectuals of the Enlightenment contributed substitute rationales for slavery, because they began studying world racial categories, and it became eminently possible to use this new 'science' as the basis for finding certain races inferior in characteristics and ripe for enslavement – especially if one despised the creation stories of Genesis, which did give all humankind a common ancestry in Adam and Eve. So both Christianity and the Enlightenment could lead Westerners in opposite directions on slavery. Far less equivocal than the *philosophes* were Pennsylvania Quakers, whose tradition enabled them to be less reverent towards biblical authority (see pp. 782–3). They anticipated Sewall by twelve years, with a petition against slavery in Pennsylvania from some Dutch Quakers in 1688. Their brethren at that stage chose to ignore the initiative, but, tempted in the early eighteenth century to join their fellow colonists in using the growing number of slaves to sustain their Quaker haven, the Pennsylvania authorities now displayed their usual consecrated cussedness and came down firmly against slavery of any sort in 1758, the first Christians corporately to do so.

One Pennsylvania Friend at the heart of these discussions, Anthony Benezet, devoted himself to publicizing the Pennsylvania decision, and he drew on the transatlantic character of international Protestantism. His message was heard in the mother country – in particular, by an Anglican gentleman, Granville Sharp, who entered prolonged and enthusiastic correspondence with him. Sharp came to hate slavery as much as he hated Roman Catholicism, an equal threat to British liberty in his eyes, and he revealed a genius for organized campaigns against both.[13] Grandson of a High Church Archbishop of York who had been patron to John Wesley's father, Sharp was a prolific biblical critic, turning his scriptural scholarship to constructing a case against slavery which would have a biblical base. Selectively he gathered from scripture a message in favour of equality and freedom, looking past the Bible's package of assumptions about the inequality of society. Yet Sharp's greatest triumph came not actually through any biblical argument but by his success in backing an English lawsuit in 1772, 'Somersett's Case'. In the judgement on this case, Lord Chief Justice Mansfield found in favour of an escaped slave, James Somersett, against his master, a customs officer of Boston, Massachusetts. Mansfield refused to accept that the institution of slavery existing in eighteenth-century England could be linked to the historic legal status of serfdom or villeinage recognized in English common law: logically, therefore, slavery had no legal existence in England.[14] Thus the useful rigidity and traditionalism of English law became the basis for a swelling campaign against slavery, just as it had brought the Jews back to England in 1656 after three and a half centuries (see pp. 773-4).

Mansfield's judgement in Somersett's Case proclaimed that only a decision of Parliament could legalize modern slavery in Britain. Now it became the ambition of one of Sharp's fellow Evangelicals, William Wilberforce, to do precisely the opposite, and legislate first the British slave trade and then slavery out of existence throughout the growing British Empire. Wilberforce's campaigning energies and charisma made him the dominant figure in his circle of Evangelical reformers, who gained the nickname 'the Clapham Sect' from a village south of London which was then a pleasant rural home to Wilberforce and other wealthy Evangelicals. His struggle was long and bitter, but in 1807 he achieved his first goal. When he and his friends realized that the abolition of the slave trade had not led to the weakening of slavery as they had hoped, they widened their horizons to persuade the British Parliament to cut off the institution at its root. It was only after Wilberforce's retirement from Parliament that, in 1833, the old man heard his friends had won that second victory, receiving the news just three days before he died. Like Charles Darwin later, the often-reviled reformer was now given national honour by burial in Westminster Abbey.[15]

The long struggle to abolish slavery remained throughout a curious collaboration of fervent Evangelicals, who were mostly otherwise extremely politically conservative, with radical children of the Enlightenment, many of whom had no great love of Christianity, though some were enthusiastic Unitarians (as Socinians were now more courteously known).[16] Such radicals saw an end to slavery as part of the war on oppression of which the French Revolution also formed a part. So in 1791, before that Revolution became a liability rather than a potential ally for English radicals, the adventurous Whig MP Charles James Fox – whose colourful private life certainly did not make him a natural ally for morally censorious Evangelicals – spoke forcefully in Parliament in support of one of Wilberforce's earlier unsuccessful motions against 'this shameful trade in human flesh'. 'Personal freedom,' he insisted, 'must be the first object of every human being . . . a right, of which he who deprives a fellow-creature is absolutely criminal'.[17]

There has been nearly a century of argument as to whether slavery's abolition was merely a Machiavellian outcome of the West's realization that slavery was becoming an economic liability. It is understandable that descendants of enslaved Africans should tire of hearing complacent British repetition of the famous judgement by the Victorian historian of European ethical change, W. E. H. Lecky, that the 'unwearied, unostentatious and inglorious crusade of England against slavery may probably be regarded as among the three or four perfectly virtuous acts recorded in the history of nations'. Yet after all the debate, and the research it engendered, Lecky seems vindicated: abolition was an act of moral revulsion which defied the strict commercial interests of European and anglophone nations.[18] Less frequently has it been recognized as one of the more remarkable turnarounds in Christian history: a defiance of biblical certainties, spearheaded by British Evangelicals who made it a point of principle to uphold biblical certainties. Many of their fellow Evangelicals berated them for their inconsistency and few of their allies in mainland European Protestantism showed much sympathy for their project.

It is true that other moral dimensions nuance Lecky's judgement. The ethical imperative in the circle of Sharp and Wilberforce was part of a new self-confidence and imperial assertiveness on the part of Britain, taking shape even as its North American empire was ripped in two. A direct outcome of the abolitionist movement was one of the earliest British colonies to extend the Crown's territorial ambitions beyond coastal trading forts outside America and India: Sierra Leone in West Africa. Inaugurated in 1792 after a badly conceived false start in the same area five years before, this was a cooperation between the indefatigable Evangelical abolitionist Thomas Clarkson, his ex-naval officer brother John and a West African – an Egba prince who in enslavement had taken the name Thomas Peters and then regained his freedom by fighting for the British in the American War of Independence. The venture tried to learn lessons from a second previous failed colony of 1775 on the ominously (though coincidentally) named Mosquito Coast of Central America. That had been a partnership between an English businessman and another formerly enslaved African-American, Olaudah Equiano, whose autobiography had become a transatlantic best-seller, especially among Evangelicals, and who became one of the advisers to the new Sierra Leone scheme. The Mosquito Coast venture involved using enslaved Africans to make it commercially viable, with only a vague prospect that financial success would bring them freedom: that strategy was very far from abolitionism and the slaves sought to escape, all drowning in the attempt.[19]

There was now no question but that the Sierra Leone colonists who started arriving in 1792 should be Africans to whom freedom had been restored, either liberated on the West African coast or shipped back from the Americas complete with Protestant Christian values. Thomas Peters had his own ideas as to what those values might be, and he had the temerity to demand more political rights for his black fellow settlers than Englishmen would have enjoyed back home. Against him were ranged the English directors of the Sierra Leone Company, who as in the Mosquito Coast venture linked 'the true principles of Commerce' to 'the introduction of Christianity and Civilization', and who crushed uprisings by kindred spirits to Peters after his early death.[20] Yet Peters's fellow colonists who shared his spirit of independence and self-reliance had the advantage that the tropical climate made even shorter work of British administrators than it did of returned African-Americans. The new venture soon developed a hierarchical pyramid of status groups: Christians from the New World at the top, then West Africans liberated locally (the two groups together became known as the Krio) and finally the indigenous population, who, like the inhabitants of Canaan three millennia before, had not been given any say in God's territorial gift to these new Children of Israel. It was an unhealthy imbalance in which the seeds of modern troubles were sown for Sierra Leone; the later American initiative in founding an entirely independent West African state of Liberia (from 1822) suffered from the same problem.

Sierra Leone did not make money for its proprietors, but it did survive, a rich source of African Christian leadership for all West Africa, from the many Protestant denominations it hosted. Its Krio language, a creative development of English, soon served as a lingua franca throughout the region.[21] The colony was also an interesting sign to imperial strategists that European African colonial possessions might usefully extend beyond scattered coastal outposts. From 1808 Sierra Leone was a Crown Colony, base for a remarkable practical extension of the Parliamentary Act abolishing the slave trade, a British naval squadron which intercepted slave ships and freed their captives. The British government was not unaware that this was a useful part of the war effort against the commerce of the Napoleonic Empire, but the work did not stop with Napoleon's defeat. The navy now combined a moral campaign with the steady extension of British influence. Evangelicals had produced this result, and their continuing agitation sustained British commitment – which, perhaps surprisingly, extended to the British government bringing pressure to bear on Pope Gregory XVI: an Apostolic Letter in 1839 echoed the recent British condemnation of the slave trade.[22] Out of this moral crusade emerged the potent idea that the British Crown was a partner with its subjects in the worldwide enterprise of spreading Christian civilization – a theme as useful to imperial subjects as to imperial government.[23]

A PROTESTANT WORLD MISSION: OCEANIA AND AUSTRALASIA

Rather separate from the abolitionist campaign, although likewise led by anglophone Evangelicals, was a sudden upwelling of commitment to worldwide mission. The Moravians had provided the precedent, while doing nothing to challenge slavery (see pp. 746–7); now a similar missionary fervour seized all the mainstream British Protestant Churches. The coincidental rapidity of the first moves is remarkable. Even a catalogue of dates and institutions provokes astonishment – the energetic (not to say driven) Rev. Thomas Coke appointed by the Wesleyan Conference in 1790 as general supervisor of Methodist world missions, a Baptist Missionary Society in 1792, a (Congregational-based) London Missionary Society in 1795, an (Anglican Evangelical) Church Missionary Society in 1799, a British and Foreign Bible Society in 1804, an American Board of Commissioners for Foreign Missions in 1810.

This activity had a complementary relationship with that feature of British Protestantism unique in Europe, its large sector of Churches separate from the established Churches. Their century of vigorous growth in the United Kingdom now marched in step with the growth of British missionary activity. The creation of institutions was presaged by a decade of thought and planning, so that between 1783 and 1792 public interest was generated with manifestos for missions in Africa and British India and the Caribbean by leaders as prominent as John Wesley as well as the then lesser-known Anglican chaplain in Calcutta David Brown and the downright obscure and uneducated Baptist shoemaker William Carey.[24] Equal excitement was aroused by the voyages of Captain James Cook in the Pacific Ocean, which Cook assiduously promoted by publishing the journals of his admittedly extraordinary feats of exploration and mapping. His dramatic death in the Hawaiian islands on his third voyage in 1779 only added to his celebrity.

But the 1790s added a new urgency. The events of the French Revolution suggested that a century of Evangelical expectations for the coming end might at last be fulfilled. Joanna Southcott's sensational public career (see pp. 828–9), which began in the year that the Baptist Missionary Society was founded, was just one symptom of the mood – she was a fierce and vocal opponent of the Revolution.[25] In 1798–9 the French revolutionaries' imprisonment of the Pope and his death in exile were icing on the apocalyptic cake. As is usually the case with such fervour, the passing of 1800 with relatively little obvious divine intervention did not dampen enthusiasm. It was clear that Evangelicalism was making great strides among Protestant Christians; the new propensity for the expression of emotion in Romanticism did nothing to lower the devotional temperature. By 1830, it has been plausibly suggested, around 60 per cent of British Protestants were involved in some variety of Evangelical religious practice, while between 1800 and 1840 a hundred books were published in English discussing the signs of the times, eagerly debated in a new crop of periodicals with titles like *The Morning Watch*, organizations like the Prophecy Investigation Society and regular Evangelical conferences.[26] Apocalyptic excitement was no longer common among the hierarchy of the established Church, so English bishops persisted in showing themselves almost as reluctant to get involved in missionary activity as they were resistant to invitations to open Joanna Southcott's box. It was not until 1841 that the Archbishop of Canterbury, William Howley, an aged High Churchman of distinctly old-fashioned type, finally accepted an ex-officio relationship with the Church Missionary Society, thirteen years into his archiepiscopate.

By then it would have been foolish in the extreme for the Primate of All England to ignore the anglophone worldwide mission, which paralleled Britain's political and economic position in the world. With its navy's global reach and a network of commerce feeding its then unequalled capacity in industrial production and engineering, Britain was at the height of its power – long before its territorial empire had reached its greatest extent, which was in fact not until the 1920s, in an age when Britain's real power was on the wane. There was a complex relationship between mission and this imperial expansion. In recent years, it has been common among some of the historians who know the subject best to play down the links between missionary work and colonial expansion, particularly in the British imperial story.[27] Certainly a majority of British missionaries were members of Dissenting Churches or Methodists, and they were unlikely to have an automatic sympathy with the aims of the British Establishment. Almost everywhere missionaries of whatever denomination preceded Crown colonial interventions by several decades, and Anglicans as much as others might resent official interference threatening the delicate web of local relationships which they had built up.[28] Yet the fact remains that almost everywhere where British missions flourished, British official hegemony eventually followed.

The classic case of colonial rule following missions is provided by the first major area of Christian success, the Pacific Ocean (Oceania), where in the end virtually everywhere fell under the rule of either European powers or the United States. Stirred by the triumphs and quasi-martyrdom of Captain Cook, the London Missionary Society made Pacific islands its especial priority straight away in the 1790s. Here missionary concerns were very close to the Enlightenment: the primarily Congregational leadership was from that intellectually lively Dissent which threw its enthusiasm into the scientific advances of its day, moving in the same circles as Anglican Enlightenment figures like Captain Cook's naturalist colleague and fellow explorer Joseph Banks or the agricultural writer Arthur Young. It was not a problem to combine a theology of nature, in which the believer could delight in the wonderful works of the Creator, with expectation of the approaching millennium, for which one could prepare by exploring those wonders: a form of purposeful meditation on the Last Days.[29]

Nevertheless the London Missionary Society's Evangelical outlook gave it a different perspective from Banks's fascination with an apparent oceanic paradise. Its leaders saw the Pacific hosting no primeval Edens but rather sinks of ancient corruption needing urgent Protestant remedy – not least for relaxed sexual mores, homosexuality included, qualities which to other European observers seemed so attractive.[30] So the Society planned an ambitious and imaginative project with its first voyage to Tahiti and elsewhere in 1796. An entire community of thirty-plus hardworking practical English people embarked not exactly to colonize, as Puritans had done in New England, but to set the degraded islanders a good Protestant example as a mission community whose intentions emulated the communal ideal of the Moravians. On board were all the respectable characters of a large English village (with the exception of the squire, who might bring his own sort of European corruption):

besides four clergy, there were weavers, tailors, shoemakers, a gardener. They had no doubt that they would spread the useful arts and better moral aspects of European civilization along with the good news of Christianity.[31]

The results from the settlements planted in this voyage of the *Duff* were disappointing in the extreme; the colonists exhibited some spectacular backsliding from godly ways, and the LMS did not repeat the experiment. Instead it fell back on a model of activity equally prone to chance but less in need of elaborate infrastructure: the single male who, with luck, training and prayer, would impress and motivate local leaders, who would then order their people to become Christians. It was, after all, the pattern which had worked well in bringing Christianity to Anglo-Saxon England twelve centuries before, and many missionary organizations followed suit. There were casualties: several missionaries themselves suffered Captain Cook's fate as some initially promising local situation soured, but far more numerous were native deaths, particularly as other Europeans arrived with a greater and more exciting range of Western amenities, including alcohol and its handmaid, sexually transmitted disease. As in the earlier American experience of European-borne epidemics, demographic disaster undermined faith in traditional religion and lent plausibility to those respected local leaders who decided to give the new religion their backing. Quite early, some local converts became Christian prophets who promised that their flock would be rewarded with the whole panoply of desirable objects brought by Europeans, an anticipation of the 'cargo cults' which still flourish in Melanesia.[32] Alongside such local adaptations of their message, missionaries did not forget the LMS's first emphasis on practical skills, so much continued to be on offer from the European arrivals, and not merely in trade goods.

Throughout the region, a consistent pattern developed from the example of Tahiti, the first large-scale success in founding Christian communities in the Pacific. Missions drew on the highly developed skills of Pacific peoples in seamanship, sending out local converts along old sea routes to other island groups. Rather than a detailed grasp of Christian theology, they brought charisma, a shrewd sense of what might appeal to local leaders in the Christian package and a determination to destroy the power of traditional cults. As the social disruption provoked by European contacts repeated itself across the Pacific, these were a winning combination. Various political leaders realized just how much advantage they might gain against rivals from missionary backing – often, as large-scale conversions took place, combatants in murderous wars would ally with missionaries of rival denominations, who frequently did not quite grasp how they were being used in local politics. When the Wesleyan Methodists and the LMS, in a laudable attempt to end their own rivalries, agreed in the 1830s to allot Samoa to the LMS and Tonga and Fiji to the Wesleyans, local Wesleyans on Samoa were furious. They would not compromise their Wesleyan purity even by using the same Bibles and hymn books as the LMS folk, and after twenty years of ill-will and agitation, European and Australian Wesleyan missionaries returned in some embarrassment to Samoa.[33]

The Maori in Aotearoa (the pair of major islands which Europeans have known as New Zealand) were part of the same oceanic culture. They had both a lively curiosity about European culture and an exceptional ability to exploit it: they learned the hard way that not all innovation was beneficial, when their acquisition of large quantities of muskets horrifically escalated casualties in their habitual and hitherto partly ritual warfare. Christianity in its various missionary forms offered more promising paths into adjusting to the European presence: by 1845, in under fifty years, at least half the Maori population was worshipping in Christian churches, far outnumbering European churchgoers on the two islands.[34] Maoris found much to interest them in the Bible. When, with the help of missionaries of the Church Missionary Society, they negotiated a treaty with the British Crown at Waitangi in 1840, the Maori leadership regarded it as a covenant on a biblical model, and, despite many subsequent colonial betrayals of the treaty's spirit, it endured as the basis of a more just settlement for the Maori people in recent years.

One of the most creative leaders in the generation after the treaty signatories was a devout Anglican, a chief's son baptized William Thompson (Wiremu Tamihana in Maori). Tamihana had initially followed his European missionary mentors in their hostility to traditional Maori tattooing, but by the 1850s he was pleased to proclaim to his people after his own more careful scrutiny of the biblical text that nothing in scripture forbade it. This was an important element in Maori self-assertion at that time, and formed part of Tamihana's greater political purpose in appealing to the Bible to remedy the deteriorating situation after the treaty. Thanks to him, Old Testament Israel provided the Maori with inspiration for an attempt to create a monarchy to unite all their feuding tribes in the North Island; they had no other model for kingship in their tradition. By 1860 the scheme degenerated into war with the British, and Tamihana looked back sadly on his work in a reproachful letter to the British Governor:

I considered, therefore, how this blood could be made to diminish in this island: I looked into *your books* where Israel cried to have a king for themselves to be a judge over them . . . on his being set up the blood at once ceased . . . I do not allude to this blood lately shed; it was your hasty work caused that blood.[35]

By then, the swelling number of colonizing immigrants had changed the balance of sympathy among Church leaders of European origins; most supported the military suppression of Maori aspirations. That terribly undermined existing Churches, principally the Anglicans. The gap was filled by syntheses of traditional religion with Christian practice, engineered by prophets more radical than Tamihana, along with imported alternatives to British religion such as the Mormon Church (see pp. 906–8).[36]

The saddest story of contact between Christianity and native peoples in the Pacific or Australasia is that of the aboriginal peoples of Australia. Pushed aside after 1788 by British colonial settlement which aimed (with broad success) to reproduce British patterns of life and religion in an infinitely sunnier climate, the aboriginals were left the vast expanses of their continent which the British did not want. Commonly missionaries did what they could to provide a way into European society by encouraging a new set of social patterns, as certainly seemed to work for the Maori; the missions were given grants of land in marginal territories on which aboriginals could form settled communities. But the gulf between traditional semi-nomadism and these Christian settlements was too great. Traditional leadership and cultural practices could not be sustained, and in any case, the general assumption of missionaries of whatever denomination was that it was not worth trying: aboriginals were a dying race, and it would be best if they were integrated into the modern world, without much great attempt to preserve their own languages. In an effort to destroy cultural memories which were seen as an insuperable barrier to integration, for nearly a century and a half countless children were removed from their parents for mission education: an unimaginable accumulation of separations, betraying any positive theory of Christian family life, whose consequences are still unravelling in Australian society.[37]

In the end, only one Australasian or Pacific territory, Tonga, escaped direct European or American rule, through an astute alliance with Britain by a newly established monarchy, basing its legitimacy on a unique construction which might have gladdened the heart of that High Tory John Wesley: a Methodist established Church. Christian groundwork was laid by LMS-inspired Tahitians in the 1820s, but a decade later Methodist initiatives began. Taufa'ahau, an ambitious and talented member of the Tupou family in the Tongan Ha'apai group of islands, allied with John Thomas, a Methodist minister once a blacksmith in Worcester; Taufa'ahau encouraged Thomas's mission and drew on the abilities of a Tongan aristocrat now a Methodist missionary, Pita (Peter) Vi. Between them they launched a vigorous campaign against traditional Tongan cults, which ran parallel with Taufa'ahau's growing power throughout the Tongan archipelago. In 1845 Thomas had the satisfaction of adapting English coronation rites for Taufa'ahau's enthronement as King George I, founding a royal dynasty which endures to this day.

Thirty years later there followed a written monarchical constitution for Tonga, shaped by an Australian Methodist minister, Shirley Baker, whose aspirations outran his self-restraint and brought a bizarre and sour twist to Tongan politics. Now Prime Minister of Tonga, Baker escaped the discipline of an increasingly alarmed Australasian Wesleyan Conference by resigning his ministry, and he encouraged the King to form an independent Tongan Methodist Church. Schism with Conference loyalists resulted, and between 1885 and 1887 there followed a brutal persecution of Methodists by Methodists, until the British High Commissioner intervened. By the end of George I's long reign in 1893, Baker had become a marginal figure, and the royal Church of the Tupou dynasty had returned to a less bloodthirsty Methodism. Queen Sālote, majestic and generously proportioned heir to the light-touch British Protectorate established in 1900, was a much-appreciated visitor to England at her fellow monarch Elizabeth II's coronation in 1953.[38]

AFRICA: AN ISLAMIC OR A PROTESTANT CENTURY?

Nowhere else in the world was the relationship of Christianity to colonial expansion so straightforward as in the Pacific, partly because elsewhere Europeans encountered cultures based on faiths also claiming a universal message or with the potential to do so: Islam, Hinduism, Buddhism, Taoism. Of these, Islam had the widest reach, and contacts were consequently the most varied. We have already noted how a far more confrontational attitude to Christianity arose in the nineteenth-century Ottoman Empire (see pp. 854–5), but for more than a century before, there had been revivals throughout the Islamic world, reactions to the humiliation of the failing empires of the Ottomans and Mughals. In the face of growing European military success in late-eighteenth-century India, Shah Wali-Allah began considering how Muslim society might adapt for the first time in its history to losing political power. He pleaded eloquently both for Islamic social reconstruction and for a reconciliation of Sunni and Shī'a within Islam, and his son 'Abd al-'Aziz sustained and developed his movement, combining tradition with a recognition of the reality of British India.[39] On the fringes of Ottoman power in Arabia, an austere revivalism founded by Muhammad ibn 'Abd al-Wahhāb (1703–87) gained support from tribal leaders of the Sa'ūd family; al-Wahhāb rejected more than a millennium of development within various branches of Islam, to return to basic texts, in a move not unlike the Protestant Reformation. In 1803 the Sa'ūd temporarily conquered the holy city of Mecca, and thereafter remained a significant force in the politics of Arabia until eventually they became its rulers.

During the nineteenth century, this Wahhabite religious movement in a peninsula dominated by desert and with no great political or economic power seemed to have little wider importance. It was in North and West Africa that a new surge of life extended Muslim frontiers, and the agent was a very different form of Islam led by mystical Sūfī orders: the first significant sign of Islamic renewal that Christian missionaries encountered anywhere. If Christian expansion in Africa did eventually become linked to military success, reforming Islam had already set the pattern in late-eighteenth-century West Africa, through the strength and proselytizing zeal of the pastoralist Fulani people. Their establishment of a string of emirates in place of previous kingdoms was spearheaded by movements of *jihad* (struggle) to establish a purer form of Islam, the greatest of which was led from 1802 by the campaigning Sūfī scholar Shehu Usman dan Fodio. In the early nineteenth century, the most plausible picture of the future was that black Africa would have become overwhelmingly Muslim, and Muslim growth there remained spectacular all through the century.[40] In fact, Christianity came to equal Islam in outreach in Africa, and this spurt of Christian growth was in the first place a mission pushed forward by self-help. Only belatedly did it gain increasing protection from European military power; even at their apparently most powerless, Africans made their own choices within the offer of Christian faith.

There was certainly demand for the new message. People all over Africa, uprooted by local wars or the recent interference of Europeans, were as eager as industrial workers in Georgian England to find new purpose and structure for their lives. Even while missionary societies were first dispatching volunteers from Britain early in the nineteenth century, a far less formal dispersal of Christian knowledge was exuberantly travelling out of the first British Protestant coastal footholds in southern and West Africa, almost without the missionaries noticing. Through much of the continent, both trade and the need for pastoralists and arable farmers to move on from easily exhausted soils or pastures encouraged Africans to travel over long distances. Young men from inland went to find work on the coast; they returned home, having witnessed a new religion and sung its hymns. Women were the mainstay of trade in West Africa, and in Sierra Leone many Krio women highly gifted in commerce were seized by enthusiasm for Christian faith. On their far travels out of the colony, they marketed Christianity as successfully as all their other wares, like the Syrian merchants of Central Asia long before them.

As a result, it was rare in nineteenth-century Africa for a European missionary to appear in any community which had apparently never before enjoyed a visit from a white man and not find someone who recognized what he was talking about. If the personal chemistry worked between missionary and this new acquaintance, such a person could become a teacher, prepared to go on repeating and recreating the Christian message when the European moved on: speaking to Africans in African ways. It was a rediscovery of the vital role of catechists like those whom Catholic missionaries had already employed in Latin America, central Africa and China in previous centuries, and it paralleled what was going on in Christianizing the Pacific. Local voices had much more chance of conveying what the missionaries were trying to bring in an alien cultural form: joy. Dan Crawford, a missionary from the British 'Brethren' movement, came to Africa at the beginning of the twentieth century as an unusually sensitive guest. In his missionary work, he drew on the Brethren's tradition of carefully eschewing any religious hierarchy, and he watched and listened. As he observed a convert lady dancing, he grasped how great were the marvels which he himself could hardly enter:

to me, a new-comer, what a gazing-stock! The amazing, maddening mix-up of the prayer in the heart, and the prance in the feet! Asked her what it meant at all at all, and she quaintly replied, 'Oh! it is only the praise getting out at the toes.'[41]

What messages made the new Christians dance? At the risk of seeming foolishly patronizing to a multitude of different peoples across a vast continent, it is worth drawing attention to a few themes, not always those which missionaries expected or wanted converts to pick up from the good news. At the heart of Christianity is a book full of signs and wonders testifying to God's power, and Africans were accustomed to looking for those. Their religions commonly spoke of spirits and provided explanations of the mysteries of world origins and creation: so did this book. It was full of genealogies: most African societies delighted in such repetitions, when they bored or baffled pious Europeans, who had often turned to Africa precisely to make their mark unhampered by the snobbery of long-pedigreed gentry back home. In fact, Africans might take the book more seriously than the missionaries who brought it, in the sense that they confidently expected concrete results from the power of God. That was a challenge to European Evangelicals, who were likewise convinced that God wrought miracles in his world, but whose rationalism (born at whatever remove from the Enlightenment) provoked them into alarm at a literalism which differed from their own.

The Bible speaks without reserve about witches and at one point it suggests that they should not be allowed to live.[42] African societies knew witches well, and many allotted power to witch-finders. Europeans did not want to encourage these rivals in charisma, particularly when the witch-finders encouraged the killing of witches, but if Europeans expressed scepticism, indigenous Christians might ignore them and take matters into their own hands. In the twentieth century, the results grew increasingly fatal in certain parts of rural Africa, where witch-killings marched in step with the growth of African-initiated Churches.[43] This was by no means the only matter on which African Christians might look for specific action from their God beyond missionary expectations. In arid zones, missionaries were repeatedly expected to bring rain where there was no rain. They were after all travelling men preaching biblical power, and they ought to be able to do better than traditional rain-makers, who were often also charismatic wanderers, and as much their competitors as the witch-finders. Once more, even the most uncompromising European Evangelicals were likely to doubt that in God's providence the weather worked quite like that. It was particularly testing, as the Wesleyan Methodist William Shaw discovered after staging a round of sermons and prayers for rain to outface challenges from a non-Christian rainmaker, to turn off God's bounty once the recipients had had enough.[44]

Rainmaking (or rather the lack of it) ended the personal missionary career of the great Scottish missionary publicist and explorer David Livingstone. His one known convert, Sechele, King of the BaKwêna in what is now Botswana, was a perfect prize, intellectually gifted and a fine orator, but he was also his people's rainmaker, and his powers appeared to have ended when he accepted Christian baptism. To Livingstone it was folly to worry about this; to Sechele it was crucial. In his frustration, the King broke with Livingstone on another matter which from different standpoints mattered very much to both of them; he took back his multiple wives. There was general satisfaction among the BaKwêna at this. Livingstone was furious and left, never again to effect any conversions in his restless African travels. Livingstone's departure suited Sechele rather well: the King continued eloquently preaching the Gospel among his people unhindered by Europeans, he made rain and he honoured all his wives.[45]

Polygamy was one of the great stumbling blocks for Western mission, just as it had been long before for the Church of Ethiopia, and with equally inconclusive results (see p. 281). Here yet again was an issue of biblical interpretation. Polygamous African Christian men were perfectly capable of reading their Bibles and finding their ancient marital customs confirmed in the private life of the patriarchs in the Old Testament; usually in vain did Europeans redirect them to a contrary message in the Pauline sections of the New Testament. John William Colenso, a polymath with an inconvenient Cornish propensity for pointing out truths to those disinclined to see them, became first Anglican Bishop of Natal in South Africa, and he had great admiration for the equal clear-sightedness which he found in his Zulu flock. He became alarmed at their puzzlement about anomalies in the Pentateuch.[46] His struggles to satisfy their queries eventually won him ostracism within Anglicanism, but apart from his notorious (and it has to be said clumsy) championing of sensible critical analysis of the Bible, Colenso also became convinced that the Zulu had a good case on polygamy. He said so in a pamphlet of 1862 addressed to the Archbishop of Canterbury. His fellow bishops worldwide were not going to agree with a heretical troublemaker, and the Lambeth Conference of Anglican bishops (with the agreement of Samuel Ajayi Crowther, the one African present and on the relevant committee) condemned polygamy in 1888.[47] Back in Sierra Leone in the same year, Anglicans hotly debated the same issue, when one speaker bluntly said that to recognize polygamy would 'make us all honest men' – but the bookseller who had proposed the idea found himself forced to resign from the Church Finance Committee.[48]

Colenso articulated what was unannounced but general practice among Anglicans and Catholics, when with characteristic candour he made it clear that he did not force Christian converts to put away extra wives, considering it cruel and 'opposed to the plain teaching of Our Lord' (who, on any reading of scripture, showed a firm if not consistently reported hostility to divorce). Colenso's pragmatism was equalled by that of the great missionary archbishop of North African Catholicism, Cardinal Charles Lavigerie, when considering with dismay another aspect of African esteem for marriage: the difficulties which it caused in recruiting local Catholic priests in the face of the Church's rule of universal clerical celibacy. Lavigerie, an enthusiastic student of Church history who took the long view, recommended that the Pope should authorize a married priesthood for Africa, but the obvious parallel in the married clergy of the Greek Catholic Churches of eastern Europe did not impress the Curia.[49] When Churches took a hard line on such matters of sexuality, they might well find their flocks and even their clergy voting with their feet, as when, in 1917, sixty-five Yoruba ministers were expelled from the Nigerian Methodist Church for polygamy. Yorubaland, a cultural frontier where the contest between Islam, Christianity and traditional religion led people to a questioning spirit in religious matters, was not a country to breed meekness to external authority. The expelled ministers went on to found a United African Methodist Church whose 'united' character, like that of a previous 'United' Methodist Church created back in England, consisted in a sturdily united refusal to be bossed around by Wesleyan Methodists.[50]

By that period, there was a vigorous movement through most of Africa to found Churches independent of European interference: Colenso, indeed, had retained a loyal Zulu following when deposed by the Metropolitan Bishop of Cape Town, and it was half a century after his death before most of the remaining Colensoites were persuaded back into mainstream Anglicanism.[51] The movement to create African-initiated Churches further fragmented African Christianity, but it might be regarded as a logical end result from the thinking of the more imaginative early missionaries. Among them had been an outstanding leader back in London, Henry Venn, grandson of one of the original 'Clapham Sect' and for more than thirty years from 1841 General Secretary of the Church Missionary Society. He was one of the first to enunciate a policy easier for Protestants than Catholics to envisage: an African Church based on a 'three-self' principle – self-supporting, self-governing, self-propagating. Naturally, for the Anglican Venn, this was not meant to involve ecclesiastical separation, but it demanded that local leadership should be established as soon as possible. A disastrous missionary venture of 1841 in West Africa prompted the CMS into acting on his strategy: a hugely ambitious expedition in the River Niger basin, during which fever struck down 130 of 145 Europeans and killed forty of them.

The Niger catastrophe seemed to show that Africans were better suited to withstand local conditions. Among its survivors was an African clearly endowed with leadership qualities, and who during visits to England had become a personal friend of Venn: Samuel Ajayi Crowther (his English baptismal names commemorated the Samuel Crowther who was a leading figure in the CMS). Crowther was another Yoruba – indeed, through his writings, he was the main agent in popularizing this proud self-ascription for his people.[52] The British Navy had freed him from a slave ship bound for the Americas, and he then settled like so many freed Yoruba in Sierra Leone; he was eventually consecrated bishop in Canterbury Cathedral in 1864. His career, so promising and so prophetic of eventual indigenous leadership, was crippled through no fault of his own. Crowther's restrained dignity clothed a passionate hatred of slavery and ignorance. He could be unsparing in his criticism of African people, precisely because he wanted to arouse them out of the poverty and deprivation which he saw as caused by false religion as much as by slavers.[53] Although as a member of the 1888 Lambeth Conference's committee on polygamy he concurred in the committee's denunciation of the institution, his hostility anticipated modern feminist critiques of polygamy's male-centredness. He couched his critique in terms of women's rights: women had not chosen polygamy, and although they usually worked harder than men, a polygamous husband was unlikely to satisfy all their needs (in one of his memoranda to the CMS, he told a cheerfully risqué tall story to illustrate his point).[54]

After the initial visionary decision to consecrate Crowther, he was ill-served by an episcopal appointment which in reality did not at all exemplify Venn's 'three-self' principle. Allotted the diocese of the Niger rather than his own Yorubaland because of jealousy from European missionaries working among the Yoruba, Crowther did his considerable best amid an unfamiliar culture with a language not his own, but eventually he found himself facing a peculiarly ruthless trading corporation, the Royal Niger Company. His efforts to remain independent of them attracted much ill-will and resentment that an African should stand in the way of Crown and commerce. Eventually a younger generation of missionaries appeared in Crowther's territories, endowed with all the self-confidence of English public schoolboys and the brisk austerity of late Victorian Evangelicalism, plus a dose of plain racism. They were unsympathetic to Crowther's gentle style – 'a charming old man, really guileless and humble . . . but he certainly does not seem called of God to be an overseer' was the magisterial judgement of the twenty-four-year-old Graham Wilmot Brooke on the bishop more than half a century his senior. Crowther was induced to resign in 1890, and died a couple of years later.[55] He was remarkably gracious about his treatment, and some of those involved later realized how foolish they had been. But no other black African was made a diocesan bishop until 1939, and then it was the Roman Catholic Church which had taken up the challenge of African leadership.[56] In 2009, as this book goes to press, the Church of England is adorned by an Archbishop of York born and raised in Uganda, John Sentamu.

It was of course possible for indigenous rulers to make decisions about Christianity and provide leadership, just as in the Pacific. Many monarchs throughout the new British territorial empire chose Anglicanism. Perhaps the most celebrated example was the kingdom of Buganda, part of what is now the Republic of Uganda, where Anglicans fought off vigorous competition for established status from Roman Catholicism and Islam. In the process they gained a set of martyrs whose fiery deaths for refusing the orders of their Kabaka (king) to commit sodomy have left the Anglican Church in Uganda particularly sensitive to recent shifts in Western sexual mores.[57] In the end, Buganda's identification between Crown and Church was so great that when in 1953 the British Governor of Uganda exiled the Kabaka of Buganda for political reasons, the Mothers' Union of the Anglican Church was loud among the chorus of furious protest. They complained that the Kabaka's exile endangered all Christian marriage in the kingdom, since the Anglican Bishop of Uganda had presided over the marriage of the Kabaka to his people when he bestowed a ring on him at his coronation.[58]

Another powerful African kingdom, on the island of Madagascar (now Malaghasy), likewise weighed up which varieties of Christianity (if any) to persecute or encourage. Eventually in 1869 Queen Ranavalona II settled not on Anglicanism but on English Congregationalism: an analogous triumph to Methodism's in Tonga and a tribute to the astuteness and persistence of the London Missionary Society.[59] So Congregationalism had a new taste of state establishment after its recent American losses, albeit this time under an absolute monarch, but the end of the story was very different from Tonga's. The colonial power which overthrew the monarchy, late in the colonial process in 1895, was not Britain but France, and for decades a further paradox afflicted Madagascar, as anticlerical French republican governments allowed Catholic clergy a free hand they would not have tolerated at home, actively repressed Protestant congregations and confiscated Protestant churches and schools, all in aid of promoting francophone against anglophone culture.[60] This was a rather curious example of colonialism and Christianization going hand in hand, although the Congregationalists survived repression and still have a substantial presence on the island.

Elsewhere, the inglorious end of Samuel Crowther's episcopate encouraged the formation of African-initiated Churches; the late nineteenth century saw the rise of leaders asserting their charisma as Old Testament prophets had once done against the Temple priesthood. One of the classic figures, whose influence is still felt all through West Africa, was William Wade Harris (1865–1929), a product of both Methodism and American Anglicanism. As a native Liberian of the Grebo people, marginalized therefore by the African-American Liberian elite, his career began in political agitation against their misgovernment which aimed to hand Liberia over to British rule, an interesting tribute to British colonialism. Imprisoned as a subversive, Harris was granted visions of the Archangel Gabriel, who relayed God's command to begin the work of prophecy. One aspect of the command was that Harris must abandon European clothing: that resolved the tangle into which his complicated relationship with Western culture had led him. Soon he was striding barefoot through the villages of the Ivory Coast and the Gold Coast (now Ghana), dressed in a simple white robe, bearing a gourd calabash of water and a tall cross-staff (after Harris, staffs became well-nigh-indispensable kit for any African prophet). He preached the coming of Christ and the absolute necessity to destroy traditional cult objects. With him was his team of two or three women, singing and playing calabash gourd rattles to summon the Holy Spirit.[61] Little in Harris's message beyond his angelic vision and personal style could be considered alien to the mainstream Christianity he had learned in his years as an Episcopalian catechist, although colonial administrators of antiquarian tastes deplored the destruction of local art which followed his visits. He himself recommended his converts to join the Methodists, but given his own tolerance of polygamy, that caused problems.

A feature of Harris's often brief visits in his tireless preaching (no more than a few weeks in the Gold Coast in 1914, for instance) was his extraordinary ability to leave permanent Churches in his wake – in terms of missionary impact, he was more John Wesley than George Whitefield. In the Ivory Coast, previously a Roman Catholic French enclave, Protestant practice mushroomed. The rich variety of Churches he left behind was characterized by local leadership and a propensity for building their own emphases into a distinctive system, beyond anything that Harris recommended. The Twelve Apostles Church in modern Ghana, for instance, has developed predominantly female leadership. Prophetesses preside over 'gardens', complexes of open-air church, oratory and hostel rather like a monastery; the prophetess's most prized ministry is healing, centring on Friday services (for which market women have decreed themselves a day off), the whole congregation dressed in red robes to honour the blood of Christ (see Plate 66). All these are developments independent of Harris. His gourd rattles nevertheless remain crucial to the liturgy, banishing spirits of illness with their clamour, while alongside them the skills of teenage drummers are given full rein. The Bible becomes a sacramental instrument, its touch calming the noisily possessed, and the prophetess bears a replica of Harris's cross-staff. The Twelve Apostles pride themselves on being the Church of last resort in affliction, even for proud folk who affect to despise such unsophisticated approaches to illness.[62]

Harris's early effort to play off the British against the Liberian authorities followed by his sudden rejection of European styles of worship echoed wider African reactions to a political situation transformed in the last two decades of the nineteenth century. A complete partition of Africa by European powers, through the Congress of Berlin in 1884–5, resulted in the destruction of a vast number of local power structures. The only lands left governing themselves were Ethiopia and Liberia, the latter a dubious exception. In King Leopold of Belgium's new so-called Congo Free State, a vast and scandalously misgoverned personal fiefdom, there was a sad symbolism of changed times when, in the 1890s, Baptist missionaries had no compunction in quarrying the ruins of Kongo's once-splendid royal and Catholic Cathedral of São Salvador to build a new church for themselves.[63] Christian missionary organizations largely welcomed the new situation, although colonial administrators, mindful of the disaster of the Great Indian Rebellion of 1857–8 (see pp. 893–4), were generally careful to respect the large areas of Africa which were now Islamic – to the annoyance of many aspiring evangelists.

Still Christians had advantages. Now that colonial governments were

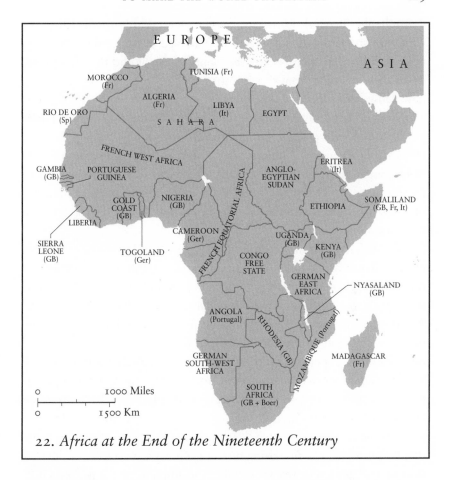

22. *Africa at the End of the Nineteenth Century*

demanding the regular collection of taxes and the filling in of forms, Western-style education was at a premium and only the Churches could offer it. In South Africa, the Xhosa word for Christians became 'School'.[64] Some Churches became alarmingly identified with the new imperialism. Catholics, Anglicans, Scots Presbyterians, Methodists, Dutch Reformed, even the Salvation Army, all accepted large grants of land from colonial promoters in 'Rhodesia' (now Zimbabwe/Zambia) and Kenya, which provoked widespread resentment against their missions.[65] Now it was possible to conceive of Christianity spanning the continent just as the British imperialist Cecil Rhodes envisaged a British-owned Cape to Cairo railway. Despite the unfortunate connotations of the image, it became common to talk about a 'chain' of missions across Africa, all belonging to some particular organization or Church. This generally European vision was to be fulfilled in a rather different fashion by African-initiated Churches.

Amid the general European ascendancy, two ancient Christian Churches stood out as not having first arrived in Africa with the slave traders. Both were Miaphysite: the Copts of Egypt and the Ethiopians. The Copts emerged from three centuries of beleaguered existence to a new prosperity, thanks to the opening up of their country to Western Christian influence in the wake of French and British clashes over Egypt in the Napoleonic period. A triangular relationship developed between the Copts, Evangelical missionaries (particularly from the Church Missionary Society) and Muhammad Ali, the Albanian Ottoman soldier of fortune turned carpet-bagging ruler of Egypt from 1805, founder of a dynasty which survived the Ottoman fall to rule Egypt into the mid-twentieth century.

All sides had something to gain. The Copts were alert to the possibility of outside help after such long isolation, the English missionaries were not only eager to save souls but excited at the prospect of contact with so venerable a Church untainted by popery, and the Muslim Muhammad Ali recognized how useful it would be to exploit a skilled indigenous people who could mediate with Western powers and provide a pool of administrative expertise. The CMS implemented a scheme to introduce European patterns of education; the Copts eagerly seized on the opportunity and were careful to take it over for themselves. The centrepiece became a Coptic Patriarchal College founded, as its name implied, by the head of the Coptic Church, Kyrillos (Cyril) IV, who initiated a wave of Church reforms, a surprising number of which survived, considering that he had only seven years in which to implement them. The CMS were disappointed in their initial hopes of mass conversions of Egyptian Muslims, but unwittingly they had aided a renaissance in an ancient Church. In the face of all the tribulations which followed for Ottoman Christians in the nineteenth and twentieth centuries, it was to prove one of the most successful in all Eastern Christianity.[66]

Ethiopia's continuing existence was the most emphatic reminder that Christianity was an ancient African faith, and the resurgence of its Church owed little to the sort of quasi-colonial assistance which benefited the Copts. In the early nineteenth century the Ethiopian Empire might have entirely disintegrated, but it was rescued by a provincial governor, Kassa, who hacked his way to power so successfully that in 1855 he was crowned Negus under the name of Tewodros (Theodore), the hero whose providential arrival as monarchical saviour had been predicted in a sixteenth-century Ethiopian Christian prophecy. Intensely pious – 'Without Christ I am nothing,' he declared – he ended the

tradition of royal polygamy and toyed with Protestant missions travelling down from Egypt, some of whom had a particular use for him in
their ability to manufacture armaments. But like several of Ethiopia's
most energetic monarchs before him, Tewodros descended into paranoia
and murderous vindictiveness; it was not good for his sanity to think
himself lineally descended from King David. His cruelty alienated his
own people, and his imperial posturing led to a British expeditionary
force which crushed his armies at Maqdala in 1868. In despair, he
turned one of his missionary-forged guns on himself.[67]

Ethiopia survived this disaster and its Church maintained its Miaphysite character. Yŏhannes IV, another provincial governor turned
Negus, imitated Constantine in presiding over a Church council in 1878
to settle long-standing disputes on Christology, although his order to tear
out the tongues of some of those challenging his decision rather outdid the
Roman Emperor's enforcement of Nicene Orthodoxy.[68] His less opinionated successor, Menelik II, brought the empire to an unprecedented size,
and delivered the most lasting defeat suffered by a colonial power during
the nineteenth century when he crushed the invading Italians at Adwa
in 1896. It was an event celebrated all over Africa: a sign (like the
Japanese victory over the Russian Empire nine years later) that Europeans were not all-powerful. It was also a triumph for authentically
African Christianity, which might now turn to Ethiopia for inspiration.

Already in 1892, far away in the Transvaal, a Methodist minister of
the Pedi people, Mangena Maake Mokone, infuriated at condescension
from his white colleagues, had founded what he called the Ethiopian
Church.[69] Here was a name for a Church which, unlike any other title –
Methodist, Anglican, even Catholic – was actually to be found in the
Bible. Mokone was mindful of the psalm-verse (68.31) 'let Ethiopia
hasten to stretch out her hands to God' – a scriptural fragment which,
in conjunction with the story in Acts 8.26–40 of Philip and the Ethiopian
eunuch, was destined to have huge repercussions through the continent
over the next century. In a remarkably deft piece of Anglican diplomacy,
the nucleus of Mokone's Ethiopian Church eventually ended up as an
'Order of Ethiopia' in union with the mainstream South African
Anglican Church, but the impulse to honour the victorious empire spread
elsewhere through a great variety of African-initiated Churches. A parallel urge to look for a truly African historic episcopal succession led some
African Christians to form congregations under the jurisdiction of the
tiny Church presided over by the Greek Orthodox Patriarch of Alexandria; but Ethiopia remained and remains the chief symbolic focus.[70]

When Fascist Italy sought to avenge the shame of Adwa in its invasion and destructive occupation of Ethiopia in 1935 (including the wrecking of historic church buildings), reaction across Africa was sharp in condemning this outrage. As far away as Nigeria, Christians sneered at the Italian Pope for his lack of condemnation of fellow Italians: 'It should be remembered that the Pope is after all a human being like the ordinary run of mankind and therefore heir to human weaknesses, in spite of the traditional claim for him by his adherents of infallibility.'[71] Equally Ethiopia has inspired many Afro-Caribbeans and African-Americans to express their pride in Africa through their adherence to Rastafari. This syncretistic religious movement takes its title from the pre-coronation name of the last Ethiopian emperor, Haile Selassie, and it meticulously grounds its beliefs in Old and New Testament, in the fashion of Christian Churches through the centuries.

INDIA: THE GREAT REBELLION AND THE LIMITS OF COLONIAL MISSION

The stories of the great Asian empires suggest that although the relationship between Christian expansion and imperial expansion could be intimate, Christianity was as likely to be disruptive as helpful. From the 1790s most British Protestants did not share the particular preoccupation of the London Missionary Society with the Pacific; they viewed former Mughal India as the flagship of mission, since it contained Britain's largest and most rapidly expanding colonial territories. The leading eighteenth-century High Churchman Bishop Samuel Horsley, though a long-standing activist in the old Society for the Propagation of the Gospel and a supporter of missions in Britain's Caribbean colonies, opposed Indian missions, because he did not consider it part of God's plan for Britain to alter the religion of another country, especially since most of India was not then ruled by agents of George III.[72] Perhaps Evangelicals should have listened to Horsley, because in the long term India was to prove the biggest failure of European missionary enterprise.

Horsley's was not the only voice raising doubts. The Honourable East India Company (which governed British India at one remove from the British Crown until 1858) was initially extremely wary of disturbing Hindu and Islamic sensibilities. It prized the fact that the admirers of the reformist Muslim scholar Shah Wali-Allah were grudgingly cooperating with British rule. The Company went out of its way to respect Hindu practice, with certain exceptions such as widow-burning which offended European notions of cruelty. Then Evangelical pressure in the British Parliament – another campaign led by William Wilberforce, culminating in success in 1813 – gave the Company no choice but to allow missionaries into its territories.[73] An Anglican bishopric was set up in Calcutta, over the next three decades acquiring a stately Gothic cathedral straight out of provincial England, designed by a military engineer. Evangelicals gradually gained influence within Company government as in other colonial territories of the British Crown's own empire. From 1805 the Company's English administrators were prepared for government in its English training college at Haileybury, among whose staff Evangelicals were prominent, and by the 1830s these boys were in positions of executive power. They were administrators of an organization which already in 1815, according to one well-informed contemporary commentator, ruled the lives of forty million people: around 65 per cent of all the people in the British Empire.[74] What a prospect opened up for Christian mission!

Company policy steadily moved towards favouring Christianity at the expense of existing Indian religion. Protestant missionaries were very willing to fund the provision of higher education, which both they and prominent members of the India Company administration increasingly saw as the way to produce a cooperative Westernized elite. By 1858 Lord Stanley's view from the India Office was that 'while professing religious neutrality we have departed widely from it in fact'. Now he was writing in reflective mood after a grave crisis for British rule the previous year: the Great Indian Rebellion, or first Indian War of Independence, long called by the British 'the Indian Mutiny'.[75] The most serious nineteenth-century uprising against any Western colonial power, it was partly triggered by efforts to promote Christianity in India, bringing Muslims and Hindus into alliance – famously, one other flashpoint for rebellion which promoted this cooperation was the rumour that bullets issued to Indian soldiers were greased with pig or cow fat, insulting both Hindus and Muslims. The figurehead for independence, the aged Bahadur Shah Zafar II, last member of the Muslim Mughal dynasty to reign in Delhi, proved a reluctant leader, but he did his best to discourage strict Muslims from alienating Hindus in the insurrection by demonstrations of their own intolerance like cow-killing.[76]

Even so, the British Indian Army overcame the rebellion partly because significant sections of Hindu and Muslim elites remained neutral in the conflict, despite having been leading voices in the hostility to Christian missions. That was a powerful incentive for the new British government of India abruptly to turn from the trajectory of supporting Christian expansion. Queen Victoria's proclamation ending Company rule in 1858 emphasized that the new government was under instruction to 'abstain from any interference with the religious belief or worship of any of our subjects', an important statement of policy on the part of a deeply serious Christian monarch whose personal feelings led in the other direction: it ran parallel to the legislation ending virtually all legal discrimination among Christians in Great Britain itself. Subject to the untidiness always associated with local implementation of policy at long distances from its origin, Christian missionaries were now stripped of official support in the largest colonial possession of the world's greatest power.[77]

By the end of the century more perceptive missionaries were realizing that Christian missionary work had not achieved the critical mass necessary to success in India. Like Catholics before them in the sixteenth and seventeenth centuries, Protestants found that the Indian caste system was a formidable barrier to promoting a religion whose rhetoric emphasized the breakdown of barriers among all those who followed Christ. British-run schools continued to flourish, but they did not deliver many converts or enough native Christian leadership to stimulate mass conversion. Indians took what they wanted from European education; Christian schools enjoyed a great success, but it was of a different order from that in similar Evangelical schools founded by the Church Missionary Societies in Egypt (see p. 890). There the intake had also been from an elite, but an elite already Christian. In India, few pupils were from Christian families, and few decided that they would take on a new faith, even while they benefited from Western culture. In fact the challenge to faith and intellect posed by the Christian onslaught had prompted Hindus to self-examination and eventually to self-confidence and pride in their heritage. They were aware and proud of a growing interest in their culture in the Christian West, ironically often as a result of their excellent education in Christian colleges.

From the beginning of the century, there had been correspondence and even meetings between a small number of outward-looking Indian religious leaders and European and American Unitarians, mutually impressed by the possibilities which their respective revolts against traditional understanding of religion might open up in their search for a common and greater religious truth, in which the constraints of particular cultures were left behind. These contacts were spearheaded by the reformist and controversially ecumenical Bengali Rammohun Roy (c. 1772–1833), who travelled across the oceans to Britain to defend the reforms of Hindu customs like widow-burning promoted by his former employees the East India Company; he died in Bristol, where the grand classical chapel built by prosperous Unitarian merchants in the city centre still proudly houses a plaque commemorating his life.[78] In the 1880s a growing self-confidence among Hindus encouraged a much wider 'Hindu renaissance' and a significant number of Hindu reconversions among Christian converts (conversion was indeed a borrowing of a Christian concept). The 'positivist' theories of the Western anticlerical philosopher Auguste Comte were among the influences in some modernizing reconstructions of Hindu faith which sought to sidestep priestly power but justify the continuing existence of the caste system.[79] Conversely Indian missionary struggles and setbacks bred a new spirit of humility among Christians. It was among Protestants in India that the impulse first arose to forget old historic differences between denominations which meant little in new settings and to seek a new unity. This was the chief origin of the twentieth-century ecumenical movement (see pp. 953–8).

CHINA, KOREA, JAPAN

The greatest Asian empire was China, ruled by the Qing dynasty. It tottered but did not quite fall during the nineteenth century, only just surviving determined efforts by first the British and then other Europeans and Americans to exploit its huge territory. The arrival of Christianity and interference by European powers identified with the Christian faith contributed to a catastrophic rebellion, and almost a century would follow from the collapse of the Qing in 1911 before the Churches could free themselves from association with imperial humiliation. The decay of the empire at the end of the eighteenth century gave opportunity both for Roman Catholics to pull together the surviving congregations of their old missions (see pp. 705–7) and for Protestants to begin their own assault on China for the first time. To this day, the official Chinese attitude to Catholicism is that it is different from 'Christianity' – that is, Protestantism – since the two religions arrived at different times in Chinese history. Protestant penetration was made possible by a series of treaties with European powers initiated by the British in 1842, the result of wars presenting a different face of Britain from that so lauded in Lecky's pronouncement on abolitionism. Simultaneous with that 'perfectly virtuous' act was a policy illustrating the selective imperial morality of the British, who made up their trade deficit with China by exporting opium grown in India.

The trade grew huge, and it led to a crisis of addiction throughout the Chinese Empire which the imperial authorities desperately tried to contain, chiefly with efforts to prohibit imports and destroy shipments of drugs as they arrived. Britain went to war in 1839 to defend its profits, and its technological superiority ensured military and naval victory. Missionaries arrived in association with this less than perfectly virtuous result, because the Treaty of Nanjing opening the trade once more in 1842 also reversed an imperial prohibition on Christian belief proclaimed a century before. A good many missionaries arrived entangled with the opium trade, sailing above holds stacked with chest on chest of the drug, and generally mission finances were kept afloat by the credit network maintained by the opium merchants – let alone funds which missions received directly from firms connected with the trade (that is, virtually any Western commercial enterprise trading with China).[80] For both Chinese people and their government, missionaries became associated with assaults on their fundamental assumptions about the world. The knowledge of military defeat and the social misery caused by the opium trade made ordinary Chinese not only hostile to missionaries but disgusted with their own regime; many remembered that the ruling Qing dynasty, Manchu in origin, was actually as foreign as their British and French tormentors.

A contradictory mixture of popular anger and fascination with Western culture fuelled the Taiping Rebellion, which broke out in 1850. Its first ideologue and leader, Hong Xiuquan, had four times failed in that traditionally indispensable key to success in China, the examinations necessary to enter the civil service. In a state of nervous breakdown, he took to reading Christian books, encouraged by a young American missionary. He became convinced that he was chosen by God for leadership, and he preached of his vision and of the redemptive power of Jesus. His movement embodied an incendiary combination of nostalgia for the Ming dynasty, traditional rebellious zeal to end corruption and a mélange of notions from Christian sources, including a drive to social equality – all united by Hong's continuing visions from God.[81] All over the world in mid-century, the sudden escalation of Western interference in traditional culture led to such ideological fusions, in which the Christian idea of the Last Days was a favourite galvanizing force, usually with devastating results. So in the same decade that saw the Taiping explosion, the Xhosa of South Africa tried to slaughter all their cattle; they were convinced by prophecies from the young girl Nongqawuse that they must remedy their impurities, in preparation for the return of a former Xhosa leader, allegedly now commanding the Russians against the British in the Crimean War, who would bring them a new abundance. Yet the Xhosa had found that only horrific hunger and death rewarded their delusional devotion; the same reward awaited the Taiping.[82]

China's huge scale magnified the effects of apocalypticism in the Taiping Rebellion. It took over most of central China, and proved far more traumatic even than India's Great Rebellion. Taiping means 'Great Peace', but this was the most destructive civil war in world history, far outstripping the contemporary American Civil War, and little outdone in mayhem by the Second World War a century later. The Taiping created an entire governmental structure, with a formidable army, but Hong Xiuquan's rapid accretion of power did nothing for his fragile mental state. He lapsed into passivity and withdrawal, his favourite reading the new Chinese translation of John Bunyan's Protestant classic *Pilgrim's Progress*. His Protestant cousin Hong Rengan, arriving at the Taiping capital of Nanjing in 1859 after years of residence in British-ruled Hong Kong, tried to pull the movement out of its antipathy to foreigners and create a more rational organization, combining the best in traditionally meritocratic government with what attracted him in European culture: this would be a thoroughly modernized China, based on the Taiping's new syncretistic faith and the Chinese version of the King James Bible. Even when Taiping military power collapsed in the wake of Hong Xiuquan's final illness in 1864, Hong Rengan, now a prisoner of the Imperial Army, obstinately reaffirmed his pride in his cousin and the 'display of divine power' which had sustained the movement for fourteen years. Flare-ups of resistance persisted for years, and although a combination of dogged provincial-led armies proved a good deal more effective against the rebels than central forces, the empire never recovered. Even while the war raged, a new round of unequal treaties with external powers in 1858–60 gave new freedoms to missionary work within the imperial boundaries.[83]

Chinese cultural misapprehensions were equalled by those of many missionaries who began work after 1842. Like Catholics before them, they mostly found the basic task of mastering the fearful complexity of the Chinese language humiliatingly difficult, and often their reaction was to externalize their own shortcomings. When they were not blaming the workings of Satan in Chinese culture, they were prone to deplore the inadequacies of Chinese languages to express subtle abstract concepts, rather than their own inability to do so in Chinese. More than Catholics, Protestant missionaries took a very negative view of the religion which Chinese culture had bred, so full of ritual and idolatry (just as bad as the papists, indeed). When the missionaries encountered Buddhism in China, with its rules on vegetarian diet and its monastic celibacy, they were especially reminded of the false vows with which the Catholic Church tyrannized its adherents. Heroic Western men battling with very real dangers in mission, they were comforted by the male stereotypes of their own world, taking great satisfaction in the eating of meat, which contrasted satisfyingly for them with feminized vegetarianism.[84]

Yet from the beginning, some missionaries did try to learn from earlier Catholic successes and failures, or discovered for themselves the same problems of working in a vastly alien culture. An early arrival in the British-occupied city of Amoy in the south-west coastal province of Fujian was the American Reformed minister John Talmage. He and a few like-minded colleagues created one of the earliest fully fledged Chinese Protestant Churches, including the first Protestant church building in China – but there was more than the accumulation of 'firsts' in Talmage's work. From as early as 1848 he determined to make foreign missionaries redundant and his congregations indigenous: at the same time as Henry Venn was not very successfully propagating the 'three-self' goal in West Africa (see pp. 884–6), Talmage was without fuss putting the principle into effect in Amoy. That was made easier by the openness of locals to outsiders: Amoy had been one of the earliest entry points for Europeans three centuries before, and now it was one of the treaty ports opened up by the Nanjing Treaty in 1847. Soon his congregations, fortified by a sensible amalgamation of American and English Presbyterian foundations, were electing Chinese elders in classic Presbyterian style, struggling towards self-support and taking on themselves the founding of new congregations.[85]

Talmage's indigenization strategy was repeated in much more publicized form by the Englishman Hudson Taylor, whom no Church missionary structure could control until he had created his own, not beholden to any Church – a creative reinterpretation of the zestfully schism-prone English Methodism of his youth. Breaking with the floundering Christian missionary society which had brought him to China, in 1865 he set up his own, the China Inland Mission, which would be based in China and seek no support but that of God himself. Taylor declared his organization's uncompromising hostility to the opium trade. His Mission would not allow itself to drift into debt, but neither would it campaign for funds through collections or appeals. Its missionaries would wear Chinese dress – including the women, a difficult matter for Europeans at the time – and its schools alongside its hospitals at Yantai (Chefoo) were designed to produce a new generation of children from Mission families who were to receive their education in China, rather than as was otherwise almost universally the norm, being sent back to Europe.[86]

In practice, the ideals were rather difficult to sustain. Such institutions as the Chefoo schools naturally require an infrastructure not that different in nature from other missionary societies, particularly when in later years the CIM claimed with some plausibility to be the largest missionary organization in the world – and it was odd that the Chefoo schools did not offer instruction in Chinese until 1917.[87] Taylor spent much of his time on publicity tours in Britain, somehow producing both missionaries and money despite himself. Yet the rhetoric was important. Behind it was Taylor's generosity of spirit: for instance, when his Mission suffered alongside others in the next great outburst of Chinese fury against foreigners, the Boxer Rebellion of 1900, he refused the compensation extorted from the imperial government for European organizations. And his missionaries followed Catholics into the expanses of China's countryside, rather than targeting cities, the scene of most Protestant missionary activity. His organization did maintain the distinctive feature that its workers could not expect to get a regular salary, and it continued to be good at enrolling those who were not by temperament natural team players.[88]

Beyond China were two kingdoms which had retreated into deliberate isolation during the seventeenth century, but were now forced to open their borders: Korea and Japan. Their relationship had always been tense, and Korea's experience of Japan was from repeated invasion; yet even given that history, the contrast in their reception of Christianity is extraordinary. When the American Commodore Perry brought his naval squadron to force openness on Japan in 1853, it was the beginning of a revolution in Japanese society which led to the restoration of imperial government in 1868, the end of two centuries of the Tokugawa shoguns' monopoly on real power. The arrival of the Americans was also followed by the surprised recognition that against all the odds, in quiet corners, a form of Christianity had survived the repression of the once flourishing Catholic Church in the archipelago (see pp. 707–9). Yet this revelation did not lead and has never yet led to a new flowering of Christianity in Japan. When the Japanese enthusiastically made selections from the Protestant West, those included their purchase of Japanese-language Bibles in very large quantities, which nevertheless inspired very few to make the leap into Christian conversion. A clue to the popularity of Bibles is to be found in the fact that Samuel Smiles's famous *Self-Help* also sold a million copies in its Japanese edition in the same period, far outclassing its sales in Britain and the USA. These books were part of a crash-course in the useful aspects of modernity, just as Japanese bureaucrats adopted Western dress when they went to work, and as Buddhist vegetarianism was violated by a fashion for eating beef, since beef seemed to have done so much good for the building up of empires by Westerners.[89]

Christian origins in Korea are a curious sport from the worldwide Christian expansion in the Counter-Reformation, which was experienced here remarkably late, just when elsewhere the Catholic tide had ebbed, and a mere decade before the great Protestant 'take-off' of the 1790s. Christianity was indigenously propagated in Korea from the unlikely base of the struggling and only semi-legal Catholic mission in the Chinese imperial capital, Beijing.[90] It experienced intense suffering and persecution such as Christianity had not known since the Japanese and Canadian missions of the seventeenth century; in the same decade that French Revolutionaries committed atrocities against Catholic Christians, Catholics were here pitted also against a hostile state. The Korean monarchy patronized a native shamanism much cross-fertilized by Buddhism and its guiding philosophy was a form of Confucianism long ago imported from China. By the late eighteenth century, the Korean state was in trouble, and seemed to be incapable of reconstruction after a series of natural disasters which, in combination with chronic misgovernment, saw the population actually falling. What did that say about Korean religion's capacity to protect this inward-looking kingdom? The question much perplexed reformist-minded members of Korea's scholar-bureaucrat elite (*yangban*), who, in Confucian fashion, regarded themselves as the divinely appointed guides of the realm.

One *yangban*, Yi Sŭng-hun, provided a new answer to this crisis of authority: while in Beijing serving as a diplomat, he was baptized a Catholic Christian and went home to propagate his faith. He was met with outrage (including from his father), accused of betraying his social position and proper respect for his ancestors, but it was by using family connections and social links with other reformists that he spread his faith.[91] At first the government regarded Catholicism as 'no more than a collateral sect of Buddha' and merely burned its books. 'Alas!' it lamented, in a fashion that later Korean Protestants might have found congenial. 'How could one replicate so easily the form of the Divine Being that is so far away and silent and orderless? What other crime could be more desecrating than the crime of worshipping a portrait of another human being in place of the Divine Being and calling it "Jesus"?'[92] The authorities were soon forced into more drastic action. From Yi Sŭng-hun's return in 1784 to the first great persecution of 1801, Korean Catholicism spread beyond its elite *yangban* origins to gain around ten thousand adherents – this with the help of just one resident Chinese priest from 1795, martyred in 1801. It was a distinctively lay beginning for a branch of the Church. The next priest did not surmount the formidable problems of entry to Korea till 1833; by now Rome had placed Korea under the auspices of the French Missions Etrangères de Paris, and it may have helped the acceptability of Catholic Christianity that France had no great military presence in East Asia. The contrast with the power of the Chinese and Japanese empires which had threatened to annihilate Korea for centuries was significant.

While Christianity expanded into the wider population still seeking deliverance from Korea's ongoing deprivations, the monarchy continued to pursue the total destruction of the alien religion. Thousands died or were tortured, the worst phase being the latest, in 1866–71. The many who faced suffering with extraordinary bravery had available to them the heritage of Tridentine Catholicism, with its stories of earlier martyrdoms and its world-denying ethos, but it is interesting to look past the emphases in contemporary Catholic accounts of persecutions to see what Christian activists did not take from the Tridentine heritage. Lifelong celibacy was not high among their goals; as in Africa, Korea's social structure made it both unacceptable and difficult to practise. For instance, only nine female virgins can be counted among the stories of sixty-three adult women martyrs and confessors gathered from the persecution of the Korean year *Kihae* (1839–40).[93] Given that clergy normally had to remain completely hidden before 1871, most of the burden of teaching fell on Catholic laity. This was a Catholicism in which the Latin Mass was necessarily an infrequent experience. The practice of lay baptism, which the Church has not always treated with much enthusiasm despite its theoretical acceptability, now became essential and common. Some lay baptizers also became preoccupied with baptizing the babies of non-Christian parents who were expected to die soon: not a matter which the Church authorities had urged on them.

Very early, Korean Christians showed a pride in their own cultural heritage, which they could contrast with the imported Chinese culture dominating the royal Court. To spread their message as widely as possible, they championed the use of the distinctive *han'gul* alphabetic script, invented in Korean Court circles in the fifteenth century, and they developed their own literature in this alphabet, so different from the Chinese pictogrammic system and long despised by the Korean elite. Christian vernacular use was the prelude to the general revival of *han'gul* in twentieth-century Korea. When (mainly American) Protestants arrived in the aftermath of the monarchy's belated and reluctant decision in the 1870s to open Korea's borders, they learned from the Catholic example, and emphasized local people's part in building the Church; in 1907 Presbyterians united to form a single national Presbytery, independent and self-governing. Christianity might have been associated, as in China, with the humiliation of a decaying and ineptly Westernizing monarchy by Western powers, but already it had established its indigenous character. It is not surprising that both Catholics and Protestants were significant in maintaining Korean national identity in the decades after Japanese armies had seized their country in 1910. Their defiance brought them new persecution before the liberation of 1945 and Koreans did not forget that. Christianity's place in Korean life and its capacity to reflect the nation's suffering and pride contrasted with the faith's lack of penetration in the culture of the occupying power, Japan. Here, then, Christianity was a symbol of resistance to colonialism, not its accompaniment. That consciousness has shaped the extraordinary dynamism of Korean Christianity in the last half-century.

AMERICA: THE NEW
PROTESTANT EMPIRE

In visiting the Christian experiences of East Asia, we have been exchanging the dominance of British activity for intervention by the new world Protestant power, the United States of America. Struggling at the beginning of the nineteenth century to the extent that the British dealt a humiliating defeat in the war of 1812 (with surprisingly little long-term repercussion), by the century's end the USA had spanned its own continent and was becoming a trans-Pacific power, on the verge of still greater things. As Federal government expanded west, Christianity experienced growth as vigorous as any in the nineteenth century. At the time of the Revolution, despite all the bustle of the Great Awakenings, only around 10 per cent of the American population were formal Church members, and a majority had no significant involvement in Church activities.[94] In 1815 active Church membership had grown to around a quarter of the population; by 1914 it was approaching half – this in a country which in the same period through immigration and natural growth had seen its numbers balloon from 8.4 million to 100 million. That growth reflected the dynamism, freedom, high literacy rates and opportunity available in this society, and the Christian religion seemed to owe its success to a competitive and innovative spirit as much as did American commerce and industry.[95] Americans were justifiably proud of themselves. It was easy to cast their pride in the language of their religion (and all the more reason to ignore the feelings of the Native Americans who stood in the way of further achievement blessed by providence). Even the laying down of the railroad could be part of God's grand design – witness a paean to its providential character in 1850 from a Yankee revivalist turned Episcopalian, Calvin Colton:

As the human family, at a very remote period of antiquity, was scattered about over the face of the earth, from the base of the Tower of Babel . . . so the people of all those languages, thus created, are now coming together again to enter another and a perpetual monument, not of human pride against heaven but of freedom against despotism; and to perfect this work, they require to be chained to us by a band of iron across this continent.[96]

The majority of the Republic's churchgoers, and the overwhelming majority in positions of power, were Protestants of some description, although the Roman Catholic Church also benefited hugely from immigration during the century and by around 1850 became America's largest single denomination. It is not surprising that, in the wake of the Revolution, entirely new Churches began to be founded – perhaps more puzzling, in fact, is that hardly any brand-new denominations had been created before 1776.[97] American Methodism was in effect the first of the new foundations, since it stonily ignored John Wesley's annoyance and gave itself episcopal organization in 1787, its Conference pointedly dropping its undertaking to follow the great man's commands in the matter. Methodists enjoyed with Baptists the lion's share of a new Protestant growth over several decades, which those looking back on it christened a Second Great Awakening. While Episcopalians mostly stood aloof, Puritan Churches in the north-east were partly drawn in.

New England Congregationalists were disorientated by their loss of established status and cultural leadership after playing such a crucial role in the Revolution, and they were divided in their attitude to their Reformed theological inheritance. Many of their influential leaders were still children of the Enlightenment, seeking a rational faith for a new Republic, and they led their congregations into Unitarianism. Others resisted that drift, took their stand on a generous reshaping of Reformed predestinarianism, and emphasized various campaigns for moral and social improvement which would Christianize the idealism of the Declaration of Independence. That was the Awakening for them. There was plenty for both sides to campaign about, especially slaveholding in the South (the North being spared the economic attractions of such exploitation) and alcohol temperance or total abstention. This latter cause, as elsewhere particularly beloved of women, entailed Evangelicals undertaking some heroic exegetical explaining away of Jesus's miracle of Cana turning water into wine. Prohibition was to have a fateful later consequence in the USA.[98]

Matters were less genteel in the South and in the growing tide of settlements west of the Appalachian Mountains. Here the revivals of the first Awakening were seen again, sweeping congregations past their ministers' expectations in wordless but often highly noisy expressions of apparent liturgical nihilism. Crowds gathered for communion in the frontier 'camp meeting' tradition stretching back to seventeenth-century Scotland and Ulster, but now they were running, singing, even barking in what were significantly termed 'exercises'. Protestantism was rediscovering physicality and spontaneity after its two-century diet of preachers' words and planned music, and the discovery came within an Evangelical mode which generally valued a common fervent style and proclamation of sin and redemption more than confessional background or history. Revivalism was firmly in Methodist, Baptist and Presbyterian culture already, so not only could they happily accommodate all this, but as ministers grappled to harness their congregations' startling releases of emotional energy, it was not worth worrying too much about denominational labels. In one of the first of these devotional explosions at Gasper River in Kentucky in 1800, a Presbyterian was host minister, but the preacher stirring the fire was a Methodist – Reformed and

Arminian side by side in front of the wailing crowd, Amazing Grace indeed to astonish Calvin or Melanchthon.[99] The voices of deist Founding Fathers seemed far away. Urban elites in Washington, Philadelphia and Boston would have to start taking notice of these people, because after all an increasing number of the menfolk among them had votes. American politicians have done well to keep an eye on the Evangelical constituency ever since.

Now among a proliferation of joyfully jerry-built churches, witnessing to new birth and discipline amid harsh and lawless farmscapes, with a dread of some very angry dispossessed Native Americans lurking on the horizon, there developed increasingly original forms of Christian experience. It was predictable that American Evangelical excitement should again look to the Last Days – if crowded and crapulous Regency England could produce apocalyptic fervour, how much more could a pure and open frontier? Surely America and not Old Europe was to be the setting for God's final drama: had not the great Jonathan Edwards given his blessing to that thought? One of those who gave an answer emphatically in the affirmative, William Miller, was himself a one-man exemplar of Protestant America's spiritual trajectory: rejecting his Baptist upbringing for the reasonable faith of deism in Vermont's remote New England farming country, moving into revivalism via his anxious search for evidence of the Last Days in his King James Bible (noting Archbishop Ussher's dates in its margins), ordained by the Baptists, preaching his startling message through the nation that the Advent of Christ was due in 1843 – much excitement – then 1844 – even more excitement – and then followed the Great Disappointment.

For true apocalypticists there is no giving up hope, although Miller, now scorned by the Baptists, retired to Vermont to contain his chagrin with a handful of followers. A welter of arguments over a decade produced one of the nineteenth century's many visionary teenage girls, the prophetess Ellen G. Harmon (soon to be the bride of Adventist James White). Cut-price printing presses aided Mrs White's urgent campaign to share roughly two thousand of her visions with the public, not to mention her decided opinions about sensible diet. What now became known as Seventh-Day Adventism flourished once more; like the Seventh-Day Baptists before it, it observed as its holy day of rest not Sunday but Saturday, the Jewish Sabbath. Modern vegetarianism, a cause earlier championed by radical English Evangelicals, now found its master salesman in Mrs White's Adventist benefactor and collaborator, Dr John H. Kellogg, whose breakfast cereals and benevolence brought lasting and worldwide prosperity to the Adventist Church.[100] Miller's prophecies have continued to fertilize the imaginations of drifting but compelling personalities like himself. One Millerite schism produced the Jehovah's Witnesses: millenarian, pacifist and with strong views against blood transfusions. Another recent prophet, Vernon Howell, was driven to rename himself David Koresh (that is the Persian King Cyrus, liberator of the Jews from Babylon), and he brought his own terrible Last Days on those who believed in him at Waco in Texas in 1993. Beyond that hideously mismanaged clash between Koresh's followers and the Federal government came Timothy McVeigh's equally ghastly act of revenge for Koresh two years later in the Oklahoma City bombing: a grim legacy for Miller alongside the corn flakes.[101]

There was plenty more creative reconstruction of Christianity in this most industrious and ingenious of Western societies. Spiritualism and the Church of Christ Scientist (products of yet more visionary women) both spread themselves from the USA through the Western world and beyond. Yet of all new departures amid the Second Awakenings, the most radical was the work of Joseph Smith, who may be seen as one of a chain of gifted young people in the nineteenth century applying their gifts to escaping the deprivation and social uncertainty in which they found themselves, both exploiting and inspired by the polychrome religious turbulence of their age.[102] Hong Xiuquan, nine years younger than Smith, was another (see pp. 896–7). Smith's creation of a Heavenly Kingdom proved more long-lasting and less destructive than the Taiping, though likewise it brought him premature and violent death. Born in rural poverty in Vermont (not far from where Miller was beginning his married life) and pursued by poverty in his New York State childhood which deprived him of a decent education, Smith developed a keen interest in treasure-hunting amid a landscape haunted by Native American earthworks, devouring what conversation and what books (the Bible naturally among them) came his way. The boy, both dreamer and likeable extrovert, on the edge of so many cultures – Evangelicalism, self-improvement, popular history and archaeology, Freemasonry – constructed out of them a lost world as wonderful as that future paradise which confronted Hong Xiuquan.[103]

Shortly after Smith's marriage in 1827, he had the first of a series of visits from a heavenly being in white, Moroni, who, according to Smith, was a former inhabitant of the Americas. Moroni took him to a secret store of inscribed golden plates. Smith was the only person definitely to view the plates, and their eventual removal was as angelic as their excavation; but the message which the semi-literate twenty-two-year-old translated into King James Bible English (his newly wed and devoted wife, Emma, and later two friends taking his dictation the other side of a curtain) was a formidably long text. It was published in 1830. The Book, written long before largely by Moroni's father, Mormon, was the story of God's people, their enemies and their eventual extinction in the fourth century CE. Yet these were no Israelites or Philistines, but Americans, and the enemies who destroyed them were the native peoples whom Smith's society called Red Indians.[104] Now the spiritual descendants of Mormon were called to restore their heritage before the Last Days. Fawn M. Brodie, whose classic life of Smith earned her excommunication from the Mormon Church, saw the Book of Mormon as 'one of the earliest examples of frontier fiction, the first long Yankee narrative that owes nothing to English literary fashions'.[105] There was quite a genre of 'lost race' novels at the time. A century on, J. R. R. Tolkien's *Lord of the Rings* saga formed an English Catholic parallel, conscious or unconscious, to Smith's work. Tolkien's story-telling has many of the same characteristics as the Book of Mormon, although most people today would find Tolkien's prose a good deal more readable.

So with Smith's inspiration, the Mormons took shape: the Church of Jesus Christ of Latter-Day Saints, regarding itself as a restoration of an authentic Christianity otherwise lost. It moved en bloc, as so many utopian groups then did, to found a new ideal community on the frontier. The first stop in Ohio proved only one in a series of moves, because Smith and his leadership were prone to involve themselves deeply in state politics and risky business ventures, and their ambitions for power frightened and infuriated their neighbours. Finally Smith, now in charge of his own private army in Illinois, was fortified by fresh revelations to declare his candidacy in the 1844 presidential election. After further confrontations with the forces of unbelief, vigilantes shot him and his brother dead in an Illinois jail, while he was awaiting trial on charges of intimidating a hostile local newspaper out of existence. Yet this was not the end for the Mormons. One of Smith's long-standing lieutenants, Brigham Young, Hong Rengan to Smith's Hong Xiuquan, seized the initiative and led the battered faithful on the final journey which would save their movement, at a cost of a hundred days' westwards travel by wagon to Utah. Young would have liked a territory to rival the Taiping conquest in scale, but he had to settle for the wilderness that the United States government allowed him. There was a long and stormy path to wary acceptance by wider American society, not least because of one of

Smith's later revelations, posthumously released to the public in 1852, which had interesting resonances with the battles then going on in Protestant missions in Africa. He had been told that he must authorize polygamy.

Brigham Young reminisced in later life that he 'desired the grave' when first informed of this in 1843, but he later implemented it thoroughly in his own life, with as much public decorum as the nineteenth century would wish. As one of his less reverential biographers observed, Young's home in Salt Lake City 'resembled a New England household on a larger scale. Instead of one superficially forbidding lady in blacks or grays, there were nineteen of them'. The widowed Mrs Emma Smith, previously much tried by Prophet Smith's own clandestine accumulation of wives, married again; but not to a Mormon.[106] It was 1890 before the mainstream of the Church laid polygamy aside, and plenty of Mormons did not acknowledge that decision (some still do not, in carefully maintained seclusion in Utah and Arizona), but Utah still became a full state in 1896.[107]

If polygamy proved a casualty of external nineteenth-century social assumptions, the end of the twentieth century saw another incursion of external liberal values when, in 1978, a revelation allowed men of Negro descent to take their place among whites in the universal priesthood allotted to all adult Mormon men – the original ban is of contested origin.[108] Wholesome prosperity such as the youthful Smith might have envied has become a worldwide Mormon speciality, together with a systematic approach to spreading the message which has hardly been equalled in the Christianity which reserves itself the description Evangelical. The Mormons' doctrinal interest in genealogy, motivated by their belief in posthumous baptism of ancestors, has exercised a powerful appeal on those whose history is based on migration from another country. In the United States, its growth has been such that it has a good claim to be America's fourth-largest Christian denomination.[109]

Behind all this nationwide outburst of energetic service of a Protestant God, a shadow lay across the expanding Republic. The British Parliament resolved the question of slavery in 1833; it took a civil war to do so in America. Before that, the Evangelical nation which shared the same rhetoric of redemption and sang the same hymns was split three ways: a white grouping (with its strength in the Northern States) repeated the arguments of eighteenth-century abolitionists with increasing anger; an equally angry defence of white Southerners' slaveholding recycled all the arguments that the Bible and the Enlightenment had provided; and lastly African-American Churches, which served both the enfranchised and the enslaved, made common cause with white Northern abolition-ists. Among Southern whites, the defence of slavery slid into a defence of white supremacy, since that was a useful way to unite the white population behind a coherent ideology; most Southerners did not actually own slaves, and had no necessary interest in defending that institution alone.[110]

Some American Churches split over the issue, including the largest, the Methodists and the Baptists, in the 1840s.[111] The border was very clearly marked out by state boundaries, with the Quaker fountainhead of abolitionism, Pennsylvania, next to slaveholding Maryland. The ten-sions exploded into fighting between the Federal government and the Confederate Southern States in 1861, ostensibly not about slavery but about individual states' rights to make decisions on slavery for them-selves. The Republican president who led the Federal war effort, Abraham Lincoln, was a rationalist Unitarian who had left behind his childhood strict Calvinist Baptist faith for something more like the cool creeds of the most prominent Founding Fathers, but that did not lessen his commitment to the war as a profoundly Christian moral cause.[112] Already the rhetoric of the struggle had been cast in terms of Christian moral crusade, thanks to the barely sane actions of a fervent Calvinist from a family long committed to the abolitionist cause, John Brown.

Brown came from the same generation as Joseph Smith, and he remains just as controversial a figure, though nature endowed him with more potential than Smith for looking like an Old Testament prophet (see Plate 64). Proud of a New England Puritan heritage but unusual among abolitionists in embracing violence for the cause amid the rising tide of violence in the Midwest, he reversed the dictum of the High Priest Caiaphas on the death of Jesus, proclaiming that 'it was better that a score of bad men should die than that one man who came here to make Kansas a Free State should be driven out'. Accordingly in 1856 he was responsible for the kidnapping and murder of five pro-slavery activists, but despite that hardly defensible crime, his Northern canonization as an abolitionist martyr came as a result of his seizure of an undefended Federal arsenal at Harpers Ferry three years later.[113] When the raid failed to arouse a black insurrection, Brown sat tight in the arsenal and waited to be martyred, which the Commonwealth of Virginia duly did, for the moment casting oblivion over the crazy character of his campaign. A Massachusetts newspaper editorial picked up the mood: 'no event . . . could so deepen the moral hostility of the people of the free states to slavery as this execution'.[114] The Northern soldiers' spontaneously composed verses about John Brown's body, with their unforgettably jaunty camp meeting tune, were turned during the course of the war towards the Boston abolitionist Julia Ward Howe's more decorous but still stirring 'Battle Hymn of the Republic', in which her words about Christ might be reapplied to Brown: 'As he died to make men holy, let us die to make men free.'[115]

During the course of the war, a presidential proclamation declared slavery abolished (though only in the Confederate States fighting the Northerners), a move ratified and extended throughout the Union by Congress after the final defeat of the South, in the Thirteenth Amendment to the American Constitution. The suddenness of the change in Southern society, the freeing of four million human beings, was a deep trauma to add to the sheer destructiveness and death of the war itself: the end of an institution which in 1861 had seemed to be flourishing and even expanding. After the Confederate surrender, many angry defeated Southerners took revenge on black Christians, even though they shared their Evangelical faith. They still saw them as inferior beings to whites, and still used the old biblical and Enlightenment arguments to justify themselves. They also viewed their own plight as that of an endangered victim culture. For the prominent Southern Baptist pastor in South Carolina and Alabama E. T. Winkler, that sense justified his defence of the Ku Klux Klan to Northern Baptists in 1872 as an example of necessary 'temporary organizations for the redress of intolerable grievances'. It was unlikely that he would apply the same argument to any temporary organizations which threatened blacks might form.[116] White control of the South and the allotting of second-class status to African-Americans were not effectively challenged until the 1950s, and much of the challenge arose from the black Churches, which now remained the only institution through which African-Americans could have any effect on politics. The scars persist in American society to this day.

Yet in the decades after the Civil War, movements arose which eventually gathered together all the varied strands of American religion and culture into a new force: Pentecostalism. Pentecostals take their name from the incident described in the Book of Acts when, at the Jewish feast of Pentecost, the Holy Spirit descended on the Apostles and they 'began to speak in other tongues', so that the huge variety of pilgrims gathered in Jerusalem could all hear them speaking in every language represented in the crowds.[117] Their roots are in the extraordinary variety of American Protestant religion and they have no single origin. Echoing in Pentecostalism are the jerking, barking, running 'exercises' of the Kentucky

Léonard Limosin, *Triumph of the Faith*, Limoges French enamel, 1560s. The chariot of
[A]ntoinette de Bourbon (1498–1583) is drawn by a heavenly cloud and doves of peace. Although
[she i]s a woman, her steadfast Catholic faith entitles her to hold a chalice and consecrated host;
[John] Calvin and Theodore Beza are among the heretics trampled below. This private propaganda
[piece] for the Guise dynasty reflects its hostility to the Valois royal family and religious compromises
[sought] by the Queen Mother Catherine de' Medici amid escalating French civil wars.

[D]uring the Emperor Charles V's controversial Interim settlement in 1554, the Croy Tapestry, now
[at G]reifswald University, Germany, was commissioned from Peter Heymans by Philipp I of Pomerania,
[son-]in-law of the defiant Lutheran Duke Johann the Constant. Based on a Lukas Cranach woodcut
[of 1]546, it shows Luther preaching, with the Pope in Hell, and contrasts conservative Duke Georg of
[Saxo]ny under the Ten Commandments with his cousin Johann the Constant under the Crucifix.

56. The Transfiguration of Christ, here depicted in an icon created for the cathedral of the Transfiguration in Pereslavl-Zallesky, Russia, in 1408 by the Byzantine immigrant Theophan the Greek, is a principal symbol of Hesychast spirituality. The disciples Peter, John and James lie in sleep, Peter just waking fearfully to behold the transfigured Lord conversing with Moses and Elijah about his coming death (Luke 9.28–35).

57. In the Capilla Real (Chapel Royal) in Granada, Spain, which houses the tombs of the conquerors Fernando and Isabel, the early sixteenth-century high altar reredos has scenes depicting their reconquest of the Moorish kingdom in 1492, including the mass baptism of defeated Muslims.

58. The seventeenth-century iconostasis in the Church of Saint Simeon Stylites in the Arbat district of Moscow, with its five tiers of icons, represents an advanced stage in elaboration of the iconostasis in the Russian Orthodox tradition.

59. The wedding of Martín García de Loyola (nephew of Ignatius) and Beatriz, great-niece to the Inka Tupac Amaru, in the Jesuit church in Cuzco: a symbol of the continuing status of the Inka élite in a Catholic setting and of the unpredictable impact of the *Conquistadores* on the New World.

60. The eighteenth-century village church of Our Lady of Tonantzintla, Mexico, built by local people, is one of the most exuberant products of the Baroque fusion between Tridentine Catholicism and indigenous central American culture. Tonantzin ('Little Mother') was a pre-conquest corn goddess who happily blended with the mother of the Christian God.

(*left*) 61. Saint Patrick, portrayed in Hounfor, a vodou temple in La Plaine on the northern outskirts of Port-au-Prince, Haiti. Patrick in Haiti continues to banish the Irish snakes beneath his feet. African enslaved peoples appreciated the fact that he too had been taken across the seas as a slave. The Catholic cult of saints proved malleable to religions brought to the New World from Africa.

(*below*) 62. Proudly displayed in the Moravian Archive building, Herrnhut, Germany, is Johann Valentin Haidt's portrait (1751) of a family shaped by the Moravian Brethren's worldwide mission. Rebekka, a mixed-race woman born into slavery in Antigua, had great trouble in obtaining baptism, from a Catholic priest. She founded the first Protestant African congregation in the New World. Her interracial marriage in the West Indies to Mattheus Freundlich, a missionary from Herrnhut, led to their imprisonment. Here she is shown with their daughter Anna-Maria and her West African second husband and fellow-missionary, Christian Protten.

63. William Holman Hunt's *Hireling Shepherd* (1851–2) can be read at many levels: charming pastoral, risqué seduction scene (for which it was criticized at the time) or allegory of Victorian England's religious divisions. Hunt explained that his wayward shepherd was a 'type' of 'muddle headed pastors who instead of performing their services to their flock .. discuss vain questions of no value to any human soul'.

64. J. Steuart Curry's *The Tragic Prelude* (1942), a terrifying mural in the State Capitol, Kansas City, is a rueful American meditation on the passions and Christian rhetoric lying behind the Civil War nearly a century before. It was not initially appreciated by all in Kansas, a reflection of the continuing fissures within American society. The Abolitionist John Brown brandishes a bible inscribed Alpha and Omega, as well as a rifle.

65. Subverting many devotional themes of Christian art, the Virgin Mary spanks the Christ Child, 1926. Watching through a window are the artist, Max Ernst, and his Surrealist friends André Breton and Paul Éluard. Symptomatic of modern doubt, it nevertheless reflects very ancient apocryphal Christian traditions about the childhood of Christ.

66. In a suburb of Accra, Ghana, the Twelve Apostles Church customarily holds its healing service on Fridays, dominated by women market traders, who have awarded themselves the day off. Gourd-calabashes banish evil spirits, and teenage drummers lead the music.

67. The Temple of Saint Sava, Belgrade, was begun in 1935 in the style of
Hagia Sophia in Constantinople, and work resumed under the rule of Slobodan
Milošević in 1985. A fine example of modern Christian political architecture, it
self-consciously embodies Serbian Orthodox nationhood. Here the congregation
mourns the assassinated Serbian Prime Minister Zoran Djindjić in 2003.

68. The Yoido Full Gospel Church, Seoul, South Korea, founded by Pentecostal
Pastor David Yonggi Cho, claims the largest single congregation in the world and
over three quarters of a million members worldwide, having started from a service
attended by six in 1958. The main auditorium can seat 26,000; there are several
packed services on Sundays.

camp meeting, which had their precedent in the extrovert emotion of the Moravians, but there is much more.

Besides the revivals of the years around 1800, a 'Holiness' movement sprang out of the teaching of the early Methodists, proclaiming that the Holy Spirit could bring an intense experience of holiness or sanctification into the everyday life of any believing Christian. While John Wesley had preached a doctrine of Christian perfection, it seems to have been John Fletcher, an Anglican priest of Swiss origins whom Wesley would have liked to have made his successor in leading the English Methodist Connexion, who first popularized a view of sanctification in the Christian life as being effected by a 'baptism with the Holy Ghost'. In the next century, the much-travelling American revivalist Mrs Phoebe Palmer developed these themes into a doctrine expressed in dramatic language of 'entire' or instant sanctification. Mainstream American Methodism did not find it easy to contain the Holiness Movement, which created yet more institutions in order to express itself.[118]

Reformed Christians, heirs of Jonathan Edwards, were also fascinated by the idea of this 'Baptism of the Holy Spirit' or 'Second Blessing', but their Reformed tradition made them wary of Wesleyan Holiness teaching about the possibility of instant perfection in the Christian life. They made a different contribution. Many continued to proclaim, like Edwards, that Christ would be returning soon in association with a thousand-year rule of perfection. However, they significantly modified his views on the millennium, developing a set of ideas generated by that strange Reformed byway which we have already encountered in British Evangelicalism: the self-styled 'Catholic Apostolic Church' inspired by Edward Irving (see p. 829). In its conferences at Albury the CAC had evolved a tidy scheme of a series of 'dispensations' structuring world history, a scheme just as comprehensive as the pronouncements of Joachim of Fiore; the dispensations would culminate (and that quite soon) in Christ's Second Coming before the millennium. Deeply interested in this dispensationalist scheme was a former Irish Anglican priest, John Nelson Darby, who left his Church for a loose grouping called the Brethren, among whom he became the most prominent leader.

Disillusioned with Anglicanism, Darby saw the future pattern of history in terms of apocalyptic and imminent struggle. He made two crucial assertions about millenarianism. First, in a notable innovation, he looked at Matthew 24.36–44 and saw there Jesus's prophecy of a 'Rapture' in which one man would be taken and one man left.[119] Second, completing the 'dispensations', he asserted that Christ would return to reveal the final mystery in this Rapture and lead the saints in the last thousand years, just as the Albury conferences had envisaged. So, to uncover a further specimen of theological in-talk, Darby's picture of Christ's coming was 'premillennial' and not post-millennial like Edwards's (see p. 759), and it did not encourage any sunny Enlightenment optimism about human prospects: only Christ could effectively change the world, not human effort. Premillennialism stressed division and separation within society, to gather in the elect, and its frostiness to Enlightenment projects of social reform contributed to that peculiar process by which 'liberal' has become a word of abuse in the United States, in sharp contrast to its esteem in European society. From the 1870s, this theology was promoted through the series of semi-institutional conferences held at Niagara-on-the-Lake in Canada and Keswick in northern England, and other gatherings connected with them (or often deliberately not connected – premillennialists have a habit of falling out with each other).[120] This was the milieu which also bred the defensive proclamations of the Fundamentalist movement (see pp. 862–3).

Amid this clash of Evangelicalisms, there remained the longing of Protestant blacks for full acceptance in American society, a widespread weariness at denominational barriers amid so much shared Evangelical rhetoric and an equally widespread instinct that Protestant emphasis on sermons and the intellectual understanding of the word of God did not give enough room for human emotion. Around 1900, speaking in 'tongues' began playing a major role: in a new enactment of the first Christian Pentecost described in Acts 2, 'tongues' created messages unrecognizable to the uninitiated, and expressing praise or worship to those within the community. The precedent was once more Irving's Catholic Apostolic Church, because it had first emerged from the excitement generated by the 'tongues' exhibited by the Scottish sisters Isabella and Mary Campbell (see p. 829). When Irving broke with the Church of Scotland, his newly founded Church continued the practice of speaking in tongues until the end of the 1870s, although it began fencing the practice around in 1847. The free expression of tongues had been effectively frozen out by an unpredictable development in the Catholic Apostolics' Church life, their penchant for some of the most elaborate liturgical ritual ever invented by a Western Church.[121]

The Catholic Apostolic Church itself was gradually killed off by its apocalyptic refusal to provide for ordination of subsequent generations of clergy after the first.[122] Yet the Catholic Apostolic example was not forgotten and splinter groups from it carried on the tradition of tongues.

There were other remarkable outbreaks of the same phenomenon around the world – for instance, in the Russian Empire in the 1850s during the Crimean War – a reflection of Christianity's growing globalization and the effects of sudden change in previously stable religious landscapes.[123] Here was an unstable balance of incompatible forces (who could be more incompatible than Arminians and Reformed?). What the Pentecostals did was to kidnap the concept of Spirit Baptism from other Evangelicals in the Holiness Movement and the Keswick Conference tradition. They then made it not a Second Blessing but a *third*, beyond conversion and sanctification. This Third Blessing would invariably be signalled by the sign of speaking in tongues. A favourite image of Pentecostals was to see the gift of tongues as the royal flag which flew whenever the king was in residence.[124]

Merely cataloguing various early emergences of Pentecostal spirit in the US around 1900 would do little to explain what happened. We can pick out particular moments, like the mixed-race congregation with its opportunities for black and female leadership, meeting in a rented former African Methodist church in Azusa Street in Los Angeles from 1906, which has become something of a founding myth to equal the first Pentecost in much writing of Pentecostal history. To give a fuller picture, it would be sensible to enrich the Azusa Street story with an account of the founding role of Charles Parham, the first Church leader to emphasize the central role of the gift of tongues in 'the Third Blessing' in 1901. His work has understandably been left in the shadows by later Pentecostals, considering his overt white racism, his eventual hostility to the Azusa Street events and his last decades of embittered obscurity after accusations of homosexuality were made against him.[125] We could perhaps point to coincidental circumstances: for instance, the trauma of the great San Francisco earthquake and fire in one of America's fastest-growing and most excitable states, although the first speaking in tongues in Azusa Street actually came twelve days before the earthquake struck in 1906. More generally, the spread around the world of news about what was happening would hardly have been possible in any previous age before the telegraph, telephone and steamship. It was indeed only two decades since a great event had first been reported all round the world almost immediately: the eruption of the volcano Krakatoa in Indonesia in 1883 was a story in American newspapers only a few hours later.[126]

Eventually Pentecostalism affected the older Churches too, as some of those drawn to the movement did not leave their existing Churches and formed 'charismatic' groups within them. 'Charisma' means a gift of grace – in this case, a gift of the Holy Spirit. The distinctive feature of Pentecostalism is its emphasis on the Holy Spirit. Historically the Spirit has been the Cinderella of the Christian doctrine of the Holy Trinity: bone of contention between Orthodox and Latin West, and frequently representing unpredictability and ecstasy within Christianity. So often the institutional Church has sought to domesticate the Holy Spirit and make it intelligible: the Spirit frees the emotions, goes beyond words. Pentecostalism sets the Spirit free – often with disastrous results, as fallible human beings decide for themselves that they best speak for the Spirit, or fall in love with the power of the Spirit and apply it to their own purposes. But the rise of Pentecostalism and its Charismatic offshoots was one of the greatest surprises of twentieth-century Christianity – in a century when most of the other surprises turned out to be unpleasant.

24
Not Peace but a Sword
(1914–60)

A WAR THAT KILLED CHRISTENDOM
(1914–18)

The most prominent pieces of furniture added during the twentieth century to the fine medieval church where my father was rector were a new pipe organ and a tall sideboard-like structure bearing a list of sixteen male names in alphabetical order. Both are Wetherden's memorials to its dead in the First World War, and it is significant that in this little Suffolk village, the parish church was then felt to be the right setting for community commemoration. So it was in my father's neighbouring parish of Haughley, where a stone churchyard cross with figures of Christ crucified, Mary and John tops another list (alphabetical by regiment) of twenty-nine dead men: a crushingly large number from a small place. Not all such memorials take Christian forms, but virtually every community or old-established company, school or college in the United Kingdom has one, almost always still carefully tended and once a year the focus for one of the last national rituals widely observed in Britain, the Service of Remembrance. They were overwhelmingly paid for by public subscription: 'the biggest communal arts project ever attempted'.[1] Their presence through the rest of Europe is likewise all-pervasive, although in many places they have fared less well than in Britain, because the political institutions whose soldiers fell have long disappeared, caught up and often discredited by the long-term effects of the war itself.[2] The greatest casualty commemorated in this multitude of crosses and symbols of war is the union between Christianity and secular power: Christendom itself. By the end of the 1960s, the alliance between emperors and bishops which Constantine had first generated was a ghost; a fifteen-hundred-year-old adventure was at an end.

The war which began in August 1914, triggered by complex diplomacy and a tangle of fears and aspirations, did not seem likely to set any such new patterns. It involved four Christian emperors – German and Austrian Kaisers, the Russian Tsar and the British King-Emperor[3] – but such rulers had habitually ignored their common faith to fight each other. They went to war over a long-standing cause of instability for Christendom: the gradual disintegration of the Ottoman Empire, or, more precisely, the competition to dominate its former Balkan conquests. The heir to the Austro-Hungarian thrones, the Archduke Francis Ferdinand, a devout Catholic keenly interested in the restoration of historic church buildings, was gunned down with his wife in Sarajevo, capital of the Habsburgs' most recently acquired province, Bosnia-Herzegovina. His murderers were part of an Orthodox-inspired movement to create a Greater Serbia which would include this religiously pluralistic territory. Beyond religion were power politics, ranging the Orthodox Tsar Nicholas II alongside the Protestant (and ethnically German) King-Emperor George V, in uncomfortable entente with an anticlerical Third French Republic. They acted in defensive nervousness, hoping to quell the expansionist ambitions of the new imperial Germany, which had encouraged its Habsburg ally to pressure Serbia, in order to confront Serbia's protector Russia. Religion lurked in unpredictable ways. When the German Kaiser's armies invaded Belgium to strike at the Franco-Russian alliance, they were violating the neutrality of a state formed in the 1830s specifically to accommodate the Roman Catholic faith of its inhabitants. Britain fought ostensibly to enforce that neutrality under guarantees that it had made to Belgium in 1839.

In summer 1914 the Second Socialist International tried in vain to summon up a cross-border solidarity of workers against the growing crisis; it found that far more were swayed by the rhetoric of nationalism backed up by the institutions of Christianity, which caused a continent-wide outpouring of popular enthusiasm for war. All sides excitedly coupled the theme of Christian faith with national unity as they launched their armies, none more so than the government of Kaiser Wilhelm II, who was also supreme Bishop of the Prussian Evangelical Church (see Plate 47). 'No lust for conquest prompts us – unshakeable determination inspires us to guard the place in which God has set us and all generations to come,' he proclaimed. 'You have read, Gentlemen, what I have said to my People from the Castle balcony. Here I say again: I know parties no more, I know nothing but a German!' The Kaiser's speech from the throne of August 1914 to the leaders of the Reichstag parties echoed the public proclamation drafted for the Emperor by the Imperial Chancellor Bethmann-Hollweg, aided by the great liberal Protestant historian Adolf von Harnack, Rector of Berlin University, now Royal Librarian, and ennobled only six months before. German Protestant theologians and academics, Harnack's colleagues, had internalized the new imperial ideal with remarkable and unedifying speed after the Hohenzollern triumph of 1870–71. At no time did they trumpet that more than in 1914 – very specifically, in a Proclamation of Ninety-three German Professors to the Cultural World. It says a good deal about the legacy of Wilhelm von Humboldt (see pp. 830–31) that German professors could take themselves that seriously.[4]

Some Anglican bishops could be heard making equally remarkable statements. The Bishop of London, Arthur Winnington-Ingram, in one sermon in Advent 1915 called on the British Army 'to kill the good as well as the bad, to kill the young men as well as the old'. At least Herbert Asquith, British Prime Minister, did not share the Kaiser's enthusiasm for bellicose sentiments from scholars and clerics, and styled Winnington-Ingram with elegant distaste 'an intensely silly bishop'. But the killing on all sides was as thorough as the Bishop of London had prescribed.[5] The four years of slaughter revealed where the power lay between nationalism and religion. When Pope Benedict XV used his studied neutrality to seek a negotiated peace in 1917, both sides ignored him, despite his outstanding record as a diplomat.[6] Just as symbolic were the desperate demands by the increasingly beleaguered German government to churches to sacrifice treasured items for the war effort. German parishioners watched in misery as their bells were carried away after being rung for the last time – the very bells which had rung out so cheerfully for the outbreak of war.[7]

Then in 1917 came the first fall of a Christian empire, the seat of the Russian Orthodox Church which had so long styled itself the Third Rome. Tsar Nicholas II was amiable, pious and well intentioned, but dull-wittedly autocratic – James Joyce neatly described Nicholas even before his downfall as having 'the face of a besotted Christ'.[8] The Tsar made the mistake of appointing himself as commander-in-chief in a war which he increasingly mismanaged, thus associating the Romanov dynasty intimately with the catastrophe into which Russia descended. At the centre of the empire, the Tsarina Alexandra was prominent in home government, to equally disastrous effect. Public outrage at the sense of drift focused on the faith-healing holy man Grigorii Rasputin, who had gained a hold over the Tsar and Tsarina because of his apparent

ability to control the haemophilia of the heir to the imperial throne.
Rasputin has been an object of much sensationalist fascination, not least
because of the Grand Guignol ghastliness of his assassination by furious
aristocrats in 1916, but it is as well to appreciate his ambiguity: pilgrim
on foot from Siberia to Mount Athos, contemptuous of social hierarchy,
treated with sympathy and respect by some senior churchmen (others
loathed him). Even in his drunkenness and promiscuity, Rasputin looks
remarkably like the Holy Fools whom we have met repeatedly in their
long journey from the eastern Mediterranean – and so his many admirers
saw him. Russian folk religion was returning to take its revenge on the
autocracy which had shackled its Church in Peter the Great's Holy
Synod.[9]

Rasputin's murder did not remedy the dire situation. 'Parastatal'
organizations – local councils, representatives of business, the Red Cross
– had been increasingly filling the gap left by the government's mal-
administration, and it was a combination of their leadership and the
terrible toll of death in the war which finally forced abdication on
the Tsar in March 1917; a Provisional Government followed.[10] For the
Orthodox Church, it was a moment of opportunity. It is a tribute to the
renewal and reflection that had been going on in the Church over
the previous decades, as part of Russia's development of grass-roots
representative institutions, that Church leaders now acted so swiftly
and with such vision. By August a council of bishops, clergy and laypeople had gathered in Moscow to make decisions for the whole Church,
something unprecedented in Russia's history. They elected the first patriarch for two centuries, since Peter the Great had brought an end to the
patriarchate. Tikhon Bellavin was a bishop who had spent nine years in
the United States, where he had been responsible for the setting up of
institutional structures for the Orthodox Church; many of his proposals
might now be brought back to this newly representative Church in
Russia. A swathe of reforming measures was agreed: laywomen were
accorded unprecedented opportunities in the Church's activity and
administration, and the council even gave time to sending messages of
friendship to the Church of England.[11]

Yet as Patriarch Tikhon was elected, in the background was the
sound of gunfire and bombardment: the Kremlin was under attack from
Bolshevik socialists. The Provisional Government in St Petersburg (now
Russified as Petrograd) had made no great effort to end the war, and
popular disillusion with its rule gave the Bolsheviks their chance to seize
power in October. They made peace with the central European emperors

to consolidate their own power against a broad coalition of opposition. The Bolsheviks were not fighting tsarist autocracy: that had already been dismantled. They saw themselves as instituting a new world order, and such visions are rarely conducive to tolerance of the past, or indeed of any contrary opinion. Their attitude was summed up in the words of Boris Pilnyak, a Russian novelist who, like so many other idealists of the Bolshevik Revolution, was eventually executed by those who turned the revolution into Stalin's Russia:

Our Revolution is a rebellion in the name of the conscious, rational, purposeful and dynamic principle of life, against the elemental, senseless biological automism of life: that is, against the peasant roots of our old Russian history, against its aimlessness, its non-technological character, against the holy and idiotic philosophy of Tolstoy's Karataev in *War and Peace*.[12]

For the Bolsheviks, the Church was the embodiment of the society which they were trying to destroy. Their detestation of Christianity was as extreme as that of the Jacobins in the French Revolution; the formal separation of Church and State in January 1918 was just one first step towards death and destruction, the Romanov family's murder being symbolic of so many others. The civil war which was already raging by then, and which ended in 1922 with Bolshevik victory, marked the beginning of seventy years for the Russian Orthodox Church which represent one of the worst betrayals of hope in the history of Christianity. During those terrible decades, the destruction of life and of the material beauty of church buildings and art outdid anything in Orthodox experience since the Mongol invasions; the Orthodox faithful were made strangers amid the culture which they had shaped over centuries. Patriarch Tikhon, desperately trying to protect his Church with no real assets at his disposal apart from the ability to forgive his enemies, eventually died under house arrest in 1925. It is likely that he was murdered by thugs commanded by a Bolshevik leader who was possibly the bastard son of a priest and in early life was one of the most unpromising of seminarians. Long before Tikhon's death, this Georgian gangster, who never fulfilled his mother's hopes that he might become a bishop, had adopted the pseudonym Josef Stalin.[13]

The Bolsheviks' hatred of religious practice extended far beyond the official Church. Of all the stories of Christian suffering in Russia after 1917, that of the Mennonites can stand for others because of the peculiar moral dilemma it presented for this sect, which since the Reformation had itself rejected the ideal of Christendom now in collapse. First gathered in the Netherlands in the 1530s by Menno Simons, a Frisian former priest sickened by the blood-soaked end to the siege of Münster (see pp. 623–4), Mennonites expressed their difference from the world around them by renouncing all forms of coercion or public violence, soldiering of course included. Their hard work and orderly peaceableness made them attractive colonists for the tsars, and by the time of the revolution hundreds of thousands lived in Mennonite communities, mostly in the Volga region. Their prosperity attracted Bolshevik and anarchist raids, both out of ideological hatred of 'bourgeois' farmers, and from simple greed or necessity – but there was another intoxicating element for bullies: the Mennonites would not fight back when attacked. Men were murdered, women raped, everything was stolen. For many of them, it was too much. They fought back and sent perpetrators of the outrages packing – but now they had to face the wrath of brethren and sisters who said that they were betraying Mennonite principles. When Russian Mennonites finally had the chance, most made new lives in communities in North America; but they did not forget the controversy. Bad feeling and arguments about the Russian civil war still beset quiet places in the prairies of Canada.[14]

The end of the war on Europe's other frontiers in late 1918 brought the collapse of three more empires. The twin Protestant and Catholic heirs of the Holy Roman Empire now quit their thrones, as the pressure of central European nationalisms led to the disintegration of the Austro-Hungarian monarchy and the shock of Germany's sudden capitulation in the West precipitated the overthrow of Kaiser Wilhelm. An array of impressively bewhiskered German princelings followed in their wake. The third to fall was the Ottoman Sultan, who had entered the war on the side of Germany and Austria, and who was ejected from his palaces in 1922; the caliphate was formally abolished two years later. Of all the European imperial crowned heads, only the British King-Emperor remained.[15]

The death throes of the Ottoman Empire led to further disasters for Orthodoxy and the ancient Miaphysite and Dyophysite Churches of the East. Nineteenth-century massacres caused by the new self-consciousness of Ottoman Islam were outclassed by what now happened in Anatolia and the Caucasus. From the beginning of the war, the reformist 'Young Turk' regime in Constantinople saw the Christians of the region as fifth columnists for Russia (with some justification) and was determined to neutralize them. The measures it authorized were increasingly extreme, to the point that it is difficult to find historians outside Turkey who are not prepared to use the word genocide to

23. *Europe in 1914*

describe the deaths of more than a million Armenian Christians between
1915 and 1916. One city, Van, largely Armenian in 1914, simply does
not exist on the site that it then occupied.[16] Britain, Russia and France
appealed to the Turks during the war to end these atrocities, threatening
post-war retribution to those involved and denouncing these 'new crimes
of Turkey against humanity and civilization'. The word 'humanity' had
significantly replaced 'Christianity' in an earlier draft of the statement,
and there was little comfort for Christian victims in the peace settlements
which followed.[17] No official statement was made about the Armenian
holocaust.

24. *Europe in 1922*

FINLAND

●Leningrad

ESTONIA

LATVIA

●Moscow

LITHUANIA

SOVIET UNION

EAST
RUSSIA

POLAND

SLOVAKIA

Budapest

GARY

ROUMANIA

●Belgrade

Danube

LAVIA

BULGARIA

ALBANIA

●Istanbul

●Ankara

GREECE

TURKEY

●Athens

SYRIA
and
LEBANON

PERSIA

IRAQ

CYPRUS
(Br)

TRANS-
JORDAN

PALESTINE

SAUDI ARABIA

Besides this catastrophe was that of the Dyophysites in Mesopotamia and the mountains of eastern Turkey who, since the mid-nineteenth century, had exploited the findings of Western archaeology in the Middle East and rebranded themselves as 'Assyrian Christians'. While general war raged, they sought to carve out a national homeland to embody their new identity, in the face of massacres by Turks and Kurds. They were fortified by military victories against the Turks led by the brilliant Assyrian military leader Agha Petros, but after the war the British reneged on previous promises. Instead Assyrians found themselves part of a newly constructed multi-ethnic British puppet kingdom, Iraq, dominated by Muslims, where they fared increasingly badly at the hands of the Hashemite monarchy and its Republican successors. The two Gulf Wars at the turn of the twentieth and twenty-first centuries brought them fresh miseries, especially the second, which has sent new streams of scapegoated refugees out of Iraqi territory.[18]

The reason why the victorious Allies fell silent on the Armenians and betrayed the Assyrians had to do with a sudden post-war series of victories by Turkey. These brought further disaster for Eastern Christianity, in this case Greek Orthodoxy. With the Ottoman Empire prostrate, Greek armies occupied much of western Anatolia (Asia Minor), continuing various Balkan land-grabs from the Ottomans which they had carried out in the years immediately before 1914. They exultantly sought to enforce the terms of the Treaty of Sèvres of 1920 with the defeated empire; this allotted them substantial parts of Anatolia's west coast as part of a Greater Greece. Turkish armies then rallied under Mustapha Kemal, who would soon restyle himself as Kemal 'Atatürk', and in September 1922, as the routed Greeks fled, Smyrna, one of the greatest cities in the Greek-speaking world, was near-obliterated by fire (see Plate 51). In the flames perished Asia Minor's nineteen centuries of Christian culture, and ten earlier centuries of Greek civilization. A Treaty of Lausanne in 1923 overturned the agreements of Sèvres, and the flood of refugees in both directions across the Aegean Sea was formalized into population exchanges on the basis of religion, not language. The effect was that religious identity transmuted into national identity: Christians became Greeks regardless of what language they then spoke, and Muslims became Turks. Within a few years, virtually all the mosques of Athens had been levelled to the ground, while the toll of church ruination in Asia Minor is still all too obvious. It was a trauma so deep that in neither country has it been possible to talk freely about refugee ancestry until very recent years.[19]

The only significant exception to the general exchange, and that tragically short-lived, was Istanbul, as the wider world learned to call Constantinople in the 1930s. The Greek and Orthodox population of the city was exempted from exile, and in a commendable and surprising display of swift reconciliation, Atatürk, now leader of a Turkish Republic, and the veteran Greek Prime Minister Eleftherios Venizelos sealed this agreement in 1930. Alas, the one continuing major territorial dispute between Greece and Turkey, over the future of ethnically divided Cyprus, poisoned the deal in little more than two decades. As the British sought unhappily to scramble out of colonial rule in Cyprus in the 1950s, and Greeks demanded the island's union with the kingdom of Greece, Turkish anger mounted. In 1955 the Turkish government of Adnan Menderes, on the most charitable interpretation, did nothing to stop two days of vicious and well-organized pogroms against Greeks in Istanbul; the flashpoint was the false rumour that Atatürk's birthplace in Thessaloniki (the ancient Thessalonica) had been burned down by the Greeks. There were death and rape throughout the city, and the wrecking of most of what survived of Istanbul's heritage of Greek Orthodox churches. In their wake, a Greek citizen population of some 300,000 in 1924 and 111,200 in 1934 has now been reduced to a probable figure of two thousand or less. The present Oecumenical Patriarch is a lonely figure in his palace in the Phanar. He is an international ecclesiastical statesman rightly much respected, but like his predecessors and presumably successors, he was chosen from the now tiny native Orthodox Turkish citizen population, and he does not even possess a working seminary for the training of his clergy. This near-death of Orthodox Christianity in the Second Rome is a direct result of the First World War, just as was the martyrdom of the Third Rome.[20]

The only substantial Christian refuge to be created in the 1923 peace settlements at Lausanne owed its existence to the Third French Republic, which might seem a paradox until one remembers the Republicans' instrumental attitude to the Church in French colonies as an agent of French cultural hegemony.[21] France was anxious to maintain its traditional strong influence in the Middle East, which dated back to the seventeenth century, when the French Crown arrogated to itself the role of protector of Levantine Christians. Accordingly it secured the creation of a French mandate over a coastal and mountainous region described as the Lebanon, whose boundaries closely followed the strength of the population of Maronite Christians – an indigenous Church of the area, originally Monothelete in its views on the nature of Christ (see

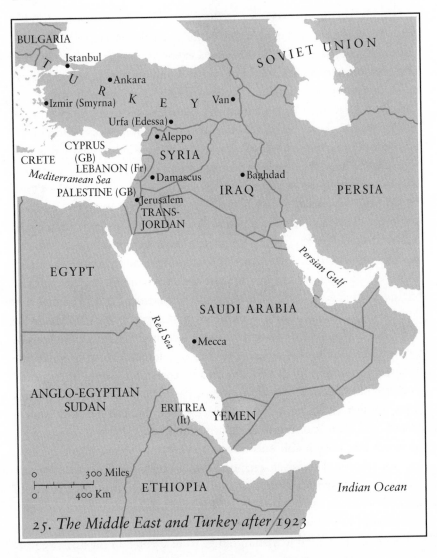

25. *The Middle East and Turkey after 1923*

pp. 441–2), but in union with Roman Catholicism since the twelfth century. When the Lebanon later gained its independence in 1943, seizing on a moment of French disarray in the Second World War, the new republic formulated a constitution carefully designed to balance the interests of Christians against other confessional groups. It succeeded for some three decades, before unravelling in civil war; the consequences of that breakdown are still unfolding.[22]

On the eastern frontier of the new Turkish Republic, the shattered remnants of Christianity were also wretchedly caught up in international politics. Virtually all remaining Armenians fled, leaving eloquent ruins of Christian churches behind them, and the Dyophysites of the Church of the East were soon mostly in Iraq. In 1924 the Miaphysite or Syriac Orthodox people of Urfa (Edessa) faced the consequences of a successful Turkish counter-attack against French invading armies. Some stayed within the new Turkish Republic, around the holy mountains of Tūr 'Abdīn, where their monasteries still do their best to guard the life of prayer dating back more than fifteen centuries. Urfa itself, cradle of Christianity's alliance with monarchy, now has virtually no Christians left. Most Urfalese Syriac Orthodox fled over the new border into what was now the French mandated territory of Syria, and there in the city of Aleppo they painfully constructed a new life and preserved as much as they could from the past, including their ancient and unique musical tradition, probably the oldest in the Christian world.

The proudly maintained Syriac Orthodox church of St George in Aleppo boasts a pastiche-Assyrian bas-relief of King Abgar receiving the *Mandylion* (see pp. 180–81), as well a reproduction of the version of the *Mandylion* in Rome, presented to the congregation by the Pope himself. There are also two touching and unexpected relics of old Edessa: the church bell and a massive crystal chandelier, both given to the Edessan Christians by Queen-Empress Victoria of the United Kingdom. What trouble it must have taken to transport these unwieldy objects over the border amid the chaos and terror of 1924! Yet one can understand why. The British Empire then seemed a possible protector for an eventual return to the homeland and these would be useful symbols for an appeal to the British. The Urfalese Christians were not to know all was not what it seemed with that great imperial power.

GREAT BRITAIN: THE LAST YEARS
OF CHRISTIAN EMPIRE

It was not yet publicly apparent that victorious Great Britain had been seriously undermined by the conflict of 1914–18. Its empire was augmented by virtually all of Germany's colonial possessions, together with large sections of the Ottoman Empire, mostly in the guise of 'mandates' from the newly established League of Nations, plus some client kingdoms. Alone among the major combatants in the European war, Britain retained its pre-war combination of monarchy and distinct national established Churches – Anglican in England, Presbyterian in Scotland –

so its Christianity, lacking the shock of defeat or regime change, had a greater inclination to enjoy the luxury of moderation than elsewhere. Yet Britain could not escape the general trauma of the war. Sensible British politicians saw that British power was not what it had been, particularly in relation to their belated war ally, the United States. As the world's largest imperial power, Britain was bound to be affected by the general perception among colonized peoples that they had been dragged into a conflict which was not their concern. Whatever moral authority their colonial masters possessed was severely tarnished, and that did not bode well for Britain's comparatively recent worldwide imperial project. Moreover, the British Isles themselves were poisoned by a civil war which the general war had only postponed, and whose origins were religious, in Ireland. The Protestants, predominant in the north-eastern Irish counties of Ulster, refused to accept any deal for Home Rule across the island which would leave them in the hands of a Roman Catholic majority, and open violence broke out only a few months after the worldwide Armistice of November 1918.

Protestant Unionists were an unstable coalition, particularly in north-eastern Ireland. Here the traditional 'Anglo-Irish' elite of the (Anglican) Church of Ireland had to make common cause with a truculently independent Ulster-Scots Presbyterianism, which shaded into a revivalism strongly linked to the fervour of the American Awakenings. Nevertheless, shared Protestant anger at British government concessions on Home Rule led significant numbers in 1914 to threaten to defend themselves by force, and when thousands of Protestant Ulstermen subsequently joined up for the British Army, their eyes were on the defence of Ulster as much as of the empire. Their slaughter in horrific numbers in the trench warfare of the Battle of the Somme in 1916, a particular holocaust of Irish regiments, only strengthened the determination of Ulster Protestants to give no ground.

As Irish nationalist support grew and shouldered aside earlier more moderate Home Rule politicians, island-wide violence mounted. Partition became inevitable, though the decision led to a further vicious civil war in the south between nationalists who accepted and those who rejected the partition deal on offer from the British government. The British Isles ceased to be a United Kingdom in 1922, although southern Ireland ungraciously accepted an increasingly threadbare figleaf of monarchical authority until 1949. Northern Ireland consolidated itself into a state where majority Protestant rule would be entrenched – not least because both Catholics and Protestants resisted the attempt of the Westminster government to create truly non-sectarian education at primary school level; thanks to the Catholic Church's firm instructions, Catholic parents overwhelmingly boycotted state secondary schools, leaving them to Protestants.[23]

Amid the crisis of Northern Ireland's birth in 1920–23, Presbyterian society was electrified by a series of revivals conducted by a classic representative of extrovert Ulster-American fundamentalism, William P. Nicholson: hardbitten, ebullient, contemptuous of nuance – full of Gospel fire, others might say. Nicholson is a problematic figure. He has been credited with saving Ulster from all-out war by turning 'born-again' gunmen away from violence, but equally, as with previous Ulster revivalists, he could be seen as confirming the siege mentality of working-class Ulster Protestantism. In later life, he gave his blessing to one in a new generation of populist Presbyterians who was destined to spend much of a long and politically charged ministry amid a further Ulster civil war. Ian Paisley, founder of a self-styled Free Presbyterian Church, reminisced that Nicholson prayed that Paisley might be given a tongue as sharp as a cow's in the service of the Gospel. Paisley if not God hearkened to that prayer, and despite the remarkable turnaround which crowned and then swiftly ended his political career in old age, he can shoulder much of the responsibility for the *immobilisme* of Ulster politics through three decades of violence at the end of the twentieth century.[24]

The virulent anti-Catholicism of interwar Northern Ireland was echoed elsewhere in the Atlantic Isles, especially in Wales and Scotland. Welsh Nonconformist Protestants were proud of their hegemony in Welsh life, but also conscious of their congregations ebbing, despite a nationwide burst of Pentecostal-related revival in 1904–5. That heightened their alarm at a growing Catholic presence in Wales, swollen by Irish and other immigrants. The Wesleyan minister Lewis Edwards in 1931 was not exceptional in his ready public affirmation, 'There is no disguising the fact that Roman Catholics are opposed to everything the Welsh people hold dear in their national life.'[25] Similar circumstances led a committee of the General Assembly of the (Presbyterian) Church of Scotland in 1923 to express fears for Scottish culture under the onslaught of Irish immigrants. They stated, with an open racism coming strangely from ethnically hybrid Scotland, 'The nations that are homogeneous in Faith and ideas, that have maintained unity of race, have ever been the most prosperous, and to them the Almighty had committed the highest tasks, and has granted the largest measure of success in achieving them.' A search for solidarity against Catholicism was an important element in a successful Reunion of 1929 between the two halves of the Church of Scotland riven in the Disruption of 1843 (see p. 844), and Reunion was combined with calls to the government to legislate to reduce Scotland's Irish immigrant community. As late as 1935 there were anti-Catholic riots in Edinburgh.[26]

Nor was England exempt from this mood, smarting as it was from the humiliating loss of one of its subordinate partners in the Atlantic archipelago. When the Church of England's bishops tried to end Anglican contention about the liturgy between Anglo-Catholics and Evangelicals by producing a new Prayer Book, their carefully calibrated efforts twenty years in preparation were twice defeated in Parliament in 1927–8, amid much talk of popery.[27] Admittedly, MPs from beyond England (and one Communist Parsee representing Battersea North) were crucial in the vote which produced this defeat on a matter which strictly speaking concerned only the English, but popular anti-Catholicism ran deep in English consciousness.[28] Respectable England was 'Church', or it was 'Chapel', and both were Protestant – with the uncomfortable complication of Anglo-Catholicism, making its own way in the Church of England (see Plate 49).

For all these groups, Rome was an alien world, liable to pollute the English way of life – although, curiously, even the most self-consciously Protestant army officer found no difficulty in calling army chaplains 'padre', since the British Indian Army had long used the term, following East India Company custom. Probably such Colonel Blimps did not realize that this popish usage had been borrowed from the Portuguese Catholic presence in India.[29] Far more acceptable than Catholicism to many 'Low Church' Anglicans was Freemasonry: Geoffrey Fisher, Archbishop of Canterbury in the late 1940s and 1950s, was an enthusiastic Mason, and fiercely protective of the organization against (generally High Church) clerical criticism.[30] Until the 1960s, the tone of English public life remained a comfortably stodgy Protestant Anglicanism. Now that seems a world away.

CATHOLICS AND CHRIST THE KING: THE SECOND AGE OF CATHOLIC MISSIONS

Ireland's independence was one compensation for Catholicism's loss of its greatest political supporter in the Habsburg emperor – but the emperor had in any case always been an ambiguous asset for the pope. Until the 1960s, the Irish Republic remained a stridently confessional Catholic state (despite a sprinkling of eminent Protestants in its leadership); it represented a spectacular gain in territory which had been lost to Protestant control in the Reformation. A similar triumph for Rome after 1919 came from the foundation of an equally fervently Catholic Polish Republic, gathered afresh out of its eighteenth-century partition between the three now-vanished European empires of the Hohenzollern, the Habsburgs and the Romanovs. It is significant that when Pope Pius XI sought to rally Catholics against what he denounced as secularism or laicism in an encyclical of 1925, *Quas primas*, the brand-new feast which he introduced as a symbol for his campaign was that of Christ the King. It was then designated to be the last Sunday in October, but Paul VI moved it in 1969 to the last Sunday in the liturgical year, late November or early December. This arbitrary shift was a clue that the new festival was not the product of any long-standing popular devotion.

The Church had never stressed Christ's kingship when Europe was full of kings of this world, but now nearly all of them had gone. The papacy, betrayed by the old European powers when it lost the Papal States, necessarily took a much wider view of Catholic fortunes than simply the devastation in Europe: Christ the King, or at least his Vicar on earth, had the task and perhaps even the prospect of integrating all society under a single monarchy. An extra incentive to take this international outlook, indeed a motive far from insignificant, was finance. Pius IX had on principled grounds refused any monetary compensation for the Papal States and its tax revenues from the Italian government, and the only way of filling the gap was by soliciting financial support from devout Catholics – what had been known in medieval Europe as 'Peter's Pence'. At first the appeal for funds had been associated with the futile military effort to defend the pope's remaining territories, but this purpose became irrelevant after Italian unification in 1870. The net was cast worldwide, and the Vatican started taking a much more detailed interest in congregations far away.[31] This was a shift as fraught with significance as that other great financial change in the Church's medieval past, the financing of parish priests by tithes (see p. 369).

The papacy was looking to every last Catholic man, woman and child for help in carrying out its task, and in return it delved much deeper into the everyday lives of the faithful. One liturgical change engineered by Pope Pius X had a huge effect on Catholics and their experience of the Church. Over the centuries there had been a seesaw of arguments as to how frequently or infrequently the laity should receive the eucharistic elements at Mass. Pius X had no doubts that the more frequent reception, the better, and issued a barrage of instructions to that end. One of these had a powerful effect: in 1907 the Pope decreed that the minimum age for first communion should be lowered from twelve or fourteen to seven. Around that 'first communion' there rapidly grew a new Catholic folk culture, a public celebration of family life in the parish church, centred on an array of proud infants dressed in innocent splendour. One might say that the modern vision of Catholic family bliss which the Church still so assiduously promotes dates from that order of 1907.[32]

The fact that financial appeals across the oceans succeeded in keeping the papacy afloat after its nineteenth-century losses of territorial revenue was an indication of the Church's overall optimism and growth. For the Catholic Church was now undergoing one of the greatest expansions in its history, especially in Africa. Whereas the nineteenth century had been the great age of Protestant mission, Catholic missions were now outstripping at least European-run Protestant initiatives. In 1910 there were more or less equal numbers of European or American Catholics and Protestants in African missions, but recruitment of Protestant missionaries from Britain was beginning to fall away – just at the time that the Irish Catholic Church, previously remarkably inward-looking, was beginning to produce great numbers of clergy and nuns prepared for mission abroad, to add to a growing stream of Catholics from mainland Europe.[33] Benedict XV (Pope 1914–22) and his successor, Pius XI (Pope 1922–39), were both keenly interested in world mission. Benedict, conscious of the political impotence revealed in his peace initiatives during the war, was further galvanized by reports from China by a Belgian Lazarist Father, Vincent Lebbe, who was deeply critical of the French government's continuing use of its historic powers over

Chinese Catholic missions to interfere with what the Church was trying to achieve.

Benedict's resulting apostolic letter of 1919, *Maximum illud*, addressed a much wider missionary canvas than simply China's. It echoed Henry Venn's 'three-self' principle, but went much further, doing a considerable amount to banish the ethos in Rome which had condemned 'Chinese Rites' long before (see p. 707). As well as looking forward to a wholly native leadership in all regions of the Church, the letter pointed out how damaging the reproduction of European nationalisms had been for work in other continents, and it urged respect for other cultures. It has been styled a 'Magna Carta' for modern missions, and it was quickly followed by moves to appoint indigenous bishops in China and Japan. *Maximum illud* heralded an age in which the Roman Catholic Church has become the largest single component in the Christian world family of Churches.[34]

Across the Atlantic, the papacy viewed contrasting situations. In North America, with its history of dominant Protestant Churches evolving away from establishment towards pluralism, the Catholic Church was a flourishing part of a denominational spectrum. In South and Central America it was still largely unchallenged by Protestantism, which remained confined to niches of immigrant communities such as the Welsh miners of Argentinian Patagonia. The successor regimes of the Spanish and Portuguese monarchies inherited the intimate relationship between Church and secular government conceded by Renaissance popes, and throughout the nineteenth century this brought confrontation with liberal regimes inclined to see the power of churchmen as a threat to progress. Colombia, for instance, had been the first independent republic recognized by the Vatican after the defeat of Spain's South American armies, in 1835, but in 1853 it had also been the first to separate Church and State, as a consequence of which, in a further insult to the Church, it had made civil marriage compulsory. The pattern had been repeated throughout Latin America.[35] It was not invariable: in late-nineteenth-century Mexico, an energetic Archbishop of Oaxaca, Eulogio Gillow, combined modernizing ideas in social and ecclesiastical matters with first-hand knowledge of what the Curia in Rome meant by modernization. He established excellent relations with Mexico's long-term dictator Porfirio Díaz (whose power base coincided with Gillow's archdiocese) and did much to overcome previous conflicts.[36]

Nevertheless the official Church in Latin America habitually competed with liberal politicians for the allegiance of the population. Each had handicaps. Leading actors in both power structures were largely drawn from an elite of Creoles who claimed pure Spanish blood. Creoles might be regarded as indifferent to the concerns of ordinary people, and they had certainly long treated native peoples as second-class citizens, rather as they themselves had once been treated by home-born Spaniards.[37] Now *mestizos* (half-bloods) and full-blooded natives were voters as well as parishioners, and they began to seek to exercise their power in church as much as in the ballot box. In 1903 Pope Pius X far away in Rome sought to impose good taste on liturgical church music, emphasizing that pipe organs honoured God in worship, while popular instruments did not. Faced with a ban on brass bands, some Mexican parishes menacingly gave their parish priests an ultimatum: no bands, no services. One Mexican priest wearily summed up the situation in 1908 when filling in a diocesan questionnaire: in reply to, 'Do all the parishioners profess the Catholic religion?' he put down, 'The Catholic religion, in a manner of their own.'[38] This might seem a symptom of Catholic weakness, but it proved an unexpected asset when matters again turned sour between Church and State in Mexico, provoking the most serious trial of strength faced by the Catholic Church worldwide in the 1920s, equalled only by the tribulations of Greek Catholics in post-1917 Soviet Ukraine.

The prolonged rule of Mexico's clericalist President Díaz provoked revolution in 1910, associated with a militant anti-Catholicism both popular and official. Churches were burned down or painted red, images destroyed and ceremonies mocked. The Church fought back for control of Mexican life: the Mexican bishops in 1914 anticipated Pope Pius XI's later move by proclaiming that Christ was King of Mexico. In retaliation a new constitution of 1917, while declaring in North American style the principle of freedom of worship for all, suppressed all Church primary education and placed drastic limits on what the clergy could do; monasteries and nunneries were forcibly closed. Education, as in the contemporary though far less violent conflict in the Third French Republic, was the chief focus for struggle, but public conflict between Catholics and anticlericals now punctuated all Mexican life. When a holy image was damaged in the stately cathedral city of Morelia in 1921, twelve people died in the resulting street violence.[39] In 1926 the Primate of Mexico used the ultimate weapon available to him when he suspended all public worship, all sacraments, in protest against the crippling of the Church's activities, particularly its loss of control over schooling. Over the next three years before an uneasy truce there was all-out warfare between

Church and Republic, in which thousands died. The Catholics who rose in rebellion against the victimization of the Church were nicknamed *Cristeros* from their Christ the King battle slogan *¡Viva Cristo Rey!* The bishops had not expected or wanted this rising, and because they were soon mostly in exile and the clergy dispersed to avoid government violence, leadership of the rebellion came overwhelmingly from laypeople.

Cristeros drew their support from those regions of Mexico where there was a long tradition of lay leadership in the Church, where local culture took for granted the synthesis between religious and local life created by the missionaries of the Counter-Reformation. Scorning the government's attempt to found a Mexican Catholic and Apostolic Church to rival the Catholic Church, they rallied to the Primate-Archbishop of Mexico's instruction that laypeople should preside at every form of Catholic rite (including, in emergency, confessions, marriages and baptisms), short of consecrating the eucharistic elements. The clergy were not always pleased at the resulting lay initiatives and loss of clerical control, but in the end the government saw that it could not outface this massive affirmation of Church life, even despite its own popular support from anticlericals. 'Those men drenched the earth with their blood, and if that wasn't enough, they gave their very lives to bring our Lord God back again,' was one proud *Cristero* reminiscence.[40] The situation was like the early days of lay Korean Catholicism (see pp. 900–902), but on an enormously larger scale. One recent historian of these events points out what a distorted retrospective picture of the revolt was provided by John Paul II's canonization in 2000 of twenty-two *Cristero* priests and only three laypeople.[41] In reality, the events of 1926–9 in Mexico set a precedent for the realignment of relationships between priest and parishioner which was to be such a striking feature of Latin American Catholicism in the aftermath of the Second Vatican Council (see pp. 975–6).

This was not the lesson which the contemporary Vatican drew from the conflict in Mexico, or from the other murderous confrontations between the Church and the Left which were simultaneously building up in Spain and Soviet Russia. Everywhere it saw the chief enemy of Christianity as socialism or Communism. The future of Europe was entrusted in 1919 to democracies, but of all the new states created by the victorious Allies, at the beginning of 1939 only Czechoslovakia was left as a functioning democratic republic, and it was about to be obliterated. The history of the interwar years is of democracy's steady subversion by authoritarian regimes. Some rulers were traditionalists trying to restore the past, such as Hungary's Catholic-dominated monarchy without a monarch, headed by the regent, Miklós Horthy, an admiral without a navy. Much more destructive were movements which despised the aristocratic past as much as they did bourgeois democracy, and espoused an extreme form of nationalism which degenerated into racism. Collectively they have taken their name from the Italian variant, which proved the most long-lasting, and which indeed seems still to have some life left in it: Fascism. The Catholic Church's record in regard to Fascists might charitably be regarded as unimpressive.

It was perhaps not surprising that the succession of Italian clerics who became popes, mostly by training civil servants of an absolute monarchy, were no more inclined to natural sympathy with democracy than Pius IX had been a friend to liberalism. They did not speak with one voice. Pius X, who popularized the word 'Modernism' as a symbol of all that was anathema to good Catholics, swept up the reformist and democratic French Catholic youth movement *Le Sillon* in his antipathies and condemned it in 1910, with much trumpeting of the virtues of hierarchy. Benedict XV was in contrast charmed by *Le Sillon*'s charismatic founder, Marc Sangnier. Not only did Benedict give no further publicity to his predecessor's fulminations, but he encouraged Sangnier's Christian Democratic activities in French politics. That allowed French Catholicism discreetly to develop political diversity in its activism over the next decades, giving it an escape route from its damaging associations with the losers in the Dreyfus Affair (see p. 827), which was to prove vital later in the twentieth century. Benedict's successor, Pius XI, went further, casting a cold eye over the beliefs and activities of Le Sillon's bitter enemy the royalist and anti-Semitic organization *Action Française*, to which Pius X had shown much favour.[42] Pius's clear-sightedness in banning *Action Française* in 1925, in the face of shocked protest from reactionary French Catholics, was aided by the fact that its journalist-founder, Charles Maurras, was an open atheist, seeing Catholicism only instrumentally as an indispensable prop for his cloudy vision of a renewed and purified monarchical France. The long history of papal attempts to come to terms with the Third French Republic and the Vatican's suspicion of nationalism enabled the Pope to take a realistic view of the French situation.

Pius XI handled events in Italy less surely after Benito Mussolini's seizure of power in 1922. The *Duce*, Mussolini, might personally be an atheist no better than Maurras, but he was able to put his annexation of the Italian state to uses of which the Pope thoroughly approved, notably in suppressing the Communist Party. Fascism's forceful destruction of trade unions in the interests of Fascist-run corporate associations in industry and commerce was gratifyingly reminiscent of the corporatist tone of Leo XIII's *Rerum novarum*, sentiments which Pope Pius was soon to reaffirm in a commemorative encyclical of 1931, *Quadragesimo anno* ('In the fortieth year . . .'). The Pope was an Italian patriot, and besides, the *Duce* patently wanted a deal to earn himself goodwill from Catholics. So in the Lateran accords of 1929, the Vatican State was born, the world's smallest sovereign power, the size of an English country-house garden, carrying with it a silver spoon in the form of 1,750 million lire, presented by the Italian government – rather less than had been on offer from the Italian monarchy to Pius IX, but still a very substantial sum.

The Pope handed over financial administration of this windfall to a suave and brilliant banker, Bernardino Nogara, naturally a good Catholic but just as importantly a fellow son of Milan, who demanded and was given a free hand in his investments. Thus unhampered by *Quadragesimo anno* or the Pope's other contemporaneous denunciations of speculative capitalism, Nogara gained more power in Catholicism than had been enjoyed by any layman since the Emperor Charles V or King Philip II of Spain. He turned the Catholic Church into what one Soviet journalist accurately described in 1948 as the 'greatest financial trust in the world'.[43] Suddenly the Vatican could afford to be generous, and that was just as well, amid the catastrophe that unfolded during the decades after this profitable supping with the Devil.

Soon outclassing Mussolini's self-inflating Italian Fascism was the rise of an infinitely more evil variant on the Fascist theme, the German National Socialist ('Nazi') party. Adolf Hitler, born a subject of the Habsburg emperor, exploited the financial and political disarray of Germany's Weimar Republic, using uninhibited violence when it suited him, and profiting from the obtuse scheming of the traditional German Rightist parties. He came to power through a nightmare manipulation of voting figures and political alliances in Germany's democratic institutions. The final barrier to his abolition of those same institutions was removed by the overtrusting agreement of Germany's Catholic Party, the Centre (*Zentrum*), who in March 1933 decided to vote for an Enabling Act in the Reichstag, giving Hitler supreme power and suspending democracy. As the Nazis exultantly put into place the apparatus of terror for a totalitarian dictatorship, Rome's chief envoy in Germany, the future Pope Pius XII, Eugenio Pacelli, negotiated a concordat with Hitler which promised to preserve freedoms for the Catholic Church in the new 'Third Reich', putative successor to the Holy Roman Empire and the Hohenzollern 'Second Reich' of 1871. The price was the dissolution of the *Zentrum* and Catholic trade unions, and a ban on any political activity on the part of the Church's clergy. With the deal secured, Hitler soon revealed his contempt for the Church into which he had been born: the poison of Nazi black propaganda and violence was visited selectively on Catholicism, as it was in more thoroughgoing and vicious form on the helpless Jewish population, the central victims of Hitler's hatred.

It was too late for Rome to go back. Pius XI, increasingly horrified by reports from Germany, did what he could. He issued an encyclical directed in German to Germany, *Mit brennender Sorge* ('With burning anxiety'), which was successfully smuggled into the country to be read simultaneously from every Catholic pulpit on Palm Sunday 1937; it denounced the harassment of the Church and condemned the presuppositions of Nazi racism. The encyclical was one of the few nationally coordinated public acts of defiance of the regime before it fell in 1945; yet it did nothing to alter the steady crescendo of wickedness which was Nazi foreign and domestic policy. Since the days of the *Kulturkampf* (see pp. 837–8), German Catholics had trumpeted their loyalty to the German state, while carving out their own devotional space within German society. The protection of that space was what they had expected from the 1933 Concordat; they had no second strategy when they discovered that Hitler was not Bismarck and that the Concordat had proved worthless.[44] The best that the Pope could do was to work behind the scenes to separate Fascist Italy from Nazi Germany, and passively express his profound disapproval when Hitler visited Mussolini in 1938. The Pope was away, there were no decorations on Rome's churches and the Vatican Museums were closed. That was a different sort of papal silence to that which had greeted Mussolini's invasion of Christian Ethiopia three years before (see pp. 891–2).[45]

Rome still saw Communism as a greater representative of evil than Fascism. In that same Holy Week of 1937 which sent *Mit brennender Sorge* to Germany, a papal encyclical addressed to the world, *Divini Redemptoris* ('Of the Divine Redeemer'), denounced Communism in far stronger terms than German congregations had heard expressed against Nazism. It was a movement which among much else 'strips man of his liberty, robs human personality of all its dignity, and removes all the moral restraints that check the eruptions of blind impulse'. At the time, the imbalance of approach seemed a reasonable if depressing calculation, contrasting Nazi harassment of the Church with the wholesale destruction and death being visited on Christianity in the Soviet Union – and also in Spain. There, the Pope was actively supporting an attack on a democratically elected government by forces strongly backed by Fascism.

The Spanish case is one of the most tragic alignments of the interwar papacy, and yet one can see precisely why the Vatican should turn against the Republican government. The Spanish Republic set up on the fall of the monarchy in 1931 mimicked amid a raft of social and economic reforms all the anticlerical policies with which the Church was familiar from Latin America and Republican France: an end, for instance, to religious education and to state financial support for church upkeep or clerical stipends. Without fully considering the effects of their actions, the Republicans charged destructively over the small certainties of everyday Catholic life, infuriating large numbers of ordinary Catholics who might not otherwise have had any special animus against the Republic or nostalgia for the exiled King Alfonso XIII. Worse still, Catholic demonstrations of outrage provoked still greater fury among anarchists and socialists. Quickly, in 1931, the burning of church buildings began.[46]

Now battle lines were drawn, and once more the newly emerged image of Christ the King became the figurehead for the political Right, as had already happened not merely in Mexico but also among militant Catholics in Belgian politics.[47] Electoral gains for a new Spanish Catholic party in 1934 provoked fury from anarchists and socialists; attacks on church buildings were now accompanied by the killing of clergy. When the parties of the Left won elections in 1936, a group of army leaders, now in alliance with a mushrooming 'Falangist' movement inspired by Fascism, determined to overturn the result by force. Among them was a primly Catholic little general from Galicia, Francisco Franco, who had been sent in semi-disgrace to the Canary Islands because of his political activities, but who eventually emerged from the rapidly moving events as chief commander. Arranging Franco's crucial flight to take command in Morocco, and providing an alibi for the British-hired plane's true purpose, was a John Buchanesque British MI6 officer, Major Hugh Pollard, undertaking this as a freelance operation because he was a devout Catholic (as well as an enthusiastic admirer of Nazism and Italian Fascism). Pollard, who subsequently publicly and indignantly defended

the Nazi obliteration bombing of the Basque capital Guernica, was
proud of having fulfilled 'the duty of a good Catholic to help fellow
Catholics in trouble'. He was duly decorated by a grateful Franco when
the Nationalists had rolled back the defenders of the Republic with
Hitler's and Mussolini's military assistance.[48]

Through three years of exceptionally brutal civil war in Spain, the
Vatican perceived only Republican atrocities, which were indeed vile:
clergy murdered, churches systematically torched and even corpses in
graves exhumed and ridiculed. Nationalist propaganda lingered over
Republicans' rape of nuns, though there is no documented case of this
occurring, the prospect apparently offending Republican notions of
military honour. What undoubtedly did take place was what one historian of the events has called 'the greatest anticlerical bloodletting
Europe has ever known'. In the Andalusian diocese of Málaga, for
instance, 115 out of 240 clergy were killed in the year before Italian
troops seized the city in 1937. Often before their deaths, clergy were
sexually tortured, or equally frequently posthumously mutilated, reflecting lay male neuroses about their celibate state and uncontrolled
lusts, ancient fears which were a standard trope of anticlericalism.[49]
Rome took less notice of the fact that in the Basque country in the north
of the peninsula, most clergy were on the side of local autonomy and
the Republic against Franco's Nationalists, and that the Nationalists brutally punished them along with all the other enemies of the
Falange.

When Franco was at last victorious in 1939, Pope Pius XII broadcast
to the Spanish people, praising Spain because it had 'once again given
to the prophets of materialist atheism a noble proof of its indestructible
Catholic faith'. Pius XI's attempt to differentiate between Hitler and
Mussolini was forgotten. No protests went up from the Vatican when
Hitler invaded the helpless remnant of Czechoslovakia, and for a while
the Catholic Church in Germany benefited accordingly.[50] At least the
Church did not advocate the restoration of the Spanish Inquisition
alongside the continuing existence of the Holy Office in Rome; but it
hardly needed to in the police state which was the Spain of the *Caudillo*
Franco (*Caudillo* means what *Führer* means in German). Franco's regime
reasserted the Spain of the 1492 expulsion, against all that had happened in the peninsula over the last hundred years: Spain was conceived
of as racially pure, deferential to paternalistic authority, corporatist,
uniformly Catholic. The dictatorship was to last with only tactical modifications of its icy authoritarianism until the *Caudillo*'s death in 1975,

by which time developments in the Catholic Church made him an increasingly embarrassing relic of the past.

THE CHURCHES AND NAZISM: THE SECOND WORLD WAR

As Franco was savouring his triumph in 1939, all Western Churches, not merely Roman Catholics, were facing the consequences of Hitler's electoral manoeuvres in 1933. Protestants came to be as soiled by the situation as Catholics. Because of its close identification with the German Empire, State Protestantism found it very difficult to adjust to the 1918 defeat and the proclamation of the Weimar Republic, which at a stroke dismissed not just the Kaiser but all the crowned heads of the empire, who, if they were Protestants, had also been heads of their State Churches. Protestant leaders shared the general sense that an undefeated German army had been betrayed by enemies of the Reich. They overwhelmingly regarded the foundation of a Republic as part of that betrayal; feeling was particularly bitter in Prussia, where the successor in 1918 to the portfolio once held by Wilhelm von Humboldt as Minister of Education and Public Worship was an anticlerical Social Democrat, Adolf Hoffmann. It has been estimated that when the Weimar Republic came into existence in 1919, 80 per cent of its Protestant clergy sympathized with its enemies, and were monarchist and angrily nationalist. This was not a good basis for mounting a critique of Nazism, which drew on the same anger and turned it to its own uses.[51]

One of the tragedies of the great tradition of liberal German Protestant theology was that some of its assumptions could turn some of its greatest practitioners into fellow-travellers with Nazi anti-Semitism. They were Lutherans: they naturally took as a basic assumption Luther's great theological contrast between Law and Gospel, or Judaism and Christianity. That had borne fruit in the nineteenth-century tradition of biblical scholarship, where, from the work of F. C. Baur onwards, scholars customarily analysed the Gospel as the product of conflict between Petrine Christians, who wished to remain close to Judaism, and Pauline Christians, who wished to take it in a new direction. In the case of Adolf von Harnack, this resulted in rejecting the whole of the Old Testament as not part of the canon of scripture, and an interest (albeit critical) in Marcion's ancient effort to do the same.[52] For other scholars in the next generation, most notoriously the celebrated New Testament scholar Gerhard Kittel, this led on to a welcome for Hitler's assumption of power, and to a number of anti-Semitic biases in one of the most monumental and still frequently consulted works of New Testament scholarship, the *Theological Dictionary of the New Testament*, of which Kittel was main editor.[53]

This intellectual background gave a superficial plausibility to the setting up of a Protestant body calling itself the German Christians, a movement supporting the aim of the Nazis to eliminate Jewish influence from the Church, and seeking to become the voice of German Protestantism. Once more it drew on an aspect of the German Protestant past, the search for reunion among Protestant Churches, which had a perfectly respectable history, but which was now perverted towards open racism. In order to account for the Saviour's origins in Galilee, German Christians suggested that the area had been an enclave of Aryan ethnic identity. Besides this borrowing from a great deal of nineteenth-century anthropological speculation and scholarship sometimes of alarmingly respectable provenance, they appealed to a selection of opinions of Luther (such as his intemperate remarks about the Jews and his theme of obedience to superior powers) in order to justify their rewriting of the faith.[54] With Nazi backing, they did well in State Church elections in July 1933, and their most prominent pastor, Ludwig Müller, gained the title *Reichsbischof*.

Who could have the imagination or the courage to stand up to the insidious mixture of seduction and intimidation? One theologian, Karl Barth, had the advantage as a Swiss of coming from outside German Protestantism, and also from a Reformed Protestant tradition, which had much more in its theological heritage than German State Lutheranism to encourage the Church into an independent or critical stance towards temporal power. Barth had been enraged by the liberal Protestant establishment's subservience to the German Empire, and as the First World War became ever more destructive, his anger had fed his perception of fraudulence in the tradition stemming from Schleiermacher, with its affirmation that reason opened a path to understanding of the divine.[55] Barth's *Commentary on Romans*, published in 1919, drew out of Paul the theme which had successively transfixed Augustine of Hippo, Luther and Calvin: humanity, its reason utterly fallen, could only reach God through divine grace mediated in Jesus Christ. Unsurprisingly, the veteran liberal scholar Adolf von Harnack was one of Barth's first opponents, while among those junior clergy seized by Barth's critique of liberalism was one of Harnack's own students in Berlin, Dietrich Bonhoeffer.[56]

The Swiss Reformed pastor and the well-connected young Lutheran Bonhoeffer were among a significant number of Reformed and Lutheran Protestants, mostly of the younger generation, who decided in 1931 that they must make an ecumenical stand against the growing nationalism of their society. Spurred by the apparent growth of the German Christians after Hitler's seizure of power, the dissidents made common cause in 1933–4 to form a 'Confessing Church'. In May 1934 the Church issued a declaration at a synod in the unglamorous industrial city of Barmen, presenting its Evangelical and Reformed faith against the 'destructive errors of the German Christians and the present national church government'. Among the array of Bible texts which it mustered, a notable absentee was the call to unequivocal obedience in Romans 13.1 which had so dominated the thought of the magisterial Reformers: 'Let every person be subject to the governing authorities. For there is no authority except from God'. Instead, the declaration fixed on obedience under the text 'Fear God, honour the Emperor' (I Peter 2.17).[57] Despite its apparent loyalism, this command has a rather more ambiguous or double quality than Romans 13.1. The balance to be struck made witnessing to Christian truth in the Confessing Church not merely dangerous, but problematic.

The Confessing Church experienced the difficulty of all well-intentioned Christians in a state dominated by an evil whose dimensions were difficult to believe, certainly to anticipate. The Barmen Declaration made no reference to the plight of the Jews (something for which Barth three decades later expressed personal regret). The Confessing Church only took an official stand on the question of racial discrimination via its ecclesiology (that is, its theology of the Church): it refused to accept that the State could determine Church membership by excluding through racist legislation ethnic Jews who had become Christians. Many Confessing Church members felt that such Christians ought to have their own separate parishes.[58] Virtually all members also continued to feel it their duty to support the lawfully elected German government. One of the senior figures in the movement was Martin Niemöller, a Lutheran pastor and former submarine commander, whose natural conservatism and patriotism wrestled uneasily with his sense of revulsion at Nazi violence and illegality. He had voted for the Nazis in the sequence of elections which brought them to power, and his brother Wilhelm, also a Confessing pastor, was a member of the Party, though neither fact prevented the Niemöllers' arrest in 1937. In April 1938 a majority of the Confessing Church's clergy were still ready to sign an oath of loyalty to Hitler as Führer in the wake of his annexation of Austria.[59] All were making decisions in a situation which positively invited moral confusion. The Nazis could never be consistent in their support of any Christian body, however closely it aspired to align itself to the Party; they were extremely good at spreading favours around as it suited them. So the small Free Church bodies in Germany, such as the Methodists and Baptists, found that the Nazis ended the discrimination that the old State Churches had maintained against their work; Hitler even paid for a new pipe organ in one Methodist church. In their pleasure at the Third Reich's encouragement of family life and campaigns against modern decadence, the German Free Churches failed to notice that they were being used to conciliate hostile opinion in their British and American sister Churches.[60]

And so as Europe fell into general war in 1939, very many Christians both Protestant and Catholic found it all too easy to fall into complicity with Nazism. There is admittedly a difference between positive support and confused mixtures of inaction and protest or even resistance. In the former category might fall those German army chaplains who were present at mass killings by the German Army after the invasion of the Soviet Union. Presiding over the German atrocities in Ukraine as its chief administrator was Erich Koch, among the most long-standing members of the Nazi Party, but also a devout Protestant who was sometime President of the Provincial Synod of the Lutheran Church in East Prussia, a great patron of *Reichsbischof* Müller.[61] One of the most unlovable churches in the world is the Martin Luther Memorial Church in the south Berlin suburb of Mariendorf. This parish church planned by nationalist Lutherans in the 1920s was taken over by the Nazis when they came to power and made into a prestige project (see Plate 48). Although its swastikas have been carefully chiselled out of the sculptures, the storm trooper carved on the font deprived of his rifle and the bust of Hitler removed, the Lutheran Church has found it hard to know what to do with this egregious place of worship, whose pipe organ was first played at a Nazi Nuremberg rally, and its future remains in doubt – in an unfortunate perversity of fate, Allied bombing spared it amid the city's devastation.

Just as difficult to excuse were the regimes emerging in the wake of Hitler's conquests which combined fervent religious commitment with enthusiasm for their own scaled-down version of Hitler's murderous racism. In Slovakia, the recovery of Slovak identity had been led by Catholic clergy, and was consciously directed against a new Czech domination after 1918. When Hitler destroyed Czechoslovakia, the Slovakian puppet regime he installed was led between 1939 and 1945 by Monsignor Jozef Tiso, who continued to act as a Catholic parish priest during his presidency, and was responsible for implementing deportations of Jews and Roma (gypsies) at Nazi bidding. In Croatia, Ante Pavelić ran a self-consciously Catholic regime, devoted to ridding a multi-ethnic state of Jews, Roma and Orthodox Serbs (though, curiously, not of Protestants or Muslims). His sadistic methods shocked even the Nazis. Nor did the Catholic Church condemn the forced conversions of the Orthodox which were part of Pavelić's programme. A Franciscan friar, Sidonje Scholz, visited concentration camps, offering Serbs conversion or death. When he was killed by Serb resisters, the newspaper sponsored by Archbishop Stepinac of Zagreb described Friar Scholz as a 'new martyr who died in the name of religion and for Catholic Croatia'. A significant number of Catholics in neighbouring Slovenia were sickened by the Croatian atrocities and drew up a protest demanding public condemnation from the Pope; it reached the Vatican in 1942 and had no public result.[62] Similar very explicit reports from Polish church leaders about Nazi outrages against the population of occupied Poland likewise left the Vatican uncomfortably wrestling with the problem of how best to make a public response.

In German-occupied Ukraine, where religious life much revived once the Red Army had been thrown back by German armies, nationalism also took religious lines, but in a terrible new combination of forces. The toxic effect of Nazi occupation was to set Pole against only recently self-identified Ukrainian, with the bizarre effect that Greek Catholic Ukrainians allied with Orthodox Ukrainians against the Roman Catholic Poles who shared Greek Catholics' allegiance to Rome – thus overturning the alignments and antipathies of the previous three centuries. In the contested territory of Volhynia, lately Polish-administered, in 1943 Ukrainians were able amid mutual genocidal conflict to identify Polish Roman Catholics because the Poles observed Christmas earlier than either Greek Catholics or Orthodox. The Poles were generally holding their Christmas celebrations in wooden churches, which burned easily, and anyone escaping these infernos was shot. Overall, around seventy thousand Poles died throughout the Ukraine in this violence, and twenty thousand Ukrainians.[63]

The case of France and its Catholicism continues to be a source of national agonizing. When in 1940 the French army fell to a devastating German attack, the Third French Republic was swiftly dismantled and its secularist appeal to the values of 1789 was cast into discredit. A new government presided over those parts of France not directly occupied by the Nazis, from the spa town of Vichy. The aged national war hero who took over as Vichy head of state, Marshal Philippe Pétain, chose to cast his vigorous conservatism around an ideology of Catholic traditionalism, despite his own lack of any great devotional fervour. The official Church was delighted to back the new national slogan, *Travail, famille, patrie* ('Work, family, country'), and the anti-Semitism of those defeated forty years before in the Dreyfus controversy (see p. 827) was not slow to ally itself with the much more radical anti-Semitism of the victorious Nazis. Only slowly did the Catholic hierarchy realize what a terrible mistake it had made; from the early days of defeat, younger and junior clergy tended to be much more suspicious of the Vichy regime, some of whose politicians combined pronounced anticlerical views with quasi-Fascist ideology.

Gradually, as the exploitative character of German occupation became clear, national resistance grew. Catholics were prominent among the resisters, and many became heroically committed to the work of saving Jews from barbaric treatment and deportation for death. Yet it is an irony of the Vichy years that among the regime's lasting memorials is one of the most beautiful works of modern Catholic liturgical music, Maurice Duruflé's *Requiem*, enfolding the plainsong melodies of the Requiem Mass in the most lush and haunting of French choral romanticism. This was commissioned by the Vichy government, from a devoutly Catholic composer, whose publisher was among Pétain's most enthusiastic supporters. For many years after the war, the origins of Duruflé's great work were conveniently shrouded in obscurity.[64]

At the centre of all this was Pope Pius XII. His part in the war has generated debate which is still not ended. Amid the noise of scholarly and less scholarly controversy, the Pope's own 'silence' is still hard to miss. It has two sides, for he was silent to the German government when he learned of an army plot to assassinate Hitler in late 1939, and discreetly communicative to the Western Allies about what he knew of it, but as the Holocaust unfolded, he was silent also about the Jews. While a variety of Vatican agencies helped thousands of Jews to escape round-ups in Italy, the Pope only once nerved himself to make a public statement about their plight, in his Christmas radio broadcast in 1942. Even then, his mention of those 'put to death or doomed to slow extinction, sometimes merely because of their race or their descent' failed to put a name to the chief sufferers. His third near-silence, that of any significant public reflection on his actions, and indeed some deliberate if understandable obfuscation, lasted through the thirteen years of his pontificate after the war had ended.[65]

The Pope's unhappy equivocations contrast with the conduct of a Catholic Church leader in an infinitely more dangerous personal situation: Andrei Sheptyts'kyi, Greek Catholic Metropolitan of Galician Ukraine since 1900, when it had been Habsburg territory. In the desperate situation of German-occupied Galicia in 1944, Sheptyts'kyi could see no other course than that a division of the Waffen-SS should become the core of an army to defend the region against the advancing Russians. That might suggest that he was another Father Tiso or a Pavelić for the Ukrainians; but despite his deep commitment to the construction of a Ukrainian nation, Sheptyts'kyi was an aristocrat whose family looked back to the old multiconfessional and multi-faith Polish-Lithuanian Commonwealth. A convert to the Greek Catholic Church from Roman Catholicism, with a brother who had helped to create the victorious Polish army in 1920, he put his own life in danger when the Germans invaded by personally sheltering Jews against deportation and setting up networks to hide them.

Sheptyts'kyi went further. As the Nazis first recruited Ukrainians to murder Jews and then encouraged them to murder Poles, the Metropolitan took the highly dangerous step of writing personally to Heinrich Himmler, pleading with him not to call up Ukrainian policemen. He then issued a pastoral letter, to be read out from every Greek Catholic pulpit in even more perilous circumstances than the distribution of *Mit brennender Sorge*: its title was 'Thou shalt not kill', and it reminded his congregations that nothing could excuse murder. It was not his only pastoral letter on the subject, and he wrote to Pius XII in 1942 to denounce Nazism as a 'system of egoism exaggerated to an absurd degree'. His Church was fortunate to have such a leader; although the old man died only a few months after Soviet tanks rolled back through Ukraine and beyond, his memory sustained Greek Catholics through half a century more of misfortune and repression.[66]

Pope Pius XII was the successor of rulers who confined their Jewish subjects to a ghetto in Rome up to the nineteenth century, yet the papacy need not alone shoulder responsibility in a religion which has institutionalized anti-Semitism for most of its existence. German Protestants did little better than the Pope in the 1950s in confronting their wartime past.[67] The taint lies throughout Chalcedonian Christianity, including the casual unthinking anti-Semitism which characterized British and American society until the late twentieth century. It will not do to point out the undoubted fact that most Nazis hated Christianity and would have done their best to destroy its institutional power if they had been victorious.[68] As the Nazi extermination machine enrolled countless thousands of European Christians as facilitators or uncomplaining bystanders of its industrialized killings of Jews, it could succeed in co-opting them in the work of dehumanizing the victims because the collaborators had absorbed eighteen centuries of Christian negative stereotypes of Judaism – not to mention the tensions visible in the text of the New Testament, which had prompted the urge to create those stereotypes, up to the most mendacious and marginalizing such as the 'blood libel' (see pp. 400–401). This is a hard burden for post-war European Christians to bear. To their credit, after unhappy half-measures in the immediate post-war period, the Churches have done their best to face facts. Like the missionary failure in India, the Holocaust has provided a useful spur to humility for Christianity.

There were also those Christians who stood out: often lonely figures, whose resistance to the apparently limitless success of the Nazis seemed baffling to most people at the time. Franz Jägerstätter was a humble man from the same area of Austria as Hitler himself, and with a not dissimilarly murky family background. What he constructed out of these personal circumstances was a firm decision to serve his little local church as sexton, a choice not to vote for the plebiscite acclaiming Hitler's absorption of Austria, and finally a fixed refusal to fight for his country in an evil cause. He was beheaded in Berlin in 1943, and the inclusion of his name on his village's war memorial after the Second World War was the subject of heated local argument.[69] From the Confessing Church, there remains the now emblematic figure of Dietrich Bonhoeffer. Although he was a marginal figure in the resistance to the Nazis, this Lutheran pastor was intimately involved in the circles of those seeking the destruction of the regime, and knew of the plans which culminated in the failed attempt to assassinate Hitler on 20 July 1944; that was why the Gestapo arrested him and took him to his final imprisonment. His situation left Christians facing anew the moral questions about the murder of tyrants which the Reformation had already raised. His execution just before the end of the war gave German Lutherans a martyr, when so many others had not been. From Bonhoeffer's time in prison, he left as the end of an industrious production of theological works a series of fragments and letters which contained phrases still echoing round Western Christian ears, as possible clues to future directions for the Church (see p. 988). His parents' quietly handsome house and garden in a leafy suburb of Berlin, from where the Gestapo escorted him to prison, remain as his memorial, but the place of his burial will probably never be known.

There were those among the Allies fighting Nazi Germany who realized that the Allies too were capable of wicked acts. George Bell, Bonhoeffer's close friend in England and an Anglican bishop with unusually wide ecumenical contacts in mainland Europe, acted as a conscience of the British governing elite, earning no gratitude from Britain's wartime Prime Minister, Winston Churchill. During the First World War he had been domestic chaplain (in effect, secretary) to Randall Davidson, Archbishop of Canterbury, who had managed to steer the Church of England's official statements away from the path of egregious patriotism represented by Bishop Winnington-Ingram. Bell, now Bishop of Chichester and, from 1938, occupying one of the Anglican episcopate's places in the British House of Lords, took Davidson's line much further; he was determined to separate out Germany from Nazism in the conduct of the war. The issue for which he came to be particularly notorious was his criticism of the systematic indiscriminate aerial bombing of German cities, made possible by the Allies' crippling of the German Air Force (the Luftwaffe) in the second half of the war. The Bishop of Coventry, whose city had been wrecked by the Luftwaffe in 1940, threw his moral weight behind the British policy of retaliatory bombing; in contrast, from 1943 Bell used his public position to denounce saturation bombing as 'a wrong deed'. It is widely held that Churchill's anger at Bell's outspokenness cost him the succession to the See of Canterbury – but inspiring moral leader as Bell was, this might not entirely have been a disaster. After the war his warm friendships with German churchmen and natural impulse to Christian forgiveness led him into some questionable judgements as to which Germans ought to escape the consequences of their involvement with the Nazis.[70]

The Second World War was at its most destructive and bestial in Eastern Europe, and it may seem strange to suggest that it brought any benefit to the Soviet Union. Yet it is difficult to see how, without the boost to Soviet prestige provided by the repelling of Nazi armies in what Russians rightly term the Great Patriotic War, Soviet Russia could otherwise have staggered on as late as the 1980s, devoid as it was of any popular legitimacy and having already ruined the lives of so many by the time of Hitler's invasion. Stalin, whose criminal complacency had blinded him to Hitler's readiness to betray their alliance, was transformed by the war into a leader comparable to the first Romanovs or Peter the Great as defender of his people. And that same patriotic war effort saved the Russian Orthodox Church from institutional extinction, although not from a great deal of moral compromise. In 1939 there were only four bishops who were still at liberty in the Soviet Union; in September 1943, with Russia fighting desperately to keep the German Army from overrunning its heartland, Stalin invited the Patriarch and three metropolitans to a meeting which was to lead to a council of the Church, the first in Russia since 1917. The council saw to it that the Church was enrolled in the war effort, urging sacrifices on its faithful. The Georgian and Armenian Churches benefited likewise from their own patriotic activities; the funds raised by the head of the Church in Armenia went to pay for two tank divisions in the Red Army.[71]

After the war was over, this institutional toleration continued. In 1946 Stalin allowed the formal extinction of the languishing rival Russian Church organization which the Soviet government had encouraged, the 'Renovationist' Church. This had started life as a genuine attempt by radical clergy to produce a reforming version of Orthodoxy during the abortive revolution of 1905 (see p. 851), but it had turned into little more than a means of disrupting Orthodox activity and parroting Communist propaganda. Stalin realized that he was better served by a subservient Orthodox leadership which would have some credibility with other worldwide Christian leaders. That is how his successors used the Moscow Patriarchate, even while they resumed vicious attempts to end any popular religious life in that same Church.[72] When the Soviets swept back into Ukraine, Stalin abruptly terminated the official life of the Greek Catholic Church, which had flourished in the wake of the Red Army's retreat before the Nazis. In 1946 a puppet synod in Ukraine declared void the Union of Brest of 1596, and the Church disappeared into a forcible union with the Orthodox Church in Moscow for nearly half a century.[73] As Soviet armies inexorably followed up the Western Allies' uncomfortable acceptance that Stalin would make Eastern Europe a Soviet sphere of influence, the various national Orthodox Churches apart from Greece followed the Moscow Patriarchate into an unhappy combination of collaboration and persecution at the hands of Communist satellite regimes. Catholics and Protestants had more external contacts to sustain them, but for that reason, they were generally more likely to be regarded as enemies of the new 'Peoples' Democracies'.

WORLD CHRISTIANITY REALIGNED:
ECUMENICAL BEGINNINGS

In 1945, Europe was a continent of ruins, in the throes of the largest population movements in its recorded history, as displaced peoples sought their homes again or sought to escape assorted retributions, while others trudged wretchedly through the devastation to conform to new political boundaries created by the victorious Allies' power deals. A number of subsidiary wars still raged in the Balkans and on the plains of Eastern Europe. A horrified consciousness was dawning, although slow to find public expression for some decades, that several million people, mostly Jews, but also Roma, homosexuals, Freemasons, Jehovah's Witnesses and others who did not conform to Nazi requirements, had disappeared, not in warfare, but cold-bloodedly herded into human abattoirs for an anonymous and casually inflicted death. A large question mark hovered over the worldwide empires created by France, Britain and their satellites during the previous three centuries. British and French prestige in East Asia had been wrecked by Japan's conquests, and France's still more by German occupation; once again, questions arose among colonial peoples as to what benefits they might now gain from their part in a war created originally in Europe. The only power whose streets and fields remained unmarked by war and whose treasury was not empty was the United States of America. In one of the most imaginative and generous international deals in recorded history, although also with an eye to upstaging rival saviours from the Communist East, the USA's Marshall Plan began the financing of a recovery programme for Europe which undoubtedly saved the European peoples from falling into new frustration, nihilism or willingness to listen to demagogues, in the fashion that had so poisoned the interwar years.[74]

This was a moment comparable to the results of the devastation of Eastern Christianity in fourteenth-century Asia by plague, Mongol destructiveness and Islamic advance (see pp. 275–7). Since that great shift, the centre of Christian activity and decision-making had been Europe. Now, although the historic power centres were still sited by the inertia of history in Istanbul, Moscow and Rome, a clear-sighted observer might recognize not only that Orthodoxy was weaker than at any stage in its existence, but that Western Christianity in its Protestant and Catholic forms was flourishing more in America, Africa and Asia than in Europe. It was certainly true that as Europe painfully pulled away from its nadir, its churchgoing benefited for more than a decade from the weary desire to find some normality and decency after the nightmare. So churches became fuller in Britain in the 1950s. Anglican theology and literary creativity had rarely seemed so impressive or cosmopolitan, and the Church of England's Evangelical wing was returning from an edgy marginality, with the aid of public missions led by one of the more thoughtful American evangelists, the young Southern Baptist Billy Graham. Roman Catholicism too was steadily becoming a contender for acceptance in British national life – in other words, it was becoming less immigrant and Irish and more middle class. In the newly declared Irish Republic, Catholicism had never been so popular or all-embracing in national life, with no sense that there might be anything amiss – that was for the future.[75]

Pius XII presided over a Catholic Church which continued vigorously to grow throughout the world. He did his best to recognize that Europe was changing through its post-war rebuilding; he gave his whole-hearted support to the formation of Christian Democratic parties, to take a full part in the chastened democratic politics now virtually unquestioned west of what was being called the 'Iron Curtain' enclosing the Soviet Union's satellites, outside the continuing authoritarian and Catholic dictatorships of Spain and Portugal. But Pius's own conservative instincts mirrored Europe's widespread longing to find comfort in the past. In 1950 he used papal infallibility to define the doctrine of the bodily Assumption of the Virgin Mary into Heaven, a move which infuriated Protestant, Orthodox and Eastern Churches alike, and which did not please those Catholic theologians who cared about the doctrine's lack of justification in the Bible or in early Church tradition. Something like the Modernist campaign of Pius X gathered momentum against those whom Pius XII regarded as dissenters against Catholic truth. In his last years, the ailing Pope presented an increasingly pitiable figure, as he tried ever more frantically to be a universal teacher: Vicar of the *Encylopaedia Britannica* rather than Vicar of Christ. Symptomatic of his conscientious but inept effort to remain in dialogue with the contemporary world was his proclamation just before his death in 1958 that St Francis's associate St Clare of Assisi was now to be the patron saint of television. This was because, on her deathbed, she had been able to attend Christmas Mass in the neighbouring basilica in the form of a vision, a miraculous medieval outside broadcast.[76]

Catholic activity in the 1950s ran in parallel to but had very little contact with the proliferation and diversification of global Protestantism. Over the previous half-century, Protestantism had developed in two different new directions which themselves had increasingly little to do with each other: on the one hand, there was a self-consciously liberal exploration of faith and social activism, and on the other, a host of newly founded Churches, many of which identified themselves as Pentecostal, and whose congregations expressed themselves in full-blooded extrovert Evangelical style. Both these Protestant impulses in fact had a common root in anglophone Evangelicalism. Eventually it may be inappropriate to see them as polarities, but that is how it seemed in the twentieth century. Between them, there remained a great spectrum of Evangelical Protestant belief, much of which, in reaction to the liberals, increasingly took to itself the label 'conservative'.

Liberal Protestantism after 1900 chose a very different path from either the Holiness/Keswick styles of the conservatives, or the proliferation of identities in the new Churches. Increasingly it seemed to dominate most of the older Protestant Churches – Lutheran, Reformed, Anglican and Methodist – while the Baptists tended to be more resistant. This new liberalism was a wider phenomenon than the liberal Protestantism whose stronghold had been in nineteenth-century Germany. It could include within its ranks such formidable critics of Schleiermacher and the older German theology as Karl Barth, whose approach to the Bible owed much to the continuing progress of critical biblical scholarship, even though he drew his own emphatic conclusions about the exclusive claims of scripture on Christian commitment. Liberals showed plenty of enthusiasm for missionary activism, but this increasingly included an emphasis on justice and equality in the world, as a necessary reflection of the Christian message – what in North America was commonly called a 'Social Gospel'.

During the twentieth century, liberal Protestantism embarked on a new adventure in Christian reunion. It elaborated a new effort to break down Church boundaries and heal the various breaches stemming from the Reformation. Liberal Protestants were open to the nuanced Catholicism of High Church Anglicans and the similar movements in northern European Lutheranism, and they saw their task as renewing an authentic Catholicism for the whole Church, just as John Calvin had once envisaged in Geneva. Hence the description of the project with a word borrowed from the first councils of the early Church, and echoing the title which the Patriarch of Constantinople had long fostered for himself: 'Ecumenical'.[77] In the end, this Ecumenical Movement was to become much wider than its Protestant origins, but that was still in the balance in the 1940s, when the Movement gained its institutional expression in a new organization, the World Council of Churches.

The Ecumenical Movement started as an outcrop of the Protestant missions of the nineteenth century. Its particular spur had been the puzzle of India: apparently the most promising missionary prospect for Christian faith but in reality the least receptive (see pp. 892–5). The leading organizer in the Ecumenical Movement for the first half of the twentieth century, J. H. Oldham, came out of this experience; he was born in India, and married the daughter of a former British Governor of Bengal, whom he had met during missionary work in Lahore. His religious experience well illustrates the trajectory of liberal Protestantism. Amorphously Evangelical in background, the young Joseph delighted his devout father by his conversion experience during the American revivalism of D. L. Moody's last English mission, and he spent time working in one of Edinburgh's leading Free Church of Scotland congregations, but his Christian commitment moved steadily away from the world of Holiness fervour, or premillennialism. His Establishment background reasserted itself, but in a remarkably creative way: he retained the Evangelical characteristic of indifference to denominational boundaries. Like many Protestants moving away from their early Evangelicalism, he began to see missionary activity as ministry not just to individual bodies but to society as a whole. Missionaries must share the good news through effective (and Western) medicine, rigorous (and Western) education and Western-style progress towards the elimination of racial discrimination or colonial exploitation. The first envoys of the London Missionary Society to the Pacific back in the 1790s would have recognized many of Oldham's preoccupations.[78]

Besides his extraordinary capacity for organization and detail, Oldham had a genius for sympathetic relationships with Church leaders and with those whom he sensed were destined to be leaders for the whole Church – Bonhoeffer and George Bell among them. He was at home in the Athenaeum, that stately London Clubland headquarters for Englishmen marked out by culture and talent rather than illustrious pedigrees – bishops flitted in and out of the doors of the club, and it served as Oldham's Vatican. A voracious reader in German theology, he reached out to the great theologians of northern Europe – Karl Barth and Barth's friendly liberal Protestant rival Emil Brunner, as well as Bonhoeffer, were among his friends – and he devoted his life to persuading as many Churches as possible to cooperate.[79] His first triumph as administrator was a Missionary Conference at Edinburgh in 1910, the largest and most comprehensive such gathering so far held. For the first time, there were invitations to Churches beyond Europe and America (and not just Protestant Churches), although these had their limits: there were no Africans on the guest list. India, with all its problems, remained at the forefront of preoccupations.

Crucially, Oldham and his fellow organizers recognized the peculiar difficulty and also the peculiar potential of Anglicanism, an episcopal Church which set great store by its episcopal structure, and which contained a battle of Protestant and Catholic identities, themselves encapsulating the great divide in the Western Church caused by the Reformation. High Church Anglicans, those who treasured Catholicity and were often suspicious of Protestants in their own Church, let alone those beyond, were persuaded to attend Edinburgh, where they were given the chance to see that there was value in working with other Protestant Churches. They could offer their own long-standing contacts with Orthodox and Catholic churchmen – some Anglo-Catholics had been seeking corporate reunion with Rome and the Orthodox since the 1850s – and that opened up possibilities for ecumenism beyond Protestant Christianity, albeit at this stage very tentative.[80] Above all, the delegates dispersed from a successful and exciting event with a recognition that it was no longer possible for Churches to work apart in spreading a message of unity and love; that insight applied to Europe as much as to India. They sent a message to 'all Christian lands' which saw the next ten years as 'a turning-point in human history' – so it proved, but not in the way that they cheerfully expected.[81] The First World War was instead another salutary call to humility for European Christianity.

Two bishops, one American Episcopal and the other Swedish, now turned the message of the conference into more permanent conversations. Charles Brent was a missionary bishop in the then American-ruled Philippines: he proposed a series of discussions and conferences which would consider issues of 'Faith and Order' – that is, what the Church believed and how it structured itself. This would help to clarify its mission in new settings, but it would have the potential to produce a coherent reaction to all that the Enlightenment had meant for Christian self-understanding, for good or ill, and such conclusions might reveal new ways of healing ancient wounds within Christianity. The Swedish Lutheran Primate, Archbishop Nathan Söderblom, concentrated on the other challenge facing the Churches in this age of dislocation and anxiety: the exploration of credible guidelines for being a Christian in modern society. Stockholm was the setting for the first conference on 'Life and Work' in 1925: another formidable task of organization for the indefatigable Oldham. Notably, a few representatives of Orthodoxy were in attendance, and their numbers grew despite the gulf in understanding which separated them from Protestant or even Anglican views of what constituted the Church.[82] These two movements eventually amalgamated in 1948 into the World Council of Churches, which, with its acquisition of an imposing headquarters in Switzerland and a central Secretariat, seemed to be bidding to become the Christian equivalent of the new United Nations, the organization created in 1945 in succession to the discredited League of Nations. Indeed, to an extent seldom remembered until recent years, the Universal Declaration of Human Rights which the United Nations proclaimed in 1948 was the product of the same ecumenical liberal Protestant nexus of clerics and laypeople which looked back to the Edinburgh Missionary Conference.[83]

Simultaneously Anglicanism was asserting its own place in the centre of ecumenical discussions, although the outcomes of its initiatives revealed a variety of drawbacks. From the 1920 Lambeth Conference of Anglican bishops, there was heard what has been called 'probably the most memorable statement of any Lambeth Conference'.[84] The bishops seem to have been shocked by the traumatic experience of the war into producing a document rather un-Anglican in its dramatic tone, one of those rare examples of official Church pronouncements which might be called prophetic. It was an *Appeal to all Christian People* to seek 'a Church, genuinely Catholic, loyal to all Truth, and gathering into its fellowship all "who profess and call themselves Christians," within whose visible unity all the treasures of faith and order, bequeathed as a heritage by the past to the present, shall be possessed in common'.[85] The problem was how to make any sense of the various responses. Many in the English Free Churches were enthusiastic, but they spent the rest of the century making little headway in the face of a constantly confused Anglican reaction to their overtures. Anglicans were always fatally divided between Anglo-Catholics and Evangelicals who could not agree on what was important about being an Anglican, alongside the 'central' Anglicans, perpetually irritated at what they regarded as the unhelpful posturing on either flank.

Equally difficult for Anglicans was to make progress with the Orthodox. Once more, there was much goodwill. Many uprooted Russian and Serb clergy and students, traumatized by war and revolution, had found a happy refuge with their wartime ally Britain. Representatives of the vacant patriarchate in Constantinople were enthusiastic witnesses of the debates at Lambeth in 1920, which came in the wake of Constantinople's own dramatic appeal for all Christians to cooperate whatever their doctrinal differences (though the delegates were less enthusiastic about most other features of the Church of England which they observed during their visit). Given the dire state of affairs in Soviet Russia, it was natural for Anglicans to look to Constantinople rather than Moscow, but the patriarchate was caught up in Ottoman Turkey's collapse and the devastation of Christianity in Asia Minor. That shrewd diplomat Archbishop Randall Davidson was aware that, as so often in the tangled three-century history of Anglican–Orthodox relations, a major consideration for the Orthodox was to grab any help they could find in a crisis.[86]

Both rival candidates to fill the patriarchal vacancy in Constantinople now made enthusiastic noises about recognizing the validity of Anglican clerical orders that had been so comprehensively rejected by the Pope in 1896 in *Apostolicae Curae*. Meletios, the successful candidate, eventually sailed into Constantinople in 1922 on a French rather than a British gunboat, but he went ahead with a declaration that he recognized Anglican orders. What seemed for a moment like a major step in reunion soon disappeared into the mire of Orthodox feuds. Meletios infuriated most of the Orthodox world, not merely by consorting with heretical Anglicans, but also because of his efforts to switch Orthodoxy to the use of the Gregorian calendar, that pernicious invention of an equally heretical pope. When the Turks engineered Meletios's dismissal a year later, the British, content with the achievement of having preserved the patriarchate in its historic setting in Constantinople, did not intervene.[87]

The one great success of the Ecumenical Movement in following up Anglican appeals to pursue corporate unity on the basis of a common episcopate took place where the Movement had begun, back in India. A statesmanlike High Churchman, Edwin Palmer, Bishop of Bombay (the modern Mumbai), won the confidence of non-episcopal Church leaders in south India. He proposed a Church which would possess the historic episcopate in succession from the Apostles, but which would take seriously decision-making by the whole body of the Church in presbyteries or synods and local congregations, and which would recognize the validity of the various ministries which came to it from Methodists, Congregationalists, Presbyterians.[88] The scheme which emerged echoed – no doubt largely unconsciously – the broadly based episcopacy which King James VI (see pp. 648–50) had long before with crafty persistence engineered in early-seventeenth-century Scotland.

Doctrinaire English Anglo-Catholics hated the plan, and their protests about it diverted a good deal of their attention from the Second World War raging around them. Bishop Palmer marshalled a terse pragmatism in its defence in a letter of 1933 to the London *Times*, using an image that would resonate with the generation who had learned realism in Flanders trenches:

> Some obscure persons in South India are making the first attempt to end that division. They are like men asking leave to go over the top. They know that they may die in the attempt and that their attempt will fail if they are not followed. In other words, it is possible that a united church may go wrong after union . . . Who is it who died, deserted by all to save all? Who is it who wants one body to complete His saving work?'[89]

Eventually in 1955 the Church of England agreed to enter (almost) full communion with the new episcopal Church of South India, which had come to fruition eight years before. It was a hard fight, and England's consent was not repeated in the case of a not dissimilar united Church in North India, which therefore continues to face procedural difficulties if its ordained ministers seek to work in Anglican settings. No other scheme of corporate union has so far sidled its way past the reluctance among opposed Anglican Church parties to surrender their respective understandings of Anglican identity.[90] Around the Christian world, it has largely been Protestant Churches of liberal tradition, whose authority is already vested in a corporate decision-making body, Presbyterians and Methodists – more sacrificially, Congregationalists – which have found it possible to overcome their historic divisions.

WORLD CHRISTIANITY REALIGNED: PENTECOSTALS AND NEW CHURCHES

The World Council of Churches has achieved much in creating understanding and communication among Christians. Around 350 Christian Churches are currently either full members in its work or in association with it; the Roman Catholic Church has not become a full member, but has a long-standing commitment to its activity. It has been an agent for channelling resources into a myriad of projects seeking to address social and political problems and redress the balance between Western wealth and the need of the developing world. Yet more than half a century after its foundation, it is clear that it has not (or at least not yet) assumed the central place in Christianity that seemed possible in its first decades. Likewise, the Ecumenical Movement's successes have not been those expected by Oldham and the other founding fathers (fathers indeed, mostly male and mostly clerical): results have been low key, local, pragmatic.

Perhaps the problem lay in the very institutions which Oldham and his colleagues excelled in creating: conferences, committees, movements with secretariats, carefully drafted and redrafted agreed statements. Liberal Protestantism was inclined to find the spontaneity of the Holy Spirit rather unnerving. Not so the mushroom-like new Church bodies which we have already noted in Africa and America at the turn of the nineteenth and twentieth centuries. As so often in the history of Christianity, at first the mainstream Churches scarcely noticed what was happening beyond them, or if they did notice, they hardly took seriously what they saw among what seemed like small groups of eccentrics. It has been argued by one of the most perceptive observers of Pentecostalism that not until the late 1950s was the wider American public made aware of its existence.[91] Indeed, it is difficult for outsiders to keep track of movements which have generated a bewildering array of names, acronyms and slogans. All were intended to express their multiform identities and zestful efforts to capture experiences life-transforming but, by their very nature, often difficult to put into words – particularly by those who lacked the benefit of higher education in the style of Oxbridge or Berlin.

Pentecostal disagreements trivial to observers, momentous to participants, threw long shadows over the future. In 1916, for instance, a significant section of American Pentecostalism split in two, in an argument which leapt back to some of the earliest recorded disputes about the Trinity. Evangelicals in the Keswick Conference tradition were inclined to invoke the name of Jesus with a frequency which would have struck a chord with late medieval northern European Catholics or Orthodox exponents of Hesychasm; yet in this case, devotional enthusiasm led to an assertion by the Canadian preacher Robert McAlister that early Christians had baptized not in the name of the Trinity, but in the name of Jesus. Did not Peter say as much in Acts 2.38? From there, McAlister developed the proposition that 'Father, Son and Holy Spirit' were only titles for the God who was named Jesus. This was a new form of that early Christian assertion of oneness in the Godhead, modalist Monarchianism (see p. 146). Since 'baptism' was a word constantly echoing through Pentecostalist conversation, there could hardly have been a more explosive intervention. Schism followed in the only recently formed Assemblies of God, and the 'Oneness' folk went their own way, preserving a commitment to racial inclusiveness which was now notably lacking among the all-white Assemblies. 'Oneness' Pentecostalism still flourishes; it may represent about a quarter of avowedly Pentecostal Churches worldwide.[92] And the emphasis on Jesus continues to resound through Pentecostal and Charismatic hymnody generally.

Mainstream Evangelicals who took a poor view of speaking in tongues noticed approvingly that the Assemblies of God had at least kept themselves true to Trinitarianism. That would be a help when later the two parties inched together. That result was not inevitable: there was an interesting problem here. In Pentecostalism's early years, Pentecostals met with extreme detestation and name-calling from more established conservative Evangelicals, perhaps all the more so because Pentecostalism's rhetorical style was unmistakably familiar. Like Evangelicalism, it combined a suspicion of modern city ways with a relish for capturing modernity from Satan. It was a leading Pentecostal Church founder, the swashbuckling Aimee Semple McPherson, who hurled handbills for God from an aeroplane in 1920, and presided over the first-known Church radio station. Taking their cue from (the sometime) Mrs McPherson's genius for showbiz, Pentecostals from Los Angeles to Seoul have subsequently shown a talent for staging worship in ways which would stand creditably beside the great Hollywood musicals of the twentieth century (see Plates 50 and 68).[93] Yet while Pentecostalism's roots were Evangelical, there was much in it which was not a natural partner for biblically based Protestantism, particularly for Protestants who looked to the Five 'Fundamentals': verbal inerrancy, Jesus Christ's divinity, the Virgin Birth, penal substitution and the physical resurrection of Christ. Pentecostalism was inclined to look instead for 'new revelation': it was intuitive, spontaneous, whereas conservative Evangelicalism was rationalist, word-based. It was also apt to give scope to female leadership, in a fashion which had always been common in the radical beginnings of nineteenth-century Protestant movements, but which in Pentecostalism showed every sign of growing rather than diminishing.

Another movement within Pentecostalism caused alarm for those Evangelicals who cared: it stood at an absolute polarity to the 'Social Gospel' of contemporary liberal Protestantism. In the American heartland, as years of catastrophic economic depression painfully inched towards recovery at the end of the 1930s, there developed a form of

Pentecostalism referring to itself as the 'Word of Faith' movement. Like some earlier American denominations, it stressed the importance of prayer in healing, but there was much more to its vision of Christian success than that, causing detractors to refer to it as the 'health and wealth' movement, or the 'Prosperity Gospel'. One of its earliest exponents, Kenneth E. Hagin, developed his ministry in Texas among the Assemblies of God, taking as a favourite text Christ's promise in Mark 11.23 that those without doubt in their hearts can move mountains. One of his associates, Oral Roberts, who became to television what Aimee Semple McPherson had been to radio, was closely involved in 1951 in a Californian multi-millionaire's foundation of a Full Gospel Business Men's Fellowship International. This organization still robustly promotes capitalism in the service of Jesus, a 'cargo cult' rebranded for the American Dream. Through Pentecostalism's global reach, many corners of the world would take up this message, so especially appealing to communities whose trajectory from poverty to prosperity seemed to vindicate the prayers they were making. There was a political corollary. Those who had suffered from Communism in a variety of settings, especially in South Korea (see Plate 68), also appreciated the firm message from the 'Word of Faith' that if capitalism represented God's will, Communism was a device of the Devil.[94]

Despite their differences, Evangelicals and Pentecostals cautiously moved together. In 1943 the (still Trinitarian) Assemblies of God joined a new umbrella organization for American conservative Evangelicalism, the National Association of Evangelicals, whose avowed goal was to fight Protestant liberalism and the Ecumenical Movement. This was a crucial alliance. It meant that Pentecostal theological education, now rapidly developing to keep pace with its proliferation of congregations which needed more pastoral understanding than fiery preaching could provide, was firmly directed into an Evangelical mode. It discouraged Pentecostalism (at least for the time being) from casting its eyes on those parts of Christianity of which conservative Evangelicals disapproved.[95] The association was a welcome reinforcement for Evangelical values at an unpromising moment. During the previous decades, conservative Evangelicals' assumption that their cultural outlook was part of the hegemony of Protestantism in mainstream America had received two serious blows, over the issues of evolutionary biology and Prohibition.

It was their hatred of Charles Darwin's theory of evolution that caused the first debacle. In the early 1920s, two states in the Midwest, Oklahoma and Tennessee, passed laws against the teaching of evolution in schools. A test case in 1925 (brought partly to boost the economy of the struggling town of Dayton, Tennessee, with a mite of free publicity) caught the imagination of pressmen across the Union; a young biology teacher, John Scopes, was found guilty, although he was not actually sure that he had got round to teaching evolution in his lessons. Leading the prosecution was the veteran Democratic politician William Jennings Bryan, who, having built his reputation on championing the concerns of ordinary decent folk from the countryside against the sophistication of the cities, was never averse in his long career to spicing his thrilling speeches with a good dose of home-cooked religion. The conviction was overturned on a technicality in the Tennessee Supreme Court, and two more states went on to pass similar laws in the aftermath, but the damage had been done.

Facing Bryan for the defence was Clarence Darrow, a lawyer who had likewise made his name championing the causes of the humble and powerless. Darrow was another masterly performer in a courtroom, unscrupulous in a good cause, and, relevant to the present case, he was that rarity in American public life, an avowed agnostic. He made the grand old man look foolish: he forced Bryan off the sure ground of parental say in children's education towards the dangerous territory of small details in the Old Testament (Darrow had more sense than to be satirical about the Gospels in public). It was all a gift for humorists, and laughter is never good news for those seeking to impose the authority of the Word of God on others. Less comic was the sudden death of Bryan, before he had the chance to leave Dayton.[96]

Far worse in its long-term effects was the experiment with total national prohibition of alcohol, which came into effect as the Eighteenth Amendment to the American Constitution in 1920, after a bitter fight, in which it had survived a presidential veto by that staunch establishment Presbyterian, Woodrow Wilson. In the nineteenth century, temperance or total abstention had not been a party issue, but a campaign involving people right across the spectrum of denominations from Catholics to Fundamentalists, especially the womenfolk. Yet as the cleavage grew between liberal Protestants and conservative Evangelicals, the Anti-Saloon League established in 1895, eventual victors in the campaign for the Amendment, seemed more and more the voice of angry small-town Evangelical America: suspicious alike of the big coastal cities and wicked old drink-sodden Europe, and determined to assert what now, after a century of temperance campaigning, seemed to be an old-time cause. Even the Southern Baptists, still nursing the grievances of the white

NOT PEACE BUT A SWORD

South from the civil war, dropped their distaste for entanglements with
hypocritical Yankee moral campaigners, in order to bring succour to
the fight for godliness.[97]

The result has often been portrayed on the cinema screen as gangster
entertainment, but it was the cause of much human tragedy, providing
a perfect opportunity for organized crime and its corruption of otherwise
law-abiding society. No issue more effectively divided conservative
Evangelicals from those among their fellow Christian Americans who
could see no harm in a glass of whiskey. It was a rerun of Cromwellian
England's bitter divisions over social regulation back in the 1650s (see
p. 652). After President Franklin D. Roosevelt presided over the repeal
of the Prohibition Amendment in 1933, for half a century conservative
Evangelicals were too cowed by the fiasco of Prohibition to try to impose
their social values on the rest of the nation by political means. They
largely left Federal politics to liberal Protestants, plus a growing number
of elite Catholics. As Washington DC's hilltop Episcopal cathedral,
which called itself 'National', steadily rose from its scaffolding to dominate northward views of the city, its cool and scholarly English Gothic
represented the low-temperature, well-mannered religion of the white
neighbourhoods in the Federal capital, in a way that Europeans would
understand. Meanwhile, Evangelicals waited. They listened to their wire-
less sets in their small towns, their unfashionable suburbs, their remote
farms, even in the barn milking, and they took comfort from the packaging
of old-time religion, syndicated and delivered by a host of
local radio stations, which had profited from the example set by Aimee
Semple McPherson. The Evangelicals' hour would come, in a more literal
historical sense than their Scofield Reference Bibles told them.[98]

As the tectonic plates of American religion shifted, so around the
world innumerable offshoots of enthusiastic Protestantisms found their
own life and style. By no means all observed the Pentecostal shibboleth
of speaking in tongues, though they were certainly charismatic in their
own fashion. Africa bred a host of prophets who owed something, if
only at a remove, to William Wade Harris (see pp. 887–8). A major
spur to their message was the great influenza epidemic which swept the
world in 1918, proving as destructive of human life as the First World
War, and in Africa almost as destructive to the reputation of the West:
the much-vaunted Western medicine seemed helpless in face of it. So two
characteristics of the new prophets were first that they left European-led
Churches which had fostered their faith, and second that they offered
their own style of healing. In West Africa their Churches were commonly

known by the Yoruba word for 'owners of prayer': *Aladura*. Prophet-led
they might be, but one of their most effective founders, the Nigerian
Josiah Olulowo Ositelu, brought from his rather High Church Anglican
background a proper respect for hierarchy, which quickly ran to twelve
categories of male officer, from Primate down to Male Cross Holders
(women could bear iron rods or crosses with the Primate's permission).
Aladura were proud of their new beginning, proclaiming in their constitution 'that Ethiopia or Africa shall raise up her own hands unto
the Great Jehovah-God under the Spiritual Guide and lead her own
indigenous sons'.[99]

That pride in an 'Ethiopian' faith, something truly African, runs
through the crowded assembly of prophets across the continent. They
could bring African solutions to African problems. That proud boast
was a great contrast with the generation of political leaders who were
to take over when European colonies in Africa became independent
countries in the 1960s. Those leaders were mostly from European-led
churches, and very commonly were Christian schoolteachers (like Kenneth Kaunda of Zambia or Robert Mugabe of Zimbabwe), with a
history of patient study in Western-style universities, often in Europe
itself. Prophets constructed alternatives. In the Zulu Isaiah Shembe's
AmaNazaretha Church, founded amid the growing racism of the white-
governed Union of South Africa, Shembe maintained that his Church
rather than the Zulu monarchy should be the source of Zulu national
identity in future. He instilled the sense that true virtue lay in avoiding
service to whites, especially amid the corrupt cities. In the worship-
dancing which his followers still perform regularly through the liturgical
week, following Shembe's instructions, broom handles are brandished
in place of the death-dealing assegais of warriors: so domestic values
triumph over traditional Zulu military posturing. The dance empowers
ancestors to dance in Heaven: it is a system of reciprocity, connecting
with the dead in as satisfying a manner as the medieval Western Purgatory industry.[100] Even if simply passive in suffering, a prophet might
have a mighty effect on people all too familiar with suffering, rather like
St Boris and St Gleb through the centuries of Russian Orthodoxy (see
pp. 508–9). Simon Kimbangu, inspired to begin healing after the 1918
influenza epidemic, had a public or rather clandestinely public ministry
for no more than five months, before he was imprisoned for life by the
authorities in the Belgian Congo on charges of subversion. His thirty
years of silence did not stop other imprisoned disciples from cherishing
his memory as good news for multitudes silenced by 'the prophets of

Satan, missionaries, the Belgian government'. Now his Church, treasuring his body enshrined at its headquarters, is one of the largest in central Africa.[101]

Africa thus presented a constant interaction between African-initiated Churches, the still-growing Churches brought earlier by Westerners and a steadily more obvious Pentecostalism. Their growth over the twentieth century was phenomenal, far outstripping that of the population. In 1914 there may have been four million Christians in Africa, by 1950 seventy-five million, and much more was to come. One wise observer who knew Africa over more than thirty years, the Swedish Lutheran bishop in Tanzania Bengt Sundkler, observed that whereas in the nineteenth century African Christianity had largely been a youth movement, in the twentieth it was a women's movement. Healing, that particular concern for women as they cared for their families, has become the great symbol of Christian success alongside education.[102] This was not confined to charismatic Protestantism. The Maasai of Kenya were long resistant to Christianity of any sort; men proud of their warrior tradition despised its message of forgiveness and sexual continence. Women contrariwise rather appreciated these propositions, and they allied with Catholic Spiritan missionaries when the priests arrived from Europe in the 1950s. Derided and obstructed by their menfolk, many women began developing a spiritual sickness called *orpeko,* which was caused by an evil spirit. It turned out that the only sure-fire permanent cure for *orpeko* was Christian baptism. There was not much that men could do in riposte to this: Catholic Christianity had arrived, but it was overwhelmingly female. Perhaps unsurprisingly, most Maasai Christians are inclined to think of the Christian God as a woman, which is not calculated to please the Spiritan Fathers.[103]

During the same period, Christianity radically diversified in other regions too. Latin America, a culture already overwhelmingly Christian, began to transform its Christianity. Catholic in outlook and Spanish or Portuguese in language in 1900, from the first few decades of the century, Latin America was gaining a Pentecostal presence which marched in step with an increasingly diverse immigrant community, but which also rapidly began penetrating existing communities. Pentecostalism was a new manifestation of its long-tangled relationship with the United States. By the 1950s, there were twenty to thirty different Pentecostal denominations in Brazil alone.[104] Then Asia was to produce Christianity's most spectacular recent success story, although that was not yet apparent in the 1950s. Korea, reduced to ruins in war between 1950 and 1953 and

partitioned with a new 'Hermit Kingdom' in its Communist north, was
to develop in the southern Republic its own mixture of old-established
Churches, Pentecostals and indigenous syncretism, which arose alongside the painful rebuilding of Korean society from wartime destitution.
Koreans did not forget the witness of premillennial Korean Protestants,
who in the last grim years of Japanese colonial rule before its collapse
in 1945 had refused to be present at state Shinto ceremonies, considering
it idolatry to worship a king who was not Jesus. This was a conjuncture
in which patriotism met apocalyptic faith. Koreans were grateful too to
the Western powers which in the Korean War had saved them from
being overwhelmed by Communism; as a result, they felt very positively
towards American-style religion, at a time when many countries in Asia
and Africa saw all varieties of Western power as oppressive colonialism.

As the 1950s reached their end, it would not have been unreasonable
for Christian leaders to feel optimism about the future of their faith
after the batterings of two world wars, yet few would have been likely
to take a wide enough view to see which parts of the world actually
justified that optimism. No one could miss the stirring of Africa, but
most attention might be drawn by the healthily full churches of Europe,
of its white dominions worldwide and of North America, or the success
of European-led Churches elsewhere which were still regarded as
'missionary'. Alongside them were obvious setbacks: the now-shackled
Churches, Orthodox, Protestant and Catholic, in Soviet Russia's sphere
of influence, and a new age of peril from 1949 for the Christianities of
China, facing a newly united, self-confident and intolerant Communist
republic. As Christian leaders renewed or extended their acquaintance,
decorously socializing around World Council of Churches committees,
and as archbishops boarded planes in Buenos Aires or Sydney to consult
the Holy Father in the Vatican, Pentecostalism was rarely the subject of
their concern. Nor was the possibility that the Enlightenment would
spring any fresh surprises on a liberal Protestantism which had adroitly
profited from it, or on a Catholicism which presented a sturdy front
against it, protected by a rampart of volumes of Thomas Aquinas.
Perspectives were, however, about to change with remarkable speed.

25
Culture Wars
(1960–Present)

THE SECOND VATICAN COUNCIL:
HALF A REVOLUTION

In 1978, on my first visit to Rome, on the eve of the enthronement of the tragically short-lived Pope John Paul I, I stared with some astonishment at the flower-decked grave of Pope John XXIII in the crypt of St Peter's Basilica. His tomb was flanked by a pair of large bronze-effect wreaths, gifts from the late General Francisco Franco of Spain. They looked like two particularly sinister minders for this most cheerily informal of twentieth-century popes, and presumably had been in place since soon after the Pope's death in 1963. I would be interested to know to what Valley of the Fallen they have now been relegated. The possibility of embarrassing memories around the tomb has otherwise ended, since the Pope himself has been reverently relocated to the customary sacred glass-fronted showcase, in the run-up to his being declared a saint.[1] Although John XXIII enjoyed one of the shorter pontificates in the papacy's history, it had a transformative effect on Christianity far beyond the boundaries of the Roman Catholic Church. It negated everything that *Caudillo* Franco had stood for – hence the glorious inappropriateness of those two bronzed wreaths. There was an unconscious symbolism about the clash of styles embodied in their presence which might make historians regret their disappearance. The last half-century of Christian experience has witnessed a war of cultures whose result still remains in doubt.

Cardinal Roncalli, a former Vatican diplomat enjoying the honourable semi-retirement of the Patriarchate of Venice, was elected John XXIII in 1958 largely because he had few enemies, and because no one involved in the election thought that he could do much harm; he was seventy-six and it was (rightly) thought that he would not enjoy a long period in office. After the last exhausted years of Pius XII, it was sensible to look for a man of peace who would give the Church a chance to find a decisive leader to set an appropriate direction for the future. Certainly Roncalli had proved good at defusing conflict throughout his career, but that might have provided a hint that he was unlikely to perpetuate the embattled, adversarial style which had characterized the papacy since its trials in the French Revolution – one need only recall the combative, denunciatory language of the *Syllabus of Errors*, or the frightened tirades against Modernism and Communism from Pius X and Pius XI.

The new pope's ebullience and boundless curiosity, so disconcerting to churchmen conscious of papal protocol, was matched by a shrewd ability to get what he wanted. What he wanted did not coincide with the wish of prominent members of the Vatican's Curia to defend old certainties without much further discussion. Instead, to the horror of Curial officials, in 1959 he threw everything open to discussion by announcing his intention of calling a new council to the Vatican.[2] The Vatican machine, resigned to the inevitable meeting, knew what to do in such circumstances: keep strict control of the agenda through the Holy Office (the more emollient term then preferred for the Roman Inquisition). The spirit would not simply be that of Vatican I but rather that of Trent, with its stern anathemas of ideas which no good Catholic should hold. As Cardinal Ottaviani of the Holy Office spelled out to the council in its early stages, 'You need to be aware that the style of councils is concise, clear, brief, and is not the same as for sermons, or for some bishop's pastoral letter, or even for the encyclicals of the Supreme Pontiff. The style proper to a council is the style that has been sanctioned by the practice of the ages.'[3]

There were three obstacles to this. One was Pope John's recall to Rome of a long-standing Vatican civil servant, Giovanni Battista Montini, who had been close to Pius XII until his broad sympathies brought him disfavour and decorous exile to the Archbishopric of Milan. Montini, now rewarded with the cardinal's hat denied him on his departure from Rome, knew how the Vatican worked, and he had good reason to find the outwitting of former colleagues a congenial task. Second was the arrival in 1962 of more than two thousand bishops in Rome, with Europe contributing less than half of their number. The bishops had been consecrated from within an ecclesiastical system paranoid about Modernism, but they brought with them a myriad of different practical experiences of what it was to be a Catholic in 1962. Third was the glare of publicity in which the council's proceedings took place. At Trent, the Holy Office had not faced the problem of journalists. Now the Vatican was forced to employ a press officer, although, with a disdainful symbolism, he was not actually given anywhere to sit during his attendance at the council's proceedings.[4]

This unprecedented gathering of Catholic leaders listened with fascination to a pope who in his inaugural address spoke excitedly of the providential guidance of the world's inhabitants to 'a new order of human relationships', and, far from lecturing the world, criticized those 'prophets of misfortune' who viewed it as 'nothing but betrayal and ruination'. It was important actually to have heard the address, since the subsequent published Latin version was substantially bowdlerized.[5] More remarkable still were invitations to and the palpable presence of Protestant observers, who would have run the risk of being burned at the stake if they had dared to set foot in Rome during the Council of Trent – and, as an afterthought, even some Catholic women, mostly nuns, were asked to attend. None of these invitees could vote, but their presence was a symbol that the Church was going to reach out beyond its traditional fortifications. All the defensive draft documents so carefully prepared by the Curia were rejected and replaced with completely different texts. Two crucial agreed documents have remained central to the council's legacy – they have provided a springboard for action to some Catholics, an obstacle course to others.

The first, *Lumen Gentium* ('The Light of Peoples'), was a decree on the nature of the Church. This document was one of those which had been transformed from the first draft prepared under the direction of Cardinal Ottaviani, the original being openly criticized for its lack of coherence by Cardinal Montini, while a Belgian cardinal dramatically expressed his scorn for its 'triumphalism', 'clericalism' and 'juridicism'.[6] The utterly different document which emerged, complete with that new title suggested by the great Belgian ecumenist Cardinal Leo Jozef Suenens, represented a significant break with previous Roman Catholic statements in its careful choice of a verb: instead of a simple identification between the Church of Christ and the Church presided over by the pope, it stated that the Church 'subsisted in' the Roman Catholic Church. What did that say about other Churches – indeed, how does 'subsist in' differ from 'is'? The decree also made a fresh attempt to tackle that question of authority which had nearly destroyed Trent, and to which Vatican I had given a partial (and partisan ultramontane) answer. Its second chapter was entitled 'The People of God', all of whom, according to the Book of Revelation, Christ the High Priest had made 'a kingdom, priests, to his God and Father' (Revelation 1.6). The ordained priesthood 'forms and rules the priestly people', but the royal priesthood of the people was exercised in a whole variety of aspects of the Church's life, both liturgical and everyday in the world. What were the implications of this for episcopacy? The decree added the concept of 'collegiality' to papal primacy: a reaffirmation of the authority of other bishops along-side that of the Bishop of Rome – or a replacement for his authority? The decree's reaffirmation of papal infallibility did not suggest the latter interpretation.[7] Cardinal Ottaviani observed with graveyard humour that the only 'collegial' act recorded in the Gospels was the flight of Jesus's disciples from the Garden of Gethsemane before his Passion.[8]

Then came *Gaudium et Spes* ('Joy and Hope'), an attempt to place the Church in the context of the modern world:

[T]his Second Vatican Council, having probed more profoundly into the mystery of the Church, now addresses itself without hesitation, not only to the sons of the Church and to all who invoke the name of Christ, but to the whole of humanity. For the council yearns to explain to everyone how it conceives of the presence and activity of the Church in the world of today . . .

The People of God believes that it is led by the Lord's Spirit, Who fills the earth. Motivated by this faith, it labours to decipher authentic signs of God's presence and purpose in the happenings, needs and desires in which this People has a part along with other men of our age. For faith throws a new light on everything, manifests God's design for man's total vocation, and thus directs the mind to solutions which are fully human.

The whole statement breathed the happy confidence, already ex-pressed in Pope John's opening address, that the Church need not fear opening discussions with those outside its boundaries, rather than lecturing them.

So much else tumbled open in conciliar statements, much of it dis-covered earlier by the separated Protestant brethren of the Western Church: the value of vernacular liturgy, an adventurous engagement with the previous two centuries of biblical scholarship, an openness to ecumenism, an affirmation of the ministry of laypeople. There was also open apology to the Jewish people for their sufferings at the hands of Christians in *Nostra aetate* ('In our age'), which in its final draft bluntly dismissed the traditional Christian idea that the Jewish people had committed deicide – the killing of God. One bishop amidst the crowds who found the whole proceedings thoroughly uncongenial and dismayingly chaotic, and whose vote was consistently in the small minority against such statements as *Gaudium et Spes*, was a Pole who during the council's sessions became Archbishop of Cracow, Karol Wojtyła. Also expressing his private disapproval of what he saw as the facile sunniness of *Gaudium et Spes* was one of the attendant German theologians, Professor Josef Ratzinger.[9]

By the time these crucial documents were agreed and promulgated by the papacy, John XXIII was dead. Even before the council had opened he had been diagnosed with cancer. He was to live only a few months more as the revolutionary programme unfolded, but the momentum which he had fostered brought a swift election of Cardinal Montini as Pope Paul VI and a resumption of the council's sittings. Pope Paul was determined to maintain the pace of change, but as he pressed on with the reforms, and later conscientiously implemented them, he repeatedly displayed a quality which his impish predecessor had once characterized as *'un po' amletico'* – 'a bit like Hamlet'.[10] The man who had seemed so exceptionally open to change in the Vatican of Pius XII now agonized about how far change should go. Perhaps unsurprisingly, the pontiff had doubts about the collegiality of all bishops, and in order to win the consent of a conservative minority to *Lumen Gentium*, he accepted 'Prefatory notes' (*Nota praevia*) added to it, which spelled out in scholastic language the limits which the main text could place on collegiality.

On his own initiative, the Pope in his closing speech to the council proclaimed Mary as Mother of the Church, after pleas from Polish bishops for an even stronger title for Mary, *Mediatrix*. His action contrasted with the fact that the idea of Mary as Mother of the Church had been relegated to some polite murmurs in *Lumen Gentium*. The Pope may have been swayed by the fact that the council's vote on the conservative proposal to consecrate the world to Mary was the most contentious and closely fought of any major decision within it. Nevertheless, the outcome was a reminder that Paul VI was not necessarily going to hold formal constitutional consultations before major public statements, even those made outside the criteria for infallibility set by Vatican I. Among those dismayed by any such Marian proclamation was Augustin Bea, the German cardinal who headed the Vatican's ecumenical Secretariat for Unity; he could easily see that the move was not calculated to win over Protestants or even necessarily the Orthodox.[11]

Motherhood, fatherhood and the family in a more general sense were to prove the preoccupations most disruptive to the revolutionary programme of Vatican II, because it was above all in matters of sexuality that the Pope drew back from the strong tide of pleas for change in the Church's practice. There was a wide expectation among those present that realities revealed by mission in Africa and provoked by ecumenical contacts elsewhere would lead to a relaxation of the Roman Church's insistence on universal celibacy for the clergy; instead Paul reaffirmed the celibacy rule. It was the beginning of a steady decline in vocations to the priesthood in the northern hemisphere, and a steady loss of priests from ministry to enter marriages. Throughout much of the rest of the world, in cultures where celibacy had never been valued, the papal rulings on this matter were frankly ignored, and in these settings, significantly, vocations continued to flourish. Even more damaging was the Pope's unmodified stand against artificial birth control: this provoked the greatest internal challenge to papal authority in the Western Church's history since Martin Luther's protests over the theology of salvation.

The technology of contraception had been transformed in the late nineteenth century. Now it was possible easily and cheaply to separate heterosexual intercourse from pregnancy, and Europeans and North Americans had not been slow to exploit the possibility. How would theologians react? The Anglican Communion was remarkably quick in coming to terms with the new situation: the change can be monitored by rapid shifts in the statements formulated by the bishops attending Lambeth Conferences. In 1908 they called on Christians 'to discountenance the use of all artificial means of restriction as demoralizing to character and hostile to national welfare', as well as being 'repugnant to Christian morality'. In 1920 they still expressed grave concern at the spread of 'theories and practices hostile to the family', and the teaching which 'encourages married people in the deliberate cultivation of sexual union as an end in itself', but they declined to lay down rules to meet every case; in 1930 they declared that 'each couple must decide for themselves, as in the sight of God, after the most careful and conscientious thought, and, if perplexed in mind, after taking competent advice, both medical and spiritual'.[12]

Much had happened in the world since the Anglican bishops had made their measured recommendations, and the council was meeting amid a cultural revolution in sexual mores in the West of the 1960s which would have astonished them. Would Roman Catholic moral teaching nevertheless follow the same trajectory as the Anglicans? A strong hint to the contrary came from the moment in 1964 when, in another example of his personal initiative, Paul VI announced that he was ending discussion on the subject before the forthcoming Third Session of the council met. Yet in 1968, it looked as if Roman Catholic teaching would indeed change. A commission of experts on natural law – including laypeople, even women – was about to publish a report on birth control after five years of deliberations, concluding that there was no good argument for banning contraceptive devices. Alarmed by the direction that the commission's thoughts had taken, Pope Paul enlarged the commission and changed the criteria for those entitled to vote, with the aim of overturning the finding; instead, it was reinforced. So the Pope finally ignored the work and issued his own statement in 1968: the encyclical *Humanae vitae* ('Of Human life'), which gave no place for artificial contraception in Catholic family life.[13] To his astonishment and dismay, the case was not closed when Rome had spoken. There were open and angry protests both lay and clerical all over the northern Catholic world, and worse still, demographics soon revealed that millions of Catholic laity paid no attention to the papal ban. They have gone on rejecting it, the first time that the Catholic faithful have ever so consistently scorned a major papal pronouncement intended to structure their lives.

The long-drawn-out battle over contraception cast a permanent shadow over Paul VI's pontificate through the 1970s. There was so much that was positive in this humane and private man's exercise of his leadership: notably generous ecumenical acts, such as the agreement with the Oecumenical Patriarch in 1965 to end the excommunications mutually proclaimed by East and West in 1054 (see p. 374), and a notably warm meeting with the endearingly saintly Archbishop Michael Ramsey of Canterbury in 1966, when the Pope presented the Anglican Primate with his own bishop's ring. Pope Paul travelled the world as no previous pope had done, and he cautiously opened dialogue with the Communist regimes of Eastern Europe, while reducing the temperature of Rome's relations with General Franco's regime to unprecedented iciness – it is reliably reported that Franco during the last year of his life came close to excommunication.[14] Around the Pope, often way beyond his control, Catholics seized on the raft of reforms and recommendations made by Vatican II and implemented them in a multitude of different forms.

Apart from the furore on contraception, nothing in the life of the Church was so universally disruptive as the changes made to public worship. These were an expression of the council's wish to stress the priesthood of all people in active participation in worship, and to encourage them to do more in the liturgy than hymn-singing. Laudable in the intention of involving the whole body of the faithful in liturgical action, the implementation of this principle represented Rome at its most woodenly centralizing. Overnight, the Tridentine rite of the Mass was virtually banned (with carefully hedged-around exceptions), and its Latin replacement was used almost universally in vernacular translations. The service of Benediction of the Blessed Sacrament, which had sustained and comforted so many for so long (see pp. 414–15), was widely discountenanced by the clergy in an effort to concentrate the minds of the laity on the Mass, and in large sections of the Catholic world it disappeared. The altar furniture that had grown with such exuberance in churches in the wake of the Council of Trent was rendered redundant by the decision to reposition the celebrant at Mass facing the people: the priest therefore stood behind the altar, which had previously been affixed to a wall of sculpture and painting and thus had been designed for celebration in the other direction. A multitude of tables often cheap in appearance if not in cost camped out in historic church buildings, while the emphasis on celebrating congregational Masses at a single main altar left the greater galaxy of side altars dusty and neglected.

With the vernacular Mass also came a musical revolution. Early-twentieth-century Catholicism had witnessed an outburst of scholarly and musical energy devoted to the proper and reverent performance of the Church's ancient plainchant. The training which had gone into such sensitivity was now as redundant as the Baroque altar, when the requirement was for congregations to perform music in their own language. Priests completely untrained in teaching music to their congregations were now forced often against their instincts to impose a musical idiom which had previously hardly existed in Catholicism and which, to begin with, had virtually no repertoire native to the Catholic Church. Overnight, outside a handful of redoubts of traditional musical excellence (plus the pope's Sistine Chapel), the acoustic guitar became the dictator of musical style in Catholicism, with the same suddenness and thoroughness that the Geneva psalm had achieved in Reformation England. Not merely plainsong but the whole heritage of Catholic musical composition centred on the Mass was relegated to the liturgical sidelines, and such music was now probably more frequently and effectively performed by Anglicans than by Catholics.[15] Although the hurt extended a good way beyond theological conservatives, the defiant and semi-clandestine celebration of the old Mass and its music became a catalyst for a slow gathering of fury among traditionalist Catholics, which in some places led to schism. Others, including Josef Ratzinger, who was appointed Archbishop of Munich in 1977 and whose elder brother at Regensburg Cathedral was one of German Catholicism's leading church musicians, swallowed their anger and bided their time.[16]

CATHOLICS, PROTESTANTS
AND LIBERATION

Another momentous development for the Church came entirely independent of the Vatican: a worldwide theological movement which has come to have an increasingly tense relationship with central Catholic authority. A huge shift in the membership of global Catholicism from north to south transformed the priorities of laity, clergy and religious in settings where the two-century-old confrontation of Church and French Revolution, or even the Russian Revolution, no longer seemed the most urgent struggle. Instead it was the fight against sheer wretched poverty in the lives of millions in Latin America, Asia, and Africa. Academic theology in the earlier part of the century had not said much about poverty, apart from being against it: rather like slaves in earlier centuries, the poor had been, with sadness, taken for granted. Now certain theologians, especially those working closely with the poor, began considering the implications of the Christian doctrine of Providence: the Father cares for humans as much as he clothes the lilies of the field.[17] They looked again at the furious debates on poverty generated by the friars in the thirteenth and fourteenth centuries, and listened again to the angry comments by friars like Bartolomé de las Casas on the early stages of Spanish colonization in America (see p. 692). They listened also to what socialism and Marxism had drawn out of the French Revolution and Christian tradition in the nineteenth century. They even listened to their congregations, humble folk like those who had fought for the Church as *Cristeros* in the Mexico of the 1920s (see pp. 934–5). They christened what they were doing liberation theology.[18]

It was not easy for the Church hierarchy in Latin America to move beyond both a long alliance with elite Creole Catholic culture and a political outlook still generally conservative and authoritarian, but there were enough clerics capable of making a new assessment of the significance of lay militancy in earlier popular Catholicism among the *Cristeros* and analogous lay movements throughout the continent. That provided the momentum for an episcopal conference called to Medellín in Colombia in 1968, whose participants sought to call the Church 'to the fulfilment of the redeeming mission to which it is committed by Christ'. Active in the preparation of the bishops' discussions at Medellín was a Peruvian theologian who combined university teaching with the work of a parish priest in a slum area of the Peruvian capital, Lima, Gustavo Gutiérrez. He later popularized a phrase first used by a further episcopal conference at Puebla in 1979, in the presence of the recently elected Pope John Paul II: a 'preferential option for the poor' in the Church's construction of its mission. This had been foreshadowed in the statements of the Medellín Conference, which had looked forward to a redistribution of world resources which would give 'preference to the poorest and most needy'.[19]

In one seminal book, *A Theology of Liberation*, which had started life as a lecture in Peruvian discussions around Medellín, and in many subsequent works, Gutiérrez employed a phrase for purposeful action guided by theory, *praxis*. To theologians of classical Catholic training, this word had a ready and negative resonance, because Karl Marx had used it to indicate a philosophy inseparable from action – but that was only half the truth. As the Greek term for structured activity by free men, it was the word embedded in the original Greek title of a book of the New Testament, and of its many subsequent imitators beyond the biblical canon, the *Acts* of the Apostles. It is notable that in Gutiérrez's discussion of poverty, he did not look back, as did some liberation theologians, to the history of Christian purposeful poverty since the first monks and hermits of the Church, as an act of solidarity with those who had not chosen to be poor. Having surveyed the biblical discussion of poverty, he simply declared material poverty as a 'subhuman situation' and 'scandalous condition', and dismissed notions of spiritual poverty as unhelpful diversions.[20]

While Catholics in Latin America were discovering new meanings for justice and equality for the powerless, Protestants in the United States turned a century of black struggle for equal political rights into an interracial campaign to make a reality of the civil war emancipation of enslaved African-Americans. Even in the worst times when white supremacists distorted the democracy of the Southern States, some white Evangelical Protestants in the South were capable of standing out against the culture round them to reach across the racial barrier within Evangelicalism. Belle Harris Bennett, epitome of well-bred white Kentucky

Methodism, was central to Southern support for overseas missions, and the founder of a college which also trained women for work at home on civil rights and social projects. She campaigned against lynching, and made sure that the great black activist W. E. B. Du Bois was invited to interracial Methodist gatherings, where she used the force of her personality to ban segregated seating.[21] When, in the 1950s, civil rights activists began to campaign against Southern racism, there was a groundswell of support which could look back to affirmations like this. Among the leadership was Martin Luther King Jr, a Baptist minister and son of another who had taken the name of Martin Luther for himself and his son, inspired by his visit to Germany. When the younger King began campaigning for civil rights, his insistence on non-violent struggle had two roots: one, the Bible; the other, the campaigns of Mahatma Gandhi, whose family he had visited in India. In King, the Evangelicalism of the South met the writings of one of the greatest exponents of the 'Social Gospel' in the USA, the theologian Reinhold Niebuhr, whose synthesis of Reformed and Lutheran theology and liberal Protestant analysis of society he much admired.

Perhaps the greatest achievement in King's career, prompting President Lyndon B. Johnson to put all the skills developed in his rather chequered political career behind an act to protect black voting rights, was a pair of marches through Alabama from Selma to the state capital Montgomery in 1965. In the first, hundreds of marchers, hastily gathered through Sunday sermons from King and his colleagues after the murder of a civil rights worker, were brutally attacked and tear-gassed by state police – fatally for the credibility of Southern government, in full view of television cameras. When King called a new march for two days later to commemorate the brutality, clergy of all denominations from across the nation, and representatives of faith beyond Christianity, poured into Selma. It was one of the most remarkable demonstrations of ecumenism and multi-faith action against injustice yet seen in the world.[22]

Faced with an order from the state authorities to turn back, King used his authority over the crowds to abandon their march rather than provoke further suffering. This might have seemed like humiliation, but once more King's enemies ruined their cause that same night by their street murder of a Unitarian minister from faraway Massachusetts, who had been among the Selma marchers. A few days later, when President Johnson – wily old Texan politician shocked into uncharacteristic moral indignation – spoke to Congress to back the Voting Rights Act, he ended incongruously but with sensational effectiveness by reciting a slogan from the song which remained the anthem of American protesters throughout the 1960s: 'We shall overcome'. Three years after that, Martin Luther King was shot dead in Memphis, Tennessee, the day after a speech in which he had likened himself to Moses, afforded no more than a glimpse of the Promised Land before the entry of Israel.[23] King joined a procession of modern Christian martyrs who were killed for their work for the powerless, at the hands of those defending unjustly wielded power.

On the other side of the world, another situation combining rapid social change and political oppression provoked the development in the 1970s of a different variety of Protestant liberation theology: the *minjung* theology of South Korea. The word means 'ordinary people', but this simple concept changed focus with the bewilderingly fast development of the republic, from factory workers through to the flexibility of the information technology industry: eventually more what might be termed a 'cognitariat' of educationally skilled workers than a 'proletariat'. Jesus was minjung and the friend of the minjung, teaching forgiveness and love of enemies, but Moses was also minjung, political leader of his people against oppression. Minjung theologians were proud of their Korean past, and saw a complex struggle not only with the authoritarian South Korean government, but with the global strategies of the United States, which maintained that regime. Those involved faced torture, imprisonment and execution from South Korea's military dictators. Given the trauma of the Korean War, with nearly a million refugees from the Communist North in their midst, even self-consciously reformist Korean theologians had little inclination to explore the terminology of Marxism in the fashion of South American liberation theologians. Although opposed to the strange dynastic Communism of Kim Il Sung in the North, minjung theologians still sought to show proper respect for the Korean ideal of self-sufficiency which lay behind North Korea's cruelty and inhumanity.[24]

As Korean democracy gradually came to maturity after three hectic decades of economic development which had taken Europe two centuries to complete, there arose a new problem for minjung theology: how to reinvent for the 'cognitariat' this movement born in political struggle. The movement contributed to the social activism of a society whose needs and problems outran the administrative capacity of government, but it found it difficult to compete with Korean Pentecostalism. Pentecostals celebrated the success of the new society, and in their vehement anti-Communism they gladly adopted a conservative evangelical style from the United States, especially the 'prosperity' message of the 'Word of Faith' movements, while scorning the 'idolatry' to be found in the Korean past. Minjung's roots were in Presbyterianism, long accustomed to respecting and exploring Korean tradition and culture. So minjung theologians in recent years have explored the Korean past to find appropriate forms for a fully involved citizenship. They look with interest to the revolutionary Donghak movement, which, in the same era as the Taiping in China, sought to synthesize religion and reform for Korea. They offer people who are in danger of being too proud of their own new success Jesus's call to principled action, which can be seen as a *praxis* for Korea: 'If any man would come after me, let him deny himself and take up his cross and follow me'.[25]

For at the heart of all these movements was a meditation on the powerlessness of the crucified Christ, and on the paradox that this powerlessness was the basis for resurrection: freedom and transformation. Christian art created in the twentieth century (beyond run-of-the-mill devotional objects) has interestingly shifted away from old priorities: even in Catholic art, the Madonna and Child appear less often, and there is a greater stress on Christ on the Cross. Against the background of power struggles which had laid empires low and ruined so many lives in two world wars and beyond, much Christian experience thus resonated with the themes of crucified weakness and the tiny scale of the mustard seed before it becomes a great tree. Protestants had discovered ecumenism in their relative failures in small villages in India. Catholics discovered liberation theology in small communities of ordinary people in Latin America. They were often facing as dire threats from military power as the Mexican *Cristeros* before them, and with what little schooling the Church could provide, they turned to the Bible to help them understand their situation. They have come to be described by the inelegant terms (which have not translated well from Iberian languages) 'basic ecclesiastical communities' or 'base groups/communities'.

Poor people throughout the global south recognized the experiences of Latin Americans and civil rights marchers in their own. They likewise looked for political liberation, but the historic context in Africa and Asia was very different from that in Latin America. From Dakar to Djakarta, the 1940s and 1950s had witnessed rapid disintegration in the enormous colonial empires built up by European colonial powers in the nineteenth century – Africa's decolonization was a particular surprise. Although the United States was initially very ready to encourage

Europe's shattered powers to shed their colonies after 1945, no one expected the virtually universal withdrawal which emerged at the end of the 1950s, postponed only by special circumstances in southern Africa. When one young liberal Catholic Belgian academic in 1956 published a work proposing that the Belgian Congo might suitably be given independence on the centenary of its cession to King Leopold in 1885, his book provoked a storm of ridicule and fury in Belgium. In fact the Congo's independence came four years after its publication. Rome had given so little consideration to providing an autonomous future for Catholicism in the vast Belgian territory that an indigenous hierarchy of bishops was only hastily established in the months between the King of Belgium announcing imminent independence in 1959 and the actual handover. The political authorities had shown no more forethought than the Church. This short-sightedness was the prelude to immeasurable human misery in the self-styled Democratic Republic of the Congo which has not yet ceased.[26]

Elsewhere, it seemed that more potential existed for a delivery of state machines into the hands of responsible politicians. The precedent was the independence won by the British Gold Coast as Ghana only three years before the Belgian Congo, but after infinitely more careful local preparation. The British government, despite major blunders like its brutally inept and demoralizing handling of the Mau Mau insurgency in Kenya through the 1950s, was generally prepared to listen to anglophone Christian missionary organizations which understood the realities of anti-colonial movements and saw positive possibilities. Max Warren, an exceptionally able secretary of the Church Missionary Society and in many ways the successor to J. H. Oldham as an international Protestant statesman, played an important role as a mediator between British officialdom and the new leadership, especially in the CMS's long-standing areas of activity in East and West Africa.[27]

Some observers in Europe and in nationalist circles in Africa confidently expected that Africans would think Christianity too closely associated with colonialism to let it flourish in the newly independent states. This was the reverse of the truth.[28] As we have seen (see pp. 963–5), beyond the European-initiated Churches there was now an extraordinary variety of African-initiated Christian practice which made Christianity even beyond its ancient north-eastern African heartlands at least as indigenous a religion as the great alternative, Islam. Moreover, the political institutions left by colonial powers at independence produced widespread disappointment. Artificially created chunks of colonial territory had been set up with democratic forms, civil services and judiciaries. Even in European society, these worked only when sustained by widespread prosperity and painfully acquired consensual norms and national identities. They rarely functioned effectively in Africa, and the generation of liberation politicians who became rulers at independence frequently succumbed to the corruption of power. People let down by government turned to the Churches for their welfare, self-expression and a chance to exercise control over their own lives. Nowhere was this more true than in the one region which did not readily succumb to decolonization, the Portuguese and British southern territories dominated by the Union of South Africa.

The Union was an amalgam of British colonies and two former republics dominated by 'Afrikaner' descendants of colonists from the Netherlands. Afrikaners were proud of more than two centuries of struggle to establish themselves in a wilderness, buoyed up by a militant Reformed Protestantism which told them that God had delivered them this land, and determined to resist any extension of power to non-whites, whether African or Asian. Indeed, as the twentieth century wore on, the Afrikaners turned their military defeat by the British in the second Boer War (1899–1902) into a gradual rebuilding of Afrikaner ascendancy, removing what political rights had existed for non-whites in some parts of the new Union. Most British settlers, and successive British governments anxious to avoid confrontation, connived at the process, which culminated in the victory of an Afrikaner Nationalist party in the 1948 all-white general election. In the intervening years, Africans had quit white-initiated Churches on a massive scale to lead their own Christian lives; the segregation of races widened inexorably. After the Nationalist victory, successive governments, with cabinets stuffed with Dutch Reformed pastors and elders, turned this de facto situation into a system with its own crazy and cruel logic, known by the Afrikaans word *apartheid*, separateness. This was often glossed by the South African government as 'separate development'. The separation of blacks, whites, Asians and 'Coloureds' was small-mindedly real; the development entirely one-sided.[29]

At the heart of apartheid was a great act of theft from the Churches: the entire mass-education system which they had built up from primary level to higher education, a beacon for Africa that had benefited students from as far away as Uganda. From 1953 all this was delivered into the hands of the government and became an instrument to hold black Africans back rather than advance them. The Roman Catholic Church resisted the confiscation the longest, but it too was eventually defeated by the effort of financing its independent schools.[30] Around the world, as the cruelty and arbitrariness of apartheid became apparent, a chorus of protest went up. From Western governments it was muted, because South Africa had a strategic importance in the 'Cold War' against Communism which had been in operation from the late 1940s (a card played to the full by the Nationalist government, which talked much of Communism as the enemy of Christian civilization). The Soviet government did indeed use the struggle against apartheid to further its own interests, but on the Western side the bulk of opposition had to come from the Churches. They alone among the coalition of activists could effectively draw on their international fellowship to keep open overseas links for South Africans and help the beleaguered liberationist political party which Christians dominated, the African National Congress.

Given the almost blanket support of the South African Dutch Reformed Church for apartheid, and its withdrawal or expulsion from ecumenical activities in worldwide Church bodies, the Anglican Church was best placed to lead the struggle in South Africa. For all the Nationalist government's efforts to shut down any sphere of cooperation between whites and non-whites, Anglicans led the Churches' resistance, and had the capacity from time to time to intimidate the ostentatiously Christian Nationalist regime – admittedly often against the wishes of many in their prosperous white congregations. Throughout all the Anglican Communion's centuries of involvement with politics and social change, its role in the liberation struggle in South Africa should perhaps give it most pride. It is a story of heroic individuals who turned what was often a personal singularity and craggy awkwardness into a stubborn refusal to compromise with evil. Exemplary was the monk Trevor Huddleston, sent out to South Africa by his Community of the Resurrection: he was tireless in his anti-apartheid work alongside the ANC and then, after a reluctantly obeyed recall from his order, he spent a lifetime in helping the struggle from afar, as an Anglican bishop and eventually archbishop. Desmond Tutu, another exceptional Anglican priest of the next generation who rose to be Archbishop of Cape Town – perhaps Anglicanism's greatest primate in the twentieth century – recalled his astonishment as a boy at witnessing Father Huddleston, the picture of Anglo-Catholic authority in his black hat and white cassock, showing an automatic English courtesy to Tutu's mother: 'I couldn't understand a white man doffing his hat to a black woman, an uneducated woman

... it made, it appeared later, a very deep impression on me and said a great deal about the person who had done this.'[31]

Perhaps most important of all for the eventual defeat of apartheid was an English Anglican priest who briefly visited South Africa only once: John Collins. Like Huddleston, Collins was an example of a type which Anglicanism has traditionally been good at fostering: an undisciplined, extrovert rebel member of England's solid middle class, for whom the Church's untidy historic legacy of niches for eccentrics provided a perch in a canonry of London's St Paul's Cathedral. Canon Collins ruined the breakfasts of many a choleric Tory reader of the *Daily Telegraph* by his pronouncements as chairman of the Campaign for Nuclear Disarmament, but his contribution to South Africa's future was the International Defence and Aid Fund, an umbrella organization which, after the South African government banned it in 1967, managed to avoid journalistic scrutiny for another quarter-century. The fund gathered money from across the northern European and North American world via a host of personal contacts; it provided a cleverly disguised financial lifeline for those struggling in the most dangerous of circumstances to resist apartheid, to fight lawsuits or survive the disappearance of their loved ones into South African jails. The South African security services, so adept at penetrating and subverting such organizations, never succeeded in infiltration here, nor did they unmask the agents who were distributing the funds: tens of thousands of people were given around £100 million. Collins's IDAF remains one of the greatest achievements of twentieth-century liberal Protestantism.[32]

Churchmen like Huddleston, Tutu and Collins played a major part alongside the imprisoned Nelson Mandela in ensuring that the African National Congress remained firmly committed to an effort to establish a genuine and all-inclusive democracy when the white minority regime eventually lost the will to resist. The liberation struggle in South Africa remained much more closely linked than elsewhere to the concerns of liberal Western Christianity for other freedoms – homosexual rights, the ordination of women – and that has been an important factor in recent travails of the Anglican Communion. Moreover, Archbishop Tutu was at the forefront of the movement to seek national healing rather than sectional revenge after the eventual defeat of apartheid and the coming of universal democracy in 1994. He headed a Truth and Reconciliation Commission which has been imitated in other places riven by long-term hatreds and atrocities. Nelson Mandela as president symbolized the commitment to a Christian reconciliation when he proclaimed that the old Afrikaner national anthem *Die Stem* ('The Call') should continue to stand alongside the serene Xhosa Christian hymn written in 1897 by a Methodist schoolteacher, *Nkosi Sikelel' iAfrika*: 'Lord, bless Africa . . . Descend, O Spirit; Descend, O Holy Spirit'.[33]

Not the least dramatic aspect of this reconciliation was the repentance shown by the official bodies of the South African Dutch Reformed Church for their part in providing ideological blessing for the lunacy of apartheid. As recently as 1982 they had responded angrily to their exclusion from the World Alliance of Reformed Churches with an emphatic assertion of their constant testing of 'the demands of Holy Scripture . . . to strive for the best practical way in which to fulfil our apostolic calling to be the Church of Jesus Christ giving due consideration to our experience within the unique South African ethnic situation'. Only eight years later, the year that Nelson Mandela was freed after twenty-seven years in jail, the Church in a declaration at Rustenburg took practical steps to restore property to the 'relocated' and provide funds for renewal and resettlement of exiles, since 'Confession and forgiveness necessarily require restitution. Without it, a confession of guilt is incomplete.'[34]

On the other side of the Atlantic five years later, in 1995, another Church actually born in racism gradually and painfully came to a similar realization. The Southern Baptists, by now America's largest Protestant denomination, in a charged and emotional meeting in Atlanta, Georgia, expressed repentance for their historic origins in a movement to oppose the abolition of slavery: twenty thousand delegates overwhelmingly passed a resolution to repudiate what they had once said on slavery and to make an official apology to African-Americans. They quoted the Bible to prove their new case for condemning slavery, albeit with more good-heartedness than profound scriptural exegesis – and it has to be said that they remain an almost entirely white denomination.[35] Other mainstream American Churches, such as the Episcopal Church of the USA, are also aware of their often inglorious role in the story of slavery and its accompanying racism. That is why they may be more sensitive to other liberation struggles than Churches elsewhere which do not have that past story.

These statements of penitence are as resonant as those made by European Churches conscious of their tarnished part in the Nazi crimes of the Second World War. They betoken a new humility in Western Christianity born of experience. Such turnarounds in the Church may encourage wariness in those inclined to make confident dogmatic pronouncements intended to lay down unchangeable truths for the future. But humility is by no means the only mood among the Churches worldwide in recent decades. Afrikaner South Africa saw the defence of its special racial system as part of a more general defence of traditional Christian values against a godless liberalism, intent on demolishing the Christian family and all the institutions dependent on it. Conservative Christians everywhere have continued to echo this wider theme: even now that apartheid is only a sour memory, a cultural battle continues. It began at the end of the 1950s, and has now become the widest fault line within Christianity – Chalcedonian, non-Chalcedonian, Catholic, Protestant, Orthodox, Pentecostal alike – casting more ancient conflicts into the shade.

A CULTURAL REVOLUTION
FROM THE SIXTIES

The nemesis of Pope Paul VI as Church reformer was a pair of issues in human sexuality. In his reaffirmation of universal clerical celibacy and ban on contraception, he had not understood the profound cultural revolution which had been occurring in the West from the early 1960s, in which new understandings and expressions of human relationships played a central role. Alongside sex was a phenomenon which began by affecting European liberal Protestantism, but which quickly spread throughout all the Churches of Western Europe, and beyond them, into their cognates in Canada and European-origin Australasia: steep falls in the number of those actively involved in corporate religious practice. The process was labelled 'secularization' by students of the sociology of religion, and during the 1970s and even early 1980s, it was confidently expected to set patterns for the whole world. The United States was also part of the cultural revolution – in fact it provided most of the symbolism of the changes, not least through the Hollywood film industry, but also through a veritable industry of youth protest centring on popular anger about America's war in Vietnam. Yet the USA has behaved differently from Europe in the matter of churchgoing and religious activism, if not in the sexual revolution. The divergence was perceptible from the early 1970s and emphatically gathered pace in the 1980s.[36]

What had happened? A starting point which may seem paradoxical is the exceptionally healthy state of the institution of marriage and the weakness of alternatives in mid-century European and American society. More people married, and they married younger. In 1960, 70 per cent of American women aged 20–24 were married. In the Republic of Ireland, extramarital births then accounted for a mere 1.6 per cent of all births, and lest it be thought that Ireland's exceptional levels of Catholic piety were responsible, comparable figures for the religiously pluralistic Netherlands were 1.4 per cent and 3.7 per cent for Lutheran Norway.[37] Clearly people were opting for the nuclear family; but this was not just a traditional Christian family. It put a great deal more emphasis on emotional and sexual fulfilment, and traditional male superiority was eroded in favour of a 'companionate' partnership of equals, where husband and wife made decisions about how many children they were willing to bring up, with the aid of artificial contraception.

The march of contraception can be instanced not only in the low rate of extramarital births, but in statistics for marriage like those of Canadian families, where the mean number of children per mother fell 3.77 to 2.33, merely through the decade of the 1960s. Fewer children exercised proportionately more emotional power; it has been said that the post-war American family has been increasingly run by and for the benefit of children. Families were getting smaller, more intimate and involved with each other. They had more possessions, more spare cash, more leisure – more choice.[38] It was personal choice which defeated *Humanae vitae*. There are echoes of that earlier emergence of social choice which in the 1690s had seen the emergence in England and the Netherlands of open companionate homosexuality in the face of every possible public social force discouraging it (see pp. 791–2).

The new-style family was not good news for Churches, whose rhetoric of support for the family had not envisaged that it might be a competitor for rather than a mainstay of Church life. An unexpected result was beginning to be felt in the United Kingdom even amid the post-war boom in churchgoing. A perceptive curate in the English Midlands, for instance, noted in 1947 that parents on his newly built housing estate in Dudley were not sending their children along to Sunday School, reluctant 'to interfere with the freedom of young people's choice'. Elsewhere in the same district, a Free Church magazine complained seventeen years later, 'Many of the newly married couples on the estates [are] concerned first and foremost with *their* pay-packets, *their* housing comforts, *their* interior decorations . . . *their* standing in the eyes of their workmates and neighbours.' There were cars for Sunday family jaunts instead of morning church; there was television around which the whole family could sit after tea instead of evening church.[39] These findings could endlessly be reproduced through European society from the early 1960s. In particular, that mainstay of Protestant Church practice from the eighteenth century, the children's Sunday School, melted away. In 1900, 55 per cent of British children attended Sunday School; the figure was still 24 per cent in 1960, but 9 per cent in 1980 and 4 per cent in 2000.[40]

Around the family, other shifts occurred. 'Companionate' marriage created high expectations which were all too frequently disappointed. In the 1970s, divorce rates began rising across Europe, and against furious protests from the Roman Catholic Church, the possibility of divorce was introduced into the law codes of Catholic countries where it had previously been outlawed – in Italy, for instance, in 1970. That was a remarkable shift from the moment in 1947 when the constitution of the new Italian Republic had only missed affirming the indissolubility of marriage by three votes in the Constituent Assembly.[41] Rates of extramarital births soared: in the nations already cited over four decades from 1960, twentyfold in Ireland, sixteenfold in the Netherlands and thirteenfold in Norway.[42] Taboos around abortion broke down, in the face of the reality of death and physical damage in clandestine illegal abortions. In country after country there was legislation to legalize abortion, most famously in the United States through a judgement of the Supreme Court in 1973, *Roe v. Wade*. Homosexuality became less a subject of public paranoia. The first stage was its decriminalization in law, a measure not designed to make homosexuality acceptable or moral in the eyes of Christians, simply to remove a major catalyst for blackmail or suicide.

It is often forgotten that in Britain, in contrast to the European-wide Catholic opposition to changes in divorce legislation, change came about in the highly contentious field of homosexuality largely through the Church. Elite liberal English Protestants, chiefly Anglicans, were at the forefront of a hard-fought struggle, way in advance of popular opinion, which led eventually to the limited decriminalization of male same-sex activity in 1967. Central to their work was the patient scholarship and advocacy of a canon of Wells Cathedral, Derrick Sherwin Bailey, a genial family man with an enthusiasm for railways which suggested the normal harmless eccentricity of Anglican clergy rather than a dangerous revolutionary spirit. Members of the British establishment beyond the Church's theological or clerical circles found all this agitation very odd, but were caught sufficiently off guard to allow the change in the law.[43] What liberal English Christians were seeking to do was actively to separate the law of the land from Christian moral prescriptions. Many, especially clergy of Anglo-Catholic sympathies, had been disgusted by the debacle caused by the Church's established status in its attempted Prayer Book revision of 1927–8, and wanted to liberate the Church in its divine mission by disentangling it from official power structures.[44] They were acknowledging, even furthering and celebrating, the death of Christendom, with a conviction that beyond it there lay better prospects for Christianity.

Behind this optimism, which might now seem quixotic, there echoed texts of Dietrich Bonhoeffer, in letters and papers written during his imprisonment before his execution in 1945: not a theological system but a series of fugitive observations about the future of Christianity, conceived in circumstances of dire isolation and in fear of death, with German society collapsing around him. Bonhoeffer anticipated themes of liberation theology such as the suffering God and the transformed Church, but with a different thrust, in seeing humanity as 'coming of age': 'God is teaching us that we must live as men who can get along very well without him . . . God allows himself to be edged out of the world and on to the cross.' Bonhoeffer criticized his friend and mentor Karl Barth for 'a positivist doctrine of revelation which says in effect "take it or leave it" ', but he still offered his own prophecy of hope and affirmation to Christianity cut loose from its practice of religion: 'The day will come when men will be called again to utter the word of God with such power as will change and renew the world. It will be a new language, which will horrify men, and yet overwhelm them by its power.'[45] Bonhoeffer, a prophet of a renewal whose outlines were not clear to him, bequeathed this idealism and anticipation to the theology of the 1960s, with a multitude of effects and fractures to come.

One notes that Bonhoeffer and his English translators in the 1950s still unselfconsciously used the language of maleness when describing the future. Part of the coming revolution would render that idiom quaintly old-fashioned, because above all the 1960s in Europe and America witnessed a profound shift in the balance of power between the sexes. It became the expectation that girls would receive as good an education as boys; indeed, over the next decades, it became apparent that in many circumstances girls achieved better results at school. Women began discovering past generations of female writers often then languishing unpublished and unstudied, and found that such pioneers as Mary Astell more than two centuries before (see pp. 793–4) had already provided the arguments which they were discovering from themselves. A word had been coined in 1882 for this consciousness: feminism.[46] Its inventor, Hubertine Auclert, had campaigned in France for women's political rights at a time when women were asserting their right to take initiatives and exercise leadership in a variety of ways, largely within the context of the Christian Church (see pp. 818–20 and 828–30). Auclert herself had left behind her family's Catholic piety for a French Republican anticlericalism. Now, a century later, feminism was decisively moving beyond its Christian roots to a 'second wave', a more general assertion, not of particular spheres of action such as prophecy or temperance campaigning, but of equality of opportunity and activity in society.

Since it was becoming less easy to see why women and men should not pursue the same occupations in later life, surely that must apply in the Church as well as beyond it? What would happen to the formation of Christian theology if women joined in what had overwhelmingly been a male task for twenty centuries? We have observed that at intervals the Holy Spirit has been described in female terms through Christian history, but it was rare for the other persons of the Trinity to be conceived without the language of Fatherhood and Sonship. Authority in the Church seemed to have been concentrated in the male gender – although careful scrutiny of the early Church's history now revealed significant exceptions to this generalization.[47] It had been difficult enough for many Churches to get past St Paul's admonitions against women holding positions of leadership or even speaking in church, but now there gathered strength a movement to open the ordained ministry of Churches to women, an impulse which had previously only appeared in the most resolutely unhierarchical of Churches, such as Quakers and Congregationalists.

Even the episcopal Anglican Communion became involved in the struggle, following a precocious precedent in 1944: in the extraordinary circumstances of the Japanese occupation of China, the Bishop of Hong Kong first conferred priestly orders on a woman, Florence Lee Tim Oi, to much worldwide Anglican surprise and episcopal scolding. With great self-abnegation, Lee Tim Oi ceased to exercise her orders and bided her time until the world and the Church changed.[48] New Zealand, a conservative, inward-looking society which has nevertheless repeatedly displayed a remarkable capacity to create social change without a great deal of fuss, first took matters further than priestly orders. Dr Penny

Jamieson, ordained priest in 1983, was Anglicanism's first woman diocesan bishop, elected by the faithful in a very traditional-minded Anglo-Catholic diocese, Dunedin, in 1989.[49] In Geneva in 2001, the Rev. Isabelle Graesslé became successor to John Calvin, the first woman Moderator of the Reformed Church of Geneva's Company of Pastors and Deacons. She has spoken to me of her delight after her election in laying a rose on the cenotaph which commemorates Calvin's unknown grave, and telling him gently, 'It's my turn now.' Graesslé was also responsible for a significant addition to Geneva's monumental Wall of the Reformers: the first female name engraved on it, that of a feisty former abbess, Marie Dentière, whose contribution to the Genevan Reformation had not given Calvin any pleasure.[50]

OLD-TIME RELIGION: AFFIRMATIONS

It is not surprising that such frighteningly rapid changes in society and the Church have provoked a strong reaction, which in fact extends beyond Christianity to all major world faiths. A sequence of political events at the end of the 1970s came to reveal over time that the narrative of advancing secularization, which during the previous decade had seemed so convincing in the seminar rooms of European and American universities, needed some modification. In 1977 the United States presidential election was a triumph for Jimmy Carter, a Southern Baptist Democrat who had openly declared himself born-again; in 1978 there came the election of Karol Wojtyła as Pope John Paul II; in 1979 Shi'ite ayatollahs seized control of the revolution which had overthrown the Shah of Iran. Throughout the world at the present day, the most easily heard tone in religion (not just Christianity) is of a generally angry conservatism. Why? I would hazard that the anger centres on a profound shift in gender roles which have traditionally been given a religious significance and validated by religious traditions. It embodies the hurt of heterosexual men at cultural shifts which have generally threatened to marginalize them and deprive them of dignity, hegemony or even much usefulness – not merely heterosexual men already in positions of leadership, but those who in traditional cultural systems would expect to inherit leadership. It has been observed by sociologists of religion that the most extreme forms of conservatism to be found in modern world

religions, conservatisms which in a borrowing from Christianity have
been termed 'fundamentalism', are especially attractive to 'literate but
jobless, unmarried male youths marginalized and disenfranchised by the
juggernaut of modernity' – in other words, those whom modernity has
created, only to fail to offer them any worthwhile purpose.[51]

That victory of Jimmy Carter in 1977 marked the return to national
American politics of Evangelicals self-exiled over the previous half-
century (see pp. 961–3). But the road to their political self-assertion was
not straightforward: Carter quickly proved a sore disappointment to
them. The problem was that Carter came from that progressive side of
Southern Evangelicalism exemplified, as we have seen, in the career of
Belle Harris Bennett, and Carter's instincts leaned dangerously towards
Protestant liberalism and ecumenism (both of which were rapidly
becoming part of the Evangelical repertoire of hate words). Carter was
equivocal on abortion, a matter which Evangelicals were increasingly
seeing as a litmus test of doctrinal soundness. On one issue he fatally
alienated the Evangelical constituency: faith schools, which Evangelicals
had founded, among other reasons, to avoid the teaching of sex education now on offer in the public (state) system. In 1978, through a
bureaucratic decision which was in fact quite independent of the new
Carter administration, the US Internal Revenue Service withdrew the
tax-exempt status of independent faith schools, claiming (on the whole
unfairly) that many were deliberately practising racial discrimination.
This was an ironic result of the civil rights campaigns which once had
involved so many Evangelicals.

Already two legal judgements had infuriated Evangelical voters: the
banning of school prayer in America's public schools in 1962, the
result of the courts trying to enforce the principle of the American
constitutional separation of Church and State, and the Roe v. Wade
judgement effectively legalizing abortion in 1973. Only now did they
begin to make the connection to the power of their vote. Sex clinched
their feelings: Carter's long-promised White House Conference on the
Family pluralized its subject to 'Families', and made thoughtful statements about gay relationships which were beyond the Evangelical pale.
Angry Evangelical leaders met in 1979 and stumbled across a resonant
title for an organization to do something about their anger: the 'Moral
Majority'. By the end of Carter's troubled period in office, he had lost
the conservative Evangelical constituency. In 1980 it helped to eject him,
voting instead for Ronald Reagan. There was plenty of irony here, for
as a Republican Reagan was – in terms of institutional politics – the heir

to the party which had defeated the South in the civil war. Moreover, he was a social libertarian of cosily amorphous religious views and his wife regularly consulted an astrologer. In all this, the Reagans were not untypical products of Hollywood, in contrast with the deeply pious Southern Democrat Carter.

Nevertheless the alliance between Republicans and conservative Evangelicals had been struck, and the Republican Party saw the huge electoral advantage of hanging on to it. The Evangelical televangelist turned politician Pat Robertson declared in 1980, 'We have enough votes to run the country . . . and when the people say, "We've had enough" we are going to take over.'[52] So far that has not happened, partly thanks to the sheer variety and perennial fissiparousness of American Evangelicalism. Yet the effect of Evangelicalism in American politics hardly needs demonstrating, baffling though it is to Europeans, who overwhelmingly disapprove of their own politicians making a public fuss of their personal religious convictions. On no political issue has this been more significant than American policy towards the State of Israel – the source of so much Arab and Muslim fury and frustration with the West.

For some years after the founding of a state of Israel in 1948, American relations with Israeli governments were dominated by power-political considerations. They were not even particularly cordial, especially at the time of the 1956 crisis, in which the Israelis aligned themselves militarily with the British and French around Egypt's nationalization of the Suez Canal. When the decisive American swing towards an alliance with Israel came in 1962, it was still motivated by power politics, and was not associated with Republicans but with President John F. Kennedy's liberal Democratic administration, which was furious at the aggressive policies adopted by President Nasser of Egypt.[53] At that stage, of course, American politicians were not generally keeping a worried eye on Evangelical political opinion. When in the 1980s they did, they discovered a large constituency emphatically in favour of Israel, for reasons related to the apocalypse. It was the same longing to bring on the Last Days which back in the 1840s had enthused the newly founded Evangelical Alliance and the promoters of the Jerusalem Bishopric (see pp. 836–7), and which derived its particular premillennialist roots from the Millerites and the dispensationalism of John Nelson Darby.[54] Millenarianism routed the widespread contrary impulse in American Protestant circles to anti-Semitism, historically seen at its worst in the racism of the Ku Klux Klan.

Now American Evangelicals made common cause with the Jewish

community in the United States, and they seemed to care little if at all for the opinions or the sufferings of their fellow Christians in the ancient Churches of the Middle East. Israeli politicians were not slow to exploit this political windfall, caring little for the fact that Evangelical apocalypticism expected the conversion of the Jews to Christianity. Likewise the Amsterdam Jews who had encouraged philo-Semitism in Puritan England in the 1650s had not been too worried about Protestant motives when Oliver Cromwell had readmitted the Jewish community to his country (see pp. 773–4). American foreign policy has for decades seemed locked into hardly questioning its support for the State of Israel, even though the consequences for its relations with the Arab and Muslim world, and with others, are almost entirely negative.[55] They have been particularly dire for the traditional Christianities of the Middle East. With the exception of Lebanon and a remarkable if complex official fostering of religious pluralism in the Syrian Republic, Christian communities are generally in steep decline in numbers through the region, and Israel/Palestine in particular. Caught between the animosities of a politics which has other concerns, Christians have every incentive to leave, whenever they can, for exile in less dangerous lands, ending a connection with homelands which goes directly back to the first generations of the followers of Christ. It is easy for them to feel abandoned and betrayed by the Christian-based cultures of the West.[56]

During the presidency of George W. Bush, the first president since Jimmy Carter to declare himself born-again, the nexus between the Republican Party and conservative Evangelical Christianity reached unprecedented proportions. It extended across the range of apocalyptic Evangelical concern (chiefly sex) and also lack of concern (chiefly the environment). Faced with the continuing world crisis over the twentieth century's newly emerged sexually transmitted disease, HIV/AIDS, the Bush administration diverted funds for prevention into abstinence-only programmes. President Bush's Pentecostal Christian Attorney-General John Ashcroft promised after his nomination to wind up a task force established by the Clinton administration to protect abortion clinics from violent protests; he had to abandon that commitment after much public alarm, but as attacks on clinics escalated, continued government protection for them was noticeably slow to materialize. In an interview with the New York Times just before his first victorious presidential election, George W. Bush also identified himself with that century-old fundamentalist angst, the status of the creation stories in the Book of Genesis, when he commented that 'the jury is still out' on evolution.[57]

It has been common for those expecting the imminent Last Days to deny the reality of global climate change or its connection with human agency. In any case, given the imminent reign of Christ, attempts to fortify humanity against such signs of the times would be pointless, not to say disrespectful to God (as well as unhelpful to some of the financial backers of the Republican Party in industry). Senator James Inhofe of Oklahoma, an Evangelical Republican who opined to the Senate on 4 March 2002 that Al Qaeda's destruction of New York's World Trade Center in 2001 was divine punishment for the inadequacy of America's support for Israel, on 28 July 2003 described global warming to the Senate as 'the greatest hoax ever perpetrated on the American people' and the Federal Environmental Protection Agency as a 'Gestapo'.[58] Nevertheless, religious movements at the moment of success tend to fragment and diversify, especially when they are already as diverse as American conservative Evangelicalism, and there have been signs that a new generation within the movement is less inclined to sign up to the agenda which won the Republicans electoral success in the first decade of the twenty-first century. Environmental concerns are one of the chief issues on which fragmentation is perceptible. What seems unlikely to shift is the vigorous presence of Evangelicalism in American public life, in a form unimaginable before 1977.

If Jimmy Carter's election marked a new phase in American politics and public religion, so did the unexpected election of Pope John Paul II the following year. His election was in a hasty conclave, subdued by the sudden death of John Paul I only a month after enthronement (a tragedy so ineptly handled by the Vatican as to give rise to a great deal of silly conspiracy theory). The choice of a Polish pope broke with more than four centuries of choices from among the Italian episcopate, and it could be taken as a fitting symbol of the rapid changes now occurring within the Catholic Church. The youngest pope at election since Pius IX in 1846, and destined to have the second-longest pontificate in the papacy's history so far, Karol Wojtyła was a heroic figure, survivor of struggles against two tyrannical regimes which were conscious enemies of the Church. He was also extrovert, articulate and a born actor. His qualities were never better demonstrated than in an assassination attempt on him in 1981, which he not only survived but turned into a notable example of forgiveness.[59]

John Paul's election was a catalyst for a renewed joyful self-confidence in the Polish Catholic Church, already the most vigorous in the Soviet bloc in its confrontation with Communism. His insistence on returning to his native country in 1979, made possible by a fatal irresolution in the Polish government, remains a moment to savour in the history of resistance to oppression as ecstatic crowds, up to a third of the population, met him in an outpouring of self-expression. Without that visit, the formation of the Solidarity movement and the process which within a decade led to a peaceful establishment of real democracy in Poland, and indeed throughout Eastern Europe, could not have happened. It is an achievement to celebrate and admire. Moreover, it was coupled with John Paul's personal ability to rise above chauvinist Polish nationalism. As the Greek Catholic Church emerged from the shadows after the fall of Communism (see pp. 1001–2), the Pope was a good deal more generous towards its efforts to rebuild its institutions and regain its church buildings than some of his fellow Polish Catholic clergy and laity. In one Galician Polish city called Przemyśl, they not only ignored his order for the restitution of a church to the Greek Catholics, but saw to the demolition of its dome on the grounds that it was unacceptably 'eastern' – it was in fact modelled on St Peter's in Rome.[60]

That incident illustrates that the Poland which Wojtyła represented was a very different country from the pluralist Commonwealth of the early modern age. Its Jews had been wiped out, its Protestantism reduced to the margins and its Catholic Church had long forgotten the sturdy conciliarism and suspicion of Rome which had characterized the medieval kingdom.[61] The Pope's very rock-like strength, so precious an asset in confronting tyranny, became less unambiguously valuable in dealing with the nuances of other cultures and societies. He took to a passionate, joyfully reckless extreme the bleak commitment expressed by Paul VI: 'my duty is too plain: decide, assume every responsibility for guiding others, even when it seems illogical and perhaps absurd'.[62] John Paul II had a liking for the word '*magisterium*', which, though not in the repertoire of biblical writers, had since the nineteenth century stealthily acquired a technical theological meaning as 'authoritative teaching', particularly thanks to Pius XII's propensity to deploy it. Now it peppered Vatican pronouncements; John Paul used it in a way which almost suggested that *magisterium* was a person, like the Holy Spirit.[63] The Pope was determined to teach Catholics what Catholicism was about, and was also determined to stop anyone else telling them something different. So within a year of John Paul's enthronement, the Swiss theologian Hans Küng, exponent of a dynamic development of the teaching of Vatican II, was deprived of his licence to teach as a Catholic. Küng's former university colleague Josef Ratzinger, his own explorations of such views long behind him, arrived in the Vatican in 1981 as Prefect of the Congregation for the Doctrine of the Faith – a title which was a further creative rebranding of the Roman Inquisition.

The Pope's instinctive anti-Communism made him react with hostility towards liberation theology, whose expression he had encountered directly at the Puebla episcopal conference early in his papacy in 1979. He had difficulties even with those Latin American clergy who had found themselves drawn, through their pastoral experiences, to campaigning for the poor. One of the most difficult cases was that of Oscar Romero, Archbishop of San Salvador, a priest of conservative instincts who nevertheless had come into increasingly bitter confrontation with the authoritarian and exploitative regime of El Salvador, to the point that he excommunicated members of the government after the murder of priests and nuns. There were representations to the Vatican from El Salvador, and Romero was about to be moved elsewhere when, in 1980, a right-wing gunman murdered him while he was celebrating Mass in his own cathedral.

The Pope could hardly ignore this outrage, so parallel to the fate of the Church's classic archiepiscopal martyr Thomas Becket (see pp. 375–6), yet he could not bring himself to use the martyr-word itself when addressing the Conference of Latin American Bishops in 1992 – he removed it from the prepared text of his speech.[64] He showed himself to be in deep conflict over the Latin American situation, because he could also recognize in it the malign work of the unbridled capitalism which he deplored as much as Communism. Notably, he was able to show respect for the Afro-Portuguese syncretism of *Candomblé*, even submitting on his visit to Brazil in 1980 to a ritual cleansing conducted by a *Candomblé* priest, a *pai de santo*. Evidently ordinary people's construction of their own religion could be tolerated, while it was dangerous to allow the same latitude to intellectuals or clergy (see Plate 53).[65]

Behind the long papacy of John Paul II was a programme which could never be made too explicit: to reverse a raft of changes launched by Vatican II. As we have seen, Wojtyła had remained at best sceptical about some of the council's major results. His right-hand man, Ratzinger, had felt his parallel doubts confirmed by the subsequent wave of European student protest in 1968 which had deeply unsettled him when he was a professor in the University of Tübingen.[66] There was a difficulty here, given the momentum that had built up since the end of the council, and the prestige which it still retained, and so official Catholic statements habitually continue to exhibit a raft of reverent references to the spirit of Vatican II. In the partly veiled struggles which revolved around that problem, a number of coded substitutes for partisanship were necessary developments. John Henry Newman, that prince among Anglican converts of the nineteenth century, Cardinal of the Church, was a name whom conservatives could hardly dismiss, yet his reservations about the first Vatican Council were clear in his writings, and the celebration of his memory could therefore well be seen as a celebration of the values of Vatican II. His cult has progressed slowly towards sainthood, after an embarrassing shortage for a considerable time of the necessary confirmatory miracles.[67]

In parallel, but in opposition, the theological stock of Hans Urs von Balthasar rose considerably during the Wojtyła papacy. Von Balthasar was an interestingly creative philosophical theologian, deeply sensitive to music, art and literature, a Swiss prepared to confront the prevailing liberalism of Swiss Catholicism just as much as he confronted the theological stance of his fellow Swiss Karl Barth. In fact he had much in common with Barth: a deep hostility to Nazism and an uncompromisingly Augustinian outlook – as a student, von Balthasar is said to have sat through the scholastic expositions of his Jesuit lectures with his ears blocked, steadily reading through the works of Augustine of Hippo. Von Balthasar found both the Jesuit and Benedictine life uncongenial, and he never held a teaching post; his close affinity with the twice-divorced visionary Adrienne von Speyr raised some clerical eyebrows, and his wide sympathies aroused the unfriendly attention of Pius XII's Curia. Yet what became a long-term asset was his coldness towards Vatican II, to which he had not been invited as a theological consultant (probably not for theological reasons). Von Balthasar's writings could openly present opinions about the council and its leading theological voice, Karl Rahner – a *bête noire* for him like Schleiermacher for Barth – which neither John Paul nor Ratzinger was prepared to express. John Paul II made von Balthasar the first recipient of the Pope Paul VI International Prize in 1984, and in his presentation speech, the Pope used the phrase 'the splendour of the truth', which later became the title of one of the most important statements of his absolutist views on moral truth, his encyclical *Veritatis Splendor* (1993). Von Balthasar died three days before he was to receive a cardinal's hat; a slew of his devotees have subsequently worn it in his stead.[68]

Pope John Paul had no time for Vatican II's discussion of collegiality in the episcopate. He sought to centralize appointments of bishops with a thoroughness which has no parallel in Catholic history, and which was often explicitly designed to override the wishes of the local diocese. Occasionally he met his match, notably in Switzerland. In the years after 1988 the quiet Swiss valleys of the Grisons, long since pioneers of religious toleration amid Reformation conflicts (see pp. 639–40), witnessed an extraordinary ecclesiastical drama over a new bishop for the diocese of Chur. Centuries of tradition gave the right of election to Chur's cathedral clergy, but the Pope did not trust the Swiss to elect a sound Catholic; he sent his own combative and ultra-conservative nominee, Wolfgang Haas, to 'assist' the old bishop in preparation to replace him on his retirement. The people of Chur were not having it. The new assistant bishop arrived at his consecration to find crowds of the faithful lying down full-length, blocking the cathedral entrance. Haas and his distinguished guests, even the Prince of Liechtenstein, had to clamber as best they could over prone parishioners for what must have been a rather muted celebration. Matters did not end there. Mothers refused to send their children to be confirmed by the Pope's bishop. Church bells tolled in protest when Bishop Haas succeeded the old bishop and appointed his own officials, and the city council even withheld the keys to his palace. Eventually the Pope grudgingly gave way and replaced his unwanted prelate, who got a newly invented archbishopric of tiny Liechtenstein as a face-saver. Haas was not much more appreciated by the good folk of the principality.[69]

The aspect of the cultural revolution of the 1960s which remained most troublesome for the Pope was the new openness in sexual mores and questioning of traditional gender roles. He gave the whole package of attitudes the striking blanket label 'a culture of death'; and he was much more consistent than most American Evangelicals in his passionate commitment to the protection of human life. Alongside his hatred of abortion, a hatred which Evangelicals shared, he bitterly opposed the death penalty for criminals, so frequently exercised in the United States, and he also discountenanced President George W. Bush by his fierce condemnation of the renewed American invasion of Iraq in the Second Gulf War. Prominent in the culture of death for the Pope was artificial contraception. There was no question of revising Paul VI's ban, even when it became apparent that the use of condoms was one of the most effective ways of curbing the worldwide spread of AIDS.[70]

John Paul's consistency (for good or ill) in all this nevertheless fatally deserted the Vatican over one of the most painful issues in sexuality, the sexual abuse of children and young people by clergy. For the world to discover how widespread this had been over the span of living memory was bad enough; what was much worse was the exposure of the Church's history of cover-up and callous treatment of those who complained, and the fact that this attitude was not effectively reversed during the 1990s. The problem sprang not simply from the defensiveness which is common to all monumental institutions. It was an inheritance from centuries of building an image of priesthood in which the priest by virtue of ordination became an objectively different being from other humans. It was easy to slide from that into an attitude which suggested that different moral rules applied to such a separate being.[71]

Particularly damaging was Pope John Paul's consistent support for an ultra-conservative Catholic activist organization, the Legion of Christ, founded in mid-twentieth-century Mexico. Persistent accusations of sexual abuse against its founder, Marcial Maciel Degollado, a participant in the *Cristero* war in his youth, were ignored in Rome to the very end of John Paul's pontificate. Not so under his successor Josef Ratzinger, Benedict XVI. In May 2006 a statement about Maciel was issued on behalf of Pope Benedict's own successor as Prefect of the Congregation for the Doctrine of the Faith, that 'considering his advanced age and his frail health, the Holy See has decided not to begin a canonical process but to "invite him to a reserved life of prayer and penance, renouncing all public ministry".'[72] At last the Vatican was taking seriously the scale of what was going on, which John Paul, with his own austere sexual integrity, seemed incapable of imaginatively appreciating. It was too late to prevent the decimation of congregations throughout the anglophone world and in Europe: an unprecedented blow to the authority of the Church in which ridicule, exemplified in the deceptively farcical Irish-made television sitcom *Father Ted*, was mixed with real fury. Whether the effects will spread into the rest of the Catholic world remains to be seen.[73]

FREEDOM: PROSPECTS AND FEARS

As John Paul's capacity to exercise his pontificate was progressively destroyed by Parkinson's disease, the consequences of his greatest achievement, hastening the collapse of repressive and unrepresentative Communist governments, continued to transform Christian fortunes in Eastern Europe and Russia. A renaissance of life in the Orthodox Churches was first borne along on the massive recovery of morale and self-confidence in the Catholic Church behind the Iron Curtain. During the years in which the will to survive drained away from the self-styled 'People's Democracies', Catholicism had the advantage of looking to the power and international prestige of the Vatican beyond the reach of the Communists. Given the precarious position of the Oecumenical Patriarch, not to mention ongoing tensions between the Phanar and the Moscow Patriarchate, the Orthodox enjoyed no comparable ally.

The impact of John Paul II's first papal visit to Poland was repeated in parallel occasions elsewhere. In Communist-run Czechoslovakia, it is instructive to compare successive celebrations of anniversaries connected with the pioneers of Slav Christianity, Cyril/Constantine and Methodios (see pp. 460–64). The first came in the regimented atmosphere of 1963–4, marking eleven hundred years since the brothers' arrival in Great Moravia. Carefully organized by the Communist state authorities, it was all very academic and low key, with public exhibitions emphasizing the pair's role as teachers and cultural ambassadors rather than bringers of Christianity. The second in 1985 commemorated eleven centuries since the death of Methodios, and this time the celebrations were firmly in the hands of the Roman Catholic Church, which presided triumphantly over a concourse of around a quarter of a million of the faithful at Methodios's tomb-shrine in the former Moravian capital, Velehrad.[74] No mass gathering like it had been seen in Czechoslovakia since the aborted hopes of a popular reformed Communist regime in the 1968 'Prague Spring' – and there was little that the government could do about it apart from feebly restricting the official guest list. The next such outpouring of popular enthusiasm would be Czechoslovakia's 'Velvet Revolution' four years later.

When that swift and bloodless overthrow of Czechoslovakia's Communist regime was complete at the end of 1989, a remarkable festivity took place in St Vitus Cathedral in Prague on 29 December, the day that the still-Communist Federal Assembly elected the dissident Václav Havel as president. Late victims of police brutality and imprisonment, parliamentary deputies and a jubilant crowd were all swept into a packed cathedral to hear Antonin Dvořák's Mass and *Te Deum*. Dvořák's adaptation of the Western Church's ancient Latin hymn of praise, performed by the Czech Philharmonic Orchestra, was staged with all the sumptuousness of nineteenth-century romantic nationalism. Sitting side by side on ornate chairs, in still-bewildered delight at the sudden eruption of freedom, were the ninety-year-old Cardinal František Tomašék, Archbishop of Prague, born under the Catholic Habsburg emperor, priest since the early days of the first Czech Republic, survivor of Nazi and Communist terror – together with the agnostic playwright President, symbol of all that 1960s culture had brought to Europe, wearing an ill-fitting suit. Behind them were the ranks of parliamentarians who a few weeks before had still been voting through the drab business of a one-party state. They were all happily aware that it was the reversal of a dishonestly conceived ceremony in 1948, when the same work had been staged in the cathedral at the behest of the new Communist leader, Klement Gottwald, to allay the fears of liberal democrats and Catholics about the new People's Republic. Perhaps only the Czechs could have so stylishly staged this solemn celebration, which was also a light-hearted juxtaposition of historical eras, reminiscences and cultural styles; yet equally, only the centuries of Western Latin ecclesiastical tradition were able to encompass the contradictions. Such happy confusions are worth enjoying and treasuring in memory before the gloomier complications of history crowd back.[75]

At the centre of the implosion of Soviet-era Communism, another religious anniversary provided the opportunity for the revival of Russian Orthodoxy. In 1988 there fell the putative millennium of Prince Vladimir of Kiev's conversion (see pp. 505–7). Mikhail Gorbachev, recently chosen General Secretary of the Communist Party, had lately been in charge of the harassment of Christianity in his capacity as head of the Soviet security service, the KGB; now he saw the anniversary as the chance to open up another front in his attempt to remould and diversify Russian Communism. The state enabled – even encouraged – celebrations of the anniversary; church buildings were reopened, religious education and religious publishing permitted once more. Not only the Orthodox benefited; for the time being all those religious groups which had survived in Russia, from Catholics to Baptists, found it possible to operate with steadily fewer restrictions.[76]

In 1990, as Gorbachev found his reforms creating freedoms which he had not envisaged, the former Metropolitan of Leningrad (St Petersburg) was elected as Patriarch Aleksii II. Born in the Baltic republic of Estonia but with a Russian mother, Aleksii brought a new energy to the patriarchate, yet his instincts in renewing the life of the Church were to return it to a selective vision of the past. He scorned the ecumenism which his Church had been tentatively exploring at the beginning of the twentieth century. It was a particular point of fury for Moscow that liberalization brought with it the re-emergence in 1989 of the Greek Catholic Church of the Ukraine from its enforced union with Moscow, and the continuing squabbles between the two Churches over property restitution and jurisdiction have mirrored the tense relationship between the newly independent Ukraine and the Russian Federation.[77] It has been remarked that as the Soviet Union finally disintegrated in 1991, the Russian Orthodox Church was left as 'arguably the most "Soviet" of all institutions' remaining in Russia.[78] One symbol of this is the remarkable circumstance that the FSB, the Russian intelligence service which has rather seamlessly succeeded the Soviet KGB, has lovingly restored a Moscow parish church for itself. In 2002 the Church of the Holy Wisdom was reconsecrated with full Orthodox pomp by no less a figure than Patriarch Aleksii, who, during the course of the day, presented the FSB's director, Nikolai Patrushev, with an icon of his name-saint, Nikolai. Stalin might have blanched – but, then again, perhaps not.[79]

The recovery of Orthodox tradition has its exhilarating stories. It is difficult not to admire the blossoming of one of Russia's most important and historic nunneries, Novodevichy, on the outskirts of Moscow, under the wise guidance of a quite exceptional personality, Mother Serafima. Born into the nobility as Varvara Vasilevna Chichagova, she had been inspired by her grandfather, a former tsarist general turned priest, who was secretly consecrated an archbishop during Stalin's purges, in which he was one of the hundreds of thousands to die. Chichagova managed to pursue a distinguished scientific career without joining the Communist Party. When the Soviet Union collapsed, now a widow and taking monastic vows, she was able to bring life back to the great semi-derelict monastic complex. Previously the brief concessions to the Church brought about by the Second World War had enabled only one chapel and a small publishing office to reopen in Novodevichy, a faint echo of all the centuries of worship, charity and education that had flourished there before 1917. Before Mother Serafima died in 1999, aged eighty-five, this tiny elderly lady had in five years galvanized an infant community with no resources. To begin with, its nuns had been forced to go on living in their old apartments round the city; now the monastery was a place of hope for women struggling with the miseries of post-Soviet life, sustaining craft shops and a farm, and at the centre of it were the refuges provided by its restored cathedrals and quiet holy places.[80]

Alongside such inspiring examples is an official Church whose relish in its renewed place of honour in Russian life is not altogether to its advantage. By 1997 a law 'On freedom of conscience and religious association' contradicted the assertion of a secular state in the 1993 constitution of the Russian Federation; it now recognized 'the special contribution of Orthodoxy to the history of Russia and to the establishment and development of Russia's spirituality and culture'. It would have been difficult for churchmen not to appreciate the sudden outpouring of money on new and restored churches throughout Russia, symbolized by the vast sums spent with the backing of the flamboyant mayor of Moscow, Iurii Luzhkov, on rebuilding Moscow's demolished landmark Cathedral of Christ the Saviour, the film of whose dynamiting by Stalin remains one of the iconic images of Soviet attacks on religion. It is noticeable that another Orthodox Cathedral of Christ the Saviour, explicitly reminiscent in its design of the Moscow Cathedral, has newly risen in the Russian Baltic detached territory of Kaliningrad, the city so thoroughly transformed from the Teutonic Knights' former East Prussian stronghold of Königsberg after 1945. Kaliningrad's Orthodox Cathedral is designed to be a dominant structure in the city centre, outdoing the ancient Lutheran cathedral recently restored from wartime ruins: it is a significant statement of political architecture.[81] One could adduce national parallels in another Orthodox-dominated state: in the multi-ethnic Transylvanian villages of Romania, every community in the first decade of the twenty-first century seemed to have a Romanian Orthodox church shrouded in scaffolding, as an enlargement or a lavish new build, alongside the older parish churches of the other ethnic communities.

In theology and social statements, the Moscow Patriarchate has likewise followed a conservative line. It did eventually rein in one of the most confrontational of its bishops, Nikon of Ekaterinburg, who on two occasions in 1994 and 1998 organized the burning of books by Orthodox writers of whose questioning spirit he did not approve. A range of charges from the diocese, some more lurid than these, earned Nikon deprivation and relocation to the Monastery of the Caves in Pskov.[82] Among the authors thus singled out as enemies of Nikon's version of Orthodoxy had been the last priest to die mysteriously in the era of Soviet rule, as late as 1990, Aleksandr Men. This theologian, of Jewish descent and ecumenical spirit, had paralleled some of the explorations of Orthodoxy made by Orthodox theologians in exile after 1917. One of the mistakes made by the Bolsheviks in the early years of the Revolution had been to allow some of the most interesting and creative theologians of the late tsarist Church to leave Russia unchallenged.[83] Out of this community of exiles had come theologians who sought to make sense of their experience of the West while remaining faithful to a dynamic version of Orthodox tradition. Two of the most prominent names, Alexander Schmemann and John Meyendorff, who both taught in North America, were among the authors whose books were thrown on the bonfires in Ekaterinburg.

A similar spirit of conservative and anti-Western nationalism has continued in the Serbian Orthodox Church. When the state which became the kingdom of Yugoslavia was established out of the torso of the Austro-Hungarian Empire in 1918, its monarchy was that of pre-war Serbia, and the Serbs were the largest ethnic group. The Orthodox Church remained central to Serb identity, while playing host to some of the more conservative elements of the Russian Orthodox Church in exile – principally those exiles who found it more congenial to come here than to be tainted by the heretical and secularist West.[84] An amalgam developed in the interwar years combining national pride, the reality of a history of Serb struggle for survival and a powerful myth adapting the Christian theme of suffering to describe that struggle. It has been christened 'Saint-Savaism' (*Svetosavlje*) after the iconic princely religious leader of the thirteenth century (see p. 479), and it was a cult much encouraged by members of the Orthodox Theology Faculty of the University of Belgrade, reinforced by exiled Russian academics.[85] Given the powerful fund of goodwill towards Serbia built up in the West through the alliance in the First World War, this ideology need not necessarily have become anti-Western, but a significant influence moving it in that direction was that of the Serb theologian and hagiographer Justin Popović, whose interwar studies in Oxford's Theology Faculty had not ended happily, when his doctorate on Dostoevskii was failed after the examiners' criticisms of its resolute hostility to Western Christianity.[86]

A man of great personal charm whose intellectual consistency led him to suffer disfavour and official isolation for decades in Communist Yugoslavia, Popović was a major force in the spiritual formation of various monks in the next generation. They then became leaders of the Serbian Church at a crucial time in the 1990s when the Yugoslav Federation began to disintegrate. At this moment, it was easy for unscrupulous demagogic politicians quitting Communism and seeking a new framework for power to draw on the more poisonous elements in the Serb past: the bitter memories of recent Serbian sufferings at the hands of Pavelić's Croatian (and Catholic) quasi-Fascists, an extremely selective reading of past Serb relations with the Ottoman Empire, and the influence of a bloodthirsty and best-selling epic poem by a nineteenth-century Orthodox Prince-Archbishop of Montenegro, *The Mountain Wreath*, which glories in a supposed seventeenth-century massacre of the Muslims of Montenegro.[87] Symbolic of the alliance between the emerging post-Communist regime and the Church is yet another piece of political architecture: the massive 'Temple' in Belgrade, now one of the city's most prominent buildings, marking (probably mistakenly) the site of the burning of the bones of St Sava by the Turks in the sixteenth century. Begun in 1935 in a style intended to recall Istanbul's Hagia Sophia, here symbolically restored to Christian hands from Turkish captivity, the Temple's construction had stopped abruptly when the Communists came to power in Yugoslavia, but work began again in 1985 (see Plate 67).[88] The consequences of this alliance in the wars of the former Yugoslavia are well known, and they are still unravelling. The Serbian Orthodox Church has not yet had the chance or the inclination to stand back and properly consider its part in what happened.[89]

The sufferings of the Orthodox and the ancient non-Chalcedonian Churches of the East through the twentieth century, combined with the mushrooming of other Christianities, have given traditional Eastern Christianity a much diminished numerical share in the contemporary spectrum of Christian activity. In 1900, the Orthodox were estimated as 21 per cent of the world's Christians; that had declined to 11 per cent at the beginning of the twenty-first century, while the Roman Catholic proportion, thanks to its growth in the south of the globe, had risen from 48 per cent to 52 per cent.[90] Yet this decline in 'market share' should be viewed in the context of the huge rise in Christian numbers generally – and more importantly, it is worth remembering that the Christian obsession with statistics, triumphalist or alarmist, is even more recent than the general Western secular fascination with them. The English are among the originators and exemplifiers of this modern neurosis, and they also demonstrate how comparatively modern it is: no more than a century and a half in duration. English politicians pioneered the uses of statistics in politics and economics in the later seventeenth century, but the Church of England did not exhibit a permanent preoccupation with them until after 1851, when the then British government decided to conduct a census of religious affiliation and church attendance alongside its customary population census. The result punctured Anglican complacency about the Church's national status, even though it also provided the remarkable affirmation that on one day in that year, a quarter of the population was still attending the established Church's services. Anglicans have not ceased to worry about or celebrate numbers ever since; they are hardly alone among Western Churches.[91]

More important in the eyes of the Orthodox or the non-Chalcedonian Churches might be an older preoccupation: the revival in the life and morale of monasticism, that institution which is so central to their life and spirituality. From the 1970s, both Mount Athos and the Coptic monasteries of Egypt have seen a sudden and unexpected revival, bringing new recruits and new hope, albeit sometimes accompanied by an ultra-traditional attitude to the modern world. A major element in this on Mount Athos was the restoration of full community life to most monasteries after centuries when monks had tended to live individually, not generally as hermits, but pursuing their own spiritual paths.[92] What remains to be seen is how this other-worldly spirituality and emphasis on an ancient liturgy can find a constructive relationship with modernity. We have seen how the Churches of the Eastern Rite and beyond found their cultures constrained in succession by two unsympathetic powers: from the fourteenth to the nineteenth centuries, the Ottoman Empire and its outliers and the Islamic monarchy of Iran, and then, in the twentieth, the short-lived but far more hostile power of Soviet Communism. Paradoxically, these oppressions were also shelters from pressing theological problems – what, in a different context, the poet Constantine Cavafy called 'a kind of solution' – for the Churches were mostly too preoccupied with survival to look beyond their walls.[93] The Western Church in its Protestant and Catholic forms had struggled with various degrees of success to find a way of addressing children of the Enlightenment – efforts frequently scorned by the Orthodox. Out of all Eastern Churches only the Russian Orthodox Church in the last years of the tsars had much chance to do this. Now that the Orthodox cannot escape the task, the effects on Eastern Christianity will be interesting.

The stories of contemporary Russia and Serbia suggest some initial misjudgements. Some may find it depressing that after seeing the collapse of traditional European Christendom, so many Christianities are still entwined with the politics of the powerful, but it is surely inevitable that any potential source of power will fascinate fallen humanity, and that religion is as likely to bring a sword as peace. The writers of Genesis who composed the story of Cain and Abel showed wisdom in recounting the first act of worship of God as immediately followed by the first murder. While no state liberated from Soviet control decided fully to re-establish a Christian Church, the Christian Right in the United States continues to play a part in American politics which is an unmistakable bid for Christian hegemony in the nation, and there are signs of a possible new Constantinian era elsewhere. In 1991 President Frederick Chiluba of Zambia, member of a Pentecostal Church and elected freely and fairly to power on a programme of reform, became the first ruler of a post-colonial African state to declare his country 'a Christian nation', submitting 'the Government and the entire nation of Zambia to the Lordship of Jesus Christ'. Although Chiluba reluctantly stepped down from further contests for the presidency in 2001, his reputation badly sullied by his conduct in office, no subsequent government, in a country where self-declared Christians reached 85 per cent of the population in 2000, has repudiated his proclamation.[94]

Most remarkable of all are some voices heard within the leadership of the People's Republic of China. After decades when all varieties of Chinese Christianity faced differing degrees of suppression or persecution, the burgeoning of Christian practice has produced a possibility as astonishing as the events which followed Constantine's victory at the Milvian Bridge. Asked in 2002 what legacy he might give to China, the Communist Party leader Jiang Zemin is reported as saying that he would propose Christianity as China's official religion. Was this one of those world-historical jokes of which senior Chinese officials have occasionally been capable?[95] Mr Jiang would remember that Sun Yat Sen, the founder of the first Chinese Republic a century before, together with his long-lived and long-revered wife, had been Methodist Christians. He might also note, with the pragmatism which has characterized Chinese policy over the last three decades, that in China and India the combined number of hidden Christians had reached an estimated 120 million, around 6 per cent of the world's total population, capable of being recognized as the world's fifth-largest religion in their own right. That was in addition to the obvious expansion of the official Churches which China had recognized over decades, albeit at first grudgingly.[96]

The same phenomenon of official favour is perceptible in South Korea, but there it has already proved counterproductive. In 2008, the government of Lee Myung-bak was embarrassed by accusations that it was discriminating against Buddhists in its partisanship towards Christians.[97] That confrontation has been one aspect of a noticeable reaction among many Koreans at the 'Prosperity Gospel' (see pp. 960–61), the doctrine of this-worldly success which has over the last few decades leached sideways out of some influential Pentecostal congregations into Protestantism generally. The result has not been a flight from Christianity itself, but a transfer of allegiance to an alternative Christianity not associated with Protestant hegemony: the national South Korean census of 2005 revealed an actual decline in Protestant numbers by around 1.5 per cent, a modest growth in Buddhism by around 3 per cent, but an astonishing growth in Catholicism by 74 per cent.[98]

It is to be hoped that if new Church establishments do develop in Asia, they have the ability to see past Augustine of Hippo's celebrated misuse of the biblical phrase 'Compel them to come in' (see p. 304). A better text to hang in the office of any Minister for Religious Affairs would be the words of a brave dissident Polish priest, Fr Jerzy Popiełusko, in one of the addresses which led to his death at the hands of Communist Poland's secret police in 1984: 'An idea which needs rifles to survive dies of its own accord.'[99] Besides the continuing involvement of politicians in Christian life and structures, there remain contests for power between and within the Churches which reflect the cultural wars within Christianity and in wider society. Most of the traditional Churches have witnessed battles patterned after the struggles within the Catholic Church in the wake of Vatican II. Southern Baptists and Australian 'Continuing' Presbyterians have both experienced determined and largely successful attempts by conservatives to take over institutional control in their Churches' decision-making bodies.

One of the most notorious and complicated stories has been the series of running battles within the Anglican Communion. Often these have been simplistically presented as a fight between a compromised and compromising liberal affluent West and a global alliance of developing countries devoted to defending old certainties. Such a narrative suits one side of the contest, but as always in Anglicanism, matters are not that simple. Much of the rhetoric and the financial muscle backing conservative self-assertions come from Evangelicals who feel that they have lost the cultural battle in the USA, Europe and anglophone ex-British dominions, but who are prepared to direct their resources elsewhere. One major powerhouse of this movement is the Australian Anglican Diocese of Sydney, heir to most of the historic endowments from the early days of Australia, when the Church of England seemed set fair for established status in the new land. Two successive (bloodless) coups d'état in the diocese created a stronghold not just of Low Church Anglicanism, but eventually of a particular variety of Reformed Protestant Evangelicalism. First of all, a good deal of hard work and attention to key committees produced the election as Archbishop of Sydney in 1933 of Howard Mowll, a Church leader of outstanding gifts, still open to mainstream ecumenism despite his steady attention to expanding

Evangelical influence in East Asia. He set the tone for the future of Sydney diocese to the end of the 1990s.[100]

In that decade, a group around two brothers called Jensen set out to harness this Sydney Evangelicalism towards a much more aggressive agenda. This was no less than altering the direction of worldwide Anglicanism towards what it might have become in a more radical sixteenth-century English Reformation, combined somewhat anachronistically with a campaigning style of evangelism borrowed from American revivalism. Though their hopes were balked in one archiepiscopal election, much lobbying secured the succession for Peter Jensen in 2001; there followed appointments of members of the Jensen family to key roles in the diocese. Despite the new archbishop's Oxford doctoral work on the Elizabethan Reformation, the Jensen circle proved as unsympathetic to the *Book of Common Prayer* as it was to Anglo-Catholicism, so Sydney's elegant St Andrew's Cathedral under Dean Phillip Jensen now shelters the minimal possible lip service to its long-standing Anglican choral tradition. Sydney stands at the centre of a worldwide campaigning network throughout Anglicanism which has made no secret of its inclination to end the role of Lambeth Palace at the centre of the Anglican Communion.[101]

The weapon of choice in this Anglican contest, as in so many others within Christianity since the 1960s, has been sexuality, and homosexuality in particular. The causes célèbres uniting Anglican conservatives around the world have been two choices of openly gay men as bishops. One failed in England through a maladroit use of the Church of England's secretive appointments system; the other, of Gene Robinson in New Hampshire, USA, was duly completed by popular open election in 2003. Sexual morality has been a good issue for conservatives to rally round, since it is about the only thing on which all can agree – not just Christians, but Muslim conservatives too. One favourite argument of that section of African Anglicanism which denounces Western attitudes to sexuality is that African Christians are ridiculed or worse by African Muslims because of their association with a Church which condones homosexuality. South African Anglicans, who are more sensitive to Western concerns through their history of liberation struggle, have taken a very different line, particularly in vehement statements from Archbishop Desmond Tutu that the acceptance of the moral integrity of same-sex relationships is 'a matter of ordinary justice'.[102]

Behind the passing conflicts of the moment lies a debate throughout Christianity about whether the Bible and Christian tradition can be

wrong and can be changed. It is also a debate about whether God's plan
for the world centres on the supremacy of heterosexual men. 'Male
headship' is one of the overriding concerns of the Sydney variant on
Anglicanism, and worldwide, those Anglicans opposed to any change
on attitudes to same-sex relationships overlap fairly snugly with those
opposed to the ordination of women to the priesthood or consecration
to the episcopate, who use the same sort of arguments. Because of the
fundamental nature of this debate, conservative Christians who look
coldly on the style of ecumenism parented by twentieth-century liberal
Protestantism, and who are frequently deeply suspicious of the World
Council of Churches, will make some religious alliances which a century
ago would have been unthinkable. So Moscow and Rome are at one in
their attitudes to such questions as homosexuality and the ordination of
women. Equally, when conservative Episcopalians met in a Dallas
hotel conference centre to discuss their future after the Robinson
consecration in 2003, these members of a heretical Protestant sect, the
Episcopal Church, were electrified to receive a message of encouragement from no less a figure than the head of the (renamed) Roman
Inquisition, Cardinal Josef Ratzinger. It assured them of his 'heartfelt
prayers for all those taking part in this convocation. The significance of
your meeting is sensed far beyond [Dallas] and even in this city, from
which St Augustine of Canterbury was sent to confirm and strengthen
the preaching of Christ's Gospel in England.'[103] A year later, a survey
on approval ratings among American Evangelicals showed that Pope
John Paul II, who would have represented Antichrist to an earlier Evangelical generation, outpolled assorted spokesmen of the Religious Right
such as Jerry Falwell or Pat Robertson.[104]

In other circumstances, this ecumenical front falters. The chief fault
line is in those areas of the world where American Protestantism is in
direct competition with Catholicism or Orthodoxy. Among the many
annoyances for the Moscow Patriarchate in Russia's crisis years in the
1990s was the arrival through the newly open borders of a vast number
of American evangelists, thirsting to spread Evangelical Christianity with
the same enthusiasm that other Americans brought venture capitalism at
the same time. Nowhere has the tension been greater than in the huge
expansion of Pentecostalism in Latin America. Pentecostalism has generally arrived with an American rhetorical style and an identification with
American cultural attitudes. In the most discreditable cases, as in the
Guatemalan civil war in the 1990s, Pentecostal missionary work became
a parallel American cultural war on older cultures in the Maya indigen-

ous population. In Guatemala, that agenda chimed in with simultaneous political and military campaigns against these peoples by the government of the born-again Pentecostal Christian Ríos Montt and a succession of similar generals which some have described as tantamount to genocide. Conversion to Pentecostalism for many of the victims was similar in nature to mass American conversions to Catholicism in the sixteenth century: a society in crisis turned to those offering prosperity and power. Catholic reaction to Pentecostalism has been divided, because Catholicism itself is divided between traditionalist elite religion and those affected by liberation theology. Perhaps the most effective potential response to Pentecostalism here and elsewhere in Latin America might have been from the popular, non-hierarchical Catholicism of liberationist 'base communities', but the Vatican was giving no support to these.[105]

Equally significant is the way in which 'old-time' religion is not quite as old-time as it seems. It is not simply that Evangelicals or Pentecostals remain as adept as ever at adapting modernity to their work of evangelization, showing, for instance, impressive mastery of the Internet. The alliance of Evangelicalism and Pentecostalism, which was extremely shaky from the first days of Pentecostalism until the 1940s (see pp. 960–61), may not be a permanent one. There is no special reason why a form of Christianity which emphasizes the renewal brought by the gifts of the Spirit should be allied to Evangelical Fundamentalism, which demands adherence to a particular set of intellectual or doctrinal propositions or a particular way of understanding texts from the past. There has indeed been a considerable 'Charismatic' movement within a very different variety of Western Christianity, the Roman Catholic Church. Pentecostalism might grow into an alliance with other forms of Christianity which have seen the Bible in more flexible and arguably more creative ways – as stories whose truth is not that of the Highway Code or a car maintenance guide. It was certainly the experience of the Quakers, from their first extrovert demonstrations in the seventeenth century, that Evangelical Christianity was a very inexact fit for their exploration of the spiritual; so it may prove with Pentecostalism.

The Ghanaian historian Kwabena Asamoah-Gyadu describes a telling incident which he witnessed in a Ghanaian indigenous Pentecostal Church. The choir, primed to sing a chorus in preparation for the sermon, simply could not stop singing. Some of them began shaking, screaming, jumping, blessing the name of the Lord; the congregation followed suit. It lasted for an hour, and the preacher decided that there was no need for a sermon: it was sufficient blessing. This is an interesting victory of liturgy – albeit not a style of liturgy traditionally familiar in the West – over the preached word. Nor need Pentecostalism's frequent alliance with American cultural forms be more than a product of its origins: much of it has other sources, and is evolving a new politics just as it takes up new modes of expression.[106]

It is observable that certain aspects of the Christian past are being jettisoned without fuss even within self-consciously traditional religion. The most notable casualty of the past century has been Hell. It has dropped out of Christian preaching or much popular concern, first among Protestants, then later among Catholics, who have also ceased to pay much attention to that aspect of Western doctrine which seemed all-consuming in the Latin Church on the eve of the Reformation, Purgatory.[107] One might see this merely as a result of European seculariz-ation: does this continent, arguably so far the world's most successfully balanced consumer society, need a Christian Heaven and Hell? It has lived through its own self-made hells in two world wars, seen the folly of blindly dogmatic belief, and now it has tried to build something less ambitious than paradise on earth, without the aid of sacred stories or absolutist ideologies.

Yet the phenomenon is wider than secular Europe. It penetrates deep into conservative as well as liberal Christianity worldwide. The disappearance of Hell represents a quiet Christian acceptance of propositions whose first prominent appearance was in nineteenth-century English Protestantism. Famously, the generous-minded theo-logian F. D. Maurice, a convert from Unitarianism to Anglicanism, lost his professorial chair at King's College, London, in 1853 for a series of theological essays which suggested that the notion of eternal punishment was a misunderstanding of the biblical message. Rather more unexpected was the near-contemporary appearance of similar ideas in premillennial Evangelicalism, in the fertile mind of Edward Irving and English disciples of his who managed to stay within the established Church, like Thomas Rawson Birks and Edward H. Bickersteth. Through these theologians, who managed to convince sympathizers of their rather implausible claim that they had not abandoned Calvinism, came the gradual lowering of temperature in the fires of Hell. They hardly flicker at all now in worldwide televangelism.[108]

A particularly surprising development in Christianity, admittedly so far noticeable mainly in the West, is the abandonment of a key aspect of Christian practice since its early days, inhumation of corpses. As hellfire receded, there advanced the literal fires of the crematorium; such fire, previously reserved by Christians for heretics, now routinely forms the liturgical climax to encomia of the good things in the life of the deceased. It will be remembered that one of the earliest public manifestations of the Christian Church was as a burial club (see p. 160), and universally archaeologists are able to detect the spread of Christian culture through the ancient and early medieval world by the excavation of corpse burials oriented east–west. The traditionalist case seems unanswerable, and was well expressed by Christopher Wordsworth, Bishop of Lincoln, in a sermon in Westminster Abbey on 5 July 1874:

Brethren, more than fourteen hundred years have now passed away, since the flames of funeral piles [*sic*], which once blazed in all parts of the Roman Empire, have been extinguished by Christianity . . . The substitution of burning for Burial would be a falling back from Christianity to Heathenism, even as Paganism itself was a lapse from primitive religion.

Cremation's earliest champions were in fact Italian liberal nationalists, who were on occasion forbidden burial in graveyards controlled by the Church, and so cremation became an anticlerical gesture in Italy.[109]

Now Bishop Wordsworth would be astonished by the victory of cremation in the face of the universal vehemence of early denunciations such as his. In 2000 cremations formed more than 70 per cent of British funerals and 25 per cent of those in the United States, starting from a basis of nil in the Christian world in the 1860s. The arguments are not so much theological as practical considerations for public health and space – particularly in crowded societies like Britain. Yet the liturgical transformation involved is huge, not least the removal of a corpse's final parting from the church, which is a community place of worship, a setting for all aspects of Christian life, to the crematorium, a specialized and often rather depressingly clinical office room for dealing with death. There are indeed signs that the disposal of ashes is creating a variety of inventive new personalized ritual, including the use of Roman candles to send the ashes of one Florida fireworks enthusiast into the heavens, and an unmanned satellite to speed various others still further from the earth. The theological implications are also profound. Death is not so much distanced as sanitized or domesticated, made part of the spectrum of consumer choice in a consumer society. The Church is robbed of what was once one of its strongest cards, its power to pronounce and give public liturgical shape to loss and bewilderment at the apparent lack of pattern in the brief span of human life.[110]

Changing attitudes to death and Hell mark a growth of this-worldly concerns in a large part of contemporary Christianity. That is as much exemplified in the concern for political justice in liberation theology as in the 'Prosperity Gospel' strand of Pentecostalism, even though the politics of both frequently stand in complete contrast. There are other contrasts: Pentecostals often seem preoccupied in their liturgy by the joy of their faith, while theologies of social justice are more inclined to remember that at the heart of Christian stories, after the birth of a helpless baby in an obscure province of the empire, there is a gallows built by the colonial power. A different sort of this-worldliness is to be found in the continuing fascination which Christian art, creativity and sacred places exercise over the Western mind, however secularized. In England, cathedrals and their choral music have never been better loved, cherished or maintained through public generosity. Their vigorous life, from Evensong to teashops, contrasts with the empty Sainte-Chapelle in Paris, in its emptiness a symbol of the troubled history of the modern French Church, and in its beauty a further twofold symbol. The Sainte-Chapelle speaks of the medieval conviction that the relics of the saints opened an entrance to Heaven (particularly for the king who paid for them), but with its modern turnstiles and sightseeing crowds, it also reflects the vague modern hope that beauty and antiquity might just open an entrance to Heaven. How does tourism relate to pilgrimage, and can the Church help tourists to become pilgrims?

It is one of the curiosities of Western society since the Enlightenment that much of its greatest sacred music (though by no means all) has been the work of those who have abandoned any structured Christian faith. Edward Elgar, who created English Catholicism's greatest modern sacred oratorio out of Cardinal Newman's poem *The Dream of Gerontius*, exclaimed at the time of its first performance that he had always believed that 'God was against art', and towards the end of his life, he lost whatever Christian faith he had. Michael Tippett, who explored the anguish of suffering humanity through Negro spirituals in *A Child of Our Time*, and stood alongside Augustine of Hippo and Monica in the garden at Ostia as they reached out to glimpse God in *The Vision of St Augustine*, never embraced any Christian affirmation. The agnosticism of the clergyman's son Ralph Vaughan Williams did not prevent him editing the finest hymn book in the English language, *The English Hymnal*, or creating even greater splendour around the Christian tradition of sacred verse in numerous song-settings and choral pieces; the passionate verse of the English parson-poet George Herbert is now almost inconceivable without Vaughan Williams. Even Nikolai Rimsky-Korsakov, so influential in the reconstruction of Russian Ortho-dox church music, which remains one of the main ambassadors of Orthodoxy beyond its boundaries, was an aggressive atheist.[111]

What do we make of this paradox? It might be seen simply as the logical historical outcome of the phenomenon which we noted as a mark of advancing secularity in eighteenth-century Enlightenment Europe, that Christian sacred music could become detached from the liturgy into the concert hall (see pp. 788–9). But that very possibility says something about the special quality of music among the arts. The writer Andreii Belïy, one of Rimsky-Korsakov's colleagues in the late-nineteenth-century artistic impulse to forge a new unworldliness for a worldly society styled the Symbolist Movement, pointed out that 'music is not concerned with the depiction of forms in space. It is, as it were, outside space.'[112] Pseudo-Dionysius, Aquinas and a host of mystics in East and West would have said the same about God, and God himself said it about himself, in the midst of a burning bush on the Sinai peninsula. Perhaps music might be one way past the impasse which has been the experience of some versions of the Protestant Reformation, tangled in the torrent of words which has flowed around the Word which dwelt among us, full of grace and truth.

This book has no ending, because, unlike Jesus Christ, historians in the Western secular tradition stemming from the Enlightenment do not think in terms of punchlines to the human story. This history can draw attention to what has gone before: an extraordinary diversity called Christianity. A couple of lines of poetry from the great English dissenting hymn-writer Isaac Watts commonly raise a smile among choirs who sing them frequently, thanks to a shift in English usage:

> Let every creature rise and bring
> *Peculiar honours* to our King.[113]

The image of a menagerie presenting a collection of bizarre objects to the enthroned Saviour in the Last Days is not what Watts was invoking, pleasing thought though it is. Watts in his eighteenth-century English wanted to talk about the glorious particularity of individual religious experience, the appropriateness of one Christian manifestation to one situation; yet all of them fixed intently on that which is outside space. So often what in one age seems bizarre – the property of a derided or persecuted sect – becomes the respected norm or variant in other, later circumstances: the abolition of slavery, the ordination of women, the

avoidance of meat-eating or tobacco.[114] Hans Urs von Balthasar reflected wisely on an aspect of the Church's history which might give
some contenders in present battles pause when he stressed the ultimate
individuality of spiritual experience: 'Nothing has ever borne fruit in
the Church without emerging from the darkness of a long period of
loneliness into the light of the community.'[115]

Most of Christianity's problems at the beginning of the twenty-first
century are the problems of success; in 2009 it has more than two billion
adherents, almost four times its numbers in 1900, a third of the world's
population, and more than half a billion more than its current nearest
rival, Islam.[116] At least Christian history offers plenty of sobering messages for overconfidence. The more interesting conundrum for Christianity is a society in which polite indifference has replaced the battles of
the twentieth century: Europe, which is not so much a continent as a state
of mind, to be found equally in Canada, Australasia and a significant part
of the United States. Can there be a new Christian message of tragedy
and triumph, suffering and forgiveness to Europeans and those who
think like them? Does secularism have to be an enemy of Christian faith,
as Nazism and Soviet Communism were enemies, or does it offer a
chance to remould Christianity, as it has been remoulded so often
before? Can the many faces of Christianity find a message which will
remake religion for a society which has decided to do without it?

Original sin is one of the more plausible concepts within the Western
Christian package, corresponding all too accurately to everyday human
experience. One great encouragement to sin is an absence of wonder.
Even those who see the Christian story as just that – a series of stories –
may find sanity in the experience of wonder: the ability to listen and
contemplate. It would be very surprising if this religion, so youthful, yet
so varied in its historical experience, had now revealed all its secrets.

Notes

Abbreviations

Ahlstrom	S. E. Ahlstrom, *A Religious History of the American People* (2nd edn, New Haven and London, 2004)
Anderson	A. Anderson, *An Introduction to Pentecostalism* (Cambridge, 2004)
Angold (ed.)	M. Angold (ed.), *The Cambridge History of Christianity 5: Eastern Christianity* (Cambridge, 2006)
ARG	*Archiv für Reformationsgeschichte*
Barrett (ed.)	C. K. Barrett (ed.), *The New Testament Background: Selected Documents* (rev. edn, London, 1987)
Baumer	C. Baumer, *The Church of the East: An Illustrated History of Assyrian Christianity* (London and New York, 2006)
Benedict	P. Benedict, *Christ's Churches Purely Reformed: A Social History of Calvinism* (New Haven and London, 2002)
Bettenson (ed.)	H. Bettenson (ed.), *Documents of the Christian Church* (2nd edn, Oxford, 1963)
Binns	J. Binns, *An Introduction to the Christian Orthodox Churches* (Cambridge, 2002)
Breward	I. Breward, *A History of the Churches in Australasia* (Oxford, 2001)
Burleigh	M. Burleigh, *Earthly Powers: The Conflict between Religion and Politics from the French Revolution to the Great War* (London, 2005)
CH	*Church History*
Chadwick	H. Chadwick, *East and West: The Making of a Rift in the Church. From Apostolic Times until the Council of Florence* (Oxford, 2003)
CWE	*Collected Works of Erasmus*, various editors: Toronto edn
Dalrymple	W. Dalrymple, *From the Holy Mountain* (London, 1997)
Doig	A. Doig, *Liturgy and Architecture from the Early Church to the Middle Ages* (Aldershot, 2008)
Duffy	E. Duffy, *Saints and Sinners: A History of the Popes* (3rd edn, New Haven and London, 2006)
EHR	*English Historical Review*
Eusebius	Eusebius, *Church History, Life of Constantine the Great, and Oration in Praise of Constantine* (NPNF new series I, 1890)

Frend   W. H. C. Frend, *The Rise of Christianity* (London, 1984)
Gilley and Stanley (eds.)   S. Gilley and B. Stanley (eds.), *Cambridge History of Christianity 8: World Christianities, c. 1815–c. 1914* (Cambridge, 2006)
Goodman   M. Goodman, *Rome and Jerusalem: The Clash of Ancient Civilisations* (London, 2006)
Handy   R. T. Handy, *A History of the Churches in the United States and Canada* (Oxford, 1976)
Harries and Mayr-Harting (eds.)   R. Harries and H. Mayr-Harting (eds.), *Christianity: Two Thousand Years* (Oxford, 2001)
Hastings   A. Hastings, *The Church in Africa 1450–1950* (Oxford, 1994)
Hastings (ed.)   A. Hastings (ed.), *A World History of Christianity* (Grand Rapids, 1999)
Herrin   J. Herrin, *Byzantium: The Surprising Life of a Medieval Empire* (London, 2007)
Hessayon and Keene (eds.)   A. Hessayon and N. Keene (eds.), *Scripture and Scholarship in Early Modern England* (Aldershot, 2006)
HJ   *Historical Journal*
Hope   N. Hope, *German and Scandinavian Protestantism, 1700–1918* (Oxford, 1995)
HTR   *Harvard Theological Review*
Hussey   J. M. Hussey, *The Orthodox Church in the Byzantine Empire* (Oxford, 1986)
JAC   *Jahrbüch für Antike und Christentum*
JEH   *Journal of Ecclesiastical History*
Jenkins   P. Jenkins, *The Lost History of Christianity: The Thousand-year Golden Age of the Church in the Middle East, Africa and Asia* (New York, 2008)
JRH   *Journal of Religious History*
JTS   *Journal of Theological Studies*
Koschorke et al. (eds.)   K. Koschorke, F. Ludwig and M. Delgado (eds.), *A History of Christianity in Asia, Africa, and Latin America 1450–1990: A Documentary Sourcebook* (Grand Rapids and Cambridge, 2007)
McClelland   J. S. McClelland, *A History of Western Political Thought* (London and New York, 1996)
MacCulloch   D. MacCulloch, *Reformation: Europe's House Divided 1490–1700* (London, 2003; US edn, *Reformation: A History*, New York, 2005)
Mitchell and Young (eds.)   M. M. Mitchell and F. M. Young (eds.), *The Cambridge History of Christianity I: Origins to Constantine* (Cambridge, 2006)
NA (PRO)   National Archives (Public Record Office of the United Kingdom), Kew, Middlesex
Naphy (ed.)   W. R. Naphy (ed.), *Documents on the Continental Reformation* (Basingstoke, 1996)
NPNF   *Nicene and Post-Nicene Fathers of the Christian Church*
ODNB   *Oxford Dictionary of National Biography*, available online in its most up-to-date form at http://www.oxforddnb.com
Parry (ed.)   K. Parry (ed.), *The Blackwell Companion to Eastern Christianity* (Oxford, 2007)
Pettegree (ed., 1992)   A. Pettegree (ed.), *The Early Reformation in Europe* (Cambridge, 1992)
Pettegree (ed., 2000)   A. Pettegree (ed.), *The Reformation World* (London, 2000)

PP	*Past and Present*
RSTC	A. W. Pollard and G. R. Redgrave, rev. W. A. Jackson and F. S. Ferguson and completed by K. F. Pantzer, *A Short Title Catalogue of Books printed in England, Scotland, and Ireland and of English Books Printed Abroad before the year 1640* (3 vols., London, 1976–91)
SCES	*Sixteenth Century Essays and Studies*
SCH	*Studies in Church History*
SCJ	*Sixteenth Century Journal*
Snyder	T. Snyder, *The Reconstruction of Nations: Poland, Ukraine, Lithuania, Belarus, 1569–1999* (New Haven and London, 2003)
Stevenson (ed., 1987)	J. Stevenson (ed.), rev. W. H. C. Frend, *A New Eusebius: Documents Illustrating the History of the Church to ad 337* (London, 1987)
Stevenson (ed., 1989)	J. Stevenson (ed.), rev. W. H. C. Frend, *Creeds, Councils and Controversies: Documents Illustrating the History of the Church ad 337–461* (London, 1989)
Stringer	M. Stringer, *A Sociological History of Christian Worship* (Cambridge, 2005)
Sundkler and Steed	B. Sundkler and C. Steed, *A History of the Church in Africa* (Cambridge, 2000)
TLS	*Times Literary Supplement*
TRHS	*Transactions of the Royal Historical Society*
Tyerman	C. Tyerman, *God's War: A New History of the Crusades* (London, 2006)
Wolffe (ed.)	J. Wolffe (ed.), *Religion in History: Conflict, Conversion and Coexistence* (Manchester, 2004)

Introduction

1 A superb analysis of this beautiful hymn is to be found in J. R. Watson, *The English Hymn: A Critical and Historical Study* (Oxford, 1999), 86–90. Its words are much enhanced by a later tune, 'Love Unknown', written by the British composer John Ireland (1879–1962). Crossman borrowed for his poem the metre of the 'Geneva' metrical version of Psalm 148 commonly sung in England in his time, 'Give laud unto the Lord', and mightily improved on the psalm version; perhaps he was trying to show that the metre could be lovely after all.

2 During a seminar at the University of Bristol, 26 February 1991. Being of a certain generation and cast of mind, his remark was phrased in the singular and with a masculine reference.

3 Two recent major studies cast complementary lights on it: M. Biddle, *The Tomb of Christ* (Stroud, 1999), and C. Morris, *The Sepulchre of Christ and the Medieval West: From the Beginning to 1600* (Oxford, 2005).

4 II Timothy 3.16.

5 G. Williams, *Recovery, Reorientation and Reformation: Wales c. 1415–1642* (Oxford, 1987), 305–31.

6 D. Dymond, 'God's Disputed Acre', *JEH*, 50 (1999), 464–97, at 465.

PART I: A MILLENNIUM OF BEGINNINGS
(1000 BCE–100 CE)

1: Greece and Rome
(*c.* 1000 BCE–100 CE)

1　John 1.1–14.

2　All four Gospels use the word 'Christ' as a name for Jesus, although fairly sparingly, with only two instances in the earliest Gospel, Mark (9.41 and 15.32, the latter being in sarcastic speech). The usage is very common in the surviving letters of Paul of Tarsus, which are generally acknowledged to predate the Gospels.

3　O. Murray, *Early Greece* (Brighton, 1980), 13–20.

4　Revelation 1.8, 21.6 and esp. 22.13.

5　J. Dillenberger, *Style and Content in Christian Art* (London, 1965), 34–6.

6　Job 38–42; Exodus 3.13–14.

7　R. G. Collingwood and J. N. L. Myres, *Roman Britain and the English Settlements* (2nd edn, Oxford, 1937), 186.

8　M. I. Finley, *The Ancient Greeks* (London, 1963), 30–53.

9　See esp. I Samuel 28.15–19.

10　See esp. Exodus 18; 34.34–5.

11　For an introduction to 'Tyrants and Lawgivers', see R. Lane Fox, *The Classical World: An Epic History of Greece and Rome* (London, 2005), Ch. 5.

12　The term 'Classical', which I will be employing, is derived not, as is sometimes asserted, from the usage of the Latin word *classis* for 'fleet', but in its meaning of 'first-class heavy infantry': see ibid., 1.

13　I am indebted to Oliver Taplin for these perceptions of Athens: *TLS*, 15 September 2006, 5. For the suggestion that Alexandria was crucial in making such choices, see p. 39.

14　R. Warner (tr.) and M. I. Finley (ed.), *History of the Peloponnesian War: Thucydides* (rev. edn, London, 1972), 152 [Bk II, Ch. 46]. The best survey of Greek homosexuality is now J. Davidson, *The Greeks and Greek Love: A Radical Reappraisal of Homosexuality in Ancient Greece* (London, 2007).

15　W. D. Desmond, *The Greek Praise of Poverty: Origins of Ancient Cynicism* (Notre Dame, 2006), esp. 6–7, 60–61, 144; on Diogenes and masturbation, H. Cherniss (ed.), *Plutarch's Moralia* (17 vols., Loeb edn, London and Cambridge, MA, 1927–2004), XIII, Pt II, 501 [*On Stoic Self-contradictions* 21]. For 'Holy Fools' in the Christian tradition, see p. 207.

16　C. Kahn, *Pythagoras and the Pythagoreans: A Brief History* (Indianapolis and Cambridge, 2001), 6–10.

17　H. N. Fowler and W. R. M. Lamb (ed.), *Plato with an English Translation I: Euthrypo; Apology; Crito; Phaedo; Phaedrus* (Loeb edn, London and Cambridge, 1953), 132–3 [*Apology*, 38a]. A good recent treatment of Socrates's trial and death is E. Wilson, *The Death of Socrates: Hero, Villain, Chatterbox, Saint* (London, 2007).

18　P. Shorey (ed.), *Plato: The Republic* (2 vols., Loeb, London, 1930), II, 118–41 [VII, 514a–519e].

19　R. G. Bury (ed.), *Plato: With an English Translation VII: Timaeus; Critias; Cleitophon; Menexenus; Epistles* (Loeb, London and Cambridge, MA, 1961), 50–53, 176–9 [*Timaeus* XXVIIIa–XXIXd; LXVIIIe–LXIXc].

20　M. Schofield, *Plato: Political Philosophy* (Oxford, 2006), esp. 40–42, 88–9.

21　H. Rackham (ed.), *Aristotle XX: The Athenian Constitution; The Eudemian Ethics; On Virtues and Vices* (Loeb edn, Harvard and London, 1971), 1–181.

22　A. D. Godley (ed.), *Herodotus, with an English Translation* (4 vols., Loeb edn, 1920–31). For Plutarch's attack, F. H. Sandbach (ed.), *Plutarch's Moralia* (17 vols., Loeb edn, London and Cambridge, 1927–2004), XI, 1–129 [*On the malice of Herodotus*]. Cicero coined the title 'Father of History': J. L. Myres, *Herodotus: Father of History* (Oxford, 1933), 19. A useful introductory discussion is J. Burrow, *A History of Histories: Epics, Chronicles,*

Romances and Inquiries from Herodotus and Thucydides to the Twentieth Century (London, 2007), 11–28.

23 For an introduction to Sparta, see Lane Fox, *The Classical World*, Ch. 6.

24 C. Forster Smith, *Thucydides, with an English translation* (4 vols., Loeb edn, London and Cambridge, 1920). Introductory discussion in Burrow, *A History of Histories*, 29–51.

25 Two good recent introductions to Alexander are P. Cartledge, *Alexander the Great: The Hunt for a New Past* (Basingstoke and Oxford, 2004), and C. Mossé, *Alexander: Destiny and Myth* (Edinburgh, 2004).

26 H. Maehler, 'Alexandria, the Mouseion, and Cultural Identity', in A. Hirst and M. Silk (eds.), *Alexandria: Real and Imagined* (Aldershot, 2004), 1–14.

27 The pioneer was the Prussian historian J.-G. Droysen: see good summary discussion on his thesis on the relationship between Christianity and the Hellenistic world in P. Cartledge, 'Introduction', in P. Cartledge, P. Garnsey and E. S. Gruen (eds.), *Hellenistic Constructs: Essays in Culture, History and Historiography* (Berkeley, 1997), 1–19, at 2–6.

28 Cartledge, *Alexander the Great*, 215–27.

29 This thesis has been contested in recent years, without being decisively controverted: see Cartledge, 'Introduction', 6–10.

30 Goodman, 43, 45, 50.

31 D. Feeney, *Caesar's Calendar: Ancient Time and the Beginnings of History* (Berkeley, 2007), 86–91.

32 Goodman, 164–5.

33 R. Rushton Fairclough (ed.), *Horace: Satires, Epistles and Ars Poetica* (Loeb edn, London and Cambridge, 1970), 408–9 [*Epistles* II.1.156–7].

34 The standard (and brilliant) account of these events is still R. Syme, *The Roman Revolution* (Oxford, 1939).

35 R. H. A. Jenkyns, *Virgil's Experience: Nature and History, Times, Names, and Places* (Oxford, 1998), 643–53.

36 H.-J. Klauck, 'The Roman Empire', in Mitchell and Young (eds.), 69–83, at 72.

37 In these remarks, I am aware of the rather different thrust in the long-influential arguments of E. R. Dodds, eloquently presented in his *Pagan and Christian in an Age of Anxiety* (Cambridge, 1965), esp. Ch. 1 and 132, that Christianity entered a vacuum in which traditional Roman religion was being emptied of emotional power and also becoming otherworldly, so that 'paganism' easily collapsed after the withdrawal of imperial favour. Dodds's theses are reaffirmed in R. Stark, *The Rise of Christianity: A Sociologist Reconsiders History* (Princeton, 1996), esp. 196–201. For an imaginative presentation of different perspectives, see K. Hopkins, *A World Full of Gods: Pagans, Jews and Christians in the Roman Empire* (London, 1999), esp. 22–31, 44–5, 78–88, and for other works stressing the vigour of traditional or non-Christian religious belief and practice persisting into the third century CE see, e.g., G. Fowden, 'The World View', in A. K. Bowman, P. Garnsey and A. Cameron (eds.), *The Cambridge Ancient History XII: The Crisis of Empire, A.D. 193–337* (2nd edn, Cambridge, 2005), 521–37, and R. Lane Fox, *Pagans and Christians in the Mediterranean World from the Second Century AD to the Conversion of Constantine* (London, 1986), esp. 669–81.

2: Israel
(c. 1000 BCE–100 CE)

1 A brilliant introduction to the city is A. Elon, *Jerusalem: City of Mirrors* (rev. edn, London, 1996).

2 Revelation 16.16.

3 Another presentation of broadly similar conclusions, lively and comprehensive, though perhaps more abrasive than this, is R. Lane Fox, *The Unauthorized Version: Truth and Fiction in the Bible* (London, 1991).

4 Genesis 13.14–17; Ch. 15; 17.5–6.

5 Genesis 32.28.

6 There is one exception to the silence, the eighth-century prophet Hosea's use of the story of Jacob's punishment, Hosea 12 – but this is the exception that proves the rule.

7 Genesis 22.20–24.

8 T. L. Thompson, *The Historicity of the Patriarchal Narratives* (New York, 1974), 75–88, 299–307, 325; J. van Seters, *Abraham in History and Tradition* (London, 1975), 29–34.

9 H. Jagersma, *History of Israel* (London, 1982), 37.

10 M. G. Hasel, '*Israel* in the Merneptah Stela', *Bulletin of the American Schools of Oriental Research*, 296 (1994), 45–61.

11 N. Naaman, '*Habiru* and Hebrews: The Transfer of a Social Term to the Literary Sphere', *Journal of Near Eastern Studies*, 45 (1986), 271–88.

12 This obscure figure who has provoked much Christian fascination over the centuries is otherwise mentioned in the Bible only at Psalm 110.4.

13 A. Alt, 'The God of the Fathers', in Alt, *Essays on Old Testament History and Religion* (Oxford, 1966), 3–65.

14 Exodus 3.14, often rendered 'I am who I am'; cf. Exodus 3.4, 15. The vocalization of 'Yahweh' around its consonants is a modern conjectural reconstruction of the original. Hebrew did not note vowel sounds in its alphabet until the medieval Massoretic scholars added them. By that time, Jews had out of reverence long ceased to pronounce the word 'YHWH', so all reconstructions of the vowel sounds in the word are conjectural and are based on transcriptions of it in the writings of early Christians. The form of Yahweh familiar to some Christians, 'Jehovah', is a mistaken late medieval Christian attempt to fill in vowel sounds to the consonants of YHWH in Hebrew. This misunderstood a convention in Jewish texts that those consonants should be completed with the vowels of an entirely different word substituted in reverence, *Adonai*, 'Lord'.

15 Exodus 6.3.

16 Alt, 'The God of the Fathers', 42–3.

17 See, e.g., the disapproving tone in the account of the people's importunate demand for a king, and Samuel's warning to them, I Samuel 8.10–20, or Samuel's open rebuke of them, I Samuel 12.17. For major later implications for seventeenth-century Europe in this material, see E. Nelson, ' "Talmudical Commonwealthsmen" and the Rise of Republican Exclusivism', *HJ*, 50 (2007), 809–36.

18 The most consistently attested contents were the original tablets of the Ten Commandments given to Moses (see pp. 61 and 1019–20): see I Kings 8.9.

19 There are too many references to this claim in the New Testament to list in summary form, but key examples are Matthew 12.23; 21.9, 15; Luke 1.27; 2.4; John 7.42; Romans 1.3.

20 For a lively treatment of possibilities, see W. G. Dever, *Did God Have a Wife? Archaeology and Folk Religion in Ancient Israel* (Grand Rapids and Cambridge, 2005), and see also J. M. Hadley, *The Cult of Asherah in Ancient Israel and Judah: Evidence for a Hebrew Goddess* (Cambridge, 2000).

21 II Kings 17–18.

22 For a useful collection of essays giving a comparative overview, see M. Nissinen, *Prophecy in Its Ancient Near Eastern Context: Mesopotamian, Biblical and Arabian Perspectives* (Atlanta, 2000), esp. H. B. Huffman, 'A Company of Prophets: Mari, Assyria, Israel', 47–70.

23 I Kings 18.19, 22, 40–45.

24 Amos 1.1; Ch. 5; 7.14–16; Hosea 1.2; 3.1.

25 Isaiah 1.11; Ch. 6.

26 Isaiah 7.3.

27 Isaiah 2.3–4. The importance of this passage was such that it was also attributed to the contemporary prophet Micah, and so it can be found in slightly varied form at Micah 4.2–3.

28 II Kings 22.1–13; II Chronicles 34.1–12.

29 Deuteronomy 13.9.

30 Cf., e.g., Genesis 17.11–14, 24; 21.4.

31 J. Barton and J. Muddiman (eds.), *The Oxford Bible Commentary* (Oxford, 2001), 136.

32 Psalm 137.1. An account of these events from the point of view of the exiles is to be found in Ezra 4.

33 Luke 10.29–37; John 4.1–45.

34 T. J. Wray and G. Mobley, *The Birth of Satan: Tracing the Devil's Biblical Roots* (Basingstoke, 2005), esp. 51–2, 66–8, 75–148.

35 Ecclesiastes 1.8–9, 18; 12.7–8.

36 Goodman, 168–71.

37 Luke 1.46–55, 68–79, and see G. Vermes, *The Nativity: History and Legend* (London, 2006), 148.

38 S. Freyne, 'Galilee and Judaea in the First Century', in Mitchell and Young (eds.), 37–51, at 39.

39 W. Horbury and D. Noy (eds.), *Jewish Inscriptions of Graeco-Roman Egypt, with an Index of the Jewish Inscriptions of Egypt and Cyrenaica* (Cambridge, 1992), e.g. 13–14, 47–9, and index of examples at 276.

40 Doig, 2; Goodman, 283–5. See also Barrett (ed.), 55–7.

41 II Esdras 14.45–6. R. A. Kraft, 'Scripture and Canon in Jewish Apocrypha and Pseudepigrapha', and S. Mason with R. A. Kraft, 'Josephus on Canon and Scriptures', in M. Saebø (ed.), *Hebrew Bible/Old Testament: The History of Its Interpretation* (3 vols., Göttingen, 1996), I, Pt I, 199–235, esp. 220–21, 228–31.

42 On the canon, see pp. 127–9.

43 A useful wider selection is given in Barrett (ed.), 316–49.

44 See this quotation of I Enoch in Jude 14; on Ethiopia, see p. 279.

45 B. Sundkler and C. Steed, *A History of the Church in Africa* (Cambridge, 2000), 8.

46 Barrett (ed.), 292–8.

47 See ibid., 251–62.

48 II Maccabees 7.28: G. O'Collins and M. Farrugia, *Catholicism: The Story of Catholic Christianity* (Oxford, 2003), 167–8.

49 W. D. Davies and L. Finkelstein (eds.), *The Cambridge History of Judaism II: The Hellenistic Age* (Cambridge, 1989), 226, 294, 302, 422, 485. For vigorous arguments for an earlier date for widespread ideas of resurrection, perhaps dangerously overstretching the argument for the literary and historical precedents, see J. D. Levenson, *Resurrection and the Restoration of Israel: The Ultimate Victory of the God of Life* (New Haven and London, 2006), esp. 191–200.

50 Good summary discussion in Goodman, 254–60.

51 Daniel 12.2–3.

52 Goodman, 311.

53 M. Goodman, 'The Function of Minim in Early Rabbinic Judaism', in H. Cancik et al. (eds.), *Geschichte-Tradition-Reflexion: Festschrift für Martin Hengel zum 70.Geburtstag* (3 vols., Tübingen, 1996), I, 501–10, esp. 501–2.

54 Matthew 22.23–40; on Paul, Acts 23.6–8.

55 The remote community which lived in the Dead Sea settlement discovered near the modern Wadi Qumran, and which probably hoarded the famous Dead Sea Scrolls, has often been seen as Essene. There is no conclusive evidence for this: Goodman, 240, though see a more positive view in G. Vermes, *Scrolls, Scriptures and Early Christianity* (London and New York, 2005), esp. 18–30. Nor is there good evidence of direct links between the Scrolls and early Christianity: G. J. Brooke, *The Dead Sea Scrolls and the New Testament: Essays in Mutual Illumination* (London, 2005), esp. xviii, 8–10, 13, 19–26, 261–71. For samples from the Qumran literature, see Barrett (ed.), 218–51.

PART II: ONE CHURCH, ONE FAITH, ONE LORD? (4 BCE–451 CE)

3: A Crucified Messiah
(4 BCE–100 CE)

1 The 'down-market' phrase is from R. A. Burridge, *What are the Gospels? A Comparison with Graeco-Roman Biography* (Cambridge, 1992), 217. Burridge nevertheless throughout stresses the Gospels' features shared with other ancient lives (*bioi*).

2 *New York Times*, 18 August 1991: 'Itchy feet: a symposium'.

3 Micah 5.2; John 7.40–43.

4 Luke 2.1, 5.

5 G. Vermes, *The Nativity: History and Legend* (London, 2006), 93–4. Much of what follows is indebted to the clear-sightedness of Vermes.

6 Matthew 1.1–17; Luke 3.23–38.

7 R. Bauckham, *Jude and the Relatives of Jesus in the Early Church* (Edinburgh, 1990), 355–9.

8 Much to be recommended as an analysis of Matthew's genealogy is a mischievous poem by the biblical scholar Michael Goulder, beginning 'Exceedingly odd is the means by which God/Has provided our path to the heavenly shore . . .' 'Tamar', first published in 1965, can be savoured in *The Reader*, 98/4 (Winter 2004), 20. For hostile comment on the Matthew genealogy from a twelfth-century rabbi, Jacob ben Reuben, see M. Rubin, *Mother of God: A History of the Virgin Mary* (London, 2009), 166–7.

9 Matthew 5.17, 21–48.

10 Matthew 1.16; Luke 3.23.

11 Isaiah 7.14; Matthew 1.23.

12 J. Jeremias, *New Testament Theology* (London, 1971), 36–7, 61–8; for 'The Lord's Prayer', Matthew 6.9–13; Luke 11.2–4. *Patēr* goes into Latin identically as *pater*, and hence the name for 'The Lord's Prayer' still widely used in the formerly Latin West, derived from its two opening words, 'Our Father' – the 'Paternoster'.

13 The reasons for Dionysius's mistaken calculations are exhaustively explored in G. Declercq, *Anno Domini: The Origins of the Christian Era* (Turnhout, 2000), but the credit for the original discoveries is austerely returned to Julius in A. A. Mosshammer, *Easter Computus and the Origins of the Christian Era* (Oxford, 2008).

14 See the references to Herod in Matthew 2 and Luke 1.5. The evidence for Herod dying in 4 BCE is exhaustively reviewed in T. D. Barnes, 'The Date of Herod's Death', *JTS*, n.s. 19 (1968), 204–9.

15 See the date in Luke 3.1–2. The only flaw in the cluster of dating evidence which Luke gives is his assertion that Annas shared the high priesthood with Caiaphas in 28–9: Vermes, *The Nativity*, 90.

16 For Jesus's baptism by John, see Matthew 4.13–17; Mark 1.9–11; Luke 3.21–2. For a variety of statements about Jesus's superiority to John, mostly put in the mouth of John himself, see Matthew 3.11–14; Mark 1.7–8; Luke 3.16–17; John 1.6–8, 35–7; 3.25–30; 4.1–2.

17 On Jesus's age at the beginning of his public ministry, see Luke 3.23.

18 Matthew 7.12; cf. Luke 6.31.

19 This cheerful summary of a textual problem which has occupied some of the sharpest minds of Western scholarship without conclusive result should be enriched by consulting, e.g., G. N. Stanton, *The Gospels and Jesus* (Oxford, 1989).

20 Mark 10.27; Luke 18.27.

21 Jeremias, *New Testament Theology*, 14–18: the phenomenon is technically known as 'antithetic parallelism'.

22 Jeremias, *New Testament Theology*, 35–6. It would be tedious to list all the many New Testament instances of 'Amen', but for the single use, see, e.g., Matthew 5.18; Mark 3.28; Luke 4.24; and for John's double form, John 1.51; 5.19, 24, 25.

23 Mark 2.27–8, with weakened versions in Matthew 12.8 and Luke 6.5.

24 The one exception to this rule, John 12.34, when 'the people' use the phrase, is echoing an earlier prediction of Jesus himself that the Son of Man will be lifted up (John 3.14).

25 Daniel 7.13.

26 B. Lindars, *Jesus, Son of Man* (London, 1983), esp. 17–28 for discussion of the Aramaic *bar enasha*, 97–100, 156–7: G. Vermes, *Jesus the Jew* (London, 1973), 160–91. For an incisive discussion which argues for a rather more positive assertion by Jesus of his Messianic status, see M. Hengel, *Studies in Early Christology* (Edinburgh, 1995), Ch. 1.

27 J. Jeremias, *Rediscovering the Parables* (London, 1966), 10. The parables are almost exclusively to be found in the Synoptic Gospels: there is only one in John's Gospel, John 10.1–6.

28 Ibid., 145.

29 Mark 12.1–12; Matthew 21.33–46; Luke 20.9–19.

30 See variations in Matthew 22.1–14 and Luke 14.16–24, usefully discussed (together with the version in the non-canonical Gospel of Thomas) in Jeremias, *Rediscovering the Parables*, 50–53, 138–42.

31 Matthew 25.1–13.

32 Luke 12.39–40; in its present form this hardly seems to be a parable, but that is what Peter calls it in response, and it may be a fragment of a larger story. For its echo in a fourth-century hymn of Ephrem the Syrian, see p. 183.

33 Matthew 20.1–16.

34 Matthew 5–7; Luke 6.17–49, with other fragments elsewhere. Much of the material is scattered through Mark's Gospel without being anthologized.

35 Matthew 5.21–6.

36 Matthew 6.7–15; Luke 11.1–4; see also Mark 11.25–6. Both the latter are abbreviated compared with the full version in Matthew.

37 Usefully discussed in T. G. Shearman, ' "Our Daily Bread" ', *Journal of Biblical Literature*, 53 (1934), 110–17 (although Shearman's conclusion may be considered too simple), and E. Lohmeyer, *'Our Father': An Introduction to the Lord's Prayer* (New York, 1965), 141–51.

38 1 Thessalonians 4.15–16; Matthew 24.30–31 (a 'Son of Man' saying). Paul in his own words has little to say about the 'kingdom' theme, and it is virtually absent from John's Gospel (exceptions are John 3.3, 5).

39 Acts 1.21–26.

40 Matthew 23.24; Matthew 8.22 (Luke 9.60).

41 For a good summary of extensive scholarly debate about the 'messianic secret', see C. Tuckett (ed.), *The Messianic Secret* (Philadelphia and London, 1983).

42 E. P. Sanders, *Jesus and Judaism* (London, 1985), 230, 256–60. Compare the absolute prohibition in Luke 16.18 with the exception for divorce for adultery in Matthew 5.31–2.

43 Good discussion of the issues in P. Bradshaw, *Eucharistic Origins* (Alcuin Club Collections 80, 2004).

44 John 18.31.

45 Matthew 27.25.

46 Mark 7.24–30; Matthew 15.21–8.

47 John 8.6, 8. It is ironic that this one instance of Jesus writing is to be found in one of the most textually insecure portions of John's Gospel (it is missing, for instance, in the text of John from Bodmer Papyrus 66, illustrated in Plate 1).

48 Hengel, *Studies in Early Christology*, 384–5.

49 Luke 24.13–35.

50 I Maccabees 4.11; Luke 24.13–49.

51 For a twentieth-century example of this, see the ceiling of the Chapel of the Ascension in the Anglican Shrine of Our Lady in Little Walsingham, England. Accounts in Mark 16.19 (in a fragment of text which seems to post-date the main text of the Gospel); Luke 24.51; Acts 1.2 (in a book generally taken as a continuation of Luke's Gospel by the same author, though the discrepancy in this detail of the Ascension does raise one's doubts about this little-challenged assumption).

52 For an interesting interchange concisely introducing many of the issues, see the correspondence of 1971 between Don Cupitt and C. F. D. Moule, *Explorations in Theology 6: Don Cupitt* (London, 1979), 27–41. Hengel, *Studies in Early Christology*, *passim* and esp. 383–9, provides a robust case for a very early and very consistent pre-Pauline exaltation of Jesus as the Son of God.

53 The question of authorship and authenticity among Paul's epistles, which is vital to sorting out which messages are his and which have been foisted on him by his admirers, is crisply dealt with in J. Barton and J. Muddiman (eds.), *The Oxford Bible Commentary* (Oxford, 2001), 1078–83, and in comment on subsequent individual epistles. Those generally agreed to be written by Paul himself are Romans, I and II Corinthians, Galatians, Philippians, I Thessalonians and Philemon. That leaves a more dubious status for Ephesians, Colossians, II Thessalonians, I and II Timothy and Titus. Hebrews has widely been recognized as by a different hand throughout the history of Christian biblical interpretation, including by Martin Luther.

54 J. M. Robinson spoke aptly of the 'domesticated Paul' to be found in the Book of Acts:

Robinson, 'Nag Hammadi: The First Fifty Years', in J. D. Turner and A. McGuire (eds.), *The Nag Hammadi Library after Fifty Years: Proceedings of the 1995 Society of Biblical Literature Commemoration* (Leiden, 1997), 3–33, at 28.

55 Acts 9.3–4.

56 Galatians 1.12–19.

57 M. M. Mitchell, 'Gentile Christianity', in Mitchell and Young (eds.), 103–24, at 109.

58 Romans 11.13. The account of Paul's arrest and trial by Felix the Roman governor in Caesarea is in Acts 24.

59 J. D. Crossan and J. L. Reed, *In Search of Paul: How Jesus's Apostle Opposed Rome's Empire with God's Kingdom* (London, 2005), esp. 23–6, 36–7, 215–34.

60 As Christ, e.g. Romans 5.6; 10.4; as Lord, e.g. the hymn, which appears to be a quotation by Paul of a text by someone else, Philippians 2.11.

61 C. F. D. Moule, *The Origin of Christology* (Cambridge, 1977), 58–60.

62 Romans 4.15; 7.8, 12.

63 E. P. Sanders, *Paul, the Law and the Jewish People* (Philadelphia, 1983), 6, 10, 13–14.

64 Romans, 1.17, with embedded quotation from Habbakuk 2.4. An excellent guide to modern discussion of Paul and the Law is D. G. Horrell, *An Introduction to the Study of Paul* (London and New York, 2000), Ch. 6.

65 Romans 2.14–15.

66 I Corinthians 15.22.

67 Paul's description of the Eucharist, I Corinthians 11.23–6, is the earliest text to assert that Jesus commanded his disciples to repeat in remembrance what he had done in the Last Supper. Among the Synoptic Gospels, the latest, Luke 22.19, picks up this reference to a command to remember and repeat the actions, which is not present in the earlier parallel descriptions in Mark 14.22 or Matthew 26.26.

68 I Corinthians 12.13, and on the variousness of the Christian community, see I Corinthians 7.7, 17; 12.27–30.

69 Genesis 1.2.

70 Romans 8.15–16, 26.

71 There is a persistent strand of argument among some modern scholars that John's Gospel was regarded in many sections of mainstream Christianity as suspect as late as the end of the second century CE. The evidential basis for this is narrow, as is demonstrated with care in C. E. Hill, *The Johannine Corpus in the Early Church* (Oxford, 2004), esp. 463–70. Equally, conservative scholarship still argues for an early dating for John: one surprising convert to this theory was J. A. T. Robinson, *The Priority of John* (London, 1985), and a recent study, generally putting the Gospels early, has been R. Bauckham, *Jesus and the Eyewitnesses: The Gospels as Eyewitness Testimony* (Grand Rapids, 2006).

72 Respectively John 6.35, 48, 51; 8.12; 9.5; 10.7; 10.11, 14; 11.25; 14.6; 15.1.

73 Mark 13.32: 'of that day or that hour no one knows, not even the angels in heaven, nor the Son, but only the Father'. This passage's concern to modify the apocalyptic urgency of the previous material suggests an addition at a very late stage in producing the final version of Mark.

74 John 1.32.

75 For the dense allusions here, see Revelation 21 and 22.

76 I Corinthians 15.5–8.

77 Galatians 2.11–14.

78 I Corinthians 10.23–32.

79 Martin Goodman has recently restated the case first made by the Jewish historian Josephus for accidental destruction: Goodman, esp. 440–44. One does not have to accept that argument to admire his masterly treatment of the era.

80 M. Goodman, 'Trajan and the Origins of Roman Hostility to the Jews', *PP*, 182 (February 2004), 28. On the genuine likelihood that the Capitoline Temple was built over the site of the crucifixion and tomb of Jesus, see J. Murphy O'Connor, *The Holy Land: An Oxford Archaeological Guide* (Oxford, 1980), 49–61.

81 Eusebius, *Church History* (*NPNF*, n.s. I, 1890), 158–9 (III.27.1–4).

82 Goodman, 103.

83 It was in this tradition that Nazi-sympathizing Christians in the twentieth century claimed

that Nazareth lay in an enclave of 'Aryanism' and that the population of Galilee was not Jewish: see p. 942 and C. Kidd, *The Forging of Races: Race and Scripture in the Protestant Atlantic World, 1600–2000* (Cambridge, 2006), Ch. 6.

84 Revelation 21.22 (see p. 104). The view which I am presenting has been challenged in recent years by scholars who argue for a much later and piecemeal separation between Judaism and Christianity, more or less complete only in the early fourth century. The case is eloquently stated in D. Boyarin, *Border Lines: The Partition of Judaeo-Christianity* (Philadelphia, 2004): see esp. xiv–xv, 192–201.

85 A useful treatment of this theme is L. W. Hurtado, *Lord Jesus Christ: Devotion to Jesus in Earliest Christianity* (Grand Rapids, 2003), esp. 1–78, 575–6.

86 C. Harline, *Sunday: A History of the First Day from Babylonia to the Super Bowl* (New York, 2007), 6–17.

87 Stringer, 42.

88 Harline, *Sunday*, 4–6.

89 Goodman, 454, 469–70, 530–31.

90 Acts 11.26; see Goodman, 539–40.

91 For a careful though not dogmatically positive account of the evidence for Peter's death in Rome, see J. Toynbee and J. Ward-Perkins, *The Shrine of St Peter and the Vatican Excavations* (London, 1956), 127–8, 133, 155–61.

4: Boundaries Defined
(50 CE–300)

1 John Rylands Library, Manchester (UK), Greek Papyrus P⁵²: for a careful dose of cold water on attempts to date the fragment more closely, see B. Nongbri, 'The Use and Abuse of P⁵²: Papyrological Pitfalls in the Dating of the Fourth Gospel', *HTR*, 98 (2005), 23–48.

2 C. Markschies, *Kaiserzeitliche christliche Theologie und ihre Institutionen: Prolegomena zu einer Geschichte der antiken christlichen Theologie* (Tübingen, 2007), 32. I am grateful to James Carleton Paget for pointing me to this reference.

3 Romans 16.5–8. On the question of authenticity in Paul's letters, see p. 1045, n, 53.

4 I Corinthians 9.14: cf. Synoptic parallels Matthew 10.10–11, Luke 10.7–8.

5 II Thessalonians 3.6 (my italics). There is a good discussion of this point in G. Theissen, *The Social Setting of Pauline Christianity: Essays on Corinth* (Edinburgh, 1982), 33–54. For a vigorously contrary view, emphasizing the poverty of Pauline Christian communities, see J. J. Meggitt, *Paul, Poverty and Survival* (Edinburgh, 1998).

6 Romans 16.23 – both men send greetings to the Christians in Rome. An inscription for Erastus, 'aedile at Corinth', may well be a reference to this same man and a testimony to his high social status: W. A. Meeks, *The First Urban Christians: The Social World of the Apostle Paul* (New Haven and London, 1983), 58–9.

7 I Corinthians 11.17–34.

8 I Corinthians 10.23–32.

9 I Corinthians 7.20.

10 Romans 13.1: cf. Jesus's ambiguous response when shown a coin of the emperor: Mark 12.17 and Matthew 22.21.

11 Galatians 3.28.

12 I Corinthians 10.21.

13 J. A. Harrill, *Slaves in the New Testament: Literary, Social and Moral Dimensions* (Minneapolis, 2006), 6–16, 177–8. A tradition about the letter has Onesimus stealing money from Philemon and then running away from his master to meet Paul, for reasons unknown (cf. ibid., 6–7). This has no basis in the text and probably arose from a desire to make sense of the letter's peculiar content. The survival of the tradition unchallenged in much modern scholarship is remarkable.

14 I Peter 2.13, 18–24: the Revised Standard Version of the Bible, like many other translations, bowdlerizes the word *oiketai* to 'servants'. It means 'house-slaves'. This material is part of the *Haustafeln*, discussed pp. 118–19.

15 G. M. E. de Ste Croix, 'Early Christian Attitudes to Property and Slavery', in D. Baker

(ed.), *Church, Society and Politics: Papers Read at the Thirteenth Summer Meeting and the Fourteenth Winter Meeting of the Ecclesiastical History Society* (*SCH*, 12, 1975), 1–38, esp. 20–21.

16 The classic statement of the case is E. Schüssler Fiorenza, *In Memory of Her: A Feminist Theological Reconstruction of Christian Origins* (London, 1983).

17 C. Tuckett, *The Gospel of Mary* (Oxford, 2007), 101 [*Gospel of Mary* 18.11–15] and see esp. 52–4, 201–3; E. Pagels and K. L. King, *Reading Judas: The Gospel of Judas and the Shaping of Christianity* (New York and London, 2007), 35–7. On the gnostics, see pp. 121–5.

18 Romans 16.1–7, 12; U. E. Eisen, *Women Officeholders in Early Christianity: Epigraphical and Literary Studies* (Collegeville, 2000), esp. on Junias, 47–8, 54, 56, and on deacons, 159–98.

19 I Corinthians 11.3–15; 14.34.

20 A classic and careful account of the arguments against Ephesians being authentically Pauline is C. L. Mitton, *The Epistle to the Ephesians: Its Authorship, Origin and Purpose* (Oxford, 1951).

21 Ephesians 2.7.

22 Ephesians 6.1–4.

23 I Timothy 2.15.

24 Ephesians 5.23. Cf. an elaborate argument by Paul about our release from the Jewish Law, based on the analogy of a wife's release from marriage by her husband's death, Romans 7.1–6.

25 I Timothy 3.7.

26 Titus 2.5.

27 C. Osiek, 'The Self-defining Praxis of the Developing *Ecclēsia*', in Mitchell and Young (eds.), 274–92, at 281; Goodman, 118, 245–8.

28 I Corinthians 7.1–9.

29 Acts 4.32–end; 5.1–11.

30 Leviticus 25.

31 I Timothy 2.11–12.

32 Stringer, 39–41; it is difficult to locate or date the *Didachē*, but scholarly opinion inclines to the late first century and a setting in Syria/Palestine.

33 D. Williams, 'Justification by Faith: A Patristic Doctrine', *JEH*, 57 (2006), 649–67, at 654.

34 D. Brakke, 'Self-differentiation among Christian Groups: The Gnostics and Their Opponents', in Mitchell and Young (eds.), 245–60, at 247–9.

35 J. D. Turner and A. McGuire (eds.), *The Nag Hammadi Library after Fifty Years: Proceedings of the 1995 Society of Biblical Literature Commemoration* (Leiden, 1997), esp. 4–8 for an account of the discovery. For a selection of gnostic texts from here and elsewhere, see Barrett (ed.), 92–119.

36 E. M. Yamauchi, 'The Issue of Pre-Christian Gnostics Reviewed in the Light of the Nag Hammadi Texts', in Turner and McGuire (eds.), *Nag Hammadi Library after Fifty Years*, 72–88, esp. 87.

37 Scholars once commonly held that early Egyptian Christianity was particularly closely associated with gnosticism, the case being first strongly argued by W. Bauer, *Rechtgläubigkeit und Ketzerei im ältesten Christentum* (Tübingen, 1934). This view has been carefully refuted by C. H. Roberts, *Manuscript, Society and Belief in Early Christian Egypt* (London, 1979), esp. Ch. 3.

38 S. Davies (ed.), *The Gospel of Thomas Annotated and Explained* (London, 2003), 54–5 [Log. 42].

39 M. Franzmann, 'A Complete History of Early Christianity: Taking the "Heretics" Seriously', *JRH*, 29 (2005), 117–28, at 120, qu. Epiphanios, *Panarion* 26.4–5.

40 A moderate (though widely criticized) exposition of gnostic opposition to authority and sympathy to female potential is E. Pagels, *The Gnostic Gospels* (New York, 1979), especially 48–69.

41 See discussion and texts in E. Pagels and K. L. King, *Reading Judas: The Gospel of Judas and the Shaping of Christianity* (London, 2007), 59, 67–8, 71–4, 113.

42 Titus 1.14.

43 Historians up to modern times have tended to follow Irenaeus of Lyons's assertion that Marcion mutilated the texts of Paul and Luke which he used: see Stevenson (ed., 1987), 92. For strong arguments to the contrary, and general discussion of Marcion's use of Luke, see A. Gregory, *The Reception of Luke and Acts in the Period before Irenaeus: Looking for Luke in the 2nd Century* (Tübingen, 2003), 175–210.

44 M. Frenschkowski, 'Marcion in arabischen Quellen', in G. May and K. Greschat (eds.), *Marcion und seine kirchengeschichtliche Wirkung* (Berlin, 2002), 39–63, at 46–9, 62.

45 On Harnack and Marcion, W. H. C. Frend, 'Church Historians of the Early Twentieth Century: Adolf von Harnack', *JEH*, 52 (2001), 83–102, at 85, 101.

46 W. R. Schoedel, *Ignatius of Antioch: A Commentary on the Letters of Ignatius of Antioch* (Philadelphia, 1985), 238, 243–4.

47 D. Trobisch, *The First Edition of the New Testament* (Oxford, 2000), esp. 6–7, 72–7, 106–7.

48 On Clement being read liturgically at Corinth and indeed elsewhere, see Eusebius, 147 [III.16]; 201 [IV.23.11].

49 D. R. Cartlidge and J. K. Elliott, *Art and the Christian Apocrypha* (London and New York, 2001), 15–18, 143–8, 169.

50 D. H. Williams, *Tradition, Scripture and Interpretation: A Sourcebook of the Ancient Church* (Grand Rapids, 2006), 82–3, qu. Irenaeus, *Proof of the Apostolic Preaching* 3.6–7.

51 See the account of their election in Acts 6.1–6.

52 Stevenson (ed., 1987), 12.

53 Ibid., 8–9. The original, Isaiah 60.17, is translated in the Revised Standard Version as 'I will make your overseers peace and your taskmasters righteousness.'

54 Various modern scholars have questioned the authenticity and early second-century date of Ignatius's letters: for summary effective replies, see A. Brent, 'The Enigma of Ignatius of Antioch', *JEH*, 57 (2006), 429–56, at 429–32.

55 Schoedel, *Ignatius of Antioch*, 238.

56 Brent, 'The Enigma of Ignatius of Antioch', 433.

57 This case is made ibid. and in A. Brent, *Ignatius of Antioch: A Martyr Bishop and the Origins of Episcopacy* (Edinburgh, 2007).

58 For the possibility that Peter's death in Rome is less secure than that of Paul, see pp. 110–11. For the earliest assertions that Peter was Bishop of Rome, in the mid-fourth century, see p. 294.

59 The first church building on the site, apart from a small shrine, was put up probably as late as 354; and for a useful summary history, including the disastrous fire and almost equally disastrous rebuilding of 1823, see M. Webb, *The Churches and Catacombs of Early Christian Rome* (Brighton and Portland, 2001), 207–13.

60 Cartlidge and Elliott, *Art and the Christian Apocrypha*, 135.

61 The evidence for the excavated shrine being the actual grave of St Peter is strong but not absolutely conclusive: see J. Toynbee and J. Ward-Perkins, *The Shrine of St Peter and the Vatican Excavations* (London, 1956), 127–8, 133, 155–61.

62 Frend, 130, 146–7.

63 A. Hastings, '150–550', in Hastings (ed.), 25–65, at 30.

64 Brakke, 'Self-differentiation among Christian Groups', in Mitchell and Young (eds.), 245–60, at 255–6.

65 Stringer, 67–8. For imitation of this stational worship in the later West, see p. 347, and in Byzantium, see p. 193.

66 V. Fiocchi Nicolai, F. Bisconti and D. Mazzoleni, *The Christian Catacombs of Rome: History, Decoration, Inscriptions* (Regensburg, 1999), 165.

67 J. Stevenson, *The Catacombs: Rediscovered Monuments of Early Christianity* (London, 1978), 31–2.

68 W. Tabbernee, *Fake Prophecy and Polluted Sacraments: Ecclesiastical and Imperial Reactions to Montanism* (Leiden and Boston, 2007), 399–400. Tabbernee was among the rediscovery team (ibid., ix, xxix, 116, 258–9); his book is now the best overview of Montanism.

69 I. Backus, *Reformation Readings of the Apocalypse: Geneva, Zürich and Wittenberg* (Oxford, 2000), xii; I. Backus, *Historical Method and Confessional Identity in the Era of*

the Reformation (1378–1615) (Leiden, 2003), 131–4, 148–52. On radicals, mainstream Protestants and the Last Days, see pp. 623–4 and 772–4.

70 This is a case well argued in A. Stewart-Sykes, 'The Original Condemnation of Asian Montanism', *JEH*, 50 (1999), 1–22.

71 G. Salmon in W. Smith and H. Wace (eds.), *Dictionary of Christian Biography* (4 vols., London, 1877–87), III, 941, s.v. Montanus.

72 Colossians 2.8.

73 A. Lukyn Williams (ed.), *Dialogue with Trypho the Jew* (London, 1930), 4–20 [Chs. 2–9].

74 Ibid., 127 [Ch. 61]. For Philo's use of *logos*, see Barrett (ed.), 262–5.

75 Stevenson (ed., 1987), 120.

76 Ibid., 167.

77 Cf. ibid., 164, 176.

78 For Tertullian's use of '*trinitas*', see M. Wellstein, *Nova Verba in Tertullians Schriften gegen die Häretiker aus montanistischer Zeit* (Stuttgart and Leipzig, 1999), 218–20.

79 Lukyn Williams (ed.), *Dialogue with Trypho the Jew*, 113 [56.11].

80 Brakke, 'Self-differentiation among Christian groups', in Mitchell and Young (eds.), 255–6; F. M. Young, 'Monotheism and Christology', in Mitchell and Young (eds.), 452–69, at 461.

81 Stevenson (ed., 1987), 184, 186.

82 Eusebius, 257 [VI.11.6].

83 Stevenson (ed., 1987), 180.

84 Ibid., 184.

85 Ibid., 187.

86 A. Le Boulluec (ed.), *Clement D'Alexandrie: Les Stromates: Stromate V (Sources Chrétiennes* 278, 1981), 38–9 [V.1.9.4]; A. Le Boulluec (ed.), *Clement D'Alexandrie: Les Stromates: Stromate VII (Sources Chrétiennes* 428, 1997), 128–9 [VII.6.34.4].

87 Stevenson (ed., 1987), 188–9.

88 J. Boswell, *Christianity, Social Tolerance and Homosexuality: Gay People in Western Europe from the Beginning of the Christian Era to the Fourteenth Century* (Chicago and London, 1980), 140, 147, 164, 355–9.

89 Eusebius, 250 [VI.2.4–6].

90 Stevenson (ed., 1987), 192–3.

91 J. N. B. Carleton Paget, 'Origen as Exegete of the Old Testament', in M. Saebø (ed.), *Hebrew Bible/Old Testament: The History of Its Interpretation* (3 vols., Göttingen, 1996), I, Pt I, 499–542.

92 There has been controversy as to whether the *Hexapla* contained the Hebrew text of the Tanakh, but see A. Grafton and M. Williams, *Christianity and the Transformation of the Book: Origen, Eusebius and the Library of Caesarea* (Cambridge, MA, and London, 2006), 92–6. On the number of books, ibid., 88, 105, on the innovative format, 17, and on Origen's hesitant Hebrew, 112. The Victorian edition was F. Field (ed.), *Origenis Hexaplorum quae supersunt; sive, Veterum interpretum Græcorum in totum Vetus Testamentum fragmenta* (2 vols., Oxford, 1867–75).

93 For a recent thorough corrective to easy assumptions that Alexandrian Christian thought should be read chiefly with reference to Plato and 'middle Platonism', see M. J. Edwards, *Origen against Plato* (Aldershot, 2002).

94 Stevenson (ed., 1987), 206. For the neo-Platonist Porphyry's hostile comments on Origen's use of allegory, see ibid., 207–8.

95 Ibid., 202.

96 Ibid., 199.

97 Commentary on John 20.28, qu. H. Chadwick, *East and West: The Making of a Rift in the Church. From Apostolic Times until the Council of Florence* (Oxford, 2003), 6.

98 G. W. Butterworth (ed.) *Origen: On First Principles* (London, 1936; reprint with further introduction, Gloucester, MA, 1973), 67–68, 110–13.

99 This doctrine is known technically as *apokatastasis*. On this and Origen's cosmic scheme, see Stevenson (ed., 1987), 201–4.

5: The Prince: Ally or Enemy?
(100–300)

1 Romans 1.19–32.

2 Useful discussion in W. V. Harris (ed.), *The Spread of Christianity in the First Four Centuries: Essays in Explanation* (Leiden, 2005), esp. 17–23, 158–60.

3 H. Chadwick, 'The Early Church', in Harries and Mayr-Harting (eds.), 1–20, at 9.

4 F. M. Young, 'Prelude: Jesus Christ, Foundation of Christianity', in Mitchell and Young (eds.), 1–35, at 14–15.

5 R. M. Grant, 'Five Apologists and Marcus Aurelius', *Vigiliae Christianae*, 42 (1988), 1–17, at 4–5.

6 H. W. Attridge et al. (eds.), *The Apostolic Tradition* (Minneapolis, 2002), 88, 90, 94.

7 F. Trombley, 'Overview: The Geographical Spread of Christianity', in Mitchell and Young (eds.), 302–23, at 310.

8 It is twice told by Eusebius in his *Church History*, 161 [III.30.6]; 187 [IV.14.6].

9 D. Trobisch, *The First Edition of the New Testament* (Oxford, 2000), esp. 19–21.

10 L. W. Hurtado, *The Earliest Christian Artifacts: Manuscripts and Christian Origins* (Grand Rapids, 2006), esp. on these *nomina sacra*, Ch. 3; Trobisch, *The First Edition of the New Testament*, 11–19.

11 A. Wypustek, 'Un aspect ignoré des persécutions des chrétiens dans l'Antiquité: les accusations de magie érotique imputées aux chrétiens aux II et III siècles', *JAC*, 42 (1999), 50–71, at 58. Cf. J. A. Hanson (ed.), *Apuleius: Metamorphoses* (2 vols., Cambridge, MA, and London, 1989), 179–85 [IX.29–31].

12 Stevenson (ed.), 1987), 1–2.

13 C. Ziwsa (ed.), *S. Optati Milevitani libri VII . . . Accedunt decem monumenta vetera ad Donatistarum historiam pertinentia* (*Corpus Scriptorum Ecclesiasticorum Latinorum*, 26, 1893), Appendix I, 186–7. On Constantine and funerary commemoration, see pp. 292–3.

14 A figure quoted by W. H. C. Frend, *JEH*, 55 (2004), 126.

15 V. Fiocchi Nicolai, F. Bisconti and D. Mazzoleni, *The Christian Catacombs of Rome: History, Decoration, Inscriptions* (Regensburg, 1999), 20–22, 35, 151–3. A further good general introduction is J. Stevenson, *The Catacombs: Rediscovered Monuments of Early Christianity* (London, 1978).

16 M. A. Tilley, 'North Africa', in Mitchell and Young (eds.), 381–96, at 391.

17 J. Huskinson, 'Pagan and Christian in the Third to the Fifth Centuries', in Wolffe (ed.), 13–41, at 22. See text in Stevenson (ed.), 1987), 44–5.

18 B. D. Shaw, 'The Passion of Perpetua', *PP*, 139 (May 1993), 3–45, at 22, and *passim* for useful comment.

19 Stevenson (ed.), 1987), 18–21.

20 H. Chadwick, *The Early Church* (London, 1967), 52n.

21 Eusebius, 201 [IV.23.4–8].

22 W. A. Meeks, 'Social and Ecclesial Life of the Earliest Christians', in Mitchell and Young (eds.), 145–73, at 171–2; M. M. Mitchell, 'From Jerusalem to the Ends of the Earth', ibid., 295–301, at 295–6. There are, however, instances of second- and early-third-century pilgrimage to the Holy Land, including such figures as Origen, Melito of Sardis and Alexander, Bishop of Cappadocia: see Stringer, 74.

23 H. Chadwick (ed.), *Contra Celsum* (rev. edn, Cambridge, 1965). We must presume that Celsus wrote his attack in Greek, the language in which it is transmitted by Origen.

24 Stevenson (ed.), 1987), 136.

25 A useful summary account of these developments is F. Millar with D. Berciu, R. N. Frye, G. Kossack and T. Talbot Rice, *The Roman Empire and Its Neighbours* (London, 1967).

26 '. . . though it was impossible that she could reconcile the practice of vice with the precepts of the gospel, she might hope to atone for the frailties of her sex and professions, by declaring herself the patroness of the Christians': E. Gibbon, *The History of the Decline and Fall of the Roman Empire* (12 vols., London, 1813), II, 446–7 [Ch. 16]. Similarly, the great French Church historian Monsignor Duchesne does not seem to have been immune to the comic aspects of her career when he observed in riposte to Gibbon, 'Her life – in such surroundings – could scarcely be in strict accord with Gospel precepts':

L. Duchesne, *Early History of the Christian Church from Its Foundation to the End of the Third Century* (London, 1914), 183, from the 4th French edn., Ch. 13, 251–2.

27 E. Cary (ed.), *Dio's Roman History* (9 vols., Loeb edn, London and Cambridge, MA, 1914–2004), IX, 271–3 [*Epitome of Book LXXVII* 14.6].

28 R. Reece, 'Town and Country: The End of Roman Britain', *World Archaeology*, 12 (1980), 77–92, at 80.

29 J. Geffcken, *The Last Days of Greco-Roman Paganism* (rev. edn, Amsterdam and London, 1978), 25–31.

30 J. G. Davies, 'Was the Devotion of Septimius Severus to Serapis the Cause of the Persecution of 202–3?', *JTS*, 5 (1954), 73–6.

31 E. R. Dodds, *Christian and Pagan in an Age of Anxiety: Some Aspects of Religious Experience from Marcus Aurelius to Constantine* (Cambridge, 1965).

32 Current archaeological opinion, however, does not favour the common idea that the famous Mithraeum from Walbrook in the City of London was deliberately desecrated by Christians: see J. D. Shepherd (ed.), *The Temple of Mithras, London: Excavations by W. F. Grimes and A. Williams at the Walbrook* (London, 1998), 227–32. For Mithraic dedications, see Barrett (ed.), 133–4.

33 On his vanishing and visions, see C. P. Jones (ed.), *Philostratus* (3 vols., Loeb edn, Cambridge, MA, and London, 2005), 322–3, 384–5, 413–15 [*Life of Apollonius of Tyana* VIII]. Vol. III contains Eusebius's refutation. Barrett (ed.), 82–5, provides economical extracts of Apollonius.

34 B. Stock, *After Augustine: The Meditative Reader and the Text* (Philadelphia, 2001), 43.

35 On Jesus as apostle, M. Franzmann, *Jesus in the Manichaean Writings* (London and New York, 2003), 15–17; on the paradoxes, ibid., 76–7.

36 S. Whitfield with U. Sims-Williams, *The Silk Road: Trade, Travel, War and Faith* (London, 2004), 121–2.

37 Stevenson (ed., 1987), 267–8.

38 I. Gardiner et al. (eds.), *Coptic Documentary Texts from Kellis I* (Oxford, 1999), 72–82, 344–57. See also M. Franzmann, 'The Syriac-Coptic Bilinguals from Ismant el-Kharab (Roman Kellis): Translation Process and Manichaean Missionary Practice', in A. van Tongerloo and L. Cirillo (eds.), *Il Manicheismo: nuove prospettive della ricerca* (Turnhout, 2005), 115–22.

39 P. McKechnie, 'Christian Grave-inscriptions from the *Familia Caesaris*', *JEH*, 50 (1999), 427–41, at 439, and see p. 167.

40 On Origen and Julia Mamaea, Stevenson (ed., 1987), 195. On Hippolytus and his imperial dedication, W. Smith and H. Wace (eds.), *Dictionary of Christian Biography* (4 vols., London, 1877–87), III, 99–100.

41 D. Magie (ed.), *The Scriptores Historiae Augustae* (3 vols., Loeb edn, London and New York, 1921–32), 234–5, 238–41 [XXIX.3, XXXI.5]. There is an equally dubious precedent in a similar story about the gnostic Carpocrates, from much the same period: Dodds, *Christian and Pagan in an Age of Anxiety*, 107.

42 McKechnie, 'Christian Grave-inscriptions from the *Familia Caesaris*', 441.

43 Stevenson (ed., 1987), 214–15. The whole episode of persecution from Valerian to Gallienus, Cyprian and Novationism is well covered ibid., 213–51. On the principle of sacrifice by heads of families, see R. Selinger, *The Mid-third Century Persecutions of Decius and Valerian* (Frankfurt am Main, 2002), 59–63.

44 For examples in summary discussion of such attitudes, Grant, 'Five Apologists and Marcus Aurelius'.

45 John 12.25; Matthew 10.23.

46 Stevenson (ed., 1987), 241–3.

47 Shaw, 'Passion of Perpetua', 15.

48 Baumer, 1–3.

49 T. Rajak, 'The Jewish Diaspora', in Mitchell and Young (eds.), 53–68, at 65; Goodman, 169–71.

50 Stringer, 83.

51 For an extraordinary long-term effect of one reading in the *Peshitta* on worldwide racist attitudes to blacks, see p. 868.

52 A good introduction is C. Hopkins, edited by B. Goldman, *The Discovery of Dura-Europos* (New Haven and London, 1979).

53 J. Gutmann, 'The Dura Europos Synagogue Paintings: The State of Research', in L. I. Levine (ed.), *The Synagogue in Late Antiquity* (Philadelphia, 1987), 61–72. A more striking instance of a cultural setting promoting the violation of Jewish prohibitions on sacred figural art, in this case the more direct violation of sculpture, is to be seen in the fine series of seventeenth- and eighteenth-century sculpted gravestones in the Portuguese Jewish cemetery at Ouderkerk aan de Amstel in the Netherlands. For Orthodox evasion of the graven-image prohibition, see p. 444.

54 Doig, 10–18.

55 Baumer, 16. It is ironic that no Christian church building now remains in its original use in Urfa: see p. 927.

56 A. Mirkovic, *Prelude to Constantine: The Abgar Tradition in Early Christianity* (Frankfurt am Main, 2004), 89–115. For the texts, see Eusebius, 100–102 [1.13].

57 For a judicious contribution to the still ill-tempered debate on the Shroud of Turin, see A. Friedlander, 'On the Provenance of the Holy Shroud of Lirey/Turin: A Minor Suggestion', *JEH*, 57 (2006), 457–77. I am grateful to Hannes Schroeder of St Cross College, Oxford, for our discussions on carbon-dating of samples from the shroud in the University of Oxford's Research Laboratory for Archaeology.

58 F. Heal, 'What Can King Lucius Do for You? The Reformation and the Early British Church', *EHR*, 120 (2005), 593–614, esp. at 595, 614.

59 Mirkovic, *Prelude to Constantine*, 22, 141–3.

60 For Eusebius's comment, see Stevenson (ed., 1987), 125.

61 Hopkins, ed. Goldman, *Discovery of Dura-Europos*, 107–8.

62 For Serapion of Antioch's description of the use of another Gospel attributed to Peter, see Stevenson (ed., 1987), 126–7.

63 On Marcion, see pp. 125–7.

64 For a sympathetic study, see E. J. Hunt, *Christianity in the Second Century: The Case of Tatian* (London, 2003), esp. 52–73, 176–8.

65 Stevenson (ed., 1987), 155.

66 Dalrymple, 175.

67 S. A. Harvey, 'Syria and Mesopotamia', in Mitchell and Young (eds.), 351–65, at 355–6.

68 K. McVey (ed.), *Ephrem the Syrian: Hymns* (New York and Mahwah, 1989), 107: Hymn 5 on the Nativity. For the parallel of burglary in a parable of Jesus, see Luke 12.39–40.

69 Dalrymple, 171–7. I much appreciate the welcome given us by the congregation of St George in 2008 and their gift of CDs of their performances of Edessan sacred music.

70 A. Gelston, *The Eucharistic Prayer of Addai and Mari* (Oxford, 1992), esp. 12, and see also B. D. Spinks, *Addai and Mari – the Anaphora of the Apostles: A Text for Students with Introduction, Translation and Commentary* (Grove Liturgical Study 24, Nottingham, 1980).

71 Baumer, 22, 59.

72 Ibid., 105–7.

73 Harvey, 'Syria and Mesopotamia', 363.

74 Baumer, 66–71.

75 Goodman, 71.

76 V. N. Nersessian, 'Armenian Christianity', in Parry (ed.), 23–47, at 25.

77 Ibid., 24–5.

78 Ibid., 27–8.

79 Stringer, 93–4.

6: The Imperial Church
(300–451)

1 Stevenson (ed., 1987), 283.

2 Ibid., 284–6.

3 Ibid., 315–16.

4 Ibid., 283–4.

5 Eusebius, 547–8, 554 (*Life of Constantine*, XXIX, LV). For further discussion of the nature of Constantine's faith, see pp. 291–3.

6 A. Grafton and M. Williams, *Christianity and the Transformation of the Book: Origen, Eusebius and the Library of Caesarea* (Cambridge, MA, 2006), 215–21.

7 A. H. M. Jones, *Constantine and the Conversion of Europe* (London, 1948), 93–4.

8 Herrin, 9.

9 For what Constantine did achieve in Rome, see pp. 291–3.

10 E. D. Hunt, 'Constantine and Jerusalem', *JEH*, 48 (1997), 405–24, at 409.

11 Herrin, 5.

12 See H. C. Evans (ed.), *Byzantium: Faith and Power (1261–1557)* (New Haven and London, 2004), 5, 523, and for comment, see p. 495.

13 Goodman, 548.

14 Stringer, 65–6.

15 Excellent accounts of this event and its consequences are provided by Hunt, 'Constantine and Jerusalem', and E. D. Hunt, *Holy Land Pilgrimage in the Later Roman Empire, AD 312–460* (Oxford, 1984), esp. Chs. 1 and 2. For the archaeology of Constantinian Jerusalem, see J. Murphy O'Connor, *The Holy Land: An Oxford Archaeological Guide* (Oxford, 1980), esp. 49–61.

16 C. Morris, *The Sepulchre of Christ and the Medieval West from the Beginning to 1600*, (Oxford, 2005), 28–31.

17 P. Walker, *Holy City, Holy Places? Christian Attitudes to Jerusalem and the Holy Land in the Fourth Century* (Oxford, 1990), esp. 371.

18 On Gregory and Jerome, B. Bitton-Ashkelony, *Encountering the Sacred: The Debate on Christian Pilgrimage in Late Antiquity* (Berkeley and London, 2005), Chs. 1 and 2, esp. 52.

19 On the gradual development of the Jerusalem pilgrimage and mixed motives of the pilgrims, see C. Mango, 'The Pilgrim's Motivation', in E. Dassmann and J. Engemann (eds.), *Akten des XII. Internationalen Kongresses für Christliche Archäologie* (2 vols. and Register, Münster, 1995), I, 1–9.

20 F. M. Young, 'Prelude: Jesus Christ, Foundation of Christianity', in Mitchell and Young (eds.), 1–35, at 5, and on crosses in texts in the form of 'staurograms' (representations of the Cross), see L. W. Hurtado, *The Earliest Christian Artifacts: Manuscripts and Christian Origins* (Grand Rapids, 2006), esp. 135–6, 139, 151–4.

21 Stevenson (ed., 1989), 258–62.

22 Matthew 24.2; Luke 19.44: cf. Jesus's predictions with a different and apparently symbolic thrust that he would destroy the Temple and rebuild it in three days, Matthew 26.61; 27.39–40; John 2.19.

23 Luke 1.52–3.

24 H. Inglebert, *Les Romains chrétiens face à l'histoire de Rome: Histoire, christianisme et romanités en Occident dans l'Antiquité tardive (IIIe–Ve siècles)* (Paris, 1996), 169–73. A balanced, not to say astringent, introduction to Eusebius as historian is F. Young, *From Nicaea to Chalcedon* (London, 1983), 1–23.

25 Stevenson (ed., 1987), 258; on Paul, see p. 175.

26 R. P. C. Hanson, 'The Liberty of the Bishop to Improvise Prayer in the Eucharist', *Vigiliae Christianae*, 15 (1961), 173–6. A very useful summary of what we can know about early liturgy is B. Spinks, 'The Growth of Liturgy and the Church Year', in A. Casiday and F. W. Norris (eds.), *The Cambridge History of Christianity II: Constantine to c. 600* (Cambridge, 2007), 601–17.

27 For the retreat to the wilderness, Matthew 4.1–11; Mark 1.12–13; Luke 4.1–13. On Nicaea, see Stevenson (ed., 1987), 339–40 (Canon 5).

28 The title of his book *The Silent Rebellion: Anglican Religious Communities, 1845–1900* (London, 1958).

29 Stevenson (ed., 1987), 146–53.

30 A. F. J. Klijn, *The Acts of Thomas: Introduction, Text, and Commentary* (2nd edn, Leiden, 2003), 70–73, 110–11 [paras. 11–16; 87–90].

31 S. A. Harvey, 'Syria and Mesopotamia', in Mitchell and Young (eds.), 351–65, at 358.

32 T. Vivian and A. N. Athanassakis with R. A. Greer (eds.), *The Life of Antony by Athanasius of Alexandria* (Kalamazoo, 2003), 60–63 [para. 3].

33 H. Chadwick, 'The Early Church', in Harries and Mayr-Harting (eds.), 1–20, at 13.

34 Good discussion of Pachomius's initiatives in J. E. Goehring, 'Withdrawing from the Desert: Pachomius and the Development of Village Monasticism in Upper Egypt', *HTR*, 89 (1996), 267–85, at 275–7.

35 E. A. Judge, 'The Earliest Use of Monachos for "Monk" (P. Coll. Youtie 77) and the Origins of Monasticism', *JAC*, 20 (1977), 72–89, at 73–4.

36 C. Stewart, *'Working the earth of the heart': The Messalian Controversy in History, Texts and Language to AD 431* (Oxford, 1991), esp. 2–4, 12–24.

37 Hastings, 6.

38 Binns, 109.

39 Vivian and Athanassakis with Greer (eds.), *The Life of Antony by Athanasius*, 68–71 [para. 6].

40 Ibid., 92–3 [para. 14.7]; cf. ibid., 78–9 [para. 8.2]. For useful discussion of the manipulation of the Egyptian story of monastic origins, see Goehring, 'Withdrawing from the Desert', 268–73.

41 Vivian and Athanassakis with Greer (eds.), *The Life of Antony by Athanasius*, 50–51.

42 For examples, see Stevenson (ed., 1989), 169–70.

43 Baumer, 112.

44 Ibid., 113.

45 D. Krueger, *Symeon the Holy Fool: Leontius's Life and the Late Antique City* (Berkeley and London, 1996), esp. 41, 43–4, 90–103. See also A. Ivanov, *Holy Fools in Byzantium and Beyond* (Oxford, 2006), esp. on Orthodox disapproval, at 2, and on Simeon in the bathhouse, at 115, and on Serbian silence, at 252–3.

46 A. Hadjar, *The Church of St. Simeon the Stylite and Other Archaeological Sites in the Mountains of Simeon and Halaqua* (Damascus, [1995]), 16–17, 22–3, 26–7, 31, 49.

47 Dalrymple, 57–60. Simeon's infant pillar-dwelling is recorded by the sixth-century historian Evagrius, who had known him: W. Smith and H. Wace (eds.), *Dictionary of Christian Biography* (4 vols., London, 1877–87), IV, 681.

48 Stevenson (ed., 1989), 99.

49 A. M. Casiday (ed.), *Evagrius Ponticus* (London, 2006), 193 ['On Prayer', 67]. Casiday provides a fine selection from Evagrius's writings.

50 L. Dysinger, *Psalmody and Prayer in the Writings of Evagrius Ponticus* (Oxford, 2005), 6, 193–5. On his enthusiastic development of medical imagery, ibid., 104–23. For his influence on John Cassian, see pp. 315–16.

51 Stevenson (ed., 1987), 277–8. For Athanasius's angrily distorted version of Melitius's break with colleagues, ibid., 357–8.

52 Events usefully summarized ibid., 297–312.

53 Ibid., 304; for these events generally, ibid., 302–7.

54 Ibid., 330.

55 R. C. Gregg and D. E. Groh, *Early Arianism: A View of Salvation* (London, 1981), esp. 14–19, 28–9, 68–70, 114–15. For a balanced assessment of Arius, see R. Williams, *Arius: Heresy and Tradition* (2nd edn, London, 2001).

56 Cf. the comments of the church historian Socrates, interestingly sympathetic to Arius, in Stevenson (ed., 1987), 321, and on Arius and Melitius, ibid., 277–8 and 321; though see doubts in Williams, *Arius*, 37–41.

57 Stevenson (ed., 1987), 334–5.

58 M. Edwards, 'The First Council of Nicaea', in Mitchell and Young (eds.), 552–67, at 561 and n.

59 The course and results of the council are usefully presented in Stevenson (ed., 1987), 338–51. The term 'oecumenical', with one of those incongruities which enrich the study of history, was (as Henry Chadwick discovered) borrowed from the title of the empire-wide association of actors and athletes given privileges by third-century emperors: Chadwick, 73.

60 See p. 428.

61 For Arius and his bishop, Stevenson (ed., 1987), 326–7.

62 The traditional picture of bishops at Nicaea voting according to the emperor's wishes and then revealing their true 'Eusebian' colours is significantly qualified in S. Parvis, *Marcellus of Ancyra and the Lost Years of the Arian Controversy, 325–345* (Oxford

2006): she detects little overlap between those voting at Nicaea and later 'Eusebian' bishops, and a good deal of evidence of ruthless politicking by Eusebius of Nicomedia after Nicaea. See esp. ibid., 5–7, 39–50, 100–107, 133, 255–64.

63 Frend, 524.

64 A. Robertson (ed.), *Select Writings and Letters of Athanasius, Bishop of Alexandria* (*NPNF*, ser. 2, IV, 1891), 329, and cf. 412–13 (*Four Discourses against the Arians*, 1.39, 3.34). For Irenaeus's formulation, see A. Roberts and J. Donaldson (eds.), *The Apostolic Fathers, Justin Martyr, Irenaeus* (*Ante-Nicene Fathers* I, 1885), 526 (Irenaeus, *Against Heresies*, bk. 5, preface): 'our Lord Jesus Christ, who did, through His transcendent love, become what we are, that He might bring us to be even what He is Himself'.

65 L. Ayres, *Nicaea and Its Legacy: An Approach to 4th-century Trinitarian Orthodoxy* (Oxford, 2004), esp. 431–2. See also D. M. Gwynn, *The Eusebians: The Polemic of Athanasius of Alexandria and the Construction of the Arian Controversy* (Oxford, 2007).

66 Various drafts and councils usefully presented in Stevenson (ed., 1989), 13–21, 39–41, 45–8.

67 An introduction to Julian with primary source material is S. Tougher, *Julian the Apostate* (Edinburgh, 2007), and a notably lively novelistic imagining of Julian is G. Vidal, *Julian: A Historical Novel* (New York, 1964). See also Stevenson (ed., 1989), 52–68.

68 Frend, 602–3.

69 J. Huskisson, 'Pagan and Christian in the Third to Fifth Centuries', in Wolffe (ed.), 13–41, at 31.

70 For another example of Epiphanius's labelling and smearing, see p. 124.

71 P. Schaff (ed.), *Basil: Letters and Select Works* (*NPNF*, ser. 2, VIII, 1895), 48 (*Oration on the Holy Spirit*, Ch. 30).

72 A fine introduction to the Cappadocian Fathers is Young, *From Nicaea to Chalcedon*, 92–122.

73 See Basil the Great's explanation of the difference: Stevenson (ed., 1989), 105.

74 For proceedings at Constantinople and Aquileia, see ibid., 111–19, 124–5.

75 A point noted by that acute and deliberately unfathomable scholar Erasmus of Rotterdam: see p. 602, and S. Snobelen, ' "To us there is but one God, the Father": Antitrinitarian Textual Criticism in Seventeenth- and Early Eighteenth-century England', in Hessayon and Keene (eds.), 116–36, at 118.

76 For this confusion in the mind of Cyril of Alexandria, see below, n. 84.

77 Stevenson (ed., 1989), 87–93, esp. 88.

78 Ibid., 150–54.

79 Ibid., 284; see Frend, 744.

80 Stevenson (ed., 1989), 77.

81 A. Hastings, '150–550', in Hastings (ed.), 25–65, at 39.

82 Stevenson (ed., 1989), 291–5.

83 For careful assessments of Cyril which some may find occasionally overgenerous in their sympathy, see T. G. Weinandy and D. A. Keating (eds.), *The Theology of St Cyril of Alexandria: A Critical Appreciation* (London, 2003). Cyril's character caused even his admirer John Henry Newman some pause, and profitable reflection on the paradoxical quality of holiness. 'David was the "man after God's own heart", but as this high glory does not oblige us to excuse his adultery or deny his treachery to his friend, so we may hold St Cyril to be a great servant of God without considering ourselves obliged to defend certain passages of his ecclesiastical career. It does not answer to call whity-brown, white': J. H. Newman, 'Trials of Theodoret', in *Historical Sketches* (3 vols., London, 1872–3), II, 303–62, at 342.

84 See Stevenson (ed., 1989), 308–9, n. on para. 73d: a treatise written by the condemned Apollinaris circulated under the name of Athanasius and Cyril therefore it took to be acceptable. Cf. also Frend, 838.

85 Cf. Theodore on *prosōpon*, Stevenson (ed., 1989), 292. See p. 218.

86 N. Constas, *Proclus of Constantinople and the Cult of the Virgin in Late Antiquity: Homilies 1–5, Texts and Translations* (2003), 52–69. For the whole sequence of events, see Stevenson (ed., 1989), 287–91, 295–308.

87 For useful comment on Antiochene horror at Nestorius's rejection of *Theotokos*, see

D. Fairbairn, 'Allies or Merely Friends? John of Antioch and Nestorius in the Christological Controversy', *JEH*, 58 (2007), 383–99, at 388–93.

88 B. Green, *The Soteriology of Leo the Great* (Oxford, 2008), ix, and see ibid., 206–8, 221–5, 230–47, 252. For documents in the affair, see Stevenson (ed., 1989), 309–21, 332–49.

89 Proceedings, and Nestorius's relation to them, summarized in Stevenson (ed., 1989), 349–68.

90 Ibid., 352–3.

91 Baumer, 49–50.

92 On Cyril and *mia physis*, T. G. Weinandy, 'Cyril and the Mystery of the Incarnation', in Weinandy and Keating (eds.), *The Theology of St Cyril of Alexandria*, 23–54. At my interview in October 2008 with His Holiness Moran Mor Ignatius Zakka I Iwas, Patriarch of Antioch and All the East (of the Syriac Orthodox Church), I was made aware of his irritation at the 'Miaphysite' label.

PART III: VANISHING FUTURES:
EAST AND SOUTH
(451–1500)

7: Defying Chalcedon: Asia and Africa
(451–622)

1 For an English translation of the Greek version, G. R. Woodward and H. Mattingly (eds.), *St. John Damascene: Barlaam and Ioasaph* (Loeb edn, London and New York, 1914); this edition retains the mistaken attribution to St John of Damascus.

2 On Fairfax, *TLS*, 28 July 2006, 15. For the Georgian version and its transmission, I. V. Abuladze (ed.; tr. D. M. Lang) *The Balavariani (Barlaam and Josaphat): A Tale from the Christian East* (London, 1966), esp. 9, 20–21, 38–9.

3 Frend, 773; for a detailed account of Proterius's troubles and ghastly fate, W. Smith and H. Wace (eds.), *Dictionary of Christian Biography* (4 vols., London, 1877–87), IV, 497–500.

4 The word derives from a Syriac word, *malko* – 'imperial', so its origins are not in Egypt.

5 B. A. Pearson, 'Egypt', in Mitchell and Young (eds.), 331–50, at 349. On the Nag Hammadi library and Manichaean papyri from Kellis, see pp. 121–2 and 171.

6 Chadwick, 46.

7 Frend, 809–13.

8 A. Hadjar, *The Church of St. Simeon the Stylite and Other Archaeological Sites in the Mountains of Simeon and Halaqua* (Damascus, [1995]), 24–6.

9 The process is well examined in V. L. Menze, *Justinian and the Making of the Syrian Orthodox Church* (Oxford, 2008).

10 Sundkler and Steed, 30–34.

11 G. M. Browne, *The Old Nubian Martyrdom of Saint George* (*Corpus Scriptorum Christianorum Orientalium, Subsidia 101*, 1998), 1–2.

12 Our understanding of this people has been revolutionized by the monumental studies by I. Shahīd, *Byzantium and the Arabs in the Sixth Century* (3 vols. so far, Washington, DC, 1995–2002). On their being written out of Byzantine sources, see ibid. I, i, 32–4.

13 I am indebted to Sebastian Brock for clarifying for me that the name 'Baradeus', often said in modern scholarship to derive from 'bar-Addai', comes from the Syriac *burd'ana*, 'having a horse-cloth (or horse-cloak)'.

14 Frend, 842–8; a more recent extended account is Shahīd, *Byzantium and the Arabs in the Sixth Century*, I, ii, 744–91.

15 'Syriac' and not 'Syrian' in English: this change was authorized by the Church's Synod in 2000 in order not to cause confusion of identity with the modern nation state called Syria.

16 Shahīd, *Byzantium and the Arabs in the Sixth Century*, II, i, 165, and ibid., 142–217.

17 J. Boswell, *The Marriage of Likeness: Same-Sex Unions in Pre-modern Europe* (London, 1996), 146–8, 151–4, 375–90, and index refs., s.v. Serge and Bacchus.

18 T. Sizgorich, 'Narrative and Community in Islamic Late Antiquity', *PP*, 185 (November 2004), 9–42, at 18. On Sergiopolis, see also Shahīd, *Byzantium and the Arabs in the Sixth Century*, II, i, 115–25.

19 C. B. Horn, *Asceticism and Christological Controversy in Fifth-century Palestine: The Career of Peter the Iberian* (Oxford, 2006), esp. Ch. 2. The use of 'Iberia' for Georgia is confusing, since the same word was used by the Romans and remains in use for the western European peninsula which contains Spain and Portugal.

20 Baumer, 71.

21 I. Dorfmann-Lazarev, *Arméniens et Byzantins à l'époque de Photius: deux débats théologiques après le triomphe de l'Orthodoxie* (*Corpus Scriptorum Christianorum Orientalium Subsidia*, 117, 2004), 102–29.

22 V. N. Nersessian, 'Armenian Christianity', in Parry (ed.), 23–47, at 29.

23 On its supposed origin, see p. 433.

24 Horn, *Asceticism and Christological Controversy in Fifth-century Palestine*, 393–4.

25 Nersessian, 'Armenian Christianity', 31–2; P. Cowe, 'The Armenians in the Era of the Crusades 1050–1350', in Angold (ed.), 404–29, at 412. For extended discussion of the place of the Cross in Miaphysite theology and devotion, see Horn, *Asceticism and Christological Controversy in Fifth-century Palestine*, Ch. 5.

26 Acts 8.26–40.

27 S. Munro-Hay, *Ethiopia, the Unknown Land: A Cultural and Historical Guide* (London, 2002), 236, 272.

28 A sour relic of the separation of 1951 can be found in that menagerie of Christian pettiness, the Church of the Holy Sepulchre in Jerusalem. The Copts then expelled the Ethiopian Christians from the rooms which they had occupied for centuries in the Coptic patriarchate in the church complex. The Ethiopians constructed a makeshift village for themselves a few yards away on the church roof, where they still live in dignified holy poverty, including the transport of all their daily water across courtyards and up two flights of stairs.

29 Munro-Hay, *Ethiopia, the Unknown Land*, 52, and on the lithic bells, cf. ibid., Pl. 50.

30 Sundkler and Steed, 35.

31 S. Munro-Hay, *The Quest for the Ark of the Covenant: The True History of the Tablets of Moses* (London, 2006), 76–9.

32 It will be appreciated that the origins and status of the Falasha are very controversial subjects, but for sensible remarks, see Hastings, 13–16, and on the wider background, ibid., 11–13.

33 On the lateness of the story of Menelik and the Ark, Munro-Hay, *Quest for the Ark of the Covenant*, 126–8, and on the late date for the *tabot*, ibid., 192–4.

34 Baumer, 140–42. Yusuf is called Masruq in Syriac and Dhu-Nuwas in Arabic.

35 Ibid., 141–2. On the dam, M. A. S. Abdel Haleem (tr. and ed.), *The Qur'an: A New Translation* (Oxford, 2004), 273 [34.16].

36 Jenkins, 18, 78.

37 Baumer, 81–4. I am grateful to Sebastian Brock for information on the present-day site of Gondeshapur.

38 On Syriac loanwords and controversy about them, A. Neuwirth, 'The Qur'an and History: A Disputed Relationship', *Journal of Qur'anic Studies*, 5 (2003), 7–10.

39 Baumer, 129. 'Mar' is the Syriac word for 'lord' or 'master' and serves as the equivalent of 'Saint'.

40 Ibid., 91–3.

41 Ibid., 169–70.

42 Ibid., 235.

43 A serviceable translation based on a not wholly satisfactory text is J. W. McCrindle (ed.), *The Christian Topography of Cosmas, an Egyptian Monk* (Hakluyt Society 1st ser. 98, 1897). See esp. ibid., 55–6, 118–20, 351–2.

44 Baumer, 29–30.

45 For cautious remarks on Sigehelm's journey, which may only have been to Rome, and

for later misidentification of him with a Bishop of Sherborne of the same name, see D. Pratt, 'The Illnesses of King Alfred the Great', *Anglo-Saxon England*, 30 (2001), 39–90, at 69–70.

46 Sebastian Brock points out to me that despite the Church of the East's deep admiration for Evagrius as a spiritual teacher, it reviles Evagrius's inspiration Origen, condemning what it regards as his irresponsible use of allegory (so foreign to the style of literal biblical scholarship deriving from Antioch), and also seeing his cosmological speculation as dangerous.

47 S. Brock (ed.), *Isaac of Nineveh (Isaac the Syrian): 'The Second Part'*, Chapters IV–XLI (Louvain, 1995), 165 [39.6].

48 R. Beulay, *L'enseignement spirituel de Jean de Dalyatha: mystique syro-oriental du VIIIe siècle* (Paris, 1990), 62, 448 (qu. Centuria 1.17, Letter 5.1; my English translations).

49 P. Brown, *The Rise of Western Christendom: Triumph and Diversity AD 200–1000* (Oxford, 1997), 174, 192.

50 Baumer, 94–5.

51 I am grateful to Martin Palmer, who materially developed earlier scholars' discussions of the monastery, for escorting me around the site and for our discussions about it. Much remains to be investigated at this fascinating place. Previous accounts of the recognition of the monastery site as Christian are in P. Y. Saeki, *The Nestorian Documents and Relics in China* (2nd edn, Tokyo, 1951), 354–99. See also Baumer, 95–8, 179–81.

52 W. A. Kaegi, *Heraclius, Emperor of Byzantium* (Cambridge, 2003), 205–7, 212–13.

53 Baumer, 97, 181.

8: Islam: The Great Realignment (622–1500)

1 I. Shahīd, *Byzantium and the Arabs in the Fifth Century* (Washington, DC, 1989), 350–60.

2 For a good summary of the issues, see A. Neuwirth, 'The Qur'an and History: A Disputed Relationship', *Journal of Qur'anic Studies*, 5 (2003), 1–18.

3 Baumer, 144.

4 M. A. S. Abdel Haleem (tr. and ed.), *The Qur'an: A New Translation* (Oxford, 2004), 66 [4.171], and see also ibid., 75 [5.73].

5 M. P. Brown, *The Lindisfarne Gospels: Society, Spirituality and the Scribe* (London, 2003), 319–21.

6 Jenkins, 194–206; see also T. Sizgorich, 'Narrative and Community in Islamic Late Antiquity', *PP*, 185 (November 2004), 9–42.

7 Cf. esp. Haleem (tr. and ed.), *The Qur'an*, 75 [5.82].

8 Z. Karabell, *People of the Book: The Forgotten History of Islam and the West* (London, 2007), 15–16; Haleem (tr. and ed.), *The Qur'an*, 16 [2.142]. The detailed exposition of this case is P. Crone and M. Cook, *Hagarism: The Making of the Islamic World* (Cambridge, 1977), 3–34.

9 Haleem (tr. and ed.), *The Qur'an*, 9 [2.62].

10 P. Grossman, 'Neue Funde aus Abū Mīnā', in E. Dassmann and J. Engemann (eds.), *Akten des XII. Internationalen Kongresses für Christliche Archäologie* (2 vols. and Register, Münster, 1995), II, 824–32, at 830–32.

11 Crone and Cook, *Hagarism*, is a quirky study which has nevertheless become fundamental to reassessing the nature and impact of the Arab conquests.

12 O. Grabar, *The Dome of the Rock* (Cambridge, MA, 2006), esp. 98–109; Crone and Cook, *Hagarism*, 8. Some sources give other versions of the surrender with a less harmonious takeover.

13 Baumer, 143, 146; see p. 247.

14 For two west Syrian apocalyptic texts of this era (one admittedly controversially dated), ed. and discussed by S. Brock, see A. Palmer (ed.), *The Seventh Century in the West Syrian Chronicles* (Liverpool, 1993), 222–53.

15 Karabell, *People of the Book*, 33–4.

16 Baumer, 151–2.

17 M. Piccirillo, 'The Christians in Palestine during a Time of Transition: 7th–9th Centuries',

in A. O'Mahony et al. (eds.), *The Christian Heritage in the Holy Land* (London, 1995), 47–51; M. Piccirillo, *The Mosaics of Jordan* (Amman, 1993), 45–7.

18 M. Smith, *Studies in Early Mysticism in the Near and Middle East* (London and New York, 1931), 120.

19 Cf. Haleem (tr. and ed.), *The Qur'an*, 75–6 [5.82] and 119 [9.31, 34].

20 Sizgorich, 'Narrative and Community in Islamic Late Antiquity', 27–9, and for a parallel story, 28 n. 47.

21 A. Zachariadou, 'Mount Athos and the Ottomans c. 1350–1550', in Angold (ed.), 154–68, at 155.

22 K. Cragg, *The Arab Christian: A History in the Middle East* (London, 1992), 77–8.

23 Baumer, 148, 153–8.

24 J. M. Bloom, *Paper before Print: The Impact and History of Paper in the Islamic World* (New Haven and London, 2002), esp. 116–23, 135–41. The traditional association of the transfer of paper-making technology with the Battle of Talas in Kyrgyzstan (751) is probably apocryphal: ibid., 42–3.

25 Jenkins, 6.

26 Ibid., 7, 91–2.

27 The inscription is translated in full in P. Y. Saeki, *The Nestorian Documents and Relics in China* (2nd edn, Tokyo, 1951), 53–77, unfortunately not easy to access: an older and less accomplished translation can be found at http://www.fordham.edu/halsall/eastasia/781nestorian.html. For useful comment on the political context of the stele, see M. Deeg, 'The Rhetoric of Antiquity: Politico-religious Propaganda in the Nestorian Stele of Chang'an', *Journal for Late Antique Religion and Culture*, 1 (2007), 17–30, esp. 27–9. See also Baumer, 179–86. A new discovery of a Tang-era funerary pillar in the former eastern imperial capital of Luoyang in 2006 promises to tell us much more about Dyophysite Chinese Christianity in this era; we await Matteo Nicolini-Zani's forthcoming article on it in *Monumenta Serica*, 2009, and I am grateful to him for sharing his findings with me in advance.

28 D. Scott, 'Christian Responses to Buddhism in Pre-medieval Times', *Numen*, 32 (1985), 88–100, esp. 92, 94, 96. For a translation of the texts and a different emphasis on their interpretation, see M. Palmer, *The Jesus Sutras: Rediscovering the Lost Scrolls of Taoist Christianity* (New York, 2001).

29 C. Humphrey and A. Hürelbaatar, 'Regret as a Political Intervention: An Essay in the Historical Anthropology of the Early Mongols', *PP*, 186 (February 2005), 3–46, at 9.

30 Baumer, 195–9; note the cross illustrated at ibid., 196.

31 Humphrey and Hürelbaatar, 'Regret as a Political Intervention', 9n.

32 P. G. Borbone, 'Syroturcica 1. The Önggüds and the Syriac Language', in G. Kiraz (ed.), *Malphono w-Rabo d-Malphone: Studies in Honor of Sebastian Brock* (Piscataway, 2008), n. 13. I am most grateful to Professor Borbone for providing me with an advance copy of this paper. See also Baumer, 199–211.

33 I am indebted to Martin Palmer for our discussions on these possibilities. For a cautious assessment of the evidence, see Baumer, 220, and see Matteo Ricci's account in 1605 of the near-disappearance – but only near-disappearance – of previous Christian activity: Koschorke et al. (eds.), 6–7.

34 Jenkins, 122.

35 Baumer, 223–7.

36 P. Jackson with D. Morgan (eds.), *The Mission of Friar William of Rubruck: His Journey to the Court of Great Khan Möngke, 1253–1255* (Hakluyt Society, 2nd ser. 173, 1990).

37 Baumer, 205.

38 Jackson with Morgan (eds.), *The Mission of Friar William of Rubruck*, 239 [Ch. 34.7].

39 The authoritative account of these events is now P. Jackson, *The Mongols and the West, 1221–1410* (Harlow, 2005), 113–28.

40 For caution in seeing Timur as particularly hostile to Christianity, see ibid., 246–7.

41 S. P. Cowe, 'The Armenians in the Era of the Crusades 1050–1350', in Angold (ed.), 404–29, at 424–9; Chadwick, 272–3.

42 Jackson with Morgan (eds.), *The Mission of Friar William of Rubruck*, 208, and see ibid., 117 n. 4.

43 Baumer, 119, 164–8, 209, 230–33.

44 Sundkler and Steed, 28–30.

45 Jenkins, 109.

46 Ibid., 98–9.

47 Crone and Cook, *Hagarism*, 114. See also F. Micheau, 'Eastern Christianities (Eleventh to Fourteenth Century): Copts, Melkites, Nestorians and Jacobites', in Angold (ed.), 373–403, at 376, 384–6, 398.

48 Hastings, 65–7. On the Council of Ferrara-Florence, see pp. 492–3.

49 A. Hessayon, 'Og, King of Bashan, Enoch and the Books of Enoch: Extra-canonical Texts and Interpretations of Genesis 6.1–4', in A. Hessayon and N. Keene (eds.), *Scripture and Scholarship in Early Modern England* (Aldershot, 2006), at 20–21. See also p. 68.

50 A. Wroe, *Pilate: The Biography of an Invented Man* (London, 1999), 3–6, 309–12, 341, 363–5.

51 For scepticism about the foundational character of the Jerusalem associations of Lalibela, see S. Munro-Hay, *Ethiopia, the Unknown Land: A Cultural and Historical Guide* (London, 2002), 190–91.

52 Hastings, 21–2.

53 Munro-Hay, *Ethiopia, the Unknown Land*, 24.

54 S. Munro-Hay, *The Quest for the Ark of the Covenant: The True History of the Tablets of Moses* (London, 2006), 82–7, although he is sceptical about the general opinion that the work is intended to boost the credentials of the Solomonic dynasty.

55 Munro-Hay, *Ethiopia, the Unknown Land*, 58.

56 Hastings, 28.

57 K. Ward, 'Africa', in Hastings (ed.), 192–237, at 200.

58 Hastings, 31. Munro-Hay is sceptical about their exact age: Munro-Hay, *Ethiopia, the Unknown Land*, 191.

59 Hastings, 34–45, provides a fine account of the reign of Zar'a Ya'qob.

60 Munro-Hay, *Ethiopia, the Unknown Land*, 54 and Pl. 1.

61 Jackson with Morgan (eds.), *The Mission of Friar William of Rubruck*, 122 [Ch. 17.2], and see also ibid., 5–6.

62 B. Wagner (ed.), *Die* Epistola presbiteri Johannis *lateinisch und deutsch: Überlieferung, Textgeschichte, Rezeption under Übertragungen im Mittelalter* (Tübingen, 2000), esp. 14, 20–25, 132–49.

PART IV: THE UNPREDICTABLE RISE OF ROME (300–1300)

9: The Making of Latin Christianity
(300–500)

1 Further discussion of the word 'Catholic' in MacCulloch, xix–xx.

2 Goodman, 550–52. On the basilican plan for churches, see pp. 197–9.

3 M. Webb, *The Churches and Catacombs of Early Christian Rome: A Comprehensive Guide* (Brighton and Portland, 2001), 240–45.

4 J. R. Curran, *Pagan City and Christian Capital: Rome in the Fourth Century* (Oxford, 2000), 105–9. Recent excavations have revealed the footings of a substantial apse possibly of Constantinian date around St Paul's shrine at San Paolo fuori le Mura, but the extent of the building is uncertain.

5 On the function of St Peter's and the probable phases of construction, see R. R. Holloway, *Constantine and Rome* (New Haven and London, 2004), 79–82.

6 J. Curran, 'Jerome and the Sham Christians of Rome', *JEH*, 48 (1997), 213–29, at 217.

7 S. Lunn-Rockliffe, 'Ambrose's Imperial Funeral Sermons', *JEH*, 59 (2008), 191–207, at 195n.

8 Doig, 41–2; see p. 160.

9 C. Morris, *The Sepulchre of Christ and the Medieval West from the Beginning to 1600* (Oxford, 2005), 31–8.

10 Holloway, *Constantine and Rome*, 73–6; Doig, 42–4.

11 Stevenson (ed., 1989), 71, 142–3.

12 Curran, *Pagan City and Christian Capital*, 148–57.

13 H. Inglebert, *Les Romains chrétiens face à l'histoire de Rome: Histoire, christianisme et romanités en Occident dans l'Antiquité tardive (IIIe–Ve siècles)* (Paris, 1996), 197–9.

14 Optatus, Bishop of Mileu or Milevis: Chadwick, 31.

15 Jerome, *Epistolae* XLV.3, qu. R. J. Goodrich, 'Vir maxime Catholicus: Sulpicius Severus' Use and Abuse of Jerome in the *Dialogi*', *JEH*, 58 (2007), 189–210, at 190. For Jerome's ministry in Rome and its abrupt termination, see Curran, 'Jerome and the Sham Christians of Rome'.

16 Jerome, Preface to Job, qu. M. H. Williams, *The Monk and the Book: Jerome and the Making of Christian Scholarship* (Chicago and London, 2006), 167.

17 Ibid., esp. 1–5, 131, 167–9, 200. On Gerasimos, Dalrymple, 296–7.

18 M. R. Salzman, *The Making of a Christian Aristocracy: Social and Religious Change in the Western Roman Empire* (Cambridge, MA, 2002), 208.

19 R. Finn, *Almsgiving in the Later Roman Empire: Christian Promotion and Practice 313–450* (Oxford, 2006), esp. 165–6, 184–8.

20 E. Bourne, 'The Messianic Prophecy in Vergil's Fourth Eclogue', *Classical Journal*, 11 (1916), 390–400.

21 S. McGill, *Virgil Recomposed: The Mythological and Secular Centos in Antiquity* (Oxford, 2005), XV, 155 n. 17, 162 n. 3.

22 Cf., e.g., *New English Hymnal*, 613; excerpts from 'Da puer plectrum, choreis ut canam fidelibus', *Cathemerinon* IX: H. J. Thomson (ed.), *Prudentius with an English Translation* (2 vols., Loeb edn, London and Cambridge, MA, 1949), I, 76 [ll. 10ff., etc.].

23 Ibid., II, 10–14; I, 154–5 [*Contra orationem Symmachi* II, 62–4; *Apotheosis*, ll. 449–54; slightly altered].

24 Stevenson (ed., 1989), 120.

25 Ibid., 132–4.

26 Ibid., 135–9.

27 Lunn-Rockliffe, 'Ambrose's Imperial Funeral Sermons', esp. at 205.

28 For a crisp and fairly minimalist summary of Augustine's knowledge of Greek, see G. Bonner, *Saint Augustine of Hippo: Life and Controversies* (2nd edn, Norwich, 1963), 394–5.

29 R. S. Pine-Coffin (ed.), *Saint Augustine: Confessions* (London, 1961), 72 [IV.2].

30 Ibid., 131 [VII.15]; see comment in P. Brown, *Augustine of Hippo: A Biography* (London, 1969), 62–3, 88–90.

31 Pine-Coffin (ed.), *Saint Augustine: Confessions*, 177–8 [VIII.12].

32 Ibid., 178–9 [VIII.12].

33 Ibid., 167–8 [VIII.6].

34 It is worth pondering the opinion of Bonner, *Saint Augustine of Hippo*, 3, contemplating the selfish intellectual Augustine revealed in the *Confessions*: 'It could fairly be maintained that whatever in Augustine's character may be called sanctity was the result of his enforced ordination.'

35 Augustine, *Enarratio in Psalmum* 57, 15, qu. Chadwick, 31.

36 The traditional picture of Donatist 'circumcellion' fanaticism and violence is likely to be largely a literary construction of the victorious Catholics: see B. D. Shaw, 'Who Were the Circumcellions?', in A. H. Merrills (ed.), *Vandals, Romans and Berbers: New Perspectives on Late Antique North Africa* (Aldershot, 2004), 227–57.

37 Luke 14.23: Augustine to Bishop Vincentius, qu. Stevenson (ed., 1989), 220–22.

38 H. Bettenson and D. Knowles (eds.), *Augustine: Concerning the City of God against the Pagans* (London, 1967), 440 [XI.9], and 479–80 [XII.7].

39 For one careful Christian critique of Augustine, see J. Hick, *Evil and the God of Love* (2nd edn, London, 1977), 38–89, esp. at 53–8.

40 Bettenson and Knowles (eds.), *Augustine*, 593 [XIV.28].

41 Quotation ibid., 596 [XV.1]. For such identifications, see ibid., 335, 524, 920 [VIII.24; XIII.16; XX.11].

42 There has been much discussion of Pelagius's origins, but Augustine himself calls him 'Brittonem': Frend, 694 n. 161.

43 See the useful discussion of the context in Curran, 'Jerome and the Sham Christians of Rome'.

44 Stevenson (ed., 1989), 232–3.

45 S. Thier, *Kirche bei Pelagius* (*Patristische Texte und Studien*, 50, Berlin and New York, 1999), 322.

46 Compare the thinking of another opponent of Augustine in a later age, Desiderius Erasmus: see pp. 600–601.

47 A point made by Bonner, *Saint Augustine of Hippo*, 4.

48 Stevenson (ed., 1989), 236.

49 Ibid., 238–9. Bonner, *Saint Augustine of Hippo*, 378, points to the catalogue of such phrases in O. Rottmanner, *Der Augustinismus. Eine dogmengeschichtliche Studie* (Munich, 1892), 8.

50 Bonner, *Saint Augustine of Hippo*, 392.

51 On Julian and Augustine, see Brown, *Augustine of Hippo*, 381–97.

52 Bettenson and Knowles (eds.), *Augustine*, 304–15 [VIII.5–15]; quotation at 313 [VIII.10].

53 Salzman, *The Making of a Christian Aristocracy*, 211–13.

54 Bettenson and Knowles (eds.), *Augustine*, 1033–48 [XXII.8–10]; for a fine treatment of this theme, see P. Brown, *The Cult of the Saints* (Chicago, 1981), esp. 55–64.

55 J. Lössl, 'Augustine in Byzantium', *JEH*, 51 (2000), 267–95, at 270–71; on Augustine's ignorance of the Council of Constantinople, Chadwick, 27.

56 J. Burnaby (ed.), *Augustine: Later Works* (*Library of Christian Classics VIII*, 1955), 71, 88 [*De Trinitate* IX.18; X.18].

57 Ibid., 85 [*De Trinitate* X.13].

58 Ibid., 157 [*De Trinitate* XV.27].

59 L.-J. Bord, *Histoire de l'abbaye Saint-Martin de Ligugé 361–2001* (Paris, 2005), Ch. 2, argues persuasively that Ligugé was from its beginnings monastic in character and not simply a hermitage for Martin.

60 F. R. Hoare (ed.), *The Western Fathers: Being the Lives of SS. Martin of Tours, Ambrose, Augustine of Hippo, Honoratus of Arles and Germanus of Auxerre* (London, 1954), 27 [Sulpicius Severus, *Vita Martini*, 13]. For comment on the contemporary controversy around Sulpicius, see Goodrich, '*Vir maxime Catholicus*', 191–3. Martin's first monastic settlement at Ligugé may have been accompanied by the first of his destructions of a cultic building on the site: see Bord, *Histoire de l'abbaye Saint-Martin de Ligugé*, 23–9, 38–9.

61 Ibid., 44, 49–51.

62 I. Backus, *Life Writing in Reformation Europe: Lives of Reformers by Friends, Disciples and Foes* (Aldershot, 2008), 17–18.

63 The account of Ninian in Bede, about which we must be cautious since it was written around three centuries later and probably reflects Bede's particular religious agenda, is L. Sherley-Price and R. E. Latham (eds.), *Bede: A History of the English Church and People* (rev. edn, London, 1968), 146 [III.4]. Other sources, equally late and unhistorical, are presented alongside valuable discussion in J. and W. MacQueen (eds.), *St Nynia: With a Translation of the Miracula Nynie episcopi and the Vita Niniani* (Edinburgh, 1990).

64 Vincent of Beauvais, *Spectrum Doctrinale*, 10.45 [my translation]: 'Adulter est in sua uxore ardentior amator. In aliena quippe uxore omnis amor turpis est, et in sua nimius.' Vincent of Beauvais, *Bibliotheca mundi. Speculum quadruplex, naturale, doctrinale, morale, historiale* … (4 vols., Douai, 1624; facsimile edn, Graz, 1964–5), I, 915. See also J. Boswell, *Christianity, Social Tolerance and Homosexuality: Gay People in Western Europe from the Beginning of the Christian Era to the Fourteenth Century* (Chicago and London, 1980), 164.

65 D. G. Hunter, *Marriage, Celibacy, and Heresy in Ancient Christianity: The Jovinianist Controversy* (Oxford, 2007), 1. See Frend, 717–19, and for comment on the ecumenically

negative afterlife of Helvidius, D. MacCulloch, 'Mary and Sixteenth-century Protestants', in R. N. Swanson (ed.), *The Church and Mary* (*SCH*, 39, 2004), 191–217, at 213.

66 Hoare (ed.), *The Western Fathers*, 137 [*Dialogue with Gallus*, 13]; and for the Priscillianist affair, Stevenson (ed., 1989), 159–63.

67 C. Stewart, *Cassian the Monk* (Oxford, 1998), 6–19. Cassian's innuendo reinforces the impression that Martin's monastic recruits included a disproportionate number from the Gallo-Roman elite.

68 Ibid., 42–3.

69 Ibid., 19–20.

70 D. Ogliari, *Gratia et certamen: The Relationship between Grace and Free Will in the Discussion of Augustine with the So-called Semipelagians* (Leuven, 2003), 106–8, 111–53. On the problems with the 'Semi-Pelagian' label, ibid., 5–6.

71 Vincent, *Commonitorium* 2.5, qu. ibid., 431 n. 12.

72 There are many translations and attempted adaptations of the Benedictine Rule. A reliable version, though without editorial annotations, is P. Barry (tr.), *Saint Benedict's Rule: A New Translation for Today* (Ampleforth, 1997).

73 C. H. Lawrence, 'St Benedict and His Rule', *History*, 67 (1982), 185–94.

10: Latin Christendom: New Frontiers
(500–1000)

1 A good discussion of this process is M. Innes, 'Land, Freedom and the Making of the Medieval West', *TRHS*, 6th ser., 16 (2006), 39–74.

2 An excellent summary account of Theoderic's Ravenna is Y. Hen, *Roman Barbarians: The Royal Court and Culture in the Early Medieval West* (Houndmills, 2007), Ch. 2.

3 K. G. Cushing, *Reform and the Papacy in the Eleventh Century: Spirituality and Social Change* (Manchester and New York, 2005), 56.

4 J. H. Burns (ed.), *The Cambridge History of Medieval Political Thought c. 350–c. 1450* (Cambridge, 1988), 288–9.

5 R. Fletcher, *The Conversion of Europe: From Paganism to Christianity 371–1386 AD* (London, 1997), 104–5.

6 Stringer, 108.

7 For the interior of the Church of Sant' Apollinare Nuovo in Ravenna, see Pl. 4. St Martin is to be seen at the eastern end of the main sequence of mosaics on the south arcade.

8 J. M. Wallace-Hadrill, *The Frankish Church* (Oxford, 1983), 56.

9 Chadwick, 53.

10 Ibid., 55–6.

11 J. Moorhead, 'On Becoming Pope in Late Antiquity', *JRH*, 30 (2006), 279–93, at 291.

12 R. A. Markus, *Gregory the Great and His World* (Cambridge, 1997), 91–4.

13 P. Brown, *The Rise of Western Christendom: Triumph and Diversity AD 200–1000* (Oxford, 1997), 145–6.

14 Gregory, *Homiliae in Hiezechielem*, 1.11.6, qu. Markus, *Gregory the Great and His World*, 25.

15 C. Thomas, *Christianity in Roman Britain to AD 500* (London, 1981), 310–14: the most likely candidate is a settlement by the fort of Birdoswald near Carlisle, which can be identified as 'Banna'.

16 For Palladius and Patrick, see Stevenson (ed., 1989), 378–84.

17 Fletcher, *The Conversion of Europe*, 87–92.

18 Stevenson (ed., 1989), 380.

19 P. Ó Riain, 'Irish Saints' Cults and Ecclesiastical Families', in A. Thacker and R. Sharpe (eds.), *Local Saints and Local Churches in the Early Medieval West* (Oxford, 2002), 290–302.

20 N. Edwards, 'Celtic Saints and Early Medieval Archaeology', in Thacker and Sharpe (eds.), *Local Saints and Local Churches in the Early Medieval West*, 225–66, at 251–2.

21 On the links to Syria, Dalrymple, 109–11, and on the *Diatessaron*, see pp. 181–2. For links of the ring-cross to Egypt via a Coptic shroud now in Minneapolis, see W. Horn, 'On the Origin of the Celtic Cross: A New Interpretation', in W. Horn, J. White Marshall

and G. D. Rourke, *The Forgotten Hermitage of Skellig Michael* (Berkeley, 1990), 89–98, esp. 92.

22 M. W. Herren and S. A. Brown, *Christ in Celtic Christianity: Britain and Ireland from the Fifth to the Tenth Century* (Woodbridge, 2002), 96–7; but see arguments by W. H. C. Frend against their main thesis that the Irish and other Christians in Britain or England took their theology directly from Pelagianism, *JEH*, 55 (2004), 140.

23 D. Bachrach, 'Confession in the *Regnum Francorum* (742–900): The Sources Revisited', *JEH*, 54 (2003), 3–22, at 9–10. On the Reformation: see Ch. 17.

24 Fletcher, *The Conversion of Europe*, 92–3.

25 Ibid., 93–6.

26 L. Sherley-Price and R. E. Latham (eds.), *Bede: A History of the English Church and People* (rev. edn, London, 1968), 66–7 [1.23].

27 Ibid., 99–100 [II.1], and J. Richards, *Consul of God: The Life and Times of Gregory the Great* (London, 1980), 238–41. The extension of the misquotation to 'Not Angels, but Anglicans' is much to be treasured: W. C. Sellar and R. J. Yeatman, *1066 and All That* (London, 1975 edn), 14.

28 T. Tatton-Brown, *Lambeth Palace: A History of the Archbishops of Canterbury and Their Houses* (London, 2000), esp. 15–20. On the still-mysterious Canterbury bridgehead in London represented by the Romanesque crypt of St Mary-le-Bow, see essays by M. Byrne and J. Schofield in M. Byrne and G. R. Bush (eds.), *St Mary-le-Bow: A History* (Barnsley, 2007), 21–9, 79–89. The final Court of Appeal of the Province of Canterbury is still associated with this church.

29 Sherley-Price and Latham (eds.), *Bede*, 132 [II.16].

30 R. Collins, *Early Medieval Europe 300–1000* (Houndmills, 1991), 170.

31 R. Meens, 'Ritual Purity and Gregory the Great', in R. N. Swanson (ed.), *Unity and Diversity in the Church* (*SCH*, 32, 1996), 31–43, at 35. Cf. Sherley-Price and Latham (eds.), *Bede*, 76–83 [I.27–28].

32 H. Mayr-Harting, *The Coming of Christianity to Anglo-Saxon England* (3rd edn, London, 1991), 15, 31; Collins, *Early Medieval Europe*, 165–6.

33 Sherley-Price and Latham (eds.), *Bede*, 104 [II.3]. Rochester Cathedral's dedication was also later changed. The pattern of dedications to Peter or Peter and Paul continued in the major churches of other Anglo-Saxon kingdoms: W. Rodwell, J. Hawkes, E. How and R. Cramp, 'The Lichfield Angel: A Spectacular Anglo-Saxon Painted Sculpture', *Antiquaries Journal*, 88 (2008), 48–108, at 50.

34 Collins, *Early Medieval Europe*, 173.

35 D. Tyler, 'Reluctant Kings and Christian Conversion in Seventh-century England', *History*, 92 (2007), 144–61, esp. at 146.

36 Fletcher, *The Conversion of Europe*, 259.

37 Ibid., 179. York was not an archiepiscopal see in the seventh century.

38 Sherley-Price and Latham (eds.), *Bede*, 94 [II.1]; P. Hayward, 'Gregory the Great as "Apostle of the English"', *JEH*, 55 (2004), 19–57.

39 Richards, *Consul of God*, 259–60, 263.

40 See the emphasis on Hertford's importance over against the more-often celebrated Synod of Whitby of 664 in P. Wormald, 'The Venerable Bede and the "Church of the English"', in G. Rowell (ed.), *The English Religious Tradition and the Genius of Anglicanism* (Wantage, 1992), 17.

41 H. Chadwick, 'Theodore, the English Church and the Monothelete Controversy', in M. Lapidge (ed.), *Archbishop Theodore: Commemorative Studies on His Life and Influence* (Cambridge, 1995), 88–95, and note his affirmation of the location of Hatfield as the place in Yorkshire rather than Hertfordshire. On Hadrian, see also M. Lapidge, 'The Career of Archbishop Theodore', ibid., 1–29, at 25–6.

42 Mayr-Harting, *The Coming of Christianity to Anglo-Saxon England*, 9.

43 Fletcher, *The Conversion of Europe*, 198, 204–13.

44 Ibid., 514–15.

45 Sherley-Price and Latham (eds.), *Bede*, 192 [III.25].

46 Ibid., 127 [II.13].

47 Richards, *Consul of God*, 264.

48 G. Graf, *Peterskirchen in Sachsen: ein patrozinienkundlicher Beitrag zum Land zwischen Saale und Neisse bis an den Ausgang des Hochmittelalters* (Frankfurt am Main, 1999).

49 R. W. Southern, *Western Society and the Church in the Middle Ages* (London, 1970), 226.

50 A. Lingas, 'Medieval Byzantine Chant and the Sound of Orthodoxy', in A. Louth and A. Casiday (eds.), *Byzantine Orthodoxies* (Aldershot, 2006), 131–50, at 142. Still later, Carolingians adopted the Byzantine eight musical modes: ibid., 142.

51 Chadwick, 64–5.

52 *Maior domus*: the same phrase as the later 'majordomo'.

53 J. L. Nelson, 'Charlemagne the Man', in J. Story (ed.), *Charlemagne: Empire and Society* (Manchester, 2005), 22–37, at 24–5; on the estates of S. Germain, C. Wickham, *Framing the Early Middle Ages: Europe and the Mediterranean 400–800* (Oxford, 2005), 399–402, 404–6.

54 M. A. Claussen, *The Reform of the Frankish Church: Chrodegang of Metz and the Regula canonicorum in the Eighth Century* (Cambridge, 2004), 27.

55 See especially ibid., Ch. 6.

56 P. Fouracre, 'The Long Shadow of the Merovingians', in Story (ed.), *Charlemagne*, 5–21, at 6–7.

57 Chadwick, 33.

58 Ibid., 77–8.

59 M. de Jong, 'Charlemagne's Church', in Story (ed.), *Charlemagne*, 103–35, at 126.

60 B. Ward and G. R. Evans, 'The Medieval West', in Hastings (ed.), 110–46, at 115; for useful commentary on the coronation and its background, J. Nelson, 'England and the Continent in the Ninth Century: IV. Minds and Bodies', *TRHS*, 6th ser., 15 (2005), 1–29, at 6–9.

61 R. Fletcher, *The Cross and the Crescent: Christianity and Islam from Muhammad to the Reformation* (London, 2003), 51.

62 R. Collins, 'Charlemagne's Imperial Coronation and the Annals of Lorsch', in Story (ed.), *Charlemagne*, 52–70, esp. 68–9.

63 S. Coupland, 'Charlemagne's Coinage', in Story (ed.), *Charlemagne*, 211–29, at 223–7.

64 Chadwick, 89–93.

65 For wise remarks on the subject, see C. Brooke, 'Approaches to Medieval Forgery', in Brooke, *Medieval Church and Society: Collected Essays* (London, 1971), 100–120.

66 For a different and later dating to the ninth century and an attribution to the same circle of forgers as pseudo-Isidore, a hypothesis which has so far not commanded general assent, see J. Fried, Donation of Constantine *and* Constitutum Constantini: *The Misinterpretation of a Fiction and Its Original Meaning. With a Contribution by Wolfram Brandes: 'The Satraps of Constantine'* (Berlin and New York, 2007). Latin text and translation are at 129–45.

67 Ibid., 95–9.

68 Doig, 112–13, 127, 130–32.

69 R. McKitterick, 'The Carolingian Renaissance of Culture and Learning', in Story (ed.), *Charlemagne*, 151–66.

70 H. Mayr-Harting, 'The Early Middle Ages', in Harries and Mayr-Harting (eds.), 44–64, at 54–5. On Josiah, see pp. 60–61.

71 A. Borst, *Die karolingische Kalendarreform* (Hannover, 1998); for the reconstruction of the original, 254–98. On the Gregorian calendar reform, see p. 683.

72 C. H. Lawrence, 'St Benedict and His Rule', *History*, 67 (1982), 185–94, at 193–4.

73 De Jong, 'Charlemagne's Church', 120–22; M. Innes, 'Charlemagne's Government', in Story (ed.), *Charlemagne*, 71–89, at 85.

74 For the reconstruction of Charlemagne's prayer book, see S. Waldhoff, *Alcuins Gebetbuch für Karl den Grossen: seine Rekonstruktion und seine Stellung in der frühmittelalterlichen Geschichte der Libelli Precum* (Münster, 2003), 341–91.

75 Mayr-Harting, 'Early Middle Ages', 47–8. On the contemporary debate between East and West on images, see pp. 442–56.

76 Ibid., 'Early Middle Ages', 49–51.

77 Nelson, 'England and the Continent in the Ninth Century: IV. Minds and Bodies', 3; Bachrach, 'Confession in the *Regnum Francorum* (742–900)', 9–10.

78 Southern, *Western Society and the Church in the Middle Ages*, 226.
79 Doig, 126–8.
80 B. Yorke, *Nunneries and the Anglo-Saxon Royal Houses* (London and New York, 2003), 17–18, 26, 31–3, 118, 153–4.
81 The definitive and truly monumental study of this is W. Horn and E. Born, *The Plan of St Gall: A Study of the Architecture & Economy of Life in a Paradigmatic Carolingian Monastery* (3 vols., Berkeley, 1979); detailed analysis and illustrations of the plan are I, 36–104.
82 J. T. Palmer, 'Rimbert's *Vita Anskarii* and Scandinavian Mission in the 9th Century', *JEH*, 55 (2004), 235–56.
83 Hayward, 'Gregory the Great as "Apostle of the English" ', at 24–5.
84 E. Gibbon, *The History of the Decline and Fall of the Roman Empire* (12 vols., London, 1813), IX, 198–9 [Ch. 49].
85 Herrin, 207–11.
86 Chadwick, 198.

11: The West: Universal Emperor or Universal Pope?
(900–1200)

1 For a notable reassessment of Aethelwold's importance, see M. Gretsch, *The Intellectual Foundations of the English Benedictine Reform* (Cambridge, 1999), esp. 425–7. For further comment on one tendentious historical legacy of Aethelwold's and Oswald's reforms, see D. Cox, 'St Oswald of Worcester at Evesham Abbey: Cult and Concealment', *JEH*, 53 (2002), 269–85. On Dunstan and Ovid's *Ars Amatoria*, see letter by D. Ganz in *TLS*, 18 May 2007, 17; the MS is Bodleian Library MS Auct.F.4.32.
2 K. G. Cushing, *Reform and the Papacy in the Eleventh Century: Spirituality and Social Change* (Manchester, 2005), 59–60.
3 Ibid., 92–3.
4 Incisive discussion of the change is R. I. Moore, *The First European Revolution, c. 970–1215* (Oxford, 2000), 45–55.
5 The process is well examined kingdom by kingdom by the essayists in N. Berend (ed.), *Christianization and the Rise of Christian Monarchy: Scandinavia, Central Europe and Rus', c. 900–1200* (Cambridge, 2008). The exception was Iceland, which acquired Christianity around 1000 without acquiring a monarchy.
6 R. N. Swanson, *The Twelfth-century Renaissance* (Manchester, 1999), 8.
7 Southern's argument is crisply summarized in a classic review article, 'Between Heaven and Hell', *TLS*, 18 June 1982, 651–2. See also G. R. Edwards, 'Purgatory: "Birth" or Evolution?', *JEH*, 36 (1985), 634–46. Both react critically to a major but flawed study by J. Le Goff, *The Birth of Purgatory* (London, 1984) – on the first use of the noun 'Purgatory', see ibid., 362–6.
8 Cushing, *Reform and the Papacy in the Eleventh Century*, 39–40.
9 Ibid., 48.
10 D. S. Bailey, *The Man–Woman Relationship in Christian Thought* (London, 1959), 89, 92–4, 114–15, 118, 139, 141.
11 Moore, *The First European Revolution, c. 970–1215*, 92–5.
12 J. Goody, *The Development of the Family and Marriage in Europe* (Cambridge, 1983), 44–7.
13 Moore, *The First European Revolution, c. 970–1215*, 65–72.
14 Cushing, *Reform and the Papacy in the Eleventh Century*, 99: for a sixteenth-century clash over this claim, see D. MacCulloch, *Thomas Cranmer: A Life* (New Haven and London, 1996), 577.
15 B. Gordon, 'Switzerland', in Pettegree (ed., 1992), 70–93, at 73n.
16 Cushing, *Reform and the Papacy in the Eleventh Century*, 63–4.
17 Chadwick, 200–213.
18 The *Dictatus papae*: see Cushing, *Reform and the Papacy in the Eleventh Century*, 78–9.
19 R. W. Southern, *Western Society and the Church in the Middle Ages* (London, 1970), 100–105.

20 Two fine biographies of Becket compete: F. Barlow, *Thomas Becket* (London, 1987) and A. Duggan, *Thomas Becket* (London, 2004).

21 S. F. Cawsey, 'Royal Eloquence, Royal Propaganda and the Use of the Sermon in the Medieval Crown of Aragon, c. 1200–1410', *JEH*, 50 (1999), 442–63, esp. 443, 446–8. For discussion of late medieval relations between monarchs and papacy, see MacCulloch, 43–6.

22 A. Bellenger and S. Fletcher, *Princes of the Church: A History of the English Cardinals* (Stroud, 2001), v–vi, comment on the more usual pious explanation for the word 'cardinal' as being a 'hinge' of the Church.

23 A. Sommerlechner et al. (eds.), *Der Register Innocenz' III* (Graz, from 1963, in progress), IX: *Pontificatsjahr, 1206/1207,* 244–5.

24 Swanson, *The Twelfth-century Renaissance*, 70.

25 Chadwick, 234; a major breakthrough in understanding the formation of 'Gratian' is now A. Winroth, *The Making of Gratian's Decretum* (Cambridge, 2000), esp. 193–6.

26 Encyclical of Pius X, *Vehementer* (1906), qu. G. O'Collins and M. Farrugia, *Catholicism: The Story of Catholic Christianity* (Oxford, 2003), 307n. For Gratian and the distinction between 'two classes of Christians', see ibid., 307, qu. *Decretum,* 2.12.1.

27 A point made by Southern, *Western Society and the Church in the Middle Ages*, 131–2.

28 G. Duby, *The Age of the Cathedrals: Art and Society 980–1420* (London, 1981), and see Doig, 169–96.

29 On the origins and connotations of the name 'Gothic', see A. Buchanan, 'Interpretations of Medieval Architecture, c. 1550–1750', in M. Hall, *Gothic Architecture and Its Meanings 1550–1830* (Reading, 2002), 27–52, esp. 29.

30 Doig, 172.

31 N. Pevsner and A. Wedgwood, *The Buildings of England: Warwickshire* (London, 1966), 251, apropos of St Michael's Coventry (Warwickshire, England), a grand fifteenth-century Gothic parish church which did indeed briefly become a cathedral in modern times before its bombing in 1940.

32 Incomparable as an essay on a church which captures the spirit of this era is H. Adams, *Mont-Saint-Michel and Chartres* (Boston, MA, 1904). For Chartres's survival through the French Revolution, thanks to the resolve of local people and officials, see M. K. Cooney, ' "May the hatchet and the hammer never damage it!": The Fate of the Cathedral of Chartres during the French Revolution', *Catholic Historical Review*, 92 (2006), 193–213.

33 H. E. J. Cowdrey, *The Cluniacs and the Gregorian Reform* (Oxford, 1970), 214–47, esp. 243–4.

34 C. Morris, *The Sepulchre of Christ and the Medieval West from the Beginning to 1600* (Oxford, 2005), 134–46. For a dissenting view on the effect of 1009, see J. France, 'The Destruction of Jerusalem and the First Crusade', *JEH*, 47 (1996), 1–17.

35 H. Houben, *Roger II of Sicily: A Ruler between East and West* (Cambridge, 2002), 20.

36 P. E. Chevedden, 'The Islamic View and the Christian View of the Crusades: A New Synthesis', *History*, 93 (2008), 181–200, esp. 184–6, 192–4.

37 T. Asbridge, *The First Crusade: A New History* (London, 2004), 29–30.

38 Tyerman, 61–3. For the background and Urban's message, Asbridge, *The First Crusade,* 16–20, 32–6.

39 Tyerman, 79, 282–6.

40 D. Hay, 'Gender Bias and Religious Intolerance in Accounts of the "Massacres" of the First Crusade', in M. Gervers and J. M. Powell (eds.), *Tolerance and Intolerance: Social Conflict in the Age of the Crusades* (Syracuse, NY, 2001), 3–10.

41 Z. Karabell, *People of the Book: The Forgotten History of Islam and the West* (London, 2007), 93.

42 Tyerman, 247, 662–3.

43 Ibid., 838–43, and M. Barber, *The Trial of the Templars* (2nd edn, Cambridge, 2006); for the sad afterlife of some ex-Templars, see A. J. Forey, 'Ex-Templars in England', *JEH*, 53 (2002), 18–37. For recent arguments that the Templars were indeed guilty of some of the blasphemies attributed to them, see J. Riley-Smith, 'Were the Templars Guilty?', in S. J. Ridyard (ed.), *The Medieval Crusade* (Woodbridge and Rochester, NY, 2004), 107–24.

44 Tyerman, 674–712.

45 For the most recent debate on the relationship between Bogomils and Cathars, still a controversial subject in which R. I. Moore is a minimalist sceptic, see essays by D. F. Callahan, B. Hamilton and M. Barber in M. Frassetto (ed.), *Heresy and the Persecuting Society in the Middle Ages: Essays on the Work of R. I. Moore* (Leiden, 2006), 31–42, 93–138. See also N. Malcolm, *Bosnia: A Short History* (London, 1994), 27–42.

46 Tyerman, 563–605.

47 Ibid., 894–905.

48 Ibid., 825–74.

49 Morris, *The Sepulchre of Christ and the Medieval West from the Beginning to 1600*, 383. The rebuilding might have taken place in association with San Lorenzo in Florence; for another piquant phase in the history of this ancient church, see pp. 664–5.

50 P. Górecki, *A Local Society in Transition: The Henryków Book and Related Documents* (Toronto, 2007), 102–3, and see also 81, 85.

51 I am grateful for clarifications of this story from Dom Gabriel van Dijck and Dom Marie-Robert Torczynski of the Grande Chartreuse, who referred me to C. E. Berseaux, *L'Ordre des chartreux et la chartreuse de Bosserville* (Nancy and Paris, 1868), 469–71, 504. A remarkable account of the last days of traditional Carthusian life in Parkminster, a twentieth-century English Charterhouse, is N. Klein Maguire, *An Infinity of Little Hours: Five Young Men and Their Trial of Faith in the Western World's Most Austere Monastic Order* (New York, 2006).

52 B. Barber and C. Thomas, *The London Charterhouse* (London, 2002), 60–65, 105–13.

53 G. Bonner, *Saint Augustine of Hippo: Life and Controversies* (2nd edn, Norwich, 1963), 386–7, provides an analysis of which texts may with confidence be attributed to Augustine.

54 Figures derived from listings in M. R. James, *Suffolk and Norfolk* (London, 1930), 28–31.

55 D. F. Wright, 'From "God-bearer" to "Mother of God" in the Later Fathers', in R. N. Swanson (ed.), *The Church and Mary* (SCH, 39, 2004), 22–30.

56 S. Hamilton, 'The Virgin Mary in Cathar Thought', *JEH*, 56 (2005), 24–49, esp. 34, 37, 48.

57 See, for instance, P. Preston, 'Cardinal Cajetan and Fra Ambrosius Catharinus in the Controversy over the Immaculate Conception of the Virgin in Italy, 1515–51', in Swanson (ed.), *The Church and Mary*, 181–90. On Bernard, see B. Sella, 'Northern Italian Confraternities and the Immaculate Conception in the Fourteenth Century', *JEH*, 49 (1998), 599–619, at 601–2.

58 H. Mayr-Harting, 'The Idea of the Assumption in the West, 800–1200', in Swanson (ed.), *The Church and Mary*, 86–111.

59 R. Marks, *Image and Devotion in Late Medieval England* (Stroud, 2004), 61, and on rededications, ibid., 38.

12: A Church for All People?
(1100–1300)

1 R. I. Moore, *The Formation of a Persecuting Society: Power and Deviance in Western Europe, 950–1250* (Oxford, 1987), 14–19.

2 On the concrete evidence for Valdes's career, P. Biller, 'Goodbye to Waldensianism?', *PP*, 192 (August 2006), 3–34, at 13–14.

3 N. Cohn, *The Pursuit of the Millennium* (3rd rev. edn, London, 1969), 148–86.

4 R. N. Swanson, *The Twelfth-century Renaissance* (Manchester, 1999), 116.

5 G. Makdisi, *The Rise of Colleges: Institutions of Learning in Islam and the West* (Edinburgh, 1981), esp. 285–91.

6 Ibid., 279–80.

7 G. Dickson, 'Revivalism as a Medieval Religious Genre', *JEH*, 51 (2000), 473–96, at 482–3.

8 Moore, *The Formation of a Persecuting Society*; J. Boswell, *Christianity, Social Tolerance and Homosexuality: Gay People in Western Europe from the Beginning of the Christian Era to the Fourteenth Century* (Chicago, 1980), esp. 288–93.

9 M. Barber, 'Lepers, Jews and Moslems: The Plot to Overthrow Christendom in 1321', *History*, 66 (1981), 1–18.

10 MacCulloch, 9, and see R. Po-chia Hsia, *The Myth of Ritual Murder: Jews and Magic in Reformation Germany* (New Haven and London, 1988).

11 P. Zutshi, 'Pope Honorius III's *Gratiarum omnium* and the Beginnings of the Dominican Order', in A. J. Duggan (ed.), *Omnia disce: Medieval Studies in Memory of Leonard Boyle, O.P.* (Aldershot, 2005), 199–210.

12 A good recent introduction to Francis's life is C. Frugoni, *Francis of Assisi: A Life* (London, 1998), and there is useful analysis in K. B. Wolf, *The Poverty of Riches: St Francis of Assisi Reconsidered* (Oxford, 2003).

13 For detailed discussion of his attitude to monasticism and to evangelism, see B. Bolton, 'The Importance of Innocent III's Gift List'; F. Andrews, 'Innocent III and Evangelical Enthusiasts: The Road to Approval', in J. C. Moore (ed.), *Pope Innocent III and His World* (Aldershot, 1999), 101–12, 229–41.

14 A fine overview is N. Tanner, 'Pastoral Care: The Fourth Lateran Council of 1215', in G. R. Evans (ed.), *A History of Pastoral Care* (London and New York, 2000), Ch. 14, repr. in N. Tanner, *The Ages of Faith: Popular Religion in Late Medieval England and Western Europe* (London and New York, 2009), 19–32.

15 G. Macy, 'The Doctrine of Transubstantiation in the Middle Ages', *JEH*, 45 (1994), 11–41; see Tanner, 'Pastoral Care', 29–30.

16 M. Rubin, *Corpus Christi: The Eucharist in Late Medieval Culture* (Cambridge, 1991), 169–76.

17 A. P. Roach, 'Penance and the Inquisition in Languedoc', *JEH*, 52 (2001), 409–33, esp. 415.

18 Biller, 'Goodbye to Waldensianism?', 5. E. Cameron, *Waldenses: Rejections of Holy Church in Medieval Europe* (Oxford, 2000), 49–62 on papal reconciliation and 264–84 on Protestant remoulding.

19 For an overview of the various new organizations, see F. Andrews, *The Other Friars: Carmelite, Augustinian, Sack and Pied Friars in the Middle Ages* (Woodbridge, 2006).

20 A. Jotischky, *The Carmelites and Antiquity: Mendicants and Their Pasts in the Middle Ages* (Oxford, 2002), esp. Ch. 1. On controversy over the scapular, see R. Copsey, 'Simon Stock and the Scapular Vision', *JEH*, 50 (1999), 652–83.

21 Qu. in T. Johnson, 'Gardening for God: Carmelite Deserts and the Sacralization of Natural Space in Counter-Reformation Spain', in W. Coster and A. Spicer (eds.), *Sacred Space in Early Modern Europe* (Cambridge, 2005), 193–210, at 206.

22 B. R. Carniello, 'Gerardo Segarelli as the Anti-Francis: Mendicant Rivalry and Heresy in Medieval Italy', *JEH*, 57 (2006), 226–51, esp. 237–9.

23 Useful samples of the writings of Joachim and the Spirituals are provided by B. McGinn (ed.), *Apocalyptic Spirituality* (London, 1979).

24 Chief among the classic works of Marjorie Reeves exploring Joachim's influence are *Joachim of Fiore and the Prophetic Future: A Medieval Study in Historical Thinking* (rev. edn, Stroud, 1999) and *The Influence of Prophecy in the Later Middle Ages: A Study in Joachimism* (Oxford, 1999); see also W. Gould and M. Reeves, *Joachim of Fiore and the Myth of the Eternal Evangel in the Nineteenth and Twentieth Centuries* (rev. edn, Oxford, 2001), esp. Chs. 9, 10, and 314–15.

25 Reeves, *The Influence of Prophecy in the Later Middle Ages*, 191–228; D. Burr, *The Spiritual Franciscans: From Protest to Persecution in the Century after St Francis* (Philadelphia, 2001). The most vivid literary evocation of this period is Umberto Eco's famous novel *The Name of the Rose*, originally published in Italian in 1980.

26 N. Housley, 'Crusading as Social Revolt: The Hungarian Peasant Uprising of 1514', *JEH*, 49 (1996), 1–28. For Franciscan promotion of anti-Semitism, see pp. 419–20.

27 The standard Latin and English edition of the *Summa Theologiae* is that created by the English Dominican Order (Blackfriars), published in sixty-one volumes from 1963.

28 Aquinas, *Summa Theologiae* 1a.13.1 [Blackfriars edition, III, 47].

29 My adaptation of a common English translation. In a major chasm in the history of Western Catholicism in the last fifty years, the service of Benediction has increasingly been

sidelined by those Church authorities who wish to pull back the faithful's attention exclusively to the Mass itself: see p. 974.

30 Quotation from F. S. Schmitt (ed.), *S. Anselmi Cantuariensis archiepiscopi opera omnia* III.6.4–9, tr. D. S. Hogg, *Anselm of Canterbury: The Beauty of Theology* (Aldershot, 2004), 29. On twelfth-century and later pseudonymous imitations of Anselm, see J.-F. Cottier, *Anima mea: prières privées et textes de devotion du moyen âge latin. Autour des* Prières ou Méditations *attribuées à saint Anselme de Cantorbéry (XIe–XIIe siècle)* (Turnhout, 2001), XCI–CXI; on *meditatio*, ibid., LVI–LVII.

31 D. Trembinski, '[Pro]passio doloris: Early Dominican Conceptions of Christ's Physical Pain', *JEH*, 59 (2008), 630–56, esp. 651, 653–5.

32 H. Oberman, 'Luther and the *Via Moderna*: The Philosophical Backdrop of the Reformation Breakthrough', *JEH*, 54 (2003), 641–70, esp. at 649.

33 *Meditaciones* 7, qu. L. Hundersmarck, 'The Use of Imagination, Emotion, and the Will in a Medieval Classic: The *Meditaciones Vite Christi*', *Logos: A Journal of Catholic Thought and Culture*, 6/2 (Spring 2003), 46–62, at 51. For a good modern edition of a lavishly illustrated MS of the work, which does not argue for a definite attribution of authorship, see I. Ragusa and R. B. Green (eds.), *Meditations on the Life of Christ: An Illustrated Manuscript of the Fourteenth Century. Paris, Bibliothèque nationale, Ms. Ital., 115* (Princeton, 1961).

34 J. Dillenberger, *Style and Content in Christian Art* (London, 1965), 78–85, and Plate 13.

35 Good discussion in R. Marks, *Image and Devotion in Late Medieval England* (Stroud, 2004), Ch. 6.

36 J. Edwards, *The Spanish Inquisition* (Stroud, 1999), 33–5. For crisp and sceptical discussion of Christian attitudes to usury, see E. Kerridge, *Usury, Interest and the English Reformation* (Aldershot, 2002), Ch. 1.

37 E. C. Parker and C. T. Little (eds.), *The Cloisters Cross: Its Art and Meaning* (New York, 1994), 151–60, 178–81, 187–9.

38 For examples of good relations, see D. Malkiel, 'Jews and Apostates in Medieval Europe: Boundaries Real and Imagined', *PP*, 194 (February 2007), 3–34, at 32–3.

39 A. Boureau, *Satan the Heretic: The Birth of Demonology in the West* (Chicago and London, 2006), 10–14, 43–67.

40 C. Wolters (ed.), *The Cloud of Unknowing, Translated into Modern English* (London, 1961), 137 [*Cloud*, Ch. 70].

41 U. Wiethaus (ed.), *Agnes Blannbekin, Viennese Beguine: Life and Revelations* (Cambridge, 2002), esp. 10, 30, 34–6, 157.

42 M. O'C. Walshe (ed.), *Meister Eckhart: Sermons and Treatises* (3 vols., Shaftesbury, 1987), II, 64 [Sermon 53]; II, 321 [Sermon 94]; II, 246 [Sermon 82].

43 N. Caciola, *Discerning Spirits: Divine and Demonic Possession in the Middle Ages* (Ithaca, NY, and London, 2003), 277–98.

PART V: ORTHODOXY: THE IMPERIAL FAITH (451–1800)

13: Faith in a New Rome
(451–900)

1 Stevenson (ed., 1989), 117.

2 A richly witty treatment of this is Archimandrite E. Lash, 'Byzantine Hymns of Hate', in A. Louth and A. Casiday (eds.), *Byzantine Orthodoxies* (Aldershot, 2006), 151–64; quotation at 155.

3 For seventh-century Byzantine burnings, J. and B. Hamilton (eds.), *Christian Dualist Heresies in the Byzantine World, c. 650–c. 1450* (Manchester and New York, 1998), 13. For the burning of Basil the Bogomil *c.* 1098, see p. 456, and on Russian burning of 'Old Believers', pp. 540–41. For the introduction of burning to Russia, G. H. Williams,

'Protestants in the Ukraine during the Period of the Polish-Lithuanian Commonwealth', *Harvard Ukrainian Studies*, 2 (1978), 41–72, at 50.

4 See the opposition to burning Manichees from Theodore the Stoudite: Hamilton (eds.), *Christian Dualist Heresies in the Byzantine World, c. 650–c. 1450*, 60–61. Note also the caution on burning expressed by Patriarch Theophylaktos (933–56) and the disapproving comments on physical punishment of heretics by the great twelfth-century Orthodox canon lawyer Balsamon: Hussey, 157–8, 165–6.

5 J. Moorhead, *Justinian* (London, 1994), 17–22.

6 G. A. Williamson (tr.), *Procopius: The Secret History* (London, 1966). There has been controversy as to whether the *Secret History* ought to be taken seriously, but there is no good reason to doubt the overall substance of what Procopius wrote.

7 Procopius, *Wars*, 1.24.32–7, qu. Moorhead, *Justinian*, 46–7.

8 Qu. J. G. Davies, *Temples, Churches and Mosques: A Guide to the Appreciation of Religious Buildings* (New York, 1982), 106–7.

9 Binns, 6.

10 N. P. Ševčenko, 'Art and liturgy in the later Byzantine Empire', in Angold (ed.), 127–53, at 143.

11 Binns, 45.

12 Stringer, 100.

13 Herrin, 72–4.

14 A. Cameron, *Christianity and the Rhetoric of Empire: The Development of Christian Discourse* (Berkeley and Los Angeles, 1994), 208–13.

15 Herrin, 15.

16 For a positive reading of a now poorly documented reign, see W. Treadgold in C. Mango (ed.), *The Oxford History of Byzantium* (Oxford, 2002), 133.

17 A. Cameron, 'Byzantium and the Past in the Seventh Century: The Search for Redefintion', in J. Fontaine and J. N. Hillgarth (eds.), *The Seventh Century: Change and Continuity* (London, 1992), 250–76, at 253; Herrin, 92, 141–7.

18 L. K. Little (ed.), *Plague and the End of Antiquity: The Pandemic of 541–750* (Cambridge, 2007), esp. H. N. Kennedy, 'Justinianic Plague in Syria and the Archaeological Evidence', 87–95, and P. Sarris, 'Bubonic Plague in Byzantium: The Evidence of Non-literary Sources', 119–32.

19 Herrin, 153–4.

20 A. Sterk, *Renouncing the World Yet Leading the Church: The Monk-bishop in Late Antiquity* (Cambridge, MA, and London, 2004), esp. 178–91.

21 Reference to this monastery as the 'Stoudion' or 'Studium' is inexact: R. Cholij, *Theodore the Stoudite: The Ordering of Holiness* (Oxford, 1996), 1n.

22 *Ladder*, 7.50 (*Patrologia Graeca*, 88.812A), qu. J. Chryssavgis, *John Climacus: From the Egyptian Desert to the Sinaite Mountain* (Oxford, 2004), 161; on Evagrius, see ibid., 183–7.

23 Maximus's origins are controversial, thanks to the discovery by Sebastian Brock of an early, circumstantial and bitterly hostile biography of him, contradicting all other accounts: see A. Louth, *Maximus the Confessor* (London and New York, 1996), 4–7.

24 See Acts 17.34. Dionysius was a common name in the Classical world, which has lent extra confusion to the Syrian mystic's identity. For instance, he has elided into a totally different Dionysius, the martyr of Gaul, who may be more familiar as the French St-Denis (see pp. 324–5).

25 Chadwick, 59–60.

26 Compare discussion of Syrian theologians Isaac of Nineveh and John of Dalyatha, pp. 250–51.

27 Pseudo-Dionysius, *Celestial Hierarchy*, 3.1f., qu. Louth (ed.), *Maximus the Confessor*, 31.

28 Maximus, *Ambiguum*, 7 (*Patrologia Graeca*, 91.1081a), qu. M. Törönen, *Union and Distinction in the Thought of St Maximus the Confessor* (Oxford, 2007), 129.

29 Maximus, *Ambiguum*, 31 (*Patrologia Graeca*, 91.1285Bf), qu. ibid., 153–4.

30 Maximus, *Ambiguum*, 21 (*Patrologia Graeca*, 91.1249B, 1253D), qu. ibid., 161.

31 N. Russell, *The Doctrine of Deification in the Greek Patristic Tradition* (Oxford, 2004), 264.

32 Maximus, *Mystagogia*, 21 (*Patrologia Graeca*, 91.697a), qu. ibid., 272, and cf. ibid., 295.

33 Matthew 26.39; D. Bathrellos, *The Byzantine Christ: Person, Nature and Will in the Christology of St Maximus the Confessor* (New York, 2004), 121–6, 189–93.

34 Louth, *Maximus the Confessor*, 56–60.

35 Herrin, 108.

36 Exodus 20.4–5. The text has its variant in the other version of the Ten Commandments, Deuteronomy 5.8–9.

37 See excellent discussion of the whole question in M. Aston, *England's Iconoclasts I. Laws against Images* (Oxford, 1988), 371–92.

38 Humanity is never consistent and naturally there are indeed sculpted icons, among a wealth of other sculpted sacred imagery of Orthodox inspiration. For an illustration of a fine eleventh-century example of an icon depicting St George, preserved in that bastion of Orthodoxy, Mount Athos, see G. Speake, *Mount Athos: Renewal in Paradise* (New Haven and London, 2002), 49.

39 T. F. Mathews, *Byzantium: From Antiquity to the Renaissance* (New York, 1998), 43–52.

40 A recent publication of the Council of Nicaea's proceedings with the statements of Hieria is D. J. Sahas (ed.), *Icon and Logos: Sources in Eighth-century Iconoclasm* (Toronto, 1986); on readings by Bishop Gregory, 38. A more comprehensive survey of what survives of iconoclast documents is T. Krannich, C. Schubert and C. Sode (eds.), *Die ikonoklastische Synod von Hieria 754: Einleitung, Text, Übersetzung und Kommentar ihres Horos* (Tübingen, 2002).

41 The argument is expressed with characteristic elegance in P. Brown, 'A Dark Age Crisis: Aspects of the Iconoclastic Controversy', in Brown, *Society and the Holy in Late Antiquity* (London, 1982), 251–301, esp. at 258–64, 272–4, 282–3.

42 K. Ware in Harries and Mayr-Harting (eds.), 251 n. 20.

43 Cameron, 'Byzantium and the Past', 261–4.

44 L. Brubaker and J. Haldon (eds.), *Byzantium in the Iconoclast Era (c. 680–850). The Sources: An Annotated Survey* (Aldershot, 2001), 30–36; M. Piccirillo, *The Mosaics of Jordan* (Amman, 1993), 41–2.

45 Brown, 'A Dark Age Crisis', 253.

46 Cholij, *Theodore the Stoudite*, 15n.

47 K. Cragg, *The Arab Christian: A History in the Middle East* (London, 1992), 77–8.

48 Dalrymple, 290. On Aquinas, see pp. 412–15.

49 A. Louth, *St John Damascene: Tradition and Originality in Byzantine Theology* (Oxford, 2002), 90–95, 252–82.

50 D. Anderson (tr.), *On the Divine Images. Three Apologies against Those Who Attack the Divine Images: St John of Damascus* (New York, 1980), 23 and 82–8, esp. 84.

51 Herrin, 101.

52 C. Barber, *Figure and Likeness: On the Limits of Representation in Byzantine Iconoclasm* (Princeton, 2002), 110, 116, 123, 132, ascribes the move to use Aristotle to the ninth-century iconophiles, but on John and Aristotle and a critique of this view, see Louth, *St John Damascene*, 40–42, 93, 100, 135, 140, and esp. 220.

53 Chadwick, 84–5.

54 H. Mayr-Harting, 'The Early Middle Ages', in Harries and Mayr-Harting (eds.), 44–64, at 47–8, and see p. 355.

55 Doig, 117; cf. the reference to I Kings 6.19 in A. Freeman (ed.), *Opus Caroli Regis contra Synodum (Libri Carolini)* (*Monumenta Germaniae Historica: Concilia 2*, Suppl. 1, 1998), 289, ll. 15–29, and Brown, 'A Dark Age Crisis', 259.

56 P. Boulhol (ed.), *Claude de Turin: un évêque iconoclaste dans l'Occident Carolingien: Etude suivie de l'édition du Commentaire sur Josué* (Paris, 2002), 16–31, 76, 87, 171–9; quotation (my translation) at 130.

57 Aston, *England's Iconoclasts*, 48–52; J. R. Payton Jr, 'Calvin and the *Libri Carolini*', *SCJ*, 28 (1997), 467–79.

58 Boulhol (ed.), *Claude de Turin*, 98.

59 Hussey, 56.

60 Brown, 'A Dark Age Crisis', 262. For the *Mandylion* legend, see A. Mirkovic, *Prelude to Constantine: The Abgar Tradition in Early Christianity* (Frankfurt am Main, 2004), 23-4.

61 Barber, *Figure and Likeness*, 138.

62 Stringer, 104-5. On Theodore and Palestine, see Cholij, *Theodore the Stoudite*, 33, 85 n. 13, 87.

63 P. Jeffrey, 'The Earliest Oktōēchoi: The Role of Jerusalem and Palestine in the Beginnings of Modal Ordering', in Jeffrey (ed.), *The Study of Medieval Chant: Paths and Bridges, East and West. In Honor of Kenneth Levy* (Cambridge, 2001), 147-225.

64 Mark 9.2-8; Matthew 17.1-9; Luke 9.28-36. The 'high mountain' is not named in the Bible, but since at least the fifth century it has been identified with Mount Tabor in Galilee.

65 The translations of the Greek are from *The Divine Liturgy of Our Father among the Saints, John Chrysostom* (Oxford, 1995), 75, 79.

66 Hamilton (eds.), *Christian Dualist Heresies in the Byzantine World*, 73, and for discussion of the movement, ibid., 1-25.

67 Ibid., 175-80.

68 N. Malcolm, *Bosnia: A Short History* (London, 1994), 27-42.

69 Chadwick, 120-21, 124.

70 W. Treadgold, 'Photius before His Patriarchate', *JEH*, 53 (2002), 1-17, at 2, 9-11.

71 Chadwick, 125, 128, 142.

72 Hussey, 92-5.

73 Ibid., 86-7; Herrin, 127.

74 I. Dorfmann-Lazarev, *Arméniens et Byzantins à l'époque de Photius: deux débats théologiques après le triomphe de l'Orthodoxie* (*Corpus Scriptorum Christianorum Orientalium Subsidia* 117, 2004), usefully summarized at 263-7.

75 Events in Bulgaria and Moravia are ably analysed in L. Simeonova, *Diplomacy of the Letter and the Cross: Photios, Bulgaria and the Papacy, 860s-880s* (Amsterdam, 1998).

76 Chadwick, 191.

77 Treadgold, 'Photius before His Patriarchate', 15, dismisses doubts about Constantine's studies with Photius.

78 A rather engagingly celebratory though scholarly account of the following is A.-E. N. Tachiaos, *Cyril and Methodios of Thessalonica: The Acculturation of the Slavs* (Thessaloniki, 2001).

79 S. Franklin, *Writing, Society and Culture in Early Rus, c. 950-1300* (Cambridge, 2002), 97.

80 Herrin, 131, 133.

81 Tachiaos, *Cyril and Methodios of Thessalonica*, 63-4.

82 Hussey, 99.

83 Lash, 'Byzantine Hymns of Hate', 164.

14: Orthodoxy: More Than an Empire
(900-1700)

1 Tyerman, 2-3.

2 Hussey, 115.

3 Stringer, 103-4.

4 C. Holmes, *Basil II and the Governance of Empire (976-1025)* (Oxford, 2005), 60-61.

5 H. Alfeyev, *St Symeon the New Theologian and Orthodox Tradition* (Oxford, 2000), esp. 23-7, where Alfeyev is perhaps a little coy about Symeon the Pious, 16-19 on confession, 140-41 on the icon of Symeon the Pious, 141, 199 on ordination; quotation from *Hymn* 21.54-68, at ibid., 40.

6 Herrin, 221.

7 P. Frankopan, 'Kinship and the Distribution of Power in Komnenian Byzantium', *EHR*, 122 (2007), 1-34, at 29.

8 Hussey, 181.

9 Chadwick, 235.
10 Hussey, 142–51.
11 Tyerman, 536.
12 J. Shepard, 'The Byzantine Commonwealth 1000–1500', in Angold (ed.), 3–52, at 7–8; S. Hackel, 'Diaspora Problems of the Russian Emigration', ibid., 539–57, at 540.
13 Tyerman, 266.
14 For a fine narrative of all these events, ibid., 501–60.
15 A. Andrea, 'Innocent III, the Fourth Crusade, and the Coming Apocalypse', in S. J. Ridyard (ed.), *The Medieval Crusade* (Woodbridge, 2004), 97–106; quotation at 104 (punctuation modified).
16 Hussey, 187.
17 N. Tanner, 'Pastoral Care: The Fourth Lateran Council of 1215', in G. R. Evans (ed.), *A History of Pastoral Care* (London and New York, 2000), Ch. 14, repr. in N. Tanner, *The Ages of Faith: Popular Religion in Late Medieval England and Western Europe* (London and New York, 2009), 19–32, at 21. On the Lateran Council in general, see pp. 401–8.
18 M. Barber, 'The Impact of the Fourth Crusade in the West: The Distribution of Relics after 1204', in d'A. Laiou (ed.), *Urbs capta: The Fourth Crusade and Its Consequences. La IVe Croisade et ses conséquences* (Paris, 2005), 326–34, at 334.
19 'Rood' is the Old and Middle English word for 'cross'.
20 Tyerman, 557–8.
21 M. Angold, *The Fourth Crusade: Event and Context* (Harlow, 2003), 225.
22 R. Fletcher, *The Cross and the Crescent: Christianity and Islam from Muhammad to the Reformation* (London, 2003), 105.
23 C. L. Striker and Y. D. Kuban, 'Work at Kalenderhane Camii in Istanbul: A Second Preliminary Report', *Dumbarton Oaks Papers*, 21 (1967), 185–93. The fragmentary frescoes are now displayed in the Archaeological Museum in Istanbul.
24 J. Gill, 'The Tribulations of the Greek Church in Cyprus, 1196–c.1280', *Byzantinische Forschungen*, 5 (1977), 73–93, at 79–81; for the context, P. W. Edbury, *The Kingdom of Cyprus and the Crusades, 1191–1374* (Cambridge, 1991), 67.
25 Chadwick, 244–5.
26 M. Angold, 'Byzantium and the West 1204–1453', in Angold (ed.), 53–78, at 56–7.
27 L. Maksimovi, 'La Serbie et les contrées voisines avant et après la IVe Croisade', in Laiou (ed.), *Urbs capta*, 269–82.
28 Shepard, 'The Byzantine Commonwealth 1000–1500', 14, 34–5.
29 F. Miklosich and J. Müller, *Acta et Diplomata Graeca medii aevi sacra et profana* (6 vols., Vienna, 1860–90), II, no. 447, p. 189, qu. Hussey, 294.
30 Shepard, 'The Byzantine Commonwealth 1000–1500', 23–7, 50.
31 Jenkins, 178.
32 E. A. Zachariadou, 'Mount Athos and the Ottomans c. 1350–1550', in Angold (ed.), 154–68, at 155–9, 162–3.
33 A. Lingas, 'Medieval Byzantine Chant and the Sound of Orthodoxy', in A. Louth and A. Casiday (eds.), *Byzantine Orthodoxies* (Aldershot, 2006), 131–50, esp. 144, 146.
34 Herrin, 278–9.
35 J. Lössl, 'Augustine in Byzantium', *JEH*, 51 (2000), 267–95, at 274, 276.
36 Herrin, 304–5.
37 Matthew 17.2; Lössl, 'Augustine in Byzantium', 277.
38 J. R. Dupuche, 'Sufism and Hesychasm', in B. Neil, G. D. Dunn and L. Cross (eds.), *Prayer and Spirituality in the Early Church III: Liturgy and Life* (Strathfield, NSW, 2003), 335–43.
39 D. Krausmüller, 'The Rise of Hesychasm', in Angold (ed.), 101–26, at 123.
40 Lössl, 'Augustine in Byzantium', 279–81.
41 R. S. Pine-Coffin (ed.), *Saint Augustine: Confessions* (London, 1961), 196–99 [IX.10].
42 Chadwick, 253–4.
43 Lössl, 'Augustine in Byzantium', 290–94.
44 Dupuche, 'Sufism and Hesychasm', 338.
45 Herrin, 288–9.
46 Hussey, 271–3.

47 R. Crowley, *Constantinople: The Last Great Siege, 1453* (London, 2nd edn, 2006), 102–3; Crowley provides a careful and vivid account of these events.

48 Ibid., 166. There is a quirky melancholy to be found in visiting the little Cornish village church of Landulph, where on the wall is a seventeenth-century monumental brass inscription bearing the double-headed eagle of the imperial insignia. It commemorates Theodore 'Palaeologus', descendant of the last emperor's brother, who died in Cornwall in 1636, having married the daughter of a Suffolk gentleman named Balls.

49 J. W. Meri (ed.), *A Lonely Wayfarer's Guide to Pilgrimage: 'Ali ibn Abî Bakr al-Harawî's Kitîb al-Ishârât ilâ Ma'rifat al-Ziyârât* (Princeton, 2004), 146.

50 G. Dufay, *Lamentatio sanctae matris ecclesiae Constantinopolitanae*; translations by Philip Weller for the Binchois Consort, reproduced by permission (and I am grateful to Dr Weller for our further discussions). Tenor text from Lamentations 1.2: interestingly, Dufay reverses the order of the biblical quotation to introduce the idea of treachery first. For Dufay's letter of 1456 to the Medici about his Constantinople motets written the previous year, see L. Holford-Strevens, 'Du Fay the Poet? Problems in the Texts of His Motets', *Early Music History*, 16 (1997), 97–165, at 98, 163–5.

51 On the Belgrade expedition, see N. Housley, 'Crusading as Social Revolt: The Hungarian Peasant Uprising of 1514', *JEH*, 49 (1998), 1–28, at 3–4, and see also J. Harris, 'Publicising the Crusade: English Bishops and the Jubilee Indulgence of 1455', *JEH*, 50 (1999), 23–37.

52 H. C. Evans (ed.), *Byzantium: Faith and Power (1261–1557)* (New Haven and London, 2004), 5, 523.

53 Herrin, 293–8.

54 The church/mosque suffered repeated fire damage, and from a state of dereliction in the early twentieth century is now stripped to the ruins of its original fifth-century basilican form.

55 Jenkins, 215–16.

56 M. Mazower, *Salonica, City of Ghosts: Christians, Muslims and Jews 1430–1950* (London, 2004), 46–65, 330–31.

57 My recalculation of figures provided by Binns, 175.

58 E. A. Zachariadou, 'The Great Church in Captivity 1453–1586', in Angold (ed.), 169–86, at 183–4.

59 Zachariadou, 'Mount Athos and the Ottomans', 166–8.

60 K. Hartnup, On the Beliefs of the Greeks: *Leo Allatios and Popular Orthodoxy* (Leiden and Boston, 2004), 199–205, 218–36.

61 On Cyprus, Jenkins, 177–8; on Asia Minor, B. Clark, *Twice a Stranger: How Mass Expulsion Forged Modern Greece and Turkey* (London, 2006), 116–18.

62 S. Michalski, *The Reformation and the Visual Arts: The Protestant Image Question in Western and Eastern Europe* (London, 1993), 102, 135.

63 K. Ware, *The Orthodox Church* (London, 1994), 96.

64 A useful account of Lucaris's career is W. S. B. Patterson, 'Cyril Lukaris, George Abbot, James VI and I, and the Beginning of Orthodox–Anglican Relations', in P. Doll (ed.), *Anglicanism and Orthodoxy 300 Years after the 'Greek College' in Oxford* (Oxford and New York, 2006), 39–56, at 40–43.

65 MacCulloch, 331–2.

66 Patterson, 'Cyril Lukaris, George Abbot, James VI and I, and the Beginning of Orthodox–Anglican Relations', 51–2.

67 For discussion of why 'Calvinism' is an inexact term to describe Reformed Protestantism, see p. 618.

68 P. M. Kitromilides, 'Orthodoxy and the West: Reformation to Enlightenment', in Angold (ed.), 187–209, at 194–9. For the wider story, see J. Pinnington, *Anglicans and Orthodox: Unity and Subversion 1559–1725* (Leominster, 2003).

15: Russia: The Third Rome
(900-1800)

1 J. Bately (ed.), *The Old English Orosius* (Early English Text Society, supplementary ser., 6, 1980), esp. p. 27, l. 15, and for discussion of authorship and dating, ibid., lxxiii–xcii. See also J. Nelson, 'England and the Continent in the Ninth Century: IV. Minds and Bodies', *TRHS*, 6th ser., 15 (2005), 1–28, at 2.

2 The apostrophe reflects pronunciation in Russian. The derivation of the name is still the subject of inconclusive controversy.

3 W. Duczko, *Viking Rus: Studies on the Presence of Scandinavians in Eastern Europe* (Leiden, 2004), esp. 34–5, 82, 101–10.

4 Herrin, 137; Chadwick, 170.

5 Herrin, 137; on the mission sponsored by Louis the Pious and Archbishop Abbo of Rheims in the 820s, see J. T. Palmer, 'Rimbert's *Vita Anskarii* and Scandinavian Mission in the 9th Century', *JEH*, 55 (2004), 235–56, esp. 235, 252.

6 Duczko, *Viking Rus*, 210–18, 257.

7 C. Holmes, *Basil II and the Governance of Empire (976–1025)* (Oxford, 2005), 513.

8 S. Franklin, *Writing, Society and Culture in Early Rus, c. 950–1300* (Cambridge, 2002), 105, 121.

9 Duczko, *Viking Rus*, 215.

10 Herrin, 213–14; Chadwick, 193–4. See also Holmes, *Basil II and the Governance of Empire (976–1025)*, 450–60, 510–11.

11 Duczko, *Viking Rus*, 10, 12, 79, 216–17. One of these Varangians has left a little graffito in runes on a parapet of the basilica of Hagia Sophia in Istanbul.

12 W. van den Bercken, *Holy Russia and Christian Europe: East and West in the Religious Ideology of Russia* (London, 1999), 38.

13 Stringer, 124–5. In Russian Orthodox usage, the word 'cathedral' has a different connotation from its usage in the West, where one church in a diocese is generally designated the cathedral church of the bishop. In Russia, a sacred area may often contain several churches designated cathedrals because of their relationship to the bishop – often quite small in ground plan, if not in architectural aspiration.

14 L. Hughes, 'Art and Liturgy in Russia: Rublev and His Successors', in Angold (ed.), 276–301, at 282.

15 K. Ware, 'Eastern Christianity', in Harries and Mayr-Harting (eds.), 65–95, at 88–9.

16 A. Vauchez, *Sainthood in the Later Middle Ages* (Cambridge, 1997), 147–56. For one mid-twelfth-century example of papal anger at wholly gratuitous popular canonization, of a Swede who was killed while he was drunk, D. Harrison, '*Quod magno nobis fuit horrori*... Horror, Power and Holiness within the Context of Canonization', in G. Klaniczay, *Procès de canonisation au moyen âge: aspects juridiques et religieux. Medieval Canonization Processes: Legal and Religious Aspects* (Rome, 2004), 39–52.

17 I am grateful to Fr Christopher Hill of the Parish of the Monastery of St Andrew in Moscow for our discussion of Orthodoxy.

18 A. Ivanov, *Holy Fools in Byzantium and Beyond* (Oxford, 2006), 244–55.

19 van den Bercken, *Holy Russia and Christian Europe*, 45, 122–6; S. Senyk, *A History of the Church in Ukraine, I: To the End of the Thirteenth Century* (Orientalia Christiana Analecta, 243, 1993), 442–3.

20 P. Engel, *The Realm of St Stephen: A History of Medieval Hungary, 895–1526* (London and New York, 2001), 101–3.

21 D. Ostrowski, 'The Mongol Origins of Muscovite Political Institutions', *Slavic Review*, 49 (1990), 525–42, at 525n. The origins of the name 'Golden Horde' are in any case uncertain.

22 Hughes, 'Art and Liturgy in Russia', 276–7.

23 Ibid., 277.

24 V. L. Lanin, 'Medieval Novgorod', in M. Perrie, *The Cambridge History of Russia, I: from Early Rus' to 1689* (Cambridge, 2006), at 188–210, esp. 196, 204, 206–7.

25 S. Rock, 'Russian Piety and Orthodox Culture 1380–1589', in Angold (ed.), 253–75, at 259.

26 S. Hackel, 'Diaspora Problems of the Russian Emigration', ibid., 539–57, at 540; on T'rnovo, see p. 473.

27 On liturgy, Ostrowski, 'Mongol Origins of Muscovite Political Institutions', 529, and on coinage, G. Alef, 'The Political Significance of the Inscriptions on Muscovite Coinage in the Reign of Vasili II', *Speculum*, 34 (1959), 1–19, at 5.

28 D. Ostrowski, *Muscovy and the Mongols: Cross-cultural Influences on the Steppe Frontier, 1304–1589* (Cambridge, 1998), 16–19. Often the rulers of Muscovy, Lithuania etc. are Englished as 'Grand Duke', but this title seems inadequate for such major powers, and 'Grand Prince' better conveys their position.

29 Snyder, 17–18.

30 P. Walters, 'Eastern Europe since the Fifteenth Century', in Hastings (ed.), 282–327, at 290; van den Bercken, *Holy Russia and Christian Europe*, 132.

31 Ostrowski, *Muscovy and the Mongols*, 23.

32 J. Shepard, 'The Byzantine Commonwealth 1000–1500', in Angold (ed.), 3–52, at 10, 29–32.

33 Hussey, 291–2.

34 Ibid., 292–3.

35 P. R. Magocsi, *A History of Ukraine* (Toronto, 1996), 163.

36 G. Alef, 'The Political Significance of the Inscriptions on Muscovite Coinage in the Reign of Vasili II', 6, although Alef prefers to relate the change to Vasilii's dynastic struggles. In a letter to the Byzantine emperor of 1451/2, the Grand Prince did not use the 'sovereign' title, while he did take care to use it for the Grand Prince of Lithuania: ibid., 8.

37 Shepard, 'The Byzantine Commonwealth 1000–1500', 44–6; Rock, 'Russian Piety and Orthodox Culture 1380–1589', 268.

38 W. B. Husband, 'Looking Backward, Looking Forward: The Study of Religion in Russia after the Fall', *JRH*, 31 (2007), 195–202, at 197.

39 Rock, 'Russian Piety and Orthodox Culture 1380–1589', 267.

40 Hughes, 'Art and Liturgy in Russia', 277, 289–91, 297.

41 Rock, 'Russian Piety and Orthodox Culture 1380–1589', 253–4.

42 Hughes, 'Art and Liturgy in Russia', 292.

43 Rock, 'Russian Piety and Orthodox Culture 1380–1589', 266–7.

44 Hughes, 'Art and Liturgy in Russia', 297.

45 Rock, 'Russian Piety and Orthodox Culture 1380–1589', 265–6.

46 G. Hosking, *Rulers and Victims: The Russians in the Soviet Union* (Cambridge, MA, 2006), 10.

47 Ostrowski, *Muscovy and the Mongols*, 222–30. On the Apollinarian heresy, see pp. 219–20.

48 Ostrowski, *Muscovy and the Mongols*, 226–7.

49 Walters, 'Eastern Europe since the Fifteenth Century', 292.

50 D. Goldfrank, 'Recentering Nil Sorskii: The Evidence from the Sources', *Russian Review*, 66 (2007), 359–76. Note in particular Goldfrank's reminder that there is no positive evidence of any debate on monastic wealth in a 'Council of Moscow' in 1503, or that Nil addressed such a council: ibid., 360n.

51 Ibid., 362, 375–6.

52 Rock, 'Russian Piety and Orthodox Culture 1380–1589', 259–60. On the Judaizers, see also G. H. Williams, 'Protestants in the Ukraine during the Period of the Polish-Lithuanian Commonwealth', *Harvard Ukrainian Studies*, 2 (1978), 41–72, at 46–56.

53 Goldfrank, 'Recentering Nil Sorskii', 367.

54 Rock, 'Russian Piety and Orthodox Culture 1380–1589', 257; Husband, 'Looking Backward, Looking Forward', 197.

55 Ivanov, *Holy Fools*, 277–9, 303–10. The common usage of St Basil's name for the Cathedral of the Intercession is as recent as the Soviet years, when the shrine of St Basil was the only part of the building which remained in use for worship for any length of time after the 1917 Revolution.

56 The Russian word *grozny* would better be translated 'awe-inspiring' or 'formidable', but the traditional English usage probably conveys more about the real Ivan, besides being more picturesque.

57 For this and what follows, I. de Madariaga, *Ivan the Terrible* (New Haven and London, 2005), Chs. 3–6.

58 F. J. Thomson, 'The Legacy of SS. Cyril and Methodios in the Counter-Reformation', in E. Konstantinou (ed.), *Methodios und Kyrillos in ihrer europäischen Dimension* (Frankfurt am Main and Oxford, 2005), 85–247, at 126–7. On the Council of Trent, see pp. 664–8.

59 de Madariaga, *Ivan the Terrible*, 293. She rejects the idea that Ivan was illiterate: ibid., 44.

60 Ibid., 382.

61 Ostrowski, *Muscovy and the Mongols*, 239, 241: quotation slightly altered.

62 Snyder, 106–7.

63 Magocsi, *A History of Ukraine*, 164. See also B. A. Gudziak, *Crisis and Reform: The Kyivan Metropolitanate, the Patriarchate of Constantinople, and the Genesis of the Union of Brest* (Cambridge, MA, 1998).

64 Snyder, 123.

65 Magocsi, *A History of Ukraine*, 166.

66 N. Davies, *God's Playground: A History of Poland. 1: The Origins to 1795* (Oxford, 1981), 174–5; J. Kłoczowski, *A History of Polish Christianity* (Cambridge, 2000), 118.

67 H. Louthan, 'Mediating Confessions in Central Europe: The Ecumenical Activity of Valerian Magni, 1586–1661', *JEH*, 55 (2004), 681–99, at 694.

68 Ibid., 696.

69 L. M. Charipova, 'Peter Mohyla's Translation of *The Imitation of Christ*', *HJ*, 46 (2003), 237–61.

70 L. M. Charipova, *Latin Books and the Eastern Orthodox Clerical Elite in Kiev, 1632–1780* (Manchester, 2006), esp. Ch. 4.

71 S. Plokhy, *The Cossacks and Religion in Early Modern Ukraine* (Oxford, 2002), esp. Ch. 2.

72 Snyder, 112–17; R. Crummey, 'Eastern Orthodoxy in Russia and Ukraine in the Age of the Counter-Reformation', in Angold (ed.), 302–24, at 323.

73 Snyder, 118–19.

74 Walters, 'Eastern Europe since the Fifteenth Century', 296.

75 Stringer, 199–200.

76 R. O. Crummey, 'Ecclesiastical Elites and Popular Belief and Practice in Seventeenth-century Russia', in J. D. Tracy and M. Ragnow (eds.), *Religion and the Early Modern State: Views from China, Russia and the West* (Cambridge, 2004), 52–79.

77 For Havvakum's autobiography, see K. N. Bostrom (tr.), *Archpriest Avvakum: The Life Written by Himself* (Ann Arbor, 1979). I have consulted the version at http://www.swentel-omania.be/avvakum/frames.html.

78 On the carnival equipment and the bears, see Crummey, 'Ecclesiastical Elites and Popular Belief and Practice in Seventeenth-century Russia', 60.

79 J. Cracraft, *The Petrine Revolution in Russian Culture* (Cambridge, 2004), 40–41, 259–60, 267, 276–83, 293–300.

80 A recent learned and ingenious attempt to show that Peter's revels were inspired by his religious vision of the Transfiguration has not won great acceptance for its central thesis: E. A. Zitser, *The Transfigured Kingdom: Sacred Parody and Charismatic Authority at the Court of Peter the Great* (Ithaca NY, 2004).

81 Binns, 191.

82 Crummey, 'Ecclesiastical Elites and Popular Belief and Practice in Seventeenth-century Russia', 77.

83 See pp. 849–50, and G. L. Freeze, 'Russian Orthodoxy: Church, People and Politics in Imperial Russia', in D. Lieven (ed.), *The Cambridge History of Russia: II: Imperial Russia, 1689–1917* (Cambridge, 2006), 284–305, at 293–4; also L. Manchester, *Holy Fathers, Secular Sons: Clergy, Intelligentsia and the Modern Self in Revolutionary Russia* (DeKalb, IL, 2008). On seminary education and its poor image, often propagated by former students, ibid., Ch. 5.

84 A good summary discussion of this is G. Hosking, 'Trust and Distrust: A Suitable Theme for Historians?', *TRHS*, 6th ser., 16 (2006), 95–116, at 98.

85 A. Sinyavsky, *Ivan the Fool. Russian Folk Belief: A Cultural History* (Moscow, 2007), 306.

86 Ibid., 369–78, 310–13.

87 Binns, 113.

PART VI: WESTERN CHRISTIANITY DISMEMBERED (1300–1800)

16: Perspectives on the True Church
(1300–1517)

1 O. J. Benedictow, *The Black Death, 1346–1353: The Complete History* (Woodbridge, 2004), 51–4, 149.

2 I. Grainger et al. (eds.), *The Black Death Cemetery, East Smithfield* (London, 2008), 25–7. To add to those the 12–25 age cohort of those identifiable by age brings the figure to 52 per cent of all burials, including those not identifiable by age.

3 G. Dickson, 'Revivalism as a Medieval Religious Genre', *JEH*, 51 (2000), 473–96, at 482–5.

4 S. K. Cohn Jr, 'The Black Death and the Burning of Jews', *PP*, 196 (August 2007), 3–36, at 36.

5 N. Largier, *In Praise of the Whip: A Cultural History of Arousal* (New York, 2007), 156–57. See also N. Cohn, *The Pursuit of the Millennium: Revolutionary Millenarians and Mystical Anarchists of the Middle Ages* (London, 1970), 131–41.

6 J. R. Banker, *Death in the Community: Memorialization and Confraternities in an Italian Commune in the Late Middle Ages* (Athens, GA, 1988), 8, 36, 173, 183–5.

7 N. Vincent, *The Holy Blood: King Henry III and the Westminster Blood Relic* (Cambridge, 2001), esp. 186–201. For further comment on the controversy, see MacCulloch, 19.

8 C. W. Bynum, 'Bleeding Hosts and Their Contact Relics in Late Medieval Northern Germany', *Medieval History Journal*, 7 (2004), 227–41; on Paris in 1290 and its unfolding consequences, M. Rubin, *Gentile Tales: The Narrative Assault on Late Medieval Jews* (New Haven and London, 1999). See also H. Joldersma, 'Specific or Generic "Gentile Tale"? Sources on the Breslau Host Desecration (1453) Reconsidered', *ARG*, 95 (2004), 6–33, esp. 9–11. The specific incident discussed was associated with the star Franciscan preacher Giovanni da Capistrano: ibid., 15.

9 For discussion of the mutuality of the Purgatory industry, see MacCulloch, 12–13. The definitive study of indulgences is R. N. Swanson, *Indulgences in Late Medieval England: Passports to Paradise?* (Cambridge, 2007).

10 See text of *Unigenitus*: Bettenson (ed.), 182–3. For a rare example of surviving diocesan evidence for the system fully in action before the Black Death, see R. N. Swanson, 'Indulgences for Prayers for the Dead in the Diocese of Lincoln in the Early 14th Century', *JEH*, 52 (2001), 197–219.

11 NA (PRO), E.135/6.56; *RSTC*, 14077c.106.

12 W. D. J. Cargill Thompson, 'Seeing the Reformation in Medieval Perspective', *JEH*, 25 (1974), 297–307, at 301.

13 S. K. Cohn Jr, 'The Place of the Dead in Flanders and Tuscany: Towards a Comparative History of the Black Death', in B. Gordon and P. Marshall (eds.), *The Place of the Dead: Death and Remembrance in Late Medieval and Early Modern Europe* (Cambridge, 2000), 14; Pettegree (ed., 2002), 17–43, at 23; J. D. Tracy, *Europe's Reformations 1450–1650* (Lanham, 2000), 42; H. Kamen, *The Phoenix and the Flame: Catalonia and the Counter-Reformation* (New Haven and London, 1993), 11–12, 19–21, 82–3, 127–9, 168–9, 194–5. On the rosary, see MacCulloch, 329, 331.

14 A. T. Thayer, 'Judge and Doctor: Images of the Confessor in Printed Model Sermon Collections, 1450–1520', in K. J. Lualdi and A. T. Thayer (eds.), *Penitence in the Age of Reformations* (Aldershot, 2000), 10–29, at 11–18; I have drawn my own conclusion from this data.

15 A good discussion of this theme and what follows is B. McGinn, 'Angel Pope and Papal Antichrist', *CH*, 47 (1978), 155–73.

16 Ockham, I *Dialogus* c. 20, 459, qu. T. Shogimen, 'From Disobedience to Toleration: William of Ockham and the Medieval Discourse on Fraternal Correction', *JEH*, 52 (2001), 599–622, at 612n (my translation).

17 McClelland, 130, 135–9; S. Lockwood, 'Marsilius of Padua and the Case for the Royal Ecclesiastical Supremacy', *TRHS*, 6th ser., 1 (1991), 89–121.

18 D. Williman, 'Schism within the Church: The Twin Papal Elections of 1378', *JEH*, 59 (2008), 29–47.

19 Bettenson (ed.), 135; translation slightly adapted.

20 For further examples, see MacCulloch, 33–4.

21 G. H. M. Posthumus Meyjes, *Jean Gerson, Apostle of Unity: His Church Politics and Ecclesiology* (Leiden, 1999); M. Rubin, 'Europe Remade: Purity and Danger in Late Medieval Europe', *TRHS*, 6th ser., 11 (2001), 101–24, at 107, 111.

22 Koschorke et al. (eds.), 13–14.

23 A fine life is C. Shaw, *Julius II: The Warrior Pope* (Oxford, 1993).

24 D. S. Chambers, *Popes, Cardinals and War: The Military Church in Renaissance and Early Modern Europe* (London, 2006), 42.

25 A fine discussion of the primer is E. Duffy, *Marking the Hours: English People and Their Prayers, 1240–1570* (New Haven and London, 2006); on printed primers, see ibid., 121–46. See also V. Reinburg, 'Liturgy and the Laity in Late Medieval and Reformation France', *SCJ*, 23 (1992), 526–64; C. Richmond, 'Religion and the Fifteenth-century English Gentleman', in R. B. Dobson (ed.), *The Church, Politics and Patronage* (Gloucester, 1984), 193–208: a comment of 1559 from England echoes Richmond's argument, NA (PRO), STAC 5 U3/34, Answer of William Siday.

26 Rubin, 'Europe Remade', at 106.

27 G. R. Evans, *John Wyclif: Myth and Reality* (Oxford, 2005), esp. 139–47, 153–7; K. B. McFarlane, *John Wycliffe and the Beginnings of English Non-conformity* (London, 1952), 60–69.

28 D. G. Denery, 'From Sacred Mystery to Divine Deception: Robert Holkot, John Wyclif and the Transformation of Fourteenth-century Eucharistic Discourse', *JRH*, 29 (2005), 129–44, esp. 132.

29 For a useful sketch of suggestive links between Wyclif's Oxford followers and later Lollards, links which some modern scholarship has regarded with scepticism, see M. Jurkowski, 'Heresy and Factionalism at Merton College in the Early Fifteenth Century', *JEH*, 48 (1997), 658–81.

30 M. Dove, *The First English Bible: The Text and Context of the Wycliffite Versions* (Cambridge, 2007), 53–8; R. Rex, *The Lollards* (Basingstoke, 2002), 75–6. For a further example of John Clopton, a wealthy and highly traditionalist East Anglian gentleman, bequeathing an English Bible to the Archdeacon of Suffolk in his will in 1496, see NA (PRO), Prerogative Court of Canterbury Wills (PROB 11), 17 Horne.

31 B. Cottret, *Calvin: A Biography* (Grand Rapids and Edinburgh, 2000), 93–4.

32 R. M. Ball, 'The Opponents of Bishop Pecock', *JEH*, 48 (1997), 230–62.

33 The best summary account is still A. Hope, 'Lollardy: The Stone the Builders Rejected?', in P. Lake and M. Dowling (eds.), *Protestantism and the National Church in 16th Century England* (London, 1987), 1–35.

34 H. Kaminsky, *A History of the Hussite Revolution* (Berkeley, 1967), 292–4.

35 For discussion of this European-wide phenomenon, see MacCulloch, 43–52.

36 E. Rummel, *The Confessionalization of Humanism in Reformation Germany* (Oxford, 2000), 10.

37 R. Rex, 'The New Learning', *JEH*, 44 (1993), 26–44.

38 The phrase, applied specifically to the city of Rome, is Stephen Wolohojian's: see *SCJ*, 31 (2000), 1117.

39 H. Baron, *The Crisis of the Early Italian Renaissance* (2 vols., Princeton, 1955).

40 M. Jurdjevic, 'Prophets and Politicians: Marsilio Ficino, Savonarola and the Valori Family', *PP*, 183 (May 2004), 41–78, at 59–61.

41 J. A. White (ed.), *Biondo Flavio: Italy Illuminated* (Cambridge, MA, 2005), 189–93.

42 H. Jones, *Master Tully: Cicero in Tudor England* (Nieuwkoop, 1998), esp. 77, and Chs. 1–4.

43 The foundation study here is F. Yates, *Giordano Bruno and the Hermetic Tradition* (London, 1964).

44 On the Dominican pioneer treatise, *Tractatus gerarchie subcoelestis*, see I. Backus, *His-*

torical Method and Confessional Identity in the Era of the Reformation (1378–1615) (Leiden, 2003), 15–16.

45 G. W. H. Lampe (ed.), *The Cambridge History of the Bible: 2. The West from the Fathers to the Reformation* (Cambridge, 1969), 301.

46 Rummel, *The Confessionalization of Humanism in Reformation Germany*, 11.

47 D. S. Ellington, *From Sacred Body to Angelic Soul: Understanding Mary in Late Medieval and Early Modern Europe* (Washington, DC, 2001), 193.

48 For examples of Catholic theologians reading Augustine afresh, see MacCulloch, 111–12.

49 B. B. Warfield, *Calvin and Augustine* (Philadelphia, 1956), 332.

50 MacCulloch, 57.

51 D. Nirenberg, 'Mass Conversion and Genealogical Mentalities: Jews and Christians in 15th Century Spain', *PP*, 174 (February 2002), 3–41, esp. 21–5.

52 J. Edwards, *The Spanish Inquisition* (Stroud, 1999), Ch. 4, well summarizes these events.

53 The cautiously revised but still massive figure for expellees is from ibid., 88.

54 M. D. Meyerson, *The Muslims of Valencia in the Age of Fernando and Isabel: Between Coexistence and Crusade* (Berkeley, 1991); J. Edwards, 'Portugal and the Expulsion of the Jews from Spain', in *Medievo hispano: estudios in memoriam del Prof. Derek W. Lomax* (Madrid, 1995), 121–39.

55 H. E. Rawlings, 'The Secularisation of Castilian Episcopal Office under the Habsburgs, c. 1516–1700', *JEH*, 38 (1987), 53–79, at 55.

56 Edwards, *The Spanish Inquisition*, 85.

57 J. R. L. Highfield, 'The Jeronimites in Spain, Their Patrons and Success, 1373–1516', *JEH*, 34 (1983), 513–33, at 531–2. For clashes between Rome and Spanish authorities over *limpieza de sangre*, see D. Fenlon, 'Pole, Carranza and the Pulpit', in J. Edwards and R. Truman (eds.), *Reforming Catholicism in the England of Mary Tudor: The Achievement of Friar Bartolomé Carranza* (Aldershot, 2005), 81–97, at 96–7, and R. Truman, 'Pedro Salazar de Mendoza and the First Biography of Carranza', ibid., 177–205, at 184.

58 R. L. Melammed, *Heretics or Daughters of Israel? The Crypto-Jewish Women of Castile* (New York, 1999), Ch. 8, and 164. On the Morisco expulsions, B. Kaplan, *Divided by Faith: Religious Conflict and the Practice of Toleration in Early Modern Europe* (Cambridge, MA, 2007), 310.

59 W. A. Christian, *Local Religion in Sixteenth-century Spain* (Princeton, 1981); W. A. Christian, *Apparitions in Late Medieval and Renaissance Spain* (Princeton, 1981).

60 J. Arrizabalaga, J. Henderson and R. French, *The Great Pox: The French Disease in Renaissance Europe* (New Haven and London, 1997), Chs. 1, 2.

61 From a sermon in the Florence Duomo in 1495: J. C. Olin (ed.), *The Catholic Reformation: Savonarola to Ignatius Loyola* (New York, 1992), 12. The 'four things' appear to be the four results which Savonarola wished his sermon to achieve, set out in its opening words (cf. ibid., 4): understanding, confirmation for the convinced, conversion of the unconvinced and confusion for the stubborn.

62 For the role of Bartolomeo Scala as mouthpiece for this innovative self-justification, see D. Wootton, 'The True Origins of Republicanism: The Disciples of Baron and the Counter-example of Venturi', in M. Albertone (ed.), *Il repubblicanesimo moderno: l'idea di Repubblica nella riflessione storica di Franco Venturi* (Naples, 2006), 271–304.

63 P. Macey, *Bonfire Songs: Savonarola's Musical Legacy* (Oxford, 1998), esp. 157, 272–302.

64 L. Polizzotto, *The Elect Nation: The Savonarolan Movement in Florence, 1494–1545* (Oxford, 1994).

65 J. W. O'Malley, *The First Jesuits* (Cambridge, MA, 1993), 262; S. T. Strocchia, 'Savonarolan Witnesses: The Nuns of San Jacopo and the Piagnone Movement in 16th-century Florence', *SCJ*, 38 (2007), 393–417, at 414.

66 M. Reeves, *Prophetic Rome in the High Renaissance Period* (Oxford, 1992), esp. essays by A. Morisi-Guera and J. M. Headley, 27–50 and 241–69.

67 There has been much modern embarrassment and obfuscation on Erasmus and Rogerus, but see sensible comment in J. Huizinga, *Erasmus of Rotterdam* (London, 1952), 11–12, and from Geoffrey Nuttall, *JEH*, 26 (1975), 403.

68 D. MacCulloch, 'Mary and Sixteenth-century Protestants', in R. N. Swanson (ed.), *The Church and Mary* (*SCH*, 39, 2004), 191–217.

69 L.-E. Halkin, *Erasmus: A Critical Biography* (Oxford, 1993), 225: cf. *Opera omnia Erasmi Roterodami* (Amsterdam, 1969–), I, 146–7. For Protestant wriggles on this subject, see MacCulloch, 'Mary and Sixteenth-century Protestants', 211–14.

70 *CWE*, XXXIX–XL: *Colloquies*, ed. C. R. Thompson (2 vols., 1997), II, 628–9; I, 198–9.

71 On the precedent in Agricola, see A. Levi in *JEH*, 34 (1983), 134.

72 For Erasmus's hard-headed attitude to his English Church pension, surviving even Henry VIII's break with Rome, see D. MacCulloch, *Thomas Cranmer: A Life* (New Haven and London, 1996), 98–9.

73 P. S. Allen, H. M. Allen and H. W. Garrod (eds.), *Opus Epistolarum Des: Erasmi Roterodami* . . . (12 vols., Oxford, 1906–58), III, no. 858, l. 561, at p. 376. Cf. a similar more extended passage in a letter to Servatius Rogerus in 1514, ibid., I, no. 296, ll. 70–88, at pp. 567–8.

74 B. Bradshaw, 'Interpreting Erasmus', *JEH*, 33 (1982), 596–610, at 597–601.

75 I Thessalonians 5.23: 'May the God of peace himself sanctify you wholly; and may your spirit and soul and body be kept sound and blameless at the coming of our Lord Jesus Christ.'

76 *CWE*, LXVI: *Spiritualia: Enchiridion; De Contemptu Mundi; De Vidua Christiana*, ed. J. W. O'Malley (1988), 3, 34, 51, 69, 108, 127.

77 A. Godin, *Erasme lecteur d'Origène* (Geneva, 1982), esp. 21–32, 34–43, 372–96, 511–21, 680–83. Quotation: Erasmus to Eck, 15 May 1518, Allen et al. (eds.), *Opus Erasmi Epistolarum*, III, no. 844, ll. 252–4, at p. 337 [my translation]. It was only just over a year before Johann Eck would achieve particular celebrity as a tormentor of Martin Luther in their confrontation at Leipzig which provoked Luther's excommunication: see MacCulloch, 127.

78 In the full form allowed into the Authorized Version of 1611, the passage reads, 'For there are three that bear record [in heaven, the Father, the Word, and the Holy Ghost: and these three are one. And there are three that bear witness in earth], the Spirit, and the water, and the blood: and these three agree in one.' Square brackets enclose the text now generally rejected by scholarship.

79 S. D. Snobelen, ' "To us there is but one God, the Father": Antitrinitarian Textual Criticism in Seventeenth- and Early Eighteenth-century England', in Hessayon and Keene (eds.), 116–36, at 117–18. On Hilary and the 'Macedonians', see pp. 219–20. M. A. Screech, *Laughter at the Foot of the Cross* (London, 1997), is a magnificent study with Erasmus's sense of humour and irony at its heart.

17: A House Divided
(1517–1660)

1 Scholarly argument (and, for what it is worth, my own opinion) sways on the fascinating but ultimately trivial question of whether the theses were actually nailed up on the door; Philipp Melanchthon asserted in 1546 that they were indeed, but that is the earliest explicit statement, and from just after Luther's death. M. Brecht, *Martin Luther: His Road to Reformation 1483–1521* (Philadelphia, 1985), 200–202, weighs the question with Teutonic thoroughness, and his cautiously positive conclusion is probably the best that we can do: the nailing on the door took place, but probably later than 31 October.

2 E. Rummel, *The Confessionalization of Humanism in Reformation Germany* (Oxford, 2000), 19.

3 Some may consider this an understatement, but see a wise little essay by A. G. Dickens, 'Luther and the Humanists', in P. Mack and M. C. Jacob (eds.), *Politics and Culture in Early Modern Europe: Essays in Honour of H. G. Koenigsberger* (Cambridge, 1987), 199–213, repr. in A. G. Dickens, *Late Monasticism and the Reformation* (London and Rio Grande, 1994), 87–100.

4 G. L. Bruns, *Hermeneutics Ancient and Modern* (New Haven and London, 1992), 139–40.

5 R. Marius, *Martin Luther: The Christian between God and Death* (Cambridge, MA, and London, 1999), Chs. 6, 7, esp. at 108. For the text, see W. Pauck (ed.), *Luther: Lectures on Romans* (Philadelphia and London: Library of Christian Classics 15, 1956).

6 Abridged version in G. Rupp and B. Drewery (eds.), *Martin Luther* (London, 1970), 5–7.

7 The Vulgate Latin of the passage is '*Justitia enim dei in eo revelatur ex fide in fidem: sicut scriptum est, "Iustus autem ex fide vivit"*'. Compare E. P. Sanders's construction of the verb 'righteoused': see pp. 100–101.

8 M. Brecht, *Martin Luther: Shaping and Defining the Reformation 1521–1532* (Minneapolis, 1990), 378–9; cf. 395–6.

9 C. M. Koslofsky, *The Reformation of the Dead: Death and Ritual in Early Modern Germany 1450–1700* (Basingstoke, 2000), 34–9.

10 See other examples in Naphy (ed.), 11–12.

11 R. L. Williams, 'Martin Cellarius and the Reformation in Strasburg', *JEH*, 32 (1981), 477–98, at 490–91.

12 B. A. Felmberg, *Die Ablasstheologie Kardijnal Cajetans (1469–1534)* (Leiden, 1998), esp. 183–6, 312–27, 387–400.

13 *The Freedom of a Christian*: J. Pelikan and H. T. Lehmann (eds.), *Luther's Works* (55 vols. and 1 companion vol., Philadelphia and St Louis, 1958–86), XXXI, 344.

14 E. Wolgast, *Die Wittenberger Luther-Ausgabe: zur überlieferungsgeschichte der Werke Luthers im 16.Jahrhundert* (Nieuwkoop, 1971), col. 122. For the speech, Rupp and Drewery (eds.), *Martin Luther*, 58–60.

15 For (perhaps Evangelically indulgent) treatment of examples of the ways in which Luther pushed the Bible's meaning towards his own priorities, see M. D. Thompson, *A Sure Ground on Which to Stand: The Relation of Authority and Interpretive Method in Luther's Approach to Scripture* (Carlisle, 2004), esp. 112–46, 235–9.

16 J. I. Packer and O. R. Johnston (eds.), *Martin Luther: The Bondage of the Will* (London, 1957), 318; *D. Martin Luthers Werke* (The *Weimarer Ausgabe*: Weimar, 1883–), XVIII, 786.

17 *CWE*, LXVI: *Hyperaspistes*, in *Controversies*, ed. C. Trinkaus (1999), 117.

18 Melanchthon's surname is an example of the Renaissance convention by which scholarly clerics and academics often adopted Latinized or cod-Greek names from their place of origin, like Johannes Pomeranus ('the Pomeranian') for Johann Bugenhagen, or as translations of their ordinary surname, like Johannes Oecolampadius for Johann Hussgen ('John House-Lamp'!). Melanchthon translates the German surname 'Schwarzerd' – 'black earth'.

19 N. Davies, *God's Playground: A History of Poland. 1: The Origins to 1795* (Oxford, 1981), 143; H. Bornkamm, *Luther in Mid-career 1521–1530* (London, 1983), Ch. 12.

20 Benedict, 17.

21 M. Aston, *England's Iconoclasts: 1. Laws against Images* (Oxford, 1988), 39–43, 378–9; S. Michalski, *The Reformation and the Visual Arts: The Protestant Image Question in Western and Eastern Europe* (London, 1993), 19, 29, 176.

22 K. H. Marcus, 'Hymnody and Hymnals in Basel, 1526–1606', *SCJ*, 32 (2001), 723–42, 731–2.

23 Benedict, 65–6.

24 L. Harder, *The Sources of Swiss Anabaptism: The Grebel Letters and Related Documents* (Scottdale, PA, 1985), [no. 63], 290.

25 The best brief account of Münster is still N. Cohn, *The Pursuit of the Millennium: Revolutionary Millenarians and Mystical Anarchists of the Middle Ages* (London, 1970 edn), 252–80.

26 An enormous amount of valuable information on radicalism is contained in G. H. Williams, *The Radical Reformation* (London, 1962). His categorization of different sorts of radicalism (ibid., xxiv–xxxi and *passim*) has not stood the test of time as well and I adopt my own approach. Another attempt at analysis is H. J. Hillerbrand (ed.), 'Radicalism in the Early Reformation: Varieties of Reformation in Church and Society', in Hillerbrand (ed.), *Radical Tendencies in the Reformation: Divergent Perspectives* (*SCES*, 9, 1988), 25–41.

27 E. Fulton, *Catholic Belief and Survival in Late Sixteenth-century Vienna: The Case of Georg Eder (1523–87)* (Aldershot, 2007), Ch. 1; M. A. Chisholm, 'The *Religionspolitik* of Emperor Ferdinand I (1521–1564): Tyrol and the Holy Roman Empire', *European History Quarterly*, 38 (2008), 551–77, at 561–5.

28 On Anne's evangelical views, see E. W. Ives, *The Life and Death of Anne Boleyn* (Oxford,

2004), Ch. 19, which is a knockout response to G. W. Bernard, 'Anne Boleyn's Religion', *HJ*, 36 (1993), 1–20.

29 Thomas Cromwell has often been caricatured as an amoral pantomime villain, the most egregious recent example being the biography by R. Hutchinson, *Thomas Cromwell: The Rise and Fall of Henry VIII's Most Notorious Minister* (London, 2007). For evidence that he displayed evangelical principle to a reckless extent and acted on it in influencing foreign policy, showing an ideological commitment which may explain his eventual fall, see D. MacCulloch, 'Heinrich Bullinger and the English-speaking World', in P. Opitz and E. Campi (eds.), *Heinrich Bullinger: Life–Thought–Influence* (2 vols., *Zürcher Beiträge zur Reformationsgeschichte* 24, 2006), II, 891–934, at 892–909.

30 Gen. 3.6–7, qu. D. Daniell, *William Tyndale: A Biography* (New Haven and London, 1994), 286, and the Deuteronomy prologue qu. ibid., 288. Daniell's is a uniquely sensitive portrait.

31 D. Daniell, 'William Tyndale, the English Bible and the English Language', in O. O'Sullivan (ed.), *The Bible as Book: The Reformation* (London, 2000), 39–50, at 47.

32 Daniell, *William Tyndale*, 1.

33 The definitive study of this often-neglected second phase is A. Kreider, *English Chantries: The Road to Dissolution* (Cambridge, MA, 1979), while the best survey of the dissolution remains D. Knowles, *Bare Ruined Choirs: The Dissolution of the English Monasteries* (Cambridge, 1976).

34 The best introduction to Henry VIII's reformation is R. Rex, *Henry VIII and the English Reformation* (2nd edn, Basingstoke, 2006). See also D. MacCulloch, *Thomas Cranmer: A Life* (London and New Haven, 1996), Chs. 3–9.

35 See various essays in Opitz and Campi (eds.), *Heinrich Bullinger*, esp. II, 755–820, 891–950. On marriage, C. Euler, 'Practical Piety: Bullinger's Marriage Theory as a Skilful Blending of Theory and Praxis', ibid., II, 661–70.

36 L. J. Abray, 'Confession, Conscience and Honour: The Limits of Magisterial Tolerance in 16th Century Strassburg', in O. Grell and B. Scribner (eds.), *Tolerance and Intolerance in the European Reformation* (Cambridge, 1996), 94–107.

37 MacCulloch, 227–9, 270–71.

38 The Schmalkaldic League had been named after the small town of Schmalkalden where the Lutheran princes and cities had reached their agreement in 1531 after Charles V had rejected their Confession at the Augsburg Diet in 1530.

39 MacCulloch, *Thomas Cranmer*, Chs. 9–11.

40 'Death us do part' was 'death us depart' when Cranmer wrote it, but the phrase has effortlessly survived the changing meaning of 'depart'.

41 The Gelasian original and Cranmer's version are helpfully laid side by side in F. E. Brightman (ed.), *The English Rite* (2 vols., London, 1915), I, 164.

42 The common image of Edward as a sickly youth is a lazy back-projection from his final illness, which was probably pneumonia. For correctives, see D. MacCulloch, *Tudor Church Militant: Edward VI and the Protestant Reformation* (London, 1999), esp. Ch. 1.

43 A fine overview of these extraordinary events, much stranger than they appear in previous historiography, is E. Ives, *Lady Jane Grey: A Tudor Mystery* (Oxford, 2009).

44 Of all the many lives of Calvin, one of the most currently fresh and interesting is B. Cottret, *Calvin: A Biography* (Grand Rapids and Edinburgh, 2000).

45 The background and excerpted text of the *Ordinances* are helpfully presented in G. R. Potter and M. Greengrass (eds.), *John Calvin: Documents of Modern History* (London, 1983), 69–76.

46 For the arrangements which Calvin made for support of poor exiles, see J. E. Olson, *Calvin and Social Welfare: Deacons and the Bourse française* (Selinsgrove, 1989), esp. 161–83.

47 For further discussion of the Servetus episode, see MacCulloch, 244–6.

48 The standard English edition of the final text is J. Calvin, ed. J. T. McNeill and F. L. Battles, *Institutes of the Christian Religion* (2 vols., Philadelphia: Library of Christian Classics XX, XXI, 1960).

49 Cf. J. Calvin, ed. F. L. Battles, *Institutes of the Christian Religion, 1536 Edition* (London, 1975), 15, with Calvin, ed. McNeill and Battles, *Institutes*, II, 35 [*Institutes* I.i.1].

50 *Commentary on Isaiah* (published 1551), 211, qu. Potter and Greengrass (ed.), *Calvin*, 36. On ubiquity, Calvin, ed. McNeill and Battles, *Institutes*, II, 1379–1403 [*Institutes* IV.xvii.16–31].

51 The key discussion here is Calvin, ed. McNeill and Battles, *Institutes*, II, 1379–1411 [*Institutes* IV.xvii.16–34].

52 Usefully discussed in P. Rorem, 'Calvin and Bullinger on the Lord's Supper', *Lutheran Quarterly*, 2 (1988), 155–84, 357–89.

53 For discussion of this development, see MacCulloch, 350–53.

54 H. P. Louthan, 'Irenicism in the Confessional Age: The Holy Roman Empire, 1563–1648', in Louthan and R. C. Zachman (eds.), *Conciliation and Confession: The Struggle for Unity in the Age of Reform, 1415–1648* (Notre Dame, IN, 2004), 228–85.

55 L. D. Bierma, *The Doctrine of the Sacraments in the Heidelberg Catechism: Melanchthonian, Calvinist, or Zwinglian? (Studies in Reformed Theology and History*, new ser., 4, 1999). The odd title of the Palatinate came from the fact that its ruler had originally been a major official in the imperial palace, and his leading position had led to him becoming one of the seven electors of the empire.

56 See conflicting etymologies in Benedict, 80, 143. On the French Wars of Religion, see pp. 675–7.

57 A superb study of Scottish Reformation society is M. Todd, *The Culture of Protestantism in Early Modern Scotland* (New Haven and London, 2002).

58 For discussion and narrative on Elizabethan England, see D. MacCulloch, *The Later Reformation in England, 1547–1603* (rev. edn, Basingstoke, 2001). The word 'Puritan' had originally been a term of abuse – *puritani* – applied to the twelfth-century Cathars, another word meaning 'pure'.

59 On confessionalization, see H. Schilling, *Religion, Political Culture and the Emergence of Early Modern Society* (Leiden, 1992); for many of the texts, M. A. Noll (ed.), *Confessions and Catechisms of the Reformation* (Leicester, 1991).

60 I. Saulle Hippenmeyer, *Nachbarschaft, Pfarrei und Gemeinde in Graubünden 1400–1600* (2 vols., Chur, 1997), esp. I, 171–82. For similar complicated arrangements in the Swiss Thurgau, see R. C. Head, 'Fragmented Dominion, Fragmented Churches: The Institutionalization of the *Landfrieden* in the Thurgau, 1531–1610', *ARG*, 96 (2005), 117–45.

61 Qu. G. Murdock, *Calvinism on the Frontier 1600–1660: International Calvinism and the Reformed Church in Hungary and Transylvania* (Oxford, 2000), 110, and see discussion, ibid., 15–16, 19–20; Murdock now provides the definitive account of the Transylvanian Reformation; and I must also acknowledge my gratitude to him and Andrew Spicer for our informed and enjoyable tours of Transylvanian churches.

62 Davies, *God's Playground*, 183. An excellent overview is G. H. Williams, 'Protestants in the Ukraine during the Period of the Polish-Lithuanian Commonwealth', *Harvard Ukrainian Studies*, 2 (1978), 41–72.

63 Naphy (ed.), 105–9, for the debates of the Synod of Iwie (now Ivye in Belarus), 1568.

64 S. Berti, 'Erudition and Religion in the Judeo-Christian Encounter: The Significance of the Karaite myth in 17th-century Europe', *Hebraic Political Studies*, 1 (2005), 110–20, at 112.

65 Williams, *The Radical Reformation*, 737, slightly altered.

66 The title of a book by J. Tazbir, *A State without Stakes: Polish Religious Toleration in the Sixteenth and Seventeenth Centuries* (New York, 1973). For exceptions to the generalization, Davies, *God's Playground*, 187–8.

67 Benedict, 224.

68 Hope, 148–9, 165–6, 256–6. On Luther's image, R. W. Scribner, 'Incombustible Luther: The Image of the Reformer in Early Modern Germany', *PP*, 110 (February 1986), 38–68, repr. in R. W. Scribner, *Popular Culture and Popular Movements in Reformation Germany* (London, 1987), 323–53.

69 For a more extended account of the British crisis of the early seventeenth century, see MacCulloch, Ch. 12.

70 On the 1590 address, A. R. MacDonald, 'James VI and I, the Church of Scotland, and British Ecclesiastical Convergence', *HJ*, 48 (2005), 885–904, at 886–7. James's apparent invention of the word 'Anglican' in 1598 is to be found in D. Calderwood, *History of the*

Church of Scotland by Mr. D. Calderwood, ed. T. Thomson (Wodrow Society, 1842–9), V, p. 694.

71 On the separate story of Dutch Arminianism, see pp. 779–80, and MacCulloch, 373–8.

72 James's organization of Scots settlement in Ulster (see pp. 756–7) was certainly another of his achievements, but it might be considered somewhat more ambiguous in its consequences.

73 A fine account is A. Nicolson, *Power and Glory: Jacobean England and the Making of the King James Bible* (London, 2003).

74 J. Morrill, 'A British Patriarchy? Ecclesiastical Imperialism under the early Stuarts', in A. Fletcher and P. Roberts (eds.), *Religion, Culture and Society in Early Modern Britain: Essays in Honour of Patrick Collinson* (Cambridge, 1994), 209–37.

75 J. Peacey, 'The Paranoid Prelate: Archbishop Laud and the Puritan Plot', in B. Coward and J. Swann (eds.), *Conspiracies and Conspiracy Theory in Early Modern Europe: From the Waldensians to the French Revolution* (Aldershot, 2004), 113–34.

76 A. Ford, *James Ussher: Theology, History, and Politics in Early Modern Ireland and England* (Oxford, 2007), 175–207, 282–4.

77 The most comprehensive overview of this period is A. Woolrych, *Britain in Revolution 1625–1660* (Oxford, 2002).

78 II Samuel 16.7.

79 The remarkably bitter modern controversy about the existence of the Ranters is judiciously surveyed in G. E. Aylmer, 'Did the Ranters Exist?', *PP*, 117 (November 1987), 208–20.

80 D. Hirst, 'The Failure of Godly Rule in the English Republic', *PP*, 132 (August 1991), 33–66. On popular attacks on Quakers during the 1650s, see J. Miller, ' "A suffering people": English Quakers and Their Neighbours c. 1650–c. 1700', *PP*, 188 (August 2005), 71–105.

81 J. Maltby, 'Suffering and Surviving: The Civil Wars, the Commonwealth and the Formation of "Anglicanism", 1642–1660', in C. Durston and J. Maltby (eds.), *Religion in Revolutionary England* (Manchester and New York, 2006), 158–80.

82 Good discussion of Latitudinarian identity in J. Spurr, ' "Latitudinarianism" and the Restoration Church', *HJ*, 31 (1988), 61–82.

83 For O'Malley's own defence of the usage amid much stimulating discussion, see his *Trent and All That: Renaming Catholicism in the Early Modern Era* (Cambridge, MA, 2000), esp. 7–9, 140–43.

18: Rome's Renewal
(1500–1700)

1 J. Edwards, 'Kindred Spirit? Alfonso de Valdés and Philip Melanchthon at the Diet of Augsburg', unpublished paper, and see also J. M. Headley, 'Rhetoric and Reality: Messianic, Humanist and Civilian Themes in the Imperial Ethos of Gattinara', in M. Reeves, *Prophetic Rome in the High Renaissance Period* (Oxford, 1992), 241–69. An excellent overview is M. Firpo, 'The Italian Reformation and Juan de Valdés', *SCJ*, 27 (1996), 353–64.

2 See the foundation document of the Genoese Oratory in J. C. Olin (ed.), *The Catholic Reformation: Savonarola to Ignatius Loyola* (New York, 1992), 18–26; note especially the 'Addition' on the administration of the associated syphilis hospice, the *Incurabili*. On syphilis, MacCulloch, 630–33.

3 For the Theatine Rule, Olin (ed.), *The Catholic Reformation*, 128–32.

4 MacCulloch, 644–6. For new light on the early years of the Ursulines, see Q. Mazzonis, *Spirituality, Gender, and the Self in Renaissance Italy: Angela Merici and the Company of St Ursula (1474–1540)* (Washington, DC, 2007).

5 F. A. James III, *Peter Martyr Vermigli and Predestination: The Augustinian Inheritance of an Italian Reformer* (Oxford, 1998), Part II. On the whitewashing in Naples, M. Firpo, *Gli affreschi di Pontormo a San Lorenzo: Eresia, politica e cultura nella Firenze di Cosimo I* (Milan, 1997), 415: I am indebted to Professor Firpo for drawing this to my attention.

6 P. Caraman, *Ignatius Loyola* (San Francisco, 1990), 80.

7 For the connections between the 1540 Bull and the Pope's family affairs, see O. Hufton, 'Altruism and Reciprocity: The Early Jesuits and Their Female Patrons', *Renaissance Studies*, 15 (2001), 328–53, esp. at 336, 340–41. For further examples of Ignatius's female diplomacy, MacCulloch, 641.

8 For more evidence of the links between Jesuits and *Spirituali*, see ibid., 222.

9 This point was made to me by Professor Massimo Firpo, and I am most grateful for our conversations.

10 P. McNair, 'Benedetto da Mantova, Marcantonio Flaminio, and the *Beneficio di Cristo*: A Developing Twentieth-Century Debate Reviewed', *Modern Language Review*, 82 (1987), 614–24. Pole's biographer Thomas Mayer makes out a rather hazy case for Cardinal Pole's direct involvement in preparing the *Beneficio*: T. F. Mayer, *Reginald Pole: Prince and Prophet* (Cambridge, 2000), 119–21.

11 On Pole and the satanic nature of the Inquisition, D. Fenlon, 'Pietro Carnesecchi and Cardinal Pole: New Perspectives', *JEH*, 56 (2005), 529–33, at 532. On Pole's general passivity or belief in his special providential role and its relation to his defeat in the 1549 conclave, the evidence may with a little effort be gathered from Mayer, *Reginald Pole*, e.g. 45, 84, 93, 98–100, 176–7, 186–7, 195, 216–17. Somewhat clearer accounts of the conclave may be found in T. Mayer, *Cardinal Pole in European Context: A via media in the Reformation* (Aldershot, 2000), Ch. 4, owing much to the text he introduces in Ch. 5.

12 Firpo, *Gli affreschi di Pontormo a San Lorenzo*, esp. 13–20, 92–102, 311–27, and see plates between pp. 200 and 201.

13 For further discussion of this, MacCulloch, 644–5.

14 J. W. O'Malley, *The First Jesuits* (Cambridge, MA, 1993), 299–300.

15 Ibid., 274–5, 278.

16 The muted tones are noted by J. W. O'Malley, *Four Cultures of the West* (Cambridge, MA, 2004), 113–14. This was the era before the large-scale eastern European unions culminating in Brest in 1596 (see pp. 533–5), but there were already Armenian, Maronite, Chaldean and Syriac Churches in communion with Rome, and sections of the liturgy in Dalmatia were customarily in Slavonic. For the tangled situation in the Church of the East at this time, see Baumer, 248–49, and for the part played by the Glagolitic Rite in the council's discussions of the vernacular, see F. J. Thomson, 'The Legacy of SS Cyril and Methodios in the Counter-Reformation', in E. Konstantinou (ed.), *Methodios und Kyrillos in ihrer europäischen Dimension* (Frankfurt am Main and Oxford, 2005), 85–247, at 102–53.

17 MacCulloch, 278.

18 Now classic analysis of Mary's religious experiment is E. Duffy, *The Stripping of the Altars: Traditional Religion in England, c.1400–c.1580* (New Haven and London, 1992), 524–63; see also essays in E. Duffy and D. Loades (eds.), *The Church of Mary Tudor* (Aldershot, 2005).

19 On the *Exercises* adapted by William Peryn, W. Wizeman, *The Theology and Spirituality of Mary Tudor's Church* (Aldershot, 2006), 33 and *passim*.

20 The best survey of this topic is J. Bossy, *The English Catholic Community, 1570–1850* (London, 1975). On the major step in dismantling the discrimination, see pp. 838–9.

21 A superb account of these events with a much wider reference than its title suggests is R. Pörtner, *The Counter-Reformation in Central Europe: Styria 1580–1630* (Oxford, 2001). See also M. A. Chisholm, 'The *Religionspolitik* of Emperor Ferdinand I (1521–1564): Tyrol and the Holy Roman Empire', *European History Quarterly*, 38 (2008), 551–77.

22 R. Taylor, 'Architecture and Magic: Considerations of the *Idea* of the Escorial', in D. Fraser, H. Hibbard and M. J. Levine (eds.), *Essays in the History of Architecture Presented to Rudolf Wittkower* (London, 1967), 81–109, at 89–97.

23 E. García Hernán, *Francisco de Borja, grande de España* (Valencia, 1999), esp. 165–75, 179–81.

24 J. Edwards and R. Truman (eds.), *Reforming Catholicism in the England of Mary Tudor: The Achievement of Friar Bartolomé Carranza* (Aldershot, 2005), esp. 177–204; on the basis of the Tridentine Catechism in Carranza's Catechism, ibid., 24; Wizeman, *The Theology and Spirituality of Mary Tudor's Church*, 11–12, 26–7.

25 V. Lincoln, *Teresa: A Woman. A Biography of Teresa of Avila* (Albany, NY, 1984), 75.

26 T. Johnson, 'Gardening for God: Carmelite Deserts and the Sacralization of Natural Space in Counter-Reformation Spain', in W. Coster and A. Spicer (eds.), *Sacred Space in Early Modern Europe* (Cambridge, 2005), 193–210, at 196.

27 'Method for the visitation of convents', qu. and tr. A. Weber, *Teresa of Avila and the Rhetoric of Femininity* (Princeton and London, 1990), 6.

28 'Camino de perfección', ibid., 41.

29 E. Allison Peers (ed.), *St. John of the Cross: Dark Night of the Soul* (London, 1976), 2 [Prologue, Stanzas of the Soul, 5–8].

30 *The Spiritual Canticle* 22.4: K. Kavanaugh and O. Rodriguez (eds.), *The Collected Works of St. John of the Cross* (Washington, DC, 1964), 497.

31 *Ascent of Mount Carmel* Bk 1, Ch. 1, sect. 2, qu. Allison Peers (ed.), *St. John of the Cross*, ix.

32 Ibid., 3 [Bk 1, preliminary exposition].

33 E. K. Rowe, 'St Teresa and Olivares: Patron Sainthood, Royal Favourites and the Politics of Plurality in 17th-century Spain', *SCJ*, 37 (2006), 721–38.

34 Statistic from M. P. Holt, *The French Wars of Religion* (Cambridge, 1995), 94.

35 On the quotation's lack of authenticity, see M. Wolfe, 'The Conversion of Henri IV and the Origins of Bourbon Absolutism', *Historical Reflections/Réflexions Historiques*, 14 (1987), 287–309, at 287.

36 G. Champeaud, 'The Edict of Poitiers and the Treaty of Nérac, or Two Steps towards the Edict of Nantes', *SCJ*, 32 (2001), 319–33.

37 N. Davies, *God's Playground: A History of Poland. 1: The Origins to 1795* (Oxford, 1981), 413–25.

38 A brilliant summary exposition of this paradox is P. Stolarski, 'Dominican–Jesuit Rivalry and the Politics of Catholic Renewal in Poland, 1564–1648', *JEH* (forthcoming). Similar tensions, which were felt all over Counter-Reformation Europe, might be much less productive wherever Catholicism was weak, as for instance in Elizabethan and early Stuart England. For an absorbing case study on the results there, see M. C. Questier, *Catholicism and Community in Early Modern England: Politics, Aristocratic Patronage and Religion, c. 1550–1640* (Cambridge, 2006).

39 S. Ditchfield, 'Text before Trowel: Antonio Bosio's *Roma sotteranea* Revisited', in R. N. Swanson (ed.), *The Church Retrospective* (*SCH*, 33, 1997), 343–60; T. Johnson, 'Holy Fabrications: The Catacomb Saints and the Counter-Reformation in Bavaria', *JEH*, 47 (1996), 274–97, esp. at 277–81.

40 On locking churches, A. Spicer, *Calvinist Churches in Early Modern Europe* (Aldershot, 2007), 228. Benedict, 436, provides a dramatic example of reduction in clerical numbers: in 1500 the bishopric of Utrecht had around eighteen thousand clergy, but in the seventeenth century the Protestant parish system in the same area had 1,524 ministers.

41 W. de Boer, *The Conquest of the Soul: Confession, Discipline and Social Order in Counter-Reformation Milan* (Leiden, 2000).

42 D. Gentilcore, ' "Adapt yourselves to the People's capabilities": Missionary Strategies, Methods and Impact in the Kingdom of Naples, 1600–1800', *JEH*, 45 (1994), 269–95.

43 For further discussion, see MacCulloch, 549–50. On Gregory's Constantinian agenda, N. Courtright, *The Papacy and the Art of Reform in 16th-century Rome: Gregory XIII's Tower of the Winds in the Vatican* (Cambridge, 2003), 33–40, 65–8.

44 M. Sharratt, *Galileo: Decisive Innovator* (Oxford, 1994), and see further summary discussion of Copernican astronomy and the Galileo affair in MacCulloch, 685–8.

45 For further discussion of Protestants and Jews in the Reformation, see ibid., 688–91.

46 For summary discussion and critique, see ibid., 604–7, but the question is magisterially discussed by the essayists of H. Lehmann and G. Roth (eds.), *Weber's Protestant ethic: Origins, Evidence, Contexts* (Cambridge, 1993).

47 MacCulloch, 650, and for discussion of marriage and the family, ibid., 651–4.

48 There is at last a decent scholarly edition of the *Malleus* with English translation: H. Institoris and J. Sprenger, ed. C. S. Mackay, *Malleus Maleficarum* (2 vols., Cambridge, 2006). For further comment on the *Malleus*, MacCulloch, 565–8.

49 For the English profile, see M. Gaskill, *Crime and Mentalities in Early Modern*

England (Cambridge, 2000), 48–66, at 78. K. Thomas, *Religion and the Decline of Magic* (2nd edn, London, 1973), 660–69, made the suggestion that witchcraft accusations generally arose from tensions over the breakdown of traditional hospitality obligations to the marginal. This may have some justification, but will not do as a general mode of explanation. For the vulnerable position of widows, see A. Rowlands, 'Witchcraft and Old Women in Early Modern Germany', *PP*, 173 (November 2001), 50–89, esp. 65, 70, 78.

50 C. Larner, *Enemies of God: The Witch-hunt in Scotland* (London, 1981), esp. 63, 107.

19: A Worldwide Faith
(1500–1800)

1 For documents on these intolerances, see Koschorke et al. (eds.), 15–16, 27–9.

2 Qu. in S. G. Payne, *A History of Spain and Portugal* (Madison, 1973), 239.

3 D. Abulafia, *The Discovery of Mankind: Atlantic Encounters in the Age of Columbus* (New Haven and London, 2008), Chs. 4–8, esp. 49–51, 67, 71, 97–8; F. Fernández-Armesto, *The Canary Islands after the Conquest* (Oxford, 1982), 10–12, 39–40, 125–9, 201–2; comment by P. E. Russell, *JEH*, 31 (1980), 115.

4 C. R. Johnson, 'Renaissance German Cosmographers and the Naming of America', *PP*, 191 (May 2006), 3–44.

5 Cf. the remarks of F. Cervantes, reviewing L. N. Rivera, *A Violent Evangelism: The Political and Religious Conquest of the Americas* (Louisville, KY, 1992), *JEH*, 45 (1994), 509.

6 Koschorke et al. (eds.), 292–3.

7 A. Hastings, 'Latin America', in Hastings (ed.), 328–68, at 340.

8 Estimates respectively in R. Bireley, *The Refashioning of Catholicism, 1450–1700* (Houndmills, 1999), 147, and P. N. Mancall, ' "The ones who hold up the world": Native American History since the Columbian Quincentennial', *HJ*, 47 (2004), 477–90, at 478.

9 This is the suggestion of J. H. Elliott, *Empires of the Atlantic World: Britain and Spain in America, 1492–1830* (New Haven and London, 2006), 79–81, 86–7.

10 T. Cummins, 'A Sculpture, a Column and a Painting: The Tension between Art and History', *Art Bulletin*, 77 (1995), 371–7, at 373–4.

11 J. Lara, *Christian Texts for Aztecs: Art and Liturgy in Colonial Mexico* (Notre Dame, IND, 2008), 20, 24, 32, 37, 81. On Augustine's mission, see pp. 336–40.

12 Lara, *Christian Texts for Aztecs*, 87, with illustration of a possible further example.

13 Elliott, *Empires of the Atlantic World*, 20.

14 J. Lara, *City, Temple, Stage: Eschatological Architecture and Liturgical Theatrics in New Spain* (Notre Dame, IN, 2004), esp. 17–21.

15 Ibid., esp. 111–50, and see also J. A. Licate, *Creation of a Mexican Landscape: Territorial Organisation and Settlement in the Eastern Puebla Basin, 1520–1605* (Chicago, 1981).

16 R. Ricard, *The Spiritual Conquest of Mexico: An Essay on the Apostolate and Evangelising Methods of the Mendicant Orders in New Spain, 1523–1572* (Berkeley, 1966), 31–6.

17 Lara, *Christian Texts for Aztecs*, 187, 194–9.

18 I. Clendinnen, *Ambivalent Conquests: Maya and Spaniard in Yucatan, 1517–1570* (Cambridge, 1987), 40–41, 72–109; Ricard, *The Spiritual Conquest* of Mexico, 264–5.

19 Bireley, *The Refashioning of Catholicism, 1450–1700*, 153–4, 158.

20 Ricard, *The Spiritual Conquest of Mexico*, 122–3.

21 Hastings, 'Latin America', 346.

22 On 'anima', see L. M. Burkhart, 'The Solar Christ in Nahuatl Doctrinal Texts of Early Colonial Mexico', *Ethnohistory*, 35 (1988), 234–56, at 242. On Hell, note the recommendations of Don Bartolomé de Alva in his *Guide to Confession Large and Small in the Mexican Language*: see the review by S. Schroeder of the modern edition of Alva's work by B. D. Sell and J. F. Schwaller with L. A. Homza (Norman, OKL, 1999), *Ethnohistory*, 48 (2001), 361–3, at 362. See also Ricard, *The Spiritual Conquest of Mexico*, 49–50.

23 Ibid., 183–7.

24 K. Burns, *Colonial Habits: Convents and the Spiritual Economy of Cuzco, Peru* (Durham, NC, 1999), 2–21, 27–37, 80, 113.

25 D. Brading, *Our Lady of Guadalupe, Image and Tradition 1531–2000* (Cambridge, 2001), 58–70, 361–8.

26 Koschorke et al. (eds.), 17–18, 24–6; P. K. Thomas, *Christians and Christianity in India* (London, 1954), 51–4.

27 Koschorke et al. (eds.), 26, 45–6, 55–6.

28 J. Brodrick, *Saint Francis Xavier (1506–1552)* (London, 1952), 239–40; on the burning of Jeronimo Dias, see Koschorke et al. (eds.), 16.

29 V. Cronin, *A Pearl to India: The Life of Roberto de Nobili* (London, 1959); Koschorke et al. (eds.), 36–8.

30 K. S. Latourette, *A History of the Expansion of Christianity* (7 vols., London, 1938–47), III, 336–66.

31 J. D. Spence, *The Memory Palace of Matteo Ricci* (London, 1984), is illuminating on Ricci's *mentalité*, and V. Cronin, *The Wise Man from the West* (London, 1955), is still worth reading.

32 Baltasar Teles (my italics): M. Brockey, *Journey to the East: The Jesuit Mission to China, 1579–1724* (Cambridge, MA, 2007), 212, 218.

33 Statistics: Latourette, *A History of the Expansion of Christianity*, III, 344, 348. For a judiciously sceptical view of Jesuit myth-making about their Chinese mission, see Brockey, *Journey to the East*, 47–56.

34 Ibid., 134–41, 172–4, 350–65, and on 'Chinese virgins', R. G. Tiedemann, 'China and Its Neighbours', in Hastings (ed.), 369–415, at 384.

35 Brockey, *Journey to the East*, 179–203; for the 1704 decree, Koschorke et al. (eds.), 39–41.

36 The best single account of the mission is C. R. Boxer, *The Christian Century in Japan, 1549–1650* (Berkeley, 1967).

37 G. Schurhammer, *Francis Xavier: His Life, His Times* (4 vols., Rome, 1973–82), IV, 269, 440, 447, 547, 555.

38 Boxer, *The Christian Century in Japan, 1549–1650*, 72–83, 89.

39 For the edict decreeing closure and the 'oath of apostasy' of 1645, see Koschorke et al. (eds.), 31–3.

40 S. Turnbull, 'Diversity or Apostasy? The Case of the Japanese "Hidden Christians"', in R. N. Swanson (ed.), *Unity and Diversity in the Church (SCH, 32, 1996)*, 441–54.

41 Sundkler and Steed, 46.

42 Bireley, *The Refashioning of Catholicism*, 162; see pp. 725 and 728.

43 Ibid., 162.

44 R. J. Morgan, 'Jesuit Confessors, African Slaves and the Practice of Confession in Seventeenth Century Cartagena', in K. J. Lualdi and A. T. Thayer (eds.), *Penitence in the Age of Reformations* (Aldershot, 2000), 222–39. On Loanda (Luanda), Hastings, 124.

45 Sundkler and Steed, 318.

46 Ibid., 51.

47 Hastings, 124–5.

48 J. K. Thornton, *The Kingdom of Kongo: Civil War and Transition, 1641–1718* (Madison, 1983), esp. 63–8.

49 Sundkler and Steed, 59–60. See the definitive study by J. K. Thornton, *The Kongolese Saint Anthony: Dona Beatriz Kimpa Vita and the Antonian Movement, 1684–1706* (Cambridge, 1998).

50 D. de Góis, *Fides, religio, moresque Aethiopum* (Louvain, 1540); I am grateful to Thomas Earle for drawing this to my attention.

51 On the Jesuit explorer Pedro Páez Xaramillo, SJ, see J. Reverte, *Dios, el Diablo y la Aventura* (Barcelona, 2001).

52 Hastings, 136–60. On nude baptisms, S. Munro-Hay, *Ethiopia, the Unknown Land: A Cultural and Historical Guide* (London, 2002), 51, and on iconography, ibid., 56.

53 For a study of this circular process, see J. L. Matory, *Black Atlantic Religion: Tradition, Transnationalism, and Matriarchy in the Afro-Brazilian Candomblé* (Princeton, 2005).

54 B. E. Schmidt, 'The Presence of Vodou in New York City: The Impact of a Caribbean

Religion on the Creolization of a Metropolis', in G. Collier and U. Fleischmann (eds.), *A Pepper-pot of Cultures: Aspects of Creolization in the Caribbean, Matatu*, 27–8 (2003), 213–34, esp. 219.

55 L. Cabrera, *El monte: (Igbo – Finda; Ewe Orisha. Vititi Nfinda: notas sobre las religiones, la magia, las supersticiones y el folklore de los negros criollos y el pueblo de Cuba* (Miami, 1975), 231–3, 243–6. Oya is also known as Iansa in Brazil. I am very grateful to Bettina Schmidt for directing me to this source.

56 L. Hurbon, *Voodoo: Truth and Fantasy* (London, 1995), 161, 77.

57 D. J. Cosentino (ed.), *Sacred Arts of Haitian Vodou* (Los Angeles, 1995), 246–59, 264–5; J. Hainard and P. Mathez (eds.), *Vodou: A Way of Life* (Geneva, 2007), 29.

58 C. R. Boxer, *The Church Militant and Iberian Expansion 1440–1770* (Baltimore, 1978), 82; on Canada, cf. e.g. L. Campeau, *La mission des Jésuites chez les Hurons 1634–1650* (Montreal, 1987), Ch. 16, esp. 298, 302.

20: Protestant Awakenings
(1600–1800)

1 Handy, 6–13. For useful sceptical comment on the Brazil and Florida ventures, see J. McGrath, 'Polemic and History in French Brazil, 1555–1560', *SCJ*, 27 (1996), 385–97.

2 N. Matar, *Turks, Moors and Englishmen in the Age of Discovery* (New York, 1999), 9, 20, 53. See also discussion of Protestant anti-papal rhetoric in relation to Islam in L. Jardine, 'Gloriana Rules the Waves: Or, the Advantage of Being Excommunicated (and a Woman)', *TRHS*, 6th ser., 14 (2004), 209–22, at 209–10, 216.

3 J. Maltby, ' "The good old way": Prayer Book Protestantism in the 1640–50s', in R. Swanson (ed.), *The Church and the Book* (*SCH*, 38, 2004), 233–56; L. Gragg, 'The Pious and the Profane: The Religious Life of Early Barbados Planters', *Historian*, 62 (2000), 264–83. I am grateful to Judith Maltby for pointing me to this reference.

4 Ahlstrom, 136.

5 Handy, 20; on North Africa, Matar, *Turks, Moors and Englishmen in the Age of Discovery*, 84–92.

6 An absorbing study of White's ministry in Dorchester and its implications for America is D. Underdown, *Fire from Heaven: The Life of an English Town in the Seventeenth Century* (London, 1992).

7 F. Bremer, *John Winthrop: America's Forgotten Founding Father* (Oxford, 2003).

8 A. Zakai, 'The Gospel of Reformation: The Origins of the Great Puritan Migration', *JEH*, 37 (1986), 584–602, at 586–7.

9 Ahlstrom, 146–7. I am grateful to Francis Bremer for our discussions on this point.

10 F. J. Bremer, *Congregational Communion: Clerical Friendship in the Anglo-American Puritan Community, 1610–1692* (Lebanon, NH, 1994).

11 S. Hardman Moore, *Pilgrims: New World Settlers and the Call of Home* (New Haven and London, 2007), esp. 143–7.

12 J. B. Bell, *The Imperial Origins of the King's Church in Early America, 1607–1783* (Houndmills and New York, 2004), 30–32. The 'King's Chapel', which still exists, turned Unitarian in the 1780s, in circumstances described in Ahlstrom, 388, and uses a remarkable version of Cranmer's Prayer Book, edited to remove any reference to the Trinity.

13 M. Winship, *Making Heretics: Militant Protestantism and Free Grace in Massachusetts, 1636–1641* (Princeton, 2002).

14 P. Bonomi, *Under the Cope of Heaven: Religion, Society and Politics in Colonial America* (New York and Oxford, 1986), 20, 23, 34.

15 Handy, 46.

16 M. Baldwin Weddle, *Walking in the Way of Peace: Quaker Pacifism in the 17th Century* (Oxford, 2001), 122–31, 162–5.

17 E. H. Ash, ' "A note and a caveat for the merchant": Mercantile Advisors in Elizabethan England', *SCJ*, 33 (2002), 1–31, at 27–9.

18 The command to Adam is at Genesis 1.28. R. W. Cogley, *John Eliot's Mission to the Indians before King Philip's War* (Cambridge, MA, 1999), 5–6, 8, 12–18, 22, 40, 51.

19 See P. Harrison, ' "Fill the Earth and Subdue it": Biblical Warrants for Colonization in Seventeenth Century England', *JRH*, 29 (2005), 3–24, esp. 4, 13–14, 22.
20 R. Strong, 'A Vision of an Anglican Imperialism: The Annual Sermons of the Society for the Propagation of the Gospel in Foreign Parts 1701–1714', *JRH*, 30 (2006), 175–98.
21 B. Wood, *Slavery in Colonial America, 1619–1776* (Lanham, MD, 2005), 4.
22 Handy, 70.
23 Sundkler and Steed, 65.
24 D. Armitage, ' "That excellent forme of Government": New Light on Locke and Carolina', *TLS*, 22 October 2004, 14–15.
25 J. Butler, *Awash in a Sea of Faith: Christianizing the American People* (Cambridge, MA, 1990), 140–41.
26 A lively treatment of this theme, although missing other ways in which New York might also foreshadow darker American legacies, is R. Shorto, *The Island at the Centre of the World: The Untold Story of Dutch Manhattan and the Founding of New York* (London, 2004), esp. 337–56.
27 Bonomi, *Under the Cope of Heaven*, 23.
28 The Amish take their name from their founder, Jakob Amman, a Swiss leader of the Anabaptists known as Mennonites, who in 1693 broke with other Mennonite groups.
29 Bonomi, *Under the Cope of Heaven*, 36.
30 A fine summary of a life's work on later Stuart Britain is J. Miller, *An English Absolutism? The Later Stuart Monarchy 1660–88* (Historical Association New Appreciations in History, 30, 1993).
31 A useful perspective is J. F. Bosher, 'The Franco-Catholic Danger, 1660–1715', *History*, 79 (1994), 5–30.
32 S. Lachenicht, 'Huguenot Immigrants and the Formation of National Identities, 1548–1787', *HJ*, 50 (2007), 309–31, at 310. The Morisco expulsions of 1609 from Spain were about twice as numerous: see p. 590.
33 An excellent narrative of this and what follows is T. Harris, *Revolution: The Great Crisis of the British Monarchy, 1685–1720* (London, 2006).
34 Judith Maltby suggests to me that he may have derived this strategy from the similar earlier Catholic toleration in Maryland: see pp. 729–30.
35 On the balance of forces in Scotland, see Harris, *Revolution*, 382–90. For the Williamite Crown's largely successful efforts to insinuate moderation into the new Presbyterian establishment, see R. K. Frace, 'Religious Toleration in the Wake of Revolution: Scotland on the Eve of Enlightenment (1688–1710s)', *History*, 93 (2008), 355–75.
36 T. Claydon, *William III and the Godly Revolution* (Cambridge, 1996), 4–6, 28–33, 83–7. McClelland, 231–5; see also R. Woolhouse, *Locke: A Biography* (Cambridge, 2008).
37 There is a huge and still-growing literature on Foxe's *Book of Martyrs*, whose actual short title is *Acts and Monuments*. The most up-to-date way to comprehend the subject is the article by T. S. Freeman, 'Foxe, John', in *ODNB*.
38 The classic exposition of British self-understanding and imperial expansion is L. Colley, *Britons: Forging the Nation, 1707–1837* (New Haven and London, 1992).
39 M. Jasanoff, 'Collectors of Empire: Objects, Conquests and Imperial Self-fashioning', *PP*, 184 (August 2004), 109–36, esp. 123–5. On the French Revolution, see pp. 806–11.
40 A masterly gathering of all the strands is W. R. Ward, *The Protestant Evangelical Awakening* (Cambridge, 1992).
41 For examples of vestigial or persistent monasteries in Lutheran lands, see O. Chadwick, *The Early Reformation on the Continent* (Oxford, 2001), 163, 168–9.
42 Ward, *The Protestant Evangelical Awakening*, 61–3.
43 Hope, 131–46; on correspondents, B. Hindmarsh, *The Evangelical Conversion Narrative: Spiritual Autobiography in Early Modern England* (Oxford, 2005), 74.
44 Ibid., esp. 58–9, 164.
45 C. Rymatzki, *Hallischer Pietismus und Judenmission: Johann Heinrich Callenbergs Institutum Judaicum und dessen Freundenkreis (1728–1736)* (Tübingen, 2004), esp. 408–10, 450–52.
46 P. Williams, *The Life of Bach* (Cambridge, 2004), 38–47.
47 Hope, 186.

48 Williams, *The Life of Bach*, 171–3, 178–81.

49 Hope, 246.

50 Hindmarsh, *The Evangelical Conversion Narrative*, 164–5.

51 On the 'side-hole', C. D. Atwood, 'Zinzendorf's 1749 Reprimand to the *Brüdergemeine*', *Transactions of the Moravian Historical Society*, 27 (1996), 59–84, at 66–7, 71, and for the postscript, see ibid., 74, 81. See also C. D. Atwood, 'Interpreting and Misinterpreting the Sichtungszeit', in M. Brecht and P. Peucker (eds.), *Neue Aspekte der Zinzendorf-Forschung* (Göttingen, 2006), 179–87, at 183. I am grateful to Jonathan Yonan for pointing me to these articles.

52 B. Singh, *The First Protestant Missionary to India: Bartholomaeus Ziegenbalg, 1683–1719* (Oxford, 1999), esp. on inter-faith dialogue, 100–145; see also Koschorke et al. (eds.), 49–53.

53 J. C. S. Mason, *The Moravian Church and the Missionary Awakening in England, 1760–1800* (London, 2001), esp. 125–42, 179–92.

54 For the usage of this term in relation to anglophone movements after 1730, which is particularly confusing for German-speakers accustomed to associating the description *evangelisch* with Lutheranism, see good discussion in D. Bebbington, *Evangelicalism in Modern Britain: A History from the 1730s to the 1980s* (London, 1989) 1–19.

55 D. Berman, *A History of Atheism in Britain from Hobbes to Russell* (London, 1988), 35–7.

56 For a London example, see M. Byrne and G. R. Bush (eds.), *St Mary-le-Bow: A History* (Barnsley, 2007), 8, 181–2.

57 T. Isaacs, 'The Anglican Hierarchy and the Reformation of Manners 1688–1738', *JEH*, 33 (1982), 391–411.

58 A splendid introduction to Wesley from the present doyen of British Methodist scholarship is J. Walsh, *John Wesley: 1703–1791. A Bicentennial Tribute* (London, 1993).

59 H. D. Rack, *Reasonable Enthusiast: John Wesley and the Rise of Methodism* (London, 1989), 48–9.

60 Wesley's Journal, 24 May 1738: W. R. Ward and R. P. Heitzenrater (eds.), *Journals and Diaries I (1735–38)* (*Works of John Wesley*, 18, 1988), 249–50.

61 Rack, *Reasonable Enthusiast*, 264–7.

62 J. Cruickshank, ' "Appear as Crucified for me": Sight, Suffering, and Spiritual Transformation in the Hymns of Charles Wesley', *JRH*, 30 (2006), 311–30.

63 The tunes are 'fuguing' because, like the musical form called the fugue, they play off musical themes against each other.

64 This great hymn offered much inspiration to composers: besides the fuguing tune 'Cranbrook', there is the magnificent 'Lyngham' and the intricate though non-fuguing 'Lydia'. Arguably the greatest fuguing tune, worthy of a Beethoven symphony, is 'Sagina', for Charles Wesley's 'And can it be that I should gain an interest in the Saviour's blood!'

65 F. Baker, *John Wesley and the Church of England* (London, 1970), esp. 319.

66 Letter of 1739: W. R. Ward and R. P. Heitzenrater (eds.), *Journals and Diaries II (1738–43)* (*Works of John Wesley*, 19, 1990), 67.

67 For approaches to the classic but dubious 'Weber–Tawney thesis', see Further Reading, p. 1128. For John Wesley and self-improvement, see p. 795.

68 A. Stott, *Hannah More: The First Victorian* (Oxford, 2004).

69 M. Snape, *The Redcoat and Religion: The Forgotten History of the British Soldier from the Age of Marlborough to the Eve of the First World War* (London, 2005), esp. 7–68.

70 R. Godbeer, *Escaping Salem: The Other Witch Hunt of 1692* (Oxford, 2005); E. Laplante, *Salem Witch Judge: The Life and Repentance of Samuel Sewall* (New York, 2007), 199–201.

71 For a fine exposition of the origins and importance of open-air Scottish Eucharists for revival, see L. E. Schmidt, *Holy Fairs: Scottish Communions and American Revivals in the Early Modern Period* (Princeton, 1989).

72 M. J. Coalter Jr, 'The Radical Pietism of Count Nicholas Zinzendorf as a Conservative Influence on the Awakener, Gilbert Tennent', *CH*, 49 (1980), 35–46.

73 *Heaven is a world of love* (1738): W. H. Kimnach, K. P. Minkema and D. A. Sweeney (eds.), *The Sermons of Jonathan Edwards: A Reader* (New Haven and London, 1999), 272.

74 For Edwards's setting in Reformed tradition, see D. A. Sweeney and B. G. Withrow, 'Jonathan Edwards: Continuator or Pioneer of Evangelical History?', in M. A. G. Haykin and K. J. Stewart (eds.), *The Emergence of Evangelicalism: Exploring Historical Continuities* (Nottingham, 2008), 278–301.

75 G. M. Marsden, *Jonathan Edwards: A Life* (New Haven and London, 2003), 160.

76 Ibid., 264.

77 N. L. Rhoden, *Revolutionary Anglicanism: The Colonial Church of England Clergy during the American Revolution* (Basingstoke, 1999), 24.

78 Bonomi, *Under the Cope of Heaven*, 119, 252–3.

79 A. D. Callahan, *The Talking Book: African Americans and the Bible* (New Haven and London, 2006), esp. xiv, 41–8, and quotation at 237. Callahan points out that not all African-Americans, let alone Africans back home, could take Christianity seriously after its association with slavery: ibid., 42.

80 Handy, 156.

81 On nakedness, K. Morgan, 'Slave Women and Reproduction in Jamaica, c. 1776–1834', *History*, 91 (2006), 231–53, at 240–41. On Evangelicals, Africans and clothing, M. Vaughan, 'Africa and the Birth of the Modern World', *TRHS*, 6th ser., 16 (2006), 143–62, at 147–51.

82 C. Harline, *Sunday: A History of the First Day from Babylonia to the Super Bowl* (New York, 2006), 323–4.

83 J. Wolffe, 'Contentious Christians: Protestant–Catholic Conflict since the Reformation', in Wolffe (ed.), 97–128, at 111. Wolffe points out that anti-popery did not stop the new Republic forming a military alliance with the Catholic French monarchy against the British.

84 H. Morrison, *John Witherspoon and the Founding of the American Republic* (Notre Dame, IN, 2005).

85 A. Phelps Stokes, *Church and State in the United States* (3 vols., New York, 1950), I, 307–8.

86 Butler, *Awash in a Sea of Faith*, 208.

87 Rhoden, *Revolutionary Anglicanism*, 106–7.

88 Handy, 138.

89 D. L. Holmes, *The Faiths of the Founding Fathers* (Oxford and New York, 2006), 53–7, 79–89; quotation at 87.

90 Ibid., 59–71; J. J. Ellis, *His Excellency: George Washington* (New York, 2004), esp. 45, 269.

91 I. Kramnick and R. L. Moore, 'The Godless Constitution', in T. S. Engeman and M. P. Zuckert (eds.), *Protestantism and the American Founding* (Notre Dame, IN, 2004), 129–42; J. Meacham, *American Gospel: God, the Founding Fathers, and the Making of a Nation* (New York, 2006), 80–83. See also F. Church, *So Help Me God: The Founding Fathers and the First Great Battle over Church and State* (Orlando, FL, 2007).

92 The rise and fall of American Church establishments are carefully discussed in L. W. Levy, *The Establishment Clause: Religion and the First Amendment* (New York and London, 1986), esp. Chs. 1–3.

93 C. S. Lewis, ed. W. Hooper, *God in the Dock* (London, 1979), 9, 100: Ch. 12, 'God in the Dock' was originally published as 'Difficulties in Presenting the Christian Faith to Modern Unbelievers', *Lumen Vitae*, 3 (September 1948), 421–6.

PART VII: GOD IN THE DOCK
(1492-PRESENT)

21: Enlightenment: Ally or Enemy?
(1492-1815)

1 On the misbehaving Christ Child, see J. Nelson Crouch, 'Misbehaving God: The Case of the Christ Child in MS Laud Misc. 108 "Infancy of Jesus Christ" ', in B. Wheeler (ed.), *Mindful Spirit in Late Medieval Literature: Essays in Honor of Elizabeth D. Kirk* (Basingstoke, 2006), 31-43.

2 E. Rummel, *The Confessionalization of Humanism in Reformation Germany* (Oxford, 2000), 90-101.

3 C. Webster, *Paracelsus: Medicine, Magic and Mission at the End of Time* (New Haven and London, 2008).

4 D. Stevenson, *The Origins of Freemasonry: Scotland's Century, 1590-1710* (Cambridge, 1988), esp. 76 and Ch. 3.

5 F. Yates, *The Rosicrucian Enlightenment* (London, 1972), esp. Ch. 4.

6 H. Hotson, *Johann Heinrich Alsted, 1588-1638: Between Renaissance, Reformation and Universal Reform* (Oxford, 2000), esp. Ch. 5; H. Hotson, *Paradise Postponed: Johann Heinrich Alsted and the Birth of Calvinist Millenarianism* (Dordrecht, 2000).

7 S. Mandelbrote, 'John Dury and the Practice of Irenicism', in N. Aston (ed.), *Religious Change in Europe 1650-1914: Essays for John McManners* (Oxford, 1997), 41-58.

8 D. S. Katz, *Philosemitism and the Readmission of the Jews to England, 1603-1655* (Oxford, 1982), esp. 235-8, 241.

9 S. D. Snobelen, ' "The true frame of nature": Isaac Newton, Heresy and the Reformation of Natural Philosophy', in J. Brooke and I. Maclean (eds.), *Heterodoxy in Early Modern Science and Religion* (Oxford, 2005), 223-62; quotation from Newton's unpublished *Theologiae gentilis origines philosophicae* ('Philosophical origins of Gentile Theology') from the 1680s, ibid., 245. See also R. S. Westfall, *Never at Rest: A Biography of Isaac Newton* (Cambridge, 1980).

10 H. Hotson, 'The Instauration of the Image of God in Man: Humanist Anthropology, Encyclopaedic Pedagogy, Baconianism and Universal Reform', in M. Pelling and S. Mandelbrote (eds.), *The Practice of Reform in Health, Medicine and Science, 1500-2000* (Aldershot, 2005), 1-21, at 4.

11 F. Bacon, *Essayes*, 'Of Atheisme' (London, 1879, reproduction of 1625 text), 64.

12 MacCulloch, 610-11.

13 J. Arrizabalaga, J. Henderson and R. French, *The Great Pox: The French Disease in Renaissance Europe* (New Haven and London, 1997), Ch. 4.

14 C. S. Dixon, 'Popular Astrology and Lutheran Propaganda in Reformation Germany', *History*, 84 (1999), 403-18; on astrology, E. Cameron, 'Philipp Melanchthon: Image and Substance', *JEH*, 48 (1997), 705-22, at 711-12, and Calvin's critique, J. Calvin, ed. J. T. McNeill and F. L. Battles, *Institutes of the Christian Religion* (2 vols., Philadelphia: Library of Christian Classics XX, XXI, 1960), 201 [*Institutes* I.xvi.3].

15 On the leadership and crucial role of Sephardic crypto-Jews at the Collège de Guyenne, P. J. McGinnis and A. H. Williamson (eds.), *George Buchanan: The Political Poetry* (Edinburgh, 1995), 6-7, 16-18, 313.

16 J. Friedman, 'The Reformation in Alien Eyes: Jewish Perceptions of Christian Troubles', *SCJ*, 13/1 (Spring 1983), 23-40.

17 Z. David, 'Hájek, Dubravius and the Jews: A Contrast in Sixteenth-century Czech Historiography', *SCJ*, 27 (1996), 997-1013, at 998, 1009.

18 J. Friedman, 'Unitarians and New Christians in Sixteenth-century Europe', *ARG*, 81 (1996), 9-37.

19 Cf. discussion of sodomy in MacCulloch, 620-29.

20 J. Edwards, 'Portugal and the Expulsion of the Jews from Spain', in *Medievo hispano: estudios in memoriam del Prof. Derek W. Lomax* (Madrid, 1995), 121-39, at 137.

21 B. J. Kaplan, ' "Remnants of the Papal Yoke": Apathy and Opposition in the Dutch Reformation', *SCJ*, 25 (1994), 653–68.

22 A. Fix, *Prophecy and Reason: The Dutch Collegiants in the Early Enlightenment* (Princeton, 1991).

23 D. M. Swetschinki, *Reluctant Cosmopolitans: The Portuguese Jews of Seventeenth-century Amsterdam* (London, 2000).

24 J. I. Israel, *Radical Enlightenment: Philosophy and the Making of Modernity 1650–1750* (Oxford, 2001), 159–74.

25 B. Spinoza, tr. S. Shirley, with introd. by B. S. Gregory, *Tractatus Theologico-Politicus* (2nd edn, Leiden, 1991), 51 [Preface].

26 B. Spinoza, ed. M. L. Morgan and tr. S. Shirley, *The Essential Spinoza*: Ethics and Related Writings (Indianapolis, 2006), 53 [Pt II, proposition 43].

27 M. Stewart, *The Courtier and the Heretic: Leibniz, Spinoza and the Fate of God in the Modern World* (New Haven and London, 2005), esp. 58–60, 65–7.

28 P. Bayle, *Miscellaneous Reflections, occasion'd by the Comet which appear'd in December 1680 . . .* (2 vols., London, 1708 [first French edn 1680]), II, 349–51.

29 J. Overhoff, 'The Theology of Thomas Hobbes's *Leviathan*', *JEH*, 51 (2000), 527–55. For a seminal study of Hobbes and his centrality to theological revision and anticlericalism, see J. A. I. Champion, *The Pillars of Priestcraft Shaken: The Church of England and Its Enemies 1660–1730* (Cambridge, 1992).

30 N. Keene, ' "A two-edged sword": Biblical Criticism and the New Testament Canon in Early Modern England', in Hessayon and Keene (eds.), 94–115, at 104–6, and on Mill, 109. On Laodiceans, see Colossians 4.16. To minimize the embarrassment of this text, the reference is translated in most Bibles as referring to a letter *from* the Laodiceans, though that does not really solve the canonical problem: see comment in E. Schweizer, *The Letter to the Colossians* (London, 1982), 242 and n. 18.

31 P. Almond, 'Adam, Pre-Adamites and Extra-terrestrial Beings in Early Modern Europe', *JRH*, 30 (2006), 163–74, esp. 164, 167; see also R. H. Popkin, *Isaac la Peyrère (1596–1676): His Life, Work and Influence* (Leiden, 1987).

32 Israel, *Radical Enlightenment*, 695–700.

33 M. Martini, SJ, *Sinicae Historiae Decas Prima* (1658), see W. Poole, 'The Genesis Narrative in the Circle of Robert Hooke and Francis Lodwick', in Hessayon and Keene (eds.), 41–57, at 48.

34 Almond, 'Adam, Pre-Adamites and Extra-terrestrial Beings in Early Modern Europe', 163–74.

35 A. Hamilton and F. Richard, *André du Ryer and Oriental Studies in 17th Century France* (Oxford, 2004), 111–12.

36 D. Gange, 'Religion and Science in Late 19th-century British Egyptology', *HJ*, 49 (2006), 1083–1104, at 1090.

37 First published in *The Spectator*, no. 465 (1712). The original text, Ps. 19.1–6, is redolent of the 'Wisdom' literary tradition in the Tanakh (see p. 67): naturally a congenial ethos for Addison.

38 A. Cunningham and O. P. Grell, *The Four Horsemen of the Apocalypse: Religion, War, Famine and Death in Reformation Europe* (Cambridge, 2000), 205, 243.

39 J. de Vries, *The Industrious Revolution: Consumer Behavior and the Household Economy, 1650 to the Present* (Cambridge, 2008), esp. 40–58. A brilliant portrait of the effect on the seventeenth-century Netherlands is S. Schama, *The Embarrassment of Riches: An Interpretation of Dutch Culture in the Golden Age* (London, 1987), esp. Ch. 5.

40 A significant though little-remarked feature of the *Messiah* is the virtually complete absence of Mary the Mother of Jesus from its text. This silence was of course predictable in anti-Catholic Georgian England, and in *Messiah*'s massive popularity with nineteenth-century Protestant Nonconformist choirs Mary would have continued to be something of a problem.

41 P. Ihalainen, *Protestant Nations Redefined: Changing Perceptions of National Identity in the Rhetoric of the English, Dutch and Swedish Public Churches, 1685–1772* (Leiden, 2005), esp. 579–99.

42 G. Ryle, *The Concept of Mind* (London, 1949), 17–24.

43 J. Locke, *An Essay Concerning Human Understanding* (Oxford, 1975; first published 1690), 525, [Bk IV, Ch. 1].

44 D. Hume, 'Of Commerce' (1752), qu. M. Berg, 'In Pursuit of Luxury: Global History and British Consumer Goods in the Eighteenth Century', *PP*, 182 (February 2004), 85–142, at 130.

45 A. Fletcher, *Gender, Sex and Subordination in England 1500–1800* (New Haven and London, 1995), esp. Pt III.

46 On the Societies for the Reformation of Manners, see p. 748. For general discussion, see R. Norton, *Mother Clap's Molly House: The Gay Subculture in England 1700–1830* (London, 1992); T. van der Meer, 'The Persecutions of Sodomites in Early Eighteenth-century Amsterdam: Changing Perceptions of Sodomy', in K. Gerard and G. Hekma (eds.), *The Pursuit of Sodomy: Male Homosexuality in Renaissance and Enlightenment Europe* (Binghamton, 1989), 263–309. It would probably be taking conspiracy theory too far to point out that the dominant political figure of the two nations in that decade, William III, was subject to much gossip about his sexuality: see *ODNB* s.v. William III and II (1650–1702): 'Marriage and Sexuality'.

47 Figures quoted by James D. Tracy, in review of W. Bergsma, *Tussen Gideonsbende en publieke kerk: een studie over gereformeerd Protestantisme in Friesland, 1580–1610* (Hilversum, 1999), in *SCJ*, 32 (2001), 893.

48 P. Crawford, *Women and Religion in England, 1500–1720* (London and New York, 1993), 143.

49 MacCulloch, 167–8, 657–9.

50 P. Matheson, *The Imaginative World of the Reformation* (Edinburgh, 2000), 130.

51 On Mather, P. Bonomi, *Under the Cope of Heaven: Religion, Society and Politics in Colonial America* (New York and Oxford, 1986), 113. Anon. [R. Allestree], *The Ladies Calling* (12th edn, Oxford, 1727; first published 1673), 107, 126, 152.

52 MacCulloch, 609–11.

53 M. Astell, *Some Reflections upon Marriage* (4th edn, London, 1730; first published 1700), Appendix, 139; M. Astell, *A Serious Proposal to the Ladies* (4th edn, London, 1697; first published 1694), 14. I am grateful to Sarah Apetrei for our discussions on these texts.

54 J. Wesley, *Primitive Physick: or an easy and natural Method of curing most Diseases* (London, 1747), Preface, ix–x, xviii. See J. Cule, 'The Rev. John Wesley M.A. (Oxon.), 1703–1791: "The Naked Empiricist" and Orthodox Medicine', *Journal of the History of Medicine and Allied Sciences*, 45 (1990), 41–63.

55 C. McC. Weis and F. Pottle (eds.), *Boswell in Extremes 1776–8* (London, 1971), 12–13.

56 I. Rivers, 'Responses to Hume on Religion by Anglicans and Dissenters', *JEH*, 52 (2001) 675–95; quotation from the Rev. Joseph Priestley at 695.

57 A fine treatment of the Catholic Enlightenment and eighteenth-century efforts at Church reform is O. Chadwick, *The Popes and European Revolution* (Oxford, 1981), Ch. 6.

58 Ibid., 247–8, 256.

59 B. Chedozeau, *Choeur clos, choeur ouvert: de l'église médiévale à l'église tridentine (France, XVIe–XVIIIe siècle)* (Paris, 1998).

60 J. Swann, 'Disgrace without Dishonour: The Internal Exile of French Magistrates in the Eighteenth century', *PP*, 195 (May 2007), 87–126, at 99.

61 D. G. Thompson, *A Modern Persecution: Breton Jesuits under the Suppression of 1762–1814* (Oxford, 1999), and D. Van Kley, *The Jansenists and the Expulsion of the Jesuits from France, 1757–1765* (New Haven and London, 1975).

62 J. McManners, *Church and Society in Eighteenth-century France* (2 vols., Oxford, 1998), II, 314, 320–23, 337–41.

63 An engaging recent study is R. Pearson, *Voltaire Almighty: A Life in Pursuit of Freedom* (London, 2005): see esp. 404–5.

64 F. Bessire, *La Bible dans la correspondance de Voltaire* (Oxford, 1999), esp. 10–13, 226–8.

65 P. Blom, *Encyclopédie: The Triumph of Reason in an Unreasonable Age* (London, 2004), esp. 54, 94–8, 143, 151–4. For a view of Mallet treating him as an ultra-conservative accepted by the editors of the *Encyclopédie* to save themselves from ecclesiastical

repression, see W. E. Rex, ' "Arche de Noé" and Other Religious Articles by Abbé Mallet in the *Encyclopédie*', *Eighteenth-Century Studies*, 9 (1976), 333–52.

66 J.-J. Rousseau, ed. M. Cranston, *The Social Contract* [*Contrat social ou Principes du droit politique*] (London, 1968; originally published 1763), 64 [Bk 1, Ch. 7].

67 D. Edmonds and J. Eidenow, *Rousseau's Dog: Two Great Thinkers at War in the Age of Enlightenment* (London, 2006), esp. 221–3, 335–42.

68 Text in J. Schmidt (ed.), *What is Enlightenment? Eighteenth-century Answers and Twentieth-century Questions* (Berkeley, CA, 1996), 58–64, at 58.

69 I. Kant, ed. P. Guyer and A. W. Wood, *Critique of Pure Reason* (Cambridge, 1998), 117 [preface to 2nd edn, 1787].

70 D. G. Steinmetz, *Reformers in the Wings: From Geiler Von Kaysersberg to Theodore Beza* (Oxford, 2001), Ch. 8.

71 An excellent concise account is D. Beales, *Prosperity and Plunder: European Catholic Monasteries in the Age of Revolution, 1650–1815* (Cambridge, 2003), 143–68.

72 Chadwick, *The Popes and European Revolution*, 385–90, and cf. other exceptions mostly in the Protestant British Empire, ibid., 377.

73 Beales, *Prosperity and Plunder*, 210–28.

74 P. Higgonet, 'Terror, Trauma and the "Young Marx" Explanation of Jacobin Politics', *PP*, 191 (May 2006), 121–64, at 155–6.

75 McManners, *Church and Society in Eighteenth-century France*, 698–701, 726–7.

76 Burleigh, 58.

77 D. Andress, *The French Revolution and the People* (London, 2004), esp. 139–41, and for what follows.

78 Burleigh, 87–8, 102–5.

79 An excellent account is still E. E. Y. Hales, *Napoleon and the Pope: The Story of Napoleon and Pius VII* (London, 1961).

80 S. Hazareesingh, *The Saint-Napoleon: Celebrations of Sovereignty in 19th-century France* (Cambridge, MA, and London, 2004), esp. 3–4, 7–11, 179–200, 227–8.

81 P. S. Wells, *Barbarians to Angels: The Dark Ages Reconsidered* (New York and London, 2008), Ch. 4.

82 Beales, *Prosperity and Plunder*, 282–90.

83 For incisive discussion of nationalism, see R. English, *Irish Freedom: The History of Nationalism in Ireland* (Basingstoke and Oxford, 2006), 1–21.

84 Burleigh, 261–3.

85 Ibid., 235–41.

86 Ibid., 247–8.

22: Europe Re-enchanted or Disenchanted?
(1815–1914)

1 N. Atkin and F. Tallett, *Priests, Prelates and People: A History of European Catholicism since 1750* (London, 2003), 91.

2 Duffy, 320. Pius X removed the possibility of this happening again in an election: ibid., 321–2.

3 V. Viaene, 'The Second Sex and the First Estate: The Sisters of St-André between the Bishop of Tournai and Rome, 1850–1886', *JEH*, 59 (2008), 447–74, at 461.

4 B. Hamnet, 'Recent Work in Mexican History', *HJ*, 50 (2007), 747–59, at 757.

5 Viaene, 'The Second Sex and the First Estate', 449.

6 K. Harrison, *Saint Thérèse of Lisieux* (London, 2003), 71–3, 186.

7 D. Blackbourn, *Marpingen: Apparitions of the Virgin Mary in Bismarckian Germany* (Oxford, 1993), 1–57.

8 J. Garnett, 'The Nineteenth Century', in Harries and Mayr-Harting (eds.), 192–217, at 199–201.

9 Blackbourn, *Marpingen*, esp. 278–81, 400–401, 405. On the *Kulturkampf*, see also Ch. 11.

10 Among the most celebrated are Anna Katherina Emmerich (from north-west Germany, stigmata from 1813), Maria Dominica Lazzari (from the Tyrol, stigmata 1835), Maria de

Moerl or von Merl (also from the Tyrol, stigmata 1839) and Louise Lateau (from Belgium, stigmata 1868). After Lateau, there was a long gap till the time of the celebrated Italian Francesco Forgione or Padre Pio (1887–1968).

11 M. A. Sells, *The Bridge Betrayed: Religion and Genocide in Bosnia* (Berkeley and Los Angeles, 1996), 98–9, 105–13.

12 J. de Maistre, *Du Pape, Discours prelim*, 24 and 7–8: qu. F. Oakley, *The Conciliarist Tradition: Constitutionalism in the Catholic Church, 1300–1870* (Oxford, 2003), 202; partly my translation.

13 O. Chadwick, *A History of the Popes 1830–1914* (Oxford, 1998), 174–6.

14 It should be pointed out that authoritarian-minded outsiders to Freemasonry of whatever political and religious complexion have found the Masons' clannishness and secretiveness threatening: nineteenth-century American Protestantism as much as Nazism and State Communism. That is what makes Freemasonry's survival in Castro's Cuba so remarkable.

15 Atkin and Tallett, *Priests, Prelates and People*, 136.

16 Handy, 121–4.

17 E. Larkin, *The Pastoral Role of the Roman Catholic Church in Pre-Famine Ireland, 1750–1850* (Dublin and Washington, DC, 2006), 5–6, 259–69. On Catholic emancipation in Britain, see pp. 838–9.

18 Hope, 316–21.

19 Burleigh, 137; Viaene, 'The Second Sex and the First Estate', esp. at 450.

20 S. Scholz, *Der deutsche Katholizismus und Polen (1830–1849): Identitätsbildung zwischen konfessioneller Solidarität und antirevolutionärer Abgrenzung* (Osnabrück, 2005), 154–63, 240–49.

21 By 1876, Our Lady had decided to clarify her syntax, and told the Marpingen visionaries (again in a local dialect), 'I am the Immaculately Conceived': Blackbourn, *Marpingen*, 2.

22 T. Taylor, ' "So many extraordinary things to tell": Letters from Lourdes, 1858', *JEH*, 46 (1995), 457–81, at 464, 472–7.

23 Atkin and Tallett, *Priests, Prelates and People*, 136–9.

24 A point eloquently made by Oakley, *The Conciliarist Tradition*, 16–19, 195.

25 B. Brennan, 'Visiting "Peter in Chains": French Pilgrimage to Rome, 1873–93', *JEH*, 51 (2000), 741–65, at 759–60. On the Pope and Bruno, see Chadwick, *A History of the Popes 1830–1914*, 303.

26 The main exception was the formidable Brooke Foss Westcott, who as Bishop of Durham successfully mediated a long-running Durham miners' dispute in 1892.

27 R. Harris, 'The Assumptionists and the Dreyfus Affair', *PP*, 194 (February 2007), 175–212, esp. 177, 192.

28 A useful introduction is J. McManners, *Church and State in France 1870–1914* (London, 1972), esp. Ch. 6.

29 Garnett, 'The Nineteenth Century', 205, 209 and Fig. 8 (217). Two versions are in St Paul's Cathedral, London and Keble College Chapel, Oxford.

30 S. Mumm, ' "A peril to the Bench of Bishops": Sisterhoods and Episcopal Authority in the Church of England, 1845–1908', *JEH*, 59 (2008), 62–78.

31 J. Hopkins, *A Woman to Deliver Her People: Joanna Southcott and English Millenarianism in an Era of Revolution* (Austin, 1982), esp. 272–3. We await the full results of the major research project being conducted on the Panacea Society of Bedford by Christopher Rowland and Jane Shaw.

32 C. G. Flegg, *'Gathered under Apostles': A Study of the Catholic Apostolic Church* (Oxford, 1992), 41–51. For the tragicomic story of a later English visionary, Mary Ann Girling, see P. Hoare, *England's Lost Eden/Lost Edens: Adventures in a Victorian Utopia* (London, 2005), and for several examples of female prophetic founders of Churches in the USA, see Ch. 23.

33 T. Larsen, ' "How many sisters make a brotherhood?" A Case Study in Gender and Ecclesiology in Early 19th-century English Dissent', *JEH*, 49 (1998), 282–92.

34 H. Mathers, 'The Evangelical Spirituality of a Victorian Feminist: Josephine Butler, 1828–1906', *JEH*, 52 (2001), 282–312, at 299, 302.

35 T. A. Howard, *Protestant Theology and the Making of the Modern German University* (Oxford, 2006), 143, 151–4.

36 Ibid., 166–72.

37 G. Spiegler, *The Eternal Covenant* (New York, 1967), 128, qu. J. Macquarrie, *Thinking about God* (London, 1975), 161.

38 B. A. Gerrish, *A Prince of the Church: Schleiermacher and the Beginnings of Modern Theology* (London, 1984), 39.

39 G. W. F. Hegel, ed. E. Moldenhauer and K. M. Michel, *Werke* (20 vols., Frankfurt am Main, 1969–71), XVI, 192, qu. P. Kennedy, *A Modern Introduction to Theology: New Questions for Old Beliefs* (London, 2006), 99.

40 L. Feuerbach, *The Essence of Christianity* (London, 1881; first published 1841), 12. The English translation, like that of Strauss's *Leben Jesu*, was by the freethinking Christian Mary Anne or Marian Evans (who used the pen name George Eliot in her novels).

41 J. Garff, *Søren Kierkegaard: A Biography* (Princeton, 2005), esp. 5–6, 102–3, 134–6, 308–16, 517–19.

42 S. Kierkegaard, ed. H. V. and E. H. Hong, *The Moment, and Late Writings* (Princeton, 1998; first published 1855), 206 [*The Moment*, no. 6].

43 S. Kierkegaard, tr. A. Hannay, *Fear and Trembling* (London, 2005; originally published pseudonymously 1843), 150 [Epilogue].

44 J. A. Moses, 'Dietrich Bonhoeffer's Repudiation of Protestant German War Theology', *JRH*, 30 (2006), 354–70, esp. 356.

45 W. Walsh, *The Secret History of the Oxford Movement* (5th edn, London, 1899), 362.

46 Hope, 340–43.

47 The monumental German Lutheran Church of the Redeemer, built between 1893 and 1898 on a site acquired by the Prussian Crown Prince in 1869 very near the Church of the Holy Sepulchre, was another eventual outcome of German religious fascination with the Holy Land. It is a notably assertive element on the Jerusalem skyline, not to that skyline's enhancement.

48 N. M. Railton, *No North Sea: The Anglo-German Evangelical Network in the Middle of the Nineteenth Century* (Leiden, 2000), esp. Ch. 8. The second Bishop of Jerusalem, Samuel Gobat, was also an enthusiastic writer on apocalyptic matters.

49 R. J. Ross, *The Failure of Bismarck's Kulturkampf: Catholicism and State Power in Imperial Germany, 1871–1887* (Washington, DC, 1998), esp. 180–90.

50 Burleigh, 263–7, and see useful summary discussion by H. McLeod in *JEH*, 54 (2003), 787–9 of L. Hölscher et al. (eds.), *Datenatlas zur religiösen Geographie im protestantischen Deutschland. Von der Mitte des 19. Jahrhunderts bis zum Zweiten Weltkrieg* (4 vols., Berlin and New York, 2001).

51 From 1873 through a personal choice of Queen Victoria, British monarchs and their family have acted as if they are members of the Church of Scotland when in Scotland, to the chagrin of many Anglican High Churchmen: on the origins of this, see O. Chadwick, 'The Sacrament at Crathie, 1873', in S. J. Brown and G. Newlands (eds.), *Scottish Christianity in the Modern World* (Edinburgh, 2000), 177–96.

52 A good treatment of the early connections is G. Johnson, 'British Social Democracy and Religion, 1881–1911', *JEH*, 51 (2000), 94–115.

53 R. Strong, *Anglicanism and the British Empire c. 1700–1850* (Oxford, 2007), 118–19, 194–7, 211. On the post-1818 'Commissioners' Churches', M. H. Port, *Six Hundred New Churches: The Church Building Commission 1818–1856* (rev. edn, Reading, 2006).

54 Extracts in Bettenson (ed.), 316–18.

55 A good introduction to Newman is I. Ker and T. Merrigan (eds.), *The Cambridge Companion to John Henry Newman* (Cambridge, 2009).

56 On the Non-Jurors, see pp. 734–5. A fine study of Non-Juror thought is C. D. A. Leighton, 'The Non-Jurors and Their History', *JRH*, 23 (2005), 241–57. The definitive study of the older High Church movement is P. Nockles, *The Oxford Movement in Context: Anglican High Churchmanship, 1760–1857* (Cambridge, 1994).

57 G. Faber, *Oxford Apostles: A Character Study of the Oxford Movement* (London, 1933) remains a sardonic masterpiece in its account of the Tractarians.

58 On the Thirty-Nine Articles, see p. 649: Newman's intellectual gymnastics in Tract XC

can be savoured in A. O. J. Cockshut, *Religious Controversies of the Nineteenth Century: Selected Documents* (London, 1966), 74–90. See Newman's protestations to his friend E. B. Pusey and to Bishop Bagot of Oxford, C. S. Dessain et al. (eds.), *Letters and Diaries of John Henry Newman* (31 vols., Oxford, 1968–2006), VIII, 97, 100.

59 J. H. Newman, ed. M. J. Svaglic, *Apologia Pro Vita Sua* (Oxford, 1967; first published 1864), 136. On Newman's sneers, tantamount to anti-Semitism, both in *Apologia* and in his correspondence at the time of the Jerusalem furore, see ibid., 133, and Dessain et al. (eds.), *Letters and Diaries of John Henry Newman*, VIII, 295, and cf. ibid., 299, 307, 314, 340.

60 Newman, ed. Svaglic, *Apologia Pro Vita Sua*, 133–5, 108. In 1841, two years later than the Monophysite insight, he was still publicly assuring Bishop Bagot of his sense of 'inestimable privilege' in being a member of the Church of England: Dessain et al. (eds.), *Letters and Diaries of John Henry Newman*, VIII, 140. Unaccountably, this assurance was not quoted in the *Apologia*.

61 A fine summary of the Gorham business is O. Chadwick, *The Victorian Church* (2 vols., 2nd edn, London, 1970–72), I, 250–71. For a previous messy case of 1844 involving Bishop Phillpotts which led to a schism in the other direction and the creation of a small Evangelical 'Free Church of England', see G. Carter, 'The Case of the Reverend James Shore', *JEH*, 47 (1996), 478–505.

62 On Manning and the London Dock Strike of 1889, see p. 826.

63 Ahlstrom, 625.

64 A fine study is R. Mullin, 'Finding a Space, Defining a Voice: John Henry Hobart and the Americanization of Anglicanism', in M. Dutton and P. Gray (eds.), *One Lord, One Faith, One Baptism: Studies in Christian Ecclesiology* (Grand Rapids, 2006), 129–43.

65 Breward, 101–2.

66 On Bishop Colenso's other unconventional views, see pp. 883–4.

67 J. Kent, *Holding the Fort: Studies in Victorian Revivalism* (London, 1978), Ch. 8.

68 An empathetic though entertainingly clear-sighted study of the latter extreme and the permeable membrane between Rome and Anglo-Catholicism is M. Yelton, *Anglican Papalism: An Illustrated History 1900–1960* (Norwich, 2005).

69 The classic study of this still often hotly denied nexus is D. Hilliard, 'UnEnglish and Unmanly: Anglo-Catholicism and Homosexuality', *Victorian Studies*, 25 (1982), 181–210.

70 P. Walters, 'Eastern Europe since the Fifteenth Century', in Hastings (ed.), 282–327, at 305.

71 R. D. Crews, *For Prophet and Tsar: Islam and Empire in Russia and Central Asia* (Cambridge, MA, and London, 2006), esp. 33–4, 52–60, 67–71. On Peter the Great and confession, see p. 543.

72 Burleigh, 119–21.

73 H. Ben-Itto, *The Lie That Wouldn't Die: 'The Protocols of the Elders of Zion'* (London, 2005), esp. 21, 77–83, 125–6, 160.

74 Snyder, 25, 45.

75 D. Beer, 'Russia in the Age of War and Revolution, 1880–1914', *HJ*, 47 (2004), 1055–68, at 1056–7.

76 G. L. Freeze, 'Russian Orthodoxy: Church, People and Politics in Imperial Russia', in D. Lieven (ed.), *The Cambridge History of Russia: II: Imperial Russia, 1689–1917* (Cambridge, 2006), 284–305, at 298–9.

77 Walters, 'Eastern Europe since the Fifteenth Century', 299–300.

78 L. Manchester, *Holy Fathers, Secular Sons: Clergy, Intelligentsia and the Modern Self in Revolutionary Russia* (DeKalb, IL, 2008), esp. Chs. 3, 4.

79 S. Dixon, 'The Russian Orthodox Church in Imperial Russia 1721–1917', in Angold (ed.), 325–47, at 339.

80 Burleigh, 299–305.

81 J. Meyendorff, *Byzantium and the Rise of Russia: A Study of Byzantino-Russian Relations in the 14th Century* (Cambridge, 1981), 25.

82 L. Murianka, 'Aleksei Khomiakov: A Study of the Interplay of Piety and Theology', in V. Tsurikov (ed.), *A. S. Khomiakov: Poet, Philosopher, Theologian* (Jordanville, NY,

2004), 20–37, at 34, and see also P. Valliere, 'The Modernity of Khomiakov', ibid., 129–44.

83 See a fine study of St Petersburg parishes, J. Hedda, *His Kingdom Come: Orthodox Pastorship and Social Activism in Revolutionary Russia* (DeKalb, IL, 2008), esp. 145–52, and Ch. 8.

84 P. M. Kitromilides, 'Orthodoxy and the West: Reformation to Enlightenment', in Angold (ed.), 187–209, at 205.

85 Burleigh, 165–8.

86 Walters, 'Eastern Europe since the Fifteenth Century', 305–6; P. M. Kitromilides, 'The Legacy of the French Revolution', in Angold (ed.), 229–75, at 242.

87 C. Finkel, *Osman's Dream: The Story of the Ottoman Empire 1300–1923* (London, 2005), 492–9.

88 N. Doumanis, 'Durable Empire: State Virtuosity and Social Accommodation in the Ottoman Mediterranean', *HJ*, 49 (2006), 953–66, at 963–4; B. Clark, *Twice a Stranger: How Mass Expulsion Forged Modern Greece and Turkey* (London, 2006), 7.

89 For the Kurdish massacres, Baumer, 255–6; on Urfa and other 1890s massacres, P. Balakian, *The Burning Tigris: The Armenian Genocide* (London, 2004), Chs. 1–10 and esp. 113–15.

90 From around 1800, there was something of an exception to this general attitude among those interested in astronomy: R. Holmes, *The Age of Wonder: How the Romantic Generation Discovered the Beauty and Terror of Science* (London, 2008), esp. 163.

91 M. J. S. Rudwick, *Bursting the Limits of Time: The Reconstruction of Geohistory in the Age of Revolution* (Chicago and London, 2005), esp. 353–88, 403–15.

92 J. A. Secord, *Victorian Sensation: The Extraordinary Publication, Reception and Secret Authorship of* Vestiges of the Natural History of Creation (Chicago and London, 2001), 85, 96. C. Darwin, *On the Origin of Species by Means of Natural Selection . . .* (London, 1902; original publication 1859), 441.

93 C. Darwin, *The Descent of Man, and Selection in Relation to Sex* (2 vols., London, 1871), II, 388, qu. A. Desmond and J. Moore, *Darwin's Sacred Cause: Race, Slavery and the Quest for Human Origins* (London, 2009), 367: Desmond and Moore provide an interesting study of Darwin as an enthusiastic abolitionist and, in Ch. 1, of his family's long-standing involvement in the cause.

94 D. N. Livingstone and R. A. Wells, *Ulster-American Religion: Episodes in the History of a Cultural Connection* (Notre Dame, IN, 1999), 49.

95 Chadwick, *The Victorian Church*, II, 23. For Chadwick's sensitive exploration of the contemporary impact of Darwin and of scientific discovery, see also O. Chadwick, *The Secularization of the European Mind in the Nineteenth Century* (Cambridge, 1975), 161–88.

96 All previous imperfect English editions of this work, which was much revised in German in 1913, are superseded by A. Schweitzer, ed. J. Bowden, *The Quest of the Historical Jesus* (London, 2000).

97 D. Gange, 'Religion and Science in Late Nineteenth-century British Egyptology', *HJ*, 49 (2006), 1083–104.

98 Memorandum to Ministerialdirektor Althoff, 1888, qu. W. H. C. Frend, 'Church Historians of the Early Twentieth Century: Adolf von Harnack (1851–1930)', *JEH*, 52 (2001), 83–102, at 91.

99 Chadwick, *The Secularization of the European Mind in the Nineteenth Century*, Pt II.

100 M. Mack, 'The Savage Science: Sigmund Freud, Psychoanalysis, and the History of Religion', *JRH*, 30 (2006), 331–53.

101 M. W. Graham, ' "The Enchanter's Wand": Charles Darwin, Foreign Missions, and the Voyage of H.M.S. Beagle', *JRH*, 31 (2007), 131–50, at 131.

102 J. Browne, *Charles Darwin: The Power of Place* (London, 2002), 484–5, 497.

103 Ibid., 403.

104 M. Bevir, 'Annie Besant's Quest for Truth: Christianity, Secularism and New Age Thought', *JEH*, 50 (1999), 62–93, esp. 62–3, 83–92.

105 Browne, *Charles Darwin*, 403–6. See also P. Lamont, 'Spiritualism and a Mid-Victorian Crisis of Evidence', *HJ*, 47 (2004), 897–920.

106 D. Cupitt, *The Sea of Faith: Christianity in Change* (London, 1984), 204–6.

107 Johann von Rist was the chief author of this hymn, which announces in v. 2 '*Gott selbst ist tot*' (bowdlerized in the customary English translation). 'The Consummate Religion' (1827), G. W. F. Hegel, ed. P. C. Hodgson et al., *Lectures on the Philosophy of Religion* (Berkeley, Los Angeles and London, 1988), 468 and n. I am very grateful to Philip Kennedy for drawing my attention to this connection.

108 F. Nietzsche, *Genealogy of Morals*, III, 27, qu. R. Schacht, *Nietzsche, Genealogy, Morality: Essays on Nietzsche's Genealogy of Morals* (Berkeley, CA, 1994), 420.

109 P. Ricoeur, *Freud and Philosophy* (New Haven and London, 1970), 32–6; cf. Kennedy, *A Modern Introduction to Theology*, 98.

23: To Make the World Protestant
(1700–1914)

1 J. Julian, *A Dictionary of Hymnology* (London, 1892), 55, comments austerely on 'Amazing Grace' that 'It is far from being a good example of Newton's work.'

2 J. Newton, *An authentic narrative of some remarkable and interesting particulars in the life of ********* communicated in a series of letters* (9th edn, London, 1799; first published 1764), 114.

3 J. Walvin, *The Trader, the Owner, the Slave: Parallel Lives in the Age of Slavery* (London, 2007), 5, 26–7, 51, 66–7, 94–5 (quotation). On Newton's nuanced Calvinism, see B. Hindmarsh, *John Newton and the English Evangelical Tradition between the Conversions of Wesley and Wilberforce* (Oxford, 1996), 119–68.

4 J. A. Harrill, *Slaves in the New Testament: Literary, Social and Moral Dimensions* (Minneapolis, 2006), and see pp. 114–16.

5 Genesis 9.20–27.

6 The allegory may not seem obvious, but Noah's nakedness represents Christ's helplessness, Ham the hypocrisy of false Christians, and Shem and Japheth the Jews and Greeks who respectively receive the Gospel. Cf. H. Bettenson and D. Knowles (eds.), *Augustine: Concerning the City of God against the Pagans* (London, 1967), 650–53 [XVI, 2].

7 D. M. Goldenberg, *The Curse of Ham: Race and Slavery in Early Judaism, Christianity and Islam* (Princeton and Oxford, 2003), 168–77. On the allegorical use of the drunkenness of Noah in soteriology, see R. Viladesau, *The Beauty of the Cross: The Passion of Christ in Theology and the Arts, from the Catacombs to the Eve of the Renaissance* (New York and Oxford, 2006), 116. A fine general survey is C. Kidd, *The Forging of Races: Race and Scripture in the Protestant Atlantic World, 1600–2000* (Cambridge, 2006).

8 D. B. Davis, *Inhuman Bondage: The Rise and Fall of Slavery in the New World* (Oxford, 2006), 55.

9 Goldenberg, *The Curse of Ham*, 178–82. The *Peshitta* Old Testament may have been written by Jews (see p. 178): it is a sad irony in the history of racism if both these motifs in justifying slavery should have originated with Jews.

10 Harrill, *Slaves in the New Testament*, 191.

11 E. Laplante, *Salem Witch Judge: The Life and Repentance of Samuel Sewall* (New York, 2007), 225–30.

12 On the *Encylopédie*, see Koschorke et al. (eds.), 179.

13 N. A. M. Rodger, 'Queen Elizabeth and the Myth of Sea-power in English History', *TRHS*, 6th ser., 14 (2004), 153–74, at 169. A fine study of Benezet is M. Jackson, *Let This Voice Be Heard: Anthony Benezet, Father of Atlantic Abolitionism* (Philadelphia, 2009).

14 S. M. Wise, *Though the Heavens May Fall: The Landmark Trial that Led to the End of Human Slavery* (London, 2006), esp. 15–16, 128, 135–6, 143, 151–2, 156, 166, 172, 180, 182.

15 W. Hague, *Wilberforce: The Life of the Great Anti-Slave Trade Campaigner* (London, 2007), 488–90, 502–4.

16 On Socinians, see p. 642.

17 *The Speeches of the Right Honourable Charles James Fox in the House of Commons* (London, 1853), 367–8: 19 April 1791. On the radical John Thelwall's leading role in abolition, see F. Felsenstein, 'Liberty Men', *TLS*, 8 September 2006.

18 W. E. H. Lecky, *A History of European Morals from Augustus to Charlemagne* (London, 1869), I, 161. A good review of the literature on abolition and its economic context is D. Richardson, 'Agency, Ideology and Violence in the History of Transatlantic Slavery', *HJ*, 50 (2007), 971–89.

19 Walvin, *The Trader, the Owner, the Slave*, 233–6. There is some doubt about Equiano's actual origins and hence the real autobiographical character of his account of his early days in West Africa – he may have been born in Carolina: ibid., 250–51.

20 Quotation: Hastings, 284. On Peters, S. Schama, *Rough Crossings: Britain, the Slaves and the American Revolution* (London, 2005), 326–30, 332–8, 377–83.

21 Sundkler and Steed, 179–92.

22 Hastings, 248.

23 D. R. Peterson, 'Culture and Chronology in African History', *HJ*, 50 (2007), 483–97, at 491.

24 I. Copland, 'Christianity as an Arm of Empire: The Ambiguous Case of India under the Company, c. 1813–1858', *HJ*, 49 (2006), 1025–54, at 1026.

25 J. Hopkins, *A Woman to Deliver Her People: Joanna Southcott and English Millenarianism in an Era of Revolution* (Austin, 1982), 195–7.

26 R. Brown, 'Victorian Anglican Evangelicalism: The Radical Legacy of Edward Irving', *JEH*, 58 (2007), 675–704, at 676, 678. One example of these meetings was the Albury conferences: see p. 829.

27 See, e.g., B. Stanley, *The Bible and the Flag: Protestant Missions and British Imperialism in the Nineteenth and Twentieth Centuries* (Leicester, 1990), 58–9; A. Porter, *Religion versus Empire? British Protestant Missionaries and Overseas Expansion, 1700–1914* (Manchester, 2004), esp. 324, 330.

28 For an excellent example of this clash in the future Nigeria, see J. H. Darch, 'The Church Missionary Society and the Governors of Lagos, 1862–72', *JEH*, 52 (2001), 313–33, esp. at 331.

29 S. Sivasundaram, *Nature and the Godly Empire: Science and Evangelical Mission in the Pacific, 1795–1850* (Cambridge, 2005), esp. 38–9, 99–102, 150–54.

30 The young Joseph Banks was among those enjoying such (heterosexual) freedom on his voyaging in the South Seas: R. Holmes, *The Age of Wonder: How the Romantic Generation Discovered the Beauty and Terror of Science* (London, 2008), Ch. 1.

31 R. Lansdown, 'Dark Parts: The Voyage of the *Duff*, 1796–1798', *TLS*, 27 August 2004, 12–13.

32 Breward, 31, 236.

33 Ibid., 32–5.

34 Ibid., 45–6.

35 L. S. Rickard, *Tamihana the Kingmaker* (Wellington and Auckland, 1963), 65, 72–3, and quotation at 118–19 (my italics).

36 D. Hilliard, 'Australasia and the Pacific', in Hastings (ed.), 508–35, at 517–18.

37 S. Morgan, ' "Upon past Ebenezers we build our Jehovah-Jireh": The Vision of the Australian Aborigines' Mission and Its Heritage in the China Inland Mission', *JRH*, 31 (2007), 169–84, at 179–81; Hilliard, 'Australasia and the Pacific', 511; Breward, 265–7.

38 Ibid., 54–9.

39 C. A. Bayly, *The Birth of the Modern World 1780–1914: Global Connections and Comparisons* (Oxford, 2004), 77, 127, 142, 338, 471.

40 Hastings, 188–94.

41 D. Crawford, *Thinking Black: 22 Years without a Break, in the Long Grass of Central Africa* (London, 1912), 55, qu. M. S. Sweetnam, 'Dan Crawford, *Thinking Black*, and the Challenge of a Missionary Canon', *JEH*, 58 (2007), 705–25, at 721; italics in the original. On the Brethren, see pp. 911–12.

42 Exodus 22.18.

43 Hastings, 329–30. The term 'African-initiated Churches' is one way of unpacking the acronym 'AIC', which can have several other interpretations – African Independent Churches, African Indigenous Churches, African Instituted Churches.

44 Sundkler and Steed, 354–5.

45 Hastings, 313–15, 320–21.

46 For the far-reaching row stirred by Colenso's views on the Bible, see O. Chadwick, *The Victorian Church* (2 vols., 2nd edn, London, 1970–72), II, 90–97. Colenso's endearingly terrier-like approach to biblical criticism can be sampled in A. O. J. Cockshut, *Religious Controversies of the Nineteenth Century: Selected Documents* (London, 1966), 217–40.

47 Hastings, 313–15, 319.

48 Sundkler and Steed, 190.

49 Hastings, 313–15, 318 (quotation from Colenso), 297.

50 Sundkler and Steed, 232. On Yoruba religious culture, see J. D. Y. Peel, *Religious Encounter and the Making of the Yoruba* (Bloomington, 2000), esp. 121–2, 213–14, 275–7, 286–9, 295–7.

51 A remnant persisted in independence as 'the Church of England in South Africa', which ironically has emphasized its Evangelical character, and hence its antipathy for what it perceives as dangerous liberalism in the mainstream Anglicanism of South Africa; it has allied with similar movements elsewhere in twentieth-century Anglicanism (see pp. 1008–10).

52 Peel, *Religious Encounter and the Making of the Yoruba*, 284.

53 M. Vaughan, 'Africa and the Birth of the Modern World', *TRHS*, 6th ser., 16 (2006), 143–62, at 148.

54 P. R. McKenzie, *Inter-religious Encounters in West Africa: Samuel Ajayi Crowther's Attitude to African Traditional Religion and Islam* (Leicester, 1976), 37, 84–5. One eminent (and male) Nigerian historian accuses Crowther of pronouncing 'irrationally' on polygamy at Lambeth and misleading his fellow bishops: E. A. Ayandele, *The Missionary Impact on Modern Nigeria 1842–1914: A Political and Social Analysis* (London, 1966), 206.

55 Ibid., 213. Among other commemorations, Crowther is depicted in stained glass in the unlikely setting of the episcopal chapel of Bishop Auckland Castle in County Durham, England; I am grateful to Judith Maltby for bringing this to my notice.

56 Hastings, 392–3.

57 Koschorke et al. (eds.), 201–2.

58 Peterson, 'Culture and Chronology in African History', 496.

59 Koschorke et al. (eds.), 198–200.

60 Sundkler and Steed, 502–9.

61 Hastings, 443–7, and on the staff, ibid., 535; Sundkler and Steed, 197–201. The gourd rattles and their power are so integral to Harrist Churches that a scheme of union between them and the British Pentecostal Apostolic Church in 1938 foundered on the British representative's insistence that gourd rattles should be replaced by tambourines: Anderson, 116.

62 C. G. Baëta, *Prophetism in Ghana: A Study of Some 'Spiritual' Churches* (2nd edn, Achimota, 2004), Ch. 2. I must thank the Church of the Twelve Apostles for their warm and courteous welcome to me in Accra.

63 Hastings, 385–6.

64 Sundkler and Steed, 358.

65 Ibid., 450, 559–61.

66 P. D. Sedra, 'John Lieder and His Mission in Egypt: The Evangelical Ethos at Work among Nineteenth-century Copts', *JRH*, 28 (2004), 219–39.

67 Hastings, 229–34; P. Marsden, *The Barefoot Emperor: An Ethiopian Tragedy* (London, 2007).

68 Sundkler and Steed, 163–4.

69 Ibid., 391, 407–8. There is competition for the honour of being the earliest 'Ethiopian' founder: see Koschorke et al. (eds.), 219–20.

70 Binns, 14; Koschorke et al. (eds.), 226–7.

71 'Back to the Land or Nationalism in Religion', *African Church Chronicle*, October–December 1935, 4f., qu. Koschorke et al. (eds.), 235–6.

72 R. Strong, *Anglicanism and the British Empire c. 1700–1850* (Oxford, 2007), 15–16.

73 Copland, 'Christianity as an Arm of Empire', 1031–3.

74 H. V. Bowen, *The Business of Empire: The East India Company and Imperial Britain, 1756–1833* (Cambridge, 2005), 5.

75 Copland, 'Christianity as an Arm of Empire', 1037, 1042–4.

76 W. Dalrymple, *The Last Mughal: The Fall of a Dynasty, Delhi, 1857* (London, 2006), 80–82, 229, 267, 295.

77 Copland, 'Christianity as an Arm of Empire': qu. at 1045.

78 G. Beckerlegge, 'The Hindu Renaissance and Notions of Universal Religion', in Wolffe (ed.), 129–60, at 134–8. Lewins Mead Unitarian Chapel in Bristol is now no longer used for worship, but the plaque remains as part of an admirably careful conversion to commercial office space.

79 On positivism and Hinduism, see Bayly, *The Birth of the Modern World 1780–1914*, 308.

80 R. G. Tiedemann, 'China and Its Neighbours', in Hastings (ed.), 369–415, at 392.

81 J. D. Spence, *God's Chinese Son: The Taiping Heavenly Kingdom of Hong Xiuquan* (London, 1996), esp. 30–32, 76–7, 115–16, 160–61.

82 J. Peires, *The Dead Will Arise: Nongqawuse and the Great Xhosa Cattle Killing Movement of 1856–57* (Johannesburg, 1989), esp. 124–38.

83 Spence, *God's Chinese Son*, esp. 141–2, 168–9, 173, 274–7, 280–81, 287, 330 (quotation).

84 E. Reinders, *Borrowed Gods and Foreign Bodies: Christian Missionaries Imagine Chinese Religion* (Berkeley and London, 2004), esp. 71–8, 109–16, 159, 161, 166, 169.

85 D. Cheung, *Christianity in Modern China: The Making of the First Native Protestant Church* (Leiden, 2004), esp. 55, 309–49.

86 R. A. Semple, *Missionary Women: Gender, Professionalism and the Victorian Idea of Christian Mission* (Woodbridge, 2005), 154–89.

87 Ibid., 187.

88 J. Cox, *The British Missionary Enterprise since 1700* (New York and London, 2008), 184, 206–7.

89 Bayly, *The Birth of the Modern World 1780–1914*, 319.

90 On what follows, see A. J. Finch, 'A Persecuted Church: Roman Catholicism in Early Nineteenth-century Korea', *JEH*, 51 (2000), 556–80, and see also A. J. Finch, 'The Pursuit of Martyrdom in the Catholic Church in Korea before 1866', *JEH*, 60 (2009), 95–118.

91 J.-K. Choi, *The Origin of the Roman Catholic Church in Korea: An Examination of Popular and Governmental Responses to Catholic Missions in the Late Chosôn Dynasty* (Cheltenham, 2006), esp. 25–6, 62–89, and see the genealogies at 364–70.

92 Ibid., 107 (directive of 1785).

93 Finch, 'A Persecuted Church', 568.

94 Handy, 145.

95 Statistics in M. A. Noll, ' "Christian America" and "Christian Canada" ', in Gilley and Stanley (eds.), 359–80, at 359. A lively discussion of the spirit of commerce in modern American religion is J. Micklethwait and A. Wooldridge, *God is Back: How the Global Revival of Faith is Changing the World* (London, 2009), 170–91.

96 C. Colton, *A Lecture on the Railroad to the Pacific* (New York, 1850), 5, qu. James D. Bratt, 'From Revivalism to Anti-revivalism to Whig Politics: The Strange Career of Calvin Colton', *JEH*, 52 (2001), 63–82, at 82.

97 The Rogerenes, a Seventh-Day Baptist sect, provide a minor exception. Founded in Connecticut in 1674 by John Rogers, they lasted less than a century: Handy, 48. On Catholicism, ibid., 197.

98 On Evangelical squirming about the miracle of Cana, see P. J. Gomes, *The Good Book: Reading the Bible with Mind and Heart* (New York, 1996), 78–83. On Prohibition, see pp. 962–3.

99 Handy, 166.

100 Ahlstrom, 479–81. On the origins of modern vegetarianism in radical Lancashire Dissent, see S. J. Calvert, 'A Taste of Eden: Modern Christianity and Vegetarianism', *JEH*, 58 (2007), 462–81.

101 Adventists naturally enough are infuriated to be reminded of this theological ancestry for Koresh's group, but the intellectual genealogy and the descent of institutional connections are undeniable. See K. G. C. Newport, *The Branch Davidians of Waco* (Oxford, 2006), esp. 11–12, 25–46, 204, 216–21, 325–6.

102 A balanced and sympathetic summary account of Mormon origins and development is provided by Ahlstrom, 501–9.

103 On Smith and Freemasonry, see D. Davies, 'Mormon History, Text, Colour, and Rites', *JRH*, 31 (2007), 305–15, at 312–14. On his possible eye problems, see F. M. Brodie, *No Man Knows My History: The Life of Joseph Smith* (New York, 1945), 405–6. For a scholarly biography from within the Mormon community, see R. L. Bushman, *Joseph Smith and the Beginnings of Mormonism* (Urbana and Chicago, 1984).

104 For a sympathetic account of the Book of Mormon, ibid., Ch. 4.

105 Brodie, *No Man Knows My History*, 67.

106 M. R. Werner, *Brigham Young* (New York, 1925), 136, 350, 195; Brodie, *No Man Knows My History*, 399.

107 For a highly coloured but circumstantial account of modern polygamous Mormon sectarianism, see J. Krakauer, *Under the Banner of Heaven: A Story of Violent Faith* (London, 2003), esp. 10–40, 259–76, 334–9.

108 Davies, 'Mormon History, Text, Colour, and Rites', 309–11; Krakauer, *Under the Banner of Heaven*, 330–31.

109 This figure is derived from E. W. Lindner (ed.), *Yearbook of American and Canadian Churches 2008*, compiled by the National Council of Churches.

110 E. Fox-Genovese and E. D. Genovese, *The Mind of the Master Class: History and Faith in the Southern Slaveholders' Worldview* (Cambridge, 2005), esp. on white supremacy, 215–24. See also M. A. Noll, *The Civil War as a Theological Crisis* (Chapel Hill, 2006), Ch. 4.

111 Handy, 189–90.

112 On Lincoln's religion, R. J. Carwardine, *Lincoln: A Life of Purpose and Power* (New York, 2006), 7–8, 32–44, 226–7, 276–7.

113 On the Kansas massacre at Pottawatomie, D. S. Reynolds, *John Brown, Abolitionist: The Man Who Killed Slavery, Sparked the Civil War and Seeded Civil Rights* (New York, 2005), Ch. 7, esp. 164–5. Quotation: ibid., 171, and cf. John 11.50. On Brown's mental state, see K. Carroll, 'A Psychological Examination of John Brown', in P. A. Russo (ed.), *Terrible Swift Sword: The Legacy of John Brown* (Athens, OH, 2005), 118–37.

114 *Springfield Republican*, qu. A. Nevins, *The Emergence of Lincoln* (2 vols., New York, 1950), II, 100.

115 Reynolds, *John Brown, Abolitionist*, 465–70.

116 See esp. P. Harvey, ' "Yankee Faith" and Southern Redemption: White Southern Baptist Ministers, 1850–1890', and H. Stout and C. Grasso, 'Civil War, Religion, and Communications: The Case of Richmond', in R. M. Miller et al. (eds.), *Religion and the American Civil War* (New York and Oxford, 1998), 167–86 (quotation at 180) and 313–59, at 346–9.

117 Acts 2.1–21.

118 Anderson, 26. E. W. Gritsch, *Born Againism: Perspectives on a Movement* (Philadelphia, 1982), 22–3; J. Kent, *Holding the Fort: Studies in Victorian Revivalism* (London, 1978), Ch. 8.

119 Cf. vv. 40–41: 'Two men will be in the field; one is taken, and one is left. Two women will be grinding at the mill; one is taken and one is left.'

120 Gritsch, *Born Againism*, 17–19.

121 C. G. Flegg, '*Gathered under Apostles': A Study of the Catholic Apostolic Church* (Oxford, 1992), 86, 102, 178, 235, 362, 434–5, 438.

122 As a graduate student in 1973, I was an occasional visitor to its small congregation in Liverpool, bravely struggling with its evening liturgy in their beautiful but half-finished Victorian building (designed according to a revelation made to one of the early clergy). Equally heroic was the heading of the notices on the porch board, 'The Church in Liverpool'.

123 Anderson, 24.

124 G. Wacker, 'Travail of a Broken Family: Evangelical Responses to Pentecostalism in America, 1906–1916', *JEH*, 47 (1996), 505–28, at 509.

125 For a balanced assessment of Azusa Street, see J. Creech, 'Visions of Glory: The Place of the Azusa Street Revival in Pentecostal History', *CH*, 65 (1996), 405–24. On Parham's last years, Anderson, 35 and Wacker, 'Travail of a Broken Family', 516.

126 *Fitchburg Sentinel, Reno Evening Gazette, New York Times*; all 28 August 1883; accessed via the website of the University of Massachusetts at Boston Newspaper Archive, http://themassmedia.newspaperarchive.com/DailyPerspectiveFullView.aspx?viewdate= 08/26/2008, accessed 17 September 2008.

24: Not Peace but a Sword
(1914–60)

1 A. Borg, *War Memorials from Antiquity to the Present* (London, 1991), ix.

2 For contrasting political fortunes of memorials, see C. Moriarty, 'Private Grief and Public Remembrance: British First World War Memorials', and W. Kidd, 'Memory, Memorials and Commemoration of War in Lorraine, 1908–88', in M. Evans and K. Lunn (eds.), *War and Memory in the Twentieth Century* (Oxford and New York, 1997), 125–62.

3 Queen Victoria had been proclaimed Empress of India in 1876; her successors formally remained emperors until 1948, the year after Indian independence.

4 G. Besier (ed.), *Die protestantischen Kirchen Europas im Ersten Weltkrieg: ein Quellen- und Arbeitsbuch* (Göttingen, 1984), 11 (my translation); on authorship, P. Porter, 'Beyond Comfort: German and English Military Chaplains and the Memory of the Great War', *JRH*, 29 (2005), 258–89, at 267. See also W. H. C. Frend, 'Church Historians of the Early Twentieth Century: Adolf von Harnack', *JEH*, 52 (2001), 83–102, at 97–8. On Harnack and the ninety-three professors, Hope, 591; the text of their Proclamation is Besier (ed.), *Die protestantischen Kirchen Europas im Ersten Weltkrieg*, 78–83.

5 On Winnington-Ingram and Asquith, A. Hastings, *A History of English Christianity 1920–1985* (London, 1986), 45.

6 N. Atkin and F. Tallett, *Priests, Prelates and People: A History of European Catholicism since 1750* (London, 2003), 197–9.

7 Hope, 601.

8 J. Joyce, *Portrait of the Artist as a Young Man* (New York, 1916), 227.

9 Binns, 141; A. Ivanov, *Holy Fools in Byzantium and Beyond* (Oxford, 2006), 358.

10 M. von Hagen, 'The First World War, 1914–1918', in R. G. Suny (ed.), *The Cambridge History of Russia III: The Twentieth Century* (Cambridge, 2006), 94–113, at 104–7.

11 B. Geffert, 'Anglican Orders and Orthodox Politics', *JEH*, 57 (2006), 270–300, at 271; C. Chulos, 'Russian Piety and Culture from Peter the Great to 1917', in Angold (ed.), 348–70, at 367; M. Bourdeaux and A. Popescu, 'The Orthodox Church and Communism', ibid., 558–79, at 558.

12 B. Pilnyak, qu. D. Nicholl, *Triumphs of the Spirit in Russia* (London, 1997), 213–14.

13 Bourdeaux and Popescu, 'The Orthodox Church and Communism', 559. On Stalin's early ecclesiastical associations, see S. Sebag Montefiore, *Young Stalin* (London, 2007), esp. 20–22, 26, 57–63. He called himself Stalin from 1912 and made it his surname from 1917: ibid., xxvii.

14 J. B. Toews, *Lost Fatherland: The Story of the Mennonite Emigration from Soviet Russia, 1921–1927* (Scottdale, 1967), esp. 26–42, 46–7, 53–5, 68–71. I am indebted to Mark Schaan, himself a Canadian Mennonite, for our conversations about the Church of his youth.

15 I except from this list the very recently minted Bulgarian Tsar Boris III, whose realm was hardly comparable to the others.

16 D. Bloxham, 'The Armenian Genocide of 1915–1916: Cumulative Radicalization and the Development of a Destruction Policy', *PP*, 181 (November 2003), 141–92. Among the vast literature on this subject, good recent contributions are P. Balakian, *The Burning Tigris: The Armenian Genocide* (London, 2004), Chs. 14–22, and a brave Turkish study by T. Akçam, *A Shameful Act: The Armenian Genocide and the Question of Turkish Responsibility* (London, 2007; first published in Turkish 1999).

17 M. Mazower, 'The Strange Triumph of Human Rights, 1933–1950', *HJ*, 47 (2004), 379–98, at 381.

18 Baumer, 260–63.

19 B. Clark, *Twice a Stranger: How Mass Expulsion Forged Modern Greece and Turkey* (London, 2006), esp. 203.

20 On the 1930 agreement, ibid., 201–2, 213–15; S. Vryonis Jr, *The Mechanism of Catas-trophe: The Turkish Pogrom of September 6–7, 1955, and the Destruction of the Greek Community of Istanbul* (New York, 2005), esp. 16, 220–25, 555–6, 565. Menderes, as Turkish prime minister at the time of the massacre, was executed in 1960 for his connivance in the affair.

21 For the example of Madagascar, see pp. 886–7.

22 Jenkins, 164.

23 D. Harkness, *Northern Ireland since 1920* (Dublin, 1983), 33–5.

24 *ODNB*, s.v. Nicholson, William Patteson. We still lack a scholarly biography of this important figure.

25 T. Owain Hughes, 'Anti-Catholicism in Wales, 1900–60', *JEH*, 53 (2002), 312–25, at 322. On the Pentecostal links of the 'Evan Roberts' revival, see R. Pope, 'Demythologising the Evan Roberts Revival, 1904–1905', *JEH*, 57 (2006), 515–34, at 526, 530, and Anderson, 36.

26 S. Brown, 'Presbyterians and Catholics in Twentieth-century Scotland', in S. J. Brown and G. Newlands (eds.), *Scottish Christianity in the Modern World* (Edinburgh, 2000), 255–81, at 256 (quotation), 265–7, 270.

27 G. I. T. Machin, 'Parliament, the Church of England, and the Prayer Book Crisis, 1927–8', *Parliamentary History*, 19 (2000), 131–47, esp. 139, 141–2.

28 When my mother was a girl in the 1920s, living in an enclave of working-class Angli-canism in Stoke-on-Trent in the Staffordshire Potteries, my devout grandfather, pillar and principal worker of his local Anglican church, and by no means an Evangelical, made it clear that he would be highly displeased if she even entered a Roman Catholic place of worship to look round.

29 M. F. Snape, *The Royal Army Chaplains' Department 1796–1953: Clergy under Fire* (Woodbridge, 2008), 15.

30 D. Kirby, 'Christianity and Freemasonry: The Incompatibility Debate within the Church of England', *JRH*, 29 (2005), 43–66. Fisher's early Victorian predecessor Archbishop Howley was also an enthusiastic Freemason.

31 J. F. Pollard, *Money and the Rise of the Modern Papacy: Financing the Vatican, 1850–1950* (Cambridge, 2005), 31–5.

32 Duffy, 322–3.

33 Sundkler and Steed, 107–8; Hastings, 419, 552, 559.

34 R. G. Tiedemann, 'China and Its Neighbours', in Hastings (ed.), 369–415, at 396; Koschorke et al. (eds.), 99–100.

35 Burleigh, 314–15.

36 E. Wright-Rios, 'Envisioning Mexico's Catholic Resurgence: The Virgin of Solitude and the Talking Christ of Tlacoxcalco 1908–1924', *PP*, 195 (May 2007), 197–240, at 201, 204–5.

37 For an early complaint (1771) by Creoles of Spanish discrimination against them, Kos-chorke et al. (eds.), 340–41.

38 Wright-Rios, 'Envisioning Mexico's Catholic Resurgence', 216n, 221.

39 M. Butler, 'The Church in "Red Mexico"': Michoacán Catholics and the Mexican Revol-ution, 1920–1929', *JEH*, 55 (2004), 520–41, at 527, 523–4.

40 Koschorke et al. (eds.), 379.

41 Butler, 'The Church in "Red Mexico"'', 532–3, 541. This is not to minimize the heroism of martyred priests: for one insouciant Jesuit reminiscence, see Koschorke et al. (eds.), 378–9.

42 G. Barry, 'Rehabilitating a Radical Catholic: Pope Benedict XV and Marc Sangnier, 1914–22', *JEH*, 60 (2009), 514–33; on *Action Française*, Duffy, 336–7.

43 Pollard, *Money and the Rise of the Modern Papacy*, esp. 143–9, 162–7, 205 (quotation).

44 Atkin and Tallett, *Priests, Prelates and People*, 217–22.

45 P. C. Kent, 'A Tale of Two Popes: Pius XI, Pius XII and the Rome–Berlin Axis', *Journal of Contemporary History*, 23 (1988), 589–608, at 598–9.

46 See a fine study of the process, M. Vincent, *Catholicism in the Second Spanish Republic: Religion and Politics in Salamanca, 1930–1936* (Oxford, 1996), Ch. 7.

47 Ibid., 231.

48 G. D. Macklin, 'Major Hugh Pollard, MI, and the Spanish Civil War', *HJ*, 49 (2006), 277–80 (quotation at 279).

49 M. Vincent, ' "The keys of the kingdom": Religious Violence in the Spanish Civil War, July–August 1936', in C. Ealham and M. Richards (eds.), *The Splintering of Spain: Cultural History and the Spanish Civil War, 1936–1939* (Cambridge, 2005), 68–89, at 68 (quotation), 86–8; M. Richards, ' "Presenting arms to the Blessed Sacrament": Civil War and Semana Santa in the City of Málaga, 1936–1939', ibid., 196–222, at 202, 211.

50 Kent, 'A Tale of Two Popes', 604.

51 Porter, 'Beyond Comfort', 258–89, at 272, 281.

52 Frend, 'Church Historians of the Early Twentieth Century', 101. For Marcion, see pp. 125–7.

53 R. P. Ericksen, *Theologians under Hitler: Gerhard Kittel, Paul Althaus and Emanuel Hirsch* (New Haven and London, 1985), esp. 50–53, 81–3, 178–84, and see M. Casey, 'Some Anti-Semitic Assumptions in the "Theological Dictionary of the New Testament" ', *Novum Testamentum*, 41 (1999), 280–91. For an interesting undergraduate personal reminiscence by a great Methodist biblical scholar of a tense moment in a visit in the late 1930s to Cambridge University by Karl Fezer, a Nazi-sympathizing German theologian, see C. K. Barrett in *Epworth Review* 13/3 (September 1986), 82.

54 Ericksen, *Theologians under Hitler*, 164–5. On the background to Christian uses of 'Aryanism', see C. Kidd, *The Forging of Races: Race and Scripture in the Protestant Atlantic World, 1600–2000* (Cambridge, 2006), Ch. 6.

55 It should be pointed out that Barth took delight in rescuing an undamaged bust of Schleiermacher from the bombed-out ruins of the Kurfürsten Schloss in Bonn when lecturing there for the first time after the war: K. Barth, *Dogmatics in Outline* (London, 1949), 7.

56 Frend, 'Church Historians of the Early Twentieth Century', 99–100; J. A. Moses, 'Dietrich Bonhoeffer's Repudiation of Protestant German War Theology', *JRH*, 30 (2006), 354–70.

57 For the text of the Barmen Declaration, and related documents, A. C. Cochrane, *The Church's Confession under Hitler* (Philadelphia, 1962), esp. 238–42; and see also ibid., Ch. 7.

58 K. H. Holtschneider, 'Christians, Jews and the Holocaust', in Wolffe (ed.), 217–48, at 234, 236–7. For Barth's regret at being inhibited by his political realism in the 1934 discussions on drafting the declaration, see M. D. Hockenos, *A Church Divided: German Protestants Confront the Nazi Past* (Bloomington, 2004), 172–3.

59 Moses, 'Dietrich Bonhoeffer's Repudiation of Protestant German War Theology', 365n. On the Niemöllers, N. Railton, 'German Free Churches and the Nazi Regime', *JEH*, 49 (1998), 117.

60 Ibid., 85–139, esp. 104–5, 129.

61 R. Steigmann-Gall, *The Holy Reich: Nazi Conceptions of Christianity* (Cambridge, 2003), 1–2, 72–3, 136, 180. By 1943 Koch had opted for the non-Church-affiliated status of *Gottgläubig* ('a believer in God'): ibid., 220.

62 On Tiso and Pavelić, Atkin and Tallett, *Priests, Prelates and People*, 247–9; on Tiso, P. Ramet, *Religion and Nationalism in Soviet and East European Politics* (Durham, NC, and London, 1989), 29, 274–5. On Croatia, E. Paris, *Genocide in Satellite Croatia 1941–45* (Chicago, 1962), esp. 154–7 (quotation at 157), 162–4, 190–91.

63 Snyder, 170, 204–5, 211.

64 J. E. Frazier, *Maurice Duruflé: The Man and His Music* (Rochester, NY, 2007), 3, 156–65, 168–9. For an introduction to the Vichy regime, see Atkin and Tallett, *Priests, Prelates and People*, 247–54.

65 Judicious recent summaries of the results of a vast field of research are Atkin and Tallett, *Priests, Prelates and People*, 244–7, and Duffy, 345–50 (quotation at 348).

66 Snyder, 124–5, 160, 165; a fine biography of Sheptyts'kyi is A. Krawchuk, *Christian Social Ethics in Ukraine: The Legacy of Andrei Sheptytsky* (Edmonton, Ottawa and Toronto, 1997), esp. xv, Ch. 5 (quotation at 213) and 266–7.

67 Hockenos, *A Church Divided*, esp. 171–7.

68 The more frequent formulation that the Nazis' ultimate aim was to destroy Christianity altogether is open to question: Steigmann-Gall, *The Holy Reich*, 261–7.

69 G. Zahn, *In Solitary Witness: The Life and Death of Franz Jägerstätter* (Springfield, IL, 1964), esp. 36–9, 46–8, 63–4, 144.

70 Hastings, *A History of English Christianity 1920–1985*, 374–80. I feel highly honoured to have been given Bishop Bell's robes as Oxford Doctor of Divinity by Mrs Anne Baelz, widow of the former Dean of Durham, and express my gratitude to her.

71 V. N. Nersessian, 'Armenian Christianity', in Parry (ed.), 23–46, at 42.

72 E. E. Roslof, *Red Priests: Renovationism, Russian Orthodoxy, and Revolution, 1905–1946* (Bloomington, 2002), esp. 198–205. For a pioneering Western account of the Orthodox Church in the decades after the Second World War, see T. Beeson, *Discretion and Valour: Religious Conditions in Russia and Eastern Europe* (London, 1974), Ch. 3.

73 Snyder, 178.

74 A superb survey of these issues is T. Judt, *Postwar: A History of Europe since 1945* (London, 2005), Chs. 1–3.

75 Hastings, *A History of English Christianity 1920–1985*, Chs. 30, 31; R. English, *Irish Freedom: The History of Nationalism in Ireland* (London, 2006), 346–55.

76 M. Pattenden, 'The Canonisation of Clare of Assisi and Early Franciscan History', *JEH*, 59 (2008), 208–26, at 226; on Pius XII's last years, see Duffy, 350–54.

77 The spelling 'Oecumenical' is now customarily reserved for the Patriarch of Constantinople and the early councils of the Church, while 'Ecumenical' describes the modern movement towards Church unity.

78 K. Clements, *Faith on the Frontier: A Life of J. H. Oldham* (Edinburgh, 1999), esp. 5–14, 18–22, 43–54. On the missionary voyage of the *Duff*, see pp. 875–6.

79 Clements, *Faith on the Frontier*, 2, 270–74, 277, 286.

80 On early aspirations to Anglican–Roman reunion, see M. D. Chapman, 'The Fantasy of Reunion: The Rise and Fall of the Association for the Promotion of the Unity of Christendom', *JEH*, 58 (2007), 49–74.

81 Koschorke et al. (eds.), 95. On the 1910 Conference, see Clements, *Faith on the Frontier*, Ch. 5.

82 D. Carter, 'The Ecumenical Movement in Its Early Years', *JEH*, 49 (1998), 465–85, esp. 477–8.

83 J. Nurser, *For All Peoples and All Nations: Christian Churches and Human Rights* (Geneva, 2005); for a different perspective bypassing this background and emphasizing Great Power politics, Mazower, 'The Strange Triumph of Human Rights, 1933–1950'.

84 Hastings, *A History of English Christianity 1920–1985*, 97.

85 *The Lambeth Conferences (1867–1948): The Reports of the 1920, 1930, and 1948 Conferences, with Selected Resolutions from the Conferences of 1867, 1878, 1888, 1897 and 1908* (London, 1948), 119–24, at 120.

86 For their beginnings in the seventeenth century, see pp. 500–501.

87 Geffert, 'Anglican Orders and Orthodox Politics', *passim*.

88 See statements in the Constitution of 1947: Koschorke et al. (eds.), 115.

89 Carter, 'Ecumenical Movement in Its Early Years', 484–5.

90 Hastings, *A History of English Christianity 1920–1985*, 468–9.

91 G. Wacker, 'Travail of a Broken Family: Evangelical Responses to Pentecostalism in America, 1906–1916', *JEH*, 47 (1996), 505–28, at 528.

92 Anderson, 47–9.

93 E. W. Gritsch, *Born Againism: Perspectives on a Movement* (Philadelphia, 1982), 76–7; T. J. Hangen, *Redeeming the Dial: Radio, Religion and Popular Culture in America* (Chapel Hill and London, 2002), Ch. 3.

94 S. Coleman, *The Globalisation of Charismatic Christianity: Spreading the Gospel of Prosperity* (Cambridge, 2000), 27–31, 42–3; Anderson, 145, 157–8, 220–21. For a critique of the 'Prosperity Gospel' in Ghanaian neo-Pentecostalism, see J. K. Asamoah-Gyadu, *African Charismatics: Current Developments within Independent Indigenous Pentecostalism in Ghana* (Leiden, 2005), Ch. 7.

95 Anderson, 247, 250.

96 M. Kazin, *A Godly Hero: The Life of William Jennings Bryan* (New York, 2006), esp. 109–18, 285–95. For Darrow's previous greatest *cause célèbre* in 1912, in which his oratory successfully swept aside an almost inevitable conviction for bribery, see G. Cowan,

The People v. Clarence Darrow: The Bribery Trial of America's Greatest Lawyer (New York, 1993), esp. 391-407.

97 Handy, 285.

98 Hangen, *Redeeming the Dial*, esp. 1-2, 8-13, 19 and Ch. 4.

99 Aladura constitution, qu. C. G. Baëta, *Prophetism in Ghana: A Study of Some 'Spiritual' Churches* (2nd edn, Achimota, 2004), 114-16.

100 Hastings, 502-4; J. Cabrita, 'Isaiah Shembe's Theological Nationalism, 1920s-1935', *Journal of Southern African Studies* (forthcoming, 2009). I am very grateful to Joel Cabrita for our discussions of Shembe.

101 Sundkler and Steed, 780-83; quotation from an early testimony after his death to the effect that he had had, Koschorke et al. (eds.), 260-61.

102 Sundkler and Steed, 408, 906.

103 D. L. Hodgson, *The Church of Women: Gendered Encounters between Maasai and Missionaries* (Bloomington, 2005), esp. 56-9, 122, 180-87, 211-22, 226.

104 Anderson, 72.

25: Culture Wars
(1960-Present)

1 That original gravesite in the crypt is now occupied by Pope John Paul II, which some might find a second irony.

2 The definitive though monumental account of the Council is provided by G. Alberigo et al. (eds.), *History of Vatican II* (5 vols., Maryknoll, 1995-2006).

3 J. W. O'Malley, 'Trent and Vatican II: Two Styles of Church', in R. F. Bulman and F. J. Parrella (eds.), *From Trent to Vatican II: Historical and Theological Investigations* (Oxford, 2006), 301-20, at 309.

4 H. Chadwick, 'Paul VI and Vatican II', *JEH*, 41 (1990), 463-9, at 464.

5 Duffy, 358-9.

6 R. P. McBrien, 'The Church (*Lumen Gentium*)', in M. A. Hayes and L. Gearon, *Contemporary Catholic Theology: A Reader* (Leominster, 1998), 279-93, at 279-80.

7 Chadwick, 'Paul VI and Vatican II', 466.

8 R. Shortt, *Benedict XVI: Commander of the Faith* (London, 2005), 37.

9 J. Cornwell, *The Pope in Winter: The Dark Face of John Paul II's Papacy* (London, 2004), 40-42; Shortt, *Benedict XVI*, 41-2.

10 V. H. H. Green, *A New History of Christianity* (Stroud, 1996), 337.

11 Chadwick, 'Paul VI and Vatican II', 468-9; M. J. Wilde, *Vatican II: A Sociological Analysis of Religious Change* (Princeton, 2007), 102-15.

12 *The Lambeth Conferences (1867-1948): The Reports of the 1920, 1930, and 1948 Conferences, with Selected Resolutions from the Conferences of 1867, 1878, 1888, 1897 and 1908* (London, 1948), 50, 200, 295.

13 Wilde, *Vatican II*, 116-25; R. McClory, *Turning Point: The Inside Story of the Papal Birth Control Commission, and How* Humanae Vitae *Changed the Life of Patty Crowley and the Future of the Church* (New York, 1995), esp. Chs. 11, 14.

14 'Mis recuerdos de Pablo VI: Entrevista con el Cardenal Vicente Enrique y Tarancón', in [no editor named], *Pablo VI y España: Giornata di studio, Madrid, 20-21 maggio 1994* (Brescia, 1996), 242-62, at 256-7.

15 For an introduction to the dimensions of the changes perhaps more irenical than my account, J. J. Boyce, 'Singing a New Song unto the Lord: Catholic Church Music', in Bulman and Parrella (eds.), *From Trent to Vatican II*, 137-59.

16 Shortt, *Benedict XVI*, 25, 39-40, 51-2.

17 Matthew 6.28-33/Luke 12.27-31.

18 P. Kennedy, *A Modern Introduction to Theology: New Questions for Old Beliefs* (London, 2006), Ch. 9.

19 A. T. Hennelly (ed.), *Liberation Theology: A Documentary History* (Maryknoll, 1990), 116, 254.

20 G. Gutiérrez, *A Theology of Liberation: History, Politics, and Salvation* (London, 1974; first published 1971), esp. 6-19, 289-91.

21 P. Harvey, *Freedom's Coming: Religious Culture and the Shaping of the South from the Civil War through the Civil Rights Era* (Chapel Hill, 2005), at 76.

22 T. Branch, *At Canaan's Edge: America in the King Years, 1965–68* (New York and London, 2006), Chs. 2–10.

23 Ibid., 114, 756–8.

24 J.-K. Kwon, 'A Sketch for a New Minjung Theology', *Madang: Journal of Contextual Theology in East Asia*, 1/1 (June 2004), 49–69; J.-K. Kwon, 'Social Movement as the Ground for Minjung Theology', *Madang: Journal of Contextual Theology in East Asia*, 4 (December 2005), 63–75.

25 Mark 8.34. V. Küster, 'Contextual Transformations: Minjung Theology Yesterday and Today', *Madang: Journal of Contextual Theology in East Asia*, 5 (June 2006), 23–43.

26 W. Manzanza Mwanangombe, *La Constitution de la hiérarchie ecclésiastique au Congo belge (10 novembre 1959): prodromes et réalisation* (Frankfurt am Main, 2002). On A. A. J. van Bilsen's *Vers l'independence du Congo et du Ruanda-Urundi* (Brussels, 1956), see Sundkler and Steed, 901–2.

27 K. Ward, 'Africa', in Hastings (ed.), 192–237, at 227.

28 T. O. Ranger (ed.), *Evangelical Christianity and Democracy in Africa* (Oxford, 2008), x and xviii n. 10.

29 Sundkler and Steed, 818–25.

30 Ibid., 992–3.

31 P. McGrandle, *Trevor Huddleston: Turbulent Priest* (New York, 2004), v.

32 D. Herbstein, *White Lies: Canon Collins and the Secret War against Apartheid* (Cape Town, 2004), esp. 21–6, 103–4, 138–41, 328.

33 A modified version of both anthems remains the official national anthem of the Republic.

34 Koschorke et al. (eds.), 265–7.

35 J. A. Harrill, *Slaves in the New Testament: Literary, Social and Moral Dimensions* (Minneapolis, 2006), 193–4. See p. 908 for similar action from the Mormons.

36 H. McLeod, *The Religious Crisis of the 1960s* (Oxford, 2007), 3. For an entertaining and perhaps surprisingly perky variety of perspectives on secularization in Britain, see J. Garnett et al. (eds.), *Redefining Christian Britain: Post-1945 Perspectives* (London, 2007).

37 G. Therborn, *Between Sex and Power: Family in the World 1900–2000* (London, 2004), 163–6, 198.

38 M. Walsh, 'Gendering Mobility: Women, Work and Automobility in the United States', *History*, 93 (2008), 376–95, at 385; McLeod, *The Religious Crisis of the 1960s*, 169–75.

39 R. Sykes, 'Popular Religion in Decline: A Study from the Black Country', *JEH*, 56 (2005), 287–307, at 297, 300 (italics in the original).

40 G. Parsons, 'How the Times They Were a-Changing: Exploring the Context of Religious Transformation in Britain in the 1960s', in Wolffe (ed.), 161–89, at 164. I can testify the same phenomenon from my own rural East Anglian boyhood in the 1950s and 1960s.

41 M. Seymour, *Debating Divorce in Italy: Marriage and the Making of Modern Italians, 1860–1974* (New York and Basingstoke, 2006), 166–8, Ch. 8.

42 Therborn, *Between Sex and Power*, 199.

43 M. Grimley, 'Law, Morality and Secularisation: The Church of England and the Wolfenden Report, 1954–1967', *JEH* 60 (2009), 744–60. In a strange oversight, Canon Sherwin Bailey has not yet been noticed by the *ODNB*: among his writings on marriage and gender relations, his study *Homosexuality and the Western Christian Tradition* (London, 1955) is a key work in the evolution of British attitudes to sexuality.

44 See, e.g., O. Chadwick, *Michael Ramsey: A Life* (Oxford, 1990), 35–6.

45 D. Bonhoeffer, *Letters and Papers from Prison* (London, 1959) 95, 122, 160.

46 Kennedy, *A Modern Introduction to Theology*, 207–8.

47 Cf., e.g., U. E. Eisen, *Women Officeholders in Early Christianity: Epigraphical and Literary Studies* (Collegeville, 2000).

48 S. Mumm, 'Women, Priesthood and the Ordained Ministry in the Christian Tradition', in Wolffe (ed.), 190–216, at 199.

49 Breward, 385.

50 M. B. McKinley, 'Marie Dentière: An Outspoken Reformer Enters the French Literary Canon', *SCJ*, 37 (2006), 401–12.

51 B. A. Brasher, *Encyclopedia of Fundamentalism* (New York and London, 2001), 18, and cf. ibid., xvii, 16–17, 292–3. Cf. the unbuttoned comment from one well-informed historian (backed up by the Evangelical politician Jerry Falwell) that a fundamentalist is 'an evangelical who is angry about something': G. M. Marsden, *Understanding Fundamentalism and Evangelicalism* (Grand Rapids, 1991), 1.

52 R. Freedman, 'The Religious Right and the Carter Administration', *HJ*, 48 (2005), 231–60, esp. 231 (quotation), 236–8.

53 W. Bass, *Support Any Friend: Kennedy's Middle East and the Making of the US–Israel Alliance* (Oxford and New York, 2003), esp. 144–50.

54 M. Northcott, *An Angel Directs the Storm: Apocalyptic Religion and American Empire* (London, 2004), 61–8.

55 J. Micklethwait and A. Wooldridge, *The Right Nation: Why America is Different* (London, 2004), 214–17. See J. J. Mearsheimer and S. M. Walt, 'The Israel Lobby and US Foreign Policy', *New York Review of Books*, 23 March 2006, and a survey of the extraordinary furore which followed the publication of this piece, M. Massing, 'The Storm over the Israel Lobby', *New York Review of Books*, 8 June 2006.

56 A point made to me forcefully outside Damascus in October 2008 by His Holiness Moran Mor Ignatius Zakka I Iwas, Syriac Orthodox Patriarch of Antioch and All the East. For the dire present plight of Christianity through much of the Middle East, see Dalrymple, *passim*, and A. Elon, *Jerusalem: City of Mirrors* (rev. edn, London, 1996), 223–34.

57 *New York Times*, 29 October 2000, main section, 18: ('For Bush, his toughest call was whether to enter the campaign'). It is only fair to add that the report went on to say that 'he does not actively disbelieve in it either, as a friend puts it, "he doesn't really care about that kind of thing"'.

58 See respectively *Congressional Record*, 4 March 2002, S1429, and Senator Inhofe's website, http://inhofe.senate.gov/pressreleases/climateupdate.htm (accessed 5 April 2009). See also G. Wills, 'A Country Ruled by Faith', *New York Review of Books*, 16 November 2006, 8–12, at 10.

59 Cornwell, *The Pope in Winter*, 84–6.

60 Snyder, 211–12, and cf. ibid., 267, 276.

61 MacCulloch, 45, 483.

62 J. Cornwell, *Breaking Faith: The Pope, the People and the Fate of Catholicism* (London, 2001), 257.

63 On '*magisterium*', see Kennedy, *A Modern Introduction to Theology*, 215.

64 Duffy, 372–3; Kennedy, *A Modern Introduction to Theology*, 196–7.

65 M. González-Wippler, *Santería: The Religion* (Woodbury, MN, 1994), 258. On *Candomblé* and its allied religions, see pp. 712–14.

66 Shortt, *Benedict XVI*, 44–9.

67 After the publicity triggered by the Church authorities' recent inept removal of Newman's remains from his Birmingham grave (which he had stipulated that his body must share with the corpse of his lifelong companion, Ambrose St John), the Cardinal's unexpected emergence as a gay icon was not an asset to the cause of his sainthood.

68 E. T. Oakes, SJ, and D. Moss (eds.), *The Cambridge Companion to Hans Urs von Balthasar* (Cambridge, 2004), esp. 4–5, 194–5, 241–2, 256–68; A. Nichols, 'An Introduction to Balthasar', *New Blackfriars*, 79 (1998), 2–10, at 9; P. Endean, 'Von Balthasar, Rahner and the Commissar', ibid., 33–8.

69 *The Tablet*, 8 January 1999.

70 Cornwell, *The Pope in Winter*, Ch. 29. The mendacious statements of some African Catholic leaders about the ineffectiveness of condoms remain one of the blots on the moral reputation of the Catholic Church in that continent.

71 I am indebted to Philip Kennedy for suggesting this *midrash* on Western theories of the ontological status of priesthood.

72 Vatican Press Office statement, 19 May 2006: translated http://nationalcatholicreporter.org/update/maciel_communique.pdf, accessed 14 September 2008. J. Berry and G. Renner, *Vows of Silence: The Abuse of Power in the Papacy of John Paul II* (New York, 2004).

73 Cornwell, *The Pope in Winter*, Ch. 28.
74 S. Albrecht, *Geschichte der Grossmährenforschung in den tschechischen Ländern und in der Slowakei* (Prague, 2003), 199–220, 236–8.
75 J. Keane, *Václav Havel: A Political Tragedy in Six Acts* (London, 1999), 382–3, though the event is there misdated.
76 A fine study of these years, albeit written before the last crisis of Gorbachev's rule, is M. Bourdeaux, *Gorbachev, Glasnost and the Gospel* (London, 1990).
77 S. Plokhy and F. E. Sysyn, *Religion and Nation in Modern Ukraine* (Edmonton, AB, 2003).
78 M. Bourdeaux and A. Popescu, 'The Orthodox Church and Communism', in Angold (ed.), 558–79, at 575.
79 C. Andrew and V. Mitrokhin, *The Mitrokhin Archive II: The KGB and the World* (London, 2005), 490–91, and Pls. 23 and 24.
80 W. L. Daniel, 'Reconstructing the "Sacred canopy": Mother Serafima and Novodevichy Monastery', *JEH*, 59 (2008), 249–71.
81 For a parallel history of Russian Orthodox imitations of architectural form, to make a more purely theological point, in Cathedrals of the Dormition, see pp. 507–8 and 524.
82 Binns, 238.
83 A classic study of this emigration and its origins is N. Zernov, *The Russian Religious Renaissance of the Twentieth Century* (London, 1963), esp. Ch. 9.
84 B. Geffert, 'Anglican Orders and Orthodox Politics', *JEH*, 57 (2006), 270–300, at 288–94.
85 K. Buchenau, '*Svetosavlje* und *Pravosavlje*: Nationales und Universales in der serbischen Orthodoxie', in M. Schulze Wessel (ed.), *Nationalisierung der Religion und Sakralisierung der Nation im östlichen Europa* (Stuttgart, 2006), 203–32, at 211–14.
86 Binns, 93; Buchenau, '*Svetosavlje* und *Pravosavlje*', 221–4.
87 B. Anzulovic, *Heavenly Serbia: From Myth to Genocide* (London, 1999), esp. 51–61. For a wise overview of the Serbian cultural formation and comparable situations, see A. Hastings, 'Holy Lands and Their Political Consequences', *Nations and Nationalism*, 9 (2003), 29–54, esp. 40–42.
88 B. Panteli, 'Nationalism and Architecture: The Creation of a National Style in Serbian Architecture and Its Political Implications', *Journal of the Society of Architectural Historians*, 56 (1997), 16–41, at 33–5.
89 A ruefully fair account by an academic of Serb descent, which does not minimize Croat or Muslim atrocities and cultural destruction, is M. A. Sells, *The Bridge Betrayed: Religion and Genocide in Bosnia* (Berkeley, CA, and Los Angeles, 1996).
90 Jenkins, 244.
91 F. Knight, *The Nineteenth-Century Church and English Society* (Cambridge, 1995), 21, 23, 31n, 35, 66; P. Slack, 'Government and Information in Seventeenth-century England', *PP*, 184 (August 2004), 33–68.
92 G. Speake, *Mount Athos: Renewal in Paradise* (New Haven and London, 2002), 173–209, and NB especially the emphasis on the restoration of community (coenobitic) life over idiorhythmic monasticism. On renewal in Coptic Egypt, see A. O'Mahony, 'Coptic Christianity in Modern Egypt', in Angold (ed.), 488–510, at 501–8.
93 C. Cavafy, 'Waiting for the Barbarians' (1904), qu. Speake, *Mount Athos*, 194: he was speaking of the paradoxical sense of moral relief which a late Roman aristocrat might have felt at the invasion of forces over the imperial borders.
94 Koschorke et al. (eds.), 273–4; I. Apawo Phiri, 'President Frederick Chiluba and Zambia: Evangelicals and Democracy in a "Christian Nation"', in Ranger (ed.), *Evangelical Christianity and Democracy in Africa*, 95–130.
95 L. Sanneh, 'Religion's Return', *TLS*, 13 October 2006, 14.
96 Jenkins, 37.
97 See, e.g., report 'President's Apology', *Korea Times*, 'Opinion', 9 September 2008, http://www.koreatimes.co.kr/www/news/opinon/2008/09/202_30800.html, accessed 25 September 2008.
98 I am grateful to Professor Sangkeun Kim of Yonsei University, Seoul, for our discussions about the significance of these figures.

99 Sermon of 1982, qu. B. Chenu et al. (eds.), *The Book of Christian Martyrs* (London, 1990), 211.

100 Breward, 253, 303–7.

101 C. McGillion, *The Chosen Ones: The Politics of Salvation in the Anglican Church* (Sydney, 2005).

102 S. Bates, *A Church at War: Anglicans and Homosexuality* (London, 2004), 129–30; see also ibid., 136–7.

103 Ibid., 198.

104 G. Wills, 'Fringe Government', *New York Review of Books*, 6 October 2005, 46–50, at 47.

105 A. Hastings, 'Latin America', in Hastings (ed.), at 365–7.

106 J. K. Asamoah-Gyadu, *African Charismatics: Current Developments within Independent Indigenous Pentecostalism in Ghana* (Leiden, 2005), 240. W. Hollenweger, *Pentecostalism: Origins and Developments Worldwide* (Peabody, MA, 1997), 200–217. For discussion of changing politics in African Evangelicalism generally, see Ranger (ed.), *Evangelical Christianity and Democracy in Africa*, esp. xii–xiii, and P. Gifford, 'Evangelical Christianity and Democracy in Africa: A Response', ibid., 225–42.

107 On the time-lag in attitudes to Hell among Catholics, Hastings, 272–3.

108 On Maurice, O. Chadwick, *The Victorian Church* (2 vols., 2nd edn, London, 1970–72), I, 545–50; on the Irving nexus, R. Brown, 'Victorian Anglican Evangelicalism: The Radical Legacy of Edward Irving', *JEH*, 58 (2007), 675–704, at 694–701. See also G. Rowell, *Hell and the Victorians: A Study of the Nineteenth-century Theological Controversies Concerning Eternal Punishment and the Future Life* (Oxford, 1974).

109 B. Parsons, *Committed to the Cleansing Flame: The Development of Cremation in Nineteenth-century England* (Reading, 2005), 39 (quotation), 51.

110 S. Prothero, *Purified by Fire: A History of Cremation in America* (Berkeley, CA, and Los Angeles, 2001), esp. 188–9, 202–12. The first American cremation was in 1876: ibid., 15. See also P. C. Jupp, *From Dust to Ashes: Cremation and the British Way of Death* (Houndmills, 2006), esp. 193–6.

111 J. Northrop Moore, *Elgar: Child of Dreams* (London, 2004), 44–5, 65–6, 70–71, 77, 130; I. Kemp, *Tippett: The Composer and His Music* (Oxford and New York, 1987), 9, 29–33, 154, 158, 386–91; P. Holmes, *Vaughan Williams: His Life and Times* (London, New York and Sydney, 1997), 35–7, 42–3; S. A. Morrison, *Russian Opera and the Symbolist Movement* (Berkeley, CA, and London, 2002), 116–17, 121–2.

112 Qu. ibid., 115.

113 I. Watts, *Psalms of David* (1719): 'Jesus shall reign where'er the sun . . .' My italics.

114 A point made with elegance by P. Jenkins, *Mystics and Messiahs: Cults and New Religions in American History* (Oxford and New York, 2000), esp. 17–18, 232–5.

115 H. U. von Balthasar, *The Moment of Christian Witness* (San Francisco, 1994; first published 1966), 32.

116 Figures provided by the *International Bulletin of Missionary Research*, 33 (2009), 32: Global Table 5.

Further Reading

This is designed to provide general introductory reading or classic works in English in the various sections of the book. Detailed reading on particular topics is cited in the notes relating to each chapter, often in works in languages other than English, and is not necessarily repeated here; the same applies to books listed in the table of abbreviations.

GENERAL READING FOR ALL CHRISTIAN HISTORY

Indispensable for reference is the present-day manifestation of a work quirkily Anglo-Catholic in flavour in its first guise half a century ago, but now transformed, E. A. Livingstone (ed.), *The Oxford Dictionary of the Christian Church* (4th edn, Oxford, 2005). Reliable too are the expert essays themed by region and Church in K. Parry (ed.), *The Blackwell Companion to Eastern Christianity* (Oxford, 2007). A work of reference which has no peer in any other culture, providing biographies of individuals connected with the British Isles/ Atlantic Isles or the British Empire, is the *Oxford Dictionary of National Biography*, best consulted in its regularly updated and corrected form as http://www.oxforddnb.com/index.js. Papal official pronouncements from the pontificate of Leo XIII are to be found on the Vatican website at http://www.vatican.va/holy_father/.

Of making surveys of Christian history, there is no end. A slightly less daunting way in than the present volume, with more emphasis on primary documents, is J. Comby with D. MacCulloch, *How to Read Church History* (2 vols., London, 1985, 1989), and an incisive and lavishly illustrated survey is O. Chadwick, *A History of Christianity* (London, 1995). R. Harries and H. Mayr-Harting (eds.), *Christianity: Two Thousand Years* (Oxford, 2001), is the concise published result of a course of public lectures by Oxford academics celebrating the millennium. More meditative, while providing a brief chronological overview, is E. Cameron, *Interpreting Christian History: The Challenge of the Churches' Past* (Oxford, 2005), and a magisterial if controversial study from a major twentieth-century combatant in Roman Catholic history is H. Küng, *Christianity: Its Essence and History* (London, 1995), translated from Küng's *Christentum: Wesen und Geschichte* (Munich, 1994). Another more reluctant combatant, Primate of All England, compellingly distils an exceptional historical imagination into R. Williams, *Why Study the Past? The Quest for the Historical Church* (London, 2005). A. F. Walls, *The Cross-cultural Process in Christian History: Studies in the Transmission and Appropriation of Faith* (Edinburgh, 2001), provides a refreshing perspective from an expert on the history of Christian mission, with an enviably wide chronological sweep.

Beyond these, there are multi-volume surveys of the field, notably the *Oxford History of the Christian Church*: a series of individually authored stand-alone studies of particular periods, still sailing as majestic in their blue livery as a twentieth-century ocean liner, and edited by the brothers O. and H. Chadwick, themselves the embodiment of one era in European church history. Fine multi-authored volumes of the *Cambridge History of Christianity* cover the whole span in nine volumes, and single-authored volumes in the *I. B. Tauris*

History of the Christian Church provide crisp surveys also aiming to span the history of the Church. I cite particular volumes from all three of these series in section bibliographies below. The same survey task is performed by expert multiple authors in a single volume: A. Hastings (ed.), *A World History of Christianity* (Grand Rapids, 1999). An astonishing, not to say daunting, multi-volume account of Christian theology by one of the princes of American liberal Protestant theology is J. J. Pelikan, *The Christian Tradition: A History of the Development of Doctrine* (5 vols., Chicago and London, 1971–89). Even more monumental, from a great Jesuit intellectual historian, is F. Copleston, *A History of Philosophy* (9 vols., London, 1946–75). Western Christianity is so inextricably tangled with Western culture that it is worth consulting the comfortingly sensible synthesis of J. S. McClelland, *A History of Western Political Thought* (London and New York, 1996). The tangle is interestingly interpreted from a classic Jesuit background in J. O'Malley, *Four Cultures of the West* (Cambridge, MA, 2004). The mystical and spiritual dimension of Christianity is dealt with in L. Bouyer, *A History of Christian Spirituality* (3 vols., London, 1968–9). The Paulist Press *Classics of Western Spirituality* series, with volumes now running into triple figures, is a user-friendly series of translations presenting a rich variety of Western spiritual writers. One tradition within the West can be sampled in G. Rowell, K. Stevenson and R. Williams, *Love's Redeeming Work: The Anglican Quest for Holiness* (Oxford, 1989).

Christian history lends itself to particular themes treated over long periods. A model of popular history covering two millennia is E. Duffy, *Saints and Sinners: A History of the Popes* (3rd edn, New Haven and London, 2006), engagingly supplemented by R. Collins, *Keepers of the Keys of Heaven: A History of the Papacy* (London, 2009), and, on an allied theme, there is wise guidance and exposition from N. P. Tanner, *The Councils of the Church: A Short History* (New York, 2001). Larded with ecclesiological documents is E. G. Jay, *The Church: Its Changing Images through Twenty Centuries* (2 vols., London, 1977–8). Two books dealing in an engaging and personal manner with the everyday Christian encounter with the Christian Bible over the centuries are J. Pelikan, *Whose Bible Is It? A History of the Scriptures through the Ages* (New York and London, 2006) and L. A. Ferrell, *The Bible and the People* (New Haven and London, 2008). As a counterbalance, one might care in prurient mood to read D. Nash, *Blasphemy in the Christian World: A History* (Oxford, 2007). C. Harline, *Sunday: A History of the First Day from Babylonia to the Superbowl* (New York, 2007) has a fine eye for changing social detail. M. Rubin, *Mother of God: A History of the Virgin Mary* (London and New York, 2009) brings a major assembly of literature and art and a sadly appropriate awareness of the relevance of anti-Semitism to her subject, to supplement the sparkling M. Warner, *Alone of All Her Sex: The Myth and Cult of the Virgin Mary* (London, 1976). J. Dillenberger, *Style and Content in Christian Art* (London, 1965) is a classic introduction to this subject, while N. MacGregor and E. Langmuir, *Seeing Salvation: Images of Christ in Art* (London, 2000) is an illuminating and often surprising survey. A thorough introduction to a related field is A. Doig, *Liturgy and Architecture from the Early Church to the Close of the Middle Ages* (Aldershot, 2008), while N. Pevsner, *An Outline of European Architecture* (London, 1990), established itself as a classic soon after publication of the original version in 1942; the *Buildings of England/ Scotland/Wales/Ireland* series initiated by Pevsner is an architectural gazetteer of which all other countries should be envious. M. Stringer, *A Sociological History of Christian Worship* (Cambridge, 2005), attempts the unenviable task of uniting sociology, history and liturgy, with fruitful results.

In regional studies attempting to span a whole chronology, English church history is decently served by D. L. Edwards, *Christian England* (rev. edn, London, 1989), while a fine team of authors providing a variety of lively spotlights on the subject is captained by S. W. Gilley and W. J. Sheils (eds.), in *A History of Religion in Britain: Practice and Belief from Pre-Roman Times to the Present* (Oxford, 1994). On the United States, a splendid if monumental study is S. E. Ahlstrom, *A Religious History of the American People* (2nd edn, New Haven and London, 2004), and is rivalled (indeed, exceeded in its coverage of Canada) by M. Noll, *A History of Christianity in the United States and Canada* (Grand Rapids, 1992). R. E. Frykenberg, *Christianity in India: From the Beginnings to the Present* (Oxford, 2009), is the best coverage of the subject. Quite brilliant, even moving, from a participant, is A. Hastings, *The Church in Africa 1450–1950* (Oxford, 1994), which is unfair competition for a wise and informative longer survey also principally authored by a European who made Africa his life, B. Sundkler and C. Steed, *A History of the Church in Africa* (Cambridge, 2000). An unusual and valuable collection of primary sources is K. Koschorke, F. Ludwig and M. Delgado (eds.), *A History of Christianity in Asia, Africa, and Latin America 1450–1990: A Documentary Sourcebook* (Grand Rapids and Cambridge, 2007).

PART I: A MILLENNIUM OF BEGINNINGS
(1000 BCE–100 CE)

General Reading

K. Armstrong, *The Great Transformation: The World in the Time of Buddha, Socrates, Confucius and Jeremiah* (London, 2006), provides a fine background survey of the great religions of ancient Europe and Asia which is not rendered redundant by being attached to the dubious concept of an 'Axial Age' in world religions. At a more detailed level, reflecting the best in contemporary scholarship, are the swarms of essayists marshalled by respectively W. D. Davies and L. Finkelstein (eds.), *The Cambridge History of Judaism II: The Hellenistic Age* (4 vols., Cambridge, 1984–2006), and M. M. Mitchell and F. M. Young (eds.), *The Cambridge History of Christianity I: Origins to Constantine* (Cambridge, 2006). A bracingly critical examination of the whole biblical text, drawing extensively on archaeology, is R. Lane Fox, *The Unauthorized Version: Truth and Fiction in the Bible* (London, 1991), while a reliable commentary both academic and devotional is J. Barton and J. Muddiman (eds.), *The Oxford Bible Commentary* (Oxford, 2001).

1: Greece and Rome
(c. 1000 BCE–100 CE)

Recent starting points in understanding are R. Lane Fox, *The Classical World: An Epic History of Greece and Rome* (London, 2005), and C. Kelly, *The Roman Empire: A Very Short Introduction* (Oxford, 2006). Among the survey works from distinguished twentieth-century classicists which have stood the test of time are O. Murray, *Early Greece* (rev. edn, London, 1992), M. I. Finley, *The Ancient Greeks* (London, 1963), and F. Millar with D. Berciu, R. N. Frye, G. Kossack and T. Talbot Rice, *The Roman Empire and Its Neighbours* (London, 1967). T. Holland, *Rubicon: The Triumph and Tragedy of the Roman Republic* (London, 2004), is a spirited modern account of the fall of the Roman Republic, but R. Syme, *The Roman Revolution* (Oxford, 1939), is the classic and epic account. Still arresting in its insights is E. R. Dodds, *The Greeks and the Irrational* (Berkeley, CA, and London, 1951).

2: Israel
(c. 1000 BCE–100 CE)

An engrossing and subtle introduction to the city which has so obsessed three world faiths is A. Elon, *Jerusalem: City of Mirrors* (rev. edn, London, 1996). A sound introduction to the history of ancient Israel is H. Jagersma, *A History of Israel in the Old Testament Period* (London, 1982), translated from Jagersma's *Geschiednis van Israël in het Oudtestamentische Tijdvak* (Kampen, 1979), while M. Goodman, *Rome and Jerusalem: The Clash of Ancient Civilizations* (London, 2006), is a majestic account of a tragic meeting of cultures. The monumentality and rigour of German scholarship on the subject is to be sampled in R. Albertz, *A History of Israelite Religion in the Old Testament Period* (2 vols., London, 1994), a translation of *Religionsgeschichte Israels in alttestamentlicher Zeit* (2 vols., Göttingen, 1992, 1996). A nuanced and user-friendly companion to the book that emerged from ancient Israel's history is J. Barton, *Reading the Old Testament* (2nd edn, London, 1996). J. Murphy O'Connor, *The Holy Land: An Oxford Archaeological Guide* (Oxford, 1980), is an indispensable companion to the physical remains of the biblical and post-biblical landscape by one who knows it intimately.

Particular themes in relation to the Tanakh/Old Testament are examined by J. Blenkinsopp, *A History of Prophecy in Israel* (London, 1984); J. L. Crenshaw, *Old Testament Wisdom: An Introduction* (2nd edn, Louisville, 1998); E. W. Nicholson, *God and His People: Covenant and Theology in the Old Testament* (Oxford, 1986). Moving from texts canonical for both Jews and Christians, the connections of the world of early Judaism with its Christian offspring are presented via primary sources in C. K. Barrett (ed.), *The New Testament Background: Selected Documents* (rev. edn, London, 1987). J. H. Charlesworth (ed.), *The Old Testament Pseudepigrapha* (2 vols., Garden City, NY, 1983–5), is the most comprehensive recent collection of Jewish sacred literature beyond the Tanakh, although H. F. D. Sparks (ed.), *The Apocryphal Old Testament* (Oxford, 1984), is also a convenient collection of these texts. To make sense of this bewildering mélange, C. Rowland, *The Open Heaven: A Study of Apocalyptic in Judaism and Early Christianity* (London, 1982), and his *Christian Origins: An Account of the Setting and Character of the Most Important Messianic Sect of Judaism* (London, 1982), are masterly accounts of the Intertestamental period of Judaism and their links to the formation of Christianity.

PART II: ONE CHURCH, ONE FAITH, ONE LORD?
(4 BCE–451 CE)

General Reading

No one interested in the period can abstain from the reading of E. Gibbon, *The History of the Decline and Fall of the Roman Empire* (first edition from 1776); Gibbon had a fine eye for the absurdities and tragedies that result from the profession of religion. H. Chadwick, *The Early Church* (London, 1967), is still an excellent and genial way to begin study of the first five centuries of Christianity, with N. Brox, *A History of the Early Church* (London, 1994), a translation of *Kirchengeschichte des Altertums* (Düsseldorf, 1986), as a useful alternative. Also vintage Chadwick, though on a larger scale, is H. Chadwick, *The Church in Ancient Society: From Galilee to Gregory the Great* (Oxford, 2001). S. G. Hall, *Doctrine and Practice in the Early Church* (London, 1991) and C. Markschies, *Between Two Worlds: Structures of Early Christianity* (London, 1999), a translation of *Zwischen den Welten Wandern: Strukturen des antiken Christentums* (Frankfurt am Main, 1997), are good next stages for exploration. Monumental yet very readable is W. H. C. Frend, *The Rise of Christianity* (London, 1984). For the whole period up to the Council of Nicaea, the indispensable collection of documents with commentary is J. Stevenson (ed.), rev. W. H. C. Frend, *A New Eusebius: Documents Illustrating the History of the Church to AD 337* (London, 1987).

3: A Crucified Messiah
(4 BCE–100 CE)

L. T. Johnson, *The Writings of the New Testament* (rev. edn, Minneapolis, 1999), is a straightforward and helpful way into the subject, from which one might progress to J. Jeremias, *New Testament Theology* (London, 1971). It will be a revelation to some readers of the Bible to see the texts of the Gospels arranged side by side to demonstrate their variant forms and development, which is most instructively done by using K. Aland (ed.), *Synopsis of the Four Gospels, Greek-English Edition of the Synopsis Quattuor Evangeliorum* (9th edn, Stuttgart, 1989), derived from the German original of 1964, K. Aland (ed.), *Synopsis quattuor Evangeliorum, locis parallelis Evangeliorum apocryphorum et patrum adhibitis*. C. M. Tuckett, *Reading the New Testament: Methods of Interpretation* (London, 1987), will help those shell-shocked by such perusal to make sense of the picture.

Three edited collections of essays are exceptionally useful introductions to twentieth-century controversies on the Gospels: G. Stanton (ed.), *The Interpretation of Matthew* (Philadelphia and London, 1983), W. Telford (ed.), *The Interpretation of Mark* (Philadelphia and London, 1985), J. Ashton (ed.), *The Interpretation of John* (Philadelphia and London,

1986). Well worth reading, although like most of the literature it assumes the unity in authorship of Luke's Gospel and the Book of Acts, is H. Conzelmann, *The Theology of Luke* (London, 1960), from the original *Die Mitte der Zeit* (Tübingen, 1953). A classic analysis of the material underlying the Synoptic Gospels is T. W. Manson, *The Sayings of Jesus as Recorded in the Gospels According to St Matthew and St Luke* (London, 1957), first published as Part II of T. W. Manson, *The Mission and Message of Jesus* (London, 1937); and G. N. Stanton, *The Gospels and Jesus* (Oxford, 1989), shows where scholarship has subsequently travelled. Engaging little accounts of crucial parts of the texts raising large questions about them are the trilogy of G. Vermes, *The Passion* (London, 2005), *The Nativity* (London, 2006) and *The Resurrection* (London, 2008). Our growing sense of the rootedness of Jesus in his culture is ably explored in J. Barclay and J. Sweet (eds.), *Early Christianity in Its Jewish Context* (Cambridge, 1996), while G. Vermes, *Jesus the Jew* (London, 1973) and E. P. Sanders, *Jesus and Judaism* (London, 1985) are both sensitive but contrasting treatments of the subject.

4: Boundaries Defined
(50 CE–300)

D. G. Horrell, *An Introduction to the Study of Paul* (London and New York, 2000), leads in to the subject, which is stimulatingly developed in E. P. Sanders, *Paul, the Law and the Jewish People* (Philadelphia, 1983). W. A. Meeks, *The First Urban Christians: The Social World of the Apostle Paul* (New Haven and London, 1983) is a helpful attempt to apply a historical and social imagination to data supplied in the Pauline letters and Acts. W. Horbury, *Jews and Christians in Contact and Controversy* (Edinburgh, 1998) emphasizes the continuing Christian relationship with Judaism. L. W. Hurtado, *The Earliest Christian Artifacts: Manuscripts and Christian Origins* (Grand Rapids, 2006), and F. Young, *The Making of the Creeds* (London, 1991), are two explorations of what began to make Christianity different. C. Markschies, *Gnosis: An Introduction* (Edinburgh, 2003), originally published as *Die Gnosis* (Munich, 2001), is a fine exposition of what we know of the alternative futures of early Christianity; more controversial, though now something of a classic for many, is E. Pagels, *The Gnostic Gospels* (New York, 1979).

5: The Prince: Ally or Enemy?
(100–300)

E. R. Dodds, *Christian and Pagan in an Age of Anxiety: Some Aspects of Religious Experience from Marcus Aurelius to Constantine* (Cambridge, 1965), is a classic exploration of an obscure period, one vital moment of which is re-examined in R. Selinger, *The Mid-third Century Persecutions of Decius and Valerian* (Frankfurt am Main, 2002). An exceptional study is R. Lane Fox, *Pagans and Christians in the Mediterranean World from the Second Century AD to the Conversion of Constantine* (London, 1986). An important time-capsule from Syria is presented in C. Hopkins, ed. B. Goldman, *The Discovery of Dura-Europos* (New Haven and London, 1979).

6: The Imperial Church
(300–451)

The turning point created by Constantine is still best encountered through a remarkable example of how to present history compellingly for novices, A. H. M. Jones, *Constantine and the Conversion of Europe* (London, 1948); thereafter, the consequences of Constantine's decision are richly depicted by the essayists of A. Casiday and F. W. Norris (eds.), *The Cambridge History of Christianity 2: Constantine to c. 1600* (Cambridge, 2007). More concise and a delightful guide to the otherwise often arid-seeming theological controversies of the age is F. Young, *From Nicaea to Chalcedon* (London, 1983). Indispensable are the primary sources and incisive commentary of J. Stevenson (ed.), rev. W. H. C. Frend, *Creeds, Councils and Controversies: Documents Illustrating the History of the Church AD 337–461* (London, 1989). A crucial episode of this period long-misrepresented in the Church's telling of its own story is sensitively reinterpreted by a master of the tradition, R. Williams, *Arius: Heresy and Tradition* (2nd edn, London, 2001), and valuably further dissected by one of Williams' admirers, L. Ayres, *Nicaea and Its Legacy: An Approach to 4th-century Trinitarian Orthodoxy* (Oxford, 2004). A vital development of the period is absorbingly reconstructed in E. D. Hunt, *Holy Land Pilgrimage in the Later Roman Empire, AD 312–460* (Oxford, 1984).

PART III: VANISHING FUTURES:
EAST AND SOUTH
(451–1500)

General Reading

As yet, the stories of the non-Chalcedonian Churches of Asia and Africa have not fully escaped into the public domain from a mound of exciting and innovative academic research, but there are useful starter essays in sections of K. Parry (ed.), *The Blackwell Companion to Eastern Christianity* (Oxford, 2007). A shining exception to the rule, on the Dyophysite Christian tradition, beautifully illustrated partly with the author's own photographs after a lifetime of travel, is C. Baumer, *The Church of the East: An Illustrated History of Assyrian Christianity* (London and New York, 2006). Two other fine introductions are I. Gillman and H.-J. Klimheit, *Christians in Asia before 1500* (Richmond, 1999), and P. Jenkins, *The Lost History of Christianity: The Thousand-year Golden Age of the Church in the Middle East, Africa and Asia* (New York, 2008).

7: Defying Chalcedon: Asia and Africa
(451–622)

Excellent background is provided in A. Cameron, *The Mediterranean World in Late Antiquity, AD 395–600* (London, 1993), and W. A. Kaegi, *Heraclius, Emperor of Byzantium* (Cambridge, 2003) is a study of the crucial moment before the coming of Islam changed all rules of the game in the Middle East. Fascinating if monumental studies of a world previously forgotten are I. Shahīd, *Byzantium and the Arabs in the Fifth Century* (Washington, DC, 1989) and I. Shahīd, *Byzantium and the Arabs in the Sixth Century* (Washington, DC, 3 vols. so far, 1995–2002).

8: Islam: The Great Realignment
(622–1500)

Two vigorous introductory surveys are R. Fletcher, *The Cross and the Crescent: Christianity and Islam from Muhammad to the Reformation* (London, 2003), and Z. Karabell, *People of the Book: The Forgotten History of Islam and the West* (London, 2007), the latter being rather consciously directed to modern American concerns. Now classic is a strange but creative text, P. Crone and M. Cook, *Hagarism: The Making of the Islamic World* (Cambridge, 1977), while a wise reflection by a lifelong episcopal enthusiast for the subject is K. Cragg, *The Arab Christian: A History in the Middle East* (London, 1992). Equally magisterial is S. H. Griffith, *The Church in the Shadow of the Mosque: Christians and Muslims in the World of Islam* (Princeton, 2008). A masterly study of the crisis caused by the Mongols with a wider perspective than its already wide title implies is P. Jackson, *The Mongols and the West, 1221–1410* (Harlow, 2005). Richly enjoyable in its no-nonsense sifting of probability from wishful thinking in Ethiopian Church history is S. Munro-Hay, *The Quest for the Ark of the Covenant: The True History of the Tablets of Moses* (London, 2006).

PART IV: THE UNPREDICTABLE RISE OF ROME
(300–1300)

General Reading

Quite magnificent in its originality and powers of synthesis is the work of the doyen of the field, P. Brown, *The Rise of Western Christendom: Triumph and Diversity AD 200–1000* (Oxford, 1997). From a master of a previous generation comes a fine introduction, R. W. Southern, *Western Society and the Church in the Middle Ages* (London, 1970). An introduction which usefully draws on social and economic history, and which takes no prisoners, is R. Collins, *Early Medieval Europe 300–1000* (Houndmills, 1991).

9: The Making of Latin Christianity
(300–500)

For the beginning of the period, see the reading for Chapter 6, but to those works should be added the particular focus on the city of Rome in J. R. Curran, *Pagan City and Christian Capital: Rome in the Fourth Century* (Oxford, 2000), also against the wider background presented with concise brilliance in P. Brown, *The Cult of the Saints: Its Rise and Function in Latin Christianity* (London, 1981). Much profit and entertainment can be derived from the essayists of A. Momigliano (ed.), *The Conflict between Paganism and Christianity in the Fourth Century: Essays* (Oxford, 1963). Augustine is perhaps the only Father of the Church whom non-Christians can read for pleasure, at least in two key works, H. Bettenson and D. Knowles (eds.), *Augustine: Concerning the City of God against the Pagans* (London, 1967), and R. S. Pine-Coffin (ed.), *Saint Augustine: Confessions* (London, 1961). Two splendid lives of this most central of Western theologians are G. Bonner, *Saint Augustine of Hippo: Life and Controversies* (2nd edn, Norwich, 1963) and P. Brown, *Augustine of Hippo: A Biography* (London, 1969). An absorbing effort to squeeze as much as possible out of the limited evidence, although there have been archaeological discoveries since, is C. Thomas, *Christianity in Roman Britain to AD 500* (London, 1981).

10: Latin Christendom: New Frontiers
(500–1000)

The period is well served for general introductions, such as G. R. Evans, *The Church in the Early Middle Ages* (London, 2007), J. Herrin, *The Formation of Christendom* (London, 1989), F. D. Logan, *A History of the Church in the Middle Ages* (London, 2002), T. F. X. Noble and J. M. H. Smith (eds.), *The Cambridge History of Christianity 4: Early Medieval Christianities, c. 600–c. 1100* (Cambridge, 2008), and C. Wickham, *The Inheritance of Rome: A History of Europe from 400 to 1000* (London and New York, 2009) – the last providing a wide sweep of perspectives including emphasis on the social and economic background. An eloquent and absorbing study, weighted before 1000, is R. Fletcher, *The Conversion of Europe: From Paganism to Christianity 371–1386 AD* (London, 1997). On a key figure, an excellent starter is R. A. Markus, *Gregory the Great and His World* (Cambridge, 1997), and there are fine essays on another key personality in J. Story (ed.), *Charlemagne: Empire and Society* (Manchester, 2005). J. M. Wallace-Hadrill, *The Frankish Church* (Oxford, 1983), is a substantial study of the section of the Western Church which transformed religious patterns on a much wider scale. H. Mayr-Harting, *The Coming of Christianity to Anglo-Saxon England* (3rd edn, London, 1991) delightfully introduces the subject, in the nature of things owing equally delightful work by an only slightly more venerable historian, L. Sherley-Price and R. E. Latham (eds.), *Bede: A History of the English Church and People* (rev. edn, London, 1968). More classic hagiographies of the period, some by Bede himself, are to be encountered in J. F. Webb (tr.) and D. H. Farmer (ed.), *The Age of Bede* (London, 1983).

11: The West: Universal Emperor or Universal Pope?
(900–1200)

After the general introductions to the whole period listed above, a refreshingly iconoclastic perspective is R. I. Moore, *The Formation of a Persecuting Society: Power and Deviance in Western Europe, 950–1250* (Oxford, 1987), expanded into a more general survey in R. I. Moore, *The First European Revolution, c. 970–1215* (Oxford, 2000). K. G. Cushing, *Reform and the Papacy in the Eleventh Century: Spirituality and Social Change* (Manchester and New York, 2005), presents a clear overview of the Gregorian Revolution, and is usefully complemented chronologically by the equally workmanlike R. N. Swanson, *The Twelfth-century Renaissance* (Manchester, 1999). J. Harvey, *The Gothic World 1100–1600: A Survey of Architecture and Art* (London, 1950), is a good place to start exploring the dominant medieval style, while its Romanesque predecessor is absorbingly catalogued in the photography of a stupendous French series of publications begun in 1955 by Benedictine monks, *La nuit des temps* (La Pierre-qui-Vire, 1955–), now running to more than ninety volumes. G. Duby, *The Age of the Cathedrals: Art and Society 980–1420* (London, 1981), originally published as *Le temps des cathédrales: l'art et la société 980–1420* (Paris, 1976), is a wonderful exposition of the importance of cathedrals in the society of the High Middle Ages, with its focus on the eleventh and twelfth century; it is a pity that the English translation is so wooden. Unequivocally a pleasure to read in its gentlemanly New England lyricism is H. Adams, *Mont-Saint-Michel and Chartres* (Boston, MA, 1904). On the Crusading phenomenon, S. Runciman, *A History of the Crusades* (3 vols., Cambridge, 1951–4) is classic. C. Tyerman, *God's War: A New History of the Crusades* (London, 2006), is a more recent summary of a lifetime's thought, complemented by the various perspectives provided by a fine crew of essayists in S. J. Ridyard (ed.), *The Medieval Crusade* (Woodbridge and Rochester, NY, 2004). A beautifully argued and illustrated survey with a wider chronological focus is particularly relevant for the Crusading period: C. Morris, *The Sepulchre of Christ and the Medieval West from the Beginning to 1600* (Oxford, 2005), while H. Houben, *Roger II of Sicily: A Ruler between East and West* (Cambridge, 2002), focuses on one of the most fascinating and unusual Western Christians of his age.

12: A Church for All People?
(1100–1300)

Much profit is provided by the essayists in M. Rubin (ed.), *The Cambridge History of Christianity 4: Christianity in Western Europe, c. 1100–c. 1500* (Cambridge, 2009). Richly enjoyable and displaying an exceptional sensitivity to visual evidence beyond its supposed boundaries is R. Marks, *Image and Devotion in Late Medieval England* (Stroud, 2004). Few other countries have had the luck to have been treated to such a study as D. Knowles, *The Religious Orders in England* (3 vols., Cambridge, 1948–59). M. Rubin, *Corpus Christi: The Eucharist in Late Medieval Culture* (Cambridge, 1991), says a great deal about the period by concentrating on one of its chief cultural products, while excellent portraits of three sharply contrasting architects of their age are to be gained from M. Reeves, *Joachim of Fiore and the Prophetic Future: A Medieval Study in Historical Thinking* (rev. edn, Stroud, 1999), J. C. Moore (ed.), *Pope Innocent III and His World* (Aldershot, 1999), and K. B. McFarlane, *John Wycliffe and the Beginnings of English Non-conformity* (London, 1952) – the last, like Jones's study of Constantine above, a superb example of how to present history to the intelligent but uninformed. N. Cohn, *The Pursuit of the Millennium* (3rd rev. edn, London, 1969) still stirs the imagination, even if some of its perspectives may now seem over-delineated.

PART V: ORTHODOXY: THE IMPERIAL FAITH
(451–1800)

General Reading

Byzantium and Orthodoxy in general have some beguiling guides. J. Herrin, *Byzantium: The Surprising Life of a Medieval Empire* (London, 2007), is an arresting place to begin, arranged topically as well as chronologically, and another splendid introduction is A. Cameron, *The Byzantines* (Oxford, 2006). A fine gateway to Orthodoxy from a magisterial historian also an Orthodox bishop is K. Ware, *The Orthodox Church* (London, 1994), and the ground is covered comprehensively albeit with some minor slips in J. Binns, *An Introduction to the Christian Orthodox Churches* (Cambridge, 2002). J. M. Hussey, *The Orthodox Church in the Byzantine Empire* (Oxford, 1986), is stodgy, but is not to be neglected. Teams of experts crowd M. Angold (ed.), *The Cambridge History of Christianity 5: Eastern Christianity* (Cambridge, 2006) and C. Mango (ed.), *The Oxford History of Byzantium* (Oxford, 2002). A sparkling set of essayists is marshalled in A. Louth and A. Casiday (eds.), *Byzantine Orthodoxies* (Aldershot, 2006), and the culminating work of a great career in historical exposition and Christian ecumenical endeavour is H. Chadwick, *East and West: The Making of a Rift in the Church. From Apostolic Times until the Council of Florence* (Oxford, 2003). A. Ivanov, *Holy Fools in Byzantium and Beyond* (Oxford, 2006), is a delightful and learned survey of a theme which may disconcert Westerners meeting the Orthodox tradition.

13: Faith in a New Rome
(451–900)

A fascinating exposition of a hitherto-neglected world catastrophe is L. K. Little (ed.), *Plague and the End of Antiquity: The Pandemic of 541–750* (Cambridge, 2007). J. Moorhead, *Justinian* (London, 1994), is the best introduction to this architect of Byzantine identity, who should also be entertainingly encountered, along with his formidable spouse, in G. A. Williamson (tr.), *Procopius: The Secret History* (London, 1966). The essayists of J. Fontaine and J. N. Hillgarth (eds.), *The Seventh Century: Change and Continuity* (London, 1992), illuminate a turning point in Byzantine history, which is explored in further detail by L. Brubaker and J. Haldon (eds.), *Byzantium in the Iconoclast Era (c. 680–850). The Sources: An Annotated Survey* (Aldershot, 2001).

14: Orthodoxy: More Than an Empire
(900–1700)

In addition to the general sources, M. Angold, *The Fourth Crusade: Event and Context* (Harlow, 2003), provides a good account of this wretched and decisive episode, while the final disaster inspires a lively presentation in R. Crowley, *Constantinople: The Last Great Siege, 1453* (London, 2005). A more upbeat story of eventual renewal, with beautiful illustrations, is G. Speake, *Mount Athos: Renewal in Paradise* (New Haven and London, 2002).

15: Russia: The Third Rome
(900–1800)

A good place to begin in the understanding of a culture very hard for Westerners properly to understand is a wise study by a great Orthodox exile, of much more general interest than its title implies, J. Meyendorff, *Byzantium and the Rise of Russia: A Study of Byzantino-Russian relations in the 14th Century* (Cambridge, 1981). Extremely lively is T. Szamuely, *The Russian Tradition* (London, 1974). W. van den Bercken, *Holy Russia and Christian Europe: East and West in the Religious Ideology of Russia* (London, 1999), a translation of *De mythe van het Oosten. Oost en West in de religieuze ideeëngeschiedenis van Rusland* (Zoetermeer,

1998), provides further general insight. G. Hosking, *Russia: People and Empire 1551–1917* (1997), is an excellent complement to the early focus of these works, and a highly engaging journey beyond high politics and elites is made in A. Sinyavsky, *Ivan the Fool. Russian Folk Belief: A Cultural History* (Moscow, 2007), a translation of this noted dissident novelist's original text. S. Plokhy, *The Cossacks and Religion in Early Modern Ukraine* (Oxford, 2002), helps to explain the tangled relationship of Russia and Ukraine, while a superb biography of a key figure is I. de Madariaga, *Ivan the Terrible* (New Haven and London, 2005).

PART VI: WESTERN CHRISTIANITY DISMEMBERED (1300–1800)

General Reading

A firework display of insights into the period is provided by J. Bossy, *Christianity in the West 1400–1700* (Oxford, 1985). D. MacCulloch, *Reformation: Europe's House Divided 1490–1700* (London, 2003), provides an overview; E. Duffy, *The Stripping of the Altars: Traditional Religion in England, c. 1400–c. 1580* (New Haven and London, 1992), evokes with elegiac elegance the world which the Reformation destroyed and the way in which one kingdom destroyed it.

16: Perspectives on the True Church (1300–1517)

The period is well introduced by N. P. Tanner, *The Church in the Later Middle Ages* (London, 2008). A passionate survey of one of its most important products, whose consequences remain still fully to be worked out, is F. Oakley, *The Conciliarist Tradition: Constitutionalism in the Catholic Church, 1300–1870* (Oxford, 2003). That giant among Dutch historians J. Huizinga produced a classic introduction to *Erasmus of Rotterdam* (London, 1952), a translation of the Dutch original of 1924; it can be triangulated with L.-E. Halkin, *Erasmus: A Critical Biography* (Oxford, 1993), and a delightful and profound meditation by M. A. Screech, *Laughter at the Foot of the Cross* (London, 1997).

17: A House Divided (1517–1660)

Varied voices of a galaxy of experts on the European Reformation are heard in A. Pettegree (ed.), *The Reformation World* (London, 2000), and R. Po-Chia Hsia (ed.), *The Cambridge History of Christianity 6: Reform and Expansion 1500–1660* (Cambridge, 2007). Textbook-style is B. Kümin (ed.), *The European World 1500–1800* (London, 2009), Part 3. A series of sure guides to the complex theological disputes of the period are furnished by D. Bagchi and D. Steinmetz (eds.), *The Cambridge Companion to Reformation Theology* (Cambridge, 2004). Of the countless biographies of the Reformation's first great personality, a variety of introductory spotlights appear in D. K. McKim (ed.), *The Cambridge Companion to Martin Luther* (Cambridge, 2003). M. Marty, *Martin Luther* (New York, 2004) is concise, and would be provocatively complemented by progressing to R. Marius, *Martin Luther: The Christian between God and Death* (Cambridge, MA, and London, 1999). All these would be a painless prelude to M. Brecht, *Martin Luther* (3 vols., London, 1985–93), translated from *Martin Luther* (3 vols., Stuttgart, 1981–7), a work conceived on a grand scale from within the Lutheran tradition, and therefore inclined to give Luther multiple benefits of the doubt. The resulting Lutheranism in Germany should be sampled in the essays of the tragically short-lived R. W. Scribner, *Popular Culture and Popular Movements in Reformation Germany* (London, 1987).

    G. R. Potter (ed.), *Huldrych Zwingli* (London, 1978), is a fine biography of this unjustly neglected Reformer, and a much better-known Reformed Protestant of the next generation is to be enjoyably encountered in the work of a fellow-Frenchman with a fine sense of Calvin's cultural context, B. Cottret, *Calvin: A Biography* (Grand Rapids and Edinburgh, 2000), translated from *Calvin: biographie* (Paris, 1995). The Reformed tradition of Protestantism which they shaped is now superbly introduced both by P. Benedict, *Christ's Churches Purely Reformed: A Social History of Calvinism* (New Haven and London, 2002) and G. Murdock, *Beyond Calvin: The Intellectual, Political and Cultural World of Europe's Reformed Churches, c. 1540–1620* (Basingstoke, 2004). The crisis which was in great measure triggered by the Reformation is presented in P. H. Wilson, *Europe's Tragedy: A History of the Thirty Years War* (London, 2009).

One national Reformation which became a very individual branch of the Reformed family is introduced in D. MacCulloch, *Thomas Cranmer: A Life* (New Haven and London, 1996), D. MacCulloch, *The Later Reformation in England, 1547–1603* (rev. edn, Basingstoke, 2001), C. Haigh, *English Reformations: Religion, Politics and Society under the Tudors* (Oxford, 1993), and P. Marshall, *Reformation England 1480–1642* (London, 2003). The contrasting Reformation which in the same islands became *plus Calviniste que Calvin* is absorbingly described in all its vitality in M. Todd, *The Culture of Protestantism in Early Modern Scotland* (New Haven and London, 2002), while the Reformation which went wrong and the Counter-Reformation which supplanted it are sympathetically evoked in R. Gillespie, *Devoted People: Belief and Religion in Early Modern Ireland* (Manchester, 1997). G. Williams, *Wales and the Reformation* (Cardiff, 1997), is one work from the master of the subject. The mid-century crisis of the whole Atlantic Isles is most comprehensively described in A. Woolrych, *Britain in Revolution 1625–1660* (Oxford, 2002).

One monumental gazetteer of 'non-magisterial' possibilities of Reformation in Europe has not yet been surpassed, even though its attempts at classification are disputable: G. H. Williams, *The Radical Reformation* (London, 1962). Classic studies of an alignment which was always problematic, but which has provoked much fruitful investigation tending to undermine the original proposition, are M. Weber, *The Protestant Ethic and the Spirit of Capitalism* (various English edns from 1930), a translation of *Die protestantische Ethik und der Geist des Kapitalismus*, 1904/5), and R. H. Tawney, *Religion and the Rise of Capitalism* (1926). More than a century of debate about the Weber–Tawney thesis is most reliably analysed in H. Lehmann and G. Roth (eds.), *Weber's Protestant Ethic: Origins, Evidence, Contexts* (Cambridge, 1993).

18: Rome's Renewal
(1500–1700)

A fine initial survey which has the advantage of taking seriously the worldwide mission of sixteenth-century Catholicism is R. Bireley, *The Refashioning of Catholicism, 1450–1700* (Houndmills, 1999), and a sprightly overview is given by one of the elder statesmen of the field in J. O'Malley, *Trent and All That: Renaming Catholicism in the Early Modern Era* (Cambridge, MA, 2000). His study of the origins of the Society of Jesus is currently the best available: *The First Jesuits* (Cambridge, MA, 1993). A rich variety of sources with commentary is provided by J. C. Olin (ed.), *The Catholic Reformation: Savonarola to Ignatius Loyola* (New York, 1992), and a lively treatment of a controversial topic is J. Edwards, *The Spanish Inquisition* (Stroud, 1999). J. Bergin, *Church, Society and Religious Change in France, 1580–1730* (New Haven and London, 2009), deals in masterly fashion with one Protestant Reformation which was eventually vanquished by Counter-Reformation. Admirably sensitive on one of the great mystics of the Christian tradition is A. Weber, *Teresa of Avila and the Rhetoric of Femininity* (Princeton and London, 1990). On the early modern witch-craze which has so fascinated post-Enlightenment Europeans for good or ill, a sensible short introduction is G. Scarre, *Witchcraft and Magic in 16th and 17th Century Europe* (Basingstoke, 1987), and a superb set of case studies is to be found in J. Barry, M. Hester and G. Roberts (eds.), *Witchcraft in Early Modern Europe: Studies in Culture and Belief* (Cambridge, 1996). K. Thomas, *Religion and the Decline of Magic* (London, 1971), provides a formidable mound of data on the subject. L. Roper, *Oedipus and the Devil: Witchcraft, Sexuality and Religion in Early Modern Europe* (London, 1994), is one thoughtful perspective on the problem, while a study of rare subtlety is S. Clark, *Thinking with Demons: The Idea of Witchcraft in Early Modern Europe* (Oxford, 1997).

19: A Worldwide Faith
(1500–1800)

The beginnings are superbly introduced in D. Abulafia, *The Discovery of Mankind: Atlantic Encounters in the Age of Columbus* (New Haven and London, 2008), and breathtaking in its ability to range across the globe is F. Fernández-Armesto, *Pathfinders: A Global History of Exploration* (Oxford, 2006). A good background survey is still J. H. Parry, *The Spanish Seaborne Empire* (London, 1966). Phenomenal in his learning on Catholic world mission and a brilliant writer was C. R. Boxer, who complements Parry in his *The Portuguese Seaborne Empire, 1415–1825* (London, 1973), sweeps over the field in *The Church Militant and Iberian Expansion 1440–1770* (Baltimore, 1978), and expounds his particular passion in *The Christian Century in Japan, 1549–1650* (Berkeley, 1967). A work equally bidding fair to achieve classic status is M. Brockey, *Journey to the East: The Jesuit Mission to China, 1579–1724* (Cambridge, MA, 2007), and a fascinating and quirky companion to the early days of Christian mission is J. D. Spence, *The Memory Palace of Matteo Ricci* (London, 1984). Authoritative on its previously neglected subject is J. K. Thornton, *The Kingdom of Kongo: Civil War and Transition, 1641–1718* (Madison, WI, 1983).

20: Protestant Awakenings
(1600–1800)

Astride the field is what may be the culmination of a scholarly career spent explicating the worldwide links of early Evangelicalism: W. R. Ward, *The Protestant Evangelical Awakening* (Cambridge, 1992). The most central composer of the Western Christian tradition is enjoyably approached through W. Mellers, *Bach and the Dance of God* (London 1980), and C. Wolff, *Bach: The Learned Musician* (New York and London, 2000); equally one might wish to contemplate Bach's achievement through the recordings conducted by Sir John Eliot Gardiner. A classic exposition of British self-understanding and imperial expansion is L. Colley, *Britons: Forging the Nation, 1707–1837* (New Haven and London, 1992). A deeply felt survey from a great Methodist historian is E. G. Rupp, *Religion in England 1688–1791* (Oxford, 1986), and a usefully different if perhaps skewed perspective may be gained from J. C. D. Clark, *English Society 1660–1832: Religion, Ideology and Politics during the Ancien Régime* (Cambridge, 2000). D. Bebbington, *Evangelicalism in Modern Britain: A History from the 1730s to the 1980s* (London, 1989, and subsequent expansions), has the same centrality for a narrower but still vast field. A splendid introduction to one of Christianity's most significant founder-churchmen from the present doyen of British Methodist scholarship is J. Walsh, *John Wesley: 1703–1791. A Bicentennial Tribute* (London, 1993), and H. D. Rack, *Reasonable Enthusiast: John Wesley and the Rise of Methodism* (London, 1989), likewise avoids Methodist hagiography. D. Hempton, *Methodism: Empire of the Spirit* (New Haven and London, 2005), helps to show why Wesley's legacy continued to be so important. A good introduction to early anglophone colonization in North America is C. Bridenbaugh, *Vexed and Troubled Englishmen, 1590–1642* (Oxford, 1968), while the relationship between Old and New Worlds is usefully complicated by F. J. Bremer, *Congregational Communion: Clerical Friendship in the Anglo-American Puritan Community, 1610–1692* (Boston, 1994), and S. Hardman Moore, *Pilgrims: New World Settlers and the Call of Home* (New Haven and London, 2007). L. E. Schmidt, *Holy Fairs: Scottish Communions and American Revivals in the Early Modern Period* (Princeton, 1989), like W. R. Ward, makes unexpected connections across the Atlantic, and is paralleled by a highly engaging and original survey, P. Bonomi, *Under the Cope of Heaven: Religion, Society and Politics in Colonial America* (New York and Oxford, 1986). Lively and wise is J. Butler, *Awash in a Sea of Faith: Christianizing the American People* (Cambridge, MA, 1990).

PART VII: GOD IN THE DOCK
(1492–PRESENT)

General Reading

D. Cupitt, *The Sea of Faith: Christianity in Change* (London, 1984), is a concise statement of this important theologian's historical reflection on the Enlightenment and its significance for Christianity, paralleled in its radical questioning and historical analysis by P. Kennedy, *A Modern Introduction to Theology: New Questions for Old Beliefs* (London, 2006). A more sober but highly useful historical account is D. Rosman, *The Evolution of the English Churches 1500–2000* (Cambridge, 2003), and a wide sweep of a central topic is N. Atkin and F. Tallett, *Priests, Prelates and People: A History of European Catholicism since 1750* (London, 2003). A counter-theme of some importance is dealt with by D. Nash, *Blasphemy in Modern Britain 1789–present* (Aldershot, 1999).

21: Enlightenment: Ally or Enemy?
(1492–1815)

There is a lack of any short introduction to the religion of the period, but a superb collection of essays is to be found in S. J. Brown and T. Tackett (eds.), *The Cambridge History of Christianity 7: Enlightenment, Reawakening and Revolution 1660–1815* (Cambridge, 2006). J. I. Israel, *Radical Enlightenment: Philosophy and the Making of Modernity 1650–1750* (Oxford, 2001), offers a superb reinterpretation of the origins of the Enlightenment which has won much approval. O. Chadwick, *The Popes and European Revolution* (Oxford, 1981), is perhaps Chadwick's most remarkable and original book; there is nothing else like it, although D. Beales, *Prosperity and Plunder: European Catholic Monasteries in the Age of Revolution, 1650–1815* (Cambridge, 2003), is a richly enjoyable and equally original treatment of one aspect of the same subject, beautifully illustrated. J. McManners, *Church and Society in Eighteenth-century France* (2 vols., Oxford, 1998), is unequalled in its treatment. Of the vast literature on the French Revolution, D. Andress, *The French Revolution and the People* (London, 2004), is one of the most interesting recent considerations.

22: Europe Re-enchanted or Disenchanted?
(1815–1914)

An absorbing survey of European religion, perhaps a little kind to Roman Catholicism, at least by omission, is M. Burleigh, *Earthly Powers: The Conflict between Religion and Politics from the French Revolution to the Great War* (London, 2005). The Oxford History of the Christian Church series serves the period well with O. Chadwick, *A History of the Popes 1830–1914* (Oxford, 1998), and N. Hope, *German and Scandinavian Protestantism, 1700–1918* (Oxford, 1995). A fine life of one who appears far more important in retrospect than he seemed at the time is J. Garff, *Søren Kierkegaard: A Biography* (Princeton, 2005), and one who was immediately recognized as exceptional is superbly portrayed in J. Browne, *Charles Darwin* (2 vols., London, 1995, 2002). Of the literature on Marian devotion in the nineteenth century, D. Blackbourn, *Marpingen: Apparitions of the Virgin Mary in Bismarckian Germany* (Oxford, 1993), is perhaps the most important case study of an extraordinary phenomenon in European society. J. McManners, *Church and State in France 1870–1914* (London, 1972), is a concise survey of a deeply riven era of French politics, whose fruits are to be sampled more seriously than a comic novel might normally promise in G. Chevallier, *Clochemerle-les-Bains*, whose French original of 1934 has various English translations. M. Angold (ed.), *The Cambridge History of Christianity 5: Eastern Christianity* (Cambridge, 2006) is a sure guide to the travails and growing ascendancy of Orthodoxy during the period.

O. Chadwick, *The Secularization of the European Mind in the Nineteenth Century* (Cambridge, 1975), is a fine survey, while on a more restricted subject, O. Chadwick, *The Victorian*

Church (2 vols., 2nd edn, London, 1970–72), is written with such lightness of touch that one hardly notices its two-volume size. Other dimensions of English religion are well served by F. Knight, *The Church in the Nineteenth Century* (London, 2008), and British theology is serviceably introduced by B. M. G. Reardon, *Religious Thought in the Victorian Age* (London, 1980); background documents are usefully gathered in A. O. J. Cockshut, *Religious Controversies of the Nineteenth Century: Selected Documents* (London, 1966). One of the most balanced accounts of the Oxford Movement and its consequences, by a primate of the allied Swedish Lutheran Church, is still Y. Brilioth, *The Anglican Revival: Studies in the Oxford Movement* (London, 1933). The character of nineteenth-century Anglicanism is beautifully traced in the works of D. Newsome, *Godliness and Good Learning: Four Studies on a Victorian Ideal* (London, 1961), on the impact of religion on education, and his *The Parting of Friends: A Study of the Wilberforces and Henry Manning* (London, 1966). Newsome also wrote an illuminating dual biography of *The Convert Cardinals: John Henry Newman and Henry Edward Manning* (London, 1993), though the standard biography of Newman is still I. Ker, *John Henry Newman* (Oxford, 1988).

23: To Make the World Protestant
(1700–1914)

In addition to the surveys of particular regions listed above under 'General Reading for All Christian History', the essayists of S. Gilley and B. Stanley (eds.), *The Cambridge History of Christianity 8: World Christianities c. 1815–c. 1914* (Cambridge, 2006), should be eagerly consulted. The greatest of world empires of the period is presented in B. Stanley, *The Bible and the Flag: Protestant Missions and British Imperialism in the Nineteenth and Twentieth Centuries* (Leicester, 1990), A. Porter, *Religion versus Empire? British Protestant Missionaries and Overseas Expansion, 1700–1914* (Manchester, 2004), and J. Cox, *The British Missionary Enterprise since 1700* (New York and London, 2008). A principal theme tangled with that story and Britain's American offshoot is magisterially discussed in both D. B. Davis, *Inhuman Bondage: The Rise and Fall of Slavery in the New World* (Oxford, 2006), and C. Kidd, *The Forging of Races: Race and Scripture in the Protestant Atlantic World, 1600–2000* (Cambridge, 2006). I. Breward, *A History of the Churches in Australasia* (Oxford, 2001), is judicious and comprehensive.

24: Not Peace but a Sword
(1914–1960)

J. Morris, *The Church in the Modern Age* (London, 2007), provides excellent shapes for the period, expanded by the essays in H. McLeod (ed.), *The Cambridge History of Christianity 9: World Christianities c. 1914–c. 2000* (Cambridge, 2006). The best guide to Western theology over the last century is P. Kennedy, *Twentieth Century Theologians: A New Introduction* (London, 2009). Admirable in its clarification of much that is complicated is A. Anderson, *An Introduction to Pentecostalism* (Cambridge, 2004), although it lacks the panache of G. Wacker, *Heaven Below: Early Pentecostals and American Culture* (Cambridge, MA, 2001). A. Hastings, *A History of English Christianity 1920–1990* (3rd edn, London, 1991), is both reflective and hugely entertaining. W. Dalrymple, *From the Holy Mountain* (London, 1997), is (in addition to being fine travel literature) a sobering account of the agony of Christianity in the Middle East over the last century.

25: Culture Wars
(1960–present)

H. McLeod, *The Religious Crisis of the 1960s* (Oxford, 2007), examines the cultural shift which sparked a turbulent half-century, from the point of view of one historian who remembers being there. As events unfold, it is difficult to provide reading which will keep pace with them, but the early twenty-first century saw a 'battle of the books' which put discussions about Christianity and religion in general back in the public sphere to a degree they have not been in some while. Developing a line of essentially anthropological thought, the biologist

Richard Dawkins argues in *The God Delusion* (London, 2006) that there is no longer any need for God and no 'evidence' to support religious belief; the professional polemicist Christopher Hitchens produced a polemical follow-on in *God is not Great: The Case against Religion* (London, 2007). Against this, A. Wooldridge, *God is Back: How the Global Revival of Faith is Changing the World* (London, 2009), makes the point that Christianity is resurgent almost everywhere except 'old Europe' and that there may already be more Christians in China than any other country in the world. In a number of subtle and impressive studies, particularly *Black Mass: Apocalyptic Religion and the Death of Utopia* (London, 2007), the philosopher John Gray has argued that whatever the level of overt Christian observance in the old world, Christianity has had a decisive influence in shaping secular movements from the Enlightenment to Communism.

A sobering analysis of the recent US story is M. Northcott, *An Angel Directs the Storm: Apocalyptic Religion and American Empire* (London, 2004). M. A. Sells, *The Bridge Betrayed: Religion and Genocide in Bosnia* (Berkeley and Los Angeles, 1996), unflinchingly examines a conflict of the period whose roots and course form one of the most shaming indictments of European religious divisions. One work from Britain's leading expert on Soviet religion which captures the moment of change in Eastern Europe as it happened is M. Bourdeaux, *Gorbachev, Glasnost and the Gospel* (London, 1990). J. Cornwell, *Breaking Faith: The Pope, the People and the Fate of Catholicism* (London, 2001), expresses many of the tensions felt in the worldwide Catholic Church. The council which helped to spark them is given a more upbeat analysis by the essayists of R. F. Bulman and F. J. Parrella (eds.), *From Trent to Vatican II: Historical and Theological Investigations* (Oxford, 2006). One controversial form of Roman Catholicism can be sampled in A. T. Hennelly (ed.), *Liberation Theology: A Documentary History* (Maryknoll, 1990). W. Hollenweger, *Pentecostalism: Origins and Developments Worldwide* (Peabody, MA, 1997), is an impressive survey by the scholar who pioneered serious study of the worldwide movement which has nurtured his own faith, and the essayists of T. O. Ranger (ed.), *Evangelical Christianity and Democracy in Africa* (Oxford, 2008), hint at a possible positive nexus between Christianity and politics in a so-far persistently troubled continent.

Index

For reasons of space, this is an abridged version of the full index, which can be found at www.stx.ox.ac.uk/general/fellows/macculloch_diarmaid. All dates are CE unless stated as BCE. Popes are listed under Rome; monarchs are gathered under their principal territory, Oecumenical Patriarchs under Constantinople and Archbishops of Canterbury under Canterbury. Monarchs and popes have (where possible) their birth date followed by the date of their accession to the throne, followed by their date of death. Members of European nobility are indexed under their surnames. Those who have been declared saints by one or other Christian Church are indexed either under their first names or their surnames, not at 'St'.